Mary Holden.

Penguin Reference Books
The Penguin World Atlas

Geographic Editor: Peter Hall

The Penguin World Atlas

Prepared by the
Cartographic Department of the Clarendon Press

Penguin Books

Penguin Books Ltd, Harmondsworth,
Middlesex, England
Penguin Books Inc., 7110 Ambassador Road,
Baltimore, Maryland 21207, U.S.A.
Penguin Books Australia Ltd, Ringwood,
Victoria, Australia

First published 1974

ISBN 014 051 059 1

Compiled, drawn and photographed by
the Cartographic Department of the Clarendon Press

Made and printed in Great Britain
Introductory text and maps:
Cook Hammond and Kell Ltd, Mitcham, Surrey
Gazetteer printed at the University Press, Oxford
by Vivian Ridler, Printer to the University

Contents

vi, vii   Key to Maps
viii–xi   Introduction, Page Area Diagrams

Ocean Maps

scale 1:60 million:
1   Indian Ocean
2,3   Atlantic Ocean
4,5   Pacific Ocean *scale 1:61·3 million approx*

The Physical Environment

scale 1:30 million:
6,7   Europe
8,9   U.S.S.R.
10,11   Southern Asia and the Nile
12,13   Far East
14,15   Australasia
16,17   North America
18,19   South America
20,21   Africa
22,23   Arctic
24,25   Antarctic

The Human Environment

scale 1:15 million:
26,27   Europe
28,29   Western U.S.S.R.
30,31   Siberia
32,33   Middle East
34,35   Central South Asia
36,37   China and Japan (inset New Zealand)
38,39   Southeast Asia
40,41   Australia
42,43   North America (Western)
44,45   North America (Eastern)
46   Mexico
47   Caribbean
48,49   Northern Andes
50,51   Brazil
52   Southern South America
53   Ethiopia
54,55   Southern Africa
56,57   West and Northwest Africa

Topographic Maps

scale 1:1·5 million:
58,59   Southeast England and the Midlands
60,61   Wales and Southwest England
62,63   North England and South Scotland

64,65   North Scotland
66,67   Ireland
scale 1:4 million:
68,69   United Kingdom and Irish Republic
70,71   Western Central Europe
72,73   Benelux, Germany
scale 1:7·5 million:
74,75   Scandinavia
76,77   Western Europe
78,79   Eastern Europe
80,81   Western U.S.S.R.
82,83   Northern India
84,85   Eastern China
86   Japan
87   New Zealand
88,89   North Pacific Coast – Alaska Panhandle
90,91   Pacific Coast – Western U.S.A.
92,93   Prairie Provinces
94,95   Great Plains
96,97   Maritime Canada
98,99   Great Lakes
100,101   U.S.A. The South

World Maps

scale 1:90 million:
102,103   Nutrition
104,105   Iron Ore / Steel
106,107   Energy
108,109   Population
110,111   Surface Communications

Urban Maps

scale 1:0·5 million:
112   London
113   Clydeside, Severnside
114   Liverpool / Manchester
115   Leeds / Birmingham
116   Barcelona, Milano, Madrid, Roma
117   Paris, Berlin
118   The Ruhr
119   Köln, Hamburg, Moskva, Leningrad
120   Sydney, Delhi, Calcutta
121   Tōkyō, Beijing (Peking), Shanghai
122   Washington, Montréal, Philadelphia, Boston
123   New York
124   Chicago
125   Toronto, Pittsburgh, Detroit
126   San Francisco, Vancouver, Seattle
127   Los Angeles
128   Mexico, Buenos Aires

Key to Maps

	pages series	1-5 60M	6-25 30M	26-57 15M	58-101 Topographic	112-128 Urban
Relief shading (land)						
Relief shading (submarine)						
Rivers	permanent					
	seasonal					
Lakes	freshwater					
	seasonal freshwater					
	salt					
	seasonal salt					
Salt pans (dry salt lakes)						
Reefs						
Dams						
Cataracts and waterfalls						
Aqueducts						
Canals						
Icecaps						
Marsh, swamp or bog						
Sandbanks or offshore mud						
International boundaries						
	over water					
	disputed *de facto*					
	other disputed					
Regional and admin. boundaries						
Limited access divided highways						
Other main roads						
Tracks used as through routes						
Railways						
Tunnels	road railway					
Airports						
Airfields						
Ferries						
Central business core						
Secondary business area						
Industrial areas						
Residential areas						
Parks						
Industrial waste						
Military installations						

SEASONAL CLIMATES on 1:30 million series
Combinations of summer and winter conditions, by mean temperature of warmest and coldest months respectively

02 No summer (below 6°C), cold winter (below 2°C)
12 Very cool summer (6°-10°C), cold winter (below 2°C)
11 Very cool summer (6°-10°C), mild winter (2°-13°C)
22 Cool summer (10°-20°C), cold winter (below 2°C)
21 Cool summer (10°-20°C), mild winter (2°-13°C)
20 Cool summer (10°-20°C), no winter (over 13°C)
32 Full summer (over 20°C), cold winter (below 2°C)
31 Full summer (over 20°C), mild winter (2°-13°C)
30 Full summer (over 20°C), no winter (over 13°C)

Arid climates
X Arid (no month receives as much as 50mm. rainfall)
Z Extremely arid (no more than 2·5mm. monthly for at least 10 months)

Seasonal temperature range for areas 21,22 and 32 outside the tropics (third small digit)

1 Oceanic (range under 12C°)
2 Sub continental (range 12-24C°)
3 Continental (range 24-36C°)
4 Very continental (range 36-48C°)
5 Extremely continental (range over 48C°)

Duration of wet and dry seasons (for areas 30 and 31 only)

a All months rainy (with over 50mm. rainfall)
b Rainy season predominant (8-11 months with over 50mm.)
c Rainy and dry seasons approx. equal (5-7 months with over 50mm.)
d Dry season predominant (1-4 months with over 50mm.)

FORESTS on 1:30 million series

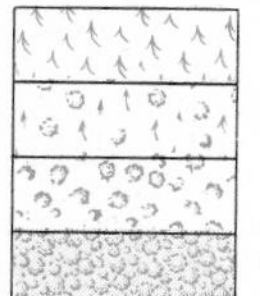

Coniferous

Mixed coniferous and deciduous

Deciduous

Tropical forest

AIR TRAFFIC on 1:15 million series
Categorized by the number of incoming flights per week

⑩ 25,600 and over
⑨ 12,800-25,599
⑧ 6,400-12,799
⑦ 3,200-6,399
⑥ 1,600-3,199
⑤ 800-1,599
④ 400-799
③ 200-399
② 100-199
① 50-99

PORTS on 1:15 million series
Categorized by tonnage handled per annum

▶ 50million and above
▶ 20.0-49.9million
▶ 5.0-19.9million
▶ 1.0-4.9million
▷ Other major ports (data not available)

MINERALS on 1:15 million series
Areas of extraction: iron coal lignite(lig) gas oil
Points of extraction: Ag (silver), Al (aluminum), Au (gold), Cu (copper), Pb (lead), Zn (zinc), Sn (tin), U (uranium), asbestos diamonds

Others of local importance sulphur nickel vanadium molybdenum manganese magnesium mica opals platinum potash

Introduction

The Penguin Atlas is based on a complete concept of map-making, developed by the Cartographic Department of the Oxford University Press. Traditionally, atlases have contained two sorts of maps: first, basic topographic maps with a restricted amount of information about relief, rivers, communications, cities and boundaries; and secondly, a much smaller number of specialized maps, usually on a very small scale, covering the whole world and giving quite separate pieces of information about such features as geology, climate, natural resources, land use and the pattern of human activities. The disadvantages of this approach are fairly obvious: each piece of specialized information is difficult to relate to the others, and because of the small scale of the special maps it is almost impossible to relate them to the basic topographic maps. This atlas uses a quite different approach.

The ideal atlas would have a simple series of maps, all on a uniform scale, each covering one part of the world, and each showing all the different types of information which the reader wanted to know. Technically, this is not possible; the maps would be too crowded to be readable. However, it is possible to put together selected elements of physical and human geography so as to obtain three main series of maps, which will together give much more information than traditional methods. That is what has been done in this atlas. There are three main series: one at the 1:30 million scale concerned with the physical environment, a second at the 1:15 million scale concerned with the human environment, and a third concerned with topography which is mapped mainly at either the 1:1·5 million scale (for the British Isles) or the 1:7·5 million scale (for the rest of the world). These, together with some ocean maps at 1:60 million, a selection of town plans at the 1:0·5 million scale and a few specialized world maps of the more traditional type, make up the contents of this atlas. Each of the three main series is concerned with one main set of topics, but certain features — boundaries, railways, urban areas, place names — recur on all of them, making cross-reference easy from one to the other.

Ocean Maps at 1:60 million, pages 1–5

The maps of the world's major oceans at the beginning of the atlas show how the features of the ocean floor are, by way of rifts and compressions, linked with volcanoes and earthquake regions.

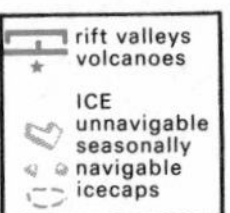

The circulation of currents and distribution of sea ice are shown, and important fishing areas are indicated by naming the main types of fish caught in each area.

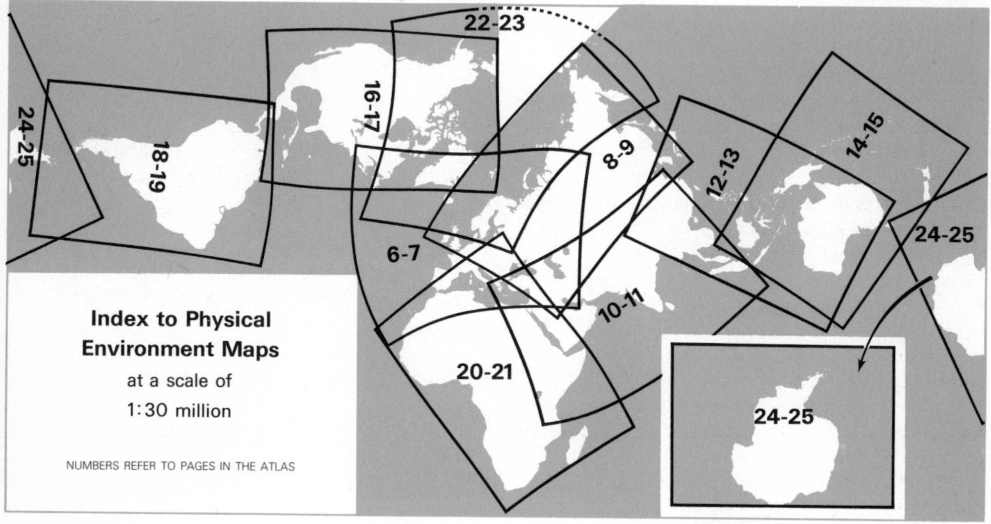

Index to Physical
Environment Maps

at a scale of
1:30 million

NUMBERS REFER TO PAGES IN THE ATLAS

These maps combine information on relief, climate and natural vegetation. Relief is shown by the same layer colouring scheme as in the Ocean Maps. Climate is given by means of superimposed information in the form of number-and-letter codes based on a classification by the late Professor David Linton, which in turn draws on work by the eminent German geographer, Professor Carl Troll. This is based fundamentally on the characteristics of summers and winters, the seasonal temperature range and the duration of the wet and dry seasons. Together, the relief and the climatic information help to explain the third main feature mapped in this series: selected elements of the natural vegetation.

Relief:
Heights and depths
in metres and feet.
Spot heights
in metres.

metres	feet
5000	16500
3000	9900
2000	6600
1000	3300
500	1650
200	660
sea level	
land depression	
200	660
3000	9900
4000	13200
5000	16500
6000	19800
7000	24750

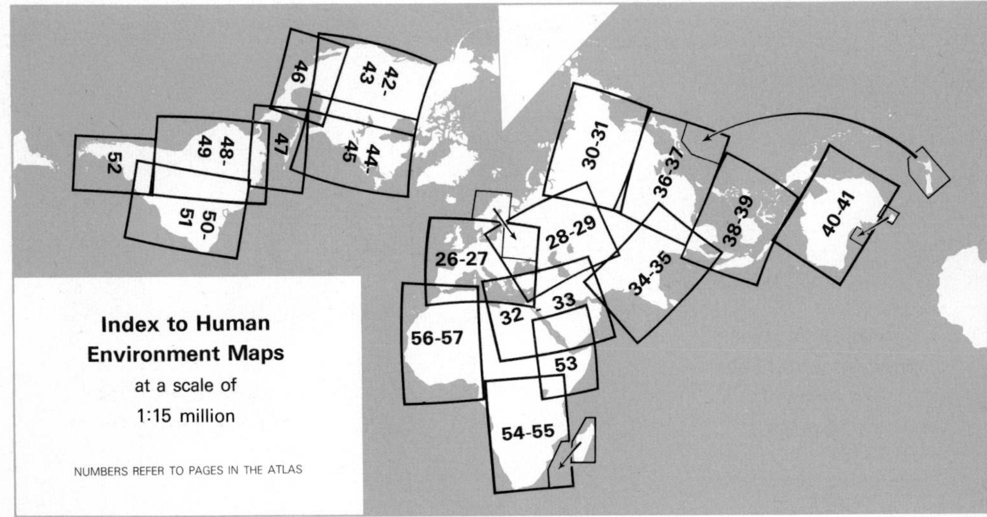

**Index to Human
Environment Maps**
at a scale of
1:15 million

NUMBERS REFER TO PAGES IN THE ATLAS

These maps cover most of the land areas of the world that are of economic significance. Together, they show aspects of man's occupation of the earth in a combined way that has never been achieved in traditional atlases.

Population is shown separately according to whether it is rural or urban. All cities with over 100,000 people have their populations shown in the form of 'stacked' yellow squares; the exact population for each city (including its suburbs) to the nearest 100,000 can be read off simply by counting the squares. The density of the rural population is shown by brown layer shading.

and airport traffic are all shown, as are occurrences of fourteen major minerals, plus additional mineral deposits of local significance. Again, basic topographic information forms the background.

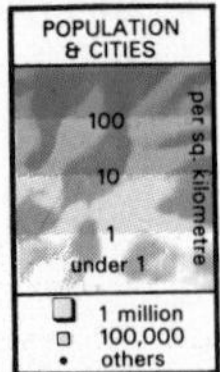

Land use and vegetation are shown by symbols. Forests and farm areas are given green symbols, while the areas of little use to man are shown in other appropriate colours. Roads, railways, port

x

Topographic Maps at scales of 1 :1·5 million, 1 :4 million and 1 :7·5 million, pages 58–101

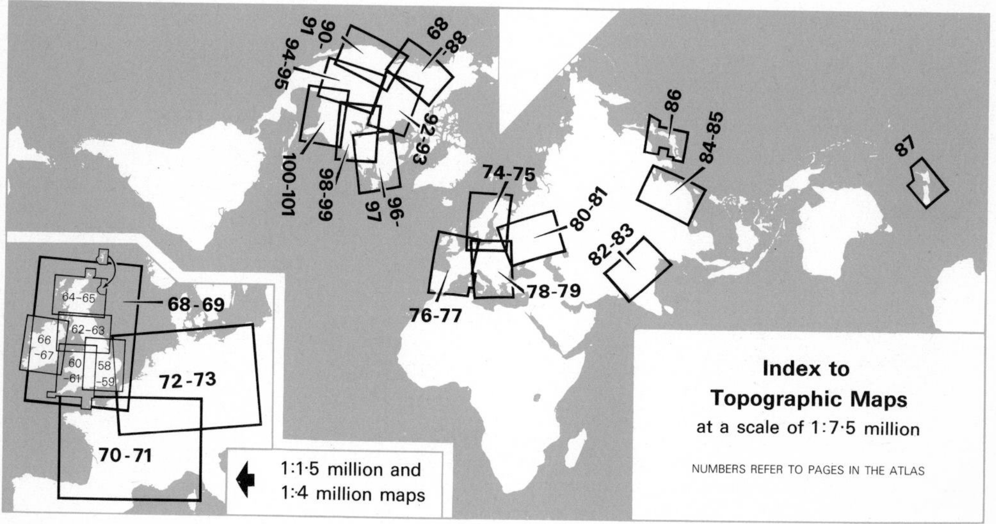

Index to
Topographic Maps
at a scale of 1:7·5 million

NUMBERS REFER TO PAGES IN THE ATLAS

1:1·5 million and
1:4 million maps

These are more conventional topographic maps covering the more densely populated parts of the world. In order to provide as much useful information as possible, the coverage and scale vary according to the density of population and the likely interest of the reader. Thus the British Isles are covered completely at the large scale of 1 :1·5 million; adjacent western and central Europe are covered at 1 :4 million; the other populous parts of the world are shown at 1 :7·5 million, with North America receiving the fullest coverage. The information on these maps (some of which is also reproduced as a basis for the other series) includes relief shown by layer shading; cities graded by size; railways, roads and airports.

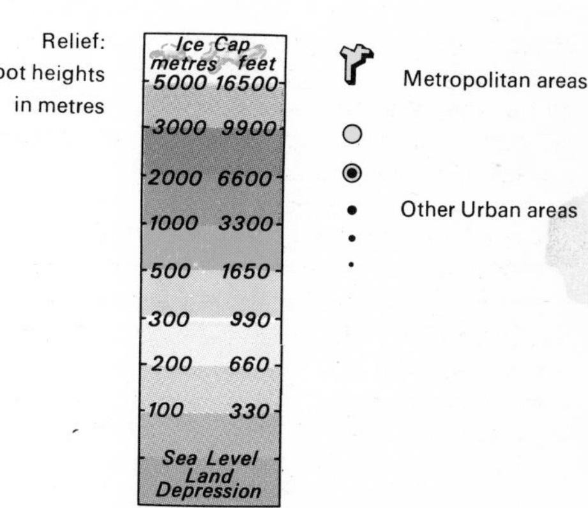

Relief:		
Spot heights in metres		

Ice Cap

metres	feet
5000	16500
3000	9900
2000	6600
1000	3300
500	1650
300	990
200	660
100	330

Sea Level
Land
Depression

Metropolitan areas

Other Urban areas

World Maps at 1 :90 million, pages 102–111
These maps show some of the critical factors affecting world development today – resources of minerals and power, population density and growth, nutrition patterns and communications. They are included here because of the importance of showing this information in a series of world-wide maps, where relationships between different parts of the world may be understood at a glance.

Urban Maps at 1 :0·5 million, pages 112–128
These cover some of the major cities and agglomerations of the world including their suburbs. All have been produced in a uniform style with a division of urban land use into major categories—industrial, commercial, residential and recreational.

Peter Hall

Countries of the World - Capital Cities, Population, Area and Land Use

COUNTRIES	CAPITAL CITY	POPULATION OF COUNTRY (to nearest thousand) a	DENSITY (per sq. mile) a÷b	AREA (in sq. miles) b	APPROX. LAND USE PERCENTAGES† Arable & orchard	Permanent meadow & pasture	Forest & woodland	Waste, city areas etc.
Afars and Issas, French Terr. of	Djibouti	81,000	10.2	8,900	—	11.1	0.4	88.5
Afghanistan	Kābul	16,516,000	66	250,000	13.7	4.9	2.3	79.1
Albania	Tiranë	2,075,000	189	11,000	17.4	25.4	43.7	13.5
Algeria	Alger	13,349,000	14	952,000	3.0	16.1	1.3	79.6
Andorra	Andorra	19,000	100	190	n.a.	n.a.	n.a.	n.a.
Angola (Port.)	Luanda	5,430,000	11	481,000	0.7	23.3	34·6	41.4
Antilles (Neth.)	–	218,000	574	380	5.2	—	—	94.8
Argentina	Buenos Aires	23,983,000	22	1,080,000	7.0	42.6	25.2	25.2
Australia	Canberra	12,296,000	4.4	2,975,000	4.6	58.1	4.6	32.7
Austria	Wien	7,371,000	230	32,000	20.6	26.9	37.9	14·6
Bahamas (U.K.)	Nassau	195,000	44	4,404	1.1	0.1	28.4	70.4
Bahrain	Al Manāmah	207,000	900	230	n.a.	n.a.	n.a.	n.a.
Bangladesh	Dacca	75,000,000	1,360.5	55,126	64.0			17.1
Barbados	Bridgetown	254,000	1,530	166	60.5	9.3	—	30.2
Belgium	Bruxelles	9,646,000	804	12,000	30.7	23.6	19.7	26.0
Bermuda (U.K.)	Hamilton	52,000	2,480	21	4.0	4.0	60.0	32.0
Bolivia	La Paz	4,804,000	11.6	415,000	2.8	10.3	42.8	44.1
Botswana	Gaborone	629,000	2.0	275,000	0.3	72.2	1.7	25.8
Brazil	Brasilia	90,840,000	30	3,286,000	3.5	12.6	60.8	23.1
Bulgaria	Sofija	8,436,000	196	43,000	41.1	11.1	32.6	15.2
Burma	Rangoon	26,980,000	106	262,000	23.4	0.5	66.8	9.3
Burundi	Bujumbura	3,475,000	315	11,000	37.3	22.6	2.5	37.6
Cameroun	Yaoundé	5,680,000	31	183,000	30.2	6.9	27.7	35.2
Canada	Ottawa	21,089,000	5.5	3,852,000	4.2	2.1	44.4	49.3
Cape Verde Is. (Port.)	Praia	250,000	162	1,560	7.4	n.a.	0.2	n.a.
Central African Rep.	Bangui	1,518,000	6.4	238,000	9.4	0.2	11.8	78.5
Chad	Fort Lamy	3,510,000	7.7	496,000	5.5	35.0	12.0	47.5
Chile	Santiago	9,566,000	33	286,000	6.1	13.6	27.9	52.4
China	Beijing	740,000,000	197	3,759,000	11.2	18.2	7.9	62.7
Colombia	Bogotá	20,463,000	47	439,000	4.4	12.8	61.0	21.0
Comoro Arch. (Fr.)	Moroni	270,000	320	838	36.9	13.8	16.1	33.2
Congo	Brazzaville	880,000	6.6	132,000	1.8	n.a.	47.5	n.a.
Costa Rica	San José	1,695,000	85	20,000	12.3	18.2	58.8	10.7
Cuba	La Habana	8,250,000	188	44,000	17.2	34.0	26.1	22.7
Cyprus	Levkosia	630,000	175	3,600	46.7	10.0	18.5	24.8
Czechoslovakia	Praha	14,418,000	292	49,000	42.5	13.9	34.8	9.2
Dahomey	Cotonou	2,640,000	58	45,000	13.7	3.9	19.2	63.2
Denmark	København	4,910,000	288	17,000	62.9	7.5	9.3	20.3
Dominican Rep.	Santo Domingo	4,174,000	222	19,000	21.9	17.8	45.7	14.6
Ecuador	Quito	5,890,000	55	106,000	10.7	8.1	54.9	26.3
Egypt	Al Qāhirah	32,501,000	84	386,000	2.7	—	—	97.3
El Salvador	San Salvador	3,390,000	414	8,200	30.3	28.2	23.7	17.8
Equatorial Guinea	Santa Isabel	286,000	26	11,000	7.9	3.7	81.6	6.8
Ethiopia	Addis Abeba	24,769,000	65	395,000	10.3	56.4	7.3	26.0
Fiji	Suva	519,000	74	7,000	16.4	44.0	38.5	1.1
Finland	Helsinki	4,703,000	36	130,000	8.1	0.4	64.6	26.9
France	Paris	50,302,000	236	213,000	38.1	24.3	21.8	15.8
Gabon	Libreville	485,000	4.7	103,000	0.5	n.a.	74.7	n.a.
Gambia, The	Bathurst	375,000	93	4,000	17.7	35.4	3.0	43.9
Germany, East	Ost-Berlin	17,097,000	407	42,000	46.2	13.3	27.2	13.3
Germany, West	Bonn	60,842,000	633	96,000	33.4	23.5	29.0	14.1
Ghana	Accra	8,600,000	93	92,000	10.7	—	10.3	n.a.
Greece	Athinai	8,835,000	173	51,000	29.2	30.0	19.7	12.1
Greenland (Dan.)	Godthaab	47,000	—	840,000	—	—	—	100.0
Guadeloupe (Fr.)	Basse-Terre	323,000	468	690	29.2	9.0	32.6	29.2
Guatemala	Guatemala	5,014,000	118	42,000	13.5	5.3	44.4	36.8
Guiana, French	Cayenne	40,000	1.1	35,000	—	0.6	95.0	4.4
Guinea	Conakry	3,890,000	40	95,000	n.a.	n.a.	4.3	n.a.
Guyana	Georgetown	742,000	8.9	83,000	0.9	11.8	84.3	3.0
Haiti	Port-au-Prince	4,768,000	476	11,000	13.4	18.0	25.2	43.4
Honduras	Tegucigalpa	2,495,000	58	43,000	7.3	30.5	26.9	35.3
Honduras, British+	Belmopan	120,000	13	8,900	1.4	0.7	45.8	52.1
Hong Kong (U.K.)	Victoria	3,990,000	9,990	400	12.6	—	9.7	77.7
Hungary	Budapest	10,295,000	286	36,000	60.7	14.0	15.3	10.0
Iceland	Reykjavik	203,000	5.0	40,000	—	22.1	—	77.9
India	New Delhi	536,984,000	425	1,263,000	49.6	4.3	17.1	29.0
Indonesia	Djakarta	115,000,000	158	736,000	9.3	*	63.8	26.9
Iran	Tehrān	27,892,000	44	628,000	7.0	4.1	7.3	81.6
Iraq	Baghdād	8,840,000	51	172,000	16.7	9.5	4.3	69.5
Irish Republic	Dublin	2,921,000	108	27,000	18.0	49.0	2.8	30.2
Israel	Yerushalayim	2,822,000	354	8,000	19.9	33.9	4.6	41.6
Italy	Roma	53,170,000	458	116,000	50.8	17.1	20.2	11.9
Ivory Coast	Abidjan	4,195,000	33	124,000	6.4	n.a.	74.4	n.a.
Jamaica	Kingston	1,959,000	445	4,400	21.1	23.4	19.2	36.3
Japan	Tōkyō	102,321,000	723	143,000	16.2	2.6	68.7	12.5
Jordan	'Ammān	2,160,000	58	37,000	11.6	2.2	0.7	85.5
Kenya	Nairobi	10,506,000	47	220,000	2.9	6.7	2.9	85.5
Khmer Republic	Phnom Penh	6,701,000	96	70,000	16.2	n.a.	73.9	n.a.
Korea, North	P'yŏngyang	13,300,000	283	47,000	15.7	n.a.	74.4	n.a.
Korea, South	Sŏul	31,139,000	820	38,000	22.9	0.2	67.1	9.8
Kuwait	Al Kuwayt	570,000	98	5,800	—	—	n.a.	n.a.
Laos	Vientiane	2,893,000	32	90,000	3.4	3.4	59.3	33.9
Lebanon	Bayrūt	2,645,000	780	3,400	28.5	1.0	9.1	61.4
Leeward Is.	–	141,000	385	418	43.0	12.0	13.0	32.0
Lesotho	Maseru	930,000	77	12,000	11.7	82.2	—	6.1
Liberia	Monrovia	1,150,000	27	43,000	34.5	2.2	32.5	30.8
Libya	Ṭarābulus	1,869,000	2.8	679,000	1.9	8.0	0.2	89.9
Liechtenstein	Vaduz	21,000	334	62	12.5	43.7	25.0	18.8
Luxembourg	Luxembourg	337,000	337	1,000	26.7	24.7	33.2	15.4
Malagasy Rep.	Tananarive	6,643,000	29	230,000	4.9	52.0	21.7	21.4
Malawi	Lilongwe	4,398,000	119	37,000	10.7	3.4	8.8	77.1
Malaysia	Kuala Lumpur	10,583,000	82	128,000	18.9	n.a.	65.7	n.a.
Maldive Islands	Male	108,000	900	115	n.a.	n.a.	n.a.	n.a.
Mali	Bamako	4,881,000	10.5	465,000	1	n.a.	3.8	n.a.
Malta	Valletta	323,000	2,608	121	50.0	—	—	50.0
Martinique (Fr.)	Fort-de-France	332,000	795	420	29.1	18.2	24.5	28.2
Mauritania	Nouakchott	1,140,000	2.7	419,000	0.2	36.2	13.9	79.7
Mauritius	Port Louis	823,000	1,160	720	50.6	16.1	21.5	11.8
Mexico	Ciudad de México	48,933,000	64	760,000	12.1	40.1	22.1	25.7
Mongolia	Ulaanbaatar	1,240,000	2.0	604,000	2.3	n.a.	16.3	n.a.
Morocco	Rabat	15,050,000	88	171,000	17.7	17.2	12.0	53.1
Mozambique (Port.)	Lourenço Marques	7,376,000	25	298,000	3.4	56.2	24.8	15.6
Nepal	Kātmāndu	10,845,000	200	54,000	13.0	14.2	32.2	40.6
Netherlands	Amsterdam	12,873,000	990	13,000	28.8	38.3	8.6	24.3
New Caledonia (Fr.)	Nouméa	98,000	13.3	7,330	4.3	21.4	14.5	59.8
New Guinea and Papua (Austl.)	–	2,315,000	12.5	184,000	0.6	—	n.a.	n.a.
New Zealand	Wellington	2,777,000	27	104,000	3.0	47.8	23.2	26.0
Nicaragua	Managua	1,915,000	34	57,000	6.2	6.6	46.2	41.1
Niger	Niamey	3,909,000	8.5	459,000	11.8	2.3	12.3	73.6
Nigeria	Lagos	63,870,000	179	357,000	23.6	n.a.	34.2	n.a.
Norway	Oslo	3,851,000	32	125,000	2.6	0.5	21.7	75.2
Oman	Masqat	565,000	6.9	82,000	n.a.	n.a.	n.a.	n.a.
Pakistan	Islāmābād	58,490,000	188.4	310,403	17.6		1.6	78.5
Panama	Panamá	1,417,000	49	29,000	7.5	11.0	80.5	1.0
Paraguay	Asunción	2,303,000	14.6	157,000	2.2	24.3	51.0	22.5
Peru	Lima	13,172,000	27	496,000	2.0	21.7	67.7	8.6
Philippines	Quezon City	37,158,000	520	116,000	26.4	11.0	41.2	21.4
Poland	Warszawa	32,555,000	274	120,000	50.3	13.7	25.8	10.2
Portugal	Lisboa	9,560,000	281	34,000	49.2	6.0	28.1	16.7
Portuguese Guinea	Bissau	530,000	37	14,000	7.3	n.a.	6.3	n.a.
Puerto Rico (U.S.A.)	San Juan	2,754,000	800	3,400	30.4	35.3	13.3	21.0
Qatar	Ad Dawḥah	100,000	250	4,000	n.a.	n.a.	—	n.a.
Réunion (Fr.)	St.-Denis	436,000	448	970	24.7	8.0	38.2	29.1
Rhodesia	Salisbury	5,090,000	33	150,000	4.7	12.5	60.0	22.8
Romania	București	20,101,000	218	92,000	44.1	18.2	26.8	10.9
Rwanda	Kigali	3,500,000	350	10.000	37.8	33.0	5.9	23.3
São Tomé and Principe (Port.)	São Tomé	66,000	186	372	31.3	n.a.	—	n.a.
Saudi Arabia	Ar Riyād	7,200,000	7.8	927,000	0.2	37.7	0.8	61.3
Senegal	Dakar	3,780,000	49	76,000	28.0	n.a.	27.1	n.a.
Seychelles (U.K.)	Victoria	51,000	318	160	42.1	1.0	12.4	44.5
Sierre Leone	Freetown	2,512,000	87	28,000	51.1	30.7	4.2	14.0
Sikkim	Gangtok	162.000	57	2,818	n.a.	n.a.	n.a.	n.a.
Singapore	Singapore	2,017,000	9,000	244	22.4	—	20.7	56.9
Somali Rep.	Mogadisho	2,730,000	11	246,000	1.5	32.3	22.6	43.6
South Africa	Pretoria	19,618,000	41	472,000	9.9	74.0	1.3	14.8
South-West Africa	Windhoek	615,000	1.9	318,000	0.8	64.2	6.4	28.6
Spain	Madrid	32,949,000	167	195,000	40.8	28.1	23.0	8.1
Spanish Sahara	El Aaiún	63,000	0.6	105,000	n.a.	7.5	n.a.	n.a.
Sri Lanka	Colombo	12.240.000	490	25.000	28.6	0.2	50.7	20.5
Sudan	Al Khurtūm	15,186,000	15	967,000	2.8	9.6	36.5	51.1
Surinam (Neth.)	Paramaribo	389,000	7.1	55,000	0.3	—	45.0	19.9
Swaziland	Mbabane	410,000	61	6,700	14.5	73.4	7.4	4.7
Sweden	Stockholm	7,978,000	46	173,260	7.1	1.2	50.0	41.7
Switzerland	Bern	6,230,000	389	16,000	16.2	42.2	23.8	23.8
Syria	Dimashq	5,866,000	81	72,000	35.9	33.0	2.4	28.7
Taiwan	T'aipei	13,800,000	985	14,000	24.7	n.a.	70.9	n.a.
Tanzania	Dar es Salaam	12,926,000	32	362,000	12.7	36.9	37.6	12.8
Thailand	Krung Thep	34,738,000	175	198,000	21.9	—	52.8	25.3
Togo	Lomé	1.815.000	86	21,000	38.2	3.5	9.4	48.9
Tonga	Nuku'alofa	87,000	32	270	n.a.	n.a.	n.a.	n.a.
Trinidad and Tobago	Port of Spain	1,040,000	515	1,980	34.1	1.0	45.0	19.9
Tunisia	Tūnis	5,027,000	79	63,362	34.6	45.2	6.7	13.5
Turkey	Ankara	34,375,000	114	296,000	33.5	36.2	13.5	16.8
Uganda	Kampala	9,500,000	102	93,981	16.0	n.a.	7.0	n.a.
United Arab Emirates	–	135,000	4.2	32,000	n.a.	n.a.	n.a.	n.a.
Union of Soviet Socialist Republics	Moskva	240,000,000	27	8,648,000	10.3	16.6	40.6	32.5
United Kingdom	London	55,534,000	620	94,500	30.7	49.7	7.4	12.2
United States of America	Washington D.C.	203,216,000	57	3,554,000	19.8	27.4	32.2	20.6
Upper Volta	Ouagadougou	5,278,000	49	106,000	17.9	n.a.	7.3	n.a.
Uruguay	Montevideo	2,852,000	37	72,000	12.0	74.1	3.2	10.7
Venezuela	Caracas	10,035,000	28	352,000	5.7	18.3	52.6	23.4
Vietnam, North	Ha Noi	21,340,000	340	63,000	12.7	n.a.	49.8	n.a.
Vietnam, South	Sài Gòn	17,867,000	272	66,000	17.2	16.8	32.8	33.2
Windward Is.	–	384,000	464	826	33.9	3.0	36.2	26.9
Yemen	Ta'iz	5,000,000	67	75,000	n.a.	n.a.	0.8	n.a.
Yemen, D.R.	Madinet al-Shaab	1,220,000	20	62,000	6.9	31.3	8.9	58.9
Yugoslavia	Beograd	20,000,000	204	99,000	32.5	25.2	34.4	7.9
Zaire	Kinshasa	17,100,000	18	906,000	20.9	1.0	42.7	35.4
Zambia	Lusaka	4,208,000	14	290,000	2.6	43.8	50.0	3.6

* Included in other groups. — None. n.a. Not Available.

+ Now Belize

† Percentages are calculated from figures given in FAO Year-Book. They do not necessarily total 100 per cent. Water is included as waste land.

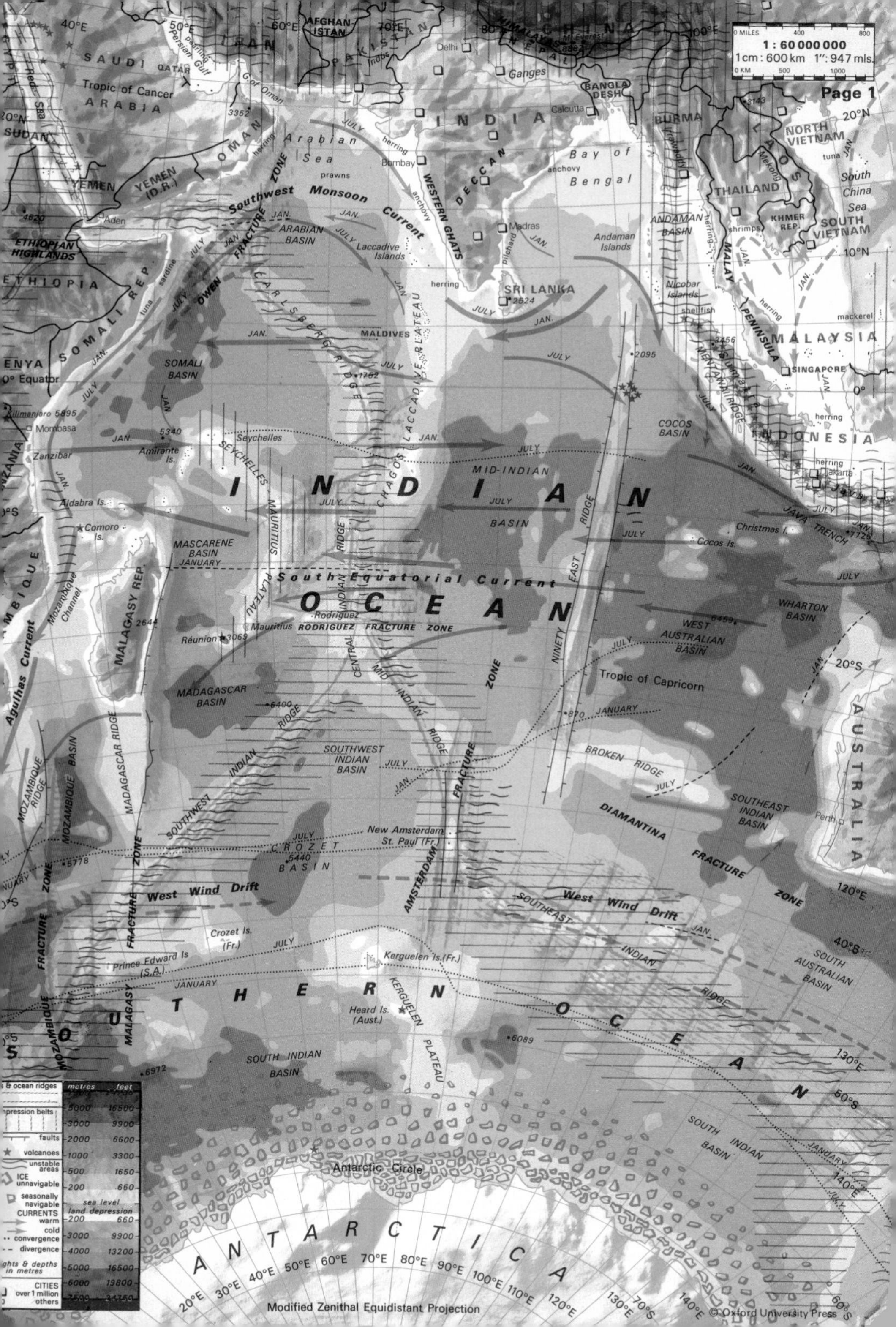

Page 1
1 : 60 000 000
1 cm : 600 km 1": 947 mls.
INDIAN OCEAN
SOUTHERN OCEAN
ANTARCTICA
South Equatorial Current
Southwest Monsoon Current
West Wind Drift
Agulhas Current
Tropic of Cancer
Tropic of Capricorn
Antarctic Circle
Equator
INDIA
ARABIA
AUSTRALIA
MALAYSIA
INDONESIA
SRI LANKA
MALAGASY REP.
SOMALI REP.
ETHIOPIA
Arabian Sea
Bay of Bengal
South China Sea
Persian Gulf
Mozambique Channel
ARABIAN BASIN
SOMALI BASIN
MASCARENE BASIN
MADAGASCAR BASIN
MID-INDIAN BASIN
WHARTON BASIN
WEST AUSTRALIAN BASIN
SOUTHWEST INDIAN BASIN
SOUTHEAST INDIAN BASIN
CROZET BASIN
SOUTH INDIAN BASIN
SOUTH AUSTRALIAN BASIN
NINETY EAST RIDGE
CARLSBERG RIDGE
CENTRAL INDIAN RIDGE
MID INDIAN RIDGE
SOUTHWEST INDIAN RIDGE
SOUTHEAST INDIAN RIDGE
BROKEN RIDGE
KERGUELEN PLATEAU
RODRIGUEZ FRACTURE ZONE
DIAMANTINA FRACTURE ZONE
AMSTERDAM FRACTURE ZONE
OWEN FRACTURE ZONE
JAVA TRENCH
Modified Zenithal Equidistant Projection
© Oxford University Press

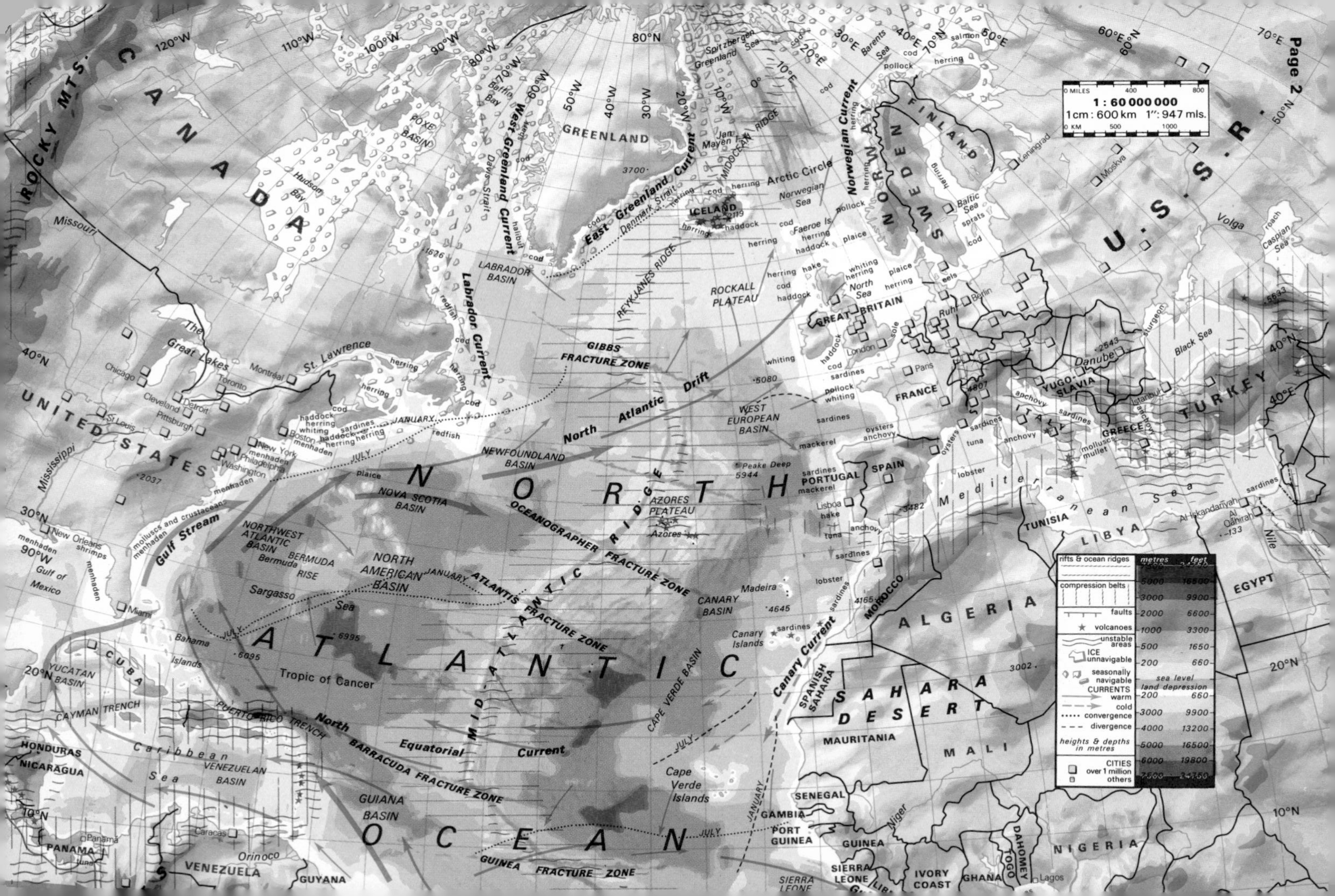
1 : 60 000 000
1cm : 600 km 1": 947 mls.
0 MILES 400 800
0 KM 500 1000
NORTH ATLANTIC OCEAN
CANADA
UNITED STATES
U.S.S.R.
GREENLAND
ICELAND
NORWAY
SWEDEN
FINLAND
GREAT BRITAIN
FRANCE
SPAIN
PORTUGAL
ITALY
YUGOSLAVIA
GREECE
TURKEY
MOROCCO
ALGERIA
TUNISIA
LIBYA
EGYPT
SPANISH SAHARA
MAURITANIA
MALI
SAHARA DESERT
SENEGAL
GAMBIA
PORT GUINEA
GUINEA
SIERRA LEONE
IVORY COAST
GHANA
TOGO
DAHOMEY
NIGERIA
CUBA
HONDURAS
NICARAGUA
PANAMA
VENEZUELA
GUYANA
ROCKY MTS.
Gulf Stream
North Atlantic Drift
Labrador Current
West Greenland Current
East Greenland Current
Norwegian Current
Canary Current
North Equatorial Current
MID-ATLANTIC RIDGE
GIBBS FRACTURE ZONE
OCEANOGRAPHER FRACTURE ZONE
ATLANTIS FRACTURE ZONE
BARRACUDA FRACTURE ZONE
GUINEA FRACTURE ZONE
REYKJANES RIDGE
MIDOCEAN RIDGE
LABRADOR BASIN
NEWFOUNDLAND BASIN
NOVA SCOTIA BASIN
NORTHWEST ATLANTIC BASIN
NORTH AMERICAN BASIN
BERMUDA RISE
WEST EUROPEAN BASIN
ROCKALL PLATEAU
AZORES PLATEAU
CANARY BASIN
CAPE VERDE BASIN
GUIANA BASIN
VENEZUELAN BASIN
YUCATAN BASIN
FOXE BASIN
CAYMAN TRENCH
PUERTO RICO TRENCH
Sargasso Sea
Tropic of Cancer
Arctic Circle
Mediterranean Sea
Black Sea
Caspian Sea
Baltic Sea
North Sea
Norwegian Sea
Barents Sea
Greenland Sea
Caribbean Sea
Gulf of Mexico
Hudson Bay
Baffin Bay
Davis Strait
Denmark Strait
Peake Deep 5944
rifts & ocean ridges
compression belts
faults
volcanoes
unstable areas
ICE unnavigable
seasonally navigable
CURRENTS warm
cold
convergence
divergence
heights & depths in metres
CITIES over 1 million
others
metres feet
5000 16500
3000 9900
2000 6600
1000 3300
500 1650
200 660
sea level
land depression
200 660
3000 9900
4000 13200
5000 16500
6000 19800
7500 24750

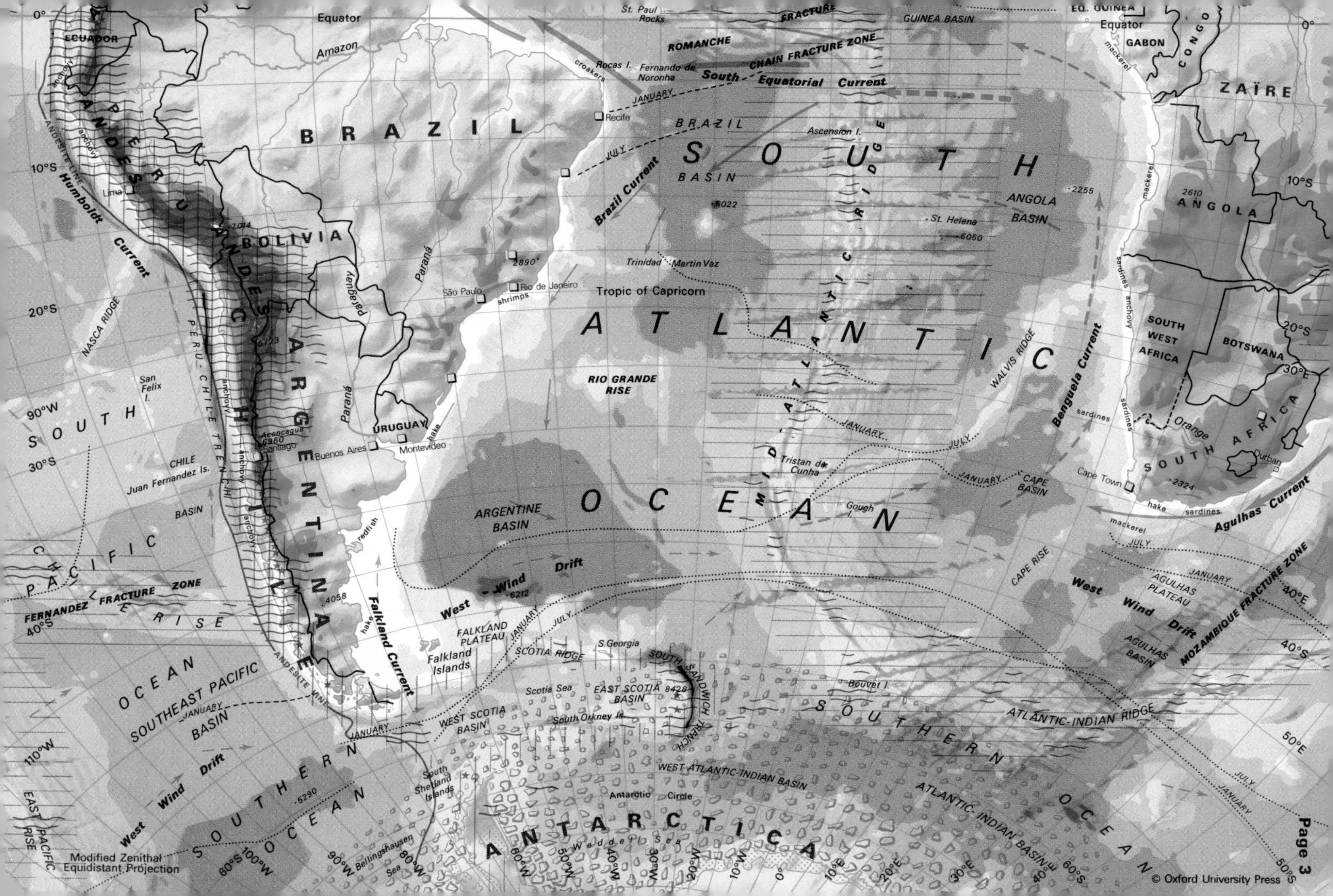

© Oxford University Press

ZAIRE

CONGO

GABON

EQ. GUINEA

Equator

ANGOLA

ZAMBIA

BOTSWANA

SOUTH WEST AFRICA

SOUTH AFRICA

Orange R.

mackerel

sardines anchovy

sardines

mackerel

sardines

hake sardines

Cape Town

CAPE BASIN

Benguela Current

Agulhas Current

Durban

AGULHAS PLATEAU

AGULHAS BASIN

MOZAMBIQUE FRACTURE ZONE

West Wind Drift

ATLANTIC-INDIAN RIDGE

ATLANTIC-INDIAN BASIN

SOUTHERN OCEAN

ATLANTIC-INDIAN BASIN

WALVIS RIDGE

ANGOLA BASIN

GUINEA BASIN

2610

2324

2255

St. Helena

Ascension I.

CAPE RISE

Gough I.

Tristan da Cunha

Bouvet I.

WEST ATLANTIC-INDIAN BASIN

Antarctic Circle

ANTARCTICA

JANUARY

JANUARY

JANUARY

JULY

JULY

ROMANCHE FRACTURE ZONE

CHAIN FRACTURE ZONE

St. Paul Rocks

Fernando de Noronha

Rocas I.

croakers

Recife

groupers

BRAZIL Current

BRAZIL

BRAZIL BASIN

MID-ATLANTIC RIDGE

6022

Trinidad

Martin Vaz

Rio de Janeiro

São Paulo

shrimps

2890'

São Paulo

Paraná

South Equatorial Current

SOUTH ATLANTIC OCEAN

6050

RIO GRANDE RISE

Tropic of Capricorn

ARGENTINE BASIN

West Wind Drift

6212

SOUTH SANDWICH TRENCH

8428

EAST SCOTIA BASIN

S. Georgia

South Orkney Is.

Scotia Sea

SCOTIA RIDGE

WEST SCOTIA BASIN

South Sandwich Islands

South Shetland Islands

Amazon

Equator

BOLIVIA

PARAGUAY

Paraguay

Paraná

URUGUAY

Montevideo

Buenos Aires

ARGENTINA

ANDES

CHILE

PERU

ECUADOR

anchovy

anchovy

Lima

ANDESITE LINE

Humboldt Current

San Felix

Juan Fernandez

NASCA RIDGE

PERU - CHILE TRENCH

4058

hake

anchovy

anchovy

Falkland Plateau

Falkland Islands

FALKLAND PLATEAU

Falkland Current

hake

Drake Passage

ANDESITE LINE

60°W

70°W

80°W

90°W

ESTE C.H

90°W

80°W

70°W

60°W

50°W

5290

SOUTH PACIFIC OCEAN

PACIFIC FRACTURE ZONE

FERNANDEZ FRACTURE ZONE

EAST PACIFIC RISE

CHILE RISE

SOUTHEAST PACIFIC BASIN

West Wind Drift

EAST PACIFIC RISE

Modified Zenithal Equidistant Projection

10°S

20°S

30°S

40°S

50°S

60°S

70°S

80°S

10°S

20°S

30°S

40°S

50°S

10°S

20°S

30°S

40°S

50°S

10°W

0°

10°E

20°E

30°E

40°E

50°E

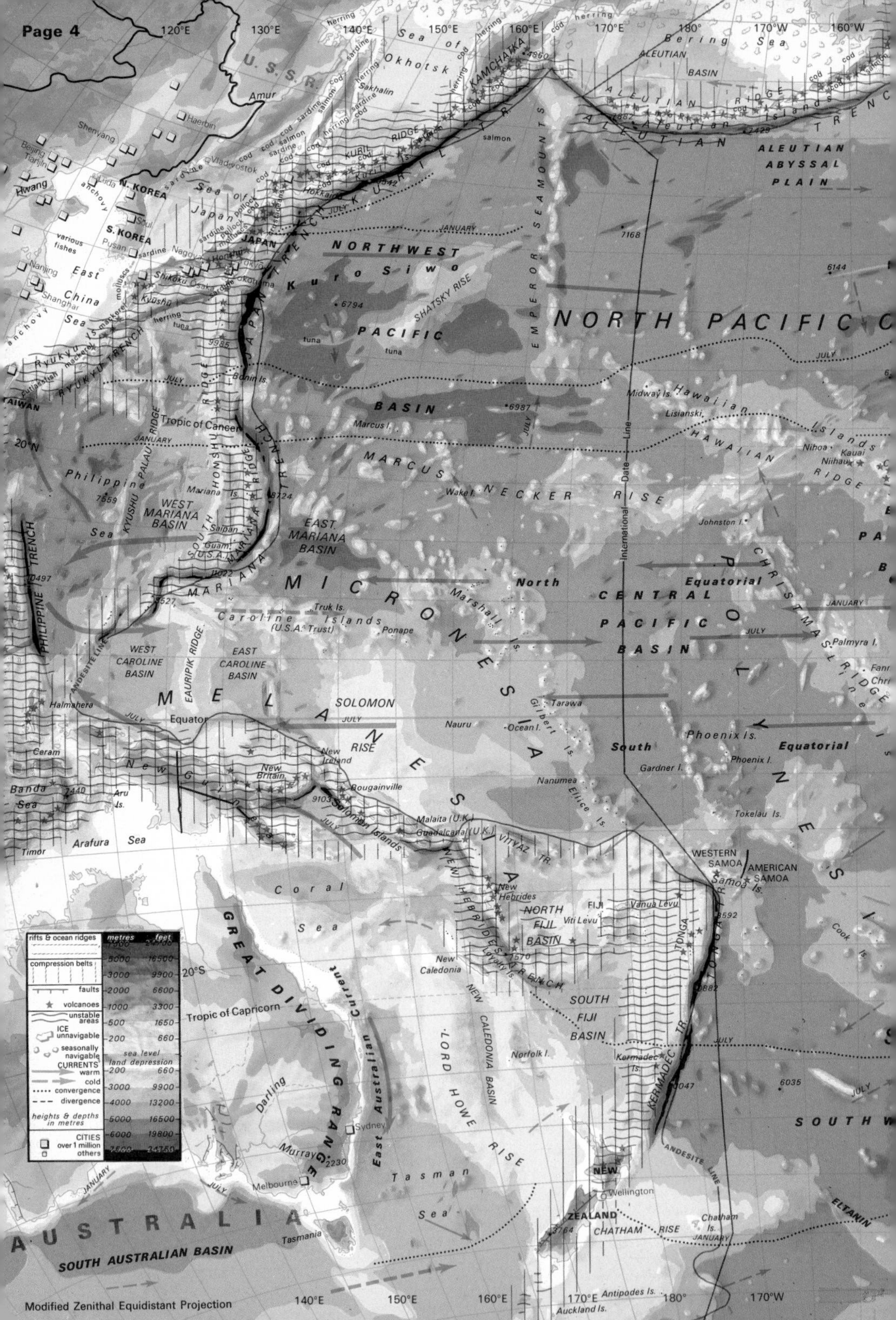
120°E
130°E
140°E
150°E
160°E
170°E
180°
170°W
160°W
U.S.S.R.
Amur
Haerbin
Shenyang
Beijing
Tianjin
Hwang
Luda
Vladivostok
N. KOREA
S. KOREA
Soul
Pusan
Nagoya
Osaka
Tokyo
Honshu
Shikoku
Kyushu
Hokkaido
Sakhalin
JAPAN
East China Sea
Shanghai
Nanjing
Sea of Japan
Sea of Okhotsk
Bering Sea
KAMCHATKA
4850
ALEUTIAN BASIN
ALEUTIAN RIDGE
Aleutian Islands
ALEUTIAN TRENCH
ALEUTIAN ABYSSAL PLAIN
7682
7428
KURIL RIDGE
KURIL TR.
Kuril Is.
JAPAN TRENCH
RYUKYU TRENCH
Ryukyu Is.
TAIWAN
herring
cod
sardine
salmon
pollock
molluscs
mackerel
anchovy
cutlassfish
tuna
various fishes
NORTHWEST PACIFIC BASIN
Kuro Siwo
SHATSKY RISE
6794
9985
EMPEROR SEAMOUNTS
7168
6144
NORTH PACIFIC
Bonin Is.
Tropic of Cancer
Marcus I.
6987
MARCUS NECKER RISE
Wake I.
Midway Is.
Lisianski
Hawaiian Islands
HAWAIIAN RIDGE
Nihoa
Kauai
Niihau
Johnston I.
International Date Line
20°N
Philippine Sea
7559
KYUSHU PALAU RIDGE
WEST MARIANA BASIN
SOUTH HONSHU RIDGE
MARIANA RIDGE
MARIANA TRENCH
Mariana Is.
8724
Saipan
Guam (U.S.A.)
EAST MARIANA BASIN
PHILIPPINE TRENCH
10497
8022
8527
MICRONESIA
North Equatorial
CENTRAL PACIFIC BASIN
Truk Is.
Caroline Islands (U.S.A. Trust)
Ponape
Marshall Is.
WEST CAROLINE BASIN
EAURIPIK RIDGE
EAST CAROLINE BASIN
ANDESITE LINE
POLYNESIA
CHRISTMAS RIDGE
Line Is.
Palmyra I.
MELANESIA
Halmahera
Equator
SOLOMON RISE
Nauru
Ocean I.
Tarawa
Gilbert Is.
South Equatorial
Phoenix Is.
Phoenix I.
Gardner I.
Ceram
New Guinea
New Britain
New Ireland
Bougainville
9103
Solomon Islands
Banda Sea
7440
Aru Is.
Timor
Arafura Sea
Nanumea
Ellice Is.
Malaita (U.K.)
Guadalcanal (U.K.)
Tokelau Is.
VITYAZ TR.
WESTERN SAMOA
AMERICAN SAMOA
Samoa Is.
Coral Sea
New Hebrides
NEW HEBRIDES TRENCH
NORTH FIJI BASIN
FIJI
Vanua Levu
Viti Levu
TONGA
TONGA TR.
8592
Cook Is.
Loyalty Is.
7570
New Caledonia
NEW CALEDONIA BASIN
SOUTH FIJI BASIN
Norfolk I.
Kermadec Is.
KERMADEC TR.
10047
6035
LORD HOWE RISE
GREAT DIVIDING RANGE
East Australian Current
Tropic of Capricorn
20°S
Darling
Murray
2230
Sydney
Melbourne
Tasman Sea
NEW ZEALAND
Wellington
3764
CHATHAM RISE
Chatham Is.
ELTANIN
SOUTH W
AUSTRALIA
Tasmania
SOUTH AUSTRALIAN BASIN
Antipodes Is.
Auckland Is.
JULY
JANUARY
rifts & ocean ridges
compression belts
faults
volcanoes
unstable areas
ICE unnavigable
seasonally navigable
CURRENTS
warm
cold
convergence
divergence
heights & depths in metres
CITIES
over 1 million
others
metres
feet
sea level
land depression
5000
16500
3000
9900
2000
6600
1000
3300
500
1650
200
660
4000
13200
6000
19800
Modified Zenithal Equidistant Projection

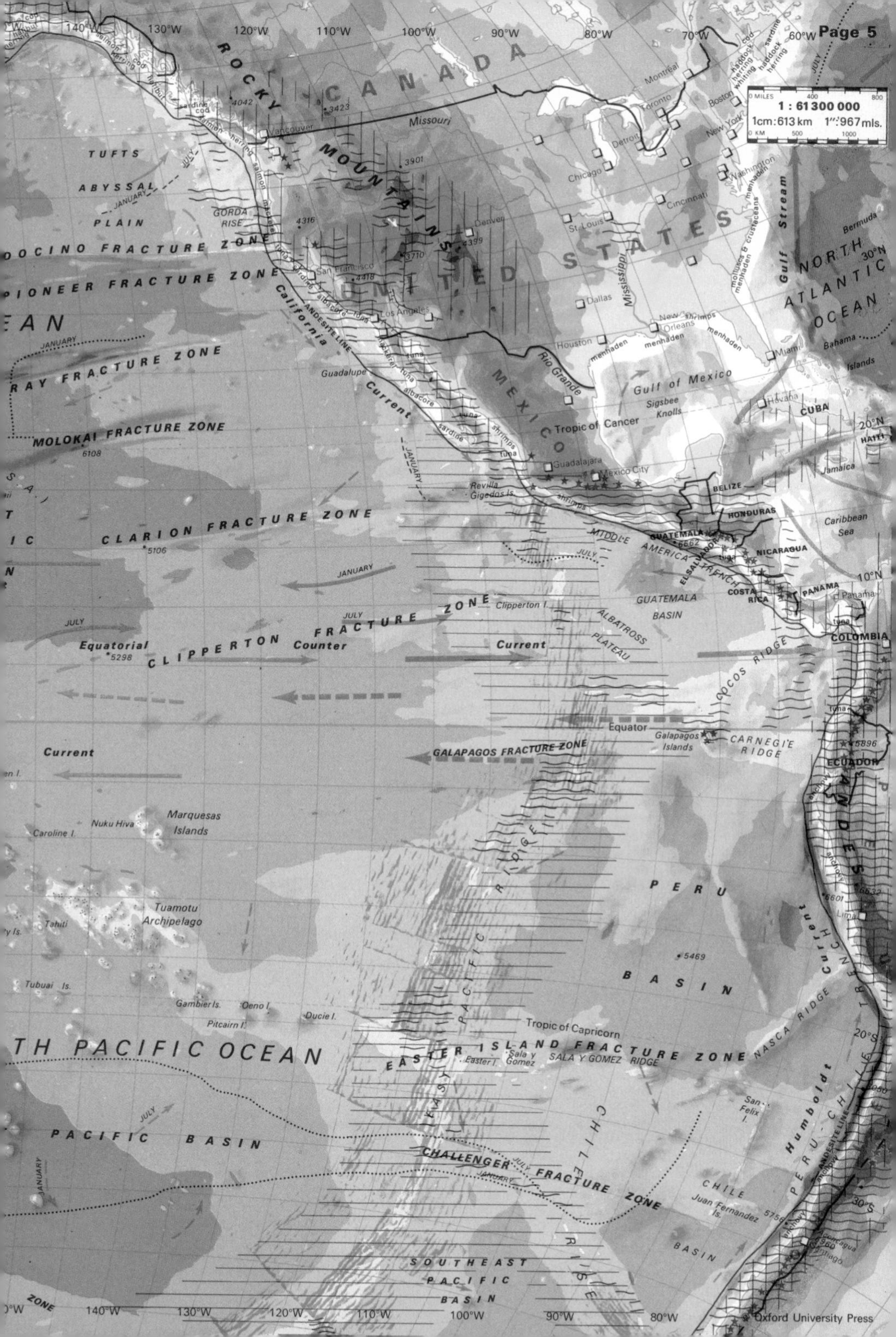

1 : 61 300 000
1cm:613 km   1":967 mls.

0 MILES   400   800

0 KM   500   1000

CANADA

ROCKY MOUNTAINS

UNITED STATES

Montreal
Toronto
Boston
New York
Detroit
Chicago
Washington
Cincinnati
St Louis
Philadelphia

Missouri
4042
3423
Vancouver
3901
Denver
3770
4399
3416
4416
San Francisco
4418
Los Angeles

Mississippi
Dallas
Houston
New Orleans

GORDA RISE
JANUARY
California Current
San Diego

ANDREAS LINE

Guadalupe
Albacore
Sardine
Tuna
shrimps

MEXICO

Rio Grande

Tropic of Cancer

Guadalajara
Mexico City
Revilla Gigedos Is.
shrimps

Gulf of Mexico
Sigsbee Knolls

NORTH
ATLANTIC
OCEAN

Gulf Stream

menhaden
shrimps
menhaden
menhaden

Bermuda

30°N

Miami
Havana
Bahama Islands

CUBA
HAITI
Jamaica

Caribbean Sea

20°N

TUFTS
ABYSSAL
PLAIN
JANUARY

MENDOCINO FRACTURE ZONE

PIONEER FRACTURE ZONE

OCEAN

MURRAY FRACTURE ZONE

MOLOKAI FRACTURE ZONE
6108

CLARION FRACTURE ZONE
5106

CLIPPERTON FRACTURE ZONE

Clipperton I.

JANUARY

JULY

JULY
Equatorial
5298
Counter
Current
Current

Current

ALBATROSS PLATEAU

MIDDLE AMERICA TRENCH
GUATEMALA
BELIZE
HONDURAS
NICARAGUA
COSTA RICA
PANAMA
Panama

GUATEMALA
BASIN

COCOS RIDGE

COLOMBIA

ECUADOR
45896

GALAPAGOS FRACTURE ZONE

Equator
Galapagos Islands
CARNEGIE RIDGE

Marquesas
Islands
Nuku Hiva
Caroline I.

Tahiti
Tuamotu
Archipelago
Tubuai Is.
Gambier Is.
Oeno I.
Pitcairn I.
Ducie I.

PACIFIC RIDGE

PERU

BASIN
5469

ANDES

Lima

NORTH PACIFIC OCEAN

EASTER ISLAND FRACTURE ZONE
Easter I.
Sala y Gomez
SALA Y GOMEZ RIDGE

Tropic of Capricorn

NASCA RIDGE

PERU-CHILE TRENCH

20°S

6601

JULY

PACIFIC BASIN
JANUARY

CHALLENGER FRACTURE ZONE
JANUARY

CHILE

San Felix

CHILE

BASIN
5745
Juan Fernandez Is.

Humboldt Current

30°S

SOUTHEAST
PACIFIC
BASIN

ZONE

140°W   130°W   120°W   110°W   100°W   90°W   80°W

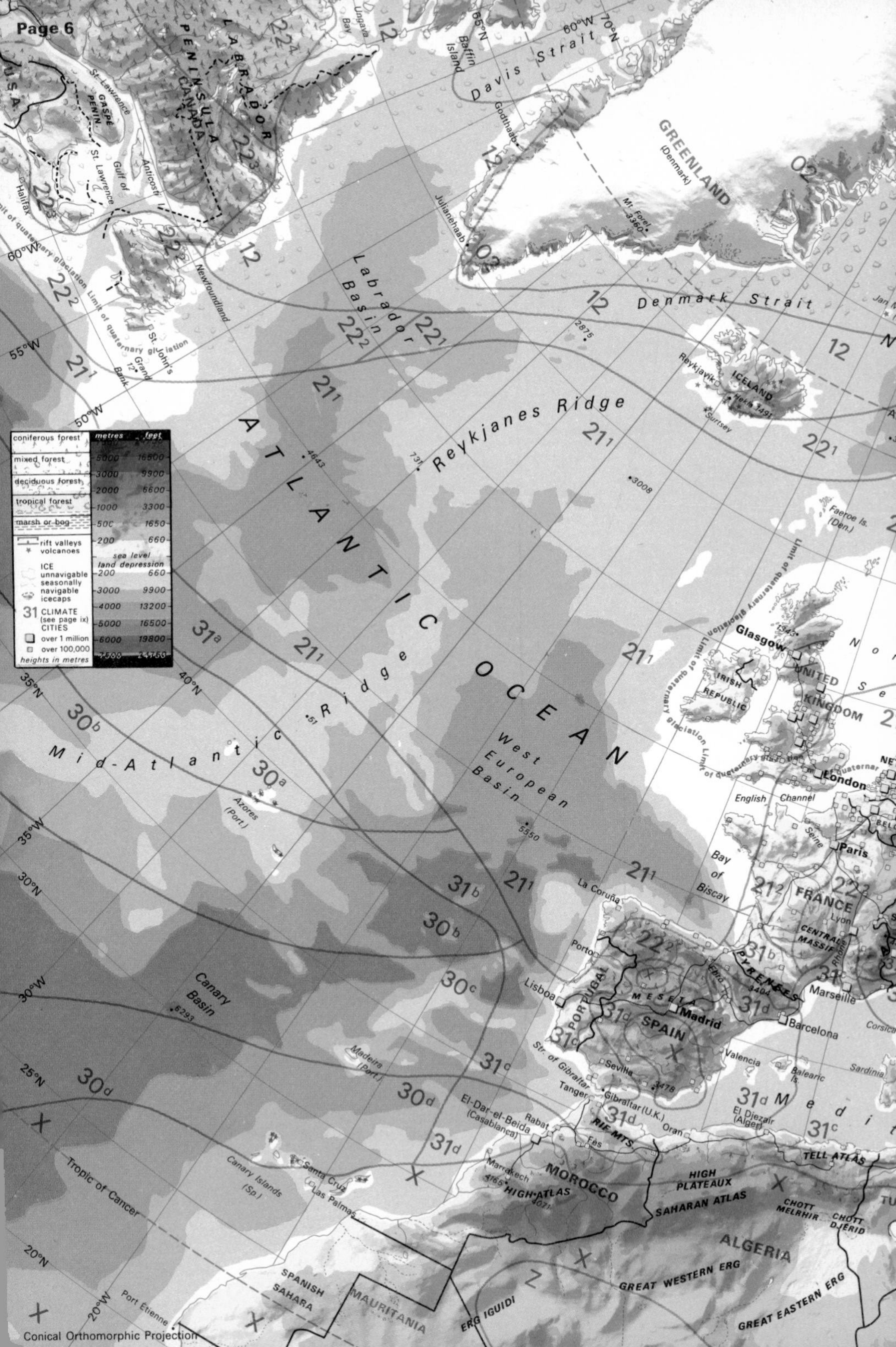

LABRADOR PENINSULA

GASPÉ PENIN.

CANADA

Ungava Bay

Baffin Island

Davis Strait

80°W 70°N

GREENLAND
(Denmark)

02

St. Lawrence

Gulf of St. Lawrence

Anticosti I.

St. John's

Godthåb

Mt. Forel
3360

Jakobshavn

12

Halifax

Limit of quaternary glaciation

Newfoundland

Grand Bank

Julianehaab

Denmark Strait

Jan Mayen I.

80°W

55°W

22

St. John's Bank

Limit of quaternary glaciation

21

50°W

Labrador Basin

22

22

21

Reykjanes Ridge

3875

3008

Reykjavík
ICELAND
Hekla 1491
Surtsey

12

22

N

A T L A N T I C

4643

731

21

Faeroe Is.
(Den.)

coniferous forest

mixed forest

deciduous forest

tropical forest

marsh or bog

rift valleys
volcanoes

ICE
unnavigable
seasonally
navigable
icecaps

31 CLIMATE
(see page ix)
CITIES
over 1 million
over 100,000

heights in metres

metres	feet
5000	16500
3000	9900
2000	6600
1000	3300
500	1650
200	660

sea level
land depression
200 660
3000 9900
4000 13200
5000 16500
6000 19800

21

21

West
European
Basin

O C E A N

North Sea

Glasgow

IRISH
REPUBLIC

UNITED
KINGDOM

2

Limit of quaternary glaciation

31a

40°N

51

Mid-Atlantic

30b

30a

Atlantic Ridge

Azores
(Port.)

31b

35°W

30b

30°N

5450

5150

21

London

English Channel

Seine

BELG.

NET.

Bay of
Biscay

21

Paris

FRANCE

22

La Coruña

Porto

22

Lyon

CENTRAL
MASSIF

30°W

30c

Canary
Basin

8251

31b

30c

Lisboa

PYRENEES

MESETA

Fès

31b

Marseille

Corsica

25°N

30d

Madeira
(Port.)

31d

Porto

SPAIN

Madrid

31d

Barcelona

Valencia

Balearic

Sardinia

El-Dar-el-Beida
(Casablanca)

Str. of Gibraltar

Sevilla
3478

Gibraltar (U.K.)

Tánger

Oran

31d Medit

31c

Rabat

Fès

RIF MTS.

El Djezair
(Alger)

TELL ATLAS

20°W

Canary Islands
(Sp.)

Santa Cruz

Las Palmas

31d

Marrakech
4165

MOROCCO

HIGH ATLAS
4021

HIGH
PLATEAUX

SAHARAN ATLAS

CHOTT
MELRHIR

CHOTT
DJERID

TU

Tropic of Cancer

X

X

X

ALGERIA

X

Port Etienne

20°N

SPANISH
SAHARA

MAURITANIA

X

ERG IGUIDI

GREAT WESTERN ERG

X

GREAT EASTERN ERG

Z

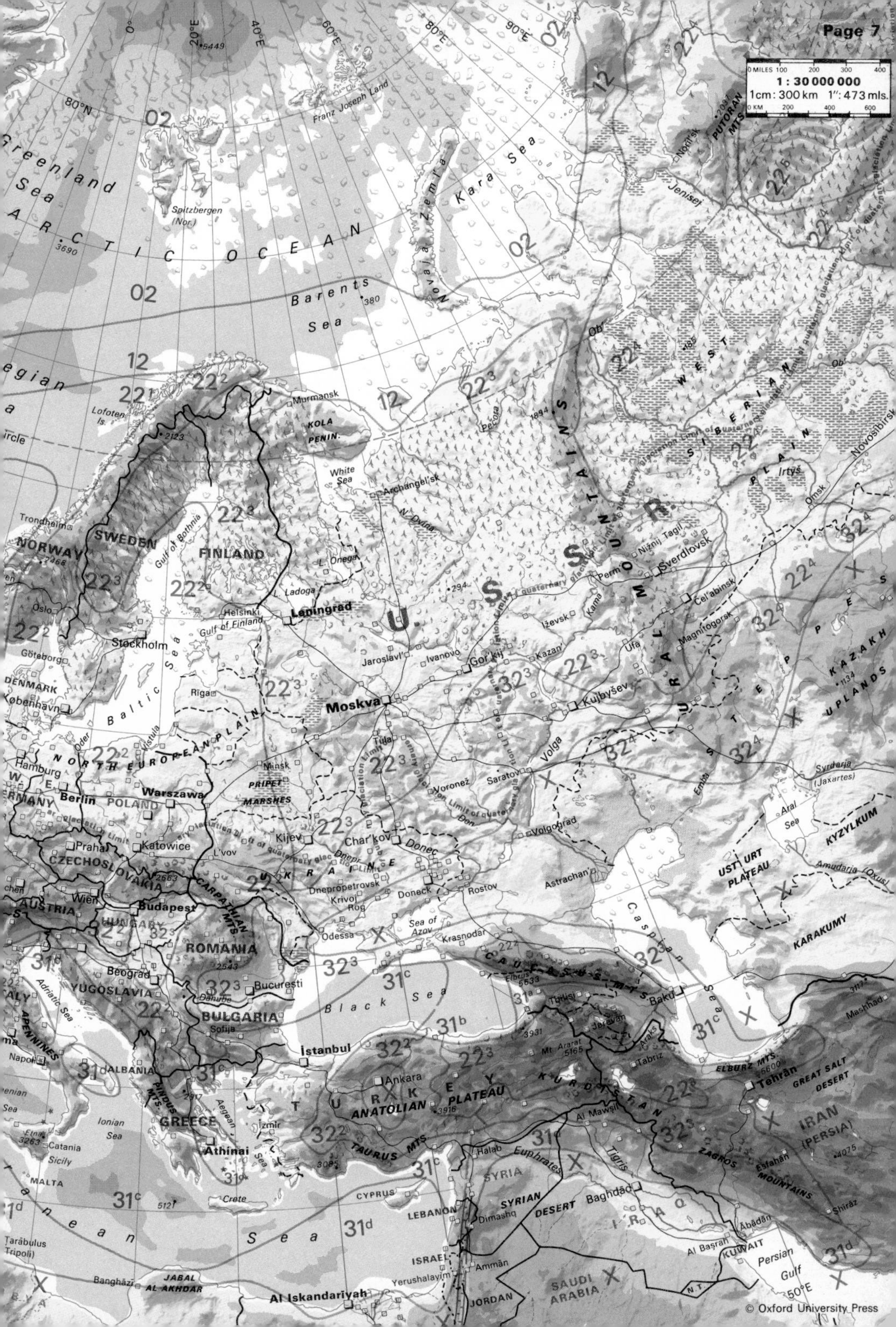

0 MILES 100   200   300   400
1 : 30 000 000
1cm : 300 km   1" : 473 mls.
0 KM 200   400   600

Greenland
Sea

ARCTIC OCEAN

Spitzbergen
(Nor.)
3690

Barents
Sea
380

Franz Joseph Land

Novaya Zemlya

Kara Sea

PUTORAN
MTS.

Jenisej

Ob

WEST

Ob
Irtyš

Omsk

Novosibirsk

egian

ircle

Trondheim
7466

NORWAY

Oslo

Göteborg

DENMARK
København

Hamburg

Berlin

Praha

CZECHOSLOVAKIA

Wien

AUSTRIA

YUGOSLAVIA

Beograd

ALY

APENNINES

Napoli

MALTA

Tarābulus
(Tripoli)

BYA

Lofoten
Is.
2123

SWEDEN

Gulf of Bothnia

Stockholm

Baltic Sea

Vistula

NORTH EUROPEAN PLAIN

POLAND

Warszawa

Katowice

L'vov

CARPATHIAN MTS.

HUNGARY

Budapest

ROMANIA
2543

Bucuresti

BULGARIA

Sofija

GREECE

Athinai

ALBANIA

Ionian
Sea

Etna
3263
Catania
Sicily

Crete
5121

Murmansk

KOLA
PENIN.

White
Sea

L. Onega

FINLAND

Helsinki

Gulf of Finland

Ladoga

Leningrad

Riga

Moskva

PRIPET
MARSHES

Minsk

Kijev

Dnepr

Char'kov

Krivoj
Rog

Dnepropetrovsk

Donbass

Doneck

Odessa

Krasnodar

Sea of
Azov

Rostov

Black Sea

İstanbul

Ankara

İzmir

ANATOLIAN PLATEAU

TURKEY

TAURUS MTS.

CYPRUS

LEBANON

ISRAEL
Yerushalayim

Al Iskandariyah

JABAL
AL AKHDAR

Banghāzī

Archangel'sk

N. Dvina

Pečora

Onega

1894

Jaroslavl'

Ivanovo

Gor'kij

Kazan'

Voronež

Don

Saratov

Volga

Volgograd

Astrachan

Caspian Sea

CAUCASUS MTS.
5633

Baku

5665
Mt. Ararat
5165

Tbilisi

Tabriz

ELBURZ MTS.
5600

Tehrān

GREAT SALT
DESERT

IRAN
(PERSIA)
4075

ZAGROS MOUNTAINS

Meshhed

Eşfahān

Shiraz

Halab
Euphrates

SYRIA

Dimashq

SYRIAN
DESERT

Baghdād

Tigris

KURDISTAN

Al Mawşil

IRAQ

Ammān

JORDAN

SAUDI
ARABIA

Al Başrah

Ābādān

KUWAIT

Persian
Gulf

U. S. S. R.

URAL MOUNTAINS

Nižnij Tagil

Sverdlovsk

Perm'

Kama

Iževsk

Ufa

Kujbyšev

Magnitogorsk

Čeljabinsk

WEST
SIBERIAN
PLAIN

STEPPES

KAZAKH
UPLANDS
1134

Syrdarja
(Jaxartes)

Aral
Sea

KYZYLKUM

USTJ URT
PLATEAU

Amudarja (Oxus)

KARAKUMY

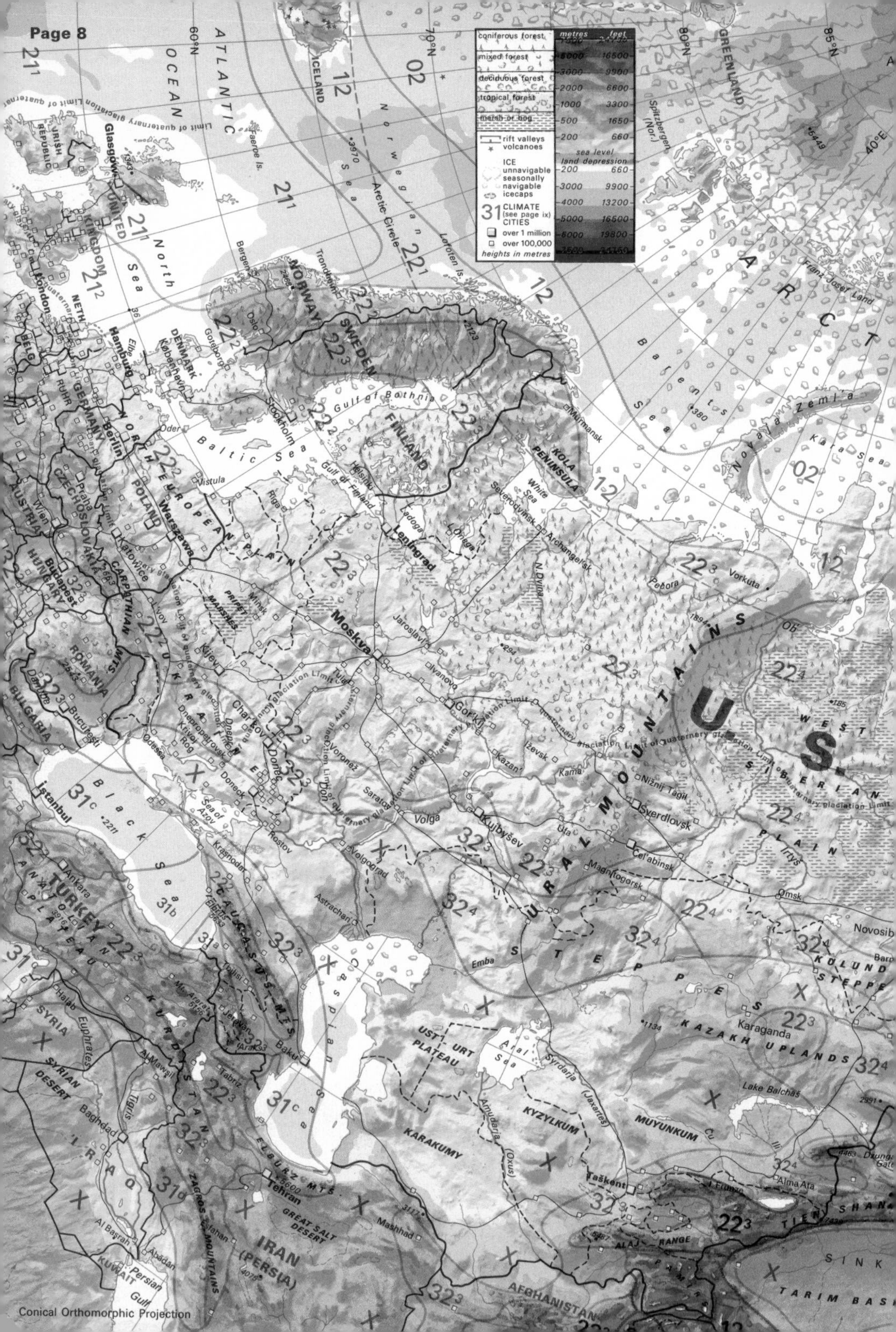

Conical Orthomorphic Projection

coniferous forest
mixed forest
deciduous forest
tropical forest
marsh or bog
rift valleys
volcanoes
ICE
unnavigable
seasonally navigable
icecaps
31 CLIMATE (see page ix)
CITIES
over 1 million
over 100,000
heights in metres
metres
feet
5000 16500
3000 9900
2000 6600
1000 3300
500 1650
200 660
sea level
land depression
200 660
3000 9900
4000 13200
5000 16500
6000 19800
ATLANTIC OCEAN
Norwegian Sea
Arctic Circle
North Sea
Baltic Sea
Gulf of Bothnia
Gulf of Finland
Barents Sea
Kara Sea
White Sea
Black Sea
Sea of Azov
Caspian Sea
Aral Sea
Persian Gulf
ICELAND
GREENLAND
Spitzbergen (Nor.)
Franz Josef Land
Novaja Zemlja
Faeroe Is.
Lofoten Is.
IRISH REPUBLIC
UNITED KINGDOM
NORWAY
SWEDEN
FINLAND
DENMARK
NETH.
BELG.
GERMANY
POLAND
CZECHOSLOVAKIA
AUSTRIA
HUNGARY
ROMANIA
BULGARIA
TURKEY
SYRIA
IRAQ
KUWAIT
IRAN (PERSIA)
AFGHANISTAN
KOLA PENINSULA
NORTH EUROPEAN PLAIN
PRIPET MARSHES
CARPATHIAN MTS
UKRAINE
URAL MOUNTAINS
WEST SIBERIAN PLAIN
CAUCASUS MTS
ANATOLIAN PLATEAU
KURDISTAN
ZAGROS MOUNTAINS
ELBURZ MTS
GREAT SALT DESERT
SYRIAN DESERT
UST URT PLATEAU
KARAKUMY
KYZYLKUM
MUYUNKUM
STEPPES
KAZAKH UPLANDS
KULUNDA STEPPE
ALAJ RANGE
TIEN SHAN
TARIM BASIN
Glasgow
London
Hamburg
Berlin
Oder
Elbe
Ruhr
Vistula
København
Göteborg
Oslo
Bergen
Trondheim
Stockholm
Helsinki
Riga
Leningrad
Ladoga
L. Onega
Murmansk
Severodvinsk
Archangel'sk
N. Dvina
Pečora
Vorkuta
Ob'
Warszawa
Praha
Wien
Katowice
Budapest
Bucuresti
Danube
Minsk
Kijev
Moskva
Jaroslavl'
Ivanovo
Gorkij
Kazan'
Kama
Izevsk
Nižnij Tagil
Sverdlovsk
Ufa
Čel'abinsk
Magnitogorsk
Omsk
Irtyš
Kujbyšev
Saratov
Volga
Volgograd
Astrachan'
Voronež
Tula
Charkov
Dnepr
Dnepropetrovsk
Krivoj Rog
Odessa
Doneck
Don
Rostov
Krasnodar
Istanbul
Ankara
Tbilisi
Jerevan
Mt Ararat
Baku
Tabriz
Tehran
Mashhad
Esfahan
Abadan
Al Basrah
Baghdad
Tigris
Euphrates
Halab
Al Mawsil
Emba
Karaganda
Lake Balchaš
Syrdarja (Jaxartes)
Amudarja (Oxus)
Taškent
Frunze
Alma Ata
Limit of quaternary glaciation

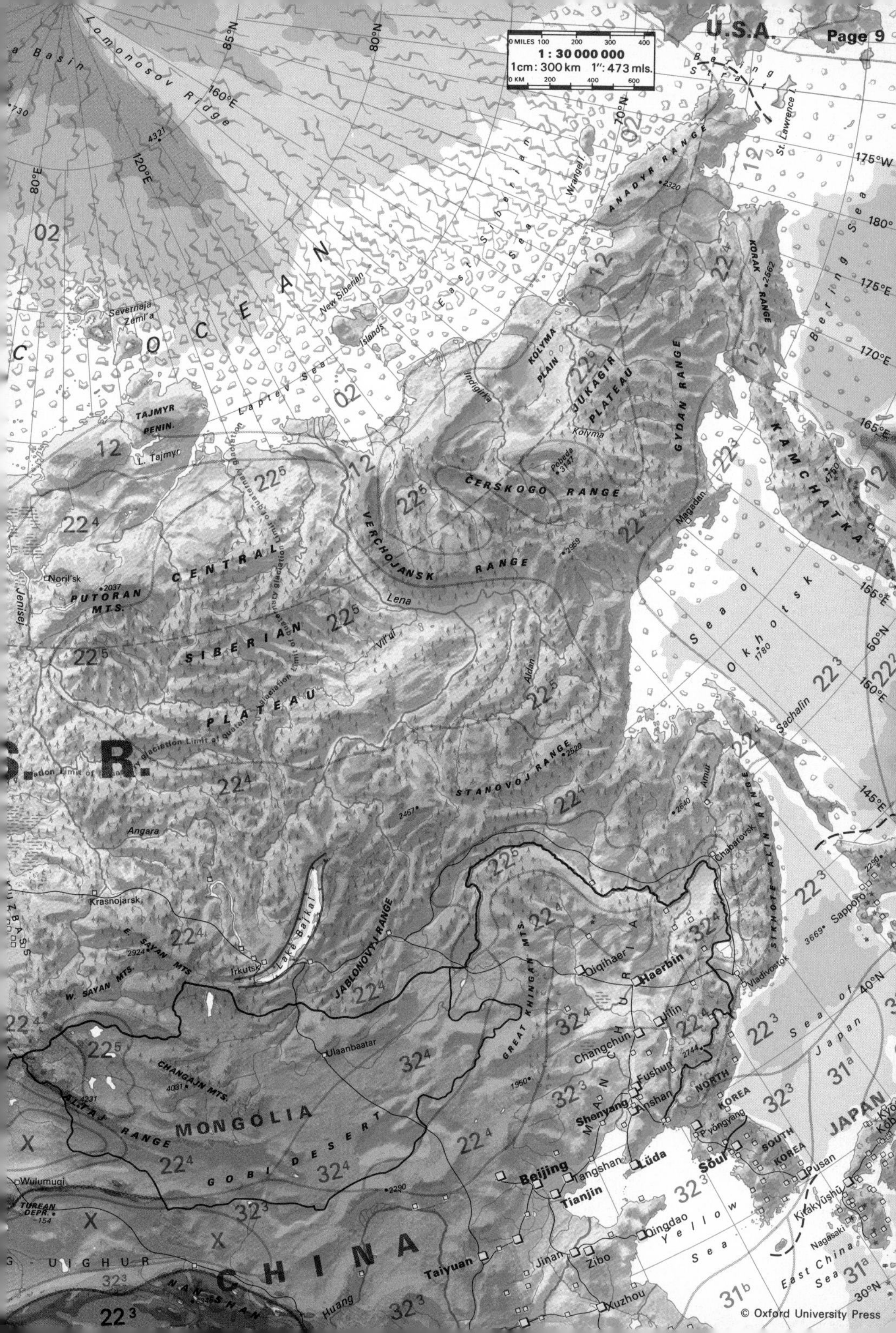

1 : 30 000 000
1cm : 300 km 1": 473 mls.

Lomonosov Ridge

Basin

C OCEAN

02

Severnaja Zeml'a

TAJMYR PENIN.

12

L. Tajmyr

22⁴

Noril'sk

CENTRAL

PUTORAN MTS.

SIBERIAN

PLATEAU

22⁵

U.S.S.R.

Angara

Krasnojarsk

E. SAYAN MTS

W. SAYAN MTS

UZBAS

22⁴

22⁵

ALTAJ RANGE

CHANGAJN MTS

MONGOLIA

TUREAN DEPR.

Wulumuqi

X

GOBI DESERT

UIGHUR

NAN SHAN

22³

CHINA

Taiyuan

Huang

Ulaanbaatar

Irkutsk

L. Baikal

JABLONOVYJ RANGE

STANOVOJ RANGE

VERCHOJANSK RANGE

Lena

Vitui

Aldan

New Siberian Islands

Laptev Sea

E S

KOLYMA PLAIN

Indigirka

Kolyma

ČERSKOGO RANGE

JUKAGIR PLATEAU

ANADYR RANGE

GYDAN RANGE

KORAK RANGE

KAMCHATKA

Magadan

22³

Sea of Okhotsk

Sachalin

22²

Chabarovsk

SICHOTE

Vladivostok

32⁴

22⁴

Qiqihaer

Haerbin

Jilin

Changchun

Fushun

22⁴

32⁴

NORTH KOREA

SOUTH KOREA

P'yongyang

Sŏul

Pusan

JAPAN

Sea of Japan

31³

40°N

32³

Shenyang

Anshan

Üda

32³

Beijing

Tianjin

Tangshan

32³

Qingdao

Jinan

Zibo

Yellow Sea

Xuzhou

31ᵇ

East China Sea 31ᵃ

30°N

© Oxford University Press

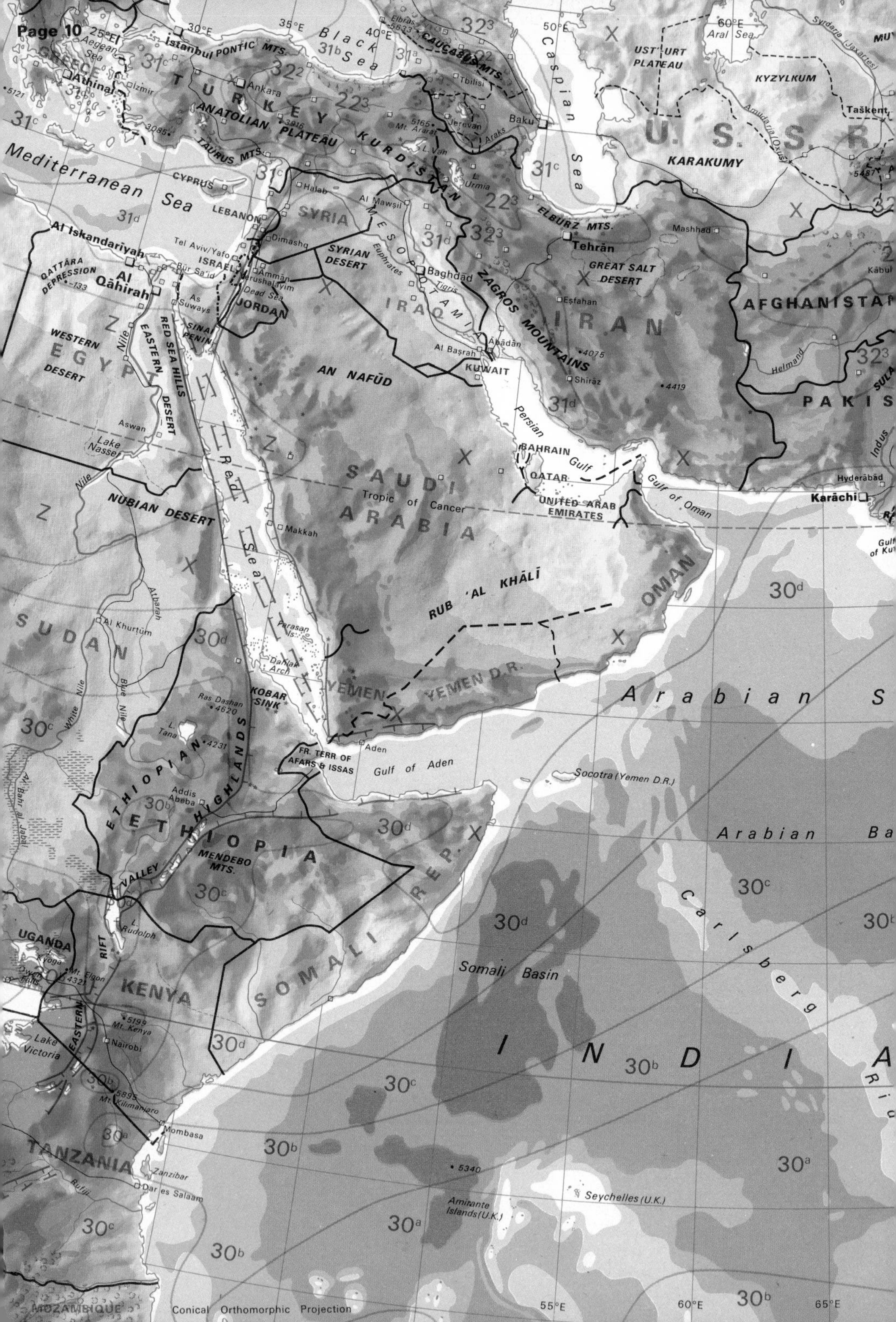
Black Sea
CAUCASUS MTS.
Elbrus 5633
Aral Sea
Syrdarja (Jaxartes)
UST'URT PLATEAU
KYZYLKUM
Taškent
Tbilisi
Caspian Sea
Baku
İstanbul
PONTIC MTS.
Aegean Sea
GREECE
Athinai
Izmir
Ankara
TURKEY
ANATOLIAN PLATEAU
KURDISTAN
Mt. Ararat
Jerevan
Araks
L. Van
L. Urmia
U.S.S.R.
Amudarja (Oxus)
KARAKUMY
TAURUS MTS.
Mediterranean Sea
CYPRUS
LEBANON
SYRIA
Halab
Al Mawşil
MESOPOTAMIA
ELBURZ MTS.
Mashhad
Tehrān
Dimashq
Tel Aviv/Yafo
ISRAEL
SYRIAN DESERT
Euphrates
Baghdād
Tigris
ZAGROS MOUNTAINS
GREAT SALT DESERT
Kābul
Al Iskandarīyah
QATTĀRA DEPRESSION
Al Qāhirah
Būr Sa'īd
'Ammān
Yerushalayim
Dead Sea
JORDAN
As Suways
SINAI PENIN.
IRAQ
Eşfahan
IRAN
AFGHANISTAN
Helmand
WESTERN DESERT
EGYPT
EASTERN DESERT
RED SEA HILLS
Nile
AN NAFŪD
Al Başrah
Ābādān
KUWAIT
Shīrāz
PAKISTAN
Aswan
Lake Nasser
Persian Gulf
BAHRAIN
QATAR
UNITED ARAB EMIRATES
Indus
Hyderābād
Karāchi
Gulf of Oman
Red Sea
SAUDI ARABIA
Tropic of Cancer
NUBIAN DESERT
Makkah
RUB 'AL KHĀLĪ
OMAN
Atbarah
Al Khurtūm
SUDAN
Farasan Is.
Dahlak Arch.
YEMEN
YEMEN D.R.
Arabian Sea
KOBAR SINK
Ras Dashan 4620
Blue Nile
White Nile
L. Tana
ETHIOPIAN HIGHLANDS
Aden
FR. TERR. OF AFARS & ISSAS
Gulf of Aden
Socotra (Yemen D.R.)
Addis Abeba
ETHIOPIA
MENDEBO MTS.
Arabian Basin
SOMALI REP.
Carlsberg Ridge
RIFT VALLEY
L. Rudolph
UGANDA
L. Kyoga
Owen Falls
Mt. Elgon 4321
KENYA
Somali Basin
Mt. Kenya 5199
Nairobi
Lake Victoria
EASTERN RIFT
INDIAN
Mt. Kilimanjaro 5895
Mombasa
TANZANIA
Zanzibar
Dar es Salaam
Rufiji
Amirante Islands (U.K.)
Seychelles (U.K.)
MOZAMBIQUE
Conical Orthomorphic Projection
30°E
35°E
40°E
50°E
55°E
60°E
65°E

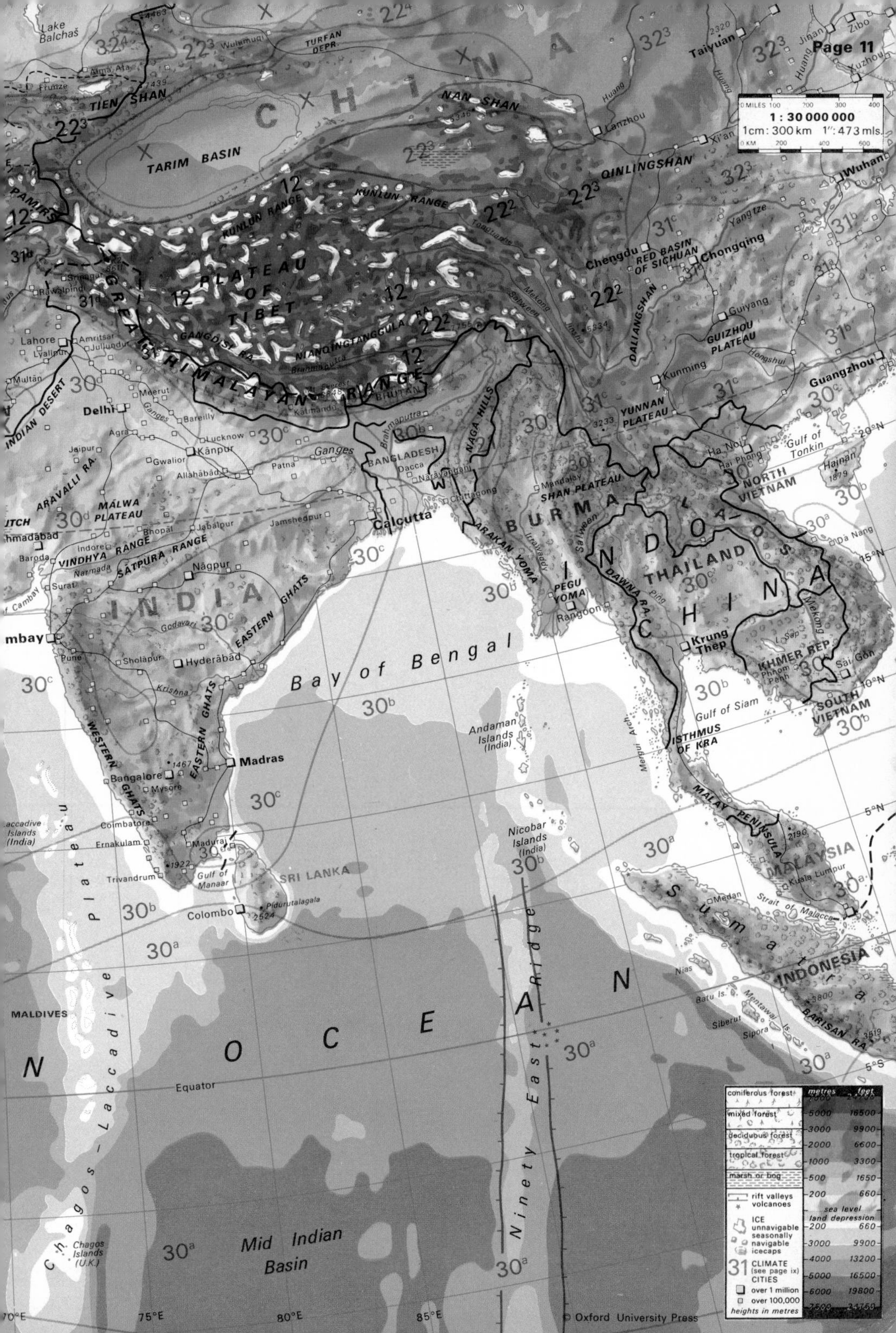
Page 11
1 : 30 000 000
1cm: 300 km 1'': 473 mls.
MILES 100 200 300 400
KM 200 400 600
CHINA
TARIM BASIN
TIEN SHAN
NAN SHAN
TURFAN DEPR.
QINLINGSHAN
KUNLUN RANGE
PLATEAU OF TIBET
GREAT HIMALAYAN RANGE
GANGDISE RA.
NIANQINGTANGGULA RA.
PAMIRS
RED BASIN OF SICHUAN
DALIANGSHAN
GUIZHOU PLATEAU
YUNNAN PLATEAU
INDIAN DESERT
ARAVALLI RA.
MALWA PLATEAU
VINDHYA RANGE
SATPURA RANGE
INDIA
EASTERN GHATS
WESTERN GHATS
BANGLADESH
NAGA HILLS
ARAKAN YOMA
PEGU YOMA
SHAN PLATEAU
BURMA
INDOCHINA
LAOS
THAILAND
DAWNA RA.
NORTH VIETNAM
SOUTH VIETNAM
KHMER REP.
ISTHMUS OF KRA
MALAY PENINSULA
MALAYSIA
Sumatra
INDONESIA
BARISAN RA.
SRI LANKA
Bay of Bengal
Gulf of Siam
Gulf of Tonkin
Gulf of Manaar
Strait of Malacca
Andaman Islands (India)
Nicobar Islands (India)
Laccadive Islands (India)
Chagos Islands (U.K.)
MALDIVES
Chagos–Laccadive Plateau
Ninety East Ridge
Mid Indian Basin
INDIAN OCEAN
Equator
Wulumuqi
Alma Ata
Frunze
Lake Balchaš
Lanzhou
Xi'an
Taiyuan
Jinan
Zibo
Xuzhou
Wuhan
Chengdu
Chongqing
Guiyang
Kunming
Guangzhou
Hainan
Ha Noi
Hai Phong
Da Nang
Mandalay
Rangoon
Krung Thep
Phnom Penh
Sai Gon
Kuala Lumpur
Medan
Nias
Siberut
Sipora
Batu Is.
Mentawai Is.
Mergui Arch.
Srinagar
Rawalpindi
Lahore
Amritsar
Jullundur
Lyallpur
Multan
Delhi
Meerut
Bareilly
Agra
Lucknow
Kanpur
Jaipur
Gwalior
Allahabad
Patna
Ganges
Brahmaputra
Dacca
Narayanganj
Chittagong
Calcutta
Jamshedpur
Jabalpur
Bhopal
Indore
Ahmadabad
Baroda
Surat
Nagpur
Narmada
Godavari
Krishna
Bombay
Pune
Sholapur
Hyderabad
Madras
Bangalore
Mysore
Coimbatore
Ernakulam
Madurai
Trivandrum
Colombo
Pidurutalagala
Katmandu
Mt Everest
BHUTAN
Irrawaddy
Salween
Mekong
Yangtze
Huang
Hongshui
Ping
L. Sap
20°N
15°N
10°N
5°N
5°S
70°E
75°E
80°E
85°E
© Oxford University Press
coniferous forest
mixed forest
deciduous forest
tropical forest
marsh or bog
rift valleys
volcanoes
ICE
unnavigable
seasonally navigable
icecaps
CLIMATE (see page ix)
CITIES
over 1 million
over 100,000
heights in metres
metres
feet
5000 16500
3000 9900
2000 6600
1000 3300
500 1650
200 660
sea level
land depression
200 660
3000 9900
4000 13200
5000 16500
6000 19800

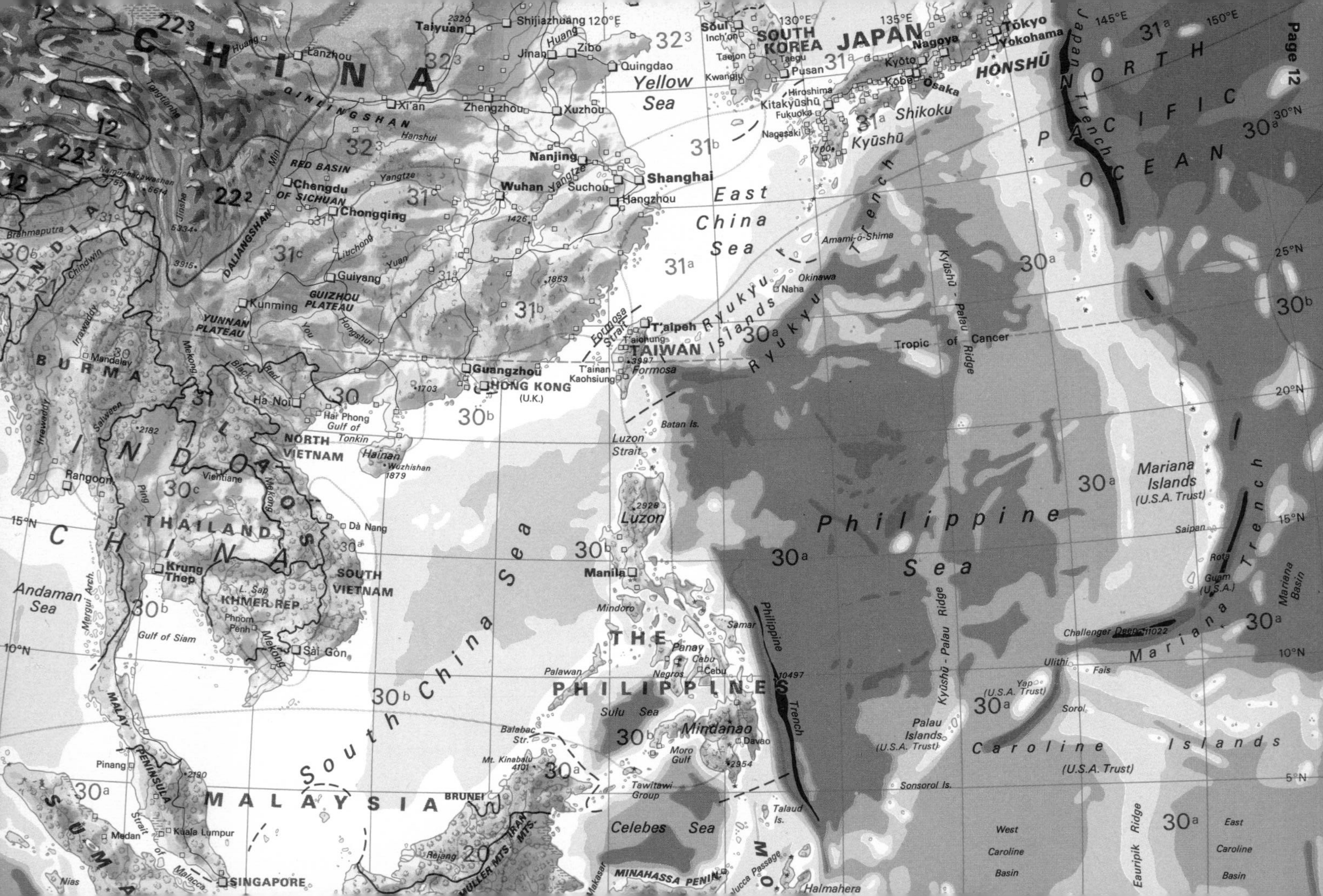
NORTH PACIFIC OCEAN
Japan Trench
Philippine Sea
Philippine Trench
Mariana Trench
Mariana Islands (U.S.A. Trust)
Mariana Basin
Challenger Deep
Saipan
Rota
Guam (U.S.A.)
Caroline Islands (U.S.A. Trust)
East Caroline Basin
West Caroline Basin
Eauripik Ridge
Kyūshū - Palau Ridge
Tropic of Cancer
Palau Islands (U.S.A. Trust)
Sonsorol Is.
Yap (U.S.A. Trust)
Ulithi
Sorol
Fais
Ryukyu Islands
Ryukyu Trench
Okinawa
Naha
Amami-ō-Shima
East China Sea
Yellow Sea
South China Sea
Celebes Sea
Sulu Sea
Andaman Sea
Gulf of Siam
Gulf of Tonkin
Luzon Strait
Formosa Strait
Strait of Malacca
Balabac Str.
Moro Gulf
JAPAN
HONSHŪ
Shikoku
Kyūshū
Tōkyo
Yokohama
Nagoya
Kyōto
Kōbe
Ōsaka
Hiroshima
Kitakyūshū
Fukuoka
Nagasaki
SOUTH KOREA
Sŏul
Inch'ŏn
Taejŏn
Taegu
Pusan
Kwangju
CHINA
Shanghai
Hangzhou
Suchou
Nanjing
Wuhan
Quingdao
Zibo
Jinan
Shijiazhuang
Xuzhou
Zhengzhou
Taiyuan
Xi'an
Lanzhou
Chengdu
Chongqing
Guiyang
Kunming
Guangzhou
HONG KONG (U.K.)
RED BASIN
OF SICHUAN
GUIZHOU PLATEAU
YUNNAN PLATEAU
QINLINGSHAN
DALIANGSHAN
Yangtze
Hanshui
Hongshui
Mekong
Salween
Irrawaddy
Chindwin
Brahmaputra
TAIWAN
T'aipeh
T'aichung
T'ainan
Kaohsiung
Formosa
Batan Is.
Hainan
Wuzhishan 1879
NORTH VIETNAM
SOUTH VIETNAM
Ha Noi
Hai Phong
Dà Nang
Sài Gòn
LAOS
Vientiane
THAILAND
Krung Thep
KHMER REP.
Phnom Penh
L. Sap
BURMA
Mandalay
Rangoon
Mergui Arch.
INDOCHINA
INDIA
THE PHILIPPINES
Luzon
Manila
Mindoro
Palawan
Panay
Negros
Cebu
Samar
Mindanao
Davao
Talaud Is.
Tawitawi Group
MALAYSIA
BRUNEI
Mt. Kinabalu 4101
Rejang
MULLER MTS.
IRAN MTS.
MALAY PENINSULA
Kuala Lumpur
SINGAPORE
Pinang
Medan
Nias
SUMATRA
MINAHASSA PENIN.
Halmahera
Makasar
Molucca Passage
150°E
145°E
135°E
130°E
120°E
30°N
25°N
20°N
15°N
10°N
5°N

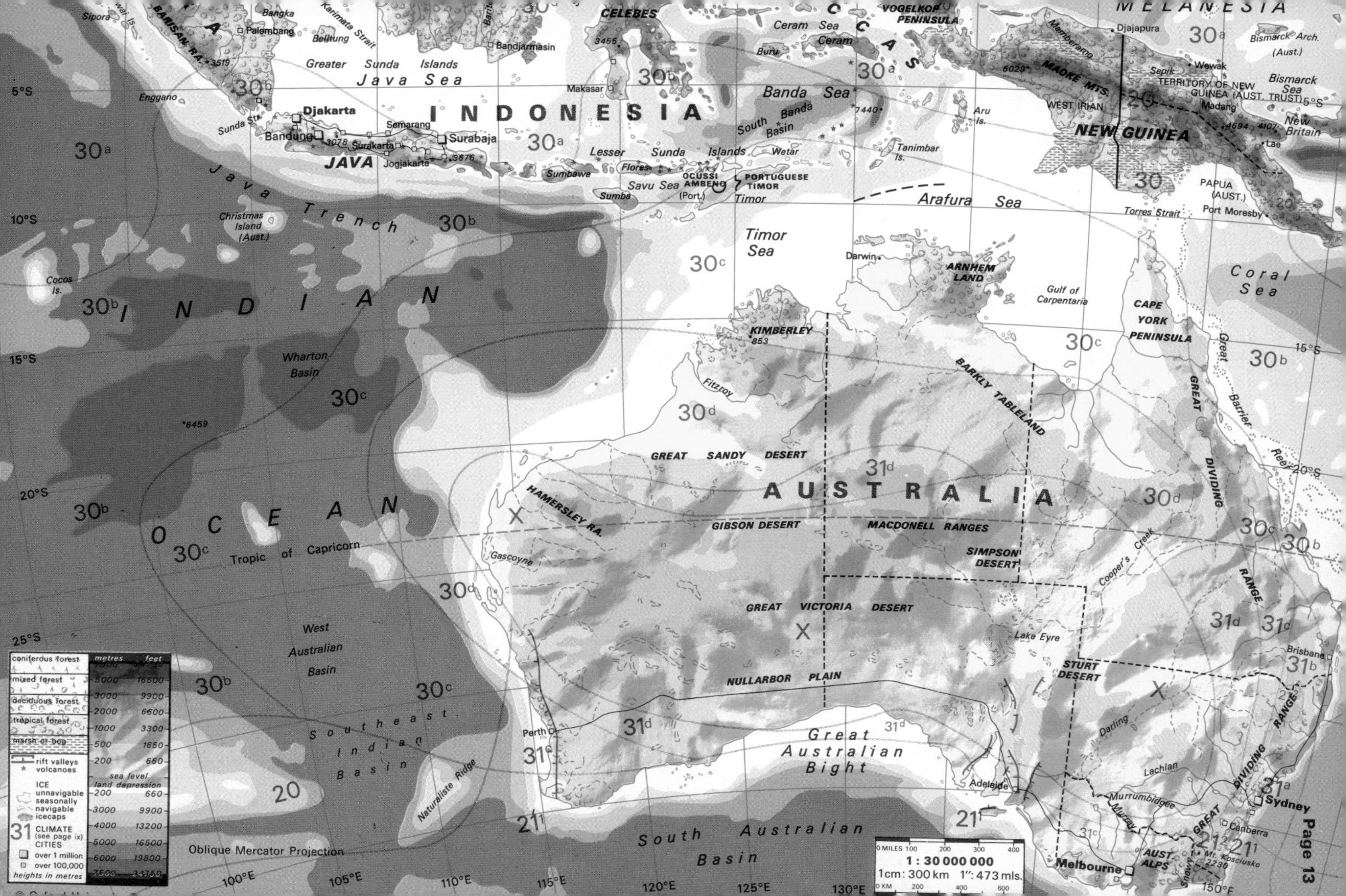
MELANESIA
INDONESIA
AUSTRALIA
INDIAN OCEAN
Java Sea
Greater Sunda Islands
Lesser Sunda Islands
Banda Sea
South Banda Basin
Ceram Sea
Ceram
Buru
Wetar
Tanimbar Is.
Aru Is.
Savu Sea
Sumba
Sumbawa
Flores
OCUSSI AMBENO (Port.)
PORTUGUESE TIMOR
Timor
Timor Sea
Arafura Sea
Java Trench
Christmas Island (Aust.)
Cocos Is.
Wharton Basin
West Australian Basin
Southeast Indian Basin
Naturaliste Ridge
South Australian Basin
Tropic of Capricorn
Sipora
Enggano
BARISAN RA.
Bangka
Palembang
Belitung
Karimata Strait
Sunda Str.
Djakarta
Bandung
Semarang
Surakarta
Jogjakarta
Surabaja
JAVA
Bandjarmasin
CELEBES
Makasar
VOGELKOP PENINSULA
Djajapura
Mamberamo
MAOKE MTS.
WEST IRIAN
NEW GUINEA
Sepik
Wewak
TERRITORY OF NEW GUINEA (AUST. TRUST)
Madang
Lae
Bismarck Arch. (Aust.)
Bismarck Sea
New Britain
PAPUA (AUST.)
Port Moresby
Torres Strait
Coral Sea
Great Barrier Reef
Gulf of Carpentaria
CAPE YORK PENINSULA
ARNHEM LAND
Darwin
KIMBERLEY
Fitzroy
BARKLY TABLELAND
GREAT SANDY DESERT
HAMERSLEY RA.
GIBSON DESERT
MACDONELL RANGES
SIMPSON DESERT
Gascoyne
GREAT VICTORIA DESERT
NULLARBOR PLAIN
Lake Eyre
Cooper's Creek
STURT DESERT
GREAT DIVIDING RANGE
Darling
Lachlan
Murrumbidgee
Murray
Snowy
AUST. ALPS
Mt. Kosciusko 2230
Brisbane
Sydney
Canberra
Melbourne
Adelaide
Perth
Great Australian Bight
5°S
10°S
15°S
20°S
25°S
100°E
105°E
110°E
115°E
120°E
125°E
130°E
150°E
coniferous forest
mixed forest
deciduous forest
tropical forest
marsh or bog
rift valleys
volcanoes
ICE
unnavigable
seasonally navigable
icecaps
31 CLIMATE (see page ix)
CITIES
over 1 million
over 100,000
heights in metres
metres feet
5000 16500
3000 9900
2000 6600
1000 3300
500 1650
200 660
sea level
land depression
200 660
3000 9900
4000 13200
5000 16500
6000 19800
Oblique Mercator Projection
1 : 30 000 000
1cm : 300 km 1'': 473 mls.

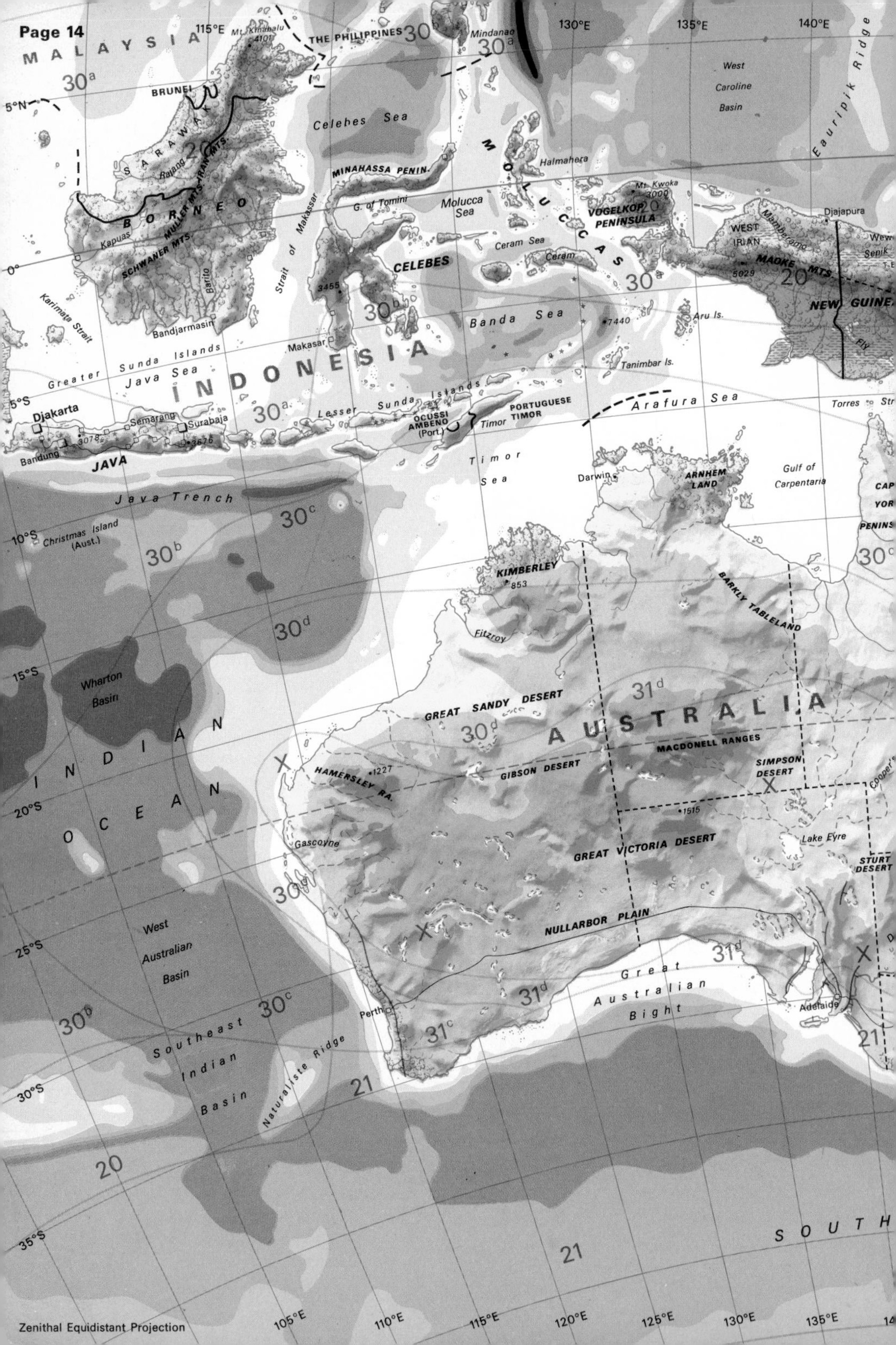

MALAYSIA

115°E   THE PHILIPPINES   30   Mindanao   30ᵃ   130°E   135°E   140°E

30ᵃ   Mt. Kinabalu 4101   5°N

BRUNEI   Celebes Sea   West Caroline Basin

SARAWAK   MINAHASSA PENIN.   MOLUCCAS   Halmahera

BORNEO   MULLER MTS   G. of Tomini   Molucca Sea   VOGELKOP PENINSULA   Mt. Kwoka 3000   20   Djajapura   Wewak Sepik   New Guinea

Kapuas   SCHWANER MTS.   CELEBES   Ceram Sea   Ceram   WEST IRIAN   MAOKE MTS.   20   0°

Karimata Strait   3455   Banda Sea   7440   Aru Is.   5029   NEW GUINEA

Bandjarmasin   Makasar   Tanimbar Is.   FLY

Greater Sunda Islands   Java Sea   INDONESIA   30ᵇ

Djakarta   Semarang   Surabaja   Lesser Sunda Islands   OCUSSI AMBENO (Port.)   Timor   PORTUGUESE TIMOR   Arafura Sea   Torres Str   5°S

Bandung   3078   3675   JAVA   30ᵃ   Timor Sea   Darwin   ARNHEM LAND   Gulf of Carpentaria   CAPE YORK PENINS

Java Trench   30ᶜ   KIMBERLEY   853   BARKLY TABLELAND   30ᵈ   10°S

Christmas Island (Aust.)   30ᵇ   Fitzroy

Wharton Basin   GREAT SANDY DESERT   30ᵈ   31ᵈ   AUSTRALIA   15°S

30ᵈ   HAMERSLEY RA.   1227   GIBSON DESERT   MACDONELL RANGES   SIMPSON DESERT   Cooper   20°S

INDIAN   Gascoyne   GREAT VICTORIA DESERT   1515   Lake Eyre   STURT DESERT

OCEAN   30ᶜ   West Australian Basin   NULLARBOR PLAIN   25°S

30ᵇ   30ᶜ   Southeast   Perth   31ᶜ   Great Australian Bight   31ᵈ   Adelaide   21

Indian   Naturaliste Ridge   31ᵈ   21

30°S   Basin   21

20   SOUTH   35°S

105°E   110°E   115°E   120°E   125°E   130°E   135°E   14

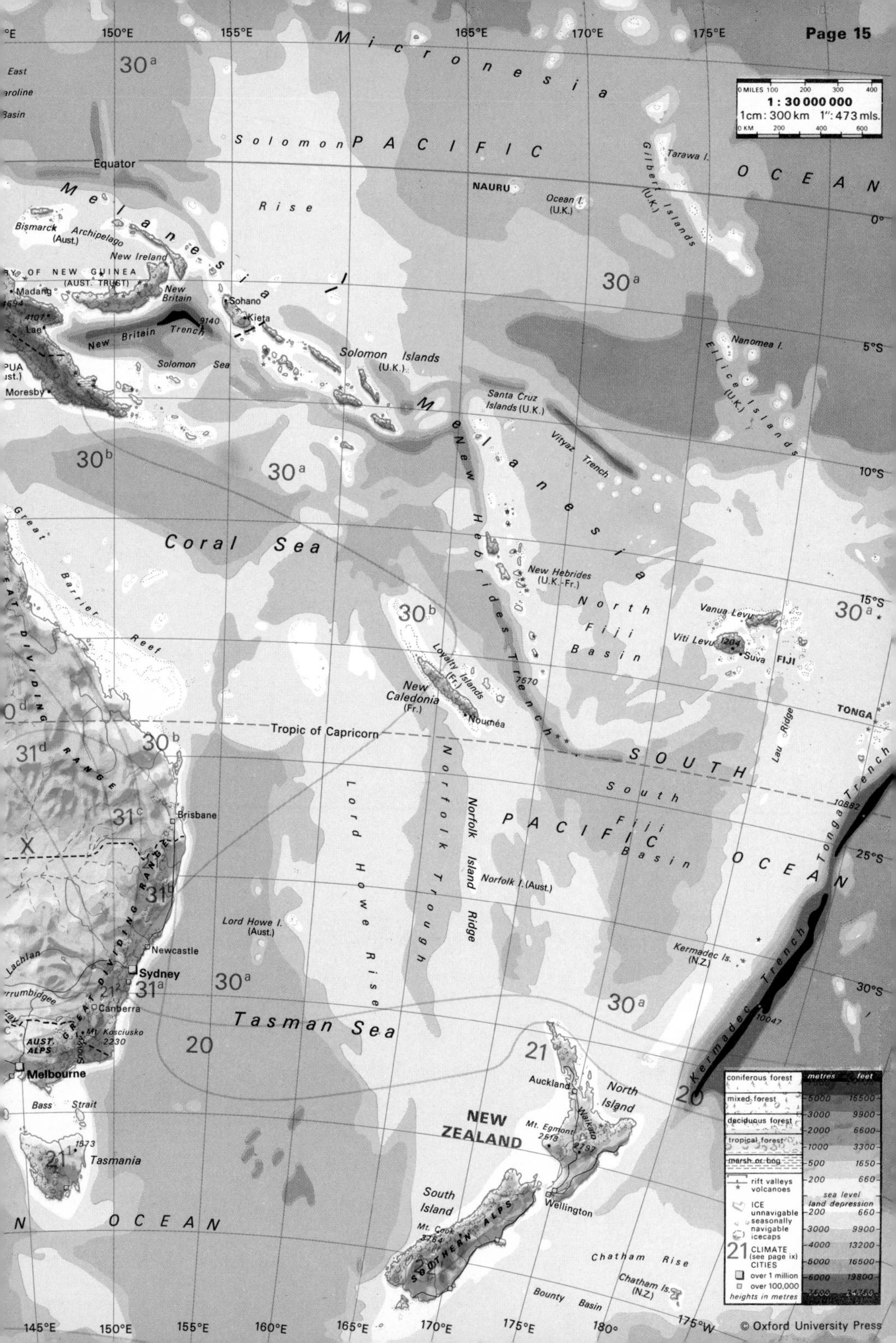

145°E   150°E   155°E   160°E   165°E   170°E   175°E   180°   175°W

°E   150°E   155°E   165°E   170°E   175°E

30ᵃ

M i c r o n e s i a

East
Caroline
Basin

Solomon P A C I F I C   O C E A N

1 : 30 000 000
0 MILES 100   200   300   400
1cm: 300 km   1″: 473 mls.
0 KM   200   400   600

Equator

Rise

NAURU

Ocean I.
(U.K.)

Tarawa I.

Gilbert Islands (U.K.)

0°

M
e
l
a
n
e
s
i
a

Bismarck Archipelago
(Aust.)

New Ireland

GULF OF NEW GUINEA
(AUST. TRUST)

Madang

4707?

Lae

PAPUA
(Aust.)

Moresby

New Britain

Sohano
Kieta

9140

New Britain Trench

Solomon Sea

30ᵃ

30ᵇ

Solomon Islands
(U.K.)

Nanomea I.

5°S

Ellice Islands (U.K.)

Santa Cruz
Islands (U.K.)

Vityaz Trench

M
e
l
a
n
e
s
i
a

New
Hebrides
Trench

New Hebrides
(U.K.-Fr.)

North
Fiji
Basin

Vanua Levu

Viti Levu
1204
Suva   FIJI

30ᵃ

Coral   Sea

30ᵇ

30ᵃ

Great
Barrier
Reef

GREAT DIVIDING RANGE

7570

Loyalty Islands
(Fr.)

New
Caledonia
(Fr.)

Nouméa

15°S

30ᵇ

Tropic of Capricorn

S O U T H

TONGA

Lau Ridge

Tonga Trench

31ᵈ

X

30ᵇ

31ᶜ

31ᵇ

Brisbane

Lord
Howe
Rise

Norfolk Trough

Norfolk Island Ridge

P A C I F I C

South

Fiji

Basin

O C E A N

10882

25°S

Lord Howe I.
(Aust.)

Norfolk I. (Aust.)

Kermadec Is.
(N.Z.)

Lachlan

Newcastle

31ᵃ

Sydney

Canberra

Murrumbidgee

30ᵃ

Tasman   Sea

30ᵃ

20

10047

Kermadec Trench

30°S

20

AUST.
ALPS
Mt Kosciusko
2230

Melbourne

21

Auckland

North
Island

Waikato

NEW
ZEALAND

Mt Egmont
2518

21

20

Bass   Strait

1573

Tasmania

21

South
Island

Mt Cook

Wellington

Chatham   Rise

SOUTHERN ALPS

Chatham Is.
(N.Z.)

N   O C E A N

Bounty   Basin

	metres	feet
coniferous forest	5000	16500
mixed forest	3000	9900
deciduous forest	2000	6600
tropical forest	1000	3300
marsh or bog	500	1650
	200	660
rift valleys	sea level	
volcanoes	land depression	
ICE	200	660
unnavigable	3000	9900
seasonally navigable icecaps	4000	13200
21 CLIMATE (see page ix)	6000	16500
CITIES	8000	19800
over 1 million		
over 100,000		
heights in metres		

© Oxford University Press

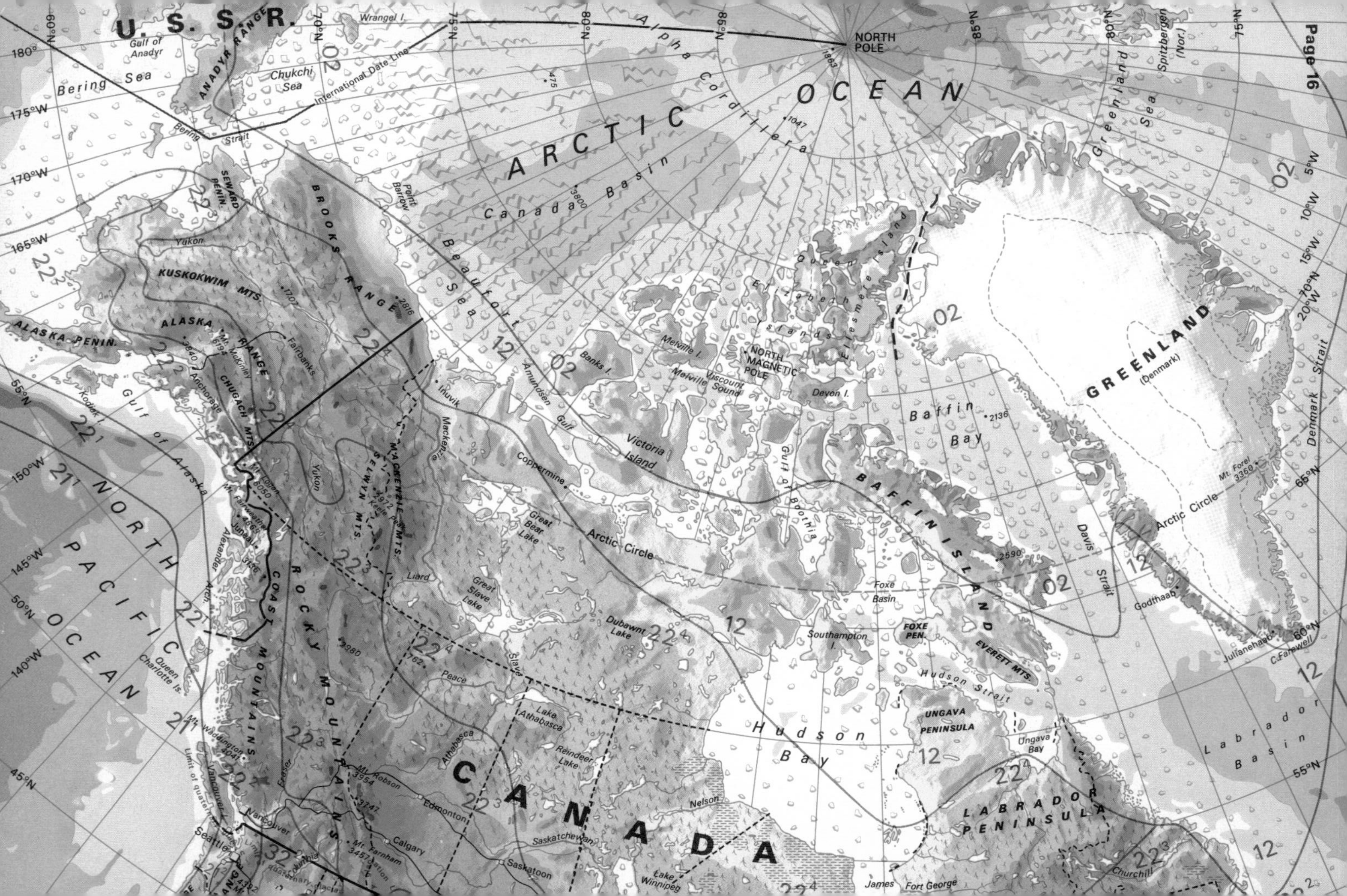
U. S. S. R.
ANADYR RANGE
Gulf of Anadyr
Bering Sea
Bering Strait
Chukchi Sea
Wrangel I.
International Date Line
ARCTIC OCEAN
NORTH POLE
Alpha Cordillera
Canada Basin
Beaufort Sea
Point Barrow
Greenland Sea
Spitzbergen (Nor.)
GREENLAND (Denmark)
Mt. Forel 3360
Denmark Strait
Arctic Circle
Godthaab
Julianehaab
C. Farewell
Labrador Basin
Davis Strait
Baffin Bay
BAFFIN ISLAND
EVERETT MTS.
Hudson Strait
Ungava Bay
UNGAVA PENINSULA
FOXE PEN.
Foxe Basin
LABRADOR PENINSULA
Churchill
Southampton I.
Hudson Bay
James
Fort George
Queen Elizabeth Islands
Ellesmere Island
Devon I.
Gulf of Boothia
NORTH MAGNETIC POLE
Viscount Melville Sound
Melville I.
Banks I.
Victoria Island
Amundsen Gulf
Coppermine
Great Bear Lake
Dubawnt Lake
Great Slave Lake
Lake Athabasca
Reindeer Lake
Lake Winnipeg
Nelson
Saskatchewan
Saskatoon
Edmonton
Calgary
Slave
Peace
Athabasca
Liard
Mackenzie
Inuvik
CANADA
MACKENZIE MTS.
Keele Pk. 2972
SELWYN MTS.
ROCKY MOUNTAINS
Mt. Robson 3954
3747
Mt. Farnham 3457
COAST MOUNTAINS
Mt. Waddington 4041
Fraser
Vancouver
Vancouver I.
Seattle
Columbia
BROOKS RANGE
2816
Yukon
Fairbanks
SEWARD PENIN.
KUSKOKWIM MTS.
ALASKA RANGE
Mt. McKinley 6194
CHUGACH MTS.
Mt. Logan 6050
Mt. Fairweather 4663
Juneau
Anchorage
Alexander Arch.
Queen Charlotte Is.
Gulf of Alaska
Kodiak I.
ALASKA PENIN.
NORTH PACIFIC OCEAN
60°N
65°N
70°N
75°N
80°N
85°N
55°N
50°N
45°N
180°
175°W
170°W
165°W
150°W
145°W
140°W
20°W
15°W
10°W
5°W

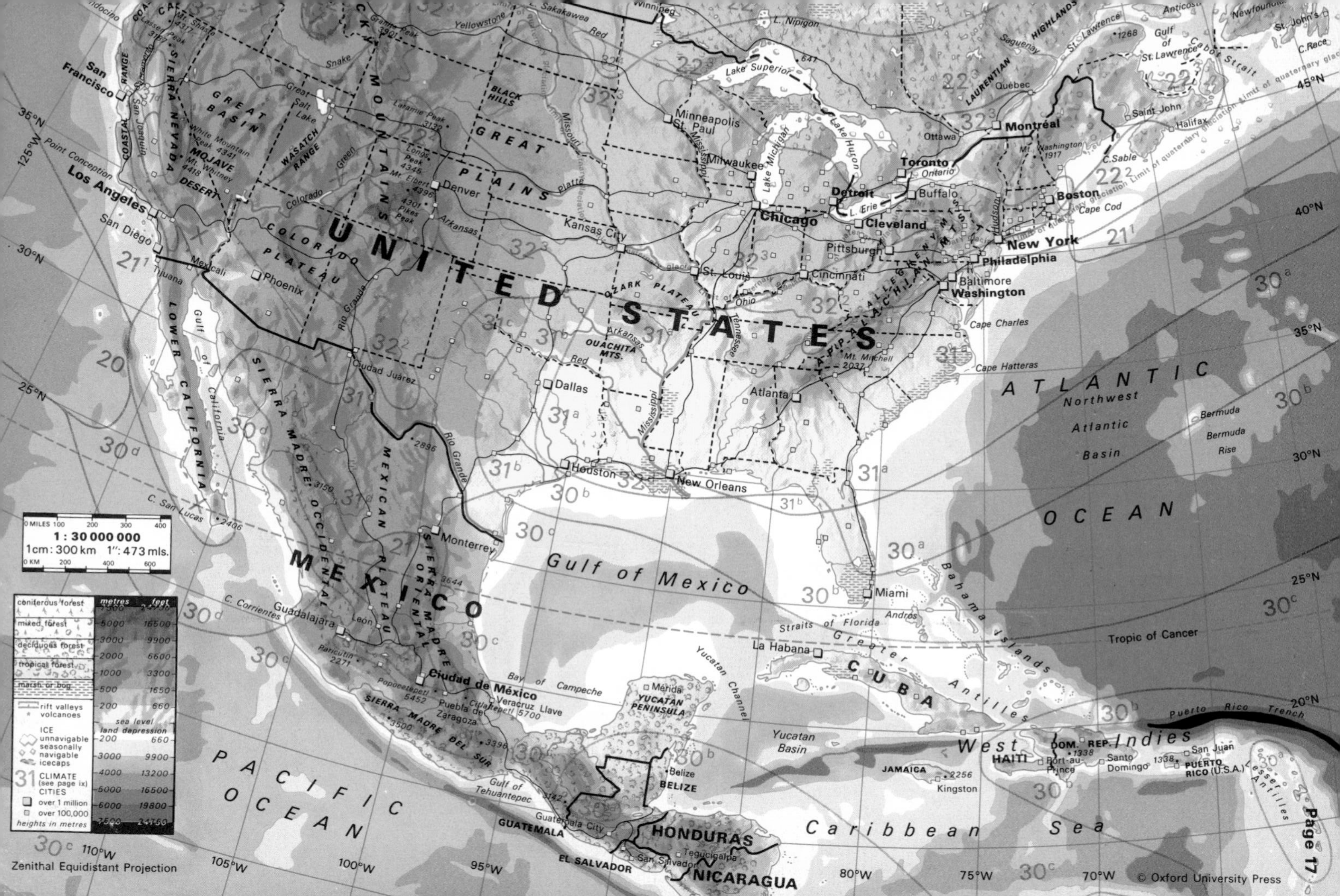

© Oxford University Press

Zenithal Equidistant Projection

1:30 000 000

1cm:300 km   1":473 mls.

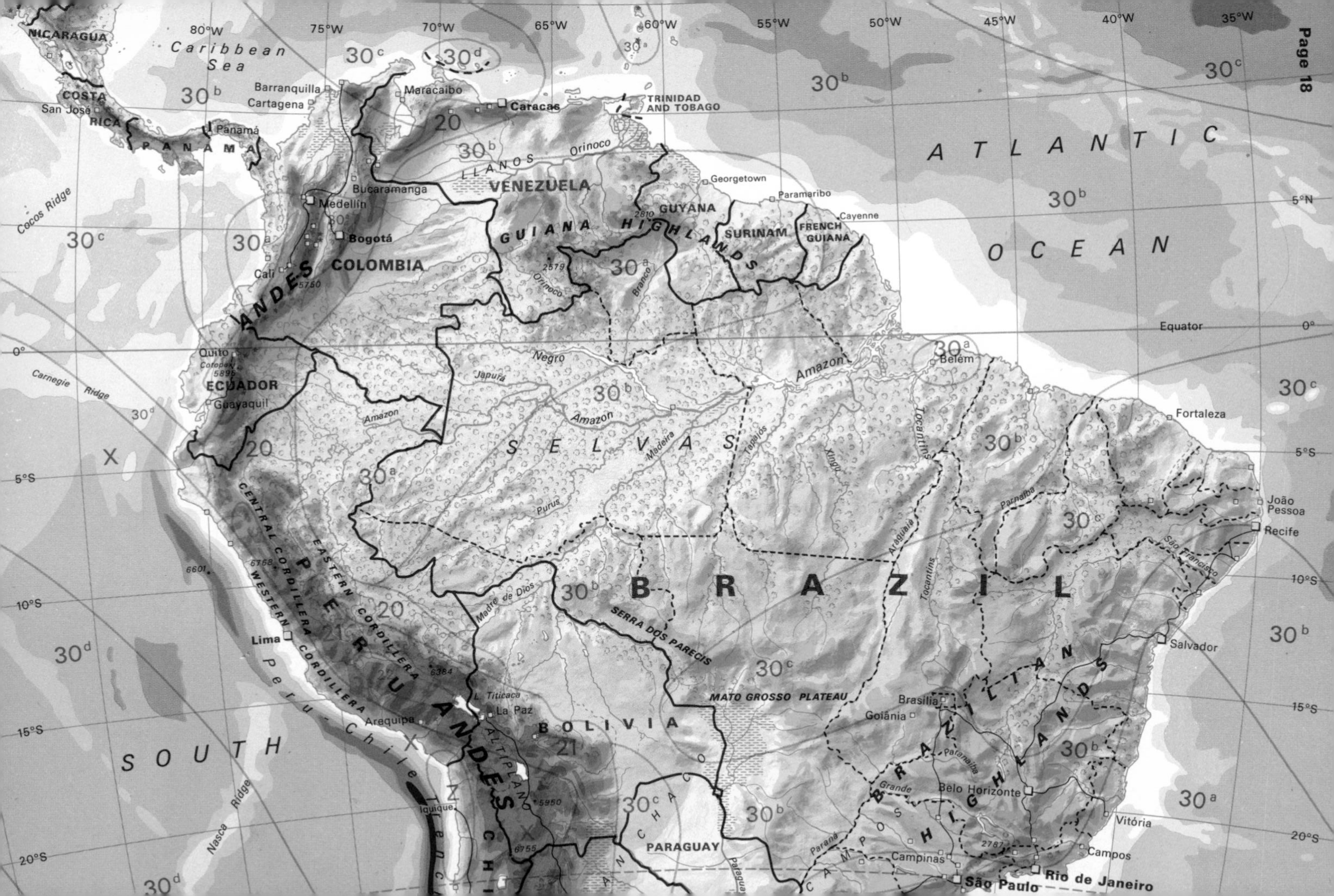
ATLANTIC OCEAN
SOUTH
Caribbean Sea
Equator
NICARAGUA
COSTA RICA
San José
PANAMA
Panamá
Barranquilla
Cartagena
Maracaibo
Caracas
TRINIDAD AND TOBAGO
VENEZUELA
LLANOS
Orinoco
GUIANA HIGHLANDS
GUYANA
Georgetown
SURINAM
Paramaribo
FRENCH GUIANA
Cayenne
COLOMBIA
Bogotá
Medellín
Bucaramanga
Cali
ANDES
ECUADOR
Quito
Cotopaxi
5896
Guayaquil
5750
2810
2579
Branco
Negro
Japurá
Amazon
Madeira
Purus
Tapajós
Xingu
Tocantins
Araguaia
Parnaíba
São Francisco
SELVAS
BRAZIL
BRAZILIAN HIGHLANDS
MATO GROSSO PLATEAU
SERRA DOS PARECIS
Belém
Fortaleza
João Pessoa
Recife
Salvador
Vitória
Campos
Rio de Janeiro
São Paulo
Campinas
Belo Horizonte
Brasília
Goiânia
Paranaíba
Grande
Paraná
Paraguai
2787
CAMPOS
BOLIVIA
La Paz
Titicaca
ALTIPLANO
5950
6755
Iquique
Arequipa
Madre de Dios
PERU
ANDES
Lima
EASTERN CORDILLERA
CENTRAL CORDILLERA
WESTERN CORDILLERA
6384
6768
6601
Peru-Chile Trench
CHACO
PARAGUAY
Cocos Ridge
Carnegie Ridge
Nasca Ridge
X
30a
30b
30c
30d
20
21
80°W
75°W
70°W
65°W
60°W
55°W
50°W
45°W
40°W
35°W
5°N
0°
5°S
10°S
15°S
20°S

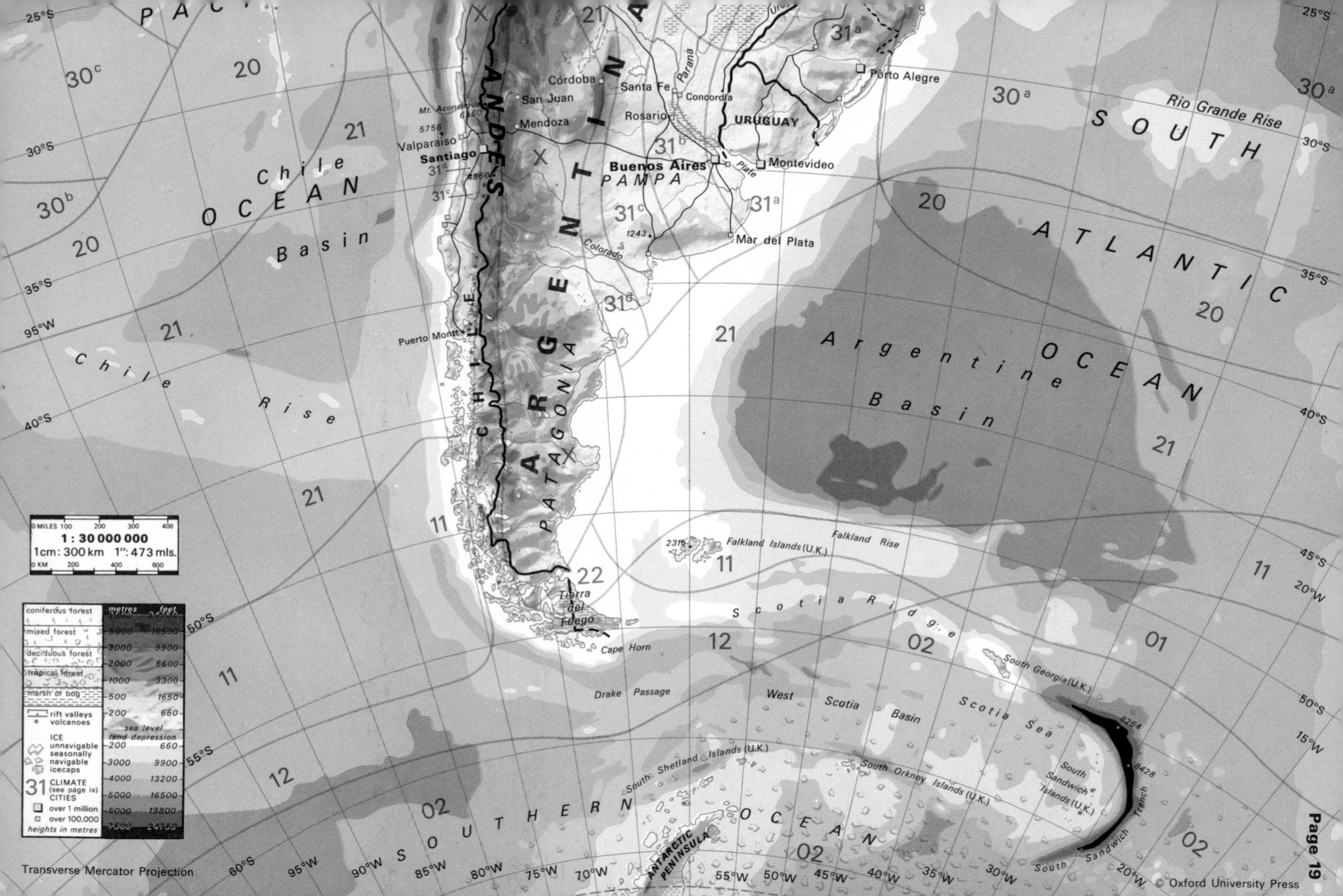
SOUTH ATLANTIC OCEAN
PACIFIC OCEAN
SOUTHERN OCEAN
Rio Grande Rise
Argentine Basin
Chile Basin
Chile Rise
Falkland Rise
Falkland Islands (U.K.)
Scotia Ridge
Scotia Sea
West Scotia Basin
South Georgia (U.K.)
South Sandwich Islands (U.K.)
South Sandwich Trench
8264
8428
South Orkney Islands (U.K.)
South Shetland Islands (U.K.)
ANTARCTIC PENINSULA
Drake Passage
Cape Horn
Tierra del Fuego
PATAGONIA
ARGENTINA
CHILE
URUGUAY
ANDES
PAMPA
Porto Alegre
Montevideo
Buenos Aires
Plate
Mar del Plata
Rosario
Santa Fe
Concordia
Paraná
Córdoba
San Juan
Mendoza
Colorado
Santiago
Valparaiso
Mt. Aconcagua 6960
5756
4860
1243
2315
Puerto Montt
1 : 30 000 000
1cm : 300 km 1": 473 mls.
0 MILES 100 200 300 400
0 KM 200 400 600
coniferous forest
mixed forest
deciduous forest
tropical forest
marsh or bog
rift valleys
volcanoes
ICE
unnavigable
seasonally navigable
icecaps
31 CLIMATE (see page ix)
CITIES
over 1 million
over 100,000
heights in metres
metres feet
5000 16500
3000 9900
2000 6600
1000 3300
500 1650
200 660
sea level
land depression
-200 660
-3000 9900
-4000 13200
-5000 16500
-6000 19800
Transverse Mercator Projection

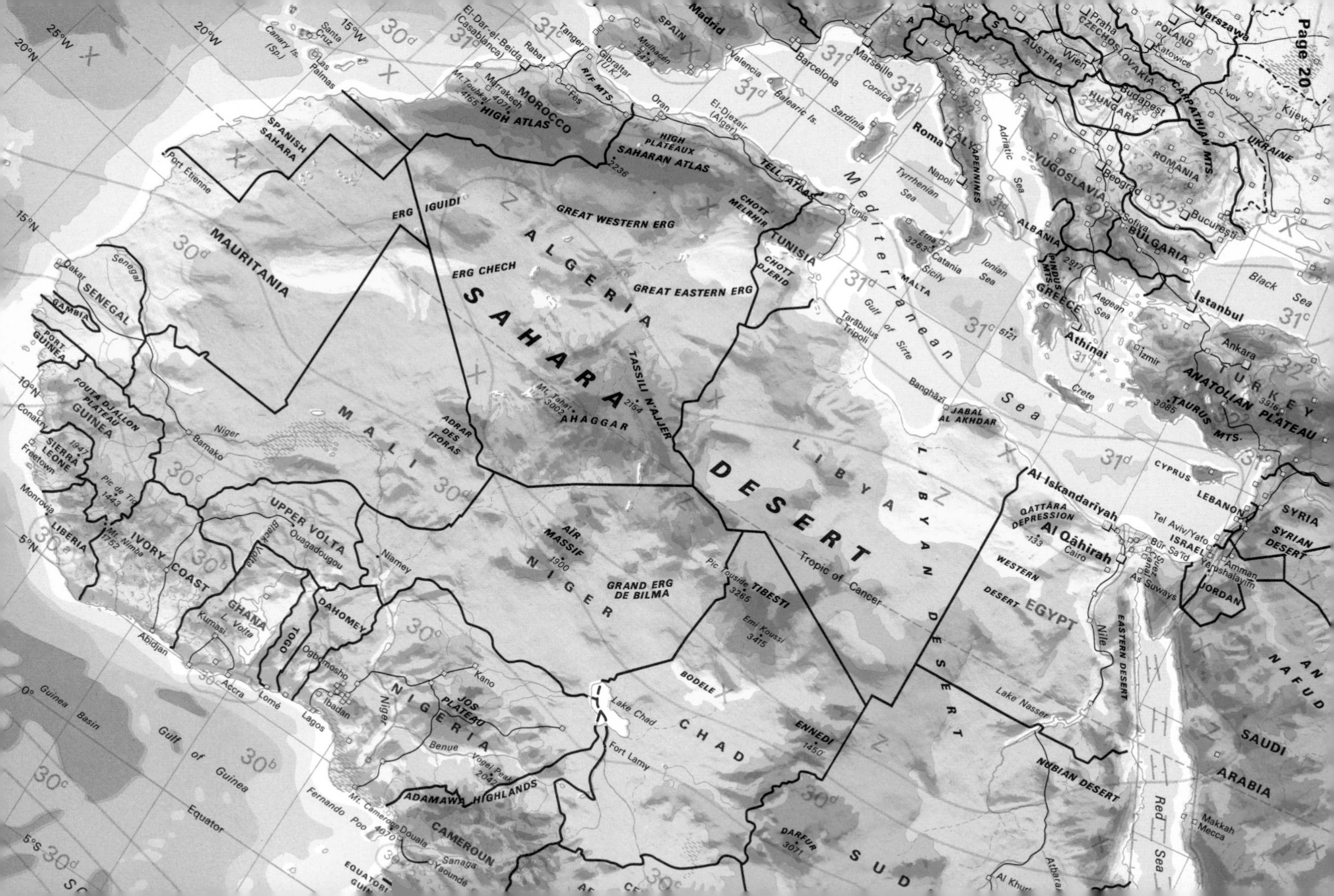
Black Sea
TURKEY
ANATOLIAN PLATEAU
TAURUS MTS.
3916
3085
Ankara
Istanbul
Izmir
SYRIA
SYRIAN DESERT
AN NAFUD
SAUDI ARABIA
Makkah
Mecca
Amman
Yerushalayim
JORDAN
LEBANON
ISRAEL
Tel Aviv/Yafo
Bûr Sa'îd
Suez Canal
As Suways
Red Sea
CYPRUS
EASTERN DESERT
Nile
NUBIAN DESERT
Atbara
Al Iskandarîyah
Al Qâhirah
Cairo
QATTÂRA DEPRESSION
-133
WESTERN DESERT
EGYPT
Lake Nasser
LIBYAN DESERT
LIBYA
DESERT
Tropic of Cancer
SUDAN
ENNEDI
1450
DARFUR
3071
TIBESTI
3265
Emi Koussi
3415
Pic Tousside
BODELE
CHAD
Lake Chad
Fort Lamy
GRAND ERG DE BILMA
AIR MASSIF
1900
NIGER
Warszawa
POLAND
Katowice
Kijev
L'vov
UKRAINE
CARPATHIAN MTS.
CZECHOSLOVAKIA
Praha
Wien
AUSTRIA
Budapest
HUNGARY
ROMANIA
Bucuresti
BULGARIA
Sofiya
Beograd
YUGOSLAVIA
ALBANIA
PINDUS MTS.
2917
GREECE
Athinai
Aegean Sea
Crete
Adriatic Sea
ITALY
APENNINES
Roma
Napoli
Tyrrhenian Sea
Ionian Sea
Etna 3263
Catania
Sicily
MALTA
Mediterranean Sea
Corsica
Sardinia
Marseille
Barcelona
Balearic Is.
Valencia
Madrid
SPAIN
Mulhacén 3478
Gibraltar (U.K.)
Tunis
TUNISIA
CHOTT DJERID
CHOTT MELRHIR
TELL ATLAS
El-Djezair (Alger)
Oran
HIGH PLATEAUX
SAHARAN ATLAS
2236
Gulf of Sirte
Tarâbulus
Tripoli
Banghâzî
JABAL AL AKHDAR
GREAT EASTERN ERG
GREAT WESTERN ERG
ALGERIA
TASSILI N'AJJER
2154
SAHARA
AHAGGAR
Mt. Tahat 3002
ERG CHECH
ERG IGUIDI
RIF MTS.
Tanger
Fès
Rabat
MOROCCO
HIGH ATLAS
Marrakech
4071
Mt. Toubkal 4165
El-Dar-el-Beida (Casablanca)
15°W
20°W
25°W
Santa Cruz
Las Palmas
Canary Is. (Sp.)
SPANISH SAHARA
MAURITANIA
Port Étienne
MALI
ADRAR DES IFORAS
Niger
Bamako
Niamey
UPPER VOLTA
Ouagadougou
Black Volta
DAHOMEY
TOGO
GHANA
L. Volta
Kumasi
Accra
Lomé
Lagos
Ibadan
Ogbomosho
Kano
JOS PLATEAU
NIGERIA
Benue
Vogel Peak 2042
ADAMAWA HIGHLANDS
CAMEROUN
Sanaga
Yaoundé
Douala
Mt. Cameroon 4070
Fernando Poo
IVORY COAST
Abidjan
Gulf of Guinea
Equator
Guinea Basin
SENEGAL
Senegal
Dakar
GAMBIA
PORT. GUINEA
FOUTA DJALLON PLATEAU
GUINEA
Conakry
SIERRA LEONE
1947
Freetown
Pic de Tio 1443
Mt. Nimba 1752
LIBERIA
Monrovia
20°N
15°N
10°N
5°N
0°
5°S

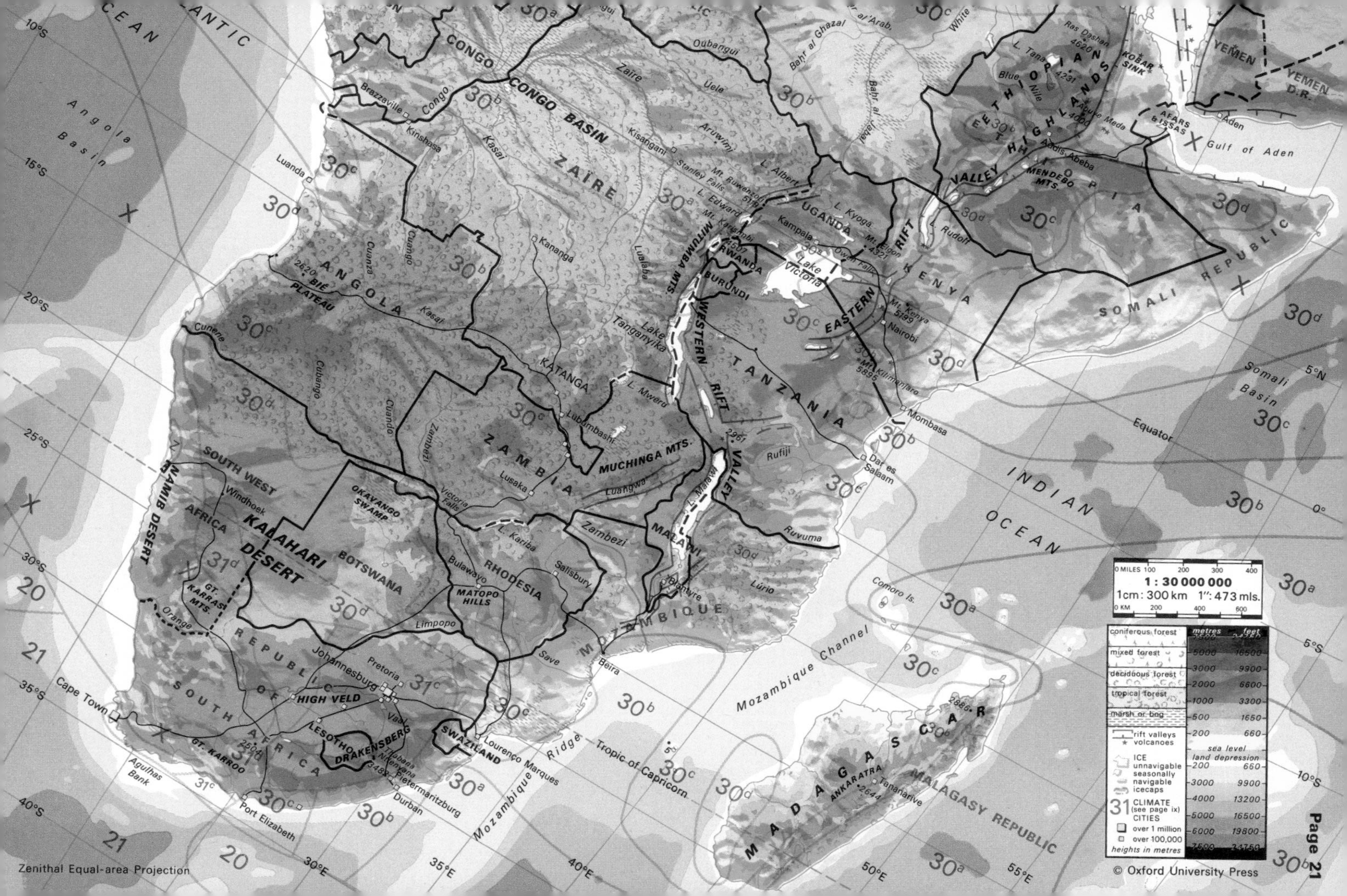

YEMEN D.R.

Gulf of Aden

AFARS ISSAS

KOBAR SINK 155 m.

Ras Casey

L. Tana 1829

Blue Nile

ETHIOPIAN HIGHLANDS

MENDEBO MTS.

ETHIOPIA

RIFT VALLEY

White Nile

Bahr al Arab

Bahr al Ghazal

Bahr al Jabal

SOMALI REPUBLIC

Somali Basin

Equator

INDIAN OCEAN

Somali Basin

SOCOTRA

KENYA

Rudolf

L. Kyoga

Kampala

UGANDA

EASTERN RIFT

Mt. Kenya 5200

L. Naivasha

Nairobi

Mt. Kilimanjaro 5895

Mombasa

Dar es Salaam

Comoro Is.

Pemba

Zanzibar

Mozambique Channel

MADAGASCAR MALAGASY REPUBLIC

ANKARATRA 2644

Tananarive

TANZANIA

Rufiji

Ruvuma

Zaire

Ubangui

Uele

Aruwimi

Kisangani Stanley Falls

Mt. Blanc

Lualaba

L. Kivu

Kigali

RWANDA

BURUNDI

MITUMBA MTS.

WESTERN RIFT VALLEY

Lake Tanganyika

L. Mweru

MUCHINGA MTS.

L. Malawi

Malawi

MALAWI

Rufiji

CONGO BASIN

ZAIRE

KATANGA

Kananga

Kasai

Lubumbashi

L. Bangweulu

ZAMBIA

Lusaka

Kafue

L. Kariba

Zambezi

Victoria Falls

Salisbury

RHODESIA

Bulawayo

MATOPO HILLS

MOZAMBIQUE

Zambezi

Beira

Save

Tropic of Capricorn

CONGO

Brazzaville Kinshasa

Congo

Kasai

Cuango

Cuanza

Luanda

ANGOLA

BIÉ PLATEAU 2620

Cubango

Cuando

OKAVANGO SWAMP

BOTSWANA

Cunene

SOUTH WEST AFRICA

Windhoek

KALAHARI DESERT

GT. KARRAS MTS.

Orange

NAMIB DESERT

REPUBLIC OF SOUTH AFRICA

Pretoria

Johannesburg

Vaal

HIGH VELD

LESOTHO

DRAKENSBERG

SWAZILAND

Lourenço Marques

Maputo

Pietermaritzburg

Durban

GT. KAROO

Port Elizabeth

Agulhas Bank

Cape Town

ATLANTIC OCEAN

Angola Basin

Zenithal Equal-area Projection

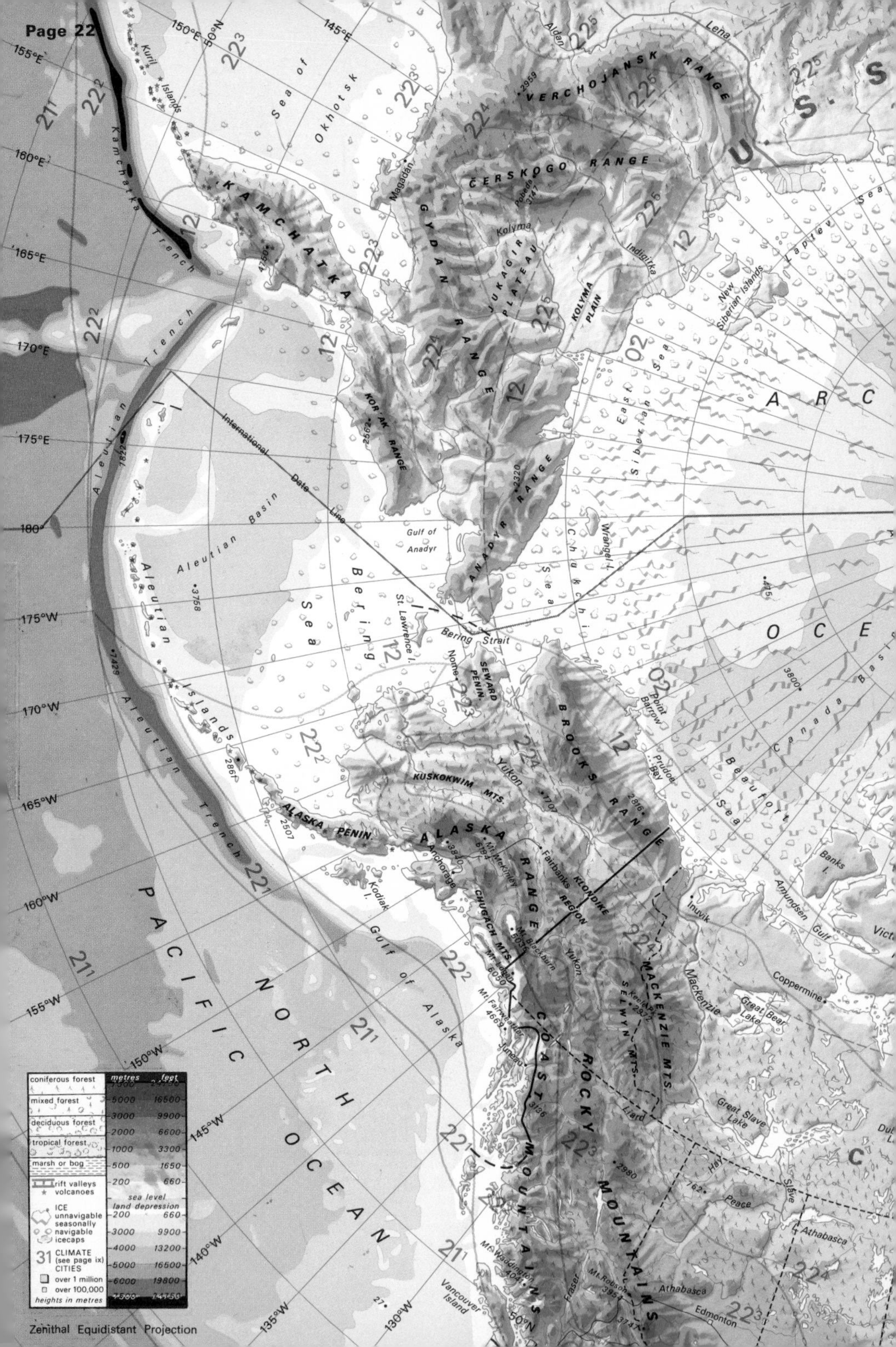

Zenithal Equidistant Projection

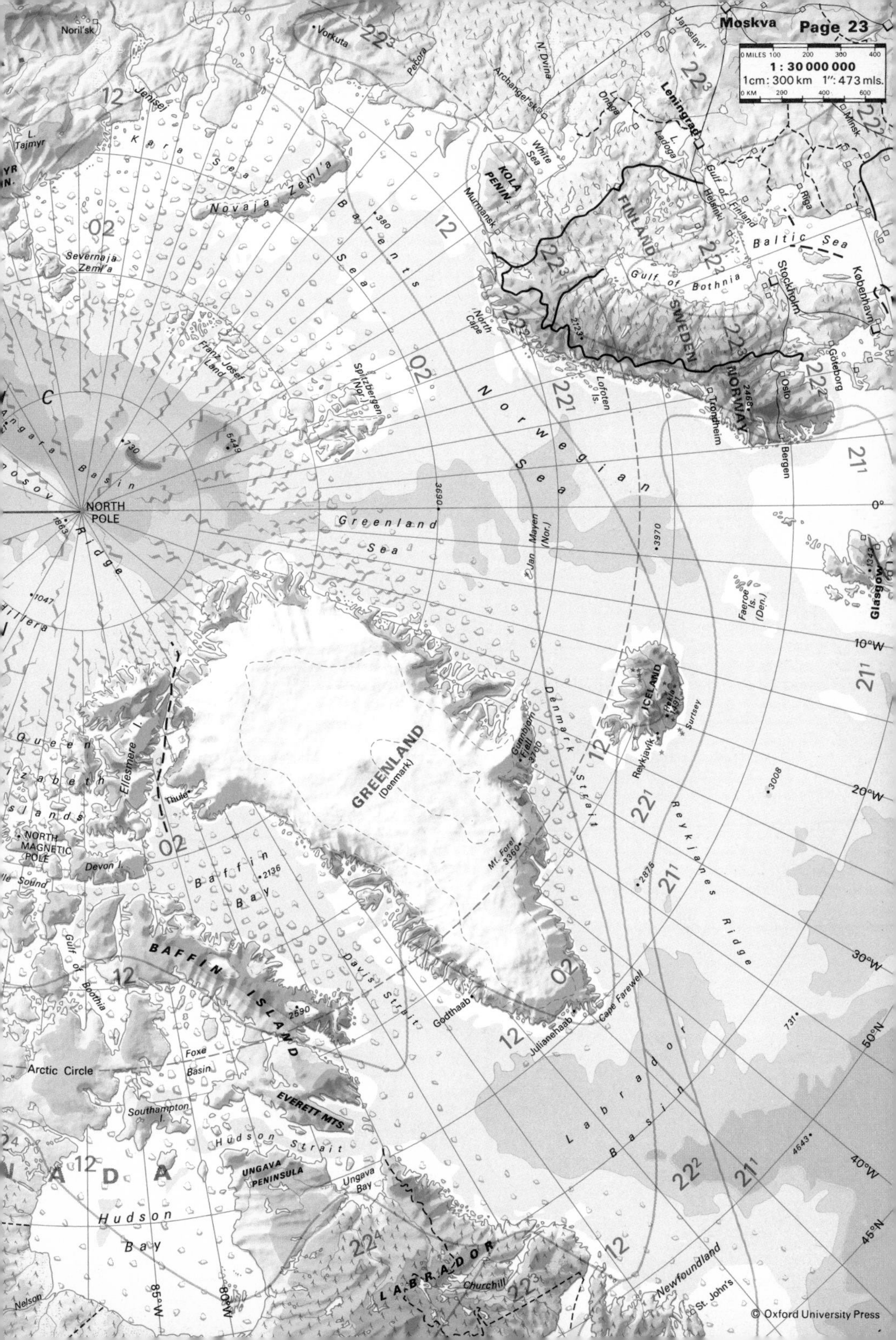

0 MILES 100   200   300   400

1 : 30 000 000
1cm: 300 km   1": 473 mls.

0 KM   200   400   600

Noril'sk

Vorkuta   22¹

12   Jenisej

L.
Tajmyr

YR   Pecora

N. Dvina

Archangel'sk

Jaroslavl'

Leningrad   223

K a r a   S e a

Novaja Zeml'a

02

Severnaja
Zeml'a

Franz Josef
Land

330

542

C

gara
Basin

onosov   Ridge

NORTH
POLE

1047

Cordillera

Queen
zabeth
Islands

NORTH
MAGNETIC
POLE

Devon I.

le Sound

Ellesmere I.

Thule

Gulf of Boothia   12

BAFFIN ISLAND

Foxe
Basin

Arctic Circle

Southampton

24

A D A   12

Hudson Bay

Nelson

85°W   80°W   75°W

B a r e n t s   S e a

380

Murmansk

KOLA
PENIN.

North
Cape

22²

2469

02   12

Spitsbergen
(Nor.)

3690

Greenland
Sea

Jan Mayen
I.(Nor.)

02

GREENLAND
(Denmark)

2135

B a f f i n
B a y

D a v i s   S t r a i t

2590

Godthaab

12   Julianehaab

Grønmmgr
Fjord

Mt. Forel
3360

2875

12   02

Capo Farewell

731

EVERETT MTS

Hudson Strait

UNGAVA
PENINSULA

Ungava
Bay

22⁴

12

LABRADOR   22³

Churchill

Finland   223

Onega

Ladoga

Gulf of Finland

Gulf of Bothnia

White
Sea

223

22²   22¹

FINLAND

SWEDEN

NORWAY

22²

Stockholm

Göteborg

Oslo

Bergen

211

0°

Trondheim

Lofoten Is.

N o r w e g i a n   S e a

3970

Faeroe
Is.
(Den.)

10°W

ICELAND

Reykjavik

Surtsey

12

221

211   Reykjanes Ridge

02

3008

20°W

30°W

Labrador   Basin

40°W

4643

45°N

211

222

22²

211

211

12

St. John's

Newfoundland

50°W

Riga

Minsk   22¹

Baltic Sea

Kobenhavn

Oland

211

Bergslag

© Oxford University Press

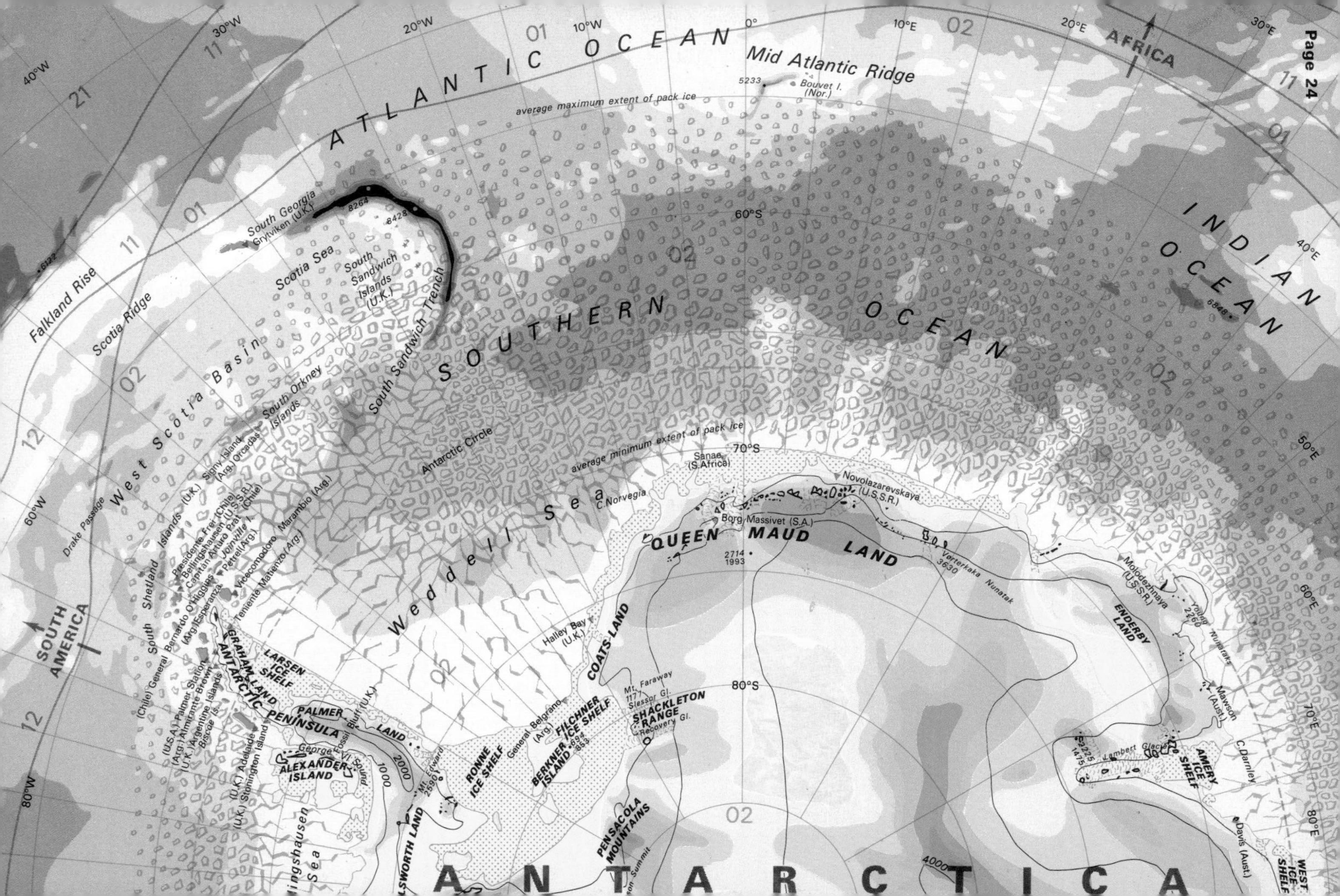
ATLANTIC OCEAN
Mid Atlantic Ridge
5233
Bouvet I. (Nor.)
average maximum extent of pack ice
AFRICA
INDIAN OCEAN
6848
SOUTHERN OCEAN
South Georgia
Grytviken (U.K.)
8264
8428
Scotia Sea
South Sandwich Islands (U.K.)
South Sandwich Trench
Falkland Rise
Scotia Ridge
West Scotia Basin
South Orkney Islands
Signy Island
(Arg.) Orcadas
Drake Passage
South Shetland Islands (U.K.)
Marambio (Arg.)
Antarctic Circle
average minimum extent of pack ice
Weddell Sea
C.Norvegia
Sanae (S.Africa)
Novolazarevskaya (U.S.S.R.)
Borg Massivet (S.A.)
QUEEN MAUD LAND
2714
1993
Vorterkaka Nunatak
3630
Molodezhnaya (U.S.S.R.)
ENDERBY LAND
Young Nunataks
2260
Mawson (Aust.)
C.Darnley
AMERY ICE SHELF
Lambert Glacier
2225
1475
Davis (Aust.)
WEST ICE SHELF
SOUTH AMERICA
GRAHAM LAND
ANTARCTIC PENINSULA
LARSEN ICE SHELF
PALMER LAND
Fossil Bluff (U.K.)
George VI Sound
ALEXANDER ISLAND
(U.K.) Adelaide
(U.K.) Stonington Island
Argentine Islands
Biscoe Is.
(U.S.A.) Palmer Station
Halley Bay (U.K.)
COATS LAND
Mt. Faraway
Slessor Gl.
SHACKLETON RANGE
Recovery Gl.
General Belgrano (Arg.)
FILCHNER ICE SHELF
BERKNER ISLAND
RONNE ICE SHELF
Mt. Edward
2000
1000
4000
PENSACOLA MOUNTAINS
Sea
ANTARCTICA
30°W
20°W
10°W
0°
10°E
20°E
30°E
40°E
50°E
60°E
70°E
80°E
40°W
60°W
80°W
60°S
70°S
80°S

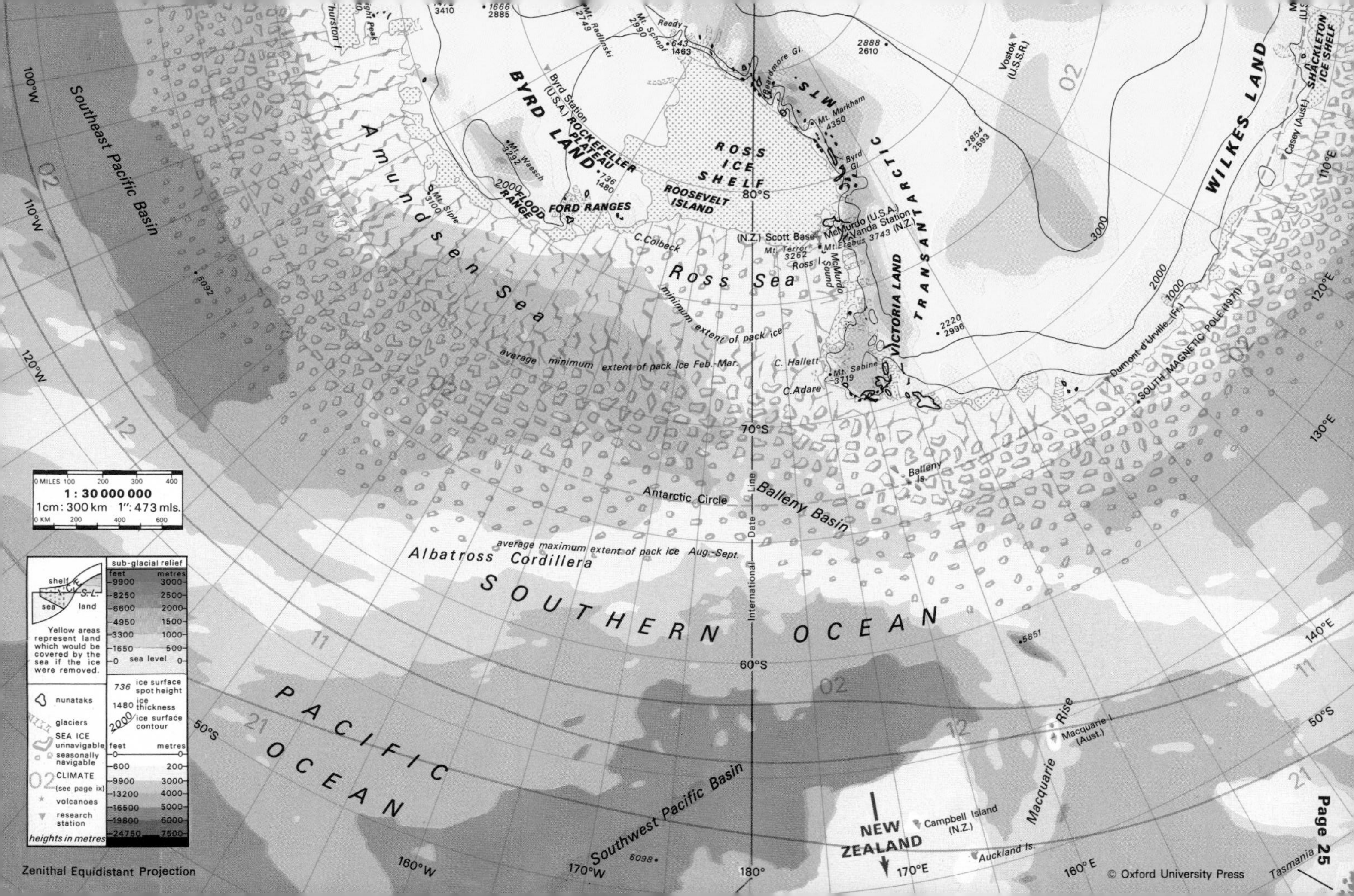

160° E © Oxford University Press

WILKES LAND

SHACKLETON ICE SHELF

Casey (Aust.)

Vostok (U.S.S.R.)

TRANSANTARCTIC

VICTORIA LAND

Dumont d'Urville (Fr.)

SOUTH MAGNETIC POLE (1971)

Balleny Is.

Macquarie Island (Aust.)

Macquarie Rise

Tasmania

NEW ZEALAND

Auckland Is. (N.Z.)

Campbell Island (N.Z.)

*2854
*2833
*2854

Mt. Markham
4292

2888
2610

*2851

Mt. Erebus 3743
Scott Base (N.Z.) McMurdo Station (U.S.A.)
McMurdo Sound
Ross I.

Mt. Terror 3262

C. Hallett
C. Adare

C. Sabine
*3119

*2996
2220
2080

T R A N S A N T A R C T I C M T S.

Mt. Meacham 4292

Mt. Fridtjof 1091

Beardmore Gl.

C. Colbeck

Ballenny Basin

ANTARCTIC
CIRCLE

Antarctic Circle

S O U T H E R N O C E A N

Date Line

International

Date Line

minimum extent of pack ice

maximum extent of pack ice Aug.–Sept.

average minimum extent of pack ice

average maximum extent of pack ice Aug.–Sept.

minimum extent of pack ice Feb.–Mar.

R o s s S e a

ROSS ICE SHELF

ROOSEVELT ISLAND

80°S

70°S

60°S

50°S

BYRD LAND

ROCKEFELLER PLATEAU

Byrd Station (U.S.A.) *736

Mt. School 2590

Mt. Radlinski 2749

1463
643

1666
2885

3410

A m u n d s e n S e a

FLOOD RANGE

Mt. Wassch 3292

Mt. Siple 3100

*6092

Thurston I.

Peak

Albatross Cordillera

P A C I F I C
O C E A N

*6098

Southwest Pacific Basin

Southeast Pacific Basin

100°W
110°W
120°W
160°W
170°W
180°
170°E

110°E
120°E
130°E
140°E
150°E

02
02
12
21
11

1:30 000 000
1cm: 300 km 1″: 473 mls.

0 MILES 100 200 300 400
0 KM 200 400 600

sub-glacial relief
feet	metres
9900	3000
8250	2500
6600	2000
4950	1500
3300	1000
1650	500
0	sea level

ice surface spot height 736
ice thickness 1480
ice surface contour 2000

feet	metres
0	sea level
1650	500
3300	1000
9900	3000
13200	4000
16500	5000
19800	6000
24750	7600

Yellow areas represent land which would be covered by the sea if the ice were removed.

shelf ice

land

sea ice

nunataks
glaciers
SEA ICE
navigable
seasonally navigable
CLIMATE see page ix
volcanoes
research station

heights in metres

Zenithal Equidistant Projection

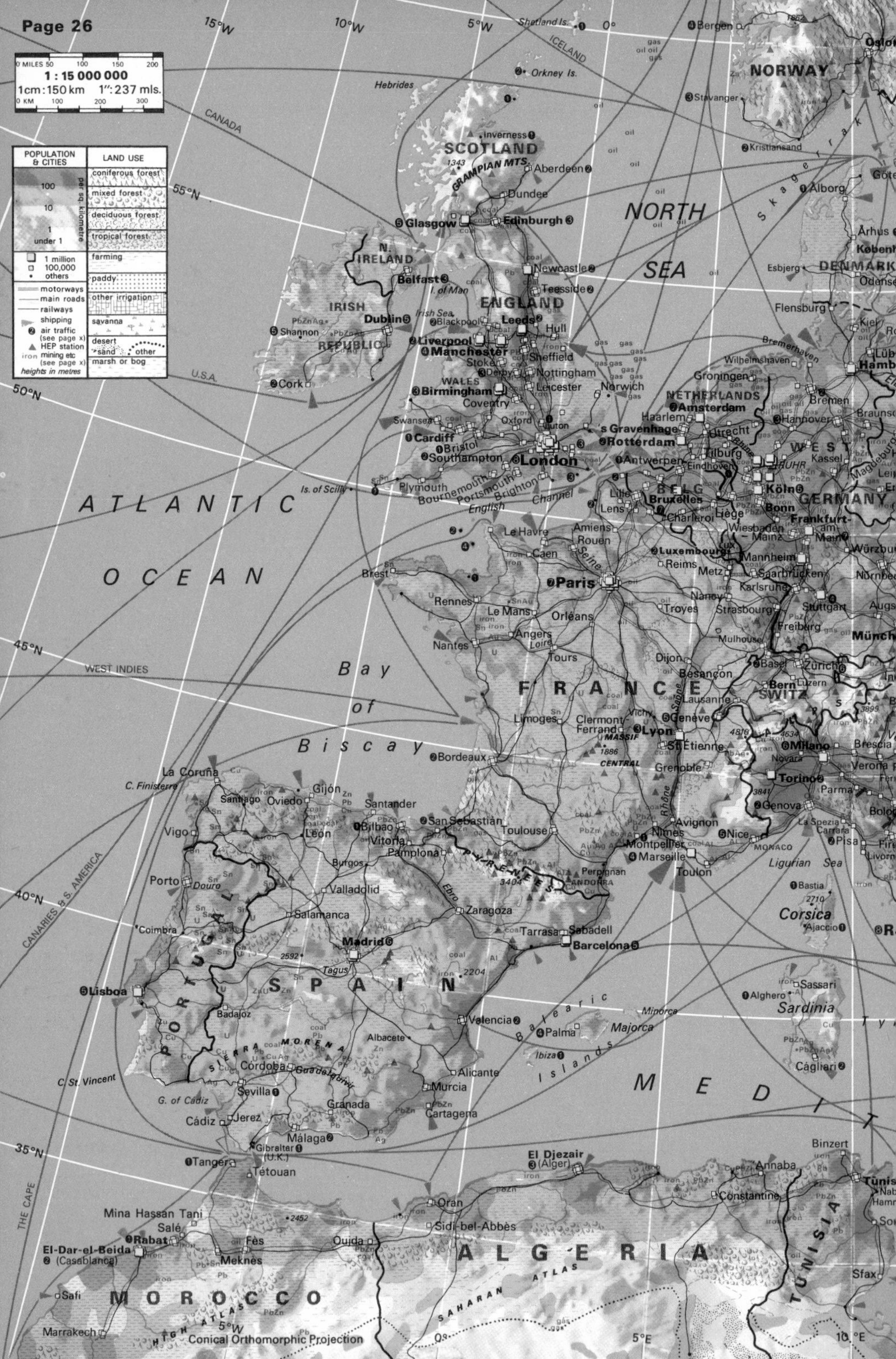

1 : 15 000 000
1cm : 150 km 1": 237 mls.
MILES 50 100 150 200
KM 100 200 300
POPULATION & CITIES
per sq. kilometre
100
10
1
under 1
1 million
100,000
others
motorways
main roads
railways
shipping
air traffic (see page x)
HEP station
iron mining etc (see page x)
heights in metres
LAND USE
coniferous forest
mixed forest
deciduous forest
tropical forest
farming
paddy
other irrigation
savanna
desert
sand
other
marsh or bog
15°W
10°W
5°W
0°
5°E
10°E
55°N
50°N
45°N
40°N
35°N
ICELAND
CANADA
U.S.A.
WEST INDIES
CANARIES & S. AMERICA
THE CAPE
Shetland Is.
Orkney Is.
Hebrides
NORWAY
Bergen
Stavanger
Kristiansand
Oslo
Skagerrak
Alborg
Århus
DENMARK
Esbjerg
Odense
SCOTLAND
GRAMPIAN MTS.
Inverness
Aberdeen
Dundee
Glasgow
Edinburgh
NORTH SEA
N. IRELAND
Belfast
I. of Man
IRISH REPUBLIC
Irish Sea
Dublin
Shannon
Cork
ENGLAND
Newcastle
Teesside
Blackpool
Leeds
Hull
Liverpool
Manchester
Sheffield
Stoke
Derby
Nottingham
Leicester
Norwich
WALES
Birmingham
Coventry
Swansea
Oxford
Luton
Cardiff
Bristol
London
Southampton
Plymouth
Bournemouth
Portsmouth
Brighton
Is. of Scilly
English Channel
ATLANTIC OCEAN
Flensburg
Kiel
Bremerhaven
Wilhelmshaven
Groningen
Bremen
NETHERLANDS
Amsterdam
Haarlem
's Gravenhage
Rotterdam
Utrecht
Hannover
Antwerpen
Tilburg
Eindhoven
Rhine
RUHR
Kassel
Magdeburg
Lille
Lens
Bruxelles
Charleroi
Liège
Köln
Bonn
GERMANY
Wiesbaden
Mainz
Frankfurt-am-Main
Würzburg
Le Havre
Amiens
Rouen
Caen
Seine
Luxembourg
Reims
Metz
Mannheim
Saarbrücken
Karlsruhe
Brest
Paris
Rennes
Le Mans
Orléans
Troyes
Nancy
Strasbourg
Stuttgart
Angers
Loire
Tours
Nantes
Freiburg
Mulhouse
Dijon
Besançon
Basel
Zürich
Bern
Luzern
SWITZ
Bay of Biscay
FRANCE
Lausanne
Limoges
Clermont-Ferrand
MASSIF CENTRAL
Vichy
Genève
Lyon
St Etienne
Grenoble
Bordeaux
Milano
Novara
Brescia
Torino
Verona
Parma
Genova
Toulouse
Avignon
Nîmes
Montpellier
Marseille
Toulon
Nice
MONACO
La Spezia
Carrara
Pisa
Livorno
Ligurian Sea
Perpignan
ANDORRA
PYRENEES
Bastia
Corsica
Ajaccio
La Coruña
C. Finisterre
Santiago
Oviedo
Gijón
Santander
San Sebastián
Bilbao
Vitoria
Pamplona
León
Vigo
Burgos
Ebro
Valladolid
Porto
Douro
Zaragoza
Salamanca
Coimbra
Tarrasa
Sabadell
Barcelona
Madrid
Tagus
PORTUGAL
SPAIN
Lisboa
Badajoz
Valencia
Balearic Islands
Minorca
Palma
Majorca
Ibiza
Albacete
SIERRA MORENA
Guadalquivir
Córdoba
Alicante
C. St. Vincent
Sevilla
Murcia
G. of Cadiz
Granada
Cartagena
Cádiz
Jerez
Málaga
Gibraltar (U.K.)
Sassari
Alghero
Sardinia
Cágliari
MEDIT
Binzert
Tanger
Tétouan
El Djezair (Alger)
Annaba
Tunis
Constantine
Oran
Mina Hassan Tani
Salé
Sidi-bel-Abbès
Rabat
Fès
Oujda
El-Dar-el-Beida (Casablanca)
Meknès
ALGERIA
TUNISIA
SAHARAN ATLAS
Sfax
Safi
MOROCCO
HIGH ATLAS
Marrakech
Conical Orthomorphic Projection

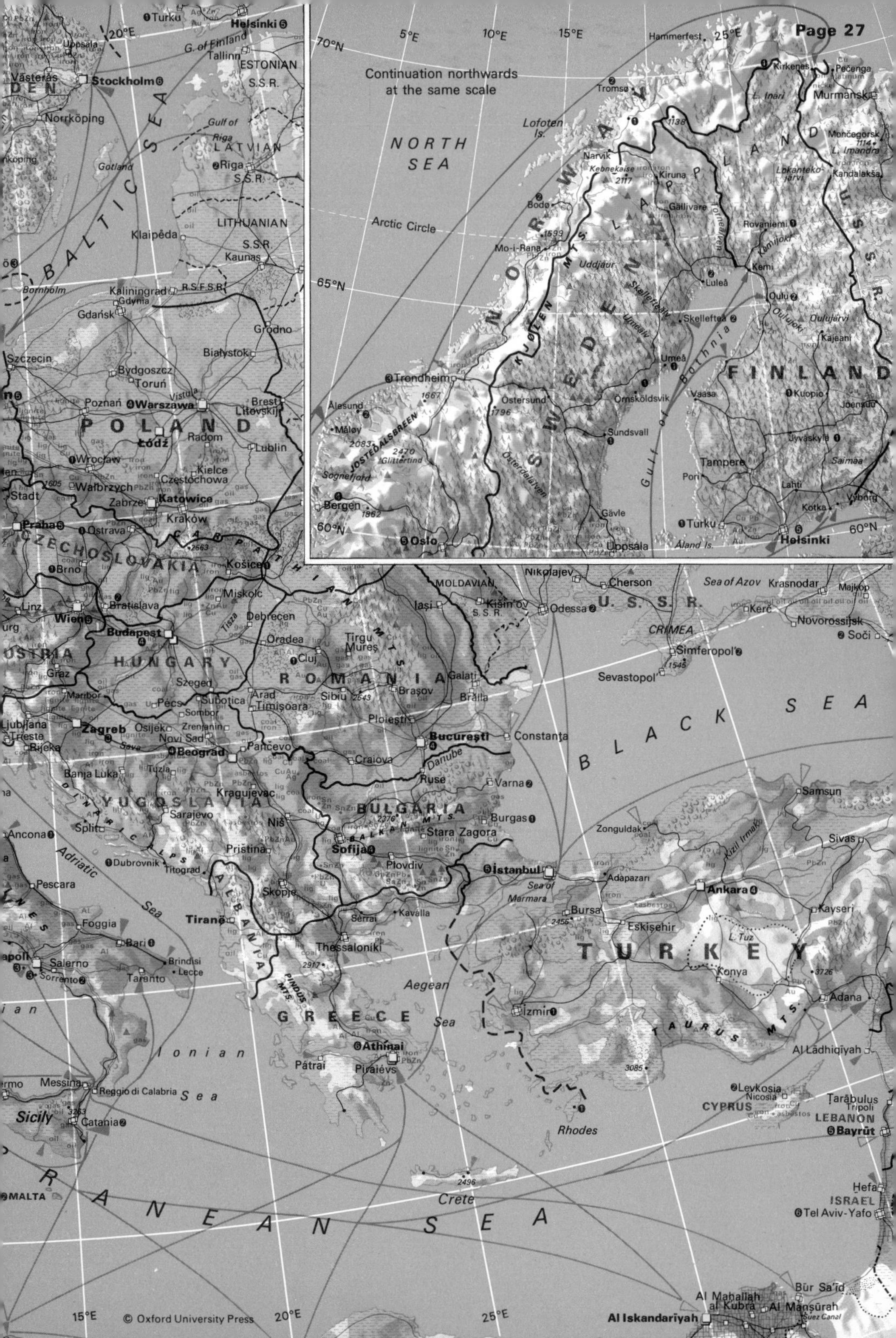

Continuation northwards
at the same scale

NORTH
SEA

Arctic Circle

65°N

60°N

BALTIC SEA

Gulf of Finland

G. of Finland

Tallinn

ESTONIAN
S.S.R.

Gulf of
Riga

Riga

LATVIAN
S.S.R.

Gotland

LITHUANIAN
S.S.R.

Klaipėda

Kaunas

Kaliningrad

R.S.F.S.R.

Bornholm

Gdynia

Grodno

Gdańsk

Białystok

Szczecin

Bydgoszcz

Toruń

Brest
Litovski

Poznań

Warszawa

POLAND

Radom

Lublin

Wrocław

Łódź

Kielce

Częstochowa

Wałbrzych

Zabrze

Katowice

Kraków

Praha

Ostrava

CZECHOSLOVAKIA

Košice

Brno

Linz

Bratislava

Miskolc

Wien

Budapest

Debrecen

Iași

OSTRIA

HUNGARY

Oradea

Tirgu
Mureș

Graz

Maribor

Szeged

Cluj

Ljubljana

Trieste

Pécs

Arad

Timișoara

ROMANIA

Brașov

Rijeka

Subotica

Sibiu

Sombor

Zagreb

Osijek

Zrenjanin

Ploiești

Banja Luka

Novi Sad

Pancevo

București

Constanța

Split

YUGOSLAVIA

Kragujevac

Craiova

Danube

Ruse

Ancona

Sarajevo

Niš

Varna

Dubrovnik

Titograd

Pristina

Stara Zagora

Burgas

Pescara

Skopje

Sofija

BULGARIA

Foggia

Tirana

Plovdiv

İstanbul

Bari

ALBANIA

Serrai

Kavalla

Sea of
Marmara

Bursa

Salerno

Brindisi

Lecce

Thessaloniki

GREECE

PINDUS MTS.

Sicily

Taranto

Reggio di Calabria

Aegean
Sea

Athinai

Pátrai

Piraiévs

Messina

Catania

Ionian
Sea

Crete

MALTA

RANEAN SEA

© Oxford University Press

NORWAY

SWEDEN

FINLAND

Hammerfest

Kirkenes

Pecanga

Tromsø

Murmansk

L. Inari

Lofoten
Is.

Narvik

Kebnekaise

Kiruna

Mončegorsk

L. Imandra

Kandalaksa

Bodö

Gällivare

Mo-i-Rana

Rovaniemi

Kemi

Luleå

Uddjaur

Skellefteå

Umeå

Oulu

Oulujärvi

Kajaani

Trondheim

Östersund

Örnsköldsvik

Vaasa

Kuopio

Joensuu

Ålesund

Måløy

Sundsvall

Tampere

Saimaa

Jyväskylä

Pori

Lahti

Sognefjord

Gävle

Kotka

Viborg

Bergen

Oslo

Uppsala

Åland Is.

Turku

Helsinki

Gulf of Bothnia

Stockholm

Norrköping

Västerås

Uppsala

Gdańsk

N
U
L
L
L
A
N
D

K
J
Ö
L
E
N

M
T
S

NORTH SEA

U.S.S.R.

MOLDAVIAN

Nikolajev

Kišin'ov

Odessa

Cherson

Sea of Azov

Krasnodar

Majkop

Kerč

CRIMEA

Simferopol'

Novorossijsk

Soči

Sevastopol'

BLACK SEA

Samsun

Zonguldak

Adapazari

Ankara

Sivas

Eskişehir

L. Tuz

Kayseri

İzmir

TURKEY

Konya

Adana

TAURUS MTS.

Al Lādhiqīyah

Rhodes

CYPRUS

Levkosia
Nicosia

Tarabulus
Tripoli

LEBANON

Bayrūt

Hefa

ISRAEL

Tel Aviv-Yafo

Al Maḥallah
al Kubra

Būr Sa'īd

Al Iskandarīyah

Al Mansūrah

Suez Canal

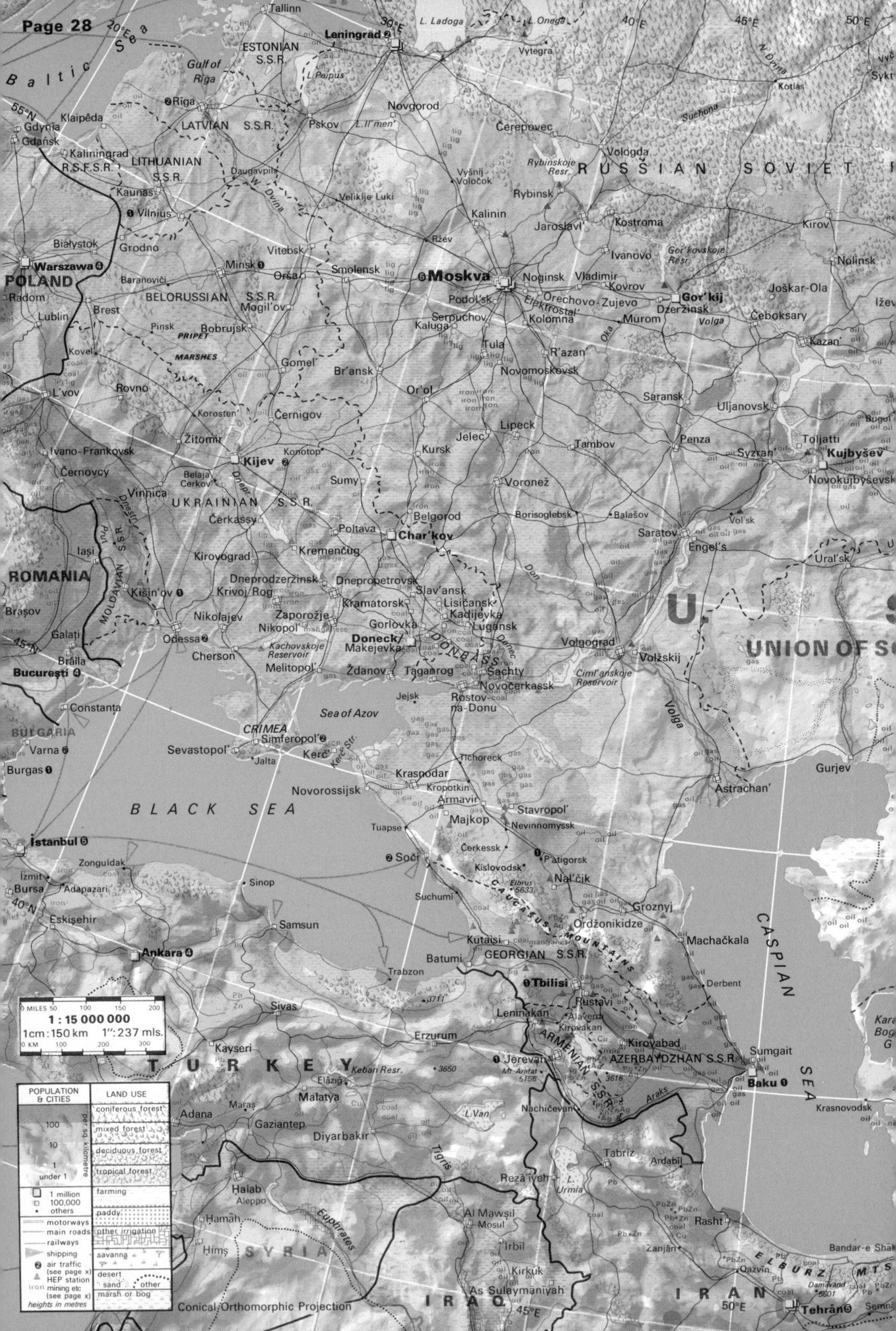
Baltic Sea
Tallinn
Leningrad
L. Ladoga
L. Onega
ESTONIAN S.S.R.
Gulf of Riga
L. Peipus
Riga
Novgorod
Vytegra
Kotlas
Suchona
Klaipėda
Gdynia
Gdańsk
Kaliningrad
R.S.F.S.R.
LATVIAN S.S.R.
Pskov
L. Il'men'
Čerepovec
Vologda
LITHUANIAN S.S.R.
Daugavpils
Kaunas
W. Dvina
Vilnius
Velikije Luki
Vyšnij Voloček
Rybinskoje Resr.
Rybinsk
RUSSIAN SOVIET
Kalinin
Jaroslavl'
Kostroma
Kirov
Białystok
Grodno
Vitebsk
Ržev
Ivanovo
Gor'kovskoje Resr.
Nolinsk
Warszawa
POLAND
Minsk
Orša
Smolensk
Moskva
Noginsk
Vladimir
Kovrov
Baranoviči
Radom
BELORUSSIAN S.S.R.
Mogil'ov
Podol'sk
Orechovo-Zujevo
Elektrostal'
Gor'kij
Dzeržinsk
Joškar-Ola
Lublin
Brest
Bobrujsk
Serpuchov
Kaluga
Kolomna
Murom
Čeboksary
Pinsk
PRIPET MARSHES
Kovel'
Gomel'
Tula
R'azan'
Oka
Volga
Kazan'
Br'ansk
Novomoskovsk
L'vov
Rovno
Or'ol
Saransk
Uljanovsk
Korosten'
Černigov
Lipeck
Žitomir
Jelec
Tambov
Penza
Toljatti
Ivano-Frankovsk
Kijev
Konotop
Kursk
Syzran'
Kujbyšev
Novokujbyševsk
Černovcy
Belaja Cerkov'
Dnepr
Sumy
Voronež
Vinnica
UKRAINIAN S.S.R.
Dnestr
Belgorod
Borisoglebsk
Balašov
Vol'sk
Čerkassy
Poltava
Char'kov
Saratov
Iași
Kremenčug
Engel's
Prut
Kirovograd
Don
Ural'sk
ROMANIA
MOLDAVIAN S.S.R.
Dneprodzeržinsk
Dnepropetrovsk
Slav'ansk
Kišin'ov
Krivoj Rog
Kramatorsk
Lisičansk
Brașov
Nikolajev
Zaporožje
Gorlovka
Kadijevka
Lugansk
Galați
Nikopol'
Doneck
Makejevka
DONBASS
Volgograd
Volžskij
UNION OF S
Odessa
Kachovskoje Reservoir
Brăila
Cherson
Melitopol'
Ždanov
Taganrog
Šachty
Novočerkassk
Ciml'anskoje Reservoir
București
Constanța
Rostov-na-Donu
Jejsk
Sea of Azov
Volga
BULGARIA
CRIMEA
Varna
Sevastopol'
Simferopol'
Kerč
Kerč Str.
Jalta
Tichoreck
Gurjev
Burgas
Krasnodar
Astrachan'
Novorossijsk
Kropotkin
Armavir
Stavropol'
BLACK SEA
Majkop
Tuapse
Nevinnomyssk
İstanbul
Čerkessk
Zonguldak
Soči
P'atigorsk
İzmit
Kislovodsk
Bursa
Adapazari
Sinop
Elbrus 5633
Nal'čik
Suchumi
CAUCASUS MOUNTAINS
Groznyj
40°N
Eskişehir
Samsun
Ordžonikidze
CASPIAN SEA
Kutaisi
Machačkala
Ankara
Batumi
GEORGIAN S.S.R.
Trabzon
Tbilisi
Derbent
Rustavi
Sivas
3711
Leninakan
Alaverdi
Kirovakan
Erzurum
Kirovabad
Sumgait
Kayseri
ARMENIAN S.S.R.
Jerevan
AZERBAYDZHAN S.S.R.
TURKEY
Keban Resr.
3650
Mt. Ararat 5156
3616
Baku
Elâzığ
Malatya
Araks
Adana
Maraș
L. Van
Nachičevan
Krasnovodsk
Gaziantep
Diyarbakır
Tigris
Tabrīz
Ardabīl
Rezā'īyeh
L. Urmia
Halab
Aleppo
Euphrates
Al Mawşil
Mosul
Hamāh
Rasht
Zanjān
Himş
SYRIA
Irbil
Bandar-e Shāh
ELBURZ MTS
Kirkūk
Qazvīn
Damāvand 5601
As Sulaymānīyah
IRAQ
IRAN
Tehrān
Semnān
Conical Orthomorphic Projection
20°E
30°E
40°E
45°E
50°E
55°N
45°N
0 MILES 50 100 150 200
1 : 15 000 000
1cm : 150 km 1'': 237 mls.
0 KM 100 200 300
POPULATION & CITIES
per sq. kilometre
100
10
1
under 1
1 million
100,000
others
motorways
main roads
railways
shipping
air traffic (see page x)
HEP station
mining etc (see page x)
heights in metres
LAND USE
coniferous forest
mixed forest
deciduous forest
tropical forest
farming
paddy
other irrigation
savanna
desert
sand
other
marsh or bog

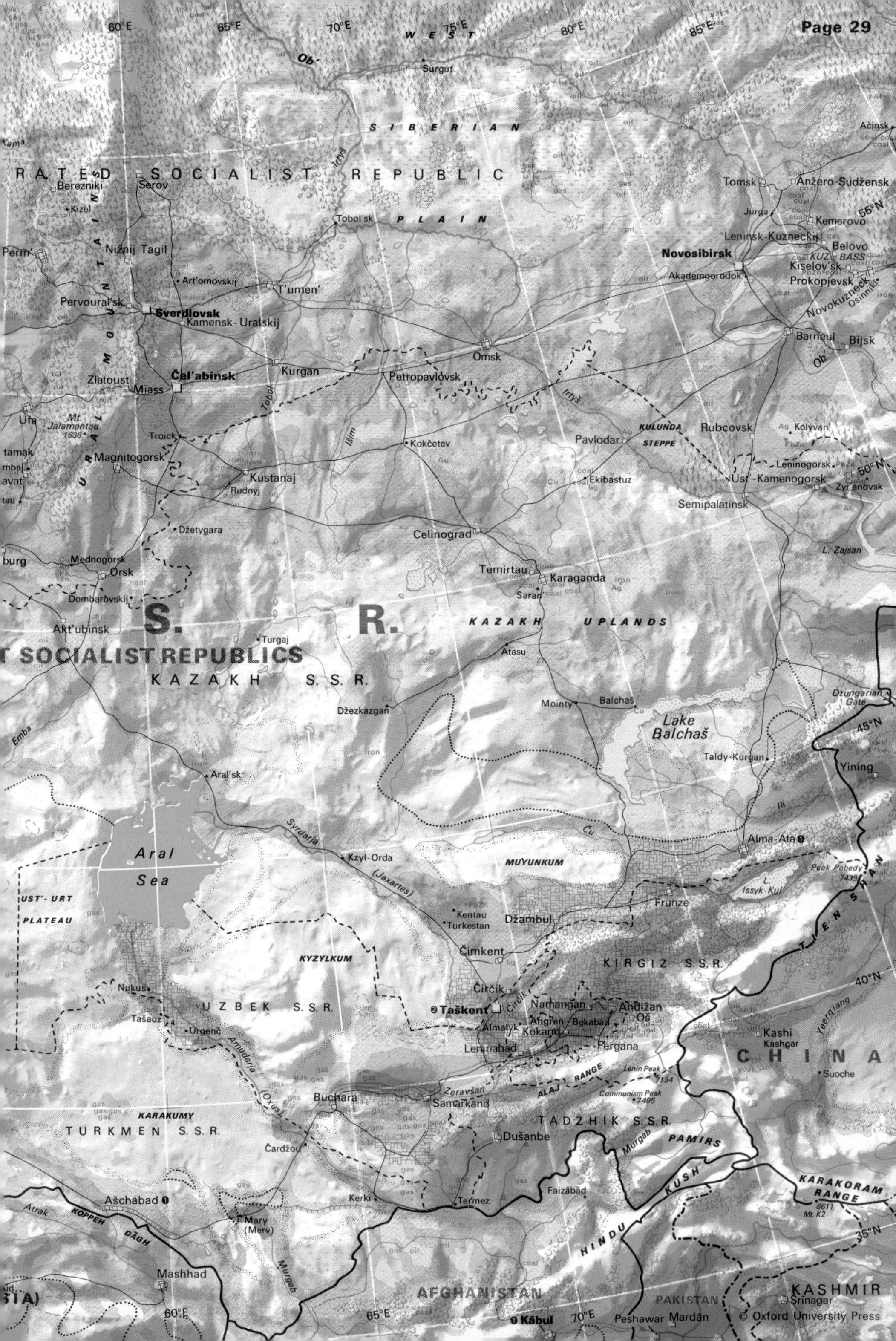

Ob·
WEST
Surgut
SIBERIAN
60°E
65°E
70°E
75°E
80°E
85°E
Ačinsk
Tomsk
Anžero-Sudžensk
Berezniki
Serov
Jurga
Kemerovo
Kizil
Tobol'sk
Leninsk-Kuzneckij
56°N
RATED SOCIALIST REPUBLIC
Perm·
Niznij Tagil
PLAIN
Novosibirsk
Belovo
KUZ
Pervoural'sk
T'umen'
Akademgorodok
Kiselov'sk
BASS
Art'omovskij
Prokopjevsk
Sverdlovsk
Kamensk-Uralskij
coal
Novokuznetsk
Osinniki
Zlatoust
Čal'abinsk
Kurgan
Omsk
Barnaul
Bijsk
Miass
Petropavlovsk
Irtyš
Ob
Mt.
Jalamantau
1638
Troick
Kokčetav
Au
Pavlodar
KULUNDA
Rubcovsk
Ag
Kolyvan'
Ufa
Ust'-Kamenogorsk
STEPPE
tamak
Magnitogorsk
Kustanaj
Ekibastuz
Cu
Leninogorsk
50°N
mbal
Rudnyj
Zyr'anovsk
avat
Džetygara
Semipalatinsk
tau
Celinograd
L. Zajsan
burg
Mednogorsk
Orsk
Temirtau
Karaganda
Dzungarian
Dombarovskij
Saran
Gate
Akt'ubinsk
KAZAKH
UPLANDS
45°N
S. S. R.
Turgaj
Atasu
Yining
T SOCIALIST REPUBLICS
Mojnty
Balchaš
Lake
KAZAKH S.S.R.
Balchaš
Džezkazgan
Taldy-Kurgan
Emba
Il
Aral'sk
Syrdarja
Alma-Ata
(Jaxartes)
Peak Pobedy
Aral
Kzyl-Orda
MUYUNKUM
Sea
UST'-URT
Frunze
L.
PLATEAU
Kentau
Issyk-Kul
Turkestan
Džambul
KYZYLKUM
Čimkent
KIRGIZ S.S.R.
40°N
Nukus
Čirčik
Namangan
Andižan
Tašent
Almalyk
Oš
Kashi
Tašauz
Afgren Bokabad
Kashgar
Urgenc
Kokand
Pergana
Suoche
UZBEK S.S.R.
Lenirabad
CHINA
Amudarja (Oxus)
Zeravšan
ALAI RANGE
Buchara
Lenin Peak
7134
Samarkand
Communism Peak
KARAKUMY
+7495
TADZHIK S.S.R.
gas
Dušanbe
PAMIRS
Čardžou
TURKMEN S.S.R.
Murgab
HINDU
Kerki
Faizābād
Atrak
Ašchabad
Kerki
Termez
KARAKORAM
KOPPEN
Mary
RANGE
DAGH
(Merv)
KUSH
8611
Mt.K2
Mashhad
AFGHANISTAN
PAKISTAN
KASHMIR
51A)
60°E
65°E
Kābul
70°E
Peshawar Mardān
Srinagar
© Oxford University Press

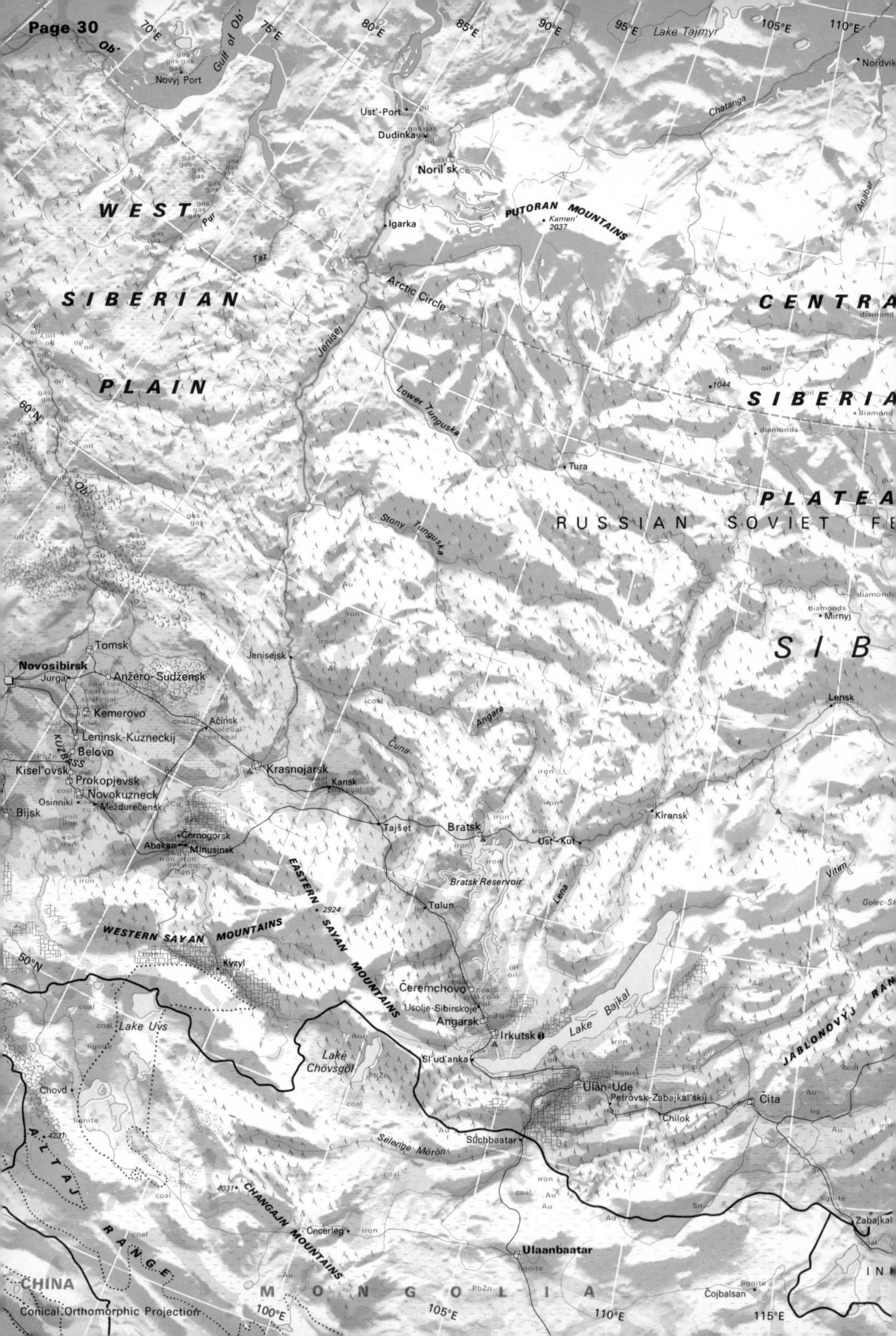

WEST SIBERIAN PLAIN
CENTRAL SIBERIAN PLATEAU
RUSSIAN SOVIET F
PUTORAN MOUNTAINS
EASTERN SAYAN MOUNTAINS
WESTERN SAYAN MOUNTAINS
CHANGAJN MOUNTAINS
ALTAJ RANGE
JABLONOVYJ RAN
KUZBASS
MONGOLIA
CHINA
Gulf of Ob'
Ob'
Pur
Taz
Jenisej
Lower Tunguska
Stony Tunguska
Angara
Čuna
Lena
Vitim
Chatanga
Anabar
Lake Tajmyr
Lake Bajkal
Bratsk Reservoir
Lake Uvs
Lake Chövsgöl
Selenge Mörön
Arctic Circle
Novyj Port
Ust'-Port
Dudinka
Noril'sk
Igarka
Nordvik
Kamen' 2037
Tura
Mirnyj
Lensk
Kirensk
Ust'-Kut
Bratsk
Tajšet
Kansk
Krasnojarsk
Jenisejsk
Ačinsk
Tomsk
Novosibirsk
Jurga
Anžero-Sudžensk
Kemerovo
Leninsk-Kuzneckij
Belovo
Kisel'ovsk
Prokopjevsk
Novokuzneck
Osinniki
Meždurečensk
Bijsk
Černogorsk
Abakan
Minusinsk
Kyzyl
Tulun
Čeremchovo
Usolje-Sibirskoje
Angarsk
Irkutsk
Sl'ud'anka
Ulan-Ude
Petrovsk-Zabajkal'skij
Chilok
Čita
Zabajkal
Suchbaatar
Ulaanbaatar
Čojbalsan
Cecerleg
Chovd
4231
4031
2924
1044
70°E
75°E
80°E
85°E
90°E
95°E
105°E
110°E
115°E
100°E
60°N
50°N
Conical Orthomorphic Projection

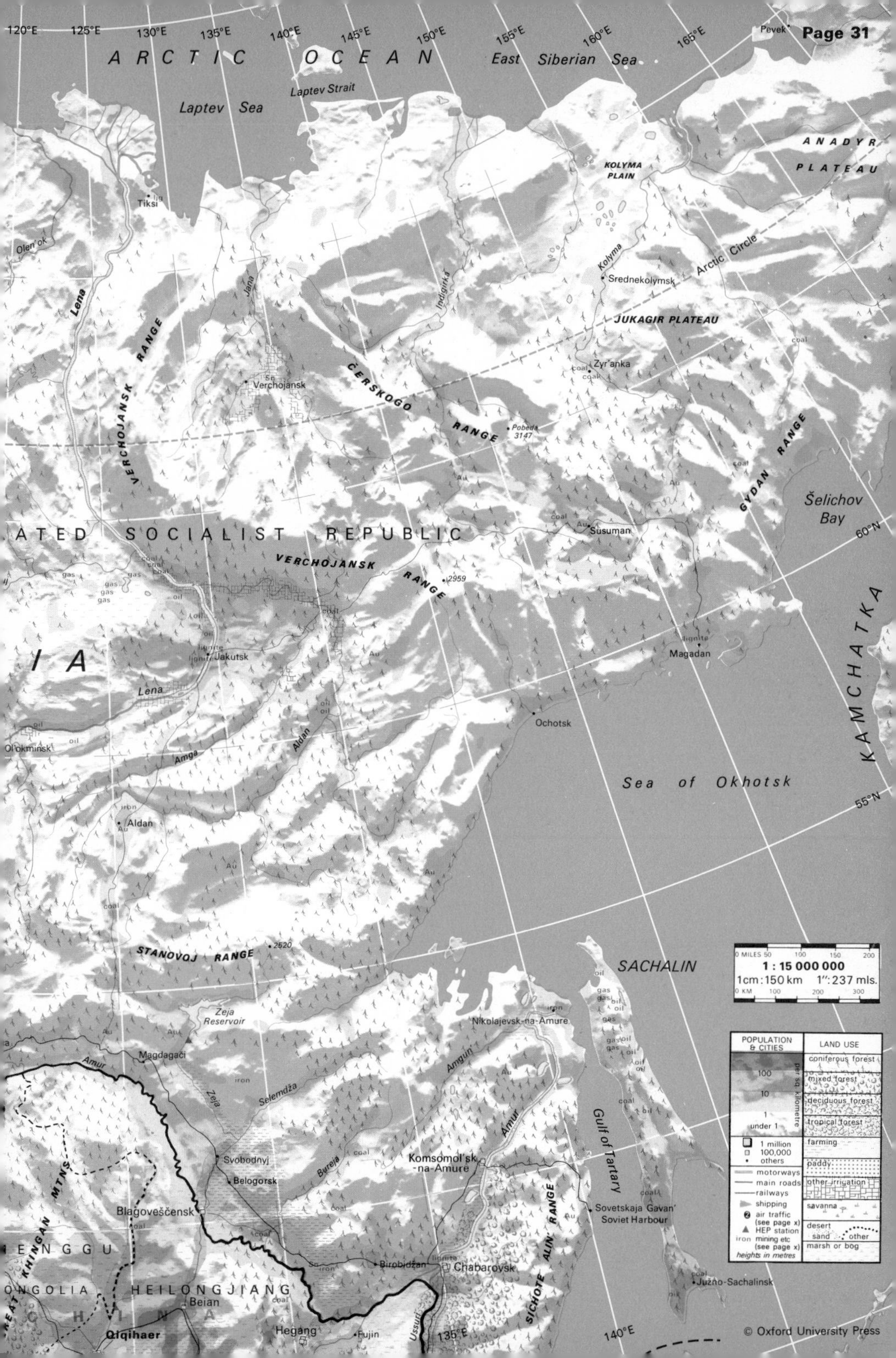

ARCTIC OCEAN
East Siberian Sea
Pevek

Laptev Strait
Laptev Sea

ANADYR PLATEAU

KOLYMA PLAIN

Tiksi

Olen'ok

Lena

Jana

Srednekolymsk
Kolyma

Arctic Circle

JUKAGIR PLATEAU

coal

Verchojansk
So

VERCHOJANSK RANGE

Zyr'anka
coal
coal

ČERSKOGO RANGE

Pobeda 3147

GYDAN RANGE

Šelichov Bay

ATED SOCIALIST REPUBLIC

coal

Susuman

60°N

gas gas
gas gas
oil
oil
oil

VERCHOJANSK RANGE

·2959

IA

Jakutsk

lignite
coal

Magadan

Lena

Ol'okminsk
oil

Amga

Aldan

oil

Ochotsk

Sea of Okhotsk

KAMCHATKA

55°N

Au

Aldan

coal

STANOVOJ RANGE
·2520

SACHALIN

1 : 15 000 000

0 MILES 50   100   150   200
1cm:150 km   1″:237 mls.
0 KM   100   200   300

Žeja Reservoir

gas
gas
oil
oil

Nikolajevsk-na-Amure

Angun

Amur

Magdagači

iron

Zeja

Selemdža

iron

Amur

Gulf of Tartary

coal

POPULATION & CITIES

LAND USE

coniferous forest
mixed forest
deciduous forest
tropical forest

100
10
1
under 1

per sq. kilometre

1 million
100,000
others

farming

paddy

other irrigation

savanna

desert
sand   other
marsh or bog

motorways
main roads
railways
shipping
air traffic (see page x)
HEP station
mining etc. (see page x)
heights in metres

Svobodnyj
Belogorsk

Bureja

Komsomol'sk-na-Amure

coal

Sovetskaja Gavan'
Soviet Harbour

SICHOTE ALIN RANGE

iron

GREAT KINGAN MTNS

Blagoveščensk

MENGGU

ONGOLIA   HEILONGJIANG

Birobidžan

Chabarovsk

Ussuri

coal

Juzno-Sachalinsk

Beian

CHINA

Qiqihaer

Hegang

Fujin

135°E

140°E

© Oxford University Press

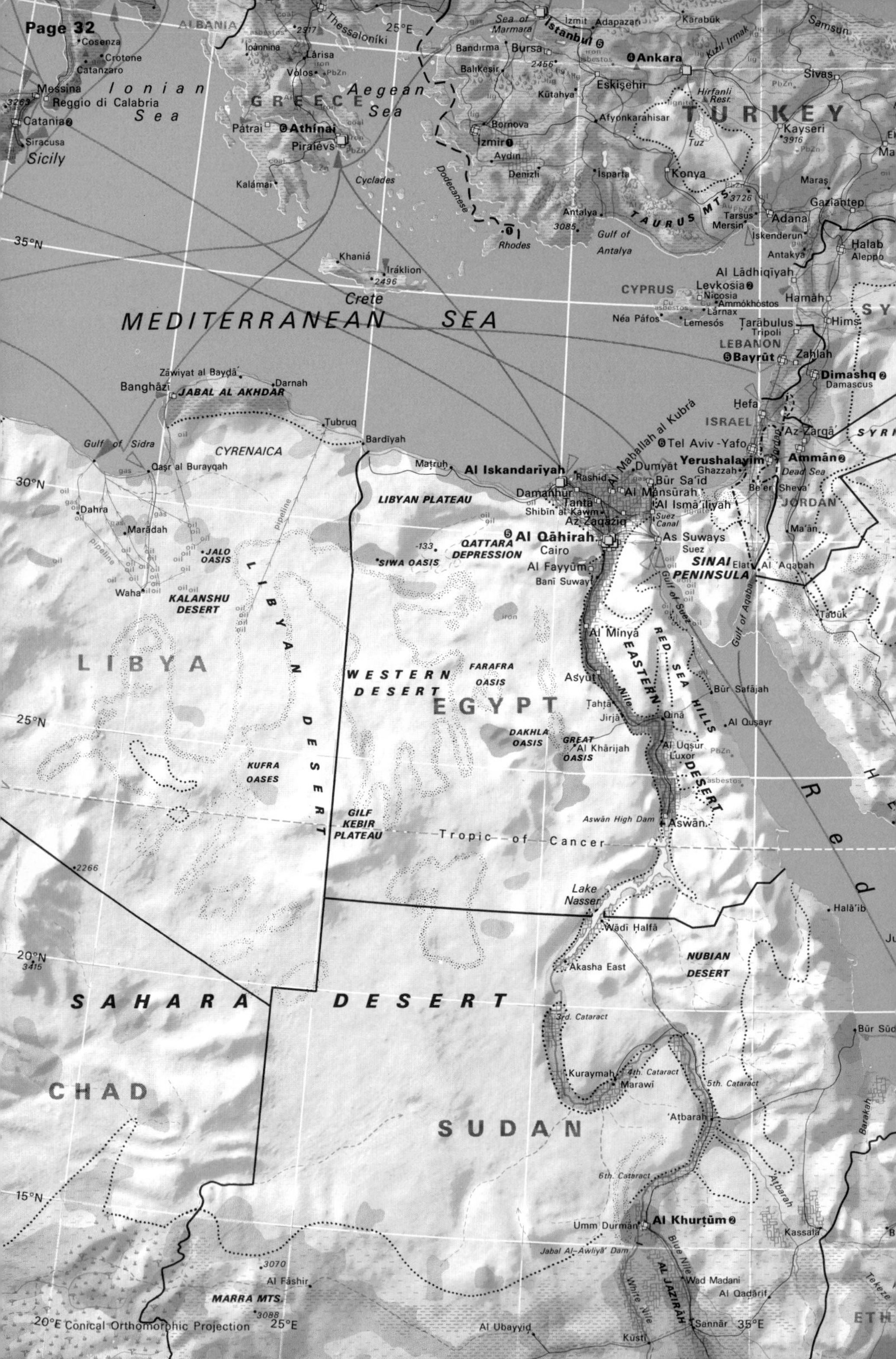
ALBANIA
Thessaloníki
25°E
Sea of Marmara
İstanbul
İzmit
Adapazarı
Karabük
Samsun
Cosenza
Crotone
Catanzaro
Ioánnina
Lárisa
Volos
Bandırma
Bursa
Balıkesir
Ankara
Kızıl Irmak
Sivas
Messina
Reggio di Calabria
Ionian Sea
Catania
Siracusa
Sicily
GREECE
Aegean Sea
Pátrai
Athínai
Piraiévs
Kalámai
Cyclades
Kütahya
Eskişehir
Hirfanli Resr.
Bornova
İzmir
Aydın
Denizli
Afyonkarahisar
TURKEY
Kayseri
3916
Tuz
Konya
Isparta
Dodecanese
Rhodes
Antalya
3085
Gulf of Antalya
TAURUS MTS.
3726
Tarsus
Mersin
Adana
Maraş
Gaziantep
İskenderun
Antakya
Halab
Aleppo
35°N
Khaniá
Iráklion
2496
Crete
Al Lādhiqīyah
Levkosia
Nicosia
Ammókhostos
Lárnax
CYPRUS
Néa Páfos
Lemesós
Hamāh
Hims
Ţarābulus
Tripoli
LEBANON
Bayrūt
Zahlah
Dimashq
Damascus
MEDITERRANEAN SEA
Zāwiyat al Baydā'
Banghāzī
Darnah
JABAL AL AKHDAR
Tubruq
Bardīyah
Ḥefa
ISRAEL
Tel Aviv-Yafo
Az-Zarqā'
Yerushalayim
Ammān
Ghazzah
Dead Sea
Be'er Sheva'
JORDAN
Gulf of Sidra
CYRENAICA
Qaşr al Burayqah
30°N
Dahra
Marādah
JALO OASIS
Waha
KALANSHU DESERT
pipeline
Maţruh
Al Iskandarīyah
Al Maḩallah al Kubrá
Rashīd
Dumyāţ
Būr Sa'īd
Damanhūr
Al Manşūrah
Ţanţā
Al Ismā'īlīyah
Shibīn al Kawm
Az Zaqāzīq
Suez Canal
LIBYAN PLATEAU
Al Qāhirah
Cairo
As Suways
Suez
QATTARA DEPRESSION
-133
SIWA OASIS
Al Fayyūm
Banī Suwayf
SINAI PENINSULA
Elat
Al 'Aqabah
Ma'ān
Gulf of Suez
Gulf of Aqaba
Tabūk
LIBYA
LIBYAN DESERT
Al Minyā
WESTERN DESERT
FARAFRA OASIS
EGYPT
Asyūţ
Nile
EASTERN DESERT
RED SEA HILLS
Būr Safājah
Ţahţā
Jirjā
Qinā
Al Quşayr
25°N
DAKHLA OASIS
GREAT OASIS
Al Khārijah
Al Uqşur
Luxor
KUFRA OASES
GILF KEBIR PLATEAU
Tropic of Cancer
Aswān High Dam
Aswān
Red
2266
Lake Nasser
Wādī Ḥalfā
Halā'ib
20°N
3415
Akasha East
NUBIAN DESERT
SAHARA DESERT
3rd. Cataract
Būr Sūdān
CHAD
Kuraymah
4th. Cataract
Marawī
5th. Cataract
'Aţbarah
SUDAN
Barakah
6th. Cataract
15°N
Al Khurţūm
Umm Durmān
Kassalā
Jabal Al-Awliyā' Dam
Blue Nile
3070
Al Fāshir
White Nile
AL JAZĪRAH
Wad Madani
Al Qaḑārif
MARRA MTS.
3088
Tekeze
20°E Conical Orthomorphic Projection 25°E
Al Ubayyid
Sannār
35°E
Kūstī

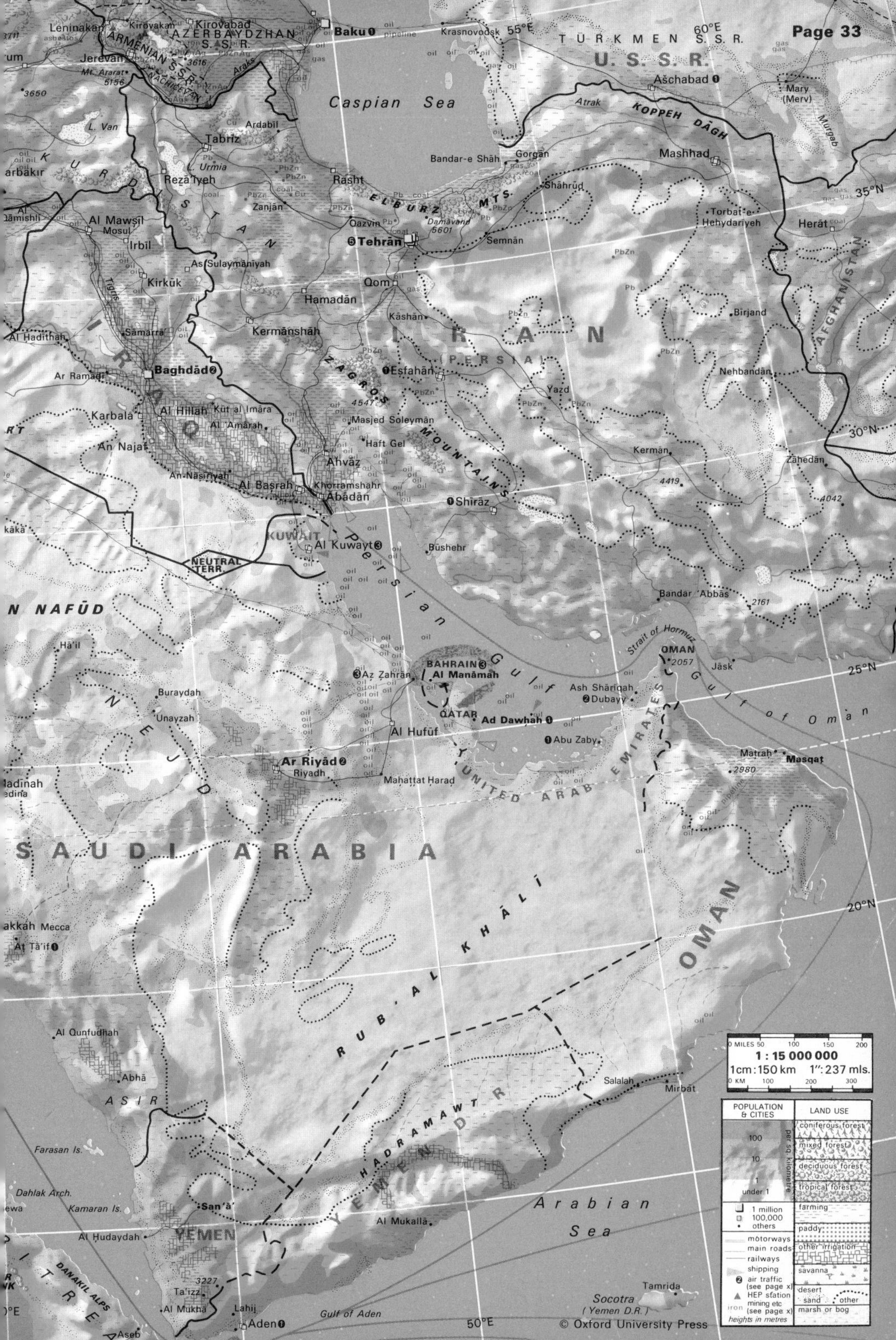

Leninakan
Kirovakan Kirovabad
AZERBAYDZHAN
ARMENIAN S.S.R.
S.S.R.
Baku
oil
pipeline
55°E
Krasnovodsk
60°E
TÜRKMEN
U.S.S.R.
S.S.R.
Aschabad
Mary
(Merv)
Murgab
Jerevan
Mt.Ararat
5156
Nachichev
3616
Caspian Sea
Atrak
KOPPEH DAGH
35°N
Ardabil
Bandar-e Shah
Gorgan
Atrak
Mashhad
Tabriz
Rasht
Shahrud
3650
L. Van
Urmia
Reza'iyeh
ELBURZ
MTS.
Torbat-e
Heydariyeh
Herat
arbakir
Zanjan
Qazvin
Damavand
5601
Semnan
KURDISTAN
coal
Tehran
AFGHANISTAN
As Sulaymaniyah
Qom
lamshli
Al Mawsil
Mosul
Irbil
Hamadan
Kashan
Birjand
Kirkuk
Kermanshah
IRAN
(PERSIA)
Yazd
Nehbandan
Samarra
Esfahan
Al Hadithah
Ar Ramadi
Baghdad
30°N
Karbala
Al Hillah
Kut al Imara
4547
ZAGROS
Kerman
Zahedan
An Najaf
Al 'Amarah
Masjed Soleyman
Haft Gel
4419
4042
An Nasiriyah
Ahvaz
MOUNTAINS
Khorramshahr
Al Basrah
Abadan
Shiraz
KUWAIT
Bushehr
Bandar 'Abbas
2161
NEUTRAL
TERR.
Al Kuwayt
Strait of Hormuz
N NAFUD
Persian
OMAN
2057
Jask
Gulf of Oman
25°N
Ha'il
BAHRAIN
Az Zahran
Al Manamah
Ash Shariqah
Dubayy
Gulf
Buraydah
QATAR
Ad Dawhah
Matrah
Masqat
Unayzah
Al Hufuf
Abu Zaby
UNITED ARAB EMIRATES
2880
ladinah
Ar Riyad
edina
Riyadh
Mahattat Harad
OMAN
NEJD
20°N
SAUDI ARABIA
RUB' AL KHALI
Al Qunfudhah
Abha
ASIR
Salalah
Mirbat
akkah Mecca
At Ta'if
Farasan Is.
HADRAMAWT
Dahlak Arch.
San'a'
Kamaran Is.
Arabian
ewa
Al Hudaydah
YEMEN
Al Mukalla
Sea
DANAKIL ALPS
3227
Ta'izz
Tamrida
Socotra
Lahij
Al Mukha
[Yemen D.R.]
Aseb
Aden
Gulf of Aden
50°E
© Oxford University Press

MILES 50   100   150   200
1 : 15 000 000
1cm:150 km   1″: 237 mls.
0 KM   100   200   300

POPULATION
& CITIES
LAND USE
coniferous forest
100
mixed forest
10
deciduous forest
under 1
tropical forest
1 million
farming
100,000
others
paddy
motorways
main roads
other irrigation
railways
shipping
savanna
air traffic
(see page x)
HEP station
desert
(see page x)
sand
other
mining etc
(see page x)
marsh or bog
heights in metres
iron

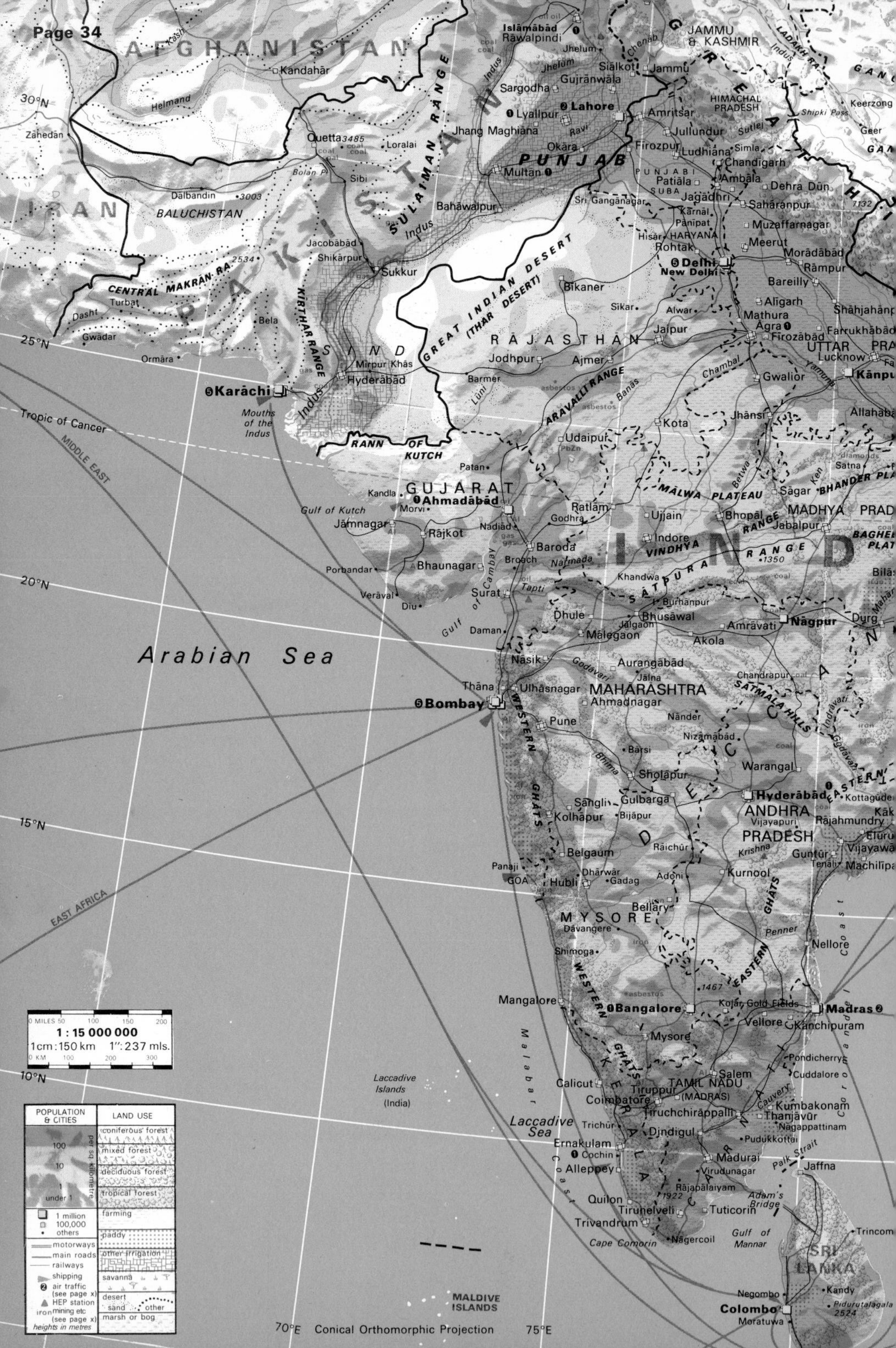

Page 34
AFGHANISTAN
Kandahār
Helmand
30°N
Zāhedān
IRAN
Quetta 3485
Loralai
Bolan P.
Sibi
Dālbandin
3003
BALUCHISTAN
Jacobābād
Shikārpur
Sukkur
CENTRAL MAKRAN RA. 2534
Turbat
Dasht
Bela
Gwadar
Ormāra
25°N
PAKISTAN
SULAIMAN RANGE
KIRTHAR RANGE
SIND
Mirpur Khās
Hyderābād
Karāchi
Mouths of the Indus
Tropic of Cancer
MIDDLE EAST
Islāmābād
Rāwalpindi
Jhelum
Sargodha
Gujrānwāla
Siālkot
Jammu
JAMMU & KASHMIR
LADAKH RA.
Lahore
Lyallpur
Jhang Maghiāna
Okāra
PUNJAB
Multān
Bahāwalpur
Indus
Chenab
Ravi
Sutlej
Amritsar
Jullundur
Firozpur
Ludhiāna
Simla
Chandigarh
Patiāla
Ambāla
Dehra Dūn
Jagādhri
Sahāranpur
HIMACHAL PRADESH
Shipki Pass
Keerzong
Geer
7132
Sri Ganganagar
Karnāl
Pānipat
Hisār
HARYANA
Rohtak
Muzaffarnagar
Meerut
Morādābād
Rāmpur
Delhi
New Delhi
Bareilly
Alīgarh
Shāhjahānp
GREAT INDIAN DESERT (THAR DESERT)
Bikaner
Sikar
Alwar
Mathura
Āgra
Firozābād
Farrukhābād
Jaipur
RĀJASTHĀN
UTTAR PRA
Lucknow
Kānpu
Jodhpur
Ajmer
Barmer
Lūni
ARAVALLI RANGE
Banās
Chambal
Gwalior
Yamuna
asbestos
Jhānsi
Allahaba
Kota
Udaipur
Betwa
Ken
Satna
RANN OF KUTCH
Patan
MĀLWA PLATEAU
Sāgar
BHANDER PLA
GUJARAT
Kandla
Ahmadābād
Morvi
Gulf of Kutch
Jāmnagar
Rājkot
Nadiād
Ratlām
Godhra
Ujjain
Bhopāl
MADHYA PRAD
Jabalpur
Baroda
Indore
VINDHYA RANGE
BAGHE PLAT
Porbandar
Bhaunagar
Broach
Narmada
Gulf of Cambay
Khandwa
SĀTPURA RANGE
1350
INDIA
Bilās
20°N
Verāval
Diu
Surat
Tapti
Burhānpur
Durg
Daman
Dhule
Jalgaon
Bhusāwal
Amrāvati
Nāgpur
Mālegaon
Akola
Arabian Sea
Nāsik
Godavari
Aurangābād
Jālna
Chandrapur
Thāna
Ulhāsnagar
MAHARASHTRA
Ahmadnagar
Bombay
WESTERN GHATS
SATMALA HILLS
Nānder
Indravati
Pune
Nizāmābād
DECCAN
Bārsi
Bhima
Sholāpur
Warangal
EASTERN
Hyderābād
Kottagude
Sāngli
Gulbarga
ANDHRA PRADESH
Kolhāpur
Bijāpur
Vijayapuri
Rājahmundry
15°N
Belgaum
Rāichūr
Krishna
Elūru
Vijayawā
Guntūr
Tenāli
Machilipa
Panaji
GOA
Hubli
Dhārwār
Gadag
Ādoni
Kurnool
EAST AFRICA
Bellary
MYSORE
Dāvangere
Penner
Shimoga
Nellore
Coromandel Coast
Mangalore
1467
Bangalore
Kolār Gold Fields
Madras
Vellore
Kānchipuram
Malabar Coast
Mysore
Pondicherry
Cuddalore
10°N
Laccadive Islands (India)
Calicut
Salem
TAMIL NADU (MADRAS)
Tiruppur
Coimbatore
Cauvery
Tiruchchirāppalli
Kumbakonam
Thanjāvūr
Nāgappattinam
Laccadive Sea
Trichūr
Dindigul
Ernakulam
Pudukkottai
Cochin
Madurai
Palk Strait
Jaffna
Alleppey
Virudunagar
KERALA
Rājapālaiyam
Adam's Bridge
Quilon
1922
Tirunelveli
Tuticorin
Trivandrum
Gulf of Mannar
Cape Comorin
Nāgercoil
Trincom
SRI LANKA
Kandy
Negombo
Colombo
Moratuwa
Pidurutalagala 2524
MALDIVE ISLANDS
0 MILES 50 100 150 200
1 : 15 000 000
1cm : 150 km 1'' : 237 mls.
0 KM 100 200 300
POPULATION & CITIES
100
10
1
under 1
per sq kilometre
1 million
100,000
others
motorways
main roads
railways
shipping
air traffic (see page x)
HEP station
iron mining etc (see page x)
heights in metres
LAND USE
coniferous forest
mixed forest
deciduous forest
tropical forest
farming
paddy
other irrigation
savanna
desert sand other
marsh or bog
70°E Conical Orthomorphic Projection 75°E

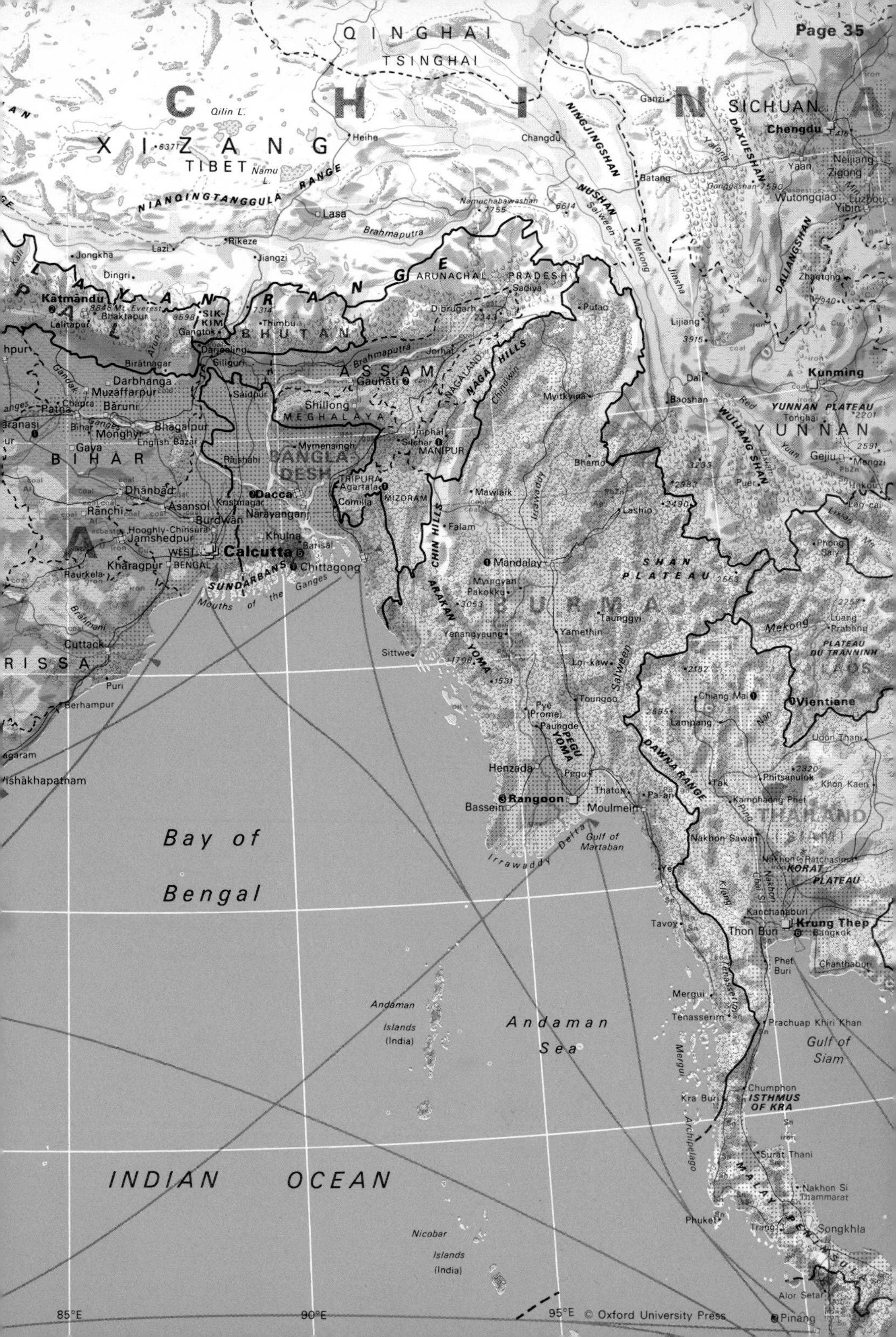

QINGHAI
TSINGHAI

C H I N A

SICHUAN

Qilin L.
Chengdu

XIZANG
TIBET

Heihe
Changdu

Neijiang
Zigong

NINGJINGSHAN

DAXUESHAN
Yaan

Wutongqiao
Yibin

Namu
L.

NIANQINGTANGGULA RANGE

Lasa

Namchabawashan
7755

Batang

Gonggashan 7590

Luzhou

6614

Brahmaputra

NUSHAN

Salween

Mekong

Jinsha

DALIANGSHAN

Zhaotong

Jongkha

Lazi

Rikeze

Jiangzi

ARUNACHAL PRADESH

Sadiya

Lijiang
3975

Dali

4940

coal

Dingri

NEPAL

Jomosom

Dibrugarh
2343

Putao

iron

Katmandu

Everest
8848

SIK-
KIM

Thimbu

Darjeeling

BHUTAN

Brahmaputra

Jorhat

Myitkyina

Baoshan

YUNNAN
PLATEAU
2201

Kunming

Lalitpur
Bhaktapur
2598

Gangtok

Siliguri

ASSAM

Gauhati

NAGALAND

NAGA HILLS

Bhamo

3293

Tonghai

Gejiu

Mangzi

YUNNAN

2591

Birâtnagar

Darbhanga

Saidpur

Shillong

MEGHALAYA

Imphal

MANIPUR

Silchar

Mawlaik

Lashio

2490

WULIANG SHAN

Phong
Saly

Muzaffarpur

Mymensingh

2865

Dali Col

Patna

BANGLA-
DESH

Dacca

Bhagalpur
Monghyr

English Bazar

Krishnagar
Narayanganj

Comilla

TRIPURA
Agartala

MIZORAM

Falam

CHIN HILLS

Mandalay

SHAN

PLATEAU

255

Luang
Prabang

Chindwin

Myingyan

Pakokku

Gaya

BIHAR

Dhânbâd

Asansol
Burdwan

Khulna

Barisal

Chittagong

Mandalay

3053

ARAKAN YOMA

Irrawaddy

Lashio

Salween

Mekong

PLATEAU
DU TRANNINH

LAOS

2192

Ranchi

Hooghly-Chinsura
Jamshedpur

WEST
BENGAL

Calcutta

SUNDARBANS

Yenangyaung

1798

BURMA

Yamethin

Loi-kaw

Chiang Mai

Lampang

Vientiane

Udon Thani

Kharagpur

Raukela

Brahmani

Mouths of the Ganges

Sittwe

PEGU YOMA

1531

Pye
(Prome)

Toungoo

885

Tak

THAILAND
SIAM

Cuttack

Puri

Henzada

Paungde

Pegu

Phitsanulok

Khon Kaen

Berhampur

ORISSA

Bassein

Rangoon

Thaton

Pa-an

Nakhon Sawan

KORAT
PLATEAU

shakhapatnam

Moulmein

Gulf of
Martaban

DAWNA RANGE

Nakhon
Ratchasima

Bay of

Bengal

Irrawaddy Delta

Kanchanaburi

Krung Thep
Bangkok

Tavoy

Thon Buri

Phet
Buri

Chanthaburi

Mergui

Tenasserim

Andaman

Islands
(India)

Andaman

Sea

TENASSERIM

Mergui

Archipelago

Prachuap Khiri Khan

Gulf of
Siam

Chumphon

Kra Buri

ISTHMUS
OF KRA

INDIAN OCEAN

Surat Thani

Nakhon Si
Thammarat

Phuket

Songkhla

Nicobar
Islands
(India)

MALAYA

Alor Setar

Pinang

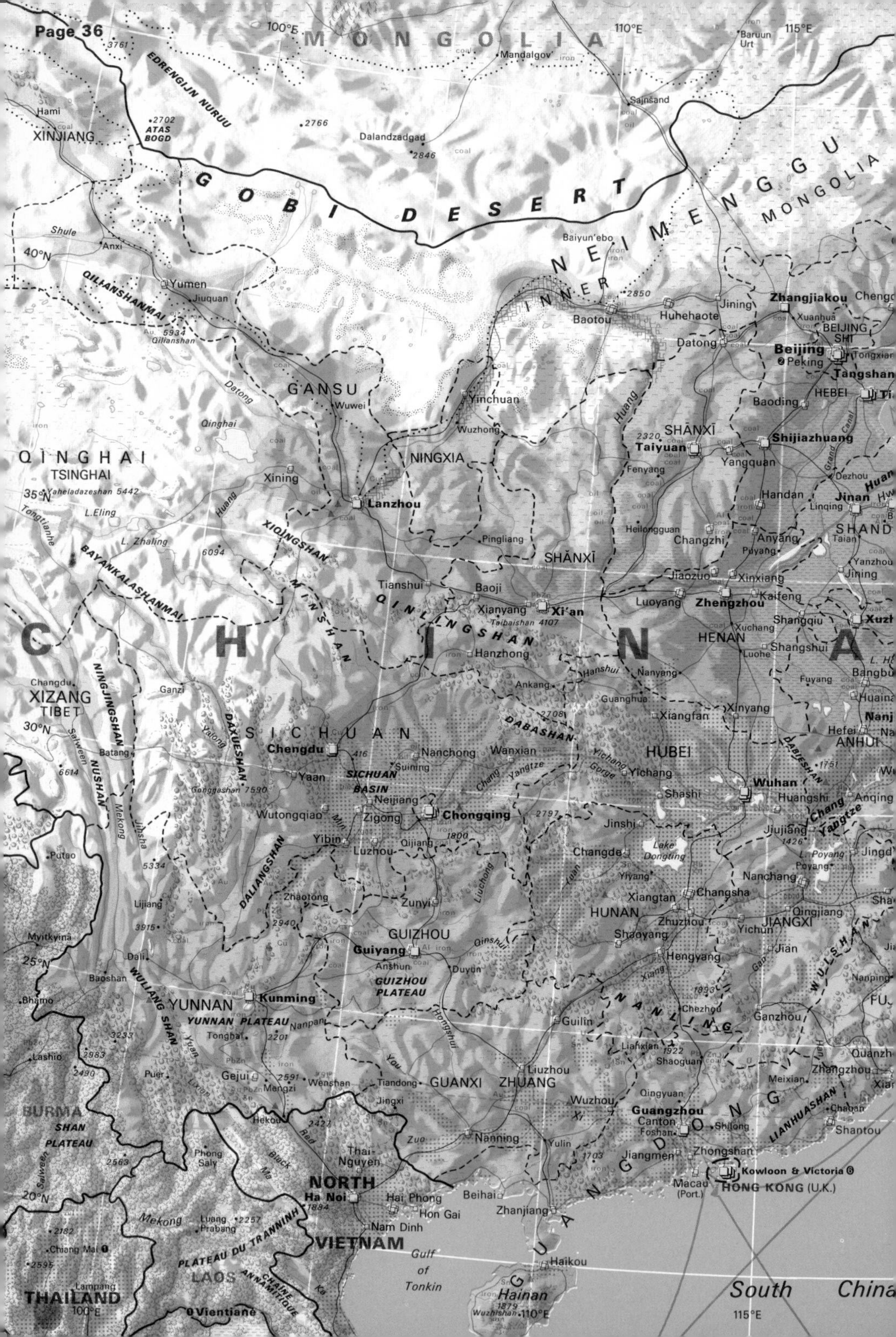

Page 36
100°E
110°E
115°E
MONGOLIA
Mandalgov'
Baruun Urt
Sajnsand
EDRENGIJN NURUU
Hami
XINJIANG
2702
ATAS BOGD
2766
Dalandzadgad
2846
GOBI DESERT
NEI MENGGU
INNER MONGOLIA
Shule
Anxi
40°N
Yumen
Jiuquan
QILIANSHANMAI
5934
Qilianshan
Baiyun'ebo
2850
Baotou
Huhehaote
Jining
Zhangjiakou
Chengde
Xuanhua
BEIJING SHI
Datong
Beijing
Peking
Tongxian
Tangshan
GANSU
Wuwei
Datong
Qinghai
Yinchuan
Wuzhong
NINGXIA
HEBEI
Baoding
Huang
SHĀNXĪ
2320
Taiyuan
Yangquan
Shijiazhuang
Grand Canal
QINGHAI
TSINGHAI
Xining
35°N
Yaheladazeshan 5442
L.Eling
Tongtianhe
L. Zhaling
6094
Lanzhou
XIQINGSHAN
BAYANKALASHANMAI
Pingliang
Fenyang
Heilongguan
Changzhi
Handan
Dezhou
Jinan
Linqing
Anyang
Puyang
Taian
Yanzhou
Jining
SHĀNXĪ
MINSHAN
Tianshui
Baoji
QINLINGSHAN
Xianyang
Xi'an
Taibaishan 4107
Jiaozuo
Xinxiang
Luoyang
Zhengzhou
Kaifeng
Shangqiu
Xuchang
HENAN
Shangshui
Luohe
CHINA
Hanzhong
Hanshui
Ankang
Nanyang
Guanghua
Changdu
XIZANG
TIBET
30°N
NINGJINGSHAN
Ganzi
DAXUESHAN
Yalong
SICHUAN
2708
DABASHAN
Xiangfan
Xinyang
Fuyang
Bangbu
Huainan
Hefei
ANHUI
DABIESHAN
1751
Batang
Salween
NUSHAN
6614
Chengdu
416
SICHUAN BASIN
Nanchong
Suining
Wanxian
Yaan
Gonggashan 7590
Chang
Yangtze
Yichang Gorge
Yichang
HUBEI
Shashi
Wuhan
Huangshi
Anqing
Mekong
Jinsha
Neijiang
Zigong
Chongqing
Wutongqiao
Min
Yibin
Luzhou
Qijiang
1800
2797
Jinshi
Lake Dongting
Changde
Yiyang
Jiujiang
Chang
Yangtze
1426
Poyang
Putao
5334
DALIANGSHAN
Zhaotong
Zunyi
Liuchong
Yuan
Xiangtan
Changsha
Nanchang
Lijiang
3915
2940
HUNAN
Zhuzhou
Qingjiang
Yichun
JIANGXI
Myitkyina
GUIZHOU
Guiyang
Qinshui
Shaoyang
Hengyang
Jian
WUISHAN
25°N
Dali
Baoshan
WULIANG SHAN
Anshun
Duyun
GUIZHOU PLATEAU
Xiang
1893
Nanping
Bhamo
YUNNAN
Kunming
YUNNAN PLATEAU
Nanpan
NANLING
Chezhou
Ganzhou
Guilin
3233
Tonghai
2201
Hongshui
Lianxian
1922
Shaoguan
Lashio
2983
2490
Puer
Gejiu
2591
Mengzi
Wenshan
Tiandong
You
GUANXI ZHUANG
Liuzhou
Meixian
Zhangzhou
Quanzhou
Jingxi
Wuzhou
Xi
Qingyuan
Guangzhou
Canton
Foshan
Shilong
LIANHUASHAN
Chaoan
Shantou
GUANGDONG
BURMA
SHAN PLATEAU
Hekou
2427
Red
Zuo
Nanning
Yulin
Phong Saly
Black
Thai-Nguyen
1703
Jiangmen
Zhongshan
Kowloon & Victoria
HONG KONG (U.K.)
Macau (Port.)
2563
Ma
NORTH
Ha Noi
1884
Hai Phong
Hon Gai
Beihai
Zhanjiang
20°N
Mekong
Luang Prabang
2257
Nam Dinh
2182
Chiang Mai
2595
VIETNAM
PLATEAU DU TRANNINH
LAOS
CHAÎNE ANNAMITIQUE
Gulf of Tonkin
Haikou
Hainan
1879
Wuzhishan
110°E
Lampang
THAILAND
100°E
Vientiane
Ka
South China
115°E
Salween
iron
coal
oil

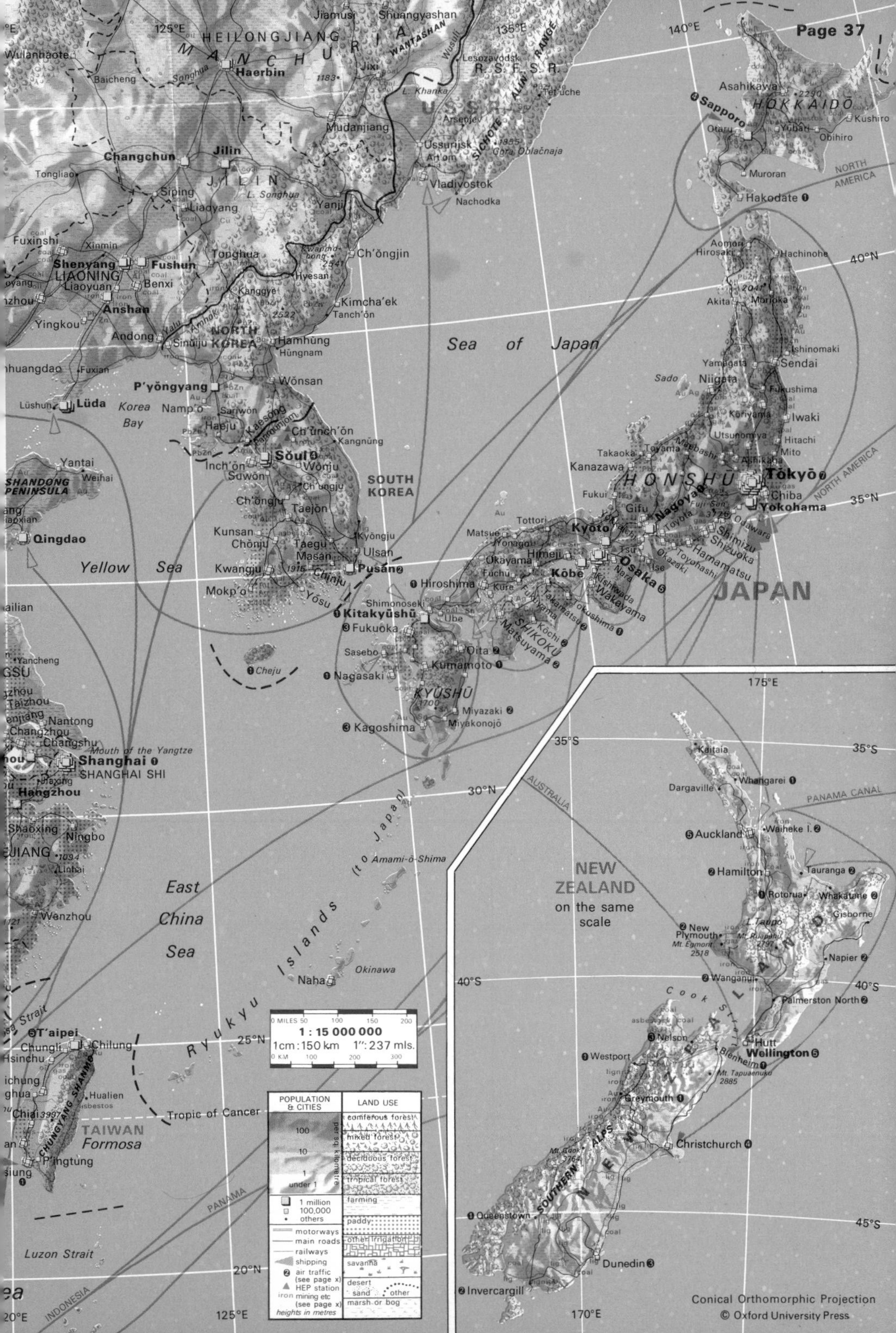

HEILONGJIANG
MANCHURIA
WANTASHAN
125°E
135°E
140°E
Jiamusi
Shuangyashan
Wulanhaote
Haerbin
Songhua
Baicheng
Jixi
Lesozavodsk
R.S.F.S.R.
L. Khanka
U.S.S.R.
SICHOTE ALIN RANGE
Tet'uche
Arsenjev
Mudanjiang
Changchun
Jilin
JILIN
Ussurijsk
Art'om
Gora Oblačnaja
Vladivostok
Nachodka
Tongliao
Siping
Liaoyang
L. Songhua
Yanji
Fuxinshi
Xinmin
Shenyang
Fushun
Tonghua
LIAONING
Benxi
Liaoyuan
Anshan
Hyesan
Kanggye
Ch'ŏngjin
Kimcha'ek
Tanch'ŏn
Yingkou
Andong
Yalu
Sinuiju
NORTH KOREA
Hamhŭng
Hŭngnam
Fuxian
P'yŏngyang
Wŏnsan
Lüshun
Lüda
Korea Bay
Namp'o
Sariwŏn
Haeju
Kaesŏng
Panmunjom
Ch'unch'ŏn
Kangnŭng
Yantai
Weihai
SHANDONG PENINSULA
Sŏul
Inch'ŏn
Suwŏn
Wŏnju
Ch'ungju
SOUTH KOREA
Ch'ŏngju
Taejŏn
Kunsan
Chŏnju
Taegu
Masan
Kyŏngju
Ulsan
Pusan
Qingdao
Yellow Sea
Kwangju
Mokp'o
Chinju
Yŏsu
Cheju
Sea of Japan
Sado
Niigata
Yamagata
Sendai
Ishinomaki
Fukushima
Koriyama
Iwaki
Utsunomiya
Hitachi
Mito
Maebashi
Ashikaga
Toyama
Takaoka
Kanazawa
HONSHŪ
Tōkyō
Chiba
Yokohama
Fukui
Gifu
Nagoya
Fuji San
Odawara
Tottori
Matsue
Yonago
Kyoto
Shimizu
Shizuoka
Hamamatsu
Toyohashi
Okazaki
Himeji
Okayama
Kōbe
Osaka
Nara
Ise
Tsu
Fuchū
Kure
Hiroshima
Kishiwada
Wakayama
Tokushima
Takamatsu
Kōchi
SHIKOKU
Matsuyama
Shimonoseki
Ube
Kitakyūshū
Fukuoka
Oita
Sasebo
Kumamoto
Nagasaki
KYŪSHŪ
Miyazaki
Miyakonojō
Kagoshima
JAPAN
Asahikawa
HOKKAIDŌ
Sapporo
Otaru
Yūbari
Obihiro
Kushiro
Muroran
Hakodate
NORTH AMERICA
Aomori
Hirosaki
Hachinohe
Akita
Morioka
40°N
35°N
30°N
25°N
20°N
Yancheng
Taizhou
Nantong
Changzhou
Changshu
Mouth of the Yangtze
Shanghai
SHANGHAI SHI
Hangzhou
Shaoxing
Ningbo
Linhai
Wenzhou
East China Sea
(to Japan)
Amami-ō-Shima
Ryukyu Islands
Okinawa
Naha
T'aipei
Chilung
Chungli
Hsinchu
Hualien
CHUNGYANG SHANMO
TAIWAN
Formosa
P'ingtung
Tropic of Cancer
Luzon Strait
PANAMA
INDONESIA
AUSTRALIA
PANAMA CANAL
125°E
170°E
175°E
35°S
40°S
45°S
NEW ZEALAND on the same scale
Kaitaia
Whangarei
Dargaville
Auckland
Waiheke I.
Hamilton
Tauranga
Rotorua
Whakatane
Gisborne
L. Taupo
Mt. Ruapehu 2797
New Plymouth
Mt. Egmont 2518
Napier
Wanganui
Cook Strait
Palmerston North
Nelson
Hutt
Wellington
Westport
Blenheim
Mt. Tapuaenuku 2885
Greymouth
Mt. Cook 3764
SOUTHERN ALPS
Christchurch
Queenstown
Dunedin
Invercargill
1 : 15 000 000
1cm : 150 km   1'': 237 mls.
POPULATION & CITIES
per sq kilometre
100
10
1
under 1
1 million
100,000
others
motorways
main roads
railways
shipping
air traffic (see page x)
HEP station
mining etc (see page x)
heights in metres
LAND USE
coniferous forest
mixed forest
deciduous forest
tropical forest
farming
paddy
other irrigation
savanna
desert
sand
other
marsh or bog
Conical Orthomorphic Projection
© Oxford University Press

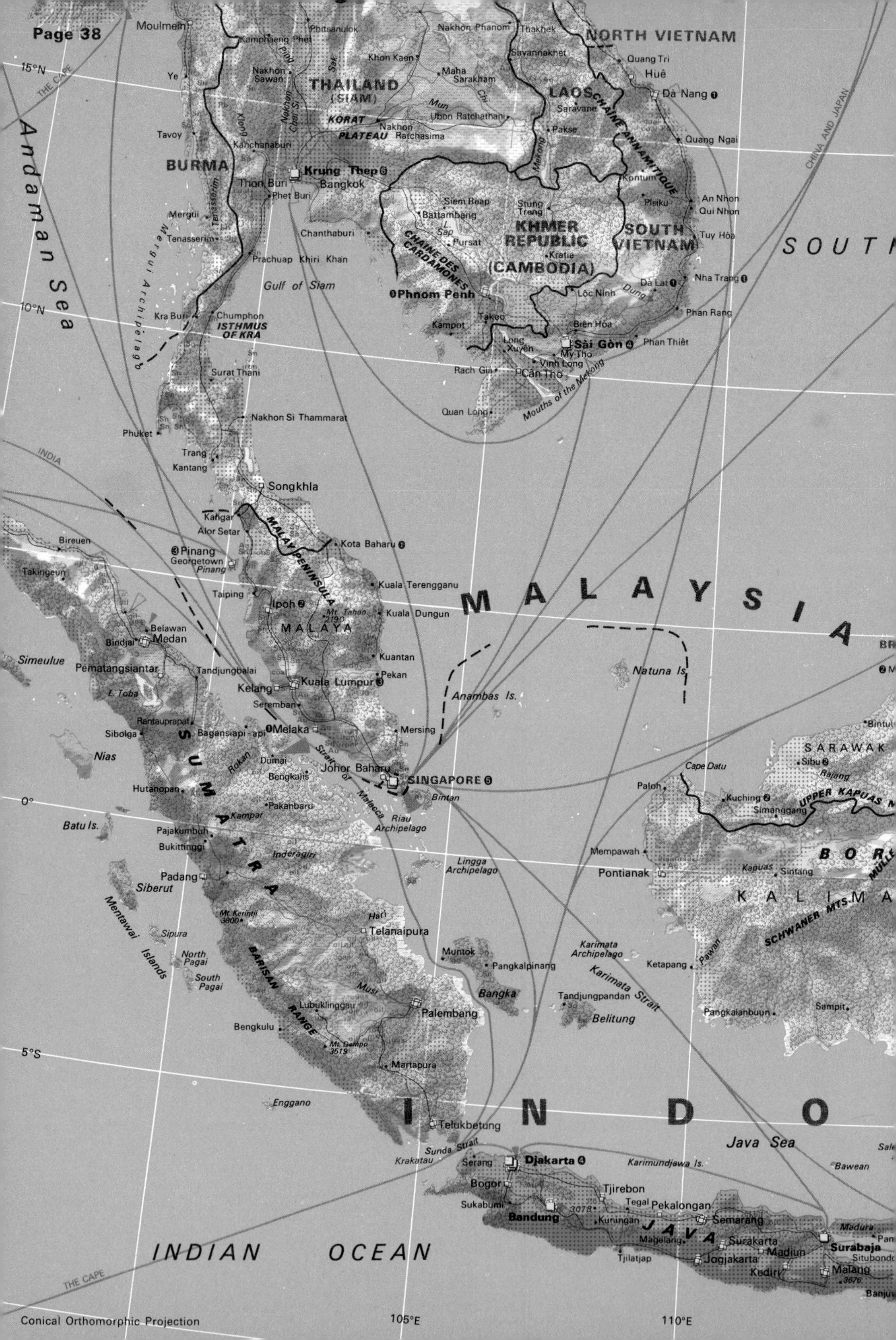

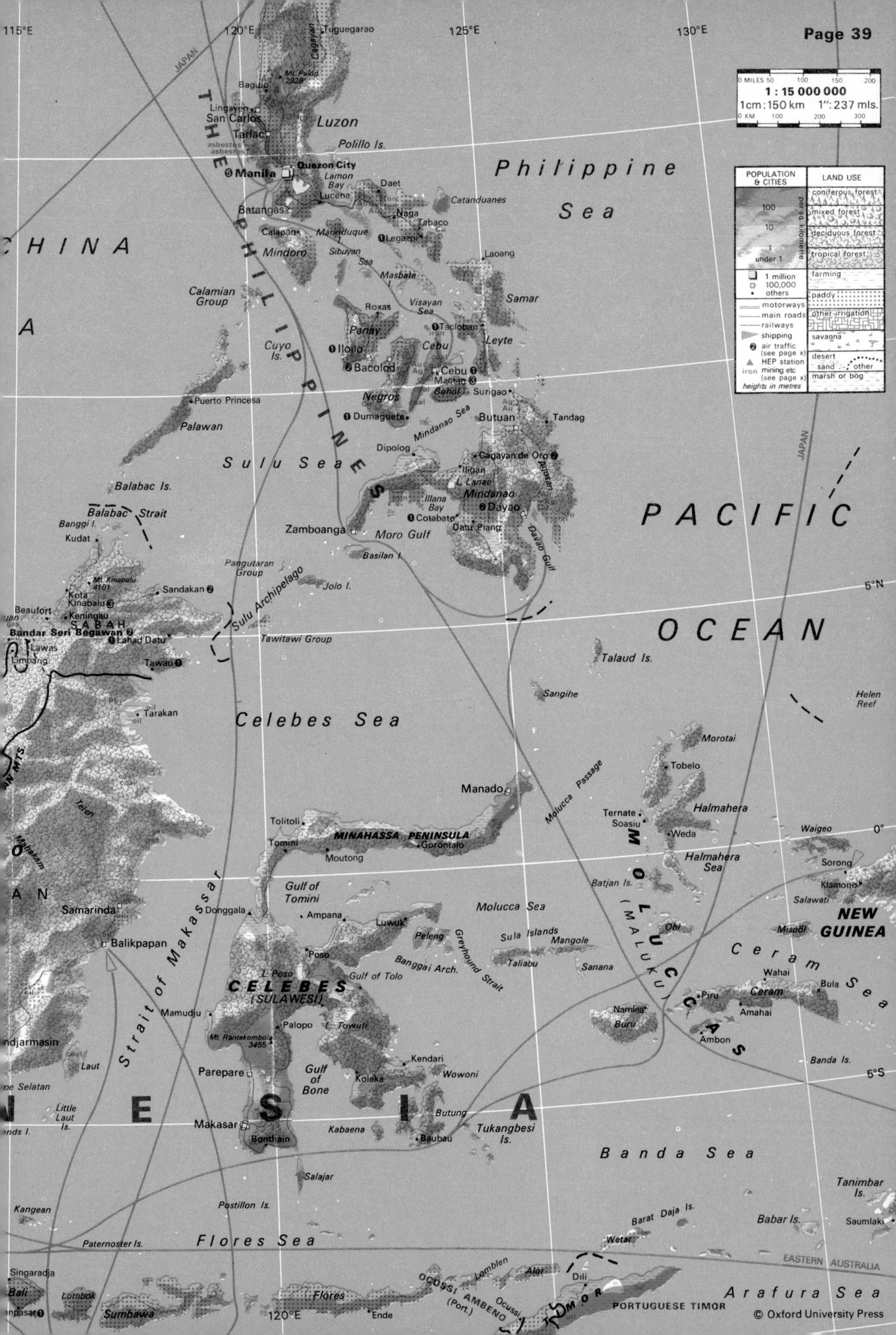

115°E   120°E   125°E   130°E

0 MILES 50   100   150   200
1 : 15 000 000
1cm:150 km   1":237 mls.
0 KM   100   200   300

POPULATION & CITIES
population per sq. kilometre
100
10
under 1
☐ 1 million
◻ 100,000
• others
— motorways
— main roads
---- railways
🚢 shipping
❷ air traffic (see page x)
❺ HEP station (see page x)
iron mining etc (see page x)
heights in metres

LAND USE
coniferous forest
mixed forest
deciduous forest
tropical forest
farming
paddy
other irrigation
savanna
desert
sand   other
marsh or bog

JAPAN

Cagayan
Tuguegarao
Mt. Pulog 2928
Baguio
Lingayen
San Carlos
Tarlac
Luzon
Polillo Is.
Manila Quezon City
Batangas
Lamon Bay
Lucena
Daet
Naga
Tabaco
Legaspi
Catanduanes

Philippine
Sea

CHINA

THE PHILIPPINES

Calapan
Mindoro
Marinduque
Sibuyan Sea
Masbate
Laoang
Samar
Calamian Group
Roxas
Visayan Sea
Panay
Cebu
Leyte
Iloilo
Bacolod
Cebu
Mactan
Bohol
Tacloban

Cuyo Is.

Puerto Princesa
Palawan

Negros
Dumaguete
Butuan
Tandag

Dipolog
Cagayan de Oro
Iligan
L. Lanao
Surigao
Mindanao Sea
Sulu Sea
Illana Bay
Mindanao
Cotabato
Dayao
Datu Piang

Balabac Is.
Balabac Strait
Banggi I.
Kudat
Pangutaran Group
Sulu Archipelago
Jolo I.
Zamboanga
Moro Gulf
Basilan I.
Davao Gulf

PACIFIC

OCEAN

Mt. Kinabalu 4101
Kota Kinabalu
Keningau
Sandakan
SABAH
Beaufort
Bandar Seri Begawan
Lawas
Limbang
Lahad Datu
Tawau
Tawitawi Group

Helen Reef

5°N

Tarakan
Celebes Sea

Talaud Is.

Sangihe

Samarinda

Morotai
Tobelo

MOLUCCAS (MALUKU)

Balikpapan
Tolitoli
Tomini
MINAHASSA PENINSULA
Gorontalo
Moutong
Manado

Ternate
Soasiu
Halmahera
Weda
Waigeo
Sorong
Klamono
Salawati
Misool

0°

NEW GUINEA

Mahakam
Teleh

Gulf of Tomini
Ampana
Luwuk
Donggala
Poso
L. Poso
Peleng
Banggai Arch.
Greyhound Strait
Sula Islands
Mangole
Taliabu
Sanana

Batjan Is.
Halmahera Sea
Obi

Ceram Sea

Wahai
Piru
Ceram
Amahai
Ambon
Bula Is.

Banjarmasin
Balikpapan
Samarinda

CELEBES (SULAWESI)
Mamudju
Mt. Rantekombola 3455
Palopo
L. Towuti
Gulf of Tolo

Kendari
Wowoni
Namlea
Buru

Banda Is.

5°S

Selatan
Little Laut Is.
Parepare
Gulf of Bone
Kolaka

Kangean
Makasar
Bonthain
Kabaena
Butung
Baubau
Tukangbesi Is.

Banda Sea

Salajar

INESIA

Postillon Is.
Paternoster Is.

Flores Sea

Barat Daja Is.
Wetar

Tanimbar Is.
Saumlaki

Babar Is.

120°E

Singaradja
Bali
Lombok
Denpasar
Sumbawa
Flores
Ende
OCUSSI AMBENO (Port.)
Lomblen
Alor
Dili
TIMOR
PORTUGUESE TIMOR
Ocussi

EASTERN AUSTRALIA

Arafura Sea

© Oxford University Press

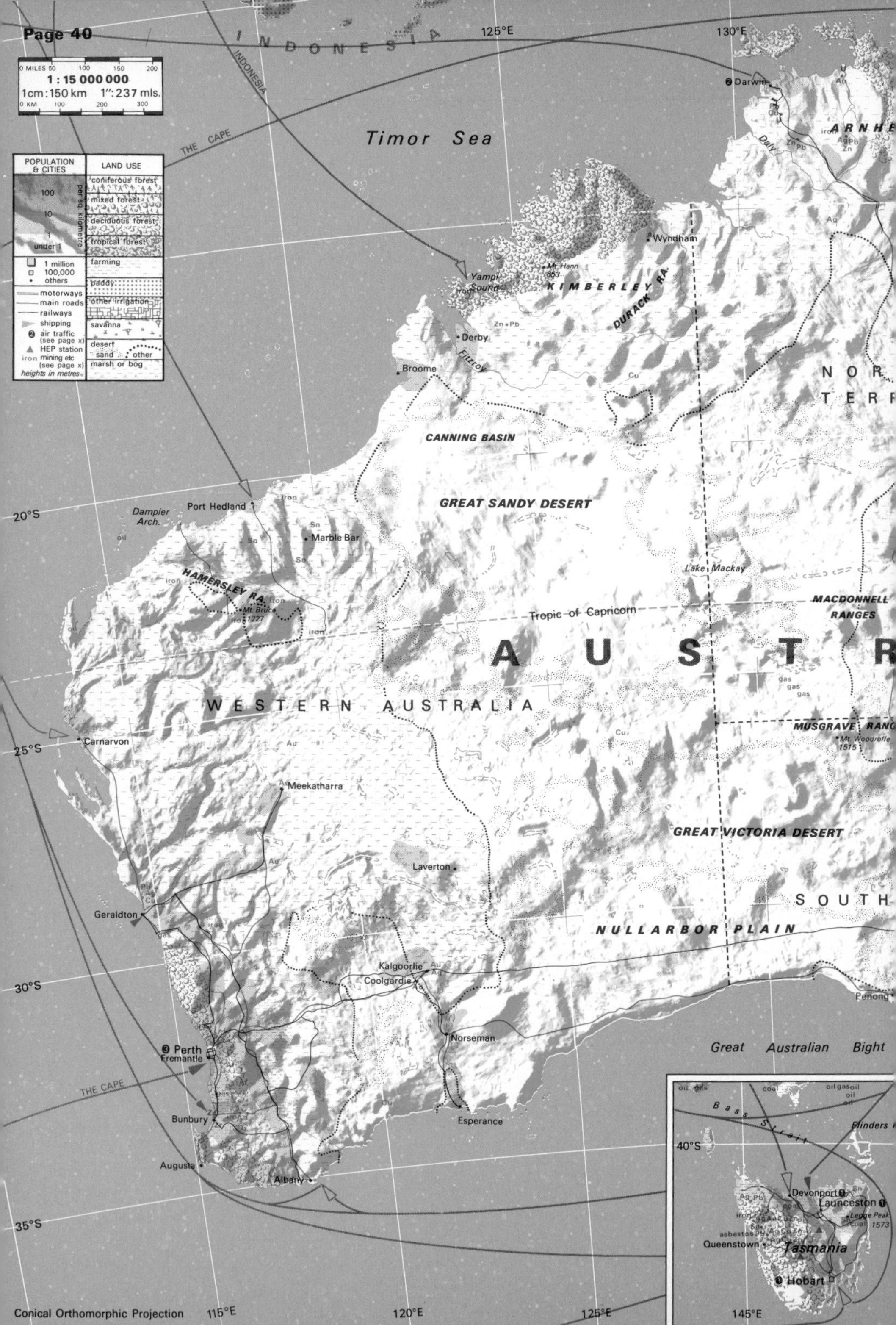

0 MILES 50   100   150   200
1 : 15 000 000
1cm:150 km   1": 237 mls.
0 KM   100   200   300

INDONESIA

Timor Sea

THE CAPE

ARNHE

Darwin

NOR
TERR

KIMBERLEY RA.

DURACK RA.

Wyndham

Mt Hann
953

Yampi
Sound

Zn • Pb

Derby

Fitzroy

Broome

Cu

CANNING BASIN

GREAT SANDY DESERT

20°S

Dampier
Arch.

Port Hedland

iron

Sn

Marble Bar

Sn

oil

HAMERSLEY RA.

iron

Mt Bruce
1227

iron

Lake Mackay

MACDONNELL
RANGES

Tropic of Capricorn

A   U   S   T   R

WESTERN AUSTRALIA

gas
gas   gas

MUSGRAVE   RANG

Mt Woodroffe
1575

Carnarvon

25°S

Au

Cu

Meekatharra

GREAT VICTORIA DESERT

Laverton

SOUTH

Geraldton

NULLARBOR PLAIN

Kalgoorlie

30°S

Coolgardie

Penong

Norseman

Great   Australian   Bight

Perth
Fremantle

Bunbury

Esperance

Augusta

Albany

35°S

115°E

120°E

125°E

145°E

130°E

125°E

**POPULATION
& CITIES**

100

10

under 1

☐ 1 million
□ 100,000
• others

— motorways
— main roads
— railways
shipping
✈ air traffic
(see page x)
▲ HEP station
iron mining etc
(see page x)
heights in metres

LAND USE

coniferous forest
mixed forest
deciduous forest
tropical forest
farming

paddy
other irrigation
savanna
desert
sand   other
marsh or bog

Bass Strait

Flinders I.

Devonport

Launceston

Ledge Peak
1573

Queenstown

asbestos

Ag • Pb

Tasmania

Hobart

40°S

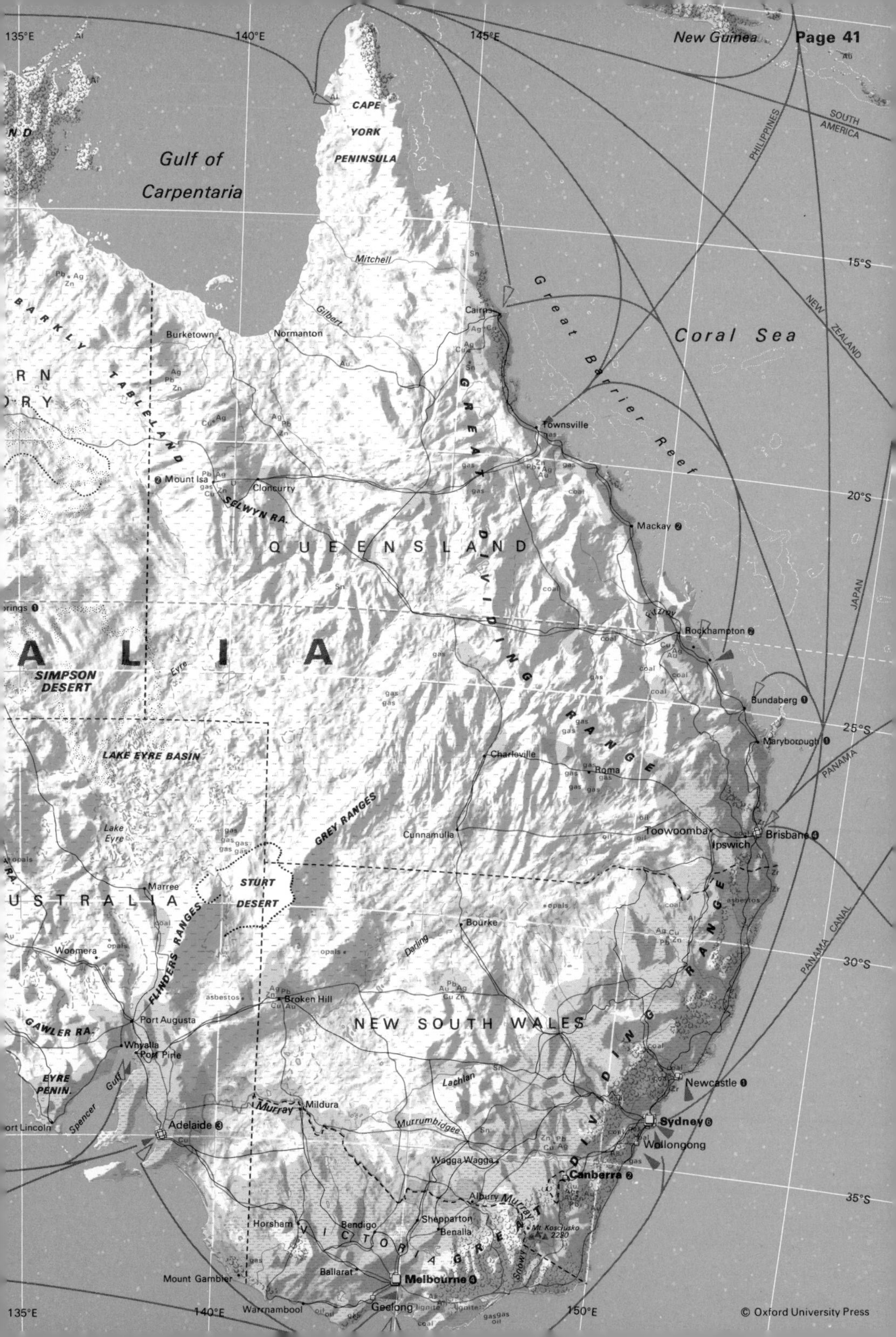

135°E   140°E   145°E

Gulf of
Carpentaria

CAPE
YORK
PENINSULA

Mitchell

Gilbert

BARKLY TABLELAND

Burketown

Normanton

Pb Ag
Zn

Ag

Ag
Zn

Cu Ag

Mount Isa

Cloncurry

SELWYN RA.

Ag

Pb Ag
Zn

Au

Coral Sea

PHILIPPINES

SOUTH
AMERICA

NEW ZEALAND

15°S

Cairns
Ag

Great Barrier Reef

GREAT

Townsville
Ag

20°S

coal

coal

gas

Mackay

JAPAN

QUEENSLAND

DIVIDING

Pb Ag
Zn

Au Ag

Ag

gas

coal

gas

coal

Rockhampton

PANAMA

ALIA

SIMPSON
DESERT

Eyre

RANGE

coal

Bundaberg

Maryborough

25°S

LAKE EYRE BASIN

Lake
Eyre

GREY RANGES

Charleville

Roma

gas

gas gas

Cunnamulla

gas

coal

Toowoomba

oil

asbestos

Brisbane

Ipswich

PANAMA CANAL

AUSTRALIA

opals

Marree

STURT
DESERT

gas
gas gas

FLINDERS RANGES

coal

Woomera

Au

Port Augusta

Whyalla
Port Pirie

GAWLER RA.

EYRE
PENIN.

rt Lincoln

Spencer Gulf

Au

asbestos

Broken Hill

Cu Au

Pb Ag
Zn

opals

Darling

Bourke

opals

NEW SOUTH WALES

Au Pb Ag
Cu Zn

Cu cu
Pb Zn

Ag cu
Pb Zn

coal

asbestos

DIVIDING RANGE

30°S

Newcastle

Lachlan

Murrumbidgee

Sn

coal

Sydney

Wollongong

Adelaide

Murray

Mildura

Wagga Wagga

Au cu
Pb Zn

Canberra

35°S

Albury

Murray

Snowy

Mt Kosciusko
2230

Horsham

VICTORIA

Bendigo

Shepparton

Benalla

GREAT

Ballarat

Mount Gambier

Melbourne

lignite

Geelong

Warrnambool

gas gas
oil

135°E   140°E   150°E   © Oxford University Press

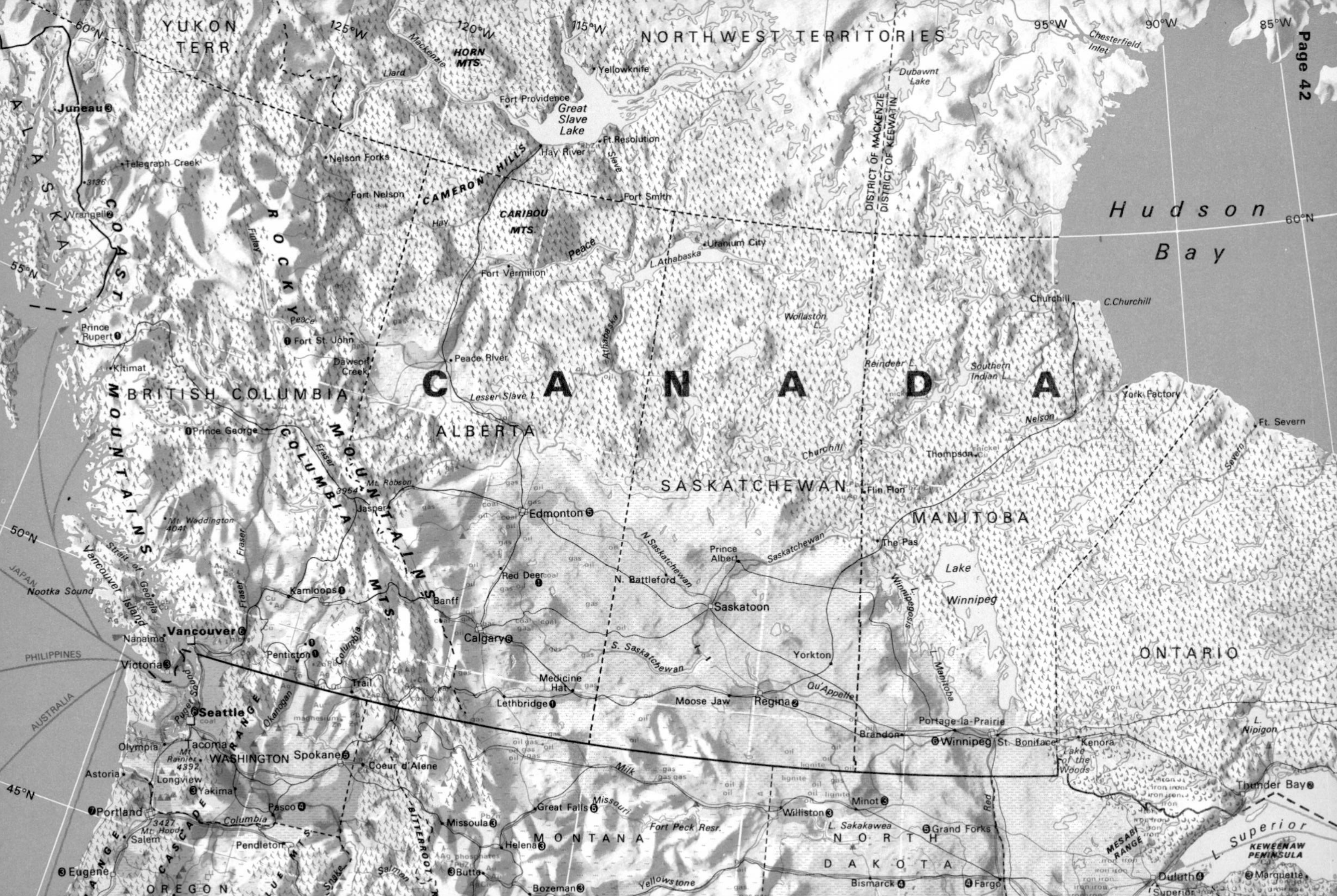
Hudson Bay
CANADA
NORTHWEST TERRITORIES
DISTRICT OF MACKENZIE
DISTRICT OF KEEWATIN
YUKON TERR.
ALASKA
BRITISH COLUMBIA
ALBERTA
SASKATCHEWAN
MANITOBA
ONTARIO
WASHINGTON
OREGON
MONTANA
NORTH DAKOTA
ROCKY MOUNTAINS
COAST MOUNTAINS
COLUMBIA MTS.
CARIBOU MTS.
CAMERON HILLS
HORN MTS.
CASCADE RANGE
BITTERROOT
MESABI RANGE
KEWEENAW PENINSULA
L. Superior
Great Slave Lake
L. Athabaska
Lake Winnipeg
L. Winnipegosis
L. Manitoba
Lake of the Woods
L. Nipigon
Lesser Slave L.
Reindeer L.
Wollaston L.
Southern Indian L.
Dubawnt Lake
Chesterfield Inlet
Vancouver Island
Strait of Georgia
Puget Sound
Nootka Sound
Fort Peck Resr.
L. Sakakawea
Mackenzie
Liard
Peace
Athabaska
Slave
Hay
Finlay
Fraser
Columbia
Okanogan
Snake
Salmon
Missouri
Yellowstone
Milk
N. Saskatchewan
S. Saskatchewan
Saskatchewan
Churchill
Nelson
Severn
Qu'Appelle
Red
Yellowknife
Fort Providence
Hay River
Ft. Resolution
Fort Smith
Uranium City
Fort Vermilion
Peace River
Fort Nelson
Nelson Forks
Fort St. John
Dawson Creek
Prince George
Prince Rupert
Kitimat
Telegraph Creek
Juneau
Wrangell
3136
Kamloops
Penticton
Trail
Vancouver
Victoria
Nanaimo
Jasper
Banff
Mt. Robson
3954
Mt. Waddington
4041
Edmonton
Red Deer
Calgary
Lethbridge
Medicine Hat
N. Battleford
Saskatoon
Prince Albert
Moose Jaw
Regina
Yorkton
Flin Flon
The Pas
Thompson
Brandon
Portage-la-Prairie
Winnipeg
St. Boniface
Kenora
Churchill
C. Churchill
York Factory
Ft. Severn
Thunder Bay
Duluth
Superior
Marquette
Grand Forks
Fargo
Minot
Bismarck
Williston
Great Falls
Helena
Missoula
Butte
Bozeman
Coeur d'Alene
Spokane
Seattle
Tacoma
Olympia
Yakima
Pasco
Pendleton
Longview
Astoria
Portland
Salem
Eugene
Mt. Rainier
4392
Mt. Hood
3427
oil
gas
coal
lignite
iron
magnesium
phosphates
PHILIPPINES
JAPAN
AUSTRALIA
60°N
55°N
50°N
45°N
85°W
90°W
95°W
115°W
120°W
125°W

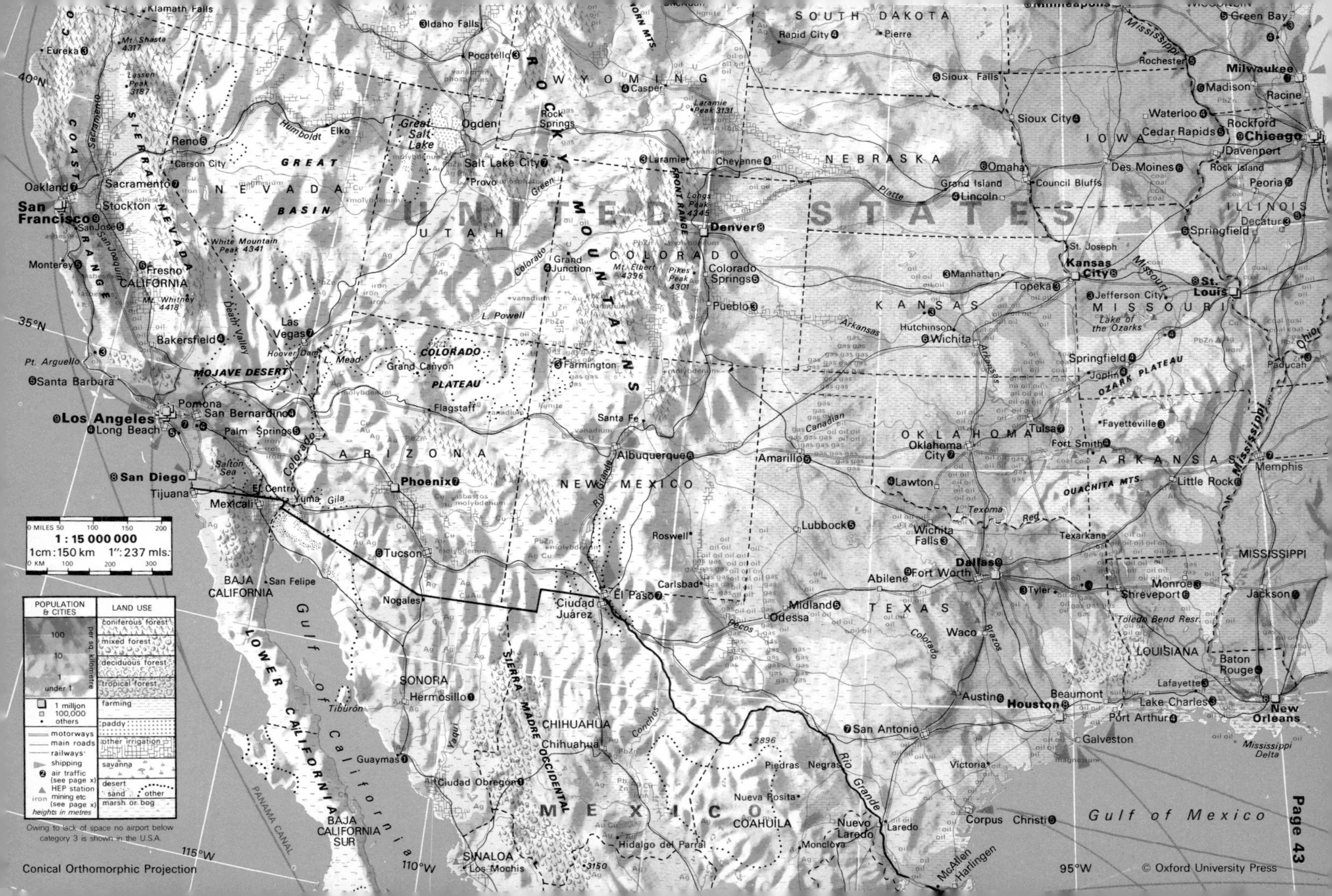

© Oxford University Press

Gulf of Mexico

Mississippi Delta

UNITED STATES

SOUTH DAKOTA

NEBRASKA

IOWA

MINNESOTA

WISCONSIN

ILLINOIS

MISSOURI

KANSAS

OKLAHOMA

ARKANSAS

MISSISSIPPI

LOUISIANA

TEXAS

COLORADO

NEW MEXICO

ARIZONA

UTAH

WYOMING

NEVADA

CALIFORNIA

MEXICO

CHIHUAHUA

COAHUILA

SONORA

SINALOA

BAJA CALIFORNIA

BAJA CALIFORNIA SUR

LOWER CALIFORNIA

Gulf of California

ROCKY MOUNTAINS

GREAT BASIN

SIERRA NEVADA

COAST RANGE

COLORADO PLATEAU

FRONT RANGE

SIERRA MADRE OCCIDENTAL

MOJAVE DESERT

Green Bay, Milwaukee, Racine, Madison, Rockford, Chicago, Waterloo, Cedar Rapids, Rochester, Rock Island, Davenport, Peoria, Decatur, Springfield, St. Louis, Jefferson City, Columbia, Paducah, Memphis, Jackson, New Orleans, Baton Rouge, Lafayette, Lake Charles, Port Arthur, Monroe, Shreveport, Galveston, Beaumont, Houston, Corpus Christi, Austin, San Antonio, Dallas, Fort Worth, Waco, Abilene, Wichita Falls, Lawton, Oklahoma City, Tulsa, Fort Smith, Fayetteville, Little Rock, Texarkana, Tyler, Laredo, Nuevo Laredo, Piedras Negras, Monclova, Nueva Rosita

Sioux City, Sioux Falls, Rapid City, Pierre, Omaha, Lincoln, Council Bluffs, Grand Island, Des Moines, Topeka, Kansas City, St. Joseph, Manhattan, Salina, Hutchinson, Wichita, Springfield, Amarillo, Lubbock, Midland, Odessa, Roswell, Carlsbad, El Paso, Ciudad Juárez, Chihuahua, Ciudad Obregón, Guaymas, Hermosillo, Los Mochis

Cheyenne, Casper, Denver, Colorado Springs, Pueblo, Laramie, Rock Springs, Grand Junction, Santa Fe, Albuquerque, Farmington, Durango, Flagstaff, Grand Canyon, Phoenix, Tucson, Nogales

Idaho Falls, Pocatello, Ogden, Salt Lake City, Provo, Elko, Reno, Carson City, Sacramento, Stockton, San Jose, Fresno, Bakersfield, Las Vegas, San Bernardino, Palm Springs, Pomona, Long Beach, Los Angeles, San Diego, Tijuana, Mexicali, Calexico, El Centro, Yuma, Klamath Falls, Eureka, Oakland, San Francisco, Monterey, Santa Barbara

PANAMA CANAL

1 : 15 000 000
1cm:150 km   1″:237 mls.

LAND USE
coniferous forest
mixed forest
deciduous forest
paddy
farming
savanna
desert
sand
other
marsh or bog

POPULATION
& CITIES
1 million
100,000
others
per sq. kilometre
100
10
1
under 1

motorways
main roads
railways
shipping
air traffic
(see page xl and airport list)
oil field
oil
gas
mining etc.

Conical Orthomorphic Projection

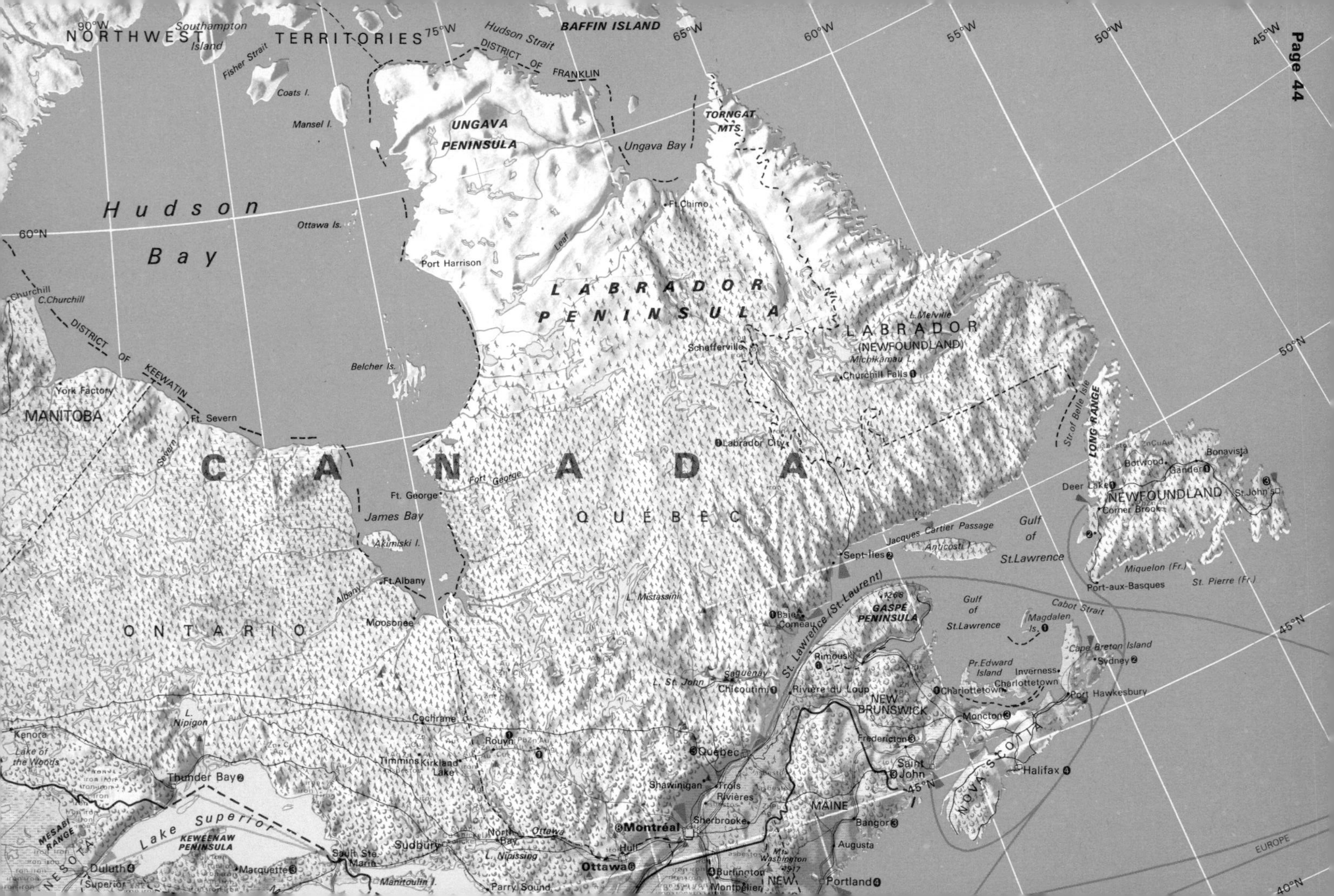

NORTHWEST TERRITORIES
Southampton Island
Fisher Strait
Coats I.
Mansel I.
Hudson Strait
DISTRICT OF FRANKLIN
BAFFIN ISLAND
UNGAVA PENINSULA
Ungava Bay
TORNGAT MTS.
Ft. Chimo
Hudson
Bay
Ottawa Is.
Port Harrison
Leaf
LABRADOR PENINSULA
L. Melville
LABRADOR (NEWFOUNDLAND)
Michikamau L.
Schefferville
Churchill Falls
Labrador City
Str. of Belle Isle
LONG RANGE
Botwood
Gander
Bonavista
Deer Lake
NEWFOUNDLAND
St. John's
Corner Brook
Port-aux-Basques
Miquelon (Fr.)
St. Pierre (Fr.)
Churchill
C.Churchill
DISTRICT OF KEEWATIN
York Factory
MANITOBA
Ft. Severn
Severn
Belcher Is.
CANADA
Fort George
Ft. George
James Bay
Akimiski I.
QUÉBEC
Jacques Cartier Passage
Anticosti
Gulf of St.Lawrence
Sept-Iles
Ft.Albany
Albany
L. Mistassini
Moosonee
ONTARIO
Baie Comeau
St. Lawrence (St. Laurent)
1268
GASPÉ PENINSULA
Gulf of St.Lawrence
Cabot Strait
Magdalen Is.
Cape Breton Island
Sydney
Rimouski
Pr.Edward Island
Inverness
Charlottetown
Saguenay
L. St. John
Chicoutimi
Rivière du Loup
NEW BRUNSWICK
Port Hawkesbury
Moncton
L. Nipigon
Cochrane
Kenora
Lake of the Woods
Rouyn
Québec
Fredericton
Timmins
Kirkland Lake
Thunder Bay
Saint John
Halifax
NOVA SCOTIA
Shawinigan
Trois Rivières
MAINE
Sherbrooke
Bangor
Montréal
Lake Superior
MESABI RANGE
KEWEENAW PENINSULA
Sudbury
North Bay
Ottawa
Hull
Augusta
L. Nipissing
Duluth
Superior
Sault Ste. Marie
Marquette
Ottawa
Mt. Washington 1917
Burlington
Manitoulin
Parry Sound
Montpelier
NEW
Portland
EUROPE
90°W
75°W
65°W
60°W
55°W
50°W
45°W
60°N
50°N
45°N
40°N

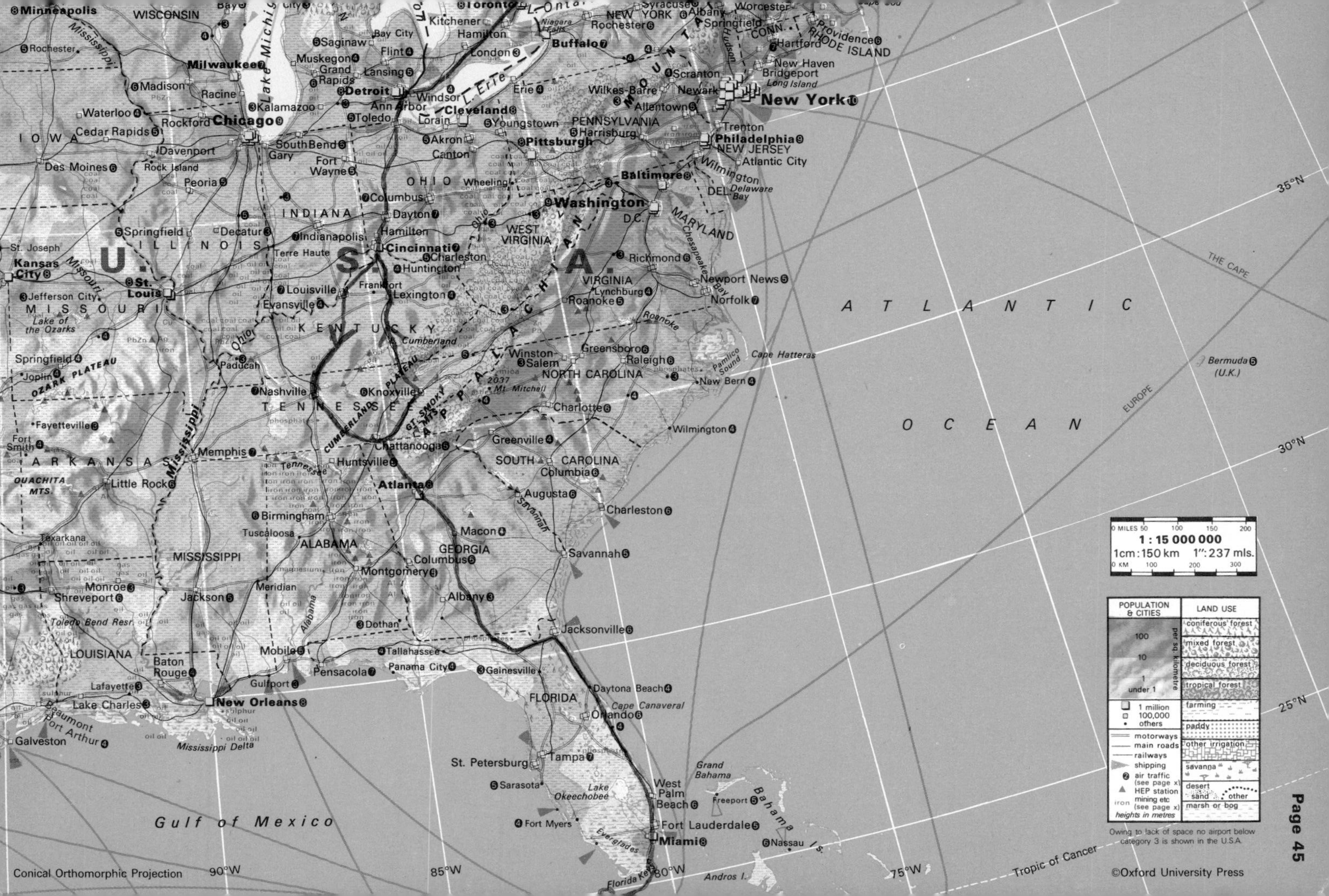

©Oxford University Press

1:15 000 000
1cm:150 km   1":237 mls.

MILES 50 100 150 200
0 KM 100 200 300

POPULATION
& CITIES
● 1 million
▪ 100,000
▫ others
per sq. kilometre
100
10
1
under 1

LAND USE
coniferous forest
mixed forest
deciduous forest
tropical forest
desert
sand   other
marsh or bog
heights in metres
farming
other irrigation
paddy
savanna

motorways
(see page 4)
main roads
railways
shipping
air traffic
(see page 4)
NEP station
mining etc
(see page 4)
iron

Owing to lack of space no airport below
category 3 is shown in the U.S.A.

THE CAPE

Bermuda
(U.K.)

EUROPE

A T L A N T I C   O C E A N

Tropic of Cancer

Conical Orthomorphic Projection

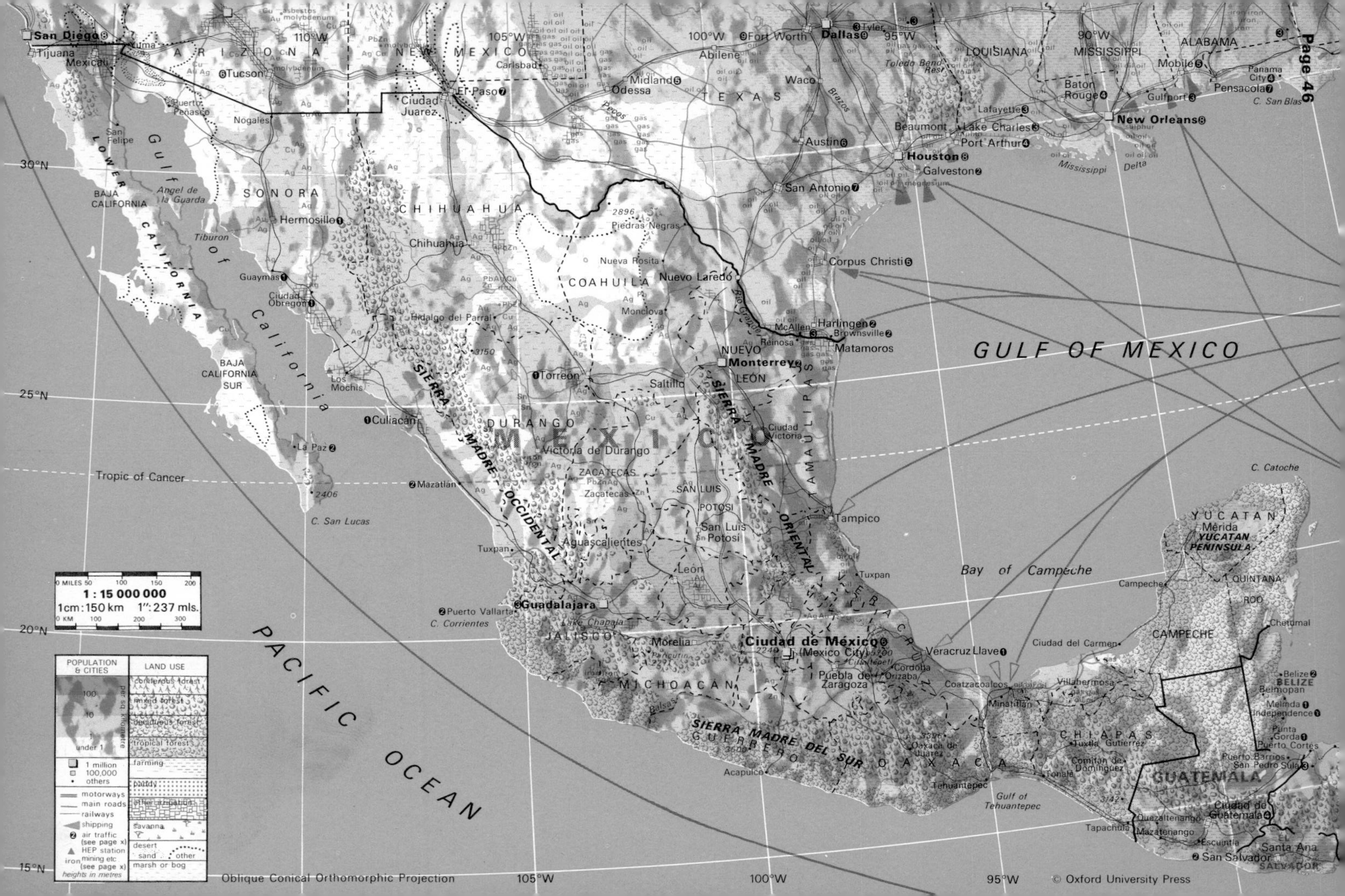

GULF OF MEXICO

Bay of Campeche

PACIFIC OCEAN

Gulf of California

LOWER CALIFORNIA

BAJA CALIFORNIA SUR

M E X I C O

SIERRA MADRE OCCIDENTAL

SIERRA MADRE ORIENTAL

SIERRA MADRE DEL SUR

TEXAS

ALABAMA
MISSISSIPPI
LOUISIANA

NEW MEXICO
ARIZONA

SONORA
CHIHUAHUA
COAHUILA
DURANGO
NUEVO LEON
TAMAULIPAS
SAN LUIS POTOSI
ZACATECAS
JALISCO
GUANAJUATO
MICHOACAN
GUERRERO
OAXACA
VERACRUZ
CHIAPAS
CAMPECHE
YUCATAN
QUINTANA ROO

YUCATAN PENINSULA

GUATEMALA
BELIZE

New Orleans
Dallas
Fort Worth
Houston
San Antonio
Austin
Waco
Abilene
Midland
Odessa
El Paso
Ciudad Juarez
Tucson
San Diego
Tijuana
Mexicali
Monterrey
Nuevo Laredo
Saltillo
Torreon
Victoria de Durango
Zacatecas
Aguascalientes
Guadalajara
Puerto Vallarta
Mazatlan
Culiacan
Ciudad Obregon
Guaymas
Hermosillo
La Paz
Tampico
Ciudad de México
México City
Puebla
Veracruz
Morelia
Acapulco
Oaxaca
Campeche
Merida
Belize
Guatemala
San Salvador

Tropic of Cancer

Rio Grande

© Oxford University Press

Oblique Conical Orthomorphic Projection

1 : 15 000 000

1cm:150 km   1":237 mls.

MILES 50   0   50   100   150   200

KM   100   0   100   200   300

LAND USE

POPULATION & CITIES

per sq kilometre

1 million
100 000
others

motorways
main roads
railways
shipping
air traffic
HEP station
iron, mining etc

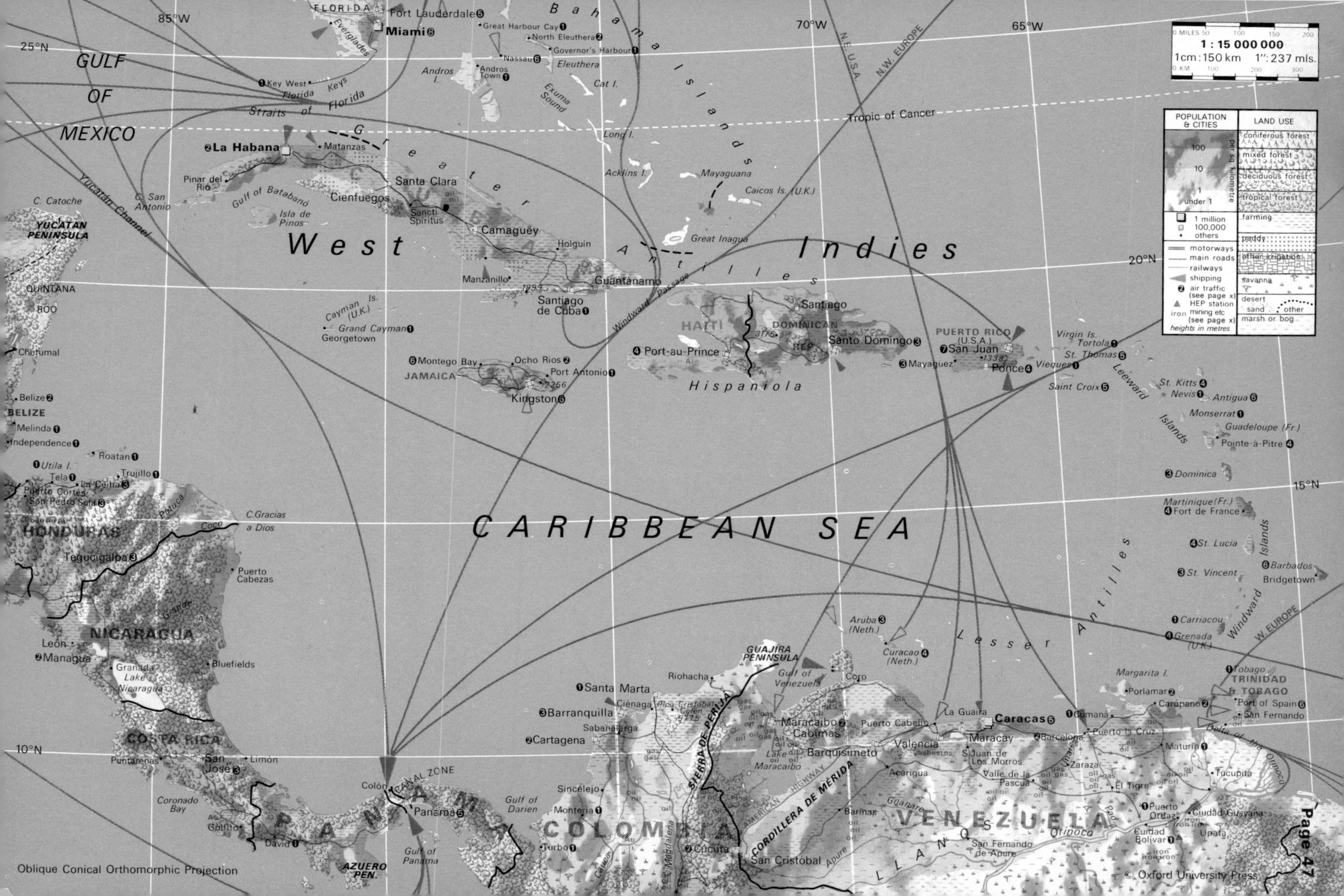
GULF OF MEXICO
Straits of Florida
Yucatan Channel
Bahama Islands
Greater Antilles
West Indies
CARIBBEAN SEA
Lesser Antilles
Leeward Islands
Windward Islands
Windward Passage
Tropic of Cancer
N.E. U.S.A.
N.W. EUROPE
W. EUROPE
FLORIDA
Everglades
Fort Lauderdale
Miami
Key West
Florida Keys
Great Harbour Cay
North Eleuthera
Governor's Harbour
Nassau
Eleuthera
Andros I.
Andros Town
Cat I.
Exuma Sound
Long I.
Acklins I.
Mayaguana
Caicos Is. (U.K.)
Great Inagua
La Habana
Matanzas
Pinar del Rio
Gulf of Batabano
Isla de Pinos
C. San Antonio
Santa Clara
Cienfuegos
Sancti Spiritus
Camagüey
Holguin
Manzanillo
Guantánamo
Santiago de Cuba
Cayman Is. (U.K.)
Grand Cayman
Georgetown
Montego Bay
Ocho Rios
Port Antonio
JAMAICA
Kingston
HAITI
Port-au-Prince
DOMINICAN REP.
Santiago
Santo Domingo
Hispaniola
PUERTO RICO (U.S.A.)
San Juan
Mayaguez
Ponce
Virgin Is.
Tortola
St. Thomas
Vieques
Saint Croix
St. Kitts
Nevis
Antigua
Monserrat
Guadeloupe (Fr.)
Pointe-à-Pitre
Dominica
Martinique (Fr.)
Fort de France
St. Lucia
St. Vincent
Barbados
Bridgetown
Carriacou
Grenada (U.K.)
Tobago
TRINIDAD & TOBAGO
Port of Spain
San Fernando
Margarita I.
Porlamar
Carúpano
Aruba (Neth.)
Curacao (Neth.)
C. Catoche
YUCATAN PENINSULA
QUINTANA ROO
Chetumal
Belize
BELIZE
Melinda
Independence
Roatan
Utila I.
Tela
La Ceiba
Trujillo
Puerto Cortes
San Pedro Sula
HONDURAS
Tegucigalpa
C. Gracias a Dios
Coco
Patuca
Puerto Cabezas
NICARAGUA
León
Managua
Granada
Lake Nicaragua
Bluefields
Grande
COSTA RICA
Puntarenas
San José
Limón
Coronado Bay
Golfito
David
PANAMA
Colón
CANAL ZONE
Panama
Gulf of Panama
AZUERO PEN.
Gulf of Darien
COLOMBIA
Turbo
Montería
Sincelejo
Cartagena
Barranquilla
Santa Marta
Ciénaga
Sabanalarga
Riohacha
GUAJIRA PENINSULA
SIERRA DE PERIJA
Cúcuta
Magdalena
Cauca
Gulf of Venezuela
Coro
Maracaibo
Cabimas
Lake Maracaibo
Barquisimeto
Puerto Cabello
Valencia
La Guaira
Caracas
Maracay
San Juan de Los Morros
Valle de la Pascua
Barcelona
Cumaná
Puerto la Cruz
Zaraza
El Tigre
Maturín
Tucupita
Delta of the Orinoco
Puerto Ordaz
Ciudad Guayana
Ciudad Bolivar
Upata
Acarigua
Barinas
Guanare
CORDILLERA DE MÉRIDA
PAN AMERICAN HIGHWAY
San Cristóbal
Apure
San Fernando de Apure
Orinoco
LLANOS
VENEZUELA
85°W
70°W
65°W
25°N
20°N
15°N
10°N
1 : 15 000 000
1cm : 150 km 1": 237 mls.
POPULATION & CITIES
per sq. kilometre
1 million
100,000
others
motorways
main roads
railways
shipping
air traffic (see page x)
HEP station
iron mining etc (see page x)
heights in metres
LAND USE
coniferous forest
mixed forest
deciduous forest
tropical forest
farming
paddy
other irrigation
savanna
desert sand other
marsh or bog
Oblique Conical Orthomorphic Projection
© Oxford University Press

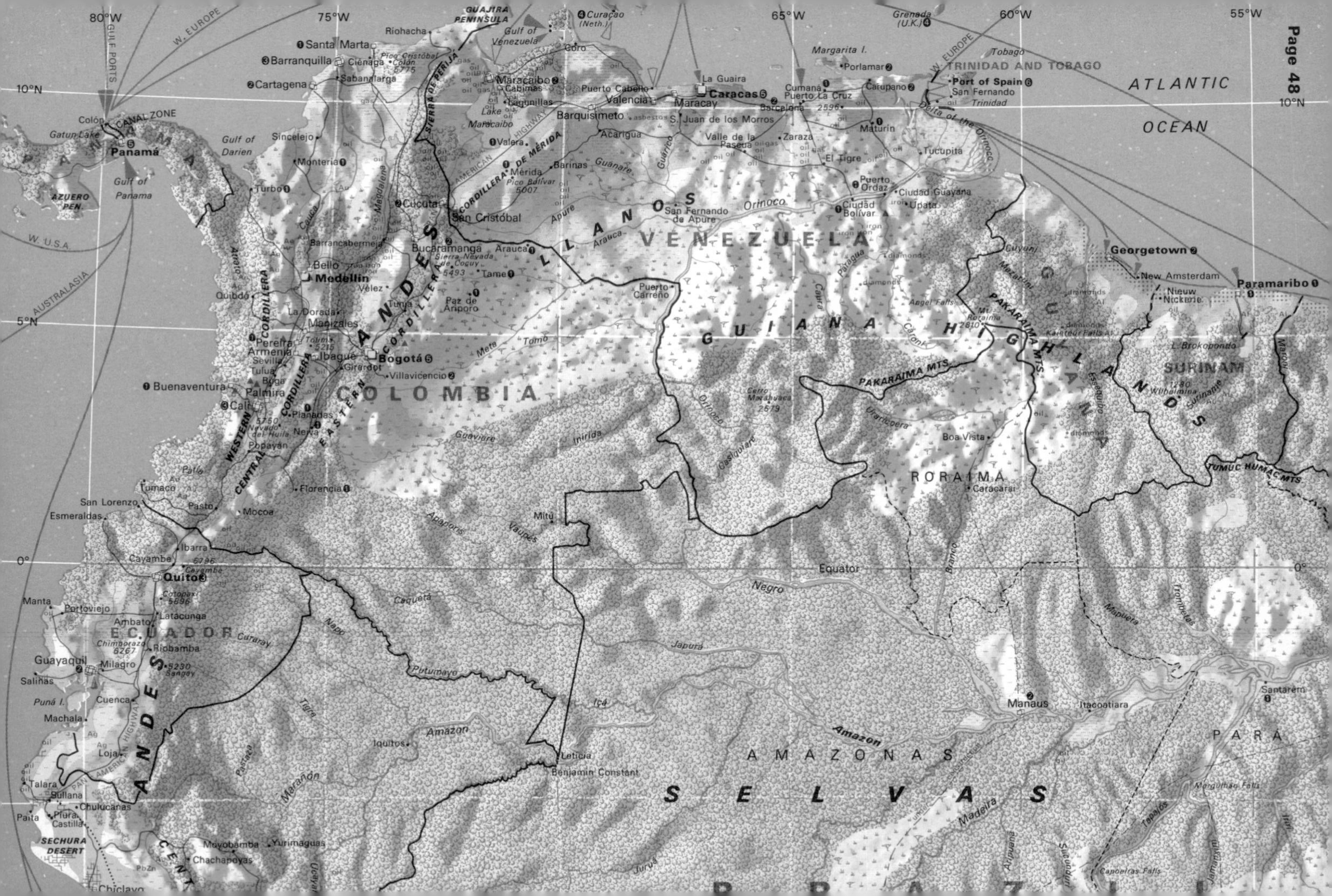
80°W
75°W
65°W
60°W
55°W
10°N
5°N
0°
ATLANTIC
OCEAN
GULF PORTS
W. EUROPE
W. U.S.A.
AUSTRALASIA
GUAJIRA PENINSULA
Gulf of Venezuela
Curaçao (Neth.)
Riohacha
Santa Marta
Barranquilla
Ciénaga
Pico Cristóbal Colón 5775
Sabanalarga
Cartagena
SIERRA DE PERIJA
Maracaibo
Cabimas
Lagunillas
Lake Maracaibo
Coro
Puerto Cabello
Valencia
Maracay
La Guaira
Caracas
Barquisimeto
S. Juan de los Morros
Acarigua
Valle de la Pascua
Zaraza
Barcelona
Cumaná
Puerto La Cruz
Margarita I.
Porlamar
Carúpano
Grenada (U.K.)
Tobago
TRINIDAD AND TOBAGO
Port of Spain
San Fernando
Trinidad
Delta of the Orinoco
Maturín
El Tigre
Tucupita
Colón
CANAL ZONE
Gatun Lake
Panamá
Gulf of Panama
AZUERO PEN.
Gulf of Darien
Sincelejo
Montería
Turbo
Valera
CORDILLERA DE MÉRIDA
Mérida
Pico Bolívar 5007
Barinas
Guanare
Guárico
Apure
Cúcuta
San Cristóbal
LLANOS
San Fernando de Apure
Orinoco
Puerto Ordaz
Ciudad Guayana
Upata
Ciudad Bolívar
VENEZUELA
Arauca
Bucaramanga
Sierra Nevada de Cocuy 5493
Tame
Barrancabermeja
Bello
Medellín
Vélez
Tunja
Paz de Ariporo
Puerto Carreño
Cuyuni
Georgetown
New Amsterdam
Nieuw Nickerie
Paramaribo
Quibdó
La Dorada
Manizales
Pereira
Armenia
Tolima 5215
Ibagué
Bogotá
Girardot
Villavicencio
Meta
Tomo
ANDES
CORDILLERA
EASTERN CORDILLERA
CENTRAL CORDILLERA
WESTERN CORDILLERA
GUIANA HIGHLANDS
Caura
Caroní
Angel Falls
Mt. Roraima 2810
PAKARAIMA MTS.
Kaieteur Falls
Mazaruni
Essequibo
L. Brokopondo
SURINAM
1280 Wilhelmina
Suriname
Maroni
Buenaventura
Palmira
Cali
Planadas
Neiva
5750 Nevado del Huila
Popayán
COLOMBIA
Guaviare
Inírida
Orinoco
Cerro Marahuaca 2579
Casiquiare
Uraricoera
Boa Vista
RORAIMA
Caracaraí
TUMUC HUMAC MTS.
Florencia
Patía
Tumaco
Pasto
Mocoa
San Lorenzo
Esmeraldas
Mitú
Apaporis
Vaupés
Ibarra
6796 Cayambe
Cayambe
Quito
Equator
Negro
Branco
Mapuera
Trombetas
Manta
Portoviejo
Cotopaxi 5896
Latacunga
Ambato
ECUADOR
Chimborazo 6267
Riobamba
Curaray
Caquetá
Napo
Guayaquil
Milagro
5230 Sangay
Salinas
Puná I.
Cuenca
Machala
Putumayo
Japurá
Içá
Tigre
Amazon
Iquitos
Leticia
Benjamin Constant
Manaus
Itacoatiara
Santarém
PARÁ
AMAZONAS
SELVAS
Madeira
Marañón
Pastaza
Loja
Talara
Sullana
Chulucanas
Paita
Piura
Castilla
SECHURA DESERT
Moyobamba
Yurimaguas
Chachapoyas
Chiclayo
Juruá
Ucayali
Aripuanã
Sucunduri
Tapajós
Jamanxim
Maranhão Falls
Capoeiras Falls
PAN AMERICAN HIGHWAY

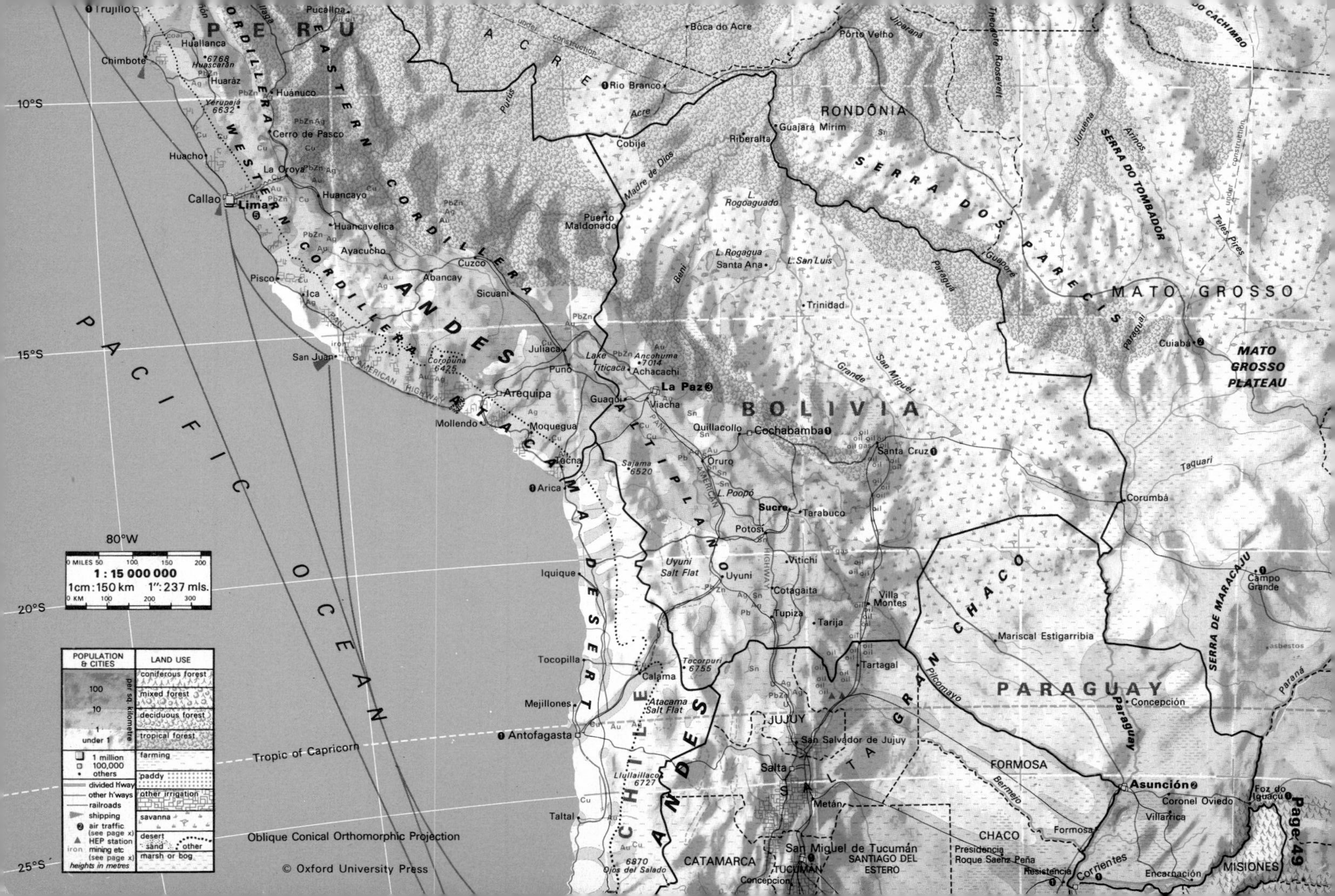

PACIFIC OCEAN

PERU

BOLIVIA

PARAGUAY

CHILE

BRAZIL

MATO GROSSO PLATEAU

SERRA DE MARACAJÚ

MATO GROSSO

SERRA DOS PARECIS

SERRA DO TOMBADOR

RONDÔNIA

ACRE

CORDILLERA

EASTERN CORDILLERA

WESTERN CORDILLERA

ANDES

ATACAMA DESERT

ALTIPLANO

GRAN CHACO

CHACO

FORMOSA

MISIONES

Asunción

Paraguay

Concepción

Coronel Oviedo

Villarrica

Encarnación

Corrientes

Resistencia

Foz do Iguaçu

Formosa

Bermejo

Pilcomayo

Mariscal Estigarribia

Presidencia Roque Sáenz Peña

Santiago del Estero

San Miguel de Tucumán

TUCUMÁN

CATAMARCA

Salta

JUJUY

San Salvador de Jujuy

Metán

Tartagal

Tarija

Tupiza

Villa Montes

Yacuiba

Cotagaita

Uyuni

Potosí

Sucre

Tarabuco

Cochabamba

Santa Cruz

Oruro

Poopó

Quillacollo

La Paz

Achacachi

Illimani 6882

Illampu 6727

Nevado de Tres Cruces 6755

Lullaillaco 6723

Ojos del Salado 6870

Ancohuma 7014

Antofagasta

Mejillones

Tocopilla

Iquique

Arica

Tacna

Moquegua

Ilo

Mollendo

Arequipa

Puno

Lake Titicaca

Juliaca

Sicuani

Cuzco

Abancay

Ayacucho

Ica

Pisco

San Juan

Lima

Callao

Huancayo

Cerro de Pasco

Huánuco

La Oroya

Huaraz

Huascarán 6768

Chimbote

Trujillo

Chiclayo

Pucallpa

Cobija

Riberalta

Santa Ana

L. Rogaguado

Trinidad

San Luis

San Miguel

Cuiabá

Corumbá

Porto Velho

Rio Branco

Guajará Mirim

Puerto Maldonado

Theodore Roosevelt

Tropic of Capricorn

80°W

10°S

15°S

20°S

25°S

ANDES

HIGHWAY

PAN AMERICAN HIGHWAY

1:15 000 000

1cm:150 km   1":237 mls.

© Oxford University Press

Oblique Conical Orthomorphic Projection

Heights in metres

MILES   50   100   150   200

KM   100   200   300

LAND USE

coniferous forest
mixed forest
deciduous forest
tropical forest
farming
paddy
savanna
desert
sand
marsh or bog

per sq. kilometre
100
10
1
under 1

POPULATION & CITIES
1 million
100,000
others
air traffic
shipping
HEP station
mining etc.
divided h'way
other h'ways
railroads

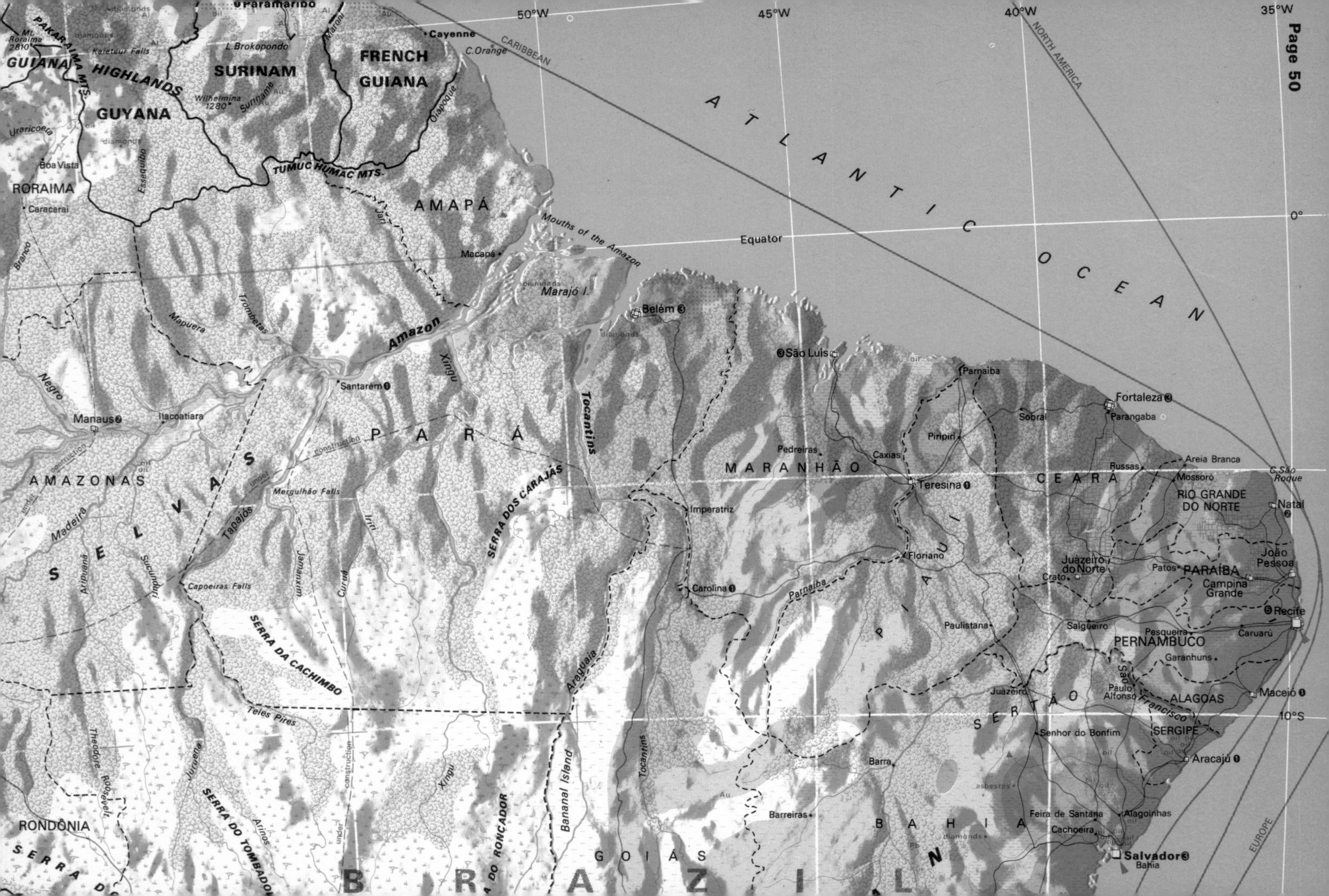

35°W

0°

EUROPE

10°S

NORTH AMERICA

40°W

45°W

50°W

Equator

ATLANTIC OCEAN

CARIBBEAN

C. Orange
Cayenne

FRENCH
GUIANA

SURINAM

Paramaribo

Brokopondo

Wilhelmina

GUYANA

PAKARAIMA HIGHLANDS

GUIANA HIGHLANDS

Kaieteur Falls

PAKARAIMA MTS.

Roraima
2810

Boa Vista

RORAIMA

Branco

Negro

Manaus

AMAZONAS

Madeira

Theodore Roosevelt

RONDÔNIA

SERRA DO TOMBADOR

Arinos

SERRA DA CACHIMBO

Teles Pires

Tapajós

Jamanxim

Sucunduri

Aripuanã

Xingu

Iriri

Curuá

Capoeiras Falls

Maguinhão Falls

Santarém

Amazon

Xingu

Jari

AMAPA

Macapá

TUMUC-HUMAC MTS.
2300

Trombetas

Maguari

Itacoatiara

Essequibo

Corantijn

Maroni

Diapoque

Mouths of the Amazon

Marajó I.

Belém

Tocantins

PARÁ

SERRA DOS CARAJÁS

Bananal Island

GOIÁS

Araguaia

SERRA DO RONCADOR

BRAZIL

Tocantins

Araguaia

Imperatriz

Carolina

MARANHÃO

São Luís

Pedreiras

Caxias

Teresina

Piripiri

Sobral

Parnaíba

Floriano

Parnaíba

Parnaguá

Fortaleza

Paracurú

Areia Branca

Mossoró

Russas

CEARÁ

RIO GRANDE DO NORTE

Natal

C. São Roque

João Pessoa

Caruaru

Recife

PARAÍBA

Campina Grande

PERNAMBUCO

Pesqueira

Garanhuns

Maceió

ALAGOAS

Arapiraca

SERGIPE

Aracajú

Juazeiro do Norte

Crato

Salgueiro

Petrolina

São Francisco

Juazeiro

Senhor do Bonfim

Feira de Santana

Barra

BAHIA

Barreiras

Bahia

Salvador

Cachoeira

Alagoinhas

Santo Amaro

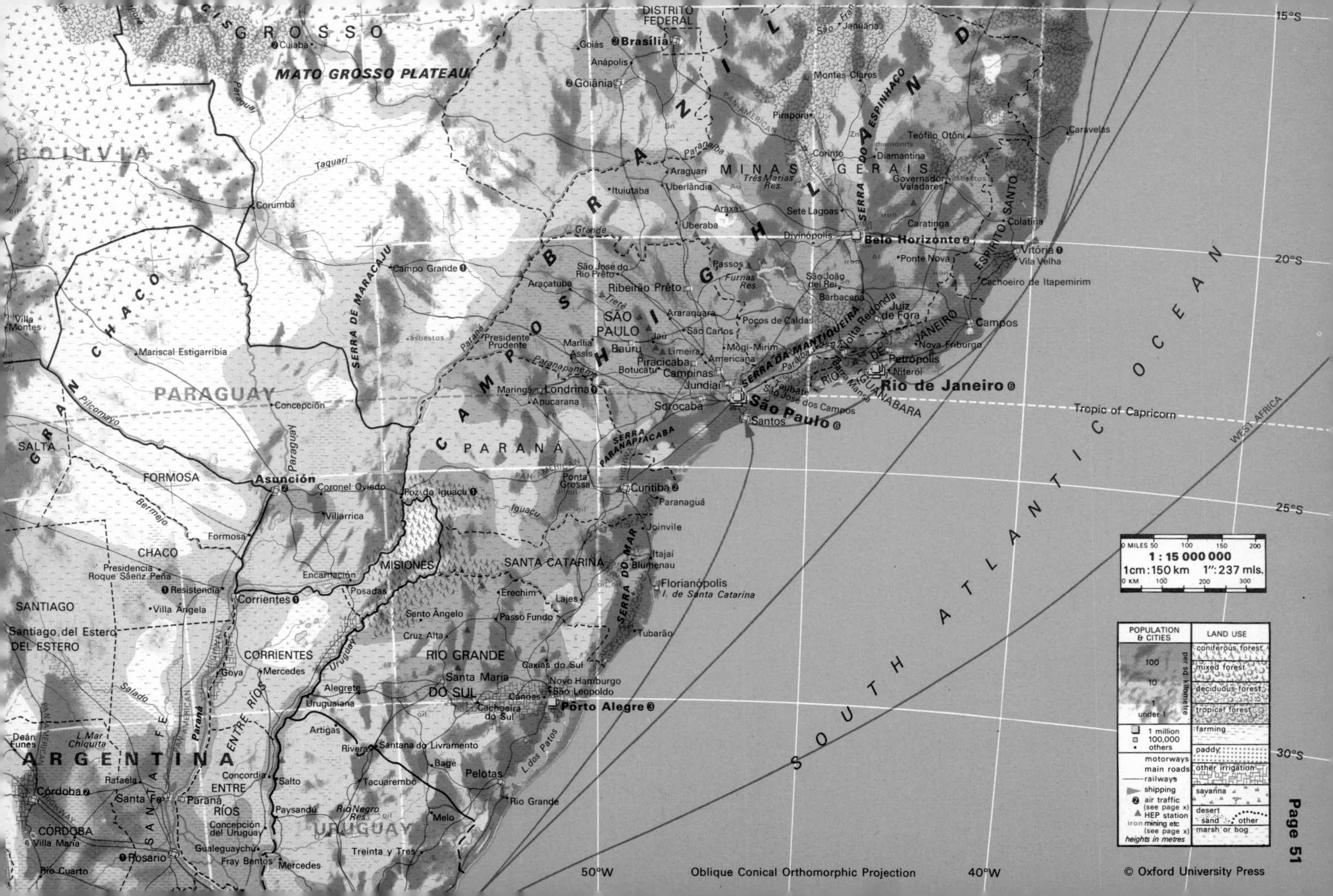

© Oxford University Press

SOUTH ATLANTIC OCEAN

Tropic of Capricorn

WEST AFRICA

15°S
20°S
25°S
30°S
40°W
50°W

1 : 15 000 000
1cm:150 km   1":237 mls.

MILES 50 0 50 100 150 200
KM 100 0 100 200 300

LAND USE
coniferous forest
mixed forest
deciduous forest
tropical forest
farming
paddy
other irrigation
savanna
desert
sand   other
marsh or bog

POPULATION & CITIES
per sq. kilometre
100
10
under 1
1 million
100,000
others
motorways
main roads
railways
iron ming etc.
shipping
air traffic   (see page x)
HEP station   (see page x)
heights in metres

Oblique Conical Orthomorphic Projection

BRAZIL

DISTRITO FEDERAL
Brasília
Anápolis
Goiás
Goiânia

MATO GROSSO PLATEAU
MATO GROSSO DO SUL

BOLIVIA

SERRA DE MARACAJU

PARAGUAY
Concepción
Mariscal Estigarribia
Presidencia Roque Sáenz Peña
Asunción
Coronel Oviedo
Villarrica
Encarnación

CHACO
Formosa
FORMOSA
Resistencia
Villa Ángela

ARGENTINA
Santiago del Estero
SANTIAGO DEL ESTERO
SALTA
SANTA FE
Santa Fe
Paraná
ENTRE RÍOS
Rosario
Mar Chiquito
CÓRDOBA
Córdoba
Río Cuarto
Rafaela

MINAS GERAIS
ESPÍRITO SANTO
Belo Horizonte
Vitória
Vila Velha
Cachoeiro de Itapemirim
Campos
Teófilo Otoni
Diamantina
Governador Valadares
Montes Claros

SERRA DO ESPINHAÇO

RIO DE JANEIRO
Rio de Janeiro
GUANABARA
Nova Friburgo
Petrópolis
Juiz de Fora

SÃO PAULO
São Paulo
Santos
Campinas
Sorocaba
Piracicaba
Ribeirão Preto
São Carlos
Araraquara
Bauru
Marília
Presidente Prudente

PARANÁ
Curitiba
Londrina
Maringá
Ponta Grossa

SANTA CATARINA
Florianópolis
I. de Santa Catarina
Joinville
Blumenau
Itajaí
Tubarão
Lajes

SERRA DO MAR

RIO GRANDE DO SUL
Porto Alegre
Novo Hamburgo
São Leopoldo
Santa Maria
Caxias do Sul
Passo Fundo
Rio Grande
Pelotas
Bagé
L. dos Patos

URUGUAY
Rivera
Salto
Paysandú
Artigas
Melo
Tacuarembó
Treinta y Tres
Mercedes
Fray Bentos

MISIONES
Posadas
CORRIENTES
Corrientes

PARANÁ
Paraná

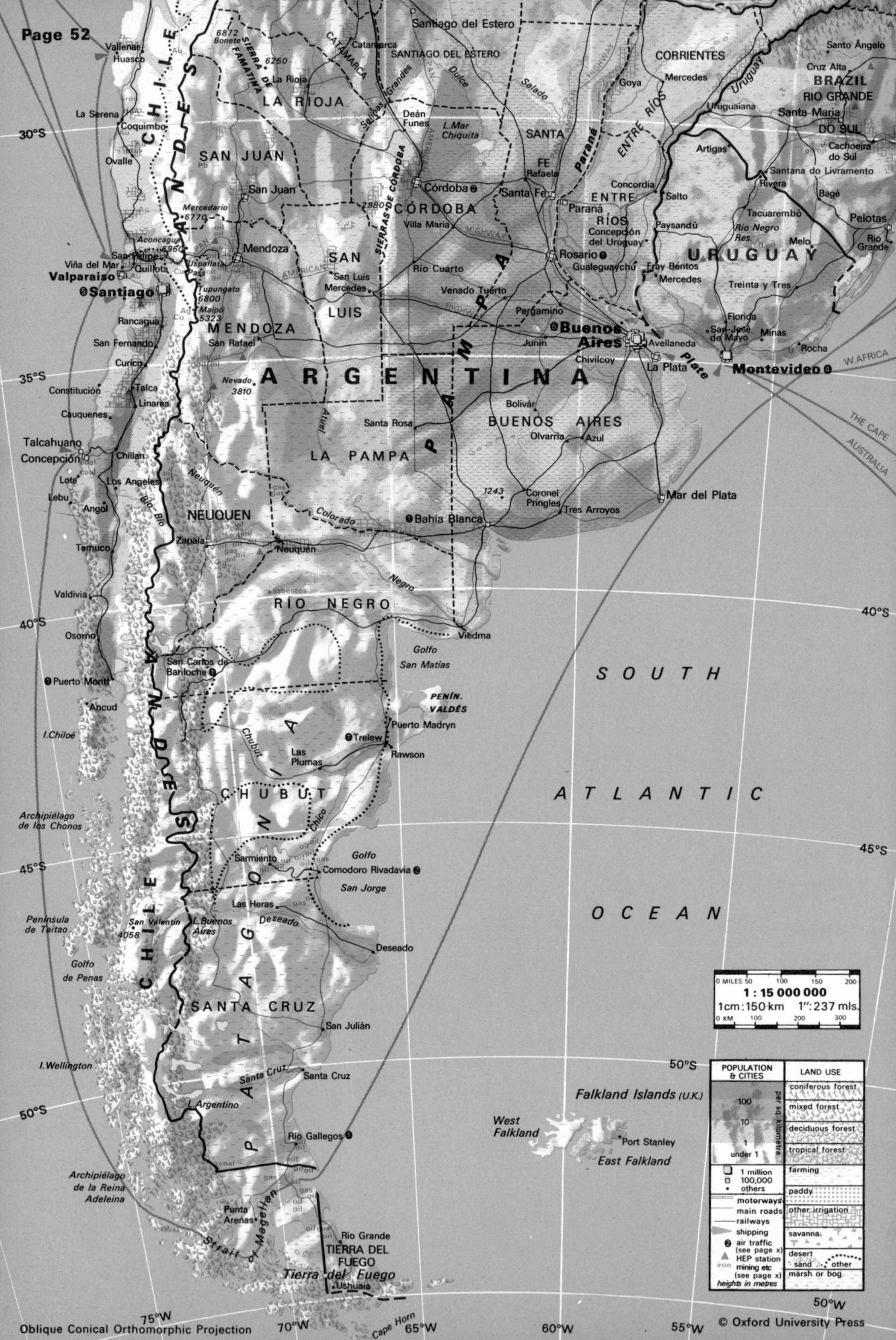
Santiago del Estero
Catamarca
SANTIAGO DEL ESTERO
CATAMARCA
6872 Bonete
SIERRA DE FAMATINA
6250
La Rioja
LA RIOJA
Salinas Grandes
Dulce
Salado
Deán Funes
L.Mar Chiquita
CORRIENTES
Goya
Mercedes
Uruguay
Uruguaiana
ENTRE RÍOS
Paraná
SANTA FE
Rafaela
Santo Ângelo
Cruz Alta
BRAZIL
RIO GRANDE DO SUL
Santa Maria
Cachoeira do Sul
Artigas
Santana do Livramento
Rivera
Bagé
Concordia
Salto
Paysandú
Tacuarembó
Rio Negro Res.
Melo
Pelotas
Rio Grande
URUGUAY
Concepción del Uruguay
Gualeguaychú
Fray Bentos
Mercedes
Treinta y Tres
Florida
San José de Mayo
Minas
Rocha
Montevideo
Plate
W.AFRICA
THE CAPE
AUSTRALIA
Vallenar
Huasco
La Serena
Coquimbo
30°S
CHILE
ANDES
SAN JUAN
Ovalle
San Juan
Mercedario 6770
Aconcagua 6960
Mendoza
San Felipe
Viña del Mar
Quillota
Valparaiso
Santiago
Uspallata Pass
Tupungato 6800
Maipo 5323
PAN-AMERICAN HIGHWAY
Córdoba
CÓRDOBA
SIERRAS DE CÓRDOBA
2880
Villa Maria
Santa Fe
Rosario
SAN LUIS
San Luis
Mercedes
Río Cuarto
Venado Tuerto
Pergamino
Buenos Aires
Avellaneda
La Plata
Junín
Chivilcoy
PAMPA
Rancagua
San Fernando
MENDOZA
San Rafael
Curico
35°S
Talca
Constitución
Linares
Nevado 3810
ARGENTINA
Cauquenes
Atuel
Santa Rosa
Bolivár
BUENOS AIRES
Olavarria
Azul
Talcahuano
Concepción
Chillan
LA PAMPA
Lota
Los Angeles
Lebu
Angol
Bio Bio
Neuquén
NEUQUEN
1243
Coronel Pringles
Tres Arroyos
Mar del Plata
Colorado
Bahía Blanca
Zapala
Neuquén
Temuco
Negro
Valdivia
asbestos
RÍO NEGRO
40°S
Osorno
Viedma
Golfo San Matías
San Carlos de Bariloche
Puerto Montt
SOUTH
Ancud
PENÍN. VALDÉS
Puerto Madryn
I.Chiloé
Chubut
Trelew
Rawson
Las Plumas
CHUBUT
ATLANTIC
Archipiélago de los Chonos
Chico
Golfo San Jorge
45°S
Sarmiento
Comodoro Rivadavia
Las Heras
Deseado
Península de Taitao
San Valentín 4058
L.Buenos Aires
OCEAN
Deseado
Golfo de Penas
PATAGONIA
0 MILES 50 100 150 200
1 : 15 000 000
1cm : 150 km 1": 237 mls.
0 KM 100 200 300
SANTA CRUZ
San Julián
I.Wellington
50°S
Santa Cruz
Santa Cruz
L.Argentino
Falkland Islands (U.K.)
West Falkland
Port Stanley
East Falkland
Río Gallegos
Archipiélago de la Reina Adeleina
Punta Arenas
Strait of Magellan
Río Grande
TIERRA DEL FUEGO
Tierra del Fuego
Ushuaia
Cape Horn
75°W
70°W
65°W
60°W
55°W
50°W
coal
oil
gas
iron
POPULATION & CITIES
per sq. kilometre
100
10
1
under 1
1 million
100,000
others
motorways
main roads
railways
shipping
air traffic (see page x)
HEP station
mining etc (see page x)
heights in metres
LAND USE
coniferous forest
mixed forest
deciduous forest
tropical forest
farming
paddy
other irrigation
savanna
desert
sand
other
marsh or bog

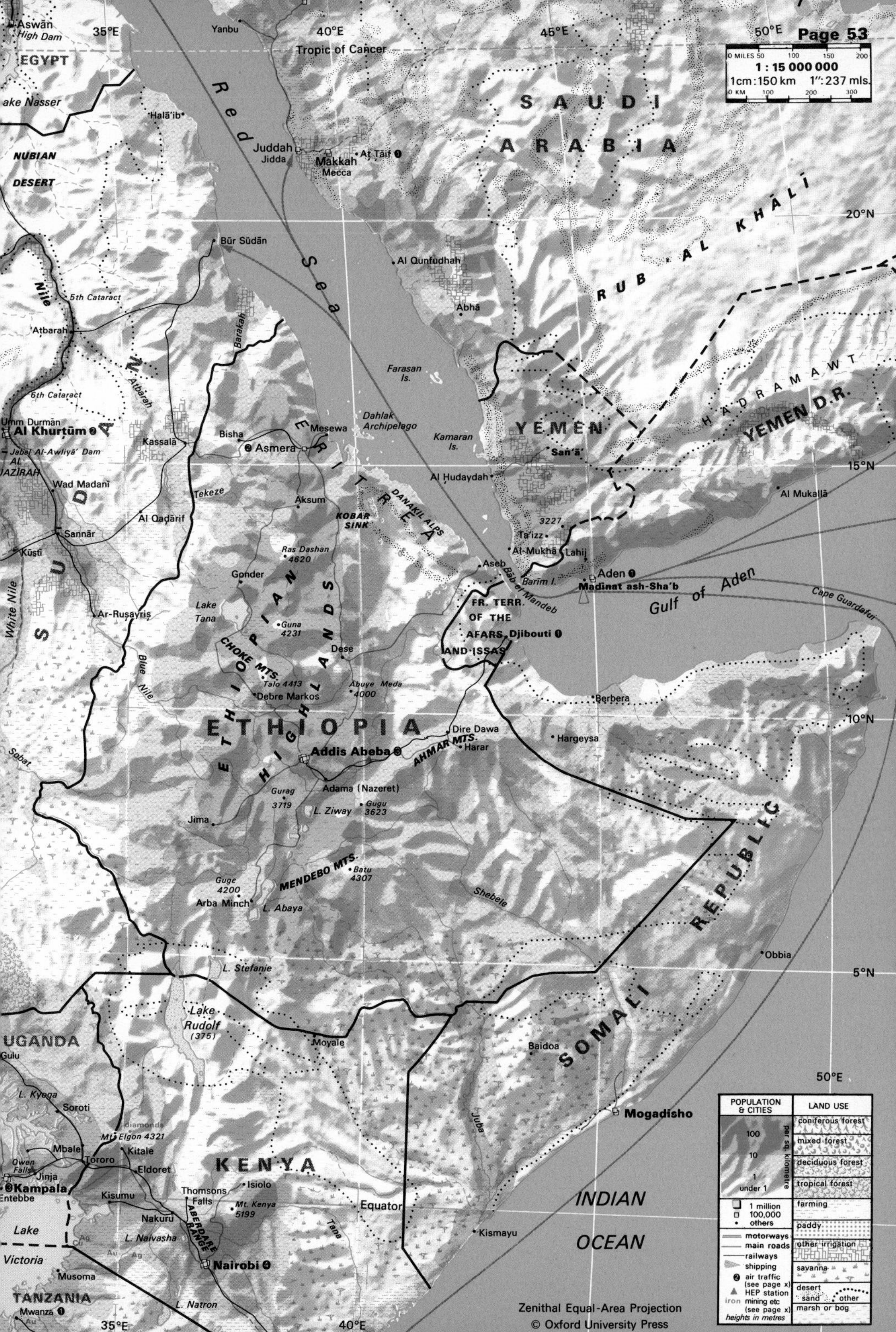

Page 53
0 MILES 50 100 150 200
1 : 15 000 000
1cm : 150 km 1'' : 237 mls.
0 KM 100 200 300
35°E
40°E
45°E
50°E
20°N
15°N
10°N
5°N
Tropic of Cancer
Aswan
High Dam
EGYPT
Lake Nasser
NUBIAN
DESERT
Halā'ib
Yanbu
Red Sea
Juddah
Jidda
Makkah
Mecca
At Tāif
SAUDI ARABIA
RUB AL KHĀLĪ
Būr Sūdān
Al Qunfudhah
Abhā
5th Cataract
Nile
Atbarah
Barakah
6th Cataract
Umm Durmān
Al Khurṭūm
Jabal Al-Awliyā' Dam
AL JAZĪRAH
SUDAN
Kassalā
Wad Madanī
Al Qaḍārif
Sannār
Kūstī
White Nile
Ar-Ruṣayriṣ
Tekeze
Bisha
Asmera
Mesewa
ERITREA
Farasan Is.
Dahlak Archipelago
Kamaran Is.
YEMEN
San'ā'
Al Hudaydah
HADRAMAWT
YEMEN D.R.
Al Mukallā
Aksum
KOBAR SINK
DANAKIL ALPS
3227
Ta'izz
Al-Mukhā
Lahij
Aseb
Barīm I.
Aden
Madinat ash-Sha'b
Bāb el Mandeb
Gulf of Aden
Cape Guardafui
Ras Dashan 4620
Gonder
Lake Tana
Guna 4231
ETHIOPIAN HIGHLANDS
CHOKE MTS.
Talo 4413
Debre Markos
Dese
Abuye Meda 4000
FR. TERR. OF THE AFARS AND ISSAS
Djibouti
Berbera
Hargeysa
Blue Nile
Sobat
ETHIOPIA
Dire Dawa
AHMAR MTS.
Harar
Addis Abeba
Adama (Nazeret)
Gurag 3719
L. Ziway
Gugu 3623
Jima
MENDEBO MTS.
Batu 4307
Guge 4200
Arba Minch
L. Abaya
Shebele
SOMALI REPUBLIC
Obbia
L. Stefanie
Lake Rudolf (375)
Moyale
Baidoa
UGANDA
Gulu
L. Kyoga
Soroti
Mt Elgon 4321
Mbale
Tororo
Kitale
Owen Falls
Jinja
Eldoret
Kampala
Entebbe
Kisumu
KENYA
Thomsons Falls
Isiolo
Mt. Kenya 5199
Equator
Juba
Mogadisho
Nakuru
ABERDARE RANGE
L. Naivasha
Tana
Kismayu
INDIAN OCEAN
Lake Victoria
Musoma
Nairobi
TANZANIA
Mwanza
L. Natron
POPULATION & CITIES
100
10
1
under 1
per sq. kilometre
1 million
100,000
others
motorways
main roads
railways
shipping
air traffic (see page x)
HEP station
iron mining etc (see page x)
heights in metres
LAND USE
coniferous forest
mixed forest
deciduous forest
tropical forest
farming
paddy
other irrigation
savanna
desert sand other
marsh or bog
Zenithal Equal-Area Projection
© Oxford University Press

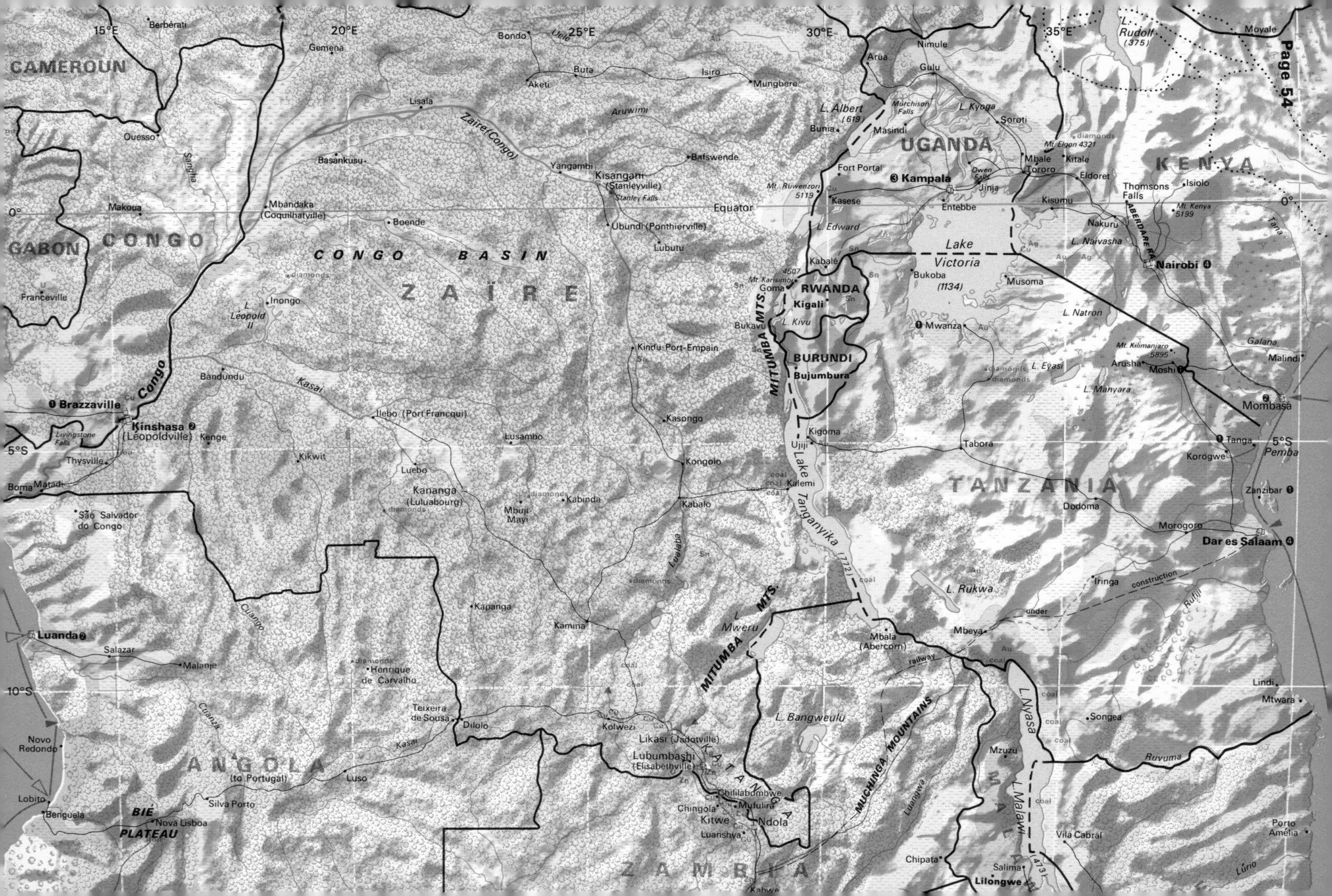
Page 54
CAMEROUN
GABON
CONGO
ZAÏRE
CONGO BASIN
UGANDA
KENYA
RWANDA
BURUNDI
TANZANIA
ANGOLA
(to Portugal)
ZAMBIA
KATANGA
15°E
20°E
25°E
30°E
35°E
0°
5°S
10°S
Equator
Berbérati
Ouesso
Makoua
Franceville
Gemena
Bondo
Buta
Aketi
Isiro
Mungbere
Lisala
Zaïre (Congo)
Aruwimi
Uele
Sangha
Basankusu
Yangambi
Kisangani
(Stanleyville)
Stanley Falls
Bafswende
Mbandaka
(Coquilhatville)
Boende
Ubundi (Ponthierville)
Lubutu
Inongo
L. Léopold II
Brazzaville
Congo
Kinshasa
(Léopoldville)
Livingstone Falls
Thysville
Boma
Matadi
Kenge
Bandundu
Kasai
Kikwit
Ilebo (Port Francqui)
Lusambo
Luebo
Kananga
(Luluabourg)
Mbuji Mayi
Kabinda
Kindu-Port-Empain
Kasongo
Kongolo
Kabalo
Kalemi
Lualaba
Kapanga
Kamina
São Salvador do Congo
Cuango
Luanda
Salazar
Malanje
Henrique de Carvalho
Teixeira de Sousa
Dilolo
Kolwezi
Likasi (Jadotville)
Lubumbashi
(Elisabethville)
Cuanza
Novo Redondo
Lobito
Benguela
Nova Lisboa
Silva Porto
Luso
BIÉ PLATEAU
Chililabombwe
Mufulira
Chingola
Kitwe
Ndola
Luanshya
Kabwe
Arua
Nimule
Gulu
L. Albert
(619)
Murchison Falls
Masindi
Bunia
L. Kyoga
Soroti
Mbale
Tororo
Mt. Elgon 4321
Kitale
Eldoret
Fort Portal
Kampala
Owen Falls
Jinja
Entebbe
Mt. Ruwenzori
5119
Kasese
L. Edward
Kabale
Mt. Karisimbi
4507
Goma
Kigali
L. Kivu
Bukavu
MITUMBA MTS.
Bujumbura
Kigoma
Ujiji
Lake Tanganyika
(772)
Lake Victoria
(1134)
Bukoba
Musoma
Mwanza
L. Natron
L. Eyasi
L. Manyara
Mt. Kilimanjaro
5895
Arusha
Moshi
L. Rudolf
(375)
Moyale
Thomsons Falls
Isiolo
Mt. Kenya
5199
Kisumu
Nakuru
L. Naivasha
ABERDARE RA.
Nairobi
Tana
Galana
Malindi
Mombasa
Tanga
Korogwe
Pemba
Zanzibar
Tabora
Dodoma
Morogoro
Dar es Salaam
Iringa
under construction
Rufiji
L. Rukwa
Mbeya
L. Mweru
MITUMBA MTS.
Mbala
(Abercorn)
railway
L. Bangweulu
MUCHINGA MOUNTAINS
Luangwa
L. Nyasa
L. Malawi
(473)
Mzuzu
Chipata
Salima
Lilongwe
Songea
Ruvuma
Lindi
Mtwara
Vila Cabral
Porto Amélia
Lúrio

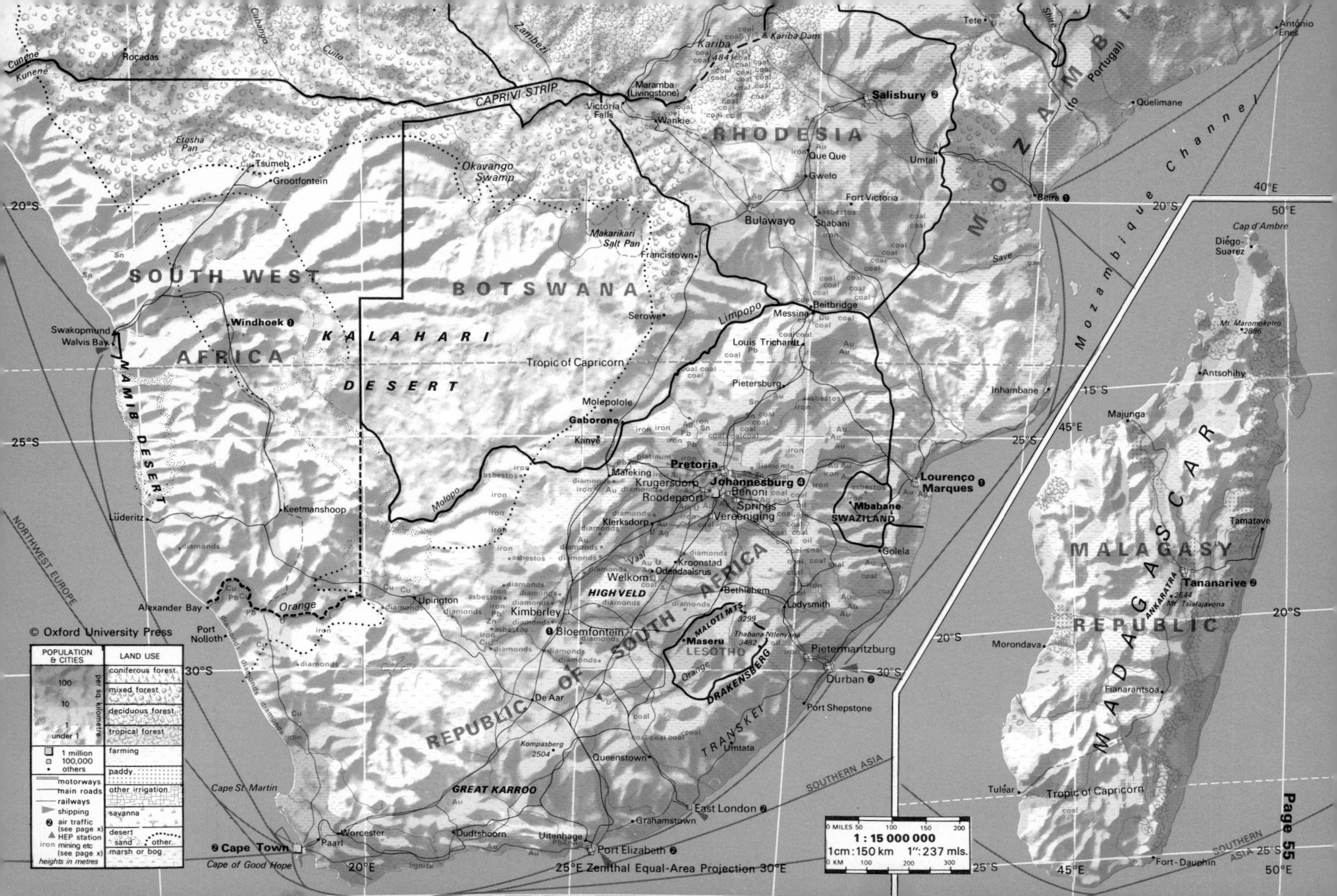
SOUTH WEST AFRICA
BOTSWANA
RHODESIA
MOZAMBIQUE
REPUBLIC OF SOUTH AFRICA
MALAGASY REPUBLIC
MADAGASCAR
LESOTHO
SWAZILAND
TRANSKEI
KALAHARI DESERT
NAMIB DESERT
GREAT KARROO
HIGH VELD
DRAKENSBERG
MALOTI MTS.
ANKARATRA
CAPRIVI STRIP
Mozambique Channel
(to Portugal)
Tropic of Capricorn
Cunene
Kunene
Cubango
Cuito
Zambezi
Limpopo
Molopo
Orange
Vaal
Save
Shire
L. Kariba
Kariba Dam
Okavango Swamp
Makarikari Salt Pan
Etosha Pan
Rocadas
Tsumeb
Grootfontein
Swakopmund
Walvis Bay
Windhoek
Keetmanshoop
Lüderitz
Alexander Bay
Port Nolloth
Cape Town
Cape of Good Hope
Cape St. Martin
Paarl
Worcester
Oudtshoorn
Uitenhage
Port Elizabeth
Grahamstown
East London
Queenstown
Umtata
Port Shepstone
Durban
Pietermaritzburg
Ladysmith
Bethlehem
Maseru
Thabana Ntlenyana 3482
Kompasberg 2504
De Aar
Kimberley
Bloemfontein
Upington
Welkom
Odendaalsrus
Kroonstad
Klerksdorp
Vereeniging
Springs
Benoni
Roodepoort
Krugersdorp
Johannesburg
Pretoria
Mafeking
Kanye
Gaborone
Molepolole
Serowe
Francistown
Victoria Falls
Maramba (Livingstone)
Wankie
Bulawayo
Gwelo
Que Que
Salisbury
Umtali
Fort Victoria
Shabani
Beitbridge
Messina
Louis Trichardt
Pietersburg
Lourenço Marques
Mbabane
Golela
Inhambane
Beira
Tete
Quelimane
António Enes
Cap d'Ambre
Diégo-Suarez
Mt. Maromokotro 2886
Antsohihy
Majunga
Tamatave
Tananarive
Mt. Tsiafajavona 2644
Morondava
Fianarantsoa
Tuléar
Fort-Dauphin
NORTHWEST EUROPE
SOUTHERN ASIA
© Oxford University Press
POPULATION & CITIES
per sq. kilometre
100
10
1
under 1
1 million
100,000
others
motorways
main roads
railways
shipping
air traffic (see page x)
HEP station
mining etc (see page x)
heights in metres
LAND USE
coniferous forest
mixed forest
deciduous forest
tropical forest
farming
paddy
other irrigation
savanna
desert sand
other
marsh or bog
1 : 15 000 000
1cm : 150 km 1": 237 mls.
25°E Zenithal Equal-Area Projection 30°E

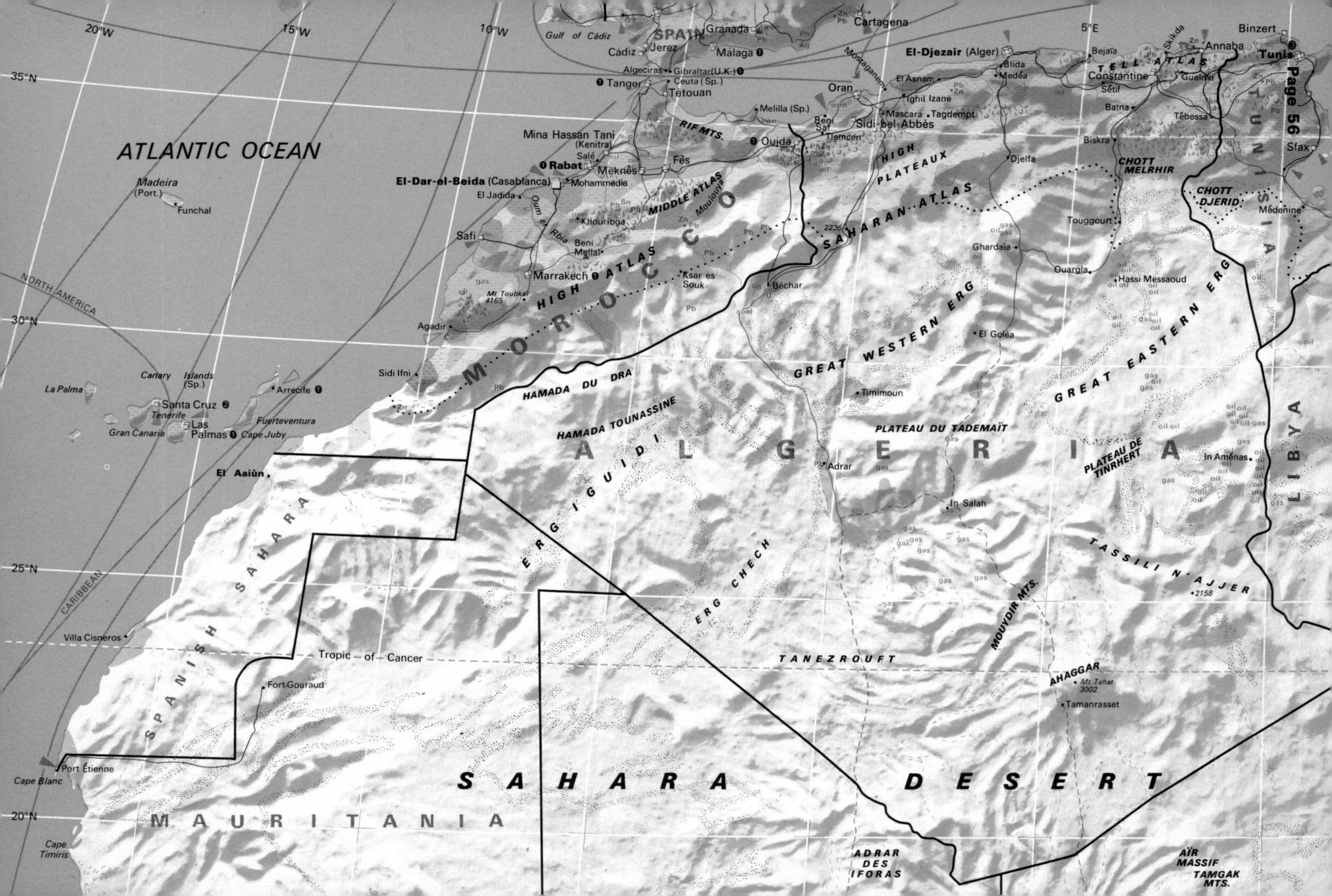

Tunis
Bizert
Annaba
T U N I S I A
Skikda
Stax
Médenine
L I B Y A

Guelma
Tébessa
TELL ATLAS
CHOTT
DJERID
In Amenas
oil

Constantine
Sétif
Batna
Biskra
CHOTT
MELRHIR
oil
oil
oil
Hassi Messoud
oil
In Amenas
oil

Bejaia
El-Djezair (Alger)
Blida
Médéa
Touggourt
oil
gas
Plateau de
Tinrhert
2158

Tlemcen
Mostaganem
El Asnam
Mascara
Tegdempt
Djelfa
Ouargla
gas
GREAT EASTERN ERG
TASSILI N'AJJER
AÏR
MASSIF
TSAMGAK
MTS.

Oran
Béni
Sidi bel-Abbès
HIGH
PLATEAUX
Ghardaïa
El Goléa
A L G E R I A
AHAGGAR
Mt. Tahat
3002
Tamanrasset

Melilla (Sp.)
Oujda
2328
SAHARAN ATLAS
El Adrar
In Salah
gas
MOUYDIR MTS.

SPAIN
Granada
Málaga
RIF MTS.
Fès
Béchar
PLATEAU DU TADEMAÏT
gas

Cádiz
Jerez
Algeciras Gibraltar (U.K.)
Tánger
Tetouán
Ceuta (Sp.)
MIDDLE ATLAS
M O R O C C O
Ksar es
Souk
Timimoun
Adrar
TANEZROUFT
A D R A R
D E S
I F O R A S

Gulf of Cádiz
Mina Hassán Tani
(Kénitra)
Salé
Rabat
Meknès
Mohammédia
Khouribga
Beni
Oum
HIGH ATLAS
HAMADA DU DRA
HAMADA TOUNASSINE
A D I L
E R G C H E C H
S A H A R A

El-Dar-el-Beida (Casablanca)
El Jadida
Marrakech
Mt. Toubkal
4165
E R G
I G U I D I
S A H A R A
D E S E R T

Safi
Oum
R'bia
Mgaun

Agadir
Sidi Ifni

ATLANTIC OCEAN
Tropic of Cancer
Fort-Gouraud
M A U R I T A N I A

Canary Islands
(Sp.)
Santa Cruz
Tenerife
Arrecife
Fuerteventura
Las Palmas
Cape Juby
El Aaiún
S P A N I S H   S A H A R A
Villa Cisneros
Cape Blanc
Port Étienne
Cape
Timiris

Madeira
(Port.)
Funchal

La Palma
Gran Canaria

NORTH AMERICA
CARIBBEAN

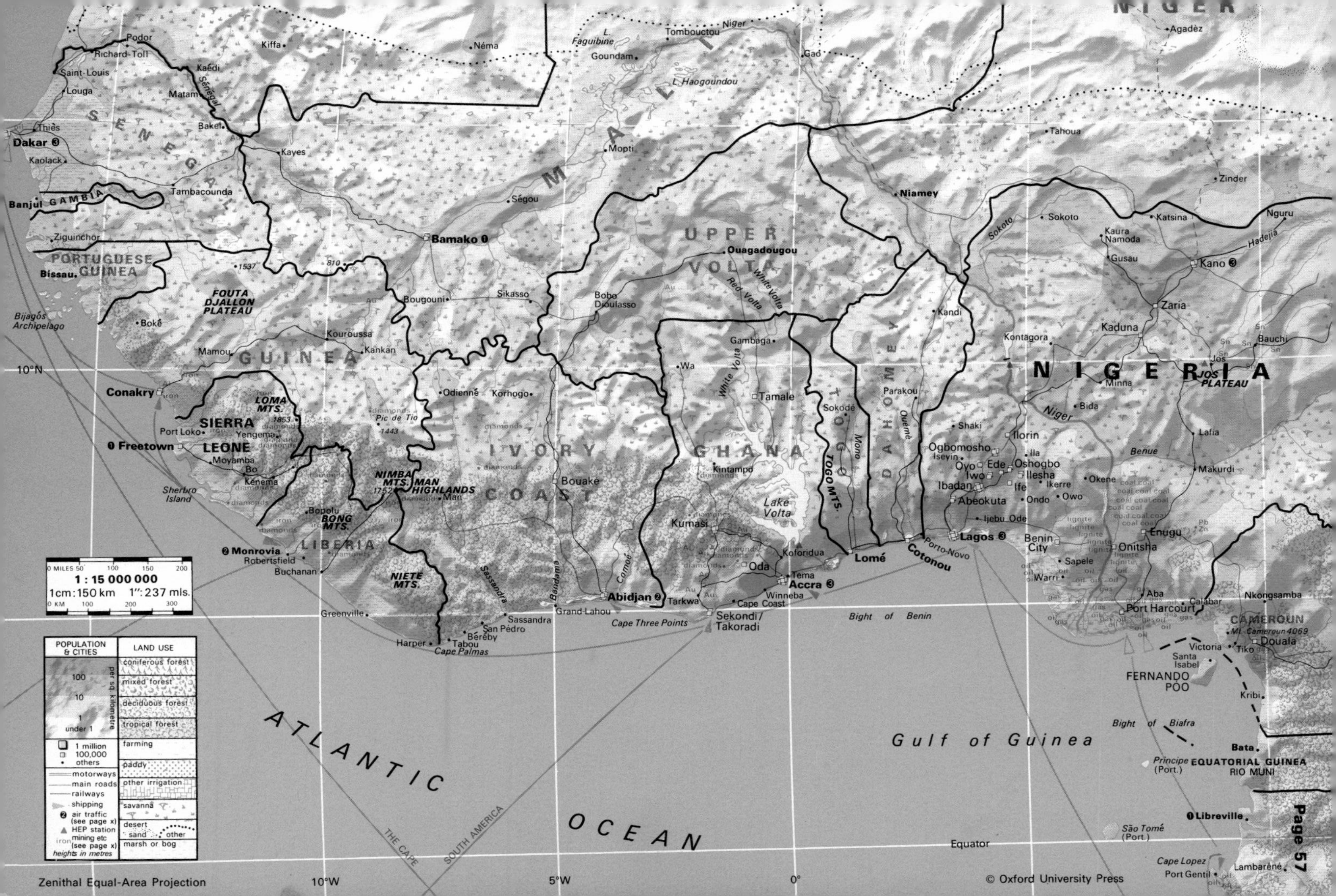

© Oxford University Press

N I G E R

Nguru
Agadez
Zinder
Bauchi
Hadejia
JOS PLATEAU
Kano ⊕
Daura
Katsina
Namoda
Kaura
Gusau
Zaria
Tahoua
Kaduna
Lafia
Makurdi
Sokoto
Minna
Bénué

N I G E R I A

Sokoto
Kandi
Bida
Okene
Owo
Onitsha
Enugu
Port Harcourt ⊕
Calabar
Nikongsamba
Victoria
Douala
Kribi
CAMEROUN
Mt. Cameroun 4069

Bata.

FERNANDO POO
Santa Isabel

EQUATORIAL GUINEA
RIO MUNI

Príncipe (Port)

São Tomé (Port)

Libreville
Cape Lopez
Port Gentil
Lambaréné

Niamey

Kontagora
Ilorin
Shaki
Oyo ⊕ Ede ⊕ Oshogbo
Iwo ⊕ Ife ⊕ Ilesha
Ogbomosho
Iseyin Ibadan ⊕ Ondo Owo
Abeokuta
Benin City
Sapele
Warri ⊕
Iwo
Bight of Biafra
Gulf of Guinea

Lagos ⊕
Porto-Novo
Cotonou
Lomé

D A H O M E Y

Parakou
Ouémé

T O G O

Sokodé
Mono

TOGO MTS.
Bight of Benin

Accra ⊕
Tema
Winneba

Equator

0°

U P P E R   V O L T A

Ouagadougou ⊕
White Volta
Red Volta

M A L I

Tombouctou
Hélgoundou
Niger
Mopti
Goundam
L. Faguibine

Gambaga
Tamale
Wa
White Volta

G H A N A

Lake Volta
Kintampo
Kumasi
Oda
Koforidua
Cape Coast
Sekondi/Takoradi

Bamako ⊕
Ségou
Sikasso
Bobo Dioulasso
Bougouni
Koutiala

I V O R Y   C O A S T

Bouaké
Bandama
Comoé
Grand Lahou
Sassandra
Cape Three Points
Tarkwa
Abidjan ⊕

Nema
Kiffa

S E N E G A L

Saint-Louis
Louga
Thiès
Dakar ⊕
Kaolack
Podor
Richard-Toll
Matam
Sénégal
Kaédi
Bakel
Kayes
Tambacounda

Banjul GAMBIA
Ziguinchor
Bissau ⊕
PORTUGUESE GUINEA
Bijagós Archipelago

G U I N E A

Kédougou
Labé
FOUTA DJALLON PLATEAU
Mamou
Kankan
Kouroussa
Kissidougou
Kindia
Conakry ⊕
Boké

Odienné
Korhogo
Pic de Tio
1143
NIMBA MTS.
MAN HIGHLANDS

S I E R R A   L E O N E

LOMA MTS.
Yengema
Makeni
Bo
Kenema
Moyamba
Port Loko
Freetown ⊕
Sherbro Island

Robertsfield
Buchanan
BONG MTS.
NIÉTÉ MTS.

L I B E R I A

Monrovia ⊕
Greenville
San Pedro
Bereby
Tabou
Cape Palmas
Harper

A T L A N T I C   O C E A N

5°W

10°W

10°N

Gulf of Guinea

SOUTH AMERICA

THE CAPE

Zenithal Equal-Area Projection

MILES
1:15 000 000
1cm:150 km 1''=237 mls.

POPULATION & CITIES
100
10
under

per sq. kilometre
1 million
100,000
others
main roads
motorways
railways
air traffic
HEP station

LAND USE
coniferous forest
mixed forest
deciduous forest
tropical forest
farming
paddy
savanna
other irrigation
desert
sand
marsh or bog

heights in metres

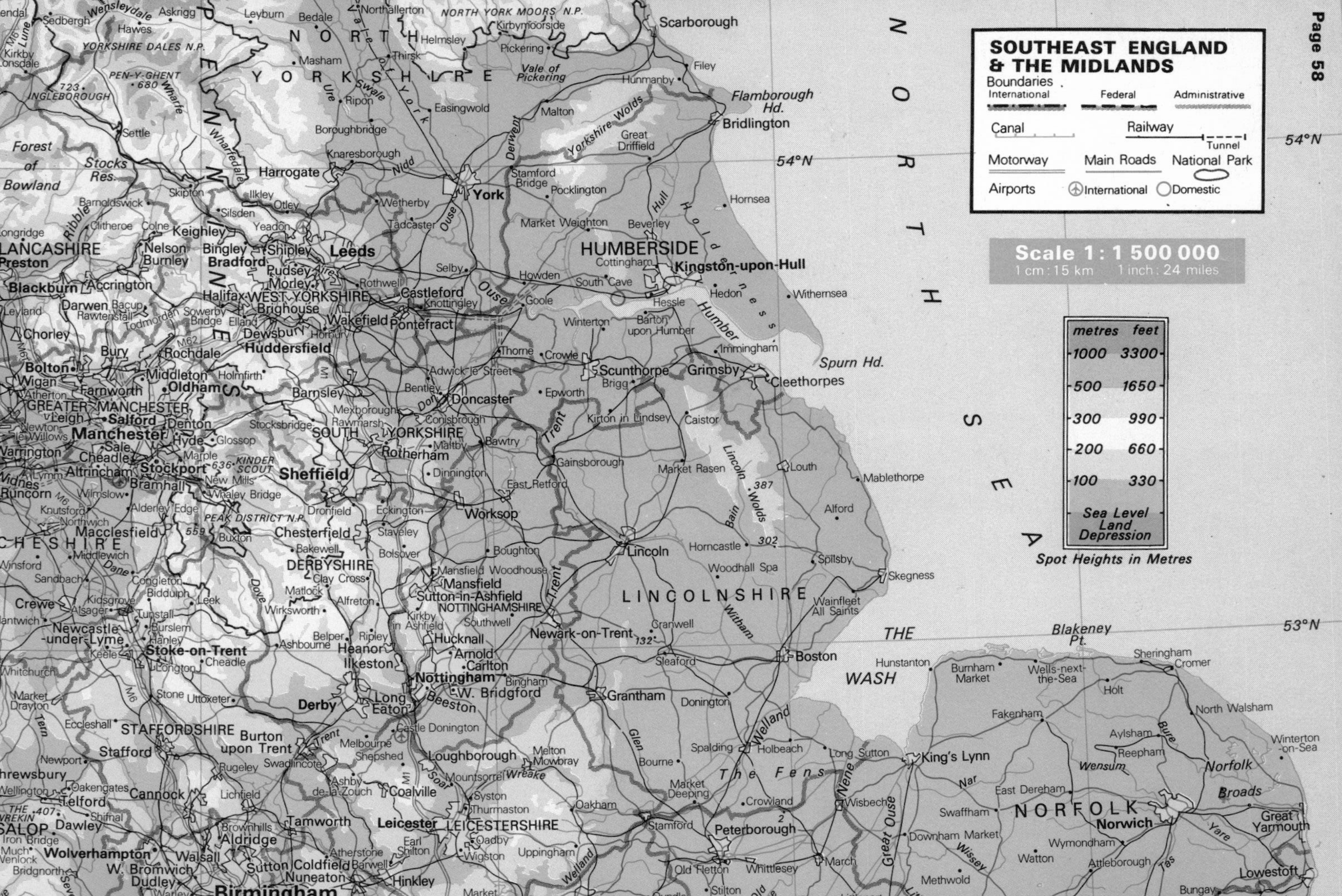

SOUTHEAST ENGLAND & THE MIDLANDS

Boundaries
International — Federal — Administrative

Canal
Motorway
Airports ⊕ International ○ Domestic

Railway
Main Roads
Tunnel ┤─┤─┤
National Park

Scale 1 : 1 500 000
1 cm : 15 km   1 inch : 24 miles

metres	feet
-1000	-3300
-500	-1650
-300	-990
-200	-660
-100	-330
Sea Level	
Land Depression	

Spot Heights in Metres

NORTH SEA

NORTH YORK MOORS N.P.

YORKSHIRE DALES N.P.

PENNINES

PEAK DISTRICT N.P.

HUMBERSIDE

LINCOLNSHIRE

THE WASH

THE FENS

NORFOLK Broads

Scarborough
Filey
Flamborough Hd.
Bridlington
Hornsea
Kingston-upon-Hull
Withernsea
Spurn Hd.
Cleethorpes
Grimsby
Immingham
Mablethorpe
Skegness
Wainfleet All Saints
Boston
Hunstanton
King's Lynn
Great Yarmouth
Lowestoft
Norwich
Cromer
Sheringham
Wells-next-the-Sea
Blakeney Pt.

York
Leeds
Bradford
Huddersfield
Sheffield
Manchester
GREATER MANCHESTER
Stockport
Derby
Nottingham
NOTTINGHAMSHIRE
Leicester
LEICESTERSHIRE
DERBYSHIRE
STAFFORDSHIRE
Stoke-on-Trent
Birmingham
WEST MIDLANDS
Wolverhampton
SALOP
Shrewsbury
Telford
Lincoln
Newark-on-Trent
Grantham
Peterborough
Stamford
Corby
March
Wisbech
Spalding

Harrogate
Knaresborough
Wetherby
Selby
Doncaster
Rotherham
Chesterfield
Worksop
Mansfield
Sutton-in-Ashfield
Loughborough
Coalville
Nuneaton
Tamworth
Cannock
Walsall
Sutton Coldfield
W. Bromwich
Dudley

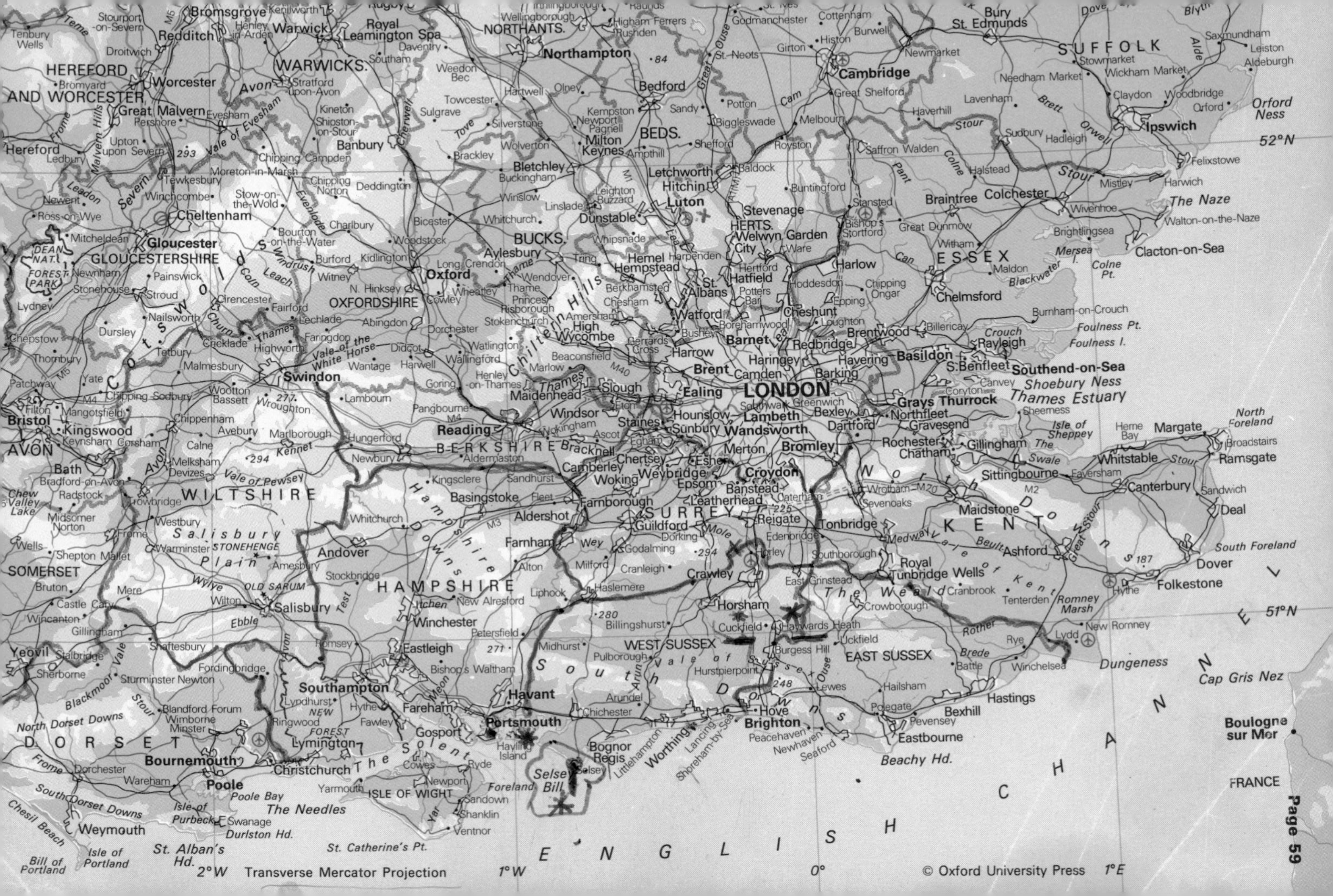

Page 59
ENGLISH CHANNEL
FRANCE
Boulogne sur Mer
Cap Gris Nez
51°N
52°N
1°E
0°
1°W
2°W
Transverse Mercator Projection
© Oxford University Press
SUFFOLK
ESSEX
KENT
SURREY
EAST SUSSEX
WEST SUSSEX
HAMPSHIRE
BERKSHIRE
WILTSHIRE
DORSET
SOMERSET
AVON
GLOUCESTERSHIRE
OXFORDSHIRE
BUCKS.
HERTS.
BEDS.
NORTHANTS.
WARWICKS.
HEREFORD AND WORCESTER
ISLE OF WIGHT
LONDON
Ipswich
Colchester
Chelmsford
Cambridge
Bury St. Edmunds
Southend-on-Sea
Thames Estuary
Margate
Ramsgate
Canterbury
Dover
Folkestone
Maidstone
Ashford
Hastings
Eastbourne
Brighton
Worthing
Portsmouth
Southampton
Winchester
Bournemouth
Poole
Weymouth
Salisbury
Swindon
Reading
Oxford
Luton
Northampton
Bedford
Milton Keynes
Gloucester
Cheltenham
Worcester
Bristol
Bath
Dungeness
Beachy Hd.
Selsey Bill
The Needles
St. Catherine's Pt.
Bill of Portland
North Foreland
South Foreland

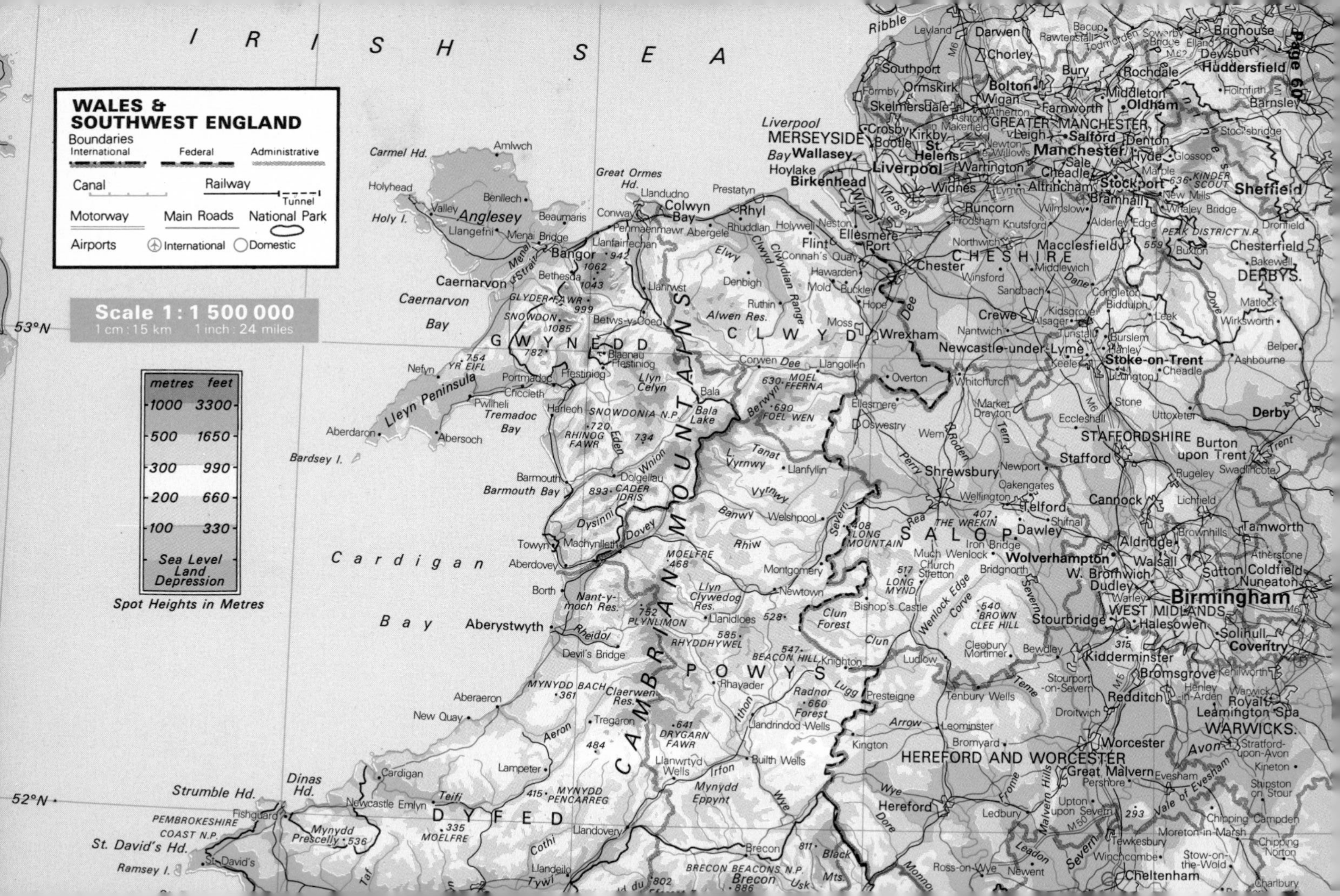
WALES & SOUTHWEST ENGLAND
Boundaries
International
Federal
Administrative
Canal
Railway
Tunnel
Motorway
Main Roads
National Park
Airports
International
Domestic
Scale 1 : 1 500 000
1 cm : 15 km
1 inch : 24 miles
metres feet
1000 3300
500 1650
300 990
200 660
100 330
Sea Level
Land Depression
Spot Heights in Metres
IRISH SEA
Page 60
53°N
52°N
Cardigan Bay
Caernarvon Bay
Barmouth Bay
Tremadoc Bay
Liverpool Bay
Anglesey
Holy I.
Bardsey I.
Ramsey I.
St. David's Hd.
Strumble Hd.
Dinas Hd.
Carmel Hd.
Great Ormes Hd.
Lleyn Peninsula
CAMBRIAN MOUNTAINS
GWYNEDD
CLWYD
POWYS
DYFED
SALOP
CHESHIRE
MERSEYSIDE
GREATER MANCHESTER
STAFFORDSHIRE
WEST MIDLANDS
HEREFORD AND WORCESTER
WARWICKS.
DERBYS.
SNOWDONIA N.P.
PEMBROKESHIRE COAST N.P.
BRECON BEACONS N.P.
PEAK DISTRICT N.P.
Liverpool
Manchester
Birmingham
Wolverhampton
Stoke-on-Trent
Sheffield
Aberystwyth
Shrewsbury
Chester
Wrexham
Hereford
Worcester
Cheltenham
Stafford
Derby
Birkenhead
Wallasey
Caernarvon
Bangor
Holyhead
Colwyn Bay
Rhyl
Cardigan
Brecon
Fishguard
St. David's

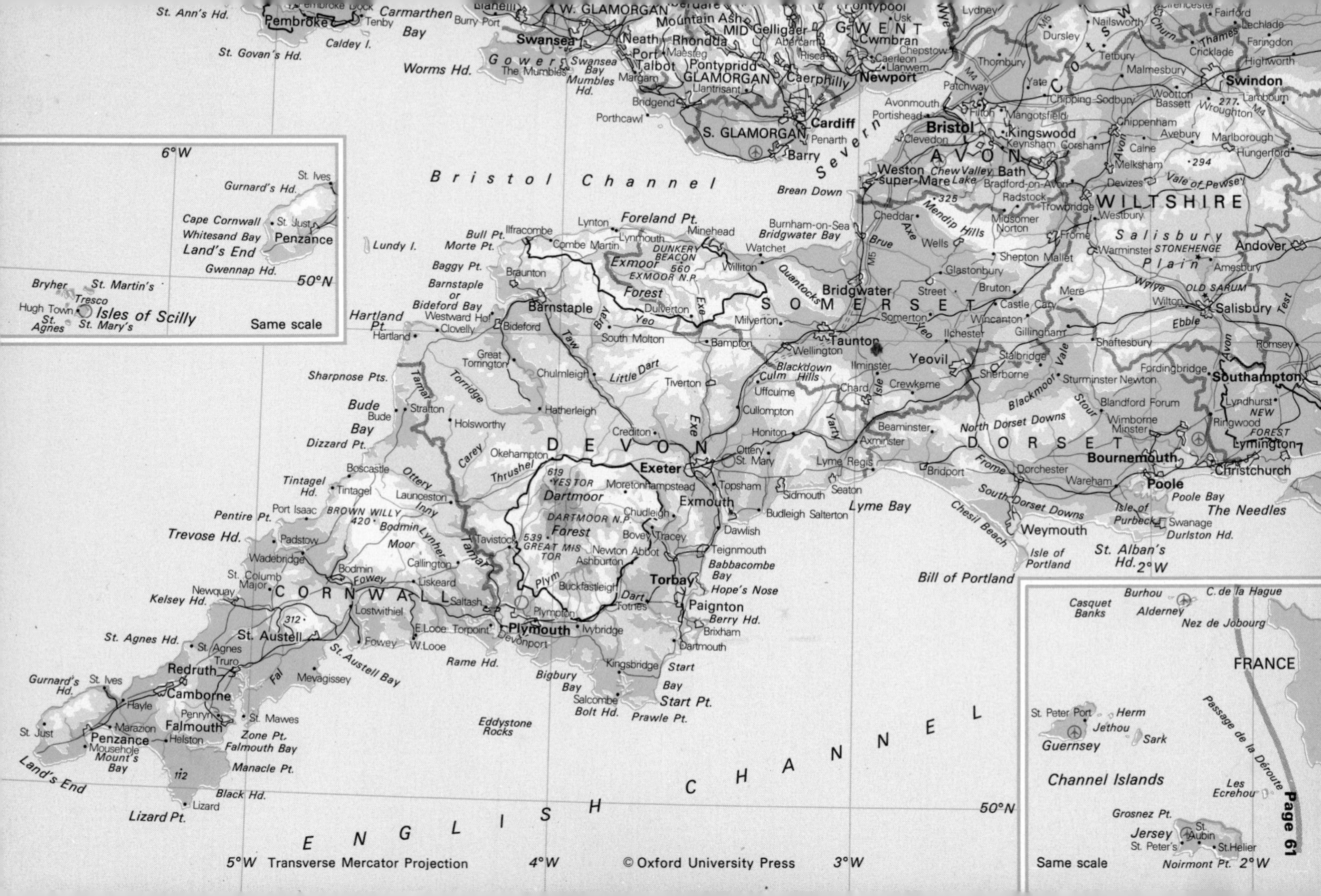
Page 61
Bristol Channel
ENGLISH CHANNEL
DEVON
CORNWALL
SOMERSET
DORSET
WILTSHIRE
AVON
GWENT
MID GLAMORGAN
S. GLAMORGAN
W. GLAMORGAN
Cotswolds
Carmarthen Bay
St. Ann's Hd.
Pembroke
Tenby
Caldey I.
St. Govan's Hd.
Worms Hd.
Burry Port
Swansea
Gower
The Mumbles
Swansea Bay
Mumbles Hd.
Neath
Port Talbot
Margam
Maesteg
Rhondda
Mountain Ash
Gelligaer
Pontypridd
Llantrisant
Bridgend
Porthcawl
Caerphilly
Cardiff
Penarth
Barry
Cwmbran
Newport
Caerleon
Llanwern
Chepstow
Usk
Lydney
Severn
Wye
Avonmouth
Portishead
Clevedon
Bristol
Kingswood
Keynsham
Bath
Weston-super-Mare
Chew Valley Lake
Brean Down
Thornbury
Patchway
Yate
Chipping Sodbury
Mangotsfield
Dursley
Nailsworth
Tetbury
Malmesbury
Cirencester
Fairford
Lechlade
Faringdon
Cricklade
Highworth
Swindon
Thames
Churn
Wootton Bassett
Wroughton
Lambourn
Chippenham
Calne
Avebury
Marlborough
Hungerford
Corsham
Melksham
Devizes
Vale of Pewsey
Bradford-on-Avon
Trowbridge
Westbury
Warminster
Frome
Radstock
Midsomer Norton
Mendip Hills
Cheddar
Axe
Wells
Shepton Mallet
Glastonbury
Street
Bruton
Castle Cary
Wincanton
Mere
Gillingham
Shaftesbury
Salisbury Plain
STONEHENGE
Amesbury
Andover
OLD SARUM
Salisbury
Wilton
Wylye
Ebble
Test
Romsey
Southampton
Fordingbridge
Lyndhurst
NEW FOREST
Ringwood
Lymington
Christchurch
Bournemouth
Poole
Poole Bay
The Needles
Wimborne Minster
Blandford Forum
Sturminster Newton
Stour
Blackmoor Vale
Sherborne
Stalbridge
Yeovil
Ilchester
Somerton
Yeo
Crewkerne
Beaminster
North Dorset Downs
Dorchester
Wareham
Isle of Purbeck
Swanage
Durlston Hd.
St. Alban's Hd.
South Dorset Downs
Weymouth
Chesil Beach
Isle of Portland
Bill of Portland
Bridport
Frome
Lyme Bay
Lyme Regis
Axminster
Chard
Isle
Ilminster
Yarty
Seaton
Sidmouth
Budleigh Salterton
Burnham-on-Sea
Bridgwater Bay
Bridgwater
Brue
Watchet
Quantocks
Williton
Minehead
Taunton
Wellington
Blackdown Hills
Culm
Milverton
Bampton
Honiton
Ottery St. Mary
Cullompton
Uffculme
Tiverton
Exe
Exeter
Topsham
Exmouth
Dawlish
Teignmouth
Babbacombe Bay
Hope's Nose
Torbay
Paignton
Berry Hd.
Brixham
Dartmouth
Start Bay
Start Pt.
Prawle Pt.
Kingsbridge
Salcombe
Bolt Hd.
Bigbury Bay
Totnes
Dart
Newton Abbot
Bovey Tracey
Chudleigh
Moretonhampstead
Crediton
Dartmoor Forest
DARTMOOR N.P.
619 YES TOR
539 GREAT MIS TOR
Ashburton
Buckfastleigh
Ivybridge
Plympton
Plymouth
Plym
Devonport
Tavistock
Okehampton
Thrushel
Foreland Pt.
Lynton
Lynmouth
Combe Martin
DUNKERY BEACON 560
Exmoor Forest
EXMOOR N.P.
Dulverton
Bray
South Molton
Little Dart
Ilfracombe
Bull Pt.
Morte Pt.
Baggy Pt.
Braunton
Barnstaple
Taw
Barnstaple or Bideford Bay
Bideford
Westward Ho!
Clovelly
Great Torrington
Torridge
Chulmleigh
Hatherleigh
Holsworthy
Lundy I.
Hartland Pt.
Hartland
Sharpnose Pts.
Tamar
Stratton
Bude
Bude Bay
Dizzard Pt.
Boscastle
Tintagel Hd.
Tintagel
Carey
Ottery
Launceston
Inny
BROWN WILLY 420
Bodmin Moor
Lynher
Callington
Liskeard
Saltash
Torpoint
Rame Hd.
E. Looe
W. Looe
Eddystone Rocks
Port Isaac
Pentire Pt.
Padstow
Trevose Hd.
Wadebridge
Bodmin
Fowey
Lostwithiel
St. Columb Major
Newquay
Kelsey Hd.
St. Austell
St. Austell Bay
Mevagissey
St. Agnes Hd.
St. Agnes
Truro
Fal
Redruth
Camborne
Penryn
Falmouth
St. Mawes
Zone Pt.
Falmouth Bay
Manacle Pt.
Helston
Black Hd.
Lizard
Lizard Pt.
Hayle
St. Ives
Gurnard's Hd.
St. Just
Penzance
Marazion
Mousehole
Mount's Bay
Land's End
Isles of Scilly
Bryher
Tresco
St. Martin's
Hugh Town
St. Mary's
St. Agnes
Gurnard's Hd.
Cape Cornwall
Whitesand Bay
Gwennap Hd.
Same scale
6°W
5°W
4°W
3°W
2°W
50°N
Channel Islands
Casquet Banks
Burhou
Alderney
C. de la Hague
Nez de Jobourg
FRANCE
Passage de la Déroute
Guernsey
St. Peter Port
Herm
Jethou
Sark
Les Ecrehou
Grosnez Pt.
Jersey
St. Peter's
St. Aubin
St. Helier
Noirmont Pt.
Transverse Mercator Projection
© Oxford University Press

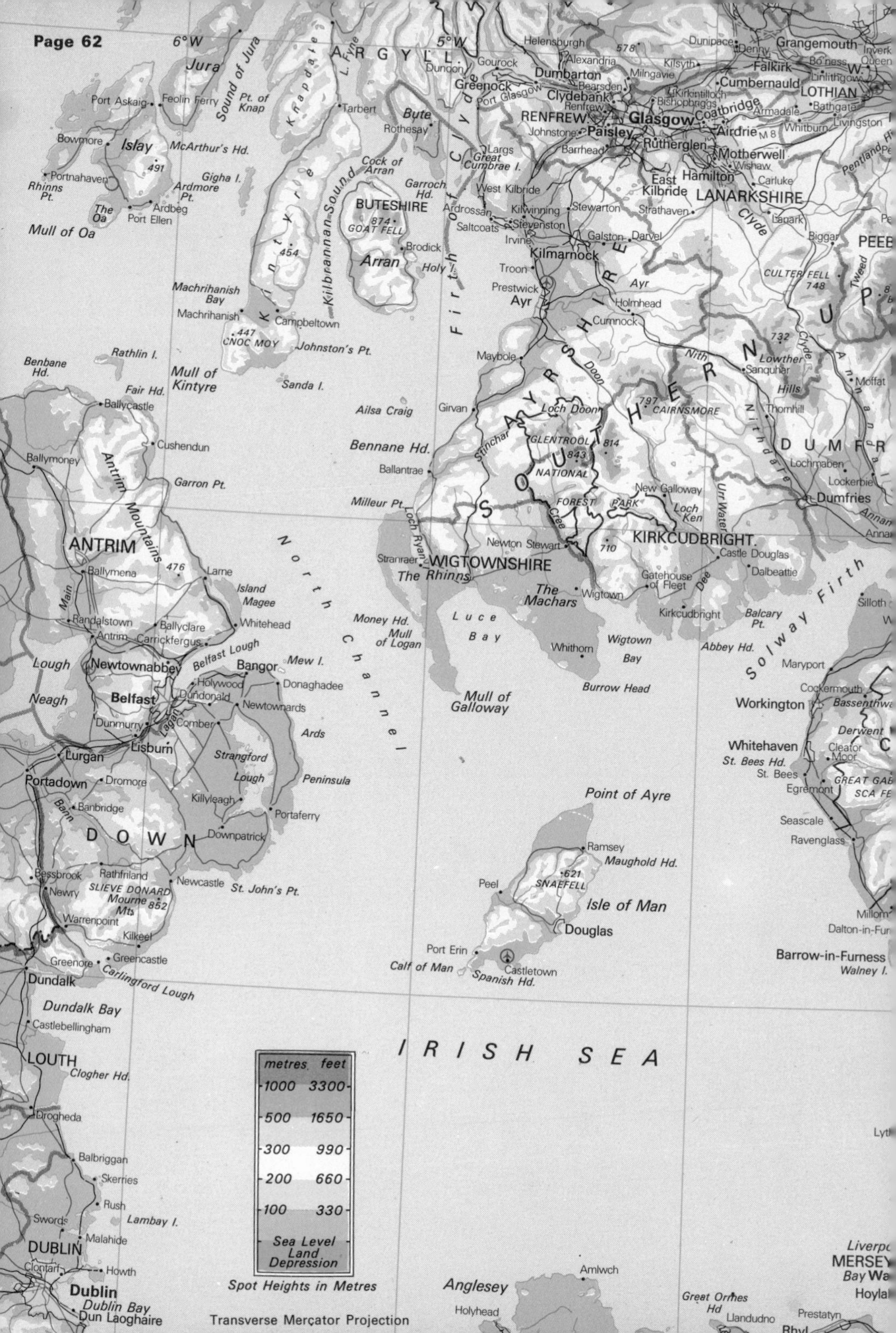

6°W

Jura

Sound of Jura

Pt. of Knap

Knapdale

ARGYLL

5°W

Helensburgh

Gourock

Dunipace

Denny

Grangemouth

Invera

Bo'ness

Queen

Dumbarton

Bearsden

Milngavie

Kilsyth

Kirkintilloch

Falkirk

Linlithgow

Cumbernauld

LOTHIAN

Armadale

Bathgate

Whitburn

Livingston

Port Askaig

Feolin Ferry

L. Fyne

Tarbert

Dunoon

Greenock

Clydebank

Bishopbriggs

Coatbridge

M8

Port Glasgow

Renfrew

Paisley

Glasgow

Rutherglen

Airdrie

Motherwell

Wishaw

Bowmore

Islay

McArthur's Hd.

491

Bute

Rothesay

Johnstone

Barrhead

East Kilbride

Hamilton

Carluke

Lanark

Portnahaven

Rhinns Pt.

Ardmore Pt.

Gigha I.

Ardbeg

Port Ellen

Great Cumbrae I.

Largs

West Kilbride

Kilwinning

Stewarton

Strathaven

Darvel

LANARKSHIRE

Biggar

PEEB

The Oa

Mull of Oa

Campbeltown

CNOC MOY

Johnston's Pt.

BUTESHIRE

874 GOAT FELL

Arran

454

Brodick

Holy I.

Ardrossan

Saltcoats

Irvine

Kilmarnock

Troon

Prestwick

Ayr

Galston

Holmhead

Cumnock

Nith

Sanquhar

Lowther Hills

Thornhill

732

Molfat

CULTER FELL 748

Tweed

Machrihanish Bay

Machrihanish

447

Rathlin I.

Fair Hd.

Ballycastle

Mull of Kintyre

Sanda I.

Ailsa Craig

Girvan

Bennane Hd.

Maybole

Loch Doon

Doon

CAIRNSMORE 797

814

GLENTROOL

843

NATIONAL

FOREST PARK

710

New Galloway

Loch Ken

Urr Water

Lochmaben

Lockerbie

Dumfries

DUMFR

Annan

Benbane Hd.

Cushendun

Ballymoney

Garron Pt.

Ballantrae

Milleur Pt.

Loch Ryan

Stinchar

Cree

Newton Stewart

KIRKCUDBRIGHT

Gatehouse of Fleet

Dee

Castle Douglas

Dalbeattie

Balcary Pt.

Solway Firth

Silloth

ANTRIM

Antrim Mountains

Ballymena

476

Larne

Island Magee

Whitehead

Randalstown

Antrim

Ballyclare

Carrickfergus

Stranraer

The Rhinns

WIGTOWNSHIRE

The Machars

Wigtown

Kirkcudbright

Abbey Hd.

Maryport

Cockermouth

Workington

Bassenthw

Lough Neagh

Newtownabbey

Bangor

Donaghadee

Mew I.

Money Hd.

Mull of Logan

Luce Bay

Whithorn

Wigtown Bay

Burrow Head

Whitehaven

St. Bees Hd.

Cleator Moor

GREAT GAB

SCA FE

St. Bees

Egremont

Belfast

Holywood

Dundonald

Newtownards

Ards

Mull of Galloway

Seascale

Ravenglass

Dunmurry

Comber

Lisburn

Strangford Lough

Peninsula

Portaferry

Point of Ayre

Ramsey

Maughold Hd.

Millom

Dalton-in-Fur

Lurgan

Dromore

Killyleagh

Portadown

Banbridge

Downpatrick

Peel

621

SNAEFELL

Isle of Man

Barrow-in-Furness

Walney I.

Bessbrook

Newry

Rathfriland

SLIEVE DONARD

Mourne Mts 852

Newcastle

St. John's Pt.

Douglas

Warrenpoint

Kilkeel

Greenore

Greencastle

Carlingford Lough

Dundalk

Port Erin

Calf of Man

Castletown

Spanish Hd.

Dundalk Bay

Castlebellingham

LOUTH

Clogher Hd.

IRISH SEA

Drogheda

Balbriggan

Skerries

Rush

Swords

Lambay I.

Malahide

DUBLIN

Clontarf

Howth

Dublin

Dublin Bay

Dun Laoghaire

Anglesey

Holyhead

Amlwch

Great Ormes Hd

Llandudno

Prestatyn

Rhyl

Liverpo

MERSEY

Bay Wa

Hoyla

Lyt

Transverse Mercator Projection

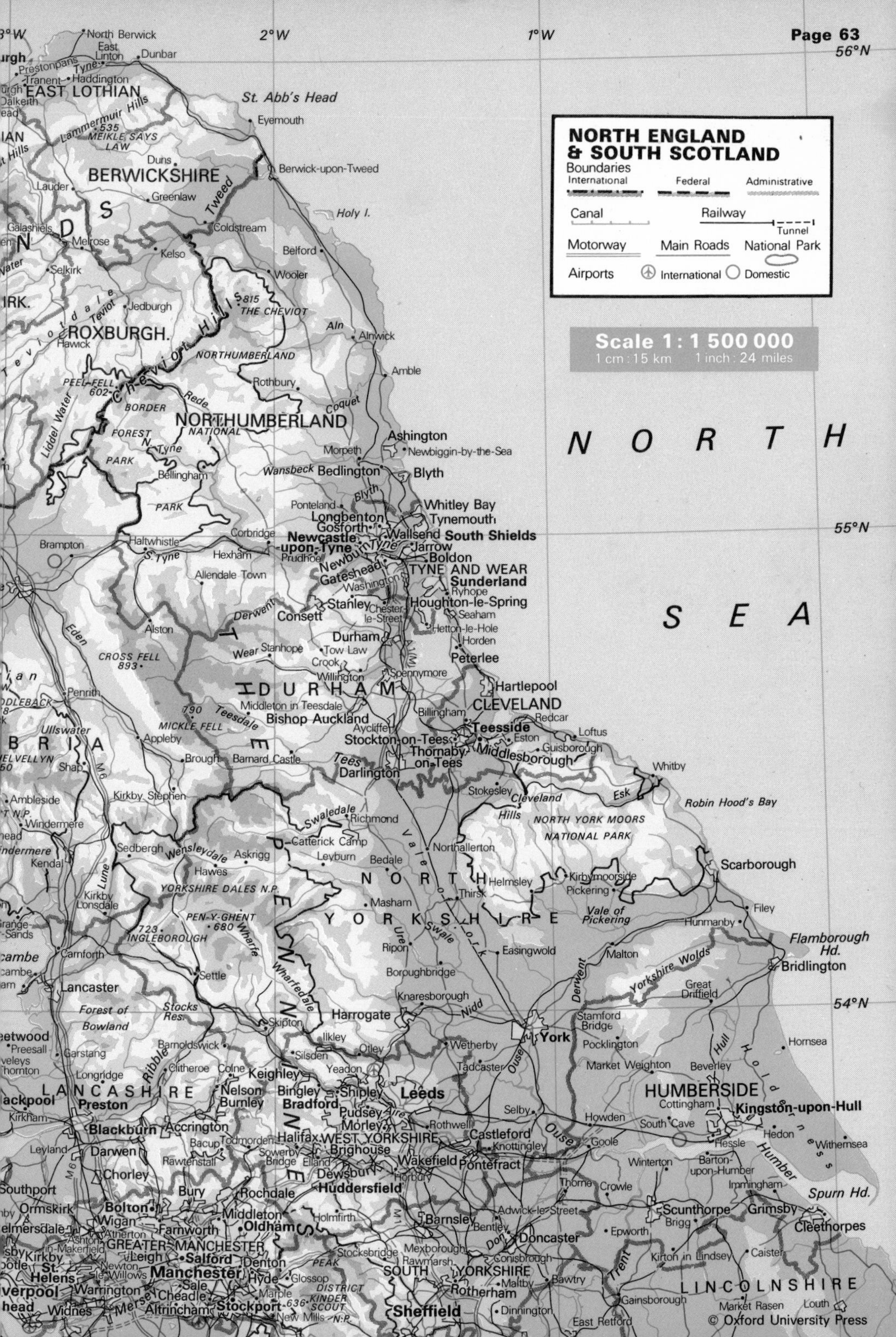
NORTH ENGLAND
& SOUTH SCOTLAND
Boundaries
International
Federal
Administrative
Canal
Railway
Tunnel
Motorway
Main Roads
National Park
Airports
International
Domestic
Scale 1 : 1 500 000
1 cm : 15 km
1 inch : 24 miles
2°W
1°W
56°N
55°N
54°N
NORTH
SEA
North Berwick
East Linton
Dunbar
Prestonpans
Tranent
Haddington
Tyne
EAST LOTHIAN
Dalkeith
St. Abb's Head
Eyemouth
Lammermuir Hills
535
MEIKLE SAYS LAW
Duns
BERWICKSHIRE
Berwick-upon-Tweed
Lauder
Greenlaw
Tweed
Holy I.
Galashiels
Melrose
Coldstream
Kelso
Belford
Selkirk
Wooler
Teviotdale
Teviot
Jedburgh
815
THE CHEVIOT
ROXBURGH.
Hawick
Cheviot Hills
Aln
Alnwick
NORTHUMBERLAND
Amble
PEEL FELL
602
Rothbury
Coquet
Rede
BORDER
NORTHUMBERLAND
NATIONAL
Liddel Water
FOREST
N. Tyne
PARK
Ashington
Newbiggin-by-the-Sea
Morpeth
Wansbeck
Bedlington
Blyth
Bellingham
PARK
Ponteland
Whitley Bay
Longbenton
Gosforth
Tynemouth
Wallsend
South Shields
Brampton
Haltwhistle
Corbridge
Newcastle-upon-Tyne
Jarrow
S. Tyne
Hexham
Prudhoe
Newburn
Boldon
Gateshead
TYNE AND WEAR
Allendale Town
Washington
Sunderland
Ryhope
Stanley
Chester-le-Street
Houghton-le-Spring
Derwent
Consett
Seaham
Alston
Hetton-le-Hole
Horden
Durham
Eden
CROSS FELL
893
Wear
Stanhope
Tow Law
Peterlee
Crook
Willington
Spennymoore
DURHAM
Hartlepool
Penrith
Middleton in Teesdale
CLEVELAND
790
Teesdale
Bishop Auckland
Billingham
Redcar
MICKLE FELL
Aycliffe
Teesside
Ullswater
Appleby
Stockton-on-Tees
Eston
Loftus
Thornaby-on-Tees
Middlesborough
Guisborough
Shap
Brough
Barnard Castle
Tees
Darlington
Whitby
M6
Esk
Ambleside
Kirkby Stephen
Stokesley
Cleveland Hills
Robin Hood's Bay
Windermere
Swaledale
Richmond
NORTH YORK MOORS
NATIONAL PARK
Catterick Camp
Vale of York
Northallerton
Sedbergh
Wensleydale
Askrigg
Leyburn
Bedale
Scarborough
Kendal
Lune
Hawes
NORTH
Helmsley
Kirbymoorside
Pickering
Kirkby Lonsdale
YORKSHIRE DALES N.P.
Thirsk
Masham
Filey
PEN-Y-GHENT
680
Wharfe
YORKSHIRE
Vale of Pickering
723
INGLEBOROUGH
Ure
Swale
Hunmanby
Flamborough Hd.
Ripon
Easingwold
Carnforth
Malton
Bridlington
Boroughbridge
Yorkshire Wolds
Derwent
Great Driffield
Settle
Lancaster
PENNINES
Wharfedale
Knaresborough
Nidd
Forest of Bowland
Stocks Res.
Harrogate
Stamford Bridge
Skipton
York
Bowland
Hull
Hornsea
Preesall
Barnoldswick
Ilkley
Wetherby
Pocklington
Garstang
Silsden
Otley
Holderness
Ribble
Clitheroe
Colne
Tadcaster
Market Weighton
Beverley
Longridge
Keighley
Yeadon
Ouse
LANCASHIRE
Nelson
Bingley
Shipley
Leeds
HUMBERSIDE
Preston
Burnley
Bradford
Cottingham
Kingston-upon-Hull
Kirkham
Pudsey
Selby
Blackburn
Accrington
Morley
Aire
Rothwell
Howden
South Cave
Hedon
Bacup
Todmorden
Halifax
WEST YORKSHIRE
Castleford
Leyland
Darwen
Brighouse
Ouse
Goole
Hessle
Withernsea
Rawtenstall
Sowerby Bridge
Elland
Knottingley
Wakefield
Pontefract
Winterton
Barton-upon-Humber
Humber
Chorley
Dewsbury
Horbury
Southport
Bury
Rochdale
Huddersfield
Thorne
Crowle
Immingham
Spurn Hd.
Ormskirk
Bolton
Wigan
Middleton
Holmfirth
M1
Barnsley
Adwick-le-Street
Scunthorpe
Grimsby
Atherton
Farnworth
Oldham
Bentley
Brigg
Ashton-in-Makerfield
Epworth
Cleethorpes
GREATER MANCHESTER
Don
Doncaster
Leigh
Salford
Stocksbridge
Mexborough
Conisbrough
St. Helens
Newton-le-Willows
Manchester
Denton
PEAK
Rawmarsh
Caister
Kirton in Lindsey
Warrington
Hyde
Glossop
SOUTH YORKSHIRE
Maltby
Bawtry
Trent
LINCOLNSHIRE
Sale
Cheadle
Marple
DISTRICT
Rotherham
Gainsborough
Widnes
Mersey
Altrincham
Stockport
636
KINDER SCOUT
New Mills
N.P.
Sheffield
Dinnington
East Retford
Market Rasen
Louth
© Oxford University Press

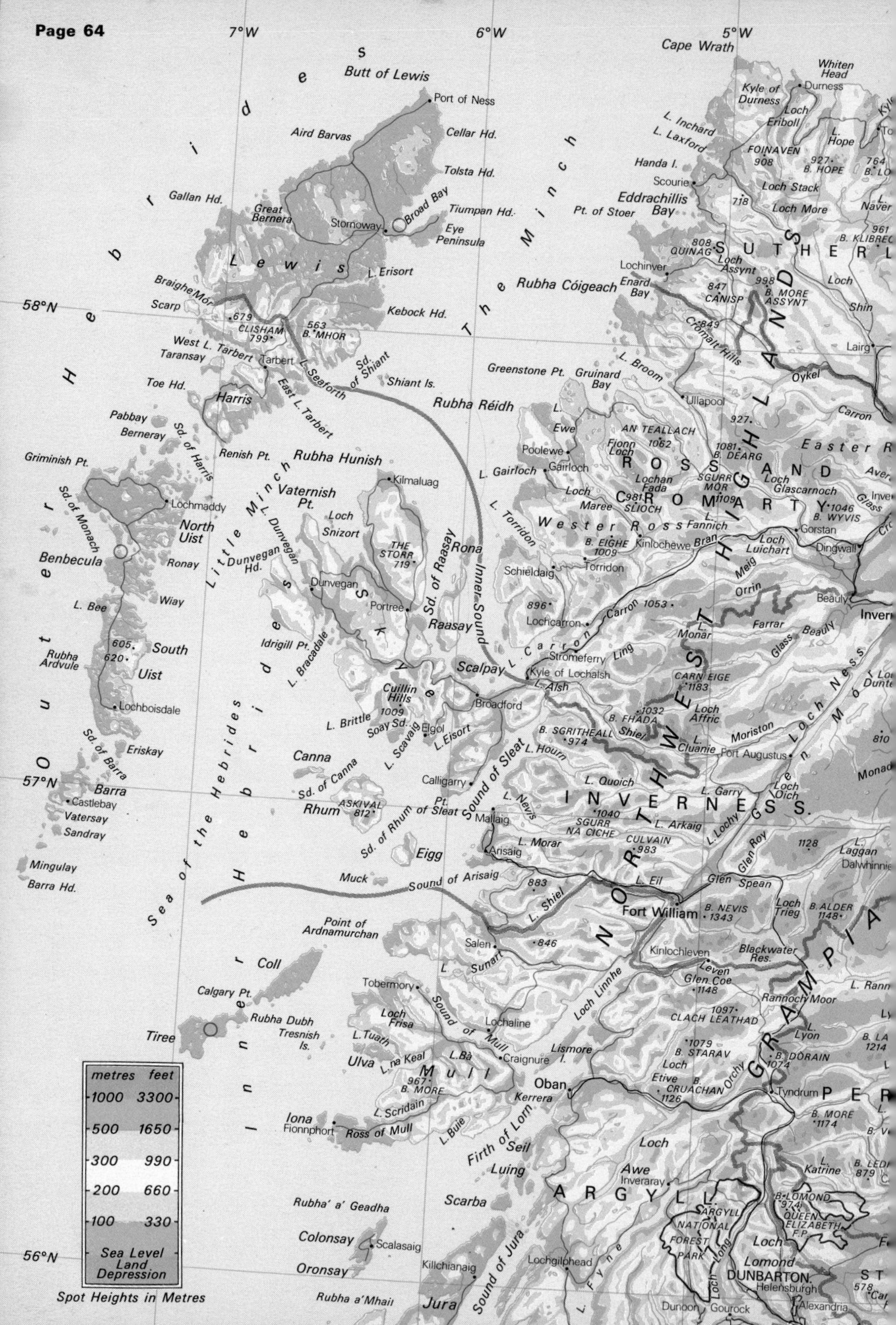
7°W
6°W
5°W
58°N
57°N
56°N
Outer Hebrides
Inner Hebrides
Butt of Lewis
Port of Ness
Aird Barvas
Cellar Hd.
Tolsta Hd.
Gallan Hd.
Great Bernera
Stornoway
Broad Bay
Tiumpan Hd.
Eye Peninsula
Lewis
L. Erisort
Braighe Mór
Scarp
Kebock Hd.
679
CLISHAM 799
563 B. MHOR
West L. Tarbert
Taransay
Tarbert
L. Seaforth
Sd. of Shiant
Shiant Is.
Toe Hd.
Harris
East L. Tarbert
Pabbay
Berneray
Sd. of Harris
Renish Pt.
Griminish Pt.
Lochmaddy
North Uist
Sd. of Monach
Benbecula
Ronay
Wiay
L. Bee
605
620
South Uist
Rubha Ardvule
Lochboisdale
Sd. of Barra
Eriskay
Barra
Castlebay
Vatersay
Sandray
Mingulay
Barra Hd.
The Minch
Little Minch
Rubha Hunish
Vaternish Pt.
Kilmaluag
Loch Snizort
THE STORR 719
L. Dunvegan
Dunvegan Hd.
Dunvegan
Portree
Sd. of Raasay
Raasay
Rona
Inner Sound
Skye
Idrigill Pt.
L. Bracadale
Scalpay
Cuillin Hills
1009
L. Brittle
Soay Sd.
Elgol
L. Scavaig
L. Eisort
Broadford
Canna
Sd. of Canna
Calligarry
Rhum
ASKIVAL 812
Sd. of Rhum
Pt. of Sleat
Sound of Sleat
Mallaig
Eigg
Muck
Sound of Arisaig
Arisaig
Sea of the Hebrides
Point of Ardnamurchan
Coll
Calgary Pt.
Rubha Dubh
Tiree
Tresnish Is.
Tobermory
Loch Frisa
L. Tuath
Sound of Mull
Lochaline
Ulva
L. na Keal
L. Bà
Craignure
Mull
967 B. MORE
L. Scridain
Iona
Fionnphort
Ross of Mull
L. Buie
Firth of Lorn
Kerrera
Oban
Seil
Luing
Scarba
Rubha' a' Geadha
Colonsay
Scalasaig
Oronsay
Killchianaig
Rubha a' Mhail
Jura
Sound of Jura
Cape Wrath
Whiten Head
Durness
Kyle of Durness
Loch Eriboll
L. Hope
L. Inchard
L. Laxford
FOINAVEN 908
927
B. HOPE
764
Handa I.
Scourie
Loch Stack
718
Loch More
Eddrachillis Bay
Pt. of Stoer
Naver
961
B. KLIBRECK
808 QUINAG
Loch Assynt
Lochinver
Enard Bay
Rubha Cóigeach
847 CANISP
998 B. MORE ASSYNT
Loch Shin
SUTHERLAND
849
Cromalt Hills
Lairg
Greenstone Pt.
Gruinard Bay
L. Broom
Oykel
Ullapool
Rubha Réidh
L. Ewe
AN TEALLACH 1062
Fionn Loch
927
Carron
Poolewe
1081 B. DEARG
Easter Ross
L. Gairloch
Gairloch
Lochan Fada
SGURR MOR 1109
Loch Glascarnoch
ROSS AND CROMARTY
Loch Maree
981 SLIOCH
L. Fannich
1046 B. WYVIS
L. Torridon
Wester Ross
B. EIGHE 1009
Kinlochewe
Bran
Loch Luichart
Gorstan
Dingwall
Torridon
Schieldaig
Meig
Orrin
896
Carron 1053
Beauly
Lochcarron
L. Monar
Farrar
L. Carron
Stromeferry
Ling
Glass
Beauly
Kyle of Lochalsh
L. Alsh
CARN EIGE 1183
Loch Ness
1032
B. FHADA
Loch Affric
L. Shiel
B. SGRITHEALL 974
L. Hourn
L. Cluanie
Moriston
Fort Augustus
810
L. Quoich
L. Garry
Loch Oich
L. Nevis
1040
SGURR NA CICHE
L. Arkaig
L. Lochy
INVERNESS
NORTH WEST HIGHLANDS
L. Morar
CULVAIN 983
Glen Roy
1128
L. Laggan
Dalwhinnie
883
L. Eil
Glen Spean
L. Shiel
Fort William
B. NEVIS 1343
Loch Treig
B. ALDER 1148
Salen
846
Kinlochleven
Blackwater Res.
L. Sunart
Leven
Glen Coe 1148
Loch Linnhe
Rannoch Moor
L. Rannoch
1097
CLACH LEATHAD
GRAMPIAN
L. Lyon
B. LAWERS 1214
1079 B. STARAV
B. DORAIN 1074
Lismore I.
Loch Etive
B. CRUACHAN 1126
Orchy
Tyndrum
B. MORE 1174
Loch Awe
Inveraray
ARGYLL
L. Katrine
B. LEDI 879
ARGYLL NATIONAL FOREST PARK
B. LOMOND 974
QUEEN ELIZABETH F.P.
Loch Lomond
Lochgilphead
L. Fyne
Loch Long
DUNBARTON
Helensburgh
Dunoon
Gourock
Alexandria
578
metres feet
1000 3300
500 1650
300 990
200 660
100 330
Sea Level
Land Depression
Spot Heights in Metres

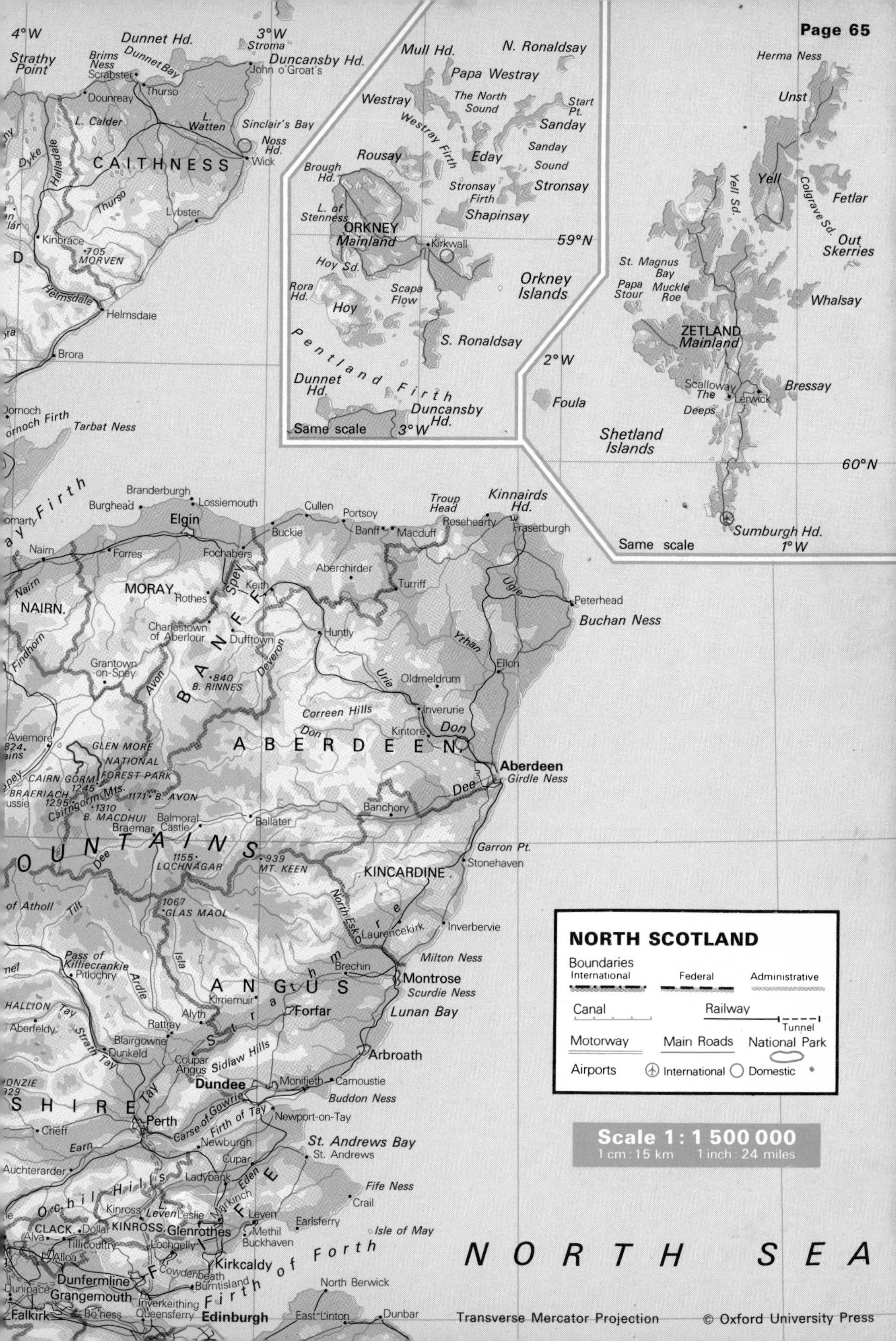

4°W 3°W
Strathy
Point
Brims
Ness Dunnet Hd.
Dunnet Bay Stroma
Scrabster Duncansby Hd.
Dounreay Thurso John o'Groat's
L. Calder
CAITHNESS L. Watten Sinclair's Bay
Thurso Noss
Hd.
Wick

Mull Hd. N. Ronaldsay

Papa Westray

Westray The North Start
Sound Pt.
Sanday
Westray Firth Sanday
Rousay Eday Sound
Brough Stronsay
Hd. Firth Stronsay
Stronsay
L. of Shapinsay
Stenness
ORKNEY Kirkwall
Mainland 59°N

Herma Ness

Unst

Yell Fetlar

Colgrave Sd. Out
Skerries

Yell Sd.
Whalsay

Kinbrace ·705
MORVEN
Helmsdale Lybster
Helmsdale
Brora

Hoy Sd.
Rora Orkney
Hd. Hoy Islands
Scapa
Flow

St. Magnus
Bay Muckle
Papa Roe
Stour
ZETLAND
Mainland

Tarbat Ness
ornoch Firth S. Ronaldsay

Pentland Firth 2°W

Dunnet Duncansby
Hd. Hd.
Same scale 3°W

Scalloway
The Lerwick
Deeps Bressay

Foula

Shetland
Islands 60°N

Same scale Sumburgh Hd.
1°W

Branderburgh Lossiemouth
Burghead Cullen Portsoy Troup Kinnairds
Elgin Buckie Banff Head Hd.
Portgordon Macduff Rosehearty Fraserburgh
Nairn Forres Fochabers
MORAY Keith Aberchirder Peterhead
Rothes Turriff Buchan Ness
NAIRN. Charlestown Dufftown
of Aberlour Huntly
Grantown- ·840 Oldmeldrum Ellon
on-Spey B. RINNES Inverurie Ythan
Correen Hills Kintore Don
Aviemore 824. Don
ains GLEN MORE ABERDEEN
CAIRN GORM NATIONAL Aberdeen
BRAERIACH 1245 FOREST PARK Girdle Ness
ussie 1295 1171·B·AVON Banchory Dee
Cairngorm Mts. 1310 B. MACDHUI Ballater
Braemar Castle Balmoral
OUNTAINS 1155· Garron Pt.
LOCHNAGAR ·939 Stonehaven
of Atholl Dee MT. KEEN KINCARDINE
1067 ·Inverbervie
·GLAS MAOL Laurencekirk
Pass of Milton Ness
Killiecrankie Brechin
Pitlochry Kirriemuir ANGUS Montrose
HALLION Aberfeldy Alyth Scurdie Ness
Tay Rattray Forfar Lunan Bay
Blairgowrie Sidlaw Hills
ONZIE Dunkeld Coupar Arbroath
929 Angus Monifieth Carnoustie
SHIRE Dundee Buddon Ness
Crieff Perth Newport-on-Tay
Earn Carse of Gowrie St. Andrews Bay
Newburgh Firth of Tay St. Andrews
Auchterarder Cupar Fife Ness
Ochil Hills Ladybank Crail
Kinross Eden Isle of May
CLACK. Dollar Leven Leslie Earlsferry
Alva KINROSS Glenrothes Leven
Tillicoultry Lochgelly Methil NORTH SEA
Alloa Kirkcaldy
Dunfermline Cowdenbeath Burntisland
Grangemouth Inverkeithing North Berwick
Falkirk Queensferry Edinburgh East Linton Dunbar

NORTH SCOTLAND

Boundaries
International Federal Administrative

Canal Railway

Motorway Main Roads National Park

Airports ⊕ International ○ Domestic ·

Scale 1 : 1 500 000
1 cm : 15 km 1 inch : 24 miles

Transverse Mercator Projection © Oxford University Press

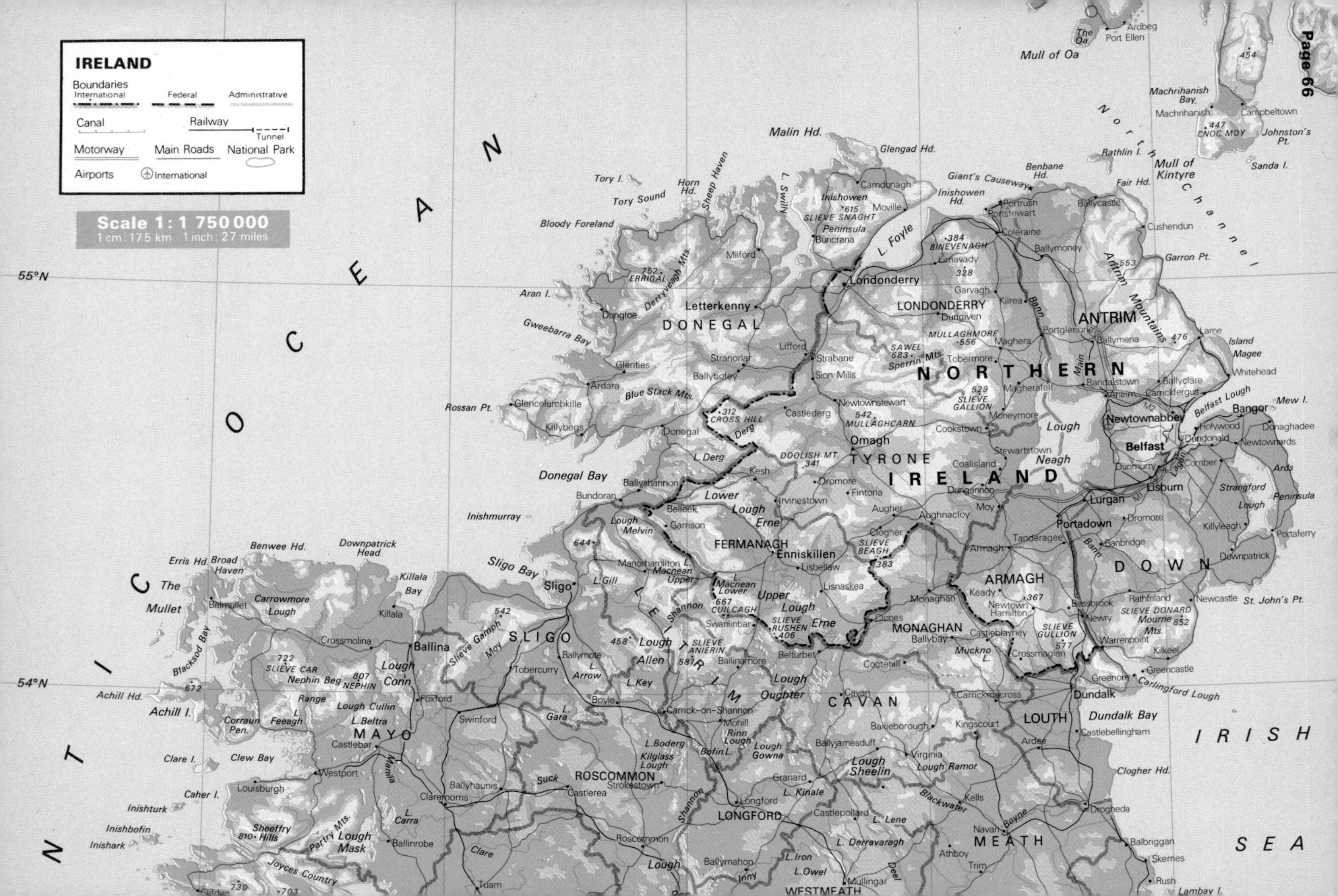
IRELAND
Boundaries
International
Federal
Administrative
Canal
Railway
Tunnel
Motorway
Main Roads
National Park
Airports
International
Scale 1: 1 750 000
1 cm : 17.5 km 1 inch : 27 miles
55°N
54°N
ATLANTIC OCEAN
IRISH SEA
North Channel
NORTHERN IRELAND
DONEGAL
LONDONDERRY
ANTRIM
TYRONE
FERMANAGH
ARMAGH
DOWN
MONAGHAN
CAVAN
LOUTH
MEATH
WESTMEATH
LONGFORD
LEITRIM
SLIGO
ROSCOMMON
MAYO
Belfast
Londonderry
Newtownabbey
Lisburn
Lurgan
Portadown
Bangor
Omagh
Enniskillen
Letterkenny
Sligo
Ballina
Dundalk
Malin Hd.
Tory I.
Tory Sound
Bloody Foreland
Horn Hd.
Sheep Haven
L. Swilly
L. Foyle
Lough Neagh
Lower Lough Erne
Upper Lough Erne
Donegal Bay
Sligo Bay
Dundalk Bay
Clew Bay
Achill I.
Mull of Kintyre
Mull of Oa
Rathlin I.
Giant's Causeway
Antrim Mountains
Sperrin Mts.
Blue Stack Mts.
Derryveagh Mts.
Mourne Mts.
Strangford Lough
Belfast Lough
Carlingford Lough
Lough Mask
Lough Conn
Lough Allen
Lough Oughter
Lough Sheelin
Lough Ramor
Inishowen Peninsula
Ards Peninsula
Campbeltown
Port Ellen
Coleraine
Ballymena
Ballymoney
Larne
Armagh
Newry
Cookstown
Dungannon
Strabane
Donegal
Ballyshannon
Bundoran
Drogheda
Cavan
Monaghan
Longford
Westport
Castlebar
Roscommon
Carrick-on-Shannon
Mullingar
Navan
Kells
Boyle
Tobercurry
Swinford
Claremorris
Ballinrobe
Belmullet
Crossmolina
Killala
Dungloe
Killybegs
Glencolumbkille
Ardara
Glenties
Milford
Buncrana
Moville
Carndonagh
Limavady
Portrush
Portstewart
Ballycastle
Cushendun
Whitehead
Carrickfergus
Holywood
Newtownards
Donaghadee
Portaferry
Downpatrick
Killyleagh
Newcastle
Kilkeel
Warrenpoint
Banbridge
Dromore
Tanderagee
Keady
Castleblayney
Carrickmacross
Kingscourt
Ardee
Castlebellingham
Balbriggan
Skerries
Rush
Lambay I.
Shannon
Bann
Erne
Moy
Boyne
Blackwater
Suck
Deel
ERRIGAL 752
SLIEVE SNAGHT 615
BINEVENAGH 384
SAWEL 683
MULLAGHMORE 556
SLIEVE GALLION 529
MULLAGHCARN 542
DOOLISH MT. 341
CROSS HILL 312
SLIEVE BEAGH 383
CUILCAGH 667
SLIEVE RUSHEN 406
SLIEVE ANIERIN 587
SLIEVE DONARD 852
SLIEVE GULLION 577
NEPHIN 807
SLIEVE CAR 722
CNOC MOY 447

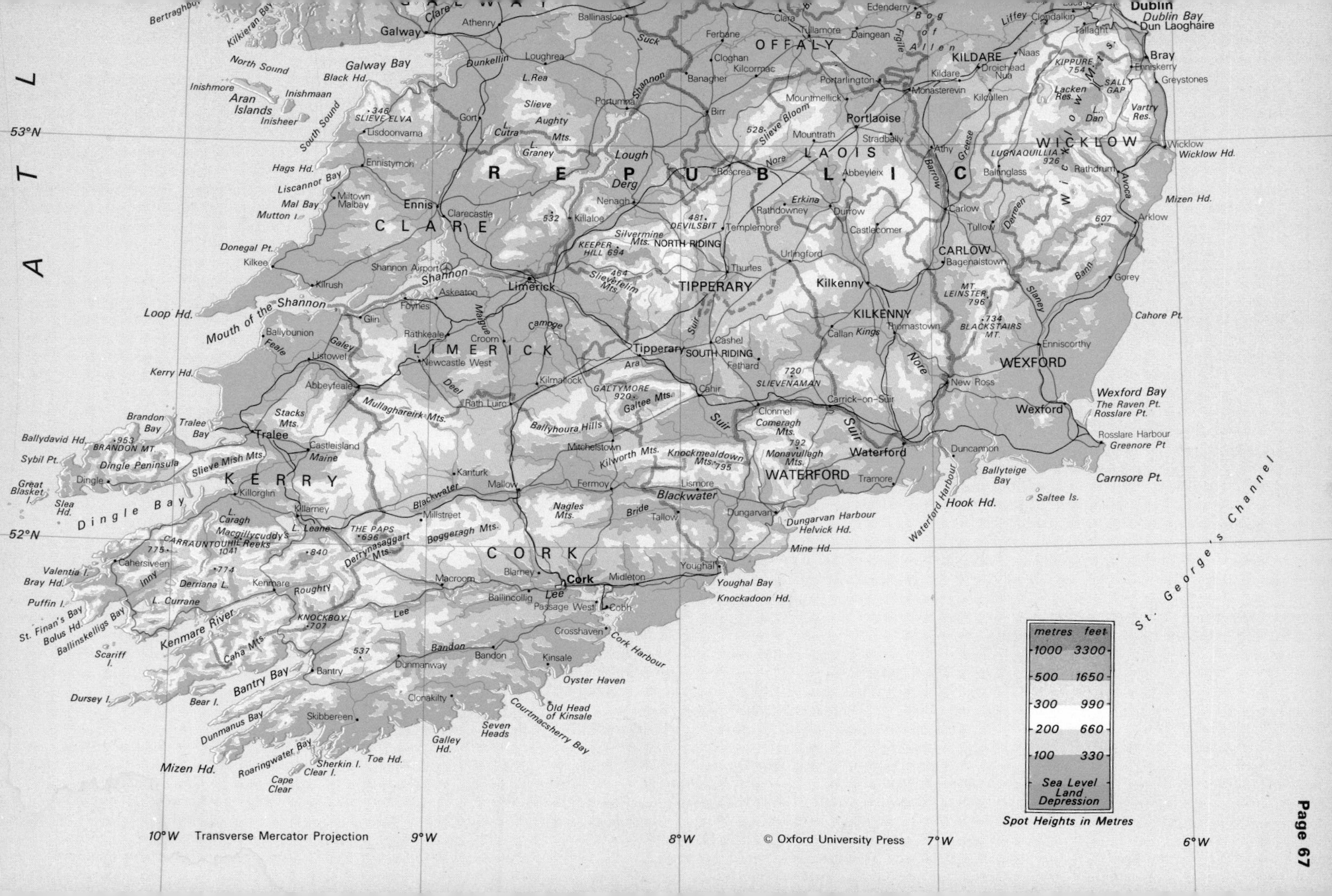

© Oxford University Press

10°W   Transverse Mercator Projection   9°W   8°W   7°W   6°W

metres	feet	
	3300	
1000	1650	
500	990	
300	660	
200	330	
100		Sea Level
		Land
		Depression

Spot Heights in Metres

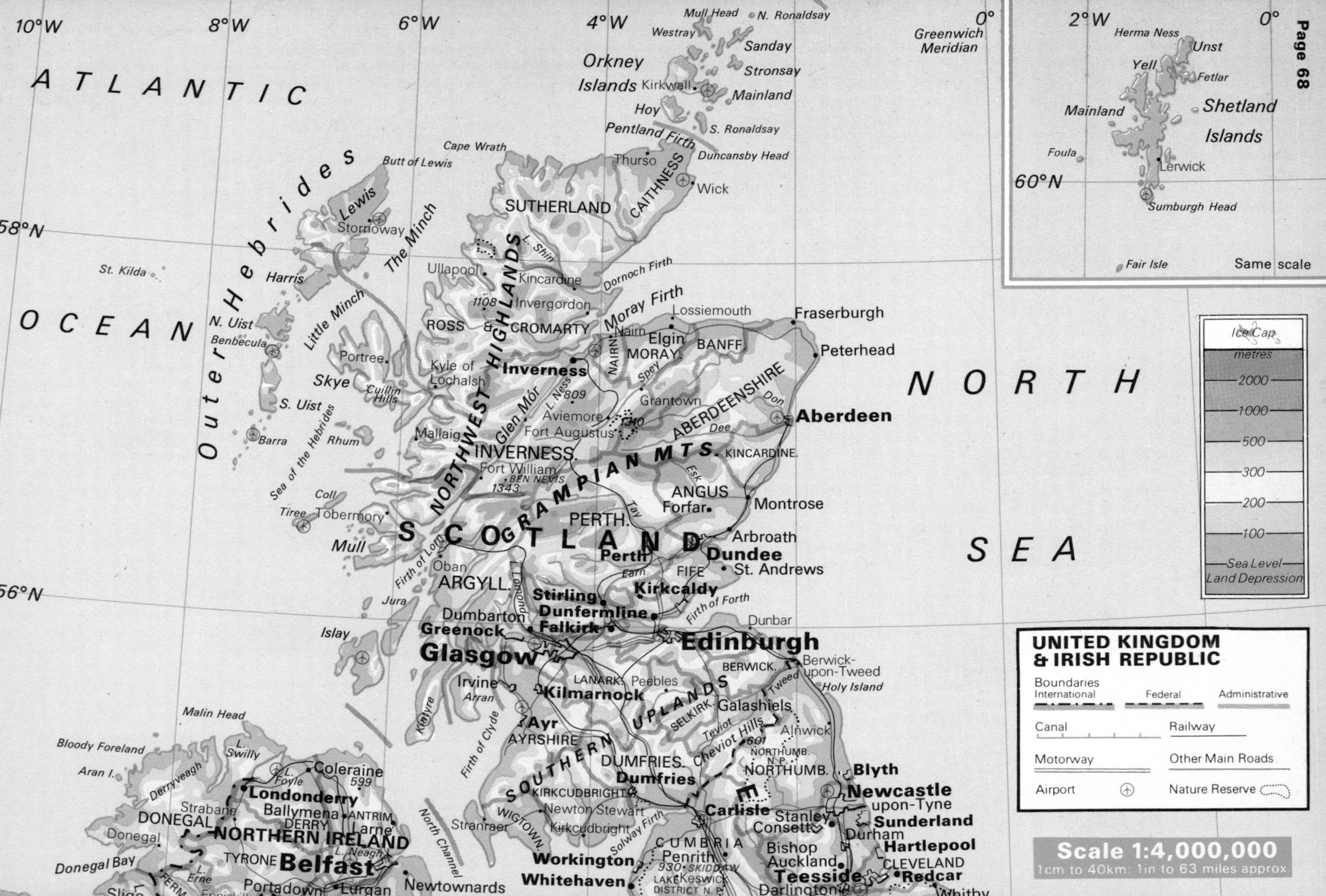

UNITED KINGDOM & IRISH REPUBLIC

Boundaries
International   Federal   Administrative

Canal   Railway

Motorway   Other Main Roads

Airport   Nature Reserve

Scale 1:4,000,000
1cm to 40km; 1 in to 63 miles approx.

metres
Ice Cap
2000
1000
500
300
200
100
Sea Level
Land Depression

Same scale

Shetland Islands

Herma Ness
Unst
Yell
Fetlar
Mainland
Lerwick
Sumburgh Head
Foula
Fair Isle

60°N

2°W   0°

Greenwich Meridian

0°

N O R T H

S E A

Fraserburgh
Peterhead
Aberdeen
ABERDEENSHIRE
Don
Dee
KINCARDINE
Montrose
Arbroath
Dundee
St. Andrews
ANGUS
Forfar
FIFE
Firth of Forth
Dunbar
Kirkcaldy
Edinburgh
Berwick-upon-Tweed
Holy Island
Peebles
Galashiels
Tweed
Alnwick
Berwick-upon-Tweed
NORTHUMB.
Newcastle upon-Tyne
Blyth
Sunderland
Hartlepool
Durham
CLEVELAND
Consett
Redcar
Bishop Auckland
Teesside
Darlington
Whitby
Stanley
Carlisle
CUMBRIA
Penrith
Lake District
N.P.
Kirk Yeth.
Dumfries
DUMFRIES
Hawick
Cheviot Hills
SOUTHERN UPLANDS
Lockerbie
Carnmore
Workington
Whitehaven
Whites

NORTH
SEA

Fraserburgh
Peterhead
Aberdeen

Lossiemouth
Elgin
Nairn
Forres
MORAY
Grantown
BANFF
Spey
Esk
Dee
Don

MORAY FIRTH
Dornoch Firth
Inverness
CROMARTY
ROSS
Glen Mor
Loch Ness
Fort Augustus
1343
Aviemore
4306
Fort William
GRAMPIAN MTS.
PERTH
Perth
Tay
L. Earn
Stirling
Dunfermline
Falkirk
Dumbarton
Greenock
Glasgow
Kilmarnock
Ayr
AYRSHIRE
LANARK
Irvine
Kilmarnock

Cape Wrath
SUTHERLAND
Kincardine
Invergordon
Kyle of Lochalsh
Mallaig
Skye
Cuillin Hills
Portree
Rhum
Coll
Tiree
Tobermory
Mull
Oban
ARGYLL
Jura
Islay
Kintyre
Arran
Firth of Clyde
North Channel
Stranraer
Newton Stewart
WIGTOWN
Kirkcudbright
KIRKCUDBRIGHT

S C O T L A N D

NORTHWEST HIGHLANDS

Loch Shin
L. Shin
Ullapool
Loch Maree
Firth of Lorn

Butt of Lewis
Stornoway
Lewis
Harris
N. Uist
Benbecula
S. Uist
Barra
The Minch
Little Minch
Sea of the Hebrides

O u t e r   H e b r i d e s

St. Kilda

A T L A N T I C

O C E A N

Mull Head
Sanday
Stronsay
N. Ronaldsay
Westray
Kirkwall
Mainland
Hoy
S. Ronaldsay
Orkney Islands
Duncansby Head
Pentland Firth
Thurso
Wick
CAITHNESS

Coleraine
Londonderry
DERRY
Ballymena
ANTRIM
Larne
Belfast
NORTHERN IRELAND
TYRONE
Portadown
Lurgan
Newtownards
Strabane
Omagh
FERM.
DONEGAL
Donegal
Donegal Bay
Sligo
Bloody Foreland
Aran Is.
Malin Head
L. Swilly
L. Foyle

Greenwich Meridian

10°W   8°W   6°W   4°W   2°W   0°

58°N

56°N

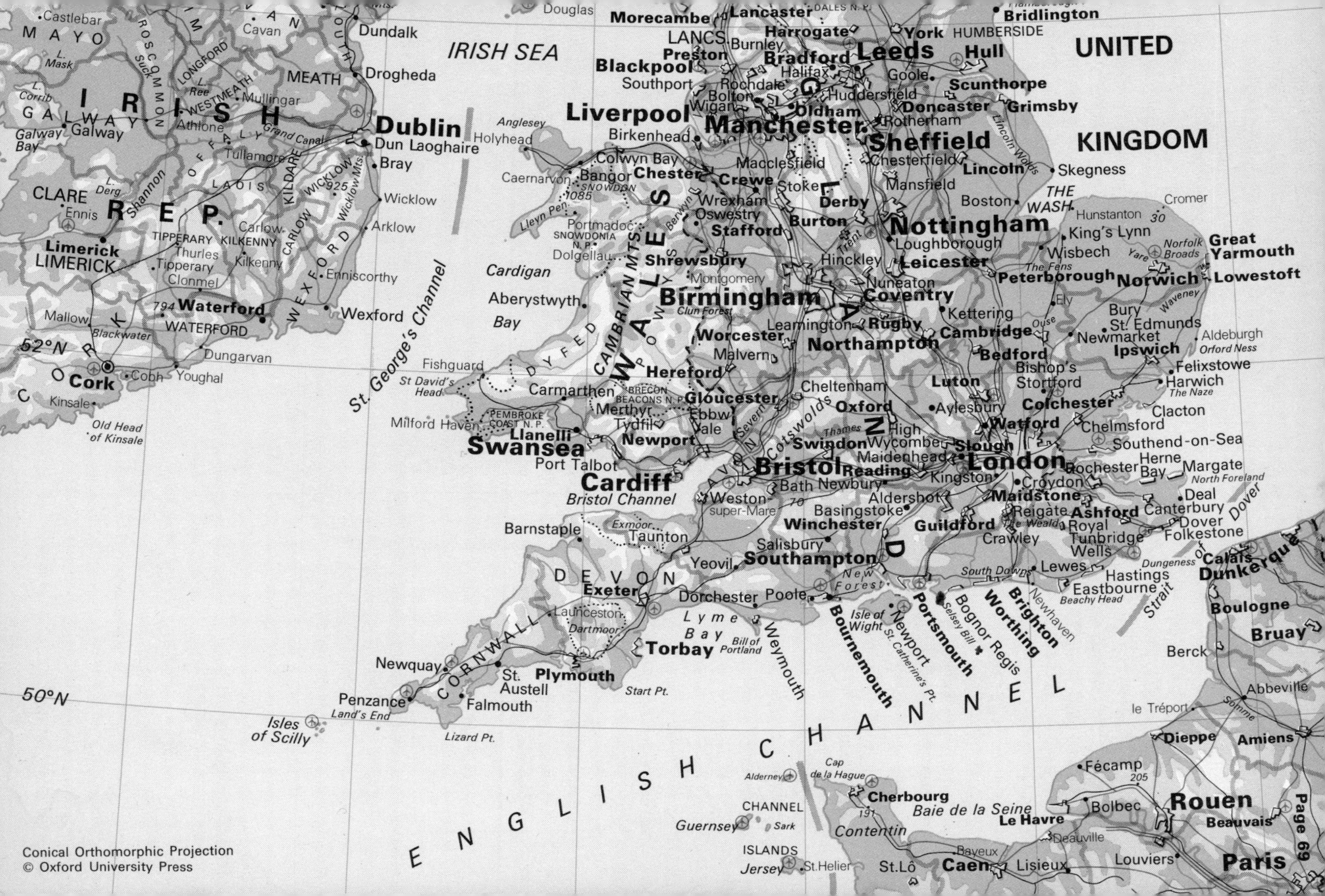

IRISH SEA
UNITED KINGDOM
IRISH REP.
WALES
ENGLAND
ENGLISH CHANNEL
St. George's Channel
Bristol Channel
Cardigan Bay
Lyme Bay
Strait of Dover
CHANNEL ISLANDS
Baie de la Seine
52°N
50°N
Dublin
Dun Laoghaire
Bray
Wicklow
Arklow
Wexford
Enniscorthy
Waterford
Dungarvan
Youghal
Cork
Cobh
Kinsale
Old Head of Kinsale
Mallow
Limerick
LIMERICK
Ennis
CLARE
Galway
Galway Bay
Castlebar
MAYO
Athlone
Mullingar
Tullamore
Kilkenny
Carlow
Clonmel
Tipperary
Thurles
Drogheda
Dundalk
Cavan
MEATH
Douglas
Holyhead
Anglesey
Caernarvon
Bangor
Colwyn Bay
Lleyn Pen.
Portmadoc
SNOWDONIA N.P.
Dolgellau
Aberystwyth
CAMBRIAN MTS
DYFED
POWYS
Fishguard
St David's Head
Milford Haven
PEMBROKE COAST N.P.
Carmarthen
Llanelli
Swansea
Port Talbot
Cardiff
Newport
Merthyr Tydfil
Ebbw Vale
BRECON BEACONS N.P.
Hereford
Shrewsbury
Liverpool
Birkenhead
Chester
Crewe
Wrexham
Oswestry
Stafford
Manchester
Blackpool
Preston
Southport
Wigan
Bolton
Rochdale
Oldham
Burnley
Morecambe
Lancaster
LANCS
Harrogate
Bradford
Leeds
Halifax
Huddersfield
York
Goole
Hull
HUMBERSIDE
Bridlington
Scunthorpe
Grimsby
Doncaster
Rotherham
Sheffield
Chesterfield
Macclesfield
Stoke
Mansfield
Lincoln
Skegness
Boston
THE WASH
Derby
Burton
Nottingham
Loughborough
Leicester
Hinckley
Nuneaton
Coventry
Birmingham
Worcester
Malvern
Gloucester
Cheltenham
Leamington
Rugby
Northampton
Kettering
Peterborough
King's Lynn
Wisbech
Hunstanton
Cromer
Norwich
Great Yarmouth
Lowestoft
Cambridge
Bedford
Bury St. Edmunds
Newmarket
Ipswich
Felixstowe
Harwich
Aldeburgh
Luton
Aylesbury
Bishop's Stortford
Colchester
Clacton
Chelmsford
Southend-on-Sea
Oxford
Swindon
High Wycombe
Watford
Slough
Maidenhead
Reading
Newbury
London
Kingston
Croydon
Bristol
Bath
Weston-super-Mare
Rochester
Herne Bay
Margate
Deal
Canterbury
Dover
Folkestone
Maidstone
Ashford
Reigate
Guildford
Aldershot
Basingstoke
Winchester
Salisbury
Southampton
Crawley
Royal Tunbridge Wells
Lewes
Hastings
Eastbourne
Beachy Head
Brighton
Newhaven
Worthing
Bognor Regis
Portsmouth
Isle of Wight
Newport
Bournemouth
Poole
Weymouth
Dorchester
Yeovil
Taunton
Barnstaple
DEVON
Exeter
Torbay
Plymouth
CORNWALL
Launceston
St. Austell
Falmouth
Newquay
Penzance
Land's End
Lizard Pt.
Isles of Scilly
Start Pt.
Alderney
Guernsey
Sark
Jersey
St.Helier
Cherbourg
Cap de la Hague
Contentin
St.Lô
Caen
Bayeux
Lisieux
Deauville
Le Havre
Bolbec
Fécamp
Dieppe
Rouen
Louviers
Paris
Beauvais
Amiens
Abbeville
le Tréport
Berck
Bruay
Boulogne
Calais
Dunkerque
Page 69
Conical Orthomorphic Projection
© Oxford University Press

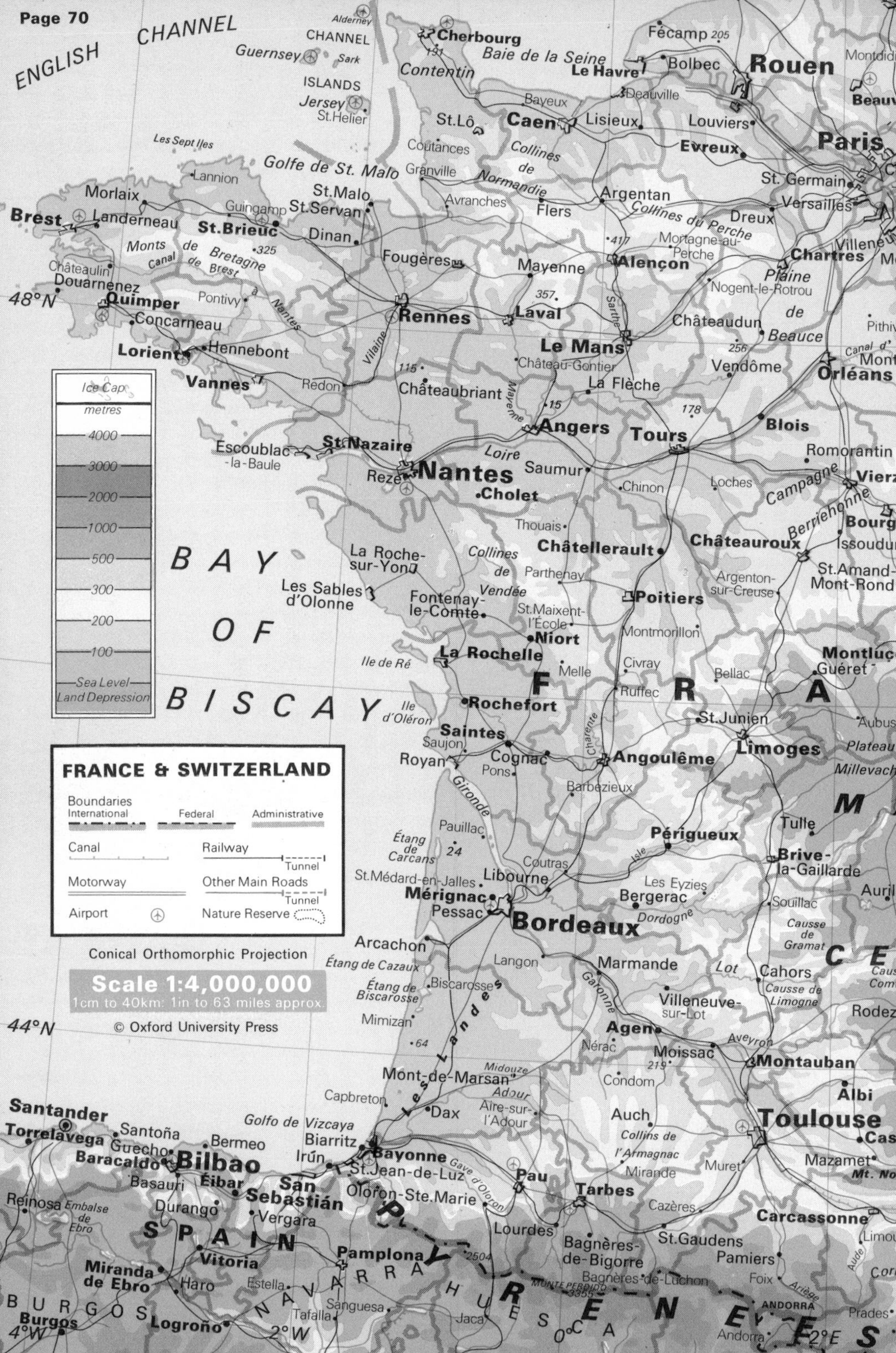
ENGLISH CHANNEL
Alderney
CHANNEL
Guernsey
Sark
ISLANDS
Jersey
St.Helier
Les Sept Iles
Cherbourg
Baie de la Seine
Contentin
Fécamp 205
Le Havre
Bolbec
Rouen
Montdidier
Beauva
Bayeux
Deauville
Caen
Lisieux
Louviers
St.Lô
Coutances
Collines de Normandie
Evreux
Paris
Golfe de St. Malo
Granville
Lannion
Morlaix
Brest
Landerneau
Guingamp
St.Malo
St.Servan
St.Brieuc
Dinan
Avranches
Flers
Argentan
Collines du Perche
Dreux
St. Germain
Versailles
Villeneuve
Monts de Bretagne
Canal de Brest à Nantes
325
Châteaulin
Douarnenez
48°N
Quimper
Concarneau
Pontivy
Fougères
Mayenne
417
Mortagne-au-Perche
Alençon
Chartres
Plaine de Beauce
Nogent-le-Rotrou
357
Rennes
Laval
Sarthe
Châteaudun
Pithivie
Lorient
Hennebont
Le Mans
256
Canal d' O
Vilaine
115
Château-Gontier
Vendôme
Orléans
Vannes
Redon
Châteaubriant
Mayenne
La Flèche
15
178
Blois
Angers
Tours
Escoublac-la-Baule
St.Nazaire
Loire
Romorantin
Rezé
Nantes
Saumur
Chinon
Loches
Campagne Berrichonne
Vierz
Cholet
Bourge
Thouais
Châtellerault
Châteauroux
Issoudun
Ice Cap
metres
4000
3000
2000
1000
500
300
200
100
Sea Level
Land Depression
BAY OF BISCAY
La Roche-sur-Yon
Collines de Vendée
Parthenay
Argenton-sur-Creuse
St.Amand-Mont-Rond
Les Sables d'Olonne
Fontenay-le-Comte
Poitiers
St.Maixent-l'École
Montmorillon
Niort
Montluçon
Guéret
Ile de Ré
La Rochelle
Melle
Civray
Bellac
Ruffec
FRANCE
Ile d'Oléron
Rochefort
St.Junien
Aubusso
Saintes
Saujon
Charente
Limoges
Plateau de Millevaches
Royan
Cognac
Angoulême
Pons
Barbezieux
Gironde
MASSIF CENTRAL
FRANCE & SWITZERLAND
Boundaries
International
Federal
Administrative
Canal
Railway
Tunnel
Motorway
Other Main Roads
Tunnel
Airport
Nature Reserve
Pauillac
Étang de Carcans
24
Tulle
Périgueux
Brive-la-Gaillarde
Coutras
Isle
St.Médard-en-Jalles
Libourne
Les Eyzies
Mérignac
Bergerac
Aurilla
Pessac
Bordeaux
Souillac
Dordogne
Causse de Gramat
Conical Orthomorphic Projection
Arcachon
Langon
Étang de Cazaux
Marmande
Lot
Cahors
Causs Comta
Scale 1:4,000,000
1cm to 40km: 1in to 63 miles approx.
Étang de Biscarosse
Biscarosse
Garonne
Causse de Limogne
Villeneuve-sur-Lot
Rodez
44°N
© Oxford University Press
Mimizan
Les Landes
Agen
64
Nérac
Aveyron
Moissac
219
Montauban
Midouze
Mont-de-Marsan
Condom
Capbreton
Adour
Albi
Santander
Dax
Aire-sur-l'Adour
Auch
Toulouse
Torrelavega
Santoña
Golfo de Vizcaya
Collins de l'Armagnac
Cast
Guecho
Bermeo
Biarritz
Baracaldo
Bilbao
Irún
Bayonne
Gave d'Oloron
Mazamet
Muret
Mt. Noir
St.Jean-de-Luz
Pau
Mirande
Basauri
Éibar
San Sebastián
Oloron-Ste.Marie
Tarbes
Reinosa
Embalse de Ebro
Durango
Cazères
Vergara
Carcassonne
SPAIN
Lourdes
Bagnères-de-Bigorre
St.Gaudens
Limoux
Vitoria
Pamplona
2504
Pamiers
Miranda de Ebro
Haro
Estella
NAVARRA
MONTE PERDIDO
3355
Bagnères-de-Luchon
Foix
Ariège
Aude
Corb
BURGOS
HUESCA
PYRENEES
ANDORRA
Prades
Burgos
Logroño
Sanguesa
Tafalla
Jaca
4°W
2°W
0°
Andorra
2°E

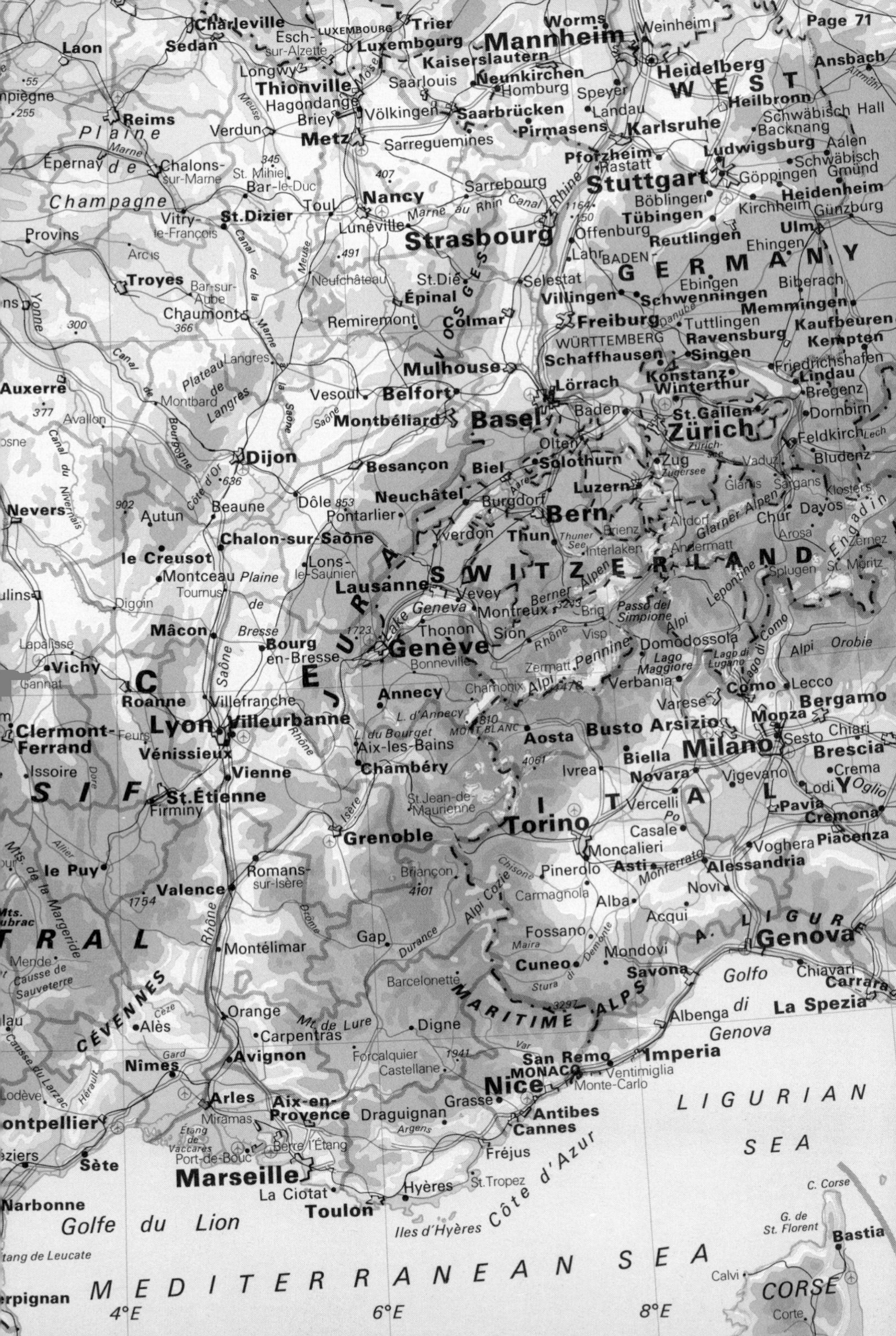
Charleville
Sedan
Laon
LUXEMBOURG
Trier
Esch-sur-Alzette
Luxembourg
Worms
Mannheim
Weinheim
Kaiserslautern
Longwy
Neunkirchen
Homburg
Heidelberg
Ansbach
Thionville
Saarlouis
Speyer
WEST
Hagondange
Völkingen
Saarbrücken
Landau
Heilbronn
Schwäbisch Hall
Reims
Briey
Verdun
Metz
Pirmasens
Karlsruhe
Backnang
Plaine
Sarreguemines
Aalen
Marne
Epernay
de
Chalons-sur-Marne
St. Mihiel
Pforzheim
Rastatt
Ludwigsburg
Schwäbisch Gmünd
Bar-le-Duc
Sarrebourg
Stuttgart
Göppingen
Champagne
Toul
Nancy
Heidenheim
Vitry-le-François
St.Dizier
Lunéville
Marne au Rhin Canal
Rhine
Böblingen
Kirchheim
Günzburg
Provins
Strasbourg
Offenburg
Tübingen
Ulm
Arcis
Lahr
BADEN
Reutlingen
Ehingen
Troyes
Bar-sur-Aube
Neufchâteau
St.Dié
Selestat
GERMANY
Ebingen
Biberach
Chaumont
Épinal
VOSGES
Villingen
Schwenningen
Memmingen
Yonne
Remiremont
Colmar
Freiburg
Danube
Tuttlingen
Kaufbeuren
WÜRTTEMBERG
Ravensburg
Kempten
Canal
Plateau de Langres
Langres
Schaffhausen
Singen
Friedrichshafen
Mulhouse
Konstanz
Lindau
Auxerre
Montbard
Vesoul
Belfort
Lörrach
Winterthur
Bregenz
Avallon
Saône
Montbéliard
Basel
Baden
St.Gallen
Dornbirn
Zürich
Feldkirch
Canal du Nivernais
Bourgogne
Dijon
Olten
Lech
Besançon
Biel
Solothurn
Zug
Vaduz
Bludenz
Zugersee
Côte d'Or
Luzern
Glarus
Sargans
Klosters
Nevers
Autun
Beaune
Dôle
Neuchâtel
Burgdorf
Pontarlier
Bern
Chur
Davos
Glarner Alpen
Brienz
Altdorf
Engadin
Chalon-sur-Saône
Yverdon
Thun
Thuner See
Interlaken
Andermatt
Arosa
Zernez
le Creusot
SWITZERLAND
Lons-le-Saunier
Splugen
St. Moritz
Montceau
Plaine
Tournus
Lausanne
Berner Alpen
Lepontine
JURA
Vevey
Digoin
Lake Geneva
Montreux
Brig
Passo del Sempione
de
Mâcon
Thonon
Sion
Rhône
Visp
Alpi
Bresse
Domodossola
Alpi Orobie
Lapalisse
Bourg-en-Bresse
Genève
Lago Maggiore
Lago di Lugano
Lago di Como
Vichy
Bonneville
Zermatt
Pennine
Gannat
Chamonix
Alpi
Verbania
Como
Lecco
Roanne
Villefranche
Annecy
Varese
Bergamo
L. d'Annecy
Lyon
Villeurbanne
Clermont-Ferrand
Feurs
L. du Bourget
MONT BLANC
Aosta
Busto Arsizio
Monza
Sesto
Chiari
Aix-les-Bains
Milano
Brescia
Vénissieux
Biella
Vienne
Chambéry
Ivrea
Novara
Vigevano
Crema
Issoire
Lodi
Oglio
St.Étienne
St.Jean-de-Maurienne
ITALY
Vercelli
Pavia
Firminy
Isère
Po
Torino
Cremona
Grenoble
Casale
Piacenza
Allier
Moncalieri
Voghera
le Puy
Romans-sur-Isère
Briançon
Pinerolo
Asti
Alessandria
Monferrato
Valence
Chisone
Novi
Mts. de la Margeride
Alpi Cozie
Carmagnola
Alba
Drôme
Acqui
Rhône
Fossano
LIGUR
CENTRAL
Gap
Durance
Maira
Genova
Montélimar
Mondovi
Mende
Cuneo
Causse de Sauveterre
Barcelonette
Stura di Demonte
Savona
Golfo
Chiavari
Carrara
CÉVENNES
MARITIME ALPS
Albenga
di
La Spezia
Cèze
Orange
Mt. de Lure
Alès
Carpentras
Digne
Genova
Gard
Forcalquier
Var
Causse du Larzac
Nîmes
Avignon
Castellane
San Remo
Imperia
MONACO
Ventimiglia
Hérault
Monte-Carlo
Lodève
Arles
Aix-en-Provence
Nice
Grasse
LIGURIAN
Montpellier
Miramas
Draguignan
Antibes
Étang de Vaccarès
Cannes
Argens
Berre l'Étang
Fréjus
SEA
Sète
Port-de-Bouc
Marseille
St.Tropez
Côte d'Azur
C. Corse
La Ciotat
Hyères
Narbonne
Toulon
G. de St. Florent
Golfe du Lion
Iles d'Hyères
Bastia
Étang de Leucate
MEDITERRANEAN SEA
Calvi
CORSE
Perpignan
Corte
4°E
6°E
8°E

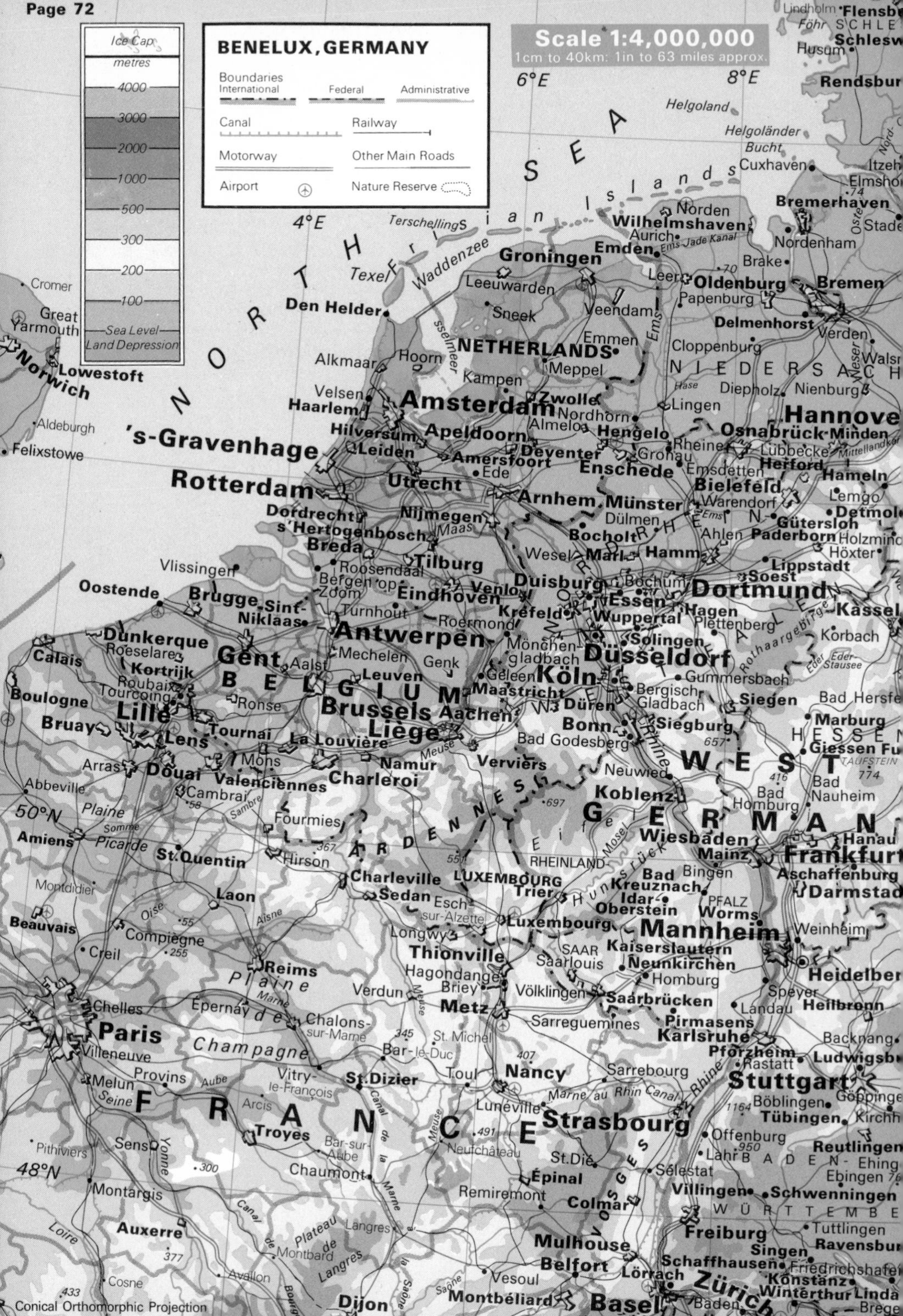
BENELUX, GERMANY
Boundaries
International
Federal
Administrative
Canal
Railway
Motorway
Other Main Roads
Airport
Nature Reserve
Ice Cap
metres
4000
3000
2000
1000
500
300
200
100
Sea Level
Land Depression
Scale 1:4,000,000
1cm to 40km: 1in to 63 miles approx.
4°E
6°E
8°E
50°N
48°N
NORTH SEA
Frisian Islands
Terschelling
Texel
Waddenzee
Helgoland
Helgoländer Bucht
Cuxhaven
Norden
Wilhelmshaven
Aurich
Emden
Ems-Jade Kanal
Bremerhaven
Nordenham
Brake
Leer
Oldenburg
Bremen
Papenburg
Delmenhorst
Verden
Cloppenburg
Diepholz
Nienburg
Lingen
NIEDERSACH
Osnabrück
Minden
Hannove
Lübbecke
Mittellandkanal
Herford
Bielefeld
Hameln
Lemgo
Detmold
Gütersloh
Paderborn
Höxter
Lippstadt
Soest
Dortmund
Kassel
Korbach
Rothaargebirge
Eder-Stausee
Flensb
Lindholm
Föhr
Schleswig
Husum
Rendsbur
Itzeh
Elmsho
Stade
Groningen
Leeuwarden
Sneek
Veendam
Emmen
NETHERLANDS
Meppel
Kampen
Zwolle
Den Helder
Alkmaar
Hoorn
IJsselmeer
Velsen
Haarlem
Amsterdam
Hilversum
Apeldoorn
Nordhorn
Almelo
Hengelo
Rheine
Gronau
Emsdetten
Warendorf
's-Gravenhage
Leiden
Amersfoort
Deventer
Enschede
Ede
Münster
Dülmen
Rotterdam
Utrecht
Arnhem
Dordrecht
s'Hertogenbosch
Nijmegen
Maas
Bocholt
Ahlen
Breda
Tilburg
Wesel
Marl
Hamm
Vlissingen
Roosendaal
Bergen op Zoom
Venlo
Eindhoven
Duisburg
Bochum
Essen
Oostende
Brugge
Sint-Niklaas
Turnhout
Roermond
Krefeld
Wuppertal
Hagen
Plettenberg
Antwerpen
Mönchengladbach
Solingen
Dunkerque
Calais
Roeselare
Kortrijk
Gent
Aalst
Mechelen
Genk
Düsseldorf
Gummersbach
Roubaix
Tourcoing
BELGIUM
Leuven
Geleen
Köln
Bergisch Gladbach
Boulogne
Lille
Ronse
Brussels
Maastricht
Aachen
Düren
Siegen
Bad Hersfe
Bruay
Lens
Tournai
La Louvière
Liège
Bonn
Siegburg
Marburg
Bad Godesberg
HESSEN
Arras
Douai
Mons
Namur
Meuse
Verviers
Giessen
Valenciennes
Charleroi
Neuwied
Koblenz
Bad Homburg
Bad Nauheim
Abbeville
Cambrai
Sambre
ARDENNES
Eifel
WEST GERMANY
Plaine Picarde
Somme
Amiens
Fourmies
Hirson
St.Quentin
Charleville
LUXEMBOURG
RHEINLAND
Mosel
Hunsrück
Wiesbaden
Mainz
Bingen
Hanau
Frankfurt
Aschaffenburg
Darmstad
Montdidier
Laon
Sedan
Trier
Bad Kreuznach
Idar-Oberstein
PFALZ
Worms
Beauvais
Oise
Aisne
Esch-sur-Alzette
Luxembourg
Mannheim
Weinheim
Compiègne
Creil
Longwy
Thionville
SAAR
Saarlouis
Kaiserslautern
Neunkirchen
Homburg
Heidelber
Reims
Hagondange
Briey
Verdun
Völklingen
Saarbrücken
Speyer
Landau
Heilbronn
Chelles
Paris
Épernay
Marne
Chalons-sur-Marne
Metz
Sarreguemines
Pirmasens
Karlsruhe
Backnang
Villeneuve
Champagne
Bar-le-Duc
St. Michel
Nancy
Pforzheim
Rastatt
Ludwigsb
Provins
Melun
Seine
Aube
Vitry-le-François
St.Dizier
Toul
Sarrebourg
Stuttgart
Göppinge
FRANCE
Arcis
Troyes
Canal de la Marne
Lunéville
Marne au Rhin Canal
Strasbourg
Böblingen
Tübingen
Kirchh
Rhine
Pithiviers
Sens
Yonne
Bar-sur-Aube
Neufchâteau
St.Dié
Offenburg
Lahr
Reutlingen
BADEN
Ebingen
Chaumont
Épinal
VOSGES
Sélestat
Montargis
Remiremont
Colmar
Villingen
Schwenningen
WÜRTTEMBE
Loire
Auxerre
Plateau de Langres
Langres
Montbard
Mulhouse
Freiburg
Tuttlingen
Singen
Ravensbur
Avallon
Bourgogne
Vesoul
Belfort
Lörrach
Schaffhausen
Friedrichshafe
Konstanz
Saône
Montbéliard
Basel
Zürich
Baden
Winterthur
Linda
Brege
Dijon
Cosne
Conical Orthomorphic Projection

Page 73

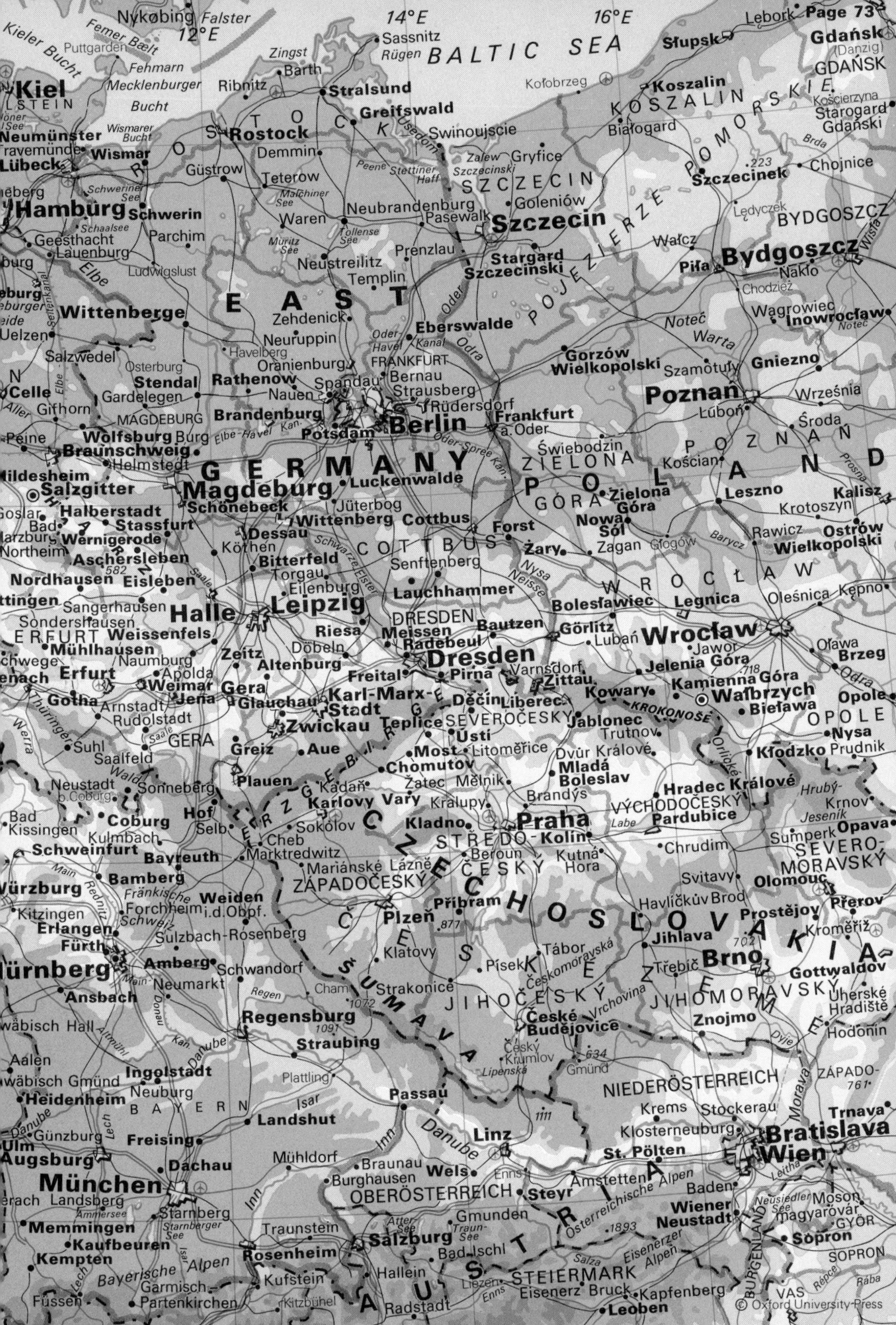
Nykøbing Falster
12°E
14°E
16°E
Lebork
Gdańsk
(Danzig)
GDAŃSK
Kieler Bucht
Femer Bælt
Puttgarden
Fehmarn
Sassnitz
Rügen
BALTIC SEA
Zingst
Barth
Słupsk
Kołobrzeg
Koszalin
KOSZALIN
Kiel
Mecklenburger Bucht
Ribnitz
Stralsund
Greifswald
Kościerzyna
Starogard Gdański
Neumünster
Wismarer Bucht
Rostock
Usedom
Swinoujscie
Białogard
POMORSKIE
Travemünde
Lübeck
Wismar
Demmin
Zalew Szczecinski
Gryfice
Brda
Güstrow
Teterow
Peene
Stettiner Haff
.223
Chojnice
Szczecinek
SZCZECIN
Schweriner See
Malchiner See
Goleniów
Hamburg
Schwerin
Neubrandenburg
Ledyczek
BYDGOSZCZ
Schaalsee
Waren
Pasewalk
Szczecin
POJEZIERZE
Geesthacht
Parchim
Müritz See
Tollense See
Lauenburg
Prenzlau
Wałcz
Wisła
Neustrelitz
Stargard Szczecinski
Piła
Bydgoszcz
Elbe
Ludwigslust
Templin
Nakło
Chodzież
Oder
EAST
Wittenberge
Zehdenick
Eberswalde
Wągrowiec
Inowrocław
Noteć
Uelzen
Oder-Havel Kanal
Odra
Neuruppin
Warta
Salzwedel
Havelberg
Gorzów Wielkopolski
Gniezno
Osterburg
Oranienburg
FRANKFURT
Szamotuły
Celle
Stendal
Rathenow
Bernau
Nauen
Spandau
Strausberg
Poznań
Września
Aller
Gifhorn
Gardelegen
Rüdersdorf
Luboń
MAGDEBURG
Brandenburg
Berlin
Frankfurt a. Oder
Środa
Peine
Wolfsburg
Burg
Elbe-Havel Kan.
Potsdam
Oder-Spree Kan.
Świebodzin
POZNAŃ
Braunschweig
Helmstedt
Kościan
Prosna
Hildesheim
GERMANY
ZIELONA
POLAND
Salzgitter
Magdeburg
Luckenwalde
Leszno
Kalisz
HARZ
Halberstadt
Schönebeck
Jüterbog
GÓRA
Zielona Góra
Krotoszyn
Goslar
Stassfurt
Wittenberg
Cottbus
Forst
Nowa Sól
Rawicz
Ostrów Wielkopolski
Bad Harzburg
Wernigerode
Dessau
Schwarze Elster
COTTBUS
Żary
Zagan
Głogów
Barycz
Northeim
Köthen
Aschersleben
582
Bitterfeld
Senftenberg
Nysa Neisse
Saale
Torgau
WROCŁAW
Nordhausen
Eisleben
Eilenburg
Lauchhammer
Oleśnica
Kępno
Göttingen
Sangerhausen
Bolesławiec
Legnica
Sondershausen
Halle
Leipzig
DRESDEN
Bautzen
ERFURT
Weissenfels
Riesa
Meissen
Görlitz
Lubań
Wrocław
Mühlhausen
Radebeul
Jawor
Oława
Eschwege
Naumburg
Zeitz
Döbeln
Brzeg
Apolda
Altenburg
Dresden
Varnsdorf
Jelenia Góra
.718
Eisenach
Erfurt
Weimar
Freital
Pirna
Zittau
Kamienna Góra
Odra
Gotha
Jena
Gera
Karl-Marx-Stadt
Děčín
Liberec
Kowary
Wałbrzych
Opole
Arnstadt
Glauchau
ERZGEBIRGE
SEVEROČESKÝ
KRKONOŠE
Jablonec
Bielawa
OPOLE
Rudolstadt
Thüringer Wald
Zwickau
Teplice
Ústí
Trutnov
Nysa
Werra
Suhl
GERA
Greiz
Aue
Most
Litoměřice
Dvůr Králové
Orlické
Kłodzko
Prudnik
Saalfeld
Chomutov
Mladá Boleslav
Neustadt b. Coburg
Sonneberg
Plauen
Kadaň
Žatec
Mělník
Hradec Králové
Hrubý-Jeseník
Krnov
Karlovy Vary
Kralupy
Brandýs
VÝCHODOČESKÝ
Bad Kissingen
Coburg
Hof
Selb
Sokolov
Kladno
Praha
Labe
Pardubice
Šumperk
Opava
Kulmbach
Cheb
STŘEDOČESKÝ
Kolín
SEVEROMORAVSKÝ
Schweinfurt
Bayreuth
Marktredwitz
Beroun
Chrudim
Main
Mariánské Lázně
Kutná Hora
Bamberg
ZÁPADOČESKÝ
CZECHOSLOVAKIA
Svitavy
Olomouc
Würzburg
Regnitz
Fränkische Schweiz
Weiden i.d. Opf.
Příbram
Havlíčkův Brod
Prostějov
Přerov
Kitzingen
Forchheim
Plzeň
.877
Kroměříž
Erlangen
Sulzbach-Rosenberg
Jihlava
702
Fürth
Klatovy
Tábor
Nürnberg
Amberg
Písek
Českomoravská Vrchovina
Třebíč
Brno
Gottwaldov
Main-Donau Kan.
Schwandorf
Neumarkt
Cham
Strakonice
Uherské Hradiště
Ansbach
Regen
ŠUMAVA
1072
JIHOČESKÝ
JIHOMORAVSKÝ
Schwäbisch Hall
Altmühl
Regensburg
1091
České Budějovice
Znojmo
Hodonín
Dyje
Aalen
Danube
Straubing
Český Krumlov
.634
Schwäbisch Gmünd
Ingolstadt
Lipenská
Gmünd
ZÁPADOSLOVENSKÝ
Plattling
NIEDERÖSTERREICH
.761
Neuburg
Passau
Morava
Heidenheim
BAYERN
Isar
Krems
Stockerau
Trnava
Danube
Lech
Landshut
1111
Günzburg
Inn
Danube
Klosterneuburg
Bratislava
Ulm
Freising
Mühldorf
Linz
Augsburg
St. Pölten
Wien
Dachau
Braunau
Wels
Enns
Amstetten
Leitha
München
Burghausen
OBERÖSTERREICH
Österreichische Alpen
Baden
Moson
Mindelheim
Landsberg
Steyr
Neusiedler See
magyaróvár
GYŐR
Ammersee
Inn
Wiener Neustadt
Starnberg
Gmunden
Memmingen
Starnberger See
Traunstein
Atter-See
Traun-See
AUSTRIA
.1893
BURGENLAND
Sopron
Kaufbeuren
Isar
Rosenheim
Salzburg
Salza
Eisenerzer Alpen
SOPRON
Kempten
Bayerische Alpen
Bad Ischl
Lech
Garmisch-Partenkirchen
Kufstein
Hallein
Liezen
STEIERMARK
Rába
VAS
Répce
Füssen
Kitzbühel
Radstadt
Enns
Eisenerz
Bruck
Kapfenberg
Leoben

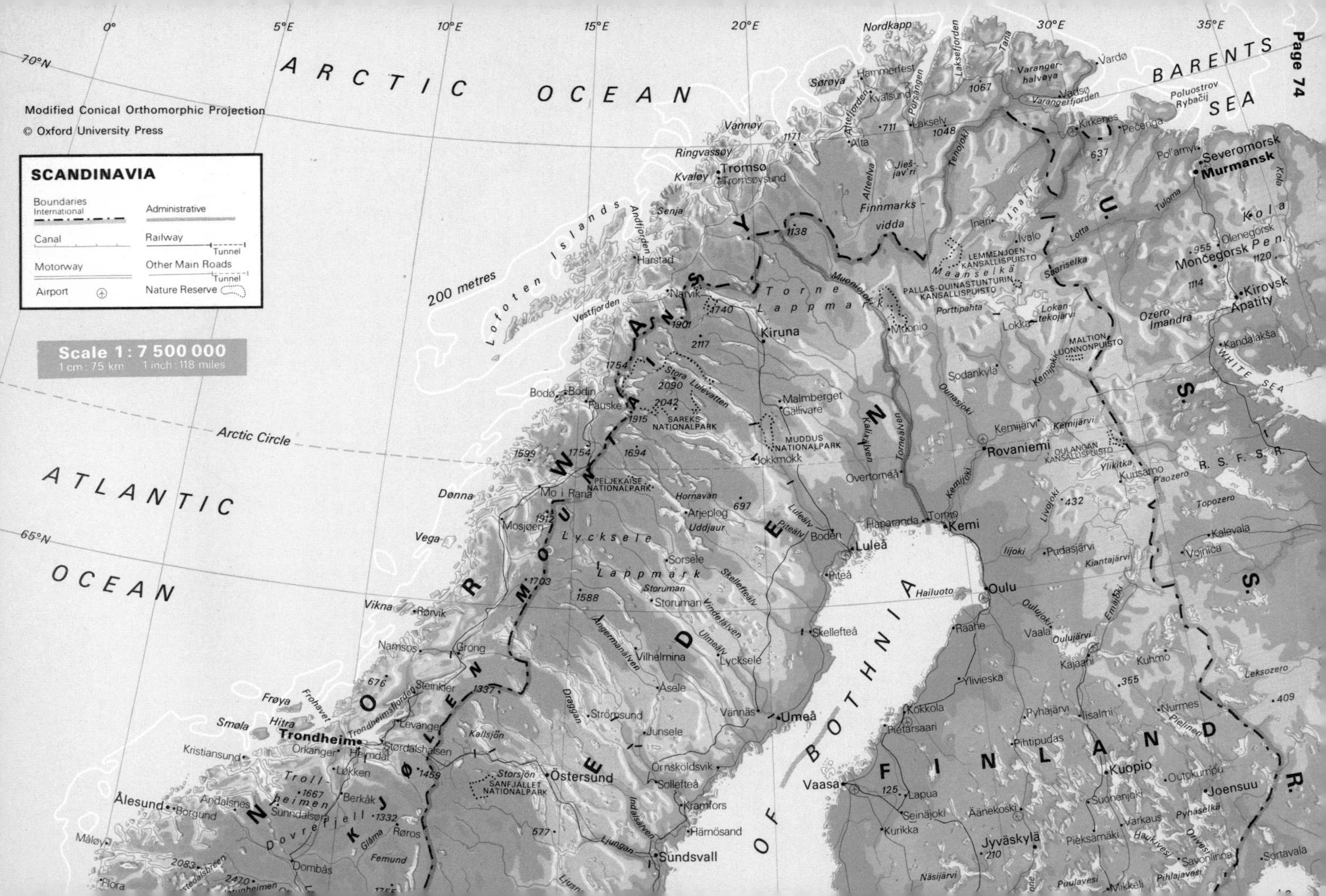
SCANDINAVIA
Boundaries
International
Administrative
Canal
Railway
Tunnel
Motorway
Other Main Roads
Tunnel
Airport
Nature Reserve
Scale 1 : 7 500 000
1 cm : 75 km 1 inch : 118 miles
Modified Conical Orthomorphic Projection
© Oxford University Press
ARCTIC OCEAN
BARENTS SEA
ATLANTIC OCEAN
GULF OF BOTHNIA
WHITE SEA
NORWAY
SWEDEN
FINLAND
U. S. S. R.
KJØLEN MOUNTAINS
Arctic Circle
200 metres
Lofoten Islands
Nordkapp
Hammerfest
Tromsø
Narvik
Kiruna
Bodø
Mo i Rana
Trondheim
Ålesund
Östersund
Sundsvall
Umeå
Luleå
Oulu
Kemi
Rovaniemi
Vaasa
Kuopio
Jyväskylä
Joensuu
Murmansk
Severomorsk
Kirovsk
Apatity
Mončegorsk
Kandalakša
Kirkenes
Vardø
Torne Lappmark
Lycksele Lappmark
Finnmarksvidda
Maanselkä
0°
5°E
10°E
15°E
20°E
30°E
35°E
70°N
65°N

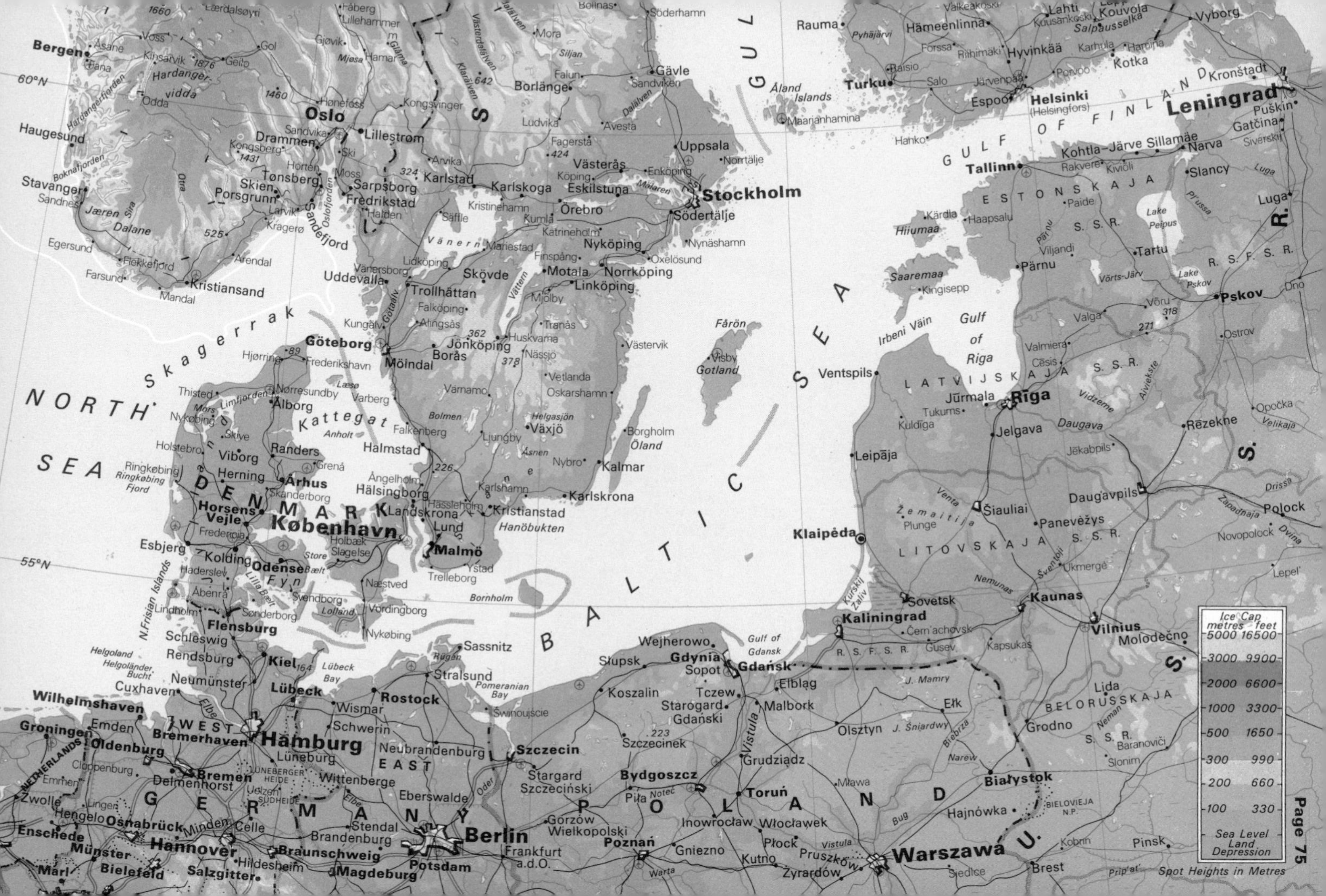
Ice Cap
metres feet
5000 16500
3000 9900
2000 6600
1000 3300
500 1650
300 990
200 660
100 330
Sea Level
Land Depression
Spot Heights in Metres
NORTH SEA
Skagerrak
Kattegat
BALTIC SEA
GULF OF FINLAND
Gulf of Riga
Gulf of Gdansk
DENMARK
POLAND
GERMANY
WEST
EAST
ESTONSKAJA S.S.R.
LATVIJSKAJA S.S.R.
LITOVSKAJA S.S.R.
BELORUSSKAJA S.S.R.
R.S.F.S.R.
Oslo
Stockholm
Helsinki
Leningrad
Tallinn
Riga
København
Berlin
Warszawa
Hamburg
Göteborg
Gdańsk
Vilnius
Kaunas
Kaliningrad
Klaipėda
Malmö
Bergen
Kristiansand
Stavanger
Turku
Tartu
Pskov
Szczecin
Bremen
Hannover
Lübeck
Kiel
Rostock
Bydgoszcz
Poznań
Toruń
Białystok
Gotland
Öland
Bornholm
Saaremaa
Hiiumaa
Åland Islands
Vänern
Vättern
Lake Peipus
Daugava
Vistula
Oder
Elbe
60°N
55°N

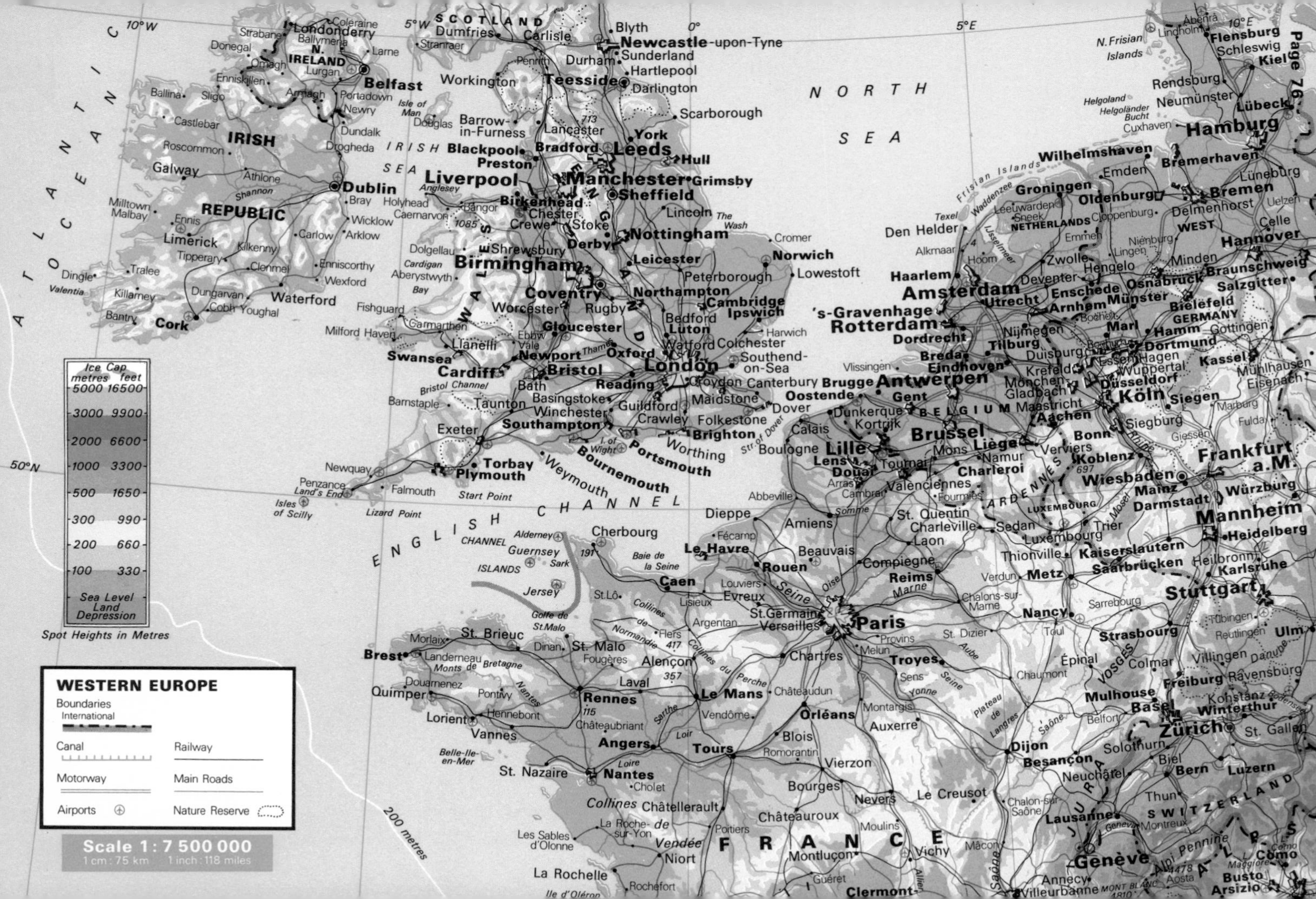

WESTERN EUROPE

Scale 1 : 7 500 000
1 cm : 75 km 1 inch : 118 miles

Boundaries
International
Canal
Motorway
Airports ⊕

Railway
Main Roads
Nature Reserve

Ice Cap
metres   feet
5000 16500
3000 9900
2000 6600
1000 3300
500 1650
300 990
200 660
100 330
Sea Level
Land
Depression

Spot Heights in Metres
200 metres

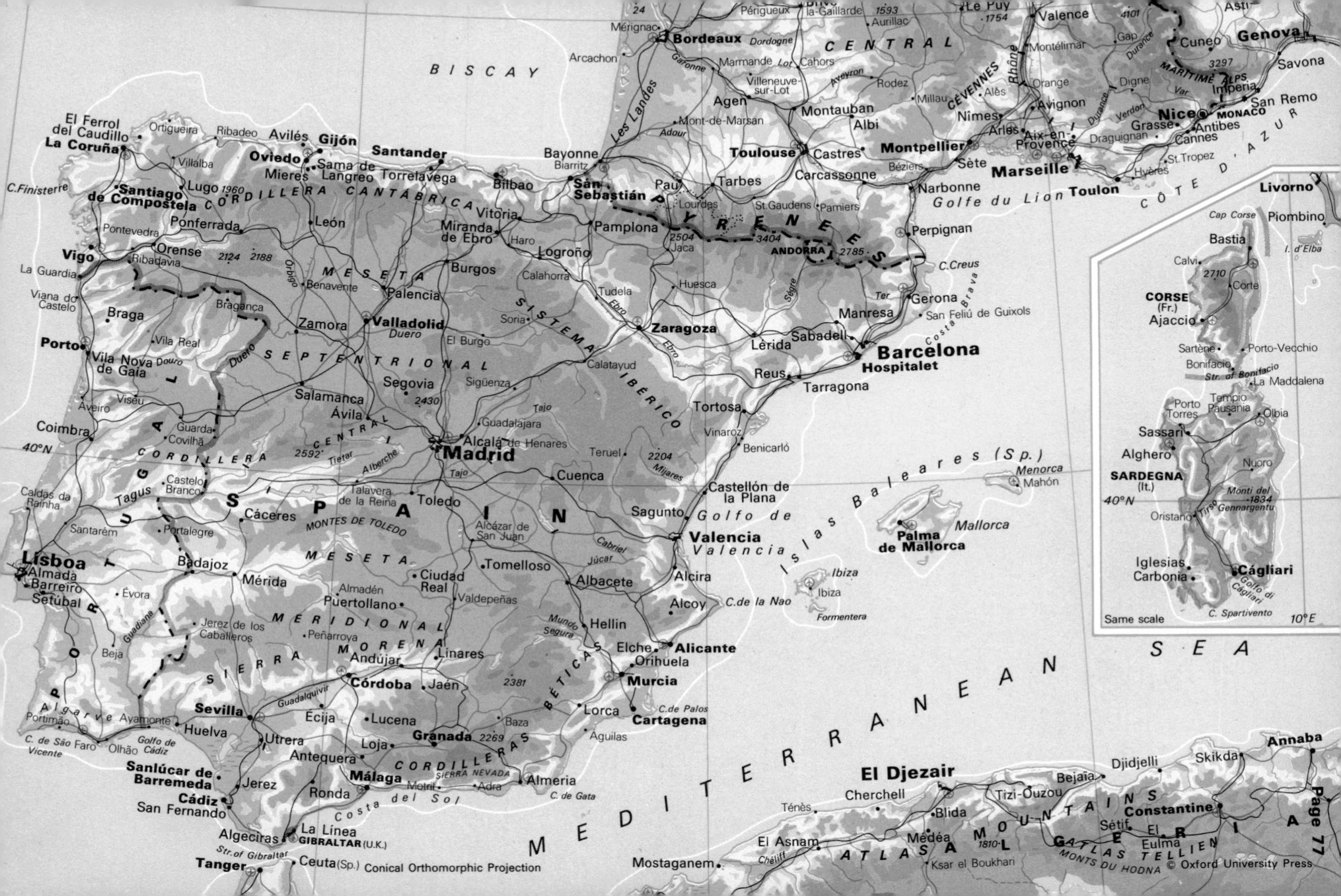
BISCAY
MEDITERRANEAN SEA
SPAIN
PORTUGAL
Madrid
Lisboa
Porto
Barcelona
Hospitalet
Valencia
Sevilla
Zaragoza
Bilbao
Valladolid
Málaga
Granada
Córdoba
Murcia
Alicante
Cartagena
Cádiz
San Fernando
Jerez
Huelva
La Coruña
El Ferrol del Caudillo
Santiago de Compostela
Vigo
Oviedo
Gijón
Avilés
Santander
San Sebastián
Pamplona
Vitoria
Burgos
León
Salamanca
Zamora
Palencia
Segovia
Ávila
Toledo
Cuenca
Albacete
Teruel
Tarragona
Lérida
Reus
Sabadell
Manresa
Gerona
Tortosa
Castellón de la Plana
Sagunto
Alcira
Alcoy
Elche
Orihuela
Lorca
Almería
Jaén
Linares
Ciudad Real
Badajoz
Mérida
Cáceres
Coimbra
Braga
Setúbal
Palma de Mallorca
Mallorca
Menorca
Ibiza
Formentera
Islas Baleares (Sp.)
Golfo de Valencia
Golfo du Lion
Côte d'Azur
CORDILLERA CANTABRICA
SISTEMA IBÉRICO
CORDILLERA CENTRAL
MESETA
SIERRA MORENA
CORDILLERAS BÉTICAS
SIERRA NEVADA
MONTES DE TOLEDO
PYRENEES
ANDORRA
GIBRALTAR (U.K.)
Str. of Gibraltar
Tanger
Ceuta (Sp.)
El Djezair
Constantine
ATLAS MOUNTAINS
ALGERIA
Bordeaux
Toulouse
Montpellier
Marseille
Toulon
Nice
MONACO
Genova
Livorno
CORSE (Fr.)
Ajaccio
Bastia
SARDEGNA (It.)
Cágliari
Sassari
Same scale
Conical Orthomorphic Projection
40°N
10°E

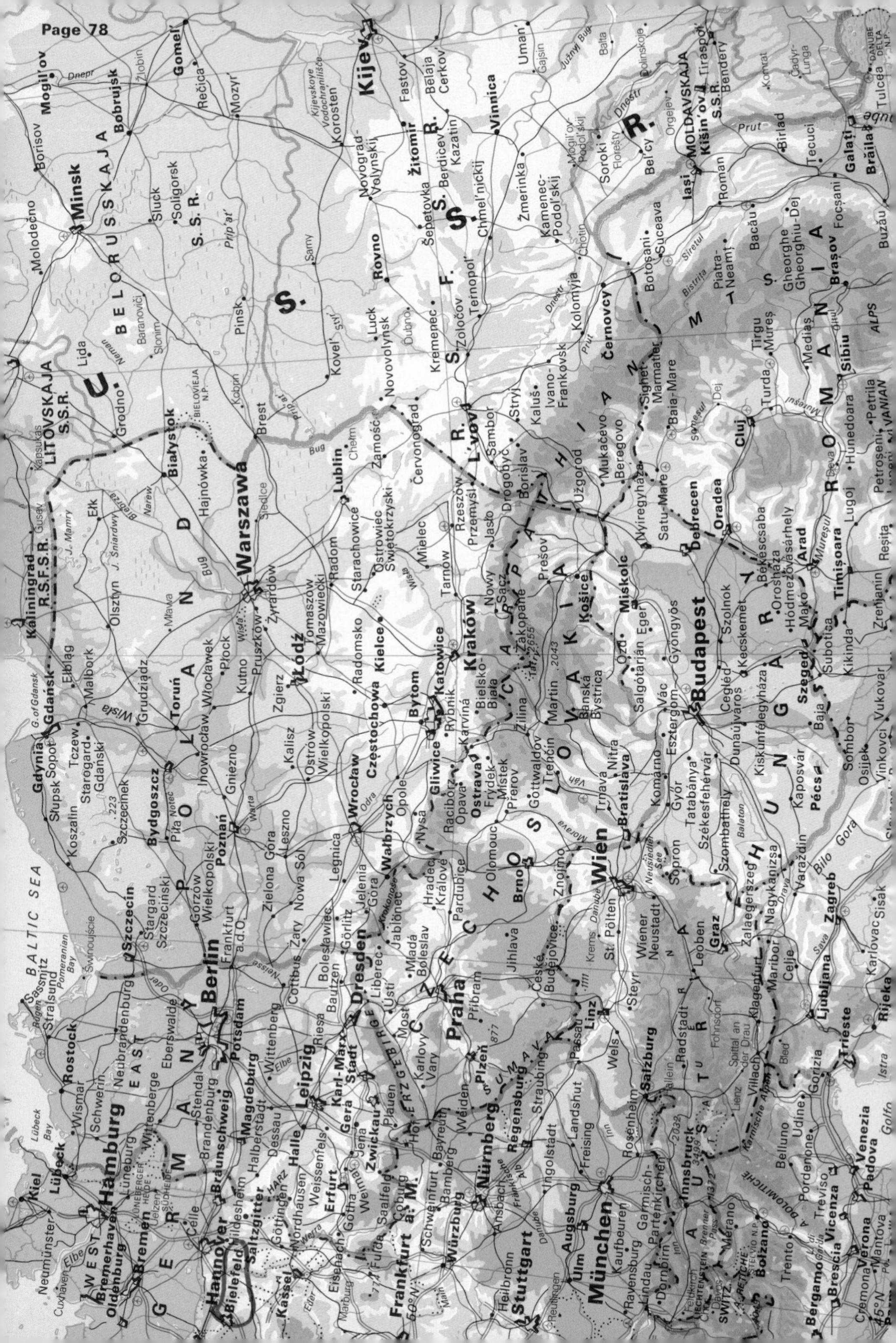

BALTIC SEA

U. S. S. R.

BELORUSSKAJA S.S.R.

LITOVSKAJA S.S.R.

R.S.F.S.R.

MOLDAVSKAJA S.S.R.

Mogilov · Gomel · Bobrujsk · Borisov · Minsk · Molodečno · Sluck · Soligorsk · Slonim · Baranoviči · Lida · Grodno · Pinsk

Kijev · Uman · Balta · Gajsin · Fastov · Bělaja Cerkov · Vinnica · Žitomir · Novograd-Volynskij · Berdičev · Žmerinka · Kamenec-Podolskij · Chmel'nickij · Ternopol' · Zoločov · Proskurov · Šepetovka · Rovno · Luck · Novovolynsk · Kovel' · Dubno · Kremenec · Soroki · Floreşti · Bălţi · Kišin'ov · Iaşi · Roman · Bacău · Suceava · Botoşani · Černovcy · Kolomyja · Ivano-Frankovsk · Stryj · Drogobyč · L'vov · Sambor · Bel'cy · Tecuci · Galaţi · Brăila · Buzău · Focşani · Gheorghe Gheorghiu-Dej · Piatra-Neamţ · Târgu-Mureş · Mediaş · Sibiu · Braşov

ROMÂNIA

Uzgorod · Mukačevo · Beregovo · Baia-Mare · Satu-Mare · Dej · Cluj · Turda · Hunedoara · Petroşeni · Petrila · Lugoj · Reşiţa

KIEV

Reč'ja · Žlobin · Mozyr · Korosten · Dnepr

POLAND / POLSKA

Kaliningrad · Gdynia · Gdańsk · Sopot · Słupsk · Koszalin · Szczecin · Szczecinek · Bydgoszcz · Toruń · Grudziądz · Malbork · Elbląg · Białystok · Łomża · Ełk · Hajnówka · Brest · Warszawa · Płock · Włocławek · Kutno · Łódź · Pabianice · Kalisz · Ostrów Wielkopolski · Poznań · Gniezno · Gorzów Wielkopolski · Zielona Góra · Leszno · Legnica · Wrocław · Opole · Częstochowa · Kielce · Radom · Lublin · Zamość · Chełm · Radomsko · Piotrków · Tomaszów Mazowiecki · Starachowice · Ostrowiec Świętokrzyski · Mielec · Tarnów · Rzeszów · Przemyśl · Jasło · Nowy Sącz · Kraków · Katowice · Bytom · Gliwice · Rybnik · Bielsko-Biała · Zakopane · Jelenia Góra · Wałbrzych · Żary · Nowa Sól · Głogów

ČESKOSLOVENSKO

Praha · Plzeň · Karlovy Vary · Ústí · Liberec · Hradec Králové · Pardubice · Mladá Boleslav · Jablonec · Brno · Jihlava · České Budějovice · Olomouc · Ostrava · Opava · Přerov · Mistek · Frýdek · Žilina · Martin · Banská Bystrica · Trenčín · Nitra · Trnava · Bratislava · Komárno · Košice · Prešov · Michalovce · Lučenec

MAGYARORSZÁG / HUNGARY

Budapest · Győr · Tatabánya · Székesfehérvár · Veszprém · Komárom · Esztergom · Vác · Salgótarján · Eger · Miskolc · Nyíregyháza · Debrecen · Oradea · Szolnok · Cegléd · Kecskemét · Szeged · Hódmezővásárhely · Békéscsaba · Orosháza · Gyula · Arad · Timişoara · Baja · Pécs · Kaposvár · Nagykanizsa · Zalaegerszeg · Szombathely · Sopron

ÖSTERREICH / AUSTRIA

Wien · St. Pölten · Krems · Wiener Neustadt · Steyr · Linz · Wels · Passau · Salzburg · Villach · Klagenfurt · Leoben · Graz · Innsbruck

DEUTSCHLAND

Berlin · Potsdam · Brandenburg · Magdeburg · Dessau · Halle · Leipzig · Karl-Marx-Stadt · Dresden · Zwickau · Gera · Jena · Erfurt · Weimar · Gotha · Eisenach · Cottbus · Bautzen · Görlitz · Riesa · Wittenberg · Frankfurt a.d.O. · Eberswalde · Neubrandenburg · Schwerin · Rostock · Wismar · Stralsund · Greifswald · Kiel · Lübeck · Hamburg · Bremen · Bremerhaven · Cuxhaven · Wilhelmshaven · Oldenburg · Hannover · Braunschweig · Salzgitter · Wolfsburg · Hildesheim · Celle · Lüneburg · Bielefeld · Osnabrück · Kassel · Göttingen · Nordhausen · Fulda · Frankfurt a.M. · Würzburg · Schweinfurt · Bamberg · Bayreuth · Nürnberg · Regensburg · Ingolstadt · Landshut · München · Augsburg · Ulm · Stuttgart · Heilbronn · Ansbach · Freising · Rosenheim · Garmisch-Partenkirchen · Kempten · Kaufbeuren · Ravensburg · Lindau · Bolzano · Trento · Verona · Vicenza · Padova · Venezia · Treviso · Belluno · Udine · Gorizia · Trieste · Cremona · Brescia · Bergamo

SCHWEIZ / SWITZ.

WEST GERMANY · EAST GERMANY

HARZ · ERZGEBIRGE · SUDETEN · ALPS · KARPATY · DOLOMITICHE

Dnestr · Prut · Siret · Wisła · Odra · Warta · Bug · Danube

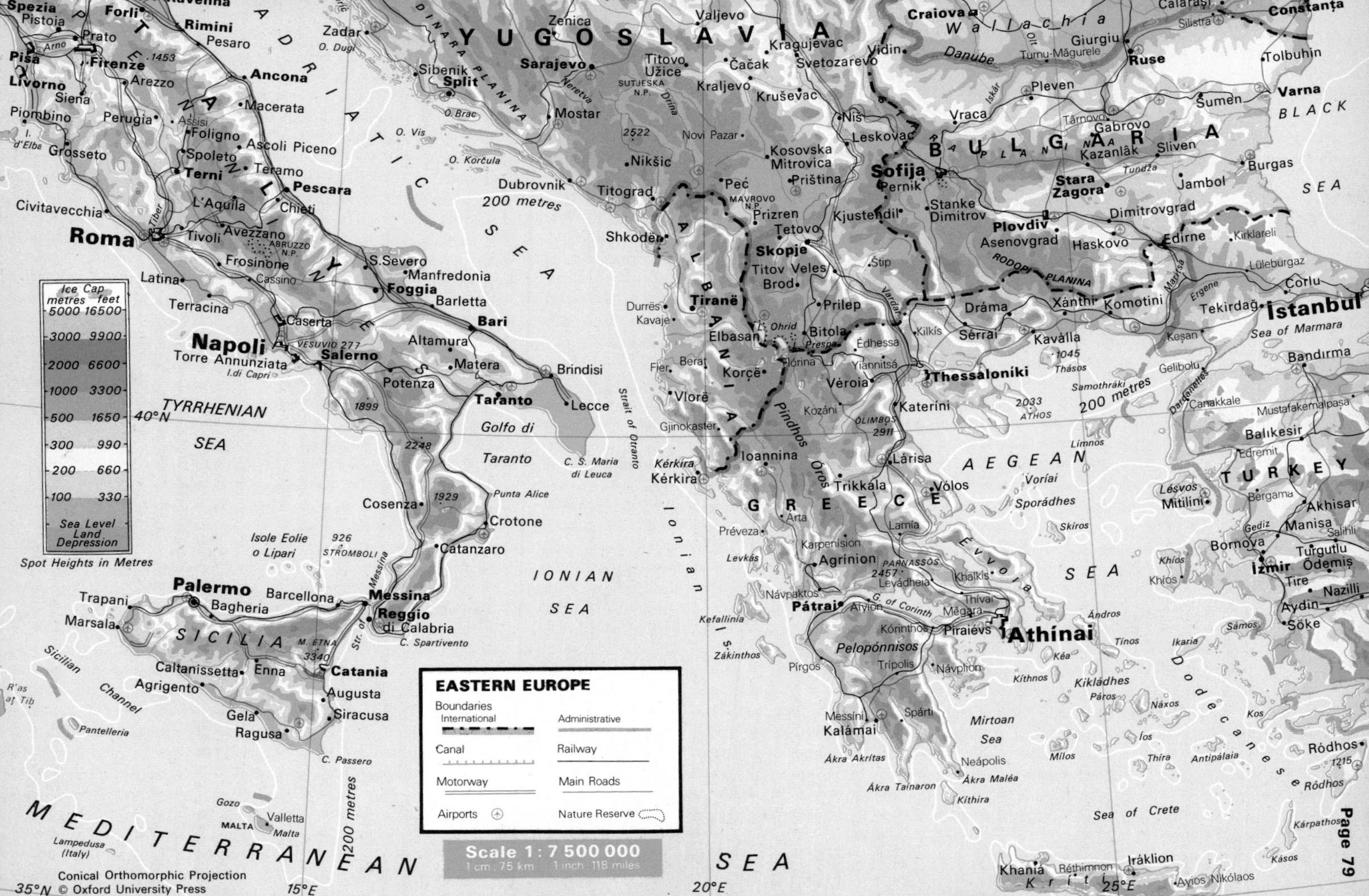

EASTERN EUROPE

Scale 1:7 500 000
1 cm 75 km · 1 inch 118 miles

Boundaries
International
Administrative
Canal
Railway
Motorway
Main Roads
Airports ⊕
Nature Reserve

Conical Orthomorphic Projection
© Oxford University Press

Spot Heights in Metres

Ice Cap
metres feet
5000 16500
3000 9900
2000 6600
1000 3300
500 1650
300 990
200 660
100 330
Sea Level
0 0
-100
-200
-300
Sea Level
and
Depression

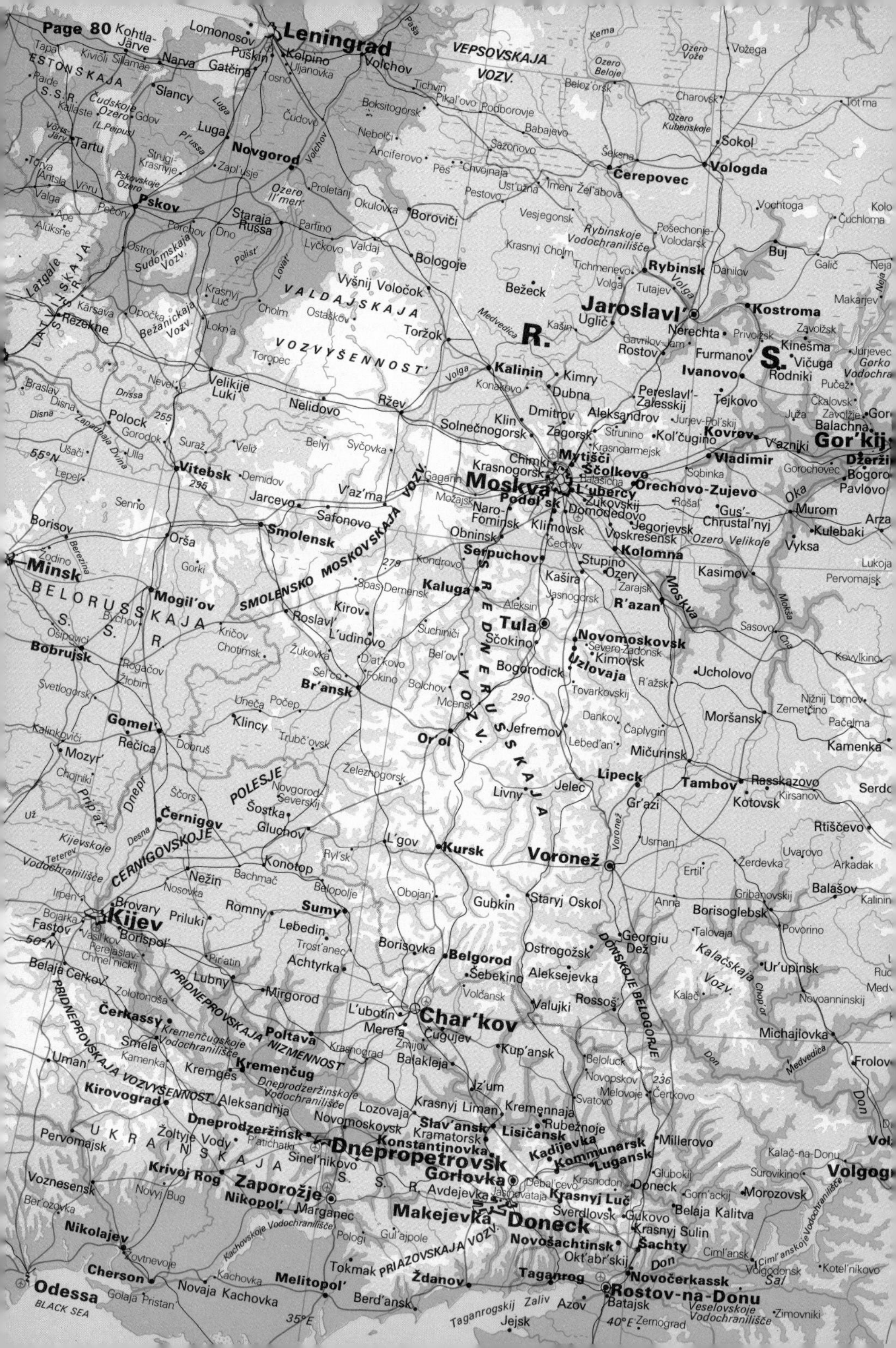
Page 80
Kohtla-Järve
Lomonosov
Leningrad
Puškin
Kolpino
Volchov
Narva
Gatčina
Tosno
Uljanovka
Sillamäe
Kiviõli
Tapa
ESTONSKAJA S.S.R.
Paide
Slancy
Čudskoje Ozero (L.Peipus)
Kallaste
Gdov
Luga
Tartu
Novgorod
Strugi-Krasnyje
Zapl'usje
Pskovskoje Ozero
Tõrva
Antsla
Võru
Valga
Pskov
Ozero Il'men'
Proletarij
Pečory
Ape
Alūksne
Staraja Russa
Porchov
Dno
Parfino
Ostrov
Sudomskaja Vozv.
Polist'
Lovat'
Lyčkovo
Valdaj
Latgale
LATVIJSKAJA S.S.R.
Kārsava
Rēzekne
Opočka
Bežanickaja Vozv.
Krasnyj Luč
Lokn'a
Cholm
Ostaškov
VALDAJSKAJA
VOZVYŠENNOST'
Toropec
Vepsovskaja Vozv.
Pаšа
Tichvin
Pikal'ovo
Boksitogorsk
Podborovje
Babajevo
Čudovo
Nebolči
Anciferovo
Pes'
Chvojnaja
Šazonovo
Pestovo
Ust'užna
Imeni Žel'abova
Okulovka
Boroviči
Bologoje
Vyšnij Voloček
Toržok
Kema
Ozero Vože
Vožega
Ozero Beloje
Belozorsk
Charovsk
Tot'ma
Ozero Kubenskoje
Sokol
Šeksna
Čerepovec
Vologda
Vochtoga
Kolo
Čuchloma
Vesjegonsk
Rybinskoje Vodochranilišče
Pošechonje-Volodarsk
Krasnyj Cholm
Tichmenevo
Rybinsk
Danilov
Buj
Galič
Neja
Volga
Tutajev
Bežeck
Medvedica
Kašin
Uglič
Jaroslavl'
Kostroma
Makarjev
R.
Nerechta
Privolžsk
Zavolžsk
Gavrilov-Jam
Rostov
Furmanov
Kinešma
Jurjevec
S.
Ivanovo
Vičuga
Rodniki
Gorko Vodochra
Pučež
Kalinin
Kimry
Konakovo
Dubna
Pereslavl'-Zalesskij
Tejkovo
Čkalovsk
Velikije Luki
Nevel'
Drissa
Braslav
Disna
Nelidovo
Ržev
Klin
Dmitrov
Aleksandrov
Jurjev-Pol'skij
Juža
Zavolžje
Polock
Gorodok
Zapadnaja Dvina
Ulla
Usači
Lepel'
55°N
Sural
Velіž
Belyj
Syčovka
Solnečnogorsk
Zagorsk
Strunino
Kol'čugino
Kovrov
Balachna
Gor'kij
V'azniki
Krasnoarmejsk
Chimki
Mytišči
Ščolkovo
Krasnogorsk
Vladimir
Dzerži
Sobinka
Gorochovec
Bogoro
Pavlovo
Vitebsk
Demidov
Gagarin
Moskva
L'ubercy
Balašicha
Orechovo-Zujevo
V'az'ma
Možajsk
Podol'sk
Žukovskij
Jarcevo
Senno
Naro-Fominsk
Domodedovo
Rošal'
Murom
Oka
Safonovo
Gus'-Chrustal'nyj
Borisov
Smolensk
Obninsk
Klimovsk
Jegorjevsk
Kulebaki
Arza
Orša
Berezina
Čechov
Voskresensk
Ozero Velikoje
Vyksa
Žodino
Serpuchov
Kolomna
Minsk
Gorki
Kondrovo
Stupino
Ozery
Kasimov
Lukoja
BELORUSSKAJA S.S.R.
Mogil'ov
SMOLENSKO MOSKOVSKAJA VOZV.
Spas-Demensk
Kaluga
Kašira
Zarajsk
Pervomajsk
Jasnogorsk
R'azan'
Moskva
Mokša
Bychov
Kirov
Aleksin
Osipoviči
Roslavl'
Tula
Sasovo
Cna
Kričov
L'udinovo
Suchiniči
Novomoskovsk
Severo-Zadonsk
Kovylkino
Bobrujsk
Chotimsk
Žukovka
D'at'kovo
Bel'ov
Ščokino
Kimovsk
Uzlovaja
Rogačov
Sel'co
Fokino
Bolchov
Bogorodick
SREDNERUSSKAJA VOZV.
Ucholovo
Žlobin
Br'ansk
R'ažsk
Svetlogorsk
Mcensk
290
Tovarkovskij
Nižnij Lomov
Uneča
Počep
Zemetčino
Gomel'
Klincy
Dankov
Čaplygin
Moršansk
Pačelma
Kalinkoviči
Rečica
Dobruš
Trubč'ovsk
Or'ol
Jefremov
Lebed'an'
Mičurinsk
Kamenka
Mozyr'
Chojniki
Dnepr
Pripat'
Železnogorsk
POLESJE
Novgorod-Severskij
Lipeck
Jelec
Tambov
Rasskazovo
Serdo
Šostka
Livny
Gr'azi
Kirsanov
Kotovsk
Už
Ščors
Černigov
Desna
Gluchov
Voronež
Usman'
Rtiščevo
Kijevskoje Vodochranilišče
ČERNIGOVSKOJE
L'gov
Kursk
Teterev
Ryl'sk
Uvarovo
Arkadak
Konotop
Ertil'
Žerdevka
Irpen'
Nežin
Bachmač
Belopolje
Obojan'
Gribanovskij
Balašov
Nosovka
Gubkin
Staryj Oskol
Anna
Kalinin
Brovary
Romny
Sumy
Borisoglebsk
Bojarka
Kijev
Priluki
Lebedin
Talovaja
Povorino
Fastov
Boryspol'
Trost'anec
Borisovka
Ostrogožsk
Georgiu Dež
Kalačskaja Vozv.
Vasil'kov
50°N
Pereiaslav-Chmel'nickij
Pir'atin
Achtyrka
Belgorod
Šebekino
DONSKOJE BELOGORJE
Ur'upinsk
Belaja Cerkov'
Lubny
Aleksejevka
Chop'or
PRIDNEPROVSKAJA VOZVYŠENNOST'
Zolotonoša
Mirgorod
Volčansk
Valujki
Rossoš
Kalač
Novoanninskij
PRIDNEPROVSKAJA NIZMENNOST'
L'ubotin
Char'kov
Čerkassy
Kremenčugskoje Vodochranilišče
Poltava
Mereфa
Čugujev
Michajlovka
Smela
Kamenka
Krasnograd
Zmijov
Kup'ansk
Medvedica
Don
Uman'
Kremges
Kremenčug
Balakleja
Beloluck
Frolov
Novopskov
Dneprodzeržinskoje Vodochranilišče
Iz'um
Melovoje
236
Kirovograd
Aleksandrija
Svatovo
Čertkovo
UKRAINSKAJA S.S.R.
Lozovaja
Krasnyj Liman
Kremennaja
Rubežnoje
Pervomajsk
Dneprodzeržinsk
Novomoskovsk
Slav'ansk
Kramatorsk
Lisičansk
Millerovo
Žoltyje Vody
P'atichatki
Dnepropetrovsk
Konstantinovka
Kadijevka
Kommunarsk
Lugansk
Vol
Sinel'nikovo
Glubokij
Kalač-na-Donu
Krivoj Rog
Zaporožje
Gorlovka
Debal'cevo
Krasnodon
Voznesensk
Novyj Bug
Avdejevka
Jasinovataja
Krasnyj Luč
Doneck
Surovikino
Volgog
Ber'ozovka
Nikopol'
Marganec
Makejevka
Doneck
Sverdlovsk
Gukovo
Gorn'ackij
Morozovsk
Belaja Kalitva
Kachovskoje Vodochranilišče
Pologi
Gul'ajpole
Krasnyj Sulin
Nikolajev
Novošachtinsk
Šachty
Ciml'ansk
Ciml'anskoje Vodochranilišče
Žovtnevoje
Tokmak
PRIAZOVSKAJA VOZV.
Okt'abr'skij
Don
Volgodonsk
Kotel'nikovo
Cherson
Kachovka
Melitopol'
Ždanov
Taganrog
Novočerkassk
Sal
Odessa
Novaja Kachovka
Berd'ansk
Rostov-na-Donu
Golaja Pristan'
Taganrogskij Zaliv
Azov
Batajsk
Veselovskoje Vodochranilišče
Zimovniki
BLACK SEA
35°E
Jejsk
40°E
Zernograd

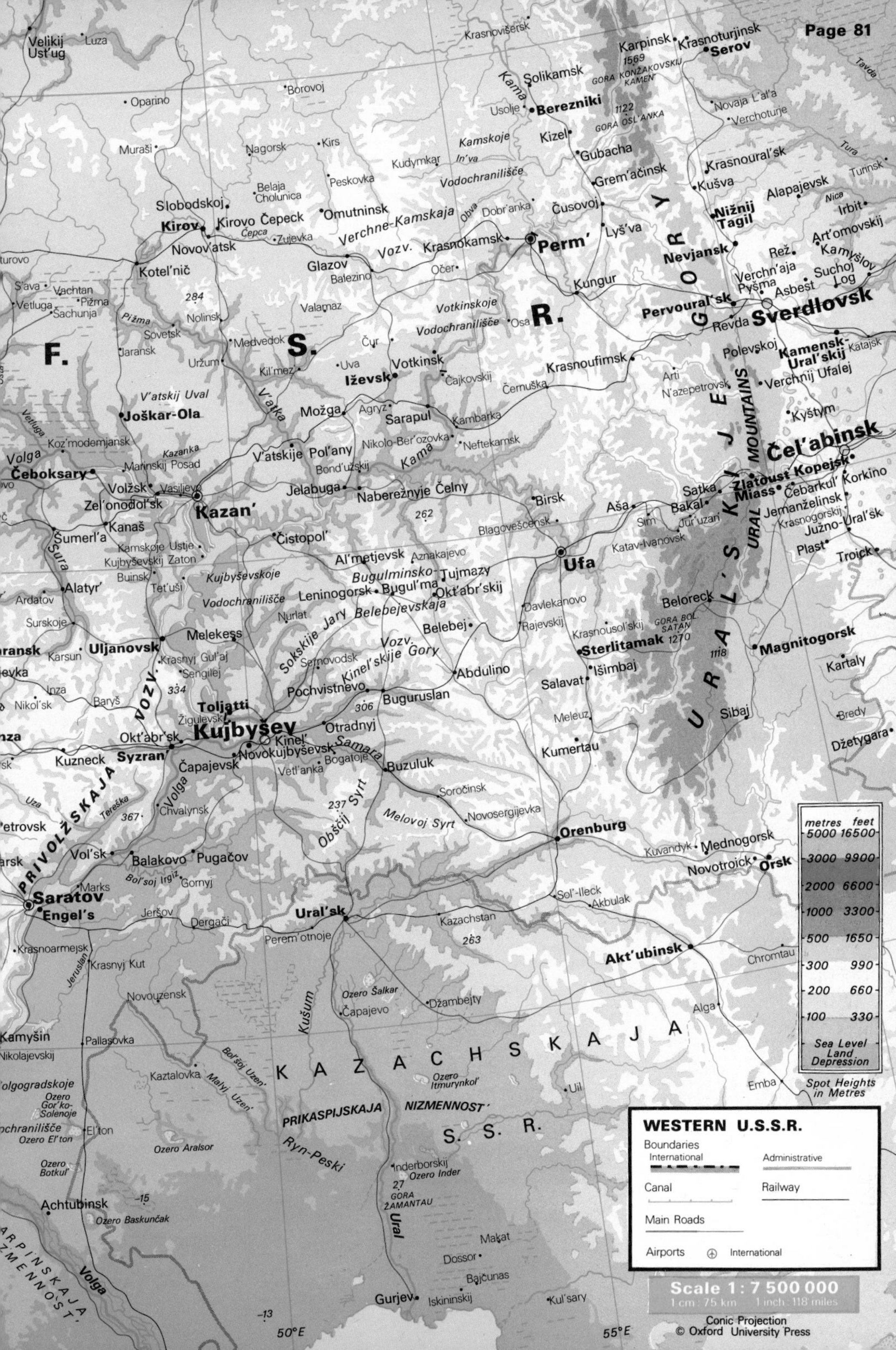

WESTERN U.S.S.R.

Boundaries
International ▬ ▪ ▬ ▪ ▬   Administrative

Canal   Railway

Main Roads

Airports   ⊕   International

metres	feet
5000	16500
3000	9900
2000	6600
1000	3300
500	1650
300	990
200	660
100	330

Sea Level
Land
Depression

Spot Heights
in Metres

Scale 1 : 7 500 000
1 cm / 75 km   1 inch = 118 miles

Conic Projection
© Oxford University Press

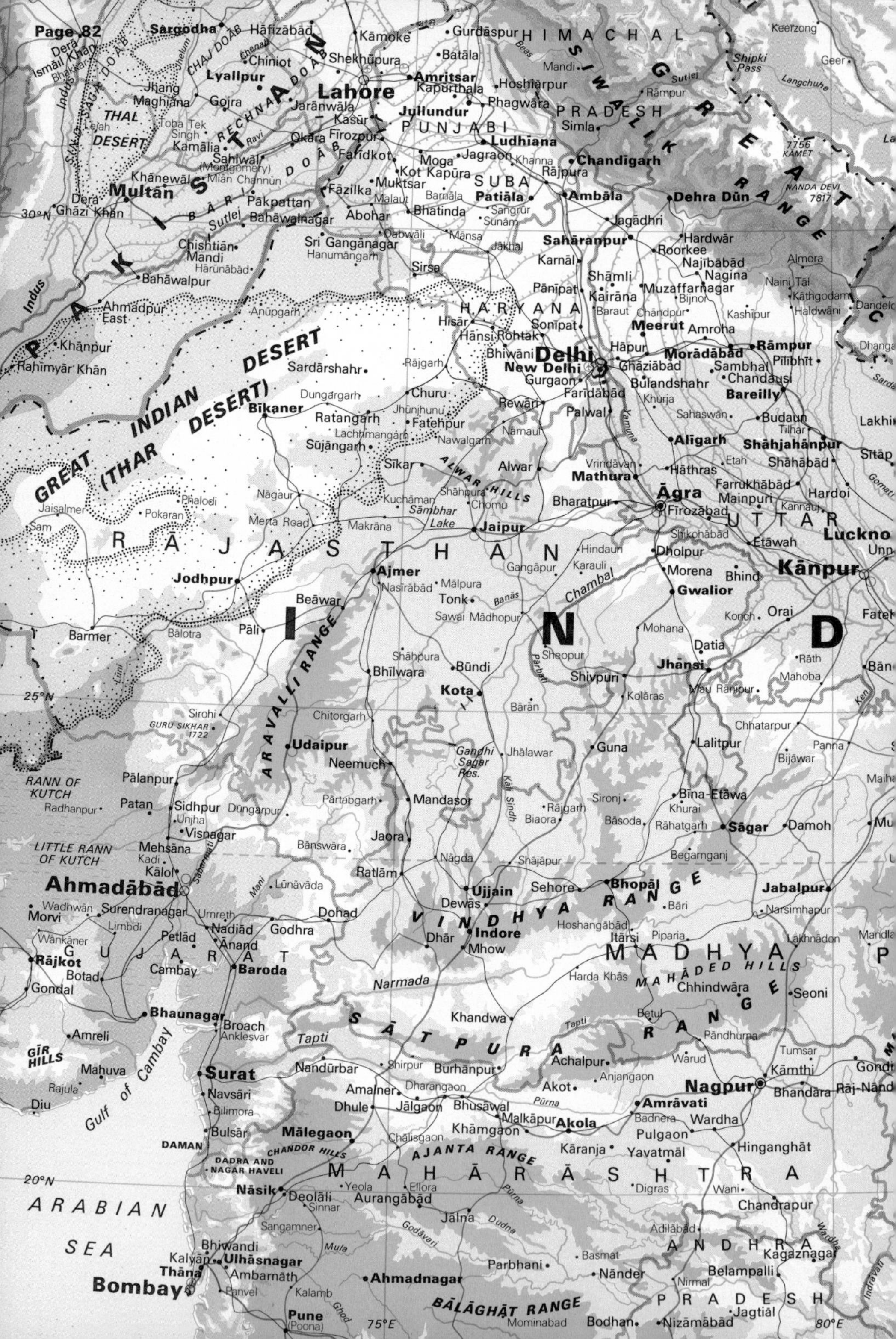
Page 82
Sargodha
Hāfizābād
Dera Ismāīl Khān
Bhakkar
Jhelum
CHAJ DOĀB
SIND SAGAR DOĀB
Chenab
Chiniot
Lyallpur
Jhang
Maghiāna
Gojra
Indus
THAL DESERT
Leiah
Toba Tek Singh
RECHNA DOĀB
Kamālia
Ravi
Sahiwāl (Montgomery)
Miān Channūn
Khānewāl
Multān
Dera Ghāzi Khān
30°N
BĀRI DOĀB
Pākpattan
Sutlej
Bahāwalnagar
Chishtiān Mandi
Hārūnābād
Bahāwalpur
Indus
Ahmadpur East
Khānpur
Rahīmyār Khān
PAKISTAN
Kāmoke
Gurdāspur
Shekhūpura
Batāla
Amritsar
Lahore
Kapurthala
Hoshiārpur
Jarānwāla
Phagwāra
Kasūr
Jullundur
Okāra
Firozpur
PUNJABI
Ludhiāna
Farīdkot
Moga
Jagraon
Khanna
Kot Kapūra
SUBA
Muktsar
Fāzilka
Malaut
Barnāla
Patiāla
Bhatinda
Sangrur
Sunām
Abohar
Dabwāli
Mānsa
Sri Gangānagar
Hanumāngarh
Jakhal
Sirsa
HIMACHAL PRADESH
Beas
Mandi
SIWALIK RANGE
Rāmpur
Simla
Chandīgarh
Rājpura
Ambāla
Dehra Dūn
Jagādhri
Sahāranpur
Hardwār
Roorkee
Karnāl
Najībābād
Nagina
Shāmli
Pānīpat
Kairāna
Muzaffarnagar
Bijnor
HARYANA
Baraut
Chāndpur
Sonīpat
Meerut
Amroha
Keerzong
Shipki Pass
Geer
Sutlej
Langchuhe
GREAT
7756 KĀMET
NANDA DEVI 7817
RANGE
Almora
Naini Tāl
Kāthgodām
Haldwāni
Kashīpur
Dandeld
Anūpgarh
GREAT INDIAN DESERT (THAR DESERT)
Sardārshahr
Rājgarh
Hisār
Hānsi
Rohtak
Bhiwāni
Delhi
New Delhi
Gurgaon
Hāpur
Ghāziābād
Moradābād
Rāmpur
Pīlībhīt
Sambhal
Chandausi
Bulandshahr
Bareilly
Dungargarh
Churu
Bīkaner
Jhūnjhunu
Rewāri
Farīdābād
Palwal
Yamuna
Khurja
Sahaswān
Budaun
Tilhar
Ratangarh
Fatehpur
Lachhmangarh
Nawalgarh
Nārnaul
Sūjāngarh
Alīgarh
Shāhjahānpur
Shāhābād
Sīkar
ALWAR HILLS
Alwar
Vrindāvan
Mathura
Hāthras
Etah
Farrukhābād
Hardoi
Nāgaur
Shāhpura
Chomu
Āgra
Mainpuri
Kannauj
Jaisalmer
Phalodi
Pokaran
Kuchāman
Sāmbhar Lake
Bharatpur
Fīrozābād
UTTAR
Sam
Merta Road
Makrāna
Jaipur
Shikohābād
Lucknow
RĀJASTHĀN
Hindaun
Karauli
Dholpur
Etāwah
Gangāpur
Ajmer
Morena
Bhind
Kānpur
Jodhpur
Nasīrābād
Mālpura
Chambal
Gwalior
Tonk
Banās
Beāwar
Sawai Mādhopur
Konch
Orai
Barmer
Pāli
Bālotra
INDIA
Mohana
ARAVALLI RANGE
Sheopur
Pārbati
Datia
Shāhpura
Bhīlwara
Būndi
Jhānsi
Rāth
Shivpuri
Mahoba
Lūni
25°N
Kota
Kolāras
Mau Rānīpur
Bārān
Sirohi
Chitorgarh
GURU SIKHAR 1722
Udaipur
Gāndhi Sāgar Res.
Jhālawar
Guna
Lalitpur
Chhatarpur
Panna
Bijāwar
Neemuch
Kāli Sindh
RANN OF KUTCH
Pālanpur
Mandasor
Sironj
Bīna-Etāwa
Radhanpur
Patan
Sidhpur
Dūngarpur
Pārtābgarh
Rājgarh
Khurai
Unjha
Biaora
Visnagar
Bāsoda
Rāhatgarh
Sāgar
Damoh
LITTLE RANN OF KUTCH
Mehsāna
Sabarmati
Bānswāra
Jaora
Kadi
Nāgda
Shājāpur
Begamganj
Kālol
Mahi
Ratlām
Ahmadābād
Lūnāvāda
Ujjain
Sehore
Bhopāl
Jabalpur
Wadhwān
Umreth
Dewās
Bāri
Morvi
Surendranagar
Dohad
Narsimhapur
Limbdi
Nadiād
Godhra
VINDHYA RANGE
Indore
Hoshangābād
Wānkāner
Petlād
Ānand
Dhār
Itārsi
Piparia
Lakhnādon
Rājkot
GUJARAT
Mhow
MADHYA
Botad
Cambay
Baroda
Gondal
Narmada
Harda Khās
MAHĀDEO HILLS
Chhindwāra
Seoni
Bhaunagar
Broach
SĀTPURA RANGE
Khandwa
Tāpti
Betul
Anklesvar
Tāpti
Pāndhurna
Amreli
Gulf of Cambay
GĪR HILLS
Mahuva
Surat
Nandūrbār
Shirpur
Burhānpur
Achalpur
Warud
Tumsar
Kāmthi
Anjangaon
Akot
Nagpur
Bhandāra
Rāj-Nāndgaon
Rajula
Navsāri
Amalner
Dharangaon
Diu
Bilimora
Dhule
Jālgaon
Bhusāwal
Pūrna
Amrāvati
Malkāpur
Akola
Badnera
Wardha
Bulsār
Mālegaon
Chālisgaon
Khāmgaon
Pulgaon
DAMAN
CHANDOR HILLS
AJANTA RANGE
Kāranja
Yavatmāl
Hinganghāt
DADRA AND NAGAR HAVELI
MAHĀRĀSHTRA
20°N
Nāsik
Yeola
Ellora
Pūrna
Digras
Wani
Deolāli
Aurangābād
Chandrapur
ARABIAN SEA
Sinnar
Jālna
Dudna
Sangamner
Godāvari
Adilābād
Wardha
Bhiwandi
Mula
ANDHRA
Kagaznagar
Kalyān
Ulhāsnagar
Parbhani
Basmat
Thāna
Ambarnāth
Nānder
Belampalli
Bombay
Ahmadnagar
Nirmal
Panvel
Kalamb
PRADESH
Ghod
Jagtiāl
BĀLĀGHĀT RANGE
Pune (Poona)
75°E
Mominabad
Bodhan
Nizāmābād
80°E
Indravati
Lakhi
Sītāpur
Gomati
Fatehpur
Bānda
Ken
Maihar
Mandla
Gondia
Dhangadhi
Sarda

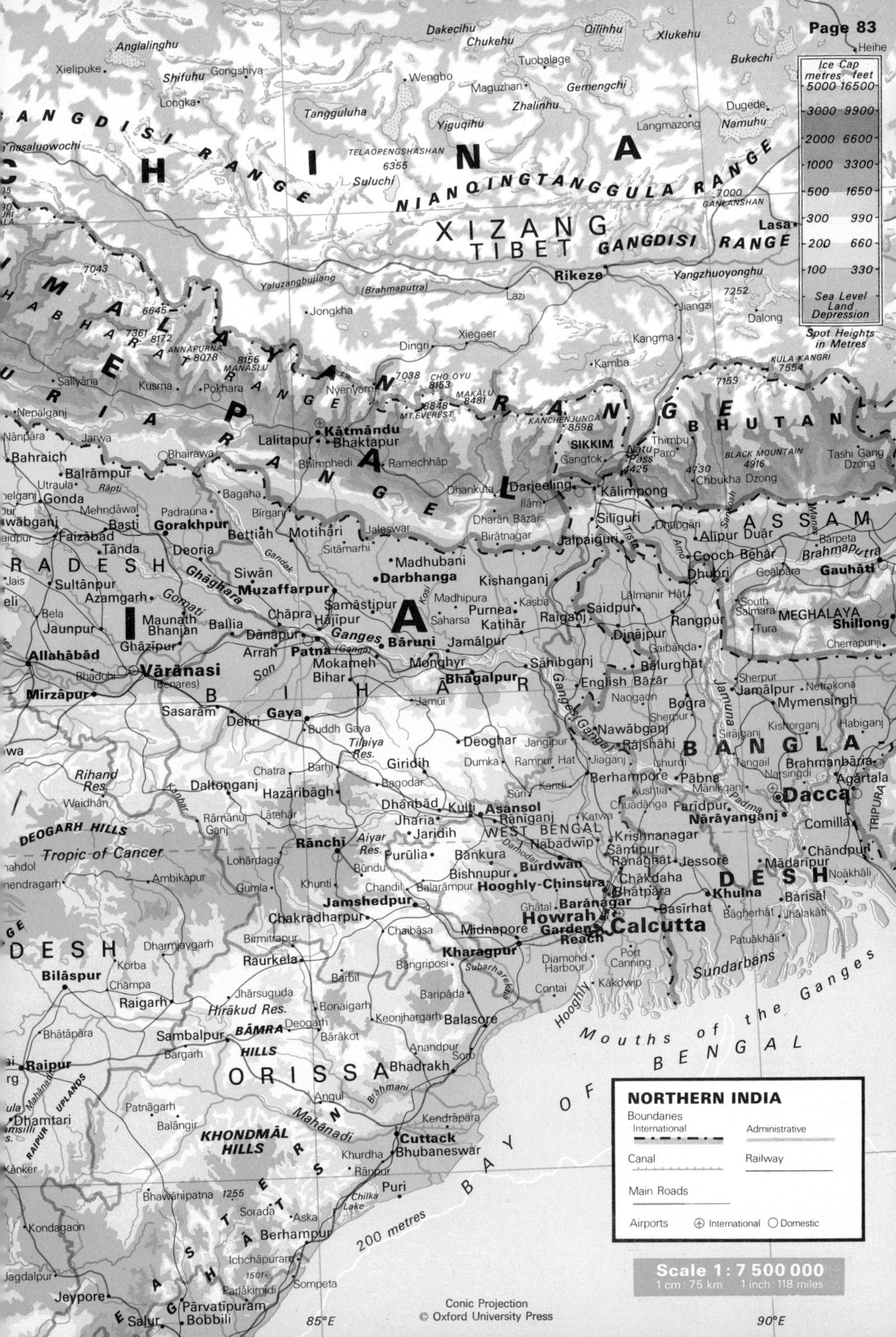

NORTHERN INDIA

Boundaries
International   Administrative

Canal   Railway

Main Roads

Airports   ⊕ International   ○ Domestic

Scale 1: 7 500 000
1 cm : 75 km   1 inch : 118 miles

Conic Projection
© Oxford University Press

Ice Cap	
metres	feet
5000	16500
3000	9900
2000	6600
1000	3300
500	1650
300	990
200	660
100	330
Sea Level	
Land	
Depression	

Spot Heights
in Metres

LIAODONG
1,132
Gaiping
Liaodong
Peninsula
Suizhong
Qinhuangdao
Xiongyuecheng
Fuxian
Xinjin
Lüshun
Changli
Lüda
Shanhaiguan
Xingcheng
Yantai (Chefoo)
Weihai
Wenden Rongcheng
Shidao
Muping
Rushan
Zhaoyuan
Fushan
Penglai
Changli
Yellow Sea

Ice Cap
metres feet
5000 16500

3000	9900	2000	6600	1000	3300	500	1650	
						300	990	
						200	660	
						100	330	Sea Level

Dot Heights in Metres
Land Depression

Bohai (Gulf of Chihli)

Qingdao

Tianjin (Tientsin)

Beijing (Peking)

HEBEI

SHANDONG

Jinan

Weifang

Zibo

Linyi

Xuzhou

JIANGSU

Nanjing (Nanking)

ANHUI

Hefei

Shijiazhuang

SHANXI

Taiyuan

Zhengzhou

HENAN

Luoyang

Kaifeng

HUBEI

Xi'an

SHAANXI

GANSU

NINGXIA

INNER MONGOLIA

NEI MENGGU

Ordos

Baotou

Huhehaote (Kweisui)

Datong

Zhangjiakou

CHINA

Qinlingshan

Dabashan

TAIBAISHAN
4107

2708

Han

Huang

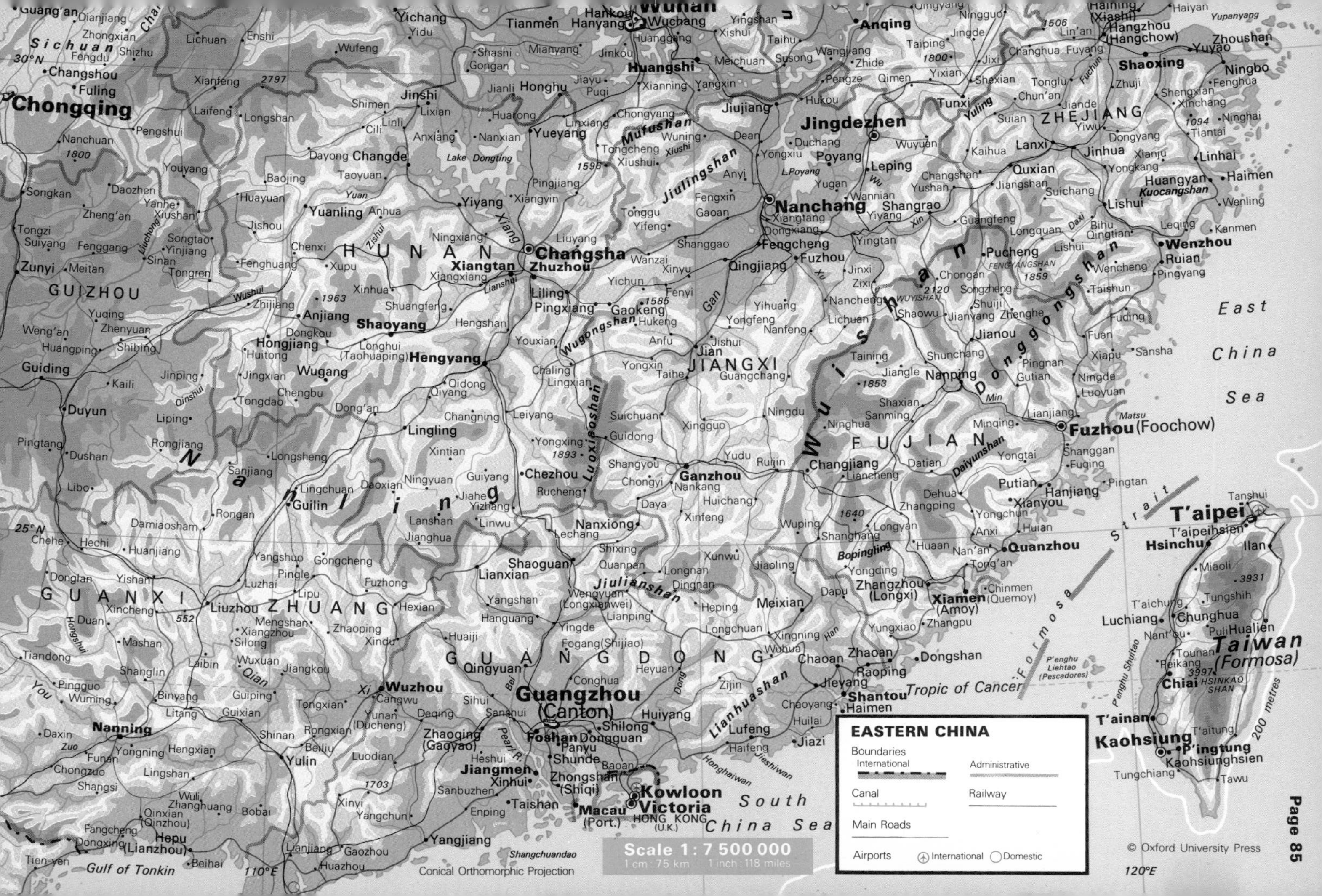

© Oxford University Press

120°E

EASTERN CHINA

Boundaries
International
Administrative

Canal
Railway

Main Roads

Airports ⊕ International ○ Domestic

Scale 1:7 500 000
1 cm = 75 km   1 inch = 118 miles

Conical Orthomorphic Projection

East   *China*   *Sea*

ZHEJIANG

FUJIAN

JIANGXI

HUNAN

GUANGDONG

GUANGXI ZHUANG

GUIZHOU

Taiwan (Formosa)

T'aipei

Kaohsiung

T'ainan

Tropic of Cancer

South China Sea

Gulf of Tonkin

Chongqing

Nanchang

Changsha

Fuzhou (Foochow)

Guangzhou (Canton)

HONG KONG (U.K.)

Kowloon

Nanning

Hengyang

Wuhan

Jingdezhen

Jiujiang

Wuzhou

Hepu (Lianzhou)

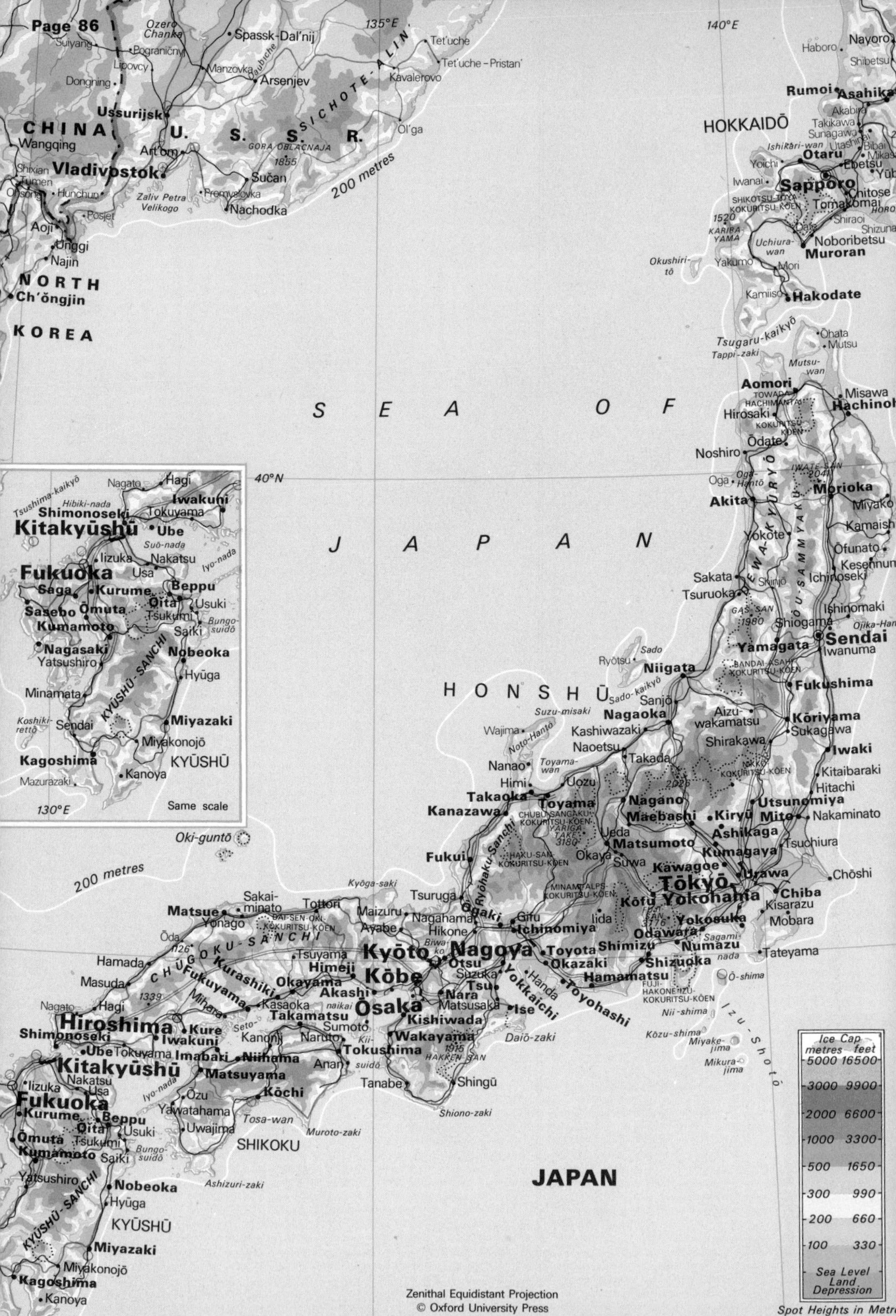

Page 86
JAPAN
SEA OF JAPAN
HONSHŪ
HOKKAIDŌ
SHIKOKU
KYŪSHŪ
CHINA
U. S. S. R.
NORTH KOREA
Tōkyō
Yokohama
Ōsaka
Nagoya
Kyōto
Kōbe
Sapporo
Sendai
Hiroshima
Kitakyūshū
Fukuoka
Same scale
200 metres
Zenithal Equidistant Projection
© Oxford University Press
Ice Cap
metres feet
5000 16500
3000 9900
2000 6600
1000 3300
500 1650
300 990
200 660
100 330
Sea Level
Land Depression
Spot Heights in Metre

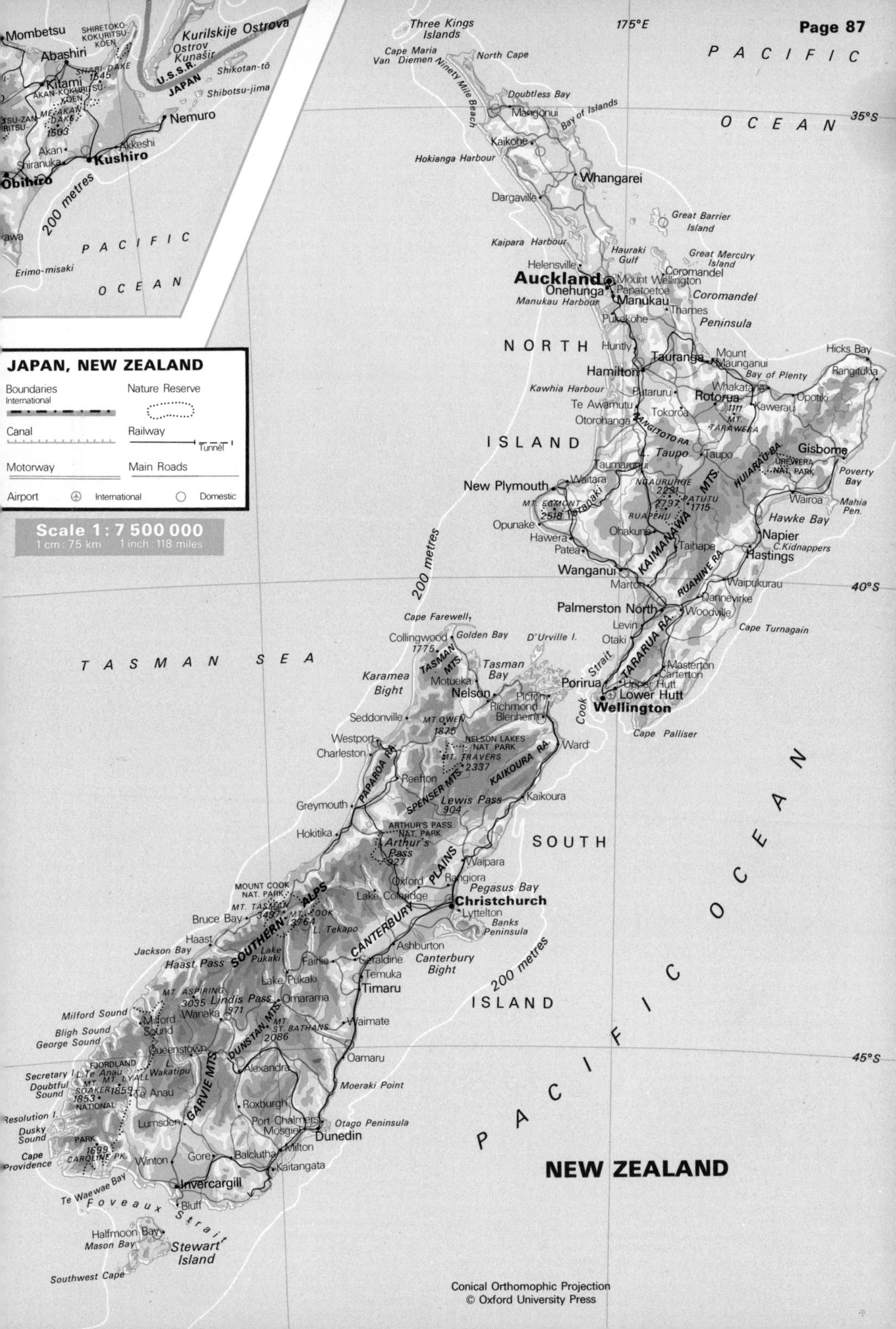

JAPAN, NEW ZEALAND

Boundaries
International

Nature Reserve

Canal

Railway

Tunnel

Motorway

Main Roads

Airport   ⊕ International   ○ Domestic

Scale 1: 7 500 000
1 cm : 75 km   1 inch : 118 miles

Conical Orthomophic Projection
© Oxford University Press

NEW ZEALAND

NORTH ISLAND

SOUTH ISLAND

TASMAN SEA

PACIFIC OCEAN

175°E

35°S

40°S

45°S

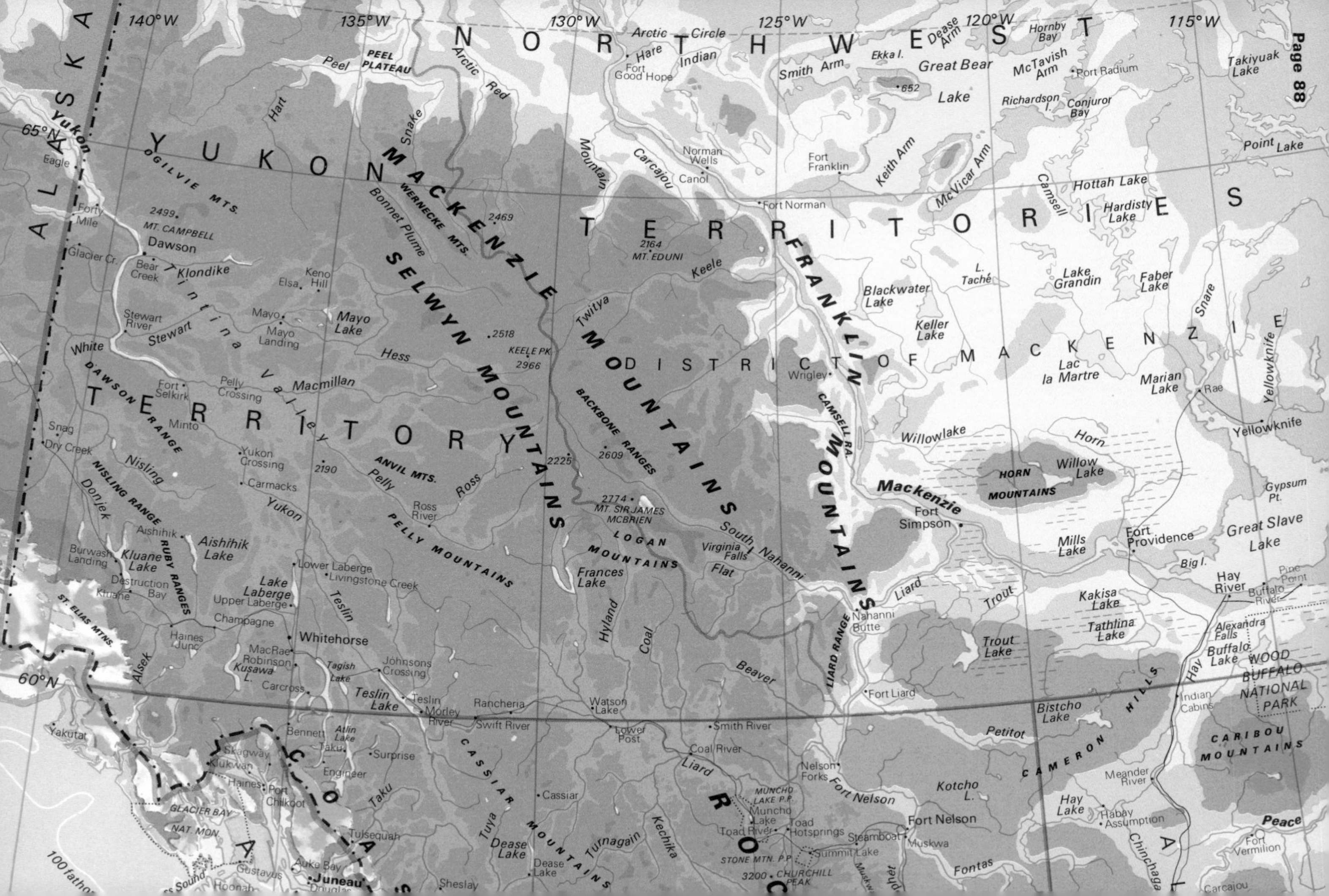
ALASKA
YUKON TERRITORY
NORTHWEST TERRITORIES
DISTRICT OF MACKENZIE
COAST
ROC
AL
140°W
135°W
130°W
125°W
120°W
115°W
65°N
60°N
Arctic Circle
Yukon
Eagle
Forty Mile
Glacier Cr.
Dawson
Bear Creek
Klondike
2499
MT. CAMPBELL
OGILVIE MTS.
Peel
PEEL PLATEAU
Hart
Snake
Arctic Red
MACKENZIE
WERNECKE MTS.
Bonnet Plume
2469
SELWYN MOUNTAINS
Keno Hill
Elsa
Mayo
Mayo Landing
Mayo Lake
Stewart River
Stewart
White
Tintina Valley
Hess
2518
KEELE PK. 2966
Fort Selkirk
Pelly Crossing
Macmillan
DAWSON RANGE
Snag
Dry Creek
Minto
Yukon Crossing
2190
Carmacks
ANVIL MTS.
Pelly
Ross
Ross River
Nisling
NISLING RANGE
Donjek
Aishihik
Aishihik Lake
RUBY RANGES
Burwash Landing
Kluane Lake
Destruction Bay
Kluane
PELLY MOUNTAINS
Lower Laberge
Livingstone Creek
Lake Laberge
Upper Laberge
Teslin
ST. ELIAS MTS.
Haines Junc.
Champagne
Whitehorse
Alsek
MacRae
Robinson
Kusawa L.
Tagish Lake
Johnsons Crossing
Carcross
Teslin Lake
Teslin
Morley River
Rancheria
Swift River
Yakutat
Bennett
Atlin Lake
Taku
Surprise
Skagway
Klukwan
Engineer
Haines
Port Chilkoot
GLACIER BAY NAT. MON.
Tulsequah
Auke Bay
Juneau
Douglas
Gustavus
Hoonah
Sound
100 fathoms
CASSIAR MOUNTAINS
Cassiar
Tuya
Dease Lake
Sheslay
Turnagain
Kechika
Watson Lake
Lower Post
Smith River
Coal River
Liard
Hyland
Coal
Frances Lake
LOGAN MOUNTAINS
2774
MT. SIR JAMES MCBRIEN
2225
2609
BACKBONE RANGES
MACKENZIE MOUNTAINS
Twitya
Keele
2164
MT. EDUNI
Mountain
Carcajou
Norman Wells
Canol
Fort Good Hope
Hare
Indian
Fort Norman
Fort Franklin
Smith Arm
Keith Arm
McVicar Arm
Ekka I.
652
Great Bear Lake
Dease Arm
Hornby Bay
McTavish Arm
Port Radium
Richardson I.
Conjuror Bay
Takiyuak Lake
Point Lake
Camsell
Hottah Lake
Hardisty Lake
FRANKLIN MOUNTAINS
CAMSELL RA.
Wrigley
Blackwater Lake
Keller Lake
L. Taché
Lake Grandin
Faber Lake
Snare
Lac la Martre
Marian Lake
Rae
Yellowknife
Willowlake
Horn
Willow Lake
HORN MOUNTAINS
Mackenzie
Fort Simpson
Gypsum Pt.
Great Slave Lake
Mills Lake
Fort Providence
Big I.
Hay River
Buffalo River
Pine Point
South Nahanni
Virginia Falls
Flat
Liard
Trout
Nahanni Butte
LIARD RANGE
Beaver
Kakisa Lake
Tathlina Lake
Trout Lake
Alexandra Falls
Buffalo Lake
WOOD BUFFALO NATIONAL PARK
Hay
Fort Liard
Indian Cabins
Bistcho Lake
HILLS
CAMERON
Petitot
CARIBOU MOUNTAINS
Nelson Forks
Fort Nelson
MUNCHO LAKE P.P.
Muncho Lake
Toad River
Toad Hotsprings
STONE MTN. P.P.
Summit Lake
3200
CHURCHILL PEAK
Steamboat
Muskwa
Fontas
Kotcho L.
Meander River
Hay Lake
Habay
Assumption
Chinchaga
Peace
Fort Vermilion
Carcajou

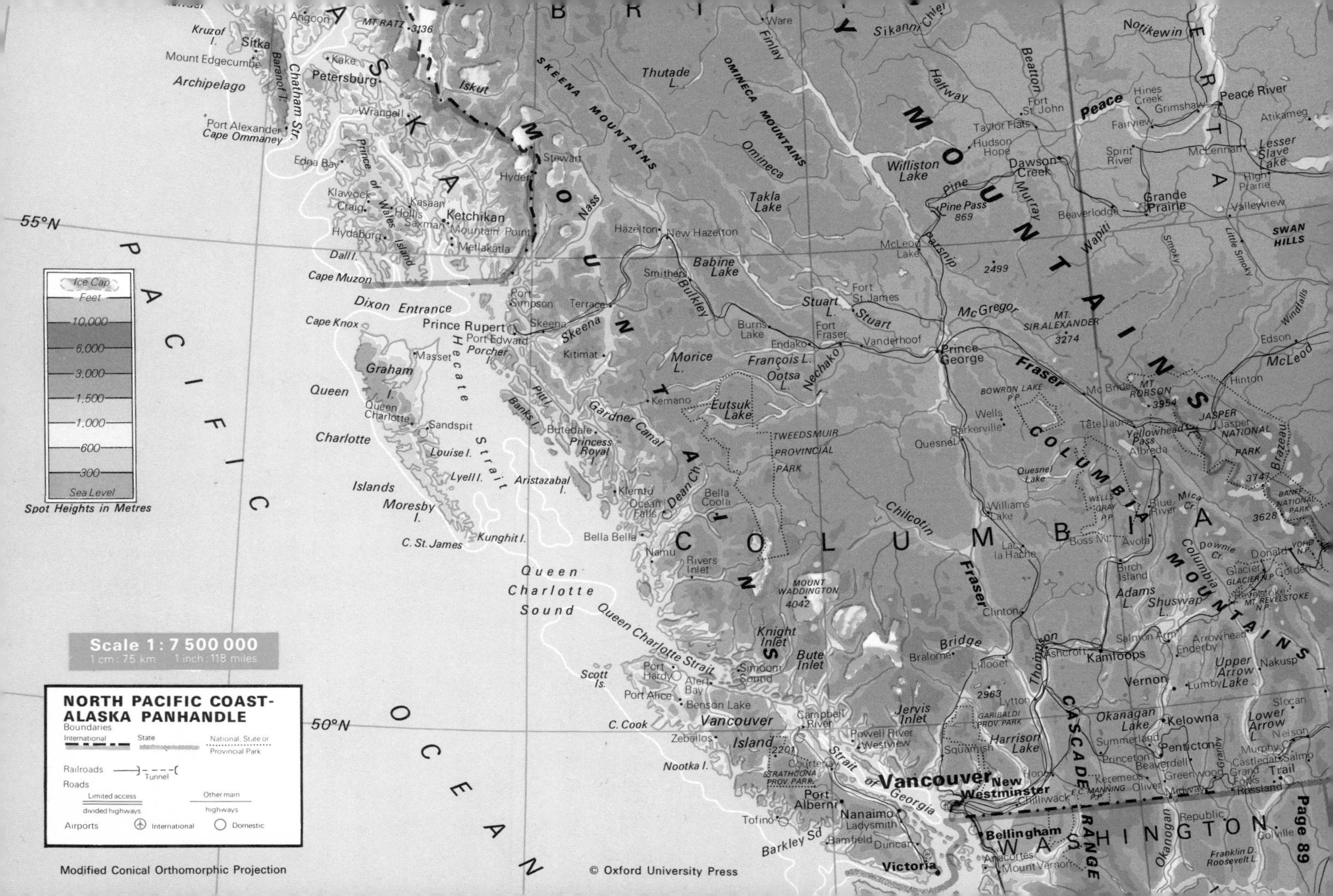

NORTH PACIFIC COAST-
ALASKA PANHANDLE

Modified Conical Orthomorphic Projection

© Oxford University Press

Scale 1 : 7 500 000
1 cm : 75 km   1 inch : 118 miles

Boundaries
International
State   National State or
                         Provincial Park
Railroads
Roads
Limited access
divided highways   Other main
                         highways
                         Tunnel
Airports
International   Domestic

Spot Heights in Metres

Feet
Ice Cap
10,000
6,000
3,000
1,500
1,000
600
300
Sea Level

PACIFIC OCEAN

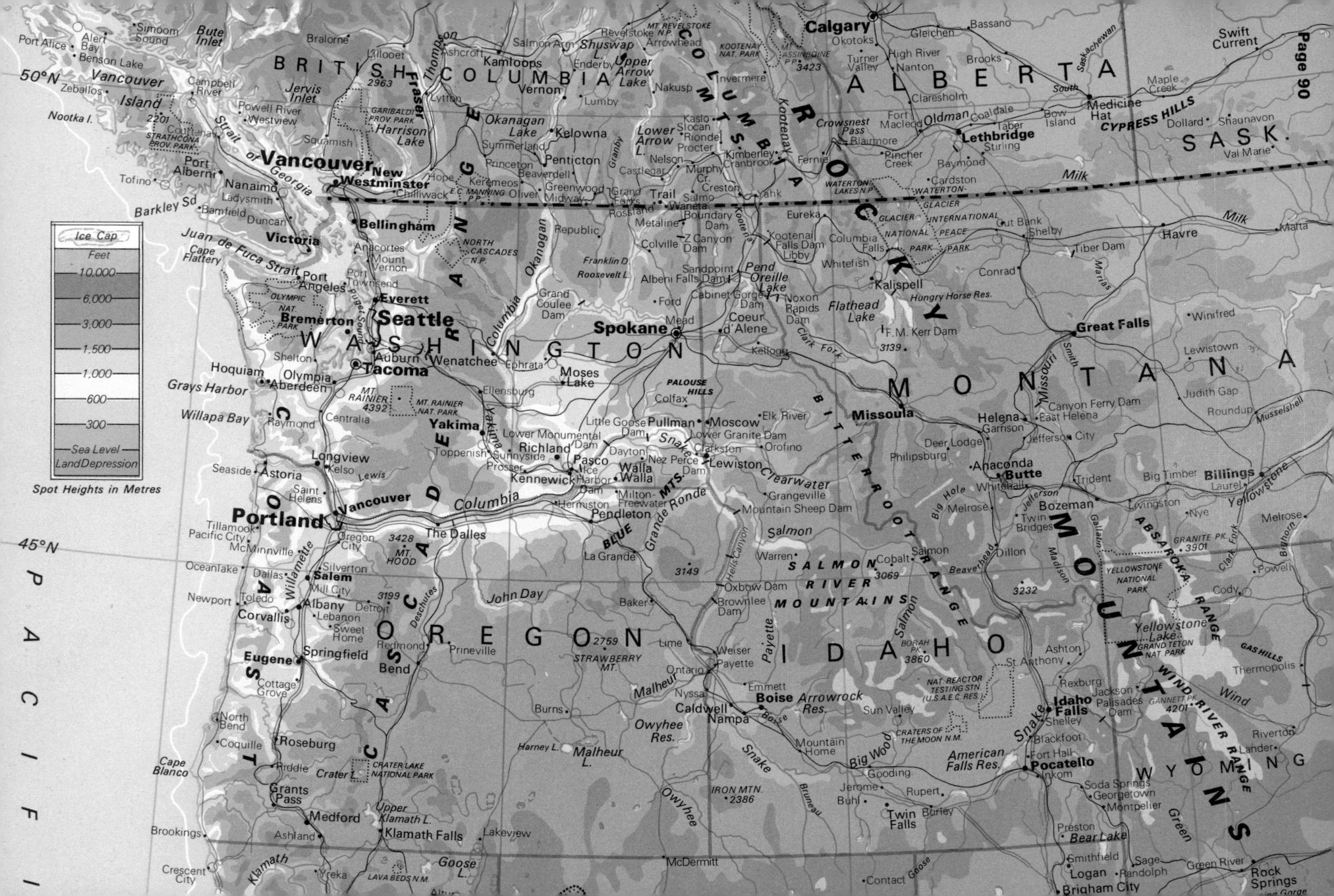
BRITISH COLUMBIA
ALBERTA
SASK.
MONTANA
WASHINGTON
OREGON
IDAHO
WYOMING
ROCKY MOUNTAINS
COLUMBIA MTS
CASCADE RANGE
COAST
BITTERROOT RANGE
SALMON RIVER MOUNTAINS
ABSAROKA RANGE
WIND RIVER RANGE
BLUE MTS.
CYPRESS HILLS
PALOUSE HILLS
GAS HILLS
P A C I F I
50°N
45°N
Vancouver Island
Nootka I.
Strait of Georgia
Juan de Fuca Strait
Puget Sound
Barkley Sd
Grays Harbor
Willapa Bay
Cape Flattery
Cape Blanco
Calgary
Medicine Hat
Lethbridge
Swift Current
Vancouver
New Westminster
Victoria
Nanaimo
Kamloops
Kelowna
Penticton
Vernon
Seattle
Tacoma
Everett
Bellingham
Olympia
Aberdeen
Bremerton
Spokane
Yakima
Wenatchee
Walla Walla
Pasco
Richland
Kennewick
Portland
Salem
Eugene
Corvallis
Albany
Medford
Klamath Falls
Bend
Pendleton
The Dalles
Astoria
Great Falls
Helena
Missoula
Butte
Billings
Bozeman
Kalispell
Havre
Boise
Nampa
Caldwell
Lewiston
Moscow
Pocatello
Idaho Falls
Twin Falls
Rock Springs
Brigham City
Flathead Lake
Yellowstone Lake
Bear Lake
Crater L.
Malheur L.
Harney L.
Goose L.
American Falls Res.
Owyhee Res.
Arrowrock Res.
Columbia
Snake
Missouri
Fraser
Thompson
Kootenay
Yellowstone
Milk
Salmon
Clearwater
Willamette
Okanogan
Deschutes
John Day
Owyhee
Malheur
Klamath
MT. RAINIER 4392
MT. HOOD 3428
BORAH PK. 3860
GRANITE PK. 3901
GANNETT PK. 4201
STRAWBERRY MT. 2759
IRON MTN. 2386
YELLOWSTONE NATIONAL PARK
GRAND TETON NAT. PARK
GLACIER NATIONAL PARK
WATERTON LAKES N.P.
OLYMPIC NAT. PARK
MT. RAINIER NAT. PARK
NORTH CASCADES N.P.
CRATER LAKE NATIONAL PARK
CRATERS OF THE MOON N.M.
LAVA BEDS N.M.
NAT. REACTOR TESTING STN. (U.S.A.E.C. RES.)
Ice Cap
Feet
10,000
6,000
3,000
1,500
1,000
600
300
Sea Level
Land Depression
Spot Heights in Metres

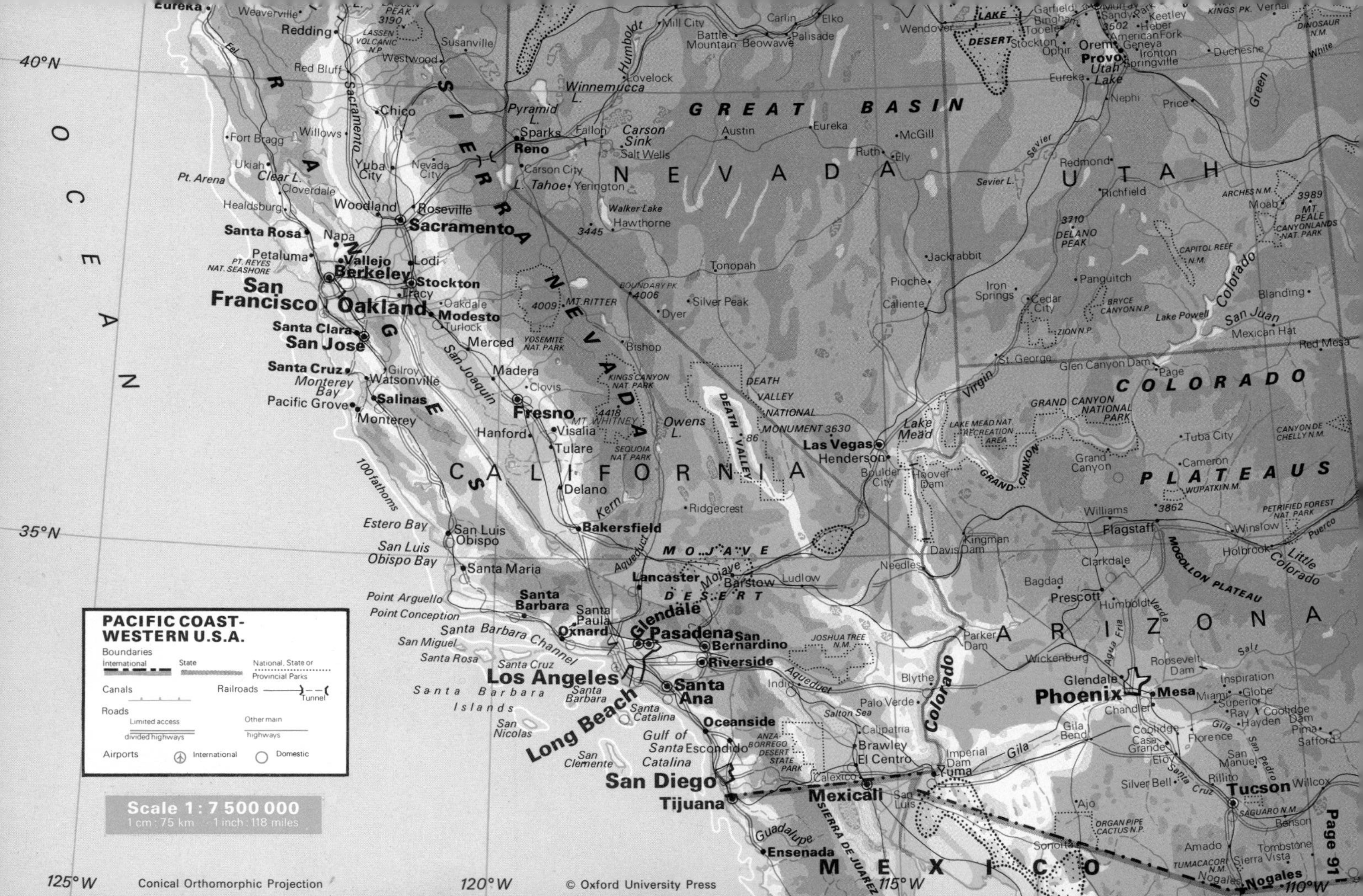

PACIFIC COAST-
WESTERN U.S.A.

Boundaries
International
State
Railroads   National, State or
                   Provincial Park
Canals   (tunnel)
Roads
  Limited access   Other main
  divided highways   Highways
Airports   International   Domestic

Scale 1 : 7 500 000
1 cm 75 km   1 inch 118 miles

Conical Orthomorphic Projection

© Oxford University Press

OCEAN

125° W

120° W

115° W

110° W

40° N

35° N

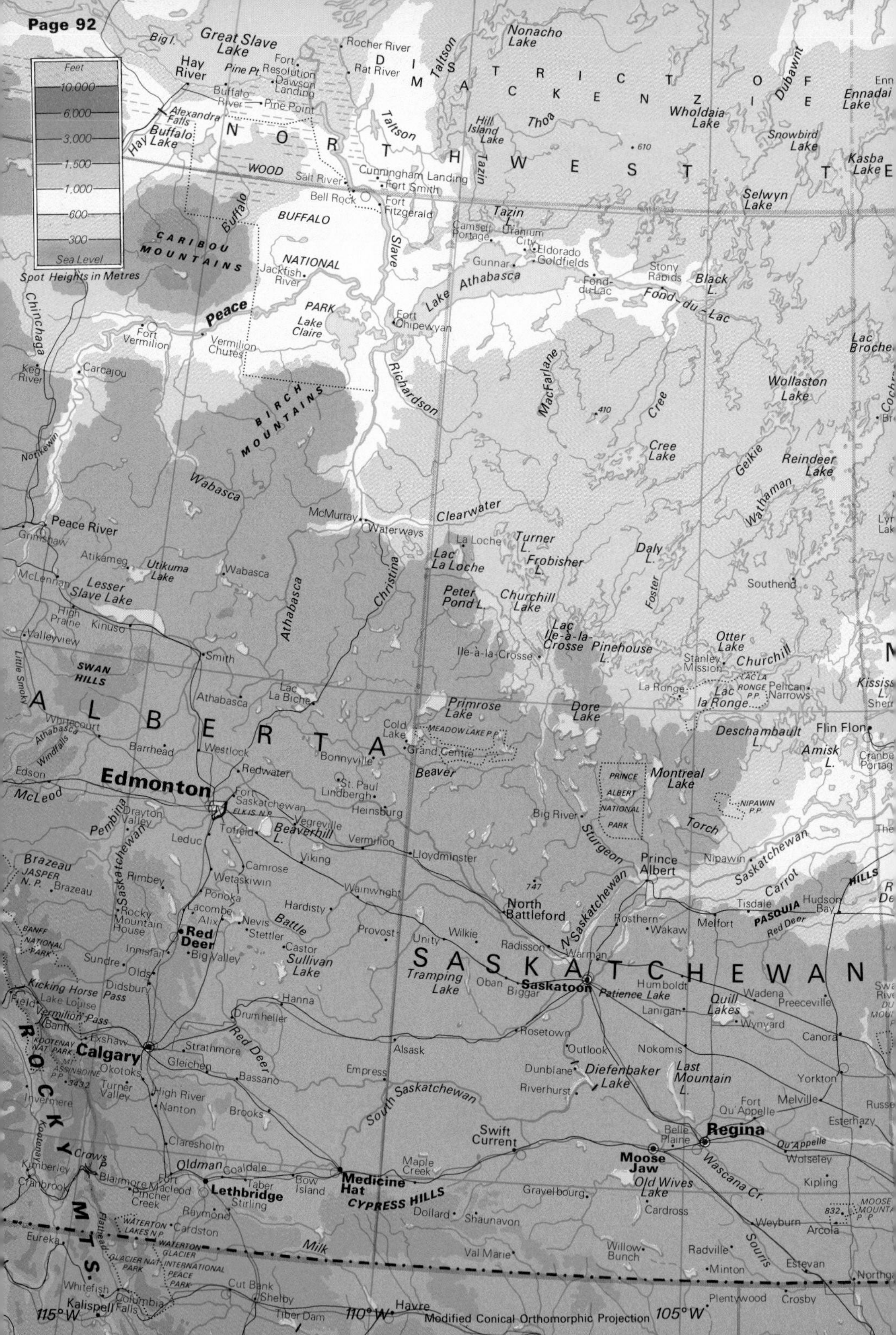
Feet
10,000
6,000
3,000
1,500
1,000
600
300
Sea Level
Spot Heights in Metres
DISTRICT OF MACKENZIE
NORTHWEST T
Great Slave Lake
Hay River
Pine Pt.
Fort Resolution
Dawson Landing
Buffalo River
Pine Point
Alexandra Falls
Buffalo Lake
Rocher River
Rat River
Nonacho Lake
Wholdaia Lake
Snowbird Lake
Kasba Lake
Ennadai Lake
Selwyn Lake
WOOD BUFFALO NATIONAL PARK
Salt River
Cunningham Landing
Fort Smith
Bell Rock
Fort Fitzgerald
Tazin L.
Uranium City
Eldorado
Goldfields
Camsell Portage
Gunnar
Lake Athabasca
Fond-du-Lac
Stony Rapids
Black L.
CARIBOU MOUNTAINS
Jackfish River
Peace
Fort Vermilion
Vermilion Chutes
Lake Claire
Fort Chipewyan
Keg River
Carcajou
BIRCH MOUNTAINS
Richardson
Wollaston Lake
Reindeer Lake
Cree Lake
McMurray
Waterways
Clearwater
Peace River
Grimshaw
La Loche
Lac La Loche
Turner L.
Frobisher L.
Daly L.
Southend
Utikuma Lake
Lesser Slave Lake
Peter Pond L.
Churchill Lake
Ile-à-la-Crosse
Pinehouse L.
Otter Lake
Churchill
Stanley Mission
La Ronge
Lac la Ronge
Pelican Narrows
SWAN HILLS
Smith
Athabasca
Lac La Biche
Primrose Lake
Dore Lake
Deschambault L.
Flin Flon
Amisk L.
ALBERTA
Whitecourt
Barrhead
Westlock
Cold Lake
Grand Centre
Bonnyville
MEADOW LAKE P.P.
PRINCE ALBERT NATIONAL PARK
Montreal Lake
NIPAWIN P.P.
Edmonton
Redwater
St. Paul
Lindbergh
Heinsburg
Fort Saskatchewan
ELK IS. N.P.
Vegreville
Beaverhill L.
Tofield
Vermilion
Lloydminster
Big River
Prince Albert
Nipawin
Saskatchewan
Leduc
Camrose
Viking
Wainwright
Wetaskiwin
Ponoka
Lacombe
Red Deer
Hardisty
Provost
Unity
Wilkie
North Battleford
Tisdale
Melfort
Hudson Bay
PASQUIA HILLS
JASPER N.P.
Brazeau
Rimbey
Rocky Mountain House
BANFF NATIONAL PARK
SASKATCHEWAN
Saskatoon
Tramping Lake
Oban
Biggar
Radisson
Warman
Rosthern
Wakaw
Humboldt
Patience Lake
Quill Lakes
Wadena
Preeceville
Lanigan
Wynyard
Canora
Kicking Horse Pass
Lake Louise
Vermilion Pass
Banff
Exshaw
Calgary
Strathmore
Gleichen
Hanna
Drumheller
Rosetown
Alsask
Outlook
Nokomis
Empress
Dunblane
Diefenbaker Lake
Last Mountain L.
Yorkton
Okotoks
Turner Valley
High River
Nanton
Bassano
Brooks
South Saskatchewan
Riverhurst
Fort Qu'Appelle
Melville
Swift Current
Regina
Moose Jaw
Belle Plaine
Claresholm
Crows P.
Blairmore
Pincher Creek
Fort Macleod
Lethbridge
Coaldale
Taber
Bow Island
Medicine Hat
CYPRESS HILLS
Maple Creek
Gravelbourg
Old Wives Lake
Wascana Cr.
Wolseley
Kipling
Raymond
Stirling
Cardston
WATERTON LAKES N.P.
WATERTON GLACIER INTERNATIONAL PEACE PARK
Dollard
Shaunavon
Cardross
Weyburn
Arcola
Milk
Val Marie
Willow Bunch
Radville
Estevan
Minton
Souris
Eureka
Whitefish
Kalispell
Columbia Falls
Cut Bank
Shelby
Havre
Tiber Dam
Plentywood
Crosby
ROCKY MTS.
115° W
110° W
105° W
Modified Conical Orthomorphic Projection

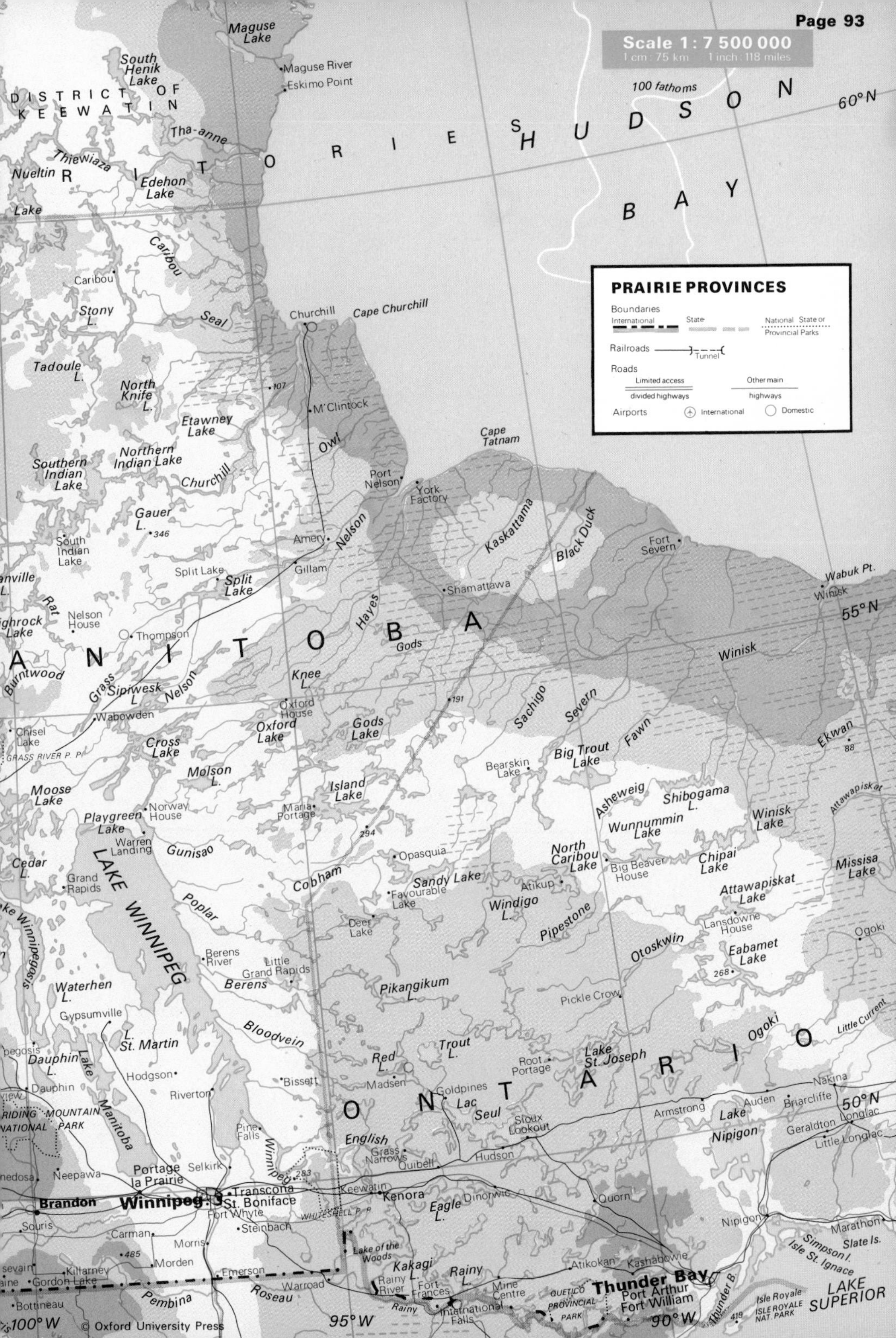

Scale 1 : 7 500 000
1 cm : 75 km   1 inch : 118 miles

100 fathoms

Maguse
Lake

• Maguse River
• Eskimo Point

DISTRICT OF
KEEWATIN

South
Henik
Lake

Tha-anne

HUDSON

BAY

60° N

Nueltin
Lake

ThlewiaZa

R
Edehon
Lake

Caribou

Caribou •

Stony
L.

Seal

Tadoule
L.

North
Knife
L.

Churchill ○   Cape Churchill

• 107

• M'Clintock

Etawney
Lake

Owl

Cape
Tatnam

Southern
Indian
Lake

Northern
Indian
Lake

Churchill

Port
Nelson

York
Factory

Kaskattama

Black Duck

Fort
Severn

PRAIRIE PROVINCES

Boundaries
International   State   National   State or
                                            Provincial Parks
Railroads ────── ─ ─ ─
                   Tunnel
Roads
Limited access   Other main
divided highways   highways
Airports   ⊕ International   ○ Domestic

Gauer
L.

• 346

Amery •

Nelson

Split Lake

Split
Lake

Gillam •

Shamattawa •

Wabuk Pt.
Winisk

55° N

South
Indian
Lake

anville

Rat

Nelson
House

Thompson •

Hayes

Gods

Winisk

ghrock
Lake

Burntwood

A N I T O B A

Knee

Split Lake

Sipiwesk

Nelson

Grass

Wabowden •

Oxford
House

• 191

Sachigo

Severn

Fawn

Ekwan

• 88

Chisel
Lake •

GRASS RIVER P. P.

Cross
Lake

Molson
L.

Oxford
Lake

Gods
Lake

Island
Lake

Bearskin
Lake •

Big Trout
Lake

Asheweig

Shibogama

Winisk
Lake

Missisa
Lake

Moose
Lake

Playgreen
Lake

• Norway
House

Maria
Portage

Wunnummin
Lake

Chipai
Lake

Attawapiskat

Cedar

Warren
Landing

Gunisao

Opasquia •

• 294

Sandy Lake

North
Caribou
Lake

Big Beaver
House

Attawapiskat
Lake

Ogoki

Grand
Rapids

L A K E   W I N N I P E G

Cobham

Favourable
Lake •

Atikup •

Windigo
L.

Pipestone

Lansdowne
House

Eabamet
Lake

ke Winnipegosis

Poplar

Deer
Lake •

• 268

Otoskwin

Waterhen
L.

Berens
River

Little
Grand Rapids

Berens

Pikangikum

Pickle Crow •

Little Current

Gypsumville •

Bloodvein

Red
L.

Trout
L.

Lake
St. Joseph

Ogoki

Nakina

L.
St. Martin

Hodgson •

Madsen •

Bissett •

Root
Portage

Goldpines •

Armstrong •

Nipigon

Lake

Auden •   Briarcliffe •

50° N

egosis

Dauphin
Lake

Dauphin •

Riverton •

English

Lac
Seul

Sioux
Lookout •

Hudson

Geraldton   Longlac

Little Longlac

RIDING MOUNTAIN
NATIONAL PARK

view

MANITOBA

Neepawa •

Pine
Falls

Grass
Narrows

Quibell •

Quorn •

Nipigon •

Marathon •

Simpson I.
Slate Is.

ndosa

Portage
la Prairie

Selkirk •

Transcona

Keewatin

Kenora

Eagle
L.

Dinorwic •

Isle St. Ignace

Brandon   **Winnipeg**   St. Boniface

Fort Whyte •

• 283

Nipigon

Slate B

Souris •

Carman •

Morris •

Steinbach •

Lake of the
Woods

WHITESHELL P. P.

Kakagi
L.

Rainy
L.

Mine
Centre •

Atikokan •

Kashabowie •

Port Arthur
Thunder Bay
Fort William

Isle Royale
ISLE ROYALE
NAT. PARK

LAKE
SUPERIOR

sevarin

Killarney •

• 485

Morden •

Emerson •

Roseau

Warroad •

Rainy
River

Fort
Frances

International
Falls

QUETICO
PROVINCIAL
PARK

• 419

ega

Gordon Lake •

Pembina

Rainy

Bottineau •

100° W   © Oxford University Press   95° W   90° W

O N T A R I O

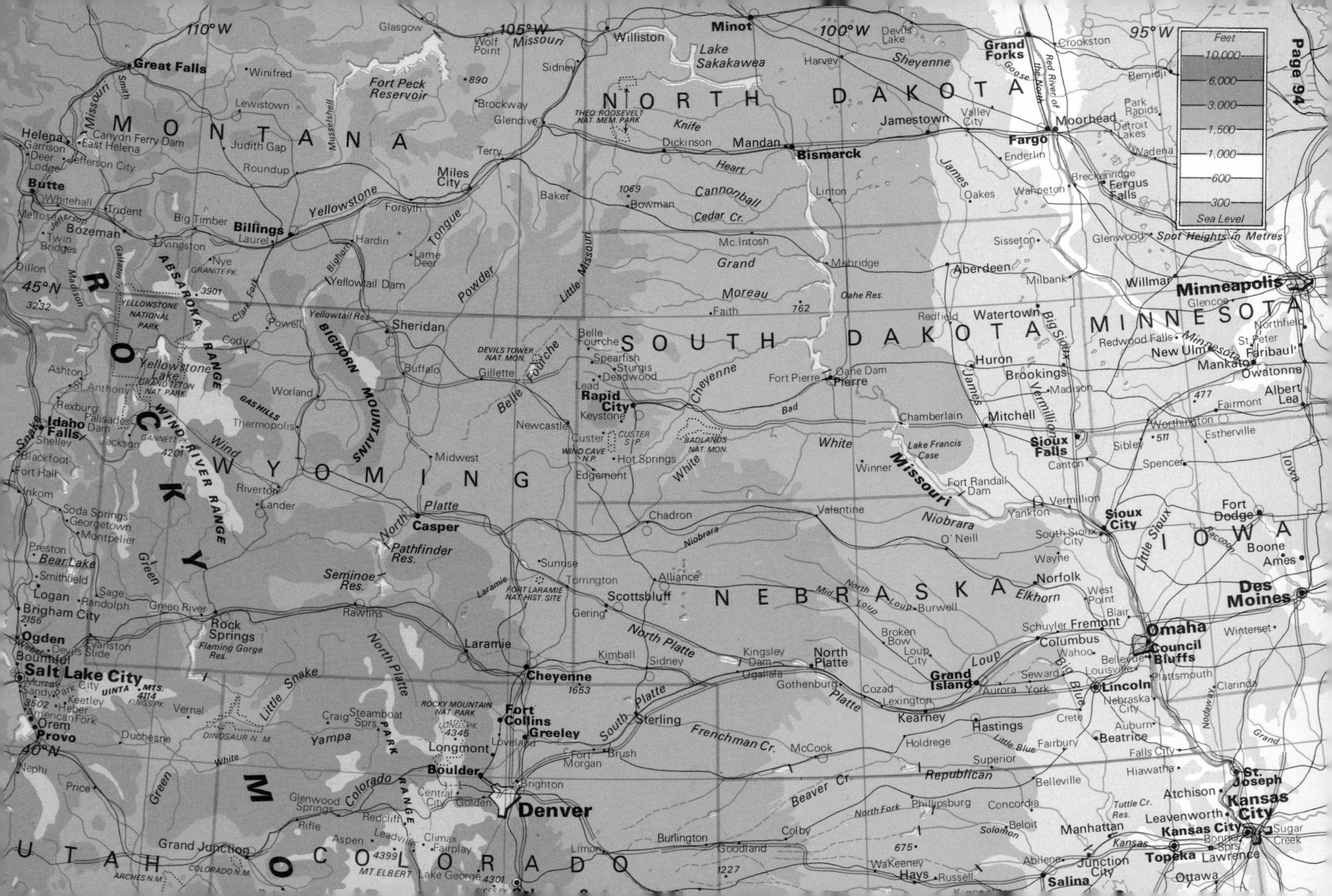
Feet
10,000
6,000
3,000
1,500
1,000
600
300
Sea Level
Spot Heights in Metres
110°W
105°W
100°W
95°W
45°N
40°N
MONTANA
NORTH DAKOTA
SOUTH DAKOTA
MINNESOTA
IOWA
NEBRASKA
WYOMING
COLORADO
UTAH
ROCKY MOUNTAINS
BIGHORN MOUNTAINS
ABSAROKA RANGE
WIND RIVER RANGE
PARK RANGE
GAS HILLS
YELLOWSTONE NATIONAL PARK
GRAND TETON NAT. PARK
THEO. ROOSEVELT NAT. MEM. PARK
DEVILS TOWER NAT. MON.
BADLANDS NAT. MON.
WIND CAVE N.P.
CUSTER S.P.
FORT LARAMIE NAT. HIST. SITE
ROCKY MOUNTAIN NAT. PARK
DINOSAUR N. M.
COLORADO N.M.
ARCHES N.M.
UINTA MTS.
Great Falls
Helena
Butte
Bozeman
Billings
Miles City
Glendive
Williston
Minot
Bismarck
Mandan
Jamestown
Fargo
Grand Forks
Moorhead
Fergus Falls
Aberdeen
Pierre
Rapid City
Huron
Brookings
Mitchell
Sioux Falls
Minneapolis
Mankato
Albert Lea
Sioux City
Fort Dodge
Des Moines
Omaha
Council Bluffs
Lincoln
Grand Island
Kearney
Hastings
North Platte
Scottsbluff
Casper
Sheridan
Cheyenne
Laramie
Rock Springs
Fort Collins
Greeley
Boulder
Denver
Grand Junction
Ogden
Salt Lake City
Provo
Idaho Falls
St. Joseph
Kansas City
Topeka
Salina
Missouri
Yellowstone
Platte
North Platte
South Platte
Niobrara
Cheyenne
Red River of the North
Lake Sakakawea
Fort Peck Reservoir
Lake Francis Case
Oahe Res.
Pathfinder Res.
Seminoe Res.
Flaming Gorge Res.
Yellowstone Lake
Bear Lake
MT. ELBERT
4399
4345
4301
4201
4114
3901
3502
3232
2156
1653
1227
1069
890
762
675
511
477

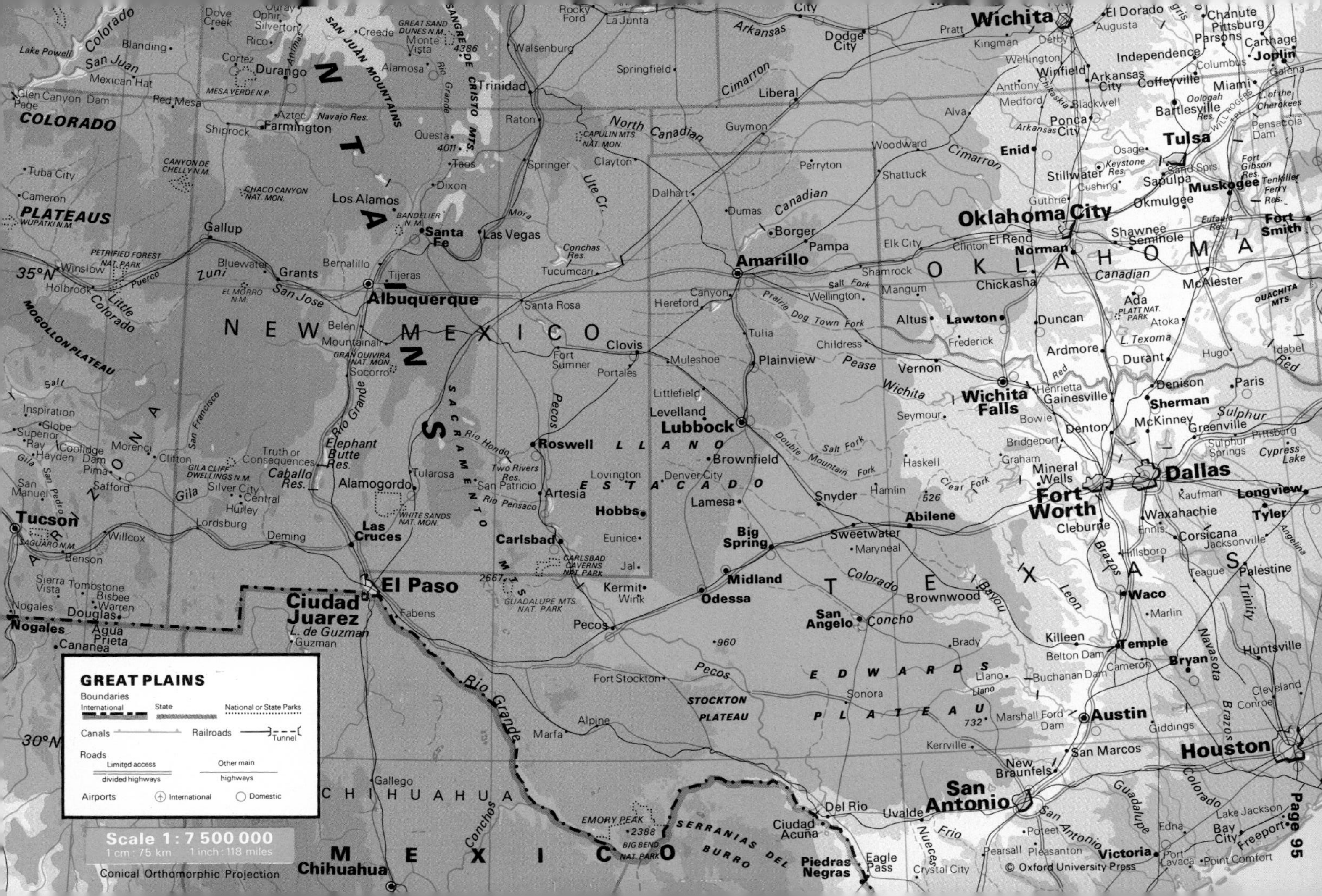

GREAT PLAINS

Boundaries
International
State   National or State Parks

Canals   Railroads
                         Tunnel

Roads
Limited access   Other main
                         highways
divided highways

Airports + International   ○ Domestic

Scale 1:7 500 000
1 cm = 75 km   1 inch = 118 miles

Conical Orthomorphic Projection

© Oxford University Press

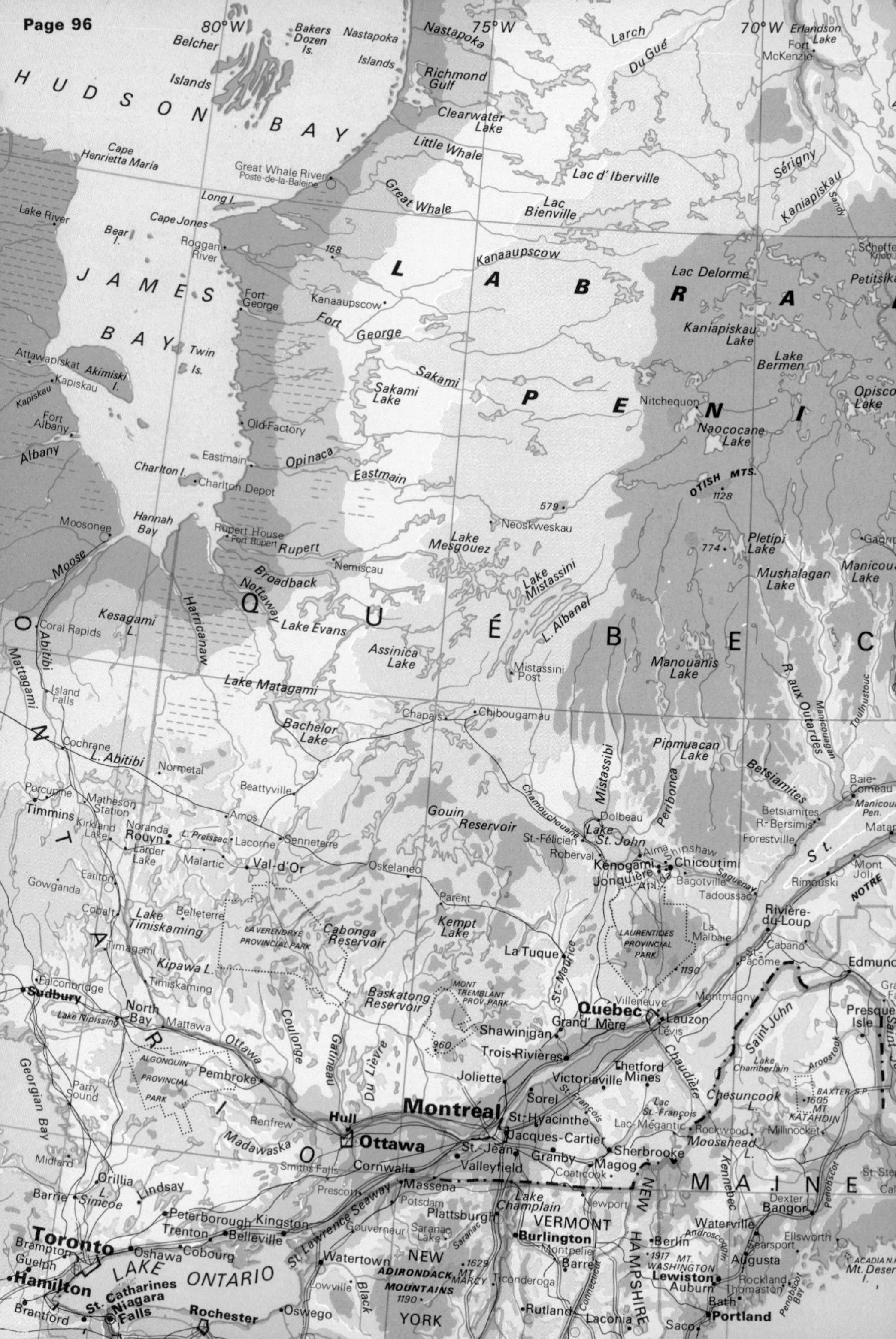

80°W
Belcher
Bakers
Dozen Is.
Nastapoka
Islands
Nastapoka
75°W
Larch
Du Gué
70°W
Erlandson
Lake
Fort
McKenzie

H U D S O N   B A Y

Richmond
Gulf

Clearwater
Lake

Little Whale

Sérigny

Lac d' Iberville

Kaniapiskau

Cape
Henrietta Maria

Great Whale River
Poste-de-la-Baleine

Great Whale

Lac
Bienville

Long I.

Cape Jones

L A B R A

Scheffe
Kjobi I

Bear
I.

Roggan
River

168

Kanaaupscow

Lac Delorme

Petitsika

Fort
George

Kanaaupscow

Fort   George

Kaniapiskau
Lake

Lake
Bermen

Opisco
Lake

J A M E S

Twin
Is.

Sakami

P E N I

Attawapiskat   Akimiski
I.

Kapiskau

Sakami
Lake

Nitchequon

Naococane
Lake

Kapiskau
Fort
Albany

Old-Factory

Eastmain

Opinaca

OTISH MTS.
1128

Albany

Charlton I.

Charlton Depot

Eastmain

579

Pletipi
Lake

Gagn

Moosonee
Hannah
Bay

Neoskweskau

774

Mushalagan
Lake

Manicou
Lake

Moose

Rupert House
Fort Rupert

Rupert

Nemiscau

Lake
Mesgouez

Lake
Mistassini

Coral Rapids

Kesagami
L.

Nottaway

Broadback

Lake Evans

L. Albanel

Manouanis
Lake

Q U É

B E

C

Mattagami

Abitibi

Island
Falls

Harricanaw

Lake Matagami

Assinica
Lake

Mistassini
Post

R. aux Outardes

Baie-
Comeau

Manicou
Pen.

Matar

Cochrane

L. Abitibi

Normetal

Chapais

Chibougamau

Pipmuacan
Lake

Betsiamites

O N T

Porcupine

Matheson
Station

Beattyville

Betsiamites
R-Bersimis

Forestville

Mont
Jol

Timmins

Kirkland
Lake

Noranda
Rouyn

Amos

Gouin

Reservoir

Dolbeau

Lake

St-Félicien

St. John

Almа

Shipshaw

Chicoutimi

Bagotville

Tadoussac

Rimouski

NOTRE

Larder
Lake

L. Preissac

Lacorne

Senneterre

Roberval

Kenogami

Jonquière

ALMA

Gowganda

Earlton

Malartic

Val-d'Or

Oskelaneo

Parent

La
Malbaie

Rivière-
du-Loup

Cabano

Edmund

Cobalt
Belleterre

LA VERENDRYE
PROVINCIAL PARK

Cabonga
Reservoir

Kempt
Lake

1190

Pacôme

Lake
Timiskaming

Kipawa L.

Timiskaming

Baskatong
Reservoir

La Tuque

Villeneuve

Montmagny

Lac
Chamberlain

Presque
Isle

Sudbury

Falconbridge

Algamami

North
Bay

Mattawa

MONT
TREMBLANT
PROV. PARK

LAURENTIDES
PROVINCIAL
PARK

Saint John

Aroostook

Ga

Lake Nipissing

ALGONQUIN
PROVINCIAL
PARK

Ottawa

960

Grand' Mère

Québec

Lauzon
Lévis

Chaudière

Chesuncook

BAXTER S.P.
MT.
KATAHDIN

Parry
Sound

Pembroke

Coulonge

Shawinigan

Trois-Rivières

Thetford
Mines

Lac
St-François

Rockwood

Moosehead
L.

Millinocket

Georgian
Bay

Renfrew

Madawaska

Du Lièvre

Gatineau

Joliette

Victoriaville

Lac
Mégantic

Sherbrooke

Kennebec

St Ste
Cal

Midland

Hull

Montreal

Sorel

St-Hyacinthe

Granby

Magog

Coaticook

M A I N E

Orillia
L.
Simcoe

Barrie

Lindsay

Smiths Falls

Ottawa

Cornwall

Jacques-Cartier

St-Jean

Valleyfield

M A I N E

Dexter
Bangor

Peterborough

Kingston

Prescott

Massena

Potsdam

Lake
Champlain

Newport

Waterville

Androscog

Ellsworth

ACADIA N
Mt. I.

Toronto

Oshawa

Cobourg

Belleville

Gouverneur

Plattsburgh
Saranac

Burlington

Montpelier

Barres

1917 MT.
WASHINGTON
1605

Augusta

Rockland

Thomaston

Guelph

Trenton

Lowville

Watertown

NEW

VERMONT

Berlin

NEW
HAMPSHIRE

Lewiston
Auburn

Searsport

Hamilton

St. Catharines

L A K E   O N T A R I O

1629 MT.
MARCY

ADIRONDACK
MOUNTAINS
1190

Ticonderoga

Laconia

Bath

Portland

Brantford

Niagara
Falls

Rochester

Oswego

Black

YORK

Rutland

Saco

Penobsc

Potosi

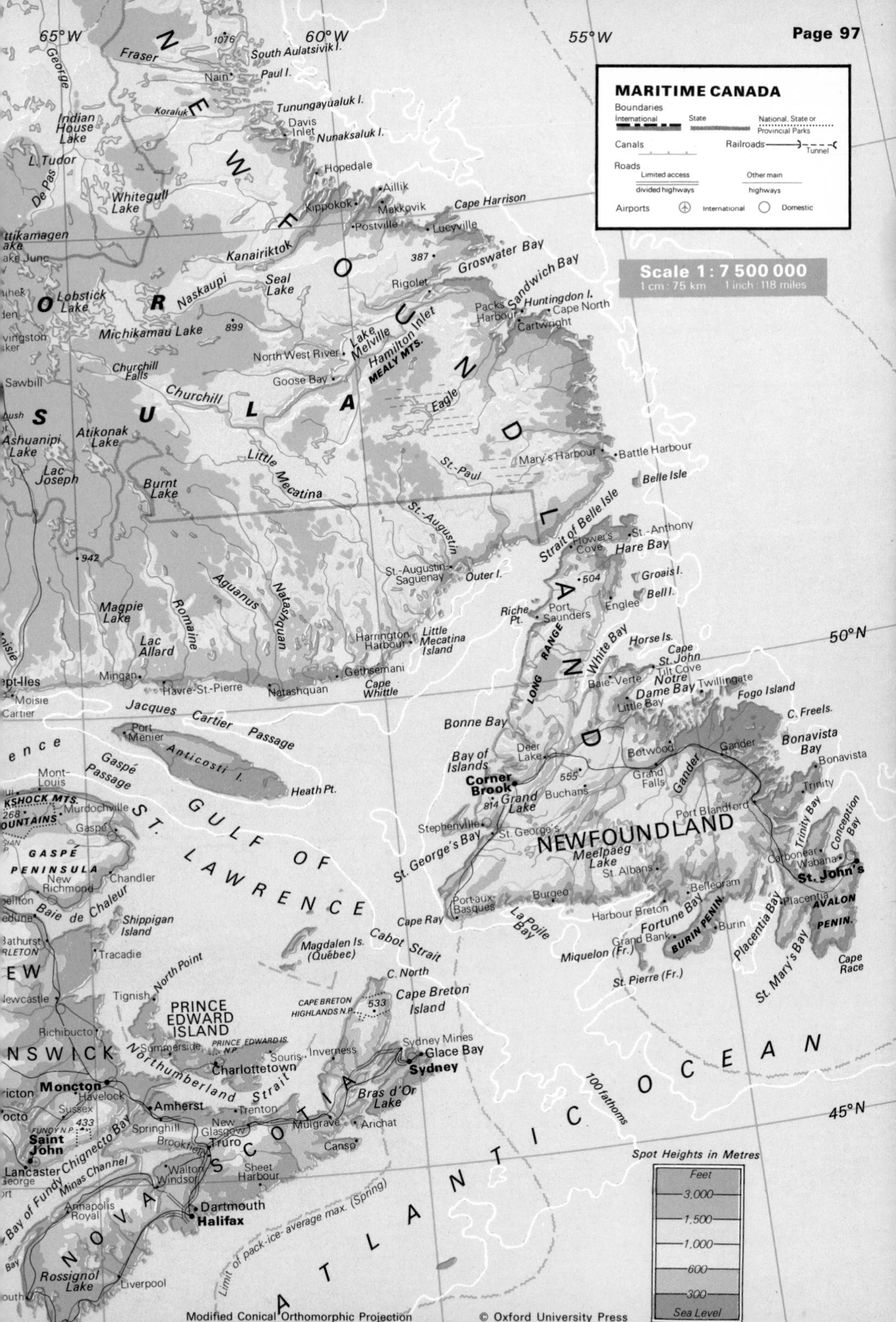
Page 97
MARITIME CANADA
Boundaries
International
State
National, State or Provincial Parks
Canals
Railroads
Tunnel
Roads
Limited access divided highways
Other main highways
Airports
International
Domestic
Scale 1 : 7 500 000
1 cm : 75 km
1 inch : 118 miles
65°W
60°W
55°W
50°N
45°N
NEWFOUNDLAND
LABRADOR
Fraser
George
Nain
Paul I.
South Aulatsivik I.
Tunungayualuk I.
Koraluk
Davis Inlet
Nunaksaluk I.
Indian House Lake
L. Tudor
De Pas
Hopedale
Whitegull Lake
Aillik
Kippokok
Makkovik
Cape Harrison
Postville
Lucyville
Kanairiktok
387
Groswater Bay
Sandwich Bay
Rigolet
Seal Lake
Naskaupi
Lobstick Lake
Michikamau Lake
899
Huntingdon I.
Packs Harbour
Cape North
Cartwright
Lake Melville
Hamilton Inlet
North West River
MEALY MTS.
Churchill Falls
Goose Bay
Churchill
Sawbill
Eagle
Ashuanipi Lake
Atikonak Lake
Lac Joseph
Burnt Lake
Little Mecatina
Mary's Harbour
Battle Harbour
St.-Paul
Belle Isle
Strait of Belle Isle
St.-Augustin
St.-Anthony
Flower's Cove
Hare Bay
942
St.-Augustin-Saguenay
Outer I.
504
Groais I.
Bell I.
Aguanus
Natashquan
Romaine
Magpie Lake
Lac Allard
Riche Pt.
Port Saunders
Englee
Harrington Harbour
Little Mecatina Island
LONG RANGE
White Bay
Horse Is.
Cape St. John
Tilt Cove
Mingan
Havre-St.-Pierre
Natashquan
Gethsemani
Cape Whittle
Baie-Verte
Notre Dame Bay
Twillingate
Fogo Island
Little Bay
C. Freels.
Moisie
Jacques Cartier Passage
Port Menier
Anticosti I.
Bonne Bay
Bonavista Bay
Bonavista
Deer Lake
Botwood
Gander
Gaspé Passage
Mont-Louis
Bay of Islands
Corner Brook
555
Grand Falls
Trinity
Heath Pt.
Murdochville
814
Grand Lake
Buchans
Port Blandford
Trinity Bay
Conception Bay
Gaspé
GULF OF ST. LAWRENCE
Stephenville
St. George's
St. George's Bay
NEWFOUNDLAND
Meelpaeg Lake
St. Albans
Carbonear
Wabana
St. John's
GASPÉ PENINSULA
Chandler
New Richmond
Port-aux-Basques
Burgeo
Belleoram
Placentia
AVALON PENIN.
Baie de Chaleur
Shippigan Island
Cape Ray
La Poile Bay
Harbour Breton
Fortune Bay
BURIN PENIN.
Burin
Placentia Bay
Bathurst
Tracadie
Magdalen Is. (Québec)
Cabot Strait
Grand Bank
Miquelon (Fr.)
St. Mary's Bay
Cape Race
North Point
C. North
St. Pierre (Fr.)
Tignish
PRINCE EDWARD ISLAND
CAPE BRETON HIGHLANDS N.P.
533
Cape Breton Island
Newcastle
Richibucto
Summerside
PRINCE EDWARD IS. N.P.
Souris
Inverness
Sydney Mines
Glace Bay
Sydney
NEW BRUNSWICK
Charlottetown
Northumberland Strait
Moncton
Havelock
Bras d'Or Lake
100 fathoms
OCEAN
Sussex
Amherst
Trenton
FUNDY N.P.
433
Springhill
New Glasgow
Mulgrave
Arichat
Saint John
Chignecto Bay
Brookfield
Truro
Canso
Lancaster
Minas Channel
Walton
Windsor
Sheet Harbour
NOVA SCOTIA
Bay of Fundy
Annapolis Royal
Dartmouth
Halifax
ATLANTIC
Limit of pack-ice - average max. (Spring)
Rossignol Lake
Liverpool
Spot Heights in Metres
Feet
3,000
1,500
1,000
600
300
Sea Level
Modified Conical Orthomorphic Projection
© Oxford University Press

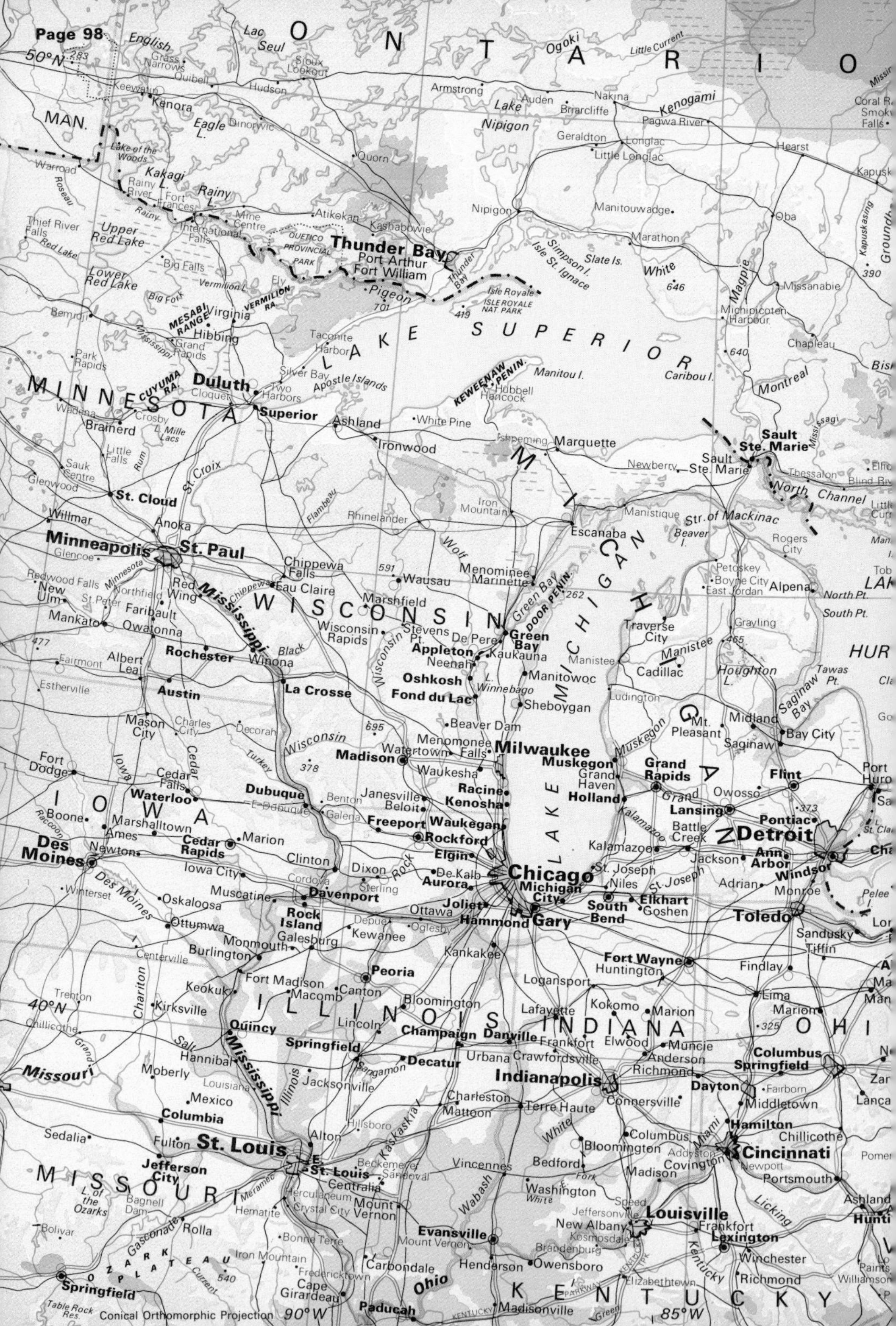

Page 98
50°N
English
Lac Seul
ONTARIO
Ogoki
Little Current
Grassy Narrows
Sioux Lookout
Quibell
Hudson
Keewatin
Kenora
Armstrong
Lake Nipigon
Auden
Nakina
Kenogami
Coral Rapids
Smoky Falls
MAN.
Eagle L.
Dinorwic
Briarcliffe
Pagwa River
Geraldton
Longlac
Little Longlac
Hearst
Lake of the Woods
Warroad
Roseau
Kakagi L.
Rainy River
Fort Frances
Rainy L.
Quorn
Kapuskasing
Nipigon
Manitouwadge
Oba
Thief River Falls
Red Lake
Upper Red Lake
Lower Red Lake
International Falls
Mine Centre
Atikokan
Kashabowie
QUETICO PROVINCIAL PARK
Thunder Bay
Port Arthur
Fort William
Simpson I.
Isle St. Ignace
Slate Is.
Marathon
White
646
Magpie
390
Big Falls
Vermilion L.
Big Fork
Ely
Pigeon
701
Isle Royale
ISLE ROYALE NAT. PARK
419
Missanabie
Bemidji
MESABI RANGE
VERMILION RA.
Virginia
Hibbing
Grand Rapids
Mississippi
Michipicoten Harbour
Taconite Harbor
LAKE SUPERIOR
Chapleau
640
Park Rapids
CUYUMA RA.
Duluth
Cloquet
Silver Bay
Two Harbors
Apostle Islands
KEWEENAW PENIN.
Manitou I.
Hubbell
Hancock
Caribou I.
Montreal
MINNESOTA
Wadena
Brainerd
Crosby
L. Mille Lacs
Superior
Ashland
White Pine
Ironwood
Ishpeming
Marquette
Sault Ste. Marie
Mississagi
Little Falls
Rum
St. Croix
Newberry
Thessalon
Sauk Centre
Glenwood
St. Cloud
Flambeau
Iron Mountain
North Channel
Willmar
Anoka
Rhinelander
Manistique
Str. of Mackinac
Escanaba
Beaver I.
Rogers City
Minneapolis
St. Paul
Glencoe
Wolf
MICHIGAN
Chippewa Falls
591
Wausau
Menominee
Marinette
Petoskey
Boyne City
East Jordan
Alpena
Redwood Falls
Minnesota
New Ulm
Northfield
St. Peter
Red Wing
Eau Claire
Chippewa
WISCONSIN
Green Bay
DOOR PENIN.
262
North Pt.
South Pt.
Faribault
Mankato
Owatonna
Mississippi
Marshfield
Wisconsin Rapids
Stevens Pt.
De Pere
Green Bay
Appleton
Kaukauna
Traverse City
Grayling
465
HURON
477
Fairmont
Albert Lea
Rochester
Winona
Black
Neenah
Oshkosh
L. Winnebago
Manitowoc
Manistee
Cadillac
Houghton L.
Tawas Pt.
Estherville
Austin
La Crosse
Fond du Lac
Sheboygan
Ludington
Saginaw Bay
Mason City
Charles City
Decorah
695
Beaver Dam
Muskegon
Mt. Pleasant
Midland
Bay City
Saginaw
Cedar
Turkey
Wisconsin
Madison
Watertown
Menomonee Falls
Milwaukee
Muskegon
Grand Haven
Grand Rapids
Flint
Port Huron
Fort Dodge
Iowa
378
Waukesha
Racine
Kenosha
Holland
Grand
Owosso
Lansing
373
IOWA
Cedar Falls
Waterloo
Dubuque
E. Dubuque
Benton
Galena
Janesville
Beloit
Kalamazoo
Battle Creek
Pontiac
Boone
Racoon
Marshalltown
Ames
Cedar Rapids
Marion
Freeport
Rockford
Waukegan
LAKE MICHIGAN
Detroit
Des Moines
Newton
Clinton
Elgin
Kalamazoo
Jackson
Ann Arbor
Windsor
Iowa City
Dixon
Rock
De Kalb
Aurora
Chicago
St. Joseph
Winterset
Des Moines
Muscatine
Cordova
Sterling
Davenport
Michigan City
Niles
St. Joseph
Adrian
Monroe
Pelee I.
Oskaloosa
Rock Island
Ottawa
Joliet
South Bend
Elkhart
Goshen
Toledo
Ottumwa
Depue
Oglesby
Kewanee
Hammond
Gary
Sandusky
Monmouth
Galesburg
Burlington
Centerville
Kankakee
Fort Wayne
Huntington
Tiffin
Findlay
Trenton
Fort Madison
Peoria
Canton
Keokuk
Macomb
Logansport
Lima
Chariton
Kirksville
40°N
Bloomington
ILLINOIS
Kokomo
Marion
Marion
Chillicothe
Grand
Quincy
Lincoln
Champaign
Danville
Lafayette
INDIANA
Frankfort
Elwood
Muncie
Anderson
325
OHIO
Salt
Springfield
Urbana
Crawfordsville
Richmond
Columbus
Springfield
Missouri
Hannibal
Mississippi
Illinois
Sangamon
Decatur
Indianapolis
Dayton
Fairborn
Moberly
Louisiana
Jacksonville
Middletown
Mexico
Charleston
Mattoon
Terre Haute
Connersville
Columbia
Kaskaskia
Hillsboro
Hamilton
Chillicothe
Sedalia
Fulton
St. Louis
Alton
White
Columbus
Bloomington
Addyston
Miami
Cincinnati
Jefferson City
E. St. Louis
Beckemeyer
Sandoval
Vincennes
Bedford
Covington
Newport
MISSOURI
Meramec
Centralia
Fork
Madison
Portsmouth
L. of the Ozarks
Bagnell Dam
Herculaneum
Crystal City
Wabash
Washington
White
Hematite
Mount Vernon
Speed
Jeffersonville
Louisville
Ashland
Licking
Bolivar
Gasconade
Rolla
Evansville
Mount Vernon
New Albany
Kosmosdale
Frankfort
Lexington
Bonne Terre
Brandenburg
OZARK PLATEAU
Iron Mountain
Henderson
Owensboro
Winchester
540
Current
Fredericktown
Carbondale
Kentucky
Springfield
Cape Girardeau
Ohio
Elizabethtown
Richmond
KENTUCKY
Table Rock Res.
Conical Orthomorphic Projection
90°W
Paducah
Madisonville
Green
85°W

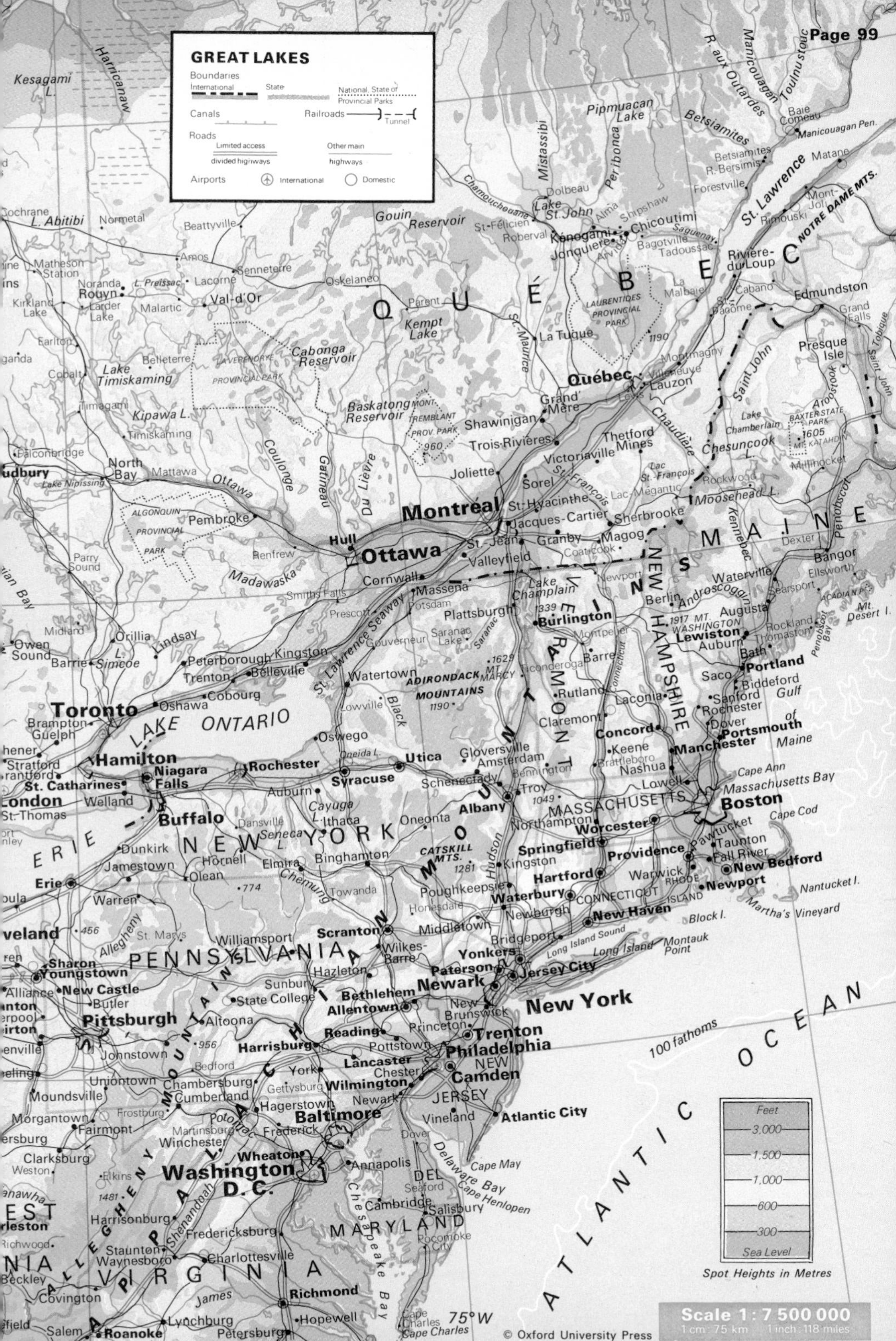

GREAT LAKES
Boundaries
International
State
National, State or Provincial Parks
Canals
Railroads
Tunnel
Roads
Limited access divided highways
Other main highways
Airports
International
Domestic
Q U É B E C
M A I N E
NEW YORK
PENNSYLVANIA
VERMONT
NEW HAMPSHIRE
MASSACHUSETTS
CONNECTICUT
RHODE ISLAND
NEW JERSEY
MARYLAND
DEL
V I R G I N I A
ATLANTIC OCEAN
LAKE ONTARIO
ERIE
APPALACHIAN MOUNTAINS
ALLEGHENY MTS.
ADIRONDACK MOUNTAINS
CATSKILL MTS.
NOTRE DAME MTS.
LAURENTIDES PROVINCIAL PARK
ALGONQUIN PROVINCIAL PARK
LAVERENDRYE PROVINCIAL PARK
MONT TREMBLANT PROV. PARK
BAXTER STATE PARK
ACADIA N.P.
Montreal
Ottawa
Hull
Québec
Lauzon
Trois-Rivières
Shawinigan
Sherbrooke
Toronto
Hamilton
Niagara Falls
St. Catharines
London
Buffalo
Rochester
Syracuse
Utica
Albany
Boston
Worcester
Springfield
Providence
Hartford
New Haven
New York
Newark
Jersey City
Yonkers
Paterson
Philadelphia
Camden
Trenton
Baltimore
Washington D.C.
Wilmington
Pittsburgh
Erie
Scranton
Allentown
Bethlehem
Reading
Harrisburg
Lancaster
Richmond
Roanoke
Portland
Manchester
Concord
Burlington
Bangor
Lewiston
Augusta
Chicoutimi
Jonquière
Kénogami
Sudbury
Kingston
Oshawa
Peterborough
Atlantic City
New Bedford
Newport
Cape Cod
Cape Ann
Massachusetts Bay
Gulf of Maine
Long Island
Long Island Sound
Martha's Vineyard
Nantucket I.
Block I.
Montauk Point
Cape May
Cape Henlopen
Delaware Bay
Chesapeake Bay
Cape Charles
100 fathoms
St. Lawrence
St. Lawrence Seaway
Ottawa
Hudson
Lake Champlain
Lake St. John
Moosehead L.
Gouin Reservoir
Cabonga Reservoir
Baskatong Reservoir
Lake Timiskaming
Lake Nipissing
L. Simcoe
Oneida L.
Cayuga L.
Seneca L.
75°W
Feet
3,000
1,500
1,000
600
300
Sea Level
Spot Heights in Metres
Scale 1 : 7 500 000
1 cm : 75 km
1 inch : 118 miles

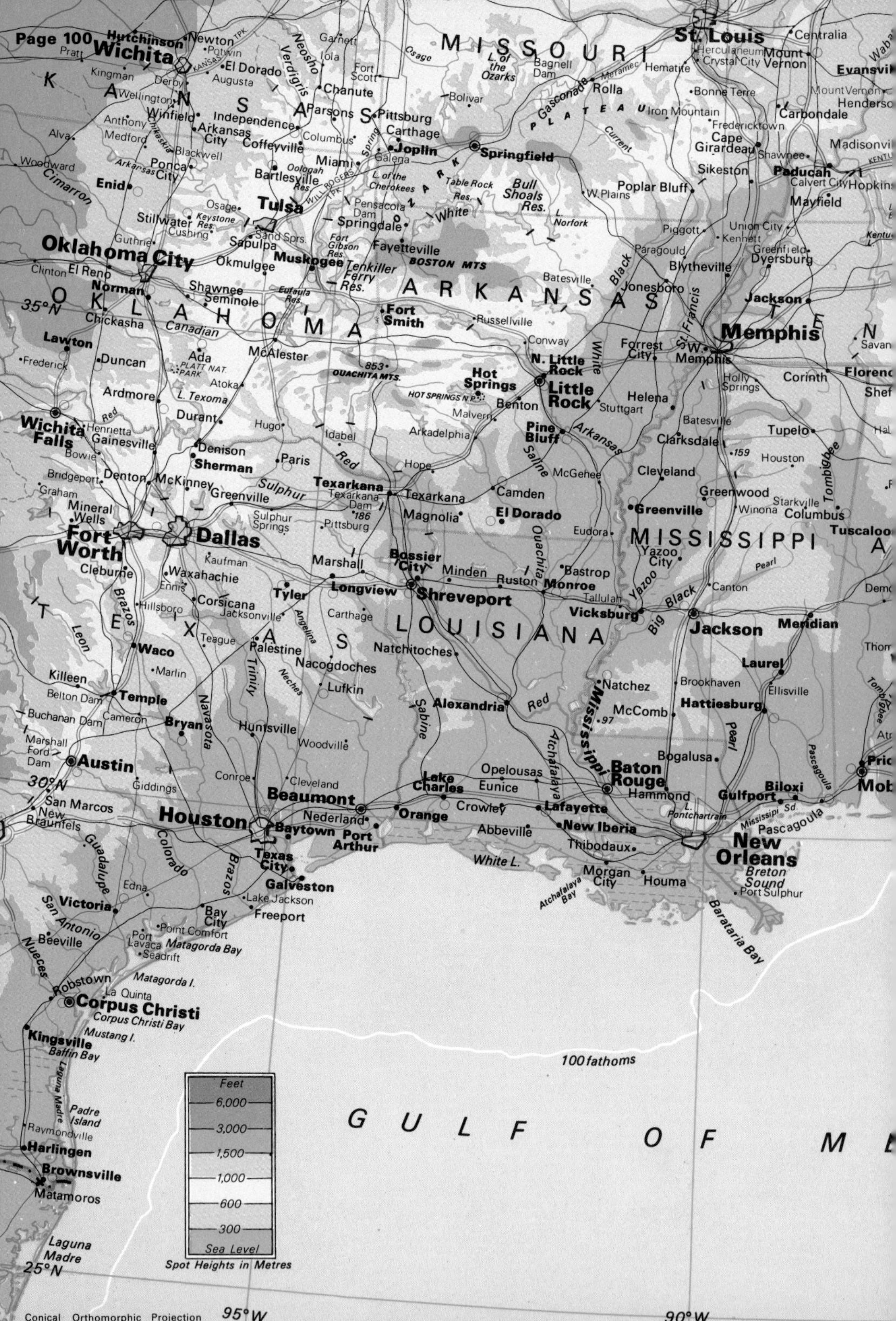

Page 100
Hutchinson
Newton
Pratt
Wichita
Potwin
KANSAS TPK.
El Dorado
Augusta
Kingman
Derby
KANSAS
Wellington
Winfield
Anthony
Independence
Arkansas City
Coffeyville
Alva
Medford
Blackwell
Woodward
Cimarron
Ponca City
Enid
Stillwater
Keystone Res.
Cushing
Osage
Guthrie
Oklahoma City
El Reno
Clinton
Norman
Shawnee
Seminole
35°N
OKLAHOMA
Chickasha
Canadian
Lawton
Frederick
Duncan
Ada
PLATT NAT. PARK
Atoka
Ardmore
L. Texoma
Durant
Wichita Falls
Henrietta
Red
Gainesville
Bowie
Denison
Sherman
Bridgeport
Denton
McKinney
Graham
Mineral Wells
Greenville
Fort Worth
Dallas
Kaufman
Cleburne
Waxahachie
Ennis
Corsicana
Brazos
Hillsboro
Jacksonville
TEXAS
Leon
Waco
Teague
Palestine
Killeen
Marlin
Belton Dam
Temple
Buchanan Dam
Cameron
Bryan
Marshall Ford Dam
Austin
30°N
Giddings
San Marcos
New Braunfels
Guadalupe
Houston
Colorado
Victoria
Edna
San Antonio
Beeville
Nueces
Port Lavaca
Matagorda Bay
Seadrift
Point Comfort
Bay City
Matagorda I.
Robstown
La Quinta
Corpus Christi
Corpus Christi Bay
Mustang I.
Kingsville
Baffin Bay
Laguna Madre
Padre Island
Raymondville
Harlingen
Brownsville
Matamoros
Laguna Madre
25°N
Garnett
Iola
Neosho
Verdigris
Osage
Fort Scott
Chanute
Parsons
Pittsburg
Columbus
Carthage
Joplin
Miami
Galena
Oologah Res.
Bartlesville
WILL ROGERS TPK.
L. of the Cherokees
Pensacola Dam
Tulsa
Sand Sprs.
Sapulpa
Okmulgee
Muskogee
Fort Gibson Res.
Tenkiller Ferry Res.
Eufaula Res.
Springdale
Fayetteville
BOSTON MTS
Fort Smith
McAlester
853
OUACHITA MTS.
Hugo
Idabel
Paris
Sulphur
Sulphur Springs
Texarkana
Texarkana Dam
186
Pittsburg
Marshall
Longview
Tyler
Carthage
Angelina
Nacogdoches
Neches
Lufkin
Trinity
Navasota
Huntsville
Woodville
Conroe
Cleveland
Beaumont
Baytown
Nederland
Port Arthur
Orange
Texas City
Galveston
Lake Jackson
Freeport
Brazos
MISSOURI
L. of the Ozarks
Bagnell Dam
Meramec
Gasconade
Rolla
Bolivar
OZARK PLATEAU
Current
Springfield
Table Rock Res.
Bull Shoals Res.
White
W. Plains
Norfolk
L. Norfolk
Poplar Bluff
ARKANSAS
Batesville
Black
Russellville
Conway
N. Little Rock
Little Rock
Hot Springs
HOT SPRINGS N.P.
Benton
Malvern
Arkadelphia
Hope
Pine Bluff
Saline
Camden
Magnolia
El Dorado
McGehee
Texarkana
Bossier City
Minden
Ruston
Shreveport
Ouachita
Bastrop
Monroe
LOUISIANA
Natchitoches
Sabine
Alexandria
Red
Lake Charles
Opelousas
Eunice
Crowley
Lafayette
New Iberia
Abbeville
White L.
Atchafalaya
Morgan City
Atchafalaya Bay
Houma
Thibodaux
St. Louis
Herculaneum
Crystal City
Hematite
Bonne Terre
Iron Mountain
Fredericktown
Cape Girardeau
Sikeston
Piggott
Paragould
Jonesboro
St. Francis
Forrest City
White
Helena
Stuttgart
Arkansas
Memphis
W. Memphis
Blytheville
Kennett
Dyersburg
Jackson
Holly Springs
Batesville
Clarksdale
159
Cleveland
Greenwood
Greenville
Eudora
MISSISSIPPI
Yazoo City
Yazoo
Tallulah
Vicksburg
Big Black
Jackson
Canton
Pearl
Natchez
Mississippi
McComb
97
Brookhaven
Baton Rouge
Hammond
Bogalusa
L. Pontchartrain
New Orleans
Breton Sound
Port Sulphur
Barataria Bay
Mississippi Sd.
Pascagoula
Gulfport
Biloxi
Hattiesburg
Laurel
Ellisville
Meridian
Centralia
Mount Vernon
Carbondale
Shawnee
Paducah
Calvert City
Mayfield
Union City
Greenfield
Corinth
Tupelo
Houston
Tombigbee
Starkville
Winona
Columbus
Tuscaloosa
Evansville
Henderson
Madisonville
Hopkins
Savannah
Florence
Pascagoula
100 fathoms
GULF OF M
Feet
6,000
3,000
1,500
1,000
600
300
Sea Level
Spot Heights in Metres
Conical Orthomorphic Projection
95°W
90°W

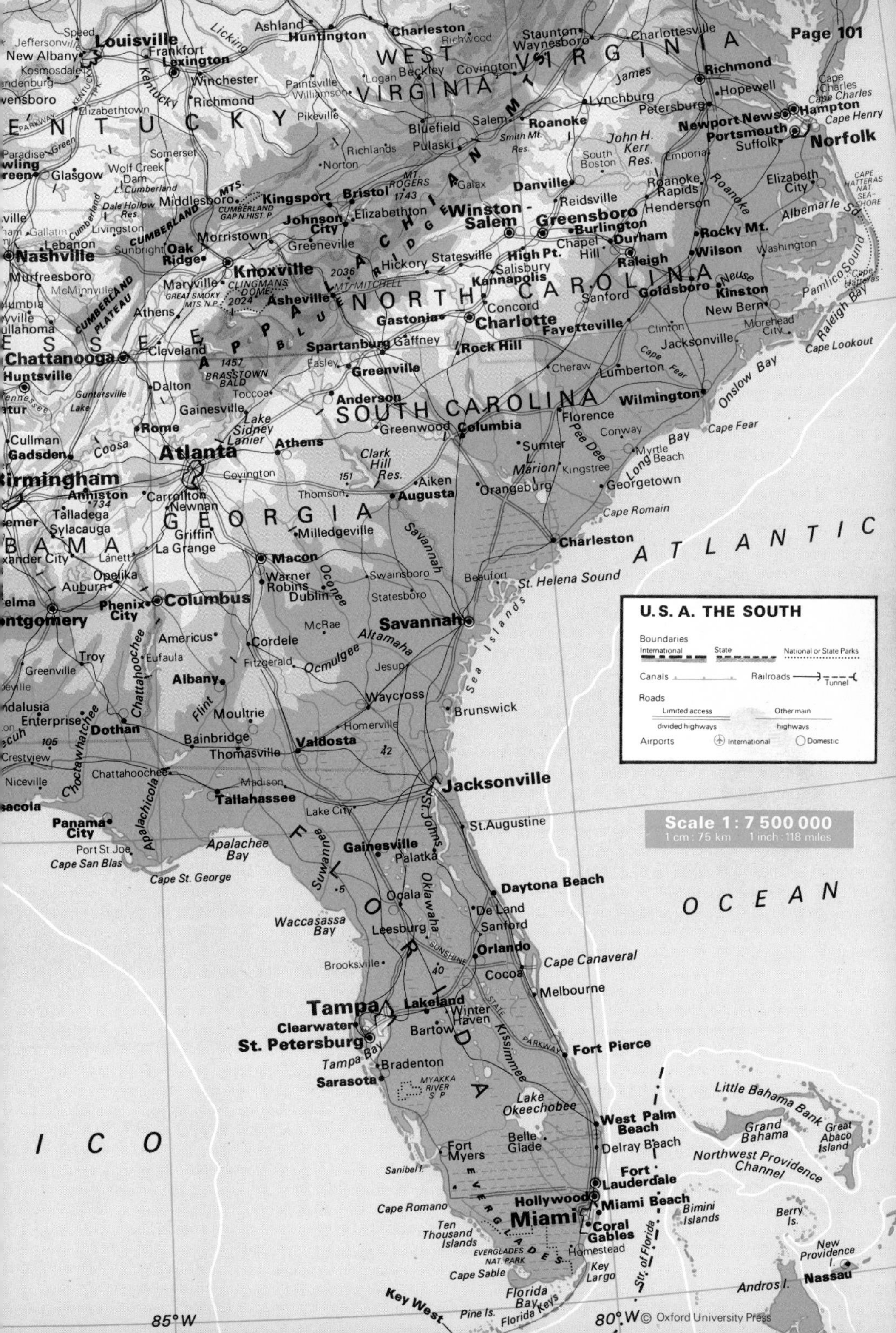
U.S.A. THE SOUTH
Boundaries
International
State
National or State Parks
Canals
Railroads
Tunnel
Roads
Limited access divided highways
Other main highways
Airports
International
Domestic
Scale 1 : 7 500 000
1 cm : 75 km
1 inch : 118 miles
KENTUCKY
WEST VIRGINIA
VIRGINIA
NORTH CAROLINA
SOUTH CAROLINA
GEORGIA
FLORIDA
APPALACHIAN MTS
BLUE RIDGE
CUMBERLAND MTS.
CUMBERLAND PLATEAU
ATLANTIC
OCEAN
Louisville
Lexington
Frankfort
New Albany
Jeffersonville
Speed
Kosmosdale
Elizabethtown
Winchester
Richmond
Ashland
Huntington
Charleston
Richwood
Paintsville
Williamson
Pikeville
Logan
Beckley
Covington
Staunton
Waynesboro
Charlottesville
Richmond
Hopewell
Petersburg
Lynchburg
James
Cape Charles
Hampton
Cape Henry
Newport News
Portsmouth
Norfolk
Suffolk
Emporia
John H. Kerr Res.
South Boston
Roanoke
Salem
Smith Mt. Res.
Bluefield
Pulaski
Richlands
Norton
Galax
MT. ROGERS 1743
Danville
Reidsville
Roanoke Rapids
Henderson
Elizabeth City
Albemarle Sd.
CAPE HATTERAS NAT. SEA-SHORE
Somerset
Wolf Creek Dam
L. Cumberland
Glasgow
Dale Hollow Res.
Middlesboro
CUMBERLAND GAP N.HIST. P.
Kingsport
Bristol
Johnson City
Elizabethton
Winston-Salem
Greensboro
Burlington
Durham
Chapel Hill
Raleigh
Rocky Mt.
Wilson
Washington
Pamlico Sound
Cape Hatteras
Goldsboro
Neuse
Kinston
New Bern
Raleigh Bay
Morehead City
Cape Lookout
Livingston
Gallatin
Lebanon
Nashville
Murfreesboro
McMinnville
Oak Ridge
Morristown
Greeneville
Knoxville
Maryville
CLINGMANS DOME 2024
GREAT SMOKY MTS N.P.
Asheville
Hickory
2036
MT. MITCHELL
Statesville
High Pt.
Salisbury
Kannapolis
Concord
Charlotte
Gastonia
Sanford
Fayetteville
Clinton
Jacksonville
Cape Fear
Lumberton
Onslow Bay
Wilmington
Cape Fear
Athens
Chattanooga
Cleveland
Huntsville
Guntersville Lake
1457
BRASSTOWN BALD
Dalton
Spartanburg
Gaffney
Rock Hill
Cheraw
Easley
Greenville
Toccoa
Anderson
Greenwood
Columbia
Florence
Conway
Sumter
Pee Dee
Myrtle Beach
Long Bay
L. Marion
Kingstree
Orangeburg
Georgetown
Cape Romain
Charleston
Gainesville
Lake Sidney Lanier
Rome
Cullman
Gadsden
Coosa
Atlanta
Athens
Clark Hill Res.
151
Aiken
Augusta
Thomson
Birmingham
Anniston
734
Carrollton
Newnan
Covington
Talladega
Sylacauga
Griffin
La Grange
Lanett
Milledgeville
Savannah
Macon
Warner Robins
Dublin
Oconee
Swainsboro
Statesboro
Beaufort
St. Helena Sound
Opelika
Auburn
Phenix City
Columbus
Montgomery
Selma
Americus
Cordele
McRae
Altamaha
Sea Islands
Troy
Eufaula
Chattahoochee
Fitzgerald
Ocmulgee
Jesup
Greenville
Albany
Flint
Waycross
Brunswick
Moultrie
Enterprise
Dothan
Andalusia
Choctawhatchee
105
Bainbridge
Thomasville
Valdosta
Homerville
42
Crestview
Niceville
Chattahoochee
Madison
Jacksonville
Tallahassee
Apalachicola
Panama City
Port St. Joe
Cape San Blas
Apalachee Bay
Cape St. George
Lake City
St. Johns
St. Augustine
Suwannee
Gainesville
Palatka
Ocala
Oklawaha
Daytona Beach
De Land
Sanford
Waccasassa Bay
Leesburg
SUNSHINE
Orlando
Cape Canaveral
Cocoa
Brooksville
40
Melbourne
Tampa
Lakeland
Winter Haven
Clearwater
St. Petersburg
Bartow
Kissimmee
STATE PARKWAY
Fort Pierce
Tampa Bay
Bradenton
Sarasota
MYAKKA RIVER S P
Lake Okeechobee
West Palm Beach
Belle Glade
Delray Beach
Fort Myers
Sanibel I.
EVERGLADES
Fort Lauderdale
Hollywood
Miami Beach
Miami
Coral Gables
Cape Romano
Ten Thousand Islands
Homestead
EVERGLADES NAT. PARK
Cape Sable
Key Largo
Florida Bay
Florida Keys
Key West
Pine Is.
Str. of Florida
Little Bahama Bank
Grand Bahama
Great Abaco Island
Northwest Providence Channel
Bimini Islands
Berry Is.
New Providence I.
Nassau
Andros I.
ICO
85°W
80°W

Nutrition

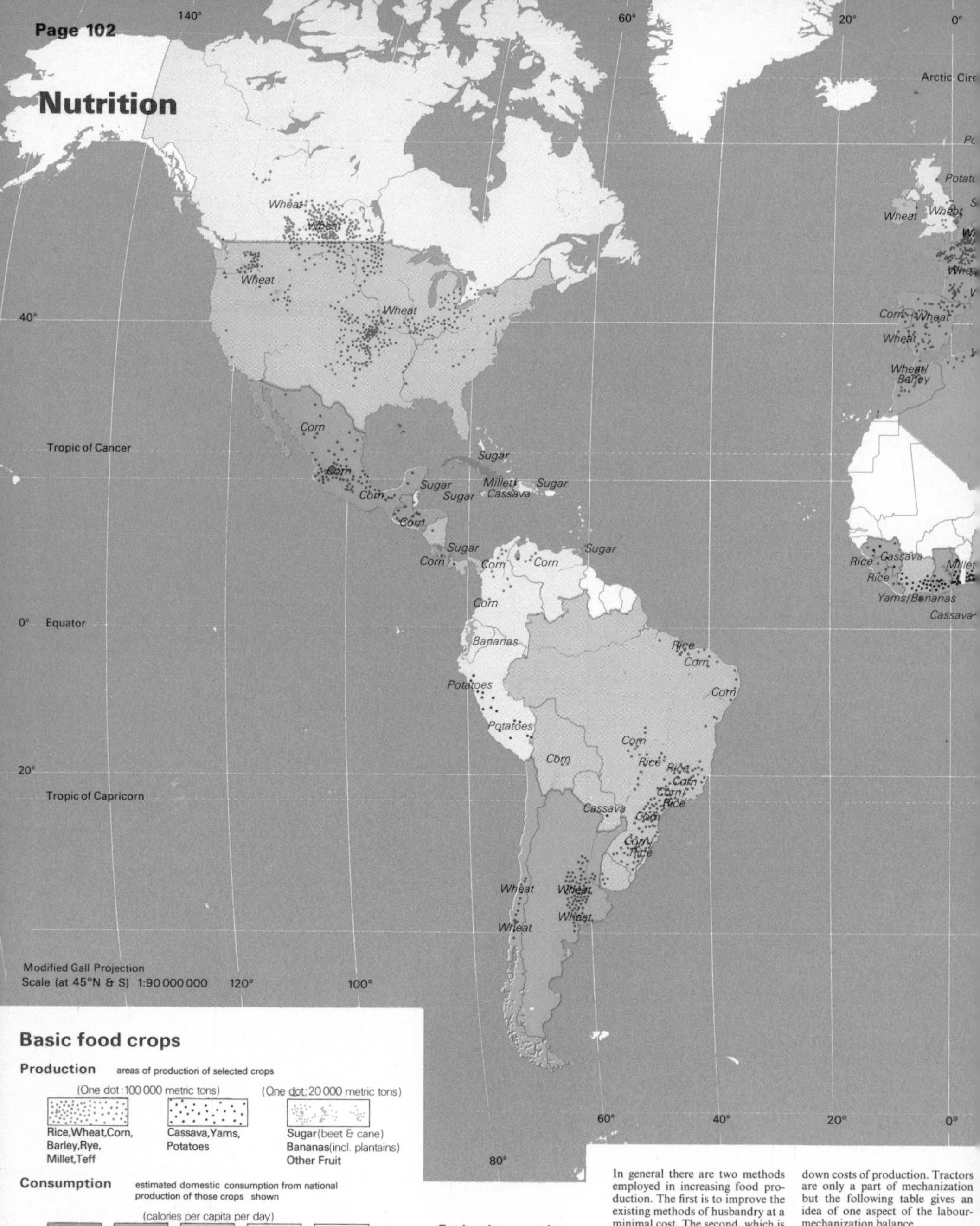

Map labels (selected): Arctic Circle, Tropic of Cancer, Equator, Tropic of Capricorn, 140°, 60°, 20°, 0°, 40°, Wheat, Corn, Sugar, Millet, Cassava, Bananas, Potatoes, Rice, Corn, Yams/Bananas, Barley

Modified Gall Projection
Scale (at 45°N & S) 1:90 000 000

Basic food crops

Production areas of production of selected crops

(One dot : 100 000 metric tons)
Rice, Wheat, Corn, Barley, Rye, Millet, Teff

(One dot : 20 000 metric tons)
Cassava, Yams, Potatoes

Sugar (beet & cane)
Bananas (incl. plantains)
Other Fruit

Consumption estimated domestic consumption from national production of those crops shown

(calories per capita per day)

| 1 660-1 220 | 1 220-750 | 750-450 | 450-160 | DATA NA |

For each country are shown per capita domestic consumption and areas of production for one or more basic food crop. The crops selected are those carbohydrates which contribute the highest number of calories per capita of any home-grown crop. Selection has been based on national averages, and does not take account of regional or other variations; for example, rice is the basic crop shown for Pakistan, but if shown regionally rice would remain the basic crop for East Pakistan although wheat would probably be more important for West Pakistan.

A further crop is shown for a country if its contribution to the national average calorific intake is at least 75% of that of the first crop selected. When this occurs, the consumption category is based on the aggregate for both crops; for example, in Brazil rice provides 394 calories per capita per day and corn 302 (76.7% of the rice). Both crops are mapped and calorific intake is given as 696 calories per capita per day.

Fat levels per capita

Selected countries
(grammes per day)

	1961-3 av.
New Zealand	157.2
U.K.	143.4
U.S.A.	142.7
Argentina	109.1
Greece	88.1
Uganda	39.0
Japan	36.3
Iraq	35.5
Bolivia	28.2
India	26.6
Malagasy R.[1]	16.8

[1]Data for 1962

In general there are two methods employed in increasing food production. The first is to improve the existing methods of husbandry at a minimal cost. The second, which is used to raise the levels of yield further, entails the breeding and selection of seeds or crops best fitted to the environment coupled with the efficient use of fertilizers, pesticides and farm mechanization. Increased productivity of the agrarian labour force is also a requirement. In some areas a high level of mechanization is essential to ensure that the crops are sown and harvested at the right times, as in the Canadian wheat belt. In other regions where, as a consequence of industrialization, farm workers must be paid high wages, mechanization is essential to keep down costs of production. Tractors are only a part of mechanization but the following table gives an idea of one aspect of the labour-mechanization balance.

	Agrarian labour as % of total	Tractors per arable 10 000 [1]
Cambodia	80.9	—
India	72.9	2
Bulgaria	64.1	133
Ghana	58.0	25
Brazil	51.6	21
Peru	49.7	25
Jordan	35.3	13
U.S.S.R.	35.2	67
Kenya	35.2	36
Japan	26.9	29
New Zealand	14.4	1 096
Netherlands	10.7	1 115
U.S.A.	6.2	250
U.K.	5.1	508

[1]Three tractors per 1 000 000 ha.

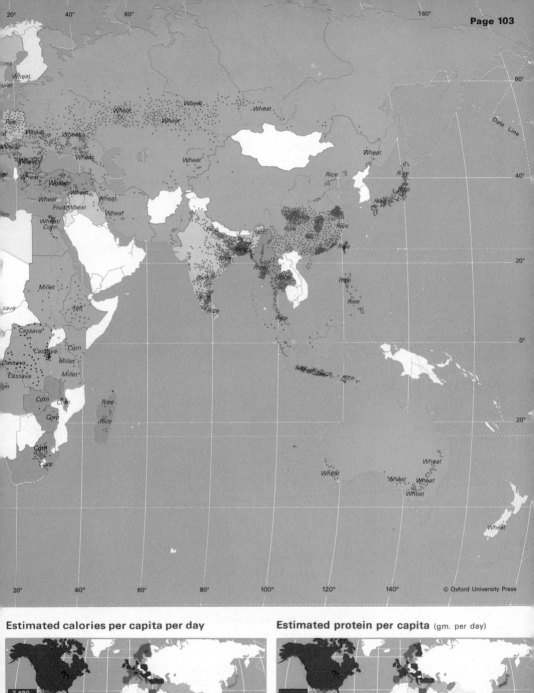

Estimated calories per capita per day

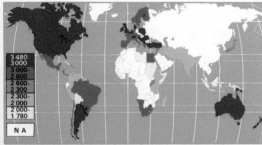

Estimated protein per capita (gm. per day)

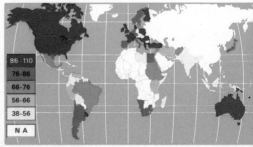

Iron Ore/Steel

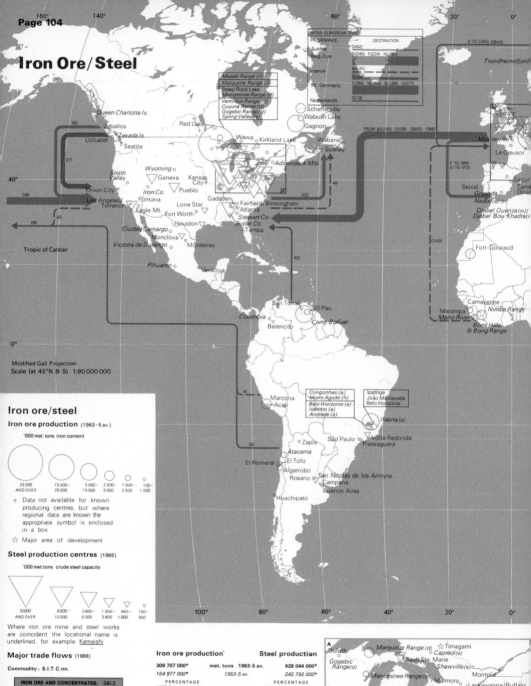

Iron ore/steel

Iron ore production (1963–5 av.)

'000 met. tons iron content

25 000 AND OVER | 15 000–25 000 | 5 000–15 000 | 2 500–5 000 | 1 000–2 500 | 100–1 000

+ Data not available for known producing centres, but where regional data are known the appropriate symbol is enclosed in a box

☆ Major area of development

Steel production centres (1965)

'000 met. tons crude steel capacity

10000 AND OVER | 6 000–10 000 | 3 800–6 000 | 1 900–3 800 | 950–1 900 | 150–950

Where iron ore mine and steel works are coincident the locational name is underlined, for example Kamaishi

Major trade flows (1966)

Commodity : S.I.T.C.no.

IRON ORE AND CONCENTRATES: –281.3

IRON AND STEEL: 67

Value ($U.S.)

0.5mm represents increments of $100 million

($ MILLIONS) — 900 / 500 / 100 — UNDER $50 MILLION / $50 MILLION / $ MILLIONS

203 — VALUE IN $ MILLIONS

Where names are boxed, a horizontal line separates names of different sized symbols, the largest symbol size being named first.

Iron ore production[1]

309 707 000* met. tons 1963–5 av.
164 977 000* 1953–5 av.

Steel production

428 044 000* 1963–5 av.
242 792 000* 1953–5 av.

	Iron ore production PERCENTAGE			Steel production PERCENTAGE	
	1953–5 av.	1963–5 av.		1963–5 av.	1953–5 av.
U.S.S.R.	23	28		20	17
U.S.A.	31	15		26	39
China	3	8		3*	1*
Canada[2]	3	6		2	1
France	8	6		4	5
Sweden[2]	6	5		1	1
Japan	1	—		9	3
W. Germany[2]	2	1		8	9
U.K.[2]	3	1		6	8
Others	20	30		21	16
	100	100		100	100

* Estimate [1]Iron content [2]The inclusion of countries whose ratings for one commodity are not grey backed, is based on their production of the other commodity.

Modified Gall Projection
Scale (at 45°N & S) 1:90 000 000

SCALE THREE TIMES THAT OF MAIN MAP

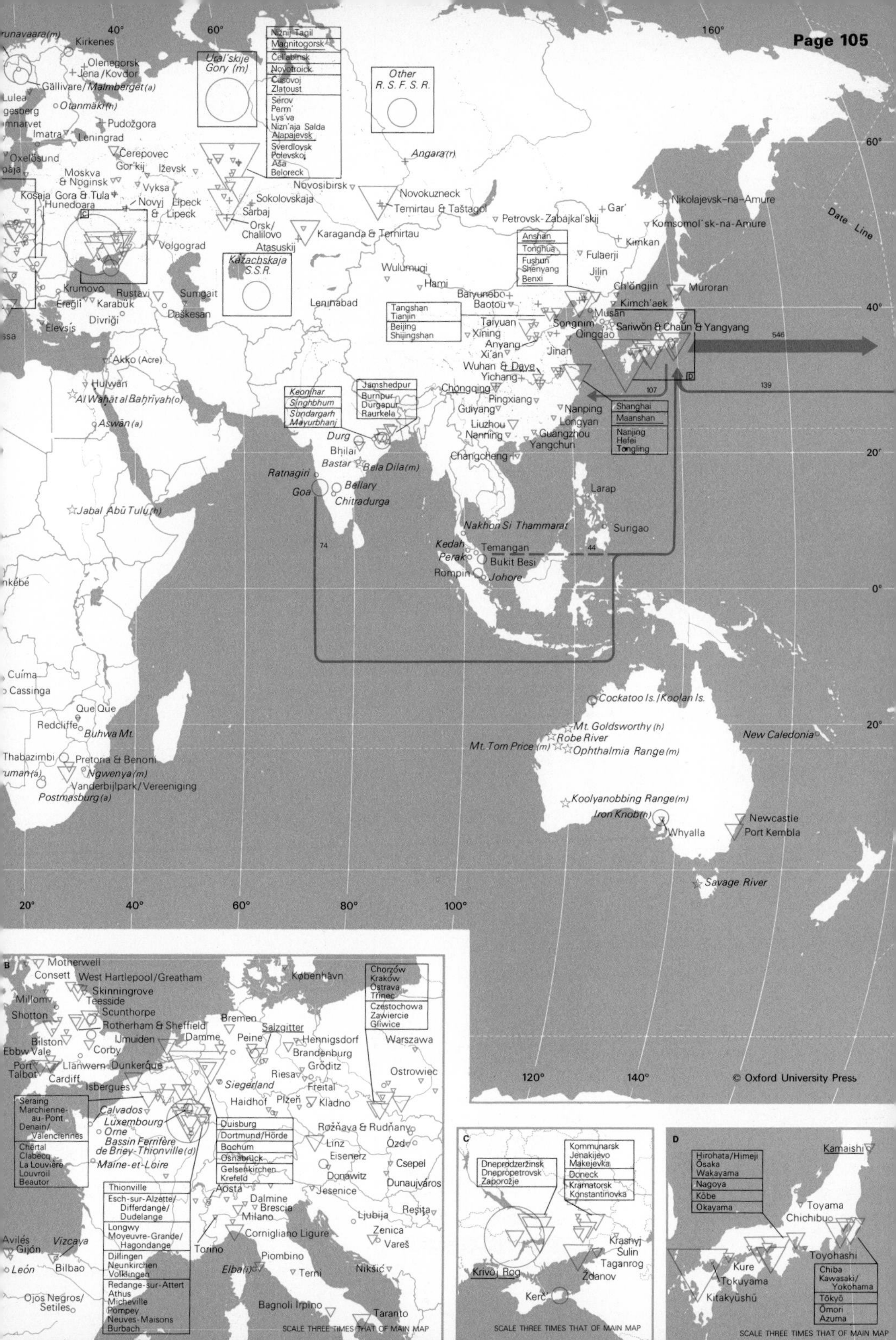
Ural'skije Gory (m)
Nižnij Tagil
Magnitogorsk
Čel'abinsk
Novotroick
Čusovoj
Zlatoust
Serov
Perm'
Lys'va
Nizn'aja Salda
Alapajevsk
Sverdlovsk
Polevskoj
Aša
Beloreck
Other R.S.F.S.R.
Kazachskaja S.S.R.
Kirkenes
Olenegorsk
Jena/Kovdor
Gällivare/Malmberget (a)
Otanmäki (h)
Pudožgora
Imatra
Leningrad
Oxelösund
Čerepovec
Gor'kij
Iževsk
Moskva & Noginsk
Vyksa
Kosaja Gora & Tula
Hunedoara
Novyj Lipeck & Lipeck
Volgograd
Sokolovskaja
Sarbaj
Orsk/Chalilovo
Atasuskij
Karaganda & Temirtau
Novosibirsk
Novokuzneck
Temirtau & Taštagol
Angara (r)
Krumovo
Ereğli
Karabük
Divriği
Rustavi
Sumgait
Daškesan
Elevsis
Leninabad
Wulumuqi
Hami
Petrovsk-Zabajkal'skij
Gar'
Nikolajevsk-na-Amure
Komsomol'sk-na-Amure
Kimkan
Date Line
Anshan
Tonghua
Fushun
Shenyang
Benxi
Fulaerji
Jilin
Ch'ŏngjin
Kimch'aek
Musan
Muroran
Songnim
Sariwŏn & Chaŭn & Yangyang
Qingdao
Baiyunebo
Baotou
Tangshan
Tianjin
Beijing
Shijingshan
Taiyuan
Xining
Anyang
Xi'an
Jinan
Wuhan & Daye
Yichang
Chongqing
Pingxiang
Guiyang
Liuzhou
Nanning
Guangzhou
Yangchun
Nanping
Longyan
Shanghai
Maanshan
Nanjing
Hefei
Tongling
Changcheng
Akko (Acre)
Hulwan
Al Wahat al Bahriyah (o)
Aswan (a)
Keonjhar
Singhbhum
Sundargarh
Mayurbhanj
Jamshedpur
Burnpur
Durgapur
Raurkela
Durg
Bhilai
Bastar
Bela Dila (m)
Ratnagiri
Goa
Bellary
Chitradurga
Jabal Abū Tulu (h)
Larap
Nakhon Si Thammarat
Surigao
Kedah
Perak
Temangan
Bukit Besi
Rompin
Johore
Cuíma
Cassinga
Que Que
Redcliffe
Buhwa Mt.
Thabazimbi
Pretoria & Benoni
Ngwenya (m)
Vanderbijlpark/Vereeniging
Postmasburg (a)
Cockatoo Is./Koolan Is.
Mt. Goldsworthy (h)
Robe River
Mt. Tom Price (m)
Ophthalmia Range (m)
New Caledonia
Koolyanobbing Range (m)
Iron Knob (h)
Whyalla
Newcastle
Port Kembla
Savage River
546
139
107
74
44
B
Motherwell
Consett
West Hartlepool/Greatham
Skinningrove
Teesside
Millom
Shotton
Scunthorpe
Rotherham & Sheffield
Bilston
Corby
IJmuiden
Ebbw Vale
Llanwern
Port Talbot
Cardiff
Dunkerque
Isbergues
Seraing
Marchienne-au-Pont
Denain/Valenciennes
Chertal
Clabecq
La Louvière
Louvroil
Beautor
Calvados
Luxembourg
Orne
Bassin Ferrifère de Briey-Thionville (d)
Maine-et-Loire
Thionville
Esch-sur-Alzette/Differdange/Dudelange
Longwy
Moyeuvre-Grande/Hagondange
Dillingen
Neunkirchen
Völklingen
Redange-sur-Attert
Athus
Micheville
Pompey
Neuves-Maisons
Burbach
Avilés
Gijón
Vizcaya
León
Bilbao
Ojos Negros/Setiles
København
Bremen
Damme
Peine
Salzgitter
Hennigsdorf
Brandenburg
Riesa
Gröditz
Freital
Siegerland
Haidhof
Plzeň
Kladno
Duisburg
Dortmund/Hörde
Bochum
Osnabrück
Gelsenkirchen
Krefeld
Aosta
Dalmine
Brescia
Milano
Torino
Cornigliano Ligure
Piombino
Elba (i)
Terni
Bagnoli Irpino
Taranto
Chorzów
Kraków
Ostrava
Třinec
Częstochowa
Zawiercie
Gliwice
Warszawa
Ostrowiec
Rožňava & Rudňany
Linz
Eisenerz
Donawitz
Ózd
Csepel
Dunaújváros
Jesenice
Ljubija
Rešita
Zenica
Vareš
Nikšić
SCALE THREE TIMES THAT OF MAIN MAP
C
Dneprodzeržinsk
Dnepropetrovsk
Zaporožje
Kommunarsk
Jenakijevo
Makejevka
Doneck
Kramatorsk
Konstantinovka
Krasnyj Sulin
Taganrog
Ždanov
Krivoj Rog
Kerč'
SCALE THREE TIMES THAT OF MAIN MAP
D
Hirohata/Himeji
Ōsaka
Wakayama
Nagoya
Kōbe
Okayama
Kamaishi
Toyama
Chichibu
Kure
Tokuyama
Kitakyūshū
Toyohashi
Chiba
Kawasaki/Yokohama
Tōkyō
Ōmori
Azuma
SCALE THREE TIMES THAT OF MAIN MAP
20°
40°
60°
80°
100°
120°
140°
160°
0°

Energy

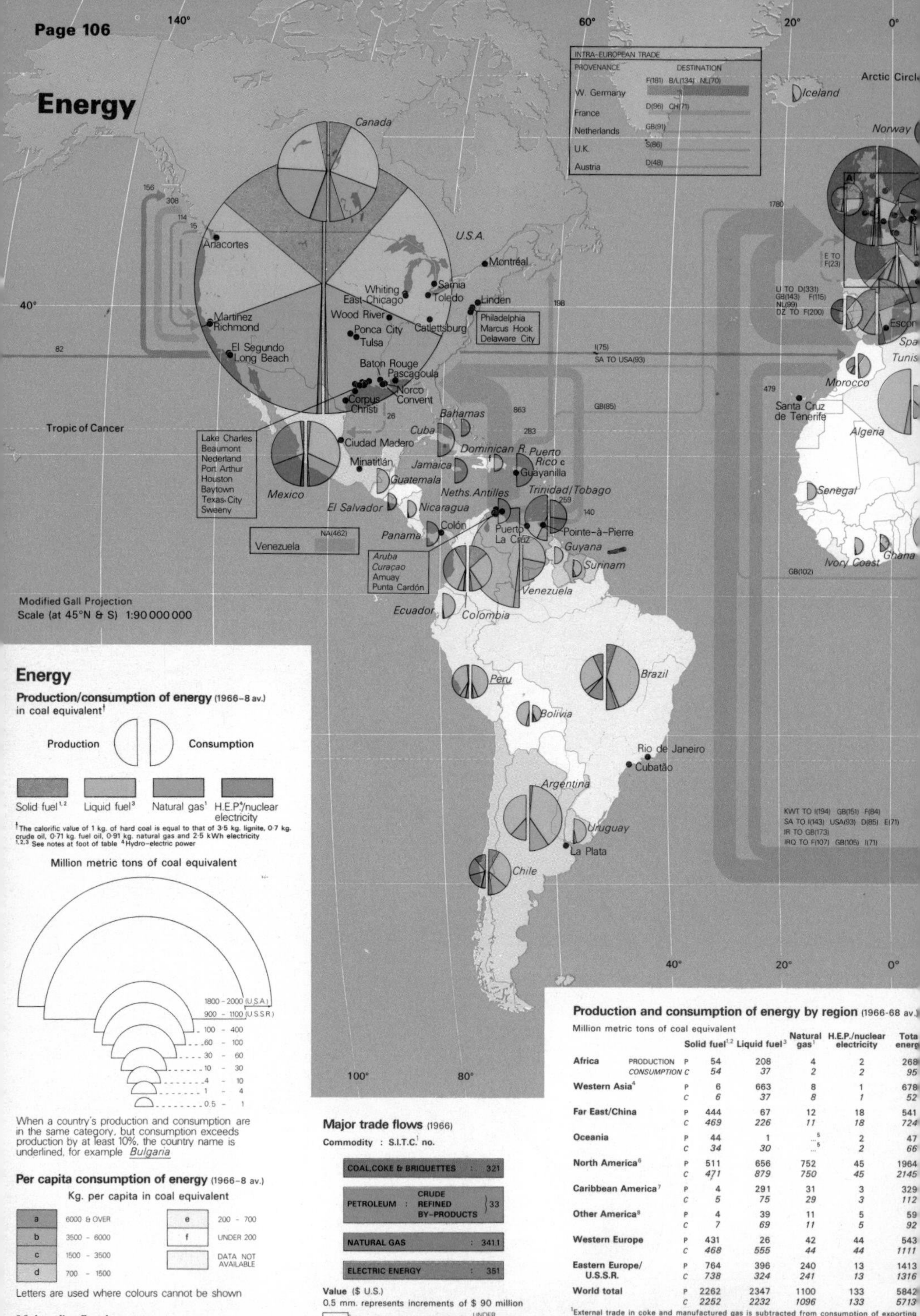

INTRA-EUROPEAN TRADE

PROVENANCE	DESTINATION
W. Germany	F(181) B/L(134) NL(70)
France	D(96) CH(7)
Netherlands	GB(91)
U.K.	S(86)
Austria	D(48)

Energy

Production/consumption of energy (1966–8 av.)
in coal equivalent[1]

Production | Consumption

Solid fuel[1,2] Liquid fuel[3] Natural gas[3] H.E.P.[9]/nuclear electricity

[1]The calorific value of 1 kg. of hard coal is equal to that of 3·5 kg. lignite, 0·7 kg. crude oil, 0·71 kg. fuel oil, 0·91 kg. natural gas and 2·5 kWh electricity
[1,2,9] See notes at foot of table [4] Hydro-electric power

Million metric tons of coal equivalent

1800 – 2000 (U.S.A.)
900 – 1100 (U.S.S.R.)
100 – 400
60 – 100
30 – 60
10 – 30
4 – 10
1 – 4
0·5 – 1

When a country's production and consumption are in the same category, but consumption exceeds production by at least 10%, the country name is underlined, for example *Bulgaria*

Per capita consumption of energy (1966–8 av.)

Kg. per capita in coal equivalent

a	6000 & OVER	e	200 – 700
b	3500 – 6000	f	UNDER 200
c	1500 – 3500		DATA NOT AVAILABLE
d	700 – 1500		

Letters are used where colours cannot be shown

Major oil refineries (1968)

● Producing centre with crude oil capacity of at least 100 000 barrels per stream day

Major trade flows (1966)

Commodity : S.I.T.C.[1] no.

COAL, COKE & BRIQUETTES	321
PETROLEUM { CRUDE / REFINED / BY-PRODUCTS }	33
NATURAL GAS	341.1
ELECTRIC ENERGY	351

Value ($ U.S.)
0.5 mm. represents increments of $ 90 million

810 ($ MILLIONS) UNDER $45 MILLION
450
90 75 VALUE IN $ MILLIONS

[1]STANDARD INTERNATIONAL TRADE CLASSIFICATION

Production and consumption of energy by region (1966–68 av.)

Million metric tons of coal equivalent

			Solid fuel[1,2]	Liquid fuel[3]	Natural gas[1]	H.E.P./nuclear electricity	Total energy
Africa	PRODUCTION	P	54	208	4	2	268
	CONSUMPTION	C	54	37	2	2	95
Western Asia[4]		P	6	663	8	1	678
		C	6	37	8	1	52
Far East/China		P	444	67	12	18	541
		C	469	226	11	18	724
Oceania		P	44	1	[5]	2	47
		C	34	30	[5]	2	66
North America[6]		P	511	656	752	45	1964
		C	471	879	750	45	2145
Caribbean America[7]		P	4	291	31	3	329
		C	5	75	29	3	112
Other America[8]		P	4	39	11	5	59
		C	7	69	11	5	92
Western Europe		P	431	26	42	44	543
		C	468	555	44	44	1111
Eastern Europe/U.S.S.R.		P	764	396	240	13	1413
		C	738	324	241	13	1316
World total		P	2262	2347	1100	133	5842
		C	2252	2232	1096	133	5713

[1]External trade in coke and manufactured gas is subtracted from consumption of exporting country and added to that of the importing country. [2]Mainly coal and lignite but includes peat where important; wood and dung excluded. [3]Consumption for energy purposes only. [4]Mainly Middle East. [5]Negligible amount. [6]Mainly U.S.A. and Canada. [7]Includes Columbia and Venezuela. [8]South America excluding Columbia and Venezuela.

Modified Gall Projection
Scale (at 45°N & S) 1:90 000 000

Canada
U.S.A.
Montréal
Whiting Sarnia
East-Chicago Toledo
Wood River Linden
Ponca City Catlettsburg Philadelphia
Tulsa Marcus Hook
Baton Rouge Delaware City
Anacortes
Martinez
Richmond
El Segundo
Long Beach
Pascagoula
Norco
Corpus Convent
Christi
Lake Charles
Beaumont
Nederland
Port Arthur
Houston
Baytown
Texas City
Sweeny
Ciudad Madero
Minatitlán
Mexico
El Salvador
Cuba
Bahamas
Jamaica Dominican R. Puerto
Guatemala Rico
Neths. Antilles Guayanilla
Nicaragua Trinidad/Tobago
Panama Puerto Pointe-à-Pierre
Colón La Cruz Guyana
Aruba Surinam
Curaçao
Amuay Venezuela
Punta Cardón
Ecuador Colombia
Peru Brazil
Bolivia Rio de Janeiro
Cubatão
Argentina
Uruguay
La Plata
Chile

Tropic of Cancer

Iceland
Norway
Arctic Circle
Escon
Spa
Tunis
Morocco
Santa Cruz
de Tenerife Algeria
Senegal
Ivory Coast Ghana

KWT TO I(194) GB(151) F(84)
SA TO I(143) USA(93) D(85) E(71)
IR TO GB(173)
IRQ TO F(107) GB(105) I(71)

E TO F(23)
LI TO D(331) GB(143) F(115)
NL(99)
DZ TO F(200)
SA TO USA(93)

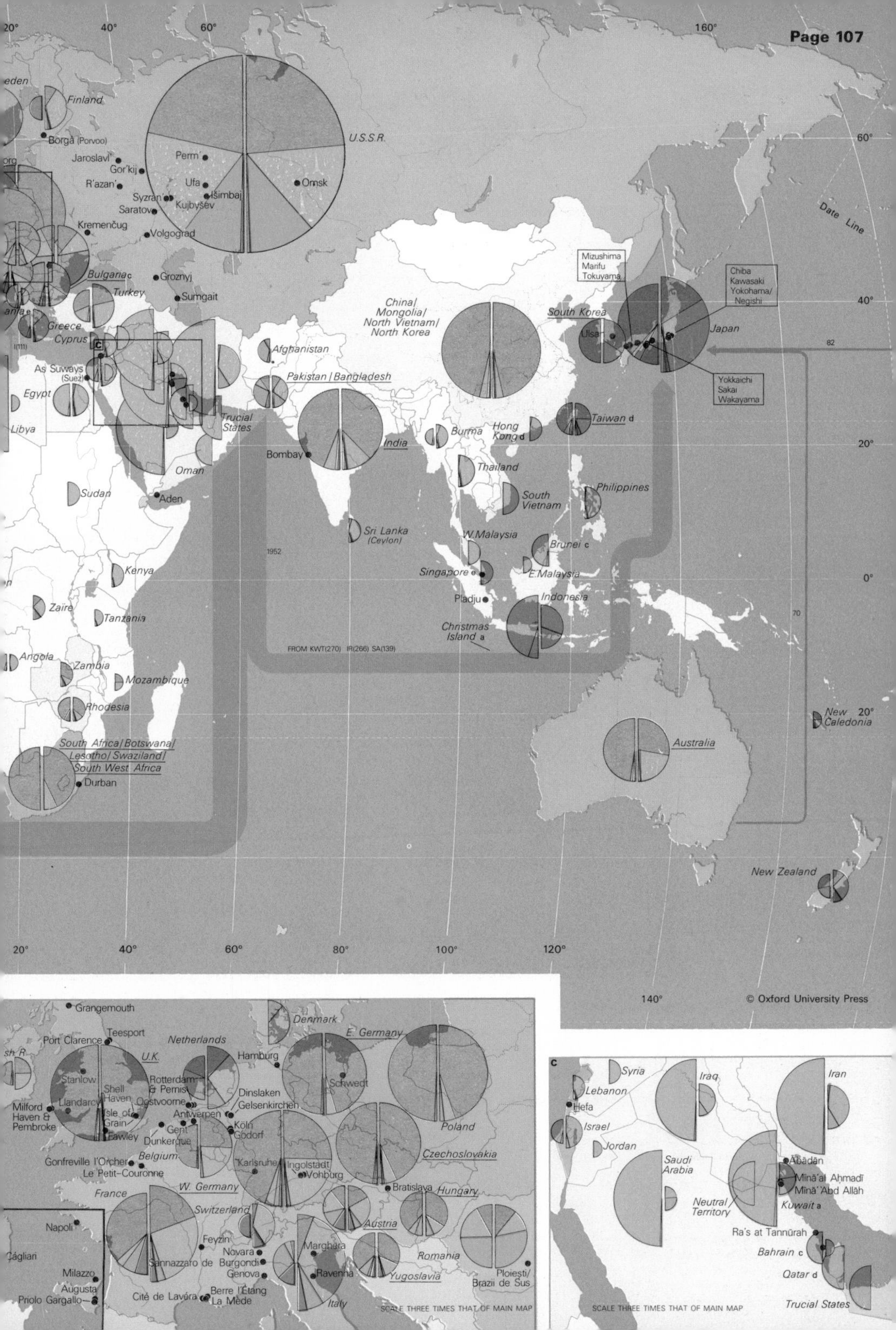

Finland
Borgå (Porvoo)
U.S.S.R.
Jaroslavl'
Gor'kij
R'azan'
Perm'
Ufa
Išimbaj
Omsk
Syzran'
Kujbyšev
Saratov
Kremenčug
Volgograd
Bulgaria c
Groznyj
Turkey
Sumgait
Greece
Cyprus
As Suways (Suez)
Egypt
Libya
Afghanistan
Pakistan / Bangladesh
China/ Mongolia/ North Vietnam/ North Korea
South Korea
Ulsan
Mizushima Marifu Tokuyama
Chiba Kawasaki Yokohama/ Negishi
Japan
Yokkaichi Sakai Wakayama
Date Line
Trucial States
India
Bombay
Burma
Hong Kong d
Taiwan d
Oman
Aden
Sudan
Thailand
South Vietnam
Philippines
Sri Lanka (Ceylon)
W. Malaysia
Brunei c
Singapore e
E. Malaysia
Pladju
Indonesia
Christmas Island a
Kenya
Zaire
Tanzania
Angola
Zambia
Mozambique
Rhodesia
South Africa / Botswana / Lesotho / Swaziland / South West Africa
Durban
Australia
New Caledonia
New Zealand
FROM KWT(270) IR(266) SA(139)
1952
82
70
© Oxford University Press
Grangemouth
Teesport
Port Clarence
Netherlands
U.K.
Hamburg
Denmark
E. Germany
Poland
Schwedt
Stanlow
Rotterdam & Pernis
Shell Haven
Milford Haven & Pembroke
Llandarcy
Isle of Grain
Fawley
Oostvoorne
Antwerpen
Gent
Dunkerque
Dinslaken
Gelsenkirchen
Köln
Godorf
Belgium
Gonfreville l'Orcher
Le Petit-Couronne
Karlsruhe
Ingolstadt
Vohburg
Czechoslovakia
Bratislava
Hungary
France
W. Germany
Switzerland
Austria
Napoli
Cágliari
Milazzo
Augusta
Priolo Gargallo
Feyzin
Sannazzaro de Burgondi
Novara
Genova
Marghera
Ravenna
Yugoslavia
Romania
Ploiesti/ Brazii de Sus
Cité de Lavéra
Berre l'Etang
La Mède
Italy
SCALE THREE TIMES THAT OF MAIN MAP
c
Syria
Lebanon
Hefa
Israel
Jordan
Iraq
Iran
Saudi Arabia
Abadan
Mīnā' al Aḥmadī
Mīnā' 'Abd Allāh
Neutral Territory
Kuwait a
Ra's at Tannūrah
Bahrain c
Qatar d
Trucial States
SCALE THREE TIMES THAT OF MAIN MAP

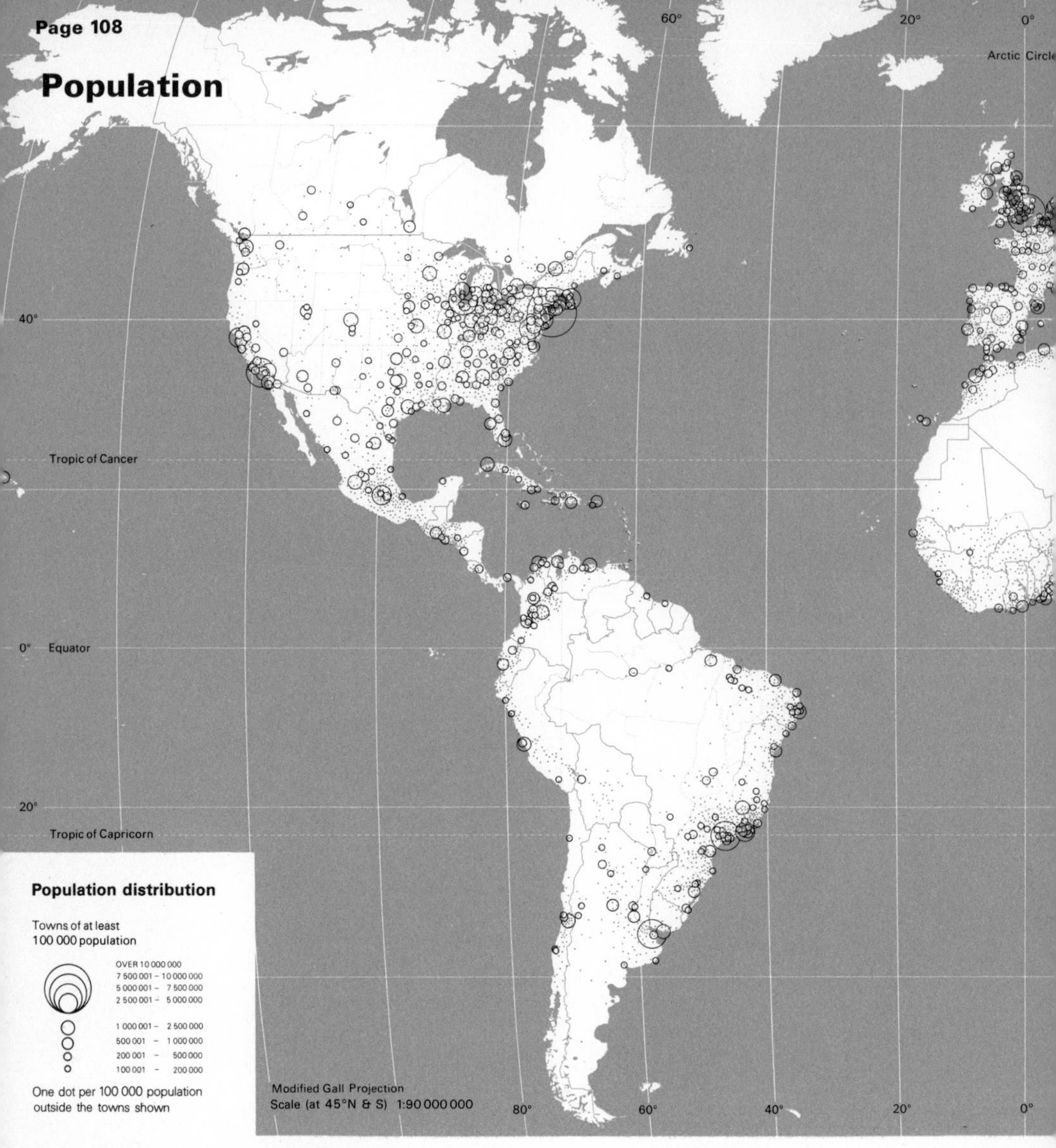

Population

40°
Tropic of Cancer
0° Equator
20°
Tropic of Capricorn
60° 20° 0°
Arctic Circle

Population distribution

Towns of at least
100 000 population

OVER 10 000 000
7 500 001 – 10 000 000
5 000 001 – 7 500 000
2 500 001 – 5 000 000

1 000 001 – 2 500 000
500 001 – 1 000 000
200 001 – 500 000
100 001 – 200 000

One dot per 100 000 population
outside the towns shown

Modified Gall Projection
Scale (at 45°N & S) 1:90 000 000

80° 60° 40° 20° 0°

Population statistics for selected countries

Latest census available in 1968

	BURMA	NIGERIA	SAUDI ARABIA	YUGO-SLAVIA	CHINA P.R.	INDIA	INDO-NESIA	ALGERIA	PHILIP-PINES	PARAGUAY	TURKEY	POLAND	U.S.S.R.	SOUTH AFRICA	MEXICO
Total population (thousands)	16 823	55 670	6 990	18 549	582 603	435 512	96 319	12 102	27 088	1 817	31 391	29 776	208 827	15 994	34 923
Population density (persons/sq. km.)[1]	38	67	3	78	75	156	74	5	116	5	42	102	11	15	23
Percentage urbanized	7	9	9	9	10	10	10	14	15	17	19	23	24	27	28
Size of largest urban agglomeration (thousands)	821	665	225	585	6 900	4 903	2 907	903	1 402	305	2 052	1 261	6 507	1 153	3 353

	TAIWAN	SWEDEN	GERMANY F.R.	FRANCE	IRAQ	U.A.R.	BRAZIL	ISRAEL	U.S.A.	NETHER-LANDS	U.K.	JAPAN	CANADA	ARGENTINA	AUSTRALIA
Total population (thousands)	13 383	7 766	53 977	46 520	8 262	25 984	70 119	2 183	179 323	11 462	52 709	98 275	18 238	23 031	11 541
Population density (persons/sq. km.)[1]	365	17	233	91	19	31	10	129	21	375	226	270	2	8	2
Percentage urbanized	29	31	32	34	34	35	36	41	45	47	49	50	52	57	63
Size of largest urban agglomeration (thousands)	1 155	1 262	2 191	7 369	1 745	4 220	5 383	390	11 410	1 048	7 914	11 005	2 437	7 000	2 445

[1]1967

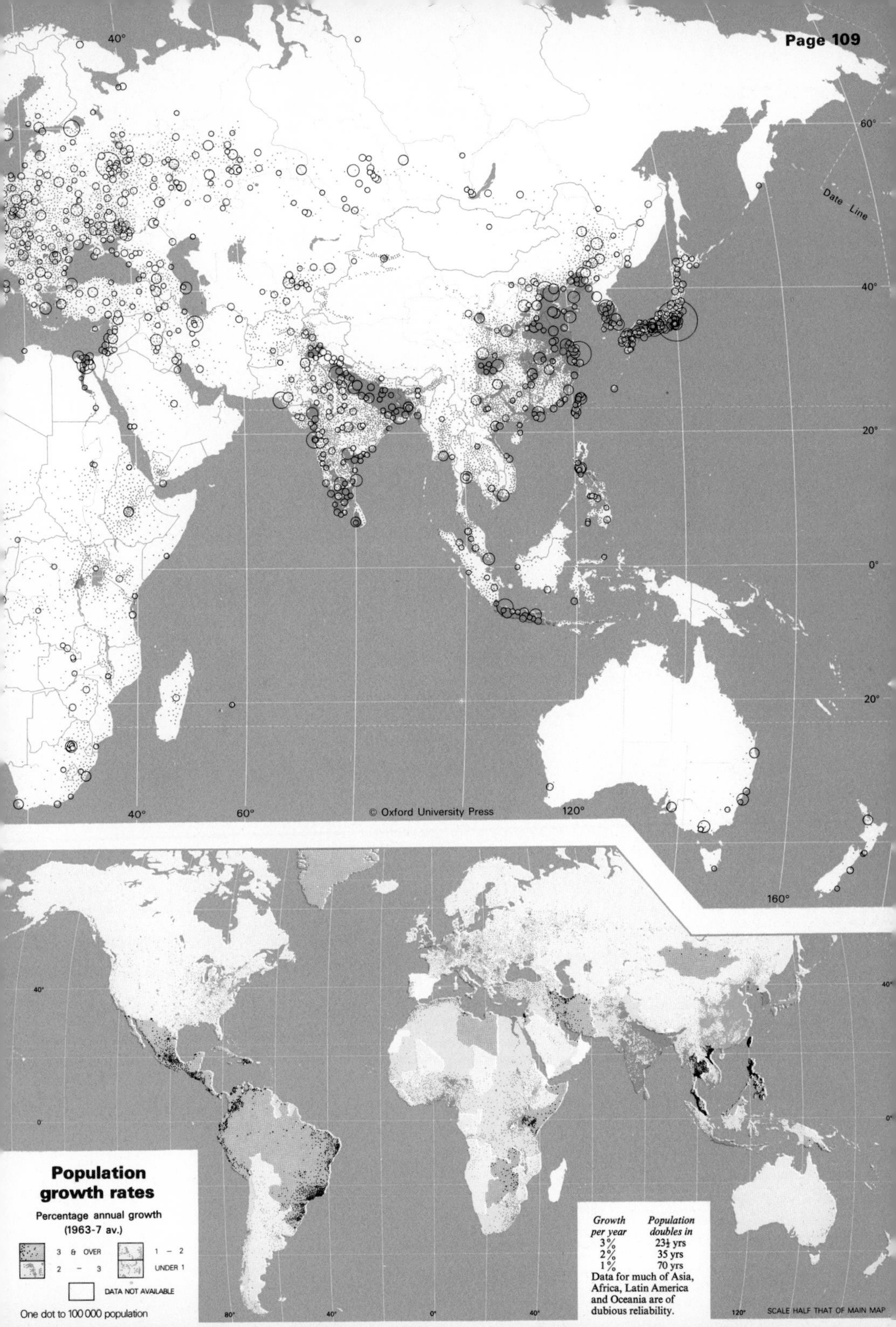

Date Line

© Oxford University Press

SCALE HALF THAT OF MAIN MAP

Population growth rates

Percentage annual growth
(1963-7 av.)

3 & OVER   1 − 2

2 − 3   UNDER 1

DATA NOT AVAILABLE

One dot to 100 000 population

Growth per year	Population doubles in
3%	23½ yrs
2%	35 yrs
1%	70 yrs

Data for much of Asia, Africa, Latin America and Oceania are of dubious reliability.

Surface Communications

Modified Gall Projection
Scale (at 45°N & S) 1:90 000 000

Surface communications

Roads

——— Principal roads

Shipping

In tons per mile on 10th March 1967

Gross registered tons per nautical mile

——— 1 - 40
——— 40 - 400

Thereafter every 200 tons is shown by 0.5 mm. thus

800 - 1 000

• Ports

Data for total shipping movements are based on a one in three sample of the 15 000 ships in *Lloyd's Shipping Index*, of which only 2 500 were at sea on the 10th March, 1967. The length of the voyage was calculated and the data adjusted to produce the number of tons per mile for each route.
The sample used gives an indication of the relative density of traffic at sea at a particular point in time, but it was not large enough to include all the ports, nor to indicate their relative importance.
The routes shown should not be regarded as precise shipping lanes since they have to a certain extent been generalized; the route followed will vary according to climatic and other conditions.
Shipping movements along inland waterways have not been shown although they are important in some areas, particularly in the U.S.A. and Canada (for example the Great Lakes and the Mississippi) and in NW. Europe (for example the Rhine/Rhône Waterway).

Railways[1]

Density (km. of track per '000 sq. km. area)[2]

110+	very dense network
65 - 110	dense network
25 - 65	moderately dense network
5 - 25	sparse network
0 - 5	very sparse network

[1] Latest available data in 1970

[2] Compiled on a national basis except in the U.S.S.R. (economic regions), Canada (provinces), the U.S.A. and Australia (states)

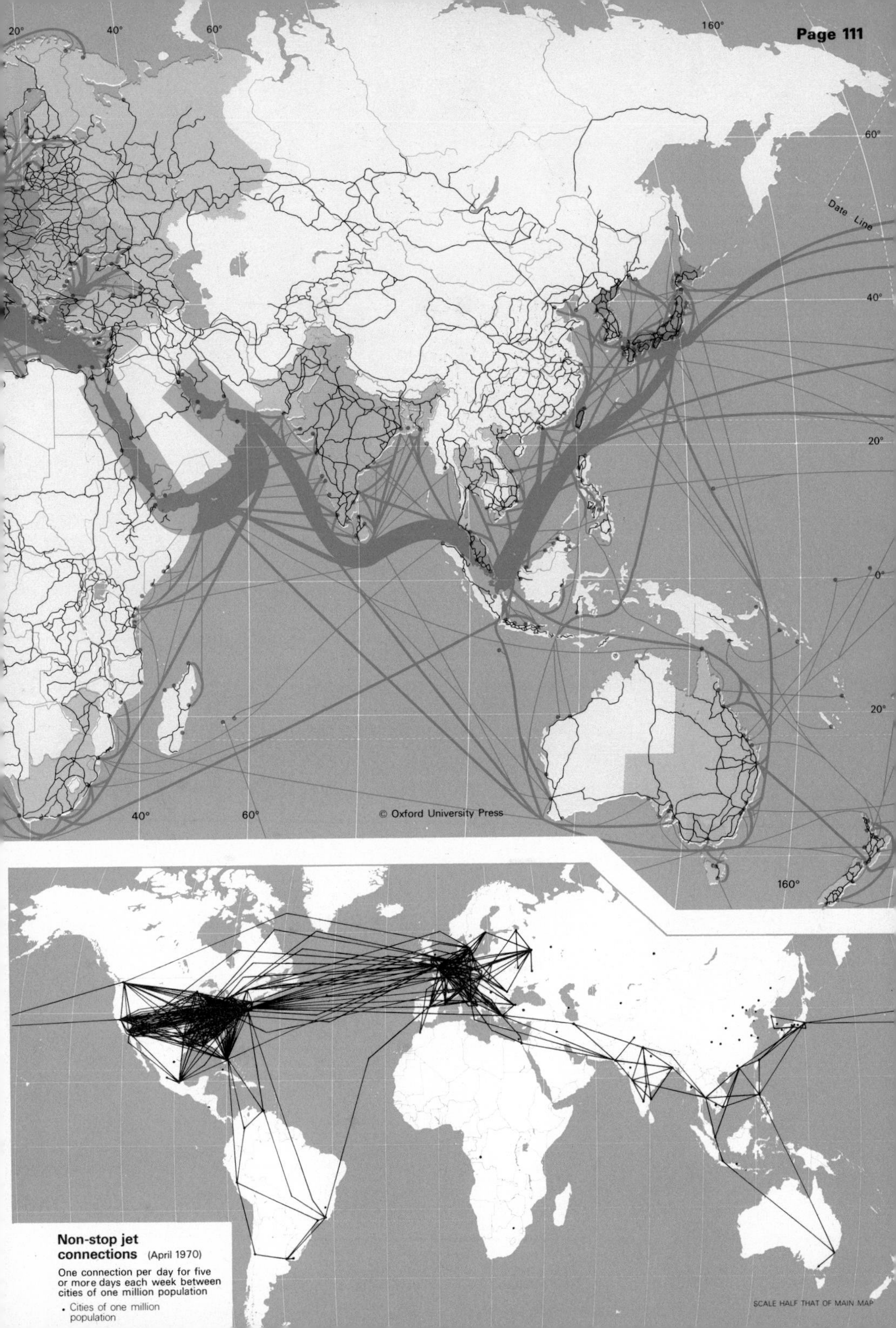

20°   40°   60°   160°

Date Line

60°

40°

20°

0°

© Oxford University Press

20°

40°   60°

160°

Non-stop jet connections (April 1970)

One connection per day for five or more days each week between cities of one million population

• Cities of one million population

SCALE HALF THAT OF MAIN MAP

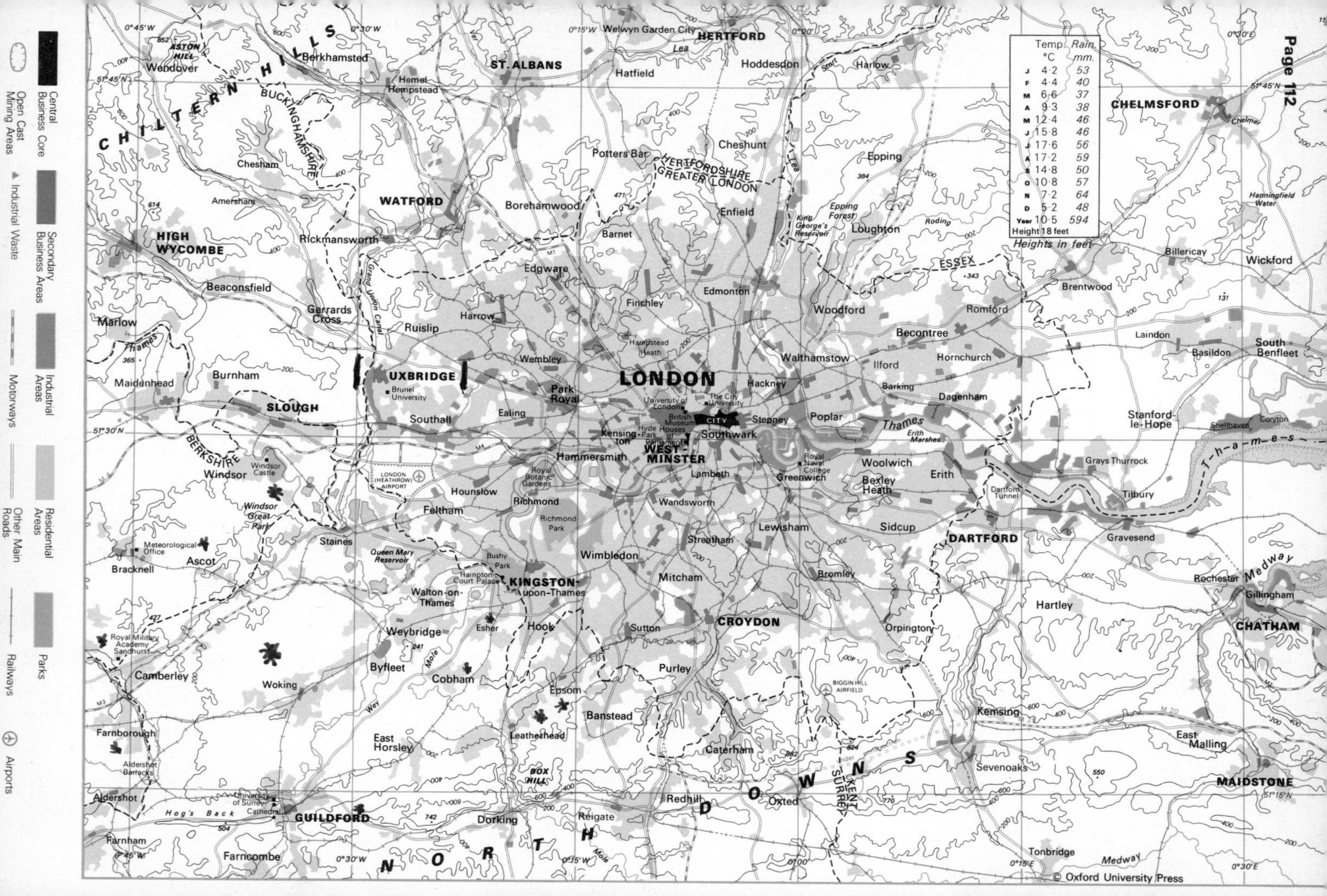

Temp.	Rain.	
°C	mm.	
J	4.2	53
F	4.4	40
M	6.6	37
A	9.3	38
M	12.4	46
J	15.8	46
J	17.6	56
A	17.2	59
S	14.8	50
O	10.8	57
N	7.2	64
D	5.2	48
Year	10.5	594
Height 18 feet		

Heights in feet

© Oxford University Press

Central Business Core   Secondary Business Areas   Industrial Areas   Residential Areas   Parks

Open Cast Mining Areas   ▲ Industrial Waste   Motorways   Other Main Roads   Railways   ⊕ Airports

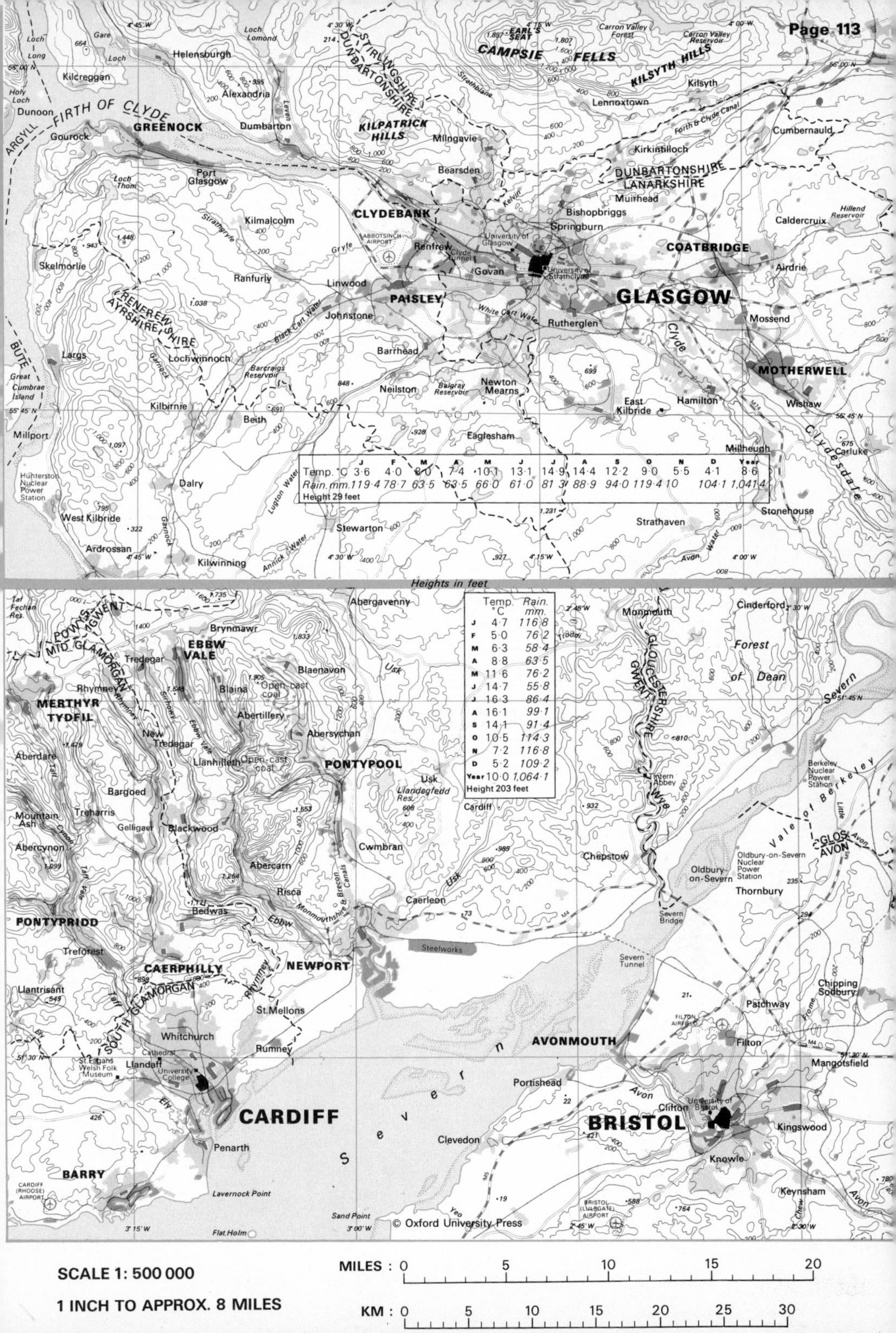

FIRTH OF CLYDE
ARGYLL
DUNBARTONSHIRE
STIRLINGSHIRE
CAMPSIE FELLS
KILSYTH HILLS
KILPATRICK HILLS
EARL'S SEAT
Carron Valley Forest
Carron Valley Reservoir
Loch Lomond
Loch Long
Gare Loch
Holy Loch
Helensburgh
Kilcreggan
Dunoon
Gourock
GREENOCK
Alexandria
Dumbarton
Leven
Strathblane
Kilsyth
Lennoxtown
Forth & Clyde Canal
Cumbernauld
Milngavie
Kirkintilloch
Bearsden
LANARKSHIRE
Muirhead
Port Glasgow
Loch Thom
CLYDEBANK
Kelvin
Bishopbriggs
Springburn
Hillend Reservoir
Caldercruix
Kilmalcolm
Strathgryfe
ABBOTSINCH AIRPORT
Renfrew
Clyde Tunnel
University of Glasgow
University of Strathclyde
COATBRIDGE
Skelmorlie
Gryfe
Govan
Airdrie
Ranfurly
Linwood
PAISLEY
GLASGOW
RENFREWSHIRE
AYRSHIRE
Black Cart Water
Johnstone
White Cart Water
Rutherglen
Clyde
Mossend
BUTE
Largs
Lochwinnoch
Barrhead
Barcraigs Reservoir
Garnock
Great Cumbrae Island
Neilston
Balgray Reservoir
Newton Mearns
MOTHERWELL
Kilbirnie
Beith
East Kilbride
Hamilton
Wishaw
Millport
Eaglesham
Clydesdale
Millheugh
Carluke
Hunterston Nuclear Power Station
Dalry
Lugton Water
Temp. °C — J 3·6, F 4·0, M 6·0, A 7·4, M 10·1, J 13·1, J 14·9, A 14·4, S 12·2, O 9·0, N 5·5, D 4·1, Year 8·6
Rain. mm. — J 119·4, F 78·7, M 63·5, A 63·5, M 66·0, J 61·0, J 81 3, A 88·9, S 94·0, O 119·4, N 10, D 104·1, Year 1,041·4
Height 29 feet
West Kilbride
Stewarton
Strathaven
Stonehouse
Ardrossan
Annick Water
Kilwinning
Avon Water
Heights in feet
Taf Fechan Res.
POWYS
GWENT
MID GLAMORGAN
Abergavenny
Brynmawr
EBBW VALE
Tredegar
Rhymney
Blaenavon
Open-cast coal
Blaina
Usk
MERTHYR TYDFIL
Sirhowy
Ebbw Vale
Abertillery
New Tredegar
Abersychan
Aberdare
Taff
Llanhilleth
PONTYPOOL
Bargoed
Usk
Llandegfedd Res.
Mountain Ash
Treharris
Gelligaer
Blackwood
Cynon
Abercynon
Abercarn
Cwmbran
Risca
Monmouthshire & Brecon Canals
Bedwas
Ebbw
Caerleon
PONTYPRIDD
Treforest
Steelworks
CAERPHILLY
Rhymney
NEWPORT
Llantrisant
SOUTH GLAMORGAN
St. Mellons
Ely
Whitchurch
Rumney
Cathedral
Llandaff
St. Fagans Welsh Folk Museum
University College
CARDIFF
Penarth
BARRY
CARDIFF (RHOOSE) AIRPORT
Lavernock Point
Sand Point
Flat Holm
Temp. °C / Rain. mm.
J 4·7 116·8
F 5·0 76·2
M 6·3 58·4
A 8·8 63·5
M 11·6 76·2
J 14·7 55·8
J 16·3 86·4
A 16·1 99·1
S 14·1 91·4
O 10·5 114·3
N 7·2 116·8
D 5·2 109·2
Year 10·0 1,064·1
Height 203 feet
Cardiff
Monmouth
Trothy
GLOUCESTERSHIRE
GWENT
Wye
Tintern Abbey
Chepstow
Cinderford
Forest of Dean
Severn
Berkeley Nuclear Power Station
Vale of Berkeley
Little Avon
GLOS
AVON
Oldbury-on-Severn Nuclear Power Station
Oldbury-on-Severn
Thornbury
Severn Bridge
Severn Tunnel
Chipping Sodbury
Patchway
FILTON AIRFIELD
Filton
Frome
AVONMOUTH
Mangotsfield
Severn
Portishead
Avon
Clifton
University of Bristol
BRISTOL
Kingswood
Clevedon
Knowle
Keynsham
Yeo
Chew
BRISTOL (LULSGATE) AIRPORT
© Oxford University Press
SCALE 1: 500 000
1 INCH TO APPROX. 8 MILES
MILES : 0 5 10 15 20
KM : 0 5 10 15 20 25 30

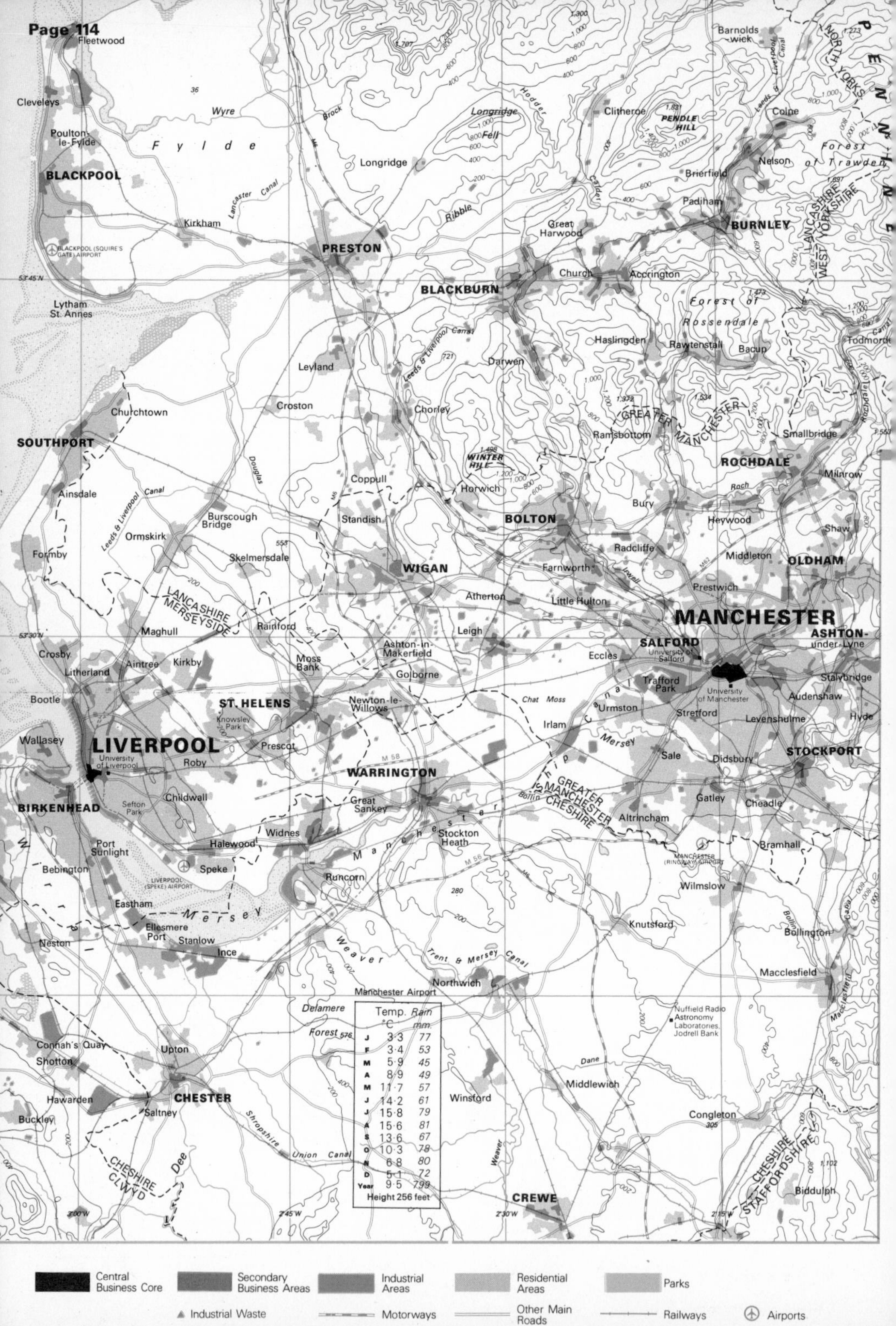

Page 114
Fleetwood
Cleveleys
Poulton-le-Fylde
BLACKPOOL
Fylde
Wyre
Kirkham
Lancaster Canal
BLACKPOOL (SQUIRE'S GATE) AIRPORT
Lytham St. Annes
53°45'N
PRESTON
Longridge
Longridge Fell
Ribble
Hodder
Brock
Clitheroe
PENDLE HILL
Barnoldswick
Great Harwood
BLACKBURN
Church
Accrington
Padiham
BURNLEY
Brierfield
Nelson
Colne
Forest of Trawden
NORTH YORKS
LANCASHIRE
WEST YORKSHIRE
Forest of Rossendale
Haslingden
Rawtenstall
Bacup
Todmorden
Leyland
Leeds & Liverpool Canal
Darwen
Croston
Chorley
Churchtown
SOUTHPORT
Ainsdale
Douglas
GREATER MANCHESTER
Ramsbottom
Smallbridge
WINTER HILL
Horwich
Coppull
ROCHDALE
Roch
Milnrow
Bury
Heywood
Burscough Bridge
Ormskirk
Standish
BOLTON
Shaw
Formby
Skelmersdale
Radcliffe
WIGAN
Farnworth
Middleton
OLDHAM
Irwell
Prestwich
LANCASHIRE
MERSEYSIDE
Atherton
Little Hulton
MANCHESTER
Maghull
Rainford
Leigh
53°30'N
SALFORD
University of Salford
ASHTON-under-Lyne
Crosby
Ashton-in-Makerfield
Eccles
Litherland
Aintree
Kirkby
Moss Bank
Golborne
Trafford Park
University of Manchester
Stalybridge
Bootle
ST. HELENS
Knowsley Park
Newton-le-Willows
Chat Moss
Ship Canal
Urmston
Stretford
Audenshaw
Levenshulme
Hyde
Irlam
Wallasey
LIVERPOOL
University of Liverpool
Prescot
Roby
Mersey
Sale
Didsbury
STOCKPORT
WARRINGTON
M 58
Childwall
BIRKENHEAD
Sefton Park
Great Sankey
GREATER MANCHESTER
CHESHIRE
Bollin
Gatley
Cheadle
Altrincham
Widnes
Stockton Heath
Halewood
Port Sunlight
Manchester
Bramhall
Bebington
Speke
LIVERPOOL (SPEKE) AIRPORT
M 56
MANCHESTER (RINGWAY) AIRPORT
Runcorn
Wilmslow
Eastham
Ellesmere Port
Stanlow
Wirral
Neston
Ince
Knutsford
Bollington
Weaver
Trent & Mersey Canal
Macclesfield
Manchester Airport
Northwich
Delamere Forest
Nuffield Radio Astronomy Laboratories, Jodrell Bank
Connah's Quay
Shotton
Upton
Dane
Middlewich
Hawarden
CHESTER
Saltney
Winsford
Buckley
Shropshire Union Canal
Congleton
CHESHIRE
CLWYD
Dee
CHESHIRE
STAFFORDSHIRE
Biddulph
CREWE
3°00'W
2°45'W
2°30'W
2°15'W
Temp. °C Rain mm.
J 3·3 77
F 3·4 53
M 5·9 45
A 8·9 49
M 11·7 57
J 14·2 61
J 15·8 79
A 15·6 81
S 13·6 67
O 10·3 78
N 6·8 80
D 5·1 72
Year 9·5 799
Height 256 feet
Central Business Core
Secondary Business Areas
Industrial Areas
Residential Areas
Parks
Industrial Waste
Motorways
Other Main Roads
Railways
Airports

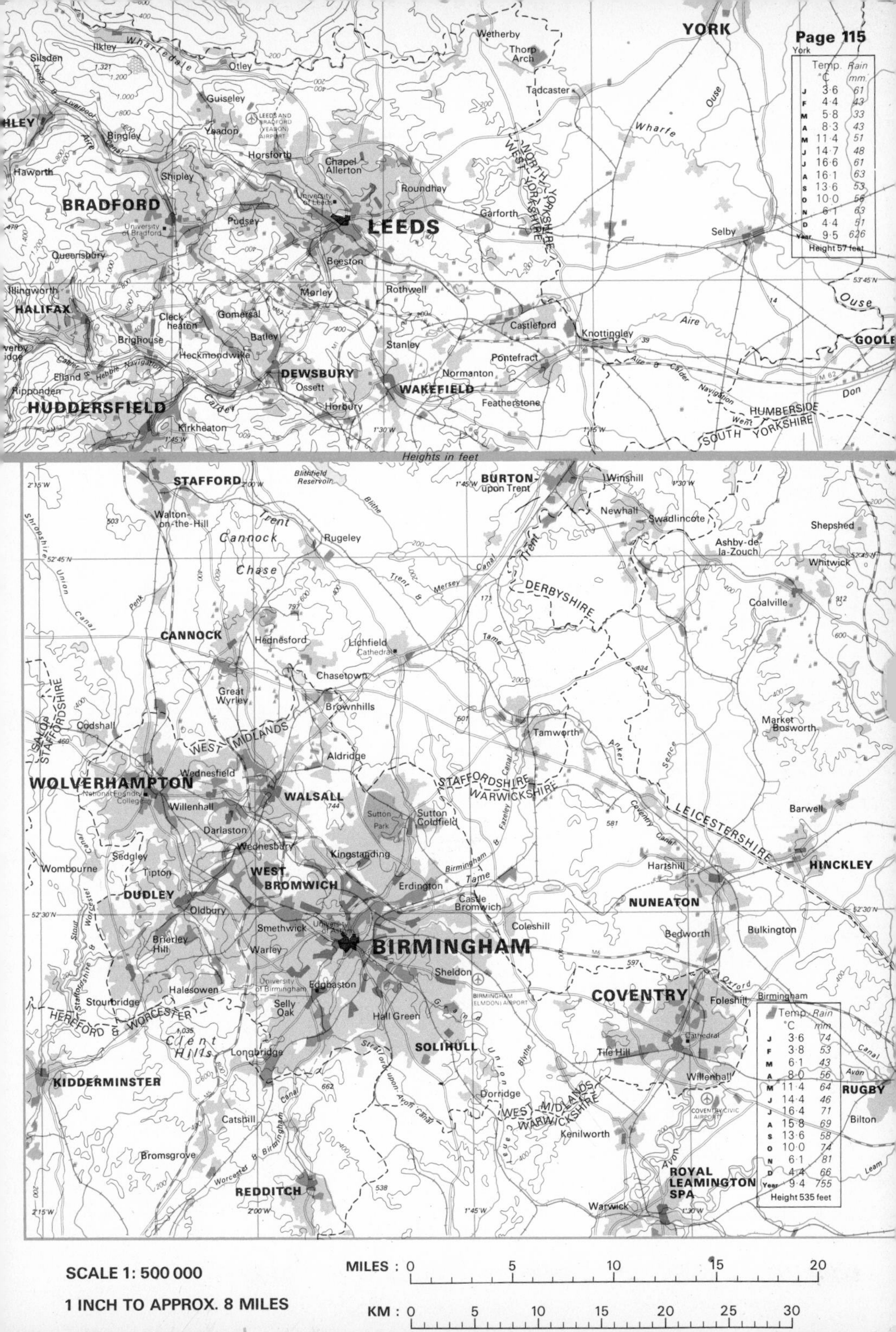
Page 115
York
Temp. °C Rain mm.
J 3·6 61
F 4·4 43
M 5·8 33
A 8·3 43
M 11·4 51
J 14·7 48
J 16·6 61
A 16·1 63
S 13·6 53
O 10·0 56
N 6·1 63
D 4·4 51
Year 9·5 626
Height 57 feet
YORK
Wetherby
Thorp Arch
Tadcaster
Ilkley
Wharfedale
Otley
Silsden
Guiseley
Yeadon
LEEDS AND BRADFORD (YEADON) AIRPORT
Bingley
Horsforth
Chapel Allerton
Roundhay
Haworth
Shipley
BRADFORD
University of Bradford
University of Leeds
LEEDS
Pudsey
Garforth
NORTH YORKSHIRE
WEST YORKSHIRE
Selby
Wharfe
Ouse
Queensbury
Beeston
Illingworth
HALIFAX
Morley
Rothwell
Cleckheaton
Gomersal
Batley
Castleford
Knottingley
Aire
GOOLE
Brighouse
Heckmondwike
Stanley
Pontefract
Elland
Calder & Hebble Navigation
DEWSBURY
Ossett
Normanton
Aire & Calder Navigation
Ripponden
HUDDERSFIELD
WAKEFIELD
Horbury
Featherstone
Don
HUMBERSIDE
SOUTH YORKSHIRE
Kirkheaton
Calder
Went
Heights in feet
STAFFORD
Blithfield Reservoir
BURTON-upon Trent
Winshill
Walton-on-the-Hill
Trent
Cannock
Chase
Rugeley
Newhall
Swadlincote
Shepshed
Ashby-de-la-Zouch
Whitwick
Shropshire Union Canal
Trent & Mersey Canal
DERBYSHIRE
Coalville
Penk
CANNOCK
Hednesford
Lichfield
Cathedral
Tame
Chasetown
Great Wyrley
Brownhills
SALOP
STAFFORDSHIRE
Codshall
WEST MIDLANDS
Tamworth
Market Bosworth
Aldridge
Anker
Sence
Wednesfield
WOLVERHAMPTON
National Foundry College
WALSALL
STAFFORDSHIRE
WARWICKSHIRE
Willenhall
Sutton Park
Sutton Coldfield
Birmingham & Fazeley Canal
Coventry Canal
LEICESTERSHIRE
Barwell
Darlaston
Wednesbury
Sedgley
Kingstanding
Wombourne
Tipton
WEST BROMWICH
Erdington
Hartshill
HINCKLEY
DUDLEY
Castle Bromwich
NUNEATON
Oldbury
Coleshill
Smethwick
University of Aston
Bulkington
Brierley Hill
Warley
BIRMINGHAM
Bedworth
Stour
Staffordshire & Worcester Canal
Sheldon
Halesowen
University of Birmingham
Edgbaston
BIRMINGHAM (ELMDON) AIRPORT
COVENTRY
Foleshill
Oxford Canal
Stourbridge
Selly Oak
HEREFORD AND WORCESTER
Hall Green
Grand Union Canal
Cathedral
Clent Hills
Longbridge
SOLIHULL
Tile Hill
Avon
Stratford-upon-Avon Canal
Blythe
KIDDERMINSTER
Willenhall
RUGBY
Dorridge
WEST MIDLANDS
WARWICKSHIRE
COVENTRY CIVIC AIRPORT
Bilton
Catshill
Kenilworth
Worcester & Birmingham Canal
Bromsgrove
Leam
ROYAL LEAMINGTON SPA
REDDITCH
Warwick
Birmingham
Temp. °C Rain mm.
J 3·6 74
F 3·8 53
M 6·1 43
A 8·0 56
M 11·4 64
J 14·4 46
J 16·4 71
A 15·8 69
S 13·6 58
O 10·0 74
N 6·1 81
D 4·4 66
Year 9·4 755
Height 535 feet
SCALE 1: 500 000
1 INCH TO APPROX. 8 MILES
MILES : 0 5 10 15 20
KM : 0 5 10 15 20 25 30

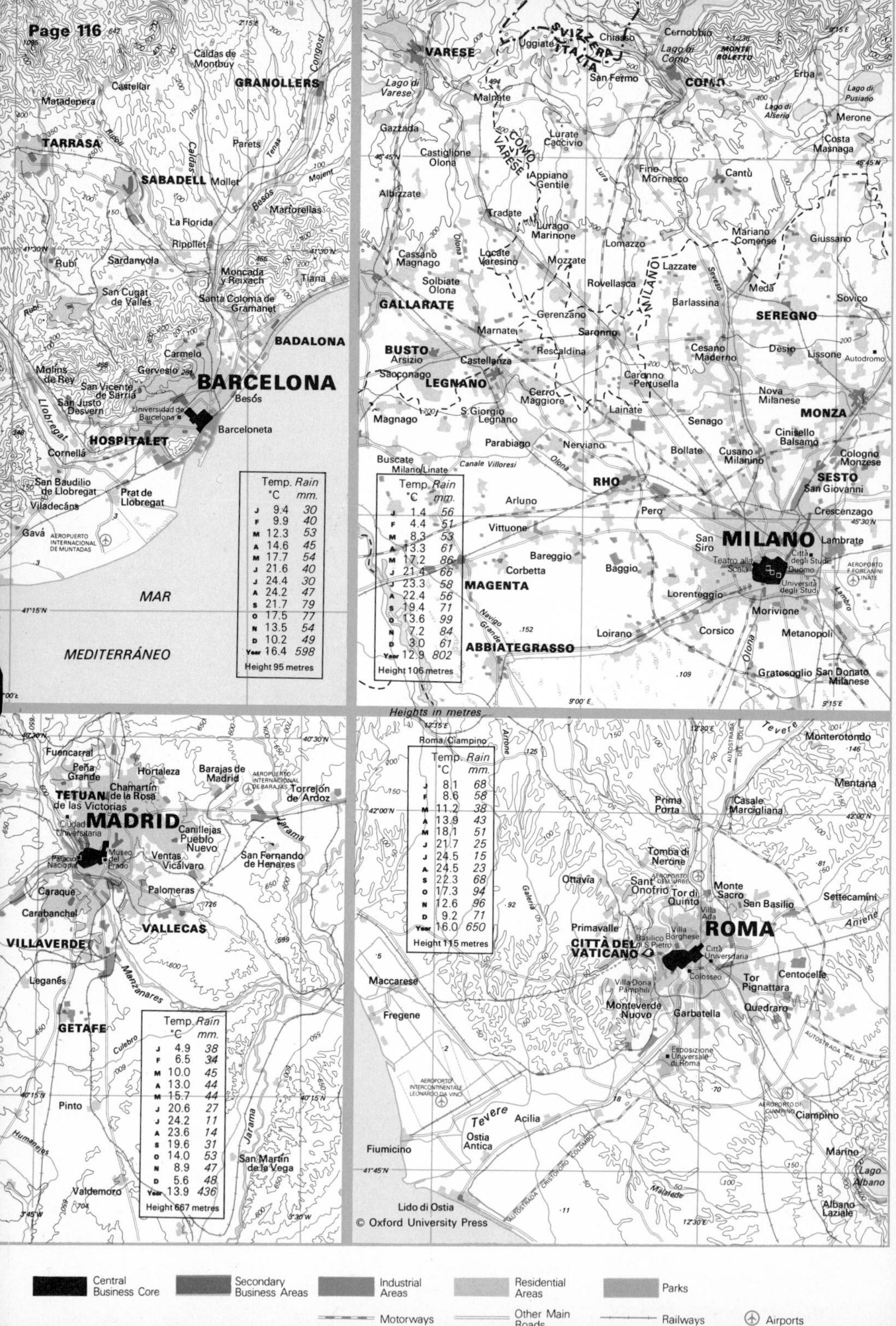

Barcelona

	Temp. °C	Rain mm.
J	9.4	30
F	9.9	40
M	12.3	53
A	14.6	45
M	17.7	54
J	21.6	40
J	24.4	30
A	24.2	47
S	21.7	79
O	17.5	77
N	13.5	54
D	10.2	49
Year	16.4	598

Height 95 metres

Milano

	Temp. °C	Rain mm.
J	1.4	56
F	4.4	51
M	8.3	53
A	13.3	61
M	17.2	86
J	21.4	66
J	23.3	58
A	22.4	56
S	19.4	71
O	13.6	99
N	7.2	84
D	3.0	61
Year	12.9	802

Height 106 metres

Madrid

	Temp. °C	Rain mm.
J	4.9	38
F	6.5	34
M	10.0	45
A	13.0	44
M	15.7	44
J	20.6	27
J	24.2	11
A	23.6	14
S	19.6	31
O	14.0	53
N	8.9	47
D	5.6	48
Year	13.9	436

Height 667 metres

Roma

	Temp. °C	Rain mm.
J	8.1	68
F	8.6	58
M	11.2	38
A	13.9	43
M	18.1	51
J	21.7	25
J	24.5	15
A	24.5	23
S	22.3	68
O	17.3	94
N	12.6	96
D	9.2	71
Year	16.0	650

Height 115 metres

Central Business Core · Secondary Business Areas · Industrial Areas · Residential Areas · Parks · Motorways · Other Main Roads · Railways · Airports

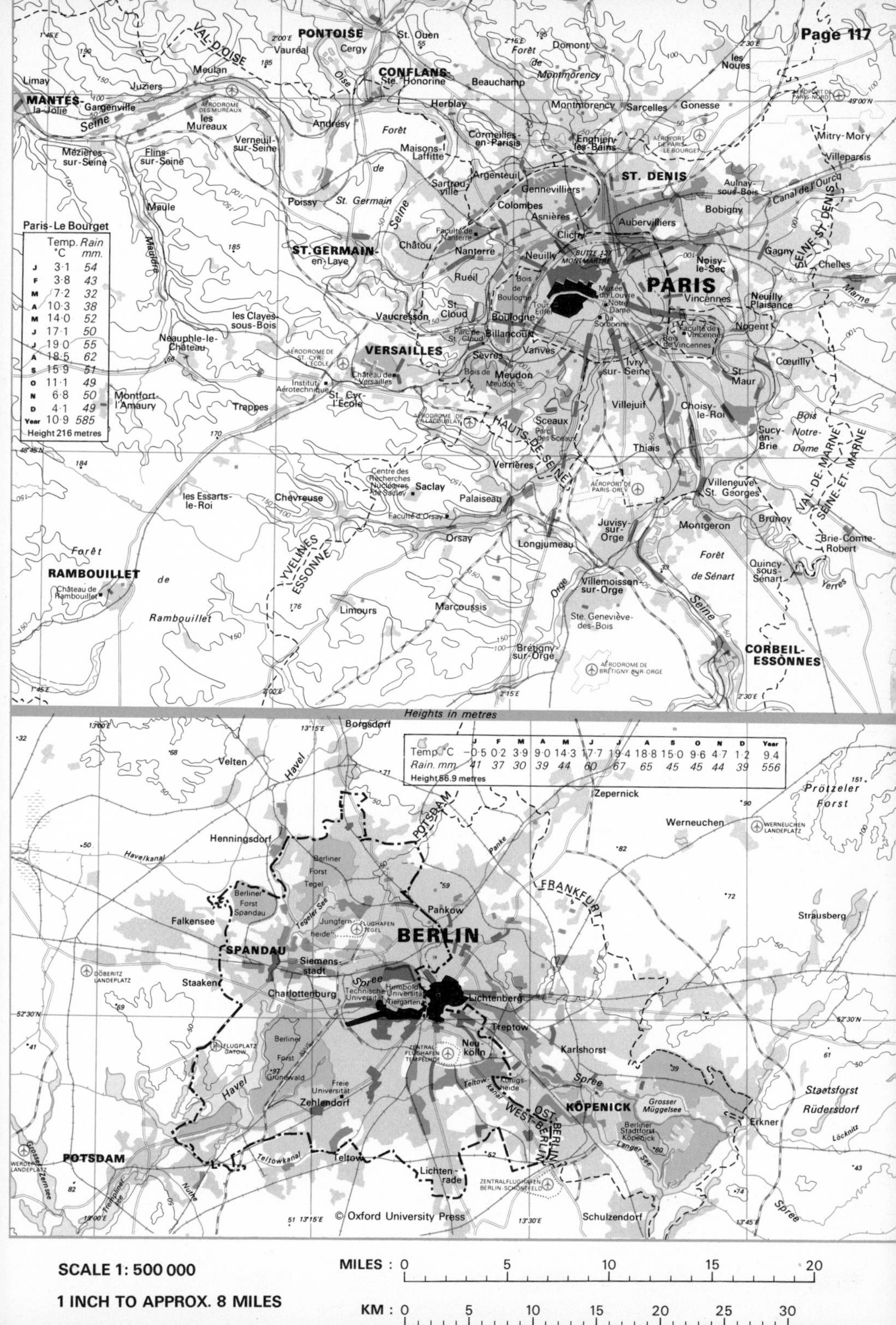

SCALE 1: 500 000

1 INCH TO APPROX. 8 MILES

© Oxford University Press

Paris-Le Bourget
	Temp. °C	Rain mm.
J	3·1	54
F	3·8	43
M	7·2	32
A	10·3	38
M	14·0	52
J	17·1	50
J	19·0	55
A	18·5	62
S	15·9	51
O	11·1	49
N	6·8	50
D	4·1	49
Year	10·9	585
Height 216 metres
	J	F	M	A	M	J	J	A	S	O	N	D	Year
Temp. °C	−0·5	0·2	3·9	9·0	14·3	17·7	19·4	18·8	15·0	9·6	4·7	1·2	9·4
Rain. mm.	41	37	30	39	44	60	67	65	45	45	44	39	556
Height 56.9 metres
MILES : 0 5 10 15 20
KM : 0 5 10 15 20 25 30

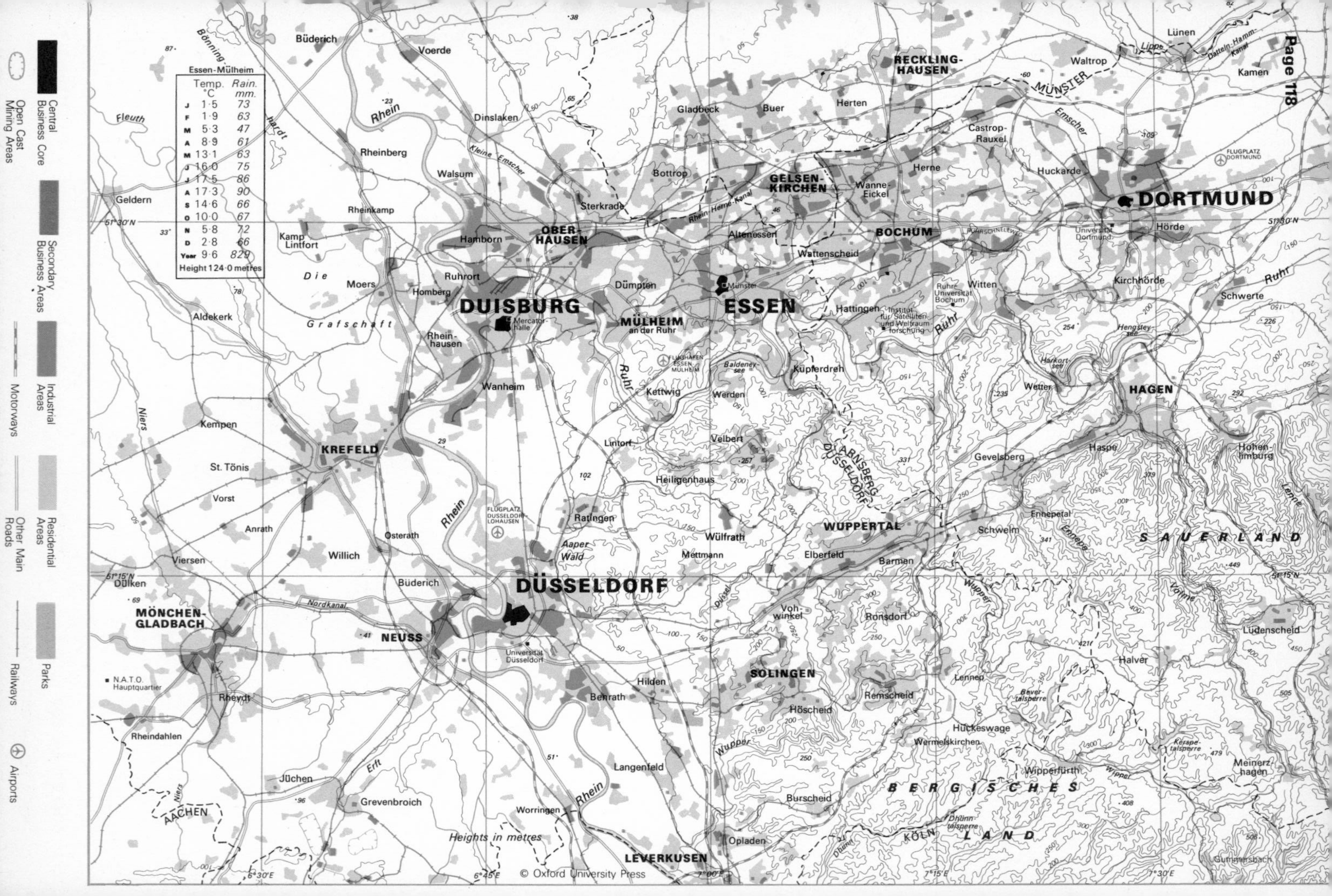

© Oxford University Press

	Central Business Core		Secondary Business Areas		Industrial Areas		Residential Areas		Parks

	Open Cast Mining Areas		Motorways		Other Main Roads		Railways		Airports

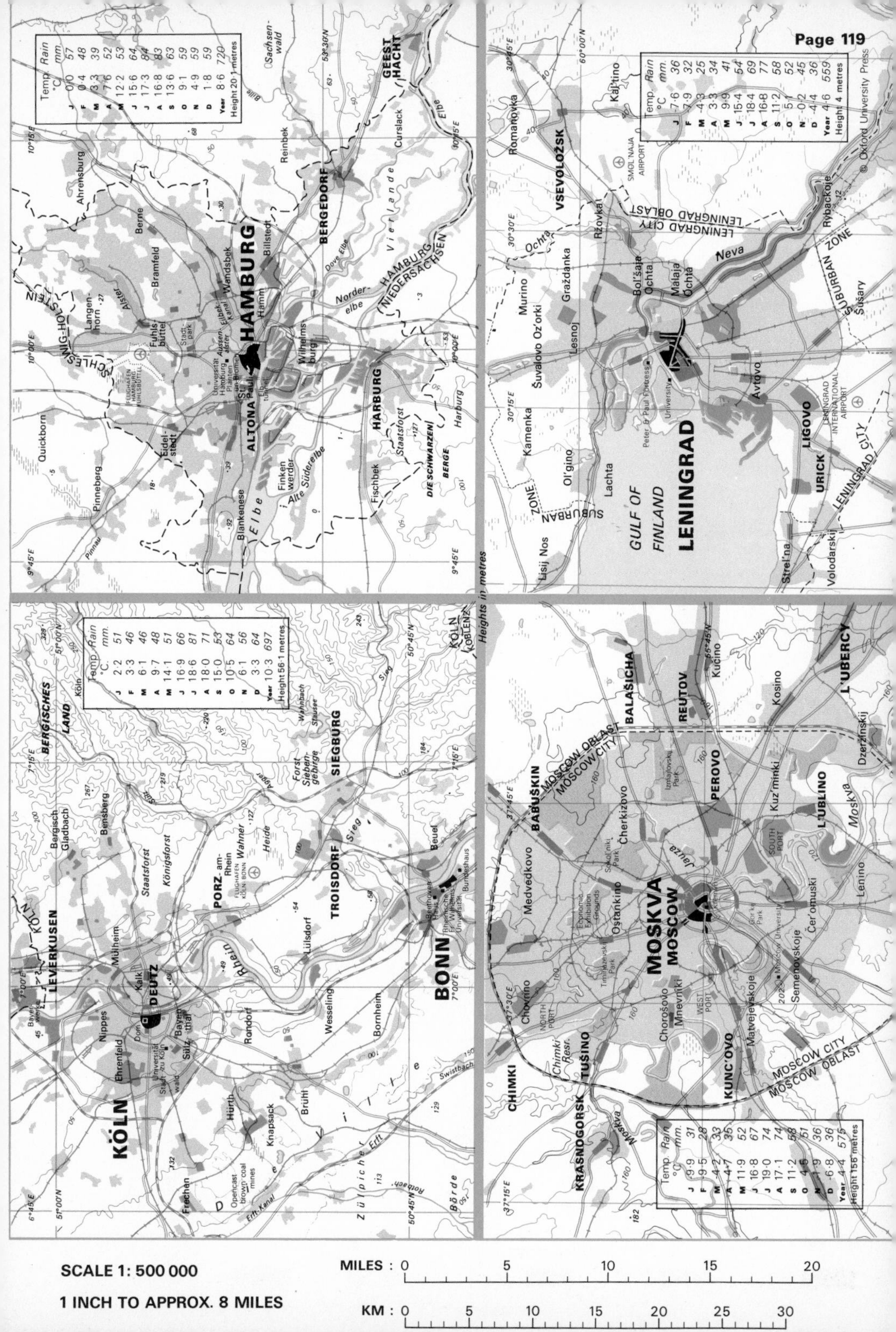

SCALE 1 : 500 000

1 INCH TO APPROX. 8 MILES

MILES : 0   5   10   15   20

KM : 0   5   10   15   20   25   30

© Oxford University Press

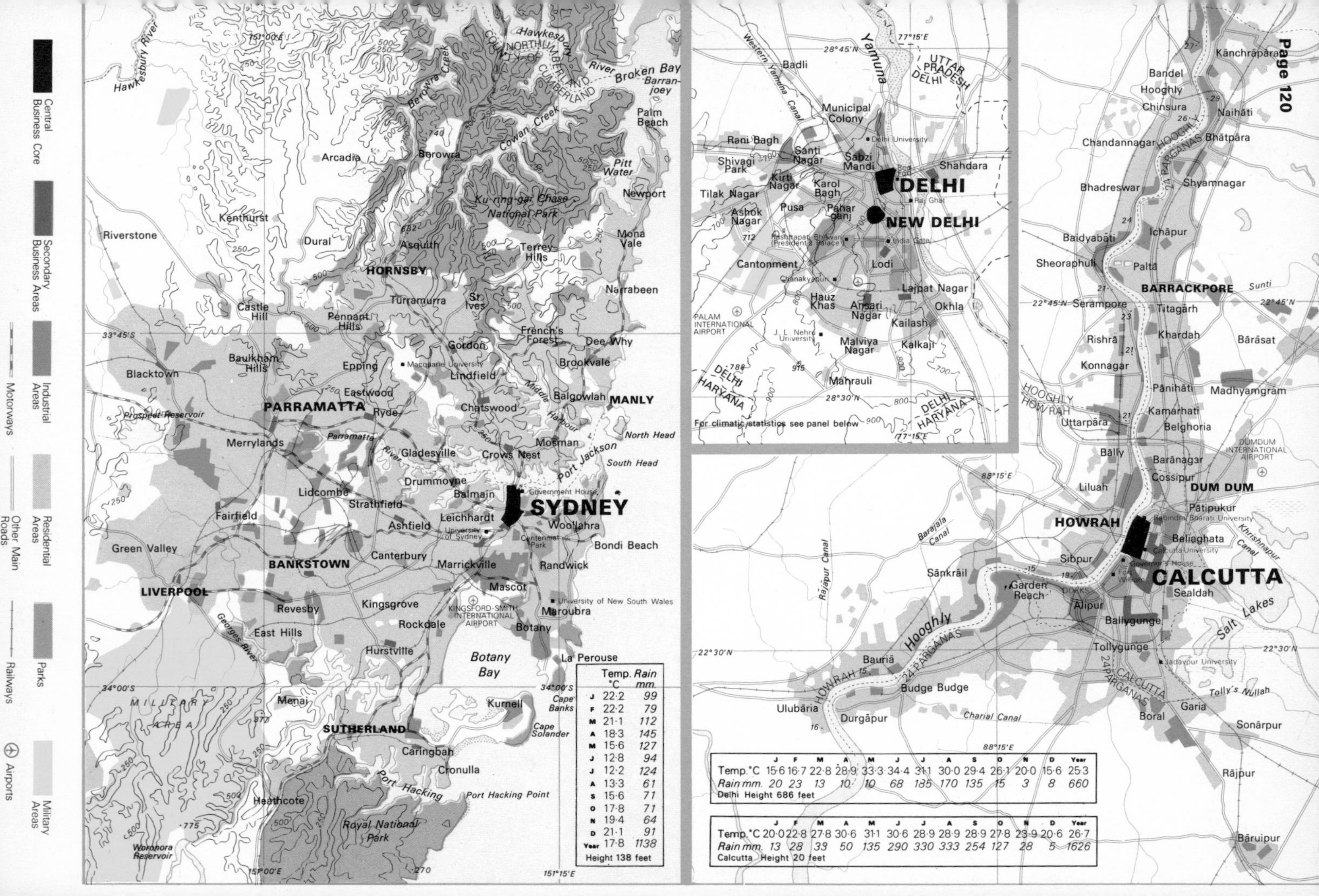

Central Business Core — Secondary Business Areas — Industrial Areas — Residential Areas — Parks — Military Areas

Motorways — Other Main Roads — Railways — Airports

	Temp. °C	Rain mm.
J	22·2	99
F	22·2	79
M	21·1	112
A	18·3	145
M	15·6	127
J	12·8	94
J	12·2	124
A	13·3	61
S	15·6	71
O	17·8	71
N	19·4	64
D	21·1	91
Year	17·8	1138
Height 138 feet
	J	F	M	A	M	J	J	A	S	O	N	D	Year
Temp. °C	15·6	16·7	22·8	28·9	33·3	34·4	31·1	30·0	29·4	26·1	20·0	15·6	25·3
Rain mm.	20	23	13	10	10	68	185	170	135	15	3	8	660
Delhi Height 686 feet
	J	F	M	A	M	J	J	A	S	O	N	D	Year
Temp. °C	20·0	22·8	27·8	30·6	31·1	30·6	28·9	28·9	28·9	27·8	23·9	20·6	26·7
Rain mm.	13	28	33	50	135	290	330	333	254	127	28	5	1626
Calcutta Height 20 feet

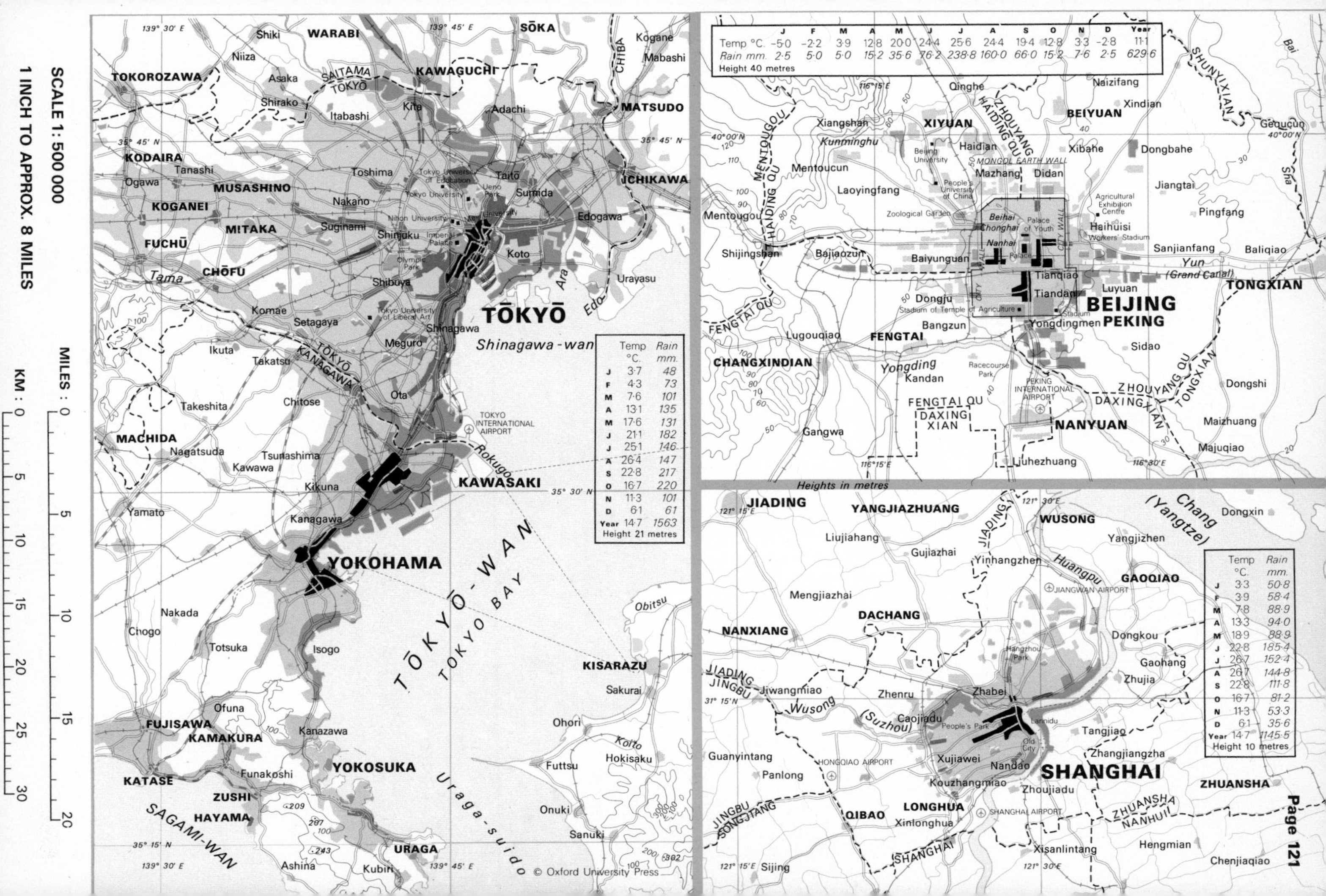

Tokyo

	Temp °C.	Rain mm.
J	3·7	48
F	4·3	73
M	7·6	101
A	13·1	135
M	17·6	131
J	21·1	182
J	25·1	146
A	26·4	147
S	22·8	217
O	16·7	220
N	11·3	101
D	6·1	61
Year	14·7	1563

Height 21 metres

Beijing

	J	F	M	A	M	J	J	A	S	O	N	D	Year
Temp °C.	-5·0	-2·2	3·9	12·8	20·0	24·4	25·6	24·4	19·4	12·8	3·3	-2·8	11·1
Rain mm.	2·5	5·0	5·0	15·2	35·6	76·2	238·8	160·0	66·0	15·2	7·6	2·5	629·6

Height 40 metres

Shanghai

	Temp °C.	Rain mm.
J	3·3	50·8
F	3·9	58·4
M	7·8	88·9
A	13·3	94·0
M	18·9	88·9
J	22·8	185·4
J	26·7	152·4
A	26·7	144·8
S	22·8	111·8
O	16·7	81·2
N	11·3	53·3
D	6·1	35·6
Year	14·7	1145·5

Height 10 metres

SCALE 1: 500 000

1 INCH TO APPROX. 8 MILES

MILES : 0 5 10 15 20

KM : 0 5 10 15 20 25 30

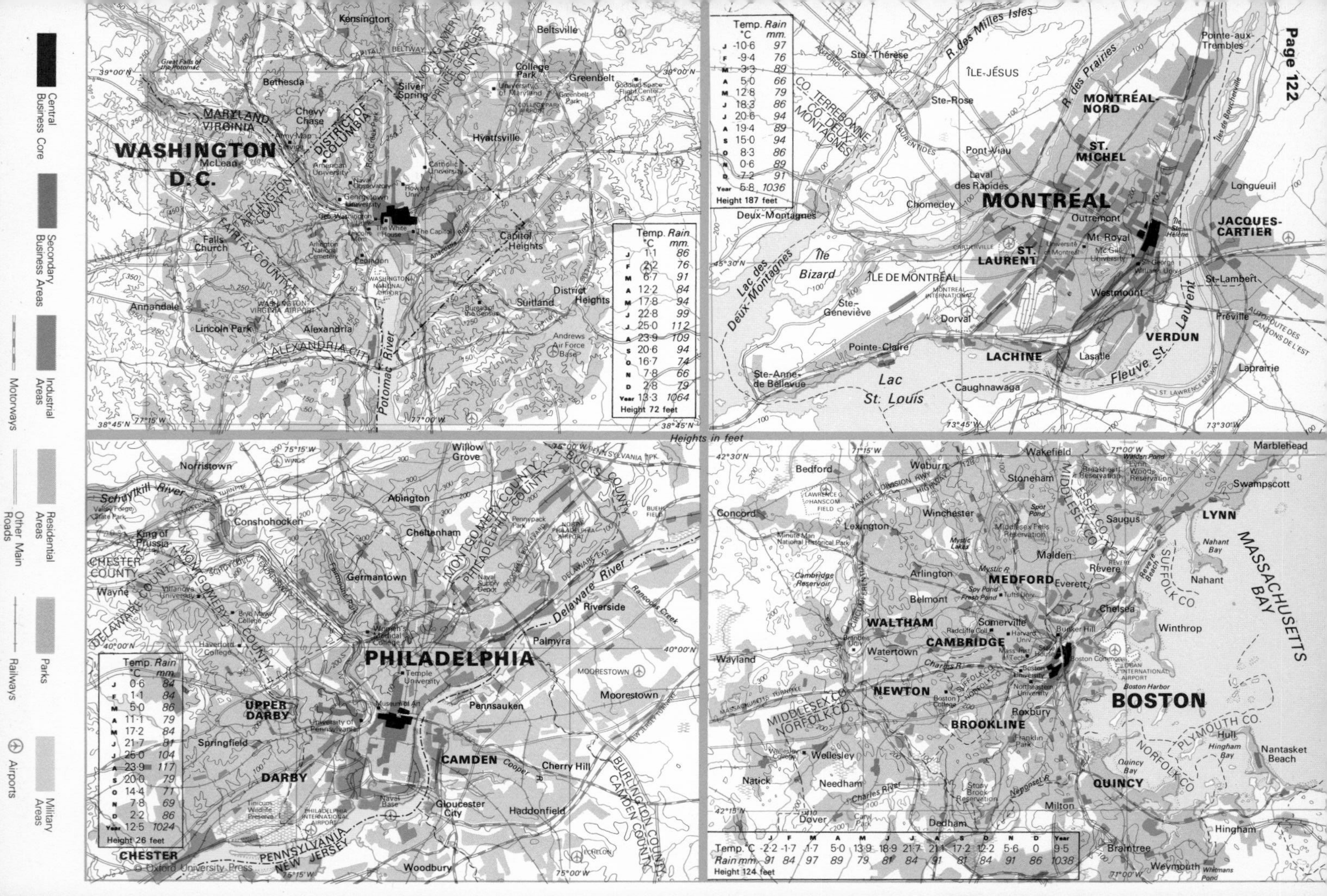

Washington

	Temp. °C	Rain mm.
J	1·1	86
F	2·2	76
M	6·7	91
A	12·2	84
M	17·8	94
J	22·8	99
J	25·0	112
A	23·9	109
S	20·6	94
O	16·7	74
N	7·8	66
D	2·8	79
Year	13·3	1064

Height 72 feet

Montréal

	Temp. °C	Rain mm.
J	-10·6	97
F	-9·4	76
M	-3·3	89
A	5·0	66
M	12·8	79
J	18·3	86
J	20·6	94
A	19·4	89
S	15·0	94
O	8·3	86
N	0·6	89
D	-7·2	91
Year	5·8	1036

Height 187 feet

Philadelphia

	Temp. °C	Rain mm.
J	0·6	84
F	1·1	84
M	5·0	86
A	11·1	79
M	17·2	84
J	21·7	81
J	25·0	104
A	23·9	117
S	20·0	79
O	14·4	71
N	7·8	69
D	2·2	86
Year	12·5	1024

Height 26 feet

Boston

	J	F	M	A	M	J	J	A	S	O	N	D	Year
Temp. °C	-2·2	-1·7	1·7	5·0	13·9	18·9	21·7	21·1	17·2	12·2	5·6	0	9·5
Rain mm.	91	84	97	89	79	81	84	91	81	84	91	86	1038

Height 124 feet

Central Business Core · Secondary Business Areas · Industrial Areas · Residential Areas · Parks · Military Areas
Motorways · Other Main Roads · Railways · Airports

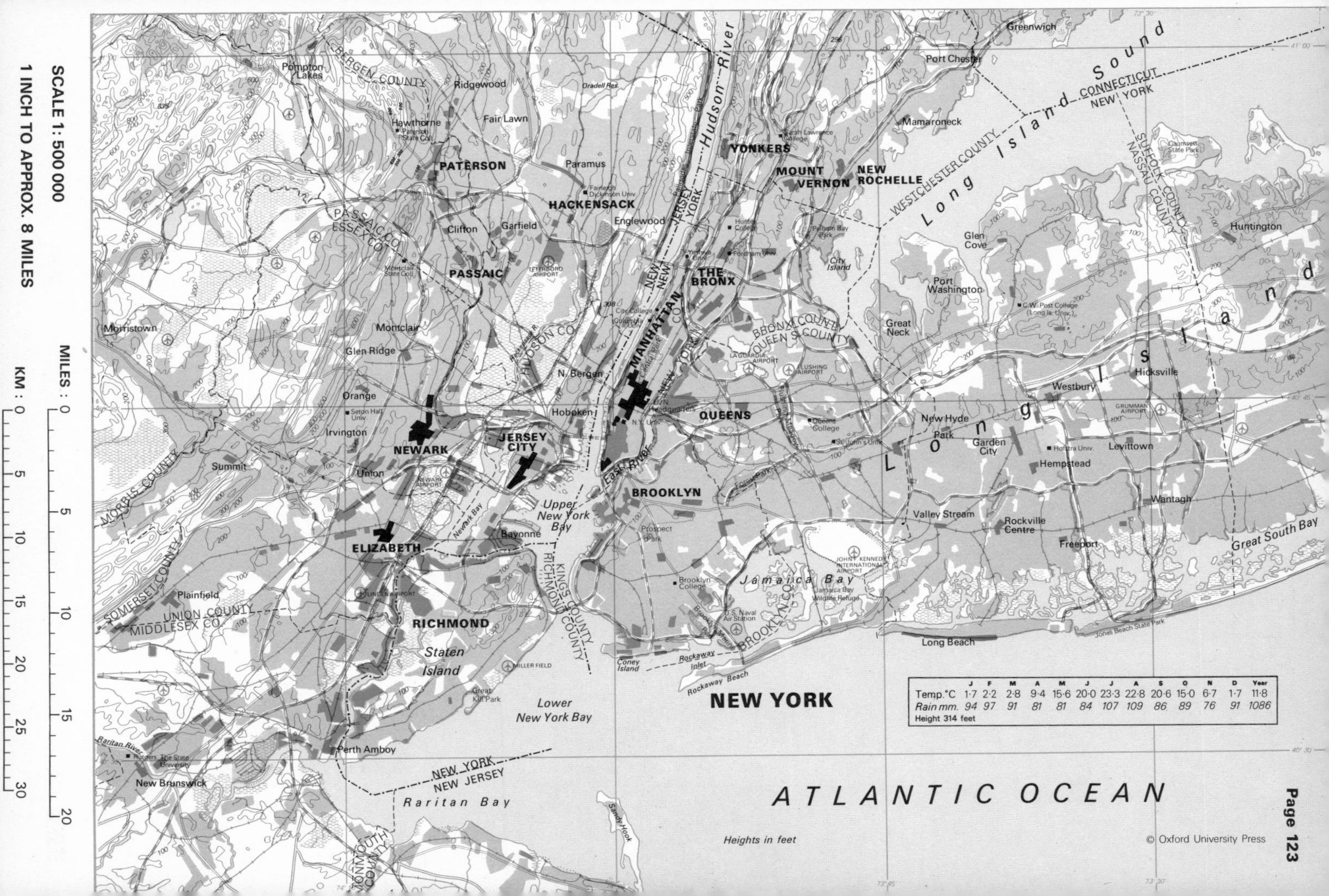

© Oxford University Press

Temp.°C	J	F	M	A	M	J	J	A	S	O	N	D
	1.7	2.2	2.8	9.4	15.6	20.0	23.3	22.8	20.6	15.0	6.7	1.7
Rain mm.	94	97	91	81	81	84	107	109	86	89	76	91
Height 314 feet												1086

NEW YORK

ATLANTIC OCEAN

Heights in feet

Long Island Sound

Connecticut
New York

Suffolk County
Nassau County

Huntington

Hicksville

Westbury

Levittown

Wantagh

Great South Bay

Long Island

Hempstead

Freeport

Rockville Centre

Valley Stream

New Hyde Park

Garden City

Long Beach

Greenwich

Port Chester

Mamaroneck

Westchester County

New Rochelle

Mount Vernon

Yonkers

Glen Cove

Port Washington

Great Neck

Jamaica Bay

Rockaway Beach

Brooklyn County

The Bronx

Manhattan

Queens

Brooklyn

Hudson River

New Jersey

New York

Hackensack

Paramus

Fair Lawn

Garfield

Paterson

Passaic

Clifton

Ridgewood

Hawthorne

Bergen County

Montclair

Glen Ridge

Orange

Irvington

Union

Newark

Jersey City

Bayonne

Elizabeth

Upper New York Bay

Kings County
Richmond County

Richmond

Staten Island

Newark Bay

Lower New York Bay

Sandy Hook

Coney Island

New York
New Jersey

Raritan Bay

Perth Amboy

Monmouth County

Summit

Plainfield

Union County

Middlesex County

Somerset County

New Brunswick

Morristown

Pompton Lakes

Passaic County
Essex County

Hudson County

Bergen County

Essex County

SCALE 1 : 500 000

1 INCH TO APPROX. 8 MILES

MILES :   0   5   10   15   20

KM :   0   5   10   15   20   25   30

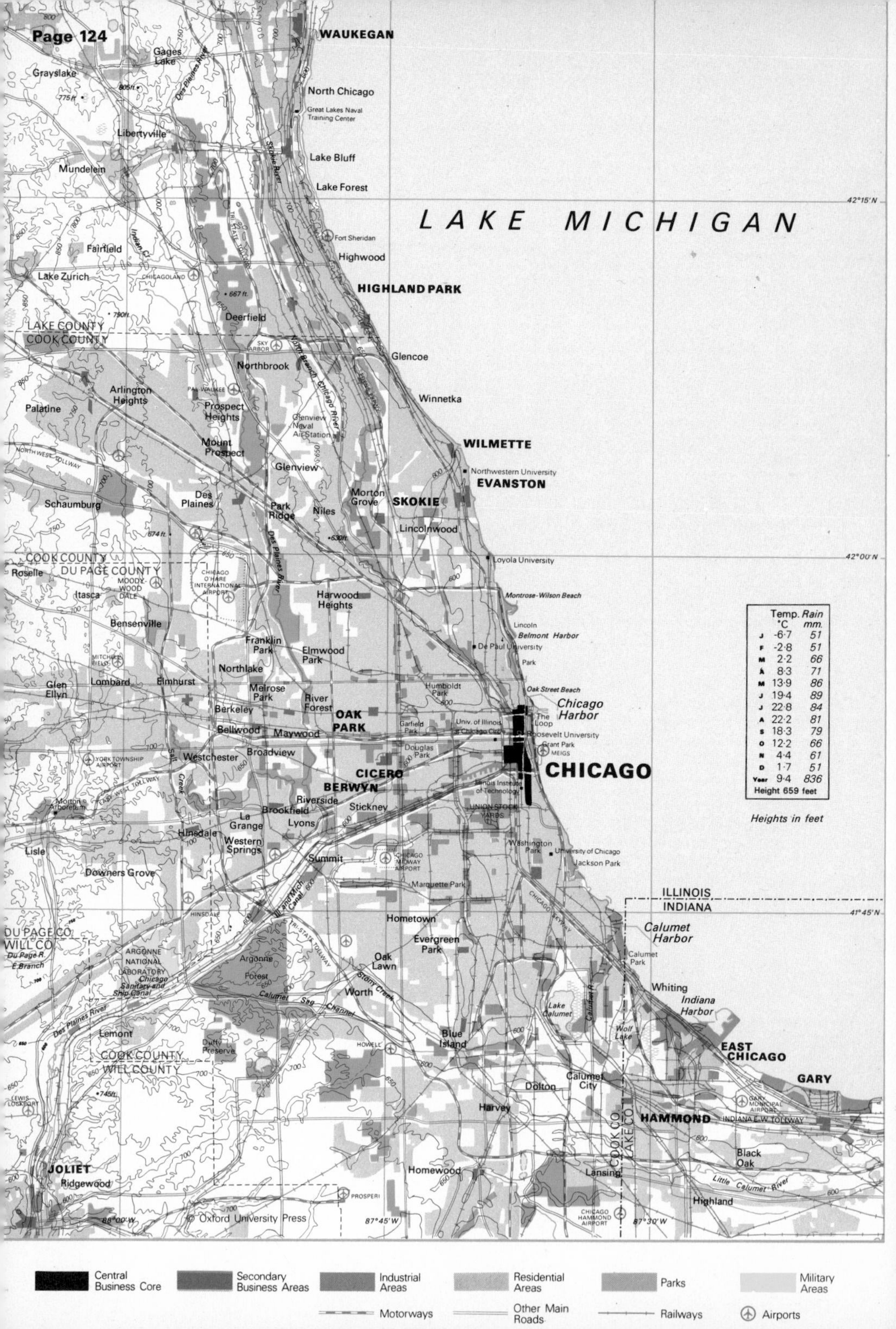

WAUKEGAN

Grayslake

Gages Lake

806 ft

North Chicago

775 ft

Great Lakes Naval
Training Center

Libertyville

Lake Bluff

Mundelein

Lake Forest

LAKE MICHIGAN

42°15'N

Fairfield

Fort Sheridan

Highwood

Lake Zurich

667 ft

HIGHLAND PARK

790 ft

CHICAGOLAND

Deerfield

Palatine

Arlington
Heights

Northbrook

Glencoe

LAKE COUNTY
COOK COUNTY

Prospect
Heights

Winnetka

Mount
Prospect

Glenview
Naval
Air Station

WILMETTE

Des
Plaines

Glenview

Northwestern University

Schaumburg

Park
Ridge

Morton
Grove

SKOKIE

EVANSTON

674 ft

Niles

Lincolnwood

630 ft

42°00'N

COOK COUNTY
DU PAGE COUNTY

CHICAGO
O'HARE
INTERNATIONAL
AIRPORT

Loyola University

Roselle

MOODY-
WOOD-
DALE

Harwood
Heights

Montrose-Wilson Beach

Itasca

Lincoln
Belmont Harbor

Bensenville

De Paul University
Park

	Temp.	Rain
	°C	mm.
J	-6·7	51
F	-2·8	51
M	2·2	66
A	8·3	71
M	13·9	86
J	19·4	89
J	22·8	84
A	22·2	81
S	18·3	79
O	12·2	66
N	4·4	61
D	1·7	51
Year	9·4	836
Height 659 feet		

Franklin
Park

Elmwood
Park

Glen
Ellyn

Lombard

Elmhurst

Northlake

Melrose
Park

Humboldt
Park

Oak Street Beach

*Chicago
Harbor*

Berkeley

River
Forest

**OAK
PARK**

Univ. of Illinois
at Chicago Circle

The
Loop

Roosevelt University

Bellwood

Maywood

Garfield
Park

Grant Park

CHICAGO

York Township
Airport

Westchester

Broadway

Douglas
Park

Illinois Institute
of Technology

Heights in feet

Mitchell's
Creek

Broadview

CICERO

Riverside

BERWYN

Brookfield

Lyons

Stickney

LINCOLN
PARK

La Grange

Hinsdale

Summit

CHICAGO
MIDWAY
AIRPORT

Washington
Park

University of Chicago

Lisle

Downers Grove

Marquette Park

Jackson Park

ILLINOIS
INDIANA

DU PAGE CO
WILL CO

ARGONNE
NATIONAL
LABORATORY
Chicago
Sanitary and
Ship Canal

Hometown

Evergreen
Park

*Calumet
Harbor*

Calumet
Park

Argonne
Forest

Oak
Lawn

Whiting

*Indiana
Harbor*

Worth

Lemont

Calumet Sag

Lake Calumet

Wolf
Lake

Blue
Island

Calumet
City

**EAST
CHICAGO**

GARY

COOK COUNTY
WILL COUNTY

7450 ft

Dolton

HAMMOND

GARY
MUNICIPAL
AIRPORT

INDIANA E.W.TOLLWAY

Harvey

Black
Oak

JOLIET

Ridgewood

Homewood

Lansing

Little Calumet River

Highland

87°45'W

© Oxford University Press

CHICAGO
HAMMOND
AIRPORT

87°30'W

■ Central Business Core	Secondary Business Areas	Industrial Areas	Residential Areas	Parks	Military Areas

Motorways   Other Main Roads   Railways   ✈ Airports

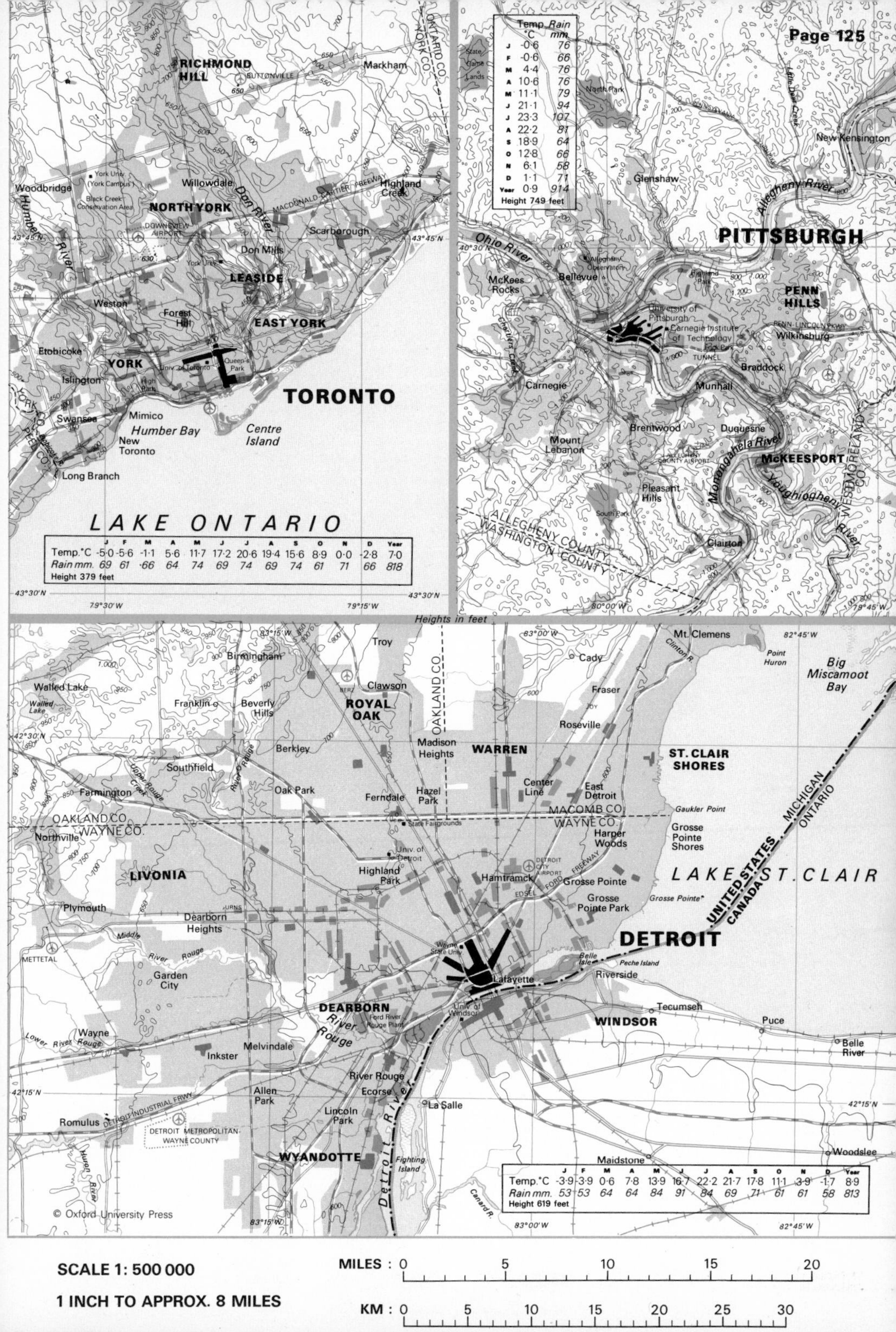

Toronto

	J	F	M	A	M	J	J	A	S	O	N	D	Year
Temp. °C	-5·0	-5·6	-1·1	5·6	11·7	17·2	20·6	19·4	15·6	8·9	0·0	-2·8	7·0
Rain mm.	69	61	·66	64	74	69	74	69	74	61	71	66	818

Height 379 feet

Pittsburgh

	Temp. °C	Rain mm
J	-0·6	76
F	-0·6	66
M	4·4	76
A	10·6	76
M	11·1	79
J	21·1	94
J	23·3	107
A	22·2	81
S	18·9	64
O	12·8	66
N	6·1	58
D	1·1	71
Year	0·9	914

Height 749 feet

Detroit

	J	F	M	A	M	J	J	A	S	O	N	D	Year
Temp. °C	-3·9	-3·9	0·6	7·8	13·9	16·7	22·2	21·7	17·8	11·1	3·9	-1·7	8·9
Rain mm.	53	53	64	64	84	91	84	69	71	61	61	58	813

Height 619 feet

SCALE 1: 500 000

1 INCH TO APPROX. 8 MILES

MILES : 0 5 10 15 20

KM : 0 5 10 15 20 25 30

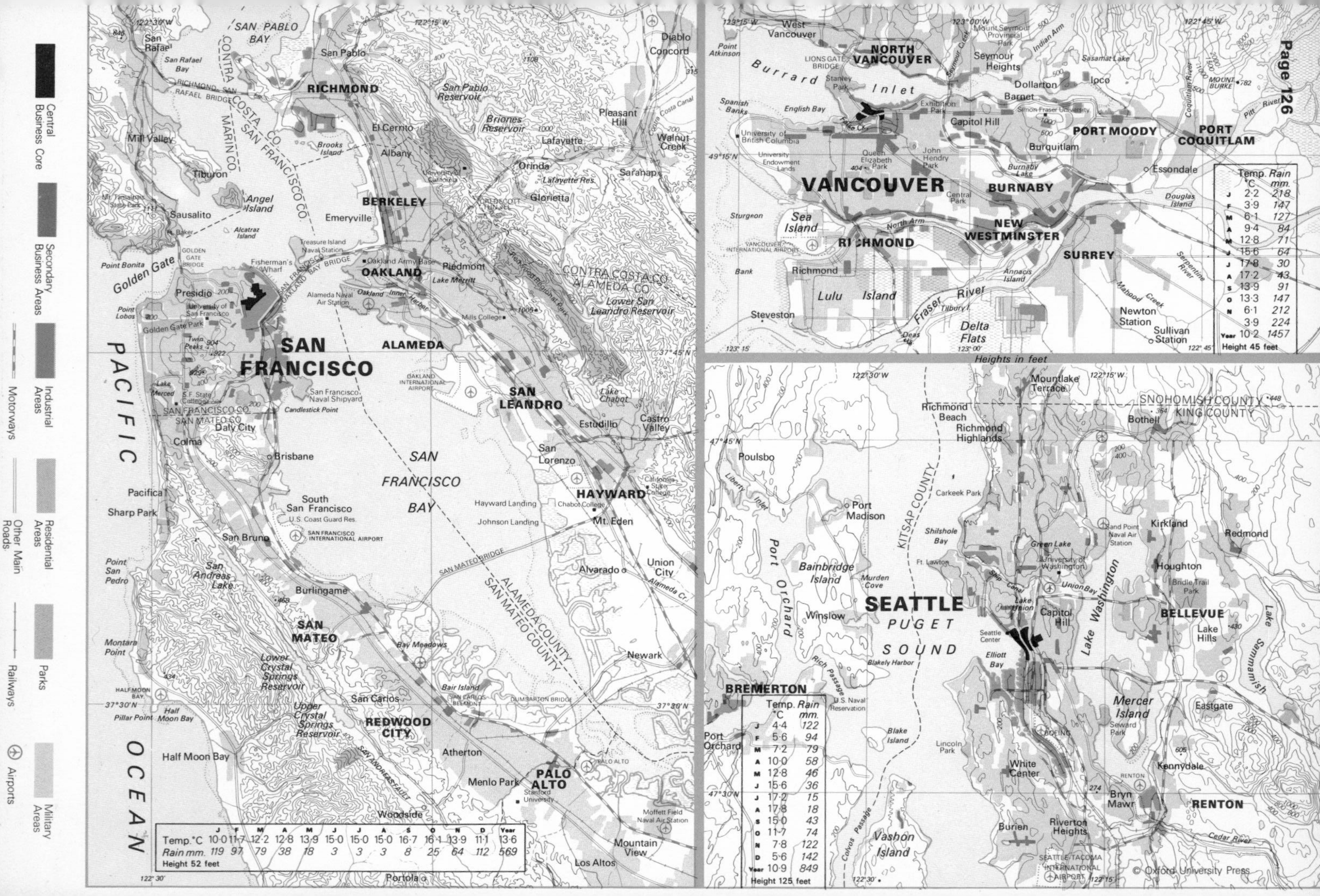

Central Business Core Secondary Business Areas Industrial Areas Residential Areas Parks Military Areas

Motorways Other Main Roads Railways Airports

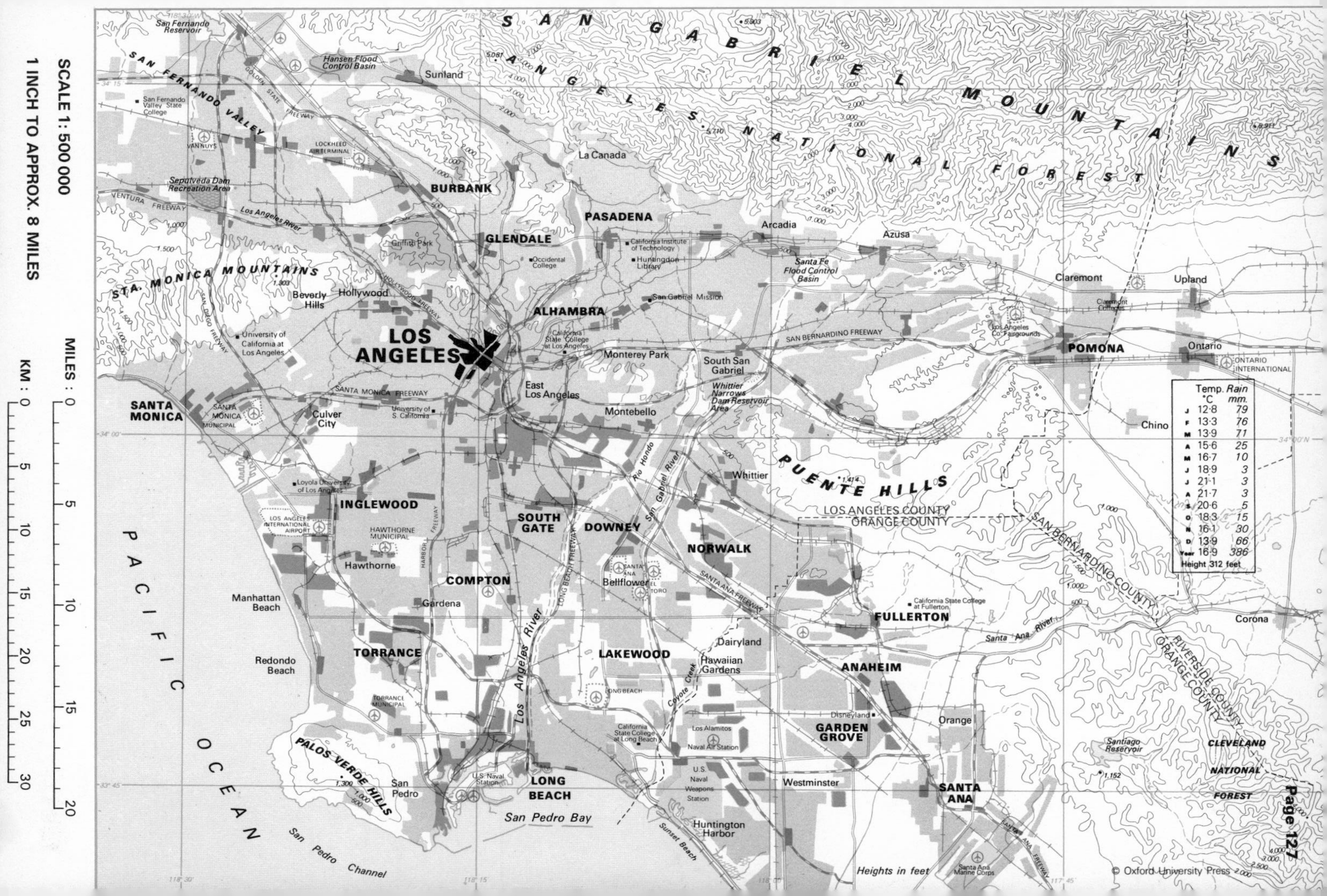

SAN GABRIEL MOUNTAINS
ANGELES NATIONAL FOREST
CLEVELAND NATIONAL FOREST
PUENTE HILLS
STA. MONICA MOUNTAINS
SAN FERNANDO VALLEY
PALOS VERDE HILLS
PACIFIC OCEAN
San Pedro Bay
San Pedro Channel
LOS ANGELES
PASADENA
GLENDALE
BURBANK
ALHAMBRA
POMONA
FULLERTON
ANAHEIM
SANTA ANA
GARDEN GROVE
NORWALK
DOWNEY
LAKEWOOD
SOUTH GATE
COMPTON
LONG BEACH
TORRANCE
INGLEWOOD
SANTA MONICA
Beverly Hills
Hollywood
Culver City
Hawthorne
Gardena
Manhattan Beach
Redondo Beach
San Pedro
Sunland
La Canada
Arcadia
Azusa
Claremont
Upland
Ontario
Chino
Corona
Orange
Westminster
Huntington Harbor
Sunset Beach
Dairyland
Hawaiian Gardens
Bellflower
Whittier
South San Gabriel
Monterey Park
Montebello
East Los Angeles
San Gabriel Mission
RIVERSIDE COUNTY
ORANGE COUNTY
SAN BERNARDINO COUNTY
LOS ANGELES COUNTY
Los Angeles River
San Gabriel River
Rio Hondo
Santa Ana River
Coyote Creek
SAN BERNARDINO FREEWAY
SANTA ANA FREEWAY
LONG BEACH FREEWAY
HARBOR FREEWAY
SANTA MONICA FREEWAY
SAN DIEGO FREEWAY
HOLLYWOOD FREEWAY
VENTURA FREEWAY
GOLDEN STATE FREEWAY
Temp. °C | Rain mm.
J 12·8 79
F 13·3 76
M 13·9 71
A 15·6 25
M 16·7 10
J 18·9 3
J 21·1 3
A 21·7 3
S 20·6 5
O 18·3 15
N 16·1 30
D 13·9 66
Year 16·9 386
Height 312 feet
Heights in feet
© Oxford University Press
SCALE 1: 500 000
1 INCH TO APPROX. 8 MILES
MILES : 0 5 10 15 20
KM : 0 5 10 15 20 25 30

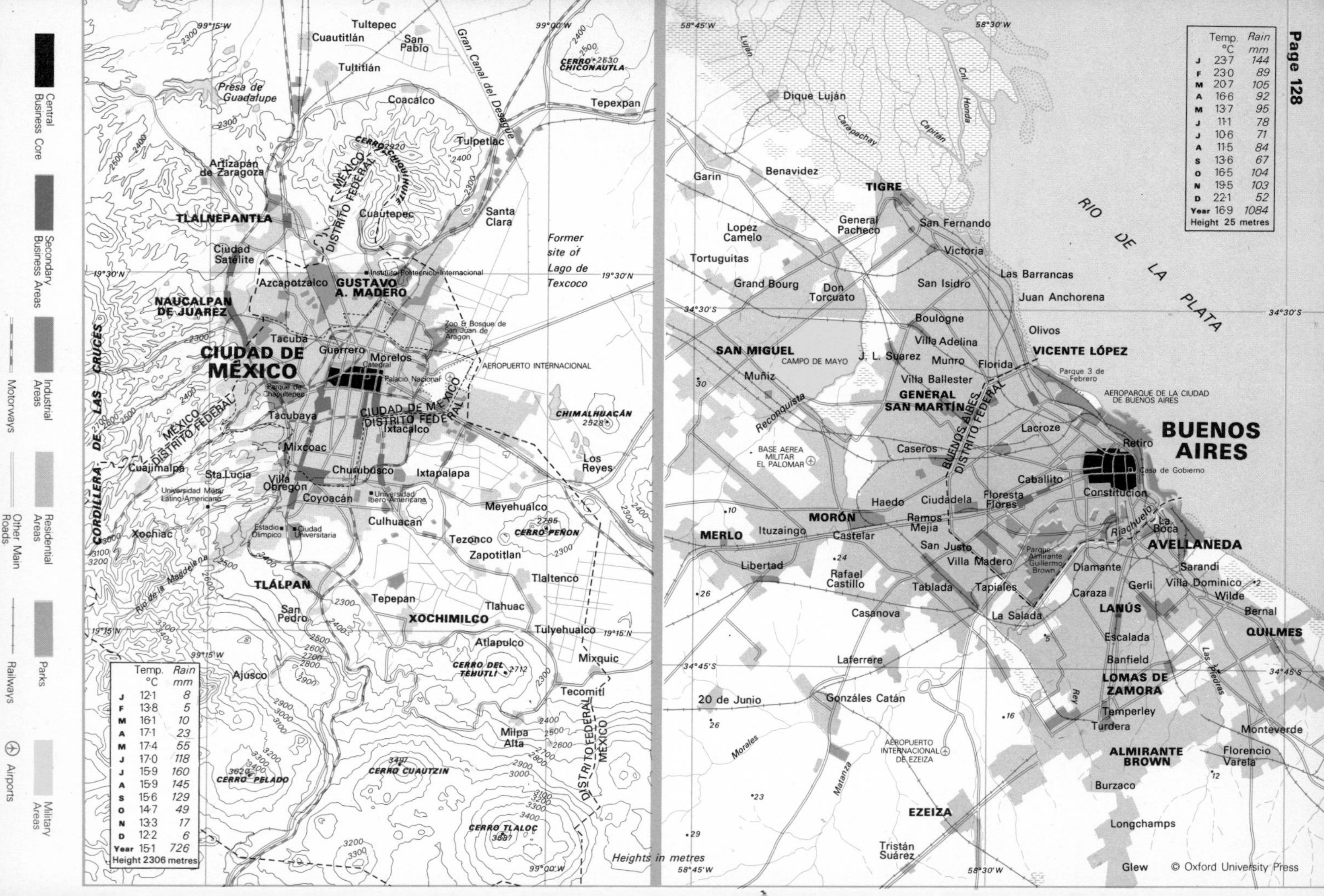
CIUDAD DE MÉXICO
Temp. °C Rain mm
J 12·1 8
F 13·8 5
M 16·1 10
A 17·1 23
M 17·4 55
J 17·0 118
J 15·9 160
A 15·9 145
S 15·6 129
O 14·7 49
N 13·3 17
D 12·2 6
Year 15·1 726
Height 2306 metres
Tultepec
Cuautitlán
San Pablo
Tultitlán
Gran Canal del Desagüe
CERRO CHICONAUTLA 2630
Tepexpan
Presa de Guadalupe
Coacalco
Artizapan de Zaragoza
CERRO CHIQUIHUITE 2920
Tulpetlac
MÉXICO DISTRITO FEDERAL
TLALNEPANTLA
Cuautepec
Santa Clara
Ciudad Satélite
Former site of Lago de Texcoco
Instituto Politecnico Internacional
Azcapotzalco
GUSTAVO A. MADERO
NAUCALPAN DE JUAREZ
Zoo & Bosque de San Juan de Aragon
Tacuba
Guerrero
Morelos
Catedral
Palacio Nacional
AEROPUERTO INTERNACIONAL
Parque de Chapultepec
CIUDAD DE MÉXICO DISTRITO FEDERAL
CHIMALHUACÁN 2528
Tacubaya
Ixtacalco
Mixcoac
Los Reyes
Cuajimalpa
Sta Lucia
Churubusco
Ixtapalapa
Villa Obregón
Universidad Militar Latino-Americano
Universidad Ibero-Americana
Coyoacán
Meyehualco
Culhuacan
Estadio Olimpico
Ciudad Universitaria
Tezonco
CERRO PEÑON 2785
Xochiac
Zapotitlan
CORDILLERA DE LAS CRUCES
Río de la Magdalena
Tlaltenco
TLÁLPAN
Tepepan
San Pedro
Tlahuac
XOCHIMILCO
Tulyehualco
Atlapulco
Ajusco
CERRO DEL TEHUTLI 2712
Mixquic
Tecomitl
Milpa Alta
DISTRITO FEDERAL MÉXICO
CERRO PELADO 3620
CERRO CUAUTZIN 3497
CERRO TLALOC 3687
Heights in metres
BUENOS AIRES
Temp. °C Rain mm
J 23·7 144
F 23·0 89
M 20·7 105
A 16·6 92
M 13·7 95
J 11·1 78
J 10·6 71
A 11·5 84
S 13·6 67
O 16·5 104
N 19·5 103
D 22·1 52
Year 16·9 1084
Height 25 metres
Luján
Dique Luján
Cnl. Honda
Capitán
Carapachay
Garin
Benavidez
TIGRE
RIO DE LA PLATA
General Pacheco
San Fernando
Lopez Camelo
Victoria
Tortuguitas
Las Barrancas
Grand Bourg
Don Torcuato
San Isidro
Juan Anchorena
Boulogne
Olivos
SAN MIGUEL
CAMPO DE MAYO
Villa Adelina
J. L. Suarez
Munro
Florida
VICENTE LÓPEZ
Muñiz
Parque 3 de Febrero
Villa Ballester
GENERAL SAN MARTIN
AEROPARQUE DE LA CIUDAD DE BUENOS AIRES
Reconquista
BUENOS AIRES DISTRITO FEDERAL
Lacroze
BASE AEREA MILITAR EL PALOMAR
Caseros
Retiro
Casa de Gobierno
Caballito
Haedo
Ciudadela
Floresta
Flores
Constitución
MORÓN
Ramos Mejia
Riachuelo
La Boca
MERLO
Ituzaingo
Castelar
AVELLANEDA
San Justo
Parque Almirante Guillermo Brown
Libertad
Rafael Castillo
Villa Madero
Diamante
Sarandi
Villa Dominico
Tablada
Tapiales
Gerli
Wilde
Caraza
LANÚS
Casanova
La Salada
Bernal
QUILMES
Escalada
Laferrere
Banfield
Las Piedras
LOMAS DE ZAMORA
20 de Junio
Gonzáles Catán
Rey
Temperley
Turdera
Monteverde
Morales
AEROPUERTO INTERNACIONAL DE EZEIZA
Matanza
ALMIRANTE BROWN
Florencio Varela
Burzaco
EZEIZA
Longchamps
Tristán Suárez
Glew
© Oxford University Press
Central Business Core
Secondary Business Areas
Industrial Areas
Residential Areas
Parks
Military Areas
Motorways
Other Main Roads
Railways
Airports

On the maps in the atlas country-names are in the Anglicized forms; physical feature names are also in the Anglicized forms where these are well known, particularly those of major features — oceans, mountain ranges, rivers, etc. — which have more than one local language form, e.g. Danube, not Donau, Dunav, Dunarea. Place names are in the forms used in the countries concerned, e.g. Firenze, not Florence: Köln, not Cologne. Exceptionally, place names are given both local and Anglicized form on some maps, e.g. As Suways and Suez, the latter in smaller type. For countries with non-Roman scripts, transliterated Roman alphabet forms follow the United States Board on Geographic Names gazetteers, except for the U.S.S.R. and China, for which the Russian Academy of Sciences and the Pin-Yin systems have been used.

The Gazetteer has entries for all the names on the maps. Additionally, it has many cross-referenced entries for alternative forms, most of which do not appear on the maps. Cross-referenced entries occur for names which have been superseded but which are still, or until recently have been, in common use, e.g. Léopoldville see Kinshasa: or Port Arthur see Thunder Bay:. They also occur where Anglicized forms are still in common use, e.g. Alexandria see Al Iskandariyah:, and where different transliteration systems result in very different forms, e.g. Peking see Beijing: or Tselinograd see Celinograd, although entries of this type have been restricted to the larger cities and towns only. The main entry in each case of cross-referencing shows the alternative form in parenthesis, e.g. Kinshasa (Léopoldville): and Beijing (Peking).

Italic type is used to distinguish physical features or administrative units from place names.

Abbreviations used in the Gazetteer

Aber.	Aberdeenshire	Glos.	Gloucestershire	na. rve.	nature reserve	riv.	river
A.C.T.		Gt.Ldn.	Greater London	nat. park	national park	Rosc.	Roscommon
	Australian Capital Territory	Gt.Man.		N.B.	New Brunswick	Rox.	Roxburghshire
			Greater Manchester	N.C.	North Carolina	rsch. stn.	research station
admin.	administrative unit	Gwyn.	Gwynedd	N.D.	North Dakota	S.	South, Southern
Ala.	Alabama	Hants.	Hampshire	Nebr.	Nebraska	S.A.	South Australia
Alta.	Alberta	harb.	harbour	Nev.	Nevada	Sask.	Saskatchewan
arch.	archipelago	Here. & Worcs.		Nfld.	Newfoundland	S.C.	South Carolina
Argyll.	Argyllshire		Hereford & Worcester	N.H.	New Hampshire	Scot.	Scotland
Ariz.	Arizona	Herts.	Hertfordshire	N.I.	North Island	S.D.	South Dakota
Ark.	Arkansas	hist. reg.	historic region	N.J.	New Jersey	sd.	sound
Arm.	Armagh	hld.	highland	N. Mex.	New Mexico	Selk.	Selkirkshire
Ayr.	Ayrshire	Humb.	Humberside	Norf.	Norfolk	S. Glam.	
Banff.	Banffshire	hwy.	highway	Northants.			South Glamorgan
B.C.	British Columbia	Ill.	Illinois		Northamptonshire	Shet. Is.	Shetland Islands
Beds.	Bedfordshire	Ind.	Indiana	Northumb.		S.I.	South Island
Ber.	Berwickshire	Inv.	Inverness		Northumberland	Som.	Somerset
Bucks.	Buckinghamshire	I. of M.	Isle of Man	Notts.	Nottinghamshire	Staffs.	Staffordshire
Bute.	Buteshire	I. of S.	Isles of Scilly	N.S.	Nova Scotia	Stirl.	Stirlingshire
Caith.	Caithness	I. of W.	Isle of Wight	N.S.W.		str.	strait
Calif.	California	is.	island, islands		New South Wales	Suff.	Suffolk
Cambs.	Cambridgeshire	Kans.	Kansas	N.T.	Northern Territory	Suther.	Sutherland
can.	canal	Kild.	Kildare	N.W.T.		S. Yorks.	
chan.	channel	Kilk.	Kilkenny		Northwest Territories		South Yorkshire
Ches.	Cheshire	Kinc.	Kincardineshire	N.Y.	New York	Tas.	Tasmania
Clack.	Clackmannanshire	Kinr.	Kinross-shire	N. Yorks.		Tenn.	Tennessee
Cleve.	Cleveland	Kirkc.	Kirkcudbrightshire		North Yorkshire	Tex.	Texas
Colo.	Colorado	Ky.	Kentucky	O.F.S.	Orange Free State	Tip.	Tipperary
Conn.	Connecticut	La.	Louisiana	Okla.	Oklahoma	Trans.	Transvaal
Corn.	Cornwall	lag.	lagoon	Ont.	Ontario	Tyr.	Tyrone
C.P.	Cape Province	Lan.	Lanarkshire	Oreg.	Oregon	U.K.	United Kingdom
D.C.	District of Columbia	Lancs.	Lancashire	Ork. Is.	Orkney Islands	Va.	Virginia
Del.	Delaware	Leics.	Leicestershire	Oxon.	Oxfordshire	val.	valley
Derby.	Derbyshire	Leit.	Leitrim	Pa.	Pennsylvania	Vic.	Victoria
des.	desert	Lim.	Limerick	Peeb.	Peeblesshire	volc.	volcano
dist.	district	Lincs.	Lincolnshire	P.E.I.		Vt.	Vermont
Don.	Donegal	Lon.	Londonderry		Prince Edward Island	W.	West, Western
Dumf.	Dumfriesshire	Long.	Longford	pen.	peninsula	W.A.	Western Australia
Dunb.	Dunbartonshire	Man.	Manitoba	Perth.	Perthshire	War.	Warwickshire
Dur.	Durham	Mass.	Massachusetts	pk.	peak	Wash.	Washington
E.	East, Eastern	Md.	Maryland	plat.	plateau	Wat.	Waterford
E.Loth.	East Lothian	Mers.	Merseyside	prehist. site		Wex.	Wexford
Eng.	England	M. Glam.	Mid Glamorgan		prehistoric site	W. Glam.	
est.	estuary	Mich.	Michigan	prom.	promontory		West Glamorgan
fd.	fjord	Midloth.	Midlothian	pt.	point	Wick.	Wicklow
Ferm.	Fermanagh	Minn.	Minnesota	Qld.	Queensland	Wig.	Wigtownshire
Fla.	Florida	Miss.	Mississippi	Qué.	Québec	Wilts.	Wiltshire
for.	forest	Mo.	Missouri	ra.	range	Wis.	Wisconsin
Ga.	Georgia	Mont.	Montana	R. & Crom.		W. Loth.	West Lothian
Gal.	Galway	Moray.	Morayshire		Ross & Cromarty	W. Mid.	West Midlands
geog. reg.		mtn., mtns.	mountain(s)	rds.	roadstead	W. Va.	West Virginia
	geographical region	mtn. reg.		reg.	region	Wyo.	Wyoming
geol. feat.			mountain region	Renf.	Renfrewshire	W. Yorks.	
	geological feature	mty.	motorway	Rep.	Republic		West Yorkshire
geol. reg.		N.	North, Northern	res.	reservoir		
	geological region	Nairn	Nairnshire	R.I.	Rhode Island		

Gazetteer

LONG *LAT* *Degrees + Minutes* (handwritten annotation)

Types of map: Ocean pp. 1-5; Physical pp. 6-25; Human pp. 26-57; Topographic pp. 58-101; World pp. 102-111; Urban pp. 112-128.

Aachen: *admin.*, W.Germany	50 30N 06 15E	72
Aalen: W.Germany	48 50N 10 07E	73
Aalst: Belgium	50 57N 04 03E	72
Äänekoski: Finland	62 36N 25 44E	75
Aaper Wald: *for.*, W.Germany	51 16N 06 50E	118
Aare: *riv.*, Switzerland	47 00N 07 15E	71
Aba: Nigeria	05 06N 07 21E	57
Ābādān: Iran	30 20N 48 15E	33 107
Abakan: U.S.S.R.	53 43N 91 26E	30
Abancay: Peru	13 37S 72 52W	49
Abashiri: Japan	44 01N 144 17E	87
Abaya, *Lake*: Ethiopia	06 30N 37 45E	53
Abbeville: France	50 06N 01 51E	72
Abbeville: La., U.S.A.	29 58N 92 09W	100
Abbeyfeale: Lim., Irish Republic	52 24N 09 18W	67
Abbey *Head*: Kirkc., Scotland	52 46N 03 58W	62
Abbeyleix: Laois, Irish Republic	52 55N 07 20W	67
Abbiategrasso: Italy	45 24N 08 55E	116
Abdulino: U.S.S.R.	53 42N 53 40E	81
Åbenrå: Denmark	55 03N 09 26E	75
Abeokuta: Nigeria	07 10N 03 26E	57
Aberaeron: Dyfed, Wales	52 15N 04 15W	60
Abercarn: Gwent, Wales	51 39N 03 08W	61 113
Aberchirder: Banff., Scotland	57 33N 02 38W	65
Abercorn see Mbala	08 50S 31 22E	54
Abercynon: M. Glam., Wales	51 38N 03 19W	113
Aberdare: M. Glam., Wales	51 43N 03 27W	61 113
Aberdare *Range*: Kenya	00 15S 36 15E	54
Aberdeen: Aber., Scotland	57 10N 02 04W	26 65
Aberdeen: S.D., U.S.A.	45 28N 98 29W	94
Aberdeen: Wash., U.S.A.	46 59N 123 50W	90
Aberdeenshire: *admin.*, Scotland	57 15N 02 45W	65
Aberdovey: Gwyn., Wales	52 33N 04 02W	60
Aberfeldy: Perth., Scotland	56 37N 03 54W	65
Abergavenny: Gwent, Wales	51 50N 03 00W	60 113
Abergele: Clwyd, Wales	53 17N 03 34W	60
Abersoch: Gwyn., Wales	52 50N 04 31W	60
Abersychan: Gwent, Wales	51 44N 03 04W	113
Abertillery: Gwent, Wales	51 45N 03 09W	61 113
Aberystwyth: Dyfed, Wales	52 25N 04 05W	60
Abhā: Saudi Arabia	18 14N 42 31E	33
Abidjan: Ivory Coast	05 19N 04 01W	57
Abilene: Kans., U.S.A.	38 55N 97 13W	94
Abilene: Tex., U.S.A.	32 28N 99 43W	43 95
Abington: Pa., U.S.A.	40 08N 75 07W	122
Abitibi: *riv.*, Ont., Canada	50 00N 81 15W	96
Abitibi, *Lake*: Canada	48 30N 79 45W	99
Åbo see Turku	60 27N 22 15E	27 75
Abohar: India	30 11N 74 14E	82
Abruzzo, *Parco Nazionale d'*: Italy	41 45N 13 45E	79
Absaroka *Range*: U.S.A.	45 00N 110 00W	94
Abu Dabi see Abū Zaby	24 28N 54 25E	33
Abuye Meda: *mtn.*, Ethiopia	10 28N 39 44E	21 53
Abū Zaby (Abu Dabi): United Arab Emirates	24 28N 54 25E	33
Acadia *National Park*: Maine, U.S.A.	44 15N 68 15W	99
Acapulco de Juárez: Mexico	16 51N 99 55W	46
Acari: Peru	15 25S 74 37W	104
Acarigua: Venezuela	09 33N 69 12W	48
Accra: Ghana	05 33N 00 15W	57
Accrington: Lancs., England	53 46N 02 21W	63 114
Achacachi: Bolivia	16 03S 68 43W	49
Achalpur (Ellichpur): India	21 19N 77 30E	82
Achill *Head*: Mayo, Irish Republic	53 59N 10 13W	66
Achill *Island*: Mayo, Irish Republic	53 45N 10 00W	66
Achinsk see Ačinsk	56 17N 90 30E	30
Achtubinsk: U.S.S.R.	48 17N 46 10E	81
Achtyrka: U.S.S.R.	50 19N 34 55E	80
Acilia: Italy	41 47N 12 22E	116
Ačinsk (Achinsk): U.S.S.R.	56 17N 90 30E	30
Acklins *Island*: Bahamas	22 30N 74 00W	47
Aconcagua: *mtn.*, Argentina	32 40S 70 02W	19 52
Acqui: Italy	44 41N 08 28E	71
Acre: Israel, see 'Akko	32 55N 35 04E	105
Acre: *admin.*, Brazil	09 15S 70 30W	48
Acre: *riv.*, Brazil	10 30S 68 15W	49
Ada: Okla., U.S.A.	34 47N 96 41W	95
Adachi: Japan	35 46N 139 47E	121

Adama (Nazeret): Ethiopia	08 39N 39 19E	53
Adamawa *Highlands* (Adamaoua, *Massif de l'*): Cameroun/Nigeria	07 00N 11 30E	20
Adamoua, *Massif de l'*: (Adamawa *Highlands*)	07 45N 13 15E	20
Adam's Bridge: *is.*, India/Sri Lanka	09 15N 79 30E	34
Adams *Lake*: B.C., Canada	51 00N 119 30W	89
Adana: Turkey	37 00N 35 19E	32
Adapazari: Turkey	40 46N 30 24E	32
Adare, *Cape*: Antarctica	71 30S 170 24E	25
Ad Dawhah (Doha): Qatar	25 17N 51 32E	33
Addis Abeba (Addis Ababa): Ethiopia	09 03N 38 42E	53
Addyston: Ohio, U.S.A.	39 08N 84 43W	98
Adelaide: S.A., Australia	34 56S 138 36E	41
Adelaide: *rsch. stn.*, Antarctica	67 46S 68 54W	24
Aden: Yemen D.R.	12 45N 45 12E	33 107
Aden, *Gulf of*	12 30N 47 15E	10 53
Adilābād: India	19 40N 78 31E	82
Adirondack *Mountains*: N.Y., U.S.A.	44 00N 74 15W	44 99 104
Ādoni: India	15 38N 77 16E	34
Adour: *riv.*, France	43 30N 01 15W	70
Adra: Spain	36 45N 03 01W	77
Adrar: Algeria	27 51N 00 19W	56
Adrar des Iforas: *mtn. reg.*, Mali	19 30N 01 30E	20 56
Adrian: Mich., U.S.A.	41 55N 84 01W	98
Adrianople see Edirne	41 40N 26 34E	79
Adriatic *Sea*	42 00N 16 00E	7 27 79
Adwick le Street: S. Yorks., England	53 34N 01 11W	63
Aegean *Sea*	39 00N 24 00E	7 27 79
Aeron: *riv.*, Dyfed, Wales	52 00N 04 00W	60
Afars and Issas, French Terr. of (French Somaliland)	11 30N 42 30E	10 53
Affric, *Loch*: Inv., Scotland	57 15N 05 00W	64
AFGHANISTAN	32 00N 65 00E	10 34 107
Afyonkarahisar: Turkey	38 45N 30 33E	32
Agadez (Agadès): Niger	17 00N 07 56E	56
Agadir: Morocco	30 30N 09 40W	56
Agartala: India	23 49N 91 15E	35 83
Agen: France	44 12N 00 38E	70
Agger: *riv.*, W.Germany	50 45N 07 00E	119
Agra: India	27 10N 78 00E	34 82
Agrigento: Sicily	37 19N 13 35E	79
Agrínion: Greece	38 38N 21 25E	78
Agryz: U.S.S.R.	56 33N 53 00E	81
Agua Fria: *riv.*, Ariz., U.S.A.	34 00N 112 00W	91
Aguanus: *riv.*, Qué., Canada	51 15N 62 15W	97
Agua Prieta: Mexico	31 20N 109 32W	95
Aguascalientes: Mexico	21 53N 102 18W	46
Águilas: Spain	37 25N 01 35W	77
Agulhas *Bank*: Indian Ocean	35 30S 21 00E	21
Agulhas *Basin*: Atlantic/Indian Ocean	45 00S 20 00E	3
Agulhas *Current*: Indian Ocean	23 00S 37 00E	1
Agulhas *Plateau*: Indian Ocean	40 00S 27 00E	3
Agusan: *riv.*, Philippines	08 00N 126 00E	39
Ahaggar (Hoggar): *mtns.*, Algeria	23 30N 05 45E	20 56
Ahlen: W.Germany	51 46N 07 53E	72
Ahmadābād: India	23 02N 72 35E	34 82
Ahmadnagar: India	19 08N 74 48E	34 82
Ahmadpur East: Pakistan	29 06N 71 14E	82
Ahmar *Mountains*: Ethiopia	09 30N 41 30E	53
Ahrensburg: W.Germany	53 41N 10 14E	119
Ahvāz: Iran	31 17N 48 43E	33
Ahvenanmaa see Åland *Islands*	60 15N 20 00E	27 75
Aiken: S.C., U.S.A.	33 34N 81 44W	101
Aillik: Nfld., Canada	55 11N 59 13W	97
Ailsa Craig: *is.*, Ayr., Scotland	55 16N 05 07W	62
Ainsdale: Mers., England	53 37N 03 03W	114
Aintree: Mers., England	53 29N 02 57W	114
Airdrie: Lan., Scotland	55 52N 03 59W	62 113
Aire: *riv.*, W. Yorks., England	53 30N 01 00W	63 115
Aire & Calder Navigation: *can.*, England	53 30N 01 00W	117
Aire-sur-l'Adour: France	43 42N 00 15W	70
Aïr *Massif*: *mtns.*, Niger	18 00N 08 30E	20 56
Aishihik: Yukon, Canada	61 34N 137 31W	88
Aishihik *Lake*: Yukon, Canada	61 34N 137 31W	88
Aiviekste: *riv.*, U.S.S.R.	57 00N 26 45E	75

Types of map: Ocean pp. 1-5; Physical pp. 6-25; Human pp. 26-57; Topographic pp. 58-101; World pp. 102-111; Urban pp. 112-128.

Aix-en-Provence: France   43 31N 05 27E   71
Aix-les-Bains: France   45 41N 05 55E   71
Aiyar *Reservoir*: India   23 30N 85 45E   83
Aíyion: Greece   38 15N 22 05E   78
Aizuwakamatsu (Wakamatsu): Japan   37 30N 139 56E   86
Ajaccio: Corsica   41 55N 08 43E   26 77
Ajanta *Range*: India   20 15N 76 00E   82
Ajmer: India   26 29N 74 40E   34 82
Ajo: Ariz., U.S.A.   32 22N 112 52W   91
Ajusco: Mexico   19 13N 99 12W   128
Akabira: Japan   43 34N 142 03E   86
Akademgorodok: U.S.S.R.   54 49N 83 09E   30
Akan: Japan   43 06N 144 10E   87
Akan-kokuritsu-kōen: *nat. park*, Japan   44 30N 144 30E   87
Akasha East: Sudan   21 05N 30 43E   32
Akashi: Japan   34 38N 134 59E   86
Akbulak: U.S.S.R.   51 01N 55 37E   81
Aketi: Zaïre   02 44N 23 46E   54
Akhdar, Jabal al: *mtns.*, Libya   32 30N 21 30E   20 32
Akhisar: Turkey   38 54N 27 50E   79
Akimiski *Island*: N.W.T., Canada   53 00N 81 00W   44 96
Akita: Japan   39 43N 140 07E   37 86
Akkeshi: Japan   43 02N 144 51E   87
'Akko (Acre): Israel   32 55N 35 04E   105
Akola: India   20 40N 77 05E   34 82
Akot: India   21 06N 77 08E   82
Ákra Akrítas: *cape*, Greece   36 43N 21 52E   79
Ákra Maléa: *cape*, Greece   36 27N 23 12E   79
Ákra Taínaron (Cape Matapan): Greece   36 23N 22 29E   79
Akrítas, Ákra: *cape*, Greece   36 43N 21 52E   79
Akron: Ohio, U.S.A.   41 04N 81 31W   45 98
Aksum: Ethiopia   14 10N 38 45E   53
Akt'ubinsk (Aktyubinsk): U.S.S.R.   50 17N 57 10E   29 81
Akyab *see* Sittwe   20 09N 92 54E   35
Alabama: *admin.*, U.S.A.   45
Alabama: *riv.*, Ala., U.S.A.   31 15N 87 45W   45 100
Alagoas: *admin.*, Brazil   09 45S 37 00W   50
Alagoinhas: Brazil   12 07S 38 26W   50
Alaj *Range* (Alai *Range*): U.S.S.R.   39 30N 71 00E   8 29
Al 'Amārah (Amara): Iraq   31 51N 47 10E   33
Alameda: Calif., U.S.A.   37 44N 122 14W   126
Alameda *Creek*: Calif., U.S.A.   37 35N 122 01W   126
Alamogordo: N.Mex., U.S.A.   32 54N 105 57W   95
Alamosa: Colo., U.S.A.   37 28N 105 52W   95
Aland: *riv.*, E.Germany   52 45N 11 30E   27
Åland Islands (Ahvenanmaa): *is. & admin.*,
   Finland   60 15N 20 00E   75
Alapajevsk: U.S.S.R.   57 52N 61 42E   81 105
Al 'Aqabah (Aqaba): Jordan   29 31N 35 00E   32
Alaska, *Gulf of*: Alaska, U.S.A.   59 00N 145 00W   16
Alaska *Peninsula*: Alaska, U.S.A.   56 30N 159 00W   16
Alaska *Range*: Alaska, U.S.A.   62 15N 152 00W   16
Alatyr': U.S.S.R.   54 51N 46 36E   81
Alatyr': *riv.*, U.S.S.R.   54 45N 45 15E   80
Alaverdi: U.S.S.R.   41 08N 44 39E   28
Alba: Italy   44 42N 08 02E   71
Albacete: Spain   39 00N 01 52W   26 77
Al-Baḥr-al-Jabal (White Nile): *riv.*, Sudan   04 15N 31 30E
   20 53
Al Baḥr al Mayyit (Dead Sea): Jordan   31 15N 35 15E   10 32
Albanel, *Lake*: Qué., Canada   50 00N 73 00W   96
ALBANIA   41 00N 20 00E   7 27 79 107
Albano, *Lago*: Italy   41 45N 12 40E   116
Albano Laziale: Italy   41 44N 12 40E   116
Albany: W.A., Australia   34 57S 117 54E   40
Albany: Calif., U.S.A.   37 53N 122 18W   126
Albany: Ga., U.S.A.   31 37N 84 00W   45 101
Albany: N.Y., U.S.A.   42 40N 73 49W   45 99
Albany: Oreg., U.S.A.   44 38N 123 06W   90
Albany: *riv.*, Ont., Canada   51 15N 84 00W   17 44 96
Al Baṣrah (Basra): Iraq   30 30N 47 50E   33
Albatross Cordillera: *ridge*, Southern Ocean
   63 00S 160 00W   25
Albatross *Plateau*: N.Pacific Ocean   07 00N 98 00W   5
Albemarle *Sound*: N.C., U.S.A.   35 45N 76 30W   101
Albenga: Italy   44 03N 08 13E   71
Albeni Falls *Dam*: Idaho, U.S.A.   48 11N 116 59W   90
Alberche: *riv.*, Spain   40 00N 04 15W   77
Albert, *Lake*: Uganda/Zaïre   01 30N 30 45E   21
Alberta: *admin.*, Canada   54 00N 115 00W   42 92
Albert Lea: Minn., U.S.A.   43 38N 93 16W   98

Albertville: Zaïre, *see* Kalemi   05 56S 29 12E   54
Albi: France   43 56N 02 08E   70
Albizzate: Italy   45 43N 08 48E   116
Alborg: Denmark   57 03N 09 56E   26 75
Albreda: B.C., Canada   52 38N 119 09W   89
Albuquerque: N.Mex., U.S.A.   35 05N 106 39W   43 95
Alcalá de Henares: Spain   40 28N 03 22W   77
Alcatraz *Island*: Calif., U.S.A.   37 50N 122 26W   126
Alcázar de San Juan: Spain   39 24N 03 12W   77
Alcira: Spain   39 10N 00 27W   77
Alcoy: Spain   38 42N 00 29W   77
Aldabra *Islands*: British Indian Ocean Terr.
   10 30S 46 30W   1
Aldan: U.S.S.R.   58 37N 125 24E   31
Aldan: *riv.*, U.S.S.R.   59 45N 133 00E   9 31
Alde: *riv.*, Suff., England   52 00N 01 15E   59
Aldeburgh: Suff., England   52 09N 01 35E   59
Aldekerk: W.Germany   51 27N 06 25E   118
Alder, Ben: *mtn.*, Inv., Scotland   56 49N 04 28W   64
Alderley Edge: Ches., England   53 18N 02 15W   58
Aldermaston: Berks., England   51 23N 01 09W   59
Alderney: *is.*, Channel Islands   49 43N 02 12W   61
Aldershot: Hants., England   51 15N 00 47W   59 112
Aldridge: W. Mid., England   52 36N 01 55W   58 115
Alegrete: Brazil   29 46S 55 46W   51
Aleksandria: U.S.S.R.   48 40N 33 07E   80
Aleksandrov: U.S.S.R.   56 24N 38 43E   80
Aleksejevka: U.S.S.R.   50 37N 38 42E   80
Aleksin: U.S.S.R.   54 31N 37 05E   80
Alençon: France   48 25N 00 05E   70
Aleppo *see* Halab   36 12N 37 10E   33
Alès: France   44 08N 04 05E   71
Alessandria: Italy   44 55N 08 37E   71
Ålesund: Norway   62 28N 06 11E   27 74
Aleutian *Abyssal Plain*: N.Pacific Ocean   47 00N 165 00W   4
Aleutian *Basin*: Bering Sea   56 00N 180 00W   4 22
Aleutian *Islands*: Bering Sea   52 00N 175 00W   4 22
Aleutian *Ridge*: Bering Sea   52 00N 175 00W   4
Aleutian *Trench*: N.Pacific Ocean   52 00N 164 00W   22
Alexander *Archipelago*: Alaska, U.S.A.   57 00N 136 00W
   16 89
Alexander Bay: C.P., Rep. of S.Africa   28 40S 16 30E   55
Alexander City: Ala., U.S.A.   32 57N 85 58W   101
Alexander *Island*: Antarctica   71 00S 70 00W   24
Alexandra: S.I., New Zealand   45 14S 169 26E   87
Alexandra *Falls*: N.W.T., Canada   60 22N 116 20W   92
Alexandria: Egypt *see* Al Iskandarīyah   31 12N 29 54E   32
Alexandria: Dunb., Scotland   55 59N 04 36W   62 113
Alexandria: La., U.S.A.   31 19N 92 29W   100
Alexandria: Va., U.S.A.   38 49N 77 06W   122
Al Fāshir (El Fasher): Sudan   13 37N 25 22E   32
Al Fayyūm: Egypt   29 19N 30 50E   32
Alford: Lincs., England   53 17N 00 11E   58
Alfreton: Derby., England   53 06N 01 23W   58
Alga: U.S.S.R.   49 46N 57 20E   81
Algarrobo: Chile   30 30S 71 07W   104
Algarve: *geog. reg.*, Portugal   37 00N 08 15W   77
Algeciras: Spain   36 08N 05 27W   56 77
Alger *see* El Djezair   36 50N 03 00E   20 56 77
ALGERIA   35 00N 03 00E   20 56 77 106
Alghero: Sardinia   40 34N 08 19E   26 77
Algiers *see* El Djezair   36 50N 03 00E   20 56 77
Algonquin *Provincial Park*: Ont., Canada   45 45N 78 30W
   99
Al Ḥadīthah (Haditha): Iraq   34 09N 42 22E   33
Alhambra: Calif., U.S.A.   34 05N 118 08W   127
Al Ḥillah (Hilla): Iraq   32 28N 44 29E   33
Al Ḥudaydah (Hodeida): Yemen   14 50N 42 58E   33
Al Ḥufūf (Hufuf): Saudi Arabia   25 20N 49 34E   33
Alicante: Spain   38 21N 00 29W   26 77
Alice: C.P., Rep. of S.Africa   32 47S 26 50E   101
Alice, *Punta*: Italy   39 24N 17 09E   79
Alice Springs: N.T., Australia   23 42S 133 52E   41
Alīgarh: India   27 54N 78 04E   34 82
Alingsås: Sweden   57 55N 12 30E   75
Ālipur: India   22 32N 88 19E   120
Alīpur Duār: India   26 28N 89 32E   83
Aliquippa: Pa., U.S.A.   40 38N 80 16W   104
Al Iskandarīyah (Alexandria): Egypt   31 12N 29 54E   32
Al Ismā'īlīyah (Ismailia): Egypt   30 35N 32 16E   32
Alix: Alta., Canada   52 25N 113 11W   92

Types of map: Ocean pp. 1-5; Physical pp. 6-25; Human pp. 26-57; Topographic pp. 58-101; World pp. 102-111; Urban pp. 112-128.

Al Jabal, Bahr: *riv.*, Sudan   04 15N 31 30E   20
Al Jawf (Jauf): Saudi Arabia   29 49N 39 52E   33
Al Jazīrah: *geog. reg.*, Sudan   15 00N 37 30E   53
Al Khārijah (El Khârga): Egypt   25 26N 30 33E   32
Al Khurṭūm (Khartoum): Sudan   15 36N 32 32E   53
Alkmaar: Netherlands   52 38N 04 44E   72
Al-Kūt (Kūt al-Imāra): Iraq   32 25N 45 49E   33
Al Kuwayt (Kuwait): Kuwait   29 20N 48 00E   33
Al Lādhiqīyah (Latakia): Syria   35 31N 35 47E   32
Allahābād: India   25 57N 81 50E   34 83
Allard, *Lac*: Qué., Canada   50 30N 63 45W   97
Allegheny: *riv.*, U.S.A.   41 15N 79 30W   99
Allegheny *Mountains*: U.S.A.   40 30N 78 30W   17 99
Allen, *Bog of*: Irish Republic   53 15N 07 00W   67
Allen, *Lough*: Irish Republic   54 00N 08 00W   66
Allendale Town: Northumb., England   54 54N 02 15W   63
Allen Park: Mich., U.S.A.   42 15N 83 11W   125
Allentown: Pa., U.S.A.   40 37N 75 30W   45 99
Alleppey: India   09 30N 76 22E   34
Aller: *riv.*, W.Germany   52 45N 09 15E   71
Alliance: Nebr., U.S.A.   42 06N 102 52W   94
Alliance: Ohio, U.S.A.   40 56N 81 06W   99
Allier: *riv.*, France   46 30N 03 00E   71
Alloa: Clack., Scotland   56 07N 03 49W   65
Alloy: W.Va., U.S.A.   38 09N 81 15W   80
Alma: Qué., Canada   48 32N 71 41W   96
Alma-Ata: U.S.S.R.   43 15N 76 57E   29
Almada: Portugal   38 40N 09 09W   77
Almadén: Spain   38 47N 04 50W   77
Al Madīnah (Medina): Saudi Arabia   24 30N 39 35E   33
Al Mahallah al Kubrā (Mahalla al Kubra): Egypt   30 59N 31 10E   32
Almalyk: U.S.S.R.   40 50N 69 38E   29
Al Manāmah (Manama): Bahrain   26 12N 50 38E   33
Al Manṣūrah: Egypt   31 03N 31 23E   32
Al Mawṣil (Mosul): Iraq   36 20N 43 08E   33
Almelo: Netherlands   52 21N 06 40E   72
Almería: Spain   36 50N 02 26W   77
Al'metjevsk: U.S.S.R.   54 53N 52 20E   81
Al Minya (El Minya): Egypt   28 06N 30 45E   32
Almirante Brown: Buenos Aires, Argentina   34 49S 58 23W   128
Almirante Brown: *rsch. stn.*, Antarctica   64 53S 62 53W   24
Almirante Guillermo Brown, *Parque*: Argentina   34 41S 58 27W   128
Almora: India   29 38N 79 41E   82
Al Mukallā (Mukalla): Yemen D.R.   14 32N 49 08E   33
Al Mukhā (Mocha): Yemen   13 19N 43 15E   33
Aln: *riv.*, Northumb., England   55 15N 01 45W   63
Alnwick: Northumb., England   55 25N 01 42W   63
Alor: *is.*, Indonesia   08 15S 124 45E   39
Alor Setar (Alorstar): Malaysia   06 07N 100 22E   38
Alpena: Mich., U.S.A.   45 04N 83 27W   98
Alpha Cordillera: *ridge*, Arctic Ocean   84 00N 160 00W   23
Alpine: Tex., U.S.A.   30 22N 103 40W   95
Alps, The: *mtns.*, Europe   46 45N 07 45E   6 26 76
Al Qaḍārif: Sudan   14 02N 35 24E   53
Al Qāhirah (Cairo): Egypt   30 03N 31 15E   32
Al Qāmishlī: Syria   37 02N 41 41E   33
Al Quds (Jerusalem): Jordan   31 47N 35 14E   32
Al Qunfudhah: Saudi Arabia   19 09N 41 07E   33
Al Quṣayr (Quseir): Egypt   26 06N 34 17E   32
Alsager: Ches., England   53 07N 02 19W   58
Alsask: Sask., Canada   51 22N 110 00W   92
Alsek: *riv.*, Canada   60 00N 137 45W   88
Alserio, *Lago di*: Italy   45 47N 09 13E   116
Alsh, *Loch*: Scotland   57 15N 05 30W   64
Alster: *riv.*, W.Germany   53 30N 10 00E   119
Alston: Cumbria, England   54 49N 02 26W   63
Alta: Norway   69 57N 23 10E   74
Altaj (Altay) *Range*: Mongolia   46 00N 93 00E   30
Altamaha: *riv.*, Ga., U.S.A.   31 45N 81 45W   101
Altamura: Italy   40 49N 16 34E   79
Altdorf: Switzerland   46 53N 08 38E   71
Alteelva: *riv.*, Norway   69 30N 23 30E   74
Altefjorden: *fd.*, Norway   70 12N 23 06E   74
Alte Land, Das: *geog. reg.*, W.Germany   53 30N 09 45E   119
Altenburg: E.Germany   50 59N 12 27E   73
Altenessen: W.Germany   51 29N 07 00E   118
Alte Süderelbe: *riv.*, W.Germany   53 30N 09 45E   119
Altiplano: *highland*, Bolivia   18 15S 67 45W   18 49

Altmühl: *riv.*, W.Germany   49 00N 11 30E   73
Alton: Hants., England   51 09N 00 59W   59
Alton: Ill., U.S.A.   38 55N 90 10W   98
Altona: W.Germany   53 34N 09 55E   119
Altoona: Pa., U.S.A.   40 32N 78 23W   99
Altrincham: Gt. Man., England   53 24N 02 21W   63 114
Altus: Okla., U.S.A.   34 38N 99 20W   95
Al Ubayyiḍ (El Obeid): Sudan   13 11N 30 13E   32
Alūksne: U.S.S.R.   57 25N 27 03E   80
Al Uqṣur (Luxor): Egypt   25 41N 32 39E   32
Alva: Clack., Scotland   56 09N 03 49W   65
Alva: Okla., U.S.A.   36 48N 98 40W   95
Alvarado: Calif., U.S.A.   37 36N 122 05W   126
Alvesta: Sweden   56 54N 14 35E   75
Al Wāḥāt al Baḥrīyah: *geog. reg.*, Egypt   28 15N 28 57E   105
Alwar: India   27 34N 76 39E   34 82
Alwar *Hills*: India   27 15N 76 00E   82
Alwen *Reservoir*: Clwyd, Wales   53 00N 03 30W   60
Alyth: Perth., Scotland   56 38N 03 14W   65
Amado: Ariz., U.S.A.   31 43N 111 04W   91
Amahai: Indonesia   03 19S 128 56E   39
Amalner: India   21 01N 75 09E   82
Amami-ō-Shima: *is.*, Ryukyu Is.   28 15N 29 30E   12 37
Amapá: *admin.*, Brazil   01 15N 52 00W   50
Amara *see* Al 'Amārah   31 51N 47 10E   33
Amarillo: Tex., U.S.A.   35 13N 101 50W   43 95
Amazon: *riv.*, S.America   01 50S 53 00W   18 50
Amazon, *Mouths of the*: Brazil   00 30N 49 30W   50
Amazonas: *admin.*, Brazil   00 00 65 15W   48
Ambāla: India   30 23N 76 49E   34 82
Ambarnāth: India   19 11N 73 11E   82
Ambato: Ecuador   01 15S 78 37W   48
Amberg: W.Germany   49 26N 11 52E   73
Ambikapur: India   23 09N 83 12E   83
Amble: Northumb., England   55 20N 01 34W   63
Ambleside: Cumbria, England   54 26N 02 58W   63
Ambon: Indonesia   03 41S 128 10E   39
Ambre, *Cap d'*: Malagasy Rep.   11 57S 49 17E   55
Americana: Brazil   22 44S 47 19W   51
American Falls *Reservoir*: Idaho, U.S.A.   42 47N 112 52W   90
American Fork: Utah, U.S.A.   40 23N 111 48W   91
AMERICAN SAMOA: S.Pacific Ocean   13 00S 170 00W   4
Americus: Ga., U.S.A.   32 04N 84 14W   101
Amersfoort: Netherlands   52 09N 05 23E   72
Amersham: Bucks., England   51 40N 00 38W   59 112
Amery: Man., Canada   56 45N 94 00W   93
Amery *Ice Shelf*: Antarctica   70 00S 72 00E   24
Ames: Iowa, U.S.A.   42 02N 93 33W   98
Amesbury: Wilts., England   51 10N 01 47W   61
Amga: *riv.*, U.S.S.R.   59 45N 128 00E   31
Amgun': *riv.*, U.S.S.R.   52 30N 137 00E   31
Amherst: N.S., Canada   45 50N 64 14W   97
Amiens: France   49 54N 02 18E   26 72
Amirante *Islands*: British Indian Ocean Terr.   06 45S 52 30E   1 10
Amisk *Lake*: Man., Canada   54 30N 102 00W   93
Amlwch: Gwyn., Wales   53 25N 04 20W   60
'Ammān: Jordan   31 57N 35 56E   32
Ammanford: Dyfed, Wales   51 48N 03 59W   60
Ammersee: *lake*, W.Germany   48 00N 11 07E   73
Ammókhóstos (Famagusta): Cyprus   35 07N 33 57E   32
Amnock (Yalu): *riv.*, China/N.Korea   40 15N 125 00E   37
Amo: *riv.*, Bhutan/India   26 15N 89 15E   83
Amos: Qué., Canada   48 34N 78 08W   96
Amour: *riv. see* Amur: *riv.*   51 00N 138 00E   9 31
Amoy *see* Xiamen   24 28N 118 07E   36 85
Ampana: Indonesia   00 54S 121 35E   39
Ampthill: Beds., England   52 02N 00 30W   59
Amrāvati (Amraoti): India   20 58N 77 50E   34 82
Amreli: India   21 36N 71 20E   82
Amritsar: India   31 39N 74 58E   34 82
Amroha: India   28 54N 78 14E   82
Amsterdam: Netherlands   52 21N 04 54E   26 72
Amsterdam: N.Y., U.S.A.   42 56N 74 12W   99
Amsterdam *Fracture Zone*: Indian Ocean   34 00S 78 00E   1
Amstetten: Austria   48 08N 14 52E   73
Amuay: Venezuela   11 47N 70 15W   106
Amudarja (Oxus): *riv.*, Afghanistan/U.S.S.R.   41 00N 62 00E   8 29

Types of map: Ocean pp. 1-5; Physical pp. 6-25; Human pp. 26-57; Topographic pp. 58-101; World pp. 102-111; Urban pp. 112-128.

Amundsen *Gulf*: N.W.T., Canada 71 00N 125 00W 16
Amundsen *Sea*: Antarctica 72 30S 112 00W 25
Amundsen-Scott: *rsch. stn.*, Antarctica 90 00S 24
Amur (Amour): *riv.*, China/U.S.S.R. 51 00N 138 00E 9 31
Anabar: *riv.*, U.S.S.R. 71 30N 113 30E 30
Anaconda: Mont., U.S.A. 46 08N 112 57W 90
Anacortes: Wash., U.S.A. 48 30N 122 37W 90 106
Anacostia: *riv.*, U.S.A. 38 45N 76 45W 122
Anadyr, *Gulf of*: U.S.S.R. 64 00N 178 00W 22
Anadyr *Plateau*: U.S.S.R. 67 00N 168 00E 31
Anadyr *Range*: U.S.S.R. 68 00N 180 00E 9
Anaheim: Calif., U.S.A. 33 50N 117 55W 127
Anaiza *see* Unayzah 26 06N 43 58E 33
Anambas *Islands*: Indonesia 03 00N 105 45E 38
Anan: Japan 33 55N 134 39E 86
Ānand: India 22 34N 73 01E 82
Anandpur: India 21 14N 86 10E 83
Anápolis: Brazil 16 20S 48 58W 50
Anatolian *Plateau*: Turkey 39 00N 34 00E 10
Anch'ing *see* Anqing 30 31N 117 04E 36 85
Anciferovo: U.S.S.R. 58 58N 34 01E 80
Ancohuma: *mtn.*, Bolivia 15 51S 68 36W 49
Ancona: Italy 43 37N 13 31E 27 79
Ancud: Chile 41 05S 73 50W 52
Åndalsnes: Norway 62 33N 07 43E 74
Andalusia: Ala., U.S.A. 31 18N 86 29W 101
Andaman *Basin*: Indian Ocean 13 00N 95 00E 1
Andaman *Islands*: Indian Ocean 12 00N 93 45E 1 11 35
Andaman *Sea* 12 00N 95 00E 12 35
Andermatt: Switzerland 46 38N 08 36E 71
Anderson: Ind., U.S.A. 40 05N 85 41W 98
Anderson: S.C., U.S.A. 34 30N 82 39W 101
Anderson *Summit*: Antarctica 85 03S 90 53W 24
Andes, Cordillera de los: *ra.*, S.America 05 00N 75 45W 18 48
Andfjorden: *fd.*, Norway 69 00N 16 15E 74
Andhra Pradesh: *admin.*, India 19 30N 79 00E 34 82
Andižan (Andizhan): U.S.S.R. 40 45N 72 22E 29
Andong (Tantung): China 40 08N 124 20E 37
ANDORRA 42 30N 01 30E 26 70
Andorra: Andorra 42 30N 01 30E 70
Andover: Hants., England 51 13N 01 28W 59
Andrade: Brazil 21 01S 42 58W 104
Andrésy: France 48 59N 02 04E 117
Ándros: *is.*, Greece 37 49N 24 54E 79
Androscoggin: *riv.*, Maine, U.S.A. 44 30N 70 30W 99
Andros *Island*: Bahamas 24 45N 78 00W 17 47 101
Andros Town: Bahamas 24 45N 77 50W 47
Andújar: Spain 38 02N 04 03W 77
Anfu: China 27 14N 114 41E 85
Angara: *riv.*, U.S.S.R. 58 45N 100 30E 9 30 105
Angara *Basin*: Arctic Ocean 88 00N 110 00E 23
Angarsk: U.S.S.R. 52 34N 103 54E 30
Angel, Salto (Angel *Falls*): Venezuela 05 57N 62 30W 48
Angel de la Guarda: *is.*, Mexico 29 15N 113 30W 46
Angeles *National Forest*: Calif., U.S.A. 34 00N 118 00W 127
Ångelholm: Sweden 56 15N 12 50E 75
Angelina: *riv.*, Tex., U.S.A. 31 30N 94 45W 100
Angel *Island*: Calif., U.S.A. 37 51N 122 20W 126
Angermanälven: *riv.*, Sweden 64 45N 16 00E 74
Angers: France 47 29N 00 32W 26 70
Anglalinghu: *lake*, China 31 30N 83 00E 83
Anglesey: *admin & is.*, Wales. Absorbed into new *admin.* of Gwynedd, 1974. 60
Anglesey: *is.*, Gwyn., Wales 53 15N 04 15W 60
Angol: Chile 37 47S 72 45W 52
ANGOLA 11 45S 18 15E 21 54 107
Angola *Basin*: S.Atlantic Ocean 15 00S 03 00E 3 21
Angoon: Alaska, U.S.A. 57 30N 134 35W 89
Angoulême: France 45 40N 00 10E 70
Angren: U.S.S.R. 41 01N 70 12E 29
Angul: India 20 48N 85 04E 83
Anguo: China 38 28N 115 20E 84
Angus: *admin.*, Scotland 56 45N 03 00W 65
Anholt: *is.*, Denmark 56 43N 11 34E 75
Anhsi *see* Anxi 40 32N 95 51E 36
Anhua: China 28 28N 111 12E 85
Anhui (Anhwei): *admin.*, China 32 15N 116 45E 36 84
Anierin, Slieve: *mtn.*, Leit., Irish Republic 54 06N 07 58W 66

Animas: *riv.*, U.S.A. 37 30N 107 30W 95
Anjangaon: India 21 11N 77 21E 82
Anji: China 30 45N 119 41E 85
Anjiang: China 27 24N 110 15E 85
Ankang: China 32 40N 109 09E 36 84
Ankara: Turkey 39 55N 32 50E 32
Ankaratra: *mtns.*, Malagasy Rep. 19 30S 47 00E 21 55
Anker: *riv.*, England 52 30N 01 30W 115
Anklesvar: India 21 38N 73 02E 82
Anlu: China 31 12N 113 41E 84
Ann, *Cape*: Mass., U.S.A. 42 39N 70 37W 99
Anna: U.S.S.R. 51 29N 40 25E 80
'Annaba (Bône): Algeria 36 55N 07 45E 56 77
Annacis *Island*: B.C., Canada 49 10N 122 57W 126
An Nafûd (Nafud): *des.*, Saudi Arabia 28 30N 41 15E 10 33
An Najaf (Najaf): Iraq 31 59N 44 19E 33
Annamitique, Chaîne: *ra.*, Indo-China 16 15N 106 45E 34
Annan: Dumf., Scotland 54 59N 03 16W 62
Annan: *riv.*, Dumf., Scotland 55 00N 03 15W 62
Annandale: Va., U.S.A. 38 50N 77 12W 122
Annandale: *val.*, Dumf., Scotland 55 15N 03 15W 62
Annapolis: Md., U.S.A. 38 59N 76 30W 99
Annapolis Royal: N.S., Canada 44 44N 65 32W 97
Annapurna: *mtn.*, Nepal 28 38N 83 50E 83
Ann Arbor: Mich., U.S.A. 42 18N 83 43W 45 98
An Nāsirīyah (Nasiriya): Iraq 31 04N 46 17E 33
Annecy: France 45 54N 06 07E 71
Annecy, *Lac d'*: France 45 52N 06 10E 71
An Nhon: S.Vietnam 13 53N 109 06E 38
Annick Water: *riv.*, Ayr., Scotland 55 30N 04 30W 113
Anniston: Ala., U.S.A. 33 39N 85 49W 101
Anoka: Minn., U.S.A. 45 11N 93 23W 98
Anping: China 38 16N 115 30E 84
Anqing (Anch'ing): China 30 31N 117 04E 36 85
Anqiu: China 36 24N 119 14E 84
Anrath: W.Germany 51 17N 06 26E 118
Ansari Nagar: India 28 34N 77 13E 120
Ansbach: W.Germany 49 18N 10 36E 73
Anshan: China 41 05N 123 00E 37 105
Anshun: China 26 19N 105 50E 36
Antakya (Antioch): Turkey 36 12N 36 10E 32
Antalya: Turkey 36 53N 30 42E 32
Antalya, *Gulf of*: Turkey 36 30N 31 15E 32
Antananarivo *see* Tananarive 18 55S 47 31E 55
Antarctica 24
Antarctic *Peninsula*: Antarctica 69 00S 65 00W 24
An Teallach: *mtn.*, R. & Crom., Scotland 57 48N 05 16W 64
Antequera: Spain 37 01N 04 34W 76
Anthony: Kans., U.S.A. 37 09N 98 02W 95
Antibes: France 43 35N 07 07E 71
Anticosti *Island*: Qué., Canada 18 00N 61 45W 44 97
Antigua: *is.*, Leeward Islands 18 00N 61 45W 1 46
Antioch: Turkey *see* Antakya 36 12N 36 10E 32
Antipodes *Islands*: Southern Ocean 49 42S 178 50E 4
Antofagasta: Chile 23 39S 70 24W 49
António Enes: Mozambique 16 12S 39 54E 55
Antrim: Antrim, N.Ireland 54 43N 06 13W 66
Antrim: *admin.*, N.Ireland 54 45N 06 00W 66
Antrim *Mountains*: Antrim, N.Ireland 55 00N 06 00W 66
Antsirane *see* Diégo-Suarez 12 16S 49 17E 55
Antsla: U.S.S.R. 57 50N 26 32E 80
Antsohihy: Malagasy Rep. 14 52S 47 59E 55
Antwerpen (Antwerp): Belgium 51 13N 04 25E 26 72 107
Anūpgarh: India 29 11N 73 12E 82
Anvil *Mountains*: Yukon, Canada 62 15N 133 00W 88
Anxi: Fujian, China 25 02N 118 17E 85
Anxi (Anhsi): Gansu, China 40 32N 95 51E 36
Anxiang: China 29 23N 112 07E 85
Anyang: China 36 03N 114 20E 36 84 105
Anyi: China 28 50N 115 39E 85
Anza-Borrego Desert *State Park*: Calif., U.S.A. 33 15N 116 15W 91
Anžero-Sudžensk (Anzhero-Sudzhensk): U.S.S.R. 56 07N 86 00E 30
Aoji: N.Korea 42 31N 130 23E 86
Aomen *see* Macau 22 17N 113 35E 36 85
Aomori: Japan 40 49N 140 45E 37 86
Aosta: Italy 45 44N 07 19E 71 105
Apalachee *Bay*: Fla., U.S.A. 29 45N 34 00W 101
Apalachicola: Fla., U.S.A. 29 43N 84 59W 101

Types of map: Ocean pp. 1-5; Physical pp. 6-25; Human pp. 26-57; Topographic pp. 58-101; World pp. 102-111; Urban pp. 112-128.

Apaporis: *riv.*, Colombia   00 00 70 15E   48
Apatity: U.S.S.R.   67 32N 33 21E   74
Ape: U.S.S.R.   57 32N 26 40E   80
Apeldoorn: Netherlands   52 13N 05 57E   72
Apennines: *ra.*, Italy   42 30N 13 30E   7 27 79
Api: *mtn.*, Nepal°   30 00N 80 56E   82
Apolda: E.Germany   51 02N 11 31E   73
Apostle *Islands*: Wis., U.S.A.   46 45N 90 30W   98
Appalachian *Mountains*: U.S.A.   41 00N 76 00W   17 45 99
Appennino Ligure: *ra.*, Italy   44 30N 09 00E   71
Appiano Gentile: Italy   45 43N 08 58E   116
Appleby: Cumbria, England   54 36N 02 29W   63
Appleton: Wis., U.S.A.   44 17N 88 24W   98
Apucarana: Brazil   23 34S 51 28W   51
Apure: *riv.*, Venezuela   07 45N 67 00W   48
Aqaba *see* Al 'Aqabah   29 31N 35 00E   32
'Aqabah, Khalīj as (Aqaba, *Gulf of*):Middle East
   28 45N 34 30E   32
Ara: *riv.*, Tip., Irish Republic   52 15N 08 00W   67
Ara: *riv.*, Japan   35 39N 139 50E   121
'Arab, Bahr al: *riv.*, Sudan   10 15N 27 45E   20
Arabian *Basin*: Indian Ocean   12 00N 63 00E   1
Arabian *Sea*   14 45N 52 45E   1 33
Aracajú: Brazil   10 55S 37 04W   50
Araçatuba: Brazil   21 12S 50 25W   51
Arad: Romania   46 10N 21 19E   27 78
Arafura *Sea*   09 30S 132 00E   14 39
Araguaia: *riv.*, Brazil   09 00S 49 45W   18 50
Araguari: Brazil   18 38S 48 11W   51
Arakan Yoma: *ra.*, Burma   21 00N 94 00E   11 35
Araks (Aras): *riv.*, Turkey/U.S.S.R.   39 45N 47 30E   8 28
Aral *Sea*: U.S.S.R.   45 00N 60 00E   8 29
Aral'sk: U.S.S.R.   46 48N 61 40E   29
Aralsor, Ozero: *lake*, U.S.S.R.   49 05N 48 12E   81
Aran *Island*: Don., Irish Rep.   55 00N 08 30W   66
Aran *Islands*: Gal., Irish Republic   53 00N 09 30W   67
Araraquara: Brazil   21 47S 48 10W   51
Ararat, *Mount*: Turkey   39 44N 44 15E   10 33
Aras: *riv.*, *see* Araks: *riv.*   39 45N 47 30E   8 28
Arauca: Colombia   07 05N 70 45W   48
Arauca: *riv.*, Colombia/Venezuela   07 00N 72 00W   48
Aravaca: Spain   40 27N 03 47W   116
Aravalli *Range*: India   25 00N 73 30E   11 34 82
Araxá: Brazil   19 35S 46 55W   51
Arba Minch: Ethiopia   06 02N 37 36E   53
Arbroath: Angus, Scotland   56 34N 02 35W   65
Arcachon: France   44 40N 01 11W   70
Arcadia: N.S.W., Australia   33 37S 151 02E   120
Arcadia: Calif., U.S.A.   34 08N 118 01W   127
Arcata: Calif., U.S.A.   40 54N 124 05W   91
Arches *National Monument*: Utah,
   U.S.A.   38 45N 109 30W   91
Arcis-sur-Aube: France   48 32N 04 09E   71
Arcola: Sask., Canada   49 37N 102 30W   92
Arctic *Ocean*   22
Arctic Red: *riv.*, N.W.T., Canada   66 00N 132 00W   88
Ardabīl: Iran   38 15N 48 18E   33
Ardara: Don., Irish Republic   54 46N 08 25W   66
Ardatov: U.S.S.R.   54 51N 46 13E   81
Ardbeg: Argyll., Scotland   55 39N 06 07W   62
Ardee: Louth, Irish Republic   53 52N 06 33W   66
Ardennes: *mtns.*, *see* Ardennais, *Haut Plateau*
   50 00N 05 30E   72
Ardle: *riv.*, Perth., Scotland   56 30N 03 15W   65
Ardmore: Okla., U.S.A.   34 10N 97 08W   95
Ardmore *Point*: Argyll., Scotland   55 42N 06 01W   62
Ardnamurchan, *Point of*: Argyll., Scotland   56 44N 06 14W
   64
Ardrossan: Ayr., Scotland   55 39N 04 49W   62 113
Ards *Peninsula*: Down, N. Ireland   54 30N 05 15W   66
Ardvule, Rubha: *cape*, Inv., Scotland   57 15N 07 28W   64
Areia Branca: Brazil   04 57S 37 08W   50
Arena *Point*: Calif., U.S.A.   38 58N 123 44W   91
Arendal: Norway   58 27N 08 56E   75
Arends *Island*: Indonesia   05 00S 114 30E   39
·Arequipa: Peru   16 25S 71 32W   49
Arezzo: Italy   43 28N 11 53E   79
Argens: *riv.*, France   43 30N 06 15E   71
Argentan: France   48 45N 00 01W   70
Argenteuil: France   48 57N 02 15E   117
ARGENTINA   19 52 106

Argentine *Basin*: S.Atlantic Ocean   43 00S 45 00W   3 19
Argentine Islands: *rsch. stn.*, Antarctica   65 15S 64 15W   24
Argentino, *Lago*: Argentina   50 15S 72 45W   52
Argenton-sur-Creuse: France   46 36N 01 30E   70
Arges: *riv.*, Romania   44 30N 25 30E   79
Argonne *Forest*: Ill., U.S.A.   41 43N 87 52W   124
Arguello, *Point*: Calif., U.S.A.   34 35N 120 39W   91
Argyll *National Forest Park*: Argyll., Scotland
   56 00N 04 45W   64
Argyllshire: *admin.*, Scotland   56 00N 05 15W   64
Århus: Denmark   56 10N 10 13E   26 75
Arica: Chile   18 29S 70 20W   49
Arichat: N.S., Canada   45 31N 61 00W   97
Ariège: *riv.*, France   42 30N 01 45E   70
Arinos: *riv.*, Brazil   12 00S 57 00W   50
Aripuanã: *riv.*, Brazil   06 15S 60 30W   50
Arisaig: Inv., Scotland   56 55N 05 51W   64
Arisaig, *Sound of*: Inv., Scotland   56 45N 05 45W   64
Arizona: *admin.*, U.S.A.   34 00N 112 00W   43 91
Arjeplog: Sweden   66 04N 18 00E   74
Arkadak: U.S.S.R.   51 58N 43 28E   80
Arkadelphia: Ark., U.S.A.   34 07N 93 03W   100
Arkaig, *Loch*: Inv., Scotland   56 45N 05 00W   64
Arkansas: *admin.*, U.S.A.   45 100
Arkansas: *riv.*, U.S.A.   34 00N 91 30W   17 43 100
Arkansas City: Kans., U.S.A.   37 04N 97 02W   95
Arklow: Wick., Irish Rep.   52 48N 06 09W   67
Arles: France   43 41N 04 38E   71
Arlington: Mass., U.S.A.   42 23N 71 09W   122
Arlington Heights: Ill., U.S.A.   42 06N 88 00W   124
Arluno: Italy   45 30N 08 56E   116
Armadale: W. Loth., Scotland   55 54N 03 42W   62
Armagh: Arm., N.Ireland   54 21N 06 39W   66
Armagh: *admin.*, N.Ireland   54 15N 06 30W   66
Armagnac, Collines de l': *hills*, France   43 30N 00 30E   70
Armavir: U.S.S.R.   45 00N 41 08E   28
Armenia: Colombia   04 32N 75 40W   49
Armenian S.S.R.: *admin.*, U.S.S.R.   40 00N 45 00E   28
Armstrong: Ont., Canada   50 20N 89 02W   98
Arnhem: Netherlands   52 00N 05 53E   72
Arnhem Land: *geog. reg.*, N.T., Australia   13 30S 134 00E
   14 40
Arno: *riv.*, Italy   43 30N 10 15E   79
Arnold: Notts., England   52 59N 01 07W   58
Arnstadt: E.Germany   50 50N 10 57E   73
Aroostook: *riv.*, Maine, U.S.A.   46 30N 68 15W   99
Arosa: Switzerland   46 47N 09 41E   71
Arrah: India   25 34N 84 40E   83
Ar Ramādī (Ramadi): Iraq   33 27N 43 19E   33
Arran: *is.*, Bute., Scotland   55 35N 05 15W   62
Arran, Cock of: *pt.*, Bute, Scotland   55 42N 05 16W   62
Arras: France   50 17N 02 46E   72
Arrecife: Canary Islands   28 57N 13 33W   56
Ar Riyāḍ (Riyadh): Saudi Arabia   24 39N 46 46E   33
Arrow: *riv.*, England/Wales   52 00N 02 45W   60
Arrow, *Lough*: Irish Republic   54 00N 08 15W   66
Arrowhead: B.C., Canada   50 43N 117 57W   89
Arrowrock *Reservoir*: Idaho, U.S.A.   43 36N 115 56W   90
Ar-Ruşayriş (Roseires): Sudan   11 51N 34 23E   53
Arsenjev: U.S.S.R.   44 10N 133 15E   37 86
Árta: Greece   39 09N 20 59E   79
Artëm *see* Art'om   43 22N 132 13E   37 86
Artëmovskiy *see* Art'omovskij   57 21N 61 54E   29 81
Artesia: N.Mexico, U.S.A.   32 51N 104 24W   95
Arthur's *Pass*: S.I., New Zealand   42 55S 171 34E   87
Arthur's Pass *National Park*: S.I., New
   Zealand   42 45S 171 45E   87
Arti: U.S.S.R.   56 26N 58 32E   81
Artigas: Uruguay   30 24S 56 28W   52
Artizapán de Zaragoza: Mexico   19 34N 99 15W   128
Art'om (Artëm): U.S.S.R.   43 22N 132 13E   37 86
Art'omovskij (Artëmovskiy): U.S.S.R.   57 21N 61 54E   29 81
Aruba: *is.*, Netherlands Antilles   12 30N 70 00W   47 106
Aru *Islands*: Indonesia   06 15S 134 15E   4
Arun: *riv.*, Asia   26 00N 87 00E   35
Arun: *riv.*, W.Sussex, England   50 45N 00 30W   58
Arunachal Pradesh: *admin.*, India   28 15N 95 00E   35
Arundel: W.Sussex, England   50 51N 00 34W   59
Arusha: Tanzania   03 21S 36 40E   54
Aruwimi: *riv.*, Zaïre   02 00N 26 00E   21 54
Arvida: Qué., Canada   48 26N 71 11W   96

Types of map: Ocean pp. 1-5; Physical pp. 6-25; Human pp. 26-57; Topographic pp. 58-101; World pp. 102-111; Urban pp. 112-128.

Arvika: Sweden 59 41N 12 38E	74
Arzamas: U.S.S.R. 55 23N 43 50E	80
Aša: U.S.S.R. 55 00N 57 16E	81 105
Asahi-dake: mtn., Japan 43 40N 142 51E	87
Asahikawa (Asahigawa): Japan 43 46N 142 22E	37 86
Asaka: Japan 35 48N 139 37E	121
Åsane: Norway 60 28N 05 18E	75
Asansol: India 23 40N 87 00E	35 83
Asbest: U.S.S.R. 57 00N 61 30E	81
Ascension Island: S.Atlantic Ocean 07 57S 14 22W	3
Ašchabad (Ashkhabad): U.S.S.R. 37 57N 58 23E	29
Aschaffenburg: W.Germany 49 58N 09 10E	72
Aschersleben: E.Germany 51 46N 11 28E	73
Ascoli Piceno: Italy 42 52N 13 35E	79
Ascot: Berks., England 51 25N 00 41W	59 112
Aseb (Assab): Ethiopia 13 01N 42 47E	53
Åsele: Sweden 64 10N 17 20E	74
Asenovgrad: Bulgaria 42 00N 24 53E	79
Ashbourne: Derby., England 53 01N 01 43W	58
Ashburton: Devon, England 50 31N 03 45W	61
Ashburton: S.I., New Zealand 43 54S 171 46E	87
Ashby-de-la-Zouch: Leics., England 52 46N 01 28W	58 115
Ashcroft: B.C., Canada 50 43N 121 17W	89
Asheville: N.C., U.S.A. 35 35N 82 35W	101
Asheweig: riv., Ont., Canada 53 30N 89 30W	93
Ashfield: N.S.W., Australia 33 53S 151 07E	120
Ashford: Kent, England 51 09N 00 53E	59
Ashikaga: Japan 36 20N 139 27E	37 86
Ashina: Japan 35 13N 139 36E	121
Ashington: Northumb., England 55 11N 01 34W	63
Ashizuri-zaki: cape, Japan 32 44N 133 01E	86
Ashkabad see Ašchabad 37 57N 58 23E	29
Ashland: Ky., U.S.A. 38 28N 82 40W	98 104
Ashland: Oreg., U.S.A. 42 14N 122 44W	90
Ashland: Wis., U.S.A. 46 34N 90 54W	98
Ashok Nagar: India 28 38N 77 07E	120
Ash Shāriqah (Sharja): United Arab Emirates 25 20N 55 26E	33
Ashtabula: Ohio, U.S.A. 41 53N 80 47W	99
Ashton: Idaho, U.S.A. 44 04N 111 27W	90
Ashton-in-Makerfield: Lancs., England 53 29N 02 39W	63 114
Ashton-under-Lyne: Gt. Man., England 53 29N 02 06W	114
Ashuanipi Lake: Nfld., Canada 52 45N 66 15W	97
Asir: admin., Saudi Arabia 17 45N 42 45E	33
Aska: India 19 38N 84 41E	83
Askeaton: Lim., Irish Republic 52 36N 08 58W	67
Askival: mtn., Inv., Scotland 56 58N 06 18W	64
Askrigg: N.Yorks., England 54 19N 02 04W	63
Asmera (Asmara): 15 20N 38 58E	53
Asnen: lake, Sweden 56 40N 14 50E	75
Asnières: France 48 55N 02 17E	117
Aspen: Colo., U.S.A. 39 11N 106 49W	94
Aspiring, Mount: S.I., New Zealand 44 23S 168 46E	87
Asquith: N.S.W., Australia 33 41S 151 07E	120
Assab see Aseb 13 01N 42 47E	53
Aş Sahrā ash Sharqīyah (Eastern Desert): Egypt 28 30N 32 15E	20 32
Assam: admin., India 25 45N 91 00E	35 83
Assiniboine: riv., Man., Canada 50 30N 101 15W	92
Assiniboine, Mount: B.C., Canada 50 51N 115 39W	92
Assinica Lake: Qué., Canada 50 15N 75 15W	96
Assis: Brazil 22 40S 50 25W	51
Assisi: Italy 43 04N 12 37E	79
As Sulaymānīyah: Iraq 35 33N 45 26E	33
Assumption: Alta., Canada 58 41N 118 48W	88
As Suways (Suez): Egypt 29 58N 32 33E	32 107
Assynt, Loch: Suther., Scotland 58 00N 05 00W	64
Asti: Italy 44 54N 08 13E	71
Astipálaia: is., Greece 36 32N 26 22E	79
Aston Hill: Bucks., England 51 48N 00 43W	112
Astoria: Oreg., U.S.A. 46 11N 123 50W	42 90
Astrachan' (Astrakhan): U.S.S.R. 46 21N 48 03E	28
Astray: Nfld., Canada 54 36N 66 42W	97
Asunción: Paraguay 25 16S 57 40W	51
Aswān: Egypt 24 05N 32 53E	32 105
Aswān High Dam: Egypt 24 04N 32 52E	32
Asyūt: Egypt 27 11N 31 11E	32
Atacama Desert: Chile/Peru 19 00S 70 00W	49 104
Atacama Salt Flat: Chile 23 30S 68 30W	49
Atas Bogd: mtn., Mongolia 43 15N 96 30E	36
Atasu: U.S.S.R. 48 42N 71 38E	29
Atasuskij: U.S.S.R. 48 42N 71 38E	105
'Aţbarah: Sudan 17 42N 33 59E	53
'Aţbarah: riv., Sudan 16 30N 35 15E	20 53
Atchafalaya: riv., La., U.S.A. 30 45N 91 45W	100
Atchafalaya Bay: La., U.S.A. 29 15N 91 15W	100
Atchison: Kans., U.S.A. 39 34N 95 07W	94
Athabasca: Alta., Canada 54 44N 113 15W	92
Athabasca, Lake: Canada 59 00N 110 00W	16 42 92
Athabasca: riv., Alta., Canada 55 45N 112 30W	16 42 92
Athboy: Meath, Irish Republic 53 37N 06 55W	66
Athenry: Gal., Irish Republic 53 18N 08 45W	67
Athens: Greece, see Athínai 38 00N 23 44E	27 79
Athens: Ga., U.S.A. 33 57N 83 24W	101
Athens: Tenn., U.S.A. 35 27N 84 38W	101
Atherstone: War., England 52 35N 01 31W	58
Atherton: Gt. Man., England 53 31N 02 31W	63 114
Atherton: Calif., U.S.A. 37 28N 122 11W	126
Athínai (Athens): Greece 38 00N 23 44E	27 79
Athlone: Westmeath, Irish Rep. 53 25N 07 56W	66
Atholl, Forest of: Perth., Scotland 56 45N 04 00W	65
Áthos: mtn., Greece 40 10N 24 19E	78
Athus: Belgium 49 34N 05 50E	105
Athy: Kild., Irish Republic 52 59N 07 00W	67
Atikameg: Alta., Canada 55 55N 115 39W	92
Atikokan: Ont., Canada 48 45N 91 37W	98
Atikonak Lake: Nfld., Canada 52 30N 64 30W	97
Atikup: Ont., Canada 52 46N 90 47W	93
Atkarsk: U.S.S.R. 51 52N 45 00E	81
Atkinson, Point: B.C., Canada 49 20N 123 16W	126
Atlanta: Ga., U.S.A. 33 45N 84 23W	45 101 104
Atlantic City: N.J., U.S.A. 39 23N 74 27W	45 99
Atlantic Ocean	2
Atlantic-Indian Basin: Southern Ocean 61 00S 25 00E	3
Atlantic-Indian Ridge: S.Atlantic Ocean 53 00S 25 00E	3
Atlantis Fracture Zone: N.Atlantic Ocean 30 00N 40 00W	2
Atlapulco: Mexico 19 15N 99 03W	128
Atlas Mountains: Algeria/Morocco 36 15N 04 00E	77
Atlas Tellien: mtns., Algeria 35 45N 04 45E	77
Atlin Lake: B.C., Canada 59 13N 133 41W	88
Atmore: Ala., U.S.A. 31 02N 87 29W	100
Atoka: Okla., U.S.A. 34 23N 96 08W	100
Atrak: riv., Iran/U.S.S.R. 38 00N 56 30E	33
Atrato: riv., Colombia 07 45N 77 00W	48
Aţ Tā'if: Saudi Arabia 21 15N 40 24E	33
Attawapiskat: Ont., Canada 53 00N 82 30W	96
Attawapiskat Lake: Ont., Canada 52 15N 87 45W	93
Atter See: lake, Austria 47 45N 13 30E	73
Attikamagen Lake: Nfld., Canada 55 00N 66 30W	97
Attleborough: Norf., England 52 31N 01 01E	58
Atuel: riv., Argentina 37 45S 65 45W	52
Aubervilliers: France 48 55N 02 24E	117
Aubrac, Montagnes d': France 44 30N 03 00E	71
Auburn: Ala., U.S.A. 32 36N 85 29W	101
Auburn: Maine, U.S.A. 44 04N 70 26W	99
Auburn: Nebr., U.S.A. 40 23N 95 51W	94
Auburn: N.Y., U.S.A. 42 57N 76 34W	99
Auburn: Wash., U.S.A. 47 18N 122 14W	90
Aubusson: France 45 58N 02 10E	70
Auch: France 43 40N 00 36E	70
Auchterarder: Perth., Scotland 56 18N 03 43W	65
Auckland: N.I., New Zealand 36 55S 174 47E	37 87
Auckland Islands: Southern Ocean 50 35S 166 00E	4 25
Aude: riv., France 42 45N 02 00E	70
Auden: Ont., Canada 50 14N 87 54W	98
Audenshaw: Gt. Man., England 53 28N 02 08W	114
Aue: E.Germany 50 35N 12 42E	73
Augher: Tyr., N.Ireland 54 26N 07 08W	66
Aughnacloy: Tyr., N.Ireland 54 25N 06 59W	66
Augsburg: W.Germany 48 21N 10 54E	26 73
Augusta: W.A., Australia 34 19S 115 09E	40
Augusta: Sicily 37 14N 15 14E	79 107
Augusta: Ga., U.S.A. 33 29N 82 00W	45 101
Augusta: Kans., U.S.A. 37 41N 96 59W	95
Augusta: Maine, U.S.A. 44 17N 69 50W	44 99
Auke Bay: Alaska, U.S.A. 58 23N 134 40W	88
Aulnay-sous-Bois: France 48 57N 02 31E	117
Aurangābād: India 19 52N 75 22E	34 82
Aurich: W.Germany 53 28N 07 29E	72

Types of map: Ocean pp. 1-5; Physical pp. 6-25; Human pp. 26-57; Topographic pp. 58-101; World pp. 102-111; Urban pp. 112-128.

Aurillac: France   44 56N 02 26E   70
Aurora: Ill., U.S.A.   41 45N 88 20W   98
Aurora: Nebr., U.S.A.   40 52N 98 00W   94
Aussenalster: *lake,* W.Germany   53 34N 10 01E   119
Austin: Minn., U.S.A.   43 40N 92 58W   98
Austin: Nev., U.S.A.   39 30N 117 04W   91
Austin: Tex., U.S.A.   30 17N 97 45W   43 95
AUSTRALIA   14 40 107
Australian Alps: *ra.,* Australia   37 00S 148 00E   15
Austral (Tubuai) *Islands:* S.Pacific Ocean   23 00S 151 00W   5
AUSTRIA   47 00N 13 30E   7 27 78 107
Autoroute des Cantons de l'Est: *hwy.,* Qué., Canada   45 15N 73 15W   122
Autoroute des Laurentides: *hwy.,* Qué., Canada   45 30N 73 45W   122
Autostrada Cristoforo Colombo: *mty.,* Italy   41 45N 12 15E   116
Autun: France   46 58N 04 18E   71
Auxerre: France   47 48N 03 35E   71
Avallon: France   47 30N 03 54E   71
Avalon *Peninsula:* Nfld., Canada   47 00N 53 15W   97
Avdejevka: U.S.S.R.   48 08N 37 46E   80
Avebury: Wilts., England   51 27N 01 51W   61
Aveiro: Portugal   40 38N 08 40W   77
Avellaneda: Argentina   34 40S 58 21W   53 128
Averon: *riv.,* R. & Crom., Scotland   57 30N 04 15W   64
Aveyron: *riv.,* France   44 00N 01 30E   70
Avezzano: Italy   42 02N 13 26E   79
Aviemore: Inv., Scotland   57 12N 03 50W   65
Avignon: France   43 56N 04 48E   26 71
Ávila: Spain   40 39N 04 42W   77
Avilés: Spain   43 33N 05 55W   77 105
Avoca: *riv.,* Wick., Irish Republic   52 45N 06 00W   67
Avola: B.C., Canada   51 47N 119 19W   89
Avon: *admin.,* England   51 15N 02 30W   61
Avon: *riv.,* Avon, England   51 15N 02 30W   61 113
Avon: *riv.,* War., England   52 00N 01 45W   59
Avon: *riv.,* Wilts., England   51 00N 01 45W   61
Avon: *riv.,* Banff., Scotland   57 15N 03 15W   65
Avon, Ben: *mtn.,* Scotland   57 06N 03 27W   65
Avonmouth: Avon., England   51 31N 02 42W   61 113
Avon Water: *riv.,* Lan., Scotland   55 30N 04 00W   113
Avranches: France   48 42N 01 21W   70
Avtovo: U.S.S.R.   59 52N 30 15E   119
Awe, *Loch:* Argyll., Scotland   56 15N 05 00W   64
Axe: *riv.,* Som., England   51 15N 02 45W   61
Axminster: Devon, England   50 47N 02 59W   61
Ayabe: Japan   35 18N 135 15E   86
Ayacucho: Peru   13 10S 74 15W   49
Ayamonte: Spain   37 13N 07 24W   77
Aycliffe: Dur., England   54 36N 01 34W   63
Aydin: Turkey   37 52N 27 50E   32 79
Áyios Nikólaos: Crete   35 12N 25 42E   79
Aylesbury: Bucks., England   51 50N 00 50W   59 112
Aylsham: Norf., England   52 49N 01 15E   58
Ayr: Ayr., Scotland   55 28N 04 38W   62
Ayr: *riv.,* Ayr., Scotland   55 30N 04 15W   62
Ayre, *Point of:* I. of M., United Kingdom   54 25N 04 22W   62
Ayrshire: *admin.,* Scotland   55 15N 04 30W   62
Azamgarh: India   26 03N 83 10E   83
Azcapotzalco: Mexico   19 24N 99 11W   128
Azerbaydzhan S.S.R.: *admin.,* U.S.S.R.   40 30N 48 00E   28
Aznakajevo: U.S.S.R.   54 53N 53 04E   81
Azores: *is.,* N.Atlantic Ocean   38 30N 28 00W   2 6
Azores *Plateau:* N.Atlantic Ocean   38 00N 28 00W   2
Azov: U.S.S.R.   47 07N 39 25E   80
Azov, *Sea of:* U.S.S.R.   46 30N 36 30E   8 28
Aztec: N.Mex., U.S.A.   36 49N 108 00W   95
Azuero *Peninsula:* Panama   07 45N 80 30W   47
Azul: Argentina   36 46S 59 50W   52
Azuma: Japan   35 56N 140 30E   105
Azur, Côte d': *coast,* France   43 15N 07 00E   71
Azusa: Calif., U.S.A.   34 08N 117 52W   127
Az Ẓahrān (Dhahran): Saudi Arabia   26 18N 50 05E   33
Az Zaqāzīq (Zagazig): Egypt   30 35N 31 31E   32
Az-Zarqā' (Zarqa): Jordan   32 04N 36 05E   32

Bà, *Loch:* Argyll., Scotland   56 15N 05 45W   64
Babajevo: U.S.S.R.   59 23N 35 56E   80
Babar *Islands:* Indonesia   08 00S 129 45E   39
Babbacombe *Bay:* Devon, England   50 30N 03 15W   61
Bāb el Mandeb: *str.,* Africa/Arabia   12 30N 43 15E   53
Babine *Lake:* B.C., Canada   54 45N 126 00W   89
Babuškin: U.S.S.R.   55 52N 37 42E   119
Bacău: Romania   46 32N 26 59E   78
Bachelor *Lake:* Qué., Canada   49 30N 76 30W   96
Bachmač: U.S.S.R.   51 13N 32 46E   80
Backbone *Ranges:* N.W.T., Canada   62 45N 128 30W   88
Backnang: W.Germany   48 57N 09 26E   72
Bacolod: Philippines   10 38N 122 58E   39
Bacup: Lancs., England   53 43N 02 12W   63 114
Bad: *riv.,* S.D., U.S.A.   44 00N 100 45W   94
Badajoz: Spain   38 53N 06 58W   26 77
Baden: Austria   48 01N 16 14E   73
Baden: Switzerland   47 28N 08 19E   71
Baden-Württemberg: *admin.,* W.Germany   49 00N 10 15E   72
Bad Godesberg: W.Germany   50 41N 07 10E   72
Bad Harzburg: W.Germany   51 53N 10 33E   73
Bad Hersfeld: W.Germany   50 53N 09 43E   72
Bad Homburg: W.Germany   50 13N 08 37E   72
Bad Ischl: Austria   47 43N 13 38E   73
Bad Kissingen: W.Germany   50 12N 10 05E   73
Bad Kreuznach: W.Germany   49 51N 07 52E   72
Badlands *National Monument:* S.D., U.S.A.   43 45N 102 15W   94
Badli: India   28 44N 77 09E   120
Bad Nauheim: W.Germany   50 21N 08 44E   72
Badnera: India   20 50N 77 47E   82
Badong: China   31 03N 110 23E   84
Baffin *Bay:* Canada/Greenland   72 00N 70 00W   2 23
Baffin *Bay:* Tex., U.S.A.   27 15N 97 30W   100
Baffin *Island:* N.W.T., Canada   65 00N 70 00W   23
Bafwasende: Zaïre   01 05N 27 16E   54
Bagaha: India   27 08N 84 04E   83
Bagansiapi-api: Indonesia   02 07N 100 53E   38
Bagdad: Iraq *see* Baghdād   33 20N 44 26E   33
Bagdad: Ariz., U.S.A.   34 35N 113 11W   91
Bagé: Brazil   31 22S 54 06W   51
Bagenalstown: Carlow, Irish Republic   52 42N 06 57W   67
Baggio: Italy   45 28N 09 05E   116
Baggy *Point:* Devon, England   51 09N 04 16W   61
Baghdād (Bagdad): Iraq   33 20N 44 26E   33
Baghelkhand *Plateau:* India   23 00N 81 30E   34
Bāgherhāt: Bangladesh   22 40N 89 48E   83
Bagheria: Sicily   38 05N 13 31E   79
Bagnell *Dam:* Mo., U.S.A.   38 13N 92 37W   98
Bagnères-de-Bigorre: France   43 04N 00 09E   70
Bagnères-de-Luchon (Luchon): France   42 48N 00 35E   70
Bagnoli Irpino: Italy   40 50N 15 04E   105
Bagodar: India   24 04N 85 50E   83
Bagotville: Qué., Canada   48 22N 70 54W   96
Baguezane *Mountains:* Niger   17 45N 08 45E   57
Baguio: Philippines   16 25N 120 37E   39
BAHAMAS   25 00N 83 00W   2 17 47 101 106
Bahāwalnagar: Pakistan   29 57N 73 23E   82
Bahāwalpur: Pakistan   29 24N 71 47E   34 82
Bahia: *see* Salvador   12 59S 38 31W   50
Bahia: *admin.,* Brazil   12 15S 42 00W   50
Bahía Blanca: Argentina   38 45S 62 15W   52
Bahraich: India   27 35N 81 36E   83
BAHRAIN   26 15N 50 30E   10 33 107
Baḥr al 'Arab: *riv.,* Sudan   10 15N 27 45E   21
Baḥr al Ghazal: *riv.,* Sudan   07 30N 27 45E   21
Baḥr-al-Jabal (White Nile): *riv.,* Sudan   04 15N 31 30E   21 53
Bai: *riv.,* China   40 03N 116 37E   121
Baia-Mare: Romania   47 39N 23 36E   78
Baicheng (Paich'eng) China   45 38N 122 46E   37
Baidoa (Iscia Baidoa): Somali Rep.   03 08N 45 34E   53
Baidyabāti: India   22 48N 88 20E   120
Baie-Comeau: Qué., Canada   49 12N 69 10W   44 96
Baie-Verte: Nfld., Canada   49 55N 56 12W   97
Baihe: China   32 48N 110 05E   84

Types of map: Ocean pp. 1-5; Physical pp. 6-25; Human pp. 26-57; Topographic pp. 58-101; World pp. 102-111; Urban pp. 112-128.

Baihekou: China   31 51N 110 13E   84
Bailieborough: Cavan, Irish Republic   53 55N 06 58W   66
Bain: riv., Lincs., England   53 15N 00 00   58
Bainbridge: Ga., U.S.A.   30 54N 84 33W   101
Bainbridge Island: Wash., U.S.A.   47 30N 122 30W   126
Bair Island: geog. reg., Calif., U.S.A.   37 31N 122 13W   126
Baiyangdian: lake, China   38 45N 116 00E   84
Baiyun'ebo: China   41 58N 109 45E   105
Baiyunguan: China   20 39 54 116 121
Baja: Hungary   46 11N 18 58E   78
Baja California: admin., Mexico   29 30N 114 30W   46
Baja California Sur: admin., Mexico   25 30N 112 00W   46
Bajan Tümen see Cojbalsan   48 04N 114 30E   30
Bajčunas: U.S.S.R.   47 14N 52 55E   81
Bajiaozun: China   39 54N 116 11E   121
Bajkal (Baykal), Lake: U.S.S.R.   53 30N 108 00E   9 30
Bakal: U.S.S.R.   54 56N 58 48E   81
Bakel: Senegal   14 54N 12 26W   57
Baker: Mont., U.S.A.   46 22N 104 17W   94
Baker: Oreg., U.S.A.   44 47N 117 50W   90
Bakers Dozen Islands: N.W.T., Canada   56 30N 78 45W   96
Bakersfield: Calif., U.S.A.   35 23N 119N 01W   43 91
Bakewell: Derby., England   53 13N 01 40W   58
Baku: U.S.S.R.   40 23N 49 51E   28
Bala: Gwyn., Wales   52 54N 03 35W   60
Balabac Islands: Philippines   08 00N 117 00E   39
Balabac Strait: Malaysia/Philippines   07 30N 117 15E   12 39
Balachna: U.S.S.R.   56 30N 43 36E   80
Bālāghat Range: India   18 45N 76 15E   82
Balakleja: U.S.S.R.   49 27N 36 52E   80
Balakovo: U.S.S.R.   52 02N 47 47E   81
Bala Lake: Gwyn., Wales   52 45N 03 30W   60
Balāngir: India   20 43N 83 30E   83
Balarāmpur: India   23 06N 86 13E   83
Balašicha: U.S.S.R.   55 49N 37 58E   80 119
Balasore: India   21 31N 86 59E   83
Balašov: U.S.S.R.   51 32N 43 08E   28 80
Balaton: lake, Hungary   46 45N 17 30E   78
Balbriggan: Dublin, Irish Republic   53 37N 06 11W   66
Balcary Point: Kirkc., Scotland   54 50N 03 50W   62
Balchaš (Balkhash): U.S.S.R.   46 49N 74 59E   29
Balchaš (Balkhash), Lake: U.S.S.R.   46 45N 76 00E   8 29
Balclutha: S.I., New Zealand   46 16S 169 46E   87
Baldeneysee: lake, W.Germany   51 24N 07 03E   118
Baldock: Herts., England   51 59N 00 12W   59
Bâle see Basel   47 33N 07 36E   26 71
Baleares, Islas (Balearic Islands): is.& Spanish admin., Mediterranean Sea   39 30N 03 00E   6 26 77
Balezino: U.S.S.R.   57 58N 53 00E   81
Balgowlah: N.S.W., Australia   33 48S 151 16E   120
Balgray Reservoir: Renf., Scotland   55 45N 04 15W   113
Bali: is., Indonesia   08 15S 115 15E   39
Balıkesir: Turkey   39 38N 27 52E   32 79
Balikpapan: Indonesia   01 15S 116 50E   39
Baliqiao: China   39 54N 116 36E   121
Balkan Mountains: Bulgaria   42 30N 25 00E   27
Balkhash see Balchaš   46 49N 74 59E   29
Balkhash, Lake see Balchaš, Lake   46 45N 76 00E   8 29
Ballantrae: Ayr., Scotland   55 06N 05 00W   62
Ballarat: Vic., Australia   37 36S 143 58E   41
Ballater: Aber., Scotland   57 03N 03 03W   65
Balleny Basin: Antarctica   66 00S 175 00E   25
Balleny Islands: Antarctica   66 35S 162 50E   25
Ballia: India   25 45N 84 09E   83
Ballina: Mayo, Irish Republic   54 07N 09 09W   66
Ballinamore: Leit., Irish Republic   54 03N 07 47W   66
Ballinasloe: Gal., Irish Republic   53 20N 08 13W   67
Ballincollig: Cork, Irish Republic   51 54N 08 35W   67
Ballinrobe: Mayo, Irish Republic   53 37N 09 13W   66
Ballinskelligs Bay: Kerry, Irish Republic   51 45N 10 00W   67
Bālly: India   22 39N 88 21E   120
Ballybay: Monaghan, Irish Republic   54 08N 06 54W   66
Ballybofey: Don., Irish Republic   54 47N 07 47W   66
Ballybunion: Kerry, Irish Republic   52 36N 09 40W   67
Ballycastle: Antrim, N.Ireland   55 12N 06 15W   66
Ballyclare: Antrim, N.Ireland   54 45N 06 00W   66
Ballydavid Head: Kerry, Irish Republic   52 13N 10 21W   67
Ballygunge: India   22 31N 88 21E   120
Ballyhaunis: Mayo, Irish Republic   53 46N 08 46W   66
Ballyhoura Hills: Irish Republic   52 15N 08 30W   67

Ballyjamesduff: Cavan, Irish Republic   53 52N 07 12W   66
Ballymahon: Long., Irish Republic   53 34N 07 45W   66
Ballymena: Antrim, N.Ireland   54 52N 06 17W   66
Ballymoney: Antrim, N.Ireland   55 04N 06 31W   66
Ballymote: Sligo, Irish Republic   54 06N 08 31W   66
Ballyshannon: Don., Irish Republic   54 30N 08 11W   66
Ballyteige Bay: Wex., Irish Republic   52 00N 06 45W   67
Balmain: N.S.W., Australia   33 51S 151 11E   120
Balmoral Castle: Aber., Scotland   57 02N 03 15W   65
Bālotra: India   25 50N 72 21E   82
Balrāmpur: India   27 25N 82 10E   83
Balsas: riv., Mexico   18 15N 102 00W   46
Balta: U.S.S.R.   47 55N 29 37E   78
Baltic Sea   56 00N 17 00E   7 27 75
Baltimore: Md., U.S.A.   39 18N 76 38W   45 99 104
Baltinglass: Wick., Irish Republic   52 57N 06 42W   67
Baluchistan: geog. reg., Pakistan   28 15N 64 30E   34
Bālurghāt: India   25 12N 88 50E   83
Bamako: Mali   12 40N 07 59W   57
Bamberg: W.Germany   49 54N 10 54E   73
Bamfield: B.C., Canada   48 50N 125 08W   89
Bampton: Devon, England   50 59N 03 29W   61
Bāmra Hills: India   21 15N 84 15E   83
Banagher: Offaly, Irish Republic   53 11N 07 59W   67
Bananal Island: Brazil   11 30S 50 30W   50
Banās: riv., India   26 00N 76 00E   34 82
Banbridge: Down, N.Ireland   54 21N 06 16W   66
Banbury: Oxon., England   52 04N 01 20W   59
Banchory: Kinc., Scotland   57 03N 02 30W   65
Bancroft: Zambia see Chililabombwe   12 20S 27 52E   54
Bānda: India   25 28N 80 20E   82
Bandai-asahi-kokuritsu-kōen: nat. park., Japan   37 45N 139 30E   86
Banda Islands: Indonesia   04 30S 130 00E   39
Bandama: riv., Ivory Coast   05 30N 04 45W   57
Bandar 'Abbās: Iran   27 12N 56 15E   33
Bandar Seri Begawan: Brunei   04 53N 114 56E   39
Banda Sea: Indonesia   06 00S 127 00E   13 39
Bandel: India   22 55N 88 24E   120
Bandelier National Monument: N.Mex., U.S.A.   35 45N 106 00W   95
Bandırma: Turkey   40 21N 27 58E   32 79
Bandjarmasin: Indonesia   03 22S 114 33E   39
Bandon: Cork, Irish Republic   51 45N 08 45W   67
Ban Don: Thailand see Surat Thani   09 09N 99 20E   35
Bandon: riv., Cork, Irish Republic   51 45N 08 45W   67
Bandundu (Banningville): Zaïre   03 20S 17 24E   54
Bandung: Indonesia   06 57S 107 34E   38
Banff: Alta., Canada   51 10N 115 34W   42 92
Banff: Banff., Scotland   57 40N 02 31W   65
Banff National Park: Alta., Canada   52 00N 116 30W   92
Banffshire: admin., Scotland   57 30N 02 45W   65
Banfield: Argentina   34 45S 58 24W   128
Bangalore: India   12 58N 77 35E   34
Bangbu (Pangfou): China   32 53N 117 29E   36 84
Banggai Archipelago: Indonesia   01 30S 123 15E   39
Banggi Island: Malaysia   07 15N 117 00E   39
Banghāzī (Benghazi): Libya   32 07N 20 05E   20 32
Bangka: is., Indonesia   02 15S 106 00E   13 38
Bangkok see Krung Thep   13 44N 100 30E   35
BANGLADESH   22 00N 89 30E   11 35 83 107
Bangor: Down, N.Ireland   54 40N 05 40W   66
Bangor: Maine, U.S.A.   44 49N 68 47W   44 99
Bangor: Gwyn., Wales   53 13N 04 08W   60
Bāngriposi: India   22 09N 86 32E   83
Bangui: Central African Rep.   04 22N 18 35E   21
Bangweulu, Lake: Zambia   11 00S 29 45E   54
Bangzun: China   39 51N 116 20E   121
Banī Suwayf (Beni Suef): Egypt   29 05N 31 05E   32
Banja Luka: Yugoslavia   44 47N 17 11E   27 79
Banjul (Bathurst): Gambia   13 28N 16 39W   57
Banjuwangi: Indonesia   08 12S 114 22E   38
Banks, Cape: N.S.W., Australia   34 00S 151 15E   120
Banks Island: B.C., Canada   53 15N 130 00W   89
Banks Island: N.W.T., Canada   73 00N 121 00W   16
Banks Peninsula: S.I., New Zealand   43 45S 173 00E   87
Bankstown: N.S.W., Australia   33 55S 151 02E   120
Bānkura: India   23 14N 87 05E   83
Bann: riv., N.Ireland   54 15N 06 15W   66
Bann: riv., Down, N.Ireland   54 15N 06 15W   66
Bann: riv., Lon., N.Ireland   54 45N 06 30W   66

Types of map: Ocean pp. 1-5; Physical pp. 6-25; Human pp. 26-57; Topographic pp. 58-101; World pp. 102-111; Urban pp. 112-128.

Bann: *riv.*, Wex., Irish Republic   52 30N 06 15W   67
Banningville *see* Bandundu   03 20S 17 24E   54
Banská Bystrica: Czechoslovakia   48 44N 19 09E   78
Banstead: Surrey, England   51 19N 00 12W   59 112
Bānswāra: India   23 32N 74 28E   82
Bantry: Cork, Irish Rep.   51 41N 09 27W   67 76
Bantry *Bay*: Cork, Irish Republic   51 30N 09 30W   67
Banwy: *riv.*, Powys, Wales   52 30N 03 30W   60
Baoan: Guangdong, China   22 37N 114 09E   85
Baoan: Hebei, China *see* Zhuolu   40 22N 115 05E   84
Baode: China   39 04N 111 11E   84
Baoding (Paoting; Qingyuan/Ch'ingyüan): Hebei, China
   38 52N 115 29E   36 84
Baofeng: China   33 44N 112 45E   84
Baoji (Paochi): China   34 20N 107 14E   36 84
Baojing: China   28 48N 109 46E   85
Baoshan (Paoshan): Yunnan, China   25 09N 99 09E   36
Baotou (Paot'ou): China   40 40N 109 59E   36 84 105
Baoying: China   33 13N 119 28E   84
Baracaldo: Spain   43 17N 02 59W   70
Barajala *Canal*: India   22 35N 88 12E   120
Barajas de Madrid: Spain   40 28N 03 35W   116
Barakah: *riv.*, Sudan   17 30N 37 30E   53
Bārākot: India   21 32N 85 02E   83
Bārān: India   25 08N 76 32E   82
Barānagar: India   22 38N 88 22E   83 120
Baranof *Island*: Alaska, U.S.A.   56 30N 134 45W   89
Baranoviči (Baranovichi): U.S.S.R.   53 40N 25 44E   28 78
Bārāsat: India   22 43N 88 29E   120
Barataria *Bay*: La., U.S.A.   29 15N 89 45W   100
Barat Daja *Islands*: Indonesia   07 30S 127 00E   39
Baraut: India   29 06N 77 15E   82
Barbacena: Brazil   21 14S 43 46W   51
BARBADOS   13 15N 58 30W   47
Barbezieux: France   45 28N 00 09W   70
Barbil: India   22 06N 85 20E   83
Barcellona: Sicily   38 10N 15 15E   79
Barcelona: Spain   41 25N 02 10E   26 77 116
Barcelona: Venezuela   10 08N 64 43W   48
Barceloneta: Spain   41 23N 02 12E   116
Barcelonnette: France   44 25N 05 55E   71
Barcraigs *Reservoir*: Renf./Ayr., Scotland   55 45N 04 30W
   113
Bardīyah (Bardia): Libya   31 44N 25 08E   32
Bardsey *Island*: Gwyn., Wales   52 46N 04 48W   60
Bareggio: Italy   45 28N 08 59E   116
Bareilly: India   28 20N 79 24E   34 82
Barents *Sea*   74 00N 40 00E   23
Bargarh: India   21 25N 83 35E   83
Bargoed: M.Glam., Wales   51 43N 03 15W   113
Barhi: India   24 19N 85 25E   83
Bāri: India   26 39N 77 37E   82
Bari: Italy   41 07N 16 52E   27 79
Bāri Doāb: *geog. reg.*, Pakistan   30 15N 72 45E   82
Barīm (Perim) *Island*: Red Sea   12 40N 43 24E   53
Barinas: Venezuela   08 36N 70 15W   48
Baripāda: India   21 52N 86 48E   83
Barisāl: Bangladesh   22 41N 90 20E   35 83
Barisan *Range*: Indonesia   03 00S 102 15E   13 38
Barito: *riv.*, Indonesia   02 15S 114 45E   13 39
Barkerville: B.C., Canada   53 06N 121 35W   89
Barking: Gt. Ldn., England   51 32N 00 05E   59 112
Barkley, *Lake*: U.S.A.   36 45N 87 45W   100
Barkley *Sound*: B.C., Canada   48 45N 125 15W   89
Barkly *Tableland*: N.T., Australia   18 30S 137 15E   14 41
Bârlad *see* Birlad   46 14N 27 40E   78
Barlassina: Italy   45 39N 09 08E   116
Bar-le-Duc: France   48 46N 05 10E   71
Barletta: Italy   41 20N 16 17E   79
Barmen: W.Germany   51 15N 07 10E   118
Barmer: India   25 43N 71 25E   34 82
Barmouth: Gwyn., Wales   52 43N 04 03W   60
Barmouth *Bay*: Gwyn., Wales   52 30N 04 00W   60
Barnāla: India   30 26N 75 33E   82
Barnard Castle: Dur., England   54 33N 01 55W   63
Barnaul: U.S.S.R.   53 22N 83 45E   29
Barnet: B.C., Canada   49 18N 122 57W   126
Barnet: Gt. Ldn., England   51 40N 00 13W   59 112
Barnoldswick: Lancs., England   53 55N 02 11W   63 114
Barnsley: S.Yorks., England   53 34N 01 28W   63
Barnstaple: Devon, England   51 05N 04 04W   61

Barnstaple (Bideford) *Bay*: Devon, England
   51 00N 04 15W   61
Baroda: India   22 19N 73 14E   34 82
Barpeta: India   26 20N 91 02E   83
Barquisimeto: Venezuela   10 03N 69 18W   48
Barra: Brazil   11 05S 43 10W   50
Barra: *is.*, Inv., Scotland   57 00N 07 15W   64
Barra, *Sound of*: Inv., Scotland   57 00N 07 15W   64
Barra *Head*: Inv., Scotland   56 47N 07 36W   64
Barrackpore: India   22 46N 88 22E   120
Barracuda *Fracture Zone*: N.Atlantic Ocean
   17 00N 50 00W   2
Barra Mansa: Brazil   22 32S 44 12W   51
Barrancabermeja: Colombia   07 06N 73 54W   48
Barranjoey: *pt.*, N.S.W., Australia   33 35S 151 20E   120
Barranquilla: Colombia   11 00N 74 50W   48
Barre: Vt., U.S.A.   44 13N 72 31W   99
Barreiras: Brazil   12 08S 45 00W   50
Barreiro: Portugal   38 40N 09 05W   77
Barrhead: Alta., Canada   54 10N 114 22W   92
Barrhead: Renf., Scotland   55 48N 04 24W   62 113
Barrie: Ont., Canada   44 22N 79 42W   99
Barrow: *riv.*, Irish Republic   52 45N 06 45W   67
Barrow, *Point*: Alaska, U.S.A.   71 24N 156 29W   16
Barrow-in-Furness: Cumbria, England   54 07N 03 14W   62
Barry: S.Glam., Wales   51 24N 03 18W   61 113
Bārsi: India   18 14N 75 48E   34
Barstow: Calif., U.S.A.   34 54N 117 01W   91
Bar-sur-Aube: France   48 14N 04 43E   71
Barth: E.Germany   54 23N 12 44E   73
Bartlesville: Okla., U.S.A.   36 45N 95 59W   95
Barton-upon-Humber: Humb., England   53 41N 00 27W
   63
Bartow: Fla., U.S.A.   27 54N 81 51W   101
Bāruipur: India   22 21N 88 26E   120
Bāruni: India   25 29N 85 59E   35 83
Baruun Urt: Mongolia   46 40N 113 12E   36
Barwell: Leics., England   52 34N 01 21W   58 115
Barycz: *riv.*, Poland   51 30N 16 45E   73
Baryš: U.S.S.R.   53 39N 47 08E   81
Basankusu: Zaïre   01 14N 19 48E   54
Basauri: Spain   43 13N 02 54W   70
Basel (Bâle; Basle): Switzerland   47 33N 07 36E   26 71
Basilan *Island*: Philippines   06 30N 122 00E   39
Basildon: Essex, England   51 34N 00 25E   59 112
Basingstoke: Hants., England   51 16N 01 05W   59
Basīrhat: India   22 38N 88 52E   83
Baskatong *Reservoir*: Qué., Canada   46 45N 75 45W   96
Baskunčak, Ozero: *lake*, U.S.S.R.   48 12N 46 54E   81
Basle *see* Basel   47 33N 07 36E   26 71
Basmat: India   19 22N 77 10E   82
Bāsoda: India   23 51N 77 56E   82
Basra *see* Al Başrah   30 30N 47 50E   33
Bassano: Alta., Canada   50 48N 112 20W   92
Bassein: Burma   16 46N 94 45E   35
Bassenthwaite *Lake*: Cumbria, England   54 30N 03 00W   62
Bass *Strait*: Australia   39 30S 145 00E   15 40
Bastar: *admin.*, India   19 00N 81 00E   105
Basti: India   26 46N 82 45E   83
Bastia: Corsica   42 41N 09 26E   26 77
Bastrop: La., U.S.A.   32 47N 91 55W   100
Basutoland *see* Lesotho   29 30S 28 15E   55
Bata: Equatorial Guinea   01 51N 09 49E   57
Batabanó, *Golfo de*: Cuba   22 15N 82 45W   47
Batajsk: U.S.S.R.   47 10N 39 44E   80
Batāla: India   31 48N 75 17E   82
Batang (Pat'ang): China   30 02N 99 02E   36
Batangas: Philippines   13 46N 121 01E   39
Batan *Islands*: Philippines   20 30N 121 45E   12
Batavia: Indonesia *see* Djakarta   06 08S 106 45E   38
Batesville: Ark., U.S.A.   35 46N 91 39W   100
Batesville: Miss., U.S.A.   34 19N 89 57W   100
Bath: Avon, England   51 23N 02 22W   61
Bath: Maine, U.S.A.   43 56N 69 50W   99
Bathgate: W.Loth., Scotland   55 54N 03 38W   62
Bathurst: N.B., Canada   47 37N 65 40W   97
Bathurst *see* Banjul   13 28N 16 39W   57
Batjan *Islands*: Indonesia   00 30S 127 30E   39
Batley: W.Yorks., England   53 44N 01 37W   115
Battle: E.Sussex, England   50 55N 00 29E   59
Batna: Algeria   35 34N 06 10E   56

Types of map: Ocean pp. 1-5; Physical pp. 6-25; Human pp. 26-57; Topographic pp. 58-101; World pp. 102-111; Urban pp. 112-128.

Baton Rouge: La., U.S.A. 30 27N 91 11W	43 100 106
Battambang: Khmer Rep. 13 06N 103 13E	38
Battle: riv., Canada 52 15N 112 00W	92
Battle Creek: Mich., U.S.A. 42 20N 85 21W	98
Battle Harbour: Nfld., Canada 52 16N 55 36W	97
Battle Mountain: Nev., U.S.A. 40 38N 116 56W	91
Batu: mtn., Ethiopia 06 55N 39 49E	53
Batu Islands: Indonesia 00 15S 98 15E	12 38
Batumi: U.S.S.R. 41 38N 41 38E	28
Baubau: Indonesia 05 30S 122 37E	39
Bauchi: Nigeria 10 16N 09 50E	57
Baulkham Hills: N.S.W., Australia 33 46S 150 59E	120
Bauriã: India 22 29N 88 10E	120
Bauru: Brazil 22 19S 49 04W	51
Bautzen: E.Germany 51 11N 14 29E	73 78
Bawean: is., Indonesia 05 45S 112 45E	38
Bawtry: S.Yorks., England 53 26N 01 01W	63
Baxian: China 39 06N 116 23E	84
Baxter State Park: Maine, U.S.A. 46 00N 69 00W	99
Bayankalashanmai (Payenk'ala Shan): ra., China 33 30N 98 00E	36
Bay City: Mich., U.S.A. 43 35N 83 52W	45 98
Bay City: Tex., U.S.A. 28 59N 95 58W	100
Bayenthal: W.Germany 50 55N 06 59E	119
Bayerische Alpen: mtns., Austria/W.Germany 47 30N 11 30E	73
Bayern: admin., W.Germany 49 00N 10 15E	73
Bayeux: France 49 16N 00 42W	70
Baykal, Lake: see Bajkal, Lake 53 30N 108 00E	9 30
Bay Meadows: geog. reg., Calif., U.S.A. 37 33N 122 15W	126
Bayonne: France 43 30N 01 28W	70
Bayonne: N.J., U.S.A. 40 39N 74 08W	123
Bayou: riv., Tex., U.S.A. 31 30N 98 45W	95
Bayreuth: W.Germany 49 27N 11 35E	73
Bayrūt (Beirut): Lebanon 33 52N 35 30E	32
Baytown: Tex., U.S.A. 29 43N 94 59W	100 106
Baza: Spain 37 30N 02 45W	77
Bazhong: China 31 51N 106 41E	84
Beachy Head: E.Sussex, England 50 44N 00 16E	59
Beacon Hill: Powys, Wales 52 23N 03 12W	60
Beaconsfield: Bucks., England 51 37N 00 39W	59 112
Beagh, Slieve: mtns., Tyr., N.Ireland 54 21N 07 12W	66
Beaminster: Dorset, England 50 49N 02 45W	61
Bear Creek: Yukon, Canada 64 02N 139 14W	88
Beardmore Glacier: Antarctica 83 45S 171 00E	25
Bear Island: N.W.T., Canada 54 20N 81 00W	96
Bear Island: Cork, Irish Republic 51 30N 09 45W	67
Bear Lake: U.S.A. 41 59N 111 21W	90
Bearsden: Dunb., Scotland 55 56N 04 20W	62 113
Bearskin Lake: Ont., Canada 53 45N 90 45W	93
Beas: riv., India 31 45N 76 15E	82
Beatrice: Nebr., U.S.A. 40 16N 96 45W	94
Beatton: riv., B.C., Canada 56 30N 120 30W	89
Beattyville: Qué., Canada 48 53N 77 10W	99
Beauce, Plaine de: France 48 15N 01 30E	70
Beauchamp: France 49 01N 02 11E	117
Beaufort: Malaysia 05 22N 115 42E	39
Beaufort: S.C., U.S.A. 32 26N 80 40W	101
Beaufort Sea: 70 30N 142 00W	22
Beauly: Inv., Scotland 57 29N 04 29W	64
Beauly: riv., Inv., Scotland 57 15N 04 30W	64
Beaumaris: Gwyn., Wales 53 16N 04 05W	60
Beaumont: Tex., U.S.A. 30 05N 94 06W	43 100 106
Beaune: France 47 02N 04 50E	71
Beautor: France 49 39N 03 20E	105
Beauvais: France 49 26N 02 05E	70
Beaver: riv., Canada 60 15N 125 30W	88
Beaver Creek: Kans., U.S.A. 39 45N 100 30W	94
Beaver Dam: Wis., U.S.A. 43 28N 88 50W	98
Beaverdell: B.C., Canada 49 26N 119 05W	89
Beaverhead: riv., Mont., U.S.A. 45 00N 113 00W	90
Beaverhill Lake: Alta., Canada 53 15N 112 30W	92
Beaver Island: Mich., U.S.A. 45 30N 85 30W	98
Beaverlodge: Alta., Canada 55 11N 119 29W	89
Beãwar: India 26 02N 74 20E	82
Bebington: Mers., England 53 22N 03 01W	114
Beccles: Suff., England 52 28N 01 34E	58
Béchar (Colomb Béchar): Algeria 31 35N 02 17W	56
Bechuanaland see Botswana	21 55 107
Beckemeyer: III., U.S.A. 38 35N 89 26W	98

Beckley: W.Va., U.S.A. 37 46N 81 12W	101
Becontree: Essex, England 51 34N 00 10E	112
Bedale: N.Yorks., England 54 17N 01 35W	63
Bedford: Beds., England 52 08N 00 29W	59
Bedford: Mass., U.S.A. 42 28N 71 17W	122
Bedford: Pa., U.S.A. 40 02N 78 31W	99
Bedfordshire: admin., England 52 00N 00 30W	59
Bedlington: Northumb., England 55 08N 01 35W	63
Bedwas: Gwent, Wales 51 36N 03 12W	113
Bedworth: War., England 52 29N 01 28W	58 115
Bee, Loch: Inv., Scotland 57 15N 07 15W	64
Be'er Sheva (Beersheba): Israel 31 14N 34 47E	32
Beeston: Notts., England 52 56N 01 12W	58
Beeston: W.Yorks., England 53 49N 01 35W	115
Beeville: Tex., U.S.A. 28 24N 97 45W	100
Begamganj: India 23 36N 78 20E	82
Bei: riv., China 23 30N 112 45E	85
Beian (Peian): China 48 15N 126 30E	31
Beida see Zãwiyat al Baydã' 32 46N 21 43E	32
Beihai (Peihai): China 21 30N 109 10E	36 85
Beihai: lake, China 39 56N 116 22E	121
Beijing (Peip'ing, Peking): China 39 55N 116 25E	36 84 121
Beijing Shi (Peking Municipality) admin., China 40 15N 116 00E	36 84
Beiliu: China 22 50N 110 26E	85
Beinn Dearg: mtn., R. & Crom., Scotland 57 47N 04 55W	64
Beinn Dorain: mtn., Argyll., Scotland 56 31N 04 44W	64
Beinn Eighe: mtn., R. & Crom., Scotland 57 35N 05 26W	64
Beinn Fhada: mtn., R. & Crom., Scotland 57 13N 05 18W	64
Beinn Mhor: mtn., R. & Crom., Scotland 57 59N 06 40W	64
Beira: Mozambique 19 50S 34 52E	55
Beirut see Bayrūt 33 52N 35 30E	32
Beitbridge: Rhodesia 22 10S 29 59E	55
Beith: Ayr., Scotland 55 45N 04 38W	113
Beiyuan: China 40 01N 116 22E	121
Beja: Portugal 38 01N 07 52W	77
Bejaïa (Bougie): Algeria 36 49N 05 03E	56 77
Bekabad: U.S.S.R. 40 37N 71 12E	29
Békéscsaba: Hungary 46 40N 21 06E	78
Bela: India 25 56N 82 00E	83
Bela: Pakistan 26 12N 66 20E	34
Bela Dila: mtn., India 18 46N 81 21E	105
Belaja Cerkov', (Belaya Tserkov'): U.S.S.R. 49 49N 30 07E	28 80
Belaja Cholunica: U.S.S.R. 58 50N 50 48E	81
Belaja Kalitva: U.S.S.R. 48 11N 40 46E	80
Belampalli: India 19 01N 79 30E	82
Belawan: Indonesia 03 46N 98 44E	38
Belaya Tserkov' see Belaja Cerkov' 49 49N 30 07E	28 80
Belcher Islands: N.W.T., Canada 56 00N 79 00W	44 96
Bel'cy (Bel'tsy): U.S.S.R. 47 46N 27 56E	78
Belebej: U.S.S.R. 54 07N 54 07E	81
Belém (Pará): Brazil 01 27S 48 29W	50
Belen: N.Mex., U.S.A. 34 40N 106 46W	95
Belencito: Colombia 05 47N 72 74W	104
Belfast: Antrim, N.Ireland 54 35N 05 55W	26 66
Belfast Lough: N.Ireland 54 30N 05 45W	66
Belford: Northumb., England 55 36N 01 49W	63
Belfort: France 47 38N 06 52E	71
Belgaum: India 15 54N 74 36E	34
Belghoria: India 22 39N 88 23E	120
BELGIUM 51 00N 04 00E	6 26 107
Belgorod: U.S.S.R. 50 36N 36 35E	28 80
Belgrade see Beograd 44 50N 20 30E	27 79
Beliaghata: India 22 35N 88 23E	120
Belitung: is., Indonesia 03 00S 108 00E	13 38
BELIZE (BRITISH HONDURAS) 17 30N 88 45W	16 46
Belize: Belize 17 29N 88 10W	46
Bella Bella: B.C., Canada 52 07N 128 05W	89
Bellac: France 46 07N 01 04E	70
Bella Coola: B.C., Canada 52 23N 126 46W	89
Bellary: India 15 11N 76 54E	34 105
Belledune: N.B., Canada 47 53N 65 45W	97
Belleek: Ferm., N.Ireland 54 29N 08 06W	66
Belle Fourche: S.D., U.S.A. 44 40N 103 51W	94
Belle Fourche: riv., U.S.A. 44 30N 104 30W	94

Types of map: Ocean pp. 1-5; Physical pp. 6-25; Human pp. 26-57; Topographic pp. 58-101; World pp. 102-111; Urban pp. 112-128.

Belle Glade: Fla., U.S.A.   26 41N 80 41W   101
Belle *Isle*: Nfld., Canada   51 45N 55 15W   97
Belle *Isle*: Mich., U.S.A.   42 21N 82 58W   125
Belle Isle, *Strait of*: Nfld., Canada   51 30N 56 30W   44 97
Belleoram: Nfld., Canada   47 32N 55 28W   97
Belle Plaine: Sask., Canada   50 25N 105 09W   92
Belle River: Ont., Canada   42 18N 82 43W   125
Belleterre: Qué., Canada   47 25N 78 41W   99
Belleville: Ont., Canada   44 10N 77 22W   99
Belleville: Kans., U.S.A.   39 50N 97 38W   94
Bellevue: Nebr., U.S.A.   41 09N 95 54W   94
Bellevue: Pa., U.S.A.   40 30N 80 03W   125
Bellevue: Wash., U.S.A.   47 37N 122 12W   126
Bellflower, Calif., U.S.A.   33 53N 118 07W   127
Bellingham: Northumb., England   55 09N 02 16W   63
Bellingham: Wash., U.S.A.   48 46N 122 29W   90
Bellingshausen: *rsch. stn.*, Antarctica   62 12S 58 56W   24
Bellingshausen *Sea*:   65 00S 90 00W   3 24
Bell *Island*: Nfld., Canada   50 45N 55 30W   97
Bello: Colombia   06 20N 75 41W   48
Bell Rock: N.W.T., Canada   60 01N 112 06W   92
Belluno: Italy   46 08N 12 13E   78
Bellwood: Ill., U.S.A.   41 51N 87 52W   124
Belmont: Mass., U.S.A.   42 22N 71 11W   122
Belmont *Harbor*: Ill., U.S.A.   41 56N 87 38W   124
Belmopan: Belize   17 13N 88 48W   46
Belmullet: Mayo, Irish Republic   54 14N 09 59W   66
Belogorsk: U.S.S.R.   50 55N 128 28E   31
Belo Horizonte: Brazil   19 55S 43 56W   51 104
Beloit: Kans., U.S.A.   39 28N 98 06W   94
Beloit: Wis., U.S.A.   42 31N 89 04W   98
Beloje, Ozero: *lake*, U.S.S.R.   60 15N 37 30E   80
Beloluck: U.S.S.R.   49 41N 39 02E   80
Belopolje: U.S.S.R.   51 09N 34 18E   80
Beloreck: U.S.S.R.   53 58N 58 24E   81 105
Belorusskaja S.S.R. (Belorussian S.S.R.): *admin.*, U.S.S.R.
   53 00N 27 30E   28 78
Bel'ov: U.S.S.R.   53 48N 36 08E   80
Belovo: U.S.S.R.   54 25N 86 18E   30
Beloz'orsk: U.S.S.R.   62 02N 37 48E   80
Belper: Derby., England   53 01N 01 29W   58
Belton *Dam*: Tex., U.S.A.   31 07N 97 29W   95
Beltra, *Lough*: Mayo, Irish Republic   53 45N 09 15W   66
Beltsville: Md., U.S.A.   39 02N 76 55W   122
Bel'tsy *see* Bel'cy   47 46N 27 56E   78
Belturbet: Cavan, Irish Republic   54 06N 07 26W   66
Belyj: U.S.S.R.   55 50N 32 56E   80
Bemidji: Minn., U.S.A.   47 29N 94 52W   98
Ben Alder: *mtn.*, Inv., Scotland   56 49N 04 28W   64
Benalla: Vic., Australia   36 35S 145 58E   41
Benares *see* Vārānasi   25 20N 83 00E   35 83
Benavente: Spain   42 00N 05 40W   77
Benavidez: Argentina   34 24S 58 42W   128
Ben Avon: *mtn.*, Scotland   57 06N 03 27W   65
Benbane *Head*: Antrim, N.Ireland   55 15N 06 29W   66
Benbecula: *is.*, Inv., Scotland   57 15N 07 15W   64
Ben Chonzie: *mtn.*, Perth., Scotland   56 26N 03 59W   65
Ben Cruachan: *mtn.*, Argyll., Scotland   56 26N 05 09W   64
Bend: Oreg., U.S.A.   44 04N 121 19W   42 90
Bendery: U.S.S.R.   46 48N 29 29E   78
Bendigo: Vic., Australia   36 48S 144 21E   41
Bengal, *Bay of*: Bangladesh/India   20 30N 88 00E   1 35 83
Benghazi *see* Banghāzī   32 07N 20 05E   20 32
Bengkalis: Indonesia   01 27N 102 10E   38
Bengkulu: Indonesia   03 46S 102 16E   38
Benguela: Angola   12 35S 13 25E   54
Benguela *Current*: S.Atlantic Ocean   33 00S 10 00E   3
Ben Hope: *mtn.*, Suther., Scotland   58 24N 04 36W   64
Beni: *riv.*, Bolivia   14 00S 67 30W   49
Benicarló: Spain   40 25N 00 25E   77
Beni Mellal: Morocco   32 22N 06 29W   56
Benin, *Bight of*: W.Africa   04 45N 02 00E   57
Benin City: Nigeria   06 18N 05 41E   57
Beni-Saf: Algeria   35 28N 01 22W   56
Beni Suef *see* Banī Suwayf   29 05N 31 05E   32
Benjamin Constant: Brazil   04 22S 70 02W   48
Ben Klibreck: *mtn.*, Suther., Scotland   58 15N 04 22W   64
Ben Lawers: *mtn.*, Perth., Scotland   56 33N 04 15W   64
Ben Ledi: *mtn.*, Perth., Scotland   56 16N 04 20W   64
Benllech: Gwyn., Wales   53 19N 04 13W   60
Ben Lomond: *mtn.*, Stirl., Scotland   56 12N 04 38W   64

Ben Macdhui: *mtn.*, Aber., Scotland   57 04N 03 40W   65
Ben More: *mtn.*, Argyll., Scotland   56 25N 06 02W   64
Ben More: *mtn.*, Perth., Scotland   56 23N 04 31W   64
Ben More Assynt: *mtn.*, Suther., Scotland   58 07N 04 52W
   64
Bennane *Head*: Ayr., Scotland   55 08N 05 00W   62
Bennett: B.C., Canada   59 49N 135 01W   88
Ben Nevis: *mtn.*, Inv., Scotland   56 48N 05 00W   64
Bennington: Vt., U.S.A.   42 54N 73 12W   99
Benoni: Trans., Rep. of S.Africa   26 12S 28 18E   55 105
Benrath: W.Germany   51 10N 06 53E   118
Ben Rinnes: *mtn.*, Banff., Scotland   57 24N 03 15W   65
Bensberg: W.Germany   50 58N 07 10E   119
Bensenville: Ill., U.S.A.   41 56N 87 56W   124
Ben Sgritheal: *mtn.*, Inv., Scotland   57 10N 05 33W   64
Benson: Ariz., U.S.A.   31 58N 110 18W   91
Benson Lake: B.C., Canada   50 20N 127 27W   89
Ben Starav: *mtn.*, Argyll., Scotland   56 32N 05 03W   64
Bentley: S.Yorks., England   53 33N 01 09W   63
Benton: Ark., U.S.A.   34 34N 92 35W   100
Benton: Wis., U.S.A.   42 34N 90 23W   98
Benue: *riv.*, Nigeria   07 45N 08 00E   20 57
Ben Vorlich: *mtn.*, Perth., Scotland   56 21N 04 13W   64
Benwee *Head*: Mayo, Irish Republic   54 21N 09 48W   66
Ben Wyvis: *mtn.*, R. & Crom., Scotland   57 40N 04 35W   64
Benxi (Pench'i): China   41 18N 123 45E   37 105
Beograd (Belgrade): Yugoslavia   44 50N 20 30E   27 79
Beowawe: Nev., U.S.A.   40 35N 116 29W   91
Beppu: Japan   33 17N 131 30E   86
Berat: Albania   40 43N 19 46E   79
Berbera: Somali Rep.   10 28N 45 02E   53
Berbérati: Central African Rep.   04 16N 15 47E   54
Berd'ansk: U.S.S.R.   46 45N 36 49E   80
Berdičev: U.S.S.R.   49 54N 28 36E   78
Béréby: Ivory Coast   04 37N 07 00W   57
Beregovo: U.S.S.R.   48 13N 22 39E   78
Berens: *riv.*, Canada   52 00N 96 15W   93
Berens River: Man., Canada   52 22N 97 00W   93
Berezina: *riv.*, U.S.S.R.   54 00N 28 45E   80
Berezniki: U.S.S.R.   59 24N 56 46E   29
Bergama: Turkey   39 08N 27 10E   79
Bergamo: Italy   45 42N 09 40E   71
Bergedorf: W.Germany   53 29N 10 13E   119
Bergen: Norway   60 23N 05 20E   26 27 75
Bergen op Zoom: Netherlands   51 30N 04 17E   72
Bergerac: France   44 50N 00 29E   70
Bergisches Land: *geog. reg.*, W.Germany   51 00N 07 15E
   118
Bergisch Gladbach: W.Germany   50 59N 07 10E   72 119
Berhampore: India   24 06N 88 18E   83
Berhampur: India   19 21N 84 51E   35 83
Bering *Sea*:   59 00N 165 00W   4 22
Bering *Strait*: U.S.A./U.S.S.R.   65 45N 169 00W   16
Berkåk: Norway   62 48N 10 03E   74
Berkeley: Calif., U.S.A.   37 53N 122 17W   91 126
Berkeley: Ill., U.S.A.   41 53N 87 56W   124
Berkeley, *Vale of*: Glos., England   51 30N 02 30W   113
Berkhamsted: Herts., England   51 46N 00 35W   59 112
Berkley: Mich., U.S.A.   42 31N 83 12W   125
Berkner *Island*: Antarctica   79 30S 50 00W   24
Berkshire: *admin.*, England   51 15N 01 15W   59
Berlin: Germany   52 30N 13 24E   27 73 117
Berlin: N.H., U.S.A.   44 27N 71 13W   99
Berlin, East (Ost-Berlin): E.Germany   52 31N 13 24E   117
Berlin, West: W.Germany   52 30N 13 20E   117
Berliner Forst Grunewald: *park*, W.Germany
   52 27N 13 14E   117
Berliner Forst Spandau: *park*, W.Germany   52 35N 13 10E
   117
Berliner Forst Tegel: *park*, W.Germany   52 36N 13 15E   117
Berliner Stadforst Köpenick: *park*, E.Germany
   52 25N 13 38E   117
Berman, *Lake*: Qué., Canada   53 30N 69 00W   96
Bermejo: *riv. see* Teuco riv.   24 00S 62 30W   49
Bermeo: Spain   43 25N 02 44W   70
BERMUDA   32 15N 64 30W   2 17 45
Bermuda *Rise*: N.Atlantic Ocean   32 00N 65 00W   2
Bern (Berne): Switzerland   46 57N 07 26E   26 71
Bernal: Argentina   34 43S 58 17W   128
Bernalillo: N.Mex., U.S.A.   35 18N 106 33W   95
Bernau: E.Germany   52 41N 13 36E   73

Types of map: Ocean pp. 1-5; Physical pp. 6-25; Human pp. 26-57; Topographic pp. 58-101; World pp. 102-111; Urban pp. 112-128.

Berneray: *is.*, Inv., Scotland 57 30N 07 00W 64
Berne: Switzerland *see* Bern 46 57N 07 26E 26 71
Berne: W.Germany 53 38N 10 08E 119
Berner *Alpen*: *mtns.*, Switzerland 46 15N 07 30E 71
Beroun: Czechoslovakia 49 58N 14 05E 73
Berowra: N.S.W., Australia 33 37S 151 09E 120
Berowra *Creek*: N.S.W., Australia 33 35S 151 08E 77
Ber'ozovka: U.S.S.R. 47 12N 30 55E 80
Berre-l'Étang: France 43 28N 05 10E 71 107
Berry *Head*: Devon, England 50 24N 03 29W 61
Berry *Islands*: Bahamas 25 30N 77 45W 101
Bersimis: *riv. see* Betsiamites 49 15N 69 30W 96
Bersimis River: Qué., Canada 48 55N 68 42W 96
Bertraghboy *Bay*: Gal., Irish Republic 53 15N 09 45W 67
Berwickshire: *admin.*, Scotland 55 45N 02 30W 63
Berwick-upon-Tweed: Northumb., England 55 46N 02 00W 63
Berwyn: Ill., U.S.A. 41 49N 87 52W 124
Berwyn: *mtns.*, Clwyd, Wales 52 45N 03 15W 60
Besançon: France 47 14N 06 02E 26 71
Besós: Spain 41 25N 02 10E 116
Besós: *riv.*, Spain 41 30N 02 15E 116
Bessbrook: Arm., N.Ireland 54 12N 06 25W 66
Bessemer: Ala., U.S.A. 33 24N 86 58W 101
Bethesda: Gwyn., Wales 53 11N 04 03W 60
Bethesda: Md., U.S.A. 39 00N 77 05W 122
Bethlehem: O.F.S., Rep. of S.Africa 28 15S 28 19E 55
Bethlehem: Pa., U.S.A. 40 36N 75 22W 99 104
Béticas, Cordilleras: *ra.*, Spain 37 00N 03 00W 77
Betsiamites: Qué., Canada 48 56N 68 40W 96
Betsiamites (Bersimis): *riv.*, Qué., Canada 49 15N 69 30W 96
Bettiah: India 26 49N 84 29E 83
Betul: India 21 54N 77 54E 82
Betwa: *riv.*, India 24 00N 78 00E 34
Betws-y-Coed: Gwyn., Wales 53 05N 03 48W 60
Beuel: W.Germany 50 44N 07 08E 119
Beult: *riv.*, Kent, England 51 00N 00 30E 59
Beverley: Humb., England 53 51N 02 26W 63
Beverly Hills: Calif., U.S.A. 34 03N 118 23W 127
Beverly Hills: Mich., U.S.A. 42 32N 83 15W 125
Bevertalsperre: *res.*, W.Germany 51 09N 07 22E 118
Bewdley: Here. & Worcs., England 52 22N 02 19W 59
Bexhill: E.Sussex, England 50 50N 00 29E 59
Bexley: Gt. Ldn., England 51 26N 00 10E 59
Bexley Heath: Gt. Ldn., England 51 26N 00 10E 112
Bežanickaja Vozvyšennost': *hld.*, U.S.S.R. 56 45N 29 30E 80
Bežeck: U.S.S.R. 57 47N 36 39E 80
Béziers: France 43 21N 03 13E 71
Bezwada *see* Vijayawāda 16 34N 80 40E 34
Bhādgāon *see* Bhaktapur 27 41N 85 26E 35 83
Bhadohi: India 25 24N 82 35E 83
Bhadrakh: India 21 05N 86 36E 83
Bhadreswar: India 22 50N 88 22E 120
Bhāgalpur: India 25 14N 86 59E 35 83
Bhairawa: Nepal 27 32N 83 23E 83
Bhakkar: Pakistan 31 40N 71 08E 82
Bhaktapur (Bhādgāon): Nepal 27 41N 85 26E 35 83
Bhamo: Burma 24 15N 97 15E 35
Bhandāra: India 21 10N 79 41E 82
Bhander *Plateau*: India 24 15N 80 45E 34
Bharatpur: India 27 14N 77 28E 82
Bhātāpāra: India 21 36N 81 56E 83
Bhatinda: India 30 10N 74 58E 82
Bhātpāra: India 22 51N 88 31E 83 120
Bhaunager: India 21 46N 72 14E 34 82
Bhawānipatna: India 19 57N 83 10E 83
Bhilai: India 21 11N 81 20E 83 105
Bhīlwara: India 25 23N 74 39E 82
Bhima: *riv.*, India 18 00N 75 15E 34
Bhīmphedi: Nepal 27 32N 85 08E 83
Bhind: India 26 33N 78 47E 82
Bhiwandi: India 19 21N 73 08E 82
Bhiwāni: India 28 47N 76 11E 82
Bhopāl: India 23 17N 77 28E 34 82
Bhubaneswar: India 20 13N 85 50E 83
Bhusāwal: India 21 01N 75 50E 34 82
BHUTAN (Druk-yul) 27 30N 90 30E 11 35 83
Biafra, *Bight of*: W.Africa 02 30N 07 30E 57
Białogard: Poland 54 00N 16 00E 73
Białystok: Poland 53 09N 23 10E 27 78
Biaora: India 23 56N 76 56E 82
Biarritz: France 43 29N 01 33W 70
Bibai: Japan 43 19N 141 52E 86
Biberach: W.Germany 48 06N 09 48E 73
Bicester: Oxon., England 51 54N 01 09W 59
Bida: Nigeria 09 06N 05 59E 57
Biddeford: Maine, U.S.A. 43 29N 70 27W 99
Biddulph: Staffs., England 53 08N 02 10W 58 114
Bideford: Devon, England 51 01N 04 13W 61
Bideford (Barnstaple) *Bay*: Devon, England 51 00N 04 15W 61
Bié *see* Silva Porto 12 25S 16 56E 54
Biebrza: *riv.*, Poland 53 30N 22 30E 78
Biel (Bienne): Switzerland 47 09N 07 16E 71
Bielawa: Poland 50 41N 16 38E 73
Bielefeld: W.Germany 52 02N 08 32E 72
Biella: Italy 45 34N 08 04E 71
Bielovieja *National Park*: U.S.S.R. 52 45N 24 30E 78
Bielsko-Biała: Poland 49 50N 19 00E 78
Biên Hoa: S.Vietnam 10 58N 106 50E 38
Bienne *see* Biel 47 09N 07 16E 71
Bienville, *Lac*: Qué., Canada 55 00N 72 30W 96
Bié *Plateau*: Angola 12 30S 15 30E 21 54
Big Beaver House: Ont., Canada 52 59N 89 50W 93
Big Bend *National Park*: Tex., U.S.A. 29 00N 103 15W 95
Big Black: *riv.*, Miss., U.S.A. 32 00N 90 45W 100
Big Blue: *riv.*, U.S.A. 41 00N 97 00W 94
Bigbury *Bay*: Devon, England 50 15N 03 45W 61
Big Falls: Minn., U.S.A. 48 12N 93 50W 98
Big Fork: *riv.*, Minn., U.S.A. 47 30N 93 30W 98
Biggar: Sask., Canada 52 03N 107 59W 92
Biggar: Lan., Scotland 55 38N 03 32W 62
Biggleswade: Beds., England 52 05N 00 17W 59
Big Hole: *riv.*, Mont., U.S.A. 45 45N 113 15W 90
Bighorn: *riv.*, U.S.A. 45 00N 108 00W 90
Bighorn *Mountains*: Wyo., U.S.A. 44 00N 107 15W 43 94
Big *Island*: N.W.T., Canada 61 00N 116 45W 92
Big Miscamoot *Bay*: Mich., U.S.A. 42 30N 82 30W 125
Big River: Sask., Canada 53 50N 107 01W 92
Big Sioux: *riv.*, S.D., U.S.A. 44 30N 96 45W 94
Big Spring: Tex., U.S.A. 32 15N 101 28W 95
Big Timber: Mont., U.S.A. 45 50N 109 57W 94
Big Trout *Lake*: Ont., Canada 53 45N 90 00W 93
Big Valley: Alta., Canada 52 03N 112 42W 92
Big Wood: *riv.*, Idaho, U.S.A. 43 00N 114 15W 90
Bihać: Yugoslavia 44 49N 15 53E 79
Bihār: India 25 13N 85 31E 35 83
Bihār: *admin.*, India 25 00N 85 00E 35 83
Bihu: China 28 19N 119 51E 85
Bijagós *Archipelago* (Bissagos *Islands*): Port. Guinea 11 00N 15 45W 57
Bijāpur: India 16 52N 75 47E 34
Bijāwar: India 24 36N 79 30E 82
Bijnor: India 29 22N 78 09E 82
Bijsk (Biysk): U.S.S.R. 52 34N 85 15E 30
Bīkaner: India 28 01N 73 22E 34 82
Bilāspur: India 22 03N 82 12E 34 83
Bilbao: Spain 43 15N 02 56W 26 70 77 105
Bilimora: India 20 46N 72 58E 82
Bille: *riv.*, W.Germany 53 03N 10 15E 119
Billericay: Essex, England 51 38N 00 25E 59 112
Billingham: Cleve., England 54 36N 01 17W 63
Billings: Mont., U.S.A. 45 47N 108 30W 42 94
Billingshurst: W.Sussex, England 51 01N 00 28W 59
Billstedt: W.Germany 53 33N 10 08E 119
Bilma, Grand Erg de: *des.*, Niger 18 45N 12 45E 20
Bilo Gora: *mtns.*, Yugoslavia 45 45N 17 00E 78
Biloxi: Miss., U.S.A. 30 24N 88 53W 100
Bilston: Staffs., England 52 34N 02 04W 105
Bilton: War., England 52 22N 01 17W 115
Bimini *Islands*: Bahamas 25 45N 79 15W 101
Bīna-Etāwa: India 24 09N 78 10E 82
Bindjai: Indonesia 03 37N 98 30E 38
Binevenagh: *mtn., Lon., N.Ireland* 55 06N 06 55W 66
Bingen: W.Germany 49 58N 07 55E 72
Bingham: Notts., England 52 57N 00 57W 58
Bingham: Utah, U.S.A. 40 32N 112 09W 91
Binghamton: N.Y., U.S.A. 42 06N 75 55W 99
Bingley: W.Yorks., England 53 51N 01 50W 63 115
Binhai (Dongkan): China 33 57N 119 51E 84

Bintulu: Malaysia   03 12N 113 01E   38
Binxian: Shandong, China   37 28N 117 56E   84
Binxian: Shǎnxī, China   34 59N 108 05E   84
Binyang: China   23 18N 108 42E   85
Binzert (Bizerta): Tunisia   37 18N 09 52E   56
Bío-Bío: riv., Chile   38 00S 71 30W   52
Birãtnagar: Nepal   26 27N 87 17E   35 83
Birch Island: B.C., Canada   51 36N 119 55W   89
Birch Mountains: Alta., Canada   57 30N 113 00W   92
Bireuen: Indonesia   05 12N 96 40E   38
Bīrganj: Nepal   27 01N 84 56E   83
Bīrjand: Iran   32 55N 59 10E   33
Birkenhead: Mers., England   53 24N 03 02W   63 114
Bîrlad (Bârlad): Romania   46 14N 27 40E   78
Birmingham: W.Mid., England   52 30N 01 50W   26 58 115
Birmingham: Ala., U.S.A.   33 31N 86 48W   45 101 105
Birmingham: Mich., U.S.A.   42 33N 83 12W   125
Birmingham & Fazeley Canal: England   52 30N 01 45W
                                                              115
Birmitrapur: India   22 15N 84 45E   83
Birobidžan: U.S.S.R.   48 48N 132 57E   31
Birr: Offaly, Irish Republic   53 05N 07 54W   67
Birsk: U.S.S.R.   55 25N 55 32E   81
Bisbee: Ariz., U.S.A.   31 27N 109 55W   95
Biscarosse: France   44 24N 01 10W   70
Biscarosse et Parentis, Étang de: lag., France
                   44 20N 01 10W   70
Biscay, Bay of: France/Spain   6 26 70 76
Biscoe Islands: Antarctica   66 00S 66 30W   24
Bisha (Biskia): Ethiopia   15 30N 37 31E   53
Bishnupur: India   23 05N 87 20E   83
Bishop: Calif., U.S.A.   37 22N 118 24W   91
Bishop Auckland: Dur., England   54 40N 01 40W   63
Bishop's Castle: Salop, England   52 29N 03 00W   60
Bishopbriggs: Lan., Scotland   55 54N 04 13W   62 113
Bishop's Stortford: Herts., England   51 53N 00 09E   59
Bishop's Waltham: Hants., England   50 58N 01 12W   59
Biskia see Bisha   15 30N 37 31E   53
Biskotasi Lake: Ont., Canada   47 00N 82 00W   98
Biskra: Algeria   34 50N 05 41E   56
Bismarck: N.D., U.S.A.   46 48N 100 47W   42 94
Bismarck Archipelago: S.Pacific Ocean   02 30S 148 00E   15
Bismarck Sea: 04 15S 148 00E   13
Bissagos Islands see Bijagós Archipelago   11 00N 15 45W
                                                               57
Bissau: Portuguese Guinea   11 52N 15 39W   57
Bissett: Man., Canada   51 01N 95 40W   93
Bistcho Lake: Alta., Canada   59 30N 118 45W   88
Bistrita: riv., Romania   47 15N 25 45E   78
Biswān: India   27 30N 81 00E   82
Bitola (Bitolj): Yugoslavia   41 01N 21 21E   79
Bitterfeld: E.Germany   51 37N 12 20E   73
Bitterroot Range: U.S.A.   45 30N 114 00W   42 90
Biwa-ko: res., Japan   35 15N 136 00E   86
Bizard,Île: Qué., Canada   45 30N 73 53W   122
Bizerta see Binzert   37 18N 09 52E   56
Black: riv., N.Vietnam see Song Da   21 30N 103 30E   12 36
Black: riv., U.S.A.   36 00N 91 15W   100 100
Black: riv., N.Y., U.S.A.   43 30N 75 15W   99
Black: riv., Wis., U.S.A.   44 00N 91 00W   98
Blackburn: Lancs., England   53 45N 02 29W   63 114
Black Cart Water: riv., Renf., Scotland   55 45N 04 30W   113
Black Creek Conservation Area: Ont., Canada
                   43 47N 79 32W   125
Blackdown Hills: England   50 45N 03 00W   61
Black Duck: riv., Canada   56 15N 89 30W   93
Blackfoot: Idaho, U.S.A.   43 11N 112 21W   90
Black Head: Corn., England   50 00N 05 05W   61
Black Head: Clare, Irish Republic   53 09N 09 16W   67
Black Hills: U.S.A.   44 00N 104 00E   17
Black Isle: dist., R. & Crom., Scotland   57 30N 04 15W   64
Black Lake: Sask., Canada   59 00N 105 00W   92
Blackmoor Vale: Dorset, England   50 45N 02 15W   61
Black Mountain: Bhutan   27 20N 90 20E   83
Black Mountains: England/Wales   52 00N 03 00W   60
Black Oak: Ind., U.S.A.   41 35N 87 25W   124
Blackpool: Lancs., England   53 50N 03 03W   26 63 114
Black Rock Desert: Nev., U.S.A.   41 00N 119 00W   90
Black Sea: 43 00N 35 00E   8 27
Blacksod Bay: Mayo, Irish Republic   54 00N 10 00W   66

Blackstairs Mountain: Carlow, Irish Republic
                   52 33N 06 49W   67
Blacktown: N.S.W., Australia   33 46S 150 55E   120
Black Volta: riv., Ghana/Upper Volta   11 00N 02 30W   20
Blackwater: riv., Essex, England   51 45N 00 45E   59
Blackwater: riv., Cork, Irish Rep.   52 00N 08 15W   67
Blackwater: riv., Meath, Irish Republic   53 45N 06 45W   66
Blackwater Lake: N.W.T., Canada   64 00N 123 00W   88
Blackwater Reservoir: Scotland   56 30N 04 45W   64
Blackwell: Okla., U.S.A.   36 48N 97 17W   95
Blackwood: Gwent, Wales   51 41N 03 13W   113
Blaenau Ffestiniog: Gwyn., Wales   52 59N 03 56W   60
Blaenavon: Gwent, Wales   51 48N 03 05W   113
Blagoveščensk: U.S.S.R.   55 01N 55 59E   81
Blagoveščensk (Blagoveshchensk): U.S.S.R.
                   50 17N 127 32E   31
Blair: Nebr., U.S.A.   41 33N 96 08W   94
Blairgowrie: Perth., Scotland   56 36N 03 21W   65
Blairmore: Alta., Canada   49 37N 114 23W   92
Blake Island: Wash., U.S.A.   47 32N 122 29W   126
Blakely Harbor: Wash., U.S.A.   47 35N 122 30W   126
Blakeney Point: Norf., England   52 58N 01 00E   58
Blanc, Cape: Mauritania   20 44N 17 05W   56
Blanc, Mont: France/Italy   45 50N 06 52E   71
Blanco, Cape: Oreg., U.S.A.   42 51N 124 34W   90
Blandford Forum: Dorset, England   50 52N 02 10W   61
Blanding: Utah, U.S.A.   37 37N 109 29W   91
Blankenese: W.Germany   53 34N 09 49E   119
Blantyre: Malawi   15 47S 35 00E   55
Blarney: Cork, Irish Republic   51 56N 08 34W   67
Bled: Yugoslavia   46 22N 14 07E   78
Blenheim: S.I., New Zealand   41 32S 173 58E   37 87
Bletchley: Bucks., England   52 00N 00 46W   59
Blida: Algeria   36 30N 02 50E   56 77
Bligh Sound: S.I., New Zealand   44 45S 167 30E   87
Blind River: Ont., Canada   46 12N 82 59W   98
Blithe: riv., Staffs., England   52 45N 01 45W   115
Blithfield Reservoir: Staffs., England   52 48N 01 54W   115
Block Island: R.I., U.S.A.   41 11N 71 34W   99
Bloemfontein: O.F.S., Rep. of S.Africa   29 07S 26 14E   55
Blois: France   47 36N 01 20E   70
Bloodvein: riv., Man., Canada   51 30N 96 00W   93
Bloody Foreland: cape, Don., Irish Rep.   55 09N 08 17W   66
Bloom, Slieve: mtns., Laois, Irish Republic
                   53 00N 07 30W   67
Bloomington: Ill., U.S.A.   40 29N 89 00W   98
Bloomington: Ind., U.S.A.   39 10N 86 31W   98
Bludenz: Austria   47 10N 09 50E   71
Bluefield: Va., U.S.A.   37 14N 81 17W   101
Bluefields: Nicaragua   12 00N 83 49W   47
Blue Island: Ill., U.S.A.   41 40N 87 42W   124
Blue Mountains: U.S.A.   45 30N 118 00W   17 42 90
Blue Nile: riv., Ethiopia/Sudan   10 30N 35 15E   21 53
Blue Ridge: U.S.A.   37 00N 80 00W   101
Blue River: B.C., Canada   52 05N 119 09W   89
Blue Stack Mountains: Don., Irish Republic
                   54 45N 08 00W   66
Bluewater: N.Mexico., U.S.A.   35 15N 107 59W   95
Bluff: S.I., New Zealand   46 38S 168 21E   87
Blumenau: Brazil   26 56S 49 03W   51
Blyth: Northumb., England   55 07N 01 30W   63
Blyth: riv., Northumb., England   55 00N 01 30W   63
Blythe: Calif., U.S.A.   33 37N 114 36W   91
Blyth: riv., Suff., England   52 15N 01 15E   59
Blythe: riv., W.Mid., England   52 15N 01 30W   115
Blytheville: Ark., U.S.A.   35 56N 89 56W   100
Bo: Sierra Leone   07 58N 11 45W   57
Boai: China   35 10N 113 00E   84
Boa Vista: Brazil   02 51N 60 43W   48
Bobai: China   22 22N 110 07E   85
Bobbili: India   18 32N 83 29E   83
Bobigny: France   48 55N 02 27E   117
Böblingen: W.Germany   48 41N 09 01E   72
Bobo Dioulasso: Upper Volta   11 11N 04 18W   57
Bobrujsk (Bobruysk): U.S.S.R.   53 09N 29 14E   28 80
Bôca do Acre: Brazil   08 45S 67 23W   49
Bocholt: W.Germany   51 49N 06 37E   72
Bochum: W.Germany   51 28N 07 11E   72 105 118
Bodelé Depression: Chad   16 45N 18 00E   20
Boden: Sweden   65 50N 21 44E   74
Boderg, Lough: Irish Republic   53 45N 07 45W   66

Types of map: Ocean pp. 1-5; Physical pp. 6-25; Human pp. 26-57; Topographic pp. 58-101; World pp. 102-111; Urban pp. 112-128.

Bodhan: India   18 40N 77 51E   82
Bodin: Norway   67 18N 14 30E   74
Bodmin: Corn., England   50 29N 04 43W   61
Bodmin *Moor*: Corn., England   50 30N 04 30W   61
Bodø: Norway   67 18N 14 26E   27 74
Boende: Zaïre   00 13S 20 52E   54
Bofin *Lough*: Irish Republic   53 45N 07 45W   66
Bogalusa: La., U.S.A.   30 47N 89 52W   100
Bogatoje: U.S.S.R.   53 04N 51 24E   81
Boggeragh *Mountains*: Cork, Irish Republic
   52 00N 08 45W   67
Bognor Regis: W.Sussex, England   50 47N 00 41W   59
Bogor: Indonesia   06 34S 106 45E   38
Bogorodick: U.S.S.R.   53 46N 38 08E   80
Bogorodsk: U.S.S.R.   56 06N 43 31E   80
Bogotá: Colombia   04 36N 74 05W   48
Bogra: Bangladesh   24 52N 89 28E   83
Bohai (Chihli, *Gulf of*): China   38 30N 120 00E   37 84
Bohaiwan: *bay*, China   38 30N 118 00E   84
Bohol: *is.*, Philippines   09 45N 124 00E   39
Bois de Boulogne: *woods*, France   48 51N 02 15E   117
Bois de Meudon: *woods*, France   48 48N 02 12E   117
Bois de Vincennes: *woods*, France   48 50N 02 26E   117
Boise: Idaho, U.S.A.   43 37N 116 13W   43 90
Boise: *riv.*, Idaho, U.S.A.   43 30N 116 00W   90
Bois Notre-Dame: *woods*, France   48 45N 02 35E   117
Boissevain: Man., Canada   49 14N 100 02W   93
Bojarka: U.S.S.R.   50 19N 30 19E   80
Boké: Guinea   10 57N 14 13W   57
Boknafjorden: *fd.*, Norway   59 10N 05 35E   75
Boksitogorsk: U.S.S.R.   59 28N 33 51E   80
Bolan *Pass*: Pakistan   29 45N 67 35E   34
Bolbec: France   49 34N 00 28E   70
Bolchov: U.S.S.R.   53 27N 36 01E   80
Boldon: Tyne & Wear, England   54 57N 01 27W   63
Bolesławiec: Poland   51 16N 15 34E   73 78
Boletto, *Monte*: Italy   45 51N 09 10E   116
Bolivár: Argentina   36 15S 61 07W   52
Bolivar: Mo., U.S.A.   37 37N 93 35W   98
Bolívar: *mtn.*, Venezuela   07 27N 63 25W   104
Bolívar (La Columna), *Pico*: Venezuela   08 35N 71 02W   48
BOLIVIA   18 49 106
Bollate: Italy   45 38N 09 07E   116
Bollin: *riv.*, England   53 15N 02 15W   114
Bollington: Ches., England   53 18N 02 06W   114
Bollnäs: Sweden   61 20N 16 25E   75
Bolmen: *lake*, Sweden   56 55N 13 45E   75
Bologna: Italy   44 30N 11 20E   26 79
Bologoje: U.S.S.R.   57 54N 34 02E   80
Bol'šaja Ochta: U.S.S.R.   59 57N 30 25E   119
Bol'šoj Irgiz: *riv.*, U.S.S.R.   51 45N 48 00E   81
Bol'šoj Satan, Gora: *mtn.*, U.S.S.R.   53 42N 57 38E   81
Bol'šoj Uzen': *riv.*, U.S.S.R.   49 30N 49 30E   81
Bolsover: Derby., England   53 14N 01 18W   58
Bolt *Head*: Devon, England   50 12N 03 47W   61
Bolton: Lancs., England   53 35N 02 26W   114
Bolus *Head*: Kerry, Irish Republic   51 47N 10 20W   67
Bolzano: Italy   46 31N 11 22E   26 78
Boma: Zaïre   05 51S 13 03E   54
Bombay: India   18 56N 72 51E   34 82 107
Bomi *Hills*: Liberia   06 54N 10 50W   104
Bon, *Cap, see* Ṭīb, R'as aṭ   37 05N 11 02E   79
Bonaigarh: India   21 47N 85 02E   83
Bonavista: Nfld., Canada   48 38N 53 08W   44 97
Bonavista *Bay*: Nfld., Canada   48 45N 53 30W   97
Bondi Beach: N.S.W., Australia   33 54S 151 17E   120
Bondo: Zaïre   03 49N 23 40E   54
Bond'užskij: U.S.S.R.   55 54N 52 20E   81
Bône *see* 'Annaba   36 55N 07 45E   56 77
Bone, *Gulf of*: Indonesia   04 00S 120 45E   39
Bo'ness: W.Loth., Scotland   56 01N 03 37W   62
Bonete: *mtn.*, Argentina   27 55S 68 41W   52
Bong *Mountains*: Liberia   06 45N 09 30W   57 104
Bonifacio: Corsica   41 23N 09 09E   77
Bonifacio, *Strait of*: Corsica/Sardinia   41 18N 09 15E   77
Bonin *Islands*: N.Pacific Ocean   27 00N 146 00E   4
Bonita, *Point*: Calif., U.S.A.   37 49N 122 32W   122
Bonn: W.Germany   50 44N 07 06E   26 72 119
Bonne *Bay*: Nfld., Canada   49 30N 57 00W   97
Bonner Springs: Kans., U.S.A.   39 03N 94 53W   94
Bonne Terre: Mo., U.S.A.   37 56N 90 33W   98

Bonnet Plume: *riv.*, Yukon, Canada   64 30N 133 30W   88
Bonneville: France   46 05N 06 25E   71
Bönninghardt: *hills*, W.Germany   51 30N 06 30E   118
Bonnyville: Alta., Canada   54 16N 110 46W   92
Bonthain: Indonesia   05 32S 119 58E   39
Boone: Iowa, U.S.A.   42 04N 93 52W   98
Boothia, *Gulf of*: N.W.T., Canada   68 30N 87 00W   16 44
Bootle: Mers., England   53 28N 03 00W   63
Bopingling: *mtns.*, China   24 45N 117 00E   85
Bopolu: Liberia   07 03N 10 32W   57
Bor: U.S.S.R.   56 22N 44 05E   80
Borah *Peak*: Idaho, U.S.A.   44 08N 113 47W   90
Boral: India   22 27N 88 22E   120
Borås: Sweden   57 44N 12 55E   75
Börde: W.Germany   50 43N 06 45E   119
Bordeaux: France   44 50N 00 34W   26 70
Border *Forest Park*: Northumb., England   55 15N 02 30W
   63
Borehamwood: Herts., England   51 40N 00 16W   59 112
Borgå (Porvoo): Finland   60 24N 25 40E   75 107
Borger: Tex., U.S.A.   35 39N 101 24W   95
Borgholm: Sweden   56 51N 16 40E   75
Borg Massivet: *rsch. stn.*, Antarctica   72 58S 03 48W   24
Borgsdorf: E.Germany   52 43N 13 15E   117
Borgund: Norway   62 28N 06 15E   74
Borislav: U.S.S.R.   49 16N 23 27E   78
Borisoglebsk: U.S.S.R.   51 23N 42 06E   28 80
Borisov: U.S.S.R.   54 15N 28 30E   80
Borisovka: U.S.S.R.   50 36N 36 01E   80
Borispol': U.S.S.R.   50 21N 30 57E   80
Borlänge: Sweden   60 29N 15 25E   75
Borneo: *is.*, S.E.Asia   00 30N 113 30E   12 38
Bornheim: W.Germany   50 46N 07 00E   119
Bornholm: *is & admin.*, Denmark   55 02N 15 00E   27 75
Bornova: Turkey   38 28N 27 14E   32 79
Boroughbridge: N.Yorks., England   54 05N 01 24W   63
Boroviči: U.S.S.R.   58 24N 33 55E   80
Borovoj: U.S.S.R.   59 55N 51 38E   81
Borth: Dyfed, Wales   52 29N 04 03W   60
Boscastle: Corn., England   50 41N 04 42W   61
Boshan (Poshan): China   36 30N 117 50E   36 84
Bosna: *riv.*, Yugoslavia   45 00N 18 15E   78
Bossier City: La., U.S.A.   32 31N 93 44W   100
Boss Mountain: B.C., Canada   51 55N 120 45W   89
Boston: Lincs., England   52 59N 00 01W   58
Boston: Mass., U.S.A.   42 20N 71 05W   45 99 122
Boston *Common*: Mass., U.S.A.   42 22N 71 04W   122
Boston *Harbor*: Mass., U.S.A.   42 15N 71 00W   122
Boston *Mountains*: Ark., U.S.A.   35 45N 93 15W   100
Botad: India   22 12N 71 44E   82
Botany: N.S.W., Australia   34 57S 151 12E   120
Botany *Bay*: N.S.W., Australia   34 04S 151 08E   120
Bothell: Wash., U.S.A.   47 44N 122 12W   126
Bothnia, *Gulf of*: Finland/Sweden   63 15N 21 00E   7 27 74
Botkul', Ozero: *lake*, U.S.S.R.   48 46N 46 40E   81
Botosani: Romania   47 44N 26 41E   78
BOTSWANA (Bechuanaland)   21 55 107
Bottineau: N.D., U.S.A.   48 50N 100 27W   93
Bottrop: W.Germany   51 31N 06 55E   118
Botucatu: Brazil   22 52S 48 26W   51
Botwood: Nfld., Canada   49 09N 55 22W   44 97
Bouaké: Ivory Coast   07 42N 05 00W   57
Boucherville, *Îles de*: Qué., Canada   45 37N 73 28W   122
Bougainville: *is.*, S.Pacific Ocean   06 00S 155 00E   4
Boughton: Notts., England   53 13N 01 00W   58
Bougie *see* Bejaïa   36 49N 05 03E   56 77
Bougouni: Mali   11 25N 07 28W   57
Boulder: Colo., U.S.A.   40 01N 105 17W   94
Boulder City: Nev., U.S.A.   35 59N 114 50W   91
Boulogne: Argentina   34 30S 58 33W   128
Boulogne, Bois de: *woods*, France   48 51N 02 15E   117
Boulogne-Billancourt: France   48 50N 02 14E   117
Boulogne-sur-Mer: France   50 43N 01 37E   72
Boundary *Dam*: Wash., U.S.A.   48 58N 117 20W   90
Boundary *Peak*: U.S.A.   37 51N 118 21W   91
Bountiful: Utah, U.S.A.   40 53N 111 53W   91
Bounty *Basin*: Southern Ocean   40 15S 177 30E   15
Bourg-en-Bresse: France   46 12N 05 13E   71
Bourges: France   47 05N 02 23E   70
Bourget, *Lac du*: France   45 43N 05 45E   71
Bourgogne, *Canal de*: France   47 45N 04 00E   71

Bourke: N.S.W., Australia   30 09S 145 59E   41
Bourne: Lincs., England   52 46N 00 23W   58
Bournemouth: Dorset, England   50 43N 01 54W   26 61
Bourton-on-the-Water: Glos., England   51 54N 01 46W   60
Bouvet *Island*: Southern Ocean   54 26S 03 24E   3
Bovey Tracey: Devon, England   50 36N 03 40W   61
Bowie: Tex., U.S.A.   33 34N 97 51W   95
Bow Island: Alta., Canada   49 53N 111 24W   92
Bowland, *Forest of:* England   53 45N 02 30W   62
Bowling Green: Ky., U.S.A.   37 00N 86 29W   101
Bowman: N.D., U.S.A.   46 11N 103 24W   94
Bowmore: Argyll., Scotland   55 45N 06 17W   62
Bowron Lake *Provincial Park*: B.C.,
   Canada   53 15N 121 45W   89
Box *Hill*: Surrey, England   51 16N 00 19W   112
Boxian: China   33 50N 115 45E   84
Boxing: China   37 10N 118 05E   84
Boyle: Rosc., Irish Republic   53 58N 08 18W   66
Boyne: *riv.*, Irish Republic   53 30N 06 30W   66
Boyne City: Mich., U.S.A.   45 13N 85 00W   98
Bozeman: Mont., U.S.A.   45 41N 111 02W   42 94
Bozhen: China   38 07N 116 40E   84
Brac, Otok: *is.*, Yugoslavia   43 19N 16 40E   79
Bracadale, *Loch*, Inv., Scotland   57 15N 06 30W   64
Brackley: Northants., England   52 02N 01 09W   59
Bracknell: Berks., England   51 26N 00 46W   59 112
Braddock: Pa., U.S.A.   40 24N 79 53W   125
Bradenton: Fla., U.S.A.   27 29N 82 33W   101
Bradford: W.Yorks., England   53 48N 01 45W   63 115
Bradford-on-Avon: Wilts., England   51 21N 02 14W   61
Brady: Tex., U.S.A.   31 09N 99 20W   95
Braemar: Aber., Scotland   57 01N 03 24W   65
Braeriach: *mtn.*, Scotland   57 05N 03 45W   65
Braga: Portugal   41 32N 08 26W   77
Bragança: Portugal   41 47N 06 46W   77
Brahmanbāria: Bangladesh   23 58N 91 04E   83
Brāhmani: *riv.*, India   20 45N 85 45E   83
Brahmaputra (Yaluzangbujiang): *riv.*, Asia   26 15N 91 15E   11 35 83
Braighe Mór: *bay*, R. & Crom., Scotland   58 00N 07 00W   64
Brăila: Romania   45 17N 27 58E   27 78
Brainerd: Minn., U.S.A.   46 20N 94 10W   98
Braintree: Mass., U.S.A.   42 14N 71 00W   122
Brake: W.Germany   53 20N 08 28E   72
Bralorne: B.C., Canada   50 47N 122 49W   89
Bramfeld: W.Germany   53 37N 10 05E   119
Bramhall: Gt. Man., England   53 23N 02 11W   58 114
Brampton: Ont., Canada   43 42N 79 46W   99
Brampton: Cumbria, England   54 57N 02 43W   63
Bran: *riv.*, R. & Crom., Scotland   57 30N 05 00W   64
Branco: *riv.*, Brazil   00 00 61 45W   48
Brandenburg: E.Germany   52 25N 12 34E   73 105
Brandenburg: Ky., U.S.A.   38 00N 86 11W   101
Branderburgh: Moray., Scotland   57 43N 03 16W   65
Brandon: Man., Canada   49 50N 99 57W   42 93
Brandon: Suff., England   52 27N 00 37E   58
Brandon *Bay*: Kerry, Irish Republic   52 15N 10 00W   67
Brandon *Mountain*: Kerry, Irish Republic   52 14N 10 15W   67
Brandýs: Czechoslovakia   50 12N 14 30E   73
Br'ansk (Bryansk): U.S.S.R.   53 15N 34 22E   28 80
Brantford: Ont., Canada   43 09N 80 17W   99
Bras d'Or *Lake*: N.S., Canada   45 45N 60 45W   97
Brasília: Brazil   15 47S 47 55W   51
Braslav: U.S.S.R.   55 38N 27 02E   80
Brasov: Romania   45 39N 25 39E   27 78
Brasstown Bald: *mtn.*, Ga., U.S.A.   34 52N 83 48W   101
Bratislava: Czechoslovakia   48 10N 17 08E   27 73 78 107
Bratsk: U.S.S.R.   56 05N 101 48E   30
Bratsk *Reservoir*: U.S.S.R.   56 00N 102 00E   30
Brattleboro: Vt., U.S.A.   42 51N 72 36W   99
Braunau: Austria   48 16N 13 03E   73
Braunschweig (Brunswick): W.Germany   52 15N 10 30E   26 73
Braunton: Devon, England   51 07N 04 10W   61
Brava, Costa: *coast*, Spain   41 45N 03 30E   77
Brawley: Calif., U.S.A.   32 59N 115 31W   91
Bray: Wick., Irish Rep.   53 12N 06 06W   67
Bray: *riv.*, *Devon, England*   51 00N 03 45W   61
Bray *Head*: Kerry, Irish Republic   51 53N 10 25W   67
Brazeau (Nordegg): Alta., Canada   52 29N 116 05W   92

Brazeau: *riv.*, Alta., Canada   52 45N 116 15W   92
Brazii de Sus: Romania   44 52N 26 01E   107
BRAZIL   18 50 106
Brazil *Basin*: S.Atlantic Ocean   10 00S 25 00W   3
Brazil *Current*: S.Atlantic Ocean   15 00S 33 00W   3
Brazilian *Highlands*: Brazil   18 00S 46 00W   18 51
Brazo Casiquiare (Casiquiare): *riv.*, Venezuela   02 30N 66 30W   48
Brazos: *riv.*, Tex., U.S.A.   30 00N 96 00W   43 100
Brazzaville: Congo   04 16S 15 17E   54
Brda: *riv.*, Poland   53 45N 17 45E   73
Breakheart *Reservation*: Mass., U.S.A.   42 29N 71 02W   122
Brean Down: *pt.*, Som., England   51 20N 03 03W   61
Brechin: Angus, Scotland   56 44N 02 40W   65
Breckenridge: Minn., U.S.A.   46 15N 96 35W   94
Brecknockshire: *admin.*, Wales. Absorbed into new *admins.* of Mid Glamorgan, Gwent & Powys, 1974.   61
Brecon (Brecknock): Powys, Wales   51 57N 03 24W   60
Brecon Beacons: *mtns.*, Powys, Wales   51 45N 03 30W   60
Brecon Beacons *National Park*: Powys, Wales   51 45N 03 30W   60
Breda: Netherlands   51 35N 04 46E   72
Bredy: U.S.S.R.   52 26N 60 21E   81
Brede: *riv.*, E.Sussex, England   50 45N 00 30E   59
Bregenz: Austria   47 31N 09 46E   71
Bremen: W.Germany   53 05N 08 48E   26 72 105
Bremerhaven: W.Germany   53 33N 08 35E   26 72
Bremerton: Wash., U.S.A.   47 34N 122 37W   90 126
Brenner Sattel: *pass*, Austria/Italy   47 02N 11 32E   78
Brent: Gt. Ldn., England   51 34N 00 17W   59
Brentwood: Essex, England   51 38N 00 18E   59 112
Brentwood: Pa., U.S.A.   40 22N 79 59W   125
Brescia: Italy   45 33N 10 13E   26 71 105
Breslau *see* Wrocław   51 05N 17 00E   27 73 78
Bressay: *is.*, Shet. Is., Scotland   60 00N 01 00W   65
Bresse, *Plaine de:* France   46 30N 05 00E   71
Brest: France   48 23N 04 30W   26 70
Brest (Brest Litovsk): U.S.S.R.   52 08N 23 40E   28 78
Brest à Nantes, *Canal de:* France   48 15N 03 30W   70
Bretagne, *Monts de:* France   48 15N 03 00W   70
Brétigny-sur-Orge: France   48 37N 02 19E   117
Breton *Sound*: La., U.S.A.   29 30N 89 15W   100
Brett: *riv.*, Suff., England   52 00N 00 45E   59
Brewton: Ala., U.S.A.   31 07N 87 04W   101
Briançon: France   44 53N 06 39E   71
Briarcliffe: Ont., Canada   50 12N 87 25W   98
Bride: *riv.*, Irish Republic   52 00N 08 00W   67
Bridge: *riv.*, B.C., Canada   50 45N 122 00W   89
Bridgend: M.Glam., Wales   51 31N 03 35W   60
Bridge of Allan: Stirl., Scotland   56 09N 05 58W   65
Bridgeport: Conn., U.S.A.   41 12N 73 12W   45 99
Bridgeport: Tex., U.S.A.   33 13N 97 45W   95
Bridgetown: Barbados   13 06N 59 37W   47
Bridgnorth: Salop, England   52 33N 02 25W   58
Bridgwater: Som., England   51 08N 03 00W   61
Bridgwater *Bay*: Som., England   51 00N 03 00W   61
Bridle Trail *Park*: Wash., U.S.A.   47 38N 122 10W   126
Bridlington: Humb., England   54 05N 00 12W   63
Bridport: Dorset, England   50 44N 02 46W   61
Brie-Comte-Robert: France   48 41N 02 37E   117
Brienz: Switzerland   46 46N 08 02E   71
Brierfield: Lancs., England   53 50N 02 14W   114
Brierley Hill: W.Mid., England   52 29N 02 07W   115
Briey: France   49 15N 05 47E   71
Briey-Thionville, Bassin Ferrifère de: *geol. feat.*, France   49 15N 06 00E   105
Brig: Switzerland   46 19N 08 00E   71
Brigg: Humb., England   53 34N 03 30W   63
Brigham City: Utah, U.S.A.   41 31N 112 01W   90
Brighouse: W.Yorks., England   53 42N 01 47W   63 115
Brightlingsea: Essex, England   51 49N 01 02E   59
Brighton: E.Sussex, England   50 50N 00 10E   26 59
Brighton: Colo., U.S.A.   39 59N 104 49W   94
Brims Ness: *cape*, Caith., Scotland   58 36N 03 37W   65
Brindaban *see* Vrindāvan   27 36N 77 41E   82
Brindisi: Italy   40 37N 17 57E   27 32 79
Briones *Reservoir*: Calif., U.S.A.   37 55N 122 12W   126
Brisbane: Qld., Australia   27 30S 153 00E   41
Brisbane: Calif., U.S.A.   37 41N 122 24W   126
Bristol: Avon, England   51 27N 02 35W   26 61 113
Bristol *Channel*: England/Wales   51 15N 03 15W   61

Types of map: Ocean pp. 1-5; Physical pp. 6-25; Human pp. 26-57; Topographic pp. 58-101; World pp. 102-111; Urban pp. 112-128.

British Columbia: *admin.*, Canada 42 89
BRITISH HONDURAS *see* BELIZE 17 30N 88 45W 17 46
British North Borneo: *admin. see* Sabah 39
Brittle, *Loch*: Inv., Scotland 57 00N 06 15W 64
Brive-la-Gaillarde: France 45 09N 01 32E 70
Brixham: Devon., England 50 24N 03 30W 61
Brno: Czechoslovakia 49 12N 16 40E 27 73 78
Broach: India 21 40N 73 02E 34 82
Broadback: *riv.*, Qué., Canada 51 00N 76 30W 96
Broad *Bay*: R. & Crom., Scotland 58 15N 06 15W 64
Broadford: Inv., Scotland 57 14N 05 54W 64
Broad Haven: *bay*, Mayo, Irish Republic 54 15N 09 45W 66
Broad Law: *mtn.*, Peeb., Scotland 55 30N 03 22W 62
Broadstairs: Kent, England 51 22N 01 27E 59
Broadview: Ill., U.S.A. 41 50N 87 51W 124
Brochet: Man., Canada 57 55N 101 40W 92
Brochet, *Lac*: Man., Canada 58 45N 101 30W 92
Brock: *riv.*, Lancs., England 53 45N 02 30W 114
Brockway: Mont., U.S.A. 47 18N 105 45W 94
Brod: Yugoslavia 41 30N 21 15E 79
Brodick: Bute., Scotland 55 35N 05 09W 62
Broken *Bay*: N.S.W., Australia 33 34S 151 20E 120
Broken Bow: Nebr., U.S.A. 41 24N 99 38W 94
Broken Hill: N.S.W., Australia 31 57S 141 30E 41
Broken Hill: Zambia, *see* Kabwe 14 27S 28 27E 54
Broken *Ridge*: Indian Ocean 1
Brokopondo, *Lake*: Surinam 04 45N 55 15W 48
Bromley: Gt. Ldn., England 51 24N 00 02E 59 112
Bromsgrove: Here. & Worcs., England 52 20N 02 03W
59 115
Bromyard: Here. & Worcs., England 52 11N 02 30W 60
Bronx, The: N.Y., U.S.A. 40 50N 73 52W 123
Brookfield: N.S., Canada 45 15N 63 18W 97
Brookfield: Ill., U.S.A. 41 48N 87 51W 124
Brookhaven: Miss., U.S.A. 31 35N 90 26W 100
Brookings: Oreg., U.S.A. 42 04N 124 17W 90
Brookings: S.D., U.S.A. 44 19N 96 48W 94
Brookline: Mass., U.S.A. 42 20N 71 07W 122
Brooklyn: N.Y., U.S.A. 40 30N 73 55W 123
Brooklyn *Marine Park*: N.Y., U.S.A. 40 35N 73 54W 123
Brooks: Alta., Canada 50 35N 111 54W 92
Brooks *Island*: Calif., U.S.A. 37 54N 122 21W 126
Brooks *Range*: Alaska, U.S.A. 68 00N 155 00W 16
Brooksville: Fla., U.S.A. 28 24N 82 24W 101
Brookvale: N.S.W., Australia 33 46S 151 16E 120
Broom, *Loch*: R. & Crom., Scotland 57 45N 05 15W 64
Broome: W.A., Australia 17 58S 122 15E 40
Brora: Suther., Scotland 58 01N 03 51W 65
Brora: *riv.*, Suther., Scotland 58 00N 04 00W 65
Brosna: *riv.*, Irish Republic 53 15N 07 15W 67
Brough: Cumbria, England 54 32N 02 19W 63
Brough *Head*: Ork. Is., Scotland 59 09N 03 19W 65
Brovary: U.S.S.R. 50 31N 30 46E 80
Brownfield: Tex., U.S.A. 33 11N 102 17W 95
Brownhills: W.Mid., England 52 39N 01 55W 58 115
Brownlee *Dam*: U.S.A. 44 50N 116 54W 90
Brownsville: Tex., U.S.A. 25 54N 97 30W 46 100
Brown Willy: *mtn.*, Corn., England 50 35N 04 36W 61
Brownwood: Tex., U.S.A. 31 43N 98 59W 95
Bruay-en-Artois: France 50 29N 02 33E 72
Bruce, *Mount*: W.A., Australia 22 36S 118 08E 40
Bruce Bay: S.I., New Zealand 43 37S 169 38E 87
Bruce *Peninsula*: Ont., Canada 45 00N 81 30W 99
Bruck: Austria 47 18N 12 49E 73
Brue: *riv.*, Som., England 51 00N 02 45W 61
Bruges: Belgium, *see* Brugge 51 13N 03 14E 72
Brugge (Bruges): Belgium 51 13N 03 14E 72
Brühl: W.Germany 50 50N 06 54E 119
Bruneau: *riv.*, U.S.A. 42 30N 115 30W 90
Brunei: *U.K. colony*, S.E. Asia 04 30N 114 30E 12 39 107
Brunoy: France 48 42N 02 31E 117
Brunswick *see* Braunschweig 52 15N 10 30E 26 73
Brunswick: Ga., U.S.A. 31 09N 81 30W 101
Brush: Colo., U.S.A. 40 15N 103 37W 94
Brussel (Bruxelles: Brussels): Belgium 50 50N 04 21E
26 72
Bruton: Som., England 51 07N 02 27W 61
Bryan: Tex., U.S.A. 30 40N 96 22W 100
Bryansk *see* Br'ansk 53 15N 34 22E 28 80
Bryce Canyon *National Park*: Utah,
U.S.A. 37 30N 112 00W 91

Bryher: *is.*, I. of S., England 49 57N 06 21W 61
Brynmawr: Gwent, Wales 51 49N 03 11W 60 113
Bryn Mawr: Wash., U.S.A. 47 29N 122 14W 126
Brzeg: Poland 50 52N 17 27E 73
Bucaramanga: Colombia 07 08N 73 10W 48
Buchanan: Liberia 05 57N 10 02W 57
Buchanan *Dam*: Tex., U.S.A. 30 45N 98 25W 95
Buchan Ness: *cape*, Aber., Scotland
57 28N 01 47W 65
Buchans: Nfld., Canada 48 49N 56 53W 97
Buchara (Bukhara): U.S.S.R. 39 48N 64 25E 29
Bucharest *see* Bucureşti 44 25N 26 07E 27 79
Buckfastleigh: Devon, England 50 29N 03 46W 61
Buckhaven: Fife, Scotland 56 11N 03 03W 65
Buckie: Banff., Scotland 57 40N 02 58W 65
Buckingham: Bucks., England 52 00N 00 59W 59
Buckinghamshire: *admin.*, England 51 45N 00 45W 59
Buckley: Clwyd, Wales 53 11N 03 04W 60 114
Bucureşti (Bucharest): Romania 44 25N 26 07E 27 79
Budapest: Hungary 47 30N 19 03E 27 78
Budaun: India 28 02N 79 07E 82
Buddh Gaya: India 24 42N 85 00E 83
Bude: Corn., England 50 50N 04 33W 61
Bude *Bay*: Corn., England 50 45N 04 30W 61
Büderich: W.Germany 51 15N 06 42E 118
Büderich: W.Germany 51 38N 06 35E 118
Budge Budge: India 22 29N 88 11E 120
Budleigh Salterton: Devon, England 50 38N 03 20W 61
Buenaventura: Colombia 03 54N 77 02W 48
Buenos Aires: Argentina 34 37S 58 24W 52 104 128
Buenos Aires: *admin.*, Argentina 35 45S 60 15W 52
Buenos Aires, *Lago*: Argentina/Chile 46 30S 72 30W 52
Buer: W.Germany 51 35N 07 03E 118
Buffalo: N.Y., U.S.A. 42 52N 78 55W 45 99 104
Buffalo: Wyo., U.S.A. 44 21N 106 42W 94
Buffalo: *riv.*, Canada 59 30N 114 30W 92
Buffalo *Lake*: N.W.T., Canada 60 15N 115 30W 92
Buffalo River: N.W.T., Canada 60 53N 115 02W 92
Bug: *riv.*, Poland/U.S.S.R. 52 30N 21 30E 78
Buga: Colombia 03 53N 76 17W 48
Bugul'ma: U.S.S.R. 54 33N 52 48E 28 81
Buguminsko–Belebejevskaja Vozvyšennost': *hld.*,
U.S.S.R. 54 30N 53 00E 81
Buguruslan: U.S.S.R. 53 39N 52 26E 81
Buhl: Idaho, U.S.A. 42 36N 114 46W 90
Buhwa *Mountain*: Rhodesia 20 38S 30 20E 105
Buie, *Loch*: Argll., Scotland 56 15N 05 45W 64
Builth Wells: Powys, Wales 52 09N 03 24W 60
Buinsk: U.S.S.R. 54 57N 48 17E 81
Buj: U.S.S.R. 58 30N 41 30E 80
Bujumbura (Usumbura): Burundi 03 22S 29 21E 54
Bukavu (Costermansville): Zaïre 02 30S 28 49E 54
Bukechi: *lake*, China 31 30N 91 00E 83
Bukhara *see* Buchara 39 48N 64 25E 29
Bukit Besi: Malaysia 04 46N 103 11E 105
Bukittinggi: Indonesia 00 18S 100 20E 38
Bukoba: Tanzania 01 20S 31 49E 54
Bula: Indonesia 03 07S 130 27E 39
Bulandshahr: India 28 30N 77 49E 82
Bulawayo: Rhodesia 20 10S 28 43E 55
BULGARIA 43 00N 25 00E 27 79 107
Bulkington: War., England 52 28N 01 26W 115
Bulkley: *riv.*, B.C., Canada 54 30N 127 00W 89
Bull *Point*: Devon, England 51 13N 04 12W 61
Bull Shoals *Reservoir*: U.S.A. 36 45N 92 30W 100
Bulsär: India 20 36N 73 03E 82
Bunbury: W.A., Australia 33 20S 115 34E 40
Buncrana: Don., Irish Republic 55 08N 07 27W 66
Bundaberg: Qld., Australia 24 50S 152 21E 41
Bündi: India 25 28N 75 42E 82
Bundoran: Don., Irish Republic 54 28N 08 17W 66
Bündu: India 23 08N 85 19E 83
Bungay: Suff., England 52 28N 01 26E 58
Bungo–suidö: *str.*, Japan 33 00N 132 00E 86
Bunia: Zaïre 01 35N 30 13E 54
Buntingford: Herts., England 51 57N 00 01W 59
Buraida *see* Buraydah 26 20N 43 59E 33
Burbach: W.Germany 49 41N 07 73E 105
Burbank: Calif., U.S.A. 34 11N 118 19W 127
Burdwän: India 23 15N 87 52E 35 83
Bure: *riv.*, Norf., England 52 30N 01 15E 58

Bureå: Sweden   64 36N 21 15E   74
Bureja (Bureya): riv., U.S.S.R.   51 00N 132 00E   31
Burford: Oxon., England   51 49N 01 38W   59
Burg: E.Germany   52 16N 11 51E   73
Burgas: Bulgaria   42 30N 27 29E   27 79
Burgdorf: Switzerland   47 09N 07 38E   71
Burgenland: admin., Austria   47 30N 16 15E   73
Burgeo: Nfld., Canada   47 37N 57 38W   97
Burgess Hill: W.Sussex, England   50 57N 00 08W   59
Burghausen: W.Germany   48 10N 12 50E   73
Burghead: Moray., Scotland   57 42N 03 30W   65
Burhou: is., Channel Islands   49 43N 02 15W   61
Burgos: Spain   42 21N 03 41W   26 70 77
Burgos: admin., Spain   42 30N 03 30W   70
Burhānpur: India   21 18N 76 08E   34 82
Burien: Wash., U.S.A.   47 27N 122 20W   126
Burin: Nfld., Canada   47 03N 55 11W   97
Burin Peninsula: Nfld., Canada   47 15N 55 30W   97
Burke, Mount: B.C., Canada   49 18N 122 43W   126
Burketown: Qld., Australia   17 43S 139 30E   41
Burley: Idaho, U.S.A.   42 32N 113 48W   90
Burlingame: Calif., U.S.A.   37 35N 122 25W   126
Burlington: Colo., U.S.A.   39 18N 102 16W   94
Burlington: Iowa, U.S.A.   40 50N 91 07W   98
Burlington: N.C., U.S.A.   36 05N 79 27W   101
Burlington: Vt., U.S.A.   44 28N 73 14W   44 99
BURMA   11 35 107
Burnaby: B.C., Canada   49 16N 122 58W   126
Burnaby Lake: B.C., Canada   49 16N 122 58W   126
Burnham: Bucks., England   51 33N 00 39W   112
Burnham Market: Norf., England   52 57N 00 44E   58
Burnham-on-Crouch: Essex, England   51 38N 00 49E   59
Burnham-on-Sea: Som., England   51 15N 03 00W   61
Burnley: Lancs., England   53 48N 02 14W   63 114
Burnpur: India   23 40N 86 55E   105
Burns: Oreg., U.S.A.   43 35N 119 03W   90
Burns Lake: B.C., Canada   54 14N 125 45W   89
Burntisland: Fife, Scotland   56 03N 03 15W   65
Burnt Lake: Qué., Canada   52 15N 63 45W   97
Burntwood: riv., Man., Canada   55 30N 99 30W   93
Burquitlam: B.C., Canada   49 16N 122 54W   126
Burrard Inlet: B.C., Canada   49 15N 123 00W   126
Burro, Serranías del: mtns., Mexico   29 00N 102 00W   95
Burrow Head: Wig., Scotland   54 41N 04 24W   62
Burry Port: Dyfed, Wales   51 42N 04 15W   61
Bursa: Turkey   40 12N 29 04E   32
Būr Safâjah: Egypt   26 44N 33 56E   32
Būr Sa'īd (Port Said): Egypt   31 16N 32 18E   32
Burscheid: W.Germany   51 06N 07 08E   118
Burscough Bridge: Lancs., England   53 37N 02 51W   114
Burslem: Staffs., England   53 02N 02 12W   58
Būr Sūdân (Port Sudan): Sudan   19 38N 37 07E   53
Burton Latimer: Northants., England   52 22N 00 41W   59
Burton upon Trent: Staffs., England   52 49N 01 36W   58 115
Buru: is., Indonesia   03 30S 126 30E   13 39
BURUNDI   03 15S 30 00E   21 54
Burwash Landing: Yukon, Canada   61 21N 139 01W   88
Burwell: Cambs., England   52 16N 00 19E   59
Burwell: Nebr., U.S.A.   41 47N 99 08W   94
Bury: Gt. Man., England   53 36N 02 17W   63 114
Bury St. Edmunds: Suff., England   52 15N 00 43E   59
Burzaco: Argentina   34 50S 58 24W   128
Buscate: Italy   45 33N 08 49E   116
Būshehr: Iran   28 59N 50 50E   33
Bushey: Herts., England   51 39N 00 22W   59
Bushy Park: Gt. Ldn., England   51 25N 00 20W   112
Busto Arsizio: Italy   45 37N 08 51E   71 116
Buta: Zaïre   02 48N 24 44E   54
Butedale: B.C., Canada   53 12N 128 45W   89
Bute Inlet: B.C., Canada   50 30N 124 45W   89
Bute: is., Bute., Scotland   55 45N 05 00W   62
Buteshire: admin., Scotland   55 30N 05 00W   62
Butler: Pa., U.S.A.   40 51N 79 55W   99
Butler County: Ga., U.S.A.   31 45N 86 50W   104
Butte: Mont., U.S.A.   46 00N 112 32W   42 94
Butte Montmartre: knoll, France   48 53N 02 20E   117
Butuan: Philippines   08 56N 125 31E   39
Butung: is., Indonesia   05 00S 123 00E   39
Buzău: Romania   45 09N 26 49E   78
Buzuluk: U.S.S.R.   52 47N 52 15E   81

Bychov: U.S.S.R.   53 32N 30 12E   80
Bydgoszcz: Poland   53 10N 18 00E   27 73 78
Byfleet: Surrey, England   51 20N 00 29W   112
Byrd Glacier: Antarctica   80 15S 160 20E   25
Byrd Land: reg., Antarctica   80 00S 120 00W   25
Byrd Station: rsch. stn., Antarctica   80 01S 119 32W   25
Bytom: Poland   50 21N 18 51E   78

Caballito: Argentina   34 37S 58 27W   128
Caballo Reservoir: N.Mex., U.S.A.   32 54N 107 18W   95
Cabano: Qué., Canada   47 40N 68 56W   96
Cabimas: Venezuela   10 26N 71 27W   48
Cabinet Gorge Dam: Idaho, U.S.A.   48 06N 116 02W   90
Cabonga Reservoir: Qué., Canada   47 15N 76 30W   99
Cabot Strait: Canada   47 15N 60 00W   17 44 97
Cabriel: riv., Spain   39 15N 01 15W   77
Čačak: Yugoslavia   43 54N 20 22E   79
Cáceres: Spain   34 29N 06 23W   77
Cachimbo, Serra do: ra., Brazil   6 50 78 96
Cachoeira: Brazil   12 36S 38 58W   50
Cachoeira do Sul: Brazil   30 03S 52 52W   51
Cachoeiro de Itapemirim: Brazil   20 51S 41 06W   51
Cader Idris: mtn., Gwyn., Wales   52 42N 03 54W   60
Cadillac: Mich., U.S.A.   44 15N 85 23W   98
Cádiz: Spain   36 32N 06 18W   26 77
Cádiz, Golfo de: Spain   37 00N 07 00W   26 77
Cady: Mich., U.S.A.   42 34N 82 57W   125
Čadyr-Lunga: U.S.S.R.   46 03N 28 47E   78
Caen: France   49 11N 00 22W   26 70
Caerleon: Gwent, Wales   51 37N 02 57W   61 113
Caernarvon: Gwyn., Wales   53 08N 04 16W   60
Caernarvon Bay: Gwyn., Wales   53 00N 04 30W   60
Caernarvonshire: admin., Wales. Absorbed into new admin. of Gwynedd, 1974   60
Caerphilly: M. Glam., Wales   51 35N 03 14W   61 113
Cagayan: riv., Philippines   17 30N 121 45E   39
Cagayan de Oro: Philippines   08 29N 124 40E   39
Cágliari: Sardinia   39 13N 09 08E   26 77 107
Cágliari, Golfo di: Sardinia   39 08N 09 11E   77
Caha Mountains: Irish Republic   51 30N 09 30W   67
Caher Island: Mayo, Irish Republic   53 43N 10 01W   66
Cahersiveen: Kerry, Irish Republic   51 57N 10 13W   67
Cahir: Tip., Irish Republic   52 22N 07 55W   67
Cahore Point: Wex., Irish Republic   52 34N 06 11W   67
Cahors: France   44 28N 01 26E   70
Caicos Islands: West Indies   21 45N 71 45W   47
Caijiazhen: China   34 10N 107 37E   84
Cairn Gorm: mtn., Inv., Scotland   57 07N 03 40W   65
Cairngorm Mountains: Scotland   57 00N 03 30W   65
Cairns: Qld., Australia   16 51S 145 43E   41
Cairnsmore: mtn., Kirkc., Scotland   55 15N 04 12W   62
Cairo: Egypt, see Al Qāhirah   30 03N 31 15E   32
Caistor: Lincs., England   53 30N 00 20W   58
Caithness: admin., Scotland   58 15N 03 30W   65
Cajamarca: Peru   07 09S 78 32W   48
Čajkovskij: U.S.S.R.   56 47N 54 09E   81
Calabar: Nigeria   04 56N 08 22E   57
Calahorra: Spain   42 19N 01 58W   77
Calais: France   50 57N 01 52E   72
Calais: Maine, U.S.A.   45 11N 67 16W   96
Calais, Pas de (Dover, Strait of): England/France   51 00N 01 30E   69
Calama: Chile   22 28S 68 56W   49
Calamian Group: is., Philippines   12 00N 120 00E   39
Calapan: Philippines   13 23N 121 10E   39
Călăraşi: Romania   44 12N 27 22E   79
Calatayud: Spain   41 21N 01 39W   77
Calcutta: India   22 35N 88 21E   35 83 120
Caldas: riv., Spain   41 30N 02 00E   116
Caldas da Rainha: Portugal   39 24N 09 08W   77
Caldas de Montbuy   41 38N 02 11E   116
Caldecott Tunnel: Calif., U.S.A.   37 51N 122 12W   126
Calder: riv., Lancs., England   53 45N 02 15W   114
Calder: riv., Yorks., England   53 30N 01 30W   115
Calder, Loch: Caith., Scotland   58 30N 03 30W   65
Calder & Hebble Navigation: can., Yorks., England   53 30N 01 45W   115
Caldercruix: Lan., Scotland   55 53N 03 55W   113

Caldey *Island*: Dyfed, Wales   51 38N 04 42W   61
Caldwell: Idaho, U.S.A.   43 40N 116 41W   90
Calexico: Calif., U.S.A.   32 40N 115 30W   91
Calf of Man: *is.*, I. of M., United Kingdom   54 03N 04 49W
                                                     62
Calgary: Alta., Canada   51 05N 114 05W   42 92
Calgary *Point*: Argyll., Scotland   56 34N 06 42W   64
Cali: Colombia   03 24N 76 30W   48
Calicut: India   11 15N 75 45E   34
Caliente: Nev., U.S.A.   37 37N 114 31W   91
California: *admin.*, U.S.A.   36 00N 118 00W   43 91
California, *Gulf of*: Mexico   28 00N 112 00W   17 46
California *Current*: N.Pacific Ocean   30 00N 120 00W   5
Calipatria: Calif., U.S.A.   33 08N 115 31W   91
Callan: Kilk., Irish Republic   52 33N 07 23W   67
Callander: Perth., Scotland   56 15N 04 13W   64
Callao: Peru   12 05S 77 08W   49
Calligarry: Inv., Scotland   57 03N 05 55W   64
Callington: Corn., England   50 30N 04 18W   61
Calne: Wilts., England   51 27N 02 00W   61
Caltanissetta: Sicily   37 29N 14 04E   79
Calumet, *Lake*: Ill., U.S.A.   41 41N 87 35W   124
Calumet City: Ill., U.S.A.   41 36N 87 32W   124
Calumet *Harbor*: Ind., U.S.A.   41 44N 87 31W   124
Calumet *Park*: Ill., U.S.A.   41 43N 87 31W   124
Calumet Sag *Channel*: Ill., U.S.A.   41 41N 87 50W 124
Calvados: *admin.*, France   49 00N 00 30W   105
Calvert City: Ky., U.S.A.   37 02N 88 22W   100
Calvi: Corsica   42 34N 08 44E   77
Cam: *riv.*, Cambs., England   52 00N 00 00   59
Camagüey: Cuba   21 23N 77 55W   47
Camayenne: Guinea   09 32N 13 41W   104
Cambay: India   22 19N 72 39E   34 82
Cambay, *Gulf of*: India   21 00N 72 00E   10 82
Camberley: Surrey, England   51 21N 00 45W   59 112
Cambodia *see* Khmer Rep.   12 38
Camborne: Corn., England   50 12N 05 19W   61
Cambrai: France   50 10N 03 14E   72
Cambrian *Mountains*: Wales   52 15N 03 45W   60
Cambridge: Cambs., England   52 12N 00 07E   59
Cambridge: Mass., U.S.A.   42 22N 71 06W   122
Cambridge: Md., U.S.A.   38 34N 76 04W   99
Cambridge *Reservoir*: Mass., U.S.A.   42 25N 71 16W 122
Cambridgeshire: *admin.*, England   52 15N 00 00   59
Camden: Gt. Ldn., England   51 33N 00 10W   59
Camden: Ark., U.S.A.   33 35N 92 50W   100
Camden: N.J., U.S.A.   39 57N 75 06W   99 122
Cameron: Ariz., U.S.A.   35 53N 111 25W   91
Cameron: Tex., U.S.A.   30 51N 96 59W   95
Cameron *Hills*: Canada   59 30N 118 30W   42 88
CAMEROUN   06 00N 12 00E   20 57
Cameroun, *Mount*: Cameroun   04 13N 09 10E   20 57
Camoge: *riv.*, Lim., Irish Republic   52 30N 08 30W 67
Campana: Argentina   34 10S 59 55W   104
Campbell, *Mount*: Yukon, Canada   64 23N 138 43W   88
Campbell Island: *rsch. stn.*, Southern Ocean
   52 33N 169 09E   25
Campbell River: B.C., Canada   50 01N 125 15W   89
Campbellton: N.B., Canada   48 00N 66 41W   97
Campbeltown: Argyll., Scotland   55 26N 05 36W   62
Campeche: Mexico   19 51N 90 32W   46
Campeche: *admin.*, Mexico   19 00N 90 00W   46
Campeche, *Bahía de*: Mexico   19 00N 94 00W   17 46
Campina Grande: Brazil   07 13S 35 53W   50
Campinas: Brazil   22 54S 47 06W   51
Campo Grande: Brazil   20 27S 54 37W   51
Campos: Brazil   21 45S 41 18W   51
Campos: *geog. reg.*, Brazil   22 45S 52 15W   18 51
Campsie Fells: *hills*, Stirl., Scotland   56 00N 04 00W
                                                 64 113
Camrose: Alta., Canada   53 01N 112 48W   92
Camsell: *riv.*, N.W.T., Canada   64 45N 118 30W   88
Camsell Portage: Sask., Canada   59 39N 109 12W   92
Camsell *Range*: N.W.T., Canada   62 45N 123 45W   88
Can: *riv.*, Essex, England   51 45N 00 15E   59
CANADA   16 42 106
Canada *Basin*: Arctic Ocean   80 00N 139 00W   22
Canadian: *riv.*, U.S.A.   34 45N 96 45W   43 95
Canakkale: Turkey   40 09N 26 25E   79
Canal Zone: *U.S.A. admin.*, Panama   09 15N 79 45W 47
Cananea: Mexico   30 59N 110 20W   95

Canary *Basin*: N.Atlantic Ocean   32 00N 24 00W   2 6
Canary *Islands*: Atlantic Ocean   28 00N 15 00W 2 20 56
Canaveral, *Cape* (*Cape* Kennedy): Fla., U.S.A.
   28 27N 80 32W   45 101
Canberra: A.C.T., Australia   35 18S 149 08E   41
Candia *see* Iráklion   35 20N 25 08E   32 79
Candlestick *Point*: Calif., U.S.A.   37 43N 122 23W 126
Canea *see* Khaniá   35 31N 24 01E   32 79
Cangwu: China   23 22N 111 15E   85
Cangzhou: China   38 19N 116 51E   84
Canillejas: Spain   40 27N 03 37W   116
Canisp: *peak*, Suther., Scotland   58 07N 05 03W   64
Canna: *is.*, Inv., Scotland   57 00N 06 30W   64
Canna, *Sound of*: Inv., Scotland   57 00N 06 30W   64
Cannes: France   43 33N 07 00E   71
Canning *Basin*: W.A., Australia   18 30S 123 45E   40
Cannock: Staffs., England   52 42N 02 01W   58 115
Cannock Chase: *hills*, Staffs., England   52 45N 02 00W 115
Cannonball: *riv.*, N.D., U.S.A.   46 15N 101 45W   94
Canoas: Brazil   29 56S 51 11W   51
Canol: N.W.T., Canada   65 13N 126 59W   88
Canon City: Colo., U.S.A.   38 27N 105 14W   94
Canora: Sask., Canada   51 38N 102 28W   92
Canso: N.S., Canada   45 20N 61 00W   97
Cantábrica, Cordillera (Cantabrian *Mountains*):
   Spain   43 00N 05 00W   77
Canterbury: N.S.W., Australia   33 55S 151 07E   120
Canterbury: Kent, England   51 17N 01 05E   59
Canterbury *Bight*: S.I., New Zealand   44 00S 172 30E 87
Canterbury *Plains*: S.I., New Zealand   43 30S 172 00E 87
Cân Tho: S.Vietnam   10 03N 105 46E   38
Canton: China, *see* Guangzhou   23 08N 113 16E 36 85 105
Canton: Ill., U.S.A.   40 33N 90 02W   98
Canton: Miss., U.S.A.   32 37N 90 02W   100
Canton: Ohio, U.S.A.   40 48N 81 23W   45 99 104
Canton: S.D., U.S.A.   43 18N 96 35W   94
Cantons de l'Est, Autoroute des: *hwy.*, Qué., Canada
   45 15N 73 15W   122
Cantù: Italy   45 45N 09 08E   116
Canvey: Essex, England   51 32N 00 35E   59
Canyon: Tex., U.S.A.   34 59N 101 55W   95
Canyon de Chelly *National Monument*: Ariz.,
   U.S.A.   36 00N 109 00W   91
Canyon Ferry *Dam*: Mont., U.S.A.   46 39N 111 07W   94
Canyonlands *National Park*: Utah, U.S.A.   38 15N 109 45W
                                                     91
Caojiadu: China   31 14N 121 24E   121
Caoxian: China   34 50N 115 38E   84
Čapajevo: U.S.S.R.   50 12N 51 10E   81
Čapajevsk (Chapayevsk): U.S.S.R.   52 58N 49 41E   81
Capbreton: France   43 38N 01 25W   70
Cape *Basin*: S.Atlantic Ocean   36 00N 10 00E   3
Cape Breton Highlands *National Park*: N.S.,
   Canada   46 45N 60 45W   97
Cape Breton *Island*: N.S., Canada   46 30N 60 45W 44 97
Cape Canaveral: Fla., U.S.A.   28 28N 80 28W   101
Cape Charles: Va., U.S.A.   37 17N 76 01W   99
Cape Coast: Ghana   05 10N 01 13W   57
Cape Fear: *riv.*, N.C., U.S.A.   34 15N 78 15W   101
Cape Girardeau: Mo., U.S.A.   37 19N 89 31W   98
Cape Hatteras *National Seashore*: N.C.,
   U.S.A.   35 30N 75 15W   101
Cape North: Nfld., Canada   53 47N 56 30W   97
Cape *Rise*: S.Atlantic Ocean   42 00S 12 00E   3
Cape Town (Kaapstad): C.P., Rep. of S.Africa
   33 56S 18 28E   55
Cape Verde *Basin*: N.Atlantic Ocean   23 00N 30 00W 2
Cape Verde *Islands*: N.Atlantic Ocean   16 00N 24 00W 2
Cape York *Peninsula*: Qld., Australia   13 15S 142 45E 14 41
Capital Beltway: *hwy.*, Md., U.S.A.   39 00N 77 00W 122
Capitán: *riv.*, Argentina   34 23S 58 33W   128
Capitán Arturo Prat: *rsch. stn.*, Antarctica   62 29S 59 38W
                                                     24
Capitol Heights: D.C., U.S.A.   38 58N 76 55W   122
Capitol Hill: B.C., Canada   49 17N 122 59W   126
Capitol Hill: Wash., U.S.A.   47 38N 122 18W   126
Capitol Reef *National Monument*: Utah,
   U.S.A.   38 00N 111 00W   91
Čaplygin: U.S.S.R.   53 14N 39 58E   80
Capoeiras *Falls*: Brazil   06 48S 58 21W   50
Capreol: Ont., Canada   46 43N 80 56W   104

148 CAPRI – CASTLE HILL

Types of map: Ocean pp. 1-5; Physical pp. 6-25; Human pp. 26-57; Topographic pp. 58-101; World pp. 102-111; Urban pp. 112-128.

Capri, *Isola di*: Italy 40 33N 14 13E 79
Caprivi Strip: *region*, S.W.Africa 17 45S 22 15E 55
Capulin Mountains *National Monument*: N.Mex., U.S.A. 36 45N 103 45W 95
Caquetá: *riv.*, Colombia 00 15S 02 45W 48
Car, Slieve: *mtn.*, Mayo, Irish Republic 54 04N 09 39W 66
Carabanchel: Spain 40 23N 03 44W 116
Caracaraí: Brazil 01 50N 61 08W 48
Caracas: Venezuela 10 35N 66 56W 48
Caragh, *Lough*: Kerry, Irish Republic 52 00N 09 45W 67
Carajás, Serra dos: *ra.*, Brazil 05 15S 51 15W 50
Carapachay: *riv.*, Argentina 34 23S 58 37W 128
Caraque: Spain 40 25N 03 43W 116
Caratinga: Brazil 19 47S 42 08W 51
Caravelas: Brazil 17 45S 39 15W 51
Caraza: Argentina 34 42S 58 24W 128
Carbondale: Ill., U.S.A. 37 43N 89 12W 98
Carbonear: Nfld., Canada 47 45N 52 16W 97
Carbonia: Sardinia 39 10N 08 31E 77
Carcajou: Alta., Canada 57 48N 117 02W 92
Carcajou: *riv.*, N.W.T., Canada 65 15N 127 45W 88
Carcans, Étang de: *lag.*, France 45 05N 01 03W 70
Carcassonne: France 43 13N 02 21E 70
Carcross: Yukon, Canada 60 11N 134 41W 88
Cardamones, Chaîne des: *ra.*, Khmer Rep. 12 15N 103 15E 38
Cardiff: S.Glam., Wales 51 30N 03 13W 26 61 105 113
Cardigan: Dyfed, Wales 52 06N 04 40W 60
Cardigan *Bay*: Dyfed, Wales 52 30N 04 45W 60
Cardiganshire: *admin.*, Wales. Absorbed into new *admin.* of Dyfed, 1974 60
Cardross: Sask., Canada 49 48N 105 39W 92
Cardston: Alta., Canada 49 14N 113 19W 92
Čardžou (Chardzhou): U.S.S.R. 39 06N 63 34E 29
Carey: *riv.*, Devon, England 50 45N 04 15W 61
Caribbean *Sea* 2 17 47
Caribou: Man., Canada 59 20N 97 50W 93
Caribou: *riv.*, Man., Canada 59 30N 96 15W 93
Caribou *Island*: Ont., Canada 47 23N 84 58W 98
Caribou *Mountains*: Alta., Canada 59 15N 116 00W 42 92
Caringbah: N.S.W., Australia 34 02S 151 08E 120
Carkeek *Park*: Wash., U.S.A. 47 42N 122 22W 126
Carleton, *Mount*: N.B., Canada 47 24N 66 52W 97
Carlin: Nev., U.S.A. 40 43N 116 07W 91
Carlingford *Lough*: Irish Republic/N. Ireland 54 00N 06 00W 66
Carlisle: Cumbria, England 54 54N 02 55W 63
Carlow: Carlow, Irish Rep. 52 50N 06 55W 67
Carlow: *admin.*, Irish Rep. 52 45N 06 45W 67
Carlsbad: N.Mex., U.S.A. 32 25N 104 14W 43 95
Carlsbad Caverns *National Park*: N.Mex., U.S.A. 32 00N 104 15W 95
Carlsberg *Ridge*: Indian Ocean 05 00N 63 00E 1
Carlton: Notts., England 53 22N 01 06W 58
Carluke: Lan., Scotland 55 45N 03 51W 62 113
Carmacks: Yukon, Canada 62 04N 136 21W 88
Carmagnola: Italy 44 51N 07 43E 71
Carman: Man., Canada 49 32N 97 59W 93
Carmarthen: Dyfed, Wales 51 52N 04 19W 60
Carmarthen *Bay*: Dyfed, Wales 51 30N 04 30W 61
Carmarthenshire: *admin.*, Wales. Absorbed into new *admin.* of Dyfed, 1974 60
Carmel *Head*: Gwyn., Wales 53 24N 04 34W 60
Carmelo: Spain 41 25N 02 10E 116
Carnarvon: W.A., Australia 24 51S 113 45E 40
Carnatic: *geog. reg.*, India 11 00N 79 00E 34
Carndonagh: Don., Irish Republic 55 15N 07 15W 66
Carnegie: Pa., U.S.A. 40 24N 80 06W 125
Carnegie *Ridge*: S.Pacific Ocean 02 00S 86 00W 5 18
Carn Eige: *mtn.*, R. & Crom., Scotland 57 18N 05 08W 64
Carnforth: Lancs., England 54 08N 02 46W 63
Carnoustie: Angus, Scotland 56 30N 02 44W 65
Carnsore *Point*: Wex., Irish Republic 52 10N 06 22W 67
Carolina: Brazil 07 20S 47 28W 50
Caroline *Islands*: N.Pacific Ocean 08 00N 150 00E 4 12
Caroline–New Guinea *Rise*: N.Pacific Ocean 02 30N 140 45E 14
Caroline *Peak*: S.I., New Zealand 45 58S 167 15E 87
Caroní: *riv.*, Venezuela 08 00N 62 45W 48
Coronno Pertusella: Italy 45 33N 09 11E 116
Carpathian *Mountains*: E.Europe 48 30N 23 30E 7 27 78

Carpentaria, *Gulf of*: Australia 14 30S 139 00E 14 41
Carpentras: France 44 03N 05 03E 71
Carra, *Lough*: Mayo, Irish Republic 53 30N 09 15W 66
Carrara: Italy 44 04N 10 06E 26 71
Carrauntouhil: *mtn.*, Kerry, Irish Republic 52 00N 09 45W 67
Carriacou: *is.*, Grenadines 12 29N 61 26W 47
Carrickfergus: Antrim, N.Ireland 54 43N 05 44W 66
Carrickmacross: Monaghan, Irish Republic 53 58N 06 43W 66
Carrick-on-Shannon: Leit., Irish Republic 53 57N 08 05W 66
Carrick-on-Suir: Tip., Irish Republic 52 21N 07 25W 67
Carrollton: Ga., U.S.A. 33 35N 85 05W 101
Carron: *riv.*, R. & Crom., Scotland 57 45N 04 15W 64
Carron: *riv.*, R. & Crom., Scotland 57 15N 05 15W 64
Carron, *Loch*: R. & Crom., Scotland 57 15N 05 30W 64
Carron Valley *Forest*: Stirl., Scotland 56 00N 04 00W 113
Carron Valley *Reservoir*: Stirl., Scotland 56 00N 04 00W 113
Carrot: *riv.*, Canada 53 15N 103 15W 92
Carrowmore *Lough*: Mayo, Irish Republic 54 00N 09 45W 66
Carse of Gowrie: *dist.*, Perth., Scotland 56 15N 06 00W 65
Carson City: Nev., U.S.A. 39 10N 119 46W 91
Carson Sink: *salt flat*, Nev., U.S.A. 39 30N 118 15W 91
Cartagena: Colombia 10 24N 75 33W 48
Cartagena: Spain 37 36N 00 59W 26 77
Carterton: N.I., New Zealand 41 01S 175 30E 87
Carthage: Mo., U.S.A. 37 10N 94 20W 95
Carthage: Tex., U.S.A. 32 09N 94 20W 100
Cartwright: Nfld., Canada 53 40N 57 00W 97
Caruaru: Brazil 08 17S 35 58W 50
Carúpano: Venezuela 10 39N 63 14W 48
Caryl *Park*: Mass., U.S.A. 41 59N 71 15W 122
Casablanca *see* El-Dar-el-Beida 33 39N 07 35W 56
Casa Grande: Ariz., U.S.A. 32 53N 111 45W 91
Casale Marcigliana: Italy 42 00N 12 31E 116
Casale Monferrato: Italy 45 08N 08 27E 71
Casanova: Argentina 34 42S 58 35W 128
Cascade *Range*: Canada/U.S.A. 17 42 90
Caseros: Argentina 34 36S 58 34W 128
Caserta: Italy 41 04N 14 20E 79
Casey: *rsch. stn.*, Antarctica 66 17S 110 32E 25
Cashel: Tip., Irish Republic 52 31N 07 53W 67
Casiquiare (Brazo Casiquiare): *riv.*, Venezuela 02 30N 66 30W 48
Casper: Wyo., U.S.A. 42 51N 106 19W 43 94
Caspian *Sea*: Iran/U.S.S.R. 42 00N 51 00E 8 28
Casquet Banks: *shoals*, Channel Islands 49 23N 02 24W 61
Cassano (Cassano Magnago): Italy 45 41N 08 50E 116
Cassiar: B.C., Canada 59 15N 129 49W 88
Cassiar *Mountains*: B.C., Canada 59 00N 130 00W 88
Cassinga: Angola 15 08S 16 05E 55 105
Cassino: Italy 41 29N 13 50E 79
Castelar: Argentina 34 39S 58 37W 128
Castellane: France 43 50N 06 30E 71
Castellanza: Italy 45 37N 08 53E 116
Castellar: Spain 41 37N 02 05E 116
Castelldefels: Spain 41 17N 01 58E 116
Castellón de la Plana: Spain 39 59N 00 03W 77
Castelo Branco: Portugal 39 50N 07 30W 76
Castera, *Canal de*: Mexico 19 42N 99 06W 128
Castiglione Olona: Italy 45 46N 08 52E 116
Castilla: Peru 05 16S 80 36W 48
Castlebar: Mayo, Irish Rep. 53 52N 09 17W 66
Castlebay: Inv., Scotland 56 58N 07 30W 64
Castlebellingham: Louth, Irish Republic 53 54N 06 23W 66
Castleblayney: Monaghan, Irish Republic 54 07N 06 44W 66
Castle Bromwich: W.Mid., England 52 30N 01 45W 115
Castle Cary: Som., England 51 06N 02 31W 61
Castlecomer: Kilk., Irish Republic 52 48N 07 12W 67
Castlederg: Tyr., N.Ireland 54 42N 07 35W 66
Castle Donington: Leics., England 52 51N 01 19W 58
Castle Douglas: Kirkc., Scotland 54 57N 03 56W 62
Castleford: W.Yorks., England 53 44N 01 21W 63 115
Castlegar: B.C., Canada 49 18N 117 41W 89
Castle Hill: N.S.W., Australia 33 44S 150 59E 120

Types of map: Ocean pp. 1-5; Physical pp. 6-25; Human pp. 26-57; Topographic pp. 58-101; World pp. 102-111; Urban pp. 112-128.

Castleisland: Kerry, Irish Republic   52 14N 09 27W   67
Castlepollard: Westmeath, Irish Republic   53 41N 07 17W
    66
Castletown: I. of M., United Kingdom   54 04N 04 38W   62
Castor: Alta., Canada   52 14N 111 54W   92
Castres: France   43 36N 02 14E   70
Castrop-Rauxel: W.Germany   51 33N 07 19E   118
Castro Valley: Calif., U.S.A.   37 46N 122 03W   126
Catamarca: Argentina   28 28S 65 46W   52
Catamarca: admin., Argentina   28 45S 65 45W   49
Catanduanes: is., Philippines   13 45N 124 15E   39
Catania: Sicily   37 31N 15 06E   27 79
Catanzaro: Italy   38 54N 16 36E   32 79
Caterham: Surrey, England   51 17N 00 04W   59 112
Cat Island: Bahamas   24 30N 75 30W   47
Catlettsburg: Ky., U.S.A.   38 24N 82 37W   106
Catoche, Cabo: Mexico   21 35N 87 05W   46
Catshill: Here. & Worcs., England   52 21N 02 04W   115
Catskill Mountains: N.Y., U.S.A.   42 00N 74 15W   99
Catterick Camp: N.Yorks., England   54 22N 01 43W   63
Cauca: riv., Colombia   09 15N 74 30W   48
Caucasus Mountains: U.S.S.R.   43 00N 43 00E   8 28
Caughnawaga: Qué., Canada   45 24N 73 44W   122
Caumsett State Park: N.Y., U.S.A.   40 55N 73 28W   123
Cauquenes: Chile   35 58S 72 22W   52
Caura: riv., Venezuela   66 45N 64 45W   48
Causse de Gramat: plat., France   44 30N 01 45E   70
Causse de Larzac: plat., France   44 00N 03 15E   71
Causse de Limogne: plat., France   44 15N 01 30E   70
Causse de Sauveterre: plat., France   44 15N 03 15E   71
Causse du Comtal: plat., France   44 15N 02 30E   70
Cauvery: riv., India   11 15N 79 30E   34
Cavan: Cavan, Irish Rep.   53 59N 07 21W   66
Cavan: admin., Irish Rep.   54 00N 07 30W   66
Cawnpore see Känpur   26 27N 80 14E   34 82
Caxias: Brazil   04 50S 43 21W   50
Caxias do Sul: Brazil   29 10S 51 11W   51
Cayambe: Ecuador   00 02N 78 08W   48
Cayambe: volc., Ecuador   00 02N 77 58W   48
Cayenne: French Guiana   04 55N 52 18W   50
Cayman Islands: Caribbean Sea   19 30N 80 30W   47
Cayman Trench: Caribbean Sea   17 00N 85 00W   2
Cayuga Lake: N.Y., U.S.A.   42 30N 76 30W   99
Cazaux, Étang de: lag., France   44 30N 01 08W   70
Cazères: France   43 13N 01 04E   70
Ceará: admin., Brazil   05 15S 39 30W   50
Čebarkul': U.S.S.R.   54 58N 60 25E   81
Čeboksary (Cheboksary): U.S.S.R.   56 09N 47 15E   28
Cebu: Philippines   10 17N 123 56E   39
Cebu: is., Philippines   10 30N 124 00E   12 39
Cecerleg: Mongolia   47 30N 101 27E   30
Čechov: U.S.S.R.   55 09N 37 27E   80
Cedar: riv., Iowa, U.S.A.   42 45N 92 15W   98
Cedar: riv., Wash., U.S.A.   47 15N 122 00W   126
Cedar City: Utah, U.S.A.   37 41N 113 04W   91
Cedar Creek: N.D., U.S.A.   46 00N 102 00W   94
Cedar Falls: Iowa, U.S.A.   42 34N 92 26W   98
Cedar Lake: Man., Canada   53 15N 100 00W   93
Cedar Rapids: Iowa, U.S.A.   41 59N 91 39W   43 98
Cegléd: Hungary   47 10N 19 48E   79
Čel'abinsk (Chelyabinsk): U.S.S.R.   55 10N 61 24E
    29 81 105
Celebes (Sulawesi): is. & admin., Indonesia
  02 15S 120 30E   13 39
Celebes Sea: Indonesia   03 15N 120 30E   12 39
Celinograd (Tselinograd): U.S.S.R.   51 10N 71 30E   29
Celje: Yugoslavia   46 15N 15 16E   78
Cellar Head: R. & Crom., Scotland   58 25N 06 11W   64
Celle: W.Germany   52 37N 10 05E   73
Centennial Park: N.S.W., Australia   33 54S 151 14E   120
Center Line: Mich., U.S.A.   42 28N 83 01W   125
Centerville: Iowa, U.S.A.   40 47N 92 51W   98
Centocelle: Italy   41 53N 12 34E   116
Central: N.Mex., U.S.A.   32 47N 108 09W   95
Central, Cordillera: ra., Portugal/Spain   40 00N 06 00W   76
Central, Massif: mtns., France   6 26
CENTRAL AFRICAN REPUBLIC   06 15N 20 30E   20
Central City: Colo., U.S.A.   39 48N 105 31W   94
Central Cordillera: ra., Colombia see Cordillera Central
  07 30N 75 15W   48
Central Cordillera: ra., Peru   08 15S 77 00W   18 48

Centralia: III., U.S.A.   38 32N 89 08W   98
Centralia: Wash., U.S.A.   46 43N 122 58W   90
Central Indian Ridge: Indian Ocean   17 30S 67 00E   1
Central Makrän Range: Pakistan   26 30N 64 00E   34
Central Massif see Massif Central   45 00N 03 00E   6 26 71
Central Pacific Basin: N.Pacific Ocean   07 00N 177 00W   4
Central Park: B.C., Canada   49 13N 123 01W   126
Central Park: N.Y., U.S.A.   40 47N 73 52W   123
Central Siberian Plateau: U.S.S.R.   67 00N 113 00E   9 30
Centre Island: Ont., Canada   43 37N 79 23W   125
Čepca: riv., U.S.S.R.   58 30N 50 45E   81
Cephalonia: is., see Kefallinía, Island   38 15N 20 30E   79
Ceram: is., Indonesia   03 00S 129 30E   13 39
Ceram Sea: Indonesia   02 30S 130 00E   13 39
Čeremchovo (Cheremkhovo): U.S.S.R.   53 09N 103 05E   30
Čerepovec (Cherepovets): U.S.S.R.   59 08N 37 54E
    28 80 105
Ceresio, Lago di see Lugano, Lago di   46 00N 09 00E   71
Cergy: France   49 02N 02 04E   117
Čerkassy (Cherkassy): U.S.S.R.   49 26N 32 04E   28 80
Čerkessk (Cherkessk): U.S.S.R.   44 14N 42 04E   28
Čerkizovo (Cherkizovo): U.S.S.R.   55 49N 37 44E   119
Černigov (Chernigov): U.S.S.R.   51 30N 31 18E   28 80
Černigovskoje Polesje: geog. reg., U.S.S.R.   51 30N 32 00E
    80
Černogorsk (Chernogorsk): U.S.S.R.   53 49N 91 18E   30
Černovcy (Chernovtsy): U.S.S.R.   48 18N 25 56E   28 78
Černuška: U.S.S.R.   56 29N 56 03E   81
Čer'omuski: U.S.S.R.   55 41N 37 35E   119
Cerro Bolívar: mtn., Venezuela   07 27N 63 25W   104
Cerro Chiconautla: mtn., Mexico   19 39N 98 58W   128
Cerro Chiquihuite: mtns., Mexico   19 35N 99 07W   128
Cerro Cuautzin: mtn., Mexico   19 09N 99 06W   128
Cerro del Tehutli: mtn., Mexico   19 13N 99 02W   128
Cerro de Pasco: Peru   10 43S 76 15W   49
Cerro Maggiore: Italy   45 36N 08 57E   116
Cerro Marahuaca: mtn., Venezuela   03 34N 65 27W   48
Cerro Pelado: mtn., Mexico   19 09N 99 13W   128
Cerro Peñon: mtn., Mexico   19 19N 99 00W   128
Cerro Tlaloc: mtn., Mexico   19 06N 99 02E   128
Čerskogo (Cherskogo) Range: U.S.S.R.   66 30N 141 00E
    9 31
Čertkovo: U.S.S.R.   49 23N 40 10E   80
Červonograd: U.S.S.R.   50 24N 24 14E   78
Cesano (Cesano Maderno): Italy   45 38N 09 08E   116
Cēsis: U.S.S.R.   57 18N 25 18E   75
České Budějovice: Czechoslovakia   49 00N 14 30E   73 79
Českézemé: province, Czechoslovakia   49 15N 15 00E   73
Českomoravská Vrchovina: mtns.,
  Czechoslovakia   49 15N 15 00E   73
Český Krumlov: Czechoslovakia   48 49N 14 20E   73
Ceuta: North Africa   35 53N 05 19W   56 76
Cévennes: mtns., France   44 00N 03 45E   71
Ceylon see Sri Lanka   07 45N 80 45E   1 11 34
Cèze: riv., France   44 15N 04 15E   71
Chabarovsk (Khabarovsk): U.S.S.R.   48 27N 135 06E   31
Chabot, Lake: Calif., U.S.A.   37 43N 122 06W   126
Chachapoyas: Peru   06 13S 77 54W   48
Chaco: admin., Argentina   27 00S 60 15W   49
Chaco Canyon National Monument: N.Mex.,
  U.S.A.   36 00N 108 15W   95
CHAD   11 00N 16 00E   20 32
Chad, Lake: Central Africa   13 30N 14 00E   20
Chadron: Nebr., U.S.A.   42 50N 103 00W   94
Chagos Islands: British Indian Ocean Terr.   06 00S 73 15E
    11
Chagos-Laccadive Plateau: Indian Ocean   00 00 73 00E   1
Chaibāsa: India   22 31N 85 50E   83
Chaîne Annamitique: ra., Indo-China   16 15N 106 45E   36
Chaîne des Cardamones: ra., Khmer Rep.   12 15N 103 15E
    38
Chain Fracture Zone: S.Atlantic Ocean   03 00S 15 00W   3
Chaj Doāb: geog. reg., Pakistan   32 00N 72 45E   82
Chākdaha: India   23 05N 88 32E   83
Chakradharpur: India   22 42N 85 38E   83
Chalcis see Khalkis   38 28N 23 36E   79
Chaleur, Baie de: Canada   47 45N 65 30W   97
Chalilovo: U.S.S.R.   51 24N 58 09E   105
Chaling: China   26 54N 113 31E   85
Chaling Hu see Zhaling, Lake   34 45N 98 00E   36
Chālisgaon: India   20 29N 75 10E   82

Types of map: Ocean pp. 1-5; Physical pp. 6-25; Human pp. 26-57; Topographic pp. 58-101; World pp. 102-111; Urban pp. 112-128.

Challenger *Deep*: N.Pacific Ocean 11 19N 142 15E 12
Challenger *Fracture Zone*: S.Pacific Ocean 34 00S 95 00W 5
Châlons-sur-Marne: France 48 58N 04 22E 71
Châlon-sur-Saône: France 46 47N 04 51E 71
Cham: W.Germany 49 13N 12 41E 73
Chamartín de la Rosa: Spain 40 28N 03 40W 116
Chambal: *riv.*, India 26 15N 77 00E 34 82
Chamberlain: S.D., U.S.A. 43 49N 99 20W 94
Chamberlain, *Lake*: Maine, U.S.A. 46 00N 69 15W 99
Chambersburg: Pa., U.S.A. 39 57N 77 40W 99
Chambéry: France 45 34N 05 55E 71
Chamonix-Mont-Blanc: France 45 55N 06 52E 71
Chamouchouane: *riv.*, Qué., Canada 49 00N 73 00W 96
Chāmpa: India 22 02N 82 42E 83
Champagne: Yukon, Canada 60 49N 136 30W 88
Champagne, *Plaine de*: France 49 00N 04 15E 71
Champagne Berriehonne: *geog. reg.*, France 47 00N 02 00E 70
Champaign: Ill., U.S.A. 40 07N 88 14W 98
Champlain, *Lake*: U.S.A. 44 30N 73 15W 99
Chanchiang *see* Zhanjiang 21 16N 110 28E 36
Chanda *see* Chandrapur 19 58N 79 21E 34 82
Chandannagar (Chandernagore): India 22 52N 88 22E 120
Chandausi: India 28 27N 78 43E 82
Chandernagore *see* Chandannagar 22 52N 88 22E 120
Chandigarh: India 30 43N 76 47E 34 82
Chandil: India 22 58N 86 04E 83
Chandler: Qué., Canada 48 21N 64 41W 97
Chandler: Ariz., U.S.A. 33 18N 111 50W 91
Chandor *Hills*: India 20 15N 74 00E 82
Chāndpur: Bangladesh 23 15N 90 40E 83
Chāndpur: India 29 08N 78 16E 82
Chandrapur (Chanda): India 19 58N 79 21E 34 82
Chang (Yangtze): *riv.*, China 31 30N 118 15E 12 36 84
Changajn *Mountains*: Mongolia 47 00N 100 00E 30
Changcheng: China 19 12N 109 01E 105
Changchiak'ou *see* Zhangjiakou 40 50N 114 53E 36 84
Ch'angchih *see* Changzhi 36 03N 113 11E 36 84
Ch'angchou *see* Changzhou 31 42N 120 00E 37 84
Changchou *see* Zhangzhou 24 33N 117 39E 36 85
Changchun: China 43 53N 125 19E 37
Changde (Ch'angte): China 29 01N 111 31E 36 85
Changdu (Ch'angt'u): China 31 11N 97 15E 36
Changgou: China 34 12N 113 47E 84
Changhua: China 30 11N 119 15E 85
Changjiang: Fujian, China 25 46N 116 20E 85
Changli: China 39 41N 119 18E 84
Changning: China 26 26N 112 21E 85
Changsha: China 28 09N 113 00E 36 85
Changshan: China 28 50N 118 32E 85
Changshou: China 29 51N 107 00E 85
Changshu: China 31 38N 120 50E 37 85
Ch'angte *see* Changde 29 01N 111 31E 36 85
Ch'angt'u *see* Changdu 31 11N 97 15E 36
Changwu: China 35 11N 107 50E 84
Changxindian: China 39 50N 116 12E 121
Changxingdao: *is.*, China 39 30N 121 15E 84
Changyuan: China 35 08N 114 39E 84
Changzhi (Ch'angchih): China 36 03N 113 11E 36 84
Changzhou (Ch'angchou): China 31 42N 120 00E 37 84
Chanka, Ozero (Khanka, *Lake*): China/U.S.S.R. 45 00N 132 30E 37 86
Channel Islands: *is. & Duchy*, United Kingdom 49 30N 02 15W 61
Chanthaburi: Thailand 12 35N 102 08E 35
Chanute: Kans., U.S.A. 37 41N 95 27W 95
Chao: *riv.*, China 41 30N 116 30E 84
Chao, *Lake*: China 31 30N 117 30E 84
Chaoan: China 23 41N 116 38E 36 85
Chaot'ung *see* Zhaotong 27 12N 103 48E 36
Chaoyang: Guangdong, China 23 18N 116 37E 85
Chaoyang: Liaoning, China 41 34N 120 28E 37
Chapais: Qué., Canada 49 47N 74 54W 96
Chapala, *Lago de*: Mexico 20 00N 103 00W 46
Chapayevsk *see* Čapajevsk 52 58N 49 41E 81
Chapel Allerton: W.Yorks., England 53 49N 01 33W 115
Chapel Hill: N.C., U.S.A. 35 55N 79 04W 101
Chapleau: Ont., Canada 47 50N 83 24W 98
Chāpra: India 25 46N 84 44E 35 83
Chapultepec, *Parque de*: Mexico 19 25N 99 12W 128
Chardzhou *see* Čardžou 39 06N 63 34E 29
Charente: *riv.*, France 45 30N 00 30W 70
Charial *Canal*: India 22 27N 88 15E 120
Chariton: *riv.*, U.S.A. 40 15N 92 30W 98
Char'kov (Khar'kov): U.S.S.R. 50 00N 36 15E 28 80
Charlbury: Oxon., England 51 53N 01 29W 59
Charleroi: Belgium 50 25N 04 27E 26 72
Charles: *riv.*, Mass., U.S.A. 42 15N 71 00W 122
Charles, *Cape*: Va., U.S.A. 37 08N 75 59W 17 101
Charles City: Iowa, U.S.A. 43 05N 92 40W 98
Charleston: S.I., New Zealand 41 55S 171 26E 87
Charleston: Ill., U.S.A. 39 30N 88 11W 98
Charleston: S.C., U.S.A. 32 48N 79 58W 45 101
Charleston: W.Va., U.S.A. 38 23N 81 40W 45 99
Charlestown of Aberlour: Banff., Scotland 57 28N 03 14W 65
Charleville: Qld., Australia 26 25S 146 13E 41
Charleville-Mézières: France 49 46N 04 43E 71
Charlotte: N.C., U.S.A. 35 03N 80 50W 45 101
Charlottenburg: W.Berlin, Germany 52 32N 13 18E 117
Charlottesville: Va., U.S.A. 38 02N 78 29W 99
Charlottetown: P.E.I., Canada 46 14N 63 09W 44 97
Charlton Depot: N.W.T., Canada 51 58N 79 19W 96
Charlton *Island*: N.W.T., Canada 52 00N 79 30W 96
Charovsk: U.S.S.R. 59 59N 40 11E 80
Chartiers *Creek*: Pa., U.S.A. 40 25N 80 05W 125
Chartres: France 48 27N 01 30E 70
Chasetown: Staffs., England 52 41N 01 56W 115
Chatanga (Khatanga): *riv.*, U.S.S.R. 72 30N 103 00E 30
Châteaubriant: France 47 43N 01 22W 70
Châteaudun: France 48 04N 01 20E 70
Château-Gontier: France 47 49N 00 42W 70
Châteaulin: France 48 12N 04 07W 70
Châteauroux: France 46 49N 01 41E 70
Châtellerault: France 46 49N 00 33E 70
Chatham: Ont., Canada 42 24N 82 11W 98
Chatham: Kent, England 51 23N 00 32E 59 112
Chatham *Islands*: S.Pacific Ocean 38 00S 177 00W 4 15
Chatham *Rise*: S.Pacific Ocean 38 00S 175 00E 4 15
Chatham *Strait*: Alaska, U.S.A. 56 30N 134 15W 89
Chat Moss: *marsh*, Gt. Man., England 53 15N 02 15W 114
Chatou: France 48 53N 02 09E 117
Chatra: India 24 14N 84 57E 83
Chatswood: N.S.W., Australia 33 48S 151 11E 120
Chattahoochee: Fla., U.S.A. 30 42N 84 51W 101
Chattahoochee: *riv.*, U.S.A. 31 30N 85 00W 101
Chattanooga: Tenn., U.S.A. 35 03N 85 19W 45 101
Chatteris: Cambs., England 52 27N 00 03E 58
Chaudière: *riv.*, Qué., Canada 46 30N 71 00W 96
Chaumont-en-Bassigny: France 48 07N 05 08E 71
Chaŭn: S.Korea 37 52N 128 00E 105
Chbukha Dzong: Bhutan 27 09N 89 36E 83
Cheadle: Gt. Man., England 53 24N 02 13W 63 114
Cheadle: Staffs., England 52 59N 01 59W 58
Cheatham *Dam*: Tenn., U.S.A. 36 18N 87 11W 101
Cheboksary *see* Čeboksary 56 09N 47 15E 28
Chech, Erg: *des.*, Algeria 25 00N 02 00W 20 56
Chechiang: *admin.* *see* Zhejiang 29 30N 120 00E 37 85
Cheddar: Som., England 51 17N 02 46W 61
Chefoo *see* Yantai 37 30N 121 22E 37 84
Chehe: China 24 53N 107 38E 85
Cheju: *is.*, S.Korea 33 30N 126 30E 37
Chéliff: *riv.*, Algeria 36 00N 00 45E 77
Chelles: France 48 53N 02 35E 70 117
Chełm: Poland 51 08N 23 29E 78
Chelmsford: Essex, England 51 44N 00 28E 59 112
Chelsea: Mass., U.S.A. 42 24N 71 02W 122
Cheltenham: Glos., England 51 54N 02 04W 60
Cheltenham: Pa., U.S.A. 40 05N 75 06W 122
Chelyabinsk *see* Čel'abinsk 55 10N 61 24E 29 81 105
Chemnitz *see* Karl-Marx-Stadt 50 50N 12 55E 27 73
Chemulpo *see* Inch'ŏn 37 28N 126 38E 37
Chemung: *riv.*, U.S.A. 42 00N 76 45W 99
Chenāb: *riv.*, Pakistan 32 15N 73 15E 34 82
Chenchiang *see* Zhenjiang 32 10N 119 30E 37 84
Cheng'an: China 36 27N 114 39E 84
Chengbu: China 26 30N 110 15E 85
Chengchou *see* Zhengzhou 34 40N 113 38E 36 84
Chengde (Ch'engte): China 41 00N 117 50E 36 84
Chengdu (Ch'engtu): China 30 39N 104 04E 36
Ch'engte *see* Chengde 41 00N 117 50E 36 84

Types of map: Ocean pp. 1-5; Physical pp. 6-25; Human pp. 26-57; Topographic pp. 58-101; World pp. 102-111; Urban pp. 112-128.

Ch'engtu *see* Chengdu 30 39N 104 04E 36
Ch'enhsien *see* Chezhou 25 47N 112 58E 36 85
Chenjiaquiao: China 31 08N 121 41E 121
Chenxi: China 28 04N 110 10E 85
Chenyüeh *see* Yiwu 29 17N 120 03E 85
Chepstow: Gwent, Wales 51 39N 02 41W 61 113
Cheraw: S.C., U.S.A. 34 41N 79 55W 101
Cherbourg: France 49 38N 01 37W 70
Cherchell: Algeria 36 36N 02 11E 77
Cheremkhovo *see* Čeremchovo 53 09N 103 05E 30
Cherepovets *see* Čerepovec 59 08N 37 54E 28 80 105
Cheribon *see* Tjirebon 06 46S 108 33E 38
Cherkassy *see* Čerkassy 49 26N 32 04E 28 80
Cherkessk *see* Čerkessk 44 14N 42 04E 28
Cherkizovo *see* Čerkizovo 55 49N 37 44E 119
Chernigov *see* Černigov 51 30N 31 18E 28 80
Chernogorsk *see* Černogorsk 53 49N 91 18E 30
Chernovtsy *see* Černovcy 48 18N 25 56E 28 78
Cherokees, *Lake of the*: Okla., U.S.A. 36 28N 95 02W 95
Cherry Hill: N.J., U.S.A. 39 55N 75 01W 122
Cherskogo *Range* *see* Čerskogo *Range* 66 30N 141 00E 9 31
Cherson (Kherson): U.S.S.R. 46 38N 32 35E 28 80
Chertal: Belgium 50 41N 05 40E 105
Chertsey: Surrey, England 51 24N 00 30W 59
Cherwell: *riv.*, Oxon., England 51 45N 01 15W 59
Chesapeake *Bay*: U.S.A. 38 00N 76 00W 45 99
Chesham: Bucks., England 51 43N 00 38W 59 112
Cheshire: *admin.*, England 53 00N 02 30W 60
Cheshunt: Herts., England 51 43N 00 02W 59 112
Chesil *Beach*: Dorset, England 50 30N 02 30W 61
Chester: Ches., England 53 12N 02 54W 60 114
Chester: Pa., U.S.A. 39 50N 75 23W 99 122
Chesterfield: Derby., England 53 15N 01 25W 58
Chesterfield *Inlet*: N.W.T., Canada 63 45N 92 00W 44
Chester-le-Street: Dur., England 54 52N 01 34W 63
Chesuncook *Lake*: Maine, U.S.A. 46 00N 69 15W 99
Chetumal: Mexico 18 30N 88 17W 46
Cheviot, The: *mtn.*, Northumb., England 55 29N 02 09W 63
Cheviot *Hills*: England/Scotland 55 15N 02 45W 63
Chevreuse: France 48 43N 02 03E 117
Chevy Chase: Md., U.S.A. 38 59N 77 05W 122
Chew: *riv.*, Avon, England 51 15N 02 30W 113
Chew Valley *Lake*: Avon, England 51 15N 02 30W 61
Cheyenne: Wyo., U.S.A. 41 08N 104 49W 43 94
Cheyenne: *riv.*, U.S.A. 44 15N 102 15W 94
Cheyenne Wells: Colo., U.S.A. 38 49N 102 21W 94
Chezhou (Ch'enhsien): China 25 47N 112 58E 36 85
Chhatarpur: India 24 54N 79 35E 82
Chhindwāra: India 22 04N 78 58E 82
Chi (Lam Chi): *riv.*, Thailand 15 30N 104 00E 38
Chiahsing *see* Jiaxing 30 46N 120 45E 37 85
Chiai: Taiwan 23 28N 120 30E 37 85
Chiamussu *see* Jiamusi 46 50N 130 21E 37
Chian *see* Jian 27 07N 115 01E 36 85
Chianghsi: *admin.* *see* Jiangxi 26 45N 115 30E 36 85
Chiang Mai: Thailand 18 48N 98 59E 35
Chiangmen *see* Jiangmen 22 37N 113 07E 36 85
Chiangsu: *admin.* *see* Jiangsu 32 45N 120 15E 37 84
Chiaohsien *see* Jiaoxian 36 18N 120 03E 37 84
Chiaotso *see* Jiaozuo 35 17N 113 12E 36 84
Chiapas: *admin.*, Mexico 16 30N 92 30W 46
Chiari: Italy 45 32N 09 55E 71
Chiasso: Switzerland 45 51N 09 02E 116
Chiavari: Italy 44 19N 09 19E 71
Chiba: Japan 35 36N 140 07E 37 86 105 107
Chibougamau: Qué., Canada 49 56N 74 24W 96
Chicago: Ill., U.S.A. 41 50N 87 45W 45 98 104 124
Chicago, North Branch: *riv.*, Ill., U.S.A. 42 00N 87 45W 124
Chicago Sanitary & Ship *Canal*: 41 30N 87 45W 124
Chicago Skyway: *hwy.*, Ill., U.S.A. 41 45N 87 30W 124
Chichagof *Island*: Alaska, U.S.A. 57 45N 135 30W 88
Chichester: W.Sussex, England 50 50N 00 48W 59
Ch'ichiang *see* Qijiang 29 02N 106 39E 36
Chichibu: Japan 35 59N 139 05E 105
Ch'ich'ihaerh *see* Qiqihaer 47 19N 123 55E 31
Chickasha: Okla., U.S.A. 35 03N 97 58W 95
Chiclayo: Peru 06 47S 79 47W 48
Chico: Calif., U.S.A. 39 46N 121 50W 91
Chico: *riv.*, Chubut, Argentina 44 45S 67 30W 52
Chiconautla, Cerro: *mtn.*, Mexico 19 39N 98 58W 128
Chicoutimi: Qué., Canada 48 26N 71 06W 44 96
Chienou *see* Jianou 27 05N 118 21E 36 85
Chieti: Italy 42 21N 14 10E 79
Chifeng: China 42 18N 119 00E 36
Chignecto *Bay*: Canada 45 30N 64 45W 97
Chihli, *Gulf of*: *see* Bohai 38 30N 120 00E 37 84
Chihsi *see* Jixi 45 17N 130 59E 37
Chihuahua: Mexico 28 38N 106 05W 46
Chihuahua: *admin.*, Mexico 27 30N 106 00W 46
Chikaskia: *riv.*, U.S.A. 37 00N 97 30W 95
Chilcotin: *riv.*, B.C., Canada 52 00N 123 15W 89
Childress: Tex., U.S.A. 34 25N 100 13W 95
Childwall: Mers., England 53 24N 02 54W 114
CHILE 19 52 106
Chile *Basin*: S.Pacific Ocean 35 00S 80 00W 5 19
Chile *Rise*: S.Pacific Ocean 42 00S 88 00W 5 19
Ch'ilien Shanmo *see* Qilianshanmai 39 30N 97 00E 36
Chililabombwe (Bancroft): Zambia 12 20S 27 52E 54
Chilin *see* Jilin 43 51N 126 33E 37 105
Chilin: *admin.* *see* Jilin 43 30N 127 00E 37
Chilka *Lake*: India 19 45N 85 15E 83
Chillán: Chile 36 37S 72 10W 52
Chillicothe: Mo., U.S.A. 39 47N 93 33W 98
Chillicothe: Ohio, U.S.A. 39 20N 82 59W 98
Chilliwack: B.C., Canada 49 10N 121 57W 89
Chiloé, *Isla*: Chile 42 30S 74 00W 52
Chilok (Khilok): U.S.S.R. 51 21N 110 28E 30
Chiltern *Hills*: England 51 45N 00 30W 59 112
Chilung (Kiirun): Taiwan 25 08N 121 44E 37
Chilwa (Shirwa), *Lake*: Malawi 15 15S 35 45E 55
Chimalhuacán: *mtn.*, Mexico 19 24N 98 57W 128
Chimborazo: *volc.*, Ecuador 01 28S 78 48W 48
Chimbote: Peru 09 04S 78 34W 49
Chimkent *see* Čimkent 42 18N 69 36E 29
Chimki: U.S.S.R. 55 56N 37 26E 80 119
Chimki *Reservoir*: U.S.S.R. 55 52N 37 28E 119
CHINA 12 36 84 106
Chinan *see* Jinan 36 40N 117 01E 36 84 105
Chinchaga: *riv.*, Alta., Canada 57 30N 119 00W 92
Chinchiang *see* Quanzhou 24 54N 118 35E 36 85
Chinchou *see* Jinzhou 41 07N 121 10E 37
Chindwin: *riv.*, Burma 25 45N 95 15E 12 35
Ch'ingchiang *see* Huaiyin 33 35N 119 04E 37 84
Chinghai *see* Qinghai 36 00N 96 00E 36
Chinghsi *see* Jingxi 23 08N 106 29E 36
Chingola: Zambia 12 32S 27 52E 54
Chingshih *see* Jinshi 29 40N 111 45E 36 85
Ch'ingshui: *riv.* *see* Qinshui 26 30N 109 00E 36 85
Ch'ingtao *see* Qindao 36 02N 120 29E 37 84 105
Chingtechen *see* Jingdezhen 29 16N 117 15E 36 85
Ch'ingyüan, Guangdong *see* Qingyuan 23 43N 113 00E 36 85
Ch'ingyüan, Hebei *see* Baoding 38 52N 115 29E 36 84
Chin *Hills*: Burma 22 30N 93 30E 35
Ch'inhuangtao *see* Qinhuangdao 39 56N 119 39E 37 84
Chining *see* Jining 35 24N 116 40E 36 84
Chiniot: Pakistan 31 40N 73 00E 82
Chinju: S.Korea 35 11N 128 05E 37
Chinmen (Quemoy): China 24 27N 118 23E 85
Chino: Calif., U.S.A. 34 01N 117 41W 127
Chinon: France 47 10N 00 15W 70
Chinsha: *riv.* *see* Jinsha 28 15N 99 30E 12 36
Chinsura: India 22 53N 88 24E 120
Chios *see* Khíos 38 23N 26 07E 79
Chipai *Lake*: Ont., Canada 52 45N 87 45W 93
Chipata (Fort Jameson): Zambia 13 39S 32 40E 54
Chippenham: Wilts., England 51 28N 02 07W 61
Chippewa: *riv.*, Wis., U.S.A. 44 30N 91 45W 98
Chippewa Falls: Wis., U.S.A. 44 56N 91 25W 98
Chipping Campden: Glos., England 52 03N 01 46W 60
Chipping Norton: Oxon., England 51 56N 01 32W 59
Chipping Ongar: Essex, England 51 43N 00 15E 59
Chipping Sodbury: Avon, England 51 33N 02 24W 61 113
Chiquihuite, Cerro: *mtns.*, Mexico 19 35N 99 07W 128
Chirchik *see* Čirčik 41 29N 69 35E 29
Chisel Lake: Man., Canada 54 52N 100 05W 93
Chisimaio *see* Kismayu 00 25S 42 31E 53
Chisone: *riv.*, Italy 45 00N 07 00E 71
Chistiān Mandi: Pakistan 29 44N 72 54E 82
Chita: U.S.S.R. *see* Čita 52 03N 113 30E 30

Chita, Sierra Nevada de *see* Sierra Nevada de Cocuy 06 25N 72 18W 48
Chitorgarh: India 24 54N 74 42E 82
Chitose: Hokkaidō, Japan 42 49N 141 39E 86
Chitose: Tokyō, Japan 35 34N 139 37E 121
Chitradurga: *admin.*, India 14 14N 76 24E 105
Chittagong: Bangladesh 22 20N 91 48E 35
Chiuchiang *see* Jiujiang 29 40N 116 04E 36 85
Chiuch'üan *see* Jiuquan 39 45N 98 34E 36
Chivilcoy: Argentina 34 55S 60 00W 52
Chkalov *see* Orenburg 51 54N 55 06E 29 81
Chmel'nickij: U.S.S.R. 49 25N 27 00E 78
Choctawhatchee: *riv.*, U.S.A. 30 45N 85 45W 101
Chodzież: Poland 53 00N 16 55E 73
Chōfu: Japan 35 39N 139 33E 121
Chogo: Japan 35 24N 139 28E 121
Choisy-le-Roi: France 48 46N 02 25E 117
Chojnice: Poland 53 30N 17 30E 73
Chojniki: U.S.S.R. 51 53N 29 56E 80
Choke *Mountains*: Ethiopia 11 00N 37 30E 53
Cholet: France 47 04N 00 53W 70
Cholm: U.S.S.R. 57 09N 31 11E 80
Chomedey: Qué., Canada 45 32N 73 44W 122
Chomu: India 27 09N 75 44E 82
Chomutov: Czechoslovakia 50 28N 13 25E 73
Chongan: China 27 45N 117 59E 85
Chonghai: *lake*, China 39 56N 116 22E 121
Ch'ŏngjin: N.Korea 41 47N 129 50E 37 86 105
Ch'ŏngju: S.Korea 39 41N 125 13E 37
Chongming: China 31 38N 121 31E 84
Chongqing (Chungking): China 29 35N 106 30E 36 85 105
Chongyang: China 29 33N 114 02E 85
Chongyi: China 25 44N 114 29E 85
Chonzie, Ben: *mtn.*, Perth., Scotland 56 26N 03 59W 65
Chonzuo: China 22 30N 107 32E 85
Chŏnju: S.Korea 35 49N 127 08E 37
Chonos *Archipelago*: Chile 45 00S 74 00W 52
Cho Oyu: *mtn.*, China/Nepal 28 06N 86 39E 83
Chop'or: *riv.*, U.S.S.R. 50 30N 42 00E 80
Chorley: Lancs., England 53 40N 02 38W 63 114
Chorošovo: U.S.S.R. 55 47N 37 28E 119
Chorzów: Poland 50 19N 18 56E 105
Chōshi: Japan 35 44N 144 50E 86
Chotimsk: U.S.S.R. 53 26N 32 35E 80
Chotin: U.S.S.R. 48 29N 26 30E 78
Chott Djerid: *salt lake*, Tunisia 33 45N 08 30E 20 56
Chott Melrhir: *salt lake*, Algeria 34 00N 06 30E 20 56
Chovd (Džargalant): Mongolia 48 01N 91 39E 30
Chovrino: U.S.S.R. 55 52N 37 30E 119
Chövsgöl, *Lake*: Mongolia 51 00N 100 30E 30
Christchurch: Dorset, England 50 44N 01 45W 61
Christchurch: S.I., New Zealand 43 33S 172 40E 37 87
Christina: *riv.*, Alta., Canada 56 00N 110 45W 92
Christmas *Island*: Indian Ocean 10 30S 105 40E 1 14 107
Christmas *Island*: N.Pacific Ocean 02 00N 157 30W 4
Christmas *Ridge*: N.Pacific Ocean 10 00N 165 00W 4
Chromtau: U.S.S.R. 50 17N 58 27E 81
Chrudim: Czechoslovakia 49 58N 15 50E 73
Chu *see* Ču 44 30N 72 45E 8 29
Chuādānga: Bangladesh 23 38N 88 52E 83
Chubut: *admin.*, Argentina 44 15S 69 00W 52
Chubut: *riv.*, Argentina 43 00S 69 30W 52
Chuchou *see* Zhuzhou 27 50N 113 07E 36 85
Chudleigh: Devon, England 50 36N 03 45W 61
Chugach *Mountains*: Alaska, U.S.A. 61 00N 145 00W 16
Chūgoku-sanchi: *mtns.*, Japan 34 45N 132 30E 86
Ch'ühsien *see* Quxian 28 58N 118 52E 36 85
Chukchi *Sea*: Arctic Ocean 67 30N 174 00W 22
Chukehu: *lake*, China 31 30N 87 45E 83
Chulmleigh: Devon, England 50 55N 03 52W 61
Chulucanas: Peru 05 08S 80 10W 48
Chumphon: Thailand 10 30N 99 11E 35
Chuna: *riv.*, *see* Čuna 57 30N 97 30E 30
Chun'an: China 29 38N 119 01E 85
Ch'ŭnch'ŏn: S.Korea 37 52N 127 43E 37
Chunghua: Taiwan 24 02N 120 32E 37 85
Ch'ungju: S.Korea 36 58N 127 58E 37
Chungking *see* Chongqing 29 35N 106 30E 36 85 105
Chungli: Taiwan 24 57N 121 13E 37
Chungshan *see* Zhongshan 22 31N 113 22E 36 85
Chungyang Shanmo: *mtns.*, Taiwan 23 45N 121 30E 37
Chur: Switzerland 46 52N 09 32E 71
Church: Lancs., England 53 46N 02 24W 114
Churchill: Man., Canada 58 45N 94 00W 42 93
Churchill: *riv.*, Man., Canada 57 00N 96 00W 42 93
Churchill: *riv.*, Nfld., Canada 53 15N 63 00W 16 97
Churchill, *Cape*: Man., Canada 58 47N 93 08W 42 93
Churchill *Falls*: Nfld., Canada 53 35N 64 18W 44 97
Churchill *Lake*: Sask., Canada 56 00N 108 15W 92
Churchill *Peak*: B.C., Canada 58 09N 125 04W 88
Church Stretton: Salop, England 52 32N 02 49W 60
Churchtown: Mers., England 53 40N 02 58W 114
Churia *Range*: Nepal 28 00N 83 00E 83
Churn: *riv.*, Glos., England 51 30N 01 45W 61
Churu: India 28 18N 75 00E 82
Churubusco: Mexico 19 21N 99 08W 128
Chusovoy *see* Čusovoj 58 17N 57 49E 81 105
Chuxian: China 32 19N 118 20E 84
Chvalynsk: U.S.S.R. 52 30N 48 07E 81
Chvojnaja: U.S.S.R. 58 54N 34 32E 80
Ciampino: Italy 41 48N 12 36E 116
Cicero: Ill., U.S.A. 41 50N 87 46W 124
Ciénaga: Colombia 11 01N 74 15W 48
Cienfuegos: Cuba 22 09N 80 27W 47
Cili: China 29 25N 110 58E 85
Cimarron: *riv.*, U.S.A. 36 15N 98 30W 95
Čimkent (Chimkent): U.S.S.R. 42 18N 69 36E 29
Ciml'ansk: U.S.S.R. 47 38N 42 04E 80
Ciml'anskoje Vodochranilišče: *res.*, U.S.S.R. 48 00N 43 00E 28 80
Cincinnati: Ohio, U.S.A. 39 10N 84 30W 45 98
Cinderford: Glos., England 51 50N 02 29W 113
Cinisello Balsamo: Italy 45 33N 09 13E 116
Čirčik (Chirchik): U.S.S.R. 41 29N 69 35E 29
Čirčik: *riv.*, U.S.S.R. 41 30N 70 00E 29
Circumferential *Highway*: Mass., U.S.A. 42 15N 71 15W 122
Cirencester: Glos., England 51 44N 01 59W 61
Čistopol': U.S.S.R. 55 21N 50 37E 81
Čita (Chita): U.S.S.R. 52 03N 113 30E 30
Cité de Lavéra: France 43 23N 05 02E 107
Citlaltépetl: *volc.*, Mexico 19 01N 97 16W 17 46
Città del Vaticano (Vatican City) 41 54N 12 27E 116
City *Island*: N.Y., U.S.A. 40 51N 73 47W 123
Ciudad Bolívar: Venezuela 08 06N 63 36W 48
Ciudad Camargo: Mexico 27 40N 105 10W 104
Ciudad de Guatemala (Guatemala): Guatemala 14 38N 90 31W 46
Ciudad del Carmen: Mexico 18 38N 91 50W 46
Ciudad de México (Mexico City): Mexico 19 24N 99 09W 46 128
Ciudadela: Argentina 34 38S 58 32W 128
Ciudad Guayana (San Tomé de Guayana): Venezuela 08 22N 62 37W 48
Ciudad Juárez: Mexico 31 42N 106 29W 46 95
Ciudad Madero: Mexico 22 16N 97 50W 106
Ciudad Obregón: Mexico 27 28N 109 59W 46
Ciudad Real: Spain 38 59N 03 55W 77
Ciudad Satélite: Mexico 19 31N 99 14W 128
Ciudad Trujillo *see* Santo Domingo 18 30N 69 57W 47
Ciudad Victoria: Mexico 23 44N 99 08W 46
Civitavecchia: Italy 42 05N 11 47E 79
Civray: France 46 09N 00 18E 70
Čkalovsk: U.S.S.R. 56 46N 43 16E 80
Clabecq: Belgium 50 41N 04 13E 105
Clach Leathad: *mtn.*, Argyll., Scotland 56 36N 04 51W 64
Clacton-on-Sea: Essex., England 51 48N 01 09E 59
Claire, *Lake*: Alta., Canada 58 30N 112 00W 92
Clairton: Pa., U.S.A. 40 17N 79 56W 125
Clár, *Loch nan*: Suther., Scotland 58 15N 04 00W 65
Clara: Offaly, Irish Republic 53 20N 07 36W 67
Clare: *admin.*, Irish Republic 52 45N 09 00W 67
Clare: *riv.*, Gal., Irish Republic 53 15N 09 00W 67
Clarecastle: Clare, Irish Republic 52 49N 08 57W 67
Clare *Island*: Mayo, Irish Republic 53 45N 10 00W 66
Claremont: Calif., U.S.A. 34 06N 117 43W 127
Claremont: N.H., U.S.A. 43 23N 72 21W 99
Claremorris: Mayo, Irish Republic 53 44N 08 59W 66
Claresholm: Alta., Canada 50 02N 113 33W 92
Clarinda: Iowa, U.S.A. 40 45N 95 01W 94
Clarion *Fracture Zone*: N.Pacific Ocean 17 00N 130 00W 5

Clarkdale: Ariz., U.S.A. 34 46N 112 03W 91
Clarke City: Qué., Canada 50 11N 66 39W 97
Clark Fork: *riv.*, Mont., U.S.A. 47 30N 115 15W 90
Clark Fork: *riv.*, Wyo., U.S.A. 45 00N 109 00W 94
Clark Hill *Reservoir*: U.S.A. 33 40N 82 12W 101
Clark *Point*: Ont., Canada 44 04N 81 46W 98
Clarksburg: W.Va., U.S.A. 39 16N 80 22W 99
Clarksdale: Miss., U.S.A. 34 12N 90 35W 100
Clarkston: Wash., U.S.A. 46 25N 117 03W 90
Clarksville: Tenn., U.S.A. 36 31N 87 21W 101
Clawson: Mich., U.S.A. 42 31N 83 08W 125
Clay Cross: Derby., England 53 10N 01 24W 58
Claydon: Suff., England 52 06N 01 07E 59
Clayton: N.Mex., U.S.A. 36 27N 103 11W 95
Clear, *Cape*: Cork, Irish Republic 51 26N 09 31W 67
Clear Fork: *riv.*, Tex., U.S.A. 32 45N 99 00W 95
Clear *Island*: Cork, Irish Republic 51 15N 09 15W 67
Clear *Lake*: Calif., U.S.A. 39 00N 122 50W 91
Clearwater: Fla., U.S.A. 27 57N 82 48W 101
Clearwater: *riv.*, Canada 56 45N 109 30W 92
Clearwater: *riv.*, Idaho, U.S.A. 46 00N 115 30W 90
Clearwater *Lake*: Qué., Canada 56 00N 74 30W 96
Cleator Moor: Cumbria, England 54 31N 03 32W 62
Cleburne: Tex., U.S.A. 32 21N 97 23W 95
Cleckheaton: W.Yorks., England 53 44N 01 43W 115
Cleethorpes: Humb., England 53 34N 00 02W 63
Clent *Hills*: Here. & Worcs., England 52 15N 02 00W 115
Cleobury Mortimer: Salop, England 52 23N 02 29W 59
Clermont-Ferrand: France 45 47N 03 05E 26 71
Clevedon: Avon, England 51 27N 02 51W 61 113
Cleveland: Miss., U.S.A. 33 45N 90 43W 100
Cleveland: Ohio, U.S.A. 41 30N 81 41W 45 99 104
Cleveland: Tenn., U.S.A. 35 10N 84 51W 101
Cleveland: Tex., U.S.A. 30 21N 95 05W 100
Cleveland: *admin.*, England 54 30N 01 00W 63
Cleveland *Hills*: N.Yorks., England 54 15N 01 00W 63
Cleveland *National Forest*: Calif., U.S.A. 33 45N 117 30W 127
Cleveleys: Lancs., England 53 53N 03 03W 63 114
Clew *Bay*: Mayo, Irish Republic 53 45N 09 45W 66
Clichy: France 48 54N 02 19E 117
Clifden: Gal., Irish Republic 53 29N 10 01W 66
Clifton: Avon, England 51 29N 02 37W 113
Clifton: Ariz., U.S.A. 33 03N 109 18W 95
Clifton: N.J., U.S.A. 40 52N 74 09W 123
Climax: Colo., U.S.A. 39 22N 106 11W 94
Clingmans Dome: *mtn.*, U.S.A. 35 34N 83 29W 101
Clinton: B.C., Canada 51 05N 121 35W 89
Clinton: Iowa, U.S.A. 41 51N 90 12W 98
Clinton: N.C., U.S.A. 35 00N 78 20W 101
Clinton: Okla., U.S.A. 35 31N 98 58W 95
Clinton: *riv.*, Mich., U.S.A. 42 34N 82 51W 125
Clipperton *Fracture Zone*: N.Pacific Ocean 07 00N 125 00W 5
Clipperton *Island*: N.Pacific Ocean 10 20N 109 13W 5
Clisham: *mtn.*, Inv., Scotland 57 58N 06 50W 64
Clitheroe: Lancs., England 53 53N 02 23W 63 114
Cloghan: Offaly, Irish Republic 53 13N 07 53W 67
Clogher: Tyr., N.Ireland 54 25N 07 10W 66
Clogher *Head*: Louth, Irish Republic 53 48N 06 13W 66
Clonakilty: Cork, Irish Republic 51 37N 08 54W 67
Cloncurry: Qld., Australia 20 41S 140 30E 41
Clondalkin: Dublin, Irish Republic 53 19N 06 24W 67
Clones: Monaghan, Irish Republic 54 11N 07 14W 66
Clonmel: Tip., Irish Republic 52 21N 07 42W 67
Clontarf: Dublin, Irish Republic 53 22N 06 12W 67
Cloppenburg: W.Germany 52 52N 08 02E 72
Cloquet: Minn., U.S.A. 46 39N 92 27W 98
Clovelly: Devon, England 51 00N 04 24W 61
Cloverdale: Calif., U.S.A. 38 46N 123 01W 91
Clovis: Calif., U.S.A. 36 49N 119 42W 91
Clovis: N.Mex., U.S.A. 34 24N 103 12W 95
Cluanie, *Loch*: Scotland 57 00N 05 00W 64
Cluj: Romania 46 47N 23 37E 27 78
Clun: *riv.*, Salop, England 52 15N 02 45W 60
Clun *Forest*: Salop, England 52 15N 03 00W 60
Clwyd: *admin.*, Wales 53 00N 03 15W 60
Clwyd: *riv.*, Clwyd, Wales 53 00N 03 15W 60
Clwydian *Range*: Clwyd, Wales 53 00N 03 15W 60
Clyde: *riv.*, Scotland 55 30N 03 45W 62 113
Clyde, Firth of: *est.*, Scotland 55 45N 05 00W 62 113
Clydebank: Dunb., Scotland 55 54N 04 24W 62 113
Clydesdale: *val.*, Lan., Scotland 55 30N 03 45W 113
Cna: *riv.*, U.S.S.R. 54 15N 42 00E 80
Cnoc Moy: *mtn.*, Argyll., Scotland 55 23N 05 46W 62
Coacalco: Mexico 19 38N 99 06W 128
Coahuila: *admin.*, Mexico 27 00N 102 00W 46
Coal: *riv.*, Canada 60 45N 127 45W 88
Coaldale: Alta., Canada 49 45N 112 38W 92
Coalisland: Tyr., N.Ireland 54 33N 06 42W 66
Coal River: B.C., Canada 59 38N 126 58W 88
Coalville: Leics., England 52 44N 01 20W 58 115
Coast *Mountains*: B.C., Canada 50 30N 124 00W 17 42 89
Coast *Ranges*: U.S.A. 16 43 90
Coatbridge: Lan., Scotland 55 52N 04 01W 62 113
Coaticook: Qué., Canada 45 08N 71 44W 96
Coats *Island*: N.W.T., Canada 62 30N 82 30W 44
Coats Land: *reg.*, Antarctica 77 00N 28 00W 24
Coatzacoalcos: Mexico 18 09N 94 25W 46
Cobalt: Ont., Canada 47 24N 79 41W 99
Cobalt: Idaho, U.S.A. 45 06N 114 14W 90
Cobh: Cork, Irish Republic 51 51N 08 17W 67
Cobham: Surrey, England 51 20N 00 25W 112
Cobham: *riv.*, Canada 53 00N 94 45W 93
Cobija: Bolivia 11 02S 68 44W 49
Cobourg: Ont., Canada 43 58N 78 11W 99
Coburg: W.Germany 50 15N 10 58E 73
Cochabamba: Bolivia 17 24S 66 09W 49
Cochrane: Ont., Canada 49 04N 81 02W 44 99
Cochrane: *riv.*, Man., Canada 58 15N 101 00W 92
Cockatoo *Island*: W.A., Australia 16 06S 123 37E 105
Cockermouth: Cumbria, England 54 40N 03 21W 62
Cock of Arran: *pt.*, Bute., Scotland 55 42N 05 16W 62
Coco: *riv.*, Honduras/Nicaragua 14 45N 84 00W 47
Cocoa: Fla., U.S.A. 28 21N 80 46W 101
Cocos *Basin*: Indian Ocean 03 00S 95 00E 1
Cocos *Islands*: Indian Ocean 11 45S 97 00E 1 13
Cocos *Ridge*: N.Pacific Ocean 05 00N 87 00W 5 18
Cocuy, Sierra Nevada de: *mtn.*, Colombia 06 25N 72 18W 48
Cod, *Cape*: Mass., U.S.A. 42 00N 70 00W 17 45 99
Codshall: Staffs., England 52 38N 02 12W 115
Cody: Wyo., U.S.A. 44 32N 109 03W 94
Coe, Glen: *val.*, Argyll., Scotland 56 30N 04 45W 64
Cœuilly: France 48 49N 02 33E 117
Coeur d'Alene: Idaho, U.S.A. 47 41N 116 46W 42 90
Coffeyville: Kans., U.S.A. 37 02N 95 37W 95
Cognac: France 45 42N 00 19W 70
Cóigeach, Rubha: *cape*, R. & Crom., Scotland 58 06N 05 25W 64
Coimbatore: India 11 00N 76 57E 34
Coimbra: Portugal 40 12N 08 25W 26 76
Čojbalsan (Bajan Tümen): Mongolia 48 04N 114 30E 30
Colatina: Brazil 19 32S 40 37W 51
Colbeck, *Cape*: Antarctica 77 00S 158 00W 25
Colby: Kans., U.S.A. 39 24N 101 03W 94
Colchester: Essex, England 51 54N 00 54E 59
Cold Lake: Alta., Canada 55 08N 110 06W 92
Coldstream: Ber., Scotland 55 39N 02 15W 63
Coleford: Glos., England 51 48N 02 37W 61
Coleraine: Lon., N.Ireland 55 08N 06 40W 66
Coleshill: War., England 52 30N 01 42W 115
Colfax: Wash., U.S.A. 46 53N 117 22W 90
Colgrave *Sound*: Shet. Is., Scotland 60 30N 00 45W 65
Coll: *is.*, Argyll, Scotland 56 30N 06 30W 64
College Park: Md., U.S.A. 39 00N 76 57W 122
Collingwood: S.I., New Zealand 40 41S 172 41E 87
Colma: Calif., U.S.A. 37 42N 122 29W 126
Colmar: France 48 05N 07 21E 71
Coln: *riv.*, Glos., England 51 45N 01 45W 61
Colne: Lancs., England 53 52N 02 09W 63 114
Colne: *riv.*, Essex, England 52 00N 00 30E 59
Colne *Point*: Essex, England 51 46N 01 04W 59
Cologne *see* Köln 50 56N 06 57E 26 72 107 119
Cologno Monzese: Italy 45 32N 09 17E 116
Colomb Béchar *see* Béchar 31 35N 02 17W 56
Colombes: France 48 55N 02 14E 117
COLOMBIA 05 15N 74 00W 18 48 104 106
Colombo: Sri Lanka 06 55N 79 52E 34
Colón: Panama 09 21N 79 54W 46 106
Colonelganj: India 27 07N 81 42E 83
Colonsay: *is.*, Argyll., Scotland 56 00N 06 00W 64

Types of map: Ocean pp. 1-5; Physical pp. 6-25; Human pp. 26-57; Topographic pp. 58-101; World pp. 102-111; Urban pp. 112-128.

Colorado: *admin.*, U.S.A.		43 94
Colorado: *riv.*, Argentina 38 30S 66 30W		19 52
Colorado: *riv.*, Mexico/U.S.A. 33 30N 114 30W		17 43 91
Colorado: *riv.*, Tex., U.S.A. 29 15N 96 15W		95
Colorado *National Monument*: Colo., U.S.A. 39 00N 108 45W		94
Colorado *Plateaus*: Ariz., U.S.A. 36 30N 111 00W		17 43 91
Colorado Springs: Colo., U.S.A. 38 50N 104 49W		43 94
Columbia: Mo., U.S.A. 38 58N 92 20W		98
Columbia: S.C., U.S.A. 34 00N 81 00W		45 101
Columbia: Tenn., U.S.A. 35 37N 87 02W		101
Columbia: *riv.*, Canada/U.S.A. 46 15N 123 45W		16 42 90
Columbia, District of: *admin.*, U.S.A. 38 45N 77 00W		45 122
Columbia Falls: Mont., U.S.A. 48 23N 114 11W		90
Columbia *Mountains*: B.C., Canada 51 00N 119 00W		42 89
Columbus: Ga., U.S.A. 32 28N 84 59W		45 101
Columbus: Ind., U.S.A. 39 12N 85 57W		98
Columbus: Kans., U.S.A. 37 10N 94 50W		95
Columbus: Miss., U.S.A. 33 30N 88 25W		100
Columbus: Nebr., U.S.A. 41 26N 97 22W		94
Columbus: Ohio, U.S.A. 39 59N 83 03W		45 98
Colville: Wash., U.S.A. 48 33N 117 54W		90
Colvos *Passage*: Wash., U.S.A. 47 15N 122 30W		126
Colwyn Bay: Clwyd, Wales 53 18N 03 43W		60
Combe Martin: Devon, England 51 13N 04 02W		61
Comber: Down, N.Ireland 54 33N 05 45W		66
Comeragh *Mountains*: Wat., Irish Republic 52 15N 07 30W		67
Comilla: Bangladesh 23 28N 91 10E		35 83
Comitán de Domínguez: Mexico 16 15N 92 08W		46
Communism *Peak*: U.S.S.R. 38 57N 72 01E		29
Como: Italy 45 49N 09 06E		71 116
Como, *Lago di*: Italy 46 00N 09 15E		71
Commodoro Rivadavia: Argentina 45 50S 67 30W		52
Comoé: *riv.*, Ivory Coast 05 45N 03 30W		57
Comorin, *Cape*: India 08 04N 77 35E		34
Comoro *Islands*: Indian Ocean 12 15S 44 15E		1 21
Compiègne: France 49 25N 02 50E		71
Compton: Calif., U.S.A. 33 55N 118 14W		127
Conakry: Guinea 09 30N 13 43W		57
Concarneau: France 47 53N 03 55W		70
Concepción: Tucumán, Argentina 27 20S 65 35W		49
Concepción: Chile 36 50S 73 03W		52
Concepción: Paraguay 23 22S 57 26W		51
Concepción del Uruguay: Argentina 32 30S 58 15W		52
Conception, *Point*: Calif., U.S.A. 34 27N 120 28W		17 91
Conception *Bay*: Nfld., Canada 47 30N 53 00W		97
Conchas *Reservoir*: N.Mex., U.S.A. 35 23N 104 11W		95
Concho: *riv.*, Tex., U.S.A. 31 30N 100 00W		95
Concord: Calif., U.S.A. 37 59N 122 04W		126
Concord: Mass., U.S.A. 42 28N 71 17W		122
Concord: N.C., U.S.A. 35 25N 80 34W		101
Concord: N.H., U.S.A. 43 13N 71 34W		99
Concordia: Argentina 31 25S 58 00W		52
Concordia: Kans., U.S.A. 39 34N 97 40W		94
Condom: France 43 58N 00 23E		70
Conecuh: *riv.*, Ala., U.S.A. 31 30N 86 15W		101
Coney *Island*: N.Y., U.S.A. 40 35N 73 59W		123
Conflans-Ste. Honorine: France 49 00N 02 05E		117
Conghua: China 23 36N 113 32E		85
Congleton: Ches., England 53 10N 02 13W		58 114
CONGO 00 30S 16 00E		21 54
Congo, Rep. of, *see* Zaïre 00 00 24 45E		21 54 107
Congo (Zaïre): *riv.*, Congo/Zaïre 01 30N 23 00E		21 54
Congo *Basin*: Zaïre 01 00S 21 15E		21 54
Congonhas: Brazil 20 30S 43 52W		104
Congost: *riv.*, Spain 41 30N 02 15E		116
Congyang: China 30 41N 117 14E		85
Conisbrough: S.Yorks., England 53 29N 01 13W		63
Conjeeveram *see* Kānchipuram 12 50N 79 44E		34
Conjuror *Bay*: N.W.T., Canada 65 45N 118 00W		88
Conn, *Lough*: Mayo, Irish Republic 54 00N 09 15W		66
Connah's Quay: Clwyd, Wales 53 13N 03 03W		60 114
Connecticut: *admin.*, U.S.A. 41 30N 72 45W		45 99
Connecticut: *riv.*, U.S.A. 44 00N 72 00W		44 99
Connemara: *geog. reg.*, Gal., Irish Republic 53 30N 09 45W		66
Connersville: Ind., U.S.A. 39 39N 85 09W		98
Conrad: Mont., U.S.A. 48 10N 111 57W		90
Conroe: Tex., U.S.A. 30 19N 95 27W		100

Consett: Dur., England 54 51N 01 49W		63 105
Conshohocken: Pa., U.S.A. 40 05N 75 18W		122
Constance *see* Konstanz 47 40N 09 10E		71
Constanţa: Romania 44 10N 28 40E		27 79
Constantine: Algeria 36 22N 06 40E		56 77
Constitución: Argentina 34 38S 58 24W		128
Constitución: Chile 35 20S 72 28W		52
Contact: Nev., U.S.A. 41 46N 114 45W		90
Contai: India 21 49N 87 46E		83
Conteville: France 49 25N 00 24E		117
Contra Costa *Canal*: Calif., U.S.A. 37 55N 122 03W		126
Convent: La., U.S.A. 29 57N 90 49W		106
Conway: Ark., U.S.A. 35 05N 92 26W		100
Conway: S.C., U.S.A. 33 51N 79 04W		101
Conway: Gwyn., Wales 53 17N 03 50W		60
Cooch Behar: India 26 18N 89 32E		83
Cook, *Cape*: B.C., Canada 50 07N 127 55W		89
Cook, *Mount*: S.I., New Zealand 43 37S 170 08E		15 37 87
Cook *Islands*: S.Pacific Ocean 20 00S 158 00W		5
Cookstown: Tyr., N.Ireland 54 39N 06 45W		66
Cook *Strait*: New Zealand 41 15S 174 30E		37 87
Coolgardie: W.A., Australia 31 01S 121 12E		40
Coolidge: Ariz., U.S.A. 32 59N 111 31W		91
Coolidge *Dam*: Ariz., U.S.A. 33 12N 110 32W		91
Cooper: *riv.*, N.J., U.S.A. 39 45N 75 00W		122
Coosa: *riv.*, U.S.A. 33 00N 86 30W		101
Cootehill: Cavan, Irish Republic 54 04N 07 05W		66
Copenhagen *see* København 55 43N 12 34E		26 75 105
Coppull: Lancs., England 53 38N 02 39W		114
Coquet: *riv.*, Northumb., England 55 15N 01 45W		63
Coquilhatville *see* Mbandaka 00 04N 18 16E		54
Coquille: Oreg., U.S.A. 43 11N 124 11W		90
Coquimbo: Chile 29 57S 71 25W		52
Coquitlam: *riv.*, B.C., Canada 49 15N 122 45W		126
Coral Gables: Fla., U.S.A. 25 44N 80 17W		101
Coral Rapids: Ont., Canada 50 13N 81 41W		96
Coral *Sea* 19 00S 150 00E		4 41
Corbeil-Essonnes: France 48 37N 02 29E		117
Corbetta: Italy 45 28N 08 55E		116
Corbières: *mtns.*, France 43 45N 02 30E		70
Corbridge: Northumb., England 54 58N 02 01W		63
Corby: Northants., England 52 29N 00 40W		58 105
Cordele: Ga., U.S.A. 31 59N 83 49W		101
Cordillera Cantábrica: *ra.*, Spain 43 00N 05 00W		77
Cordillera Central (Central Cordillera): *ra.*, Colombia 07 30N 75 15W		48
Cordillera Central: *ra.*, Portugal/Spain 40 00N 06 00W		77
Cordillera de las Cruces: *ra.*, Mexico 19 24N 99 21W		128
Cordillera de los Andes: *ra.*, S.America 05 00N 75 45W		18 48
Cordillera de Mérida: *ra.*, Venezuela 08 30N 71 00W		48
Cordillera Occidental (Western Cordillera): *ra.*, Colombia 05 00N 76 00W		18 48
Cordillera Oriental (Eastern Cordillera): *ra.*, Colombia 05 00N 73 30W		48
Cordilleras Béticas: *ra.*, Spain 37 30N 02 30W		77
Córdoba: Argentina 31 25S 64 11W		52
Córdoba: Mexico 18 53N 96 56W		46
Córdoba: Spain 37 53N 04 46W		26 77
Córdoba: *admin.*, Argentina 32 00S 63 45W		52
Córdoba, Sierra de: *ra.*, Argentina 31 45S 64 45W		52
Cordova: Ill., U.S.A. 41 42N 90 19W		98
Corfu *see* Kérkira 39 36N 19 56E		79
Corfu: *is.*, *see* Kérkira 39 30N 19 45E		79
Corinth: Greece *see* Kórinthos 37 56N 22 55E		79
Corinth: Miss., U.S.A. 34 56N 88 31W		100
Corinth, *Gulf of*: Greece 38 00N 22 30E		79
Corinto: Brazil 18 21S 44 27W		51
Cork: Cork, Irish Republic 51 54N 08 28W		26 67
Cork: *admin.*, Irish Rep. 52 00N 08 45W		67
Cork *Harbour*: Cork, Irish Republic 51 45N 08 15W		67
Çorlu: Turkey 41 11N 27 49E		79
Cormeilles-en-Parisis: France 48 58N 02 13E		117
Cornellá: Spain 41 21N 02 04E		116
Corner Brook: Nfld., Canada 48 58N 57 58W		44 97
Cornigliano Ligure: Italy 44 25N 08 53E		105
Cornwall: Ont., Canada 45 02N 74 44W		99
Cornwall: *admin.*, England 50 15N 05 00W		61
Cornwall, *Cape*: Corn., England 50 07N 05 44W		61
Coro: Venezuela 11 27N 69 41W		48
Coromandel *Coast*: India 13 00N 80 15E		34

Types of map: Ocean pp. 1-5; Physical pp. 6-25; Human pp. 26-57; Topographic pp. 58-101; World pp. 102-111; Urban pp. 112-128.

Coromandel *Peninsula*: N.I., New Zealand 37 00S 175 45E 87
Corona: Calif., U.S.A. 33 53N 117 34W 127
Coronado *Bay*: Costa Rica 11 30N 83 45W 47
Coronel Honda: *riv.*, Argentina 34 21S 58 32W 128
Coronel Oviedo: Paraguay 25 25S 56 27W 51
Coronel Pringles: Argentina 37 56S 61 25W 52
Coropuna: *mtn.*, Peru 15 30S 72 41W 49
Corpus Christi: Tex., U.S.A. 27 47N 97 26W 43 100 106
Corpus Christi *Bay*: Tex., U.S.A. 27 45N 97 15W 100
Corraun *Peninsula*: Mayo, Irish Republic 53 45N 09 45W 66
Correen *Hills*: Aber., Scotland 57 15N 02 30W 65
Corrib, *Lough*: Gal., Irish Rep. 53 15N 09 00W 66
Corrientes: Argentina 27 30S 58 48W 52
Corrientes: *admin.*, Argentina 29 00S 58 00W 51
Corrientes, *Cape*: Mexico 20 25N 105 42W 17 46
Corse (Corsica): *is. & French admin.*, Mediterranean Sea 42 00N 09 00E 6 26 77
Corse, *Cap*: Corse, France 43 00N 09 23E 77
Corsham: Wilts., England 51 26N 02 11W 61
Corsicana: Tex., U.S.A. 32 06N 96 28W 100
Corsico: Italy 45 26N 09 07E 116
Corte: Corsica 42 18N 09 09E 77
Cortez: Colo., U.S.A. 37 21N 108 35W 95
Corumbá: Brazil 19 01S 57 39W 51
Corunna: Spain *see* La Coruña 43 22N 08 24W 26 77
Corvallis: Oreg., U.S.A. 44 34N 123 16W 90
Corve: *riv.*, Salop, England 52 30N 02 30W 60
Corwen: Clwyd, Wales 52 59N 03 22W 60
Coryton: Essex, England 51 32N 00 31E 59 112
Cos: *is. see* Kos 36 45N 27 00E 79
Cosenza: Italy 39 17N 16 16E 79
Cosne-sur-Loire: France 47 25N 02 55E 71
Cossipur: India 22 37N 88 22E 120
Costa Brava: *coast*, Spain 41 45N 03 30E 77
Costa del Sol: *coast*, Spain 36 30N 04 00W 77
Costa Masnaga: Italy 45 45N 09 15E 116
COSTA RICA 10 00N 84 00W 17 47
Costermansville *see* Bukavu 02 30S 28 49E 54
Cotabato: Philippines 07 14N 124 15E 39
Cotagaita: Bolivia 20 50S 65 41W 49
Côte d'Azur: *coast*, France 43 15N 07 00E 71
Côte d'Or: *geog. reg.*, France 47 00N 04 45E 71
Cotentin: *geog. reg.*, France 49 15N 01 30W 70
Cothi: *riv.*, Dyfed, Wales 51 45N 04 00W 60
Cotonou: Dahomey 06 24N 02 31E 57
Cotopaxi: *volc.*, Ecuador 00 40S 78 28W 18 48
Cotswolds: *hills*, England 51 45N 01 45W 61
Cottage Grove: Oreg., U.S.A. 43 48N 123 03W 90
Cottbus: E.Germany 51 43N 14 21E 73 78
Cottbus: *admin.*, E.Germany 51 30N 14 00E 73
Cottenham: Cambs., England 52 18N 00 09E 59
Cottingham: Humb., England 53 47N 02 24W 63
Coulonge: *riv.*, Qué., Canada 46 15N 76 45W 99
Council Bluffs: Iowa, U.S.A. 41 14N 95 54W 43 94
Coupar Angus: Perth., Scotland 56 33N 03 17W 65
Courtenay: B.C., Canada 49 41N 125 00W 89
Courtmacsherry *Bay*: Cork, Irish Republic 51 30N 08 30W 67
Courtrai *see* Kortrijk: 50 50N 03 17E 72
Coutances: France 49 03N 01 29W 70
Coutras: France 45 02N 00 07W 70
Coventry: W.Mid., England 52 25N 01 30W 26 59 115
Coventry *Canal*: England 52 30N 01 30W 115
Covilhã: Portugal 40 17N 07 30W 77
Covington: Ga., U.S.A. 33 35N 83 52W 101
Covington: Ky., U.S.A. 39 04N 84 30W 99
Covington: Va., U.S.A. 37 48N 80 01W 101
Cowan *Creek*: N.S.W., Australia 33 37S 151 13E 120
Cowdenbeath: Fife, Scotland 56 07N 03 21W 65
Cowes: I. of W., England 50 45N 01 18W 59
Cowley: Oxon., England 51 44N 01 14W 59
Coyoacán: Mexico 19 20N 99 10W 128
Coyote *Creek*: Calif., U.S.A. 33 45N 118 00W 127
Cozad: Nebr., U.S.A. 40 52N 99 59W 94
Cozie, *Alpi*: France/Italy 44 45N 07 00E 71
Cracow *see* Kraków 50 04N 19 57E 27 78 105
Craig: Alaska, U.S.A. 55 29N 133 09W 89
Craig: Colo., U.S.A. 40 31N 107 33W 94
Craignure: Argyll., Scotland 56 28N 05 42W 64

Crail: Fife, Scotland 56 16N 02 38W 65
Craiova: Romania 44 18N 23 47E 27 79
Cranberry Portage: Man., Canada 54 36N 101 22W 92
Cranbrook: B.C., Canada 49 29N 115 48W 90
Cranbrook: Kent, England 51 06N 00 33E 59
Cranleigh: Surrey, England 51 09N 00 30W 59
Cranwell: Lincs., England 53 02N 00 30W 58
Crater *Lake*: Oreg., U.S.A. 42 45N 122 00W 90
Crater Lake *National Park*: Oreg., U.S.A. 42 45N 122 00W 90
Craters of the Moon *National Monument*: Idaho, U.S.A. 43 15N 113 15W 90
Crato: Brazil 07 14S 39 23W 50
Crawfordsville: Ind., U.S.A. 40 03N 86 54W 98
Crawley: W.Sussex, England 51 07N 00 12W 59
Crediton: Devon, England 50 47N 03 39W 61
Cree: *riv.*, Sask., Canada 58 00N 106 00W 92
Cree: *riv.*, Scotland 55 00N 04 30W 62
Creede: Colo., U.S.A. 37 51N 106 56W 95
Cree *Lake*: Sask., Canada 57 30N 106 30W 92
Creil: France 49 16N 02 29E 70
Crema: Italy 45 22N 09 41E 71
Cremona: Italy 45 08N 10 01E 71
Cres, Otok: *is.*, Yugoslavia 44 58N 14 25E 78
Crescent City: Calif., U.S.A. 41 46N 124 13W 90
Crescenzago: Italy 45 31N 09 15E 116
Creston: B.C., Canada 49 05N 116 32W 90
Crestview: Fla., U.S.A. 30 46N 86 34W 101
Crete: Nebr., U.S.A. 40 38N 96 58W 94
Crete: *is. & Greek admin. see* Kríti 35 00N 25 00E 7 27 79
Crete, *Sea of*: Greece 35 45N 25 15E 79
Creus, *Cabo*: Spain 42 19N 03 19E 77
Crewe: Ches., England 53 05N 02 27W 58 114
Crewkerne: Som., England 50 53N 02 48W 61
Criccieth: Gwyn., Wales 52 55N 04 14W 60
Cricklade: Wilts., England 51 39N 01 51W 61
Crieff: Perth., Scotland 56 23N 03 52W 65
Crimea: *pen.*, U.S.S.R. 45 00N 34 00E 28
Cripple Creek: Colo., U.S.A. 38 49N 105 11W 94
Cristóbal Colón, *Pico*: Colombia 10 53N 73 48W 48
Cristoforo Colombo, Autostrada: *mty.*, Italy 41 45N 12 15E 116
Croix-Mare: France 49 36N 00 51E 117
Cromalt *Hills*: R. & Crom., Scotland 58 00N 05 00W 64
Cromarty: R. & Crom., Scotland 57 40N 04 02W 65
Cromarty Firth: *est.*, R. & Crom., Scotland 57 30N 04 00W 64
Cromer: Norf., England 52 56N 01 18E 58
Cronulla: N.S.W., Australia 34 04S 151 09E 120
Crook: Dur., England 54 43N 01 44W 63
Crookston: Minn., U.S.A. 47 47N 96 36W 94
Croom: Lim., Irish Republic 52 31N 08 43W 67
Crosby: Mers., England 53 30N 03 02W 63 114
Crosby: Minn., U.S.A. 46 28N 93 58W 98
Crosby: N.D., U.S.A. 48 55N 103 18W 93
Cross Fell: *mtn.*, Cumbria, England 54 43N 02 29W 63
Crosshaven: Cork, Irish Republic 51 48N 08 17W 67
Cross Hill: Tyr., N.Ireland 54 42N 07 52W 66
Cross *Lake*: Man., Canada 54 30N 97 30W 93
Crossmaglen: Arm., N.Ireland 54 05N 06 36W 66
Crossmolina: Mayo, Irish Republic 54 06N 09 19W 66
Cross *Sound*: Alaska, U.S.A. 58 00N 136 30W 88
Croston: Lancs., England 53 40N 02 47W 114
Crotone: Italy 39 05N 17 08E 79
Crouch: *riv.*, Essex, England 51 30N 00 45E 59
Crowborough: E.Sussex, England 51 03N 00 09E 59
Crowland: Lincs., England 52 41N 00 11W 58
Crowle: Humb., England 53 37N 00 49W 63
Crowley: La., U.S.A. 30 13N 92 22W 100
Crows Nest: N.S.W., Australia 33 50S 151 12E 120
Crowsnest *Pass*: Canada 49 40N 114 41W 92
Croydon: Gt. Ldn., England 51 23N 00 06W 59 112
Crozet *Basin*: Indian Ocean 40 00S 62 30E 1
Crozet *Islands*: Indian Ocean 46 00S 52 30E 1
Cruachan, Ben: *mtn.*, Argyll., Scotland 56 26N 05 09W 64
Cruces, Cordillera de las: *ra.*, Mexico 19 24N 99 21W 128
Cruz Alta: Brazil 28 38S 53 38W 51
Cruzeiro do Sul: Brazil 07 38S 72 36W 49
Crystal City: Mo., U.S.A. 38 11N 90 22W 98
Crystal City: Tex., U.S.A. 28 41N 99 50W 95
Csepel: Hungary 47 25N 19 05E 105

Types of map: Ocean pp. 1-5; Physical pp. 6-25; Human pp. 26-57; Topographic pp. 58-101; World pp. 102-111; Urban pp. 112-128.

Ču (Chu): *riv.*, U.S.S.R. 4430N 7245E   8 29
Cuajimalpa: Mexico 1921N 9918W   128
Cuando (Kwando): *riv.*, Angola/Zambia 1515S 2130E
    21 55
Cuango: *riv.*, Angola/Zaïre 0830S 1800E   21 54
Cuanza: *riv.*, Angola 1030S 1700E   21 54
Cuautepec: Mexico 1932N 9908W   128
Cuautitlán: Mexico 1940N 9911W   128
Cuautzin, Cerro: *mtn.*, Mexico 1909N 9906W   128
CUBA 2230N 8000W   17 47 106
Cubango: *riv.*, Angola 1615S 1745E   21 55
Cubatão: Brazil 2353S 4626W   106
Čuchloma: U.S.S.R. 5845N 4241E   80
Cuckfield: W.Sussex, England 5100N 0009W   59
Cúcuta: Colombia 0755N 7231W   48
Cuddalore: India 1143N 7946E   34
Čudovo: U.S.S.R. 5907N 3141E   80
Čudskoje Ozero (Peipus, *Lake*): U.S.S.R. 5845N 2730E
    28 80
Cuenca: Ecuador 0253S 7859W   48
Cuenca: Spain 4004N 0207W   77
Čugujev: U.S.S.R. 4950N 3641E   80
Cuiabá: Brazil 1535S 5605W   51
Cuilcagh: *mtn.*, Cavan, N.Ireland 5412N 0749W   66
Cuillin *Hills*: Inv., Scotland 5715N 0600W   64
Cuíma: Angola 1316S 1542E   105
Cuito: *riv.*, Angola 1645S 1930E   55
Culebro: *riv.*, Spain 4015N 0330W   116
Culhuacan: Mexico 1920N 9907W   128
Culiacán: Mexico 2448N 10724W   46
Cullen: Banff., Scotland 5741N 0250W   65
Cullin, *Lough*: Mayo, Irish Republic 5345N 0900W   66
Cullman: Ala., U.S.A. 3411N 8651W   101
Cullompton: Devon, England 5052N 0324W   61
Culm: *riv.*, England 5045N 0315W   61
Culter Fell: *mtn.*, Lan., Scotland 5533N 0330W   62
Culvain: *mtn.*, Inv., Scotland 5657N 0516W   64
Culver City: Calif., U.S.A. 3401N 11824W   127
Cumaná: Venezuela 1029N 6412W   48
Cumberland: Md., U.S.A. 3940N 7847W   99
Cumberland: *admin.*, England. Absorbed into new *admin.*
  of Cumbria, 1974   63
Cumberland: *riv.*, U.S.A. 3630N 8530W   101
Cumberland, *Lake*: Ky., U.S.A. 3645N 8500W   45 101
Cumberland Gap *National Historical Park*: Ky.,
  U.S.A. 3630N 8330W   101
Cumberland *Mountains*: U.S.A. 3630N 8430W   101
Cumberland *Plateau*: Tenn., U.S.A. 3530N 8530W   45 101
Cumbernauld: Dunb., Scotland 5558N 0359W   62 113
Cumbria: *admin.*, England 5430N 0300W   62
Cumbrian *Mountains*: Cumbria, England 5430N 0300W
    63
Cumnock: Ayr., Scotland 5527N 0416W   62
Čuna (Chuna): *riv.*, U.S.S.R. 5730N 9730E   30
Cunene (Kunene): *riv.*, Angola/S.W.Africa 1715S 1300E
    21 55
Cuneo: Italy 4424N 0733E   71
Cunnamulla: Qld., Australia 2804S 14540E   41
Cunningham Landing: N.W.T., Canada 6002N 11208W   92
Cupar: Fife, Scotland 5619N 0301W   65
Čur: U.S.S.R. 5707N 5258E   81
Curaçao: *is.*, Netherlands Antilles 1211N 6900W   47 106
Curicó: Chile 3500S 7115W   52
Curitiba: Brazil 2524S 4916W   51
Currane, *Lough*: Kerry, Irish Republic 5145N 1000W   67
Current: *riv.*, Mo., U.S.A. 3715N 9115W   100
Curslack: W.Germany 5327N 1014E   119
Curuá: *riv.*, Brazil 0645S 5445W   50
Cusano Milanino: Italy 4533N 0911E   116
Cushendun: Antrim, N.Ireland 5507N 0603W   66
Cushing: Okla., U.S.A. 3559N 9646W   95
Čusovoj (Chusovoy): U.S.S.R. 5817N 5749E   81 105
Custer *State Park*: S.D., U.S.A. 4345N 10330W   94
Custer: S.D., U.S.A. 4346N 10336W   94
Cut Bank: Mont., U.S.A. 4838N 11220W   90
Cutra, *Lough*: Gal., Irish Republic 5300N 0845W   67
Cuttack: India 2026N 8556E   35 83
Cuxhaven: W.Germany 5352N 0842E   72
Cuyo *Islands*: Philippines 1045N 12100E   39
Cuyuna *Range*: Minn., U.S.A. 4645N 9330W   98 104
Cuyuni: *riv.*, Guyana/Venezuela 0630N 5900W   48

Cuzco: Peru 1332S 7157W   49
Cwmbran: Gwent, Wales 5139N 0300W   61 113
Cyclades: *is.*, *see* Kikládhes 3700N 2500E   79
Cynon: *riv.*, M.Glam., Wales 5130N 0315W   113
Cypress Hills: Canada 4930N 11000W   92
Cypress *Lake*: Tex., U.S.A. 3245N 9430W   95
CYPRUS 3500N 3300E   7 32 107
Cyrenaica: *geog. reg.*, Libya 3100N 2200E   32
Cywyn: *riv.*, Dyfed, Wales 5145N 0430W   61
CZECHOSLOVAKIA 4900N 1700E   7 27 78 107
Częstochowa: Poland 5049N 1907E   27 78 105

Da (Black): *riv.*, N.Vietnam 2145N 10400E   12 36
Dabashan: *mtns.*, China 3215N 10900E   84
Dabieshan (Tapieh Shan): *mtns.*, China 3115N 11545E
    36 84 85
Dabwāli: India 2958N 7442E   82
Dacca: Bangladesh 2342N 9022E   35 83
Dachang: China 3118N 12125E   121
Dachau: W.Germany 4815N 1126E   73
Dadra & Nagar Haveli: *admin.*, India 2000N 7300E   82
Daerhanmaoming'anqi: China 4155N 11028E   84
Daet: Philippines 1407N 12258E   39
Dafeng (Dazhongji): China 3309N 12030E   84
Dagenham: Gt. Ldn., England 5133N 0008E   112
Dagö: *is.*, *see* Hiiumaa 5845N 2230E   75
Dagu (Taku): China 3858N 11740E   84
Dahlak *Archipelago*: Red Sea   10 53
DAHOMEY 1000N 0230E   20 57
Dahra: Libya 2934N 1750E   32
Daingean: Offaly, Irish Republic 5318N 0717W   67
Daiō-zaki: *cape*, Japan 3417N 13654E   86
Dairen *see* Lüda 3853N 12135E   37 84
Dairyland: Calif., U.S.A. 3351N 11802W   127
Dai-sen-oki-kokuritsu-kōen: *nat. park*, Tottori, Japan
  3515N 13330E   86
Daixian: China 3909N 11252E   84
Daiyunshan: *mtns.*, China 2545N 11815E   85
Dakar: Senegal 1438N 1727W   57
Dakecihu: *lake*, China 3145N 8715E   83
Dakhla *Oasis*: Egypt 2515N 2900E   32
Dalälven: *riv.*, Sweden 6015N 1700E   74
Dalandzadgad: Mongolia 4335N 10430E   36
Dalane: *geog. reg.*, Norway 5830N 0615E   75
Dà Lat: S.Vietnam 1156N 10825E   38
Dālbandin: Pakistan 2856N 6430E   34
Dalbeattie: Kirkc., Scotland 5456N 0349W   62
Dale Hollow *Reservoir*: U.S.A. 3630N 8515W   101
Dalhart: Tex., U.S.A. 3604N 10231W   95
Dali (Tali): Shănxī, China 3442N 10955E   84
Dali: Yunnan, China 2538N 10009E   36
Dali: *riv.*, China 3730N 10915E   84
Daliangshan (Taliang Shan): *mtns.*, China 2800N 10245E
    12 36
Dalkeith: Midloth., Scotland 5554N 0304W   63
Dallas: Oreg., U.S.A. 4455N 12319W   90
Dallas: Tex., U.S.A. 3247N 9649W   43 100
Dalles, The: Oreg., U.S.A. 4536N 12110W   90
Dall *Island*: Alaska, U.S.A. 5445N 13300W   89
Dalmine: Italy 4539N 0936E   105
Dalry: Ayr., Scotland 5543N 0444W   113
Dalton: Ga., U.S.A. 3446N 8458W   101
Dalton-in-Furness: Cumbria, England 5409N 0311W   62
Dalwhinnie: Inv., Scotland 5656N 0415W   64
Daly: riv., N.T., Australia 1345S 13045E   40
Daly City: Calif., U.S.A. 3742N 12228W   126
Daly *Lake*: Sask., Canada 5635N 10540W   92
Daman (Damão): *admin.*, India 2015N 7245E   34 82
Damanhūr: Egypt 3103N 3028E   32
Damão *see* Daman 2015N 7245E   34 82
Damascus: Syria, *see* Dimashq 3330N 3615E   32
Damāvand (Demavend): *volc.*, Iran 3556N 5208E   33
Damiaosham: China 2506N 10912E   85
Damietta *see* Dumyāt 3126N 3148E   32
Daming: China 3617N 11503E   84
Damme: W.Germany 5230N 0812E   105
Damodar: *riv.*, India 2315N 8715E   83
Damoh: India 2350N 7930E   82

Types of map: Ocean pp. 1-5; Physical pp. 6-25; Human pp. 26-57; Topographic pp. 58-101; World pp. 102-111; Urban pp. 112-128.

Dampier *Archipelago*: W.A, Australia 20 30S 116 45E 40
Dan, *Lough*: Wick., Irish Republic 53 00N 06 15W 67
Danakil *Alps*: Ethiopia 14 00N 41 15E 53
Dà Nang (Tourane): S.Vietnam 16 04N 108 13E 38
Danāpur: India 25 08N 85 03E 83
Dandeldhura: Nepal 29 18N 80 36E 82
Dane: *riv.*, England 53 00N 02 15W 58 114
Danfeng: China 33 40N 110 10E 84
Dangshan: China 34 21N 116 29E 84
Dangtu: China 31 33N 118 32E 84
Dangyang: China 30 50N 111 39E 85
Danilov: U.S.S.R. 58 12N 40 12E 80
Dankov: U.S.S.R. 53 15N 39 08E 80
Dannevirke: N.I., New Zealand 40 12S 176 08E 87
Dansville: N.Y., U.S.A. 42 33N 77 41W 99
Danube: *riv.*, Europe 45 00N 28 00E 7 27 78
Danube Delta *National Park*: Romania 45 00N 29 00E 78
Danville: Ill., U.S.A. 40 09N 87 37W 98
Danville: Va., U.S.A. 36 34N 79 25W 101
Danxian: China 34 48N 116 10E 84
Danyang: China 31 56N 119 39E 84
Danzig *see* Gdańsk 54 22N 18 41E 27 73 79
Daoxian: China 25 33N 111 27E 85
Daozhen: China 28 42N 107 52E 85
Dapu: China 24 26N 116 42E 85
Darbhanga: India 26 10N 95 54E 35 83
Darby: Pa., U.S.A. 39 56N 75 15W 122
Dardanelles: *str.*, Turkey 40 15N 26 30E 79
Dar es Salaam: Tanzania 06 48S 39 17E 54
Darfur: *mtns.*, Sudan 13 15N 24 30E 20
Dargaville: N.I., New Zealand 35 57S 173 53E 37 87
Darién, *Golfo de*: Colombia/Panama 09 00N 77 00W 48
Darjeeling: India 27 02N 88 20E 35 83
Darlaston: W.Mid., England 52 34N 02 02W 115
Darling: *riv.*, N.S.W., Australia 33 30S 142 15E 14 41
Darlington: Dur., England 54 31N 01 34W 63
Darmstadt: W.Germany 49 52N 08 39E 72
Darnah (Derna): Libya 32 45N 22 39E 32
Darnley, *Cape*: Antarctica 67 16S 69 53E 24
Dart: *riv.*, Devon, England 50 15N 03 30W 61
Dartford: Kent, England 51 27N 00 14E 59 112
Dartmoor *Forest*: Devon, England 50 30N 03 45W 61
Dartmoor *National Park*: Devon, England 50 30N 03 45W 61
Dartmouth: N.S., Canada 44 40N 63 35W 97
Dartmouth: Devon, England 50 21N 03 35W 61
Darvel: Ayr., Scotland 55 37N 04 18W 62
Darwen: Lancs., England 53 42N 02 28W 63 114
Darwin: N.T., Australia 12 23S 130 44E 40
Das Alte Land: *geog. reg.*, W.Germany 53 30N 09 45E 119
Dashan, Ras: *mtn.*, Ethiopia 13 15N 38 27E 20 53
Dasht: *riv.*, Pakistan 25 30N 62 00E 34
Daškesan: U.S.S.R. 40 30N 46 04E 105
Date: Japan 42 27N 140 51E 86
Datia: India 25 41N 78 28E 82
Datian: China 25 42N 117 49E 85
D'at'kovo: U.S.S.R. 53 36N 34 20E 80
Datong (Tat'ung): China 40 12N 113 15E 36 84
Datong: *riv.*, China 38 00N 100 15E 36
Datteln-Hamm-*Kanal*: W.Germany 51 30N 07 30E 118
Datu, *Cape*: Malaysia 00 01S 103 49E 38
Datu Piang: Philippines 07 02N 124 30E 39
Daubiche: *riv.*, U.S.S.R. 45 00N 133 30E 86
Daugava: *riv.*, U.S.S.R. 56 30N 25 00E 75
Daugavpils: U.S.S.R. 55 53N 26 32E 28
Dauphin: Man., Canada 51 09N 100 05W 93
Dauphin *Lake*: Man., Canada 51 15N 99 45W 93
Dāvangere: India 14 30N 75 52E 34
Davao: Philippines 07 05N 125 38E 39
Davao *Gulf*: Philippines 06 30N 125 45E 39
Davenport: Iowa, U.S.A. 41 32N 90 36W 43 98
Daventry: Northants., England 52 16N 01 09W 59
David: Panama 08 26N 82 26W 47
Davis: *rsch. stn.*, Antarctica 68 35S 77 58E 24
Davis *Dam*: U.S.A. 35 11N 114 34W 91
Davis Inlet: Nfld., Canada 55 51N 60 52W 97
Davis *Strait*: Canada/Greenland 65 00N 60 00W 2 23
Davlekanovo: U.S.S.R. 54 13N 55 03E 81
Davos: Switzerland 46 50N 09 51E 71
Dawley: Salop, England 52 39N 02 28W 58
Dawlish: Devon, England 50 35N 03 28W 61

Dawna *Range*: Thailand 17 30N 98 30E 35
Dawson: Yukon, Canada 64 04N 139 24W 88
Dawson Creek: B.C., Canada 55 44N 120 15W 42 89
Dawson Landing: N.W.T., Canada 61 00N 114 08W 92
Dawson *Range*: Yukon, Canada 62 30N 139 00W 88
Dawu: China 31 32N 114 08E 84
Dax: France 43 43N 01 03W 70
Daxi: *riv.*, China 28 15N 119 45E 85
Daxian: China 31 20N 107 30E 84
Daxin: China 22 50N 107 26E 85
Daxing: China 39 41N 116 29E 84
Daxueshan (Tahsüeh Shan): *mtns.*, China 30 30N 101 30E 36
Daya: China 25 30N 114 20E 85
Daye: China 30 05N 114 57E 105
Dayishan *see* Guanyun 34 23N 119 19E 84
Dayong: China 29 10N 110 20E 85
Dayton: Ohio, U.S.A. 39 45N 84 10W 45 98
Dayton: Wash., U.S.A. 46 19N 117 59W 90
Daytona Beach: Fla., U.S.A. 29 11N 81 01W 45 101
Dazhongji *see* Dafeng 33 09N 120 30E 84
Dazhu: China 30 48N 107 12E 85
De Aar: C.P., Rep. of S.Africa 30 39S 24 00E 55
Dead Sea *ḤāMelah, Yam; Al Baḥr al Mayyit*): *lake*, Israel/Jordan 31 15N 35 15E 10 32
Deadwood: S.D., U.S.A. 44 23N 103 44W 94
Deal: Kent, England 51 14N 01 24E 59
Dean: China 29 17N 115 52E 84
Dean, *Forest of*: Glos., England 51 45N 02 30W 113
Dean *National Forest Park*: Glos., England 51 45N 02 30W 60
Dean *Channel*: B.C., Canada 52 30N 127 00W 89
Deán Funes: Argentina 30 25S 64 22W 52
Dearborn: Mich., U.S.A. 42 18N 83 14W 125
Dearborn Heights: Mich., U.S.A. 42 19N 83 14W 125
Dearg, Beinn: *mtn.*, R.& Crom., Scotland 57 47N 04 55W 64
Dease Arm: *bay*, N.W.T., Canada 66 45N 121 00W 88
Dease Lake: B.C., Canada 58 28N 130 04W 88
Dease *Lake*: B.C., Canada 58 30N 130 00W 88
Deas *Island*: B.C., Canada 49 07N 123 04W 126
Death *Valley*: Calif., U.S.A. 36 15N 116 45W 43
Death Valley *National Monument*: Calif., U.S.A. 36 15N 117 00W 91
Deauville-les-Bains: France 49 21N 00 04E 70
Debal'cevo: U.S.S.R. 48 20N 38 24E 80
Debrecen: Hungary 47 30N 21 39E 27 79
Debre Markos: Ethiopia 10 19N 37 41E 53
Decatur: Ala., U.S.A. 34 36N 86 59W 101
Decatur: Ill., U.S.A. 39 51N 88 57W 45 98
Deccan: *geog. reg.*, India 19 00N 79 00E 34
Děčín: Czechoslovakia 50 48N 14 15E 73
Decorah: Iowa, U.S.A. 43 18N 91 49W 98
Deddington: Oxon., England 51 59N 01 19W 59
Dedham: Mass., U.S.A. 42 15N 71 10W 122
Dee: *riv.*, England/Wales 53 15N 03 00W 60
Dee: *riv.*, Aber., Scotland 57 00N 02 45W 65
Dee: *riv.*, Kirkc., Scotland 54 45N 04 00W 62
Deel: *riv.*, Lim., Irish Republic 52 15N 08 45W 67
Deel: *riv.*, Westmeath, Irish Republic 53 30N 07 00W 66
Deeps, the: *bay*, Shet. Is., Scotland 60 00N 01 15W 65
Deerfield: Ill., U.S.A. 42 09N 87 50W 124
Deer Lake: Nfld., Canada 49 11N 57 27W 44 97
Deer Lake: Ont., Canada 52 40N 94 04W 93
Deer Lodge: Mont., U.S.A. 46 24N 112 44W 94
Dee Why: N.S.W., Australia 33 45S 151 17E 120
Dehra Dūn: India 30 21N 78 21E 34 82
Dehri: India 24 55N 84 11E 83
Dehua: China 25 29N 118 09E 85
Dej: Romania 47 08N 23 55E 78
De Kalb: Ill., U.S.A. 41 57N 88 45W 98
Delamere *Forest*: Ches., England 53 00N 02 30W 114
De Land: Fla., U.S.A. 29 02N 81 18W 101
Delano: Calif., U.S.A. 35 46N 119 15W 91
Delano *Peak*: Utah, U.S.A. 38 22N 112 22W 91
Delaware: *admin.*, U.S.A. 38 45N 75 30W 45 99
Delaware *Bay*: U.S.A. 39 00N 75 15W 45 99
Delaware City: Del., U.S.A. 39 35N 75 36W 106
Delaware Expressway: *hwy.*, U.S.A. 40 00N 75 00W 122
Delhi: India 28 40N 77 14E 34 82 120
Delmenhorst: W.Germany 53 03N 08 37E 72

Types of map: Ocean pp. 1-5; Physical pp. 6-25; Human pp. 26-57; Topographic pp. 58-101; World pp. 102-111; Urban pp. 112-128.

Deloraine: Man., Canada   49 11N 100 30W   93
Delorme, *Lac*: Qué., Canada   54 30N 70 00W   96
Delray Beach: Fla., U.S.A.   26 29N 80 04W   101
Del Rio: Tex., U.S.A.   29 22N 100 54W   95
Delta: Colo., U.S.A.   38 44N 108 04W   94
Delta *Flats*: B.C., Canada   49 00N 123 00W   126
Demavend: *volc.*, *see* Damāvand   35 56N 52 08E   33
Demidov: U.S.S.R.   55 16N 31 31E   80
Deming: N.Mex., U.S.A.   32 16N 107 46W   95
Demmin: E.Germany   53 55N 13 03E   73
Demopolis: Ala., U.S.A.   32 31N 87 50W   100
Dempo, *Mount*: Indonesia   04 02S 103 07E   38
Denain: France   50 19N 03 24E   105
Denbigh: Clwyd, Wales   53 11N 03 25W   60
Denbighshire: *admin.*, Wales. Absorbed into new *admins.*
  of Clwyd & Gwynedd, 1974.   60
Dengkou: China   40 09N 106 49E   84
Dengxian: China   32 47N 112 00E   84
Den Haag *see* 's-Gravenhage   52 05N 04 16E   26 72
Den Helder: Netherlands   52 58N 04 46E   72
Denison: Tex., U.S.A.   33 45N 96 33W   100
Denizli: Turkey   37 46N 29 05E   32
DENMARK   56 00N 10 00E   7 26 75 107
Denmark *Strait*: Greenland/Iceland   66 00N 24 00W   2 6
Denny: Stirl., Scotland   56 02N 03 55W   62
Denpasar: Indonesia   08 40S 115 14E   39
Denton: Gt. Man., England   53 27N 02 07W   63
Denton: Tex., U.S.A.   33 13N 97 08W   95
Denver: Colo., U.S.A.   39 44N 104 59W   43 94
Denver City: Tex., U.S.A.   32 58N 102 50W   95
Deogarh: India   21 32N 84 46E   83
Deogarh *Hills*: India   23 30N 82 15E   83
Deoghar: India   24 31N 86 42E   83
Deolāli: India   19 58N 73 54E   82
Deoria: India   26 31N 83 48E   83
De Pere: Wis., U.S.A.   44 25N 88 02W   98
Depue: Ill., U.S.A.   41 09N 89 20W   98
Deqing: China   23 09N 111 46E   85
Dera Ghāzi Khān: Pakistan   30 05N 70 44E   82
Derā Ismāil Khān: Pakistan   31 51N 70 56E   82
Derbent: U.S.S.R.   42 03N 48 18E   28
Derby: W.A., Australia   17 19S 123 38E   40
Derby: Derby., England   52 55N 01 30W   26 58
Derby: Kans., U.S.A.   37 33N 97 16W   95
Derbyshire: *admin.*, England   53 00N 01 30W   58
Derg: *riv.*, Irish Republic/N.Ireland   54 30N 07 45W   66
Derg, *Lough*: Clare, Irish Rep.   53 00N 08 15W   67
Derg, *Lough*: Don., Irish Republic   54 30N 07 45W   66
Dergači: U.S.S.R.   51 14N 48 46E   81
Derna *see* Darnah   32 45N 22 39E   32
Déroute, Passage de la: *str.*, Channel Islands/France
  49 10N 01 45W   61
Derravaragh, *Lough*: Westmeath, Irish Republic
  53 30N 07 15W   66
Derreen: *riv.*, Irish Republic   52 45N 06 30W   67
Derriana *Lough*: Kerry, Irish Republic   51 45N 10 00W   67
Derry (Londonderry): *admin.*, N.Ireland   54 45N 06 45W   66
Derrynasaggart *Mountains*: Irish Republic   52 00N 09 00W
  67
Derryveagh *Mountains*: Don., Irish Rep.   55 00N 08 00W
  66
Derwent: *riv.*, Dur., England   54 45N 02 00W   63
Derwent: *riv.*, N.Yorks., England   53 45N 00 45W   63
Derwent Water: *lake*, Cumbria, England   54 30N 03 00W
  62
Desagüe, *Gran Canal del*: Mexico   19 38N 99 03W   128
Desborough: Northants., England   52 27N 00 49W   58
Deschambault *Lake*: Sask., Canada   54 45N 103 15W   92
Deschutes: *riv.*, Oreg., U.S.A.   44 30N 121 00W   90
Dese (Dessye): Ethiopia   11 05N 39 40E   53
Deseado: Argentina   47 44S 65 56W   52
Deseado: *riv.*, Argentina   46 45S 69 00W   52
Desio: Italy   45 37N 09 12E   116
Des Moines: Iowa, U.S.A.   41 35N 93 35W   43 98
Des Moines: *riv.*, U.S.A.   41 15N 93 00W   98
Desna: *riv.*, U.S.S.R.   51 15N 31 00E   80
Des Plaines: Ill., U.S.A.   42 02N 87 54W   124
Des Plaines: *riv.*, U.S.A.   41 45N 87 45W   124
Dessau: E.Germany   51 51N 12 15E   73
Dessye *see* Dese   11 05N 39 40E   53
Destruction Bay: Yukon, Canada   61 16N 138 50W   88

Detmold: W.Germany   51 56N 08 52E   72
Detroit: Mich., U.S.A.   42 23N 83 05W   45 98 104 125
Detroit: Oreg., U.S.A.   44 44N 122 09W   90
Detroit: *riv.*, U.S.A./Canada   42 00N 83 00W   125
Detroit Industrial Freeway: *hwy.*, Mich., U.S.A.
  42 00N 83 15W   125
Detroit Lakes: Minn., U.S.A.   46 49N 95 49W   94
Deutz: W.Germany   50 56N 06 59E   119
Deux-Montagnes: Qué., Canada   45 35N 74 05W   122
Deux-Montagnes, *Lac des*: Qué., Canada   45 30N 73 45W
  122
Deva: Romania   45 53N 22 55E   78
Deventer: Netherlands   52 15N 06 10E   72
Deveron: *riv.*, Scotland   57 15N 02 45W   65
Devilsbit: *mtn.*, Tip., Irish Republic   52 49N 07 55W   67
Devil's Bridge: Dyfed, Wales   52 23N 03 51W   60
Devils Lake: N.D., U.S.A.   48 06N 98 52W   94
Devils Slide: Utah, U.S.A.   41 04N 111 33W   91
Devils Tower *National Monument*: Wyo.,
  U.S.A.   44 38N 104 40W   94
Devizes: Wilts., England   51 22N 02 00W   61
Devon: *admin.*, England   50 45N 03 45W   61
Devon *Island*: N.W.T., Canada   75 00N 85 00W   16
Devonport: Tas., Australia   41 09S 146 16E   40
Devonport: Devon, England   50 22N 04 10W   61
Dewa-kyūryō: *hills*, Japan   39 30N 140 15E   86
Dewās: India   22 59N 76 03E   82
Dewsbury: W.Yorks., England   53 42N 01 37W   63 115
Dexter: Maine, U.S.A.   45 01N 69 19W   99
Dezhou (Techou): China   37 27N 116 18E   36 84
Dhahran *see* Az̧ Z̧ahrān   26 18N 50 05E   33
Dhamtari: India   20 43N 81 36E   83
Dhānbād: India   23 47N 86 32E   35 83
Dhangarhi: Nepal   28 42N 80 36E   82
Dhankuta: Nepal   26 59N 87 20E   83
Dhār: India   22 32N 75 24E   82
Dharān Bāzār: Nepal   26 49N 87 18E   83
Dharangaon: India   21 00N 75 30E   82
Dharmjaygarh: India   22 27N 83 16E   83
Dhārwār: India   15 30N 75 04E   34
Dholpur: India   26 43N 77 54E   82
Dhubri: India   26 01N 90 00E   83
Dhule: India   20 54N 74 47E   34 82
Dhünn: *riv.*, W.Germany   51 00N 07 00E   118
Dhüntalsperre: *res.*, W.Germany   51 00N 07 15E   118
Dhupgāri: India   26 36N 88 54E   83
Diablo: Calif., U.S.A.   37 50N 121 58W   126
Diamante: Buenos Aires, Argentina   34 41S 58 25W   128
Diamantina: Brazil   18 15S 43 36W   51
Diamantina *Fracture Zone*: Indian Ocean   37 00S 105 00E
  1
Diamond Harbour: India   22 11N 88 12E   83
Dianjiang: China   30 27N 107 20E   85
Dibrugarh: India   27 29N 94 56E   35
Dickinson: N.D., U.S.A.   46 53N 102 47W   94
Dicle: *riv. see* Tigris   35 15N 43 30E   10 32
Didan: China   39 58N 116 24E   121
Didcot: Oxon., England   51 37N 01 15W   59
Didsbury: Alta., Canada   51 40N 114 06W   92
Didsbury: Gt. Man., England   53 25N 02 14W   114
Diefenbaker *Lake*: Canada   51 00N 106 55W   92
Diégo-Suarez: Malagasy Rep.   12 16S 49 17E   55
Die Grafschaft: *geog. reg.*, W.Germany   51 15N 06 30E   118
Diepholz: W.Germany   52 37N 08 22E   72
Die Schwarzen Berge: *mtns.*, W.Germany   53 15N 09 45E
  119
Die Ville: *geog. reg.*, W.Germany   50 45N 06 45E   119
Differdange: Luxembourg   49 32N 05 53E   105
Digne: France   44 05N 06 14E   71
Digoin: France   46 29N 03 54E   71
Digras: India   20 06N 77 48E   82
Dijlah: *riv, see* Tigris   35 15N 43 30E   10 32
Dijon: France   47 20N 05 02E   26 71
Dili: Portuguese Timor   08 35S 125 35E   39
Dillingen: W.Germany   49 21N 06 44E   105
Dillon: Mont., U.S.A.   45 13N 112 38W   94
Dilolo: Zaïre   10 42S 22 20E   54
Dimashq (Damascus): Syria   33 30N 36 15E   32
Dimitrovgrad: Bulgaria   42 03N 23 54E   79
Dinājpur: Bangladesh   25 38N 88 44E   83
Dinan: France   48 27N 02 02W   70

Types of map: Ocean pp. 1-5; Physical pp. 6-25; Human pp. 26-57; Topographic pp. 58-101; World pp. 102-111; Urban pp. 112-128.

Dinara Planina (Dinaric Alps): *mtns.*, Yugoslavia
 44 00N 16 30E   27 79
Dinaric *Alps see* Dinara Planina   44 00N 16 30E   27 79
Dinas *Head*: Dyfed, Wales   52 02N 04 55W   60
Dindigul: India   10 23N 78 00E   34
Dingle: Kerry, Irish Rep.   52 08N 10 15W   67 76
Dingle *Bay*: Kerry, Irish Republic   52 00N 10 00W   67
Dingle *Peninsula*: Kerry, Irish Republic   52 00N 10 00W   67
Dingbian: China   37 36N 107 38E   84
Dingnan: China   24 31N 114 44E   85
Dingri: China   28 35N 86 38E   35 83
Dingshan: China   31 13N 119 57E   84
Dingtao: China   35 04N 115 39E   84
Dingwall: R. & Crom., Scotland   57 35N 04 26W   64
Dingxian: China   38 32N 114 58E   84
Dingyuan: China   32 29N 117 41E   84
Dinnington: S.Yorks., England   53 22N 01 12W   63
Dinorwic: Ont., Canada   49 42N 92 30W   98
Dinosaur *National Monument*: U.S.A.   40 30N 108 45W   94
Dinslaken: W.Germany   51 34N 06 43E   107 118
Dipolog: Philippines   08 34N 123 28E   39
Dique Luján: Argentina   34 21S 58 41W   128
Dire Dawa: Ethiopia   09 35N 41 50E   53
Disna: U.S.S.R.   55 53N 28 10E   80
Disna: *riv.*, U.S.S.R.   55 15N 27 30E   80
Diss: Norf., England   52 23N 01 06E   59
District Heights: Md., U.S.A.   38 50N 76 55W   122
District of Columbia: *admin.*, U.S.A.   38 45N 77 00W   122
Distrito Federal: *admin.*, Brazil   15 15S 48 15W   51
Diu: India   20 41N 71 03E   34 82
Divinópolis: Brazil   20 09S 44 54W   51
Divriği: Turkey   39 23N 38 07E   105
Dixon: Ill., U.S.A.   41 52N 89 30W   98
Dixon: N.Mex., U.S.A.   36 12N 105 53W   95
Dixon Entrance: *str.*, Canada/U.S.A.   54 15N 132 00W   89
Diyarbakir: Turkey   37 55N 40 14E   33
Dizzard *Point*: Corn., England   50 45N 04 38W   61
Djajapura (Kotabaru, Sukarnapura): Indonesia
 02 32S 140 42E   13
Djakarta (Jakarta, Batavia): Indonesia   06 08S 106 45E   38
Djambi *see* Telanaipura   01 36S 103 37E   38
Djebel Bou Khadra: *mtn.*, Algeria   35 45N 08 00E   104
Djebel Ouenza: *mtn.*, Algeria   35 57N 08 06E   104
Djelfa: Algeria   34 43N 03 14E   104
Djerid, Chott: *salt lake*, Tunisia   33 45N 08 30E   20 56
Djerissa: Tunisia   35 51N 08 38E   104
Djibouti: French Terr. of Afars & Issas   11 35N 43 11E   53
Djidjelli: Algeria   36 50N 05 43E   77
Dmitrov: U.S.S.R.   56 21N 37 31E   80
Dnepr: *riv.*, U.S.S.R.   51 45N 30 30E   8 28 80
Dneprodzeržinsk: U.S.S.R.   48 30N 34 37E   28 80 105
Dneprodzeržinskoje Vodochranilišče: *res.*,
 U.S.S.R.   48 45N 34 00E   80
Dnepropetrovsk: U.S.S.R.   48 27N 34 59E   28 80 105
Dnestr: *riv.*, U.S.S.R.   47 45N 29 00E   28 78
Dno: U.S.S.R.   57 50N 29 59E   80
Döbeln: E.Germany   51 07N 13 07E   73
Dobr'anka: U.S.S.R.   58 27N 56 24E   81
Dobruš: U.S.S.R.   52 25N 31 19E   80
Dodecanese: *is. see* Sporádhes   36 30N 26 30E   79
Dodge City: Kans., U.S.A.   37 45N 100 01W   95
Dodoma: Tanzania   06 11S 35 45E   54
Doha, Qatar *see* Ad Dawhah   25 17N 51 32E   33
Dohad: India   22 48N 74 18E   82
Dôle: France   47 05N 05 30E   71
Dolgellau: Gwyn., Wales   52 44N 03 53W   60
Dolinskoje: U.S.S.R.   47 32N 29 55E   78
Dollar: Clack., Scotland   56 09N 03 41W   65
Dollard: Sask., Canada   49 38N 108 38W   92
Dollarton: B.C., Canada   49 19N 122 58W   126
Dolomitiche, *Alpi* (Dolomites): Italy   46 15N 11 45E   78
Dolores: *riv.*, U.S.A.   38 30N 108 45W   91
Dolton: Ill., U.S.A.   41 36N 87 36W   124
Dombarovskij: U.S.S.R.   50 46N 59 32E   29
Dombås: Norway   62 05N 09 07E   75
Dominica: *is.*, Windward Islands   15 15N 61 15W   47
DOMINICAN REPUBLIC   19 00N 70 00W   17 47 106
Domnarvet: Sweden   60 30N 15 27E   105
Domodedovo: U.S.S.R.   55 26N 37 46E   80
Domodossola: Italy   46 08N 08 17E   71
Domont: France   49 02N 02 20E   117

Don: *riv.*, Ont., Canada   43 45N 79 15W   125
Don: *riv.*, S.Yorks., England   53 30N 00 45W   63 115
Don: *riv.*, Aber., Scotland   57 15N 02 15W   65
Don: *riv.*, U.S.S.R.   47 30N 40 45E   8 28 80
Donaghadee: Down, N.Ireland   54 39N 05 33W   66
Donald: B.C., Canada   51 29N 117 11W   89
Donard, Slieve: *mtn.*, Down, N.Ireland   54 11N 05 55W   66
Donawitz: Austria   47 22N 15 04E   105
Donbass: *geog. reg.*, U.S.S.R.   48 00N 39 00E   28
Doncaster: S.Yorks., England   53 32N 01 07W   63
Donec: *riv.*, U.S.S.R.   48 30N 41 00E   8 28
Doneck (Donetsk): Ukrainskaja S.S.R., U.S.S.R.
 48 00N 37 48E   28 80 105
Doneck: R.S.F.S.R., U.S.S.R.   48 21N 40 02E   80
Donegal: Don., Irish Rep.   54 39N 08 06W   66
Donegal: *admin.*, Irish Rep.   54 45N 08 00W   66
Donegal *Bay*: Don., Irish Republic   54 30N 08 45W   66
Donegal *Point*: Clare, Irish Republic   52 44N 09 38W   67
Donetsk *see* Doneck   48 00N 37 48E   28 80 105
Dong: *riv.*, China   23 30N 114 45E   85
Dong'an: China   26 22N 111 11E   85
Dongbahe: China   39 58N 116 27E   121
Donggala: Indonesia   00 38S 119 45E   39
Donggongshan: *mtns.*, China   27 15N 119 15E   85
Dongguan: China   23 03N 113 45E   85
Dongguang: China   37 56N 116 31E   84
Donghai (Haizhou): China   34 34N 119 09E   84
Dongju: China   39 53N 116 14E   121
Dongkan *see* Binhai   33 57N 119 51E   84
Dongkou: Hunan, China   27 06N 110 35E   85
Dongkou: Shanghai Shi, China   31 17N 121 34E   121
Donglan: China   24 35N 107 23E   85
Dongming: China   35 14N 115 08E   84
Dongning: China   44 04N 131 07E   86
Dongping: China   35 52N 116 20E   84
Dongping, *Lake*: China   35 45N 116 15E   84
Dongshan: China   23 44N 117 31E   85
Dongsheng: China   39 50N 110 00E   84
Dongshi: China   39 49N 116 34E   121
Dongtai: China   32 48N 120 20E   84
Dongting, *Lake* (Tungt'ing Hu): China   28 45N 112 30E
   36 85
Dongxiang: China   28 18N 116 35E   85
Dongxin: China   31 24N 121 41E   121
Dongxing: China   21 35N 107 59E   85
Dongyang: China   29 12N 120 15E   85
Donington: Lincs., England   52 55N 00 12W   58
Donjek: *riv.*, Yukon, Canada   61 30N 139 30W   88
Don Mills: Ont., Canada   43 45N 79 22W   125
Dønna: *is.*, Norway   66 00N 12 30E   74
Donskoje Belogorje: *mtns.*, U.S.S.R.   50 30N 40 00E   80
Don Torcuato: Argentina   34 29S 58 38W   128
Doolish *Mountain*: Tyr., N.Ireland   54 35N 07 31W   66
Doon: *riv.*, Ayr., Scotland   55 15N 04 15W   62
Doon, *Loch*: Ayr., Scotland   55 15N 04 15W   62
Door *Peninsula*: Wis., U.S.A.   45 00N 87 15W   98
Dorain, Beinn: *mtn.*, Argyll., Scotland   56 31N 04 44W   64
Dorchester: Dorset, England   50 43N 02 26W   61
Dorchester: Oxon., England   51 39N 01 10W   59
Dordogne: *riv.*, France   44 45N 00 30E   70
Dordrecht: Netherlands   51 48N 04 40E   72
Dore: *riv.*, Here. & Worcs., England   52 00N 02 45W   60
Dore: *riv.*, France   45 30N 03 45E   71
Dore, *Mont*: France   45 30N 02 45E   71
Dore *Lake*: Sask., Canada   54 45N 107 15W   92
Dorking: Surrey, England   51 14N 00 20W   59 112
Dornbirn: Austria   47 25N 09 46E   71
Dornoch: Suther., Scotland   57 52N 04 02W   65
Dornoch Firth: *est.*, Suther., Scotland   57 45N 04 00W   65
Dorridge: W.Mid., England   52 22N 01 45W   115
Dorset: *admin.*, England   50 45N 02 15W   61
Dortmund: W.Germany   51 32N 07 27E   72 105 118
Dorval: Qué., Canada   45 27N 73 46W   122
Dossor: U.S.S.R.   47 32N 53 01E   81
Dothan: Ala., U.S.A.   31 13N 85 24W   45 101
Douai: France   50 22N 03 05E   72
Douala: Cameroun   04 04N 09 43E   57
Douaria: Tunisia   37 00N 09 11E   104
Douarnenez: France   48 05N 04 20W   70
Double Mountain Fork: *riv.*, Tex., U.S.A.   33 00N 101 00W
   95

Types of map: Ocean pp. 1-5; Physical pp. 6-25; Human pp. 26-57; Topographic pp. 58-101; World pp. 102-111; Urban pp. 112-128.

Doubtful *Sound*: S.I., New Zealand   45 15S 166 45E   87
Doubtless *Bay*: N.I., New Zealand   34 45S 173 15E   87
Douglas: I. of M., United Kingdom   54 09N 04 29W   62
Douglas: Alaska, U.S.A.   58 17N 134 24W   88
Douglas: Ariz., U.S.A.   31 21N 109 33W   95
Douglas: *riv.*, Lancs., England   53 30N 02 45W   114
Douglas *Island*: B.C., Canada   49 13N 122 46W   126
Douglas *Park*: Ill., U.S.A.   41 51N 87 42W   124
Dounreay: Caith., Scotland   58 33N 03 42W   65
Douro (Duero): *riv.*, Portugal/Spain   41 00N 07 15W   26 77
Dove: *riv.*, Derby., England   53 00N 01 45W   58
Dove: *riv.*, Suff., England   52 15N 01 00E   59
Dove Creek: Colo., U.S.A.   37 46N 108 54W   95
Dove Elbe: *riv.*, W.Germany   53 15N 10 00E   119
Dover: Kent, England   51 08N 01 19E   59
Dover: Del., U.S.A.   39 10N 75 32W   99
Dover: Mass., U.S.A.   42 15N 71 17W   122
Dover: N.H., U.S.A.   43 12N 70 55W   99
Dover, *Strait of* (Calais, Pas de):
   England/France   51 00N 01 30E   69
Dovey: *riv.*, Wales   52 30N 03 45W   60
Dovrefjell: *mtns.*, Norway   62 30N 09 00E   74
Down: *admin.*, N.Ireland   54 15N 06 00W   66
Downers Grove: Ill., U.S.A.   41 47N 88 00W   124
Downey: Calif., U.S.A.   33 56N 118 08W   127
Downham Market: Norf., England   52 36N 00 23E   58
Downie *Creek*: B.C., Canada   51 30N 118 15W   89
Downpatrick: Down, N.Ireland   54 20N 05 43W   66
Downpatrick *Head*: Mayo, Irish Republic   54 20N 09 20W
                                                       66
Dra, Hamada du: *geog. reg.*, Algeria   29 30N 06 00W   56
Draggan: *lake*, Sweden   64 00N 15 15E   74
Draguignan: France   43 32N 06 28E   71
Drakensberge: *mtns.*, Lesotho/Rep. of S.Africa
   30 00S 29 00E   21 55
Drake *Passage*: Southern Ocean   57 45S 65 00W   19
Dráma: Greece   41 10N 24 11E   79
Drammen: Norway   59 45N 10 15E   75
Drava: *riv.*, Hungary/Yugoslavia   46 15N 16 15E   78
Drayton Valley: Alta., Canada   53 15N 115 00W   92
Dresden: E.Germany   51 03N 13 45E   27 73 78
Dresden: *admin.*, E.Germany   51 15N 14 00E   73
Dreux: France   48 44N 01 23E   70
Drina: *riv.*, Yugoslavia   43 15N 19 30E   79
Drissa: *riv.*, U.S.S.R.   55 45N 29 00E   80
Drogheda: Louth, Irish Republic   53 43N 06 21W   66
Drogobyč: U.S.S.R.   49 21N 23 30E   78
Droichead Nua: Kild., Irish Republic   53 11N 06 48W   67
Droitwich: Here. & Worcs., England   52 16N 02 09W   59
Drôme: *riv.*, France   44 30N 05 30E   71
Dromore: Down, N.Ireland   54 25N 06 09W   66
Dromore: Tyr., N.Ireland   54 31N 07 28W   66
Dronfield: Derby., England   53 19N 01 27W   58
Druk-yul *see* Bhutan   27 30N 90 30E   11 35 83
Drummheller: Alta., Canada   51 28N 112 40W   92
Drummoyne: N.S.W., Australia   33 51S 151 09E   120
Dry Creek: Yukon, Canada   62 10N 140 40W   88
Drygarn Fawr: *mtn.*, Powys, Wales   52 12N 03 41W   60
Duan: China   24 04N 108 09E   85
Dubawnt: *riv.*, N.W.T., Canada   61 15N 104 15W   92
Dubawnt *Lake*: N.W.T., Canada   63 00N 101 30W   16 42
Dubayy: United Arab Emirates   25 14N 55 17E   33
Dubh, Rubha: *cape*, Argyll., Scotland   56 32N 06 24W   64
Dublin: Dublin, Irish Republic   53 20N 06 15W   26 67
Dublin: Ga., U.S.A.   32 31N 82 54W   101
Dublin: *admin.*, Irish Republic   53 15N 06 15W   66
Dublin *Bay*: Dublin, Irish Republic   53 15N 06 00W   67
Dubna: U.S.S.R.   56 44N 37 10E   80
Dubno: U.S.S.R.   50 26N 25 44E   78
Dubovka: U.S.S.R.   49 03N 44 50E   80
Dubrovnik: Yugoslavia   42 40N 18 07E   27 79
Dubuque: Iowa, U.S.A.   42 31N 90 41W   98
Duchang: China   29 15N 116 13E   85
Ducheng *see* Yunan   23 11N 111 29E   85
Duchesne: Utah, U.S.A.   40 10N 110 24W   91
Ducie *Island*: S.Pacific Ocean   24 40S 124 48W   5
Duck: *riv.*, Tenn., U.S.A.   35 45N 87 45W   101
Duck Mountain *Provincial Park*: Man.,
   Canada   51 30N 101 15W   92
Duddon: *riv.*, Cumbria, England   54 15N 03 00W   62
Dudelange: Luxembourg   49 28N 06 05E   105

Dudinka: U.S.S.R.   69 25N 86 15E   30
Dudley: W.Mid., England   52 30N 02 05W   58 115
Dudna: *riv.*, India   19 30N 76 15E   82
Duero (Douro): *riv.*, Spain/Portugal   41 15N 06 15W   26 77
Dufftown: Banff., Scotland   57 27N 03 09W   65
Duffy Preserve: *park*, Ill., U.S.A.   41 39N 87 54W   124
Dugede: China   30 54N 90 48E   83
Dugi, Otok: *is.*, Yugoslavia   44 00N 15 00E   79
Duisburg: W.Germany   51 26N 06 45E   72 105 118
Dulce: *riv.*, Argentina   30 00S 62 45W   52
Du Lièvre: *riv.*, Qué., Canada   45 35N 75 25W   96
Dülken: W.Germany   51 16N 06 20E   118
Dülmen: W.Germany   51 49N 07 17E   72
Duluth: Minn., U.S.A.   46 45N 92 10W   42 98 104
Dulverton: Som., England   51 03N 03 33W   61
Dumaguete: Philippines   09 20N 123 18E   39
Dumai: Indonesia   01 39N 101 28E   38
Dumas: Tex., U.S.A.   35 52N 101 58W   95
Dumbarton: Dunb., Scotland   55 57N 04 35W   62 113
Dumbarton *Bridge*: Calif., U.S.A.   37 30N 122 05W   126
Dum Dum: India   22 38N 88 25E   120
Dumfries: Dumf., Scotland   55 04N 03 37W   62
Dumfriesshire: *admin.*, Scotland   55 15N 03 30W   62
Dumka: India   24 17N 87 15E   83
Dumont d'Urville: *rsch. stn.*, Antarctica   66 40S 140 01E   25
Dümpten: W.Germany   51 27N 06 54E   118
Dumyât (Damietta): Egypt   31 26N 31 48E   32
Dunaújváros: Hungary   46 58N 18 57E   78 105
Dunbar: E.Loth., Scotland   56 00N 02 31W   63
Dunblane: Sask., Canada   51 12N 106 53W   92
Dunblane: Perth., Scotland   56 12N 03 59W   65
Dunboyne: Meath, Irish Republic   53 25N 06 29W   66
Duncan: B.C., Canada   48 47N 123 42W   89
Duncan: Okla., U.S.A.   34 30N 97 57W   95
Duncannon: Wex., Irish Republic   51 13N 06 55W   67
Duncansby *Head*: Caith., Scotland   58 39N 03 01W   65
Dundalk: Louth, Irish Republic   54 01N 06 25W   66
Dundalk *Bay*: Louth, Irish Republic   53 45N 06 15W   66
Dundee: Angus, Scotland   56 28N 03 00W   26 65
Dundonald: Down, N.Ireland   54 36N 05 48W   66
Dunedin: S.I., New Zealand   45 52S 170 30E   37 87
Dunfermline: Fife, Scotland   56 04N 03 29W   65
Dung (Sông Dông Nai): *riv.*, S.Vietnam   11 45N 108 00E   38
Dungannon: Tyr., N.Ireland   54 31N 06 46W   66
Dungarpur: India   28 05N 74 09E   82
Dungarvan: Wat., Irish Republic   52 05N 07 37W   67
Dungarvan *Harbour*: Wat., Irish Republic   52 00N 07 30W
                                                       67
Dungeness: *cape*, Kent, England   50 55N 00 58E   59
Dungiven: Lon., N.Ireland   54 55N 06 55W   66
Dungloe: Don., Irish Republic   54 57N 02 22W   66
Dunipace: Stirl., Scotland   56 02N 03 55W   62
Dunkeld: Perth., Scotland   56 33N 03 36W   65
Dunkellin: *riv.*, Gal., Irish Republic   53 00N 08 45W   67
Dunkerque (Dunkirk): France   51 02N 02 23E   72 105 107
Dunkery Beacon: *mtn.*, Som., England   51 11N 03 35W   61
Dunkirk: N.Y., U.S.A.   42 29N 79 21W   99
Dun Laoghaire: Dublin, Irish Republic   53 17N 06 08W   67
Dunmanus *Bay*: Cork, Irish Republic   51 30N 09 30W   67
Dunmanway: Cork, Irish Republic   51 43N 09 07W   67
Dunmurry: Antrim, N.Ireland   54 33N 06 00W   66
Dunnet *Bay*: Caith., Scotland   58 30N 03 15W   65
Dunnet *Head*: Caith., Scotland   58 39N 03 23W   65
Dunoon: Argyll., Scotland   55 57N 04 56W   62 113
Duns: Ber., Scotland   55 47N 02 20W   63
Dunstable: Beds., England   51 53N 00 32W   59
Dunstan *Mountains*: S.I., New Zealand   40 30S 16 30E   87
Duntelchaig, *Loch*: Inv., Scotland   57 15N 04 15W   64
Dunvegan: Inv., Scotland   57 26N 06 35W   64
Dunvegan, *Loch*: Inv., Scotland   57 30N 06 30W   64
Dunvegan *Head*: Inv., Scotland   57 30N 06 41W   64
Du Page East Branch: *riv.*, Ill., U.S.A.   41 30N 88 00W   124
Duquesne: Pa., U.S.A.   40 23N 79 53W   125
Durack *Range*: W.A., Australia   16 45S 127 45E   40
Dural: N.S.W., Australia   33 41S 151 02E   120
Durance: *riv.*, France   43 45N 05 15E   71
Durango: Spain   43 10N 02 38W   70
Durango: *admin.*, Mexico   24 30N 105 00W   46
Durango: Colo., U.S.A.   37 17N 107 53W   95
Durant: Okla., U.S.A.   34 00N 96 23W   100

Types of map: Ocean pp. 1-5; Physical pp. 6-25; Human pp. 26-57; Topographic pp. 58-101; World pp. 102-111; Urban pp. 112-128.

Durban: Natal, Rep. of S.Africa   29 53S 31 00E   55 107
Düren: W.Germany   50 48N 06 30E   72
Durg: India   21 12N 81 20E   34 83 105
Durgāpur: India   22 28N 88 08E   105 120
Durham: Dur., England   54 47N 01 34W   63
Durham: N.C., U.S.A.   36 00N 78 54W   101
Durham: *admin.*, England   54 30N 01 45W   63
Durlston *Head*: Dorset, England   50 35N 01 57W   61
Durness: Suther., Scotland   58 33N 04 45W   64
Durness, Kyle of: *sea loch,* Suther., Scotland
   58 30N 04 45W   64
Durrës: Albania   41 18N 19 28E   79
Durrow: Laois, Irish Republic   52 51N 07 23W   67
Dursey *Island*: Kerry, Irish Republic   51 30N 10 00W   67
Dursley: Glos., England   51 42N 02 21W   61
D'Urville *Island*: S.I., New Zealand   40 45S 173 45E   87
Dušanbe (Dushanbe): U.S.S.R.   38 35N 68 48E   29
Dushan: China   25 50N 107 31E   85
Dushanbe *see* Dušanbe   38 35N 68 48E   29
Dushui: *riv.*, China   32 15N 110 15E   84
Dusky *Sound*: S.I., New Zealand   45 45S 166 30E   87
Düssel: *riv.*, W.Germany   51 00N 07 00E   118
Düsseldorf: W.Germany   51 13N 06 47E   72 118
Duyun (Tuyün): China   26 20N 107 29E   36 85
Dvina, North: *riv.*, U.S.S.R.   62 30N 44 00E   8 28
Dvina, Western *see* Zapadnaja Dvina   55 15N 29 00E   28 80
Dvúr Králové: Czechoslovakia   50 27N 15 50E   73
Dyer: Nev., U.S.A.   37 41N 118 05W   91
Dyersburg: Tenn., U.S.A.   36 02N 89 23W   100
Dyfed: *admin.*, Wales   52 00N 04 15W   60
Dyje: *riv.*, Czechoslovakia   48 45N 16 45E   73
Dyke: *riv.*, Suther., Scotland   58 15N 03 45W   65
Dysinni: *riv.*, Gwyn., Wales   52 30N 03 45W   60
Džambejty: U.S.S.R.   50 16N 52 35E   81
Džambul (Dzhambul): U.S.S.R.   42 54N 71 22E   29
Džargalant *see* Choud   48 01N 91 39E   30
Dzaudzhikau *see* Ordžonikidze   43 03N 44 40E   28
Dzeržinsk (Dzerzhinsk): U.S.S.R.   56 15N 43 24E   28 80
Dzeržinskij: U.S.S.R.   55 38N 37 50E   119
Džetygara: U.S.S.R.   52 11N 61 12E   29 81
Džezkazgan: U.S.S.R.   47 47N 67 46E   29
Dzhambul *see* Džambul   42 54N 71 22E   29
Dzungarian Gates: *pass*, China/U.S.S.R.   45 25N 82 25E
   8 29

Eabamet *Lake*: Ont., Canada   51 30N 88 00W   93
Eagle: Alaska, U.S.A.   64 46N 141 20W   88
Eagle: *riv.*, Nfld., Canada   53 15N 58 00W   97
Eagle *Lake*: Ont., Canada   49 30N 93 00W   98
Eagle *Mountain*: Calif., U.S.A.   33 50N 115 30W   104
Eagle Pass: Tex., U.S.A.   28 43N 100 30W   95
Eaglesham: Renf., Scotland   55 44N 04 17W   113
Ealing: Gt. Ldn., England   51 31N 00 20W   59 112
Earlsferry: Fife, Scotland   56 11N 02 50W   65
Earl Shilton: Leics., England   52 34N 01 18W   58
Earl's Seat: *mtn.*, Stirl., Scotland   56 02N 04 18W   113
Earlton: Ont., Canada   47 43N 79 49W   99
Earn: *riv.*, Perth., Scotland   56 15N 03 30W   65
Earn, *Loch*: Perth., Scotland   56 15N 04 00W   64
Easingwold: N.Yorks., England   54 07N 01 11W   63
Easley: S.C., U.S.A.   34 50N 82 34W   101
East: *riv.*, N.Y., U.S.A.   40 52N 73 59W   123
East Australian *Current*: S.Pacific Ocean   4
East Berlin *see* Ost-Berlin   52 31N 13 24E   117
Eastbourne: E.Sussex, England   50 46N 00 17E   59
East Caroline *Basin*: N.Pacific Ocean   05 00N 142 00E   4
East Chicago: Ind., U.S.A.   41 38N 87 27W   104 106 124
East China *Sea*:   32 00N 125 00E   4 12 37 85
East Dereham: Norf., England   52 41N 00 56E   58
East Detroit: Mich., U.S.A.   42 29N 82 57W   125
East Dubuque: Ill., U.S.A.   42 30N 90 37W   98
Easter *Island*: S.Pacific Ocean   27 05S 109 20W   5
Easter Island *Fracture Zone*: S.Pacific Ocean
   25 00S 100 00W   5
Eastern Cordillera: *ra.*, Colombia *see* Cordillera Oriental
   05 00N 73 30W   48
Eastern Cordillera: *ra.*, Peru   12 00S 73 45W   18 49
Eastern *Desert, see* Aş Sahrā ash Sharqīyah
   28 30N 32 15E   20 32

Eastern Ghāts: *ra.*, India   19 00N 84 00E   11 34 83
Eastern Rift *Valley*: E.Africa   02 30N 35 30E   20
Eastern Sayan (Sajan) *Mountains*: U.S.S.R.
   53 00N 98 00E   9 30
Easter Ross: *dist.*, R. & Crom., Scotland
   57 45N 04 15W   64
East Falkland: *is.*, Falkland Is.   51 30S 58 45W   52
Eastgate: Wash., U.S.A.   47 34N 122 08W   126
EAST GERMANY   52 30N 12 00E   3 7 78 107 261
East Greenland *Current*: N.Atlantic Ocean   68 00N 30 00W
   2
East Grinstead: Sussex, England   51 08N 00 01W   59
Eastham: Mers., England   53 19N 02 58W   114
East Helena: Mont., U.S.A.   46 35N 111 56W   94
East Hills: N.S.W., Australia   33 58S 150 59E   120
East Horsley: Surrey, England   51 16N 00 26W   112
East Jordan: Mich., U.S.A.   45 09N 85 09W   98
East Kilbride: Lan., Scotland   55 46N 04 10W   62 113
Eastleigh: Hants., England   50 58N 01 22W   59
East Linton: E.Loth., Scotland   55 59N 02 39W   63
East Liverpool: Ohio, U.S.A.   40 38N 80 36W   99
East Loch Tarbert: *lake*, Inv., Scotland   57 45N 06 45W   64
East London (Oos-Londen): C.P., Rep. of S.Africa
   33 00S 27 54E   55
East Looe: Corn., England   50 22N 04 27W   61
East Los Angeles: Calif., U.S.A.   34 01N 118 09W   127
East Lothian: *admin.*, Scotland   55 45N 02 45W   63
East-Main: Qué., Canada   52 10N 78 30W   96
Eastmain: *riv.*, Qué., Canada   52 00N 76 15W   96
East Malaysia: *admin.*, Malaysia   02 00N 114 00E   107
East Malling: Kent, England   51 18N 00 26E   112
East Mariana *Basin*: N.Pacific Ocean   15 00N 152 00E   4
East Pacific *Basin*: N.Pacific Ocean '   20 00N 155 00W   4
East Pacific *Ridge*: S.Pacific Ocean   20 00S 110 00W   5
East Pakistan *see* Bangladesh   22 00N 89 30E   11 35 83 107
Eastport: Maine, U.S.A.   44 55N 67 01W   96
East Retford: Notts., England   53 19N 00 56W   58
East St. Louis: Ill., U.S.A.   38 34N 90 04W   98
East Scotia *Basin*: Southern Ocean   53 00S 35 00W   3
East Siberian *Sea*: U.S.S.R.   72 00N 158 00E   22 31
East Sussex: *admin.*, England   50 45N 00 15E   59
East-West Tollway: *hwy.*, Ill., U.S.A.   41 45N 88 00W   124
Eastwood: N.S.W., Australia   33 48S 151 05E   120
East York: Ont., Canada   43 43N 79 20W   125
Eau Claire: Wis., U.S.A.   44 50N 91 30W   98
Eauripik *Ridge*: N.Pacific Ocean   05 00N 142 00E   4
Ebble: *riv.*, Wilts., England   51 00N 01 45W   61
Ebbw: *riv.*, Gwent, Wales   51 30N 03 00W   113
Ebbw Vale: Gwent, Wales   51 47N 03 12W   61 105 113
Eberswalde: E.Germany   52 50N 13 50E   73 78
Ebetsu: Japan   43 07N 141 34E   86
Ebingen: W.Germany   48 13N 09 02E   72
Ebro: *riv.*, Spain   41 15N 00 15W   6 26 77
Ebro, Embalse de: *res.*, Spain   43 00N 03 58W   70
Eccles: Gt. Man., England   53 29N 02 21W   114
Eccleshall: Staffs., England   52 52N 02 15W   58
Ecija: Spain   37 33N 05 04W   77
Eckington: Derby., England   53 19N 01 21W   58
Ecorse: Mich., U.S.A.   42 15N 83 09W   125
ECUADOR   01 15S 78 15W   18 48 106
Eday: *is.*, Ork. Is., Scotland   59 00N 02 30W   65
Eddrachillis *Bay*: Suther., Scotland   58 15N 05 00W   64
Eddystone *Rocks*: England   50 10N 04 16W   61
Ede: Netherlands   52 03N 05 40E   72
Ede: Nigeria   07 44N 04 31E   57
Edehon *Lake*: N.W.T., Canada   60 15N 97 00W   93
Eden: *riv.*, Cumbria, England   54 45N 02 45W   63
Eden: *riv.*, Fife, Scotland   56 15N 03 30W   65
Eden: *riv.*, Gwyn., Wales   52 45N 03 45W   60
Edenbridge: Kent, England   51 12N 00 04E   59
Edenderry: Offaly, Irish Republic   53 21N 07 03W   67
Edens Expressway: *hwy.*, Ill., U.S.A.   42 00N 87 45W   124
Eder: *riv.*, W.Germany   51 00N 09 15E   72
Eder-Stausee: *lake*, W.Germany   51 00N 09 00E   72
Edgbaston: W.Mid., England   52 26N 01 56W   115
Edgemont: S.D., U.S.A.   43 18N 103 50W   94
Edgware: Gt. Ldn., England   51 37N 00 17W   112
Édhessa: Greece   40 48N 22 03E   79
Edinburgh: Midloth., Scotland   55 57N 03 13W   26 63
Edirne (Adrianople): Turkey   41 40N 26 34E   79
Edmonton: Alta., Canada   53 34N 113 25W   42 92

Edmonton: Gt. Ldn., England 51 37N 00 02W 112
Edmundston: N.B., Canada 47 22N 68 20W 97
Edna: Tex., U.S.A. 28 59N 96 39W 100
Edna Bay: Alaska, U.S.A. 55 57N 133 40W 89
Edo: *riv.*, Japan 35 38N 139 52E 121
Edogawa: Japan 35 41N 139 51E 121
Edremit: Turkey 39 34N 27 01E 79
Edrengijn Nuruu: *ra.*, Mongolia 44 00N 98 00E 36
Edsel-Ford Freeway: *hwy.*, Mich., U.S.A. 42 15N 83 00W 125
Edson: Alta., Canada 53 36N 116 28W 92
Eduni, *Mount*: N.W.T., Canada 64 14N 128 02W 88
Edward, *Lake*: Uganda/Zaïre 00 15S 29 45E 21 54
Edward, *Mount*: Antarctica 75 12S 69 33W 24
Edwards *Plateau*: Tex., U.S.A. 30 30N 100 00W 95
Eel: *riv.*, Calif., U.S.A. 39 45N 123 15W 91
Eger: Hungary 47 53N 20 22E 78
Egersund: Norway 58 27N 06 01E 75
Egham: Surrey, England 51 26N 00 34W 59
Egmont, *Mount*: N.I., New Zealand 39 18S 174 05E 15 37 87
Egremont: Cumbria, England 54 29N 03 33W 62
EGYPT 29 30N 31 15E 20 32 107
Ehingen: W.Germany 48 17N 09 45E 72
Ehrenfeld: W.Germany 50 57N 06 55E 119
Éibar: Spain 43 11N 02 28W 70
Eidelstedt: W.Germany 53 36N 09 55E 119
Eifel: *mtns.*, W.Germany 50 00N 06 45E 72
Eigg: *is.*, Inv., Scotland 56 45N 06 00W 64
Eighe, Beinn: *mtn.*, R. & Crom., Scotland 57 35N 02 26W 64
Eil, *Loch*: Scotland 56 45N 05 15W 64
Eilat *see* Elat 29 33N 34 57E 32
Eilbek-*Kanal*: W.Germany 53 30N 10 00E 119
Eilenburg: E.Germany 51 28N 12 38E 73
Eindhoven: Netherlands 51 26N 05 30E 26 72
Eisenach: E.Germany 50 59N 10 19E 73
Eisenerz: Austria 47 32N 14 53E 73 105
Eisenerzer *Alpen*: Austria 47 30N 15 00E 73
Eisleben: E.Germany 51 32N 11 33E 73
Eisort, *Loch*: Inv., Scotland 57 00N 05 45W 64
Ekibastuz: U.S.S.R. 51 42N 75 22E 29
Ekka *Island*: N.W.T., Canada 66 19N 122 21W 88
Ekwan: *riv.*, Ont., Canada 53 30N 85 30W 93
El Aaiùn (El Aiun): Spanish Sahara 27 10N 13 12W 56
El Asnam (Orléansville): Algeria 36 10N 01 20E 56 77
Elat (Eilat): Israel 29 33N 34 57E 32
Elâziğ: Turkey 38 41N 39 14E 32
Elba, *Isola d'*: Italy 42 45N 10 15E 79 105
Elbasan: Albania 41 07N 20 05E 79
Elbe: *riv.*, E.Germany/W.Germany 53 30N 10 00E 7 27 73
Elbe-Havel *Kanal*: E.Germany 52 15N 11 45E 73
Elberfeld: W.Germany 51 15N 07 10E 118
Elbert, *Mount*: Colo., U.S.A. 39 07N 106 26W 17 43 94
Elbe-Seitenkanal: *can.*, W.Germany 50 30N 10 30E 73
Elblag: Poland 54 10N 19 25E 78
Elbrus: *mtn.*, U.S.S.R. 43 21N 42 26E 8 28
El Burgo: Spain 41 35N 03 04W 77
Elburz *Mountains*: Iran 36 15N 52 15E 10 33
El Centro: Calif., U.S.A. 32 48N 115 34W 43 91
El Cerrito: Calif., U.S.A. 37 55N 122 18W 126
Elche: Spain 38 16N 00 41W 77
El-Dar-el-Beida (Casablanca): Morocco 33 39N 07 35W 56
El Djezair (Alger, Algiers): Algeria 36 50N 03 00E 20 56 77
Eldorado: Sask., Canada 59 36N 108 28W 92
El Dorado: Ark., U.S.A. 33 12N 92 40W 100
El Dorado: Kans., U.S.A. 37 49N 96 52W 95
Eldoret: Kenya 00 31N 35 17E 54
Elektrostal': U.S.S.R. 55 47N 38 28E 28
Elephant Butte *Reservoir*: N.Mex., U.S.A. 33 09N 107 11W 95
El Eulma: Algeria 36 08N 05 40E 77
Eleuthera: *is.*, Bahamas 25 15N 76 15W 47
Elevsís: Greece 38 02N 23 33E 105
El Fasher *see* Al Fāshir 13 37N 25 22E 32
El Ferrol del Caudillo: Spain 43 29N 08 14W 77
Elgin: Moray., Scotland 57 39N 03 20W 65
Elgin: Ill., U.S.A. 42 03N 88 19W 98
Elgol: Inv., Scotland 57 09N 06 07W 64
El Goléa: Algeria 30 35N 02 51E 56
Elgon, *Mount*: Kenya/Uganda 01 07N 34 35E 21 53
Eling, *Lake* (Oling Hu): China 34 45N 97 30E 36
Elisabethville *see* Lubumbashi 11 40S 27 28E 54
Elizabeth: N.J., U.S.A. 40 40N 74 13W 123
Elizabeth City: N.C., U.S.A. 36 18N 76 16W 101
Elizabethton: Tenn., U.S.A. 36 22N 82 15W 101
Elizabethtown: Ky., U.S.A. 37 41N 85 51W 101
El Jadida (Mazagan): Morocco 33 16N 08 30W 56
Ełk: Poland 53 51N 22 20E 78
Elk City: Okla., U.S.A. 35 25N 99 25W 95
El Khârga *see* Al Khārijah 25 26N 30 33E 32
Elkhart: Ind., U.S.A. 41 52N 85 56W 98
Elkhorn: *riv.*, Nebr., U.S.A. 41 45N 97 15W 94
Elkins: W.Va., U.S.A. 38 56N 79 53W 99
Elk Island *National Park*: Alta., Canada 53 30N 112 45W 92
Elko: Nev., U.S.A. 40 50N 115 46W 91
Elk River: Idaho, U.S.A. 46 47N 116 11W 90
Elland: W.Yorks., England 53 41N 01 50W 63 115
Ellensburg: Wash., U.S.A. 47 00N 120 32W 90
Ellesmere: Salop, England 52 54N 02 54W 60
Ellesmere *Island*: Canada 80 00N 80 00W 23
Ellesmere Port: Ches., England 53 17N 02 54W 60 114
Ellice *Islands*: S.Pacific Ocean 07 00S 177 00E 4 15
Ellichpur *see* Achalpur 21 19N 77 30E 82
Elliott *Bay*: Wash., U.S.A. 47 36N 122 22W 126
Ellisville: Miss., U.S.A. 31 36N 89 12W 100
Ellon: Aber., Scotland 57 22N 02 05W 65
Ellora: India 20 04N 75 15E 82
Ellore *see* Elūru 16 45N 81 10E 34
Ellsworth: Maine, U.S.A. 44 34N 68 24W 99
Ellsworth Land: *reg.*, Antarctica 76 00S 80 00W 24
Elmhurst: Ill., U.S.A. 41 54N 87 56W 124
El Minya *see* Al Minya 28 06N 30 45E 32
Elmira: N.Y., U.S.A. 42 06N 76 50W 99
El Morro *National Monument*: N.Mex., U.S.A. 35 04N 108 25W 95
Elmshorn: W.Germany 53 46N 09 40E 72
Elmwood Park: Ill., U.S.A. 41 54N 87 49W 124
El Obeid *see* Al Ubayyiḍ 13 11N 30 13E 53
Eloy: Ariz., U.S.A. 32 45N 111 33W 91
El Pao: Venezuela 08 01N 62 38W 104
El Paso: Tex., U.S.A. 31 45N 106 29W 43 95
El Reno: Okla., U.S.A. 35 32N 97 57W 95
El Romeral: Chile 29 43S 71 15W 104
Elsa: Yukon, Canada 63 55N 135 29W 88
EL SALVADOR 13 45N 89 00W 17 46 106
El Segundo: Calif., U.S.A. 33 55N 118 25W 106
Eltanin *Fracture Zone*: S.Pacific Ocean 45 00S 155 00W 5
El Tigre: Venezuela 08 44N 64 18W 48
El Tofo: Chile 29 27S 71 15W 104
El'ton: U.S.S.R. 49 08N 46 50E 81
El'ton, Ozero: *lake*, U.S.S.R. 49 16N 46 35E 81
Elūru (Ellore): India 16 45N 81 10E 34
Elva, Slieve: *mtn.*, Clare, Irish Republic 53 05N 09 16W 67
Elverum: Norway 60 54N 11 33E 75
Elwood: Ind., U.S.A. 40 17N 85 51W 98
Elwy: *riv.*, Clwyd, Wales 53 00N 03 30W 60
Ely: Cambs., England 52 24N 00 16E 59
Ely: Nev., U.S.A. 39 15N 114 54W 91
Ely: *riv.*, Glam., Wales 51 15N 03 00W 113
Emäjoki: *riv.*, Finland 64 30N 28 30E 74
Emba: U.S.S.R. 48 50N 58 08E 81
Emba: *riv.*, U.S.S.R. 44 45N 56 00E 8 29
Emden: W.Germany 53 23N 07 13E 72 76
Emerson: Man., Canada 49 00N 97 11W 93
Emeryville: Calif., U.S.A. 37 50N 122 19W 126
Emi Koussi: *mtn.*, Chad 19 52N 18 31E 20
Emmen: Netherlands 52 47N 06 55E 72
Emmett: Idaho, U.S.A. 43 52N 116 30W 90
Emory *Peak*: Tex., U.S.A. 29 15N 103 18W 95
Emperor *Seamounts*: N.Pacific Ocean 40 00N 170 00E 4
Emporia: Kans., U.S.A. 38 25N 96 11W 94
Emporia: Va., U.S.A. 36 42N 77 33W 101
Empress: Alta., Canada 50 56N 110 01W 92
Ems: *riv.*, W.Germany 53 15N 07 15E 72
Emscher: *riv.*, W.Germany 51 30N 07 15E 118
Emsdetten: W.Germany 52 11N 07 32E 72
Ems-Jade *Kanal*: W.Germany 53 15N 07 45E 72
Enard *Bay*: R. & Crom., Scotland 58 00N 05 15W 64
Encarnación: Paraguay 27 19S 55 53W 51
Endako: B.C., Canada 54 10N 125 21W 89

Ende: Indonesia 08 51S 121 40E   39
Enderby: B.C., Canada 50 32N 119 10W   89
Enderby Land: reg., Antarctica 69 00S 53 00E   24
Enderlin: N.D., U.S.A. 46 38N 97 36W   94
Enfield: Gt. Ldn., England 51 40N 00 05W   112
Engadin: geog. reg., Switzerland   71
Engel's: U.S.S.R. 51 30N 46 07E   28 81
Enggano: is., Indonesia 05 30S 102 15E   13 38
Enghien-les-Bains: France 48 58N 02 19E   117
Engineer: B.C., Canada 59 30N 134 15W   88
ENGLAND   26 69
Englee: Nfld., Canada 50 45N 56 05W   97
Englewood: N.J., U.S.A. 40 55N 73 59W   123
English: riv., Canada 50 15N 94 30W   93
English Bay: B.C., Canada 49 15N 123 00W   126
English Bāzār: India 25 00N 88 12E   35 83
English Channel: England/France 50 00N 02 00W
                                                    6 26 69 70
Enid: Okla., U.S.A. 36 24N 97 53W   95
Enköping: Sweden 59 38N 17 07E   75
Enna: Sicily 37 34N 14 17E   79
Ennadai: N.W.T., Canada 61 05N 101 00W   92
Ennadai Lake: N.W.T., Canada 61 00N 101 30W   92
Ennedi: mtns., Chad 17 00N 22 30E   20
Ennell, Lough: Westmeath, Irish Republic 53 30N 07 15W
                                                             66
Ennepe: riv., W.Germany 51 15N 07 15E   118
Ennepetal: W.Germany 51 18N 07 22E   118
Ennis: Clare, Irish Republic 52 50N 08 59W   67
Ennis: Tex., U.S.A. 32 20N 96 38W   100
Enniscorthy: Wex., Irish Republic 52 30N 06 34W   67
Enniskerry: Wick., Irish Republic 53 12N 06 10W   67
Enniskillen: Ferm., N.Ireland 54 21N 07 38W   66
Ennistymon: Clare, Irish Republic 52 57N 09 13W   67
Enns: Austria 48 13N 14 28E   73
Enns: riv., Austria 47 30N 14 30E   73
Enping: China 22 12N 112 20E   85
Enschede: Netherlands 52 13N 06 55E   72
Enshi: China 30 19N 109 28E   85
Entebbe: Uganda 00 05N 32 29E   53
Enterprise: Ala., U.S.A. 31 19N 85 51W   101
Entre Ríos: admin., Argentina 32 00S 59 15W   52
Entre Ríos: geog. reg., Argentina 30 00S 58 45W   52
Enugu: Nigeria 06 20N 07 29E   57
Eolie o Lipari, Isole (Lipari Islands): Sicily 38 30N 14 45E
                                                             79
Épernay: France 49 02N 03 58E   71
Ephrata: Wash., U.S.A. 47 19N 119 33W   90
Épinal: France 48 10N 06 28E   71
Epping: N.S.W., Australia 33 46S 151 05E   120
Epping: Essex, England 51 42N 00 07E   59 112
Epping Forest: Essex, England 51 30N 00 00   112
Epsom: Surrey, England 51 20N 00 16W   59 112
Epworth: Humb., England 53 32N 00 49W   63
Equatorial Counter Current: N.Atlantic Ocean
  03 00N 10 00W   2
Equatorial Counter Current: N.Pacific Ocean
  06 00N 125 00W   5
EQUATORIAL GUINEA 01 30N 10 00E   20 57
Erba: Italy 45 48N 09 14E   116
Erbil see Irbīl 36 11N 44 01E   33
Erdington: W.Mid., England 52 32N 01 54W   115
Erebus, Mount: volc., Antarctica 77 40S 167 20E   25
Erechim: Brazil 27 35S 52 15W   51
Ereğli: Turkey 41 17N 31 25E   105
Erft: riv., W.Germany 51 00N 06 30E   118
Erft-Kanal: W.Germany 50 45N 06 45E   119
Erfurt: E.Germany 50 58N 11 02E   3 261
Erfurt: admin., E.Germany 51 00N 10 45E   73
Erg Chech: des., Algeria 25 00N 02 00W   20 56
Ergene: riv., Turkey 41 15N 26 45E   79
Erg Iguidi: des., Algeria/Mauritania 27 00N 06 00W   20 56
Eriboll, Loch: Suther., Scotland 58 30N 04 30W   64
Erie: Pa., U.S.A. 42 07N 80 05W   45 99
Erie, Lake: Canada/U.S.A.   17 45 99
Erimo-Misaki: cape., Japan 41 55N 143 15E   87
Eriskay: is., Inv., Scotland 57 00N 07 15W   64
Erisort, Loch: R. & Crom., Scotland 58 00N 06 30W   64
Erith: Gt. Ldn., England 51 29N 00 11E   112
Erith Marshes: Gt. Ldn., England 51 30N 00 00   112
Eritrea: geog. reg., Ethiopia 14 30N 40 00E   53

Erkina: riv., Laois, Irish Republic 52 45N 07 30W   67
Erkner: E.Germany 52 25N 13 46E   117
Erlandson Lake: Qué., Canada 57 15N 68 30W   96
Erlangen: W.Germany 49 36N 11 02E   73
Ernakulam: India 10 00N 76 16E   34
Erne, Lower Lough: Ferm., N.Ireland 54 15N 07 45W   66
Erne, Upper Lough: Ferm., N.Ireland 54 00N 07 30W   66
Errigal: mtn., Don., Irish Republic 55 02N 08 07W   66
Erris Head: Mayo, Irish Republic 54 19N 10 00W   66
Ertil': U.S.S.R. 51 51N 40 49E   80
Erzgebirge: mtns., Czechoslovakia/E.Germany
  50 30N 13 00E   73
Erzurum: Turkey 39 57N 41 17E   33
Esbjerg: Denmark 55 28N 08 27E   26 75
Escalada: Argentina 34 44S 58 24W   128
Escanaba: Mich., U.S.A. 45 47N 87 04W   98
Esch-sur-Alzette: Luxembourg 49 30N 05 59E   72 105
Eschwege: W.Germany 51 11N 10 03E   73
Escombreras: Spain 37 34N 00 57W   106
Escondido: Calif., U.S.A. 33 07N 117 05W   91
Escoublac-la-Baule: France 47 18N 02 21W   70
Escuintla: Guatemala 14 18N 90 47W   46
Eşfahān (Isfahan): Iran 32 41N 51 41E   33
Esher: Surrey, England 51 23N 00 22W   59 112
Esk: riv., England/Scotland 55 00N 03 00W   63
Esk: riv., N.Yorks., England 54 30N 00 30W   63
Esker: Nfld., Canada 53 55N 66 28W   97
Eskilstuna: Sweden 59 22N 16 31E   75
Eskimo Point: N.W.T., Canada 61 10N 94 04W   93
Eskişehir: Turkey 39 46N 30 32E   32
Esmeraldas: Ecuador 00 59N 79 42W   48
Esperance: W.A., Australia 33 49S 121 52E   40
Esperanza: rsch. stn., Antarctica 63 24S 57 00W   24
Espinhaço, Serra do: ra., Brazil 18 15S 43 45W   51
Espírito Santo: admin., Brazil 19 45S 40 45W   51
Espoo: Finland 60 13N 24 40E   75
Essen: W.Germany 51 27N 06 57E   72 118
Essequibo: riv., Guyana 05 30N 58 45W   48
Essex: admin., England 51 45N 00 30E   59
Essondale: B.C., Canada 49 15N 122 49W   126
Estacado, Llano: plat., U.S.A. 33 15N 103 00W   95
Estella: Spain 42 41N 02 02W   70
Esterhazy: Sask., Canada 50 40N 102 02W   92
Estero Bay: Calif., U.S.A. 35 15N 120 45W   91
Estevan: Sask., Canada 49 09N 103 00W   92
Estherville: Iowa, U.S.A. 43 28N 94 49W   98
Eston: Cleve., England 54 34N 01 07W   63
Estonskaja S.S.R. (Estonian S.S.R.): U.S.S.R.
  59 00N 26 00E   29 75
Estudillo: Calif., U.S.A. 37 42N 122 06W   126
Esztergom: Hungary 47 46N 18 44E   78
Etah: India 27 33N 78 39E   82
Étang de Biscarosse et de Parentis: lag., France
  44 20N 01 10W   70
Étang de Carcans: lag., France 45 05N 01 03W   70
Étang de Cazaux: lag., France 44 30N 01 08W   70
Étang de Leucate: lag., France 42 50N 03 00E   71
Étang de Vaccarès: lag., France 43 32N 04 35E   71
Etāwah: India 26 45N 79 01E   82
Etawney Lake: Man., Canada 57 45N 96 45W   93
ETHIOPIA 04 50N 39 00E   21 53
Ethiopian Highlands: Ethiopia 10 15N 38 00E   21 53
Etive, Loch: Argyll., Scotland 56 15N 05 00W   64
Etna, Monte: volc., Sicily 37 45N 15 00E   7 79
Etobicoke: Ont., Canada 43 38N 79 30W   125
Etobicoke: riv., Ont., Canada 43 30N 79 30W   125
Eton: Berks., England 51 31N 00 37W   59
Etosha Pan: salt lake, S.W.Africa 18 30S 16 15E   55
Etuokeqi: China 39 11N 107 59E   84
Euboea see Évvoia 38 30N 23 30E   79
Eudora: Ark., U.S.A. 33 07N 91 16W   100
Eufaula: Ala., U.S.A. 31 54N 85 09W   101
Eufaula Reservoir: Okla., U.S.A. 35 17N 95 35W   100
Eugene: Oreg., U.S.A. 44 05N 123 04W   42 90
Eunice: La., U.S.A. 30 30N 92 25W   100
Eunice: N.Mex., U.S.A. 32 26N 103 10W   95
Euphrates: riv., Middle East 35 30N 40 15E   10 33
Eureka: Calif., U.S.A. 40 49N 124 10W   43 91
Eureka: Mont., U.S.A. 48 53N 115 03W   90
Eureka: Nev., U.S.A. 39 31N 115 58W   91
Eureka: Utah, U.S.A. 39 58N 112 07W   91

Types of map: Ocean pp. 1-5; Physical pp. 6-25; Human pp. 26-57; Topographic pp. 58-101; World pp. 102-111; Urban pp. 112-128.

Eutsuk *Lake*: B.C., Canada 53 15N 126 30W 89
Evans, *Lake*: Qué., Canada 50 45N 77 00W 96
Evanston: Ill., U.S.A. 42 02N 87 41W 124
Evanston: Wyo., U.S.A. 41 16N 110 58W 94
Evansville: Ind., U.S.A. 38 00N 87 33W 45 98
Evelix: *riv.*, Suther., Scotland 57 45N 04 15W 64
Evenlode: *riv.*, England 51 45N 01 30W 59
Everest, *Mount*: China/Nepal 27 58N 86 57E 11 35 83
Everett: Mass., U.S.A. 42 23N 71 03W 122
Everett: Wash., U.S.A. 47 59N 122 12W 90
Everett *Mountains*: N.W.T., Canada 62 45N 68 00W 16
Everglades, The: *swamps*, Fla., U.S.A. 25 45N 80 45W 45 101
Everglades *National Park*: Fla., U.S.A. 25 30N 80 45W 101
Evergreen Park: Ill., U.S.A. 41 43N 87 42W 124
Evesham: Here. & Worcs., England 52 06N 01 56W 59
Evesham, *Vale of*: England 52 00N 01 45W 59
Évora: Portugal 38 34N 07 54W 77
Evreux: France 49 03N 01 11E 70
Évvoia (Euboea): *is.*, Greece 38 30N 23 30E 79
Ewe, *Loch*: R.& Crom., Scotland 57 45N 05 30W 64
Exe: *riv.*, England 50 45N 03 30W 61
Exeter: Devon, England 50 43N 03 31W 61
Exhibition *Park*: B.C., Canada 49 17N 123 02W 126
Exmoor *Forest*: England 51 00N 03 45W 61
Exmoor *National Park*: England 51 00N 03 30W 61
Exmouth: Devon, England 50 37N 03 25W 61
Exshaw: Alta., Canada 51 07N 115 08W 92
Exuma *Sound*: Bahamas 24 15N 76 00W 47
Eyasi, *Lake*: Tanzania 03 30S 35 00E 54
Eye: Suff., England 52 19N 01 09E 59
Eyemouth: Ber., Scotland 55 52N 02 06W 63
Eye *Peninsula*: R. & Crom., Scotland 58 00N 06 00W 64
Eyre: *riv.*, Qld., Australia 25 00S 138 45E 41
Eyre, *Lake*: S.A., Australia 28 30S 137 15E 14 41
Eyre *Peninsula*: S.A., Australia 33 45S 135 45E 40
Ezeiza: Argentina 34 51S 58 32W 128

Fabens: Tex., U.S.A. 31 30N 106 10W 95
Fåberg: Norway 61 10N 10 22E 75
Faber *Lake*: N.W.T., Canada 63 45N 117 00W 88
Fada, Lochan: *lake*, R.& Crom., Scotland 57 30N 05 15W 64
Faden: Nfld., Canada 54 12N 66 30W 97
Færoe *Islands see* Føroyar 62 00N 07 00W 2 6
Fagersta: Sweden 59 59N 15 49E 75
Faguibine, *Lake*: Mali 16 30N 04 00W 56
Fairborn: Ohio, U.S.A. 39 48N 84 03W 98 98
Fairbury: Nebr., U.S.A. 40 08N 97 11W 94
Fairfield: N.S.W., Australia 33 52S 150 57E 120
Fairfield: Ala., U.S.A. 33 29N 86 59W 104
Fairfield: Ill., U.S.A. 42 13N 88 03W 124
Fairford: Glos., England 51 54N 01 47W 61
Fair *Head*: Antrim, N.Ireland 55 13N 06 09W 66
Fair *Isle*: Shet. Is., Scotland 59 32N 01 38W 68
Fair Lawn: N.J., U.S.A. 40 56N 74 08W 123
Fairless Hills: Pa., U.S.A. 40 10N 74 53W 104
Fairlie: S.I., New Zealand 44 05S 170 50E 87
Fairmont: Minn., U.S.A. 43 39N 94 27W 98
Fairmont: W.Va., U.S.A. 39 28N 80 08W 99
Fairmount *Park*: Pa., U.S.A. 40 03N 75 12W 122
Fairplay: Colo., U.S.A. 39 14N 106 00W 94
Fairview: Alta., Canada 56 03N 118 28W 89
Fais: *is.*, Caroline Is. 09 46N 140 31E 12
Faith: S.D., U.S.A. 45 02N 102 02W 94
Faizābād: Afghanistan 37 06N 70 34E 29
Faizābād (Fyzabad): India 26 46N 82 08E 34 83
Fakenham: Norf., England 52 50N 00 51E 58
Fal: *riv.*, Corn., England 50 15N 04 45W 61
Falam: Burma 22 58N 93 45E 35
Falconbridge: Ont., Canada 46 35N 80 48W 99
Falkenberg: Sweden 56 55N 12 30E 75
Falkensee: E.Germany 52 35N 13 06E 117
Falkirk: Stirl., Scotland 56 00N 03 48W 62
Falkland *Current*: S.Atlantic Ocean 50 00S 74 00W 3
Falkland *Islands* (Malvinas, *Islas*): *U.K. colony*, S.Atlantic Ocean 51 30S 59 30W 3 19 52
Falkland *Plateau*: S.Atlantic Ocean 52 00S 53 00W 3
Falkland *Rise*: S.Atlantic Ocean 51 00S 47 00W 19
Falköping: Sweden 58 10N 13 32E 75
Fallon: Nev., U.S.A. 39 29N 118 47W 91
Fall River: Mass., U.S.A. 41 42N 71 08W 99
Falls Church: Va., U.S.A. 38 54N 77 11W 122
Falls City: Nebr., U.S.A. 40 03N 95 36W 94
Falmouth: Corn., England 50 08N 05 04W 61
Falmouth *Bay*: Corn., England 50 00N 05 00W 61
Falster: *is.*, Denmark 54 45N 12 00E 73 75
Falun: Sweden 60 37N 15 40E 75
Famagusta *see* Ammókhóstos 35 07N 33 57E 32
Famatina, Sierra de: *ra.*, Argentina 28 30S 68 00W 52
Fana: Norway 60 15N 05 23E 75
Fangcheng: Guanxi Zhuang, China 21 47N 108 22E 85
Fangcheng: Henan, China 33 17N 112 58E 84
Fangxian: China 32 05N 110 43E 84
Fannich, *Loch*: R. & Crom., Scotland 57 30N 05 00W 64
Fanning *Island*: N.Pacific Ocean 03 52N 159 22W 4
Fanxian: China 35 52N 115 39E 84
Fanzhi: China 39 12N 113 10E 84
Farafra *Oasis*: Egypt 26 45N 28 30E 32
Farasan *Islands*: Red Sea 16 45N 42 00E 10 33
Faraway, *Mount*: Antarctica 79 12S 28 49W 24
Fareham: Hants., England 50 51N 01 10W 59
Farewell, *Cape*: Greenland 59 45N 44 00W 16
Farewell, *Cape*: S.I., New Zealand 40 30S 172 42E 87
Fargo: N.D., U.S.A. 46 53N 96 48W 42 94
Faribault: Minn., U.S.A. 44 19N 93 15W 98
Farīdābād: India 28 24N 77 18E 82
Farīdkot: India 30 42N 74 47E 82
Farīdpur: Bangladesh 23 29N 89 31E 83
Faringdon: Oxon., England 51 40N 01 35W 59
Farmington: Mich., U.S.A. 42 29N 83 22W 125
Farmington: N.Mex., U.S.A. 36 44N 108 12W 43 95
Farnborough: Hants., England 51 17N 00 46W 59 112
Farnham: Surrey, England 51 13N 00 49W 59 112
Farnham, *Mount*: Alta., Canada 50 27N 116 37W 16
Farnworth: Gt. Man., England 53 33N 02 24W 63 114
Faro: Portugal 37 01N 07 56W 77
Fårön: *is.*, Sweden 57 56N 19 08E 75
Farrar: *riv.*, Inv., Scotland 57 15N 04 45W 64
Farrukhābād: India 27 24N 79 37E 34 83
Farsund: Norway 58 05N 06 49E 75
Fastov: U.S.S.R. 50 06N 29 55E 80
Fatehpur: Rājasthān, India 27 59N 75 01E 82
Fatehpur: Uttar Pradesh, India 25 56N 80 55E 82
Fatthpur: Uttar Pradesh, India 27 10N 81 13E 83
Fauske: Norway 67 17N 15 25E 74
Faversham: Kent, England 51 20N 00 53E 59
Favourable Lake: Ont., Canada 52 50N 93 38W 93
Fawley: Hants., England 50 49N 01 20W 59 107
Fawn; *riv.*, Ont., Canada 54 00N 89 00W 93
Fayette: Ala., U.S.A. 33 41N 87 50W 100
Fayetteville: Ark., U.S.A. 36 04N 94 10W 43 100
Fayetteville: N.C., U.S.A. 35 03N 78 53W 101
Fāzilka: India 30 26N 74 04E 82
Feale: *riv.*, Kerry, Irish Republic 52 15N 09 30W 67
Fear, *Cape*: N.C., U.S.A. 33 51N 77 59W 101
Featherstone: W.Yorks., England 53 41N 01 21W 115
Fécamp: France 49 45N 00 23E 70
Feeagh, *Lough*: Mayo, Irish Republic 53 45N 09 30W 66
Fehmarn: *is.*, W.Germany 54 28N 11 08E 73
Feicheng: China 36 18N 116 46E 84
Feira de Santana: Brazil 12 15S 38 57W 50
Feixi: China 31 41N 117 14E 84
Feldkirch: Austria 47 15N 09 38E 71
Felixstowe: Suff., England 51 58N 01 20E 59
Feltham: Gt. Ldn., England 51 27N 00 25W 112
Femer Bælt: *str.*, Denmark/W.Germany 54 30N 11 15E 73
Femund: *lake*, Norway 62 00N 11 45E 75
Fen: *riv.*, China 36 30N 111 45E 84
Fengcheng: China 28 10N 115 47E 85
Fengdu: China 29 59N 107 45E 84
Fenggang: China 27 59N 107 43E 85
Fenghua: China 29 40N 121 29E 85
Fenghuang: Hunan, China 27 58N 109 30E 85
Fenglehe: China 31 28N 112 29E 84
Fengqiu: China 34 57N 114 21E 84
Fengtai: Anhui, China 32 44N 116 45E 84
Fengtai: Beijing Shi, China 39 51N 116 16E 121
Fengt'ien *see* Shenyang 41 48N 123 30E 37 105

Fengxian: Jiangsu, China   34 42N 116 40E   84
Fengxian: Shǎnxī, China   33 57N 106 40E   84
Fengxin: China   28 43N 115 29E   85
Fengyangshan: *mtn.*, China   27 47N 119 15E   85
Fengzhen: China   40 29N 113 10E   84
Fens, The: *geog. reg.*, England   52 45N 00 00   58
Fenyang: China   37 11N 111 41E   36 84
Fenyi: China   27 44N 114 40E   85
Feolin Ferry: Argyll., Scotland   55 51N 06 06W   62
Ferbane: Offaly, Irish Republic   53 16N 07 49W   67
Fergana: U.S.S.R.   40 23N 71 46E   29
Fergus Falls: Minn., U.S.A.   46 18N 96 07W   94
Fermanagh: *admin.*, N.Ireland   54 15N 07 45W   66
Fermoy: Cork, Irish Republic   52 08N 08 16W   67
Fernandez *Fracture Zone*: S.Pacific Ocean   40 00S 90 00W
                                                   3
Fernando de Noronha: *is.*, S.Atlantic Ocean
   03 50S 32 25W   3
Fernando Póo: *see* Macias Nguema Biyogo
   03 30N 08 45E   20 57
Ferndale: Mich., U.S.A.   42 26N 83 08W   125
Fernie: B.C., Canada   49 30N 115 00W   90
Ferozepore *see* Firozpur   30 55N 74 38E   34 82
Ferrara: Italy   44 50N 11 38E   26 78
Fertő: *lake see* Neusiedler See   47 45N 16 45E 78
Fès (Fez): Morocco   34 05N 05 00W   56
Fethard: Tip., Irish Republic   52 28N 07 41W   67
Fetlar: *is.*, Shet. Is., Scotland   60 30N 00 45W 65
Feurs: France   45 44N 04 13E   71
Feyzin: France   45 40N 04 51E   107
Fez *see* Fès   34 05N 05 00W   56
Fezzan: *geog. reg.*, Libya   26 30N 15 00E   32
Ffestiniog: Gwyn., Wales   52 58N 03 55W   60
Fforest Fawr: *mtns.*, Powys, Wales   51 45N 03 30W 60
Fhada, Beinn: *mtn.*, R. & Crom., Scotland   57 13N 05 18W
                                                   64
Fianarantsoa: Malagasy Rep.   21 26S 47 05E   55
Field: Alta., Canada   51 24N 116 29W   92
Fier: Albania   40 44N 19 33E   79
Fife: *admin.*, Scotland   56 15N 03 00W   65
Fife Ness: *cape*, Fife, Scotland   56 17N 02 36W 65
Fighting *Island*: Ont., Canada   42 13N 83 07W 125
Figile: *riv.*, Irish Republic   53 15N 07 00W   67
FIJI   17 00S 178 00E   4 15
Filchner *Ice Shelf*: Antarctica   79 00S 40 00W 24
Filey: N.Yorks., England   54 12N 00 17W   63
Filton: Avon, England   51 31N 02 35W   61 113
Finchley: Gt. Ldn., England   51 37N 00 11W   112
Findhorn: *riv.*, Scotland   57 15N 03 45W   65
Findlay: Ohio, U.S.A.   41 02N 83 40W   98
Finisterre, *Cabo*: Spain   42 52N 09 16W   26 77
Finkenwerder: W.Germany   53 32N 09 52E   119
FINLAND   7 74 107
Finland, *Gulf of*: Finland/U.S.S.R.   60 00N 26 00E 7 75
Finlay: *riv.*, B.C., Canada   56 30N 124 30W 42 89
Finlay Forks: B.C., Canada   56 00N 123 59W   89
Finnmarksvidda: *plat.*, Norway   69 30N 25 00E   74
Fino Mornasco: Italy   45 44N 09 03E   116
Finspång: Sweden   58 42N 15 45E   75
Fintona: Tyr., N.Ireland   54 30N 07 18W   66
Fionn *Loch*: R. & Crom., Scotland   57 45N 05 15W 64
Fionnphort: Argyll., Scotland   56 19N 06 22W   64
Firenze (Florence): Italy   44 47N 11 15E   26 79
Firminy: France   45 23N 04 18E   71
Fīrozābad: India   27 09N 78 24E   34 82
Firozpur (Ferozepore): India   30 55N 74 38E   34 82
Firth of Clyde: *est.*, Scotland   55 45N 05 00W 62 113
Firth of Forth: *est.*, Scotland   56 00N 03 00W 65
Firth of Lorne: *est.*, Argyll., Scotland   56 15N 05 30W 64
Firth of Tay: *est.*, Scotland   56 15N 03 00W   65
Fischbek: W.Germany   53 28N 09 50E   119
Fisherman's *Wharf*: Calif., U.S.A.   37 48N 122 27W 126
Fisher *Strait*: N.W.T., Canada   63 00N 84 00W   44
Fishguard: Dyfed, Wales   51 59N 04 59W   60
Fitzgerald: Ga., U.S.A.   31 43N 83 16W   101
Fitzroy: *riv.*, W.A., Australia   17 45S 123 45E 14 40
Fiumicino: Italy   41 46N 12 14E   116
Fjordland *National Park*: S.I., New Zealand   45 45S 167 00E
                                                   87
Flagstaff: Ariz., U.S.A.   35 12N 111 39W   43 91
Flambeau: *riv.*, Wis., U.S.A.   45 30N 90 45W   98

Flamborough *Head*: Humb., England   54 06N 00 04W 63
Flaming Gorge *Reservoir*: Wyo., U.S.A.   40 55N 109 25W
                                                   94
Flat: *riv.*, N.W.T., Canada   61 15N 126 00W   88
Flathead: *riv.*, Canada/U.S.A.   49 00N 114 30W 92
Flathead *Lake*: Mont., U.S.A.   47 51N 114 08W   90
Flat Holm: *is.*, Bristol Channel, England   51 15N 03 00W
                                                  113
Flattery, *Cape*: Wash., U.S.A.   48 23N 124 29W 90
Fleet: Hants., England   51 16N 00 50W   59
Fleet: *riv.*, Suther., Scotland   57 45N 04 00W 65
Fleetwood: Lancs., England   53 56N 03 01W   63 114
Flekkefjord: Norway   58 17N 06 40E   75
Flensburg: W.Germany   54 47N 09 27E   26 72 76
Flers: France   48 45N 00 34W   70
Fleuth: *riv.*, W.Germany   51 30N 06 15E   118
Flinders *Island*: Tas., Australia   40 00S 148 15E 40
Flinders *Range*: S.A., Australia   31 00S 138 30E 41
Flin Flon: Man., Canada   54 47N 101 51W   42 92
Flins-sur-Seine: France   48 58N 01 52E   117
Flint: Mich., U.S.A.   43 03N 83 40W   45 98
Flint: Clwyd, Wales   53 15N 03 07W   60
Flint: *riv.*, Ga., U.S.A.   31 00N 84 30W   101
Flintshire: *admin.*, Wales. Absorbed into new *admin.* of
   Clwyd, 1974.   60
Flood *Range*: Antarctica   76 00S 134 30W   25
Flora: Norway   61 36N 05 00E   75
Florence: Italy *see* Firenze   43 47N 11 15E 26 79
Florence: Ala., U.S.A.   34 48N 87 41W   100
Florence: Ariz., U.S.A.   33 02N 111 23W   91
Florence: Colo., U.S.A.   38 23N 105 08W   95
Florence: S.C., U.S.A.   34 12N 79 44W   101
Florencia: Colombia   01 37N 75 37W   48
Florencio Varela: Argentina   34 49S 58 17W   128
Flores: Guatemala   16 56N 89 53W   46
Flores: *is.*, Indonesia   08 30S 120 45E   13 39
Flores *Sea*: Indonesia   07 15S 119 30E   39
Floresta Flores: Argentina   34 38S 58 29W   128
Florešty: U.S.S.R.   47 53N 28 17E   78
Floriano: Brazil   06 47S 43 01W   50
Florianópolis: Brazil   27 35S 48 31W   51
Florida: Argentina   34 32S 58 29W   128
Florida: Uruguay   34 04S 56 14W   52
Florida: *admin.*, U.S.A.   29 00N 82 00W   45 101
Florida, *Straits of*: Bahama Is./U.S.A.
   25 00N 80 00W   47
Florida *Bay*: Fla., U.S.A.   25 00N 80 45W   101
Florida Keys: *is.*, Fla., U.S.A.   25 00N 80 30W 45 101
Flórina: Greece   40 48N 21 26E   79
Flower's Cove: Nfld., Canada   51 18N 56 41W   97
Flushing: Netherlands *see* Vlissingen   51 27N 03 35E 72
Flushing Meadow *Park*: N.Y., U.S.A.   40 45N 73 50W 123
Fly: *riv.*, Papua   08 00S 141 45E   13
Fochabers: Moray., Scotland   57 37N 03 07W   65
Focşani: Romania   45 41N 27 12E   78
Foel Wen: *mtn.*, Clwyd, Wales   52 54N 03 23W   60
Fogang (Shijiao): China   23 54N 113 30E   85
Foggia: Italy   41 28N 15 33E   27 79
Fogo *Island*: Nfld., Canada   49 30N 54 15W   97
Fohnsdorf: Austria   47 13N 14 40E   78
Föhr: *is.*, W.Germany   54 30N 08 30E   72
Foinaven: *pk.*, Suther., Scotland   58 24N 04 53W 64
Foix: France   42 57N 01 35E   70
Fokino: U.S.S.R.   53 27N 34 24E   80
Foleshill: W.Mid., England   52 26N 01 28W   115
Foligno: Italy   42 57N 12 43E   79
Folkestone: Kent, England   51 05N 01 11E   59
Fond-du-Lac: Sask., Canada   59 20N 107 09W   92
Fond du Lac: Wis., U.S.A.   43 48N 88 27W   98
Fond-du-Lac: *riv.*, Sask., Canada   59 00N 105 00W 92
Fontana: Calif., U.S.A.   34 06N 117 26W   104
Fontas: *riv.*, B.C., Canada   58 15N 121 15W   88
Fontenay-le-Comte: France   46 28N 00 48W   70
Foochow *see* Fuzhou   26 06N 119 23E   37 85
Forcalquier: France   43 56N 05 46E   71
Forchheim: W.Germany   49 43N 11 05E   73
Ford: Wash., U.S.A.   47 55N 117 49W   90
Fordingbridge: Hants., England   50 56N 01 47W   59
Ford *Ranges*: Antarctica   77 00S 145 00W   25
Forel, *Mount*: Greenland   66 56N 36 48W   16
Foreland: *cape*, I. of W., England   50 41N 01 04W 59

Types of map: Ocean pp. 1-5; Physical pp. 6-25; Human pp. 26-57; Topographic pp. 58-101; World pp. 102-111; Urban pp. 112-128.

Foreland *Point*: Devon, England 51 16N 03 47W 61
Forest Hill: Ont., Canada 43 42N 79 27W 125
Forest *Park*: N.Y., U.S.A. 40 57N 73 52W 123
Forestville: Qué., Canada 48 45N 69 04W 96
Forli: Italy 44 13N 12 02E 79
Formby: Mers., England 53 34N 03 07W 63 114
Formentera: *is.*, Balearic Islands 38 30N 01 30E 77
Formosa *see* Taiwan 23 30N 120 45E 12 37 85 107
Formosa: Argentina 26 07S 58 14W 49
Formosa: *admin.*, Argentina 24 15S 61 00W 49
Formosa *Strait* (T'aiwan Haihsia): China/Taiwan 24 30N 119 30E 12 37 85
Føroyar (Færoe *Islands*): N.Atlantic Ocean 62 00N 07 00W 2 6
Forres: Moray., Scotland 57 37N 03 38W 65
Forrest City: Ark., U.S.A. 35 01N 90 47W 100
Forssa: Finland 60 49N 23 40E 75
Forst: E.Germany 51 46N 14 39E 73
Forsyth: Mont., U.S.A. 46 16N 106 41W 94
Fort Albany: Ont., Canada 52 15N 81 35W 44 96
Fortaleza: Brazil 03 43S 38 30W 50
Fort Augustus: Inv., Scotland 57 09N 04 41W 64
Fort Bayard *see* Zhanjiang 21 16N 110 28E 36
Fort Bragg: Calif., U.S.A. 39 29N 123 46W 91
Fort Chimo: Qué., Canada 58 10N 68 15W 44
Fort Chipewyan: Alta., Canada 58 46N 111 09W 92
Fort Collins: Colo., U.S.A. 40 35N 105 05W 94
Fort-Dauphin: Malagasy Rep. 25 02S 47 00E 55
Fort-de-France: Martinique 14 36N 61 05W 47
Fort Dodge: Iowa, U.S.A. 42 31N 94 10W 98
Fort Fitzgerald: Alta., Canada 59 51N 111 41W 92
Fort Frances: Ont., Canada 48 37N 93 23W 98
Fort Franklin: N.W.T., Canada 65 10N 123 30W 88
Fort George: Qué., Canada 53 50N 79 01W 44 96
Fort George: *riv.*, Qué., Canada 53 30N 77 00W 16 44 96
Fort Gibson *Reservoir*: Okla., U.S.A. 35 52N 95 14W 95
Fort Good Hope: N.W.T., Canada 66 16N 128 37W 88
Fort-Gouraud: Mauritania 22 40N 12 41W 56 104
Forth: *riv.*, Scotland 56 00N 04 00W 64
Forth, Firth of: *est.*, Scotland 56 00N 03 00W 65
Fort Hall: Idaho, U.S.A. 43 02N 112 26W 90
Forth & Clyde *Canal*: Scotland 55 45N 04 00W 113
Fort Hertz *see* Putao 27 22N 97 27E 35
Fort Jameson *see* Chipata 13 39S 32 40E 54
Fort Laramie *National Historical Site*: Wyo., U.S.A. 42 13N 104 31W 94
Fort Lauderdale: Fla., U.S.A. 26 08N 80 08W 45 101
Fort Liard: N.W.T., Canada 60 14N 123 28W 88
Fort McKenzie: Qué., Canada 56 50N 69 00W 96
Fort Macleod: Alta., Canada 49 44N 113 24W 92
Fort Madison: Iowa, U.S.A. 40 38N 91 21W 98
Fort Morgan: Colo., U.S.A. 40 15N 103 48W 94
Fort Myers: Fla., U.S.A. 26 39N 81 51W 45 101
Fort Nelson: B.C., Canada 58 48N 122 44W 42 88
Fort Nelson: *riv.*, B.C., Canada 59 00N 123 30W 88
Fort Norman: N.W.T., Canada 64 55N 125 29W 88
Fort Peck *Reservoir*: Mont., U.S.A. 47 45N 106 30W 42 94
Fort Pierce: Fla., U.S.A. 27 28N 80 20W 101
Fort Pierre: S.D., U.S.A. 44 21N 100 22W 94
Fort Portal: Uganda 00 40N 30 17E 54
Fort Providence: N.W.T., Canada 61 03N 117 40W 42 88
Fort Qu'Appelle: Sask., Canada 50 46N 103 54W 92
Fort Randall *Dam*: S.D., U.S.A. 48 04N 98 34W 94
Fort Resolution: N.W.T., Canada 61 10N 113 39W 42 92
Fortrose: R. & Crom., Scotland 57 34N 04 09W 65
Fort Rupert *see* Rupert House 51 29N 78 45W 96
Fort St. James: B.C., Canada 54 26N 124 15W 89
Fort St. John: B.C., Canada 56 14N 120 55W 42 89
Fort Saskatchewan: Alta., Canada 53 42N 113 12W 92
Fort Scott: Kans., U.S.A. 37 50N 94 42W 95
Fort Selkirk: Yukon, Canada 62 46N 137 23W 88
Fort Severn: Ont., Canada 56 00N 87 40W 44 93
Fort Sibut: Central African Rep. 05 44N 19 05E 54
Fort Simpson: N.W.T., Canada 61 46N 121 15W 88
Fort Smith: N.W.T., Canada 60 01N 111 55W 42 92
Fort Smith: Ark., U.S.A. 35 23N 94 25W 43 100
Fort Stockton: Tex., U.S.A. 30 53N 102 53W 95
Fort Sumner: N.Mex., U.S.A. 34 28N 104 15W 95
Fortune *Bay*: Nfld., Canada 47 30N 55 15W 97
Fort Vermilion: Alta., Canada 58 22N 115 59W 42 92
Fort Victoria: Rhodesia 20 10S 30 49E 55
Fort Wayne: Ind., U.S.A. 41 05N 85 08W 45 98
Fort Whyte: Man., Canada 49 49N 97 30W 93
Fort William: Canada *see* Thunder Bay 48 24N 89 14W 44 98
Fort William: Inv., Scotland 56 49N 05 07W 64
Fort Worth: Tex., U.S.A. 32 45N 97 18W 43 95 104
Forty Mile: Yukon, Canada 64 24N 140 31W 88
Foshan: China 23 03N 113 09E 36 85
Fossano: Italy 44 33N 07 43E 71
Fossil Bluff: *rsch stn.*, Antarctica 71 20S 68 17W 24
Foster: *riv.*, Sask., Canada 56 00N 105 30W 92
Fougères: France 48 21N 01 12W 70
Fouhsin *see* Fuxinshi 42 03N 121 46E 37
Foula: *is.*, Shet. Is., Scotland 60 08N 02 05W 65
Foulness *Island*: Essex, England 51 30N 00 45E 59
Foulness *Point*: Essex, England 51 38N 00 57E 59
Fourmies: France 50 01N 04 03E 72
Fournaise, Piton de la: *mtn.*, Réunion 21 14S 55 43E 1
Fouta Djallon *Plateau*: Guinea 11 30N 12 00W 20 57
Fouyang *see* Fuyang 32 52N 115 52E 36 85
Foveaux *Strait*: New Zealand 41 30S 168 00E 87
Fowey: Corn., England 50 20N 04 38W 61
Fowey: *riv.*, Corn., England 50 15N 04 30W 61
Foxe *Basin*: N.W.T., Canada 68 00N 78 00W 23
Foxe *Peninsula*: N.W.T., Canada 64 45N 77 00W 16
Foxford: Mayo, Irish Republic 53 59N 09 07W 66
Foyle, *Lough*: Irish Rep./N.Ireland 55 05N 07 10W 66
Foynes: Lim., Irish Republic 52 37N 09 06W 67
Foz do Iguaçú: Brazil 25 33S 54 35W 51
FRANCE 6 26 70 76 107
Frances *Lake*: Yukon, Canada 61 15N 129 12W 88
Franceville: Gabon 01 38S 13 35E 54
Francis Case, *Lake*: S.D., U.S.A. 43 04N 98 34W 94
Francistown: Botswana 21 11S 27 32E 55
François *Lake*: B.C., Canada 53 45N 125 30W 89
Frankfort: Ind., U.S.A. 40 16N 86 31W 98
Frankfort: Ky., U.S.A. 38 11N 84 53W 45 101
Frankfurt: *admin.*, E.Germany 52 45N 13 45E 73
Frankfurt am Main: W.Germany 50 06N 08 41E 26 72
Frankfurt an der Oder: E.Germany 52 20N 14 32E 73 78
Fränkische Alb: *mtns.*, W.Germany 49 00N 11 15E 78
Fränkische Schweiz: *geog. reg.*, W.Germany 49 45N 11 15E 73
Franklin: Mich., U.S.A. 42 30N 83 19W 125
Franklin, District of: *admin.*, Canada 68 00N 102 00W 44
Franklin D. Roosevelt *Lake*: Wash., U.S.A. 47 57N 118 59W 90
Franklin *Mountains*: N.W.T., Canada 63 00N 123 00W 88
Franklin Park: Ill., U.S.A. 41 50N 87 52W 124
Franklin *Park*: Mass., U.S.A. 42 18N 71 05W 122
Franz Josef Land: *is.*, Arctic Ocean 81 00N 55 00E 23
Fraser: Mich., U.S.A. 42 31N 82 57W 125
Fraser: *riv.*, B.C., Canada 51 15N 122 15W 42 89
Fraser: *riv.*, Nfld., Canada 56 45N 63 30W 97
Fraserburgh: Aber., Scotland 57 42N 02 00W 65
Fray Bentos: Uruguay 33 10S 58 20W 52
Frechen: W.Germany 50 54N 06 48E 119
Fredericia: Denmark 55 34N 09 47E 74
Frederick: Md., U.S.A. 39 25N 77 25W 99
Frederick: Okla., U.S.A. 34 23N 99 01W 95
Fredericksburg: Va., U.S.A. 38 18N 77 30W 99
Fredericktown: Mo., U.S.A. 37 33N 90 19W 98
Fredericton: N.B., Canada 45 57N 66 40W 44 97
Frederikshavn: Denmark 57 28N 10 33E 75
Fredrikstad: Norway 59 15N 10 55E 75
Freels, *Cape*: Nfld., Canada 49 13N 53 29W 97
Freeport: Bahamas 26 30N 78 47W 47
Freeport: Ill., U.S.A. 42 17N 89 38W 98
Freeport: N.Y., U.S.A. 40 40N 73 35W 123
Freeport: Tex., U.S.A. 28 57N 95 21W 100
Freetown: Sierra Leone 08 30N 13 17W 57
Fregene: Italy 41 51N 12 12E 116
Freiburg im Breisgau: W.Germany 48 00N 07 52E 26 72
Freising: W.Germany 48 24N 11 45E 73
Freital: E.Germany 51 01N 13 39E 73 105
Fréjus: France 43 26N 06 44E 71
Fremantle: W.A., Australia 32 07S 115 44E 40
Fremont: Nebr., U.S.A. 41 26N 96 30W 94
FRENCH GUIANA 04 00N 53 00W 18 50
Frenchman *Creek*: U.S.A. 40 30N 102 00W 94
French's Forest: N.S.W., Australia 33 45S 151 14E 120

French Somaliland *see* Afars and Issas, French Territory of		
11 30N 42 30E	10 53	
Fresh *Pond*: Mass., U.S.A. 42 24N 71 09W	122	
Fresno: Calif., U.S.A. 36 44N 119 47W	43	
Fresno: *riv.*, Calif., U.S.A. 37 00N 119 45W	91	
Frick *Park*: Pa., U.S.A. 40 26N 79 54W	125	
Friedrichshafen: W.Germany 47 39N 09 29E	72	
Frio: *riv.*, Tex., U.S.A. 29 00N 99 30W	95	
Frisa, *Loch*: Argyll., Scotland 56 30N 06 00W	64	
Frisian *Islands*: Netherlands/W.Germany 53 30N 06 00E		
	72 76	
Frobisher *Lake*: Sask., Canada 56 15N 108 15W	42 92	
Frodsham: Ches., England 53 18N 02 44W	60	
Frohavet: *bay*, Norway 63 45N 09 00E	74	
Frolovo: U.S.S.R. 49 47N 43 39E	80	
Frome: Som., England 51 14N 02 20W	61	
Frome: *riv.*, Avon, England 51 30N 02 15W	113	
Frome: *riv.*, Dorset, England 50 45N 02 30W	61	
Frome: *riv.*, Here. & Worcs., England 52 00N 02 30W	59	
Front *Range*: Colo., U.S.A. 40 15N 105 45W	43	
Frosinone: Italy 41 38N 13 22E	79	
Frostburg: Md., U.S.A. 39 39N 78 56W	99	
Frøya: *is.*, Norway 63 45N 08 45E	74	
Frunze: U.S.S.R. 42 54N 74 36E	29	
Frýdek-Místek: Czechoslovakia 49 42N 18 20E	78	
Fuan: China 27 04N 119 41E	85	
Fuchien *see* Fujian 26 00N 117 30E	36 85	
Fuchin *see* Fujin 47 14N 132 00E	31	
Fuchou *see* Fuzhou 26 06N 119 23E	37 85	
Fuchū: Hiroshima, Japan 34 34N 133 14E	37	
Fuchū: Tōkyō, Japan 35 40N 139 29E	121	
Fuchun: *riv.*, China 29 45N 120 00E	85	
Fuding: China 27 19N 120 12E	85	
Fuencarral: Spain 40 30N 03 41W	116	
Fuerteventura: *is.*, Canary Is. 28 30N 14 00W	56	
Fugou: China 34 08N 114 20E	84	
Fuhlsbüttel: W.Germany 53 37N 10 00E	119	
Fuhsien *see* Fuxian 39 37N 122 04E	37 84	
Fujian (Fuchien): *admin.*, China 26 00N 117 30E	36 85	
Fuji-hakone-izu-kokuritsu-kōen: *nat. park*,		
Japan 34 45N 139 00E	86	
Fujin (Fuchin): China 47 14N 132 00E	31	
Fuji-san (Fujiyama): *mtn.*, Japan 35 22N 138 44E	37 86	
Fujisawa: Japan 35 22N 139 29E	121	
Fujiyama: *mtn.*, *see* Fuji-san 35 22N 138 44E	37 86	
Fukui: Japan 36 04N 136 13E	37 86	
Fukuoka: Japan 33 35N 130 24E	37 86	
Fukushima: Japan 37 45N 140 28E	37 86	
Fukuyama: Japan 34 29N 133 22E	37 86	
Fulaerji: China 47 15N 123 40E	105	
Fulda: W.Germany 50 33N 09 41E	72	
Fulda: *riv.*, W.Germany 51 00N 09 30E	72	
Fuling: China 29 42N 107 22E	85	
Fullerton: Calif., U.S.A. 33 53N 117 56W	127	
Fulton: Mo., U.S.A. 38 50N 91 57W	98	
Funabashi: Japan 35 18N 139 33E	121	
Funan: China 22 40N 107 58E	85	
Funchal: Madeira Islands 32 40N 16 55W	56	
Fundy, *Bay of*: Canada 45 00N 66 00W	97	
Fundy *National Park*: N.B., Canada 45 30N 65 15W	97	
Funing: China 33 42N 119 52E	84	
Fuping: China 34 42N 109 07E	84	
Fuqing: China 25 41N 119 28E	85	
Furmanov: U.S.S.R. 57 15N 41 07E	80	
Furnas *Reservoir*: Brazil 20 45S 46 15W	51	
Fürth: W.Germany 49 28N 11 00E	73	
Fushan: China 37 29N 121 19E	84	
Fushun: China 41 52N 123 53E	37 105	
Füssen: W.Germany 47 35N 10 43E	73	
Futtsu: Japan 35 18N 139 49E	121	
Fuxian (Fuhsien): China 39 37N 122 04E	37 84	
Fuxinshi (Fouhsin): China 42 03N 121 46E	37	
Fuyang: Zhejiang, China 30 03N 119 58E	84	
Fuyang (Fouyang): Anhui, China 32 52N 115 52E	36 85	
Fuyung: *riv.*, China 37 45N 115 30E	84	
Fuzhong: China 24 30N 111 09E	85	
Fuzhou: Jiangxi, China 28 01N 116 18E	85	
Fuzhou (Foochow): Fujian, China 26 06N 119 23E	37 85	
Fylde: *geog. reg.*, Lancs., England 53 50N 02 45W	114	
Fyn: *is. & admin.*, Denmark 55 15N 10 15E	75	
Fyne, *Loch*: Argyll., Scotland 56 00N 05 15W	64	

Fyzabad *see* Faizābād 26 46N 82 08E	34 83	
Gaberones *see* Gaborone 24 45S 25 55E	55	
GABON 01 30S 10 30E	21 57 107	
Gaborone (Gaberones): Botswana 24 45S 25 55E	55	
Gabrovo: Bulgaria 42 52N 25 19E	79	
Gadag: India 15 26N 75 42E	34	
Gadsden: Ala., U.S.A. 34 01N 86 01W	101 104	
Gaffney: S.C., U.S.A. 35 03N 81 40W	101	
Gagarin (Gzhatzk): U.S.S.R. 55 33N 35 00E	80	
Gages Lake: Ill., U.S.A. 42 21N 87 59W	124	
Gagnon: Qué., Canada 51 56N 68 16W	96 104	
Gagny: France 48 53N 02 33E	117	
Gaibānda: Bangladesh 25 21N 89 36E	83	
Gainesville: Fla., U.S.A. 29 37N 82 21W	45 101	
Gainesville: Ga., U.S.A. 34 17N 83 50W	101	
Gainesville: Tex., U.S.A. 33 38N 97 08W	95	
Gainsborough: Lincs., England 53 24N 00 46W	58	
Gaiping: China 40 21N 122 20E	84	
Gairloch: R. & Crom., Scotland 57 43N 05 40W	64	
Gairloch, *Loch*: R.& Crom., Scotland 57 30N 05 45W	64	
Gajsin: U.S.S.R. 48 48N 29 24E	78	
Galana: *riv.*, Kenya 03 00S 39 30E	54	
Galapagos *Fracture Zone*: S.Pacific Ocean		
02 00S 110 00W	5	
Galapagos *Islands*: S.Pacific Ocean 00 00 91 00W	5	
Galashiels: Selk., Scotland 55 37N 02 49W	63	
Galaţi (Galatz): Romania 45 27N 28 02E	27 78	
Galatz *see* Galaţi 45 27N 28 02E	27 78	
Galax: Va., U.S.A. 36 40N 80 56W	101	
Galena: Ill., U.S.A. 42 25N 90 26W	92	
Galena: Kans., U.S.A. 37 04N 94 38W	95	
Galeria: *riv.*, Italy 41 45N 12 15E	116	
Galesburg: Ill., U.S.A. 40 58N 90 22W	98	
Galey: *riv.*, Irish Republic 52 30N 09 15W	67	
Galič: U.S.S.R. 58 23N 42 21E	80	
Gallan *Head*: R. & Crom., Scotland 58 14N 07 01W	64	
Gallarate: Italy 45 39N 08 37E	116	
Gallatin: Tenn., U.S.A. 36 22N 82 28W	101	
Gallatin: *riv.*, Mont., U.S.A. 45 15N 111 00W	94	
Gallego: Mexico 29 50N 106 23W	95	
Galley *Head*: Cork, Irish Republic 51 32N 08 57W	67	
Gallion, Slieve: *mtn.*, Lon., N.Ireland 54 45N 06 45W	66	
Gallipoli: Turkey *see* Gelibolu 40 26N 26 40E	79	
Gällivare: Sweden 67 10N 20 40E	27 74 105	
Galloway, Mull of: *cape*, Wig., Scotland 54 39N 04 52W	62	
Gallup: N.Mex., U.S.A. 35 31N 108 45W	95	
Galston: Ayr., Scotland 55 36N 04 24W	62	
Galtee *Mountains*: Irish Republic 52 15N 08 00W	67	
Galtymore: *mtn.*, Lim., Irish Republic 52 23N 08 11W	67	
Galveston: Tex., U.S.A. 29 18N 94 48W	43 100	
Galway: Gal., Irish Republic 53 16N 09 03W	67	
Galway: *admin.*, Irish Republic 53 15N 09 00W	67	
Galway *Bay*: Irish Republic 53 00N 09 15W	67	
Gambaga: Ghana 10 31N 00 22W	57	
GAMBIA, THE 13 30N 15 00W	20 57	
Gambier *Islands*: S.Pacific Ocean 23 10S 135 00W	5	
Gamph, Slieve: *mtns.*, Irish Republic 54 00N 08 45W	66	
Gan (Kan): *riv.*, China 27 30N 115 15E	36 85	
Gandak: *riv.*, India 26 15N 84 45E	35 83	
Gander: Nfld., Canada 48 58N 54 34W	44 97	
Gander: *riv.*, Nfld., Canada 48 45N 55 15W	97	
Gandhi Sagar *Reservoir*: India 24 15N 75 30E	82	
Ganga (Ganges): *riv.*, Bangladesh/India 24 45N 88 00E		
	11 35 83	
Gangāpur: India 26 30N 76 49E	82	
Gangdisi *Range*: China 29 30N 90 00E	11 34 83	
Ganges (Ganga): *riv.*, Bangladesh/India 24 45N 88 00E		
	11 35 83	
Ganges, *Mouths of the*: Bangladesh/India 21 30N 89 00E		
	35 83	
Ganglingshan: *ra.*, China 32 30N 82 00E	34	
Gangtok: Sikkim 27 20N 88 39E	35 83	
Gangwa: China 39 48N 116 10E	121	
Ganlanshan: *mtn.*, China 29 54N 90 02E	83	
Gannat: France 46 06N 03 11E	71	
Gannet *Peak*: Wyo., U.S.A. 43 11N 109 39W	94	
Gansu (Kansu): *admin.*, China 35 45N 108 00E	36 84	

Types of map: Ocean pp. 1-5; Physical pp. 6-25; Human pp. 26-57; Topographic pp. 58-101; World pp. 102-111; Urban pp. 112-128.

Ganyu: China   34 50N 119 10E   84
Ganzhou (Kanchou): China   25 50N 114 52E   36 85
Ganzi: China   31 40N 100 01E   36
Gao: Mali   16 19N 00 09W   56
Gaoan: China   28 28N 115 25E   85
Gaohang: China   31 17N 121 36E   121
Gaokeng: China   27 32N 113 59E   85
Gaoping: China   35 47N 113 00E   84
Gaoqiao: China   31 21N 121 34E   121
Gaoyao *see* Zhaoqing   23 03N 112 27E   85
Gaoyi: China   37 33N 114 32E   84
Gaoyou: China   32 47N 119 30E   84
Gaoyou, *Lake*: China   33 00N 119 15E   84
Gaozhou: China   21 47N 110 55E   85
Gap: France   44 33N 06 05E   71
Gar': U.S.S.R.   52 35N 129 08E   105
Gara, *Lough*: Sligo, Irish Republic   53 45N 08 15W   66
Garanhuns: Brazil   08 54S 36 29W   50
Garbatella: Italy   41 52N 12 29E   116
Gard: *riv.*, France   44 00N 04 00E   71
Garda, *Lago di*: Italy   45 40N 10 41E   78
Gardelegen: E.Germany   52 33N 11 24E   73
Gardena: Calif., U.S.A.   33 53N 118 19W   127
Garden City: Kans., U.S.A.   37 58N 100 53W   95
Garden City: Mich., U.S.A.   42 18N 83 20W   125
Garden City: N.Y., U.S.A.   40 36N 73 44W   123
Garden Grove: Calif., U.S.A.   33 46N 117 57W   127
Garden Reach: India   22 33N 88 17E   83 120
Gardner *Canal*: B.C., Canada   53 15N 128 15W   89
Gardner *Island*: S.Pacific Ocean   04 40S 174 32W   4
Gare *Loch*: Dunb., Scotland   56 00N 04 45W   113
Garfield: N.J., U.S.A.   40 53N 74 07W   123
Garfield: Utah, U.S.A.   40 44N 112 11W   91
Garfield *Park*: Ill., U.S.A.   41 52N 87 42W   124
Garforth: W.Yorks., England   53 48N 01 24W   115
Gargenville: France   49 00N 01 49E   117
Garia: India   22 28N 88 23E   120
Garibaldi *Provincial Park*: B.C., Canada   49 45N 122 45W   89
Garin: Argentina   34 25S 58 45W   128
Garmisch-Partenkirchen: W.Germany   47 30N 11 05E   73
Garnett: Kans., U.S.A.   38 17N 95 14W   94
Garnock: *riv.*, Ayr., Scotland   55 45N 04 30W   113
Garonne: *riv.*, France   44 30N 00 15W   70
Garrison: Ferm., N.Ireland   54 25N 08 05W   66
Garrison: Mont., U.S.A.   46 31N 112 49W   94
Garrison *Reservoir see* Sakakawea, *Lake*   47 30N 101 25W   17 42 94
Garroch *Head*: Bute., Scotland   55 43N 05 02W   62
Garron *Point*: Antrim, N.Ireland   55 03N 05 58W   66
Garron *Point*: Kinc., Scotland   56 59N 02 09W   65
Garry: *riv.*, Perth., Scotland   56 45N 04 00W   65
Garry, *Loch*: Inv., Scotland   57 00N 05 00W   64
Garstang: Lancs., England   53 55N 02 47W   63
Garvagh: Lon., N.Ireland   54 59N 06 41W   66
Garvie *Mountains*: S.I., New Zealand   45 30S 169 00E   87
Gary: Ind., U.S.A.   41 34N 87 20W   45 98 104 124
Gasconade: *riv.*, Mo., U.S.A.   37 45N 92 00W   98
Gascoyne: *riv.*, W.A., Australia   24 30S 114 30E   14
Gas *Hills*: Wyo., U.S.A.   43 45N 108 45W   94
Gaspé: Qué., Canada   48 50N 64 30W   97
Gaspé *Passage*: Qué., Canada   49 15N 64 30W   97
Gaspé *Peninsula*: Qué., Canada   48 30N 65 30W   44 97
Gaspesian *Provincial Park*: Qué., Canada   48 45N 66 00W   97
Gas-san: *mtn.*, Japan   38 32N 140 01E   86
Gastonia: N.C., U.S.A.   34 14N 81 12W   101
Gata, *Cabo de*: Spain   36 44N 02 10W   77
Gatčina: U.S.S.R.   59 34N 30 08E   80
Gatehouse of Fleet: Kirkc., Scotland   54 53N 04 11W   62
Gateshead: Tyne & Wear, England   54 58N 01 35W   63
Gatineau: *riv.*, Qué., Canada   46 00N 76 00W   96
Gatley: Gt. Man., England   53 23N 02 14W   114
Gatun *Lake*: Panama   09 15N 79 45W   48
Gauer *Lake*: Man., Canada   57 00N 97 45W   93
Gauhāti: India   26 10N 91 45E   35 83
Gaukler *Point*: Mich., U.S.A.   42 27N 82 52W   125
Gavá: Spain   41 18N 02 00E   116
Gävle: Sweden   60 41N 17 10E   27 75
Gavrilov-Jam: U.S.S.R.   57 18N 39 51E   80
Gawler *Range*: S.A., Australia   32 45S 136 00E   40

Gaya: India   24 48N 85 00E   35 83
Gaza *see* Ghazzah, Egypt   31 30N 34 28E   32
Gaziantep: Turkey   37 04N 37 21E   32
Gazzada: Italy   45 46N 08 48E   116
Gdańsk (Danzig): Poland   54 22N 18 41E   27 73 78
Gdańsk: *admin.*, Poland   54 00N 18 15E   73
Gdańsk, *Gulf of*: Poland   54 15N 19 15E   78
Gdov: U.S.S.R.   58 44N 27 48E   80
Gdynia: Poland   54 31N 18 30E   27 78
Geadha, Rubh' a': *cape*, Argyll., Scotland   56 08N 06 09W   64
Gediz: *riv.*, Turkey   38 30N 27 00E   79
Geelong: Vic., Australia   38 10S 144 26E   41
Geer: China   31 44N 80 21E   34 82
Geesthacht: W.Germany   53 26N 10 23E   73 119
Geikie: *riv.*, Sask., Canada   57 30N 104 00W   92
Geilo: Norway   60 32N 08 11E   75
Gejiu (Kochiu): China   23 22N 103 06E   36
Gela: Sicily   37 04N 14 15E   79
Geldern: W.Germany   51 31N 06 19E   118
Geleen: Netherlands   50 58N 05 45E   72
Gelibolu (Gallipoli): Turkey   40 26N 26 40E   79
Gelligaer: M.Glam., Wales   51 40N 03 18W   61 113
Gelsenkirchen: W.Germany   51 30N 07 05E   105 107 118
Gemena: Zaïre   03 15N 19 46E   54
Gemengchi: *lake*, China   31 00N 89 00E   83
General Belgrano: *rsch. stn.*, Antarctica   77 58S 38 48W   24
General Bernardo O'Higgins: *rsch. stn.*, Antarctica   63 19S 57 54W   24
General Pacheco: Argentina   34 27S 58 37W   128
General San Martín: Argentina   34 34S 58 33W   128
Geneva: Switzerland *see* Genève   46 13N 06 09E   26 71
Geneva: Utah, U.S.A.   40 19N 111 45W   91 104
Geneva, *Lake of see* Léman, *Lac*   46 15N 06 30E   71
Genève (Geneva): Switzerland   46 13N 06 09E   26 71
Genk: Belgium   50 58N 05 30E   72
Gennargentu, *Monti del*: Sardinia   40 00N 09 30E   77
Gennevilliers: France   48 56N 02 17E   117
Genoa: Italy *see* Genova   44 24N 08 56E   26 71 107
Genova (Genoa): Italy   44 24N 08 56E   26 71 107
Genova, *Golfo di*: Italy   43 45N 09 00E   71
Gent (Ghent): Belgium   51 02N 03 42E   72 107
George: *riv.*, Qué., Canada   57 15N 65 15W   97
Georges: riv., N.S.W., Australia   33 58S 150 59E   120
George *Sound*: S.I., New Zealand   44 45S 167 15E   87
George VI *Sound*: Antarctica   71 00S 68 00W   24
Georgetown: Cayman Is.   19 20N 81 23W   47
Georgetown: Guyana   06 46N 58 10W   48
George Town: Malaysia *see* Pinang   05 25N 100 20E   38
Georgetown: Idaho, U.S.A.   42 29N 111 22W   90
Georgetown: S.C., U.S.A.   33 23N 79 18W   101
Georgia: *admin.*, U.S.A.   33 00N 83 00W   45 101
Georgia, *Strait of*: B.C., Canada   49 30N 124 30W   89
Georgian *Bay*: Ont., Canada   45 30N 81 00W   44 99
Georgian S.S.R.: *admin.*, U.S.S.R.   42 00N 43 00E   28
Georgiu Dež (Liski): U.S.S.R.   50 59N 39 30E   80
Gera: E.Germany   50 51N 12 11E   73
Gera: *admin.*, E.Germany   50 30N 11 30E   73
Geraldine: S.I., New Zealand   44 04S 171 12E   87
Geraldton: W.A., Australia   28 49S 114 36E   40
Geraldton: Ont., Canada   49 44N 86 59W   98
Gerenzano: Italy   45 38N 09 00E   116
Gering: Nebr., U.S.A.   41 50N 103 40W   94
Gerli: Argentina   34 42S 58 22W   128
Germantown: Pa., U.S.A.   40 03N 75 11W   122
GERMANY, EAST   3 7 78 261
GERMANY, WEST   7 26 72 76
Gerona: Spain   41 59N 02 49E   77
Gerrards Cross: Bucks., England   51 35N 00 34W   59 112
Gethsémani: Qué., Canada   50 14N 60 40W   97
Gettysburg: Pa., U.S.A.   39 50N 77 16W   99
Gevelsberg: W.Germany   51 19N 07 20E   118
Ghāghara: *riv.*, India   26 15N 84 00E   83
GHANA   20 57 106
Ghardaïa: Algeria   32 20N 03 40E   56
Ghātal: India   22 40N 87 44E   83
Ghazal, Bahr al: *riv.*, Sudan   07 30N 27 45E   20
Ghāziābād: India   28 39N 77 26E   82
Ghāzīpur: India   25 36N 83 36E   83
Ghazzah (Gaza): Egypt   31 30N 34 28E   32
Ghent *see* Gent   51 02N 03 42E   72 107

Types of map: Ocean pp. 1-5; Physical pp. 6-25; Human pp. 26-57; Topographic pp. 58-101; World pp. 102-111; Urban pp. 112-128.

Gheorghe Gheorghiu–Dej: Romania   46 14N 26 22E   78
Ghod: *riv.*, India   18 45N 74 30E   82
Giant's Causeway: *prom.*, Antrim, N.Ireland
  55 14N 06 32W   66
Gibbs *Fracture Zone*: N.Atlantic Ocean   53 00N 35 00W   2
GIBRALTAR: *U.K. Colony*: S.W.Europe   36 09N 05 21W
  26 77
Gibraltar, *Strait of*: Africa/Europe   35 45N 05 30W   6 77
Gibson *Desert*: W.A., Australia   24 00S 126 00E   14
Giddings: Tex., U.S.A.   30 11N 96 56W   100
Giessen: W.Germany   50 35N 08 42E   72
Gifhorn: W.Germany   52 28N 10 33E   73
Gifu: Japan   35 25N 136 45E   37 86
Gigha *Island*: Argyll., Scotland   55 30N 05 30W   62
Gijón: Spain   43 32N 05 40W   26 77 105
Gila: *riv.*, U.S.A.   32 45N 113 30W   43 91
Gila Bend: Ariz., U.S.A.   32 57N 112 43W   91
Gila Cliff Dwellings *National Monument*: N.Mex.,
  U.S.A.   33 16N 108 13W   95
Gilbert: *riv.*, Qld., Australia   17 15S 142 00E   41
Gilbert *Islands*: Pacific Ocean   01 00S 175 00E   4 15
Gilf Kebir *Plateau*: Egypt   23 30N 25 30E   32
Gill, *Lough*: Irish Republic   54 15N 08 15W   66
Gillam: Man., Canada   56 25N 94 45W   93
Gillette: Wyo., U.S.A.   44 18N 105 30W   94
Gillingham: Dorset, England   51 02N 02 17W   61
Gillingham: Kent, England   51 24N 00 33E   59 112
Gilroy: Calif., U.S.A.   37 00N 121 34W   91
Girardot: Colombia   04 19N 74 47W   48
Girdle Ness: *cape*, Aber., Scotland   57 08N 02 02W   65
Gīr *Hills*: India   21 15N 70 45E   82
Giridih: India   24 10N 86 20E   83
Gironde: *est.*, France   45 30N 00 45W   70
Girton: Cambs., England   52 14N 00 05E   59
Girvan: Ayr., Scotland   55 15N 04 51W   62
Gisborne: N.I., New Zealand   38 41S 178 02E   37 87
Giurgiu: Romania   43 53N 25 58E   79
Giussano: Italy   45 43N 09 12E   116
Gjirokastër: Albania   40 05N 20 10E   79
Gjøvik: Norway   60 48N 10 42E   75
Glace Bay: N.S., Canada   46 11N 59 58W   97
Glacier: B.C., Canada   51 16N 117 31W   88
Glacier Bay *National Monument*: Alaska,
  U.S.A.   58 45N 136 00W   88
Glacier Creek: Yukon, Canada   64 01N 140 42W   88
Glacier *National Park*: B.C., Canada   51 00N 117 30W   89
Glacier *National Park*: Mont., U.S.A.   48 15N 113 15W   90
Gladbeck: W.Germany   51 34N 06 59E   118
Gladesville: N.S.W., Australia   33 50S 151 08E   120
Glåma: *riv.*, Norway   60 45N 11 30E   75
Glamorgan: *admin.*, Wales *see* Mid. Glamorgan; South
  Glamorgan; West Glamorgan   61
Glarner *Alpen*: Switzerland   46 45N 09 00E   71
Glarus: Switzerland   47 03N 09 04E   71
Glascarnoch, *Loch*: R. & Crom., Scotland   57 30N 04 45W
  64
Glasgow: Lan., Scotland   55 53N 04 15W   26 62 113
Glasgow: Ky., U.S.A.   36 59N 85 56W   101
Glasgow: Mont., U.S.A.   48 12N 106 38W   94
Glas Maol: *mtn.*, Angus, Scotland   56 52N 03 22W   65
Glass: *riv.*, Inv., Scotland   57 15N 04 45W   64
Glass: *riv.*, R. & Crom., Scotland   57 30N 04 15W   64
Glastonbury: Som., England   51 09N 02 43W   61
Glauchau: E.Germany   50 48N 12 32E   73
Glazov: U.S.S.R.   58 09N 52 40E   81
Gleichen: Alta., Canada   50 54N 113 02W   92
Glen: *riv.*, Lincs., England   52 45N 00 30W   58
Glen Canyon *Dam*: Ariz., U.S.A.   36 55N 111 29W   91
Glencoe: Ill., U.S.A.   42 07N 87 45W   124
Glencoe: Minn., U.S.A.   44 45N 94 10W   98
Glen Coe: *val.*, Argyll., Scotland   56 30N 04 45W   64
Glencolumbkille: Don., Irish Republic   54 42N 08 44W   66
Glen Cove: N.Y., U.S.A.   40 53N 73 36W   123
Glendale: Ariz., U.S.A.   33 32N 112 11W   91
Glendale: Calif., U.S.A.   34 09N 118 15W   91 127
Glendive: Mont., U.S.A.   47 07N 104 42W   94
Glen Ellyn: Ill., U.S.A.   41 51N 88 04W   124
Glengad *Head*: Don., Irish Republic   55 20N 07 11W   66
Glen More *National Forest Park*: Scotland   57 00N 03 30W
  65
Glen Ridge: N.J., U.S.A.   40 48N 74 12W   123

Glenrothes: Fife, Scotland   56 12N 03 10W   65
Glen Roy: *val.*, Inv., Scotland   56 45N 04 45W   64
Glenshaw: Pa., U.S.A.   40 31N 79 57W   125
Glen Spean: *val.*, Inv., Scotland   56 45N 04 45W   64
Glenties: Don., Irish Republic   54 47N 08 17W   66
Glentrool *National Forest Park*: Scotland   55 00N 04 30W
  62
Glenview: Ill., U.S.A.   42 05N 87 49W   124
Glenwood: Minn., U.S.A.   45 39N 95 22W   98
Glenwood Springs: Colo., U.S.A.   39 33N 107 19W   94
Glew: Argentina   34 53S 58 23W   128
Glin: Lim., Irish Republic   52 34N 09 17W   67
Glittertind: *mtn.*, Norway   61 39N 08 33E   27
Gliwice: Poland   50 20N 18 40E   78 105
Globe: Ariz., U.S.A.   33 24N 110 47W   91
Głogów: Poland   51 40N 16 06E   73
Glorietta: Calif., U.S.A.   37 52N 122 10W   126
Glossop: Derby., England   53 27N 01 57W   58
Gloucester: Glos., England   51 53N 02 14W   60
Gloucester City: N.J., U.S.A.   39 53N 75 08W   122
Gloucestershire: *admin.*, England   51 45N 02 15W   60
Gloversville: N.Y., U.S.A.   43 03N 74 21W   99
Glubokij: U.S.S.R.   48 31N 40 19E   80
Gluchov: U.S.S.R.   51 41N 33 53E   80
Glyder Fawr: *mtn.*, Gwyn., Wales   53 06N 04 01W   60
Gmünd: Niederösterreich, Austria   48 47N 14 59E   73 78
Gmunden: Austria   47 56N 13 48E   73
Gniezno: Poland   52 32N 17 32E   73 78
Goa: *admin.*, India   15 30N 75 45E   34 105
Goålpāra: India   26 10N 90 38E   83
Goat Fell: *mtn.*, Bute., Scotland   55 38N 05 12W   62
Gobi: *des.*, China/Mongolia   41 45N 107 00E   9 36
Godalming: Surrey, England   51 11N 00 37W   59
Godāvari: *riv.*, India   19 30N 75 15E   11 34 82
Goderich: Ont., Canada   43 43N 81 43W   98
Godhra: India   22 49N 73 40E   34 82
Godmanchester: Cambs., England   52 19N 00 11W   59
Godorf: W.Germany   50 51N 06 59E   107
Gods: *riv.*, Man., Canada   55 15N 92 45W   93
Gods *Lake*: Man., Canada   54 30N 94 00W   93
Godwin Austen, *Mount see* K2, *Mount*   35 53N 76 30E
  11 29
Gogebic *Range*: Wis., U.S.A.   46 30N 89 45W   104
Goiânia: Brazil   16 40S 49 16W   50
Goiás: Brazil   15 56S 50 08W   51
Goiás: *admin.*, Brazil   13 00S 48 30W   50
Gojra: Pakistan   31 10N 72 43E   82
Gol: Norway   60 43N 08 55E   75
Golaja Pristan': U.S.S.R.   46 31N 32 31E   80
Golborne: Gt. Man., England   53 29N 02 36W   114
Golden: B.C., Canada   51 19N 116 58W   89
Golden: Colo., U.S.A.   39 46N 105 13W   94
Golden *Bay*: S.I., New Zealand   40 30S 173 00E   87
Golden Gate: *str.*, Calif., U.S.A.   37 45N 122 15W   126
Golden Gate *Bridge*: Calif., U.S.A.   37 49N 122 28W   126
Golden Gate *Park*: Calif., U.S.A.   37 46N 122 29W   126
Golden State Freeway: *hwy.*, Calif., U.S.A.
  34 15N 118 15W   127
Goldfields: Sask., Canada   59 28N 108 31W   92
Goldpines: Ont., Canada   50 38N 93 10W   93
Goldsboro: N.C., U.S.A.   35 23N 78 00W   101
Goldsworthy *Mount*: W.A., Australia   20 21S 119 32E   105
Golec-Skalistyj (Golets-Skalistyy): *mtn.*, U.S.S.R.
  56 24N 119 12E   30
Golela: Natal, Rep. of S.Africa   27 20S 31 55E   55
Goleniów: Poland   53 34N 14 50E   73
Golets-Skalistyy: *mtn.*, *see* Golec-Skalistyj
  56 24N 119 12E   30
Golfito: Costa Rica   08 42N 83 10W   47
Goma: Zaïre   01 40S 29 10E   54
Gomati: *riv.*, India   26 00N 83 30E   82
Gomel': U.S.S.R.   52 25N 31 00E   28 80
Gomersal: W.Yorks., England   53 43N 01 41W   115
Gonda: India   27 08N 81 58E   83
Gondal: India   21 59N 70 52E   82
Gonder (Gondar): Ethiopia   12 39N 37 29E   53
Gondia: India   21 23N 80 14E   82
Gonesse: France   48 59N 02 27E   117
Gonfreville l'Orcher: France   49 30N 00 14E   107
Gongan: China   30 02N 112 15E   85
Gongcheng: China   24 52N 110 38E   85

Types of map: Ocean pp. 1-5; Physical pp. 6-25; Human pp. 26-57; Topographic pp. 58-101; World pp. 102-111; Urban pp. 112-128.

Gonggashan (Kungka Shan): *mtn.*, China   29 35N 101 51E
36
Gongshiya: China   31 25N 84 37E   83
Gongxian: China   34 48N 112 58E   84
Gonzáles Catán: Argentina   34 46S 58 38W   128
Good Hope, *Cape of*: C.P., Rep. of S.Africa   34 20S 18 25E
55
Gooding: Idaho, U.S.A.   42 53N 114 43W   90
Goodland: Kans., U.S.A.   39 21N 101 43W   94
Goole: Humb., England   53 42N 00 52W   63 115
Goose: *riv.*, N.D., U.S.A.   47 30N 97 15W   94
Goose: *riv.*, U.S.A.   41 45N 114 00W   90
Goose Bay: Nfld., Canada   53 15N 60 20W   97
Goose *Lake*: U.S.A.   41 45N 120 15W   90
Göppingen: W.Germany   48 43N 09 39E   72
Gora Bol'šoj Šatan: *mtn.*, U.S.S.R.   53 42N 57 38E   81
Gorakhpur: India   26 45N 83 23E   35 83
Gora Konžakovskij Kamen': *mtn.*, U.S.S.R.   59 38N 59 08E
81
Gora Oblačnaja (Gora Oblachnaya): *mtn.*, U.S.S.R.
43 42N 134 10E   37 86
Gora Osl'anka: *mtn.*, U.S.S.R.   59 10N 58 33E   81
Gora Žamantau: *mtn.*, U.S.S.R.   48 20N 51 50E   81
Gorda *Rise*: N.Pacific Ocean   42 00N 128 00W   5
Gordon: N.S.W., Australia   33 46S 151 09E   120
Gordon Lake: Man., Canada   49 04N 100 15W   93
Gore: S.I., New Zealand   46 06S 168 58E   87
Gorelovo: U.S.S.R.   59 47N 30 08E   119
Gorey: Wex., Irish Republic   52 40N 06 18W   67
Gorgān: Iran   36 50N 54 29E   33
Goring: Oxon., England   51 32N 01 09W   59
Gorizia: Italy   45 57N 13 37E   78
Gorki: U.S.S.R.   54 17N 30 59E   80
Gor'kij (Gorki, Gor'kiy): U.S.S.R.   56 20N 44 00E
28 80 105 107
Gor'kij (Gorki, Gor'kiy) *Park*: U.S.S.R.   55 43N 37 35E   119
Gor'ko-Solenoje, Ozero: *lake*, U.S.S.R.   49 20N 46 05E   81
Gor'kovskoje Vodochranilišče (Gor'kovskoje *Reservoir*):
U.S.S.R.   57 00N 43 15E   28 80
Görlitz: E.Germany   51 09N 15 00E   73 78
Gorlovka: U.S.S.R.   48 18N 38 03E   28 80
Gorn'ackij: U.S.S.R.   48 17N 40 55E   80
Gornyj: U.S.S.R.   51 46N 48 34E   81
Gorochovec: U.S.S.R.   56 12N 42 40E   80
Gorodec: U.S.S.R.   56 38N 43 30E   80
Gorodok: U.S.S.R.   55 28N 29 59E   80
Gorontalo: Indonesia   00 33N 123 05E   39
Gorstan: R. & Crom., Scotland   57 38N 04 43W   64
Gort: Gal., Irish Republic   53 04N 08 50W   67
Gorzów Wielkopolski: Poland   52 42N 15 12E   73 78
Gosforth: Tyne & Wear, England   55 01N 01 36W   63
Goshen: Ind., U.S.A.   41 34N 85 49W   98
Goslar: W.Germany   51 54N 10 26E   73
Gosport: Hants., England   50 48N 01 08W   59
Götaälv: *riv.*, Sweden   58 00N 12 00E   75
Göteborg (Gothenburg): Sweden   57 45N 12 00E
26 75 107
Gotha: E.Germany   50 57N 10 43E   73
Gothenburg: Sweden *see* Göteborg   57 45N 12 00E
26 75 107
Gothenburg: Nebr., U.S.A.   40 56N 100 10W   94
Gotland: *is & admin.*, Sweden   57 30N 18 30E   27 75
Göttingen: W.Germany   51 32N 09 57E   73
Gottwaldov (Zlín): Czechoslovakia   49 14N 17 40E   73 78
Gough *Island*: S.Atlantic Ocean   40 20S 10 00W   3
Gouin *Reservoir*: Qué., Canada   48 30N 74 45W   96
Goundam: Mali   16 27N 03 39W   56
Gourock: Renf., Scotland   55 58N 04 49W   62 113
Gouverneur: N.Y., U.S.A.   44 21N 75 29W   99
Govan: Lan., Scotland   55 51N 04 20W   113
Governador Valadares: Brazil   18 51S 41 56W   51
Governor's Harbour: Bahamas   25 13N 76 15W   47
Gower: *pen.*, W. Glam., Wales   51 30N 04 00W   61
Gowganda: Ont., Canada   47 41N 80 46W   99
Gowna, *Lough*: Irish Republic   53 45N 07 30W   66
Gowrie, Carse of: *dist.*, Perth., Scotland   56 15N 03 00W   65
Goya: Argentina   29 10S 59 15W   52
Gozo: *is.*, Malta   36 00N 14 15E   79
Gracias a Dios, *Cape*: Honduras/Nicaragua
15 00N 83 10W   47
Grafschaft, Die: *geog. reg.*, W.Germany   51 15N 06 30E   118

Graham: Tex., U.S.A.   33 06N 98 35W   95
Graham *Island*: B.C., Canada   53 30N 132 30W   89
Graham Land: *reg.*, Antarctica   66 00S 65 00W   24
Grahamstown: C.P., Rep. of S.Africa   33 19S 26 32E   55
Gramat, Causse de: *plat.*, France   44 30N 01 45E   70
Grampian *Mountains*: Scotland   56 45N 04 00W   26 64
Granada: Nicaragua   11 58N 85 59W   47
Granada: Spain   37 10N 03 35W   26 77 104
Granard: Long., Irish Republic   53 47N 07 30W   66
Granby: Qué., Canada   45 23N 72 44W   96
Granby: *riv.*, Canada/U.S.A.   49 15N 118 30W   89
Gran Canaria: *is.*, Canary Is.   28 00N 15 30W   56
Gran Chaco: *geog. reg.*, Argentina/Paraguay
23 45S 60 45W   18 51
Grand: *riv.*, Mich., U.S.A.   42 45N 85 00W   98
Grand: *riv.*, Mo., U.S.A.   40 00N 94 15W   98
Grand: *riv.*, S.D., U.S.A.   45 30N 101 30W   94
Grand Bahama: *is.*, Bahamas   26 38N 78 25W   47 101
Grand Bank: Nfld., Canada   47 06N 55 48W   97
Grand Bourg: Argentina   34 29S 58 42W   128
Grand *Canal*: China   38 15N 116 30E   36 84 121
Grand *Canal*: Irish Republic   53 15N 06 45W   69
Grand Canyon: Ariz., U.S.A.   36 03N 112 09W   43 91
Grand Canyon: Ariz., U.S.A.   36 00N 113 00W   91
Grand Canyon *National Park*: Ariz.,
U.S.A.   36 15N 112 30W   91
Grand Cayman: *is.*, Cayman Is.   19 15N 81 00W   47
Grand Centre: Alta., Canada   54 25N 110 13W   92
Grand Coulee *Dam*: Wash., U.S.A.   47 57N 118 59W   90
Grande: *riv.*, Brazil   19 45S 50 00W   51
Grande: *riv.*, Nicaragua   13 00N 84 30W   47
Grande, Navigo: *can.*, Italy   45 15N 08 45E   116
Grande, Río: *riv.*, Bolivia   16 15S 63 45W   49
Grande, Río: *riv.*, Mexico/U.S.A.   26 45N 99 15W 43 95
Grande Prairie: Alta., Canada   55 10N 118 52W   89
Grand Erg de Bilma: *des.*, Niger   18 45N 12 45E   20
Grande Ronde: *riv.*, Oreg., U.S.A.   45 30N 117 45W   90
Grandes, Salinas: *salt lakes*, Argentina
29 30S 65 00W   52
Grand Falls: N.B., Canada   47 02N 67 46W   96
Grand Falls: Nfld., Canada   48 57N 55 40W   97
Grand Forks: B.C., Canada   49 02N 118 30W   89
Grand Forks: N.D., U.S.A.   47 55N 97 03W   42 94
Grand Haven: Mich., U.S.A.   43 04N 86 13W   98
Grandin, *Lake*: N.W.T., Canada   63 45N 118 45W   88
Grand Island: Nebr., U.S.A.   40 55N 98 21W   43 94
Grand Junction: Colo., U.S.A.   39 04N 108 33W   43 94
Grand-Lahou: Ivory Coast   05 09N 05 01W   57
Grand *Lake*: Nfld., Canada   48 45N 57 30W   97
Grand Manan *Island*: N.B., Canada   44 45N 66 45W   97
Grand' Mère: Qué., Canada   46 36N 72 41W   96
Grand Rapids: Man., Canada   53 12N 99 19W   93
Grand Rapids: Mich., U.S.A.   42 57N 85 40W   45 98
Grand Rapids: Minn., U.S.A.   47 13N 93 30W   98
Grand Teton *National Park*: Wyo., U.S.A.   43 45N 110 30W
94
Grandview: Man., Canada   51 11N 100 51W   93
Graney, *Lough*: Clare, Irish Republic   52 45N 08 30W 67
Grangemouth: Stirl., Scotland   56 01N 03 44W   62 107
Grange-over-Sands: Cumbria, England   54 12N 02 55W
63
Grängesberg: Sweden   60 05N 14 59E   105
Grangeville: Idaho, U.S.A.   45 56N 116 07W   90
Granite City: Ill., U.S.A.   38 42N 90 08W   104
Granite *Peak*: Mont., U.S.A.   45 10N 109 48W   17 42 94
Granollers: Spain   41 37N 02 18E   116
Gran Quivira *National Monument*: N.Mex.,
U.S.A.   34 14N 106 15W   95
Grantham: Lincs., England   52 55N 00 39W   58
Grantown-on-Spey: Moray., Scotland   57 20N 03 38W   65
Grant *Park*: Ill., U.S.A.   41 52N 87 36W   124
Grants: N.Mex., U.S.A.   35 09N 107 52W   95
Grants Pass: Oreg., U.S.A.   42 26N 123 20W   90
Granville: France   48 50N 01 35W   70
Granville *Lake*: Man., Canada   56 15N 100 15W   93
Grass: *riv.*, Man., Canada   55 15N 98 15W   93
Grasse: France   43 40N 06 56E   71
Grass Narrows: Ont., Canada   50 14N 94 01W   93
Grass River *Provincial Park*: Man.,
Canada   54 35N 100 40W   93
Gratosoglio: Italy   45 24N 09 08E   116

Gravelbourg: Sask., Canada	49 53N 106 33W	92
Gravesend: Kent, England	51 27N 00 24E	59 112
Grayling: Mich., U.S.A.	44 40N 84 43W	98
Grays *Harbor*: Wash., U.S.A.	46 45N 124 00W	90
Grayslake: Ill., U.S.A.	42 21N 88 02W	124
Grays Thurrock: Essex, England	51 28N 00 20E	59 112
Graz: Austria	47 05N 15 22E	27 78
Grażdanka: U.S.S.R.	60 00N 30 24E	119
Gr'azi: U.S.S.R.	52 29N 39 57E	80
Great Abaco *Island*: Bahamas	26 15N 77 00W	47 101
Great Australian *Bight*: Australia	33 15S 129 45E	14 40
Great Barrier *Island*: N.I., New Zealand	36 15S 175 15E	87
Great Barrier *Reef*: Qld., Australia	19 30S 149 00E	15 41
Great *Basin*: U.S.A.	39 45N 116 00W	17 43 91
Great Bear *Lake*: N.W.T., Canada	66 00N 121 00W	16 88
Great Bend: Kans., U.S.A.	38 22N 98 46W	94
Great Bernera: *is.*, R. & Crom., Scotland	58 00N 06 45W	64
Great Blasket *Island*: Kerry, Irish Republic	52 00N 10 30W	67
Great Britain *see* United Kingdom		6 26 69
Great Cumbrae *Island*: Bute., Scotland	55 45N 04 45W	62 113
Great Dividing *Range*: Australia		15 41
Great Driffield: Humb., England	54 01N 00 26W	63
Great Dunmow: Essex, England	51 53N 00 22E	59
Great Eastern Erg: *des.*, Algeria	30 00N 07 00E	20 56
Greater Antilles: *is.*, Caribbean Sea	21 00N 75 00W	17 47
Greater London: *admin.*, England	51 30N 00 00E	112
Greater Manchester: *admin.*, England	53 30N 02 15W	63 114
Greater Sunda *Islands*: Indonesia	04 00S 110 00E	13
Great Falls: Mont., U.S.A.	47 30N 111 17W	42 94
Great Gable: *mtn.*, Cumbria, England	54 29N 03 13W	62
Great Glen *see* Glen Mór	57 00N 04 45W	64
Greatham: Dur., England	54 39N 01 14W	105
Great Harbour Cay: Bahamas	25 45N 77 50W	47
Great Harwood: Lancs., England	53 48N 02 24W	114
Great Himalayan *Range*: Asia		11 34 83
Great Inagua: *is.*, Bahamas	21 00N 73 15W	47
Great Indian (Thar) *Desert*: India	28 00N 72 30E	11 34 82
Great Karras *Mountains*: S.W.Africa	27 00S 19 00E	21
Great Karroo *see* Groot-Karoo	32 30S 23 00E	21 55
Great Khingan *Mountains* (Tahsinganling Shanmo): China	49 30N 122 00E	9 31
Great Kill *Park*: N.Y., U.S.A.	40 32N 74 07W	123
Great Malvern: Here. & Worcs., England	52 07N 02 19W	59
Great Mercury *Island*: N.I., New Zealand	36 30S 175 45E	87
Great Mis Tor: *mtn.*, Devon, England	50 34N 04 01W	61
Great Neck: N.Y., U.S.A.	40 49N 73 43W	123
Great *Oasis*: Egypt	25 30N 31 00E	32
Great Ormes *Head*: Gwyn., Wales	53 21N 03 53W	60
Great Ouse: *riv.*, Norfolk, England	52 30N 00 15E	58
Great *Plains*: U.S.A.	40 00N 103 00W	17
Great Salt *Desert*: Iran	34 30N 55 00E	10
Great Salt *Lake*: Utah, U.S.A.	41 00N 112 30W	17 43 91
Great Salt Lake *Desert*: Utah, U.S.A.	40 45N 113 15W	91
Great Sand Dunes *National Monument*: Colo., U.S.A.	37 45N 105 30W	95
Great Sandy *Desert*: W.A., Australia	21 00S 124 30E	14 40
Great Sankey: Ches., England	53 23N 02 37W	114
Great Shelford: Cambs., England	52 09N 00 09E	59
Great Slave *Lake*: N.W.T., Canada	61 30N 114 00W	16 42 88
Great Smoky *Mountains*: U.S.A.	35 30N 84 00W	45
Great Smoky Mountains *National Park*: U.S.A.	35 30N 83 30W	101
Great South *Bay*: N.Y., U.S.A.	40 30N 73 15W	123
Great Stour: *riv.*, Kent, England	51 00N 00 45E	59
Great Torrington: Devon, England	50 57N 04 09W	61
Great Victoria *Desert*: Australia	28 30S 129 45E	14 40
Great *Wall*: China	40 15N 118 45E	84
Great Western Erg: *des.*, Algeria	30 00N 01 00E	20 56
Great Whale: *riv.*, Qué., Canada	55 00N 76 00W	96
Great Whale River (Poste-de-la-Baleine): Qué., Canada	55 20N 77 50W	96
Great Wyrley: Staffs., England	52 41N 02 01W	115
Great Yarmouth: Norf., England	52 37N 01 44E	58
GREECE	39 00N 21 30E	7 27 79 107
Greeley: Colo., U.S.A.	40 25N 104 42W	94
Green: *riv.*, Ky., U.S.A.	37 15N 86 00W	101
Green: *riv.*, U.S.A.	39 45N 109 45W	17 43 91
Green Bay: Wis., U.S.A.	44 30N 88 00W	45 98
Green *Bay*: U.S.A.	45 00N 87 30W	98
Greenbelt: Md., U.S.A.	39 00N 76 53W	122
Greenbelt *Park*: Md., U.S.A.	38 59N 76 53W	122
Greencastle: Down, N.Ireland	54 02N 06 06W	66
Greeneville: Tenn., U.S.A.	36 10N 82 50W	101
Greenfield: Tenn., U.S.A.	36 09N 88 48W	100
Green *Lake*: Wash., U.S.A.	47 40N 122 20W	126
GREENLAND		2 23
Greenland *Sea*	78 00N 05 00W	23
Greenlaw: Ber., Scotland	55 43N 02 28W	63
Greenock: Renf., Scotland	55 57N 04 45W	62 113
Greenore: Louth, Irish Republic	54 02N 06 08W	66
Greenore *Point*: Wex., Irish Republic	52 15N 06 18W	67
Green River: Wyo., U.S.A.	41 32N 109 28W	94
Greensboro: N.C., U.S.A.	36 03N 79 50W	45 101
Greenstone *Point*: R. & Crom., Scotland	57 55N 05 37W	64
Green Valley: N.S.W., Australia	33 54S 150 52E	120
Greenville: Liberia	05 01N 09 03W	57
Greenville: Ala., U.S.A.	31 50N 86 38W	101
Greenville: Miss., U.S.A.	33 24N 91 04W	100
Greenville: S.C., U.S.A.	34 52N 82 25W	45 101
Greenville: Tex., U.S.A.	33 08N 96 07W	100
Greenwich: Gt. Ldn., England	51 28N 00 00	112
Greenwich: N.Y., U.S.A.	43 07N 73 30W	123
Greenwood: B.C., Canada	49 08N 118 41W	89
Greenwood: Miss., U.S.A.	33 31N 90 11W	100
Greenwood: S.C., U.S.A.	34 11N 82 10W	101
Greese: *riv.*, Kild., Irish Republic	53 00N 06 45W	67
Greifswald: E.Germany	54 06N 13 24E	73
Greiz: E.Germany	50 40N 12 11E	73
Grem'ačinsk: U.S.S.R.	58 34N 57 51E	81
Grenà: Denmark	56 25N 10 53E	75
GRENADA	12 00N 61 45W	47
Grenoble: France	45 11N 05 43E	26 71
Gretna: Dumf., Scotland	54 59N 03 04W	63
Grevenbroich: W.Germany	51 06N 06 36E	118
Greyhound *Strait*: Indonesia	02 00S 124 00E	39
Greymouth: S.I., New Zealand	42 28S 171 12E	37 87
Grey *Range*: Qld., Australia	28 00S 143 00E	41
Greystones: Wick., Irish Republic	53 09N 06 04W	67
Gribanovskij: U.S.S.R.	51 27N 41 58E	80
Griffin: Ga., U.S.A.	33 15N 84 17W	101
Griffith *Park*: Calif., U.S.A.	34 08N 118 17W	127
Griminish *Point*: Inv., Scotland	57 40N 07 29W	64
Grimsby: Humb., England	53 35N 00 05W	63
Grimshaw: Alta., Canada	56 11N 117 37W	92
Gris Nez, *Cap*: France	50 52N 01 35E	59
Groais *Island*: Nfld., Canada	50 45N 55 30W	97
Gröditz: E.Germany	51 25N 13 27E	105
Grodno: U.S.S.R.	53 40N 23 50E	28 78
Gronau: W.Germany	52 13N 07 02E	72
Grong: Norway	64 27N 12 19E	74
Groningen: Netherlands	53 13N 06 35E	26 72
Grootfontein: S.W.Africa	19 32S 18 05E	55
Groot-Karoo (Great Karroo): *plat.*, C.P., Rep. of S.Africa	32 30S 23 00E	21 55
Grosnez *Point*: Channel Islands	49 15N 02 15W	61
Grosse Pointe: Mich., U.S.A.	42 22N 82 59W	125
Grosse *Pointe*: Mich., U.S.A.	42 25N 82 53W	125
Grosse Pointe Park: Mich., U.S.A.	42 23N 82 56W	125
Grosse Pointe Shores: Mich., U.S.A.	42 25N 83 08W	125
Grosser Plöner See: *lake*, W.Germany	54 08N 10 25E	73
Grosser Müggelsee: *lake*, E.Germany	52 15N 13 30E	117
Grosser Zernsee: *lake*, E.Germany	52 15N 12 45E	117
Grosseto: Italy	42 46N 11 07E	79
Groswater *Bay*: Nfld., Canada	54 15N 57 30W	97
Groundhog: *riv.*, Ont., Canada	49 00N 82 00W	98
Groznyj (Groznyy): U.S.S.R.	43 20N 45 42E	28 107
Grudziądz: Poland	53 29N 18 45E	78
Gruinard *Bay*: R. & Crom., Scotland	57 45N 05 30W	64
Gryfe: *riv.*, Renf., Scotland	55 45N 04 30W	113
Gryfice: Poland	53 55N 15 11E	73
Grytviken: *rsch. stn.*, South Georgia	54 17S 36 30W	24
Guadalajara: Mexico	20 40N 103 20W	46
Guadalajara: Spain	40 37N 03 10W	77
Guadalcanal: *is.*, S.Pacific Ocean	09 30S 160 00E	4

Types of map: Ocean pp. 1-5; Physical pp. 6-25; Human pp. 26-57; Topographic pp. 58-101; World pp. 102-111; Urban pp. 112-128.

Guadalquivir: *riv.*, Spain   37 30N 05 15W   26 76
Guadalupe: *is.*, N.Pacific Ocean   29 00N 118 00W   5
Guadalupe: *riv.*, Tex., U.S.A.   29 15N 97 15W   95
Guadalupe, Presa de: *res.*, Mexico   19 38N 99 16W   128
Guadalupe Mountains *National Park*: Tex.,
    U.S.A.   32 00N 104 45W   95
Guadeloupe: *is.*, Leeward Is.   16 30N 61 30W   47
Guadiana: *riv.*, Portugal/Spain   38 15N 07 15W   77
Guajará Mirim: Brazil   10 48S 65 22W   49
Guajira, *Península de la*: Colombia   12 00N 71 45W   48
Gualeguaychú: Argentina   33 03S 58 31W   52
Guam: *is.*, Philippine Sea   13 30N 144 40E   4 12
Gu'an: China   39 26N 116 19E   84
Guanabara: *admin.*, Brazil   23 30S 43 15W   51
Guanare: Venezuela   09 04N 69 45W   48
Guang'an: China   30 32N 106 37E   85
Guangchang: China   26 45N 116 08E   85
Guangde: China   30 50N 119 28E   85
Guangdong (Kuangtung): *admin.*, China   23 45N 113 45E
                                                    36 85
Guangfeng: China   28 20N 118 14E   85
Guanghua (Kuanghua): China   32 21N 111 39E   36 84
Guangling: China   39 47N 114 13E   84
Guangshan: China   32 02N 115 00E   84
Guangzhou (Kuangchou, Canton): China   23 08N 113 16E
                                                    36 85 105
Guangzong: China   37 06N 115 08E   84
Guantánamo: Cuba   20 08N 75 12W   47
Guanting *Dam*: China   40 25N 115 21E   84
Guanxian: China   36 26N 115 23E   84
Guanxi Zhuang (Kuanghsichuangtsu): *admin.*, China
    24 30N 109 00E   36 85
Guanyun (Dayishan): China   34 23N 119 19E   84
Guaporé: *riv.*, Bolivia/Brazil   13 45S 60 30W   49
Guaqui: Bolivia   16 35S 68 51W   49
Guarda: Portugal   40 32N 07 17W   77
Guardafui, *Cape*: Somali Rep.   11 50N 51 16E   53
Guárico: *riv.*, Venezuela   08 30N 67 30W   48
GUATEMALA   15 30N 90 45W   17 46 106
Guatemala: *city see* Ciudad de Guatemala   14 38N 90 31W
                                                    46
Guatemala *Basin*: N.Pacific Ocean   09 00N 95 00W   5
Guaviare: *riv.*, Colombia   03 03N 69 00W   48
Guayanilla: Puerto Rico   18 01N 66 47W   106
Guayaquil: Ecuador   02 10S 79 50W   48
Guaymas: Mexico   27 59N 110 54W   46
Gubacha: U.S.S.R.   58 52N 57 36E   81
Gubkin: U.S.S.R.   51 18N 37 32E   80
Gucheng: Hebei, China   37 25N 116 00E   84
Gucheng: Hubei, China   32 18N 111 30E   84
Gué, du: *riv.*, Qué., Canada   57 00N 71 15W   96
Guecho: Spain   43 21N 03 01W   70
Guelma: Algeria   36 29N 07 25E   56
Guelph: Ont., Canada   43 34N 80 16W   99
Guéret: France   46 10N 01 52E   70
Guernsey: *is.*, Channel Is.   49 15N 02 30W   61
Guerrero: Mexico   19 27N 99 09W   128
Guerrero: *admin.*, Mexico   18 00N 100 00W   46
Guge: *mtn.*, Ethiopia   06 16N 37 25E   53
Gugu: *mtn.*, Ethiopia   08 10N 40 00E   53
Guiana *Basin*: N.Atlantic Ocean   17 00N 54 00W   2
Guiana *Highlands*: S.America   05 15N 61 30W   18 48
Guiding: China   26 38N 107 10E   85
Guidong: China   26 10N 113 57E   85
Guildford: Surrey, England   51 14N 00 35W   59 112
Guilin (Kueilin): China   25 24N 110 11E   36 85
GUINEA   10 00N 10 00W   20 57
Guinea, *Gulf of*: W.Africa   01 30N 00 00   20 57
Guinea *Basin*: N.Atlantic Ocean   00 00 06 00W   3 20
Guinea *Fracture Zone*: N.Atlantic Ocean   09 00N 38 00W   2
Guingamp: France   48 34N 03 09W   70
Guiping: China   23 24N 110 07E   85
Guisborough: Cleve., England   54 32N 01 04W   63
Guiseley: W.Yorks., England   53 53N 01 42W   115
Guixian: China   23 06N 109 41E   85
Guiyang (Kueiyang): Guizhou, China   26 38N 106 38E
                                                    36 85 105
Guizhou (Kueichou): *admin.*, China   27 30N 107 45E   36 85
Guizhou *Plateau* (Kweichow *Plateau*): China
    25 45N 106 30E   12 36
Gujarat: *admin.*, India   23 30N 71 00E   34 82

Gujiazhai: China   31 21N 121 23E   121
Gujrānwāla: Pakistan   32 06N 74 11E   34
Gukovo: U.S.S.R.   48 03N 39 56E   80
Gul'ajpole: U.S.S.R.   47 38N 36 16E   80
Gulbarga: India   17 22N 76 47E   34
Gulfport: Miss., U.S.A.   30 22N 89 06W   45 100
Gulf Stream: *current*, N.Atlantic Ocean   32 00N 77 00W   2
Gullion, Slieve: *mtn.*, Arm., N.Ireland   54 06N 06 25W   66
Gulu: Uganda   02 46N 32 21E   53
Gumla: India   23 03N 84 36E   82
Gummersbach: W.Germany   51 02N 07 34E   72
Guna: India   24 39N 77 18E   82
Guna: *mtn.*, Ethiopia   11 40N 38 20E   53
Gunisao: *riv.*, Man., Canada   53 30N 97 00W   93
Gunnar: Sask., Canada   59 25N 108 50W   92
Gunnison: Colo., U.S.A.   38 33N 106 56W   94
Gunnison: *riv.*, Colo., U.S.A.   38 30N 107 00W   94
Guntersville *Lake*: Ala., U.S.A.   34 25N 86 23W   101
Guntūr: India   16 20N 80 27E   34
Günzberg: W.Germany   48 27N 10 18E   73
Guo: *riv.*, China   33 30N 116 30E   84
Guoxian: China   38 52N 112 44E   84
Guoyang: China   33 28N 116 12E   84
Gurag: *mtn.*, Ethiopia   08 15N 38 21E   53
Gurdāspur: India   32 04N 75 28E   82
Gurgaon: India   28 27N 77 01E   82
Gurjev (Gur'yev): U.S.S.R.   47 07N 51 56E   28 81
Gurnard's *Head*: Corn., England   50 11N 05 36W   61
Gur'yev *see* Gurjev   47 07N 51 56E   28 81
Gusau: Nigeria   12 12N 06 40E   57
Gus'–Chrustal'nyj: U.S.S.R.   55 37N 40 40E   80
Gusev: U.S.S.R.   54 36N 22 12E   78
Gushi: China   32 10N 115 45E   84
Gustavo A. Madero: Mexico   19 29N 99 08W   128
Gustavus: Alaska, U.S.A.   58 25N 135 44W   88
Güstrow: E.Germany   53 48N 12 11E   73
Gütersloh: W.Germany   51 54N 08 22E   72
Guthrie: Okla., U.S.A.   35 53N 97 25W   95
Gutian: China   26 36N 118 52E   85
GUYANA   05 45N 60 00W   18 48 106
Guymon: Okla., U.S.A.   36 41N 101 29W   95
Guyuan: China   35 55N 106 45E   84
Guzhen: China   33 19N 117 21E   84
Guzman: Mexico   31 14N 107 24W   95
Guzman, *Lago de*: Mexico   31 30N 107 20W   95
Gwādar: Pakistan   25 09N 62 21E   34
Gwalior: India   26 12N 78 09E   34 82
Gweebarra *Bay*: Don., Irish Republic   54 45N 08 15W   66
Gwelo: Rhodesia   19 27S 29 49E   55
Gwennap *Head*: Corn., England   50 02N 05 43W   61
Gwent: *admin.*, Wales   51 30N 02 45W   61
Gwynedd: *admin.*, Wales   53 00N 04 00W   60
Gyangtse *see* Jiangzi   28 57N 89 35E   35 83
Gydan *Range*: U.S.S.R.   62 30N 157 00E   9 31
Gyöngyös: Hungary   47 46N 19 57E   78
Győr: Hungary   47 42N 17 38E   78
Gypsum *Point*: N.W.T., Canada   61 52N 114 36W   88
Gypsumville: Man., Canada   51 47N 98 38W   93
Gzhatzk *see* Gagarin   55 33N 35 00E   80
Győr Sopron: *admin.*, Hungary   47 30N 17 00E   73

Haapsalu: U.S.S.R.   58 58N 23 32E   75
Haard, Die: *hills*, W.Germany   51 30N 07 15E   118
Haarlem: Netherlands   52 23N 04 38E   72
Haast: S.I., New Zealand   43 53S 169 04E   87
Haast *Pass*: S.I., New Zealand   44 05S 169 22E   87
Habay: Alta., Canada   58 48N 118 40W   88
Habiganj: Bangladesh   24 24N 91 25E   83
Haboro: Japan   44 22N 141 42E   86
Hachinohe: Japan   40 30N 141 29E   37 86
Hackensack: N.J., U.S.A.   40 54N 74 03W   123
Hackensack: *riv.*, N.J., U.S.A.   40 48N 74 05W   123
Hackney: Gt. Ldn., England   51 33N 00 03W   112
Haddington: E.Loth., Scotland   55 58N 02 47W   63
Haddonfield: N.J., U.S.A.   39 54N 75 02W   122
Hadejia: Nigeria   12 30N 10 03E   57
Haderslev: Denmark   55 15N 09 30E   75
Hadhramaut: *geog. reg. see* Hadramawt   16 30N 49 15E   33

Types of map: Ocean pp. 1-5; Physical pp. 6-25; Human pp. 26-57; Topographic pp. 58-101; World pp. 102-111; Urban pp. 112-128.

Haditha see Al Ḥadīthah   34 09N 42 22E   33
Hadleigh: Suff., England   52 02N 00 57E   59
Hadramawt (Hadhramaut): geog. reg., Yemen D.R.
  16 30N 49 15E   33
Haedo: Argentina   34 38S 58 35W   128
Haeju: N.Korea   38 02N 125 42E   37
Haerbin (Harbin): China   45 45N 126 41E   37
Hāfizābād: Pakistan   32 03N 73 42E   82
Haft Gel: Iran   31 28N 49 35E   33
Hagen: W.Germany   51 22N 07 27E   72 118
Hagerstown: Md., U.S.A.   39 39N 77 44W   99
Hagi: Japan   34 24N 131 25E   86
Hagondange: France   49 16N 06 11E   71 105
Hags Head: Clare, Irish Republic   52 57N 09 28W   67
Hague, Cap de la: France   49 44N 01 56W   61
Haian: China   32 30N 120 30E   84
Haidhof: W.Germany   49 41N 11 13E   105
Haidian: China   39 59N 116 18E   121
Haifa see Hefa   32 49N 34 59E   32 107
Haifeng: China   22 58N 115 36E   85
Haihuisi: China   39 56N 116 26E   121
Haikou: China   20 06N 110 21E   36
Hā'il: Saudi Arabia   27 31N 41 45E   33
Hailaer (Hailaerh): China   49 12N 119 42E   30
Hailsham: E. Sussex, England   50 52N 00 16E   59
Hailuoto: is., Finland   65 02N 24 42E   74
Haimen: Guangdong, China   23 13N 116 40E   85
Haimen: Zheijiang, China   28 38N 121 30E   85
Hainandao (Hainan): is., China   19 15N 109 30E   12 36
Haines: Alaska, U.S.A.   59 11N 135 23W   88
Haines Junction: Yukon, Canada   60 45N 137 21W   88
Haining (Xiashi): China   30 32N 120 42E   85
Hai Phong: N.Vietnam   20 50N 106 41E   36
HAITI   18 30N 74 30W   17 47
Haiyan: China   30 31N 121 00E   85
Haizhou see Donghai   34 34N 119 09E   84
Hājīpur: India   25 41N 85 13E   83
Hajnówka: Poland   52 45N 23 32E   78
Hakken-san: mtn., Japan   34 10N 135 54E   86
Hakodate: Japan   41 45N 140 43E   37 86
Haku-san-kokuritsu-kōen: nat. park,
  Japan   36 00N 136 30E   86
Ḥalab (Aleppo): Syria   36 12N 37 10E   33
Ḥalā'ib: Sudan   22 13N 36 38E   53
Halberstadt: E.Germany   51 54N 11 04E   73
Halden: Norway   59 08N 11 13E   75
Haldwāni: India   29 13N 79 33E   82
Halesowen: W.Mid., England   52 26N 02 05W   58 115
Halesworth: Suff., England   52 21N 01 30E   59
Halewood: Mers., England   53 22N 02 50W   114
Haleyville: Ala., U.S.A.   34 14N 87 37W   100
Halfmoon Bay: Stewart I., New Zealand   46 54S 168 08E   87
Half Moon Bay: Calif., U.S.A.   37 28N 122 26W   126
Half Moon Bay: Calif., U.S.A.   37 29N 122 29W   126
Halfway: riv., B.C., Canada   56 30N 122 15W   89
Halifax: N.S., Canada   44 38N 63 35W   44 97
Halifax: W.Yorks., England   53 44N 01 52W   63 115
Halladale: riv., Suther., Scotland   58 15N 03 45W   65
Halle: E.Germany   51 28N 11 58E   26 73
Hallein: Austria   47 41N 13 06E   73
Hallett, Cape: Antarctica   72 19S 170 18E   25
Halley Bay: rsch. stn., Antarctica   75 31S 26 38W   24
Hall Green: W.Mid., England   52 25N 01 50W   115
Halmahera: is., Indonesia   00 45N 128 00E   12 39
Halmahera Sea: Indonesia   00 15S 128 45E   39
Halmstad: Sweden   56 41N 12 55E   75
Hälsingborg: Sweden   56 05N 12 45E   75
Halstead: Essex, England   51 57N 00 38E   59
Haltwhistle: Northumb., England   54 58N 02 27W   63
Halver: W.Germany   51 12N 07 28E   118
Hamada: Japan   34 53N 132 05E   86
Hamada du Dra: geog. reg., Algeria   29 30N 06 00W   56
Hamadān: Iran   34 46N 48 30E   33
Hamada Tounassine: geog. reg., Algeria   28 30N 05 00W
    56
Hamāh: Syria   35 08N 36 45E   33
Hamamatsu: Japan   34 42N 137 44E   37 86
Hamar: Norway   60 57N 10 55E   75
Hamborn: W.Germany   51 29N 06 46E   118
Hamburg: W.Germany   53 33N 10 00E   26 73 107 119
Hämeenlinna: Finland   61 00N 24 25E   75
Hameln (Hamelin): W.Germany   52 06N 09 21E   72
Hamersley Range: W.A., Australia   22 00S 117 30E   14 40
Hamhŭng: N.Korea   39 54N 127 32E   37
Hami: China   42 47N 93 32E   36 105
Hamilton: Ont., Canada   43 15N 79 50W   45 99 104
Hamilton: N.I., New Zealand   37 46S 175 18E   37 87
Hamilton: Lan., Scotland   55 47N 04 03W   62 113
Hamilton: Ohio, U.S.A.   39 23N 84 33W   45 98
Hamilton Inlet: Nfld., Canada   53 45N 59 00W   97
Hamina: Finland   60 33N 27 15E   75
Hamlin: Tex., U.S.A.   32 53N 100 08W   95
Hamm: Arnsberg, W.Germany   51 40N 07 49E   72
Hamm: Hamburg, W.Germany   53 33N 10 05E   119
Hammamet: Tunisia   36 25N 10 40E   26
Hammerfest: Norway   70 40N 23 44E   27 74
Hammersmith: Gt. Ldn., England   51 30N 00 14W   112
Hammond: Ind., U.S.A.   41 37N 87 30W   98 124
Hammond: La., U.S.A.   30 30N 90 28W   100
Hampshire: admin., England   51 00N 01 15W   59
Hampshire Downs: hills, Hants., England   51 15N 01 00W
    59
Hampstead Heath: Gt. Ldn., England   51 34N 00 12W   112
Hampton: Va., U.S.A.   37 02N 76 23W   101
Hamtramck: Mich., U.S.A.   42 26N 83 02W   125
Han: riv., China   24 00N 116 30E   36 85
Hanau am Main: W.Germany   50 08N 08 56E   72
Hancheng: China   35 24N 110 25E   84
Hanchung see Hanzhong   33 06N 107 02E   36 84
Hancock: Mich., U.S.A.   47 08N 88 32W   98
Handa: Japan   34 53N 136 56E   86
Handa Island: Suther., Scotland   58 15N 05 00W   64
Handan (Hantan): China   36 37N 114 28E   36 84
Hanford: Calif., U.S.A.   36 20N 119 39W   91
Hangchow see Hangzhou   30 15N 120 10E   37 85
Hangjinqi: China   39 57N 108 33E   84
Hangu: China   39 18N 117 44E   84
Hanguang: China   24 16N 113 09E   85
Hangzhou (Hangchow): China   30 15N 120 10E   37 85
Hangzhou Park: China   31 17N 121 29E   121
Hanjiang: China   25 30N 119 09E   85
Hanko: Finland   59 50N 23 00E   75
Hankou: China   30 36N 114 17E   85
Hanley: Staffs., England   53 01N 02 10W   58
Hann, Mount: W.A., Australia   15 55S 125 54E   40
Hanna: Alta., Canada   51 38N 111 56W   92
Hannah Bay: Ont., Canada   51 15N 80 00W   96
Hannibal: Mo., U.S.A.   39 41N 91 20W   98
Hanningfield Water: lake, Essex, England   51 30N 00 30E
    112
Hannover (Hanover): W.Germany   52 23N 09 44E   26 72
Hanöbukten: bay, Sweden   55 45N 14 45E   75
Ha Noi: N.Vietnam   21 01N 105 52E   36
Hanover: W.Germany see Hannover   52 23N 09 44E   26
Hansen Flood Control Basin: Calif., U.S.A.
  34 16N 118 22W   127
Hanshan: China   31 44N 118 08E   84
Hanshui: riv., China   31 15N 112 30E   12 36 84
Hänsi: India   29 06N 76 01E   82
Hantan see Handan   36 37N 114 28E   36 84
Hanumāngarh: India   29 33N 74 21E   82
Hanyang: China   30 33N 114 16E   85
Hanyin: China   32 56N 108 41E   84
Hanzhong (Hanchung): China   33 06N 107 02E   36 84
Haogoundou, Lake: Mali   15 45N 02 30W   57
Haoli see Hegang   47 24N 130 17E   31
Haparanda: Sweden   65 50N 24 10E   74
Hāpur: India   28 43N 77 47E   82
Hárad see Maḥaṭṭat Harad   24 08N 49 04E   33
Harar: Ethiopia   09 20N 42 10E   53
Harbin see Haerbin   45 45N 126 41E   37
Harbour Breton: Nfld., Canada   47 39N 55 50W   97
Harburg: W.Germany   53 28N 09 57E   73 119
Harburg, Staatsforst: for., W.Germany   53 15N 09 45E   119
Harda Khās: India   22 22N 77 08E   82
Hardangerfjorden: fd., Norway   60 00N 06 00E   75
Hardangervidda: plat., Norway   60 00N 08 00E   75
Hardin: Mont., U.S.A.   45 44N 107 37W   94
Hardisty: Alta., Canada   52 42N 111 19W   92
Hardisty Lake: N.W.T., Canada   64 30N 117 45W   88
Hardwār: India   29 58N 78 09E   82
Hare: riv., N.W.T., Canada   66 30N 128 15W   88

Types of map: Ocean pp. 1-5; Physical pp. 6-25; Human pp. 26-57; Topographic pp. 58-101; World pp. 102-111; Urban pp. 112-128.

Hare *Bay*: Nfld., Canada   51 15N 55 45W   97
Hargeysa (Hargeisa): Somali Rep.   09 31N 44 02E   53
Hari: *riv.*, Indonesia   01 15S 104 00E   38
Haringey: Gt. Ldn., England   51 35N 00 07W   59
Harkortsee: *lake*, W.Germany   51 15N 07 15E   118
Harlech: Gwyn., Wales   52 52N 04 07W   60
Harleston: Norf., England   52 24N 01 18E   58
Harlingen: Tex., U.S.A.   26 12N 97 43W   46 100
Harlow: Essex, England   51 47N 00 08E   59 112
Harney *Lake*: Oreg., U.S.A.   43 14N 119 08W   90
Härnösand: Sweden   62 37N 17 55E   74
Haro: Spain   42 34N 02 52W   70 77
Harpenden: Herts., England   51 49N 00 22W   59
Harper: Liberia   04 25N 07 43W   57
Harper Woods: Mich., U.S.A.   42 25N 82 57W   125
Harricanaw: *riv.*, Canada   50 30N 79 00W   96
Harrington Harbour: Qué., Canada   50 31N 59 30W   97
Harris: *dist.*, Inv., Scotland   57 45N 07 00W   64
Harris, *Sound of*: Inv., Scotland   57 45N 07 00W   64
Harrisburg: Pa., U.S.A.   40 17N 76 54W   45 99
Harrison, *Cape*: Nfld., Canada   54 55N 58 00W   97
Harrisonburg: Va., U.S.A.   38 27N 78 54W   99
Harrison *Lake*: B.C., Canada   49 30N 121 45W   89
Harrogate: N.Yorks., England   54 00N 01 33W   63
Harrow: Gt. Ldn., England   51 35N 00 21W   59 112
Harstad: Norway   68 48N 16 30E   74
Hart: *riv.*, Yukon, Canada   65 30N 136 45W   88
Hartford: Conn., U.S.A.   41 46N 72 40W   45 99
Hartland: Devon, England   50 59N 04 29W   61
Hartland *Point*: Devon, England   51 02N 04 31W   61
Hartlepool: Cleve., England   54 42N 01 11W   63 105
Hartley: Kent, England   51 23N 00 18E   112
Hartshill: War., England   52 37N 01 32W   115
Hartwell: Northants., England   52 08N 00 52W   59
Hārūnābād: Pakistan   29 37N 73 08E   82
Harvey: Ill., U.S.A.   41 38N 87 40W   124
Harvey: N.D., U.S.A.   47 47N 99 56W   94
Harwell: Oxon., England   51 37N 01 18W   59
Harwich: Essex, England   51 57N 01 17E   59
Harwood Heights: Ill., U.S.A.   41 59N 87 48W   124
Haryana: *admin.*, India   29 00N 76 00E   34 82
Harz: *mtns.*, E.Germany/W.Germany   51 30N 10 45E   73
Hase: *riv.*, W.Germany   52 30N 08 00E   72
Haskell: Tex., U.S.A.   33 10N 99 44W   95
Haskovo (Khaskovo): Bulgaria   41 56N 25 33E   79
Haslemere: Surrey, England   51 06N 00 43W   59
Haslingden: Lancs., England   53 43N 02 18W   114
Haspe: W.Germany   51 21N 07 26E   118
Hassi Messaoud: Algeria   31 43N 06 05E   56
Hässleholm: Sweden   56 09N 13 45E   75
Hastings: E.Sussex, England   50 51N 00 36E   59
Hastings: N.I., New Zealand   39 39S 176 52E   87
Hastings: Nebr., U.S.A.   40 35N 98 23W   94
Hatfield: Herts., England   51 46N 00 13W   59 112
Hatherleigh: Devon, England   50 49N 04 04W   61
Hāthras: India   27 36N 78 02E   82
Hatteras, *Cape*: N.C., U.S.A.   35 14N 75 31W   17 45 101
Hattiesburg: Miss., U.S.A.   31 20N 89 17W   100
Hattingen: W.Germany   51 24N 07 10E   118
Haugesund: Norway   59 25N 05 16E   75
Haukivesi: *lake*, Finland   62 00N 28 30E   74
Hauraki *Gulf*: N.I., New Zealand   36 30S 175 00E   87
Hauz Khas: India   28 34N 77 11E   120
Havana, Cuba *see* La Habana   23 08N 82 22W   47
Havant: Hants., England   50 51N 00 59W   59
Havelberg: E.Germany   52 50N 12 05E   73
Havelkanal: *can.*, E.Germany   52 30N 13 00E   117
Havelock: N.B., Canada   45 59N 65 20W   97
Haverfordwest: Dyfed, Wales   51 49N 04 58W   60
Haverhill: Suff., England   52 05N 00 26E   59
Havering: Gt. Ldn., England   51 37N 00 11E   59
Havlíčkův Brod: Czechoslovakia   49 38N 15 36E   73
Havre: Mont., U.S.A.   48 33N 109 41W   90
Havre-St.-Pierre: Qué., Canada   50 16N 63 36W   97
Hawaii: *is.*, Hawaii, U.S.A.   19 00N 155 00W   5
Hawaiian Gardens: Calif., U.S.A.   33 50N 118 04W   127
Hawaiian *Ridge*: N.Pacific Ocean   22 00N 165 00W   4
Hawarden: Clwyd, Wales   53 11N 03 02W   60 114
Hawera: N.I., New Zealand   39 35S 174 19E   87
Hawes: N.Yorks., England   54 18N 02 12W   63
Hawick: Rox., Scotland   55 25N 02 47W   63

Hawke *Bay*: N.I., New Zealand   39 00S 177 15E   87
Hawkesbury: *riv.*, N.S.W., Australia   33 34S 150 53E   120
Hawkshead: Cumbria, England   54 23N 03 00W   63
Haworth: W.Yorks., England   53 50N 01 57W   115
Hawthorne: Calif., U.S.A.   33 55N 118 21W   127
Hawthorne: Nev., U.S.A.   38 32N 118 38W   91
Hawthorne: N.J., U.S.A.   40 57N 74 09W   123
Hay: *riv.*, Canada   60 00N 116 45W   42 92
Hayama: Japan   35 16N 139 34E   121
Hayden: Ariz., U.S.A.   33 00N 110 47W   91
Hayes: *riv.*, Man., Canada   55 45N 93 15W   93
Hay *Lake*: Alta., Canada   58 45N 119 00W   88
Hayle: Corn., England   50 10N 05 25W   61
Hayling Island: Hants., England   50 48N 00 59W   59
Hay River: N.W.T., Canada   60 51N 115 42W   42 92
Hays: Kans., U.S.A.   38 53N 99 20W   94
Hayward: Calif., U.S.A.   37 40N 122 07W   126
Haywards Heath: W.Sussex, England   51 00N 00 06W   59
Hazāribāgh: India   24 00N 85 23E   83
Hazel Park: Mich., U.S.A.   42 27N 83 05W   125
Hazelton: B.C., Canada   55 16N 127 18W   89
Hazleton: Pa., U.S.A.   40 58N 75 59W   99
Healdsburg: Calif., U.S.A.   38 36N 122 53W   91
Heanor: Derby., England   53 01N 01 22W   58
Heard *Island*: Southern Ocean   53 07S 73 20E   1
Hearst: Ont., Canada   49 42N 83 40W   98
Heart: *riv.*, N.D., U.S.A.   46 30N 101 45W   94
Heathcote: N.S.W., Australia   34 05S 151 01E   120
Heath *Point*: Qué., Canada   49 05N 61 42W   97
Hebei (Hopeh): *admin.*, China   38 45N 115 30E   36 84
Heber: Utah., U.S.A.   40 31N 111 25W   91
Hebi: China   35 53N 114 09E   84
Hebrides, Inner: *is.*, Scotland   57 00N 06 30W   64
Hebrides, Outer: *is.*, Scotland   57 30N 07 00W   26 64
Hebrides, *Sea of the*: Scotland   57 00N 07 00W   64
Hecate *Strait*: B.C., Canada   53 15N 131 00W   89
Hechi: China   24 51N 107 45E   85
Heckmondwike: W.Yorks., England   53 42N 01 40W   115
Hednesford: Staffs., England   52 43N 02 00W   115
Hedon: Humb., England   53 44N 00 12W   63
Hefa (Haifa): Israel   32 49N 34 59E   32 107
Hefei (Hofei): China   31 51N 117 19E   36 84 105
Hegang (Haoli): China   47 24N 130 17E   31
Heidelberg: W.Germany   49 25N 08 42E   72
Heidenheim: W.Germany   48 41N 10 10E   73
Heihe: China   31 34N 92 00E   35 83
Heilbronn: W.Germany   49 08N 09 14E   72
Heiligenhaus: W.Germany   51 19N 06 59E   118
Heilongjiang (Heilungkuan): China   36 09N 111 11E   36 84
Heilongjiang (Heilungkiang): *admin.*, China
   46 15N 127 00E   37
Heilungkuan *see* Heilongguan   36 09N 111 11E   36 84
Heimdal: Norway   63 21N 10 22E   74
Heinola: Finland   61 13N 26 05E   75
Heinsburg: Alta., Canada   53 47N 110 30W   92
Hejaz: *admin.*, Saudi Arabia   23 45N 39 00E   33
Hejian: China   38 28N 116 03E   84
Hekla: *volc.*, Iceland   64 01N 19 39W   6
Hekou (Hok'ou): China   22 38N 103 56E   36
Helena: Ark., U.S.A.   34 32N 90 36W   100
Helena: Mont., U.S.A.   46 36N 112 02W   42 94
Helen *Reef*: Caroline Is.   02 45N 131 45E   39
Helensburgh: Dunb., Scotland   56 01N 04 44W   62
Helensville: N.I., New Zealand   36 40S 174 29E   87
Helgasjön: *lake*, Sweden   56 58N 14 45E   75
Helgoland (Heligoland): *is.*, W.Germany   54 09N 07 52E
                                                          72 76
Helgoländer Bucht (Heligoland Bight): W.Germany
   53 45N 08 15E   72
Hellín: Spain   38 31N 01 43W   77
Hells *Canyon*: U.S.A.   45 15N 116 30W   90
Helmand: *riv.*, Afghanistan   32 45N 65 15E   10
Helmsdale: Suther., Scotland   58 07N 03 40W   65
Helmsdale: *riv.*, Scotland   58 00N 03 45W   65
Helmsley: N.Yorks., England   54 14N 01 04W   63
Helmstedt: W.Germany   52 14N 11 01E   73
Helsingfors *see* Helsinki   60 08N 25 00E   27 75
Helsinki (Helsingfors): Finland   60 08N 25 00E   27 75
Helston: Corn., England   50 05N 05 16W   61
Helvellyn: *mtn.*, Cumbria, England   54 32N 03 02W   61
Helvick *Head*: Wat., Irish Republic   52 03N 07 32W   67

Types of map: Ocean pp. 1-5; Physical pp. 6-25; Human pp. 26-57; Topographic pp. 58-101; World pp. 102-111; Urban pp. 112-128.

Hematite: Mo., U.S.A. 38 11N 90 26W	98
Hemel Hempstead: Herts., England 51 46N 00 28W	
	59 112
Hempstead: N.Y., U.S.A. 40 42N 73 37W	123
Henan (Honan): admin., China 34 15N 113 00E	36 84
Henderson: Ky., U.S.A. 37 49N 87 35W	100
Henderson: N.C., U.S.A. 36 20N 78 26W	101
Henderson: Nev., U.S.A. 36 02N 114 59W	91
Hengelo: Netherlands 52 16N 06 46E	72
Hengmian: China 31 09N 121 38E	121
Hengshan: Hunan, China 27 17N 112 46E	84
Hengshan: Shǎnxī, China 37 54N 108 57E	85
Hengshui: China 37 43N 115 41E	84
Hengsteysee: lake, W.Germany 51 15N 07 15E	118
Hengxian: China 22 42N 109 23E	85
Hengyang: China 26 56N 112 30E	36 85
Henley-in-Arden: War., England 52 17N 01 46W	59
Henley-on-Thames: Oxon., England 51 32N 00 56W	59
Henlopen, Cape: Del., U.S.A. 38 48N 75 05W	99
Hennebont: France 47 48N 03 16W	70
Hennigsdorf: E.Germany 52 39N 13 13E	105 117
Henrietta: Tex., U.S.A. 33 49N 98 12W	95
Henrietta Maria, Cape: Ont., Canada 55 10N 82 20W	96
Henrique de Carvalho: Angola 09 39S 20 24E	54
Henry, Cape: Va., U.S.A. 36 56N 76 00W	101
Henzada: Burma 17 36N 95 26E	35
Heping: China 24 24N 114 59E	85
Hepu (Lianzhou): China 21 39N 109 13E	85
Hequ: China 39 21N 111 22E	84
Herāt: Afghanistan 34 20N 62 10E	33
Hérault: riv., France 43 45N 03 30E	71
Herblay: France 49 00N 02 09E	117
Herculaneum: Mo., U.S.A. 38 16N 90 24W	98
Hereford: Here. & Worcs., England 52 04N 02 43W	60
Hereford: Tex., U.S.A. 34 49N 102 24W	95
Hereford & Worcester: admin., England 52 00N 02 30W	
	60
Herefordshire: admin., England. Absorbed into new admin.	
of Hereford & Worcester, 1974.	60
Herford: W.Germany 52 07N 08 40E	72
Herm: is., Channel Islands 49 28N 02 27W	61
Herma Ness: cape, Shet. Is., Scotland 60 50N 00 54W	65
Hermiston: Oreg., U.S.A. 45 51N 119 17W	90
Hermosillo: Mexico 29 15N 110 59W	46
Herne: W.Germany 51 32N 07 12E	118
Herne Bay: Kent, England 51 23N 01 08E	59
Herning: Denmark 56 08N 08 59E	75
Herten: W.Germany 51 36N 07 08E	118
Hertford: Herts., England 51 48N 00 05W	59 112
Hertfordshire: admin., England 51 45N 00 15W	59
Heshui: China 22 48N 112 31E	85
Heshun: China 37 21N 113 35E	84
Hess: riv., Yukon, Canada 63 15N 133 30W	88
Hessen: admin., W.Germany 51 00N 08 45E	72
Hessle: Humb., England 53 44N 00 26W	63
Hetton-le-Hole: Dur., England 54 50N 01 27W	63
Hexham: Northumb., England 54 58N 02 06W	63
Hexian: China 24 22N 111 29E	85
Heyang: China 35 12N 110 02E	84
Heysham: Lancs., England 54 02N 02 54W	63
Heyuan: China 23 42N 114 46E	85
Heywood: Gt. Man., England 53 36N 02 13W	114
Heze: China 35 15N 115 30E	84
Hiawatha: Kans., U.S.A. 39 51N 95 32W	94
Hibbing: Minn., U.S.A. 47 25N 92 55W	98
Hibiki-nada: sea, Japan 34 00N 130 45E	86
Hickory: N.C., U.S.A. 35 44N 81 23W	101
Hicks Bay: N.I., New Zealand 37 36S 178 21E	87
Hicksville: N.Y., U.S.A. 40 47N 73 32W	123
Hidalgo del Parral: Mexico 26 56N 105 40W	46
Higham Ferrers: Northants., England 52 18N 00 36W	59
High Atlas: mtns., Morocco 31 30N 06 00W	20 56
Highland: Ind., U.S.A. 41 32N 87 27W	124
Highland Creek: Ont., Canada 43 47N 79 12W	125
Highland Park: Ill., U.S.A. 42 10N 87 48W	124
Highland Park: Mich., U.S.A. 42 26N 83 05W	125
Highland Park: Pa., U.S.A. 40 29N 79 50W	125
High Park: Ont., Canada 43 39N 79 27W	125
High Plateaux: Algeria 34 00N 01 00E	20 56
High Point: N.C., U.S.A. 35 58N 80 00W	101
High Prairie: Alta., Canada 55 27N 116 28W	92
High River: Alta., Canada 50 35N 113 50W	92
Highrock Lake: Man., Canada 55 45N 100 30W	93
High Veld: geog. reg., Rep. of S.Africa 28 30S 25 45E	
	21 55
Highwood: Ill., U.S.A. 42 13N 87 50W	124
Highworth: Oxon., England 51 38N 01 43W	59
High Wycombe: Bucks., England 51 38N 00 46W	59 112
Hiiumaa (Dagö): is., U.S.S.R. 58 45N 22 30E	75
Hikone: Japan 35 15N 136 15E	86
Hilden: W.Germany 51 10N 06 56E	118
Hildesheim: W.Germany 52 09N 09 58E	73
Hilla see Al Hillah 32 28N 44 29E	33
Hillend Reservoir: Lan., Scotland 55 52N 03 50W	113
Hill Island Lake: N.W.T., Canada 60 30N 109 45W	92
Hillsboro: Ill., U.S.A. 39 10N 89 28W	98
Hillsboro: Tex., U.S.A. 32 01N 97 08W	95 95
Hilversum: Netherlands 52 14N 05 10E	72
Himachal Pradesh: admin., India 32 00N 77 00E	34 82
Himalayas see Great Himalayan Range	11 34 83
Himeji: Japan 34 49N 134 42E	37 86 105
Himi: Japan 36 51N 136 59E	86
Hims (Homs): Syria 34 45N 36 45E	33
Hinckley: Leics., England 52 33N 01 21W	115
Hindaun: India 26 44N 77 02E	82
Hindley: Lancs., England 53 32N 02 35W	114
Hindu Kush: ra., Asia 36 30N 72 00E	29
Hines Creek: Alta., Canada 56 13N 118 39W	89
Hinganghāt: India 20 32N 78 52E	82
Hingham: Mass., U.S.A. 42 15N 70 53W	122
Hingham Bay: Mass., U.S.A. 42 15N 70 45W	122
Hinsdale: Ill., U.S.A. 41 48N 87 55W	124
Hinton: Alta., Canada 53 34N 117 35W	89
Hirākud Reservoir: India 21 30N 83 45E	83
Hirfanli Reservoir: Turkey 39 15N 33 45E	32
Hirohata: Japan 34 48N 134 38E	105
Hirosaki: Japan 40 35N 140 28E	37 86
Hiroshima: Japan 34 24N 132 27E	37
Hirson: France 49 56N 04 05E	72
Hisār: India 29 10N 75 45E	34 82
Hispaniola: is., West Indies 19 00N 71 00W	47
Histon: Cambs., England 52 15N 00 06E	59
Hitachi: Japan 36 36N 140 39E	37 86
Hitchin: Herts., England 51 57N 00 17W	59
Hità: is., Norway 63 30N 08 45E	74
Hjørring: Denmark 57 28N 09 59E	75
Hobart: Tas., Australia 42 54S 147 18E	40
Hobbs: N.Mex., U.S.A. 32 42N 103 08W	95
Hoboken: N.J., U.S.A. 40 45N 74 02W	123
Hodder: riv., Lancs., England 53 45N 02 15W	114
Hoddesdon: Herts., England 51 46N 00 01W	59 112
Hodeida see Al Ḥudaydah 14 50N 42 58E	33
Hodgson: Man., Canada 51 13N 97 35W	93
Hódmezővásárhely: Hungary 46 25N 20 22E	78
Hodna, Monts du: Algeria 35 45N 05 30E	77
Hodonín: Czechoslovakia 48 52N 17 10E	73
Hof: W.Germany 50 19N 11 56E	73
Hofei see Hefei 31 51N 117 19E	36 84 105
Hoggar: mtns., see Ahaggar 23 30N 05 45E	20 56
Hog's Back: ridge, Surrey, England 51 00N 00 30W	112
Hohenlimburg: W.Germany 51 22N 07 34E	118
Höhscheid: W.Germany 51 06N 07 08E	118
Hokianga Harbour: N.I., New Zealand 35 30S 173 15E	87
Hokisaku: Japan 35 18N 139 55E	121
Hokitika: S.I., New Zealand 42 42S 170 59E	87
Hokkaidō: is., Japan 43 30N 143 00E	4 37 86
Hok'ou see Hekou 22 38N 103 56E	36
Holbæk: Denmark 55 43N 11 44E	75
Holbeach: Lincs., England 52 49N 00 01E	58
Holbrook: Ariz., U.S.A. 34 54N 110 10W	91
Holderness: pen., Humb., England 53 45N 00 00	63
Holdrege: Nebr., U.S.A. 40 26N 99 22W	94
Holguín: Cuba 20 53N 76 15W	47
Holland: Mich., U.S.A. 42 46N 86 06W	98
Hollick-Kenyon Plateau: Antarctica 78 00S 93 00W	25
Hollis: Alaska, U.S.A. 55 27N 132 41W	89
Holly Springs: Miss., U.S.A. 34 46N 89 27W	100
Hollywood: Calif., U.S.A. 34 07N 118 25W	127
Hollywood: Fla., U.S.A. 26 01N 80 09W	101
Hollywood Freeway: hwy., Calif., U.S.A. 34 00N 118 15W	
	127
Holmfirth: W.Yorks., England 53 35N 01 46W	63

Types of map: Ocean pp. 1-5; Physical pp. 6-25; Human pp. 26-57; Topographic pp. 58-101; World pp. 102-111; Urban pp. 112-128.

Holmhead: Ayr., Scotland   55 27N 04 16W   62
Holstebro: Denmark   56 22N 08 38E   75
Holsworthy: Devon, England   50 49N 04 21N   61
Holt: Norf., England   52 55N 01 05E   58
Holyhead: Gwyn., Wales   53 19N 04 38W   60
Holy *Island* (Lindisfarne): Northumb., England
    55 41N 01 48W   63
Holy *Island*: Bute., Scotland   53 32N 05 05W   62
Holy *Island*: Gwyn., Wales   53 15N 04 30W   60
Holy Loch: Argyll., Scotland   55 45N 04 45W   113
Holywell: Clwyd, Wales   53 17N 03 13W   60
Holywood: Down, N.Ireland   54 38N 05 50W   66
Holzminden: W.Germany   51 49N 09 26E   72
Homberg: W.Germany   51 27N 06 41E   118
Homburg: W.Germany   49 20N 07 20E   72
Homerville: Ga., U.S.A.   31 02N 82 44W   101
Homestead: Fla., U.S.A.   25 29N 80 29W   101
Hometown: Ill., U.S.A.   41 44N 87 44W   124
Homewood: Ill., U.S.A.   41 33N 87 40W   124
Homs *see* Himş   34 45N 36 45E   33
Honan: *admin. see* Henan   34 15N 113 00E   36 84
Hondo, *Rio*: Calif., U.S.A.   33 45N 118 00W   127
Hondo, *Rio*: N.Mex., U.S.A.   30 15N 105 00W   95
HONDURAS   14 30N 87 30W   17 47
Hønefoss: Norway   60 10N 10 16E   75
Honesdale: Pa., U.S.A.   41 34N 75 15W   99
Hong (Red): *riv.*, China/N.Vietnam   21 45N 104 30E   12 36
Hon Gai: N.Vietnam   20 57N 107 06E   36
Hongan: China   31 18N 114 40E   84
Hongdong: China   36 14N 111 39E   84
Honghaiwan: *bay*, China   22 45N 115 15E   85
Honghu: China   29 48N 113 27E   85
Hongjiang: China   27 10N 109 51E   85
HONG KONG: *U.K. colony*, S.E.Asia   22 15N 114 15E
    12 36 85 107
Hongshui (Hungshui): *riv.*, China   24 00N 107 45E   12 36 85
Hongze: China   33 19N 118 50E   84
Hongze (Hungtse) *Lake*: China   33 15N 118 45E   36 84
Honiton: Devon, England   50 48N 03 13W   61
Honshū: *is.*, Japan   37 00N 137 00E   12 37 86
Hood, *Mount*: Oreg., U.S.A.   45 23N 121 42W   16 42 90
Hooghly: India   22 54N 88 24E   120
Hooghly: *riv.*, India   21 45N 87 45E   83
Hooghly-Chinsura: India   22 53N 88 25E   35 83
Hook: Gt. Ldn., England   51 22N 00 19W   112
Hook *Head*: Wex., Irish Republic   52 07N 06 55W   67
Hoonah: Alaska, U.S.A.   58 07N 135 27W   88
Hoorn: Netherlands   52 38N 05 03E   72
Hoover *Dam*: U.S.A.   36 01N 114 44W   43 91
Hope: B.C., Canada   49 23N 121 26W   89
Hope: Ark., U.S.A.   33 40N 93 36W   100
Hope: Clwyd, Wales   53 07N 03 02W   60
Hope, Ben: *mtn.*, Suther., Scotland   58 24N 04 36W   64
Hope, *Loch*: Suther., Scotland   58 15N 04 30W   64
Hopedale: Nfld., Canada   55 30N 60 10W   97
Hopeh: *admin. see* Hebei   38 45N 115 30E   36 84
Hope's Nose: *pt.*, Devon, England   50 28N 03 28W   61
Hopewell: Va., U.S.A.   37 17N 77 19W   101
Hopkinsville: Ky., U.S.A.   36 50N 87 30W   100
Hoquiam: Wash., U.S.A.   46 59N 123 53W   90
Horbury: W.Yorks., England   53 41N 01 33W   63 115
Hörde: W.Germany   51 29N 07 30E   105 118
Horden: Dur., England   54 46N 01 18W   63
Horley: W.Sussex, England   51 11N 00 11W   59
Hormuz, *Strait of*: Iran/Oman   26 45N 56 15E   33
Horn: *riv.*, N.W.T., Canada   62 30N 118 15W   88
Horn, *Cape*: Chile   56 00S 67 15W   19 52
Hornavan: *lake*, Sweden   66 00N 17 30E   75
Hornby *Bay*: N.W.T., Canada   66 30N 118 00W   88
Horncastle: Lincs., England   53 13N 00 07W   58
Hornchurch: Gt. Ldn., England   51 34N 00 13E   112
Hornell: N.Y., U.S.A.   42 19N 77 39W   99
Horn *Head*: Don., Irish Republic   55 13N 07 59W   66
Horn *Mountains*: N.W.T., Canada   62 00N 120 00W   42 88
Hornsby: N.S.W., Australia   33 42S 151 06E   120
Hornsea: Humb., England   53 55N 00 10W   63
Horoshiri-dake: *mtn.*, Japan   43 00N 142 41E   87
Horse *Islands*: Nfld., Canada   50 00N 55 45W   97
Horsens: Denmark   55 53N 09 53E   75
Horsforth: W.Yorks., England   53 51N 01 39W   115
Horsham: Vic., Australia   36 45S 142 15E   41

Horsham: W.Sussex, England   51 04N 00 21W   59
Hortaleza: Spain   40 28N 03 39W   116
Horten: Norway   59 25N 10 30E   75
Horwich: Gt. Man., England   53 37N 02 33W   114
Hoshangābād: India   22 44N 77 45E   82
Hoshiarpur: India   31 30N 78 59E   82
Hospitalet: Spain   41 21N 02 06E   77 116
Hot Springs: Ark., U.S.A.   34 31N 93 03W   100
Hot Springs: N.Mex. *see* Truth or
    Consequences   33 08N 107 15W   95
Hot Springs: S.D., U.S.A.   43 26N 103 29W   94
Hot Springs *National Park*: Ark., U.S.A.   34 30N 93 00W
    100
Hottah *Lake*: N.W.T., Canada   64 45N 116 30W   88
Houghton: Wash., U.S.A.   47 40N 122 12W   126
Houghton *Lake*: Mich., U.S.A.   44 15N 84 45W   98
Houghton-le-Spring: Tyne & Wear, England
    54 51N 01 28W   63
Houma: China   35 34N 111 19E   84
Houma: La., U.S.A.   29 36N 90 43W   100
Hounslow: Gt. Ldn., England   51 29N 00 22W   59 112
Hourn, *Loch*: Inv., Scotland   57 00N 05 30W   64
Houston: Miss., U.S.A.   33 54N 89 00W   100
Houston: Tex., U.S.A.   29 46N 95 22W   43 100 104 106
Hove: E.Sussex, England   50 49N 00 10W   59
Howden: Humb., England   53 45N 00 52W   63
Howrah: India   22 35N 88 20E   83 120
Howth: Dublin, Irish Republic   53 23N 06 04W   67
Höxter: W.Germany   51 47N 09 22E   72
Hoy: *is.*, Ork. Is., Scotland   58 45N 03 15W   65
Høyanger: Norway   61 13N 06 05E   75
Hoylake: Mers., England   53 23N 03 11W   62
Hoy *Sound*: Ork. Is., Scotland   58 45N 03 15W   65
Hradec Králové: Czechoslovakia   50 13N 15 50E   73 78
Hrubý-Jeseník: *mtns.*, Czechoslovakia   50 00N 17 15E   73
Hsiamen *see* Xiamen   24 28N 118 07E   36 85
Hsian *see* Xi'an   34 15N 108 52E   36 84 105
Hsiang: *riv. see* Xiang   28 15N 112 45E   36 85
Hsiangfan *see* Xiangfan   32 03N 112 01E   36 84
Hsiangt'an *see* Xiangtan   27 51N 112 47E   36 85
Hsienyang *see* Xianyang   34 22N 108 42E   36 84
Hsiling Hsia *see* Yichang *Gorge*   30 45N 110 00E   36
Hsinchu: Taiwan   24 48N 121 01E   37 85
Hsinhsiang *see* Xinxiang   35 16N 113 51E   36 84
Hsining *see* Xining   36 38N 101 55E   36 105
Hsinkao Shan: *mtn.*, Taiwan   23 25N 121 00E   85
Hsinmin *see* Xinmin   42 00N 122 48E   37
Hsinyang *see* Xinyang   32 10N 114 07E   36 84
Hsüch'ang *see* Xuchang   34 03N 113 48E   36 84
Huaan: China   24 58N 117 32E   85
Huachipato: Chile   36 45S 73 07W   104
Huacho: Peru   11 14S 77 35W   49
Huaian: Jiangsu, China   33 28N 119 12E   84
Huaiji: China   24 01N 112 05E   85
Huailai: China   40 23N 115 30E   84
Huainan: China   32 39N 117 02E   36 84
Huairou: China   40 19N 116 34E   84
Huaiyang: China   33 44N 114 58E   84
Huaiyin (Ch'ingchiang): China   33 35N 119 04E   37 84
Huaiyuan: China   32 57N 117 15E   84
Hualien: Taiwan   23 57N 121 38E   37 85
Huallaga: *riv.*, Peru   08 00S 76 30W   49
Huallanca: Peru   08 47S 77 53W   49
Huancavelica: Peru   12 45S 75 03W   49
Huancayo: Peru   12 05S 75 12W   49
Huang (Hwang, Yellow): *riv.*, China   37 15N 118 00E
    12 36 84
Huangchuan: China   32 13N 115 09E   84
Huanggang: China   30 27N 114 50E   85
Huang Hai *see* Yellow *Sea*   35 30N 123 00E   12 37
Huanghua: China   38 22N 117 15E   84
Huanglong: China   35 30N 109 54E   84
Huangping: China   26 57N 107 51E   85
Huangpu: *riv.*, China   31 20N 121 32E   121
Huangshi: China   30 10N 115 05E   36 85
Huangxian: China   37 38N 120 32E   84
Huangyan: China   28 39N 121 21E   85
Huanjiang: China   24 50N 108 18E   85
Huánuco: Peru   09 55S 76 11W   49
Huanxian: China   36 37N 107 19E   84
Huaráz: Peru   09 33S 77 31W   49

Types of map: Ocean pp. 1-5; Physical pp. 6-25; Human pp. 26-57; Topographic pp. 58-101; World pp. 102-111; Urban pp. 112-128.

Huarong: China   29 30N 112 30E   85
Huascaran: mtn., Peru   09 08S 77 36W   49
Huasco: Chile   28 30S 71 15W   52
Huaxian: Henan, China   35 27N 114 32E   84
Huaxian: Shănxī, China   34 30N 109 42E   84
Huayuan: China   28 40N 109 27E   85
Huazhou: China   21 30N 110 38E   85
Hubbell: Mich., U.S.A.   47 10N 88 27W   98
Hubei (Hupeh): admin., China   31 30N 112 15E   36 84
Hubli: India   15 20N 75 14E   34
Huckarde: W.Germany   51 32N 07 24E   118
Hückeswagen: W.Germany   51 09N 07 20E   118
Hucknall: Notts., England   53 02N 01 11W   58
Huddersfield: W.Yorks., England   53 39N 01 47W   63 115
Hudiksvall: Sweden   61 45N 17 10E   74
Hudson: Ont., Canada   50 06N 92 09W   93
Hudson: riv., U.S.A.   42 00N 74 00W   17 45 99
Hudson Bay: Sask., Canada   52 51N 102 23W   92
Hudson Bay: Canada   60 00N 88 00W   16 44 93
Hudson Hope: B.C., Canada   56 03N 121 59W   89
Hudson Strait: Canada   62 30N 72 00W   16 44
Hue: S.Vietnam   16 28N 107 35E   38
Huelva: Spain   37 15N 06 56W   77
Huesca: Spain   42 08N 00 25W   77
Huesca: admin., Spain   42 00N 00 00   70
Hufuf see Al Hufūf   25 20N 49 34E   33
Hugh Town: I. of S., England   49 55N 06 19W   61
Hugo: Okla., U.S.A.   34 01N 95 31W   100
Huhehaote (Kweisui): China   40 48N 111 40E   36 84
Huian: China   25 02N 118 50E   85
Huiarau Range: N.I., New Zealand   38 45S 177 00E   87
Huichang: China   25 29N 115 41E   85
Huilai: China   23 04N 116 20E   85
Huimin: China   37 32N 117 30E   84
Huitong: China   27 02N 109 38E   85
Huiyang: China   23 09N 114 29E   85
Hukeng: China   27 20N 114 19E   85
Hukou: China   29 40N 116 22E   85
Hull: Qué., Canada   45 26N 75 45W   44 96
Hull: England see Kingston-upon-Hull   53 45N 00 20W
                                                             26 63
Hull: Mass., U.S.A.   42 19N 70 54W   122
Hull: riv., Humb., England   43 45N 00 15W   63
Ḥulwān: Egypt   29 51N 31 20E   105
Humanejos: riv., Spain   40 00N 03 45W   116
Humber: riv., Ont., Canada   43 45N 79 30W   125
Humber: riv., Humb., England   53 30N 00 15W   63
Humber Bay: Ont., Canada   43 30N 79 15W   125
Humberside: admin., England   53 45N 00 30W   63
Humboldt: Sask., Canada   52 13N 105 09W   92
Humboldt: Ariz., U.S.A.   34 30N 112 14W   91
Humboldt: riv., Nev., U.S.A.   40 15N 118 15W   43 91
Humboldt (Peru) Current: S.Pacific Ocean   20 00S 76 00W
                                                              5
Humboldt Park: Ill., U.S.A.   41 54N 87 42W   124
Hunan: admin., China   28 15N 111 30E   36 85
Hunchun: China   42 54N 130 22E   86
Hunedoara: Romania   45 45N 22 54E   78 105
HUNGARY   46 30N 19 00E   7 27 78 107
Hungerford: Berks., England   51 26N 01 30W   59
Hŭngnam: N.Korea   39 50N 127 38E   37
Hunish, Rubha: cape, Inv., Scotland   57 42N 06 21W   64
Hungry Horse Reservoir: Mont., U.S.A.   48 21N 114 01W
                                                             90
Hungshui: riv. see Hongshui   24 00N 107 45E   12 36 85
Hungtse, Lake see Hongze   33 15N 118 45E   36 84
Hunmanby: N.Yorks., England   54 11N 00 19W   63
Hunsrück: mtns., W.Germany   49 45N 07 00E   72
Hunstanton: Norf., England   52 57N 00 30E   58
Huntingdon: Cambs., England   52 20N 00 12W   59
Huntingdon Island: Nfld., Canada   53 45N 57 00W   97
Huntingdonshire: admin., England. Absorbed into
   Cambridgeshire, 1974.   59
Huntington: Ind., U.S.A.   40 54N 85 30W   98
Huntington: N.Y., U.S.A.   40 53N 73 25W   123
Huntington: W.Va., U.S.A.   38 24N 82 26W   45 98
Huntington Harbor: Calif., U.S.A.   33 43N 118 04W   127
Huntly: N.I., New Zealand   37 35S 175 10E   87
Huntly: Aber., Scotland   57 27N 02 47W   65
Huntsville: Ala., U.S.A.   34 44N 86 35W   45 101
Huntsville: Tex., U.S.A.   30 43N 95 33W   100

Hunyuan: China   39 40N 113 41E   84
Huoqiu: China   32 20N 116 16E   84
Huoshan: China   31 22N 116 26E   84
Huoxian: China   36 31N 111 45E   84
Hupeh: admin. see Hubei   31 30N 112 15E   36 84
Hurley: N.Mex., U.S.A.   32 42N 108 08W   95
Huron: S.D., U.S.A.   44 22N 98 13W   94
Huron, Lake: Canada/U.S.A.   17 44 98
Huron, Point: Mich., U.S.A.   42 34N 82 47W   125
Hurstpierpoint: W.Sussex, England   50 56N 00 11W   59
Hurstville: N.S.W., Australia   33 58S 151 06E   120
Hürth: W.Germany   50 52N 06 52E   119
Huskvarna: Sweden   57 47N 14 15E   75
Husum: W.Germany   54 29N 09 04E   72
Hutanopan: Indonesia   00 40N 99 46E   38
Hutchinson: Kans., U.S.A.   38 05N 97 56W   43 95
Hutt: N.I., New Zealand   41 12S 174 54E   37
Hutuo: riv., China   38 30N 113 30E   84
Huxian: China   34 05N 108 32E   84
Huzhou (Wuhsing): China   30 55N 120 06E   37 85
Hwang: riv. see Huang, China   37 15N 118 00E   12 36 84
Hyattsville: Md., U.S.A.   38 57N 76 56W   122
Hydaburg: Alaska, U.S.A.   55 12N 132 50W   89
Hyde: Gt. Man., England   53 27N 02 04W   63 114
Hyde Park: Gt. Ldn., England   51 20N 00 10W   112
Hyder: Alaska, U.S.A.   55 55N 130 02W   89
Hyderābād: India   17 22N 78 26E   34
Hyderābād: Pakistan   25 23N 68 24E   34
Hyères: France   43 07N 06 08E   71
Hyères, Iles d': France   43 01N 06 25E   71
Hyesan: N.Korea   41 23N 128 12E   37
Hyland: riv., Canada   60 45N 128 30W   88
Hythe: Hants., England   50 51N 01 24W   59
Hythe: Kent, England   51 05N 01 05E   59
Hyūga: Japan   32 25N 131 38E   86
Hyvinkää: Finland   60 37N 24 50E   75

Iar Connaught: geog. reg., Gal., Irish Republic
   53 15N 09 15W   67
Iaşi: Romania   47 09N 27 38E   27 78
Ibadan: Nigeria   07 23N 03 56E   57
Ibagué: Colombia   04 35N 75 30W   48
Ibarra: Ecuador   00 23N 78 05W   48
Ibérico, Sistema (Iberian Mountains):
   Spain   41 00N 01 00W   77
Iberville, Lac d': Qué., Canada   55 30N 73 15W   96
Ibiza (Iviza): Balearic Is.   38 54N 01 26E   77
Ibiza (Iviza): is., Balearic Is.   39 00N 01 15E   26 77
Ica: Peru   14 05S 75 43W   49
Içá: riv., Brazil   02 45S 69 00W   48
Ice Harbor Dam: Wash., U.S.A.   46 15N 118 53W   90
ICELAND   65 00N 20 00W   2 6 106
Ich'ang see Yichang   30 42N 111 22E   36 85 105
Ichāpur: India   22 48N 88 22E   120
Ichchāpuram: India   19 10N 84 43E   83
Ichikawa: Chiba, Japan   35 44N 139 54E   121
Ichinomiya: Japan   35 18N 136 48E   86
Ichinoseki: Japan   38 55N 141 08E   86
Ich'un see Yichun   27 42N 114 22E   36 85
Idabel: Okla., U.S.A.   33 54N 94 50W   100
Idaho: admin., U.S.A.   44 00N 115 00W   43 90
Idaho Falls: Idaho, U.S.A.   43 30N 112 02W   43 90
Idar-Oberstein: W.Germany   49 43N 07 19E   72
Idrigill Point: Inv., Scotland   57 19N 06 33W   64
Ife: Nigeria   07 33N 04 34E   57
Iforas, Adrar des: mtn. reg., Mali   19 30N 01 30E   20 56
Igarka: U.S.S.R.   67 28N 86 35E   30
Ighil Izane: Algeria   35 44N 00 30E   56
Iglesias: Sardinia   39 19N 08 32E   77
Iguaçu: riv., Brazil   25 30S 53 30W   51
Iguidi, Erg: des., Algeria/Mauritania   27 00N 06 00W   20 56
Iida: Japan   35 31N 137 50E   86
Iijoki: riv., Finland   65 15N 26 00E   74
Iisalmi: Finland   63 33N 27 14E   74
Iizuka: Japan   33 38N 130 41E   86
Ijebu Ode: Nigeria   06 47N 03 58E   57
IJmuiden: Netherlands   52 28N 04 38E   105
IJsselmeer: lake, Netherlands   52 45N 05 15E   72

Ikaría: *is.*, Greece 37 30N 26 00E	79	
Ikerre: Nigeria 07 30N 05 19E	57	
Ikuta: Japan 35 36N 139 33E	121	
Ila: Nigeria 08 01N 04 54E	57	
Ilâm: Nepal 26 55N 87 55E	83	
Ilan: Taiwan 24 42N 121 44E	85	
Ilchester: Som., England 51 01N 02 41W	61	
Ile-à-la-Crosse: Sask., Canada 55 28N 107 53W	92	
Ile-à-la-Crosse, *Lac*: Sask., Canada 55 30N 107 45W	92	
Ilebo (Port Francqui): Zaïre 04 19S 20 35E	54	
Île de Montréal: *admin.*, Qué., Canada 45 15N 73 45W	122	
Île-Jésus: *admin.*, Qué., Canada 45 30N 73 30W	122	
Ilesha: Nigeria 07 39N 04 38E	57	
Ilford: Gt. Ldn., England 51 33N 00 06E	112	
Ilfracombe: Devon, England 51 13N 04 08W	61	
Ilhéus: Brazil 14 49S 39 02W	51	
Ili: *riv.*, U.S.S.R. 44 00N 78 30E	8 29	
Iligan: Philippines 08 12N 124 13E	39	
Ilkeston: Derby., England 52 59N 01 18W	58	
Ilkley: W.Yorks., England 53 55N 01 50W	63 115	
Illana *Bay*: Philippines 07 30N 123 45E	39	
Illingworth: W.Yorks., England 53 45N 01 54W	115	
Illinois: *admin.*, U.S.A. 40 00N 89 00W	45 98 98	
Illinois: *riv.*, Ill., U.S.A. 39 15N 90 30W	98	
Illinois & Michigan *Canal*: Ill., U.S.A. 41 45N 87 45W	124	
Il'men', Ozero: *lake*, U.S.S.R. 58 15N 31 15E	28 80	
Ilminster: Som., England 50 56N 02 55W	61	
Iloilo: Philippines 10 41N 122 33E	39	
Ilorin: Nigeria 08 32N 04 34E	57	
Imabari: Japan 34 03N 133 00E	86	
Imandra, Ozero: *lake*, U.S.S.R. 67 30N 32 45E	27 74	
Imatra: Finland 61 14N 28 50E	75 105	
Imeni Žel'abova: U.S.S.R. 58 57N 36 36E	80	
Immingham: Humb., England 53 37N 00 14W	63	
Imperatriz: Brazil 05 32S 47 29W	50	
Imperia: Italy 43 52N 08 01E	71	
Imperial *Dam*: U.S.A. 32 53N 114 28W	91	
Imphâl: India 24 47N 93 55E	35	
In Aménas: Algeria 28 05N 09 23E	56	
Inari: Finland 68 54N 27 05E	74	
Inari: *lake*, Finland 68 54N 27 05E	27 74	
Ince: Ches., England 53 17N 02 50W	114	
Inchard, *Loch*: Suther., Scotland 58 15N 05 00W	64	
Inch'ŏn (Chemulpo): S.Korea 37 28N 126 38E	37	
Indalsälven: *riv.*, Sweden 62 45N 16 30E	74	
Independence: British Honduras 16 30N 88 28W	46	
Independence: Kans., U.S.A. 37 14N 95 42W	95	
Inder, Ozero: *lake*, U.S.S.R. 48 27N 51 54E	81	
Inderagiri: *riv.*, Indonesia 00 15S 102 15E	38	
Inderborskij: U.S.S.R. 48 33N 51 44E	81	
INDIA	11 34 82 107	
Indian: *riv.*, N.W.T., Canada 66 15N 127 00W	88	
Indiana: Pa., U.S.A. 40 39N 79 11W	45	
Indiana: *admin.*, U.S.A. 40 00N 86 00W	45 98 98	
Indiana East-West *Toll Road*: Ind., U.S.A. 41 45N 85 30W	124	
Indiana Harbor: Ind., U.S.A. 41 40N 87 27W	124	
Indianapolis: Ind., U.S.A. 39 45N 86 10W	45 98	
Indian Arm: *inlet*, B.C., Canada 49 15N 122 45W	126	
Indian Cabins: Alta., Canada 59 50N 117 04W	88	
Indian *Creek*: Ill., U.S.A. 42 00N 87 45W	124	
Indian House *Lake*: Qué., Canada 56 00N 64 45W	97	
Indian *Ocean*	1	
Indigirka: *riv.*, U.S.S.R. 68 15N 145 00E	9 31	
Indo-China: *geog. reg.*, S.E.Asia 14 00N 104 00E	12 38	
INDONESIA	13 38 107	
Indore: India 22 42N 75 54E	34 82	
Indrāvati: *riv.*, India 19 00N 80 15E	34 82	
Indus: *riv.*, India/Pakistan 28 45N 70 15E	11 34 82	
Indus, *Mouths of the*: Pakistan 24 15N 67 15E	34	
Ingleborough: *mtn.*, N.Yorks., England 54 10N 02 23W	63	
Inglewood: Calif., U.S.A. 33 58N 118 22W	127	
Ingolstadt: W.Germany 48 46N 11 27E	73 107	
Inhambane: Mozambique 23 51S 35 29E	55	
Inírida: *riv.*, Colombia 03 15N 68 00W	48	
Inishark: *is.*, Gal., Irish Republic 53 37N 10 16W	66	
Inishbofin: *is.*, Don., Irish Republic 53 30N 10 00W	66	
Inisheer: *is.*, Gal., Irish Republic 53 00N 09 30W	67	
Inishmaan: *is.*, Gal., Irish Republic 53 00N 09 30W	67	
Inishmore: *is.*, Gal., Irish Republic 53 00N 09 30W	67	
Inishmurray: *is.*, Sligo, Irish Republic 54 26N 08 40W	66	

Inishowen *Head*: Don., Irish Republic 55 09N 06 56W	66	
Inishowen *Peninsula*: Don., Irish Republic 55 00N 07 15W	66	
Inishturk: *is.*, Mayo, Irish Republic 53 30N 10 00W	66	
Inkom: Idaho, U.S.A. 42 48N 112 15W	90	
Inkster: Mich., U.S.A. 42 16N 83 18W	125	
Inland *Sea see* Seto-naikai 34 00N 133 00E	86	
Inn: *riv.*, W.Europe 48 00N 12 00E	78	
Inner Hebrides: *is.*, Scotland 57 00N 06 30W	64	
Innerleithen: Peeb., Scotland 55 38N 03 05W	63	
Inner Mongolia *see* Neimenggu 41 30N 109 00E	36 84	
Inner *Sound*: Scotland 57 30N 05 45W	64	
Innisfail: Alta., Canada 52 01N 113 59W	92	
Innsbruck: Austria 47 17N 11 25E	26 78	
Inny: *riv.*, Corn., England 50 30N 04 15W	61	
Inny: *riv.*, Kerry, Irish Republic 51 45N 10 00W	67	
Inny: *riv.*, Long., Irish Republic 53 30N 07 45W	66	
Inongo: Zaïre 01 57S 18 16E	54	
Inowrocław : Poland 52 49N 18 12E	73 78	
In Salah: Algeria 27 12N 02 29E	56	
Inspiration: Ariz., U.S.A. 33 23N 110 52W	91	
Interlaken: Switzerland 46 42N 07 52E	71	
International Falls: Minn., U.S.A. 48 38N 93 26W	98	
In'va: *riv.*, U.S.S.R. 59 00N 55 15E	81	
Inverary: Argyll., Scotland 56 13N 05 05W	64	
Inverbervie: Kinc., Scotland 56 51N 02 17W	65	
Invercargill: S.I., New Zealand 46 26S 168 21E	37 87	
Invergordon: R. & Crom., Scotland 57 42N 04 10W	64	
Inverkeithing: Fife, Scotland 56 02N 03 25W	62	
Invermere: B.C., Canada 50 30N 116 00W	90	
Inverness: N.S., Canada 46 14N 61 19W	44 97	
Inverness: Inv., Scotland 57 27N 04 15W	26 64	
Inverness-shire: *admin.*, Scotland 56 45N 05 00W	64	
Inverurie: Aber., Scotland 57 17N 02 23W	65	
Inza: U.S.S.R. 53 51N 46 21E	81	
Ioánnina: Greece 39 40N 20 51E	32 79	
Ioca: B.C., Canada 49 19N 122 54W	126	
Iola: Kans., U.S.A. 37 55N 95 24W	95	
Iona: *is.*, Argyll., Scotland 56 15N 06 15W	64	
Ionian *Islands*: Greece 38 30N 19 45E	79	
Ionian *Sea* 38 30N 18 15E	7 27 79	
Íos (Nios): *is.*, Greece 36 43N 25 17E	79	
Iowa: *admin.*, U.S.A. 42 00N 93 00W	43 98	
Iowa: *riv.*, Iowa, U.S.A. 42 30N 93 15W	98	
Iowa City: Iowa, U.S.A. 41 39N 91 31W	98	
Ipatinga: Brazil 19 30S 42 32W	104	
Ipin *See* Yibin 28 47N 104 38E	36	
Ipoh: Malaysia 04 36N 101 02E	38	
Ipswich: Qld., Australia 27 38S 152 40E	41	
Ipswich: Suff., England 52 04N 01 10E	59	
Iquique: Chile 20 12S 70 10W	49	
Iquitos: Peru 03 51S 73 13W	48	
Iráklion (Candia): Crete 35 20N 25 08E	32 79	
IRAN (Persia)	10 33 107	
Iran *Mountains*: Indonesia 02 00N 115 00E	12 39	
IRAQ 32 45N 44 15E	10 33 107	
Irbeni Väin: *str.*, U.S.S.R. 57 45N 22 15E	75	
Irbīl (Erbil): Iraq 36 11N 44 01E	33	
Irbit: U.S.S.R. 57 41N 63 03E	81	
Irfon: *riv.*, Powys, Wales 52 00N 03 30W	60	
Iringa: Tanzania 07 46S 35 42E	54	
Iriri: *riv.*, Brazil 05 30S 54 15W	50	
IRISH REPUBLIC	6 26 67 107	
Irish *Sea*: 53 45N 05 00W	26 69	
Irkutsk: U.S.S.R. 52 16N 104 20E	30	
Irlam: Gt. Man., England 53 28N 02 25W	114	
Iron, *Lough*: Westmeath, Irish Republic 53 30N 07 15W	66	
Iron Bridge: Salop, England 52 38N 02 30W	58	
Iron *County*: Utah, U.S.A. 38 00N 113 00W	104	
Iron Gates: *defile*, Romania 44 45N 22 45E	79	
Iron Knob: S.A., Australia 32 44S 137 08E	105	
Iron *Mountain*: Idaho, U.S.A. 42 43N 116 45W	90	
Iron Mountain: Mich., U.S.A. 45 49N 88 04W	98	
Iron Mountain: Mo., U.S.A. 37 42N 90 38W	98 104	
Iron Springs: Utah, U.S.A. 37 45N 113 14W	91	
Ironton: Utah, U.S.A. 40 12N 111 37W	91	
Ironwood: Mich., U.S.A. 46 25N 90 08W	98	
Irpen': U.S.S.R. 50 31N 30 15E	80	
Irrawaddy: *riv.*, Burma 23 30N 96 00E	11 35	
Irrawaddy *Delta*: Burma 16 30N 94 30E	35	
Irthlingborough: Northants., England 52 20N 00 37W	59	

Irtyš (Irtysh): *riv.*, U.S.S.R.   53 30N 75 30E   8 29
Irún: Spain   43 20N 01 48W   70
Irvine: Ayr., Scotland   55 37N 04 40W   62
Irvinestown: Ferm., N.Ireland   54 29N 07 38W   66
Irvington: N.J., U.S.A.   40 43N 74 15W   123
Irwell: *riv.*, Gt. Man., England   53 30N 02 15W   114
Isar: *riv.*, W.Germany   48 30N 12 45E   73
Isbergues: France   50 37N 02 27E   105
Iscia Baidoa *see* Baidoa   03 08N 43 34E   53
Ise (Uji-yamada): Japan   34 29N 136 42E   37 86
Isère: *riv.*, France   45 15N 05 30E   71
Iserlohn: W.Germany   51 23N 07 42E   118
Iseyin: Nigeria   07 59N 03 40E   57
Isfahan *see* Eşfahān   32 41N 51 41E   33
Ishikari-wan: *bay*, Japan   43 15N 141 00E   86
Ishim: *riv.*, see Išim   55 45N 67 45E   29
Ishimbay *see* Išimbaj   53 28N 56 02E   29 81 107
Ishinomaki: Japan   38 25N 141 18E   37 86
Ishpeming: Mich., U.S.A.   46 29N 87 40W   98
Ishurdi: Bangladesh   24 10N 89 04E   83
Išim (Ishim): *riv.*, U.S.S.R.   53 45N 67 45E   29
Išimbaj (Ishimbay): U.S.S.R.   53 28N 56 02E   29 81 107
Isiolo: Kenya   00 20N 37 36E   54
Isiro (Paulis): Zaïre   02 48N 27 41E   54
Iskår: *riv.*, Bulgaria   43 30N 24 00E   79
Iskenderun: Turkey   36 37N 36 08E   32
Iskininskij: U.S.S.R.   47 13N 52 41E   81
Iskut: *riv.*, B.C., Canada   56 30N 131 00W   89
Isla: *riv.*, Angus, Scotland   56 45N 03 15W   65
Islāmābād: Pakistan   33 40N 73 08E   34
Island Falls: Ont., Canada   49 36N 81 21W   99
Island Lake: Man., Canada   53 45N 94 30W   93
Islands, *Bay of*: Nfld., Canada   49 00N 58 15W   97
Islands, *Bay of*: N.I., New Zealand   35 15S 174 15E   87
Islay: *is.*, Argyll., Scotland   55 45N 06 15W   62
Isle: *riv.*, Som., England   50 45N 02 45W   61
Isle: *riv.*, France   45 00N 00 00   70
Isle of Grain: Kent, England   51 27N 00 42E   107
Isle of Man: *admin. & is.*, United Kingdom   54 15N 04 30W
                                                               62
Isle of Purbeck: *dist.*, Dorset, England   50 30N 02 00W   61
Isle of Wight: *admin. & is.*, England   50 30N 01 15W   59
Islington: Ont., Canada   43 39N 79 32W   125
Ismailia *see* Al Ismāʻīlīyah   30 35N 32 16E   32
Isogo: Japan   35 23N 139 37E   121
Isparta: Turkey   37 46N 30 33E   32
ISRAEL   31 00N 34 45E   10 32 107
Issoire: France   45 33N 03 15E   71
Issoudun: France   46 57N 01 59E   70
Issyk-Kulʻ, *Lake*: U.S.S.R.   42 30N 77 15E   29
İstanbul: Turkey   41 02N 28 59E   27 79
Istra (Istria): *pen.*, Yugoslavia   45 15N 14 00E   78
Istria: *pen. see* Istra   45 15N 14 00E   78
Itabashi: Japan   35 45N 139 39E   121
Itabira: Brazil   19 37S 43 13W   104
Itabirito: Brazil   20 15S 43 48W   104
Itabuna: Brazil   14 48S 39 16W   51
Itacoatiara: Brazil   03 08S 58 25W   50
Itajaí: Brazil   26 50S 48 39W   51
ITALY   7 27 79 107
Itārsi: India   22 39N 77 48E   82
Itasca: Ill., U.S.A.   41 56N 88 00W   124
Itchen: *riv.*, Hants., England   51 00N 01 15W   59
Ithaca: N.Y., U.S.A.   42 26N 76 30W   99
Ithon: *riv.*, Powys, Wales   52 15N 03 15W   60
Itmurynkol', Ozero: *lake*, U.S.S.R.   49 30N 52 22E   81
Ituiutaba: Brazil   18 58S 49 28W   51
Iturup: *is.*, U.S.S.R.   45 15N 148 00E   31
Ituzaingo: Buenos Aires, Argentina   34 40S 58 40W   128
Itzehoe: W.Germany   53 56N 09 32E   72
Ivalo: Finland   68 41N 27 30E   74
Ivano-Frankovsk: U.S.S.R.   48 55N 24 43E   28 78
Ivanovo: U.S.S.R.   57 00N 40 59E   28 80
Iviza *see* Ibiza   38 54N 01 26E   77
Iviza: *is. see* Ibiza   39 00N 01 15E   26 77
IVORY COAST   08 00N 05 30W   20 57 106
Ivrea: Italy   45 28N 07 52E   71
Ivry-sur-Seine: France   48 49N 02 24E   117
Ivybridge: Devon, England   50 23N 03 56W   61
Iwaki (Taira): Japan   37 03N 140 55E   37 86
Iwakuni: Japan   34 09N 132 11E   86

Iwanai: Japan   42 58N 140 30E   86
Iwanuma: Japan   38 06N 140 52E   86
Iwate-san: *mtn.*, Japan   39 51N 141 00E   86
Iwo: Nigeria   07 38N 04 11E   57
Ixtacalco: Mexico   19 23N 99 06W   128
Ixtapalapa: Mexico   19 21N 99 05W   128
Iyang *see* Yiyang   28 36N 112 10E   36 85
Iyo-nada: *sea*, Japan   33 30N 132 00E   86
Iževsk (Izhevsk): U.S.S.R.   56 51N 53 14E   28 81 105
Izmajlovskij *Park*: U.S.S.R.   55 46N 37 47E   119
İzmir (Smyrna): Turkey   38 25N 27 10E   32 79
Iz'um: U.S.S.R.   49 12N 37 19E   80
Izu-shotō: *arch.*, Japan   34 00N 139 30E   86

Jabal, Baḥr al (White Nile): *riv.*, Sudan   04 15N 31 30E
                                                               20 53
Jabal Abū Tulu: *hill*, Sudan   11 41N 28 40E   105
Jabal al Akhdar: *mtns.*, Libya   32 30N 21 30E   20 32
Jabal Al-Awliyā' *Dam*: Sudan   15 18N 32 30E   53
Jabalpur (Jubbulpore): India   23 10N 79 59E   34 82
Jablonec: Czechoslovakia   50 44N 15 10E   73 78
Jablonovyj (Yablonovyy) *Range*: U.S.S.R.   54 00N 117 00E
                                                               9 30
Jaca: Spain   42 34N 00 33W   70 77
Jackfish River: Alta., Canada   59 03N 112 50W   92
Jackrabbit: Nev., U.S.A.   38 17N 114 29W   91
Jackson: Mich., U.S.A.   42 15N 84 24W   98
Jackson: Miss., U.S.A.   32 18N 90 12W   45 100
Jackson: Tenn., U.S.A.   35 37N 88 49W   100
Jackson: Wyo., U.S.A.   43 29N 110 46W   94
Jackson *Bay*: S.I., New Zealand   44 00S 168 45E   87
Jackson Creek: Nev., U.S.A.   41 29N 118 40W   90
Jackson *Park*: Ill., U.S.A.   41 47N 87 34W   124
Jacksonville: Fla., U.S.A.   30 20N 81 40W   45 101
Jacksonville: Ill., U.S.A.   39 44N 90 14W   98
Jacksonville: N.C., U.S.A.   34 45N 77 26W   101
Jacksonville: Tex., U.S.A.   31 58N 95 17W   100
Jacobābād: Pakistan   28 15N 68 30E   34
Jacques Cartier: Qué., Canada   45 31N 73 31W   96 122
Jacques Cartier *Passage*: Qué., Canada   50 00N 63 00W
                                                               44 97
Jade Hate *see* Yumen   39 56N 97 51E   36
Jadotville *see* Likasi   10 59S 26 44E   54
Jaén: Spain   37 46N 03 48W   77
Jaeren: *geog. reg.*, Norway   58 45N 06 15E   75
Jaffa-Tel Aviv *see* Tel Aviv - Yafo   32 04N 34 46E   32
Jaffna: Sri Lanka   09 38N 80 02E   34
Jagādhri: India   30 11N 77 18E   34 82
Jagdalpur: India   19 04N 82 05E   83
Jagraon: India   30 48N 75 36E   82
Jagtiāl: India   18 48N 78 55E   82
Jaipur: India   26 54N 75 50E   34 82
Jais: India   26 15N 81 32E   82
Jaisalmer: India   26 52N 70 55E   82
Jakarta *see* Djakarta   06 08S 106 45E   38
Jākhal: India   29 46N 75 51E   82
Jakutsk (Yakutsk): U.S.S.R.   62 13N 129 49E   31
Jal: N.Mex., U.S.A.   32 07N 103 12W   95
Jaleswar: Nepal   26 40N 85 48E   83
Jālgaon: India   21 01N 75 39E   35 82
Jalisco: *admin.*, Mexico   20 15N 104 00W   46
Jālna: India   19 50N 75 58E   34 82
Jalo *Oasis see* Jālū *Oasis*   29 02N 21 32E   32
Jalpaiguri: India   26 30N 88 50E   83
Jalta (Yalta): U.S.S.R.   44 30N 34 10E   28
Jālū (Jalo) *Oasis*: Libya   29 02N 21 32E   32
JAMAICA   18 00N 77 15W   17 47 106
Jamaica *Bay*: N.Y., U.S.A.   40 30N 73 45W   123
Jamaica Bay *Wildlife Refuge*: N.Y., U.S.A.   40 37N 73 48W
                                                               123
Jamālpur: Bangladesh   24 54N 89 57E   83
Jamālpur: India   25 19N 86 30E   83
Jamantau (Yamantau) *Mount*: U.S.S.R.   54 15N 58 06E   29
Jamanxim: *riv.*, Brazil   06 30S 55 45W   50
Jambol: Bulgaria   42 29N 26 30E   79
James: *riv.*, U.S.A.   44 00N 98 00W   94
James: *riv.*, Va., U.S.A.   37 00N 76 45W   101
James *Bay*: Canada   53 30N 81 00W   16 44 96

Types of map: Ocean pp. 1-5; Physical pp. 6-25; Human pp. 26-57; Topographic pp. 58-101; World pp. 102-111; Urban pp. 112-128.

Jamestown: N.D., U.S.A.   46 54N 98 42W   94
Jamestown: N.Y., U.S.A.   42 05N 79 15W   99
Jammu: India   32 43N 74 54E   34
Jammu and Kashmir: *admin.*, India/Pakistan
  32 45N 76 45E   34
Jāmnagar (Navanagar): India   22 28N 70 06E   34
Jamshedpur: India   22 47N 86 12E   35 83 105
Jamuna: *riv.*, Bangladesh   24 45N 89 45E   83
Jana (Yana): *riv.*, U.S.S.R.   69 30N 134 15E   31
Janesville: Wis., U.S.A.   42 42N 89 02W   98
Jangipur: India   24 28N 88 08E   83
Jan Mayen *Island*: Norwegian Sea   71 00N 08 20W   2 6
Januária: Brazil   15 29S 44 22W   51
Jaochou *see* Poyang   29 00N 116 40E   36 85
Jaora: India   23 40N 75 10E   82
JAPAN   37 86 107
Japan, *Sea of*:   40 00N 135 00E   37 86
Japurá: *riv.*, Brazil   01 45S 67 15W   18 48
Jaransk: U.S.S.R.   57 19N 47 54E   81
Jarānwāla: Pakistan   31 20N 73 26E   82
Jarcevo: U.S.S.R.   55 04N 32 41E   80
Jari: *riv.*, Brazil   01 00N 53 30W   50
Jaridih: India   23 38N 86 04E   83
Jaroslavl' (Yaroslavl'): U.S.S.R.   57 37N 39 52E   28 80 107
Jarrow: Tyne & Wear, England   54 59N 01 29W   63
Järvenpää: Finland   60 29N 25 06E   75
Jarwa: India   27 38N 82 32E   83
Jasinovataja: U.S.S.R.   48 08N 37 51E   80
Jāsk: Iran   25 40N 57 46E   33
Jasło: Poland   49 45N 21 28E   78
Jasnogorsk: U.S.S.R.   54 29N 37 42E   80
Jasper: Alta., Canada   52 55N 118 05W   89
Jasper: Ala., U.S.A.   33 50N 87 17W   101
Jasper *National Park*: Alta., Canada   52 45N 117 45W   89
Jaú: Brazil   22 18S 48 33W   51
Jauf *see* Al Jawf   29 49N 39 52E   33
Jaunpur: India   25 44N 82 41E   83
Jauza: *riv.*, U.S.S.R.   55 46N 37 41E   119
Java: *is. & admin.*, Indonesia   07 15S 110 00E   38
Java *Sea*: Indonesia   05 00S 111 00E   38
Jawor: Poland   51 01N 16 11E   73
Jaxartes: *riv. see* Syrdarja   45 30N 64 30E   8 29
Jedburgh: Rox., Scotland   55 29N 02 34W   63
Jefferson: *riv.*, Mont., U.S.A.   45 45N 112 00W   94
Jefferson City: Mo., U.S.A.   38 33N 92 10W   43 98
Jefferson City: Mont., U.S.A.   46 24N 112 02W   94
Jeffersonville: Ind., U.S.A.   38 16N 85 45W   98
Jefremov: U.S.S.R.   53 09N 38 07E   80
Jegorjevsk: U.S.S.R.   55 23N 39 02E   80
Jejsk (Yeysk): U.S.S.R.   46 42N 38 16E   28 80
Jēkabpils: U.S.S.R.   56 29N 25 51E   75
Jelabuga: U.S.S.R.   55 47N 52 04E   81
Jelec (Yelets): U.S.S.R.   52 37N 38 30E   28 80
Jelenia Góra: Poland   50 55N 15 45E   73 78
Jelgava: U.S.S.R.   56 39N 23 40E   75
Jemanželinsk: U.S.S.R.   54 45N 61 20E   81
Jena: E.Germany   50 56N 11 35E   73
Jena: U.S.S.R.   67 36N 31 10E   105
Jenakijevo (Ordzhonikidze): U.S.S.R.   48 14N 38 13E   105
Jenisej (Yenisey): *riv.*, U.S.S.R.   64 30N 87 30E   9 30
Jenisejsk (Yeniseysk): U.S.S.R.   58 27N 92 10E   30
Jequié: Brazil   13 51S 40 05W   50
Jérémie: Haiti   18 40N 74 09W   11
Jerevan (Yerevan): U.S.S.R.   40 11N 44 30E   28
Jerez: Spain   36 41N 06 08W   26 77
Jerez de los Caballeros: Spain   38 20N 06 45W   77
Jerome: Idaho, U.S.A.   42 44N 114 31W   90
Jersey: *is.*, Channel Islands   49 13N 02 07W   61
Jersey City: N.J., U.S.A.   40 44N 74 04W   99 123
Jeršov: U.S.S.R.   51 20N 48 17E   81
Jerusalem: Israel *see* Yerushalayim   31 47N 35 14E   32
Jerusalem: Jordan *see* Al Quds   31 47N 35 14E   32
Jeruslan: *riv.*, U.S.S.R.   50 45N 47 00E   81
Jervis *Inlet*: B.C., Canada   50 00N 123 45W   89
Jesenice: Yugoslavia   46 26N 14 02E   105
Jesselton *see* Kota Kinabalu   05 59N 116 04E   39
Jessore: Bangladesh   23 10N 89 12E   83
Jesup: Ga., U.S.A.   31 36N 81 54W   101
Jethou: *is.*, Channel Islands   49 28N 02 28W   61
Jeypore: India   18 51N 82 41E   83
Jezioro Mamry: *lake*, Poland   54 00N 21 30E   78

Jezioro Śniardwy: *lake*, Poland   53 45N 21 45E   78
Jhālakāti: Bangladesh   22 38N 90 10E   83
Jhālawar: India   24 37N 76 12E   82
Jhang Maghiāna: Pakistan   31 19N 72 22E   34 82
Jhānsi: India   25 27N 78 34E   34 82
Jharia: India   23 45N 86 26E   83
Jhārsuguda: India   21 56N 84 04E   83
Jhelum: Pakistan   32 58N 73 45E   34
Jhelum: *riv.*, Pakistan   31 45N 72 15E   34 82
Jhūnjhunu: India   28 05N 75 30E   82
Jiading: China   31 23N 121 15E   121
Jiaganj: India   24 16N 88 19E   83
Jiahe: China   25 30N 112 10E   85
Jiamusi (Chiamussu): China   46 50N 130 21E   37
Jian (Chian): China   27 07N 115 01E   36 85
Jiande: China   29 32N 119 33E   85
Jianghua: China   25 01N 111 44E   85
Jiangkou: China   23 37N 110 10E   85
Jiangle: China   26 50N 117 30E   85
Jiangmen (Chiangmen): China   22 37N 113 07E   36 85
Jiangshan: China   28 43N 118 40E   85
Jiangsu (Chiangsu): *admin.*, China   32 45N 120 15E   37 84
Jiangtai: China   39 57N 116 30E   121
Jiangxi (Chianghsi): *admin.*, China   26 45N 115 30E   36 85
Jiangyan: China   32 29N 120 09E   84
Jiangyin: China   31 50N 120 19E   84
Jiangzi (Gyangtse): China   28 57N 89 35E   35 83
Jianli: China   29 48N 112 50E   85
Jianou (Chienou): China   27 05N 118 21E   36 85
Jianshi: China   30 42N 109 42E   85
Jianyang: China   27 22N 118 04E   85
Jiaocheng: China   37 33N 112 12E   84
Jiaoling: China   24 41N 116 10E   85
Jiaoxian (Chiaohsien): China   36 18N 120 03E   37 84
Jiaozuo (Chiaotso): China   35 17N 113 12E   36 84
Jiashan: Anhui, China   32 47N 118 00E   84
Jiashan: Zhejiang, China   30 51N 120 58E   85
Jiawang: China   34 25N 117 27E   84
Jiaxian: Henan, China   33 57N 113 05E   84
Jiaxian: Shănxĭ, China   38 08N 110 31E   84
Jiaxing (Chiahsing): China   30 46N 120 45E   37 85
Jiayu: China   29 58N 113 57E   85
Jiazi: China   22 55N 116 04E   85
Jidda *see* Juddah   21 30N 39 10E   33
Jieshiwan: *bay*, China   22 45N 115 45E   85
Jieshou: China   33 18N 115 29E   84
Jiešjav'ri: *lake*, Norway   69 45N 24 15E   74
Jiexiu: China   36 57N 111 51E   84
Jieyang: China   23 30N 116 21E   85
Jihlava: Czechoslovakia   49 24N 15 35E   73 78
Jihočeský: *admin.*, Czechoslovakia   49 00N 14 30E   73
Jihomoravský: *admin.*, Czechoslovakia   49 00N 16 30E   73
Jilantai: China   39 45N 105 46E   84
Jilin (Chilin, Kirin): China   43 51N 126 33E   37 105
Jilin (Chilin, Kirin): *admin.*, China   43 30N 127 00E   37
Jima (Jimma): Ethiopia   07 39N 36 47E   53
Jimma *see* Jima   07 39N 36 47E   53
Jimo: China   36 23N 120 31E   84
Jinan (Chinan): China   36 40N 117 01E   36 84 105
Jing: *riv.*, China   35 45N 108 00E   84
Jingde: China   30 19N 118 32E   85
Jingdezhen (Chingtechen): China   29 16N 117 15E   36 85
Jinghai: China   38 56N 116 55E   84
Jingjiang: China   31 59N 120 20E   84
Jingmen: China   31 00N 112 09E   85
Jingxi (Chinghsi): China   23 08N 106 29E   36
Jingxian: Anhui, China   30 42N 118 31E   85
Jingxian: Hunan, China   26 45N 109 33E   85
Jingxing, China   38 00N 114 09E   84
Jingyuan: China   35 30N 106 45E   84
Jinhua: China   29 05N 119 41E   85
Jining: Neimenggu, China   40 58N 113 04E   84
Jining (Chining): Shandong, China   35 24N 116 40E   36 84
Jinja: Uganda   00 27N 33 14E   53
Jinkou: China   30 20N 114 13E   85
Jinping: China   26 44N 109 06E   85
Jinsha (Chinsha): *riv.*, China   28 15N 99 30E   12 36
Jinshi (Chingshih): China   29 40N 111 45E   36 85
Jintan: China   31 41N 119 34E   84
Jinxi: Jiangxi, China   27 52N 116 50E   85
Jinxian: Liaoning, China   39 04N 121 47E   84

Jinxiang: China 35 05N 116 20E 84
Jinzhou (Chinchou): China 41 07N 121 10E 37
Jiparaná: *riv.*, Brazil 08 45S 62 30W 49
Jirjā: Egypt 26 20N 31 53E 32
Jishou: China 28 17N 109 40E 85
Jishui: China 27 11N 115 12E 85
Jiujiang (Chiuchiang): China 29 40N 116 04E 36 85
Jiulianshan: *mtns.*, China 24 30N 114 15E 85
Jiulingshan: *mtns.*, China 28 45N 115 15E 85
Jiulong *see* Kowloon 22 21N 114 15E 36 85
Jiuquan (Chiuch'üan): China 39 45N 98 34E 36
Jiwangmiao: China 31 15N 121 16E 121
Jixi: Anhui, China 30 04N 118 36E 85
Jixi (Chihsi): Heilongjiang, China 45 17N 130 59E 37
Jixian: Henan, China 35 26N 114 04E 84
Jixian: Hopeh, China 40 03N 117 21E 84
Jiyuan: China 35 04N 112 29E 84
João Monlevade: Brazil 19 50S 43 08W 104
João Pessoa: Brazil 07 07S 34 52W 50
Jobourg, Nez de: *pt.*, France 49 41N 01 54W 61
Jodhpur: India 26 18N 73 08E 34 82
Joensuu: Finland 62 35N 29 45E 27 74
Jogjakarta: Indonesia 07 48S 110 24E 38
Johannesburg: Trans., Rep. of S.Africa 26 10S 28 02E 55
John Day: *riv.*, Oreg., U.S.A. 44 45N 120 00W 90
John Hendry *Park*: B.C., Canada 49 15N 123 03W 126
John H. Kerr *Reservoir*: U.S.A. 36 30N 78 30W 101
John o' Groat's: Caith., Scotland 58 39N 03 02W 65
Johnson City: Tenn., U.S.A. 36 20N 82 23W 101
Johnsons Crossing: Yukon, Canada 60 29N 133 17W 88
Johnstone: Renf., Scotland 55 50N 04 31W 62 113
Johnston *Island*: N.Pacific Ocean 16 45N 169 42W 4
Johnston's *Point*: Argyll., Scotland 55 22N 05 31W 62
Johnstown: Pa., U.S.A. 40 20N 78 56W 99 104
Johor Baharu: Malaysia 01 29N 103 44E 38
Johore: *admin.*, Malaysia 02 00N 103 30E 105
Joinvile: Brazil 26 20S 48 49W 51
Joinville *Island*: Antarctica 63 15S 55 45W 24
Jokkmokk: Sweden 66 37N 19 50E 74
Joliet: Ill., U.S.A. 41 32N 88 05W 98 124
Joliette: Qué., Canada 46 02N 73 27W 96
Jolo *Island*: Philippines 06 00N 121 00E 39
Jones, *Cape*: Qué., Canada 54 35N 79 50W 96
Jones Beach *State Park*: N.Y., U.S.A. 40 35N 73 32W 123
Jonesboro: Ark., U.S.A. 35 50N 90 42W 100
Jongkha: China 28 57N 85 12E 35 83
Jönköping: Sweden 57 45N 14 10E 27 75
Jonquière: Qué., Canada 48 25N 71 16W 97
Joplin: Mo., U.S.A. 37 04N 94 31W 43 100
JORDAN 30 45N 35 30E 32 107
Jordan (Urdunn, Nahr al): *riv.*, Israel/Jordan 32 00N 35 30E 32
Jorhāt: India 26 45N 94 12E 35
Jos: Nigeria 09 54N 08 53E 57
José León Suárez: Argentina 34 32S 58 35W 128
Joseph, *Lac*: Nfld., Canada 52 45N 65 15W 97
Joshua Tree *National Monument*: Calif., U.S.A. 33 45N 116 00W 91
Joškar-Ola (Yoshkar-Ola): U.S.S.R. 56 38N 47 52E 28 81
Jos *Plateau*: Nigeria 09 45N 09 45E 20 57
Jostedalsbreen: *ice-cap*, Norway 61 45N 07 15E 27 74
Jotunheimen: *mtns.*, Norway 61 30N 09 00E 74
Joyces Country: *geog. reg.*, Gal., Irish Republic 53 30N 09 30W 66
Juan Anchorena: Argentina 34 29S 58 29W 128
Juan de Fuca, *Strait of*: Canada/U.S.A. 48 15N 124 00W 90
Juan Fernandez *Islands*: S.Pacific Ocean 38 00S 79 00W 5
Juàzeiro: Brazil 09 25S 40 30W 50
Juàzeiro do Norte: Brazil 07 12S 39 20W 50
Juba: *riv.*, E.Africa 01 45N 42 30E 53
Jubbulpore *see* Jabalpur 23 10N 79 59E 34 82
Juby, *Cape*: Morocco 27 57N 12 55W 56
Júcar: *riv.*, Spain 39 00N 01 15W 77
Jüchen: W.Germany 51 06N 06 30E 118
Juddah (Jidda): Saudi Arabia 21 30N 39 10E 33
Judith Gap: Mont., U.S.A. 46 41N 109 45W 94
Juiz de Fora: Brazil 21 45S 43 20W 51
Jujuy: *admin.*, Argentina 24 00S 65 00W 49
Jukagir (Yukagir) *Plateau*: U.S.S.R. 66 00N 155 00E 9 31
Juliaca: Peru 15 29S 70 09W 49

Jullundur: India 31 18N 75 40E 34 82
Junction City: Kans., U.S.A. 39 02N 96 50W 94
Jundiaí: Brazil 23 10S 46 54W 51
Juneau: Alaska, U.S.A. 58 18N 134 25W 42 88
Jungfernheide: *heath*, W.Germany 52 30N 13 15E 117
Junín: Argentina 34 34S 60 55W 52
Junsele: Sweden 63 40N 16 55E 74
Junxian: China 32 40N 111 06E 84
Jura: *is.*, Argyll., Scotland 56 00N 05 45W 62
Jura: *mtns.*, France/Switzerland 47 00N 07 00E 71
Jura, *Sound of*: Argyll., Scotland 55 45N 05 45W 62
Jurga (Yurga): U.S.S.R. 55 42N 84 51E 30
Jurjev *see* Tartu 58 23N 26 43E 80
Jurjevec: U.S.S.R. 57 18N 43 06E 80
Jurjev-Pol'skij: U.S.S.R. 56 30N 39 41E 80
Jūrmala: U.S.S.R. 56 58N 23 42E 75
Juruá: *riv.*, Brazil 06 30S 68 15W 48
Juruena: *riv.*, Brazil 10 30S 58 30W 50
Jur'uzan': U.S.S.R. 54 52N 58 26E 81
Jüterbog: E.Germany 51 59N 13 05E 73
Jutland: *pen.*, *see* Jylland 55 45N 09 00E 75
Juvisy-sur-Orge: France 48 42N 02 23E 117
Juxian: China 35 35N 118 55E 84
Juye: China 35 23N 116 08E 84
Juža: U.S.S.R. 56 35N 42 01E 80
Juziers: France 49 00N 01 51E 117
Južno-Sachalinsk (Yuzhno-Sakhalinsk): U.S.S.R. 46 58N 142 42E 31
Južno-Ural'sk: U.S.S.R. 54 26N 61 15E 81
Južnyj Bug: *riv.*, U.S.S.R. 48 15N 30 00E 78
Jylland (Jutland): *pen.*, Denmark 55 45N 09 00E 75
Jyväskylä: Finland 62 16N 25 50E 27 74

K₂ (Godwin Austen), *Mount*: China/India 35 53N 76 30E 11 29
Ka: *riv.*, Laos/N.Vietnam 19 00N 105 15E 36
Kaapstad *see* Cape Town 33 56S 18 28E 55
Kabaena: *is.*, Indonesia 05 15S 122 00E 39
Kabale: Uganda 01 15S 30 00E 54
Kabalo: Zaïre 06 03S 26 55E 55
Kabinda: Zaïre 06 08S 24 29E 54
Kābul: Afghanistan 34 30N 69 11E 29
Kabwe (Broken Hill): Zambia 14 27S 28 27E 54
Kachovka: U.S.S.R. 46 47N 33 30E 80
Kachovskoye Vodokhranilišče (Kakhovskoye Vodokhranilishche): *res.*, U.S.S.R. 47 30N 34 30E 28 80
Kadaň: Czechoslovakia 50 23N 13 15E 73
Kadi: India 23 20N 72 22E 82
Kadijevka (Kadiyevka): U.S.S.R. 48 34N 38 40E 28 80
Kadiyevka *see* Kadijevka 48 34N 38 40E 28 80
Kaduna: Nigeria 10 28N 07 25E 57
Kaesŏng: N.Korea 37 59N 126 33E 37
Kafue: *riv.*, Zambia 15 30S 26 45E 55
Kaganovich *see* Tovarkovskiy 53 40N 38 14E 80
Kagaznagar: India 19 18N 79 50E 82
Kagoshima: Japan 31 36N 130 33E 37 86
Kaieteur *Falls*: Guyana 05 09N 59 29W 48
Kaifeng: China 34 44N 114 21E 36 84
Kaihua: China 29 08N 118 23E 85
Kaijiang: China 31 09N 107 52E 84
Kaikoura: S.I., New Zealand 42 24S 173 41E 87
Kaikoura *Range*: S.I., New Zealand 42 00S 173 45E 87
Kailash: India 28 33N 77 16E 120
Kaili: China 26 37N 107 59E 85
Kaimanawa *Mountains*: N.I., New Zealand 39 30S 175 45E 87
Kaipara *Harbour*: N.I., New Zealand 36 30S 175 15E 87
Kaiping: China 39 41N 118 14E 84
Kairāna: India 29 24N 77 12E 82
Kaiserslautern: W.Germany 49 27N 07 47E 72
Kaitaia: N.I., New Zealand 35 08S 173 18E 37
Kaitangata: S.I., New Zealand 46 18S 169 52E 87
Kajaani: Finland 64 14N 27 37E 27 74
Kakagi *Lake*: Ont., Canada 49 00N 93 15W 98
Kākdwip: India 21 52N 88 11E 83
Kake: Alaska, U.S.A. 56 59N 133 57W 89
Kakhovskoye Vodokhranilishche: *res.*, *see* Kachovskoje Vodokhranilišče 47 30N 34 30E 28 80

Types of map: Ocean pp. 1-5; Physical pp. 6-25; Human pp. 26-57; Topographic pp. 58-101; World pp. 102-111; Urban pp. 112-128.

Kākināda: India   16 59N 82 20E   34
Kakisa *Lake*: N.W.T., Canada   60 55N 117 40W   88
Kalač: U.S.S.R.   50 25N 41 01E   80
Kalač-na-Donu: U.S.S.R.   48 43N 43 31E   80
Kalačskaja Vozvyšennost': *hld.*, U.S.S.R.   50 45N 41 30E   80
Kalahari *Desert*: Botswana/S.W.Africa   23 00S 22 00E   21 55
Kalámai: Greece   37 02N 22 07E   32 79
Kalamazoo: Mich., U.S.A.   42 17N 85 36W   45 98
Kalamazoo: *riv.*, Mich., U.S.A.   42 30N 86 00W   98
Kalamb: India   19 00N 73 45E   82
Kalanshu *Desert*: Libya   28 00N 21 15E   32
Kalemi (Albertville): Zaïre   05 56S 29 12E   54
Kalevala: U.S.S.R.   65 13N 31 08E   74
Kalgan *see* Zhangjiakou   40 50N 114 53E   36 84
Kalgoorlie: W.A., Australia   30 49S 121 29E   40
Kāli: *riv.*, Nepal   29 00N 83 45E   35
Kalimantan: *admin.*, Indonesia   00 15S 113 00E   38
Kālimpong: India   27 02N 88 34E   83
Kalinin (Tver'): U.S.S.R.   56 52N 35 55E   28 80
Kaliningrad (Königsberg): U.S.S.R.   54 43N 20 30E   28 78
Kalininsk: U.S.S.R.   51 30N 44 28E   80
Kalinkoviči: U.S.S.R.   52 08N 29 21E   80
Kāli Sindh: *riv.*, India   24 00N 76 15E   82
Kalispell: Mont., U.S.A.   48 12N 114 19W   90
Kalisz: Poland   51 46N 18 02E   73 78
Kalixälven: *riv.*, Sweden   66 15N 22 30E   74
Kalk: W.Germany   50 57N 07 01E   119
Kalkaji: India   28 32N 77 15E   120
Kallaste: U.S.S.R.   58 39N 27 09E   80
Kallsjön: *lake*, Sweden   63 30N 13 00E   74
Kalmar: Sweden   56 39N 16 20E   75
Kālol: India   23 15N 72 32E   82
Kal'tino: U.S.S.R.   59 58N 30 40E   119
Kaluga: U.S.S.R.   54 31N 36 16E   28 80
Kaluš: U.S.S.R.   49 03N 24 23E   78
Kalyān: India   19 17N 73 11E   82
Kama: *riv.*, U.S.S.R.   56 00N 53 30E   8 28 81
Kamaishi: Japan   39 16N 141 53E   86 105
Kamakura: Japan   35 19N 139 33E   121
Kamālia: Pakistan   30 41N 72 40E   82
Kamaran *Islands*: Red Sea   15 30N 42 45E   33
Kamarhati: India   22 40N 88 22E   120
Kamba: China   28 13N 88 32E   83
Kambarka: U.S.S.R.   56 17N 54 12E   81
Kamchatka: *pen.*, U.S.S.R.   56 00N 159 00E   9 31
Kamchatka *Trench*: N.Pacific Ocean   50 00N 160 00E   22
Kamen: W.Germany   51 36N 07 39E   118
Kamen': *mtn.*, U.S.S.R.   69 06N 94 48E   30
Kamenec-Podol'skij: U.S.S.R.   48 41N 26 36E   78
Kamenka: U.S.S.R.   60 01N 30 12E   119
Kamenka: U.S.S.R.   53 13N 44 03E   80
Kamenka: U.S.S.R.   49 02N 32 06E   80
Kamensk-Ural'skij: U.S.S.R.   56 28N 61 54E   29 81
Kāmet: *mtn.*, India   30 56N 79 40E   82
Kamienna Góra: Poland   50 48N 16 00E   73
Kamiiso: Japan   41 49N 140 39E   86
Kamina: Zaïre   08 44S 25 00E   54
Kamloops: B.C., Canada   50 40N 120 20W   89
Kamloops *Lake*: B.C., Canada   50 45N 120 30W   42
Kāmoke: Pakistan   31 58N 74 13E   82
Kampala: Uganda   00 19N 32 35E   53
Kampar: *riv.*, Indonesia   00 15N 101 00E   38
Kampen: Netherlands   52 33N 05 55E   72
Kamphaeng Phet: Thailand   16 28N 99 31E   35
Kamp-Lintfort: W.Germany   51 30N 06 32E   118
Kampot: Khmer Rep.   10 37N 104 11E   38
Kamskoje Ustje: U.S.S.R.   55 13N 49 16E   81
Kamskoje Vodochranilišče: *res.*, U.S.S.R.   58 52N 56 15E   81
Kāmthi: India   21 12N 79 16E   82
Kamyšin: U.S.S.R.   50 06N 45 24E   81
Kamyšlov: U.S.S.R.   56 52N 62 43E   81
Kan: *riv.*, *see* Gan   27 30N 115 15E   36 85
Kanaaupscow: Qué., Canada   54 00N 76 40W   96
Kanaaupscow: *riv.*, Qué., Canada   54 30N 74 00W   96
Kanagawa: Japan   35 28N 139 39E   121
Kanairiktok: *riv.*, Nfld., Canada   54 30N 61 30W   97
Kananga (Luluabourg): Zaïre   05 54S 22 25E   54
Kanaš: U.S.S.R.   55 31N 47 30E   81
Kanazawa: Ishikawa, Japan   36 34N 136 39E   37 86

Kanazawa: Kanagawa, Japan   35 21N 139 37E   121
Kanchanaburi: Thailand   14 02N 99 32E   35
Kanchenjunga: *mtn.*, Nepal/Sikkim   27 44N 88 11E   83
Kanchou *see* Ganzhou   25 50N 114 52E   36
Kandahār: Afghanistan   31 36N 65 47E   34
Kandalakša: U.S.S.R.   67 09N 32 31E   27 74
Kandan: China   39 49N 116 16E   121
Kandi: Dahomey   11 05N 02 59E   57
Kandi: India   23 57N 88 04E   83
Kandla: India   23 03N 70 11E   34
Kandy: Sri Lanka   07 17N 80 40E   34
Kangean: *is.*, Indonesia   07 00S 115 15E   39
Kanggye: N.Korea   40 58N 126 34E   37
Kangma: China   28 32N 89 41E   83
Kangnüng: S.Korea   37 45N 128 54E   37
Kanhar: *riv.*, India   24 00N 83 30E   83
Kaniapiskau: *riv.*, Qué., Canada   55 15N 69 00W   96
Kaniapiskau *Lake*: Qué., Canada   54 00N 69 45W   96
Kankaanpää: Finland   61 47N 22 25E   74
Kankakee: Ill., U.S.A.   41 08N 87 52W   98
Kankan: Guinea   10 22N 09 11W   57
Känker: India   20 17N 81 30E   83
Kanmen: China   28 06N 120 20E   85
Kannapolis: N.C., U.S.A.   35 30N 80 36W   101
Kannauj: India   27 02N 79 56E   82
Kano: Nigeria   12 00N 08 31E   57
Kanonji: Japan   34 07N 133 39E   86
Kanopolis: Kans., U.S.A.   38 43N 98 09W   94
Kanoya: Japan   31 23N 130 51E   86
Kānpur (Cawnpore): India   26 27N 80 14E   34 82
Kansas: *admin.*, U.S.A.   43 94
Kansas: *riv.*, Kans., U.S.A.   39 00N 96 15W   94
Kansas City: Kans., U.S.A.   39 07N 94 38W   43 94 104
Kansas City: Mo., U.S.A.   39 02N 94 33W   45 94
Kansas Turnpike: *hwy.*, Kans., U.S.A.   38 15N 96 30W   95
Kansk: U.S.S.R.   56 13N 95 41E   30
Kansu: *admin. see* Gansu   35 45N 108 00E   36 84
Kantang: Thailand   07 25N 99 30E   38
Kanturk: Cork, Irish Republic   52 10N 08 55W   67
Kanye: Botswana   24 59S 25 19E   55
Kaohsiung: Taiwan   22 38N 120 20E   37 85
Kaohsiunghsien: Taiwan   22 38N 120 26E   85
Kaolack: Senegal   14 09N 16 08W   57
Kapanga: Zaïre   08 21S 22 35E   54
Kapfenberg: Austria   47 27N 15 18E   73
Kapiskau: Ont., Canada   52 50N 82 01W   96
Kapiskau: *riv.*, Ont., Canada   52 00N 83 15W   96
Kaposvár: Hungary   46 21N 17 49E   78
Kapsukas (Marijampole): U.S.S.R.   54 31N 23 20E   78
Kapuas: *riv.*, Indonesia   00 00 110 45E   12 38
Kapūrthala: India   31 20N 75 26E   82
Kapuskasing: Ont., Canada   49 25N 82 26W   98
Kapuskasing: *riv.*, Ont., Canada   49 00N 82 30W   98
Kara-Bogaz-Gol: *gulf*, U.S.S.R.   41 30N 53 00E   28
Karabük: Turkey   41 12N 32 36E   32 105
Karāchi: Pakistan   24 51N 67 02E   34
Karaganda: U.S.S.R.   49 50N 73 10E   29 105
Karakoram *Range*: China/Kashmir   36 00N 77 30E   29
Karakumy: *des.*, U.S.S.R.   40 00N 60 00E   8 29
Karamea *Bight*: S.I., New Zealand   41 00S 172 00E   87
Kāranja: India   20 28N 77 32E   82
Kara *Sea*: Arctic Ocean   74 00N 75 00E   23
Karauli: India   26 30N 77 00E   82
Karbalā (Kerbela): Iraq   32 37N 44 03E   33
Kärdla: U.S.S.R.   59 00N 22 42E   75
Kareima *see* Kuraymah   18 33N 31 51E   32
Karhula: Finland   60 29N 26 58E   75
Kariba, *Lake*: Rhodesia/Zambia   17 00S 27 45E   21 55
Kariba *Dam*: Rhodesia/Zambia   16 31S 28 50E   55
Kariba-yama: *mtn.*, Japan   42 36N 139 56E   86
Karimata *Archipelago*: Indonesia   01 45S 108 45E   38
Karimata *Strait*: Indonesia   02 15S 108 45E   13 38
Karimundjawa *Islands*: Indonesia   05 45S 110 15E   38
Karisimbi, *Mount*: Zaïre   01 31S 29 25E   21 54
Karl-Marx-Stadt (Chemnitz): E.Germany   50 50N 12 55E   27 73
Karlovac: Yugoslavia   45 30N 15 34E   78
Karlovy Vary: Czechoslovakia   50 14N 12 53E   73
Karlshamn: Sweden   56 10N 14 50E   75
Karlshorst: E.Germany   52 29N 13 32E   117
Karlskoga: Sweden   59 19N 14 33E   75

Types of map: Ocean pp. 1-5; Physical pp. 6-25; Human pp. 26-57; Topographic pp. 58-101; World pp. 102-111; Urban pp. 112-128.

Karlskrona: Sweden　56 10N 15 35E　75
Karlsruhe: W.Germany　49 00N 08 24E　26 72 107
Karlstad: Sweden　59 24N 13 32E　75
Karnāl: India　29 41N 76 58E　34 82
Karnāli: *riv.*, India　28 00N 81 15E　83
Karnische *Alpen*: Austria　47 30N 13 00E　78
Karol Bagh: India　28 39N 77 12E　120
Kárpathos: *is.*, Greece　35 31N 27 13E　79
Karpenísion: Greece　38 55N 21 47E　79
Karpinsk: U.S.S.R.　59 45N 60 01E　81
Kārsava: U.S.S.R.　56 47N 27 40E　80
Karsun: U.S.S.R.　54 11N 46 59E　81
Kartaly: U.S.S.R.　53 03N 60 40E　81
Karviná: Czechoslovakia　49 50N 18 30E　78
Kasaan: Alaska, U.S.A.　55 32N 132 24W　89
Kasai: *riv.*, Africa　03 45S 19 15E　21 54
Kasaoka: Japan　34 30N 133 30E　86
Kasba: India　25 51N 87 32E　83
Kasba *Lake*: N.W.T., Canada　60 15N 102 15W　92
Kasese: Uganda　00 10N 30 06E　54
Kash: *riv.*, Afghanistan　32 15N 63 30E　34
Kashabowie: Ont., Canada　48 40N 90 26W　98
Kāshān: Iran　33 59N 51 35E　33
Kashi (Kashgar): China　39 29N 75 59E　29
Kashīpur: India　29 13N 78 58E　82
Kashiwazaki: Japan　37 22N 138 33E　86
Kashmir: *admin. see* Jammu and Kashmir　32 45N 76 45E
　　35
Kasimov: U.S.S.R.　54 56N 41 24E　80
Kašin: U.S.S.R.　57 21N 37 37E　80
Kašira: U.S.S.R.　54 51N 38 10E　80
Kaskaskia: *riv.*, Ill., U.S.A.　39 00N 89 00W　98
Kaskattama: *riv.*, Man., Canada　56 30N 90 30W　93
Kaslo: B.C., Canada　49 54N 116 57W　90
Kasongo: Zaïre　04 27S 26 40E　54
Kásos: *is.*, Greece　35 15N 26 45E　79
Kassalā: Sudan　15 28N 36 24E　53
Kassel: W.Germany　51 18N 09 30E　26 72
Kasūr: Pakistan　31 07N 74 30E　82
Katahdin, *Mount*: Maine, U.S.A.　45 55N 68 57W　99
Katajsk: U.S.S.R.　56 18N 62 35E　81
Katanga: *reg.*, Zaïre　11 45S 28 00E　21 54
Katase: Japan　35 19N 139 29E　121
Katav-Ivanovsk: U.S.S.R.　54 45N 58 12E　81
Kateríni: Greece　40 15N 22 30E　79
Kāthgodam: India　29 15N 79 32E　82
Kātmāndu: Nepal　27 42N 85 19E　35 83
Katni *see* Murwāra　23 49N 80 28E　82
Katowice: Poland　50 15N 18 59E　27 78
Katrine, *Loch*: Perth., Scotland　56 15N 04 30W　64
Katrineholm: Sweden　58 59N 16 15E　75
Katrina: Nigeria　13 00N 07 32E　57
Kattegat: *str.*, Denmark/Sweden　56 45N 11 00E　75
Katwa: India　23 39N 88 08E　83
Kauai: *is.*, Hawaii, U.S.A.　22 00N 159 30W　4
Kaufbeuren: W.Germany　47 53N 10 37E　73
Kaufman: Tex., U.S.A.　32 35N 96 19W　100
Kaukauna: Wis., U.S.A.　44 20N 88 16W　98
Kaunas (Kovno): U.S.S.R.　54 52N 23 55E　28 75
Kaura Namoda: Nigeria　12 39N 06 38E　57
Kavajë: Albania　41 11N 19 33E　79
Kavalerovo: U.S.S.R.　44 15N 135 04E　86
Kaválla: Greece　40 56N 24 25E　27 79
Kawagoe: Japan　35 55N 139 29E　86
Kawaguchi: Japan　35 47N 139 42E　121
Kawasaki: Kanagawa, Japan　35 32N 139 43E　105 107 121
Kawawa: Japan　35 31N 139 33E　121
Kawerau: N.I., New Zealand　38 03S 176 43E　87
Kawhia *Harbour*: N.I., New Zealand　38 03S 174 50E　87
Kayes: Mali　14 26N 11 28W　57
Kayseri: Turkey　38 42N 35 28E　32
Kazachskaja S.S.R. (Kazakh S.S.R.): *admin.*, U.S.S.R.
　49 30N 55 00E　29 81 105
Kazachstan: U.S.S.R.　51 09N 53 00E　81
Kazakh S.S.R. *see* Kazachskaja S.S.R.　49 30N 55 00E
　　29 81 105
Kazakh *Uplands*: U.S.S.R.　49 00N 73 00E　8 29
Kazan': U.S.S.R.　55 45N 49 08E　28 81
Kazan: *riv.*, N.W.T., Canada　61 45N 100 30W　92
Kazanka: *riv.*, U.S.S.R.　56 00N 49 00E　81
Kazanlâk: Bulgaria　42 38N 25 21E　79

Kazatin: U.S.S.R.　49 43N 28 50E　78
Kaztalovka: U.S.S.R.　49 46N 48 42E　81
Kéa: *is.*, Greece　37 38N 24 20E　79
Keady: Arm., N.Ireland　54 15N 06 42W　66
Keal, *Loch na*: Argyll., Scotland　56 15N 06 00W　64
Kearney: Nebr., U.S.A.　40 42N 99 05W　94
Kearns: Utah, U.S.A.　40 39N 112 00W　91
Keban *Reservoir*: Turkey　38 45N 39 15E　32
Kebnekaise: *mtn.*, Sweden　67 53N 18 33E　27
Kebock *Head*: R.& Crom., Scotland　58 02N 06 22W　64
Kechika: *riv.*, B.C., Canada　58 45N 127 15W　88
Kecskemét: Hungary　46 55N 19 44E　78
Kedah: *admin.*, Malaysia　06 00N 100 40E　105
Kediri: Indonesia　07 45S 112 01E　38
Keele: Staffs., England　53 00N 02 17W　58
Keele: *riv.*, N.W.T., Canada　64 15N 126 30W　88
Keele *Peak*: Yukon, Canada　63 25N 130 17W　88
Keen, *Mount*: Angus, Scotland　56 58N 02 59W　65
Keene: N.H., U.S.A.　42 55N 72 17W　99
Keeper *Hill*: Tip., Irish Republic　52 45N 08 16W　67
Keerzong: China　32 11N 79 59E　34 82
Keetley: Utah, U.S.A.　40 38N 111 25W　91
Keetmanshoop: S.W.Africa　26 36S 18 08E　55
Keewatin: Ont., Canada　49 47N 94 30W　98
Keewatin, District of: *admin.*, Canada　61 00N 98 00W
　　42 93
Kefallinía (Cephalonia): *is.*, Greece　38 15N 20 30E　79
Keg River: Alta., Canada　57 51N 117 55W　92
Keighley: W.Yorks., England　53 52N 01 54W　63 115
Keith: Banff., Scotland　57 32N 02 57W　65
Keith Arm: *bay*, N.W.T., Canada　65 15N 122 30W　88
Kelan: China　38 44N 111 30E　84
Kelang: Malaysia　03 02N 101 27E　38
Keller *Lake*: N.W.T., Canada　63 45N 121 30W　88
Kellogg: Idaho, U.S.A.　47 32N 116 07W　90
Kells: Meath, Irish Republic　53 44N 06 53W　66
Kelowna: B.C., Canada　49 53N 119 29W　42 89
Kelsey *Head*: Corn., England　50 24N 05 08W　61
Kelso: Rox., Scotland　55 36N 02 25W　63
Kelso: Wash., U.S.A.　46 09N 122 54W　90
Kelvin: *riv.*, Lan., Scotland　55 45N 04 15W　113
Kema: *riv.*, U.S.S.R.　60 30N 37 30E　80
Kemano: B.C., Canada　53 39N 127 58W　89
Kemerovo: U.S.S.R.　55 20N 86 05E　30
Kemi: Finland　65 46N 24 34E　27 74
Kemijärvi: Finland　66 42N 27 30E　74
Kemijärvi: *lake*, Finland　66 42N 27 30E　74
Kemijoki: *riv.*, Finland　66 00N 24 45E　27 74
Kempen: W.Germany　51 22N 06 25E　118
Kempston: Beds., England　52 07N 00 30W　59
Kempten: W.Germany　47 44N 10 19E　73
Kempt *Lake*: Qué., Canada　47 15N 74 15W　96
Kemsing: Kent, England　51 18N 00 14E　112
Ken: *riv.*, India　25 00N 80 15E　34 82
Ken, *Loch*: Kirkc., Scotland　55 00N 04 00W　62
Kendal: Cumbria, England　54 20N 02 45W　63
Kendari: Indonesia　03 57S 122 36E　39
Kendrāpāra: India　20 30N 89 29E　83
Kenema: Sierra Leone　07 57N 11 11W　57
Kenge: Zaïre　04 52S 16 59E　54
Kenilworth: War., England　52 21N 01 34W　59 115
Keningau: Malaysia　05 21N 116 11E　39
Kenitra *see* Mina Hassan Tani　34 16N 06 36W　56
Kenmare: Kerry, Irish Republic　51 53N 09 35W　67
Kenmare *River*: Kerry, Irish Republic　51 45N 09 45W　67
Kennebec: *riv.*, Maine, U.S.A.　45 00N 69 45W　99
Kennedy, *Cape see* Canaveral, *Cape*:　28 27N 80 32W
　　45 101
Kennet: *riv.*, England　51 15N 01 45W　59
Kennett: Mo., U.S.A.　36 15N 90 04W　100
Kennewick: Wash., U.S.A.　46 12N 119 07W　90
Kennydale: Wash., U.S.A.　47 31N 122 11W　126
Kénogami: Qué., Canada　48 26N 71 16W　96
Kénogami: *riv.*, Ont., Canada　50 00N 85 30W　98
Keno Hill: Yukon, Canada　63 58N 135 22W　88
Kenora: Ont., Canada　49 47N 94 26W　44 98
Kenosha: Wis., U.S.A.　42 34N 87 50W　98
Kensington: Gt, Ldn., England　51 30N 00 12W　112
Kensington: Md., U.S.A.　39 01N 77 05W　122
Kent: *admin.*, England　51 00N 00 45E　59
Kent, *Vale of*: Kent, England　51 00N 00 30E　59

Kentau: U.S.S.R.   43 36N 68 36E   29
Kenthurst: N.S.W., Australia   33 40S 151 01E   120
Kentucky: *admin.*, U.S.A.   37 30N 85 00W   45 101
Kentucky: *riv.*, Ky., U.S.A.   37 45N 84 45W   101
Kentucky *Lake*: U.S.A.   36 30N 88 00W   100
Kentucky Parkway: *hwy.*, Ky., U.S.A.   37 15N 87 30W   101
Kentucky Turnpike: *hwy.*, Ky., U.S.A.   37 45N 85 45W   101
KENYA   00 45N 37 30E   21 54 107
Kenya, *Mount*: Kenya   00 10S 37 19E   21 54
Keokuk: Iowa, U.S.A.   40 23N 91 25W   98
Keonjhar: *admin.*, India   22 00N 85 30E   105
Keonjhargarh: India   21 38N 85 40E   83
Kępno: Poland   51 18N 17 59E   73
Kerala: *admin.*, India   10 30N 76 30E   34
Kerbela *see* Karbalā   32 37N 44 03E   33
Kerč' (Kerch'): U.S.S.R.   45 22N 36 27E   28 105
Kerč' *Strait* (Kerch' *Strait*): U.S.S.R.   45 22N 36 38E   28
Keremeos: B.C., Canada   49 12N 119 50W   89
Kerguelen *Islands*: Indian Ocean   48 00S 69 00E   1
Kerguelen *Plateau*: Southern Ocean   55 00S 77 00E   1
Kerintji, *Mount*: Indonesia   01 43S 101 15E   38
Kerki: U.S.S.R.   37 50N 65 12E   29
Kérkira (Corfu): Corfu, Greece   39 36N 19 56E   79
Kérkira (Corfu): *is.*, Greece   39 30N 19 45E   79
Kermadec *Islands*: S.Pacific Ocean   30 00S 178 30W   4 15
Kermadec *Trench*: S.Pacific Ocean   30 00S 176 00W   4
Kermān: Iran   30 18N 57 05E   33
Kermānshāh: Iran   34 19N 47 04E   33
Kermit: Tex., U.S.A.   31 52N 103 06W   95
Kern: *riv.*, Calif., U.S.A.   35 30N 118 30W   91
Kerrera: *is.*, Argyll., Scotland   56 15N 05 30W   64
Kerrville: Tex., U.S.A.   30 03N 99 08W   95
Kerry: *admin.*, Irish Republic   52 15N 09 15W   67
Kerry *Head*: Kerry, Irish Republic   52 25N 09 57W   67
Kerspetalsperre: *res.*, W.Germany   51 00N 07 30E   118
Kesagami *Lake*: Ont., Canada   50 15N 80 15W   96
Keşan: Turkey   40 52N 26 38E   79
Kesennuma: Japan   38 54N 141 35E   86
Kesh: Ferm., N.Ireland   54 31N 07 43W   66
Keswick: Cumbria, England   54 37N 03 08W   63
Ketapang: Indonesia   01 50S 109 59E   38
Ketchikan: Alaska, U.S.A.   55 21N 131 39W   89
Kettering: Northants., England   52 24N 00 44W   59
Kettwig: W.Germany   51 22N 06 55E   118
Kewanee: Ill., U.S.A.   41 14N 89 56W   98
Keweenaw *Peninsula*: Mich., U.S.A.   47 00N 88 15W   44 98
Key, *Lough*: Rosc., Irish Republic   54 00N 08 15W   66
Key Largo: *is.*, Fla., U.S.A.   25 11N 80 21W   101
Keynsham: Avon, England   51 26N 02 30W   61 113
Keystone: S.D., U.S.A.   43 54N 103 25W   94
Keystone *Reservoir*: Okla., U.S.A.   36 09N 96 16W   95
Key West: Fla., U.S.A.   24 34N 81 48W   47 101
Khabarovsk *see* Chabarovsk   48 27N 135 06E   31
Khalkís (Chalcis): Greece   38 28N 23 36E   79
Khāmgaon: India   20 42N 76 40E   82
Khandwa: India   21 49N 76 23E   34 82
Khānewāl: Pakistan   30 17N 72 00E   82
Khaniá (Canea): Crete   35 31N 24 01E   32 79
Khanka, *Lake* (Ozero Chanka): China/U.S.S.R.   45 00N 132 30E   37 86
Khanna: India   30 42N 76 15E   82
Khānpur: Pakistan   28 38N 70 40E   82
Kharagpur: India   25 07N 86 33E   35 83
Khardah: India   22 44N 88 22E   120
Khar'kov *see* Char'kov   50 00N 36 15E   28 80
Khartoum *see* Al Khurṭūm   15 36N 32 32E   53
Khaskovo *see* Haskovo   41 56N 25 33E   79
Khatanga: *riv.*, *see* Chatanga   72 30N 103 00E   30
Kherson *see* Cherson   46 38N 32 35E   28 80
Khilok *see* Chilok   51 21N 110 28E   32
Khíos (Chios): Greece   38 23N 26 07E   79
Khíos: *is.*, Greece   38 23N 26 08E   79
Khiuri Khala: *mtn.*, Nepal   29 58N 81 18E   83
KHMER REPUBLIC (Cambodia)   13 15N 104 45E   12 38
Khondmāl *Hills*: India   20 15N 84 15E   83
Khong (Mékôngk, Mekong): *riv.*, Indo-China   10 30N 105 30E   12 35
Khon Kaen: Thailand   16 26N 102 50E   38
Khorramshahr (Khurramshahr): Iran   30 25N 48 09E   33
Khouribga: Morocco   32 54N 06 57W   56
Khrishnapur *Canal*: India   22 35N 88 27E   120

Khulna: Bangladesh   22 49N 89 34E   35 83
Khunti: India   23 02N 85 19E   83
Khurai: India   24 04N 78 18E   82
Khurdha: India   20 10N 85 42E   83
Khurja: India   28 15N 77 51E   82
Khurramshahr *see* Khorramshahr   30 25N 48 09E   33
Kiantajärvi: *lake*, Finland   65 00N 29 00E   74
Kicking Horse *Pass*: Canada   51 28N 116 23W   92
Kidderminster: Here. & Worcs., England   52 23N 02 14W   59 115
Kidlington: Oxon., England   51 50N 01 17W   59
Kidnappers, *Cape*: N.I., New Zealand   39 29S 177 17E   87
Kidsgrove: Staffs., England   53 05N 02 16W   58
Kidwelly: Dyfed, Wales   51 45N 04 18W   61
Kiel: W.Germany   54 20N 10 08E   26 73 76
Kiel *Canal*: W.Germany   54 00N 09 15E   75
Kielce: Poland   50 51N 20 39E   27 78
Kieler Bucht: *bay*, W.Germany   54 30N 10 30E   73
Kierunavaara: *mtn.*, Sweden   67 50N 20 12E   105
Kieta: Terr. of New Guinea   06 13S 155 38E   15
Kiev *see* Kijev   50 26N 30 31E   28 80
Kiffa: Mauritania   16 38N 11 28W   56
Kigali: Rwanda   01 59S 30 05E   54
Kigoma: Tanzania   04 52S 29 38E   54
Kiirun *see* Chilung   25 08N 121 44E   37
Kii–suidō: *str.*, Japan   33 45N 134 45E   86
Kijev (Kiev): U.S.S.R.   50 26N 30 31E   28 80
Kijevskoje Vodochranilišče: *res.*, U.S.S.R.   51 00N 30 30E   80
Kikinda: Yugoslavia   45 50N 20 30E   78
Kikládhes (Cyclades): *is.*, Greece   37 00N 25 00E   79
Kikuna: Japan   35 30N 139 38E   121
Kikwit: Zaïre   05 02S 18 49E   54
Kilbeggan: Westmeath, Irish Republic   53 22N 07 30W   67
Kilbirnie: Ayr., Scotland   55 46N 04 41W   113
Kilbrannan *Sound*: Scotland   55 30N 05 15W   62
Kilcock: Kild., Irish Republic   53 24N 06 40W   67
Kilcormac: Offaly, Irish Republic   53 10N 07 43W   67
Kilcreggan: Dunb., Scotland   55 59N 04 50W   113
Kilcullen: Kild., Irish Republic   53 08N 06 45W   67
Kildare: Kild., Irish Republic   53 10N 06 55W   67
Kildare: *admin.*, Irish Republic   53 00N 06 45W   67
Kilglass *Lough*: Rosc., Irish Republic   53 45N 08 00W   66
Kilimanjaro, *Mount*: Tanzania   03 02S 37 20E   21 54
Kilkee: Clare, Irish Republic   52 41N 09 38W   67
Kilkeel: Down, N.Ireland   54 04N 06 00W   66
Kilkenny: Kilk., Irish Republic   52 39N 07 15W   67
Kilkenny: *admin.*, Irish Republic   52 30N 07 15W   67
Kilkieran *Bay*: Gal., Irish Republic   53 15N 09 30W   67
Kilkis: Greece   40 59N 22 22E   79
Killala: Mayo, Irish Republic   54 13N 09 13W   66
Killala *Bay*: Irish Republic   54 15N 09 00W   66
Killaloe: Clare, Irish Republic   52 48N 08 27W   67
Killarney: Man., Canada   49 12N 99 40W   93
Killarney: Kerry, Irish Republic   52 03N 09 30W   67
Killchianaig: Argyll., Scotland   56 02N 05 48W   64
Killeen: Tex., U.S.A.   31 07N 97 44W   95
Killiecrankie, *Pass of*: Perth., Scotland   56 43N 03 40W   65
Killorglin: Kerry, Irish Republic   52 06N 09 47W   67
Killybegs: Don., Irish Republic   54 38N 08 27W   66
Killyleagh: Down, N.Ireland   54 24N 05 39W   66
Kilmalcolm: Renf., Scotland   55 54N 04 38W   113
Kilmallock: Lim., Irish Republic   52 25N 08 35W   67
Kilmaluag: Inv., Scotland   57 41N 06 19W   64
Kilmarnock: Ayr., Scotland   55 37N 04 30W   62
Kil'mez': U.S.S.R.   57 01N 51 22E   81
Kilpatrick *Hills*: Dunb., Scotland   55 45N 04 15W   113
Kilrea: Lon., N.Ireland   54 57N 06 34W   66
Kilrush: Clare, Irish Republic   52 39N 09 29W   67
Kilsyth: Stirl., Scotland   55 59N 04 04W   62 113
Kilsyth *Hills*: Stirl., Scotland   56 00N 04 00W   113
Kilwinning: Ayr., Scotland   55 40N 04 42W   62 113
Kilworth *Mountains*: Irish Republic   52 00N 08 15W   67
Kimball: Nebr., U.S.A.   41 14N 103 40W   94
Kimberley: B.C., Canada   49 40N 115 58W   90
Kimberley: C.P., Rep. of S.Africa   28 45S 24 46E   55
Kimberley: *geog. reg.*, W.A., Australia   16 30S 126 45E   14 40
Kimch'aek (Sŏngjin): N.Korea   40 41N 129 12E   37 105
Kimkan: U.S.S.R.   48 58N 131 26E   105
Kimovsk: U.S.S.R.   53 58N 38 32E   80

Types of map: Ocean pp. 1-5; Physical pp. 6-25; Human pp. 26-57; Topographic pp. 58-101; World pp. 102-111; Urban pp. 112-128.

Kimry: U.S.S.R.   56 52N 37 21E   80
Kinabalu, *Mount*: Malaysia   06 03N 116 32E   12 39
Kinale, *Lough*: Long., Irish Republic   53 45N 07 15W   66
Kinbrace: Suther., Scotland   58 15N 03 56W   65
Kincardineshire: *admin.*, Scotland   56 45N 02 30W   65
Kinder Scout: *mtn.*, Derby., England   53 23N 01 52W   58
Kindu-Port-Empain: Zaïre   02 57S 25 56E   54
Kinel': U.S.S.R.   53 14N 50 39E   81
Kinel'skije Gory: *mtns.*, U.S.S.R.   54 00N 53 00E   81
Kinešma: U.S.S.R.   57 26N 42 09E   80
Kineton: War., England   52 10N 01 30W   59
King George's *Reservoir*: England   51 30N 00 00   112
Kingisepp: Estonskaja S.S.R., U.S.S.R.   58 12N 22 30E   75
Kingman: Ariz., U.S.A.   35 12N 114 04W   91
Kingman: Kans., U.S.A.   37 39N 98 07W   95
King of Prussia: Pa., U.S.A.   40 05N 75 23W   122
Kings: *riv.*, Irish Republic   52 30N 07 15W   67
Kingsbridge: Devon, England   50 17N 03 46W   61
Kings Canyon *National Park*: Calif., U.S.A.
   36 45N 118 30W   91
Kingsclere: Hants., England   51 20N 01 14W   59
Kingscourt: Cavan., Irish Republic   53 55N 06 48W   66
Kingsgrove: N.S.W., Australia   33 57S 151 06E   120
Kingsley *Dam*: Nebr., U.S.A.   41 15N 101 40W   94
King's Lynn: Norf., England   52 45N 00 24E   58
Kings *Peak*: Utah, U.S.A.   40 46N 110 23W   91
Kingsport: Tenn., U.S.A.   36 33N 82 34W   101
Kingstanding: W.Mid., England   52 32N 01 54W   115
Kingston: Ont., Canada   44 14N 76 30W   44 99
Kingston: Jamaica   17 58N 76 48W   47
Kingston: N.Y., U.S.A.   41 55N 74 00W   99
Kingston-upon-Hull (Hull): Yorks., England
   53 45N 00 20W   26 63
Kingston upon Thames: Surrey, England   51 25N 00 17W
   112
Kingstree: S.C., U.S.A.   33 40N 79 50W   101
Kingsville: Tex., U.S.A.   27 32N 97 53W   100
Kingswood: Avon, England   51 27N 02 22W   61 113
Kington: Here. & Worcs., England   52 12N 03 01W   60
Kingussie: Inv., Scotland   57 05N 04 04W   65
Kinlochewe: R.& Crom., Scotland   57 36N 05 18W   64
Kinlochleven: Inv., Scotland   56 43N 04 58W   64
Kinnairds *Head*: Aber., Scotland   57 42N 02 00W   65
Kinross: Kinr., Scotland   56 13N 03 27W   65
Kinross-shire: *admin.*, Scotland   56 00N 03 15W   65
Kinsale: Cork, Irish Republic   51 42N 08 32W   67
Kinsale, *Old Head of*: Cork, Irish Republic   51 36N 08 32W
   67
Kinsarvik: Norway   60 22N 06 44E   75
Kinshasa (Léopoldville): Zaïre   04 18S 15 18E   21 54
Kinston: N.C., U.S.A.   35 15N 77 34W   101
Kintampo: Ghana   08 06N 01 40W   57
Kintore: Aber., Scotland   57 14N 02 21W   65
Kintyre: *pen.*, Argyll., Scotland   55 30N 05 30W   62
Kintyre, Mull of: *cape*, Argyll., Scotland   55 18N 05 45W   62
Kinuso: Alta., Canada   55 22N 115 20W   92
Kipawa *Lake*: Qué., Canada   46 45N 79 00W   99
Kipling: Sask., Canada   50 08N 102 40W   92
Kippokok: Nfld., Canada   55 05N 59 35W   97
Kippure: *mtn.*, Dublin, Irish Republic   53 11N 06 20W   67
Kirbymoorside: N.Yorks., England   54 16N 00 55W   63
Kirchheim unter Teck: W.Germany   48 39N 09 28E   72
Kirchhörde: W.Germany   51 27N 07 27E   118
Kirensk: U.S.S.R.   57 46N 108 08E   30
Kirgiz S.S.R.: *admin.*, U.S.S.R.   41 30N 74 00E   29
Kirin *see* Jilin   43 51N 126 33E   37 105
Kirin: *admin. see* Jilin   43 30N 127 00E   37
Kirkby: Mers., England   53 29N 02 54W   63 114
Kirkby in Ashfield: Notts., England   53 06N 01 16W   58
Kirkby Lonsdale: Cumbria, England   54 13N 02 36W   63
Kirkby Stephen: Cumbria, England   54 28N 02 20W   63
Kirkcaldy: Fife, Scotland   56 07N 03 10W   65
Kirkcudbright: Kirkc., Scotland   54 50N 04 03W   62
Kirkcudbrightshire: *admin.*, Scotland   55 00N 04 00W   62
Kirkenes: Norway   69 41N 30 05E   27 74 105
Kirkham: Lancs., England   53 47N 02 53W   63 114
Kirkheaton: W.Yorks., England   53 39N 01 44W   115
Kirkintilloch: Dumb., Scotland   55 57N 04 10W   62 113
Kirkland: Wash., U.S.A.   47 41N 122 13W   126
Kirkland Lake: Ont., Canada   48 10N 80 02W   44 99 104
Kirklareli: Turkey   41 45N 27 12E   79

Kirksville: Mo., U.S.A.   40 12N 92 35W   98
Kirkūk: Iraq   35 28N 44 26E   33
Kirkwall: Ork. Is., Scotland   58 59N 02 58W   65
Kirov: U.S.S.R.   58 33N 49 42E   28 80
Kirov: U.S.S.R.   54 05N 34 20E   81
Kirovabad: U.S.S.R.   40 40N 46 22E   28
Kirovaken: U.S.S.R.   40 48N 44 30E   28
Kirovo Čepeck: U.S.S.R.   58 33N 50 01E   81
Kirovograd: U.S.S.R.   48 30N 32 18E   28 80
Kirovsk: U.S.S.R.   67 37N 33 39E   74
Kirriemuir: Angus, Scotland   56 41N 03 01W   65
Kirs: U.S.S.R.   59 21N 52 14E   81
Kirsanov: U.S.S.R.   52 38N 42 43E   80
Kīrthar *Range*: Pakistan   26 00N 67 30E   34
Kirti Nagar: India   28 39N 77 09E   120
Kirton in Lindsey: Humb., England   52 56N 00 04W   63
Kiruna: Sweden   67 53N 20 15E   27 74
Kiryū: Japan   36 24N 139 20E   86
Kisangani (Stanleyville): Zaïre   00 30N 25 12E   54
Kisarazu: Japan   35 23N 139 55E   86 121
Kisel'ovsk (Kiselëvsk): U.S.S.R.   54 00N 86 39E   30
Kishanganj: India   26 06N 87 57E   83
Kishinëv *see* Kišin'ov   47 00N 28 50E   28 78
Kishiwada: Japan   34 28N 135 22E   37 86
Kishorganj: Bangladesh   24 26N 90 46E   83
Kišin'ov (Kishinëv): U.S.S.R.   47 00N 28 50E   28 78
Kiskunfélegyháza: Hungary   46 41N 19 51E   78
Kislovodsk: U.S.S.R.   43 55N 42 44E   28
Kismayu (Chisimaio): Somali Rep.   00 25S 42 31E   53
Kissimmee: *riv.*, Fla., U.S.A.   27 15N 81 00W   101
Kississing *Lake*: Man., Canada   55 00N 101 15W   92
Kisumu: Kenya   00 03S 34 47E   54
Kita: Japan   35 46N 139 43E   121
Kitaibaraki: Japan   36 48N 140 45E   86
Kitakyūshū: Japan   33 53N 130 50E   37 86 105
Kitale: Kenya   01 01N 35 01E   54
Kitami: Japan   43 48N 143 54E   87
Kitchener: Ont., Canada   43 27N 80 30W   45 99
Kíthira: *is.*, Greece   36 15N 22 45E   79
Kíthnos: *is.*, Greece   37 25N 24 25E   79
Kitimat: B.C., Canada   54 05N 128 38W   42 89
Kitwe: Zambia   12 49S 28 15E   54
Kitzbühel: Austria   47 27N 12 23E   73
Kitzingen: W.Germany   49 45N 10 11E   73
Kiviöli: U.S.S.R.   59 21N 26 57E   80
Kivu, *Lake*: Rwanda/Zaïre   02 00S 29 00E   54
Kizel: U.S.S.R.   59 03N 57 40E   29 81
Kızıl Irmak: *riv.*, Turkey   40 45N 34 00E   32
Kizil Khoto *see* Kyzyl   51 42N 94 27E   30
Kjølen *Mountains*: Norway/Sweden   27 74
Kjustendil: Bulgaria   42 17N 22 41E   79
Kladno: Czechoslovakia   50 10N 14 05E   73 105
Klagenfurt: Austria   46 38N 14 20E   78
Klaipėda (Memel): U.S.S.R.   55 43N 21 07E   28 75
Klamath: *riv.*, U.S.A.   41 15N 123 45W   90
Klamath Falls: Oreg., U.S.A.   42 14N 121 47W   43 90
Klamono: Indonesia   01 08S 131 28E   39
Klarälven: *riv.*, Sweden   60 30N 13 15E   75
Klatovy: Czechoslovakia   49 24N 13 20E   73
Kleine-Emscher: *can.*, W.Germany   51 30N 06 45E   118
Klemtu: B.C., Canada   52 36N 128 31W   89
Klerksdorp: Trans., Rep. of S.Africa   26 52S 26 39E   55
Klibreck, Ben: *mtn.*, Suther., Scotland   58 15N 04 22W   64
Klimovsk: U.S.S.R.   55 22N 37 32E   80
Klin: U.S.S.R.   56 20N 36 44E   80
Klincy: U.S.S.R.   52 47N 32 14E   80
Kłodzko: Poland   50 28N 16 40E   73
Klondike: *riv.*, Yukon, Canada   64 00N 137 45W   88
Klondike *Region*: Canada/U.S.A.   64 00N 141 00W   22
Klong: *riv.*, Thailand   14 45N 99 15E   35
Klosterneuburg: Austria   48 19N 16 20E   73
Klosters: Switzerland   46 54N 09 54E   71
Kluane: Yukon, Canada   60 59N 138 22W   88
Kluane *Lake*: Yukon, Canada   61 00N 138 45W   88
Klukwan: Alaska, U.S.A.   59 24N 135 54W   88
Knap, *Point of*: Argyll., Scotland   55 53N 05 41W   62
Knapdale: *dist.*, Argyll., Scotland   55 45N 05 30W   62
Knapsack: W.Germany   50 52N 06 51E   119
Knaresborough: N.Yorks., England   54 00N 01 27W   63
Knee *Lake*: Man., Canada   55 00N 94 30W   93
Knife: *riv.*, N.D., U.S.A.   47 00N 102 15W   94

Types of map: Ocean pp. 1-5; Physical pp. 6-25; Human pp. 26-57; Topographic pp. 58-101; World pp. 102-111; Urban pp. 112-128.

Knight *Inlet*: B.C., Canada   50 45N 125 30W   89
Knighton: Powys, Wales   52 21N 03 03W   60
Knob Lake *see* Schefferville   54 50N 67 00W   44 96 104
Knob Lake Junction: Nfld., Canada   54 50N 67 00W   97
Knockadoon *Head*: Cork, Irish Republic   51 53N 07 52W   67
Knockboy: *mtn.*, Cork, Irish republic   51 48N 09 27W   67
Knockmealdown *Mountains*: Irish Republic
  52 00N 07 45W   67
Knottingley: W.Yorks., England   53 43N 01 14W   63 115
Knowle: Avon, England   51 26N 02 34W   113
Knox, *Cape*: B.C., Canada   54 09N 133 05W   89
Knoxville: Tenn., U.S.A.   36 00N 83 57W   45 101
Knutsford: Ches., England   53 18N 02 23W   58 114
Kobar Sink: *depression*, Ethiopia   14 00N 40 00E   21 53
Kōbe: Japan   34 41N 135 10E   86 105
København (Copenhagen): Denmark   55 43N 12 34E
  26 75 105
Koblenz: W.Germany   50 21N 07 36E   72
Kobrin: U.S.S.R.   52 16N 24 22E   78
Kōchi: Japan   33 33N 133 33E   37 86
Kochiu *see* Gejiu   23 22N 103 06E   36
Kodaira: Japan   35 44N 139 30E   121
Kodiak *Island*: Alaska, U.S.A.   57 30N 153 00W   16
Koforidua: China   06 01N 00 12W   57
Kōfu: Japan   35 39N 138 35E   86
Kogane: Japan   35 49N 139 56E   121
Koganei: Japan   35 43N 139 28E   121
Kohtla-Järve: U.S.S.R.   59 24N 27 15E   80
Koito: *riv.*, Japan   35 19N 139 54E   121
Kokand: U.S.S.R.   40 33N 70 57E   29
Kokčetav (Kokchetav): U.S.S.R.   53 17N 69 25E   29
Kokkola: Finland   63 50N 23 07E   74
Kokomo: Ind., U.S.A.   40 30N 86 09W   98
Koko Nor *see* Qinghai   37 00N 100 30E   36
Kola: *riv.*, U.S.S.R.   68 30N 35 30E   74
Kolaka: Indonesia   04 04S 121 38E   39
Kola *Peninsula*: U.S.S.R.   68 00N 35 00E   8 74
Kolāras: India   25 14N 77 36E   82
Kolar *Gold Fields*: India   11 00N 79 00E   34
Kol'čugino: U.S.S.R.   56 18N 39 23E   80
Kolding: Denmark   55 29N 09 30E   75
Kolhāpur: India   16 42N 74 13E   34
Köln (Cologne): W.Germany   50 56N 06 57E   26 72 107 119
Kołobrzeg: Poland   54 10N 15 35E   73
Kologriv: U.S.S.R.   58 51N 44 17E   80
Kolomna: U.S.S.R.   55 05N 38 49E   28 80
Kolomyja: U.S.S.R.   48 32N 25 04E   78
Kolpin, Staatsforst: *for.*, E.Germany   52 15N 13 45E   117
Kolpino: U.S.S.R.   59 45N 30 36E   80
Kolwezi: Zaïre   10 43S 25 28E   54
Kolyma: *riv.*, U.S.S.R.   67 45N 154 30E   9 31
Kolyma *Plain*: U.S.S.R.   69 00N 157 00E   9 31
Kolyvan': U.S.S.R.   51 18N 82 34E   29
Komae: Japan   35 37N 139 35E   121
Komárno: Czechoslovakia   47 46N 18 07E   78
Kommunarsk (Voroshilovsk): U.S.S.R.   48 30N 38 47E
  80 105
Komotiní: Greece   41 06N 25 25E   79
Kompasberg: mtn., C.P., Rep of S.Africa   31 45S 24 32E   55
Komrat: U.S.S.R.   46 18N 28 38E   78
Komsomol'sk-na-Amure: U.S.S.R.   50 35N 137 02E   31 105
Konakovo: U.S.S.R.   56 42N 36 46E   80
Konch: India   25 59N 79 08E   82
Kondagaon: India   19 36N 81 40E   83
Kondrovo: U.S.S.R.   54 48N 35 56E   80
Kongolo: Zaïre   05 23S 27 00E   54
Kongsberg: Norway   59 42N 09 39E   75
Kongsvinger: Norway   60 13N 11 59E   75
Königsberg *see* Kaliningrad   54 43N 20 30E   28 78
Königsforst, Staatsforst: *for.*, W.Germany   50 45N 07 00E
  119
Königsheide: *heath*, E.Germany   52 27N 13 28E   117
Konnagar: India   22 42N 88 22E   120
Konotop: U.S.S.R.   51 14N 33 12E   28 80
Konstantinovka: U.S.S.R.   48 32N 37 43E   80 105
Konstanz (Constance): W.Germany   47 40N 09 10E   71
Kontagora: Nigeria   10 24N 05 22E   57
Kontum: S.Vietnam   14 23N 108 00E   38
Konya: Turkey   37 51N 32 30E   32
Konžakovskij Kamen', Gora: *mtn.*, U.S.S.R.   59 38N 59 08E
  81

Koolan *Island*: Australia   16 08S 123 45E   105
Koolyanobbing: W.A., Australia   30 48S 119 43E   105
Kootenai: *riv.*, Canada/U.S.A.   48 45N 116 15W   90
Kootenai Falls *Dam*: Mont., U.S.A.   48 31N 116 00W   90
Kootenay: *riv.*, B.C., Canada   49 45N 115 45W   90
Kootenay *National Park*: B.C., Canada   50 30N 116 00W   90
Kopejsk: U.S.S.R.   55 07N 61 37E   81
Köpenick: E.Germany   52 27N 13 36E   117
Köping: Sweden   59 31N 16 01E   75
Koppang: Norway   61 34N 11 04E   74
Koppeh Dāgh: *mtns.*, Iran   37 30N 58 45E   33
Kor'ak (Koryak) *Range*: U.S.S.R.   61 30N 169 00E   9
Koraluk: *riv.*, Nfld., Canada   56 00N 63 00W   97
Korat *Plateau*: Thailand   15 00N 101 30E   38
Korba: India   22 22N 82 46E   83
Korbach: W.Germany   51 16N 08 53E   72
Korçë (Koritsa): Albania   40 38N 20 44E   79
Korea *Bay*: China/N.Korea   38 45N 123 30E   37
Korhogo: Ivory Coast   09 22N 05 31W   57
Kórinthos (Corinth): Greece   37 56N 22 55E   79
Koritsa *see* Korçë   40 38N 20 44E   79
Kōriyama: Japan   37 24N 140 23E   37 86
Korkino: U.S.S.R.   54 54N 61 23E   81
Korogwe: Tanzania   05 10S 38 30E   54
Koromo *see* Toyota   35 05N 137 09E   37 86
Korosten': U.S.S.R.   50 57N 28 39E   28 78
Kortrijk (Courtrai): Belgium   50 50N 03 17E   72
Koryak *Range see* Kor'ak *Range*   61 30N 169 00E   9
Kos (Cos): *is.*, Greece   36 45N 27 00E   79
Kosaja Gora: U.S.S.R.   54 07N 37 33E   105
Kościan: Poland   52 05N 16 38E   73
Kościerzyna: Poland   54 08N 17 58E   73
Kosciusko, *Mount*: N.S.W., Australia   36 28S 148 17E
  15 41
Koshiki-rettō: *arch.*, Japan   31 45N 129 45E   86
Kosi: *riv.*, India   26 00N 86 30E   83
Košice: Czechoslovakia   48 43N 21 14E   27 78
Kosino: U.S.S.R.   55 43N 37 52E   119
Kosmosdale: Ky., U.S.A.   38 02N 85 54W   101
Kosovska Mitrovica: Yugoslavia   42 54N 20 52E   79
Kosti *see* Küstī   13 10N 32 40E   53
Kostroma: U.S.S.R.   57 46N 40 55E   29 80
Koszalin: Poland   54 10N 16 10E   73 78
Koszalin: *admin.*, Poland   54 00N 16 30E   73
Kota: India   25 11N 75 58E   34 82
Kota Baharu: Malaysia   06 07N 102 15E   38
Kotabaru *see* Djajapura   02 32S 140 42E   13
Kota Kinabalu (Jesselton): Malaysia   05 59N 116 04E   39
Kotcho *Lake*: B.C., Canada   59 05N 121 10W   88
Kotel'nič: U.S.S.R.   58 18N 48 20E   81
Kotel'nikovo: U.S.S.R.   47 38N 43 09E   80
Köthen: E.Germany   51 46N 11 59E   73
Kotka: Finland   60 26N 26 55E   27 75
Kot Kapūra: India   30 35N 74 44E   82
Kotlas: U.S.S.R.   61 16N 46 35E   29
Koto: Japan   35 40N 139 48E   121
Kotovo: U.S.S.R.   50 18N 44 50E   80
Kotovsk: U.S.S.R.   52 36N 41 32E   80
Kottagūdem: India   17 32N 80 39E   34
Kouroussa: Guinea   10 40N 09 50W   57
Kouvola: Finland   60 54N 26 45E   75
Kouzhangmiao: China   31 11N 121 25E   121
Kovdor: U.S.S.R.   67 34N 30 28E   105
Kovel': U.S.S.R.   51 12N 24 48E   28 78
Kovno *see* Kaunas   54 52N 23 55E   28 75
Kovrov: U.S.S.R.   56 25N 41 18E   28 80
Kovylkino: U.S.S.R.   54 02N 43 56E   80
Kowary: Poland   50 49N 15 51E   73
Kowloon (Jiulong): Hong Kong   22 21N 114 15E   36 85
Kozáni: Greece   40 18N 21 48E   79
Koz'modemjansk: U.S.S.R.   56 20N 46 36E   81
Kōzu-shima: *is.*, Japan   34 13N 139 10E   86
Kra, *Isthmus of*: Burma/Thailand   10 30N 99 00E   12 35
Kra Buri: Thailand   10 25N 98 48E   35
Kragerø: Norway   58 54N 09 25E   75
Kragujevac: Yugoslavia   44 01N 20 55E   27 79
Krakatau (Krakatoa): *is.*, Indonesia   06 15S 105 30E   38
Kraków (Cracow): Poland   50 04N 19 57E   27 78 105
Kraljevo: Yugoslavia   43 44N 20 41E   79
Kralupy: Czechoslovakia   50 14N 14 19E   73
Kramatorsk: U.S.S.R.   48 43N 37 32E   28 80 105

Kramfors: Sweden 62 55N 17 50E 74
Krasnoarmejsk: U.S.S.R. 56 08N 38 08E 80
Krasnoarmejsk: U.S.S.R. 51 02N 45 42E 81
Krasnodar: U.S.S.R. 45 02N 39 00E 28
Krasnodon: U.S.S.R. 48 17N 39 48E 80
Krasnogorsk: U.S.S.R. 55 50N 37 20E 80 119
Krasnogorskij: U.S.S.R. 54 36N 61 15E 81
Krasnograd: U.S.S.R. 49 22N 35 27E 80
Krasnojarsk (Krasnoyarsk): U.S.S.R. 56 01N 92 50E 30
Krasnokamsk: U.S.S.R. 58 04N 55 48E 81
Krasnoturjinsk: U.S.S.R. 59 46N 60 12E 81
Krasnoufimsk: U.S.S.R. 56 37N 57 46E 81
Krasnoural'sk: U.S.S.R. 58 21N 60 03E 81
Krasnousol'skij: U.S.S.R. 53 54N 56 27E 81
Krasnovišersk: U.S.S.R. 60 23N 56 59E 81
Krasnovodsk: U.S.S.R. 40 00N 53 00E 28
Krasnyj Cholm: U.S.S.R. 58 03N 37 07E 80
Krasnyj Gul'aj: U.S.S.R. 54 01N 48 22E 81
Krasnyj Kut: U.S.S.R. 50 57N 46 58E 81
Krasnyj Liman: U.S.S.R. 48 59N 37 49E 80
Krasnyj Luč: R.S.F.S.R., U.S.S.R. 57 04N 30 05E 80
Krasnyj Luč: Ukrainskaja S.S.R., U.S.S.R. 48 08N 38 56E 80
Krasnyj Sulin: U.S.S.R. 47 54N 40 03E 80 105
Kratie: Khmer Rep. 12 30N 106 03E 38
Krefeld: W.Germany 51 20N 06 32E 72 105 118
Kremenčug (Kremenchug): U.S.S.R. 49 04N 33 25E 28 80 107
Kremenčugskoje Vodochranilišče: *res.*, U.S.S.R. 49 15N 32 30E 80
Kremenec: U.S.S.R. 50 07N 25 45E 78
Kremennaja: U.S.S.R. 49 03N 38 14E 80
Kremges: U.S.S.R. 49 04N 33 15E 80
Krems: Austria 48 25N 15 36E 73 78
Kribi: Cameroun 02 56N 09 56E 57
Kričov: U.S.S.R. 53 42N 31 43E 80
Krishna: *riv.*, India 16 00N 78 45E 10 34
Krishnanagar: India 23 22N 88 32E 35 83
Kristiansand: Norway 58 08N 08 01E 26 75
Kristianstad: Sweden 56 02N 14 08E 75
Kristiansund: Norway 63 06N 07 58E 74
Kristinehamn: Sweden 59 17N 14 09E 75
Kríti (Crete): *is. & Greek admin.*, Mediterranean Sea 35 00N 25 00E 7 27 78
Krivoj Rog (Krivoy Rog): U.S.S.R. 47 55N 33 21E 28 80 105
Krk, Otok: *is.*, Yugoslavia 45 02N 14 34E 78
Krnov: Czechoslovakia 50 05N 17 40E 73
Krokonoše: *mtns.*, Czechoslovakia/Poland 50 45N 15 45E 73 78
Kroměříž: Czechoslovakia 49 19N 17 27E 73
Kronštadt: U.S.S.R. 60 00N 29 40E 75
Kroonstad: O.F.S., Rep. of S.Africa 27 40S 27 15E 55
Kropotkin: U.S.S.R. 45 26N 40 34E 28
Krotoszyn: Poland 51 41N 17 27E 73
Krugersdorp: Trans., Rep. of S.Africa 26 06S 27 46E 55
Krumovo: Bulgaria 42 16N 26 24E 105
Krung Thep (Bangkok, Phra Nakhon): Thailand 13 44N 100 30E 35
Kruševac: Yugoslavia 43 34N 21 20E 79
Kruzof *Island*: Alaska, U.S.A. 57 10N 135 40W 89
Ksar el Boukhari: Algeria 35 51N 02 52E 77
Ksar es Souk: Morocco 31 58N 04 25W 56
Kuala Dungun: Malaysia 04 45N 103 24E 38
Kuala Lumpur: Malaysia 03 08N 101 42E 38
Kuala Terengganu: Malaysia 05 20N 103 07E 38
Kuangchou: *admin. see* Guangzhou 23 08N 113 16E 36 85 105
Kuanghsichuangtsu *see* Guanxi Zhuang 24 30N 109 00E 36 85
Kuanghua *see* Guanghua 32 21N 111 39E 36 84
Kuangtung: *admin. see* Guangdong 23 45N 113 45E 36 85
Kuantan: Malaysia 03 50N 103 19E 38
Kubenskoje, Ozero: *lake*, U.S.S.R. 59 45N 39 30E 80
Kubiri: Japan 35 14N 139 43E 121
Kuchāman: India 27 10N 74 54E 82
Kuching: Malaysia 01 32N 110 20E 38
Kučino: U.S.S.R. 55 45N 37 58E 119
Kudat: Malaysia 06 54N 116 47E 39
Kudymkar: U.S.S.R. 59 01N 54 37E 81
Kueichou *see* Guizhou 27 30N 107 45E 36 85
Kueilin *see* Guilin 25 24N 110 11E 36 85
Kueiyang *see* Guiyang 26 38N 106 38E 36 85 105
Kufra *Oases*: Libya 24 45N 23 15E 32
Kufstein: Austria 47 36N 12 11E 73
Kuhmo: Finland 64 04N 29 30E 74
Kujbyšev (Kuybyshev): U.S.S.R. 53 12N 50 09E 28 81 107
Kujbyševskij Zaton: U.S.S.R. 55 09N 49 12E 81
Kujbyševskoje Vodochranilišče: *res.*, U.S.S.R. 54 30N 48 45E 81
Kula Kangri: *mtn.*, China 28 14N 90 37E 83
Kuldīga: U.S.S.R. 56 58N 21 58E 75
Kuldja *see* Yining 43 55N 81 14E 29
Kulebaki: U.S.S.R. 45 24N 42 32E 80
Kulmbach: W.Germany 50 06N 11 28E 73
Kul'sary: U.S.S.R. 46 59N 54 01E 81
Kulti: India 23 45N 86 50E 83
Kulunda *Steppe*: U.S.S.R. 52 00N 78 00E 8 29
Kumagaya: Japan 36 08N 139 23E 86
Kumamoto: Japan 32 48N 130 43E 37 86
Kumasi: Ghana 06 45N 01 35W 57
Kumbakonam: India 10 59N 79 24E 34
Kumertau: U.S.S.R. 52 46N 55 47E 29 81
Kumla: Sweden 59 08N 15 09E 75
Kunašir, Ostrov: *Is.*, Kuril Is., U.S.S.R. 44 00N 145 45E 87
Kunc'ovo: U.S.S.R. 55 44N 37 26E 119
Kunene (Cunene): *riv.*, Angola/S.W.Africa 17 15S 13 00E 21 55
Kungälv: Sweden 57 54N 12 00E 75
Kunghit *Island*: B.C., Canada 52 02N 131 02W 89
Kungka Shan *see* Gonggashan 29 35N 101 51E 36
Kungur: U.S.S.R. 57 25N 56 57E 81
Kuningan: Indonesia 07 02S 108 30E 38
Kunlun *Range*: China 35 45N 94 00E 11
Kunming: China 25 05N 102 40E 36
Kunminghu: *lake*, China 39 59N 116 16E 121
Kunsan: S.Korea 35 58N 126 41E 37
Kunshan: China 31 20N 121 00E 84
Kuocangshan: *mtns.*, China 28 30N 120 45E 85
Kuopio: Finland 62 51N 27 30E 27 74
Kup'ansk: U.S.S.R. 49 42N 37 38E 80
Kupferdreh: W.Germany 51 23N 07 05E 118
Kurashiki: Japan 34 35N 133 46E 86
Kuraymah (Kareima): Sudan 18 33N 31 51E 32
Kurdistan: *geog. reg.*, Iran/Turkey 37 00N 45 00E 10 33
Kure: Japan 34 14N 132 34E 37 86 105
Kurgan: U.S.S.R. 55 26N 65 18E 29
Kurikka: Finland 62 36N 22 25E 74
Kuril *Islands*: U.S.S.R. 47 00N 152 00E 22
Kuril *Ridge*: Sea of Okhotsk 47 00N 150 00E 4
Kuril (Kuril-Kamchatka) *Trench*: N.Pacific Ocean 45 00N 155 00E 4
Ku-ring-gai Chase *National Park*: N.S.W., Australia 33 40S 151 12E 120
Kurisches Haff: *lag. see* Kurskij Zaliv 55 00N 21 00E 75
Kurnell: N.S.W., Australia 34 01S 151 12E 120
Kurnool: India 15 51N 78 01E 34
Kuro Siwo *Current*: N.Pacific Ocean 37 00N 155 00E 4
Kursk: U.S.S.R. 51 42N 36 12E 28 80
Kurskij Zaliv (Kurisches Haff): *lag.*, U.S.S.R. 55 00N 21 00E 75
Kuruman: C.P., Rep. of S.Africa 27 28S 23 27E 104
Kurume: Japan 33 19N 130 31E 86
Kusawa *Lake*: Yukon, Canada 60 15N 136 00W 88
Kushiro: Japan 42 58N 144 23E 37 87
Kushtia: Bangladesh 23 54N 89 07E 83
Kuskokwim *Mountains*: Alaska, U.S.A. 61 45N 156 30W 16
Kusma: Nepal 28 14N 83 41E 83
Kustanaj (Kustanay): U.S.S.R. 53 10N 63 35E 29
Kūstī (Kosti): Sudan 13 10N 32 40E 53
Kušum: *riv.*, U.S.S.R. 50 15N 50 30E 81
Kušva: U.S.S.R. 58 18N 59 45E 81
Kütahya: Turkey 39 25N 29 56E 32
Kutaisi: U.S.S.R. 42 15N 42 40E 28
Kūt al-Imāra (Al-Kūt): Iraq 32 25N 45 49E 33
Kutch, *Gulf of*: India 22 30N 69 30E 10 34
Kutch, Little Rann of: *geog. reg.*, India 23 15N 71 15E 82
Kutch, Rann of: *geog. reg.*, India 24 00N 70 00E 11 34 82
Kutná Hora: Czechoslovakia 49 58N 15 18E 73
Kutno: Poland 52 13N 19 20E 78
Kuusamo: Finland 65 57N 29 15E 74
Kuusankoski: Finland 60 55N 26 42E 75

Types of map: Ocean pp. 1-5; Physical pp. 6-25; Human pp. 26-57; Topographic pp. 58-101; World pp. 102-111; Urban pp. 112-128.

Kuvandyk: U.S.S.R. 51 28N 57 21E   81
KUWAIT 29 30N 47 30E   10 33 107
Kuwait *see* Al Kuwayt 29 20N 48 00E   33
Kuybyshev *see* Kujbyšev 53 12N 50 09E   28 81 107
Kuzbass: *reg.,* U.S.S.R. 54 15N 86 00E   9 30
Kuz'minki: U.S.S.R. 55 42N 37 48E   119
Kuzneck (Kuznetsk): U.S.S.R. 53 07N 46 36E   81
Kvaløy: *is.,* Norway 70 35N 23 50E   74
Kvalsund: Norway 70 30N 24 00E   74
Kvarnerić: *gulf,* Yugoslavia 44 30N 14 45E   79
Kwando: *riv. see* Cuando 15 15S 21 30E   21 55
Kwangju: S.Korea 35 09N 126 54E   37
Kwanmo-bong: *mtn.,* N.Korea 41 42N 129 13E   37
Kweichow *Plateau see* Guizhou *Plateau* 25 45N 106 30E   12 36
Kweisui *see* Huhehaote 40 48N 111 40E   36 84
Kwoka, *Mount:* Indonesia 00 40S 132 24E   13
Kyle of Durness: *sea loch,* Suther., Scotland 58 30N 04 45W   64
Kyle of Lochalsh: R. & Crom., Scotland 57 17N 05 43W   64
Kyle of Tongue: *sea loch,* Suther., Scotland 58 30N 04 15W   64
Kyoga, *Lake:* Uganda 01 30N 32 45E   21 53
Kyōga-saki: *cape,* Japan 35 46N 135 13E   86
Kyŏmip'o *see* Songnim 38 44N 125 38E   105
Kyŏngju: S.Korea 35 51N 129 14E   37
Kyŏngsŏng *see* Sŏul 37 33N 126 58E   37
Kyōto: Japan 35 00N 135 45E   37 86
Kyštym: U.S.S.R. 55 42N 60 34E   81
Kyūshū: *is.,* Japan 33 00N 131 00E   12 37 86
Kyushu Palau *Ridge:* Philippine Sea 20 00N 136 00E   4
Kyūshū-sanchi: *mtns.,* Japan 32 30N 131 00E   86
Kyzyl (Kizil Khoto): U.S.S.R. 51 42N 94 27E   30
Kyzylkum: *des.,* U.S.S.R. 43 00N 64 00E   8 29
Kzyl-Orda: U.S.S.R. 44 48N 65 28E   29

Labe: *riv.,* Czechoslovakia 50 00N 15 30E   73
Laberge, *Lake:* Yukon, Canada 61 00N 135 00W   88
La Boca: Argentina 34 39S 58 21W   128
Labrador: *reg.,* Nfld., Canada 54 00N 62 00W   44
Labrador Basin: N.Atlantic Ocean 59 00N 53 00W   2 23
Labrador City: Nfld., Canada 52 54N 66 50W   44 97
Labrador Current: N.Atlantic Ocean 54 00N 55 00W   2
Labrador Peninsula: Canada   16 44 96
Labuan: *is.,* Malaysia 05 30N 115 15E   39
La Canada: Calif., U.S.A. 34 12N 118 12W   126
Laccadive *Islands:* Indian Ocean 11 00N 72 30E   1 11 34
Laccadive *Sea* 10 15N 74 45E   34
La Ceiba: Honduras 15 47N 86 50W   47
Lachen *Reservoir:* Wick., Irish Republic 53 00N 06 30W   67
Lachhmangarh: India 27 48N 75 06E   82
Lachine: Qué., Canada 45 27N 73 41W   122
Lachlan: *riv.,* N.S.W., Australia 34 00S 144 30E   15 41
Lachta: U.S.S.R. 60 00N 30 09E   119
La Ciotat: France 43 10N 05 36E   71
Lackawanna: N.Y., U.S.A. 42 49N 78 49W   104
Lac La Biche: Alta., Canada 54 46N 111 59W   92
Lac la Hache: B.C., Canada 51 50N 121 29W   89
Lac la Ronge *Provincial Park:* Sask., Canada 55 00N 104 00W   92
Lac-Mégantic: Qué., Canada 45 34N 70 53W   96
La Columna: *pk. see* Bolívar, Pico 08 35N 71 02W   48
Lacombe: Alta., Canada 52 30N 113 42W   92
Laconia: N.H., U.S.A. 43 32N 71 29W   99
Lacorne: Qué., Canada 48 22N 78 00W   99
La Coruña (Corunna): Spain 43 22N 08 24W   26 77
La Crosse: Wis., U.S.A. 43 48N 91 04W   98
Lacroze: Argentina 34 35S 58 27W   128
La Cumbre *Pass see* Uspallata *Pass* 32 43S 69 24W   52
Ladakh *Range:* India 32 30N 78 30E   34
Ladoga, *Lake:* U.S.S.R. 61 00N 31 00E   8 28 74
La Dorada: Colombia 05 28N 74 43W   48
Ladybank: Fife, Scotland 56 17N 03 08W   65
Ladysmith: B.C., Canada 49 00N 123 49W   89
Ladysmith: Natal, Rep. of S.Africa 28 34S 29 47E   55
Lae; New Guinea 06 45S 147 00E   15
Lærdalsøyri: Norway 61 06N 07 28E   75
Læsø: *is.,* Denmark 57 15N 11 00E   75

Lafayette: Calif., U.S.A. 37 53N 122 07W   126
Lafayette: Ind., U.S.A. 40 25N 86 54W   98
Lafayette: La., U.S.A. 30 14N 92 01W   43 100
Lafayette: Mich., U.S.A. 42 20N 83 01W   125
Lafayette *Reservoir:* Calif., U.S.A. 37 52N 122 08W   126
Laferrere: Argentina 34 45S 58 35W   128
Lafia: Nigeria 08 30N 08 34E   57
La Flèche: France 47 42N 00 04W   70
La Florida: Spain 41 31N 02 12E   116
Lagan: *riv.,* N.Ireland 54 30N 05 45W   66
Lagechi: *lake,* China 30 45N 81 00E   82
Lågen: *riv.,* Norway 61 45N 09 45E   74
Laggan, *Loch:* Inv., Scotland 56 45N 04 30W   64
Lagos: Nigeria 06 27N 03 28E   57
La Grande: Oreg., U.S.A. 45 20N 118 05W   90
La Grange: Ga., U.S.A. 33 02N 85 02W   101
La Grange: Ill., U.S.A. 41 47N 87 53W   124
La Guaira: Venezuela 10 38N 66 55W   48
La Guardia: Spain 41 54N 08 53W   77
Lagunillas: Venezuela 10 07N 71 16W   48
La Habana (Havana): Cuba 23 08N 82 22W   47
Lahad Datu: Malaysia 05 01N 118 20E   39
Lahij: Yemen D.R. 13 02N 44 54E   33
Lahore: Pakistan 31 34N 74 22E   34 82
Lahr: W.Germany 48 21N 07 52E   72
Lahti: Finland 61 00N 25 40E   27 75
Laibin: China 23 46N 109 18E   85
Laifeng: China 29 35N 109 20E   85
Lainate: Italy 45 34N 09 02E   116
Laindon: Essex, England 51 34N 00 26E   112
Lairg: Suther., Scotland 58 01N 04 25W   64
Laixi: China 36 49N 120 31E   84
Laiyang: China 36 58N 120 40E   84
Laizhouwan: *bay,* China 37 30N 119 30E   84
Lajes: Brazil 27 48S 50 20W   51
Lajpat Nagar: India 28 34N 77 14E   120
La Junta: Colo., U.S.A. 37 59N 103 33W   95
Lake Bluff: Ill., U.S.A. 42 16N 87 50W   124
Lake Charles: La., U.S.A. 30 14N 93 13W   43 100 106
Lake City: Fla., U.S.A. 30 12N 82 39W   101
Lake Coleridge: S.I., New Zealand 43 22S 171 33E   87
Lake District *National Park:* Cumbria, England 54 30N 03 00W   63
Lake Eyre *Basin:* S.A., Australia 28 00S 137 30E   41
Lake Forest: Ill., U.S.A. 42 15N 87 50W   124
Lake George: Colo., U.S.A. 38 59N 105 22W   94
Lake Hills: Wash., U.S.A. 47 36N 122 08W   126
Lake Jackson: Tex., U.S.A. 29 03N 95 27W   100
Lakeland: Fla., U.S.A. 28 02N 81 59W   101
Lake Louise: Alta., Canada 51 26N 116 10W   92
Lake Mead *National Recreation Area:* U.S.A. 36 00N 114 00W   91
Lake Pukaki: S.I., New Zealand 44 12S 170 11E   87
Lake River: Ont., Canada 54 30N 82 30W   96
Lakeview: Oreg., U.S.A. 42 13N 120 21W   90
Lakewood: Calif., U.S.A. 33 50N 118 08W   127
Lake Zurich: Ill., U.S.A. 42 11N 88 05W   124
Lakhimpur: India 27 57N 80 47E   82
Lakhnādon: India 22 34N 79 38E   82
Laksefjorden: *fd.,* Norway 70 45N 27 00E   74
Lakselv: Norway 70 03N 25 06E   74
La Línea: Spain 36 10N 05 21W   77
Lalitapur: Nepal 27 40N 85 20E   35 83
Lalitpur: India 24 42N 78 24E   82
Lālmanir Hāt: Bangladesh 25 51N 89 34E   83
La Loche: Sask., Canada 56 31N 109 27W   92
La Louvière: Belgium 50 29N 04 12E   72 104
La Maddalena: Sardinia 41 13N 09 24E   77
La Malbaie (Murray Bay): Qué., Canada 47 39N 70 11W   96
Lamar: Colo., U.S.A. 38 05N 102 37W   95
Lambaréné: Gabon 00 41S 10 13E   57
Lambay *Island:* Dublin, Irish Republic 53 29N 06 01W   66
Lambert *Glacier:* Antarctica 71 00S 70 00E   24
Lambeth: Gt. Ldn., England 51 30N 00 07W   59 112
Lambourn: Berks., England 51 31N 01 31W   59
Lambrate: Italy 45 29N 09 15E   116
Lam Chi (Chi): *riv.,* Thailand 15 30N 104 00E   38
La Mède: France 43 24N 05 07E   107
Lame Deer: Mont., U.S.A. 45 37N 106 40W   94
Lamesa: Tex., U.S.A. 32 44N 101 58W   100
Lamía: Greece 38 55N 22 26E   79

Types of map: Ocean pp. 1-5; Physical pp. 6-25; Human pp. 26-57; Topographic pp. 58-101; World pp. 102-111; Urban pp. 112-128.

Lammermuir *Hills*: Scotland   55 45N 02 30W   63
Lamon *Bay*: Philippines   14 30N 122 00E   39
Lampang: Thailand   18 16N 99 30E   36
Lampedusa: *is.*, Mediterranean Sea   35 15N 12 30E   79
Lampeter: Dyfed, Wales   52 07N 04 05W   60
Lanao, *Lake*: Philippines   07 45N 124 00E   39
Lanark: Lan., Scotland   55 41N 03 48W   62
Lanarkshire: *admin.*, Scotland   55 30N 04 00W   62
Lancashire: *admin.*, England   53 30N 02 30W   63
Lancaster: N.B., Canada   45 16N 66 06W   97
Lancaster: Lancs., England   54 03N 02 48W   63
Lancaster: Calif., U.S.A.   34 42N 118 08W   91
Lancaster: Ohio, U.S.A.   39 43N 82 37W   98
Lancaster: Pa., U.S.A.   40 01N 76 19W   99
Lancaster *Canal*: Lancs., England   53 45N 02 45W   114
Lanchou *see* Lanzhou   36 03N 103 41E   36
Lancing: W.Sussex, England   50 47N 00 20W   59
Landau in der Pfalz: W.Germany   49 12N 08 07E   72
Lander: Wyo., U.S.A.   42 50N 108 44W   94
Landerneau: France   48 27N 04 16W   70
Landes, Les: *geog. reg.*, France   44 00N 01 00W   70
Landsberg am Lech: W.Germany   48 05N 10 55E   73
Land's End: *cape*, Corn., England   50 03N 05 44W   61
Landshut: W.Germany   48 31N 12 10E   73
Landskrona: Sweden   55 53N 12 50E   75
Lanett: Ala., U.S.A.   32 52N 85 12W   101
Langchuhe (Sutlej): *riv.*, Asia   30 00N 72 45E   82
Langenfeld: W.Germany   51 06N 06 57E   118
Langenhorn: W.Germany   53 39N 10 01E   119
Langer See: *lake*, E.Germany   52 15N 13 30E   117
Langholm: Dumf., Scotland   55 09N 03 00W   63
Langmazong: China   30 50N 89 50E   83
Langon: France   44 33N 00 15W   70
Langres: France   47 53N 05 20E   71
Langres, *Plateau de*: France   47 30N 05 00E   71
Lanigan: Sask., Canada   51 50N 105 01W   92
Lankao: China   34 48N 114 49E   84
Lannidu: China   31 14N 121 29E   121
Lannion: France   48 44N 03 27W   70
Lansdowne House: Ont., Canada   52 05N 88 00W   93
Lanshan: China   25 20N 111 59E   85
Lanshantou: China   35 04N 119 25E   84
Lansing: Ill., U.S.A.   41 33N 87 33W   124
Lansing: Mich., U.S.A.   42 44N 83 34W   45 98
Lantian: China   34 03N 109 18E   84
Lan-ts'ang Chiang *see* Mekong: *riv.*,   10 30N 105 30E
                                                                        12 35
Lanús: Argentina   34 43S 58 24W   128
Lanxi: China   29 09N 119 28E   85
Lanzhou (Lanchou): China   36 03N 103 41E   36
Laoang: Philippines   12 35N 125 02E   39
Lao-cai: N.Vietnam   22 30N 104 00E   35
Laois: *admin.*, Irish Rep.   53 00N 07 15W   67
Laon: France   49 34N 03 37E   71
La Oroya: Peru   11 36S 75 54W   49
LAOS   17 45N 105 00E   12 35
Little Snake: *riv.*, U.S.A.   40 45N 108 00W   94
Laoyingfang China   39 57N 116 16E   121
Lapalisse: France   46 15N 03 44E   71
La Palma: *is.*, Canary Islands   28 30N 17 45W   56
La Pampa: *admin.*, Argentina   37 15S 65 45W   52
La Paz: Bolivia   16 30S 68 09W   49
La Paz: Mexico   24 10N 110 17W   46
La Perouse: N.S.W., Australia   33 59S 151 14E   120
La Plata: Argentina   34 52S 57 55W   52 106
La Poile *Bay*: Nfld., Canada   47 30N 58 15W   97
Lappeenranta (Villmanstrand): Finland   61 04N 28 11E   75
Lappland: *geog. reg.*, Scandinavia   67 30N 21 00E   27
La Prairie: Qué., Canada   45 24N 73 29W   122
Laptev *Sea*: U.S.S.R.   74 00N 131 00E   22 31
Laptev *Strait*: U.S.S.R.   73 00N 142 00E   31
Lapua: Finland   62 57N 23 00E   74
L'Aquila: Italy   42 22N 13 24E   79
La Quinta: Tex., U.S.A.   27 59N 97 08W   100
Laramie: Wyo., U.S.A.   41 19N 105 35W   43 94
Laramie: *riv.*, Wyo., U.S.A.   42 00N 105 15W   94
Laramie *Peak*: Wyo., U.S.A.   42 18N 105 26W   17 43
Larap: Philippines   14 07N 122 55E   105
Larch: *riv.*, Qué., Canada   57 00N 72 00W   96
Larder Lake: Ont., Canada   48 06N 79 44W   99
Laredo: Tex., U.S.A.   27 32N 99 22W   43

Largs: Ayr., Scotland   55 48N 04 52W   62 113
La Rioja: Argentina   29 26S 66 50W   52
La Rioja: *admin.*, Argentina   30 00S 66 00W   52
Lárisa: Greece   39 38N 22 25E   32 79
Lark: *riv.*, England   52 15N 00 30E   59
Lárnax (Larnaca): Cyprus   34 55N 33 36E   32
Larne: Antrim, N.Ireland   54 51N 05 49W   66
Larned: Kans., U.S.A.   38 11N 99 06W   95
La Rochelle: France   46 10N 01 10W   70
La Roche-sur-Yon: France   46 40N 01 25W   70
La Ronge: Sask., Canada   55 07N 105 18W   92
Larsen *Ice Shelf*: Antarctica   68 30S 63 00W   24
Larvik: Norway   59 04N 10 02E   75
Larzac, Causse de: *plat.*, France   44 00N 03 15E   71
Lasa (Lhasa): China   29 41N 91 10E   35 83
La Salada: Argentina   34 43S 58 29W   128
La Salle: Ont., Canada   42 15N 83 05W   125
Lasalle: Qué., Canada   45 26N 73 40W   122
Las Animas: Colo., U.S.A.   38 04N 103 14W   95
Las Barrancas: Argentina   34 28S 58 29W   128
Las Cruces: N.Mex., U.S.A.   32 19N 106 47W   95
La Serena: Chile   29 54S 71 18W   52
Las Heras: Argentina   32 48S 68 50W   52
Lashio: Burma   22 58N 97 48E   35
Las Palmas: Canary Islands   28 08N 15 27W   56
La Spezia: Italy   44 07N 09 48E   26 71
Las Piedras: *riv.*, Argentina   34 45S 58 19W   128
Las Plumas: Argentina   43 43S 67 16W   52
Lassen *Peak*: Calif., U.S.A.   40 30N 121 30W   17 43 91
Lassen *Volcanic National Park*: Calif., U.S.A.
                                      40 30N 121 15W   91
Last Mountain *Lake*: Sask., Canada   51 00N 105 00W   92
Lastoursville: Gabon   00 49S 12 42E   54
Las Vegas: Nev., U.S.A.   36 10N 115 09W   43 91
Latacunga: Ecuador   00 56S 78 37W   48
Latakia *see* Al Lādhiqīyah   35 31N 35 47E   32
Lātehär: India   23 55N 84 30E   83
Latgale: *hist. reg.*, U.S.S.R.   56 45N 27 00E   80
Latina: Italy   41 28N 12 53E   79
La Tuque: Qué., Canada   47 26N 72 47W   96 96
Latvijskaja S.S.R. (Latvian S.S.R.): *admin.*, U.S.S.R.
                                      57 15N 24 00E   28 75
Lauchhammer: E.Germany   51 30N 13 48E   73
Lauder: Ber., Scotland   55 43N 02 45W   63
Lauenburg: W.Germany   53 23N 10 33E   73
Launceston: Tas., Australia   41 25S 147 07E   40
Launceston: Corn., England   50 38N 04 21W   61
Laurel: Miss., U.S.A.   31 41N 89 08W   100
Laurencekirk: Kinc., Scotland   56 50N 02 29W   65
Laurentian *Highlands*: Qué., Canada   48 30N 73 00W   17
Laurentides, Autoroute des: *hwy.*, Qué., Canada
                                      45 30N 73 45W   122
Laurentides *Provincial Park*: Qué., Canada   47 30N 71 30W
                                                                        96
Lau *Ridge*: S.Pacific Ocean   21 00S 179 00W   15
Lausanne: Switzerland   46 32N 06 39E   26 71
Laut: *is.*, Indonesia   03 45S 116 15E   39
Lauzon: Qué., Canada   46 49N 71 10W   96
Lava Beds *National Monument*: Calif., U.S.A.
                                      41 45N 121 30W   90
Laval: France   48 04N 00 45W   70
Laval des Rapides: Qué., Canada   45 33N 73 43W   122
Lavenham: Suff., England   52 06N 00 47E   59
Lavernock *Point*: S.Glam., Wales   51 24N 03 11W   113
Laverton: W.A., Australia   28 49S 122 25E   40
Lawas: Malaysia   04 50N 115 25E   39
Lawers, Ben: *mtn.*, Perth., Scotland   56 33N 04 15W   64
Lawrence: Kans., U.S.A.   38 58N 95 14W   94
Lawton: Okla., U.S.A.   34 37N 98 25W   43 95
Laxford, *Loch*: Suther., Scotland   58 15N 05 00W   64
Lazi: China   29 10N 87 42E   35 83
Lazzate: Italy   45 40N 09 05E   116
Lea: *riv.*, England   51 30N 00 00   59
Leach: *riv.*, Glos., England   51 45N 01 45W   61
Lead: S.D., U.S.A.   44 21N 103 46W   94
Leadon: *riv.*, Glos., England   51 45N 02 15W   60
Leadville: Colo., U.S.A.   39 15N 106 18W   94
Leaf: *riv.*, Qué., Canada   58 00N 72 30W   44
Leam: *riv.*, War., England   52 15N 01 15W   115
Leamington Spa, Royal: War., England   52 18N 01 31W
                                                                        59 115

Types of map: Ocean pp. 1-5; Physical pp. 6-25; Human pp. 26-57; Topographic pp. 58-101; World pp. 102-111; Urban pp. 112-128.

Leane, *Lough*: Kerry, Irish Republic   52 00N 09 30W   67
Leaside: Ont., Canada   43 43N 79 23W   125
Leatherhead: Surrey, England   51 18N 00 20W   59 112
Leavenworth: Kans., U.S.A.   39 19N 94 55W   94
LEBANON   33 45N 35 30E   10 32 107
Lebanon: Oreg., U.S.A.   44 32N 122 55W   90
Lebanon: Tenn., U.S.A.   36 11N 86 19W   101
Lebed'an': U.S.S.R.   53 01N 39 09E   80
Lebedin: U.S.S.R.   50 36N 34 30E   80
Lębork: Poland   54 32N 17 43E   73
Lebu: Chile   37 38S 73 43W   52
Lecce: Italy   40 21N 18 11E   27 79
Lecco: Italy   45 52N 09 20E   71
Lech: *riv.*, Austria/W.Germany   48 30N 10 45E   73
Lechang: China   25 09N 113 19E   85
Lechlade: Glos., England   51 43N 01 41W   61
le Creusot: France   46 48N 04 26E   71 104
Ledbury: Here.& Worcs., England   52 02N 02 25W   60
Ledi, Ben: *mtn.*, Perth., Scotland   56 15N 04 20W   64
Leduc: Alta., Canada   53 17N 113 30W   92
Lędyczek: Poland   53 31N 17 01E   73
Lee: *riv.*, Cork, Irish Republic   51 45N 08 30W   67
Leeds: W.Yorks., England   53 50N 01 35W   26 63 115
Leeds & Liverpool *Canal*: England   53 30N 02 45W   114
Leek: Staffs., England   53 06N 02 01W   58
Leer: W.Germany   53 14N 07 27E   72
Leesburg: Fla., U.S.A.   28 49N 81 54W   101
Leeuwarden: Netherlands   53 12N 05 48E   72
Leeward *Islands*: Caribbean Sea   17 30N 61 45W   47
Leganés: Spain   40 19N 03 45W   116
Legazpi (Legaspi): Philippines   13 10N 123 45E   39
Legge *Peak*: Tas., Australia   41 32S 147 41E   40
Leghorn *see* Livorno   43 33N 10 18E   26 79
Legnano: Italy   45 36N 08 54E   116
Legnica: Poland   51 12N 16 02E   73 79
Le Havre: France   49 30N 00 06E   26 70
Leiah: Pakistan   30 59N 70 58E   82
Leicester: Leics., England   52 38N 01 05W   26 58
Leicestershire: *admin.*, England   52 30N 01 15W   58
Leichhardt: N.S.W., Australia   33 53S 151 09E   120
Leiden: Netherlands   52 10N 04 30E   72
Leigh: Gt. Man., England   53 30N 02 33W   63 114
Leighton Buzzard: Beds., England   51 55N 00 40W   59
Leine: *riv.*, W.Germany   52 30N 09 30E   73
Leinster, *Mount*: Carlow, Irish Republic   52 37N 06 47W   67
Leipzig: E.Germany   51 20N 12 20E   26 73
Leiston: Suff., England   52 13N 01 34E   59
Leith: Midloth., Scotland   55 59N 03 10W   63
Leitha: *riv.*, Austria   47 30N 16 60E   73
Leitrim: *admin.*, Irish Rep.   54 00N 08 00W   66
Leixlip: Kild., Irish Republic   53 22N 06 30W   67
Leiyang: China   26 27N 112 45E   85
Leksozero: *lake*, U.S.S.R.   64 45N 31 00E   74
Leling: China   37 45N 117 12E   84
Le Mans: France   48 00N 00 12E   26 70
Lemesós (Limassol): Cyprus   34 40N 33 03E   32
Lemgo: W.Germany   52 02N 08 54E   72
Lemmenjoen Kansallispuisto: *na. rve.*,
   Finland   68 30N 26 00E   74
Lemnos: *is. see* Límnos   39 45N 25 15E   79
Lemont: III., U.S.A.   41 39N 87 59W   124
Lena: *riv.*, U.S.S.R.   69 30N 124 30E   9 31
Lene, *Lough*: Westmeath, Irish Republic   53 30N 07 00W
       66
Leninabad: U.S.S.R.   40 56N 72 01E   105
Leninabad: U.S.S.R.   40 17N 69 37E   29
Leninakan: U.S.S.R.   40 48N 43 50E   28
Leningrad (Petrograd): U.S.S.R.   59 55N 30 15E
       28 80 105 119
Lenino: U.S.S.R.   55 37N 37 41E   119
Leninogorsk: R.S.F.S.R., U.S.S.R.   54 36N 52 30E   81
Leninogorsk: Kazakh S.S.R., U.S.S.R.   50 27N 83 32E   29
Lenin *Peak*: U.S.S.R.   39 20N 72 55E   29
Leninsk-Kuzneckij (Leninsk-Kusnetskiy): U.S.S.R.
   54 38N 86 10E   30
Lenne: *riv.*, W.Germany   51 15N 07 30E   118
Lennep: W.Germany   51 11N 07 16E   118
Lennoxtown: Stirl., Scotland   55 59N 04 12W   113
Lens: France   50 26N 02 50E   26 72
Lensk: U.S.S.R.   61 00N 114 50E   30
Leoben: Austria   47 23N 15 06E   73 78

Leominster: Here.& Worcs., England   52 14N 02 45W   60
León: Mexico   21 07N 101 40W   46
Léon: Nicaragua   12 26N 86 54W   47
León: Spain   42 35N 05 34W   26 77
León: *admin.*, Spain   42 40N 06 00W   105
Léopold II, *Lake*: Zaïre   02 00S 18 15E   54
Léopoldville *see* Kinshasa   04 18S 15 18E   21 54
Lepel': U.S.S.R.   54 53N 28 42E   80
Le Petit-Couronne: France   49 23N 01 01E   107
Leping: China   28 57N 117 10E   85
Lepontine, *Alpi*: Switzerland   46 15N 08 45E   71
Le Puy: France   45 03N 03 53E   71
Leqing: China   28 08N 121 02E   85
Lérida: Spain   41 37N 00 38E   77
Lerwick: Shet. Is., Scotland   60 09N 01 09W   65
Lesbos: *is. see* Lésvos   39 00N 26 15E   79
les Clayes-sous-Bois: France   48 49N 01 59E   117
Les Ecrehou: *is.*, Channel Islands   49 17N 01 56W   61
les Essarts-le-Roi: France   48 43N 01 55E   117
Les Eyzies-de-Tayac: France   44 56N 01 01E   70
Leskovac: Yugoslavia   43 00N 21 57E   79
Leslie: Fife, Scotland   56 13N 03 13W   65
les Mureaux: France   49 00N 01 55E   117
Lesnoj: U.S.S.R.   60 00N 30 19E   119
les Noues: France   49 02N 02 28E   117
LESOTHO (Basutoland)   29 30S 28 15E   21 55 107
Lesozavodsk: U.S.S.R.   45 28N 133 27E   37
Les Sables-d'Olonne: France   46 30N 01 47W   70
Lesser Antilles: *is.*, Caribbean Sea   12 00N 65 00W   17 47
Lesser Slave *Lake*: Alta., Canada   55 15N 115 30W   42 92
Lesser Sunda *Islands*: Indonesia   08 00S 122 00E   13
Lésvos (Lesbos): *is.*, Greece   39 00N 26 15E   79
Leszno: Poland   51 51N 16 35E   73 78
Letchworth: Herts., England   51 58N 00 14W   59
Lethbridge: Alta., Canada   49 43N 112 48W   42 92
Leticia: Colombia   04 09S 69 57W   48
Leting: China   39 22N 118 57E   84
Letterkenny: Don., Irish Republic   54 57N 07 44W   66
Leucate, Étang de: *lag.*, France   42 50N 03 00E   71
Leuven (Louvain): Belgium   50 53N 04 42E   72
Levádhia: Greece   38 26N 22 53E   79
Levanger: Norway   63 44N 11 20E   74
Levelland: Tex., U.S.A.   33 35N 102 23W   95
Leven: Fife, Scotland   56 12N 03 00W   65
Leven: *riv.*, Argyll./Inv., Scotland   56 30N 04 45W   64
Leven: *riv.*, Dunb., Scotland   55 45N 04 45W   113
Leven, *Loch*: Kinr., Scotland   56 00N 03 15W   65
Levenshulme: Gt. Man., England   53 27N 02 10W   114
Leverkusen: W.Germany   51 02N 06 59E   119
Levin: N.I., New Zealand   40 37S 175 18E   87
Lévis: Qué., Canada   46 47N 71 12W   96
Levittown: N.Y., U.S.A.   40 44N 73 32W   123
Levkás: *is.*, Greece   38 50N 20 42E   79
Levkosia (Nicosia): Cyprus   35 11N 33 23E   27
Lewes: E.Sussex, England   50 52N 00 01E   59
Lewis: *is.*, R. & Crom., Scotland   58 00N 06 45W   64
Lewis: *riv.*, Wash., U.S.A.   46 00N 121 45W   90
Lewis, Butt of: *pt.*, R.& Crom., Scotland   58 31N 06 15W   64
Lewisham: Gt. Ldn., England   51 27N 00 01W   112
Lewis *Pass*: S.I., New Zealand   42 22S 172 27E   87
Lewiston: Idaho, U.S.A.   46 25N 117 01W   90
Lewiston: Maine, U.S.A.   44 06N 70 14W   99
Lewistown: Mont., U.S.A.   47 04N 109 26W   94
Lexington: Ky., U.S.A.   38 02N 84 30W   45 101
Lexington: Mass., U.S.A.   42 26N 71 13W   122
Lexington: Nebr., U.S.A.   40 47N 99 45W   94
Leyburn: N.Yorks., England   54 19N 01 49W   63
Leyland: Lancs., England   53 42N 02 42W   63 114
Leyte: *is.*, Philippines   11 00N 124 45E   39
L'gov: U.S.S.R.   51 43N 35 17E   80
Lhasa *see* Lasa   29 41N 91 10E   35 83
Liancheng: China   25 42N 116 46E   85
Lianhuashan: *mtns.*, China   23 15N 115 30E   36 85
Lianjiang: Fujian, China   26 12N 119 34E   85
Lianjiang: Guangdong, China   21 39N 110 20E   85
Lianping: China   24 19N 114 29E   85
Lianshui: China   33 47N 119 21E   84
Lianshui: *riv.*, China   27 45N 112 45E   85
Lianxian (Lienhsien): China   24 48N 112 28E   36 85
Lianyun'gang: China   34 41N 119 30E   84
Lianzhou *see* Hepu   21 39N 109 13E   85

Types of map: Ocean pp. 1-5; Physical pp. 6-25; Human pp. 26-57; Topographic pp. 58-101; World pp. 102-111; Urban pp. 112-128.

Liaocheng: China 36 27N 115 58E	84	
Liaodong *Peninsula*: China 39 45N 122 15E	84	
Liaodongwan (Liaotung, *Gulf of*): China 40 30N 121 30E		
	84	
Liaoning: *admin.*, China 41 15N 121 00E	37 84	
Liaotung, *Gulf of see* Liaodongwan 40 30N 121 30E	84	
Liaoyang: China 41 17N 123 14E	37	
Liaoyuan: China 42 54N 125 07E	37	
Liard: *riv.*, Canada 61 00N 122 30W	16 42 88	
Liard *Range*: N.W.T., Canada 60 30N 124 00W	88	
Libby: Mont., U.S.A. 48 23N 115 33W	90	
Liberal: Kans., U.S.A. 37 03N 100 55W	95	
Liberec: Czechoslovakia 50 48N 15 05E	73 78	
LIBERIA 06 30N 09 30W	20 57	
Libertad: Argentina 34 41S 58 47W	128	
Liberty *Inlet*: Wash., U.S.A. 47 43N 122 39W	126	
Libertyville: Ill., U.S.A. 42 16N 88 02W	124	
Libo: China 25 28N 107 51E	85	
Libourne: France 44 55N 00 14W	70	
Libreville: Gabon 00 23N 09 27E	57	
LIBYA	20 32 107	
Libyan *Desert*: Egypt/Libya 26 45N 24 00E	20 32	
Libyan *Plateau*: Egypt 30 30N 26 45E	32	
Licheng: China 36 21N 113 30E	84	
Lichfield: Staffs., England 52 42N 01 48W	58 115	
Lichiang *see* Lijiang 26 57N 100 15E	36	
Lichtenberg: E.Germany 52 31N 13 30E	117	
Lichtenrade: W.Germany 52 23N 13 24E	117	
Lichuan: Hubei, China 30 22N 108 51E	85	
Lichuan: Jiangxi, China 27 18N 116 50E	85	
Licking: *riv.*, Ky., U.S.A. 38 15N 83 45W	101	
Lida: U.S.S.R. 53 53N 25 18E	78	
Lidcombe: N.S.W., Australia 33 52S 151 03E	120	
Liddel Water: *riv.*, Scotland 55 15N 02 45W	63	
Lidköping: Sweden 58 30N 13 10E	75	
Lido di Ostia: Italy 41 43N 12 17E	116	
LIECHTENSTEIN 47 00N 09 30E	78	
Liège: Belgium 50 38N 05 35E	26 72	
Lienhsien *see* Lianxian 24 48N 112 28E	36 85	
Lienyünchiang *see* Xinhailian 34 37N 119 16E	36 84	
Lienz: Austria 46 51N 12 50E	78	
Liepāja: U.S.S.R. 56 30N 21 00E	75 105	
Lièvre, du: *riv.*, Qué., Canada 46 00N 75 30W	99	
Liezen: Austria 47 35N 14 15E	73	
Liffey: *riv.*, Irish Republic 53 15N 06 30W	67	
Lifford: Don., Irish Republic 54 50N 07 29W	66	
Ligovo: U.S.S.R. 59 50N 30 12E	119	
Ligurian *Sea* 43 00N 08 00E	26 71	
Lihsien: *riv. see* Lixian 23 00N 102 00E	36	
Lijiang (Lichiang): China 26 57N 100 15E	36	
Likasi (Jadotville): Zaïre 10 59S 26 44E	54	
Liling: China 27 40N 113 30E	85	
Lille: France 50 39N 03 05E	26 72	
Lille Bælt: *str.*, Denmark 55 15N 09 45E	75	
Lillehammer: Norway 61 06N 10 27E	75	
Lillestrøm: Norway 59 58N 11 05E	75	
Lillooet: B.C., Canada 50 42N 121 56W	89	
Lilongwe: Malawi 13 59S 33 47E	54	
Liluah: India 22 37N 88 20E	120	
Lima: Peru 12 06S 77 03W	49	
Lima: Ohio, U.S.A. 40 43N 84 06W	98	
Limassol *see* Lemesós 34 40N 33 03E	32	
Limavady: Lon., N.Ireland 55 03N 06 57W	66	
Limay: France 49 00N 01 44E	117	
Limbang: Sarawak, Malaysia 04 45N 115 00E	39	
Limbdi: India 22 36N 72 00E	82	
Lime: Oreg., U.S.A. 44 24N 117 19W	90	
Limeira: Brazil 22 34S 47 25W	51	
Limerick: Lim., Irish Rep. 52 40N 08 38W	67	
Limerick: *admin.*, Irish Rep. 52 30N 08 45W	67	
Limfjorden: *fd.*, Denmark 56 45N 09 00E	75	
Límnos (Lemnos): *is.*, Greece 39 45N 25 15E	79	
Limoges: France 45 50N 01 15E	26 70	
Limogne, Causse de: *plat.*, France 44 15N 01 30E	70	
Limón: Costa Rica 10 00N 83 01W	47	
Limon: Colo., U.S.A. 39 16N 103 41W	94	
Limours: France 48 39N 02 05E	117	
Limoux: France 43 03N 02 13E	70	
Limpopo: *riv.*, Africa 24 30S 32 45E	21 55	
Lin'an: China 30 14N 119 43E	85	
Linares: Chile 35 47S 71 40W	52	

Linares: Spain 38 05N 03 38W	77	
Linchiang *see* Qingjiang 28 00N 115 23E	36 85	
Linch'ing *see* Linqing 36 53N 115 41E	36 84	
Lincoln: Lincs., England 53 14N 00 33W	58	
Lincoln: Ill., U.S.A. 40 10N 89 21W	98	
Lincoln: Nebr., U.S.A. 40 49N 96 41W	43 94	
Lincoln *Park*: Ill., U.S.A. 41 56N 87 38W	124	
Lincoln Park: Mich., U.S.A. 42 13N 83 10W	125	
Lincoln Park: Va., U.S.A. 38 49N 77 10W	122	
Lincoln *Park*: Wash., U.S.A. 47 32N 122 24W	126	
Lincolnshire: *admin.*, England 53 00N 00 15W	58	
Lincoln Wolds: *hills*, Lincs., England 53 15N 00 00	58	
Lincolnwood: Ill., U.S.A. 42 00N 87 44W	124	
Lindbergh: Alta., Canada 53 53N 110 40W	92	
Linden: N.J., U.S.A. 40 38N 74 15W	106	
Lindfield: N.S.W., Australia 33 47S 151 10E	120	
Lindholm: W.Germany 54 46N 08 52E	72 76	
Lindi: Tanzania 10 00S 39 43E	54	
Lindis *Pass*: S.I., New Zealand 44 43S 169 31E	87	
Lindsay: Ont., Canada 44 21N 78 44W	99	
Line *Islands*: Pacific Ocean 00 00 157 00W	5	
Linfen: China 36 05N 111 32E	84	
Ling: *riv.*, R. & Crom., Scotland 57 15N 05 15W	64	
Lingayen: Philippines 16 02N 120 14E	39	
Lingchuan: Guangxizhuang, China 25 36N 110 15E	85	
Lingchuan: Shānxī, China 35 42N 113 25E	84	
Lingen: W.Germany 52 32N 07 19E	72	
Lingga *Archipelago*: Indonesia 00 15S 104 45E	38	
Lingling: China 26 14N 111 33E	85	
Lingqiu: China 39 24N 114 07E	84	
Lingshan: China 22 28N 109 13E	85	
Lingshi: China 36 49N 111 45E	84	
Lingshou: China 37 18N 114 22E	84	
Lingwu: China 38 02N 106 28E	84	
Lingxian: Hunan, China 26 40N 113 46E	85	
Lingxian: Shandong, China 37 21N 116 34E	84	
Linhai: China 28 51N 121 13E	37 85	
Linhuanji: China 33 42N 116 31E	84	
Lini: Shandong *see* Linyi 35 04N 118 22E	36 84	
Lini: Shandong *see* Linyi 37 11N 116 51E	84	
Linköping: Sweden 58 25N 15 35E	75	
Linli: China 29 23N 111 30E	85	
Linlithgow: W.Loth., Scotland 55 59N 03 37W	62	
Linnhe, *Loch*: Argyll., Scotland 56 30N 05 15W	64	
Lin'ovo: U.S.S.R. 50 53N 44 51E	80	
Linqing (Linch'ing): China 36 53N 115 41E	36 84	
Linqu: China 36 30N 118 30E	84	
Linru: China 34 11N 112 44E	84	
Linslade: Beds., England 51 55N 00 41W	59	
Linton: N.D., U.S.A. 46 16N 100 14W	94	
Lintong: China 34 21N 109 09E	84	
Lintorf: W.Germany 51 21N 06 50E	118	
Linwood: Renf., Scotland 55 48N 04 30W	113	
Linwu: China 25 18N 112 25E	85	
Linxian: Henan, China 35 58N 113 50E	84	
Linxian: Shānxī, China 37 57N 110 58E	84	
Linxiang: China 29 34N 113 29E	85	
Linyi (Lini): Shandong, China 35 04N 118 22E	36 84	
Linyi (Lini): Shandong, China 37 11N 116 51E	84	
Linz: Austria 48 19N 14 18E	27 73 78 105	
Lion, *Golfe du*: France 43 00N 04 00E	71	
Lipari *Islands see* Eolie o Lipari, *Isole* 38 30N 14 45E	79	
Lipeck (Lipetsk): U.S.S.R. 52 37N 39 35E	28 80 105	
Lipenská: *lake*, Czechoslovakia 48 45N 14 00E	73	
Liphook: Hants., England 51 05N 00 49W	59	
Liping: China 26 17N 109 00E	85	
Lipovcy: U.S.S.R. 44 11N 131 44E	86	
Lippstadt: W.Germany 51 41N 08 20E	72	
Lipu: China 24 29N 110 19E	85	
Lisala: Zaïre 02 09N 21 31E	54	
Lisbellaw: Ferm., N.Ireland 54 19N 07 32W	66	
Lisboa (Lisbon): Portugal 38 44N 09 08W	26 77	
Lisburn: Antrim, N. Ireland 54 31N 06 03W	66	
Liscannor *Bay*: Clare, Irish Republic 52 45N 09 15W	67	
Lisdoonvarna: Clare, Irish Republic 53 02N 09 17W	67	
Lishi: China 37 27N 111 07E	84	
Lishui: Jiangsu, China 31 39N 119 03E	84	
Lishui: Zhejiang, China 28 27N 120 01E	85	
Lishui: Zhejiang, China 28 06N 119 39E	85	
Lisianski: *is.*, Hawaii, U.S.A. 26 04N 173 58W	4	
Lisičansk (Lisichansk): U.S.S.R. 48 55N 38 26E	28 80	

Types of map: Ocean pp. 1-5; Physical pp. 6-25; Human pp. 26-57; Topographic pp. 58-101; World pp. 102-111; Urban pp. 112-128.

Lisieux: France   49 09N 00 14E   70
Lisij Nos: U.S.S.R.   60 01N 30 00E   119
Liskeard: Corn., England   50 28N 04 28W   61
Liski *see* Georgiu Dež   50 59N 39 30E   80
Lisle: Ill., U.S.A.   41 48N 88 05W   124
Lismore: Wat., Irish Republic   52 08N 07 55W   67
Lismore *Island*: Argyll., Scotland   56 30N 05 30W   64
Lisnaskea: Ferm., N.Ireland   54 15N 07 26W   66
Lissone: Italy   45 37N 09 14E   116
Listowel: Kerry, Irish Republic   52 27N 09 29W   67
Litang: China   23 11N 109 09E   85
Litherland: Mers., England   53 28N 02 59W   114
Lithuanian S.S.R. *see* Litovskaja S.S.R.   55 30N 24 00E
                                                  28 78
Litoměřice: Czechoslovakia   50 33N 14 10E   73
Litovskaja S.S.R. (Lithuanian S.S.R.): *admin.*, U.S.S.R.
   55 30N 24 00E   28 78
Little Avon: *riv.*, Glos., England   51 30N 02 15W   113
Little Bahama *Bank*: Bahamas   26 45N 77 45W   101
Little Bay: Nfld., Canada   49 38N 55 48W   97
Little Blue: riv., U.S.A.   40 15N 97 45W   94
Little Calumet: *riv.*, U.S.A.   41 30N 87 15W   124
Little Colorado: riv., Ariz., U.S.A.   34 30N 109 45W   91
Little Current: Ont., Canada   45 57N 81 57W   98
Little Current: *riv.*, Ont., Canada   50 45N 86 00W   98
Little Dart: *riv.*, Devon, England   50 45N 03 45W   61
Little Deer *Creek*: Pa., U.S.A.   40 30N 79 45W   125
Little Falls: Minn., U.S.A.   45 58N 94 20W   98
Littlefield: Tex., U.S.A.   33 55N 102 20W   95
Little Goose *Dam*: Wash., U.S.A.   46 34N 117 54W   90
Little Grand Rapids: Man., Canada   52 03N 95 29W   93
Littlehampton: W.Sussex, England   50 48N 00 33W   59
Little Hulton: Gt. Man., England   53 32N 02 26W   114
Little Kanawha: *riv.*, W.Va., U.S.A.   38 45N 81 15W   99
Little Laut *Islands*: Indonesia   04 45S 115 45E   39
Little Longlac: Ont., Canada   49 42N 86 58W   98
Little Mecatina: riv., Canada   52 15N 61 30W   97
Little Mecatina *Island*: Qué., Canada   50 30N 59 15W   97
Little Minch: *chan.*, Inv., Scotland   57 30N 06 45W   64
Little Missouri: *riv.*, N.D., U.S.A.   45 30N 103 45W   94
Little Ouse: *riv.*, England   52 15N 00 30E   58
Littleport: Cambs., England   52 28N 00 19E   58
Little Rann of Kutch: *geog. reg.*, India   23 15N 71 15E   82
Little Rock: Ark., U.S.A.   34 45N 92 17W   43 100
Little Sioux: *riv.*, Iowa, U.S.A.   42 15N 95 45W   94
Little Smoky: *riv.*, Alta., Canada   54 30N 117 00W   92
Little Snake: *riv.*, U.S.A.   40 45N 108 00W   94
Little Whale: *riv.*, Qué., Canada   55 45N 75 30W   96
Liuan: China   31 44N 116 31E   84
Liuchong (Liuch'ung): *riv.*, China   28 15N 108 15E   12 36 85
Liuchou *see* Liuzhou   24 20N 109 19E   36 85 105
Liuch'ung: *riv. see* Liuchong   28 15N 108 15E   12 36 85
Liuhe: China   32 19N 118 50E   84
Liuhezhuang: China   39 46N 116 22E   121
Liujiahang: China   31 21N 121 38E   121
Liuyang: China   28 09N 113 38E   85
Liuzhou (Liuchou): China   24 20N 109 19E   36 85 105
Liverpool: N.S.W., Australia   33 56S 150 55E   120
Liverpool: N.S., Canada   44 03N 64 43W   97
Liverpool: Mers., England   53 25N 02 55W   26 63 114
Liverpool *Bay*: Mers., England   53 15N 03 15W   63
Livingston: Nfld., Canada   53 58N 66 27W   97
Livingston: W.Loth., Scotland   55 53N 03 34W   62
Livingston: Mont., U.S.A.   45 40N 110 34W   94
Livingston: Tenn., U.S.A.   36 22N 85 20W   101
Livingstone *see* Maramba   17 51S 25 52E   55
Livingstone Creek: Yukon, Canada   61 20N 134 21W   88
Livingstone *Falls*: Zaïre   04 50S 14 30E   54
Livny: U.S.S.R.   52 25N 37 37E   80
Livojoki: *riv.*, Finland   65 45N 27 15E   74
Livonia: Mich., U.S.A.   42 25N 83 23W   125
Livorno (Leghorn): Italy   43 33N 10 18E   26 79
Lixian: China   29 39N 111 39E   85
Lixian (Lihsien): *riv.*, China   23 00N 102 00E   36
Liyang: China   31 24N 119 30E   84
Lizard: Corn., England   49 57N 05 13W   61
Lizard *Point*: Corn., England   49 56N 05 13W   61
Ljubija: Yugoslavia   44 57N 16 38E   105
Ljubljana: Yugoslavia   46 04N 14 28E   27 78
Ljungan: *riv.*, Sweden   62 15N 16 30E   74
Ljungby: Sweden   56 49N 13 55E   75

Ljusdal: Sweden   61 49N 16 09E   74
Ljusnan: *riv.*, Sweden   62 00N 15 15E   74
Llandaff: S.Glam., Wales   51 30N 03 14W   113
Llandarcy: Glam., Wales   51 38N 03 48W   107
Llandegfedd *Reservoir*: Gwent, Wales   51 41N 02 58W   113
Llandeilo: Dyfed, Wales   51 53N 03 59W   60
Llandovery: Dyfed, Wales   51 59N 03 48W   60
Llandrindod Wells: Powys, Wales   52 15N 03 23W   60
Llandudno: Gwyn., Wales   53 19N 03 49W   60
Llanelli: Dyfed, Wales   51 42N 04 10W   61
Llanfairfechan: Gwyn., Wales   53 15N 03 58W   60
Llanfyllin: Powys, Wales   52 46N 03 17W   60
Llangefni: Gwyn., Wales   53 16N 04 18W   60
Llangollen: Clwyd, Wales   52 58N 03 10W   60
Llanhilleth: Gwent, Wales   51 42N 03 07W   113
Llanidloes: Powys, Wales   52 27N 03 32W   60
Llano: Tex., U.S.A.   30 45N 98 41W   95
Llano: *riv.*, Tex., U.S.A.   20 30N 99 00W   95
Llano Estacado: *plat.*, U.S.A.   33 15N 103 00W   95
Llanos: *geog. reg.*, Colombia/Venezuela   07 30N 74 00W
                                                  18 48
Llanrwst: Gwyn., Wales   53 08N 03 48W   60
Llantrisant: M.Glam., Wales   51 33N 03 23W   61 113
Llanwern: Gwent, Wales   51 35N 02 55W   61 105
Llanwrtyd Wells: Powys, Wales   52 07N 03 38W   60
Lleyn *Peninsula*: Gwyn., Wales   52 45N 04 30W   60
Llobregat: *riv.*, Spain   41 15N 02 00E   116
Lloydminster: Sask., Canada   53 18N 110 00W   92
Llullaillaco: *volc.*, Argentina/Chile   24 43S 68 33W   49
Llyn Celyn: *lake*, Gwyn., Wales   52 45N 03 30W   60
Llyn Clywedog *Reservoir*: Powys, Wales   52 30N 03 30W
                                                  60
Loanhead: Midloth., Scotland   55 53N 03 09W   63
Lobito: Angola   12 20S 13 34E   54
Lobos, *Point*: Calif., U.S.A.   37 47N 122 31W   126
Lobstick *Lake*: Nfld., Canada   54 00N 65 00W   97
Locate Varesino: Italy   45 41N 08 56E   116
Lochaline: Argyll., Scotland   56 32N 05 47W   64
Lochboisdale: Inv., Scotland   57 09N 07 19W   64
Lochcarron: R. & Crom., Scotland   57 25N 05 36W   64
Loche, *Lac la*: Canada   56 15N 110 00W   92
Loches: France   47 08N 01 00E   70
Lockgelly: Fife, Scotland   56 08N 03 19W   65
Lochgilphead: Argyll., Scotland   56 03N 05 26W   64
Lochinver: Suther., Scotland   58 09N 05 15W   64
Lochmaben: Dumf., Scotland   55 08N 03 27W   62
Lochmaddy: Inv., Scotland   57 36N 07 10W   64
Lochnagar: *mtn.*, Aber., Scotland   56 57N 03 15W   65
Lochwinnoch: Renf., Scotland   55 48N 04 39W   113
Lochy, *Loch*: Inv., Scotland   56 45N 04 45W   64
Lockerbie: Dumf., Scotland   55 07N 03 22W   62
Lóc Ninh: S.Vietnam   11 51N 106 35E   38
Lodève: France   43 44N 03 19E   71
Lodi: India   28 36N 77 14E   120
Lodi: Italy   45 19N 09 30E   71
Lodi: Calif., U.S.A.   38 07N 121 18W   91
Łódź: Poland   51 49N 19 28E   27 78
Lofoten *Islands*: Norway   68 15N 14 00E   7 27 74
Loftus: Cleve., England   54 33N 00 53W   63
Logan: Utah, U.S.A.   41 44N 111 50W   90
Logan: W.Va., U.S.A.   37 52N 82 00W   101
Logan, *Mount*: Yukon, Canada   60 31N 140 22W   16
Logan, Mull of: *cape*, Wig., Scotland   54 44N 04 59W   62
Logan *Mountains*: Canada   61 30N 128 00W   88
Logansport: Ind., U.S.A.   40 45N 86 25W   98
Longroño: Spain   42 28N 02 26W   70 77
Lohärdaga: India   23 27N 84 42E   83
Loho *see* Luohe   33 32N 114 02E   36 84
Loi-kaw: Burma   19 40N 97 17E   35
Loirano: Italy   45 25N 09 03E   116
Loire: *riv.*, France   47 15N 02 00W   26 70
Loja: Ecuador   04 00S 79 13W   48
Loja: Spain   37 10N 04 09W   77
Lokantekojärvi: *lake*, Finland   67 45N 27 30E   27 74
Lokka: Finland   67 49N 27 45E   74
Løkken: Norway   63 06N 09 43E   74
Lokn'a: U.S.S.R.   56 50N 30 09E   80
Lolland: *is.*, Denmark   54 45N 11 15E   75
Loma *Mountains*: Sierra Leone   09 15N 11 00W   57
Lomas de Zamora: Argentina   34 46S 58 24W   128
Lomazzo: Italy   45 42N 09 02E   116

Types of map: Ocean pp. 1-5; Physical pp. 6-25; Human pp. 26-57; Topographic pp. 58-101; World pp. 102-111; Urban pp. 112-128.

Lombard: Ill., U.S.A. 41 52N 88 00W 124
Lomblen: *is.*, Indonesia 08 30S 123 30E 39
Lombok: *is.*, Indonesia 08 30S 116 15E 39
Lomé: Togo 06 08N 01 14E 57
Lomond, Ben: *mtn.*, Stirl., Scotland 56 12N 04 38W 64
Lomond, *Loch*: Scotland 56 00N 04 30W 64 113
Lomonosov: U.S.S.R. 59 55N 29 46E 80
Lomonosov *Ridge*: Arctic Ocean 89 00N 145 00E 23
London: Ont., Canada 42 58N 81 15W 45 99
London: England 51 30N 00 10W 26 59 112
Londonderry: Lon., N.Ireland 55 00N 07 19W 66
Londonderry (Derry): *admin.*, N.Ireland 54 45N 06 45W 66
Londrina: Brazil 23 18S 51 09W 51
Lone Star: Tex., U.S.A. 32 55N 94 43W 104
Long, *Loch*: Argyll., Scotland 56 00N 04 45W 64 113
Long *Bay*: U.S.A. 33 30N 78 30W 101
Long Beach: Calif., U.S.A. 33 47N 118 11W 43 91 106 127
Long Beach: N.Y., U.S.A. 40 35N 73 40W 123
Longbenton: Tyne & Wear, England 55 01N 01 34W 63
Long Branch: Ont., Canada 43 35N 79 32W 125
Longbridge: W.Mid., England 52 25N 01 56W 115
Longchamps: Argentina 34 51S 58 24W 128
Longchuan: China 24 02N 115 15E 85
Long Crendon: Bucks., England 51 47N 01 01W 59
Long Eaton: Derby., England 52 54N 01 15W 58
Longford: Long., Irish Republic 53 44N 07 47W 66
Longford: *admin.*, Irish Rep. 53 45N 07 45W 66
Longhua: Shanghai Shi, China 31 10N 121 27E 121
Longhui (Toahuaping): China 27 10N 111 02E 85
Long *Island*: Bahamas 23 15N 75 15W 47
Long *Island*: N.W.T., Canada 54 45N 79 15W 96
Long *Island*: N.Y., U.S.A. 40 45N 72 45W 45 99
Long Island *Sound*: U.S.A. 41 00N 73 00W 99
Longjumeau: France 48 42N 02 18E 117
Longka: China 31 10N 84 00E 83
Longlac: Ont., Canada 49 47N 86 34W 98
Longmont: Colo., U.S.A. 40 10N 105 06W 94
Long *Mountain*: Powys, Wales 53 39N 03 04W 60
Long Mynd: *hill*, Salop, England 52 35N 02 48W 60
Longnan: China 24 43N 114 35E 85
Longquan: China 28 08N 119 18E 85
Long *Range*: Nfld., Canada 50 15N 57 15W 44 97
Longridge: Lancs., England 53 51N 02 36W 63 114
Longridge Fell: *hill*, Lancs., England 53 51N 02 36W 114
Longshan: China 29 30N 109 28E 85
Longsheng: China 25 55N 109 58E 85
Longs *Peak*: Colo., U.S.A. 40 15N 105 37W 17 43 94
Long Sutton: Lincs., England 52 47N 00 08E 58
Longton: Staffs., England 52 59N 02 08W 58
Longueuil: Qué., Canada 45 32N 73 31W 122
Longview: Tex., U.S.A. 32 30N 94 44W 100
Longview: Wash., U.S.A. 46 08N 122 57W 42 90
Longwy: France 49 32N 05 46E 71 105
Longxi *see* Zhangzhou 24 33N 117 39E 36 85
Longxian: China 34 50N 106 53E 84
Longxianwei *see* Wengyuan 24 31N 114 10E 85
Long Xuyên: S.Vietnam 10 23N 105 25E 38
Longyan: China 25 08N 117 02E 85 105
Lons-le-Saunier: France 46 41N 05 33E 71
Lookout, *Cape*: N.C., U.S.A. 34 34N 76 34W 101
Loop *Head*: Clare, Irish Republic 52 34N 09 56W 67
Lopez, *Cape*: Gabon 00 36S 08 45E 57
López Camelo: Argentina 34 27S 58 41W 128
Lorain: Ohio, U.S.A. 41 28N 82 11W 45 98 104
Loralai: Pakistan 30 20N 68 41E 34
Lorca: Spain 37 40N 01 41W 77
Lord Howe *Island*: S.Pacific Ocean 31 28S 159 09E 15
Lord Howe *Rise*: S.Pacific Ocean 30 00S 162 00E 4
Lordsburg: N.Mex., U.S.A. 32 21N 108 43W 95
Lorenteggio: Italy 45 27N 09 07E 116
Lorient: France 47 45N 03 21W 70
Lorn, Firth of: *est.*, Argyll., Scotland 56 15N 05 30W 64
Lörrach: W.Germany 47 37N 07 40E 72
Los Alamos: N.Mex., U.S.A. 35 53N 106 19W 95
Los Altos: Calif., U.S.A. 37 24N 122 07W 126
Los Angeles: Chile 37 28S 72 23W 52
Los Angeles: Calif., U.S.A. 34 04N 118 15W 43 91 104 127
Los Angeles: *riv.*, Calif., U.S.A. 33 45N 118 00W 127
Los Mochis: Mexico 25 48N 109 00W 46
Los Reyes: Mexico 19 21N 98 59W 128
Lossiemouth: Moray., Scotland 57 43N 03 18W 65
Lostwithiel: Corn., England 50 25N 04 40W 61
Lot: *riv.*, France 44 15N 00 45E 70
Lota: Chile 37 07S 73 10W 52
Lotta: *riv.*, Finland/U.S.S.R. 68 30N 29 30E 74
Louga: Senegal 15 31N 16 13W 57
Loughborough: Leics., England 52 47N 01 11W 58
Loughrea: Gal., Irish Republic 53 12N 08 34W 67
Loughton: Essex, England 51 39N 00 03E 59 112
Louisburgh: Mayo, Irish Republic 53 46N 09 48W 66
Louise *Island*, B.C., Canada 52 59N 131 50W 89
Louisiana: Mo., U.S.A. 39 27N 91 02W 98
Louisiana: *admin.*, U.S.A. 43 100
Louis Trichardt: Trans., Rep. of S.Africa 23 01S 29 43E 55
Louisville: Ky., U.S.A. 38 13N 85 48W 45 101
Louisville: Nebr., U.S.A. 41 00N 96 10W 94
Loup: *riv.*, Nebr., U.S.A. 41 15N 98 00W 94
Loup City: Nebr., U.S.A. 41 17N 98 58W 94
Lourdes: France 43 06N 00 02W 70
Lourenço Marques: Mozambique 25 58S 32 35E 55
Louth: Lincs., England 53 22N 00 01W 58
Louth: *admin.*, Irish Rep. 53 45N 06 15W 66
Louvain *see* Leuven 50 53N 04 42E 72
Louviers: France 49 13N 01 11E 70
Louvroil: France 50 16N 03 58E 105
Lovat': *riv.*, U.S.S.R. 57 30N 31 30E 80
Loveland: Colo., U.S.A. 40 24N 105 05W 94
Lovelock: Nev., U.S.A. 40 11N 118 28W 90
Lovington: N.Mex., U.S.A. 32 57N 103 21W 95
Lowell: Mass., U.S.A. 42 38N 71 19W 99
Lower Arrow *Lake*: B.C., Canada 49 30N 118 00W 89
Lower California: *pen.*, Mexico 29 00N 114 00W 17 46
Lower Crystal Springs *Reservoir*: Calif., U.S.A. 37 32N 122 22W 126
Lower Granite *Dam*: Wash., U.S.A. 46 42N 117 24W 90
Lower Hutt: N.I., New Zealand 41 12S 174 54E 87
Lower Laberge: Yukon, Canada 61 24N 135 13W 88
Lower Lough Erne: *lake*, Ferm., N.Ireland 54 15N 07 45W 66
Lower Monumental *Dam*: Wash., U.S.A. 46 33N 118 30W 90
Lower New York *Bay*: N.Y., U.S.A. 40 30N 74 00W 123
Lower Post: B.C., Canada 59 56N 128 09W 88
Lower Red *Lake*: Minn., U.S.A. 47 45N 94 45W 98
Lower Rouge: *riv.*, Mich., U.S.A. 42 15N 83 15W 125
Lower San Leandro *Reservoir*: Calif., U.S.A. 37 47N 122 06W 126
Lower Tunguska: *riv.*, U.S.S.R. 64 30N 93 00E 30
Lowestoft: Suff., England 52 29N 01 45E 58
Lowther *Hills*: Scotland 55 15N 03 30W 62
Lowville: N.Y., U.S.A. 43 47N 75 30W 99
Loyalty *Islands*: Coral Sea 21 00S 167 00E 4 15
Loyang *see* Luoyang 34 41N 112 24E 36 84
Lozovaja: U.S.S.R. 48 54N 36 20E 80
Lozva: *riv.*, U.S.S.R. 60 00N 61 30E 81
Lualaba: *riv.*, Zaïre 07 15S 27 00E 21 54
Luan: *riv.*, China 39 30N 119 00E 36 84
Luanda: Angola 08 48S 13 14E 54
Luang Prabang: Laos 19 53N 102 10E 35
Luangwa: *riv.*, Zambia 12 30S 32 15E 21 54
Luanshya: Zambia 13 08S 28 24E 54
Luanxian: China 39 45N 118 50E 84
Lubań: Poland 51 07N 15 17E 73
Lübbecke: W.Germany 52 19N 08 37E 72
Lubbock: Tex., U.S.A. 33 35N 101 51W 43 95
Lübeck: W.Germany 53 52N 10 40E 26 73
Lübeck *Bay*: Germany 54 00N 11 30E 78
L'ubercy: U.S.S.R. 55 41N 37 53E 80 119
Lublin: Poland 51 18N 22 31E 27 78
L'ublino: U.S.S.R. 55 41N 37 44E 119
Lubny: U.S.S.R. 50 01N 33 00E 80
Luboń: Poland 52 23N 16 54E 73
L'ubotin: U.S.S.R. 49 57N 35 57E 80
Lubuklinggau: Indonesia 03 24S 102 56E 38
Lubumbashi (Elisabethville): Zaïre 11 40S 27 28E 54
Lubutu: Zaïre 00 44S 26 35E 54
Lucan: Dublin, Irish Republic 53 22N 06 27W 67
Luce *Bay*: Wig., Scotland 54 45N 04 45W 62
Lucena: Philippines 13 57N 121 36E 39
Lucena: Spain 37 25N 04 29W 77
Lucerne *see* Luzern 47 03N 08 17E 26 71
Luchiang: Taiwan 24 00N 120 26E 85

Types of map: Ocean pp. 1-5; Physical pp. 6-25; Human pp. 26-57; Topographic pp. 58-101; World pp. 102-111; Urban pp. 112-128.

Luchon, Bagnères-de-: France 42 48N 00 35E	70
Luchou see Luzhou 28 54N 105 27E	36
Lucin: Utah, U.S.A. 41 21N 113 54W	90
Luck (Lutsk): U.S.S.R. 50 44N 25 20E	78
Luckenwalde: E.Germany 52 05N 13 11E	73
Lucknow: India 26 50N 80 54E	34 82
Lucyville: Nfld., Canada 54 46N 58 28W	97
Lüda (Lüta; Dairen): China 38 53N 121 35E	37 84
Lüdenscheid: W.Germany 51 13N 07 38E	118
Lüderitz: S.W.Africa 26 38S 15 10E	55
Ludhīana: India 30 56N 75 52E	34 82
Ludington: Mich., U.S.A. 43 58N 86 27W	98
L'udinovo: U.S.S.R. 53 52N 34 27E	80
Ludlow: Salop, England 52 22N 02 43W	60
Ludlow: Calif., U.S.A. 34 43N 116 10W	91
Ludvika: Sweden 60 08N 15 14E	75
Ludwigsburg: W.Germany 48 54N 09 12E	72
Ludwigslust: E.Germany 53 20N 11 30E	73
Luebo: Zaïre 05 21S 21 25E	54
Lufeng: China 22 57N 115 38E	85
Lufkin: Tex., U.S.A. 31 21N 94 44W	100
Luga: U.S.S.R. 58 44N 29 52E	80
Luga: riv., U.S.S.R. 59 00N 29 30E	80
Lugano, Lago di (Ceresio, Lago di): Italy/Switzerland	
46 00N 09 00E	71
Lugansk (Voroshilovgrad): U.S.S.R. 48 34N 39 20E 28 80	
Lugg: riv., England/Wales 52 15N 03 00W	60
Lugnaquilla: mtn., Wick., Irish Republic 52 58N 06 27W 67	
Lugo: Spain 43 00N 07 33W	77
Lugoj: Romania 45 41N 21 57E	78
Lugouqiao: China 39 50N 116 13E	121
Luichart, Loch: R. & Crom., Scotland 57 30N 04 45W	64
Lugton Water: riv., Ayr., Scotland 55 30N 04 30W	113
Luing: is., Argyll., Scotland 56 15N 05 30W	64
Luján: riv., Argentina 34 19S 58 43W	128
Lukojanov: U.S.S.R. 55 02N 44 30E	80
Luleå: Sweden 65 35N 22 10E 27 74 105	
Luleälv: riv., Sweden 66 15N 21 00E	74
Lüleburgaz: Turkey 41 25N 27 22E	79
Lulong: China 39 54N 118 52E	84
Lülsdorf: W.Germany 50 50N 07 00E	119
Luluabourg see Kananga 05 54S 22 25E	54
Lulu Island: B.C., Canada 49 00N 123 00W	126
Lumberton: N.C., U.S.A. 34 37N 79 03W	101
Lumsden: S.I., New Zealand 45 45S 168 27E	87
Lunan Bay: Angus, Scotland 56 30N 02 15W	65
Lūnāvāda: India 23 08N 73 40E	82
Lund: Sweden 55 42N 13 10E	75
Lundy Island: Devon, England 51 11N 04 40W	61
Lune: riv., England 54 15N 02 30W	63
Lüneburg: W.Germany 53 15N 10 24E	73
Lüneburger Heide: geog. reg., W.Germany 53 00N 10 15E	
	73
Lünen: W.Germany 51 37N 07 31E	118
Lunéville: France 48 35N 06 30E	71
Lūni: riv., India 25 45N 72 00E	34 82
Luo: riv., China 36 15N 109 15E	84
Luodian: Guangdong, China 22 42N 111 31E	85
Luohe (Loho): China 33 32N 114 02E	36 84
Luonan: China 34 08N 110 04E	84
Luoning: China 34 20N 111 37E	84
Luoshan: China 32 13N 114 32E	84
Luotian: China 30 48N 115 29E	85
Luoxiaoshan: mtns., China 26 15N 113 45E	85
Luoyang (Loyang): China 34 41N 112 24E	36 84
Luoyuan: China 26 27N 119 35E	85
Lupeni: Romania 45 20N 23 10E	78
Lura: riv., Italy 45 30N 09 00E	116
Lurago Marinone: Italy 45 45N 08 59E	116
Lurate Caccivio: Italy 45 45N 08 59E	116
Lure, Montagne de: France 44 06N 05 46E	71
Lurgan: Arm., N.Ireland 54 28N 06 20W	66
Lúrio: riv., Mozambique 14 45S 39 15E	21 54
Lusaka: Zambia 15 25S 28 17E	55
Lusambo: Zaïre 04 58S 23 27E	54
Lushan: China 33 35N 112 39E	84
Lushi: China 33 59N 111 01E	84
Lüshun (Port Arthur): China 38 47N 121 20E	37 84
Luso: Angola 11 48S 19 55E	54
Lüta see Lüda 38 53N 121 35E	37 84
Luton: Beds., England 51 53N 00 25W	26 59

Lutsk see Luck 50 44N 25 20E	78
Lutterworth: Leics., England 52 28N 01 10W	58
Luwuk: Indonesia 00 56S 122 47E	39
LUXEMBOURG 49 45N 06 00E	26 72 105
Luxembourg: Luxembourg 49 37N 06 08E	26 72
Luxor see Al Uqşur 25 41N 32 39E	32
Luyuan: China 39 54N 116 29E	121
Luza: U.S.S.R. 60 39N 47 10E	81
Luzern (Lucerne): Switzerland 47 03N 08 17E	26 71
Luzhai: China 24 35N 109 30E	85
Luzhou (Luchou): China 28 54N 105 27E	36
Luzon: is., Philippines 16 30N 121 15E	12 39
Luzon Strait: Philippines/Taiwan 20 30N 121 00E	12 37
L'vov (Lwów): U.S.S.R. 49 50N 24 00E	28 78
Lyall, Mount: S.I., New Zealand 45 17S 167 36E	87
Lyallpur: Pakistan 31 25N 73 09E	34 82
Lybster: Caith., Scotland 58 18N 03 18W	65
Lyčkovo: U.S.S.R. 57 55N 32 24E	80
Lycksele: Sweden 64 34N 18 40E	74
Lycksele Lappmark: geog. reg., Sweden 65 15N 16 30E	74
Lydd: Kent, England 50 57N 00 55E	59
Lydney: Glos., England 51 44N 02 32W	61
Lyell Island: B.C., Canada 52 30N 131 30W	89
Lyles Wrigley: Tenn., U.S.A. 35 50N 87 21W	101
Lyme Bay: England 50 30N 03 00W	61
Lyme Regis: Dorset, England 50 44N 02 57W	61
Lymington: Hants., England 50 46N 01 33W	59
Lymm: Ches., England 53 23N 02 28W	58
Lynchburg: Va., U.S.A. 37 24N 79 09W	45 101
Lyndhurst: Hants., England 50 52N 01 34W	59
Lynher: riv., Corn., England 50 30N 04 15W	61
Lynmouth: Devon, England 51 15N 03 50W	61
Lynn Lake: Man., Canada 56 51N 101 01W	92
Lynn Wood Reservation: Mass., U.S.A. 42 29N 70 59W	
	122
Lynton: Devon, England 51 15N 03 50W	61
Lyon: France 45 46N 04 50E	26 71
Lyon, riv., Perth., Scotland 56 30N 04 15W	64
Lyon, Loch: Perth., Scotland 56 30N 04 15W	64
Lyons: Ill., U.S.A. 41 48N 87 49W	124
Lyons: Kans., U.S.A. 38 21N 98 12W	94
Lyskovo: U.S.S.R. 56 04N 45 02E	81
Lyś'va: U.S.S.R. 58 07N 57 47E	81 105
Lytham St. Annes: Lancs., England 53 45N 03 01W 63 114	
Lyttelton: S.I., New Zealand 43 36S 172 42E	87
Lytton: B.C., Canada 50 14N 121 34W	89

Ma: riv., Laos/N.Vietnam 21 00N 103 45E	35
Ma'ān: Jordan 30 12N 35 44E	32
Maanselkä: hills, Finland 65 45N 28 45E	74
Maanshan: China 31 48N 118 35E	84 105
Maarianhamina (Mariehamn): Finland 60 06N 19 56E	75
Maas: riv., Netherlands 51 45N 05 30E	72
Maastricht: Netherlands 50 51N 05 42E	72
Mabashi: Japan 35 48N 139 55E	121
Mablethorpe: Lincs., England 53 21N 00 15E	58
McAlester: Okla., U.S.A. 34 56N 95 46W	100
McAllen: Tex., U.S.A. 26 13N 98 14W	43
Macapá: Brazil 00 02N 51 03W	50
McArthur's Head: Argyll., Scotland 55 46N 06 03W	62
Macau (Aomen): Port. colony, China 22 17N 113 35E	
	36 85
McBride: B.C., Canada 53 21N 120 19W	89
Maccarese: Italy 41 53N 12 13E	116
Macclesfield: Ches., England 53 16N 02 07W 58 114	
Macclesfield Canal: Ches., England 53 15N 02 00W	114
McComb: Miss., U.S.A. 31 15N 90 27W	100
McCook: Nebr., U.S.A. 40 12N 100 38W	94
McDermitt: Nev., U.S.A. 42 00N 117 43W	90
Macdhui, Ben: mtn., Aber., Scotland 57 04N 03 40W	65
Macdonald-Cartier Freeway: hwy., Ont., Canada	
43 45N 79 15W	125
Macdonnell Ranges: N.T., Australia 23 30S 132 15E 14 40	
Macduff: Banff., Scotland 57 40N 02 29W	65
Maceió: Brazil 09 40S 35 43W	50
Macerata: Italy 43 18N 13 27E	79
MacFarlane: riv., Sask., Canada 58 15N 107 45W	92
McGehee: Ark., U.S.A. 33 38N 91 24W	100

Types of map: Ocean pp. 1-5; Physical pp. 6-25; Human pp. 26-57; Topographic pp. 58-101; World pp. 102-111; Urban pp. 112-128.

McGill: Nev., U.S.A.   39 23N 114 47W   91
Macgillycuddy's Reeks: *mtns.*, Kerry, Irish Republic
  52 00N 09 30W   67
McGregor: *riv.*, B.C., Canada   54 00N 122 00W   89
Machačkala (Makhachkala): U.S.S.R.   42 58N 47 30E   28
Machala: Ecuador   03 16S 79 58W   48
Machars, The: *dist.*, Wig., Scotland   54 45N 04 30W   62
Macheng: China   31 10N 115 05E   84
Machida: Japan   35 32N 139 27E   121
Machilīpatnam (Masulipatam): India   16 11N 81 08E   34
Machrihanish: Argyll., Scotland   52 26N 05 44W   62
Machrihanish *Bay*: Argyll., Scotland   55 15N 05 30W   62
Machynlleth: Powys, Wales   52 35N 03 51W   60
Macias Nguema Biyogo (Fernando Póo): *is.*, & *admin.*,
  Equatorial Guinea   03 30N 08 45E   20 57
McIntosh: S.D., U.S.A.   45 53N 101 21W   94
Mackay: Qld., Australia   21 00S 149 10E   41
Mackay, *Lake*: Australia   22 30S 129 00E   40
McKeesport: Pa., U.S.A.   40 21N 79 52W   125
McKees Rocks: Pa., U.S.A.   40 29N 80 10W   125
Mackenzie: *riv.*, N.W.T., Canada   62 00N 122 00W   16 42 88
Mackenzie, District of: *admin.*, Canada   61 00N 109 00W
  42 92
Mackenzie *Mountains*: Canada   64 00N 130 00W   16 88
Mackinac, *Straits of*: Mich., U.S.A.   45 45N 84 45W   98
McKinley, *Mount*: Alaska, U.S.A.   63 02N 151 01W   16
McKinney: Tex., U.S.A.   33 12N 96 37W   100
McLean: Va., U.S.A.   38 57N 77 13W   122
McLennan: Alta., Canada   55 42N 116 50W   92
Madhyamgrām: India   22 42N 88 27E   120
Madhya Pradesh: *admin.*, India   22 00N 80 00E   34 82
Madīnat ash-Sha'b: Yemen D.R.   12 50N 44 56E   53
Madison: Fla., U.S.A.   30 28N 83 25W   101
Madison: Ind., U.S.A.   38 46N 85 22W   98
Madison: S.D., U.S.A.   44 00N 97 07W   94
Madison: Wis., U.S.A.   43 04N 89 22W   45 98
Madison: *riv.*, Mont., U.S.A.   45 00N 111 30W   94
Madison Heights: Mich., U.S.A.   42 29N 83 05W   125
Madisonville: Ky., U.S.A.   37 20N 87 30W   100
Madiun: Indonesia   07 37S 111 33E   38
Madras: India   13 05N 80 18E   34
Madras: *admin. see* Tamil Nadu   11 30N 78 00E   34
Madre, *Laguna*: Tex., U.S.A.   26 30N 97 15W   100
Madre de Dios: *riv.*, Bolivia/Peru   11 45S 68 15W   49
Madre del Sur, Sierra: *ra.*, Mexico   17 15N 98 30W   17 46
Madre Occidental, Sierra: *ra.*, Mexico   25 00N 105 45W
  17 46
Madre Oriental, Sierra: *ra.*, Mexico   21 00N 100 00W   17 46
Madrid: Spain   40 25N 03 43W   26 77 116
Madsen: Ont., Canada   50 58N 93 55W   93
Madura: *is.*, Indonesia   07 00S 113 15E   38
Madurai (Mathurai): India   09 55N 78 07E   34
Maebashi: Japan   36 23N 139 04E   37 86
Maesteg: M.Glam., Wales   51 37N 03 40W   61
Mafeking: C.P., Rep. of S.Africa   25 53S 25 39E   55
Magadan: U.S.S.R.   59 34N 150 48E   31
Magdagači: U.S.S.R.   53 27N 125 48E   31
Magdalena: *riv.*, Colombia   10 30N 74 45W   48
Magdalena, Río de la: *riv.*, Mexico   19 17N 99 17W   128
Magdalen *Islands*: Qué., Canada   47 30N 61 45W   44 97
Magdeburg: E.Germany   52 08N 11 37E   26 73
Magdeburg: *admin.*, E.Germany   52 15N 11 30E   73
Magee, *Island*: Antrim, N.Ireland   54 45N 05 30W   66
Magelang: Indonesia   07 28S 110 11E   38
Magellan, *Strait of*: Chile   54 00S 71 00W   52
Magenta: Italy   45 28N 08 52E   116
Maggiore, *Lago*: Italy/Switzerland   46 00N 08 30E   71
Maghera: Lon., N.Ireland   54 51N 06 40W   66
Magherafelt: Lon., N.Ireland   54 45N 06 36W   66
Maghull: Mers., England   53 32N 02 57W   114
Magnago: Italy   45 35N 08 48E   116
Magnitogorsk: U.S.S.R.   53 27N 59 04E   29 81 105
Magnolia: Ark., U.S.A.   33 16N 93 14W   100
Magog: Qué., Canada   45 16N 72 09W   96
Magpie: *riv.*, Ont., Canada   48 15N 84 30W   98
Magpie *Lake*: Qué., Canada   51 00N 64 30W   97
Maguse *Lake*: N.W.T., Canada   61 30N 94 45W   93
Maguse River: N.W.T., Canada   61 20N 94 05W   93
Maguzhan: China   31 15N 88 00E   83
Mahabharat *Range*: Nepal   28 45N 83 00E   83
Mahāded *Hills*: India   22 00N 78 30E   83

Mahakam: *riv.*, Indonesia   00 45N 115 15E   39
Mahalla el Kubra *see* Al Mahallah al Kubrā   30 59N 31 10E
  32
Mahānadi: *riv.*, India   20 30N 85 00E   34 83
Mahārāshtra: *admin.*, India   20 00N 77 00E   34 82
Maha Sarakham: Thailand   16 12N 103 16E   38
Mahaṭṭat Ḥaraḍ (Ḥaraḍ): Saudi Arabia   24 08N 49 04E   33
Mahia *Peninsula*: N.I., New Zealand   39 00S 178 00E   87
Mahoba: India   25 18N 79 53E   82
Mahón: Balearic Islands   39 54N 04 15E   77
Mahood *Creek*: B.C., Canada   49 08N 122 48W   126
Mahrauli: India   28 31N 77 11E   120
Mahuva: India   21 03N 71 50E   82
Maidenhead: Berks., England   51 32N 00 44W   59
Maidstone: Ont., Canada   42 13N 82 53W   125
Maidstone: Kent, England   51 17N 00 32E   59 112
Maigue: *riv.*, Lim., Irish Republic   52 30N 08 45W   67
Maihar: India   24 14N 80 50E   82
Maikala *Range*: India   22 00N 81 00E   83
Main: *riv.*, Antrim, N.Ireland   54 45N 06 15W   66
Main: *riv.*, W.Germany   49 45N 09 00E   73
Main-Donau *Kanal*: W.Germany   49 00N 11 15E   73
Maine: *admin.*, U.S.A.   45 00N 69 00W   44 96
Maine: *riv.*, Kerry, Irish Republic   52 00N 09 15W   67
Maine, *Gulf of*: U.S.A.   43 00N 69 30W   99
Maine-et-Loire: *admin.*, France   47 30N 00 30W   105
Mainland: *is.*, Orkney Is., Scotland   59 00N 03 00W   65
Mainland: *is.*, Shetland Is., Scotland   60 15N 01 15W   65
Mainpuri: India   27 14N 79 01E   82
Mainz: W.Germany   50 00N 08 16E   26 72
Maipo: *mtn.*, Argentina/Chile   34 10S 69 52W   52
Maira: *riv.*, Italy   44 15N 07 00E   71
Maisons-Laffitte: France   48 57N 02 08E   117
Maizhuang: China   39 48N 116 36E   121
Maizuru: Japan   35 27N 135 20E   86
Majkop (Maykop): U.S.S.R.   44 35N 40 07E   28
Majorca: *is.*, *see* Mallorca   39 30N 03 00E   26 77
Majunga: Malagasy Rep.   15 43S 46 19E   55
Majuqiao: China   39 46N 116 32E   121
Makālu: *mtn.*, China/Nepal   27 54N 87 06E   83
Makarikari: *salt pan*, Botswana   20 30S 25 45E   55
Makarjev: U.S.S.R.   57 52N 43 48E   80
Makasar: Indonesia   05 07S 119 24E   39
Makassar, *Strait of* (Makasar Selat): Indonesia
  01 30S 118 00E   13 39
Makat: U.S.S.R.   47 39N 53 19E   81
Makejevka (Makeyevka): U.S.S.R.   48 02N 37 58E
  28 80 105
Makhachkala *see* Machačkala   42 58N 47 30E   28
Makkah (Mecca): Saudi Arabia   21 26N 39 49E   33
Makkovik: Nfld., Canada   55 00N 59 10W   97
Makó: Hungary   46 11N 20 31E   78
Makoua: Congo   00 01N 15 39E   54
Makrāna: India   27 02N 74 44E   82
Makurdi: Nigeria   07 44N 08 35E   57
Malabar *Coast*: India   10 15N 74 45E   34
Malabo (Santa Isabel): Macias Nguema Biyogo
  03 45N 08 48E   57
Malacca *see* Melaka   02 12N 102 15E   38
Malacca, *Strait of*: S.E.Asia   01 30N 102 45E   12 38
Malafede: *riv.*, Italy   41 30N 12 15E   116
Malahide: Dublin, Irish Republic   53 27N 06 09W   66
Málaga: Spain   36 43N 04 25W   26 77
Malagasy *Fracture Zone*: Indian Ocean   45 00S 42 00E   1
MALAGASY REPUBLIC   1 21 55
Malaita: *is.*, S.Pacific Ocean   09 00S 161 00E   4
Malaja Ochta: U.S.S.R.   59 56N 30 24E   119
Malang: Indonesia   07 59S 112 45E   38
Malanje: Angola   09 32S 16 20E   54
Mälaren: *lake*, Sweden   59 15N 17 00E   75
Malartic: Qué., Canada   48 09N 78 09W   99
Malatya (Milid): Turkey   38 22N 38 18E   32
Malaut: India   30 12N 74 40E   82
MALAWI   13 00S 34 15E   21 54
Malawi (Nyasa), *Lake*: E.Africa   11 45S 34 30E   21 54
Malaya: *admin.*, Malaysia   04 15N 102 00E   38
Malay *Peninsula*: Malaysia/Thailand   06 00N 101 30E
  12 38
MALAYSIA   05 00N 109 00E   12 38
Mal *Bay*: Clare, Irish Republic   52 45N 09 15W   67
Malbork (Marienburg): Poland   54 02N 19 01E   78

Types of map: Ocean pp. 1-5; Physical pp. 6-25; Human pp. 26-57; Topographic pp. 58-101; World pp. 102-111; Urban pp. 112-128.

Malchiner See: *lake*, E.Germany   53 30N 12 30E   73
Malden: Mass., U.S.A.   42 24N 71 04W   122
Malden *Island*: S.Pacific Ocean   04 03S 154 59W   5
MALDIVES, REPUBLIC OF   04 00N 72 30E   1 11 34
Maldon: Essex, England   51 45N 00 40E   59
Maléa, Ákra: *cape*, Greece   36 26N 23 12E   79
Mālegaon: India   20 32N 74 38E   34 82
Malheur: *riv.*, Oreg., U.S.A.   43 45N 117 45W   90
Malheur *Lake*: Oreg., U.S.A.   43 20N 118 48W   90
MALI   20 57
Malindi: Kenya   03 14S 40 08E   54
Malines *see* Mechelen   51 02N 04 29E   72
Malin *Head*: Don., Irish Rep.   55 23N 07 24W   66
Malkāpur: India   20 52N 76 18E   82
Mallaig: Inv., Scotland   57 00N 05 50W   64
Mallorca (Majorca): *is.*, Balearic Islands   39 30N 03 00E   26 77
Mallow: Cork, Irish Republic   52 08N 08 39W   67
Malmberget: Sweden   67 11N 20 40E   74 105
Malmesbury: Wilts., England   51 36N 02 06W   61
Malmö: Sweden   55 35N 13 00E   27 75
Malnate: Italy   45 48N 08 52E   116
Maloti *Mountains*: Lesotho   29 00S 28 15E   55
Måløy: Norway   61 57N 05 06E   27 74
Mālpura: India   26 19N 75 24E   82
MALTA   35 45N 14 15E   7 27 79
Malta: Mont., U.S.A.   48 21N 107 52W   90
Maltby: S.Yorks., England   53 26N 01 11W   63
Maltion Luonnonpuisto: *na. rve.*, Finland   67 15N 28 30E   75
Malton: N.Yorks., England   54 08N 00 48W   63
Maluku: *is. & admin. see* Moluccas   01 30S 127 30E   13 39
Malvern: Here.& Worcs., *see* Great Malvern, England   52 07N 02 19W   59
Malvern: Ark., U.S.A.   34 22N 92 49W   100
Malvern *Hills*: Here.& Worcs., England   52 00N 02 15W   59
Malvinas, Islas *see* Falkland *Islands*   51 30S 59 30W   3 19 52
Malviya Nagar: India   28 32N 77 13E   120
Mālwa *Plateau*: India   23 45N 77 00E   11 34
Malyi Uzen': *riv.*, U.S.S.R.   49 30N 49 00E   81
Mamaroneck: N.Y., U.S.A.   40 57N 73 44W   123
Mamberamo: *riv.*, Indonesia   03 00S 139 00E   13
Mamou: Guinea   10 24N 12 05W   57
Mamry, Jezioro: *lake*, Poland   54 00N 21 30E   78
Mamudju: Indonesia   02 41S 118 55E   39
Man: Ivory Coast   07 31N 07 37W   57
Man, Calf of: *is.*, I. of Man., United Kingdom   54 03N 04 49W   62
Man, Isle of: *is. & admin.*, United Kingdom   54 15N 04 30W   62
Manaar, *Gulf of*: India/Sri Lanka   08 15N 79 00E   11 34
Manacle *Point*: Corn., England   50 03N 05 02W   61
Manado (Menado): Indonesia   01 32N 124 55E   39
Manáes *see* Manaus   03 08S 60 01W   50
Managua: Nicaragua   12 06N 86 18W   47
Manama *see* Al Manāmah   26 12N 50 38E   33
Manas: *riv.*, Bhutan/India   26 30N 91 00E   83
Ma'nasaluowochi: *lake*, China   30 45N 81 15E   83
Manāslu: *mtn.*, Nepal   28 33N 84 33E   83
Manaus (Manáes): Brazil   03 08S 60 01W   50
Manchester: Gt. Man., England   53 30N 02 15W   26 63 114
Manchester: N.H., U.S.A.   42 59N 71 28W   99
Manchester *Ship Canal*: England   53 15N 02 30W   114
Manchuria: *reg.*, China   46 00N 133 00E   37
Mandal: Norway   58 02N 07 30E   75
Mandalay: Burma   21 57N 96 04E   35
Mandalgov': Mongolia   45 45N 106 20E   36
Mandan: N.D., U.S.A.   46 50N 100 54W   94
Mandasor: India   24 03N 75 10E   82
Mandi: India   31 43N 76 55E   82
Mandla: India   22 35N 80 28E   82
Manendragarh: India   23 12N 82 20E   83
Manfredonia: Italy   41 37N 15 55E   79
Mangalore: India   12 54N 74 51E   34
Mangole: *is.*, Indonesia   01 45S 125 45E   39
Mangonui: N.I., New Zealand   35 00S 173 34E   87
Mangotsfield: Avon, England   51 29N 02 29W   61 113
Mangum: Okla., U.S.A.   34 53N 99 30W   95
Manhattan: Kans., U.S.A.   39 11N 96 35W   43 94
Manhattan: N.Y., U.S.A.   40 45N 73 58W   123

Manhattan Beach: Calif., U.S.A.   33 54N 118 24W   127
Man *Highlands*: Ivory Coast   07 30N 07 30W   57
Mani: *riv.*, India   23 00N 73 30E   82
Manicouagan: *riv.*, Qué., Canada   50 00N 68 30W   96
Manicouagan *Lake*: Qué., Canada   51 15N 68 30W   96
Manicouagan *Peninsula*: Qué., Canada   49 00N 68 15W   96
Mānikganj: Bangladesh   23 52N 90 00E   83
Manila: Philippines   14 36N 120 59E   39
Manila: *riv.*, Mayo, Irish Republic   53 45N 09 00W   66
Manipur: *admin.*, India   24 30N 93 45E   35
Manisa: Turkey   38 37N 27 29E   79
Manistee: Mich., U.S.A.   44 14N 86 20W   98
Manistee: *riv.*, Mich., U.S.A.   44 30N 85 30W   98
Manistique: Mich., U.S.A.   45 58N 86 17W   98
Manitoba: *admin.*, Canada   55 30N 95 00W   42 93
Manitoba, *Lake*: Man., Canada   51 00N 98 30W   42 93
Manitou *Island*: Mich., U.S.A.   47 25N 87 36W   98
Manitoulin *Island*: Ont., Canada   45 45N 82 30W   44 98
Manitouwadge: Ont., Canada   49 08N 85 47W   98
Manitowoc: Wis., U.S.A.   44 04N 87 40W   98
Manizales: Colombia   05 03N 75 32W   48
Mankato: Minn., U.S.A.   44 10N 94 00W   98
Manly: N.S.W., Australia   33 48S 151 17E   120
Mannheim: W.Germany   49 30N 08 28E   26 72
Manning, E.C.: *provincial park*, B.C., Canada   49 00N 120 45W   89
Manorhamilton: Leit., Irish Republic   54 18N 08 10W   66
Mano *River*: Liberia   06 56N 11 31W   104
Manouanis *Lake*: Qué., Canada   50 45N 70 45W   96
Manresá: Spain   41 43N 01 50E   77
Mānsa: India   29 59N 75 23E   82
Mansel *Island*: N.W.T., Canada   62 00N 80 00W   44
Mansfield: Notts., England   53 09N 01 11W   58
Mansfield: Ohio, U.S.A.   40 46N 82 31W   98
Mansfield Woodhouse: Notts., England   53 10N 01 11W   58
Manta: Ecuador   00 57S 80 44W   48
Mantes-la-Jolie: France   48 59N 01 43E   117
Mantiqueira, Serra da: *ra.*, Brazil   22 15S 45 15W   51
Mantova (Mantua): Italy   45 10N 10 47E   78
Manturovo: U.S.S.R.   58 20N 44 46E   81
Manukau: N.I., New Zealand   37 03S 174 32E   87
Manukau *Harbour*: N.I., New Zealand   37 00S 174 45E   87
Manyara, *Lake*: Tanzania   03 45S 35 45E   54
Manzanillo: Cuba   20 21N 77 07W   47
Manzanillo: Mexico   19 03N 104 20W   46
Manzovka: U.S.S.R.   44 12N 132 26E   86
Maoke *Mountains*: Indonesia   04 30S 139 00E   13
Maple Creek: Sask., Canada   49 55N 109 28W   92
Mapuera: *riv.*, Brazil   00 30N 58 15W   50
Mar, Serra do: *ra.*, Santa Catarina, Brazil   26 15S 49 15W   51
Maracaibo: Venezuela   10 44N 71 37W   48
Maracaibo, *Lago de*: Venezuela   10 00N 71 30W   48
Maracaju, Serra de: *ra.*, Brazil   23 45S 55 30W   51
Maracay: Venezuela   10 20N 67 28W   48
Marādah: Libya   29 15N 19 14E   32
Marahuaca, Cerro: *mtn.*, Venezuela   03 37N 65 25W   48
Marajó *Island*: Brazil   01 00S 49 45W   50
Maramba (Livingstone): Zambia   17 51S 25 52E   55
Marampa: Sierra Leone   08 41N 12 28W   104
Maramsilli *Reservoir*: India   20 30N 81 45E   83
Maranhão: *admin.*, Brazil   04 45S 45 15W   50
Marañón: *riv.*, Peru   04 30S 75 30W   48
Maraş: Turkey   37 34N 36 54E   33
Marathon: Ont., Canada   48 44N 86 23W   98
Marawi (Merowe): Sudan   18 29N 31 49E   53
Marazion: Corn., England   50 07N 05 29W   61
Marble Bar: W.A., Australia   21 16S 119 45E   40
Marblehead: Mass., U.S.A.   42 30N 70 50W   122
Marburg an der Lahn: W.Germany   50 49N 08 36E   72
March: Cambs., England   52 33N 00 06E   58
Marchienne-au-Pont: Belgium   50 24N 04 23E   105
Mar Chiquita, *Laguna*: Argentina   30 45S 62 30W   52
Marcona: Peru   15 10S 75 02W   104
Marcoussis: France   48 38N 02 14E   117
Marcus Hook: Pa., U.S.A.   39 50N 72 25W   106
Marcus *Island*: N.Pacific Ocean   24 18N 153 58E   4
Marcus Necker *Rise*: N.Pacific Ocean   20 00N 170 00E   4
Marcy, *Mount*: N.Y., U.S.A.   44 07N 73 56W   99
Mardān: Pakistan   34 12N 72 02E   29

Types of map: Ocean pp. 1-5; Physical pp. 6-25; Human pp. 26-57; Topographic pp. 58-101; World pp. 102-111; Urban pp. 112-128.

Mar del Plata: Argentina   38 00S 57 32W   52
Mardin: Turkey   37 19N 40 43E   33
Maree, *Loch*: R. & Crom., Scotland   57 30N 05 30W   64
Marfa: Tex., U.S.A.   30 19N 104 01W   95
Margam: W.Glam., Wales   51 34N 03 44W   61
Marganec: U.S.S.R.   47 38N 34 40E   80
Margarita, *Isla de*: Venezuela   11 00N 64 00W   48
Margate: Kent., England   51 24N 01 24E   59
Margeride, *Monts de la*: France   44 45N 03 30E   71
Marghera: Italy   45 28N 12 14E   107
Marguerite: *riv.*, Qué., Canada   50 45N 66 45W   97
Mariana *Islands*: Philippine Sea   17 00N 145 00E   4 12
Mariana *Ridge*: N.Pacific Ocean   17 00N 147 00E   4
Mariana *Trench*: N.Pacific Ocean   15 00N 147 00E   4
Marian *Lake*: N.W.T., Canada   63 00N 116 00W   88
Mariano (Mariano Comense): Italy   45 42N 09 10E   116
Mariánské Lázně: Czechoslovakia   49 59N 12 40E   73
Maria Portage: Man., Canada   53 54N 94 57W   93
Marias: *riv.*, Mont., U.S.A.   48 00N 110 30W   90
Maria Van Diemen, *Cape*: N.I., New
    Zealand   34 29S 172 39E   87
Maribor: Yugoslavia   46 35N 15 40E   27 78
Mariehamn *see* Maarianhamina   60 06N 19 56E   75
Marienburg *see* Malbork   54 02N 19 01E   78
Mariestad: Sweden   58 44N 13 50E   75
Marifu: Japan   34 23N 132 30E   107
Marijampole *see* Kapsukas   54 31N 23 20E   78
Marília: Brazil   22 13S 49 58W   51
Marinduque *Island*: Philippines   13 15N 122 00E   39
Marinette: Wis., U.S.A.   45 06N 87 38W   98
Maringá: Brazil   23 25S 51 55W   51
Marino: Italy   41 46N 12 40E   116
Marinskij Posad: U.S.S.R.   56 07N 47 43E   81
Marion: Ind., U.S.A.   40 33N 85 40W   98
Marion: Iowa, U.S.A.   42 02N 91 36W   98
Marion: Ohio, U.S.A.   40 35N 83 08W   98
Marion, *Lake*: S.C., U.S.A.   33 30N 80 15W   101
Mariscal Estigarribia: Paraguay   22 03S 60 35W   51
Maritimes, *Alpes*: France   44 00N 07 00E   71
Maritsa: *riv.*, Greece/Turkey   41 15N 26 15E   79
Mariupol' *see* Ždanov   47 06N 37 33E   28 80 105
Market Bosworth: Leics., England   52 37N 01 24W   115
Market Deeping: Lincs., England   52 41N 00 19W   58
Market Drayton: Salop, England   52 54N 02 29W   58
Market Harborough: Leics., England   52 29N 00 55W   58
Market Rasen: Lincs., England   53 24N 00 21W   58
Market Weighton: Humb., England   53 52N 00 40W   63
Markham: Ont., Canada   43 54N 79 16W   125
Markham, *Mount*: Antarctica   82 45S 160 25E   25
Markinch: Fife, Scotland   56 12N 03 09W   65
Marks: U.S.S.R.   51 42N 46 46E   81
Marktredwitz: W.Germany   50 00N 12 06E   73
Marl: W.Germany   51 39N 07 05E   72
Marlborough: Wilts., England   51 26N 01 43W   61
Marlin: Tex., U.S.A.   31 18N 96 54W   95
Marlow: Bucks., England   51 35N 00 48W   59 112
Marmande: France   44 30N 00 10E   70
Marmara, *Sea of*: Turkey   40 45N 28 15E   27 79
Marmora: Ont., Canada   44 29N 77 40W   104
Marnate: Italy   45 38N 08 54E   116
Marne: *riv.*, France   49 00N 03 45E   71
Marne à la Saône, *Canal de la*: France   48 00N 05 15E   71
Marne au Rhin, *Canal de la*: France   48 30N 05 30E   71
Maromokotro, *Mount*: Malagasy Rep.   14 01S 48 58E   55
Maroni: *riv.*, French Guiana/Surinam   05 15N 54 15W   50
Maroubra: N.S.W., Australia   33 57S 151 15E   120
Marple: Gt. Man., England   53 24N 02 03W   63
Marquesas *Islands*: S.Pacific Ocean   09 00S 139 00W   5
Marquette: Mich., U.S.A.   46 33N 87 23W   98
Marquette *Park*: Ill., U.S.A.   41 45N 87 42W   124
Marquette *Range*: Mich., U.S.A.   46 30N 87 15W   104
Marrakech: Morocco   31 49N 08 00W   56
Marra *Mountains*: Sudan   13 30N 24 00E   32
Marree: S.A., Australia   29 40S 138 04E   41
Marrickville: N.S.W., Australia   33 55S 151 09E   120
Marsa el Brega *see* Qaṣr al Burayqah   30 25N 19 34E   32
Marsala: Sicily   37 48N 12 27E   79
Marseille: France   43 18N 05 22E   26 71
Marshall: Tex., U.S.A.   32 33N 94 23W   100
Marshall Ford *Dam*: Tex., U.S.A.   30 12N 98 01W   95
Marshall *Islands*: N.Pacific Ocean   07 00N 167 00E   4

Marshalltown: Iowa, U.S.A.   42 05N 92 54W   98
Marshfield: Wis., U.S.A.   44 40N 90 11W   98
Marsh Harbour: Bahamas   26 31N 77 05W   47
Marsoui: Qué., Canada   49 13N 66 05W   97
Martaban, *Gulf of*: Burma   16 00N 96 30E   35
Martapura: Indonesia   04 20S 104 22E   38
Martha's Vineyard: *is.*, Mass., U.S.A.   41 15N 70 70W   99
Martin: Czechoslovakia   49 04N 18 55E   78
Martinez: Calif., U.S.A.   38 00N 122 10W   106
Martinique: *is.*, Windward Islands   14 30N 61 00W   47
Martinsburg: W.Va., U.S.A.   39 28N 77 59W   99
Martin Vaz: *is.*, S.Atlantic Ocean   20 30S 28 51W   3
Marton: N.I., New Zealand   40 04S 175 25E   87
Martorellas: Spain   41 32N 02 14E   116
Martre, *Lac la*: N.W.T., Canada   63 15N 118 00W   88
Mary (Merv): U.S.S.R.   37 36N 61 50E   29
Maryborough: Qld., Australia   25 32S 152 36E   41
Maryland: *admin.*, U.S.A.   38 30N 76 30W   45 99
Maryneal: Tex., U.S.A.   32 14N 100 27W   95
Maryport: Cumbria, England   54 43N 03 30W   62
Mary's Harbour: Nfld., Canada   52 18N 55 51W   97
Maryville: Tenn., U.S.A.   35 45N 83 59W   101
Masan: S.Korea   35 11N 128 32E   37
Masbate *Island*: Philippines   12 15N 123 15E   39
Mascara: Algeria   35 20N 00 09E   56
Mascarene *Basin*: Indian Ocean   14 00S 53 00E   1
Mascot: N.S.W., Australia   33 56S 151 12E   120
Maseru: Lesotho   29 19S 27 29E   55
Masham: N.Yorks., England   54 13N 01 40W   63
Mashan: China   23 51N 108 16E   85
Mashhad: Iran   36 16N 59 34E   33
Masjed Soleymān: Iran   31 59N 49 18E   33
Mask, *Lough*: Mayo, Irish Rep.   53 35N 09 20W   66
Mason *Bay*: Stewart I., New Zealand   47 00S 167 45E   87
Mason City: Iowa, U.S.A.   43 10N 93 10W   98
Masqaṭ (Muscat): Oman   23 37N 58 38E   33
Massachusetts: *admin.*, U.S.A.   42 15N 72 30W   45 99
Massachusetts *Bay*: Mass., U.S.A.   42 15N 70 45W   99
Massachusetts Turnpike: *hwy.*, Mass., U.S.A.
    42 15N 73 15W   122
Massawa *see* Mesewa   15 37N 39 28E   53
Massena: N.Y., U.S.A.   44 56N 74 57W   99
Masset: B.C., Canada   54 00N 132 09W   89
Massif Central: *mtns.*, France   45 00N 03 00E   6 26 71
Massillon: Ohio, U.S.A.   40 48N 81 32W   98
Masterton: N.I., New Zealand   40 57S 175 39E   87
Masuda: Japan   34 40N 131 51E   86
Masulipatam *see* Machilīpatnam   16 11N 81 08E   34
Matadepera: Spain   41 36N 02 02E   116
Matadi: Zaïre   05 49S 13 27E   54
Matagami, *Lake*: Qué., Canada   49 45N 77 15W   96
Matagorda *Bay*: Tex., U.S.A.   28 30N 96 15W   100
Matagorda *Island*: Tex., U.S.A.   28 00N 96 45W   100
Matam: Senegal   15 40N 13 18W   57
Matamoros: Tamaulipas, Mexico   25 53N 97 30W   46
Matane: Qué., Canada   48 50N 67 31W   96
Matanza: *riv.*, Argentina   34 50S 58 37W   128
Matanzas: Cuba   23 03N 81 35W   47
Matapan, *Cape see* Taínaron, Ákra   36 23N 22 29E   79
Matera: Italy   40 40N 16 37E   79
Matheson Station: Ont., Canada   48 33N 80 23W   99
Mathura: India   27 30N 77 42E   34 82
Mathurai *see* Madurai   09 55N 78 07E   34
Matlock: Derby., England   53 07N 01 34W   58
Mato Grosso: *admin.*, Brazil   22 00S 55 00W   51
Mato Grosso *Plateau*: Brazil   16 15S 54 45W   18 50
Matopo *Hills*: Rhodesia   20 45S 28 30E   21
Maṭraḥ: Oman   23 37N 58 34E   33
Maṭrūḥ (Mersa Maṭrūḥ): Egypt   31 21N 27 14E   32
Matsu: *is.*, Taiwan   26 15N 120 00E   85
Matsudo: Japan   35 48N 139 54E   121
Matsue: Japan   35 28N 133 04E   37 86
Matsumoto: Japan   36 14N 137 58E   86
Matsusaka: Japan   34 34N 136 32E   86
Matsuyama: Japan   33 50N 132 45E   37 86
Mattagami: *riv.*, Ont., Canada   49 30N 81 30W   98
Mattawa: Ont., Canada   46 19N 78 42W   99
Mattoon: Ill., U.S.A.   39 29N 88 21W   98
Maturín: Venezuela   09 45N 63 10W   48
Matvejevskoje: U.S.S.R.   55 43N 37 21E   119
Maughold *Head*: I. of M., United Kingdom   54 18N 04 20W

Types of map: Ocean pp. 1-5; Physical pp. 6-25; Human pp. 26-57; Topographic pp. 58-101; World pp. 102-111; Urban pp. 112-128.

	62
Mauldre: *riv.*, France 48 45N 01 45E	116
Maule: France 48 55N 01 51E	116
Maunath Bhanjan: India 25 57N 83 34E	83
Mau Ranīpur: India 25 14N 79 07E	82
MAURITANIA	20 56
Mavrovo *National Park*: Yugoslavia 42 17N 20 32E	79
Mawlaik: Burma 23 40N 94 26E	35
Mawson: *rsch. stn.*, Antarctica 67 36S 62 53E	24
May, *Cape*: N.J., U.S.A. 38 58N 74 55W	99
May, *Isle of*: Scotland 56 12N 02 32W	65
Mayaguana: *is.*, Bahamas 22 30N 73 00W	47
Mayagëz: Puerto Rico 18 13N 67 09W	47
Maybole: Ayr., Scotland 55 21N 04 41W	62
Mayenne: France 48 18N 00 37W	70
Mayenne: *riv.*, France 47 30N 00 30W	70
Mayfield: Ky., U.S.A. 36 45N 88 40W	100
Maykop *see* Majkop 44 35N 40 07E	28
Maynooth: Kild., Irish Republic 53 23N 06 35W	67
Mayo: Yukon, Canada 63 34N 135 52W	88
Mayo: *admin.*, Irish Rep. 53 45N 09 00W	66
Mayo *Lake*: Yukon, Canada 63 45N 135 00W	88
Mayo Landing: Yukon, Canada 63 35N 135 49W	88
Mayurbhanj: *admin.*, India 21 50N 86 30E	105
Maywood: Ill., U.S.A. 41 51N 87 48W	124
Mayyit, Al Baḥr al (Dead Sea): *lake*, Jordan 31 15N 35 15E	
	10 32
Mazagan *see* El Jadida 33 16N 08 30W	56
Mazamet: France 43 29N 02 22E	70
Mazaruni: *riv.*, Guyana 05 45N 59 30W	48
Mazatenango: Guatemala 14 13N 91 30W	46
Mazatlán: Mexico 23 13N 106 25W	46
Mazhang: China 39 58N 116 22E	121
Mazurazaki: Japan 31 16N 130 19E	86
Mbabane: Swaziland 26 20S 31 08E	55
Mbala (Abercorn): Zambia 08 50S 31 22E	54
Mbale: Uganda 01 04N 34 12E	53
Mbandaka (Coquilhatville): Zaïre 00 04N 18 16E	54
Mbeya: Tanzania 08 54S 33 27E	54
Mbuji-Mayi: Zaïre 06 09S 23 36E	54
Mcensk: U.S.S.R. 53 17N 36 35E	80
McLeod: *riv.*, Alta., Canada 53 15N 116 30W	92
McLeod Lake: B.C., Canada 54 59N 123 02W	89
M'Clintock: Man., Canada 57 48N 94 12W	93
Macmillan: *riv.*, Yukon, Canada 62 45N 135 00W	88
McMinnville: Oreg., U.S.A. 45 13N 123 12W	90
McMinnville: Tenn., U.S.A. 35 41N 85 46W	101
McMurdo: *rsch. stn.*, Antarctica 70 51S 166 37W	25
McMurdo *Sound*: Antarctica 77 00S 165 00E	25
McMurray: Alta., Canada 56 45N 111 27W	92
Macnean, *Lower Lough*: Ferm., N.Ireland 54 15N 07 45W	
	66
Macnean, *Upper Lough*: Irish Republic/N.Ireland 54 15N 07 45W	66
Macomb: Ill., U.S.A. 40 27N 90 40W	98
Mâcon: France 46 18N 04 50E	71
Macon: Ga., U.S.A. 32 49N 83 37W	45 101
McPherson: Kans., U.S.A. 38 22N 97 40W	94
Macquarie Island: *rsch. stn.*, Southern Ocean 54 30S 158 57E	25
Macquarie *Rise*: Southern Ocean 53 00S 160 00E	25
MacRae: Yukon, Canada 60 36N 135 00W	88
McRae: Ga., U.S.A. 32 02N 82 55W	101
Macroom: Cork, Irish Republic 51 54N 08 57W	67
Mactan: Philippines 10 16N 123 58E	39
McTavish Arm: *bay*, N.W.T., Canada 66 15N 118 30W	88
McVicar Arm: *bay*, N.W.T., Canada 65 00N 120 30W	88
Madagascar: *is. see* Malagasy Rep.	1 21 55
Madagascar *Basin*: Indian Ocean 25 00S 54 00E	1
Madagascar *Ridge*: Indian Ocean 30 00S 44 00E	1
Madang: Terr. of New Guinea 05 15S 145 50E	15
Madanīyīn (Médenine): Tunisia 33 24N 10 25E	56
Mādarīpur: Bangladesh 23 09N 90 11E	83
Madawaska: *riv.*, Ont., Canada 45 15N 77 15W	99
Madeira: *is.*, N.Atlantic Ocean 32 45N 17 00W	2 6 56
Madeira: *riv.*, Brazil 05 15S 60 45W	18 50
Madera: Calif., U.S.A. 36 57N 120 04W	91
Madhipura: India 25 56N 86 48E	83
Madhubani: India 26 21N 86 05E	83
Mead: Wash., U.S.A. 47 46N 117 21W	90
Mead, *Lake*: Nev., U.S.A. 36 00N 114 15W	43 91
Meadow Lake *Provincial Park*: Sask., Canada 54 15N 109 00W	92
Me–Akan-dake: *mtn.*, Japan 43 23N 144 01E	87
Mealy *Mountains*: Nfld., Canada 53 30N 59 15W	97
Meander River: Alta., Canada 59 02N 117 42W	88
Meath: *admin.*, Irish Rep. 53 30N 06 45W	66
Mecca: Saudi Arabia *see* Makkah 21 26N 39 49E	33
Mechelen (Malines): Belgium 51 02N 04 29E	72
Mecklenburger Bucht: *bay*, Germany 54 15N 11 30E	73
Meda: Italy 45 40N 09 09E	116
Medan: Indonesia 03 35N 98 39E	38
Médéa: Algeria 36 15N 02 48E	56 77
Medellín: Colombia 06 15N 75 36W	48
Médenine *see* Madanīyīn 33 24N 10 25E	56
Medford: Mass., U.S.A. 42 25N 71 05W	122
Medford: Okla., U.S.A. 36 48N 97 44W	95
Medford: Oreg., U.S.A. 42 20N 122 52W	43 90
Medgidia: Romania 44 15N 28 16E	79
Mediaş: Romania 46 10N 24 21E	78
Medicine Hat: Alta., Canada 50 03N 110 41W	42 92
Medina: Saudi Arabia *see* Al Madīnah 24 30N 39 35E	33
Mediterranean *Sea*	7 27
Mednogorsk: U.S.S.R. 51 24N 57 37E	29 81
Medvedica: *riv.*, U.S.S.R. 49 45N 42 45E	80
Medvedica: *riv.*, U.S.S.R. 57 15N 36 00E	80
Medvedickij: U.S.S.R. 50 47N 44 43E	80
Medvedkovo: U.S.S.R. 55 47N 37 38E	119
Medvedok: U.S.S.R. 57 23N 50 05E	81
Medway: *riv.*, Kent, England 51 15N 00 15E	59
Meekatharra: W.A., Australia 26 35S 118 30E	40
Meelpaeg *Lake*: Nfld., Canada 48 15N 56 30W	97
Meerut: India 29 00N 77 42E	34 82
Mégara: Greece 38 00N 23 20E	79
Meghalaya: *admin.*, India 25 15N 91 00E	35
Meguro: Japan 35 36N 139 42E	121
Mehndāwal: India 26 59N 83 06E	83
Mehsāna: India 23 37N 72 28E	82
Meichuan: China 30 04N 115 36E	85
Meig: *riv.*, R. & Crom., Scotland 57 30N 04 45W	64
Meihsien *see* Meixian 24 18N 116 14E	36 85
Meikle Says Law: *mtn.*, E.Loth., Scotland 55 55N 02 40W	
	63
Meinerzhagen: W.Germany 51 07N 07 40E	118
Meissen: E.Germany 51 10N 13 28E	73
Meitan: China 27 46N 107 25E	85
Meixian (Meihsien): China 24 18N 116 14E	36 85
Mejillones: Chile 23 06S 70 27W	49
Meknès: Morocco 33 53N 05 37W	56
Mekong (Khong, Lan-ts'ang Chiang, Mékôngk): *riv.*, Indo–China 10 30N 105 30E	12 5
Mekong *Delta* (*Mouths of the*): S.Vietnam 10 00N 106 30E	38
Melaka (Malacca): Malaysia 02 12N 102 15E	38
Melanesia: *geog. reg.*, Pacific Ocean 05 00S 160 00E	4 15
Melbourn: Cambs., England 52 05N 00 01E	59
Melbourne: Vic., Australia 37 45S 144 58E	41
Melbourne: Derby., England 52 49N 01 25W	58
Melbourne: Fla., U.S.A. 28 04N 80 38W	47 101
Melekess: U.S.S.R. 54 14N 49 39E	81
Meleuz: U.S.S.R. 52 58N 55 55E	81
Melfort: Sask., Canada 52 52N 104 38W	92
Melilla: North Africa 35 17N 02 57W	56
Melinda: British Honduras 17 00N 88 18W	46
Melitopol': U.S.S.R. 46 50N 35 22E	28 80
Melksham: Wilts., England 51 23N 02 09W	61
Melle: France 46 13N 00 08W	70
Mělník: Czechoslovakia 50 22N 14 30E	73
Melo: Uruguay 32 22S 54 10W	52
Melovoje: U.S.S.R. 49 22N 40 06E	80
Melovoj Syrt: *ridge*, U.S.S.R. 52 15N 52 30E	81
Melrhir, Chott: *salt lake*, Algeria 34 00N 06 30E	20 56
Melrose: Rox., Scotland 55 36N 02 44W	63
Melrose: Mont., U.S.A. 45 38N 112 41W	94
Melrose Park: Ill., U.S.A. 41 52N 87 51W	124
Melton Mowbray: Leics., England 52 46N 00 53W	58
Melun: France 48 32N 02 40E	70
Melville: Sask., Canada 50 57N 102 49W	92
Melville, *Lake*: Nfld., Canada 53 45N 59 45W	44 97
Melville *Island*: N.W.T., Canada 75 30N 110 00W	22
Melvin, *Lough*: Irish Republic/N.Ireland 54 15N 08 00W	66

Types of map: Ocean pp. 1-5; Physical pp. 6-25; Human pp. 26-57; Topographic pp. 58-101; World pp. 102-111; Urban pp. 112-128.

Melvindale: Mich., U.S.A.   42 17N 83 15W   125
Memel *see* Klaipėda   55 43N 21 07E   28 75
Memmingen: W.Germany   47 59N 10 11E   73
Mempawah: Indonesia   00 23N 108 56E   38
Memphis: Tenn., U.S.A.   35 08N 90 03W   45 100
Menado *see* Manado   01 32N 124 55E   39
Menai: N.S.W., Australia   34 01S 151 01E   120
Menai Bridge: Gwyn., Wales   53 14N 04 10W   60
Menai *Strait*: Gwyn., Wales   53 00N 04 15W   60
Mende: France   44 32N 03 30E   71
Mendebo *Mountains*: Ethiopia   06 45N 39 00E   21 53
Mendip *Hills*: Som., England   51 15N 02 30W   61
Mendocino, *Cape*: Calif., U.S.A.   40 26N 124 24W 16
Mendocino *Fracture Zone*: N.Pacific Ocean
   40 00N 145 00W   5
Mendoza: Argentina   32 48S 68 52W   52
Mendoza: *admin.*, Argentina   34 15S 68 30W   52
Mengcheng: China   33 17N 116 32E   85
Mengheyi: China   35 51N 115 02E   84
Mengjiazhai: China   31 19N 121 20E   121
Mengshan: China   24 10N 110 30E   85
Mengtzu *see* Mengzi   23 22N 103 20E   36
Mengyin: China   35 40N 117 57E   84
Mengzi (Mengtzu): China   23 22N 103 20E   36
Menihek: Nfld., Canada   54 15N 66 30W   97
Menihek *Lakes*: Nfld., Canada   53 45N 66 30W   97
Menlo Park: Calif., U.S.A.   37 27N 122 11W   126
Menominee: Mich., U.S.A.   45 07N 87 37W   98
Menomonee Falls: Wis., U.S.A.   43.11N 88 09W   98
Menorca (Minorca): *is.*, Balearic Islands   40 00N 04 00E
                                                 26 77
Mentana: Italy   42 02N 12 39E   116
Mentawai *Islands*: Indonesia   02 00S 99 30E   13 38
Mentawai *Ridge*: Indian Ocean   00 00 94 00E   1
Mentoucun: China   39 59N 116 13E   121
Mentougou: China   39 57N 116 06E   121
Meon: *riv.*, Hants., England   50 45N 01 15W   59
Meppel: Netherlands   52 42N 06 12E   72
Meramee: *riv.*, Mo., U.S.A.   38 15N 90 45W   98
Merano: Italy   46 41N 11 10E   78
Merced: Calif., U.S.A.   37 17N 120 29W   91
Merced, *Lake*: Calif., U.S.A.   37 43N 122 29W   126
Mercedario: *mtn.*, Argentina   31 59S 70 10W   52
Mercedes: Corrientes, Argentina   29 15S 58 05W   52
Mercedes: San Luis, Argentina   33 41S 65 28W   52
Mercedes: Uruguay   33 16S 58 05W   52
Mercer *Island*: Wash., U.S.A.   47 30N 122 00W   126
Mere: Wilts., England   51 06N 02 16W   61
Merefa: U.S.S.R.   49 49N 36 03E   80
Mergui: Burma   12 26N 98 34E   12 35
Mergui *Archipelago*: Burma   10 30N 98 00E   35
Mergulhão *Falls*: Brazil   04 42S 56 18W   50
Mérida: Mexico   20 58N 89 37W   46
Mérida: Spain   38 55N 06 20W   77
Mérida: Venezuela   08 24N 71 08W   48
Mérida, Cordillera de: *ra.*, Venezuela   08 30N 71 00W   48
Meridian: Miss., U.S.A.   32 22N 88 42W   45 100
Meridional, Meseta: *plat.*, Spain   39 00N 04 30W 77
Mérignac: France   44 50N 00 38W   70
Merionethshire: *admin.*, Wales. Absorbed into new *admins.*
   of Clwyd & Gwynedd, 1974.   60
Merlo: Argentina   34 40S 58 44W   128
Merone: Italy   45 47N 09 15E   116
Merowe *see* Marawi   18 29N 31 49E   53
Merritt, *Lake*: Calif., U.S.A.   37 48N 122 15W   126
Merrylands: N.S.W., Australia   33 50S 150 59E   120
Mersa Maṭrūḥ *see* Maṭrūḥ   31 21N 27 14E   32
Mersea *Island*: Essex, England   51 45N 00 45E   59
Mersey: *riv.*, England   53 15N 02 45W   63
Merseyside: *admin.*, England   53 15N 02 45W   63 114
Mersin: Turkey   36 47N 34 37E   32
Mersing: Malaysia   02 25N 103 50E   38
Merta Road: India   26 42N 73 54E   82
Merthyr Tydfil: M.Glam., Wales   51 46N 03 23W   61 113
Merton: Gt. Ldn., England   51 25N 00 12W   59
Merv *see* Mary   37 36N 61 50E   29
Mesa: Ariz., U.S.A.   33 25N 111 50W   91
Mesabi *Range*: Minn., U.S.A.   47 30N 93 00W   42 98 104
Mesa Verde *National Park*: Colo., U.S.A.   37 11N 108 29W
                                                    95
Meseta Meridional: *plat.*, Spain   39 00N 04 30W   77

Meseta Septentrional: *plat.*, Spain   41 00N 04 30W   77
Mesewa (Massawa): Ethiopia   15 37N 39 28E   53
Mesgouez, *Lake*: Qué., Canada   51 15N 74 45W   96
Mesopotamia: *geog. reg.*, Iraq/Syria   33 00N 45 00E 10
Messina: Trans., Rep. of S.Africa   22 23S 30 00E   55
Messina: Sicily   38 13N 15 33E   27 79
Messina, *Strait of*: Italy   38 00N 15 30E   79
Messíni: Greece   37 03N 22 00E   79
Meta: *riv.*, Colombia/Venezuela   06 00N 68 00W   48
Metaline: Wash., U.S.A.   48 51N 117 22W   90
Metán: Argentina   25 29S 64 57W   49
Metanopoli: Italy   45 25N 09 16E   116
Methil: Fife, Scotland   56 12N 03 01W   65
Methwold: Norf., England   52 31N 00 33E   58
Metlakatla: Alaska, U.S.A.   55 08N 131 35W   89
Mettmann: W.Germany   51 15N 06 58E   118
Metz: France   49 07N 06 11E   26 71
Meudon: France   48 49N 02 15E   117
Meudon, Bois de: *woods*, France   48 45N 02 12E   117
Meulan: France   49 00N 01 55E   117
Meuse: *riv.*, Belgium/France   49 45N 04 30E   72
Mevagissey: Corn., England   50 16N 04 48W   61
Mew *Island*: Down, N.Ireland   54 42N 05 32W   66
Mexborough: S.Yorks., England   53 30N 01 17W   63
Mexicali: Mexico   32 36N 115 30W   91
Mexican Hat: Utah, U.S.A.   37 09N 109 52W   91
Mexican *Plateau*: Mexico   25 00N 102 30W   17
MEXICO   17 46 106
Mexico: Mo., U.S.A.   39 10N 91 53W   98
Mexico, *Gulf of*   17 46 100
Mexico City *see* Ciudad de Mexico   19 24N 99 09W 46 128
Meyehualco: Mexico   19 20N 99 03W   128
Meždurečensk (Mezhdurechensk): U.S.S.R.
   53 42N 88 03E   30
Mezhdurechensk *see* Meždurečensk   53 42N 88 03E   30
Mézières-sur-Seine: France   48 58N 01 47E   117
Mhail, Rubha a': *pt.*, Argyll., Scotland   55 56N 06 07W 62
Mhor, Beinn: *mtn.*, R. & Crom., Scotland   57 59N 06 40W
                                                    64
Mhow: India   22 32N 75 49E   82
Mi: *riv.*, China   36 45N 118 30E   84
Miami: Ariz., U.S.A.   33 24N 110 52W   91
Miami: Fla., U.S.A.   25 45N 80 15W   45 101
Miami: Okla., U.S.A.   36 52N 94 53W   95
Miami: *riv.*, Ohio, U.S.A.   39 00N 84 30W   98
Miami Beach: Fla., U.S.A.   25 47N 80 07W   101
Miān Channūn: Pakistan   30 24N 72 27E   82
Mianchi: China   34 48N 111 49E   84
Mianxian: China   33 12N 106 31E   84
Mianyang: China   30 20N 113 39E   85
Miaodaoqundao: *is.*, China   38 15N 120 45E   84
Miaoli: Taiwan   24 30N 120 52E   85
Miass: U.S.S.R.   54 59N 60 06E   29 81
Mica *Creek*: B.C., Canada   52 00N 118 28W   89
Micangshan: *mtns.*, China   32 30N 107 30E   84
Michajlovka: U.S.S.R.   50 05N 43 15E   80
Micheville: France   49 28N 05 56E   105
Michigan: *admin.*, U.S.A.   45 00N 86 00W   45 98
Michigan, *Lake*: U.S.A.   17 45 98
Michigan City: Ind., U.S.A.   41 43N 86 54W   98
Michikamau *Lake*: Nfld., Canada   54 00N 64 00W 44 97
Michipicoten Harbour: Ont., Canada   47 57N 84 55W 98
Michoacán: *admin.*, Mexico   18 30N 102 00W   46
Mickle Fell: *mtn.*, Dur., England   54 38N 02 18W 63
Micronesia: *geog. reg.*, Pacific Ocean   05 00N 165 00E 4 15
Mičurinsk: U.S.S.R.   52 54N 40 30E   80
Mid-Atlantic *Ridge*: Atlantic Ocean   2
Middle America *Trench*: N.Pacific Ocean   12 00N 93 00W 5
Middle Atlas: *mtns.*, Morocco   33 00N 04 00W   56
Middle East: *geog. reg.*   33
Middle *Harbour*: N.S.W., Australia   33 48S 151 14E 120
Middle Rouge: *riv.*, Mich., U.S.A.   42 15N 83 15W 125
Middlesboro: Ky., U.S.A.   36 37N 83 43W   101
Middlesbrough *see* Teesside   54 30N 01 15W   26 105
Middlesbrough: Cleve., England   54 35N 01 14W   63
Middlesex Fells *Reservation*: Mass., U.S.A.
   42 27N 71 07W   122
Middleton: Gt. Man., England   53 33N 02 12W   63 114
Middleton in Teesdale: Dur., England   54 38N 02 04W 63
Middletown: N.Y., U.S.A.   41 26N 74 26W   99
Middletown: Ohio, U.S.A.   39 31N 84 13W   98 104

Middlewich: Ches., England 53 11N 02 27W	58 114	
Mid Glamorgan: *admin.*, Wales 51 30N 03 15W	61	
Midhurst: W.Sussex, England 50 59N 00 45W	59	
Mid-Indian *Basin*: Indian Ocean 10 00S 81 00E	1	
Mid-Indian *Ridge*: Indian Ocean 28 00N 73 00E	1	
Midland: Ont., Canada 44 45N 79 53W	99	
Midland: Mich., U.S.A. 43 38N 84 14W	98	
Midland: Pa., U.S.A. 40 38N 80 28W	104	
Midland: Tex., U.S.A. 32 00N 102 05W	43 95	
Midleton: Cork, Irish Republic 51 55N 08 10W	67	
Midlothian: *admin.*, Scotland 55 45N 03 15W	62	
Mid Loup: *riv.*, Nebr., U.S.A. 41 45N 100 15W	94	
Midnapore: India 22 25N 87 24E	83	
Midocean *Ridge*: N.Atlantic Ocean 70 00N 10 00W	2	
Midouze: *riv.*, France 43 45N 00 00	70	
Midsomer Norton: Avon, England 51 17N 02 29W	61	
Midway: B.C., Canada 49 02N 118 45W	89	
Midway *Islands*: Hawaii, U.S.A. 28 15N 177 25W	4	
Midwest: Wyo., U.S.A. 43 25N 106 16W	94	
Mielec: Poland 50 18N 21 25E	78	
Mieres: Spain 43 15N 05 46W	77	
Mihara: Japan 34 24N 133 05E	86	
Mijares: *riv.*, Spain 40 00N 00 30W	77	
Mikasa: Japan 43 20N 141 40E	86	
Mikkeli: Finland 61 44N 27 15E	74	
Mikura-jima: *is.*, Japan 33 52N 139 36E	86	
Milagro: Ecuador 02 07S 79 36W	48	
Milan: Italy *see* Milano 45 28N 09 12E	26 71 105 116	
Milano (Milan): Italy 45 28N 09 12E	26 71 105 116	
Milazzo: Italy 38 13N 15 14E	107	
Milbank: S.D., U.S.A. 45 13N 96 38W	94	
Mildenhall: Suff., England 52 21N 00 30E	59	
Mildura: Vic., Australia 34 14S 142 13E	41	
Miles City: Mont., U.S.A. 46 25N 105 51W	94	
Milford: Surrey, England 51 10N 00 40W	59	
Milford: Don., Irish Republic 55 05N 07 42W	66	
Milford Haven: Dyfed, Wales 51 44N 05 02W	61 107	
Milford Sound: S.I., New Zealand 44 41S 167 56E	87	
Milford *Sound*: S.I., New Zealand 44 30S 167 45E	87	
Mil'id *see* Malatya 38 22N 38 18E	32	
Milk: *riv.*, Canada/U.S.A. 48 15N 108 30W	42 90	
Millau: France 44 06N 03 05E	71	
Mill City: Nev., U.S.A. 40 41N 118 04W	91	
Mill City: Oreg., U.S.A. 44 45N 122 29W	90	
Milledgeville: Ga., U.S.A. 33 04N 83 13W	101	
Mille Lacs, *Lake*: Minn., U.S.A. 46 00N 93 30W	98	
Millerovo: U.S.S.R. 48 55N 40 25E	80	
Milles Isles: *riv.*, Qué., Canada 45 30N 73 45W	122	
Milleur *Point*: Wig., Scotland 55 01N 05 06W	62	
Millevaches, *Plateau de*: France 45 45N 02 00E	70	
Millheugh: Lan., Scotland 55 44N 03 59W	113	
Millinocket: Maine, U.S.A. 45 42N 68 43W	99	
Millom: Cumbria, England 54 13N 03 18W	62 105	
Millport: Bute., Scotland 55 46N 04 55W	113	
Mills *Lake*: N.W.T., Canada 61 15N 118 15W	88	
Millstreet: Cork, Irish Republic 52 03N 09 04W	67	
Milltown Malbay: Clare, Irish Rep. 52 52N 09 23W	76	
Mill Valley: Calif., U.S.A. 37 54N 122 34W	126	
Milngavie: Dunb., Scotland 55 57N 04 19W	62 113	
Milnrow: Gt. Man., England 53 37N 02 06W	114	
Mílos: *is.*, Greece 36 44N 24 25E	79	
Milpa Alta: Mexico 19 11N 99 01W	128	
Milton: S.I., New Zealand 46 08S 169 59E	87	
Milton: Mass., U.S.A. 42 16N 71 05W	122	
Milton-Freewater: Oreg., U.S.A. 45 56N 118 23W	90	
Milton Keynes: Bucks., England 52 03N 00 42W	59	
Milton Ness: *cape*, Kinc., Scotland 56 46N 02 22W	65	
Miltown Malbay: Clare, Irish Republic 52 52N 09 23W	67	
Milverton: Som., England 51 02N 03 16W	61	
Milwaukee: Wis., U.S.A. 43 03N 87 56W	45 98	
Mimico: Ont., Canada 43 37N 79 30W	125	
Mimizan: France 44 12N 01 14W	70	
Min: *riv.*, Jiangxi, China 26 30N 118 30E	85	
Min: *riv.*, Sichuan, China 29 00N 104 15E	12 36	
Mīnā' 'Abd Allāh: Kuwait 29 01N 48 10E	107	
Mīnā'al Ahmadī: Kuwait 29 04N 48 02E	107	
Mina Hassan Tani (Kenitra, Port Lyautey): Morocco 34 16N 06 36W	56	
Minahassa *Peninsula*: Indonesia 00 45N 122 15E	12 39	
Minamata: Japan 32 13N 130 24E	86	
Minami-alps-kokuritsu-kōen: *nat. park,*		

Japan 35 30N 138 00E	86	
Minas: Uruguay 34 20S 55 15W	52	
Minas *Channel*: N.S., Canada 45 00N 64 45W	97	
Minas Gerais: *admin.*, Brazil 22 00S 44 45W	51	
Minatitlán: Mexico 17 59N 94 31W	46 106	
Minch, The: *chan.*, Scotland 58 00N 06 00W	64	
Mindanao: *is.*, Philippines 07 30N 125 00E	12 39	
Mindanao *Sea*: Philippines 09 00N 124 00E	39	
Minden: La., U.S.A. 32 37N 93 17W	100	
Minden: W.Germany 52 18N 08 54E	72	
Mindoro: *is.*, Philippines 13 00N 121 00E	12 39	
Mine Centre: Ont., Canada 48 48N 92 37W	99	
Minehead: Som., England 51 13N 03 29W	61	
Mine *Head*: Wat., Irish Republic 52 00N 07 35W	67	
Mineral Wells: Tex., U.S.A. 32 48N 98 07W	95	
Mingan: Qué., Canada 50 19N 64 02W	97	
Mingulay: *is.*, Inv., Scotland 56 45N 07 30W	64	
Minkébé: Gabon 01 46N 12 48E	105	
Minna: Nigeria 09 39N 06 32E	57	
Minneapolis: Minn., U.S.A. 45 00N 93 15W	43 98	
Minnedosa: Man., Canada 50 14N 99 51W	93	
Minnesota: *admin.*, U.S.A. 46 30N 94 00W	42 98	
Minnesota: *riv.*, U.S.A. 44 30N 95 00W	98	
Minorca: *is. see* Menorca 40 00N 04 00E	26 77	
Minot: N.D., U.S.A. 48 14N 101 18W	42 94	
Minqing: China 26 10N 118 50E	85	
Minquan: China 34 40N 115 09E	84	
Minshan: *mtns.*, China 33 30N 103 30E	36	
Minsk: U.S.S.R. 53 54N 27 34E	28 80	
Minto: Yukon, Canada 62 34N 136 50W	88	
Minton: Sask., Canada 49 11N 104 38W	92	
Minusinsk: U.S.S.R. 53 43N 91 42E	30	
Minute Man *National Historical Park*: Mass., U.S.A. 42 26N 71 20W	122	
Miquelon: *is.*, N.Atlantic Ocean 47 00N 56 15W	44 97	
Miramas: France 43 33N 05 02E	71	
Miranda de Ebro: Spain 42 41N 02 57W	70 77	
Mirande: France 43 31N 00 25E	70	
Mirbāţ: Oman 16 58N 54 42E	33	
Mirgorod: U.S.S.R. 49 58N 33 36E	80	
Miri: Malaysia 04 28N 114 00E	38	
Mirik, *Cape see* Timiris, *Cape* 19 21N 16 29W	56	
Mirny: *rsch. stn.*, Antarctica 66 33S 93 01E	25	
Mirnyj (Mirnyy): U.S.S.R. 62 33N 113 53E	30	
Mīrpur Khās: Pakistan 25 33N 69 05E	34	
Mirtoan *Sea*: Greece 37 00N 23 30E	79	
Mirzāpur: India 25 09N 82 34E	35 83	
Misawa: Japan 40 41N 141 24E	86	
Misiones: *admin.*, Argentina 26 45S 54 30W	51	
Miskolc: Hungary 48 06N 20 48E	27 79	
Misoöl: *is.*, Indonesia 02 00S 130 00E	39	
Missanabie: Ont., Canada 48 20N 84 06W	98	
Missinaibi: *riv.*, Ont., Canada 50 15N 82 45W	98	
Mississagi: *riv.*, Ont., Canada 46 45N 83 15W	98	
Mississippi: *admin.*, U.S.A.	45 100	
Mississippi: *riv.*, U.S.A. 31 45N 91 15W	17 43 100	
Mississippi *Delta*: La., U.S.A. 29 30N 90 00W	45 100	
Mississippi *Sound*: Miss., U.S.A. 30 15N 88 45W	100	
Missoula: Mont., U.S.A. 46 52N 114 01W	42 90	
Missouri: *admin.*, U.S.A. 38 00N 92 00W	43 98	
Missouri: *riv.*, U.S.A. 39 00N 94 00W	17 45 98	
Mistassibi: *riv.*, Qué., Canada 49 15N 72 00W	96	
Mistassini, *Lake*: Qué., Canada 51 00N 73 30W	44 96	
Mistassini Post: Qué., Canada 50 20N 73 50W	96	
Mistley: Essex, England 51 57N 01 05E	59	
Mitaka: Japan 35 41N 139 33E	121	
Mitcham: Gt. Ldn., England 51 24N 00 09W	112	
Mitcheldean: Glos., England 51 53N 02 30W	60	
Mitchell: S.D., U.S.A. 43 43N 98 02W	94	
Mitchell: *riv.*, Qld., Australia 16 00S 142 45E	41	
Mitchell, *Mount*: N.C., U.S.A. 35 47N 82 16W	17 45 101	
Mitchelstown: Cork, Irish Republic 52 16N 08 16W	67	
Mitilíni (Mytilene): Greece 39 06N 26 33E	79	
Mito: Japan 36 22N 140 28E	37 86	
Mitry-Mory: France 48 59N 02 38E	117	
Mittellandkanal: *can.*, W.Germany 52 15N 08 30E	72	
Mitú: Colombia 01 07N 70 05W	48	
Mitumba *Mountains*: Zaïre 02 45S 28 45E	21 54	
Mixcoac: Mexico 19 23N 99 11W	128	
Mixian: China 34 28N 113 15E	84	
Mixquic: Mexico 19 13N 98 58W	128	

Miyake-jima: *is.*, Japan 34 05N 139 32E 86
Miyako: Japan 39 38N 141 57E 86
Miyakonojō: Japan 31 44N 131 04E 37 86
Miyazaki: Japan 31 54N 131 26E 37 86
Miyun: China 40 22N 116 50E 84
Mizen *Head*: Cork, Irish Republic 51 27N 09 49W 67
Mizen *Head*: Wick., Irish Republic 52 52N 06 03W 67
Mizhi: China 37 48N 110 02E 84
Mizoram: *admin.*, India 23 30N 92 45E 35
Mizushima: Japan 34 35N 133 50E 107
Mjölby: Sweden 58 19N 15 10E 75
Mjosa: *lake*, Norway 60 30N 11 00E 75
Mladá Boleslav: Czechoslovakia 50 26N 14 55E 73 78
Mława: Poland 53 08N 20 20E 78
Mnevniki: U.S.S.R. 55 45N 37 28E 119
Moab: Utah, U.S.A. 38 35N 109 33W 91
Moate: Westmeath, Irish Republic 53 24N 07 58W 67
Mobara: Japan 35 25N 140 18E 86
Moberly: Mo., U.S.A. 39 25N 92 25W 98
Mobile: Ala., U.S.A. 30 41N 88 03W 45 100
Mobridge: S.D., U.S.A. 45 32N 100 26W 94
Moçambique: Mozambique 15 03S 40 45E 54
Mocha *see* Al Mukhā 13 19N 43 15E 33
Mocoa: Colombia 01 07N 76 38W 48
Modena: Italy 44 39N 10 55E 78
Modesto: Calif., U.S.A. 37 37N 121 00W 91
Moel Fferna: *mtn.*, Clwyd, Wales 52 57N 03 18W 60
Moelfre: *mtn.*, Dyfed, Wales 51 58N 04 26W 60
Moelfre: *mtn.*, Powys, Wales 52 34N 03 42W 60
Moeraki *Point*: S.I., New Zealand 45 23S 170 52E 87
Moers: W.Germany 51 27N 06 36E 118
Moffat: Dumf., Scotland 55 20N 03 27W 62
Moga: India 30 49N 75 13E 82
Mogadisho (Mogadiscio): Somali Rep. 02 02N 45 21E 53
Mogil'ov (Mogilëv): U.S.S.R. 53 54N 30 21E 28 80
Mogil'ov-Podol'skij: U.S.S.R. 48 27N 27 48E 78
Mogi-Mirim: Brazil 22 26S 46 57W 51
Mogoča: US.S.R. 53 44N 119 44E 30
Mogollon *Plateau*: Ariz., U.S.A. 34 30N 111 00W 91
Mohammedia: Morocco 33 44N 07 24W 56
Mohana: India 25 55N 77 46E 82
Mohill: Leit., Irish Republic 53 55N 07 52W 66
Mointy: U.S.S.R. 47 13N 73 21E 29
Mo i Rana: Norway 66 19N 14 10E 27 74 105
Moisie: Qué., Canada 50 12N 66 06W 97
Moisie: *riv.*, Qué., Canada 50 45N 66 15W 97
Moissac: France 44 07N 01 05E 70
Mojave: *riv.*, Calif., U.S.A. 34 45N 117 00W 91
Mojave *Desert*: Calif., U.S.A. 35 00N 117 00W 17 43 91
Mojent: *riv.*, Spain 41 30N 02 15E 116
Mokameh: India 25 24N 85 55E 83
Mokp'o: S.Korea 34 48N 126 22E 37
Mokša: *riv.*, U.S.S.R. 54 30N 42 00E 80
Mold: Clwyd, Wales 53 10N 03 08W 60
Moldavskaja S.S.R. (Moldavian S.S.R.): *admin.*, U.S.S.R. 47 00N 29 00E 28 78
Mole: *riv.*, Surrey, England 51 15N 00 15W 59 112
Molepolole: Botswana 24 25S 25 30E 55
Molíns de Rey: Spain 41 25N 02 01E 116
Mollendo: Peru 17 00S 72 00W 49
Mollet: Spain 41 32N 02 13E 116
Mölndal: Sweden 57 40N 12 00E 75
Molodečno: U.S.S.R. 54 16N 26 50E 78
Molodezhnaya: *rsch. stn.*, Antarctica 67 40S 45 51E 24
Molokai *Fracture Zone*: N.Pacific Ocean 25 00N 140 00W 5
Molopo: *riv.*, Botswana/Rep. of S.Africa 25 30S 22 45E 55
Molotov *see* Perm' 58 00N 56 15E 29 81 105 107
Molson *Lake*: Man., Canada 54 00N 96 45W 93
Molucca *Passage*: Indonesia 01 30N 126 00E 12 39
Moluccas (Maluku): *is. & admin.*, Indonesia 01 30S 127 30E 13 39
Molucca *Sea*: Indonesia 00 45S 124 45E 12 39
Mombasa: Kenya 04 04S 39 40E 54
Mombetsu: Japan 44 21N 143 22E 87
Mominabad: India 18 44N 76 23E 82
Monach, *Sound of*: Inv., Scotland 57 30N 07 30W 64
MONACO 43 45N 07 15E 26 71
Monadhliath *Mountains*: Inv., Scotland 57 00N 04 00W 64
Monaghan: Monaghan, Irish Republic 54 15N 06 58W 66
Monaghan: *admin.*, Irish Rep. 54 00N 07 00W 66
Monar, *Loch*: R.& Crom., Scotland 57 15N 05 00W 64
Monasterevin: Kild., Irish Republic 53 08N 07 03W 67
Mona Vale: N.S.W., Australia 33 41S 151 18E 120
Monavullagh *Mountains*: Wat., Irish Republic 52 00N 07 30W 67
Moncada y Reixach: Spain 41 29N 02 11E 116
Moncalieri: Italy 45 00N 07 41E 71
Mončegorsk: U.S.S.R. 67 55N 33 01E 27 74
Mönchengladbach: W.Germany 51 12N 06 26E 72 118
Monclova: Mexico 26 54N 101 25W 46 104
Moncton: N.B., Canada 46 04N 64 50W 44 97
Mondeville: France 49 10N 00 19W 104
Mondoví: Italy 44 23N 07 49E 71
Monessen: Pa., U.S.A. 40 08N 79 54W 104
Money *Head*: Wig., Scotland 54 48N 05 03W 62
Moneymore: Lon., N.Ireland 54 42N 06 40W 66
Monferrato: *hills*, Italy 44 45N 08 00E 71
Monghyr: India 25 24N 86 29E 35 83
MONGOLIA 30 107
Mongu: Zambia 15 15S 23 09E 55
Monifieth: Angus, Scotland 56 29N 02 50W 65
Monmouth: Ill., U.S.A. 40 54N 90 39W 98
Monmouth: Gwent, Wales 51 50N 02 43W 60 113
Monmouthshire: *admin.*, Wales. Absorbed into new Welsh *admins.* of Gwent, Mid Glamorgan & South Glamorgan, 1974. 61
Monmouthshire & Brecon *Canals*: S.Wales 51 30N 03 00W 113
Monnow: *riv.*, England/Wales 51 45N 02 45W 60
Mono: *riv.*, Togo 08 15N 01 30E 57
Monongahela: *riv.*, U.S.A. 40 15N 80 00W 125
Monroe: La., U.S.A. 32 30N 92 07W 43 100
Monroe: Mich., U.S.A. 41 56N 83 21W 98
Monroeville: Ala., U.S.A. 31 31N 87 20W 101
Monrovia: Liberia 06 20N 10 46W 57
Mons: Belgium 50 28N 03 58E 72
Monserrat: *is.*, Leeward Islands 16 45N 62 15W 47
Montana: *admin.*, U.S.A. 47 00N 109 00W 42 94
Montara *Point*: Calif., U.S.A. 37 33N 122 31W 126
Montargis: France 48 00N 02 44E 70
Montauban: Tarn-et-Garonne, France 44 01N 01 20E 70
Montauk *Point*: N.Y., U.S.A. 41 04N 71 51W 99
Montbard: France 47 38N 04 20E 71
Montbéliard: France 47 31N 06 48E 71
Montceau-les-Mines: France 46 40N 04 23E 71
Montclair: N.J., U.S.A. 40 49N 74 13W 123
Mont-de-Marsan: France 43 54N 00 30W 70
Montdidier: France 49 39N 02 35E 70
Montebello: Calif., U.S.A. 34 01N 118 07W 127
Monte-Carlo: Monaco 43 44N 07 25E 71
Montego Bay: Jamaica 18 27N 77 56W 47
Montélimar: France 44 33N 04 45E 71
Monterey: Calif., U.S.A. 36 37N 121 55W 43 91
Monterey *Bay*: Calif., U.S.A. 36 45N 121 45W 91
Monterey Park: Calif., U.S.A. 34 04N 118 07W 127
Montería: Colombia 08 45N 75 54W 48
Monterotondo: Italy 42 03N 12 38E 116
Monterrey: Mexico 25 40N 100 19W 46 104
Monte Sacro: Italy 41 56N 12 32E 116
Montes Claros: Brazil 16 43S 43 52W 50
Monteverde: Argentina 34 48S 58 17W 128
Monteverde Nuovo: Italy 41 51N 12 27E 116
Montevideo: Uruguay 34 55S 56 10W 52
Monte Vista: Colo., U.S.A. 37 35N 106 09W 95
Montfort-l'Amaury: France 48 47N 01 49E 116
Montgeron: France 48 42N 02 27E 116
Montgomery: Pakistan *see* Sahiwāl 30 41N 73 11E 82
Montgomery: Ala., U.S.A. 32 23N 86 19W 45 101
Montgomery: Powys, Wales 52 34N 03 10W 60
Montgomeryshire: *admin.*, Wales. Absorbed into new *admin.* of Powys, 1974. 60
Mont-Joli: Qué., Canada 48 36N 68 14W 96
Mont-Louis: Qué., Canada 49 15N 65 46W 97
Montluçon: France 46 20N 02 36E 70
Montmagny: Qué., Canada 46 58N 70 33W 96
Montmartre, Butte: *knoll*, France 48 53N 02 21E 117
Montmorency: France 48 59N 02 19E 117
Montmorency, *Forêt de*: France 49 00N 02 15E 117
Montmorillon: France 46 26N 00 52E 70
Montpelier: Idaho, U.S.A. 42 19N 111 18W 90
Montpelier: Vt., U.S.A. 44 16N 72 34W 44 99

Montpellier: France   43 36N 03 53E   26 71
Montréal: Qué., Canada   45 30N 73 36W
                                    44 96 104 106 122
Montréal: riv., Ont., Canada   47 15N 84 00W   98
Montreal Lake: Sask., Canada   54 15N 105 30W   92
Montréal Nord: Qué., Canada   45 36N 73 38W   122
Montreux: Switzerland   46 27N 06 55E   71
Montrose: Angus, Scotland   56 43N 02 29W   65
Montrose: Colo., U.S.A.   38 29N 107 53W   94
Montrose-Wilson Beach: III., U.S.A.   41 58N 87 38W   124
Mont Royal: Qué., Canada   45 32N 73 38W   122
Mont Tremblant Provincial Park: Qué., Canada
    46 30N 74 30W   96
Monza: Italy   45 35N 09 16E   71 116
Moorestown: N.J., U.S.A.   39 58N 74 54W   122
Moorfoot Hills: Midloth., Scotland   55 45N 03 00W   63
Moorhead: Minn., U.S.A.   46 51N 96 44W   94
Moose: riv., Ont., Canada   50 45N 81 15W   96
Moosehead Lake: Maine, U.S.A.   45 30N 69 30W   99
Moose Jaw: Sask., Canada   50 23N 105 35W   42 92
Moose Lake: Man., Canada   54 00N 100 00W   93
Moose Mountain Provincial Park: Sask.,
    Canada   49 45N 102 30W   92
Moosonee: Ont., Canada   51 18N 80 40W   44 96
Mopti: Mali   14 29N 04 10W   57
Moquegua: Peru   17 07S 70 55W   49
Mór, Glen (Great Glen): val., Inv., Scotland
    57 00N 04 45W   64
Mora: Sweden   61 00N 14 30E   75
Mora: riv., N.Mex., U.S.A.   35 45N 104 45W   95
Morādābād: India   28 50N 78 45E   34 82
Morales: riv., Argentina   34 49S 58 43W   128
Morar, Loch: Inv., Scotland   56 45N 05 30W   64
Moratuwa: Sri Lanka   06 47N 79 53E   34
Morava: riv., Czechoslovakia   48 45N 17 00E   73 78
Moray Firth: est., Scotland   57 30N 04 00W   65
Morayshire: admin., Scotland   57 30N 03 30W   65
Morden: Man., Canada   49 12N 98 05W   93
More, Ben: mtn., Argyll., Scotland   56 25N 06 02W   64
More, Ben: mtn., Perth., Scotland   56 23N 04 31W   64
More, Loch: Suther., Scotland   58 15N 04 45W   64
More Assynt, Ben: mtn., Suther., Scotland
    58 07N 04 52W   64
Moreau: riv., S.D., U.S.A.   45 00N 101 30W   94
Morecambe: Lancs., England   54 04N 02 53W   63
Morecambe Bay: England   54 00N 03 00W   63
Morehead City: N.C., U.S.A.   34 43N 76 44W   101
Morelia: Mexico   19 42N 101 07W   46
Morelos: Mexico   19 26N 99 07W   128
Morena: India   26 24N 78 04E   82
Morena, Sierra: ra., Spain   38 00N 05 00W   26 77
Morenci: Ariz., U.S.A.   33 05N 109 22W   95
Moresby Island: B.C., Canada   52 15N 131 15W   89
Moretonhampstead: Devon, England   50 40N 03 45W   61
Moreton-in-Marsh: Glos., England   51 59N 01 42W   60
Morgan City: La., U.S.A.   29 42N 91 12W   100
Morgantown: W.Va., U.S.A.   39 38N 79 57W   99
Mori: Japan   42 06N 140 35E   86
Morice Lake: B.C., Canada   53 45N 127 30W   89
Morioka: Japan   39 42N 141 09E   37 86
Moriston: riv., Inv., Scotland   57 00N 04 45W   64
Morivione: Italy   45 26N 09 12E   116
Morlaix: France   48 35N 03 50W   70
Morley: W.Yorks., England   53 46N 01 36W   63 115
Morley River: Yukon, Canada   60 00N 132 09W   88
MOROCCO   34 30N 05 00W   20 56 77 106
Morogoro: Tanzania   06 49S 37 40E   54
Moro Gulf: Philippines   07 00N 123 00E   12 39
Morón (Seis de Septiembre): Argentina   34 39S 58 38W
                                    128
Morondava: Malagasy Rep.   20 17S 44 17E   55
Morotai: is., Indonesia   02 15N 128 30E   39
Morozovsk: U.S.S.R.   48 22N 41 50E   80
Morpeth: Northumb., England   55 10N 01 41W   63
Morris: Man., Canada   49 22N 97 21W   93
Morristown: N.J., U.S.A.   40 48N 74 29W   123
Morristown: Tenn., U.S.A.   36 13N 83 18W   101
Morro Agudo: hill, Brazil   20 42S 42 09W   104
Mors: is., Denmark   56 45N 08 45E   75
Moršansk: U.S.S.R.   53 26N 41 49E   80
Mortagne-au-Perche: France   48 32N 00 33E   70

Morte Point: Devon, England   51 11N 04 13W   61
Morton Arboretum: III., U.S.A.   41 49N 88 04W   124
Morton Grove: III., U.S.A.   42 01N 87 47W   124
Morven: mtn., Caith., Scotland   58 13N 03 42W   65
Morvi: India   25 50N 70 52E   34 82
Moscow: Idaho, U.S.A.   46 44N 117 00W   90
Moscow: U.S.S.R. see Moskva   55 45N 37 35E
                                    28 80 105 119
Moscow: riv. see Moskva: riv.   54 45N 40 00E   80 119
Mosel: riv., W.Germany   50 00N 07 15E   72
Moses Lake: Wash., U.S.A.   47 10N 119 21W   90
Mosgiel: S.I., New Zealand   45 54S 170 21E   87
Moshi: Tanzania   03 20S 37 21E   54
Mosjøen: Norway   65 50N 13 12E   75
Moskva (Moscow): U.S.S.R.   55 45N 37 35E   28 80 105 119
Moskva (Moscow): riv., U.S.S.R.   54 45N 40 00E   80 119
Mosman: N.S.W., Australia   33 50S 151 14E   120
Mosonmagyaróvár: Hungary   47 51N 17 17E   73
Moss: Norway   59 26N 10 41E   75
Moss: Clwyd, Wales   53 04N 03 02W   60
Moss Bank: Mers., England   53 29N 02 44W   114
Mossend: Lan., Scotland   55 49N 03 59W   113
Mossoró: Brazil   05 11S 37 20W   50
Most: Czechoslovakia   50 31N 13 39E   73 78
Mostaganem: Algeria   35 54N 00 05E   56 77
Mostar: Yugoslavia   43 20N 17 50E   79
Mosul see Al Mawşil   36 20N 43 08E   33
Motala: Sweden   58 34N 15 05E   75
Motherwell: Lan., Scotland   55 48N 04 00W   62 105 113
Motihāri: India   26 40N 84 55E   83
Motril: Spain   36 45N 03 31W   77
Motueka: S.I., New Zealand   41 08S 173 01E   87
Moudjéria: Mauritania   17 51N 12 28W   56
Moulins: France   46 34N 03 20E   71
Moulmein: Burma   16 30N 97 39E   35
Moulouya: riv., Morocco   33 00N 03 30W   56
Moultrie: Ga., U.S.A.   31 11N 83 47W   101
Moundsville: W.Va., U.S.A.   39 54N 80 44W   99
Mountain: riv., N.W.T., Canada   65 15N 129 00W   88
Mountainair: N.Mex., U.S.A.   34 31N 106 15W   95
Mountain Ash: M.Glam., Wales   51 42N 03 24W   61 113
Mountain Home: Idaho, U.S.A.   43 08N 115 41W   90
Mountain Point: Alaska, U.S.A.   55 18N 131 32W   89
Mountain Sheep Dam: U.S.A.   45 40N 116 38W   90
Mountain View: Calif., U.S.A.   37 23N 122 04W   126
Mount Assiniboine Provincial Park: B.C.,
    Canada   50 30N 115 30W   90
Mount Clemens: Mich., U.S.A.   42 35N 82 55W   125
Mount Cook National Park: S.I., New
    Zealand   43 30S 170 00E   87
Mount Desert Island: Maine, U.S.A.   44 15N 68 15W   99
Mount Eden: Calif., U.S.A.   37 38N 122 06W   126
Mount Edgecumbe: Alaska, U.S.A.   57 03N 135 21W   89
Mount Gambier: S.A., Australia   37 51S 140 50E   41
Mount Goldsworthy: hill, W.A., Australia   20 21S 119 32E
                                    105
Mount Isa: Qld., Australia   20 50S 139 29E   41
Mountlake Terrace: Wash., U.S.A.   47 47N 122 18W   126
Mount Lebanon: Pa., U.S.A.   40 23N 80 03W   125
Mount Maunganui: N.I., New Zealand   37 38S 176 12E   87
Mountmellick: Laois, Irish Republic   53 07N 07 20W   67
Mount Pleasant: Mich., U.S.A.   43 36N 84 46W   98
Mount Prospect: III., U.S.A.   42 02N 87 55W   124
Mount Rainier National Park: Wash., U.S.A.
    46 45N 121 45W   90
Mountrath: Laois, Irish Republic   53 00N 07 28W   67
Mount Revelstoke National Park: B.C.,
    Canada   51 00N 118 00W   89
Mount's Bay: Corn., England   50 00N 05 15W   61
Mount Seymour Provincial Park: B.C., Canada
    49 20N 122 58W   126
Mountsorrel: Leics., England   52 44N 01 07W   58
Mount Tamalpais State Park: Calif., U.S.A.
    37 53N 122 33W   126
Mount Vernon: III., U.S.A.   38 19N 88 52W   98
Mount Vernon: Ind., U.S.A.   37 55N 87 55W   98
Mount Vernon: N.Y., U.S.A.   40 55N 73 51W   123
Mount Vernon: Wash., U.S.A.   48 25N 122 20W   90
Mount Wellington: N.I., New Zealand   37 15S 174 45E   87
Mouping: China   37 20N 121 39E   84
Mourne Mountains: Down, N.Ireland   54 00N 06 00W   66

Types of map: Ocean pp. 1-5; Physical pp. 6-25; Human pp. 26-57; Topographic pp. 58-101; World pp. 102-111; Urban pp. 112-128.

Types of map: Ocean pp. 1-5; Physical pp. 6-25; Human pp. 26-57; Topographic pp. 58-101; World pp. 102-111; Urban pp. 112-128.

Mousehole: Corn., England   50 05N 05 33W   61
Moutong: Indonesia   00 28N 121 13E   39
Mouydir *Mountains*: Algeria   24 45N 04 00E   56
Moville: Don., Irish Republic   55 11N 07 03W   66
Moy: Tyr., N.Ireland   54 27N 06 42W   66
Moy: *riv.*, Sligo, Irish Republic   54 00N 08 45W   66
Moyale: Ethiopia   03 34N 39 04E   53
Moyamba: Sierra Leone   08 04N 12 03W   57
Moyeuvre-Grande: France   49 15N 06 02E   105
Moyobamba: Peru   06 04S 76 56W   48
Możajsk: U.S.S.R.   55 30N 36 01E   80
MOZAMBIQUE   23 00S 33 30E   21 55 107
Mozambique *Basin*: Indian Ocean   33 00S 49 00E   1
Mozambique *Channel*: Malagasy Rep./Mozambique
   20 00S 37 15E   1 55
Mozambique *Fracture Zone*: Indian Ocean   45 00S 30 00E
                                                    1
Mozambique *Ridge*: Indian Ocean   32 00N 35 00E   1 21
Możga: U.S.S.R.   56 27N 52 13E   81
Mozyr': U.S.S.R.   52 03N 29 14E   80
Mozzate: Italy   45 41N 08 52E   116
Mtwara: Tanzania   10 16S 40 11E   54
Muchinga *Mountains*: Zambia   11 15S 31 30E   21 54
Much Wenlock: Salop, England   52 36N 02 34W   58
Muck: *is.*, Inv., Scotland   56 45N 06 15W   64
Muckle Roe: *is.*, Shet. Is., Scotland   60 15N 01 15W   65
Muckno *Lough*: Monaghan, Irish Republic   54 00N 06 30W
                                                    66
Muddus *Nationalpark*: Sweden   67 15N 20 15E   74
Mufulira: Zambia   12 33S 28 14E   54
Mufushan: *mtns.*, China   29 30N 114 30E   85
Mühldorf: W.Germany   48 14N 12 33E   73
Mühlhausen: E.Germany   51 13N 10 28E   73
Muirhead: Lan., Scotland   55 55N 04 06W   113
Mukačevo: U.S.S.R.   48 27N 22 45E   78
Mukalla *see* Al Mukallā   14 32N 49 08E   33
Mukden *see* Shenyang   41 48N 123 30E   37 105
Muktsar: India   30 30N 74 34E   82
Mula: *riv.*, India   19 15N 74 15E   82
Muleba: Tanzania   01 49S 31 40E   74
Muleshoe: Tex., U.S.A.   34 13N 102 43W   95
Mulgrave: N.S., Canada   45 36N 61 25W   97
Mülheim: W.Germany   50 58N 07 00E   119
Mülheim an der Ruhr: W.Germany   51 25N 06 50E   118
Mulhouse: France   47 45N 07 21E   26 71
Mull: *is.*, Argyll., Scotland   56 30N 06 00W   64
Mull, Ross of: *dist.*, Argyll., Scotland   56 15N 06 00W   64
Mull, *Sound of*: Argyll., Scotland   56 30N 05 45W   64
Mullaghareirk *Mountains*: Irish Republic   52 15N 09 00W
                                                    67
Mullaghcarn: *mtn.*, Tyr., N.Ireland   54 40N 07 13W   66
Mullaghmore: *mtn.*, Lon., N.Ireland   54 52N 06 50W   66
Müller *Mountains*: Indonesia   01 00N 113 45E   12 38
Mullet, The: *pen.*, Mayo, Irish Republic   54 00N 10 00W   66
Mull *Head*: Ork. Is., Scotland   59 23N 02 53W   65
Mullingar: Westmeath, Irish Republic   53 32N 07 20W   66
Mull of Galloway: *cape*, Wig., Scotland   54 39N 04 52W   62
Mull of Kintyre: *cape*, Argyll., Scotland   55 18N 05 45W   62
Mull of Logan: *cape*, Wig., Scotland   54 44N 04 59W   62
Mull of Oa: *cape*, Argyll., Scotland   55 36N 06 21W   62
Multān: Pakistan   30 11N 71 29E   34 82
Mumbles: W.Glam., Wales   51 35N 03 59W   61
Mumbles *Head*: W.Glam., Wales   51 35N 03 59W   61
Mun: *riv.*, Thailand   15 15N 102 30E   35
München (Munich): W.Germany   48 08N 11 35E   26 73
Muncho Lake: B.C., Canada   59 00N 125 46W   88
Muncho Lake *Provincial Park*: B.C.,
   Canada   59 15N 125 30W   88
Muncie: Ind., U.S.A.   40 11N 85 22W   98
Mundelein: Ill., U.S.A.   42 16N 88 00W   124
Mundo: *riv.*, Spain   38 30N 01 45W   76
Mungbere: Zaïre   02 40N 28 25E   54
Munhall: Pa., U.S.A.   40 24N 79 54W   125
Munich *see* München   48 08N 11 35E   26 73
Municipal Colony: India   28 42N 77 12E   120
Muñiz: Argentina   34 33S 58 42W   128
Munro: Argentina   34 32S 58 32W   128
Münster: Münster, W.Germany   51 58N 07 37E   72
Muntok: Indonesia   02 04S 105 11E   38
Muonio: Finland   67 58N 23 40E   74
Muoniojoki: *riv.*, Finland   78 15N 22 30E   74

Muraši: U.S.S.R.   59 24N 48 55E   81
Murchison *Falls*: Uganda   02 17N 31 41E   54
Murcia: Spain   37 59N 01 08W   26 76
Murden *Cove*: Wash., U.S.A.   47 39N 122 30W   126
Murdochville: Qué., Canada   48 57N 65 30W   97
Mureşul: *riv.*, Romania   46 00N 21 45E   78
Muret: France   43 28N 01 19E   70
Murfreesboro: Tenn., U.S.A.   35 51N 86 24W   101
Murgab: *riv.*, Afghanistan/U.S.S.R.   38 00N 72 00E   29
Murino: U.S.S.R.   60 03N 30 27E   119
Müritz See: *lake*, E.Germany   53 15N 12 45E   73
Murmansk: U.S.S.R.   68 59N 33 08E   27 74
Murom: U.S.S.R.   55 34N 42 02E   28 81
Muroran: Japan   42 18N 140 59E   37 86 105
Muroto-zaki: *cape*, Japan   33 15N 134 11E   86
Murphy Creek: B.C., Canada   49 28N 117 30W   89
Murray: Utah, U.S.A.   40 40N 111 53W   91
Murray: *riv.*, Australia   34 15S 139 30E   15 41
Murray: *riv.*, B.C., Canada   55 15N 121 00W   89
Murray Bay *see* La Malbaie   47 39N 70 11W   96
Murray *Fracture Zone*: N.Pacific Ocean   30 00N 145 00W   5
Murrumbidgee: *riv.*, N.S.W., Australia   34 30S 146 00E
                                                    15 41
Murwāra (Katni): India   23 49N 80 28E   82
Musan: N.Korea   42 14N 129 13E   105
Musashino: Japan   35 43N 139 34E   121
Muscat *see* Masqaţ   23 37N 58 38E   33
Muscat and Oman *see* OMAN   20 00N 56 00E   10 33 107
Muscatine: Iowa, U.S.A.   41 25N 91 03W   98
Musgrave *Ranges*: Australia   26 15S 132 30E   40
Mushalagan *Lake*: Qué., Canada   51 15N 69 00W   96
Musi: *riv.*, Indonesia   02 45S 103 45E   38
Muskegon: Mich., U.S.A.   43 13N 86 15W   45 98
Muskegon: *riv.*, Mich., U.S.A.   43 15N 86 00W   98
Muskogee: Okla., U.S.A.   35 45N 95 22W   100
Muskwa: B.C., Canada   58 45N 122 41W   88
Muskwa: *riv.*, B.C., Canada   58 15N 123 30W   88
Musoma: Tanzania   01 31S 33 48E   54
Musselburgh: Midloth., Scotland   55 57N 03 04W   62
Musselshell: *riv.*, Mont., U.S.A.   47 00N 107 45W   94
Mustafakemalpasa: Turkey   40 42N 28 25E   79
Mustang *Island*: Tex., U.S.A.   27 15N 97 15W   100
Mutsu: Japan   41 17N 141 10E   86
Mutsu-wan: *bay*, Japan   41 00N 141 00E   86
Mutton *Island*: Clare, Irish Republic   52 45N 09 30W   67
Muyunkum: *des.*, U.S.S.R.   44 00N 71 00E   8 29
Muzaffarpur: India   26 08N 85 24E   35 83
Muzaffarnagar: India   29 28N 77 42E   34 82
Muzon, *Cape*: Alaska, U.S.A.   54 41N 132 40W   89
Mwanza: Tanzania   02 30S 32 54E   54
Mweru, *Lake*: Zaïre/Zambia   09 00S 28 45E   21 54
Myakka River *State Park*: Fla., U.S.A.   27 15N 82 15W   101
Myingyan: Burma   21 25N 95 20E   35
Myitkyinā: Burma   25 24N 97 25E   35
Mymensingh: Bangladesh   24 45N 90 23E   35 83
Mynydd Bach: *mtns.*, Dyfed, Wales   52 15N 04 00W   60
Mynydd du: *mtns.*, Dyfed, Wales   51 45N 03 45W   60
Mynydd Eppynt: *mtns.*, Powys, Wales   52 00N 03 30W   60
Mynydd Pencarreg: *mtn.*, Dyfed, Wales   52 04N 04 04W   60
Mynydd Prescelly: *mtn.*, Dyfed, Wales   51 58N 04 42W   60
Myrtle Beach: S.C., U.S.A.   33 42N 78 54W   101
Mysore: India   12 18N 76 37E   34
Mysore: *admin.*, India   14 45N 75 30E   34
Mystic: *riv.*, Mass., U.S.A.   42 15N 71 00W   122
Mystic *Lakes*: Mass., U.S.A.   42 26N 71 09W   122
Mỹ Tho: S.Vietnam   10 21N 106 21E   38 39
Mytilene *see* Mitilíni   39 06N 26 33E   79
Mytišči: U.S.S.R.   55 55N 37 46E   80
Mzuzu: Malawi   11 27S 33 55E   54

Naas: Kild., Irish Republic   53 13N 06 39W   67
Nabadwīp: India   23 24N 88 23E   83
Naberežnyje Čelny: U.S.S.R.   55 42N 52 19E   81
Nabeul: Tunisia   36 30N 10 44E   26
Nacala: Mozambique   14 33S 40 40E   54
Nachičevan' (Nakhichevan'): U.S.S.R.   39 13N 45 24E   28
Nachodka (Nakhodka): U.S.S.R.   42 48N 132 52E   37 86
Nacogdoches: Tex., U.S.A.   31 36N 94 39W   100

Types of map: Ocean pp. 1-5; Physical pp. 6-25; Human pp. 26-57; Topographic pp. 58-101; World pp. 102-111; Urban pp. 112-128.

Nadiād: India　22 42N 72 55E　　　　　　34 82
Næstved: Denmark　55 14N 11 47E　　　　　75
Nafud: *des. see* An Nafūd　28 30N 41 15E　10 33
Naga: Philippines　13 36N 123 12E　　　　39
Nagahama: Shiga, Japan　35 23N 136 16E　86
Nāgā *Hills*: Burma/India　26 15N 95 00E　11 35
Nāgāland: *admin.,* India　26 15N 94 15E　35
Nagano: Japan　36 39N 138 11E　　　　　86
Nagaoka: Niigata, Japan　37 27N 138 51E　86
Nāgappattinam: India　10 45N 79 50E　　34
Nagasaki: Japan　32 48N 129 55E　　　37 86
Nagasu *see* Usa　33 31N 131 22E　　　　86
Nagato: Japan　34 21N 131 10E　　　　　86
Nagatsuda: Japan　35 31N 139 30E　　　121
Nāgaur: India　27 12N 73 48E　　　　　　82
Nāgda: India　23 30N 75 29E　　　　　　82
Nāgercoil: India　08 11N 77 30E　　　　34
Nagina: India　29 26N 78 27E　　　　　82
Nagles *Mountains*: Cork, Irish Republic　52 00N 08 15W　67
Nagorsk: U.S.S.R.　59 18N 50 48E　　　　81
Nagoya: Japan　35 10N 136 55E　　　37 86 105
Nagpur: India　21 10N 79 12E　　　　　34 82
Nagykanizsa: Hungary　46 27N 17 00E　　78
Naha: Ryukyu Islands　26 13N 127 40E　　37
Nahanni Butte: N.W.T., Canada　61 03N 123 31W　88
Nahant: Mass., U.S.A.　42 24N 70 55W　　122
Nahant *Bay*: Mass., U.S.A.　42 15N 70 45W　122
Nahr al Urdunn (Jordan): *riv.,* Israel/Jordan
　32 00N 35 30E　　　　　　　　　　32
Naibandan *see* Nehbandān　31 32N 60 04E　33
Naihāti: India　22 53N 88 25E　　　　　120
Nailsworth: Glos., England　51 42N 02 14W　61
Nain: Nfld., Canada　56 30N 61 45W　　　97
Naini Tāl: India　29 22N 79 26E　　　　82
Nairn: Nairn., Scotland　57 35N 03 53W　65
Nairn: *riv.,* Scotland　57 30N 03 45W　　65
Nairnshire: *admin.,* Scotland　57 30N 03 45W　65
Nairobi: Kenya　01 17S 36 50E　　　　　54
Naivasha: Kenya　00 44S 36 26E　　　　53
Naivasha, *Lake*: Kenya　00 46S 36 21E　52
Naizifang: China　40 02N 116 26E　　　121
Najaf *see* An Najaf　31 59N 44 19E　　33
Najībābād: India　29 37N 78 19E　　　　82
Najin: N.Korea　42 15N 130 18E　　　　86
Nakada: Japan　35 24N 139 30E　　　　121
Nakaminato: Japan　36 21N 140 36E　　86
Nakano: Japan　35 42N 139 39E　　　　121
Nakatsu: Japan　33 34N 131 13E　　　　86
Nakhichevan' *see* Nachičevan'　39 13N 45 24E　28
Nakhodka *see* Nachodka　42 48N 132 52E　37 86
Nakhon Chai Si: *riv.,* Thailand　14 45N 100 00E　35
Nakhon Phanom: Thailand　17 22N 104 45E　38
Nakhon Ratchasima: Thailand　15 00N 102 06E　35
Nakhon Sawan: Thailand　15 42N 100 04E　35
Nakhon Si Thammarat: Thailand　08 24N 99 58E　35 105
Nakło: Poland　53 08N 17 35E　　　　　73
Nakina: Ont., Canada　50 11N 86 43W　98
Nakuru: Kenya　00 16S 36 04E　　　　54
Nakusp: B.C., Canada　50 15N 117 48W　89
Nal'čik (Nal'chik): U.S.S.R.　43 29N 43 37E　28
Namangan: U.S.S.R.　41 00N 71 40E　　29
Nam Dinh: N.Vietnam　20 25N 106 12E　36
Namib *Desert*: S.W.Africa　25 00S 15 00E　21 55
Namibia *see* South West Africa　　　21 55 107
Namlea: Indonesia　03 15S 127 07E　　39
Nampa: Idaho, U.S.A.　43 34N 116 34W　90
Namp'o: N.Korea　38 45N 125 23E　　　37
Nampula: Mozambique　15 07S 39 15E　55
Namsos: Norway　64 28N 11 30E　　　　74
Namu: B.C., Canada　51 52N 127 52W　89
Namuchabawashan (Namuchopaerhwa Shan): *mtn.,* China
　29 38N 95 04E　　　　　　　　12 35
Namuhu (Namu): *lake,* China　31 30N 90 30E　35 83
Namur: Belgium　50 28N 04 52E　　　　72
Nan: *riv.,* Thailand　18 00N 100 45E　　35
Nanaimo: B.C., Canada　49 10N 123 56W　42 89
Nan'an: China　24 54N 118 29E　　　　85
Nanao: Japan　37 03N 136 58E　　　　86
Nanchang: China　28 39N 115 58E　　36 85
Nancheng: China　27 33N 116 35E　　　85
Nanching *see* Nanjing　32 01N 118 47E　36 84 105

Nanchong (Nanch'ung): China　30 48N 106 04E　36
Nanchuan: China　29 08N 107 15E　　　85
Nanch'ung *see* Nanchong　30 48N 106 04E　36
Nancy: France　48 42N 06 12E　　　　26 71
Nanda Devi: *mtn.,* India　30 21N 79 50E　82
Nandao: China　31 12N 121 29E　　　　121
Nänder: India　19 11N 77 21E　　　　34 82
Nandūrbar: India　21 22N 74 18E　　　82
Nanfeng: China　27 13N 116 25E　　　85
Nangong: China　37 24N 115 20E　　　84
Nan Hai *see* South China *Sea*　22 15N 115 45E　12 38 85
Nanhai: *lake,* China　39 55N 116 22E　　121
Nanjiang: China　32 22N 106 47E　　　84
Nanjing (Nanching; Nanking): China　32 01N 118 47E
　　　　　　　　　　　　　36 84 105
Nankang: China　25 40N 114 44E　　　85
Nanking *see* Nanjing　32 01N 118 47E　36 84 105
Nanling: *mtns.,* China　25 30N 110 45E　36 85
Nanning: China　22 51N 108 20E　　36 85 105
Nanpan: *riv.,* China　24 30N 104 15E　36
Nānpāra: India　27 51N 81 30E　　　　83
Nanping: China　26 38N 118 11E　　36 85 105
Nan Shan: *ra.,* China　39 00N 98 30E　11
Nantasket Beach: Mass., U.S.A.　42 17N 70 52W　122
Nanterre: France　48 53N 02 13E　　　117
Nantes: France　47 14N 01 35W　　　26 70
Nanton: Alta., Canada　50 21N 113 45W　92
Nantong (Nant'ung): China　32 02N 120 57E　37 84
Nant'ou: China　23 50N 120 41E　　　85
Nantucket *Island*: Mass., U.S.A.　41 15N 70 00W　99
Nant'ung *see* Nantong　32 02N 120 57E　37 84
Nantwich: Ches., England　53 04N 02 32W　58
Nant-y-moch *Reservoir*: Dyfed, Wales　52 15N 03 45W　60
Nanumea: *is.,* S.Pacific Ocean　06 00S 176 00E　4 15
Nanxian: China　29 20N 112 21E　　　85
Nanxiang: China　31 17N 121 18E　　121
Nanxiong: China　25 12N 114 20E　　85
Nanyang: China　33 02N 112 30E　　36 84
Nanyang, *Lake*: China　35 15N 116 45E　84
Nanyuan: China　39 48N 116 23E　　　121
Nanzhang: China　31 48N 111 41E　　84
Nao, *Cabo de la*: Spain　38 44N 00 14E　77
Naococane *Lake*: Qué., Canada　52 45N 70 30W　96
Naoetsu: Japan　37 11N 138 15E　　　86
Naogaon: Bangladesh　24 49N 88 59E　83
Napa: Calif., U.S.A.　38 19N 122 18W　91
Napier: N.I., New Zealand　39 29S 176 58E　37 87
Naples: Italy *see* Napoli　40 50N 14 15E　27 79 107
Napo: *riv.,* Ecuador/Peru　00 30S 76 30W　48
Napoli (Naples): Italy　40 50N 14 15E　27 79 107
Nar: *riv.,* Norf., England　52 30N 00 30E　58
Nara: Japan　34 41N 135 50E　　　　37 86
Narberth: Dyfed, Wales　51 48N 04 45W　60
Narbonne: France　43 11N 03 00E　　71
Narew: *riv.,* Poland　53 00N 22 45E　　78
Narmada: *riv.,* India　22 00N 75 00E　11 34 82
Nārnaul: India　28 04N 76 10E　　　　82
Naro-Fominsk: U.S.S.R.　55 23N 36 43E　80
Narrabeen: N.S.W., Australia　33 43S 151 18E　120
Narsimhapur: India　23 00N 79 15E　　82
Narsingdi: Bangladesh　23 56N 90 40E　83
Naruto: Japan　34 11N 134 37E　　　　86
Narva: U.S.S.R.　59 23N 28 12E　　　　80
Narvik: Norway　68 26N 17 25E　　　27 74
Nasca *Ridge*: S.Pacific Ocean　20 00S 80 00W　5 18
Naseby: Northants., England　52 24N 00 59W　59
Nashua: N.H., U.S.A.　42 44N 71 28W　99
Nashville: Tenn., U.S.A.　36 10N 86 50W　45 101
Näsijärvi: *lake,* Finland　61 45N 23 45E　74
Nāsik: India　20 00N 73 52E　　　　34 82
Nasīrābād: India　21 00N 75 43E　　　82
Nasirya *see* An Nāsirīyah　31 04N 46 17E　33
Naskaupi: *riv.,* Nfld., Canada　54 15N 60 30W　97
Nass: *riv.,* B.C., Canada　55 30N 128 45W　89
Nassau: Bahamas　25 05N 77 20W　　47 101
Nasser, *Lake*: Egypt/Sudan　23 00N 32 45E　20 32
Nässjö: Sweden　57 39N 14 40E　　　　75
Nastapoka: *riv.,* Qué., Canada　56 45N 75 45W　96
Nastapoka *Islands*: N.W.T., Canada　56 45N 76 30W　96
Natal: Brazil　05 47S 35 13W　　　　50
Natal *Basin*: Indian Ocean　33 30S 39 00E　21

Natashquan: Qué., Canada 50 10N 61 50W 97
Natashquan: *riv.*, Canada 51 00N 61 30W 97
Natchez: Miss., U.S.A. 31 34N 91 24W 100
Natchitoches: La., U.S.A. 31 46N 93 05W 100
Natick: Mass., U.S.A. 42 17N 71 21W 122
Natron, *Lake*: Tanzania 02 15S 36 00E 54
Natuna *Island*: Indonesia 04 00N 108 15E 38
Naturaliste *Ridge*: Indian Ocean 33 30S 110 00E 14
Naucalpan de Juarez: Mexico 19 28N 99 14W 128
Naumburg: E.Germany 51 09N 11 48E 73
Nauru: *is.*, S.Pacific Ocean 00 31S 166 56E 4 15
Navajo *Reservoir*: N.Mex., U.S.A. 36 48N 107 36W 95
Navan: Meath, Irish Republic 53 39N 06 40W 66
Navanagar *see* Jämnagar 22 28N 70 06E 34
Navarra: *admin.*, Spain 42 30N 01 30W 70
Navasota: *riv.*, Tex., U.S.A. 30 45N 96 15W 100
Naver: *riv.*, Suther., Scotland 58 15N 04 15W 64
Naver, *Loch*: Suther., Scotland 58 15N 04 15W 64
Navigo Grande: *can.*, Italy 45 15N 08 45E 116
Návpaktos: Greece 38 23N 21 50E 79
Návplion: Greece 37 34N 22 48E 79
Navsāri: India 20 58N 73 01E 82
Nawābganj: Bangladesh 24 35N 88 21E 83
Nawābganj: India 26 52N 82 09E 83
Nawalgarh: India 27 50N 75 15E 82
Náxos: *is.*, Greece 37 07N 25 25E 79
Nayoro: Japan 44 21N 142 28E 86
Naze, The: *cape*, Essex, England 51 53N 01 16E 59
N'azepetrovsk: U.S.S.R. 56 03N 59 36E 81
Nazeret *see* Adama 08 39N 39 19E 53
Nazilli: Turkey 37 54N 28 21E 79
Ndola: Zambia 12 58S 28 38E 54
Neagh, *Lough*: N.Ireland 54 40N 06 25W 66
Néa Páfos: Cyprus 34 45N 32 23E 32
Neápolis: Greece 36 31N 23 03E 79
Neath: W.Glam., Wales 51 40N 03 38W 61
Neauphle-le-Château: France 48 49N 01 54E 117
Nebolči: U.S.S.R. 59 08N 33 18E 80
Nebraska: *admin.*, U.S.A. 41 30N 100 00W 43 94
Nebraska City: Nebr., U.S.A. 40 41N 95 52W 94
Nechako: *riv.*, B.C., Canada 53 30N 124 45W 89
Neches: *riv.*, Tex., U.S.A. 30 50N 94 00W 100
Nederland: Tex., U.S.A. 29 59N 94 00W 100 106
Needham: Mass., U.S.A. 42 17N 71 14W 122
Needham Market: Suff., England 52 09N 01 03E 59
Needles: Calif., U.S.A. 34 51N 114 37W 91
Needles, The: *cape*, I. of W., England 50 39N 01 34W 59
Neemuch (Nimach): India 22 27N 74 56E 82
Neenah: Wis., U.S.A. 44 10N 88 29W 98
Neepawa: Man., Canada 50 14N 99 29W 93
Neftekamsk: U.S.S.R. 56 06N 54 17E 81
Nefyn: Gwyn., Wales 52 57N 04 31W 60
Negishi: Japan 35 26N 139 37E 107
Negombo: Sri Lanka 07 13N 79 51E 34
Negro: *riv.*, Argentina 40 00S 64 45W 52
Negro: *riv.*, Amazonas, Brazil 00 15S 63 45W 18 48
Negros: *is.*, Philippines 10 00N 123 00E 12 39
Nehbandān (Naibandan): Iran 31 32N 60 04E 33
Neichiang *see* Neijiang 29 35N 105 03E 36
Neijiang (Neichiang): China 29 35N 105 03E 36
Neilston: Renf., Scotland 55 47N 04 27W 113
Neimenggu (Inner Mongolia): *admin.*, China
    41 30N 109 00E 36 84
Neiqiu: China 37 17N 114 30E 84
Neisse (Nysa): *riv.*, E.Germany/Poland 51 45N 14 30E
    73 78
Neiva: Colombia 02 58N 75 15W 48
Neixiang: China 33 09N 111 45E 85
Neja: U.S.S.R. 58 18N 43 54E 80
Neja: *riv.*, U.S.S.R. 58 00N 43 45E 80
Nejd: *admin.*, Saudi Arabia 25 15N 44 00E 33
Nelidovo: U.S.S.R. 56 31N 32 46E 80
Nellore: India 14 29N 80 00E 34
Nelson: B.C., Canada 49 29N 117 17W 89
Nelson: Lancs., England 53 51N 02 13W 63 114
Nelson: S.I., New Zealand 41 18S 173 17E 37 87
Nelson: *riv.*, Man., Canada 56 30N 93 30W 16 42 93
Nelson Forks: B.C., Canada 59 30N 124 00W 42 88
Nelson House: Man., Canada 55 49N 98 51W 93
Nelson Lakes *National Park*: S.I., New
    Zealand 41 45S 172 30E 87

Néma: Mauritania 16 32N 07 12W 56
Neman: *riv.*, U.S.S.R. 53 30N 25 15E 78
Nemiscau: Qué., Canada 51 19N 76 54W 96
Nemunas: *riv.*, U.S.S.R. 55 00N 23 30E 75
Nemuro: Japan 43 20N 145 35E 87
Nenagh: Tip., Irish Republic 52 52N 08 12W 67
Nene: *riv.*, England 52 30N 00 00 58
Neosho: *riv.*, U.S.A. 38 00N 95 30W 95
Neoskweskau: Qué., Canada 51 53N 74 17W 96
NEPAL 28 00N 84 00E 11 35 83
Nepalganj: Nepal 28 02N 81 38E 83
Nephi: Utah, U.S.A. 39 43N 111 50W 91
Nephin: *mtn.*, Mayo, Irish Republic 54 01N 09 22W 66
Nephin Beg *Range*: Mayo, Irish Republic 54 00N 09 30W
    66
Neponset: *riv.*, Mass., U.S.A. 42 16N 71 06W 122
Nérac: France 44 08N 00 21E 70
Nerechta: U.S.S.R. 57 28N 40 34E 80
Neretva: *riv.*, Yugoslavia 43 30N 18 00E 79
Nerviano: Italy 45 33N 08 58E 116
Ness, *Loch*: Inv., Scotland 57 15N 04 30W 64
Neston: Ches., England 53 18N 03 04W 60 114
NETHERLANDS 52 45N 06 00E 6 26 72 107
NETHERLANDS ANTILLES 106
Netherlands Guiana *see* Surinam 04 30N 56 15W
    18 50 106
Netrakona: Bangladesh 24 52N 90 46E 83
Neubrandenburg: E.Germany 53 33N 13 16E 73
Neuburg an der Donau: W.Germany 48 44N 11 12E 73
Neuchâtel: Switzerland 47 00N 06 56E 71
Neufchâteau: France 48 21N 05 42E 71
Neuilly: France 48 53N 02 16E 117
Neuilly-Plaisance: France 48 52N 02 31E 117
Neukölln: W.Germany 52 29N 13 28E 117
Neumarkt in der Oberpfalz: W.Germany 49 17N 11 29E 73
Neumünster: W.Germany 54 05N 09 59E 73
Neunkirchen: W.Germany 49 21N 07 12E 72 105
Neuquén: Argentina 38 55S 68 55W 52
Neuquén: *admin.*, Argentina 38 15S 69 45W 52
Neuquén: *riv.*, Argentina 37 30S 70 00W 52
Neuruppin: E.Germany 52 56N 12 49E 73
Neuse: *riv.*, N.C., U.S.A. 35 15N 77 00W 101
Neusiedler See (Fertő): *lake*, Austria/Hungary
    47 45N 16 45E 73 78
Neuss: W.Germany 51 12N 06 42E 118
Neustadt bei Coburg: W.Germany 50 20N 11 08E 73
Neustrelitz: E.Germany 53 22N 13 05E 73
Neutral Zone: *admin.*, Iraq/Saudi Arabia 29 00N 45 30E
    107
Neuves-Maisons: France 48 37N 06 07E 105
Neuwied: W.Germany 50 26N 07 28E 72
Neva: *riv.*, U.S.S.R. 60 00N 30 30E 119
Nevada: *admin.*, U.S.A. 39 00N 117 00W 91
Nevada, Sierra: *ra.*, Spain 36 45N 03 00W 77
Nevada, Sierra: *ra.*, Calif., U.S.A. 38 00N 119 00W
    17 43 91
Nevada City: Calif., U.S.A. 39 16N 121 00W 91
Nevada de Cocuy, Sierra: *mtn.*, Colombia 06 28N 72 18W
    48
Nevado: *mtn.*, Argentina 35 35S 68 32W 52
Nevado del Huila: *mtn.*, Colombia 03 00N 76 00W 48
Nevel': U.S.S.R. 56 02N 29 55E 80
Nevers: France 47 00N 03 09E 71
Nevinnomyssk: U.S.S.R. 44 38N 41 56E 28
Nevis: Alta., Canada 52 22N 113 01W. 92
Nevis: *is.*, Leeward Islands 17 15N 62 30W 47
Nevis, Ben: *mtn.*, Inv., Scotland 56 48N 05 00W 64
Nevis, *Loch*: Inv., Scotland 57 00N 05 30W 64
Nevjansk: U.S.S.R. 57 32N 60 13E 81
New Albany: Ind., U.S.A. 38 17N 85 50W 98
New Alresford: Hants., England 51 06N 01 10W 59
New Amsterdam: Guyana 06 18N 57 30W 48
New Amsterdam: *is.*, Indian Ocean 37 55S 77 40E 1
Newark: Calif., U.S.A. 37 31N 122 03W 126
Newark: Del., U.S.A. 39 42N 75 45W 99
Newark: N.J., U.S.A. 40 44N 74 11W 99 123
Newark: Ohio, U.S.A. 40 03N 82 25W 98
Newark *Bay*: N.J., U.S.A. 40 40N 74 08W 123
Newark-on-Trent: Notts., England 53 05N 00 49W 58
New Bedford: Mass., U.S.A. 41 38N 70 55W 99
New Bern: N.C., U.S.A. 35 05N 77 04W 45 101

Types of map: Ocean pp. 1-5; Physical pp. 6-25; Human pp. 26-57; Topographic pp. 58-101; World pp. 102-111; Urban pp. 112-128.

Newberry: Mich., U.S.A.   46 22N 85 30W   98
Newbiggin-by-the-Sea: Northumb., England
   55 11N 01 30W   63
New Braunfels: Tex., U.S.A.   29 42N 98 08W   95
New Britain: *is.*, S.Pacific Ocean   05 00S 150 00E   4 15
New Britain *Trench*: S.Pacific Ocean   07 00S 152 00E   15
New Brunswick: N.J., U.S.A.   40 29N 74 27W   99 123
New Brunswick: *admin.*, Canada   47 00N 66 00W   44 97
Newburgh: Fife, Scotland   56 21N 03 15W   65
Newburgh: N.Y., U.S.A.   41 30N 74 00W   99
Newburn: Tyne & Wear, England   54 58N 01 44W   63
Newbury: Berks., England   51 25N 01 20W   59
New Caledonia: *is.*, Coral Sea   21 00S 166 00E
   4 15 105 107
New Caledonia *Basin*: S.Pacific Ocean   30 00S 165 00E   4
Newcastle: N.S.W., Australia   32 55S 151 46E   41 105
Newcastle: N.B., Canada   47 01N 65 36W   97
Newcastle: Down, N.Ireland   54 12N 05 54W   66
New Castle: Pa., U.S.A.   41 00N 80 22W   99
Newcastle: Wyo., U.S.A.   43 50N 104 11W   94
Newcastle Emlyn: Dyfed, Wales   52 02N 04 28W   60
Newcastle-under-Lyme: Staffs., England   53 00N 02 14W
   58
Newcastle-upon-Tyne: Tyne & Wear, England
   54 59N 01 35W   26 63
Newcastle West: Lim., Irish Republic   52 27N 09 03W   67
New Delhi: India   28 37N 77 13E   34 82 120
Newent: Glos., England   51 56N 02 24W   60
New *Forest*: Hants., England   50 45N 01 30W   59
Newfoundland: *admin.*, Canada   44 97
Newfoundland: *is.*, Nfld., Canada   49 00N 56 00W   17 44 97
Newfoundland *Basin*: N.Atlantic Ocean   44 00N 45 00W   2
New Galloway: Kirkc., Scotland   55 05N 04 10W   62
New Glasgow: N.S., Canada   45 36N 62 38W   97
New Guinea: *is.*, S.Pacific Ocean   05 00S 141 00E   4 13 39
NEW GUINEA, AUSTRALIAN TRUST TERR. OF
   04 00S 143 00E   15
Newhall: Derby., England   42 48N 01 34W   115
New Hampshire: *admin.*, U.S.A.   44 00N 71 15W   44 99
Newhaven: E.Sussex, England   50 47N 00 03E   59
New Haven: Conn., U.S.A.   41 18N 72 55W   45 99
New Hazelton: B.C., Canada   55 15N 127 35W   89
New Hebrides: *is.*, Coral Sea   15 00S 167 00E   4 15
New Hebrides *Trench*: Coral Sea   17 00S 167 00E   4
New Hyde Park: N.Y., U.S.A.   40 45N 73 44W   123
New Iberia: La., U.S.A.   30 01N 91 49W   100
New Ireland: *is.*, S.Pacific Ocean   03 00S 153 00E   4 15
New Jersey: *admin.*, U.S.A.   40 00N 74 30W   45 99
New Jersey Turnpike: *hwy.*, N.J., U.S.A.   40 00N 74 45W
   122
Newmarket: Suff., England   52 15N 00 25E   59
New Mexico: *admin.*, U.S.A.   34 30N 106 00W   43 95
New Mills: Derby., England   52 23N 02 00W   58
Newnan: Ga., U.S.A.   33 23N 84 48W   101
Newnham: Glos., England   51 49N 02 27W   60
New Orleans: La., U.S.A.   29 58N 90 04W   45 100
New Plymouth: N.I., New Zealand   39 03S 174 04E   37 87
Newport: N.S.W., Australia   33 39S 151 19E   120
Newport: I. of W., England   50 42N 01 18W   59
Newport: Salop, England   52 47N 02 22W   58
Newport: Ky., U.S.A.   39 06N 84 29W   98
Newport: Oreg., U.S.A.   44 38N 124 03W   90
Newport: R.I., U.S.A.   41 30N 71 19W   99
Newport: Vt., U.S.A.   44 56N 72 13W   99
Newport: Gwent, Wales   51 35N 03 00W   61 113
Newport News: Va., U.S.A.   36 59N 76 26W   45 101
Newport-on-Tay: Fife, Scotland   56 27N 02 56W   65
Newport Pagnell: Bucks., England   52 05N 00 44W   59
New Providence *Island*: Bahamas   25 00N 77 15W   101
Newquay: Corn., England   50 25N 05 05W   61
New Quay: Dyfed, Wales   52 13N 04 22W   60
New Richmond: Qué., Canada   48 12N 65 52W   97
New Rochelle: N.Y., U.S.A.   40 55N 73 47W   123
New Romney: Kent, England   50 59N 00 57E   59
New Ross: Wex., Irish Republic   52 24N 06 56W   67
Newry: Down, N.Ireland   54 11N 06 20W   66
New Siberian *Islands*: U.S.S.R.   75 00N 145 00E   22
New South Wales: *admin.*, Australia   41
Newton: Iowa, U.S.A.   41 41N 93 02W   98
Newton: Kans., U.S.A.   38 03N 97 21W   95
Newton: Mass., U.S.A.   42 20N 71 13W   122

Newton Abbot: Devon, England   50 32N 03 36W   61
Newton-le-Willows: Mers., England   53 28N 02 37W
   63 114
Newton Mearns: Renf., Scotland   55 46N 04 18W   113
Newton Station: B.C., Canada   49 08N 122 54W   126
Newton Stewart: Wig., Scotland   54 57N 04 29W   62
New Toronto: Ont., Canada   43 35N 79 32W   125
Newtown: Powys, Wales   52 32N 03 19W   60
Newtownabbey: Antrim, N.Ireland   54 40N 05 57W   66
Newtownards: Down, N.Ireland   54 36N 05 41W   66
Newtown Hamilton: Arm., N.Ireland   54 12N 06 35W   66
Newtownstewart: Tyr., N.Ireland   54 43N 07 22W   66
New Tredegar: M.Glam., Wales   51 43N 03 14W   113
New Ulm: Minn., U.S.A.   44 19N 94 28W   98
New Westminster: B.C., Canada   49 12N 122 55W   89 126
New York: N.Y., U.S.A.   40 40N 73 50W   45 99 123
New York: *admin.*, U.S.A.   42 30N 77 00W   99
NEW ZEALAND   15 37 87 107
Neyland: Dyfed, Wales   51 43N 04 57W   61
Nez de Jobourg: *pt.*, France   49 33N 01 48W   61
Nežin: U.S.S.R.   51 03N 31 54E   80
Nez Perce *Dam*: U.S.A.   46 17N 117 00W   90
Ngauruhoe: *mtn.*, N.I., New Zealand   39 10S 175 40E   87
Ngo Chu: *riv. see* Salween   19 30N 97 30E   11 35
Nguru: Nigeria   12 53N 10 30E   57
Ngwenya: *mtn.*, Swaziland   26 11S 31 02E   105
Nha Trang: S.Vietnam   12 15N 109 11E   38
Niagara Falls: N.Y., U.S.A.   43 06N 79 04W   99
Niagara *Falls*: Canada/U.S.A.   43 05N 79 05W   45
Niamey: Niger   13 32N 02 05E   57
Nianqingtanggula *Range*: China   30 00N 88 00E   11 35 83
Nias: *is.*, Indonesia   01 00N 97 45E   12 38
Nica: *riv.*, U.S.S.R.   57 30N 64 15E   81
NICARAGUA   13 00N 85 30W   18 47 106
Nicaragua, *Lake*: Nicaragua   11 30N 85 30W   17 47
Nice: France   43 42N 07 16E   26 71
Niceville: Fla., U.S.A.   30 31N 86 29W   101
Nicobar *Islands*: Indian Ocean   08 00N 93 30E   1 11 35
Nicosia *see* Levkosia   35 11N 33 23E   27
Nidd: *riv.*, N.Yorks., England   53 45N 01 15W   63
Niederösterreich: *admin.*, Austria   48 30N 16 00E   73
Niedersachsen: *admin.*, W.Germany   52 15N 07 15E   72
Nienburg: W.Germany   52 38N 09 13E   72
Niete *Mountains*: Liberia   05 30N 08 00W   57
Nieuw Nickerie: Surinam   05 52N 57 00W   48
NIGER   14 00N 08 00E   20 56
Niger: *riv.*, W.Africa   05 45N 06 30E   20 57
NIGERIA   20 57 106
Nihoa: *is.*, Hawaiian Islands   23 03N 161 55W   4
Niigata: Japan   37 55N 139 03E   37 86
Niihama: Japan   33 58N 133 16E   86
Niihau: *is.*, Hawaii, U.S.A.   21 50N 160 11W   4
Nii-shima: *is.*, Japan   34 22N 139 16E   86
Niiza: Japan   35 48N 139 33E   121
Nijmegen: Netherlands   51 50N 05 52E   72
Nikko-kokuritsu-kōen: *nat. park.*, Japan   37 00N 139 45E
   86
Nikolajev (Nikolayev): U.S.S.R.   46 58N 32 00E   28 80
Nikolajevskij: U.S.S.R.   50 01N 45 28E   81
Nikolajevsk-na-Amure (Nikolayevsk-na-Amure): U.S.S.R.
   53 08N 140 44E   31 105
Nikolo-Ber'ozovka: U.S.S.R.   56 08N 54 09E   81
Nikol'sk: U.S.S.R.   53 45N 46 05E   81
Nikopol': U.S.S.R.   47 35N 34 25E   28 80
Nikšić: Yugoslavia   42 48N 18 56E   79 105
Nil, Nahr an (Nile): *riv.*, Africa   29 15N 31 15E   20 32
Nile: *riv., see* Nil, Nahr an   29 15N 31 15E   20 32
Niles: Ill., U.S.A.   42 00N 87 48W   124
Niles: Mich., U.S.A.   41 51N 86 15W   98
Nimach *see* Neemuch   22 27N 74 56E   82
Nimba *Mountains*: Guinea   07 45N 08 15W   20 57 104
Nîmes: France   43 50N 04 21E   26 71
Nimule: Sudan   03 35N 32 04E   54
Ninety East *Ridge*: Indian Ocean   15 00S 88 00E   1
Ninety Mile *Beach*: N.I., New Zealand   34 45S 173 00E   87
Ningbo (Ningpo): China   29 52N 121 29E   37 85
Ningde: China   26 40N 119 33E   85
Ningdu: China   26 20N 115 50E   85
Ningguo: China   30 33N 118 58E   85
Ninghai: China   29 17N 121 28E   85
Ninghua: China   26 10N 116 31E   85

Types of map: Ocean pp. 1-5; Physical pp. 6-25; Human pp. 26-57; Topographic pp. 58-101; World pp. 102-111; Urban pp. 112-128.

Ningjingshan (Ning Ting Shan): *mtns.*, China
    30 45N 98 15E   36
Ningpo *see* Ningbo   29 52N 121 29E   37 85
Ningshan: China   33 15N 108 29E   84
Ningsia: *admin. see* Ningxia   37 30N 106 45E   36 84
Ning Ting Shan: *mtns. see* Ningjingshan   30 45N 98 15E
                                                                    36
Ningwu: China   38 58N 112 21E   84
Ningxia (Ningsia): *admin.*, China   37 30N 106 45E   36 84
Ningxiang: China   28 19N 112 30E   85
Ningyuan: China   25 37N 111 47E   85
Niobrara: *riv.*, U.S.A.   42 45N 98 30W   94
Niort: France   46 19N 00 27W   70
Nios: *is. see* los   36 43N 25 17E   79
Nipawin: Sask., Canada   53 23N 104 01W   92
Nipawin *Provincial Park*: Sask., Canada   54 00N 104 15W
                                                                    92
Nipigon: Ont., Canada   49 02N 88 26W   98
Nipigon, *Lake*: Ont., Canada   49 45N 88 30W   17 44 98
Nipissing, *Lake*: Ont., Canada   46 15N 79 45W   44 99
Nippes: W.Germany   50 58N 06 57E   119
Nirmal: India   19 04N 78 21E   82
Niš: Yugoslavia   43 20N 21 54E   27 79
Nisling: *riv.*, Yukon, Canada   61 45N 138 30W   88
Nilsing *Range*: Yukon, Canada   61 45N 139 00W   88
Nitchequon: Qué., Canada   53 10N 70 58W   96
Niterói: Brazil   22 53S 43 07W   51
Nith: *riv.*, Scotland   55 15N 04 00W   62
Nithdale: *val.*, Dumf., Scotland   55 00N 03 45W   62
Nitra: Czechoslovakia   48 19N 18 05E   78
Nivernais, *Canal du*: France   47 15N 03 30E   71
Nizāmābād: India   18 40N 78 05E   34 82
Nizhniy Tagil *see* Nižnij Tagil   57 55N 59 57E   29 81 105
Nižn'aja Salda: U.S.S.R.   58 05N 60 43E   105
Nižnij Lomov: U.S.S.R.   53 32N 43 41E   80
Nižnij Tagil (Nizhniy Tagil): U.S.S.R.   57 55N 59 57E
                                                              29 81 105
Nkongsamba: Cameroun   04 57N 09 56E   57
Noākhāli: Bangladesh   22 51N 91 06E   83
Nobeoka: Japan   32 35N 131 40E   86
Noboribetsu: Japan   42 27N 141 11E   86
Nodaway: *riv.*, U.S.A.   40 15N 95 00W   94
Nogales: Mexico   31 20N 111 00W   46 95
Nogales: Ariz., U.S.A.   31 20N 110 56W   91
Nogent: France   48 50N 02 29E   117
Nogent-le-Rotrou: France   48 19N 00 50E   70
Noginsk: U.S.S.R.   55 51N 38 27E   28 105
Noire, *Montagne*: France   43 28N 02 18E   70
Noirmont *Point*: Channel Islands   49 10N 02 03W   61
Noisy-le-Sec: France   48 54N 02 27E   117
Nokia: Finland   61 29N 23 31E   75
Nokomis: Sask., Canada   51 30N 105 00W   92
Nolinsk: U.S.S.R.   57 33N 49 57E   28 81
Nonacho *Lake*: N.W.T., Canada   61 45N 109 30W   92
Nootka *Island*: B.C., Canada   49 45N 126 50W   89
Nootka *Sound*: B.C., Canada   49 30N 126 30W   43
Noranda: Qué., Canada   48 16N 79 03W   99
Norco: La., U.S.A.   30 00N 90 25W   106
Nordegg *see* Brazeau   52 29N 116 05W   92
Norden: W.Germany   53 36N 07 13E   72
Nordenham: W.Germany   53 30N 08 29E   72
Norderelbe: *riv.*, W.Germany   53 15N 10 00E   119
Nordhausen: E.Germany   51 31N 10 48E   73
Nordhorn: W.Germany   52 27N 07 05E   72
Nordkanal: *can.*, W.Germany   51 00N 06 30E   118
Nordkapp (North Cape): Norway   71 11N 25 40E   23 74
Nord-Ostsee *Kanal*: W.Germany   54 00N 09 30E   72
Nordrhein–Westfalen: *admin.*, W.Germany
    52 15N 07 15E   72
Nordvik: U.S.S.R.   74 02N 111 32E   30
Nore: *riv.*, Irish Republic   52 15N 07 00W   67
Norfolk: Nebr., U.S.A.   42 02N 97 25W   94
Norfolk: Va., U.S.A.   36 54N 76 18W   45 101
Norfolk: *admin.*, England   52 30N 01 00E   58
Norfolk Broads: *geog. reg.*, England   52 30N 01 15E   58
Norfolk *Island*: S.Pacific Ocean   29 05S 167 59E   4
Norfolk Island *Ridge*: S.Pacific Ocean   28 00S 168 00E   15
Norfork, *Lake*: Ark., U.S.A.   36 13N 92 14W   100
Noril'sk: U.S.S.R.   69 20N 88 06E   30
Norman: Okla., U.S.A.   35 13N 97 26W   95
Normandie, Collines de: *hills*, France   48 45N 00 45W   70

Normanton: Qld., Australia   17 40S 141 05E   41
Normanton: W.Yorks., England   53 42N 01 25W   115
Norman Wells: N.W.T., Canada   65 19N 126 46W   88
Normetal: Qué., Canada   48 59N 79 21W   99
Nørresundby: Denmark   57 04N 09 56E   75
Norristown: Pa., U.S.A.   40 07N 75 20W   122
Norrköping: Sweden   58 35N 16 10E   27 75
Norrtälje: Sweden   59 46N 18 43E   75
Norseman: W.A., Australia   32 15S 121 47E   40
North, *Cape*: N.S., Canada   47 03N 60 24W   97
Northallerton: N.Yorks., England   54 20N 01 26W   63
North American *Basin*: N.Atlantic Ocean   33 00N 55 00W   2
Northampton: Northants., England   52 14N 00 54W   59
Northampton: Mass., U.S.A.   42 19N 72 38W   99
Northamptonshire: *admin.*, England   52 15N 01 00W   59
North Arm: *riv.*, B.C., Canada   49 12N 123 20W   126
North Atlantic *Drift*: N.Atlantic Ocean   48 00N 30 00W   2
North Atlantic *Ocean*   2
North Battleford: Sask., Canada   52 47N 108 19W   42 92
North Bay: Ont., Canada   46 20N 79 28W   42 99
North Bend: Oreg., U.S.A.   43 24N 124 14W   90
North Bergen: N.J., U.S.A.   40 48N 74 03W   123
North Berwick: E.Loth., Scotland   56 04N 02 44W   63
North Branch Chicago: *riv.*, Ill., U.S.A.   42 00N 87 45W   124
Northbrook: Ill., U.S.A.   42 07N 87 49W   124
North Canadian: *riv.*, U.S.A.   36 45N 103 00W   95
North *Cape*: N.I., New Zealand   34 23S 173 04E   87
North *Cape*: Norway *see* Nordkapp   71 11N 25 40E   23 74
North Caribou *Lake*: Ont., Canada   52 45N 90 30W   93
North Carolina: *admin.*, U.S.A.   36 00N 79 00W   45 101
North Cascades *National Park*: Wash., U.S.A.
    48 45N 121 15W   90
North *Channel*: Ont., Canada   46 00N 83 00W   98
North *Channel*: N.Ireland/Scotland   54 45N 05 15W   62
North Chicago: Ill., U.S.A.   42 18N 87 52W   124
North Dakota: *admin.*, U.S.A.   47 00N 100 00W   42 94
North Dorset Downs: *hills*, Dorset, England
    50 45N 02 30W   61
North Downs: *hills*, Kent, England   51 15N 00 15E   59
North Dvina: *riv.*, U.S.S.R.   62 30N 44 00E   8 28
Northeim: W.Germany   51 43N 09 59E   73
North Eleuthera: Bahamas   25 30N 76 45W   47
North Equatorial *Current*: N.Atlantic Ocean
    18 00N 50 00W   2
North Equatorial *Current*: N.Pacific Ocean
    12 00N 170 00W   4
Northern Indian *Lake*: Man., Canada   56 45N 97 00W   93
NORTHERN IRELAND   54 45N 06 45W   26 66
Northern Sporades: *is. see* Voríai
    Sporádhes   39 00N 24 00E   79
Northern Territory: *admin.*, Australia   18 30S 133 30E   40
North Esk: *riv.*, Scotland   56 45N 02 30W   65
North European *Plain*   53 00N 19 00E   7
Northfield: Minn., U.S.A.   44 28N 93 10W   98
North Fiji *Basin*: S.Pacific Ocean   17 00S 172 00E   4 15
Northfleet: Kent, England   51 27N 00 20E   59
North Foreland: *cape*, Kent, England   51 23N 01 27E   59
North Fork Solomon: *riv.*, Kans., U.S.A.   39 30N 99 45W   94
North Frisian *Islands*:
    Denmark/W.Germany   55 00N 08 15E   75
Northgate: Sask., Canada   49 02N 102 18W   92
North *Head*: N.S.W., Australia   33 49S 151 18E   120
North Hinksey: Oxon., England   51 45N 01 16W   59
North *Island*: New Zealand   38 00S 175 00E   15 41 87
North Knife *Lake*: Man., Canada   58 00N 96 45W   93
NORTH KOREA   41 30N 129 00E   12 37 86 107
Northlake: Ill., U.S.A.   41 52N 87 56W   124
North Little Rock: Ark., U.S.A.   34 45N 92 16W   100
North Loup: *riv.*, Nebr., U.S.A.   41 45N 99 30W   94
North Magnetic *Pole* (1971): Arctic   76 02N 101 00W   23
North Pacific *Ocean*   4
North Pagai: *is.*, Indonesia   02 45S 100 00E   38
North *Park*: Pa., U.S.A.   40 36N 80 01W   125
North Platte: Nebr., U.S.A.   41 08N 100 46W   94
North Platte: *riv.*, U.S.A.   41 30N 103 00W   94
North *Point*: P.E.I., Canada   47 03N 64 00W   97
North *Point*: Mich., U.S.A.   45 02N 83 17W   98
North *Pole*: Arctic   90 00N   23
North *Riding*: *dist.*, Tip., Irish Republic   52 45N 08 00W   67
North Ronaldsay: *is.*, Ork. Is., Scotland   59 25N 02 30W   65
North Saskatchewan: *riv.*, Canada   53 00N 106 45W   42 92

North *Sea*   6 26 68
North *Sound*: Gal., Irish Republic   53 00N 09 30W   67
North Sound, The: Ork. Is., Scotland   59 15N 02 45W   65
North Tyne: *riv.*, Northumb., England   55 00N 02 15W   63
North Uist: *is.*, Inv., Scotland   57 37N 07 22W   64
Northumberland: *admin.*, England   55 15N 02 00W   63
Northumberland *National Park*: England   55 15N 02 15W
                                                    63
Northumberland *Strait*: Canada   46 00N 63 00W   97
North Vancouver: B.C., Canada   49 19N 123 04W   126
NORTH VIETNAM   19 00N 106 15E   12 36 107
Northville: Mich., U.S.A.   42 24N 83 28W   125
North Walsham: Norf., England   52 50N 01 24E   58
Northwest Atlantic *Basin*: N.Atlantic Ocean
    34 00N 70 00W   2
Northwest *Highlands*: Scotland   57 00N 05 00W   64
Northwest Pacific *Basin*: N.Pacific Ocean   4
Northwest Providence *Channel*: Bahamas   26 00N 78 00W
                                                    101
North West River: Nfld., Canada   53 30N 60 10W   97
Northwest Territories: *admin.*, Canada   42 92
Northwest Tollway: *hwy.*, Ill., U.S.A.   42 00N 88 00W   124
Northwich: Ches., England   53 16N 02 32W   58 114
North York: Ont., Canada   43 44N 79 26W   125
North York Moors *National Park*: N.Yorks., England
    54 15N 01 00W   63
North Yorkshire: *admin.*, England   54 15N 01 30W   63
Norton: Va., U.S.A.   36 56N 82 37W   101
Norvegia, *Cape*: Antarctica   71 28S 12 25W   24
Norwalk: Calif., U.S.A.   33 56N 118 04W   127
NORWAY   7 27 74 106
Norway House: Man., Canada   53 59N 97 50W   93
Norwegian *Current*: N.Atlantic Ocean   68 00N 10 00E   2
Norwegian *Sea*   65 00N 00 00   2 6
Norwich: Norf., England   52 38N 01 18E   26 58
Noshiro: Japan   40 12N 140 02E   86
Nosovka: U.S.S.R.   50 55N 31 35E   80
Noss *Head*: Caith., Scotland   58 28N 03 03W   65
Noteć: *riv.*, Poland   53 00N 17 15E   73 78
Notikewin: *riv.*, Alta., Canada   57 00N 118 00W   92
Noto-Hantō: *pen.*, Japan   37 15N 137 00E   86
Notre-Dame, Bois: *woods*, France   48 45N 02 35E   117
Notre Dame *Bay*: Nfld., Canada   49 45N 55 30W   97
Notre Dame *Mountains*: Qué., Canada   48 30N 67 00W   96
Nottaway: *riv.*, Qué., Canada   50 45N 78 00W   96
Nottingham: Notts., England   52 58N 01 10W   26 58
Nottingham *Island*: N.W.T., Canada   63 30N 78 00W   44
Nottinghamshire: *admin.*, England   53 00N 01 00W   58
Nouadhibou *see* Port Étienne   20 54N 17 01W   56
Nouakchott: Mauritania   18 09N 15 58W   56
Nova Freixo: Mozambique   14 49S 36 33E   54 55
Nova Friburgo: Brazil   22 16S 42 32W   51
Nova Goa *see* Panaji   15 29N 73 50E   34
Novaja Kachovka: U.S.S.R.   46 45N 33 23E   80
Novaja L'al'a: U.S.S.R.   59 03N 60 36E   81
Novaja Zeml'a: *is.*, U.S.S.R.   74 00N 58 00E   23
Nova Lisboa: Angola   12 44S 15 47E   54
Nova Milanese: Italy   45 35N 09 12E   116
Novara: Italy   45 27N 08 37E   26 71 107
Nova Scotia: *admin.*, Canada   45 00N 63 00W   44 97
Nova Scotia Basin: N.Atlantic Ocean   38 00N 55 00W   2
Novgorod: U.S.S.R.   58 31N 31 17E   28 80
Novgorod-Severskij: U.S.S.R.   51 59N 33 16E   80
Novi Ligure: Italy   44 46N 08 47E   71
Novi Pazar: Yugoslavia   43 09N 20 29E   79
Novi Sad: Yugoslavia   45 15N 19 51E   27 78
Novoanninskij: U.S.S.R.   50 32N 42 41E   80
Novočerkassk (Novocherkassk): U.S.S.R.   47 25N 40 06E
                                                    28 80
Novograd-Volynskij: U.S.S.R.   50 36N 27 36E   78
Novo Hamburgo: Brazil   29 37S 51 07W   51
Novokujbyševsk (Novokuybyshevsk): U.S.S.R.
    53 07N 49 58E   28 81
Novokuzneck (Novokuznetsk, Stalinsk): U.S.S.R.
    53 45N 87 06E   30 105
Novolazarevskaya: *rsch. stn.*, Antarctica   70 46S 11 50E   24
Novomoskovsk (Stalinogorsk): U.S.S.R.   54 05N 38 13E
                                                    28 80
Novomoskovsk: U.S.S.R.   48 37N 35 12E   80
Novopolock: U.S.S.R.   55 31N 28 38E   75
Novopskov: U.S.S.R.   49 33N 39 05E   80

Novo Redondo: Angola   11 13S 13 50E   54
Novorossijsk (Novorossiysk): U.S.S.R.   44 45N 37 45E   28
Novošachtinsk: U.S.S.R.   47 47N 39 56E   80
Novosergijevka: U.S.S.R.   52 06N 53 39E   81
Novosibirsk: U.S.S.R.   55 02N 82 55E   30 105
Novotroick: U.S.S.R.   51 12N 58 20E   81 105
Novouzensk: U.S.S.R.   50 28N 48 08E   81
Novov'atsk: U.S.S.R.   58 29N 49 44E   81
Novovolynsk: U.S.S.R.   50 44N 24 09E   78
Novyj Bug: U.S.S.R.   47 41N 32 30E   80
Novyj Lipeck: U.S.S.R.   52 35N 39 37E   105
Novyj Port (Novyy Port): U.S.S.R.   67 40N 72 52E   30
Nowa Sól: Poland   51 49N 15 41E   73 78
Nowy Sącz: Poland   49 39N 20 40E   78
Noxon Rapids *Dam*: Mont., U.S.A.   47 59N 115 48W   90
Nubian *Desert*: Sudan   21 00N 33 15E   20 53
Nueces: *riv.*, Tex., U.S.A.   28 15N 97 45W   100
Nueltin *Lake*: N.W.T., Canada   60 15N 99 30W   93
Nueva Rosita: Mexico   27 57N 101 13W   46
Nuevo Laredo: Mexico   27 30N 99 31W   46
Nuevo León: *admin.*, Mexico   26 00N 100 00W   46
Nuku Hiva: *is.*, S.Pacific Ocean   08 56S 140 00W   5
Nukus: U.S.S.R.   42 50N 59 29E   29
Nullarbor *Plain*: Australia   30 30S 128 30E   14 40
Numazu: Japan   35 06N 138 52E   86
Nunaksaluk *Island*: Nfld., Canada   55 48N 60 20W   97
Nuneaton: War., England   52 32N 01 28W   58 115
Nuoro: Sardinia   49 19N 09 20E   77
Nuremberg *see* Nürnberg   49 27N 11 05E   26 73
Nurlat: U.S.S.R.   54 26N 50 46E   81
Nurmes: Finland   63 31N 29 10E   74
Nürnberg (Nuremberg): W.Germany   49 27N 11 05E   26 73
Nushan: *mtns.*, China   29 00N 98 30E   36
Nuthe: *riv.*, E.Germany   52 15N 13 00E   117
Nyasa (Malawi), *Lake*: E.Africa   11 45S 34 30E   21 54
Nybro: Sweden   56 44N 15 55E   75
Nye: Mont., U.S.A.   45 23N 109 53W   94
Nyenyam: China   28 11N 85 58E   83
Nyíregyháza: Hungary   47 57N 21 43E   79
Nykøbing: Denmark   54 47N 11 53E   74
Nyköping: Sweden   58 45N 17 03E   75
Nynäshamn: Sweden   58 54N 17 55E   75
Nysa: Poland   50 30N 17 20E   73 78
Nysa: *riv. see* Neisse   51 45N 14 45E   73
Nyssa: Oreg., U.S.A.   43 53N 117 00W   90

Oa, Mull of: *cape*, Argyll., Scotland   55 36N 06 21W   62
Oa, The: *dist.*, Argyll., Scotland   55 30N 06 15W   62
Oadby: Leics., England   52 36N 01 04W   58
Oahe *Dam*: S.D., U.S.A.   44 27N 100 24W   94
Oahe *Reservoir*: U.S.A.   45 30N 100 15W   43 94
Oahu: *is.*, Hawaii, U.S.A.   21 30N 158 00W   4
Oakdale: Calif., U.S.A.   37 45N 120 50W   91
Oakengates: Salop, England   52 42N 02 28W   58
Oakes: N.D., U.S.A.   46 08N 98 06W   94
Oakham: Leics., England   52 40N 00 43W   58
Oakland: Calif., U.S.A.   37 50N 122 15W   43 91 126
Oakland *Inner Harbor*: Calif., U.S.A.   37 47N 122 15W   126
Oak Lam: Ill., U.S.A.   41 42N 87 45W   124
Oak Park: Ill., U.S.A.   41 52N 87 47W   124
Oak Park: Mich., U.S.A.   42 26N 83 09W   125
Oak Ridge: Tenn., U.S.A.   36 02N 84 12W   101
Oak Street *Beach*: Ill., U.S.A.   41 54N 87 37W   124
Oamaru: S.I., New Zealand   45 07S 170 58E   87
Oaxaca: *admin.*, Mexico   16 30N 96 45W   46
Oaxaca de Juárez: Mexico   17 03N 96 43W   46
Ob': *riv.*, U.S.S.R.   66 15N 66 00E   8 30
Ob', *Gulf of*: U.S.S.R.   68 30N 74 00E   30
Oba: Ont., Canada   49 04N 84 07W   98
Oban: Sask., Canada   52 09N 108 09W   92
Oban: Argyll., Scotland   56 25N 05 29W   64
Obbia: Somali Rep.   05 20N 48 30E   53
Oberhausen: W.Germany   51 27N 06 50E   118
Oberösterreich: *admin.*, Austria   48 15N 14 00E   73
Obi: *is.*, Indonesia   01 30S 127 30E   39
Obihiro: Japan   42 55N 143 12E   37 87
Obitsu: *riv.*, Japan   35 24N 139 55E   121
Oblačnaja (Oblachnaya), Gora: *mtn.*, U.S.S.R.
    43 42N 134 10E   37 86

Types of map: Ocean pp. 1-5; Physical pp. 6-25; Human pp. 26-57; Topographic pp. 58-101; World pp. 102-111; Urban pp. 112-128.

Obninsk: U.S.S.R.   55 05N 36 37E   80
Obojan': U.S.S.R.   51 13N 36 16E   80
Obščij Syrt: *ridge*, U.S.S.R.   52 15N 51 30E   81
Obva: *riv.*, U.S.S.R.   58 30N 55 15E   81
Ocala: Fla., U.S.A.   29 11N 82 09W   101
Occidental, Cordillera: *ra.*, Colombia   05 00N 76 00W   48
Oceanlake: Oreg., U.S.A.   44 59N 124 00W   90
Ocean Falls: B.C., Canada   52 24N 127 42W   89
Ocean *Island*: S.Pacific Ocean   00 52S 169 35E   4 15
Oceanographer *Fracture Zone* N.Atlantic Ocean
   35 00N 35 00W   2
Oceanside: Calif., U.S.A.   33 12N 117 23W   91
Očer: U.S.S.R.   57 53N 54 42E   81
Ochil *Hills*: Scotland   56 15N 03 30W   65
Ocho Rios: Jamaica   18 24N 77 06W   47
Ochotsk (Okhotsk): U.S.S.R.   59 23N 143 18E   31
Ochta: *riv.*, U.S.S.R.   59 57N 30 24E   119
Ocmulgee: *riv.*, Ga., U.S.A.   31 45N 83 00W   101
Oconee: *riv.*, Ga., U.S.A.   32 30N 82 45W   101
Ocussi: Ocussi Ambeno   09 15S 124 23E   39
Ocussi Ambeno: *Port. colony*, Timor   09 15S 124 15E
                                                     13 39
Oda: Ghana   05 55N 00 56W   57
Ōda: Japan   35 11N 132 30E   86
Ōdate: Japan   40 16N 140 34E   86
Odawara: Japan   35 15N 139 10E   37 86
Odda: Norway   60 03N 06 34E   75
Ödemiş: Turkey   38 11N 27 58E   79
Odendaalsrus: O.F.S., Rep. of S.Africa   27 52S 26 42E   55
Odense: Denmark   55 24N 10 25E   26 75
Oder (Odra): *riv.*, E.Germany/Poland   53 00N 14 15E
                                                7 27 73 78
Oder-Havel *Kanal*: E.Germany   52 45N 13 30E   73
Oder-Spree *Kanal*: E.Germany   52 15N 14 15E   73
Odessa: Tex., U.S.A.   31 52N 102 23W   43 95
Odessa: U.S.S.R.   46 28N 30 44E   28 80
Odienné: Ivory Coast   09 36N 07 32W   57
Odra (Oder): *riv.*, Poland/E.Germany   50 45N 17 30E
                                                7 27 73 78
Oeno *Island*: S.Pacific Ocean   23 55S 130 45W   5
Oer-Erkenschwick: W.Germany   51 38N 07 15E   118
Offaly: *admin.*, Irish Republic   53 15N 07 30W   67
Offenburg: W.Germany   48 29N 07 57E   72
Ōfuna: Japan   35 21N 139 32E   121
Ōfunato: Japan   39 04N 141 43E   86
Oga: Japan   39 53N 139 51E   86
Oga-hantō: *pen.*, Japan   39 45N 139 45E   86
Ōgaki: Gifu, Japan   35 21N 136 37E   86
Ogallala: Nebr., U.S.A.   41 08N 101 43W   94
Ogawa: Tōkyō, Japan   35 45N 139 28E   121
Ogbomosho: Nigeria   08 05N 04 11E   57
Ogden: Utah, U.S.A.   41 13N 111 58W   43 90
Ogilvie *Mountains*: Yukon, Canada   64 45N 138 30W   88
Oglesby: Ill., U.S.A.   41 16N 89 02W   98
Oglio: *riv.*, Italy   45 00N 10 30E   71
Ogoki: Ont., Canada   51 35N 86 00W   93
Ogoki: *riv.*, Ont., Canada   50 45N 87 45W   93
Ōhakune: N.I., New Zealand   39 24S 175 25E   87
Ōhata: Japan   41 24N 141 10E   86
Ohio: *admin.*, U.S.A.   45 98
Ohio: *riv.*, U.S.A.   17 45 98
Ohori: Japan   35 20N 139 51E   121
Ohrid, *Lake*: Albania/Yugoslavia   41 00N 20 45E   79
Oiapoque: *riv.*, Brazil/French Guiana
   03 15N 52 15W   50
Oich, *Loch*: Inv., Scotland   57 00N 04 45W   64
Oise: *riv.*, France   49 00N 02 00E   71
Ōita: Japan   33 14N 131 36E   37 86
Ojika-Hantō: *pen.*, Japan   38 15N 141 30E   86
Ojos del Salado: *mtn.*, Argentina   27 06S 68 32W   49
Ojos Negros: Spain   40 44N 01 30W   105
Oka: *riv.*, U.S.S.R.   55 45N 42 15E   28 80
Okanagan *Lake*: B.C., Canada   50 00N 119 30W   89
Okanogan: *riv.*, Canada/U.S.A.   48 30N 119 30W   42 90
Okāra: Pakistan   30 49N 73 31E   34 82
Okavango *Swamp*: Botswana   19 15S 22 45E   21 55
Okaya: Japan   36 03N 138 03E   86
Okayama: Japan   34 39N 133 55E   37 86 105
Okazaki: Japan   34 57N 137 10E   37 86
Okeechobee, *Lake*: Fla., U.S.A.   27 00N 80 45W   45 101
Okehampton: Devon, England   50 44N 04 00W   61

Okene: Nigeria   07 31N 06 14E   57
Okhla: India   28 34N 77 18E   120
Okhotsk *see* Ochotsk   59 23N 143 18E   31
Okhotsk, *Sea of*: U.S.S.R.   55 00N 148 00E   9 31
Oki-guntō: *is.*, Japan   36 00N 133 00E   86
Okinawa: *is.*, Ryukyu Is.   26 30N 128 00E   12 37
Oklahoma: *admin.*, U.S.A.   35 00N 98 00W   43 95
Oklahoma City: Okla., U.S.A.   35 30N 97 30W   43 95
Oklawaha: *riv.*, Fla., U.S.A.   29 15N 81 45W   101
Okmulgee: Okla., U.S.A.   35 37N 95 58W   100
Okotoks: Alta., Canada   50 46N 113 57W   92
Okt'abr'sk: U.S.S.R.   53 11N 48 40E   81
Okt'abr'skij: U.S.S.R.   54 28N 53 28E   81
Okt'abr'skij: U.S.S.R.   47 28N 40 04E   80
Okulovka: U.S.S.R.   58 26N 33 18E   80
Okushiri-tō: *is.*, Japan   42 00N 139 30E   86
Öland: *is.*, Sweden   56 45N 16 45E   75
Olavarría: Argentina   36 54S 60 17W   52
Oława: Poland   50 57N 17 18E   73
Olbia: Sardinia   40 55N 09 31E   77
Oldbury: W.Mid., England   52 30N 02 00W   115
Oldbury-on-Severn: Avon, England   51 29N 02 31W   113
Oldenburg: W.Germany   53 08N 08 13E   72
Old Factory: Qué., Canada   52 37N 78 49W   96
Old Fletton: Cambs., England   52 33N 00 15W   58
Oldham: Gt. Man., England   53 33N 02 07W   63 114
Oldman: *riv.*, Alta., Canada   49 45N 113 00W   92
Oldmeldrum: Aber., Scotland   57 20N 02 20W   98
Old Nene: *riv.*, Cambs., England   52 30N 00 00   58
Olds: Alta., Canada   51 50N 114 06W   92
Old Sarum: *prehist. site*, Wilts., England   51 07N 01 48W
                                                      61
Old Wives *Lake*: Sask., Canada   50 00N 106 00W   92
Olean: N.Y., U.S.A.   42 05N 78 26W   99
Olëkminsk *see* Ol'okminsk   60 24N 120 24E   30
Olenegorsk: U.S.S.R.   68 04N 33 15E   74 105
Olen'ok (Olenëk): *riv.*, U.S.S.R.   70 30N 121 00E   31
Oléron, *Ile d'*: France   45 55N 01 16W   70
Oleśnica: Poland   51 12N 17 21E   73
Ol'ga: U.S.S.R.   43 45N 135 18E   86
Ol'gino: U.S.S.R.   60 00N 30 09E   119
Olhão: Portugal   37 01N 07 50W   77
Ólimbos (Olympus, *Mount*): Greece   40 05N 22 21E   79
Oling Hu *see* Eling, *Lake*   34 45N 97 30E   36
Oliver: B.C., Canada   49 11N 119 33W   89
Olivos: Argentina   34 31S 58 29W   128
Olney: Bucks., England   52 09N 00 43W   59
Ol'okminsk (Olëkminsk): U.S.S.R.   60 24N 120 24E   31
Olomouc: Czechoslovakia   49 38N 17 15E   73 78
Olona: *riv.*, Italy   45 15N 09 00E   116
Oloron, Gave d': *riv.*, France   43 15N 00 45W   70
Oloron-Ste. Marie: France   43 12N 00 35W   70
Olsztyn: Poland   53 49N 20 29E   78
Olt: *riv.*, Romania   44 00N 24 30E   79
Olten: Switzerland   47 22N 07 55E   71
Oltul: *riv.*, Romania   45 45N 25 00E   78
Olympia: Wash., U.S.A.   47 03N 122 53W   42 90
Olympic *National Park*: Wash., U.S.A.   47 45N 123 45W   90
Olympic *Park*: Japan   35 40N 139 41E   121
Olympus, *Mount*: Greece *see* Ólimbos   40 05N 22 21E   79
Omagh: Tyr., N.Ireland   54 36N 07 18W   66 76
Omaha: Nebr., U.S.A.   41 17N 96 01W   43 94
OMAN   20 00N 56 00E   10 33 107
Oman, *Gulf of*:   24 30N 58 30E   1 10 33
Omarama: S.I., New Zealand   44 29S 169 59E   87
Omdurman *see* Umm Durmān   15 37N 32 29E   53
Omineca: *riv.*, B.C., Canada   55 45N 125 45W   89
Omineca *Mountains*: B.C., Canada   56 30N 126 00W   89
Ommaney, *Cape*: Alaska, U.S.A.   56 10N 134 40W   89
Ōmori: Japan   35 50N 140 09E   105
Omsk: U.S.S.R.   55 00N 73 24E   29
Ōmuta: Japan   33 02N 130 27E   86
Omutninsk: U.S.S.R.   58 40N 52 12E   81
Ondo: Nigeria   07 05N 04 55E   57
Onega, *Lake*: U.S.S.R.   62 00N 35 30E   8 28
Onehunga: N.I., New Zealand   36 56S 174 48E   87
Oneida, *Lake*: N.Y., U.S.A.   43 00N 75 45W   99
O'Neill: Nebr., U.S.A.   42 27N 98 39W   94
Oneonta: N.Y., U.S.A.   42 28N 75 04W   99
Onitsha: Nigeria   06 10N 06 47E   57
Onslow *Bay*: N.C., U.S.A.   34 15N 77 00W   101

Types of map: Ocean pp. 1-5; Physical pp. 6-25; Human pp. 26-57; Topographic pp. 58-101; World pp. 102-111; Urban pp. 112-128.

Onsong: N.Korea 42 55N 129 59E		86
Ontario: Calif., U.S.A. 34 04N 117 39W		127
Ontario: Oreg., U.S.A. 44 02N 116 58W		90
Ontario: admin., Canada		44 98
Ontario, Lake: Canada/U.S.A.		17 45 99
Onuki: Japan 35 16N 139 51E		121
Oologah Reservoir: Okla., U.S.A. 36 26N 95 41W		95
Oos-Londen see East London 33 00S 27 54E		55
Oostende (Ostend): Belgium 51 13N 02 55E		72
Oostvoorne: Netherlands 51 55N 04 06E		107
Oosta Lake: B.C., Canada 53 30N 126 00W		89
Oparino: U.S.S.R. 59 52N 48 17E		81
Opasquia: Ont., Canada 53 16N 93 34W		93
Opava: Czechoslovakia 49 57N 17 54E		73 78
Opelika: Ala., U.S.A. 32 39N 85 23W		101
Opelousas: La., U.S.A. 30 32N 92 05W		100
Ophir: Colo., U.S.A. 37 50N 107 52W		95
Ophir: Utah, U.S.A. 40 23N 112 15W		91
Ophthalmia Range: W.A., Australia 23 17S 119 30E		105
Opinaca: riv., Qué., Canada 52 15N 77 30W		96
Opiscoteo Lake: Qué., Canada 53 09N 68 10W		96
Opladen: W.Germany 51 04N 07 00E		118
Opočka: U.S.S.R. 56 43N 28 38E		80
Opole: Poland 50 40N 17 56E		73 78
Opole: admin., Poland 50 30N 18 00E		73
Oporto see Porto 41 09N 08 37W		26 77
Opotiki: N.I., New Zealand 38 00S 177 18E		87
Opunake: N.I., New Zealand 39 27S 173 52E		87
Or, Côte d': geog. reg., France 47 00N 04 45E		71
Oradea: Romania 47 03N 21 55E		27 78
Oradell Reservoir: N.J., U.S.A. 40 48N 74 00W		123
Orai: India 26 00N 79 26E		82
Oran (Ouahran): Algeria 35 45N 00 38W		56
Orange: France 44 08N 04 48E		71
Orange: Calif., U.S.A. 33 47N 117 51W		127
Orange: N.J., U.S.A. 40 47N 74 15W		123
Orange: Tex., U.S.A. 30 06N 93 44W		100
Orange: riv., see Oranje 23 45S 18 15E		21 55
Orange, Cabo: Brazil 04 24N 51 33W		50
Orangeburg: S.C., U.S.A. 33 28N 80 53W		101
Oranienburg: E.Germany 52 45N 13 15E		73
Oranje (Orange): riv., Southern Africa 23 45S 18 15E		21 55
Órbigo: riv., Spain 42 00N 05 45W		77
Orcadas: rsch. stn., Antarctica 60 45S 44 43W		24
Orchy: riv., Argyll., Scotland 56 30N 04 45W		64
Ordos: plat., China 39 45N 108 15E		84
Ordzhonikidze see Jenakijevo 48 14N 38 13E		105
Ordžonikidze (Dzaudzhikau, Ordzhonikidze): U.S.S.R. 43 03N 44 40E		28
Örebro: Sweden 59 17N 15 13E		75
Orechovo-Zujevo (Orekhovo-Zuyevo): U.S.S.R. 55 49N 38 59E		28 80
Oregon: admin., U.S.A. 44 00N 120 00W		42 90
Oregon City: Oreg., U.S.A. 45 21N 122 36W		90
Orekhovo-Zuyevo see Orechovo-Zujevo 55 49N 38 59E		28 80
Orël see Or'ol 52 59N 36 05E		28 80
Orem: Utah, U.S.A. 40 19N 111 42W		91
Orenburg (Chkalov): U.S.S.R. 51 54N 55 06E		29 81
Orense: Spain 42 20N 07 52W		77
Orford: Suff., England 52 06N 01 31E		59
Orford Ness: cape., Suff., England 52 05N 01 34E		59
Organ Pipe Cactus National Park: Ariz., U.S.A. 32 00N 112 45W		91
Orgejev: U.S.S.R. 47 23N 28 48E		78
Oriental, Cordillera: ra., Colombia 05 00N 73 30W		48
Orihuela: Spain 38 05N 00 56W		77
Orillia: Ont., Canada 44 36N 79 26W		99
Orinoco: riv., Venezuela 07 30N 66 00W		18 48
Orinoco, Delta of the: Venezuela 09 00N 61 30W		48
Orissa: admin., India 21 00N 85 00E		35 83
Oristano: Sardinia 39 54N 08 36E		77
Orivesi: lake, Finland 62 15N 29 15E		74
Orizaba: Mexico 18 51N 97 06W		46
Orkanger: Norway 63 17N 09 52E		74
Orkney Islands: is. & admin., Scotland 59 00N 03 00W		26 65
Orlando: Fla., U.S.A. 28 33N 81 21W		45 101
Orléans: France 47 54N 01 54E		26 70
Orléans, Canal d': France 47 45N 02 15E		70
Orléansville see El Asnam 36 10N 01 20E		56 77
Orlické: mtns., Czechoslovakia/Poland 50 15N 16 30E		73
Ormāra: Pakistan 25 12N 64 39E		34
Ormskirk: Lancs., England 53 35N 02 54W		63 114
Orne: admin., France 48 30N 00 00		105
Örnsköldsvik: Sweden 63 19N 18 45E		27 74
Orobie, Alpi: Italy 46 00N 09 45E		71
Orofino: Idaho, U.S.A. 46 29N 116 15W		90
Or'ol (Orël): U.S.S.R. 52 59N 36 05E		28 80
Oromocto: N.B., Canada 45 50N 66 28W		97
Oronsay: is., Argyll., Scotland 56 00N 06 15W		64
Oroshāza: Hungary 46 33N 20 40E		78
Orpington: Gt. Ldn., England 51 23N 00 06E		112
Orrin: riv., R. & Crom., Scotland 57 30N 04 45W		64
Orša (Orsha): U.S.S.R. 54 30N 30 24E		28 80
Orsay: France 48 42N 02 12E		117
Orsha see Orša 54 30N 30 24E		28 80
Orsk: U.S.S.R. 51 12N 58 34E		29 81 105
Ortigueira: Spain 43 41N 07 51W		77
Oruro: Bolivia 17 59S 67 09W		49
Orwell: riv., Suff., England 52 00N 01 00E		59
Oš (Osh): U.S.S.R. 40 33N 72 48E		29
Osa: U.S.S.R. 57 17N 55 26E		81
Osage: Okla., U.S.A. 36 26N 96 26W		95
Osage: riv., U.S.A. 38 00N 94 00W		100
Ōsaka: Japan 34 40N 135 30E		37 86 105
Ösel: is, see Saaremaa 58 15N 22 30E		75
Osh see Oš 40 33N 72 48E		29
Oshawa: Ont., Canada 43 53N 78 51W		99
Ō-Shima: is., Chiba, Japan 34 30N 139 15E		86
Oshkosh: Wis., U.S.A. 44 01N 88 32W		98
Oshogbo: Nigeria 07 50N 04 35E		57
Osijek: Yugoslavia 45 33N 18 42E		27 78
Osinniki: U.S.S.R. 53 37N 87 21E		30
Osípoviči: U.S.S.R. 53 18N 28 38E		80
Oskaloosa: Iowa, U.S.A. 41 16N 92 40W		98
Oskarshamn: Sweden 57 16N 16 25E		75
Oskelaneo: Qué., Canada 48 07N 75 14W		99
Osl'anka, Gora: mtn., U.S.S.R. 59 10N 58 33E		81
Oslo: Norway 59 56N 10 45E		27 75
Oslofjorden: fd., Norway 59 15N 10 30E		75
Osnabrück: W.Germany 52 17N 08 03E		72
Osnabrück: admin., W.Germany 52 30N 07 15E		105
Osorno: Chile 40 35S 73 14W		52
Ossett: W.Yorks., England 53 41N 01 35W		115
Ostankino: U.S.S.R. 55 49N 37 37E		119
Ostaškov: U.S.S.R. 57 09N 33 06E		80
Ost-Berlin (East Berlin): E.Germany 52 31N 13 24E		117
Oste: riv., W.Germany 53 30N 09 00E		72
Ostend see Oostende 51 13N 02 55E		72
Osterath: W.Germany 51 16N 06 37E		118
Osterburg: E.Germany 52 48N 11 45E		73
Österdalälven: riv., Sweden 61 30N 13 45E		27 75
Österreichische Alpen: mtns., Austria 47 45N 15 00E		73
Östersund: Sweden 63 10N 14 40E		27 74
Ostia (Ostia Antica): Italy 41 46N 12 18E		116
Ostrava: Czechoslovakia 49 50N 18 13E		27 78 105
Ostrogožsk: U.S.S.R. 50 52N 39 05E		80
Ostrov: U.S.S.R. 57 20N 28 22E		80
Ostrov Kunašir: is., Kuril Is., U.S.S.R. 44 00N 145 45E		87
Ostrowiec Świętokrzyski: Poland 50 58N 21 22E		78 105
Ostrów Wielkopolski: Poland 51 39N 17 43E		73 78
Oswego: N.Y., U.S.A. 43 27N 76 31W		99
Oswestry: Salop, England 52 52N 03 04W		60
Ota: Japan 35 34N 139 42E		121
Otago Peninsula: S.I., New Zealand 45 45S 170 30E		87
Otaki: N.I., New Zealand 40 45S 175 09E		87
Otanmäki: hill, Finland 64 08N 27 06E		105
Otaru: Japan 43 13N 141 00E		37 86
Otish Mountains: Qué., Canada 52 15N 70 30W		96
Otley: W.Yorks., England 53 54N 01 41W		63 115
Otok Krk: is., Yugoslavia 45 02N 14 34E		78
Otorohanga: N.I., New Zealand 38 10S 175 14E		87
Otoskwin: riv., Ont., Canada 51 45N 89 15W		93
Otpor see Zabajkal'sk 49 38N 117 19E		30
Otra: riv., Norway 59 00N 07 30E		75
Otradnyj: U.S.S.R. 53 22N 51 21E		81
Otranto, Strait of: Albania/Italy 40 00N 19 00E		79
Ōtsu: Japan 35 00N 135 52E		86
Otta: Norway 61 46N 09 33E		74
Ottavia: Italy 41 58N 12 24E		116

Types of map: Ocean pp. 1-5; Physical pp. 6-25; Human pp. 26-57; Topographic pp. 58-101; World pp. 102-111; Urban pp. 112-128.

Ottawa: Ont., Canada   45 25N 75 44W   44 99
Ottawa: Ill., U.S.A.   41 21N 88 51W   98
Ottawa: Kans., U.S.A.   38 37N 95 16W   94
Ottawa: riv., Canada   46 00N 77 15W   44 96
Ottawa Islands: N.W.T., Canada   59 00N 80 00W   44
Otter Lake: Sask., Canada   55 30N 104 30W   92
Ottery: riv., Corn., England   50 30N 04 15W   61
Ottery St. Mary: Devon, England   50 45N 03 17W   61
Ottumwa: Iowa, U.S.A.   41 02N 92 26W   98
Ouachita: riv., U.S.A.   33 15N 92 30W   100
Ouachita Mountains: U.S.A.   34 30N 94 00W   17 43 100
Ouagadougou: Upper Volta   12 20N 01 40W   57
Ouahran see Oran   35 45N 00 38W   56
Ouargla: Algeria   32 00N 05 16E   57
Oubangui (Ubangi): riv., Africa   04 30N 21 15E   21 54
Oudtshoorn: C.P., Rep. of S.Africa   33 35S 22 12E   55
Ouémé: riv., Dahomey   08 45N 02 30E   57
Ouesso: Congo   01 37N 16 04E   54
Oughter, Lough: Cavan, Irish Republic   54 00N 07 15W   66
Oujda: Morocco   34 41N 01 45W   56
Oujiamiao: China   31 55N 112 10E   84
Oulangan Kansallispuisto: na. rve., Finland   66 15N 29 15E   74
Oulu: Finland   65 02N 25 27E   27 74
Oulujärvi: lake, Finland   64 15N 27 00E   27 74
Oulujoki: riv., Finland   64 15N 26 30E   27 74
Oum er Rbia: riv., Morocco   32 45N 07 30W   56
Ounasjoki: riv., Finland   67 00N 25 00E   74
Oundle: Northants., England   52 29N 02 29W   58
Ouray: Colo., U.S.A.   38 01N 107 40W   95
Oureq, Canal de l': France   48 45N 02 30E   117
Ou-sammyaku: ra., Japan   39 00N 140 30E   86
Ouse: riv., Norfolk, see Great Ouse   52 30N 00 15E   58
Ouse: riv., E.Sussex, England   50 45N 00 00   59
Ouse: riv., N.Yorks., England   53 30N 00 45W   63 115
Outardes, aux: riv., Qué., Canada   50 00N 69 00W   96
Outer Hebrides: is., Scotland   57 30N 07 00W   64
Outer Island: Qué., Canada   51 10N 58 30W   97
Outlook: Sask., Canada   51 30N 107 03W   92
Outokumpu: Finland   62 43N 29 05E   74
Outremont: Qué., Canada   45 32N 73 37W   122
Out Skerries: is., Shet. Is., Scotland   60 25N 00 46W   65
Ovalle: Chile   30 33S 71 16W   52
Overton: Clwyd, Wales   52 58N 02 56W   60
Övertorneå: Sweden   66 22N 23 40E   74
Oviedo: Spain   43 21N 05 50W   26 77
Owatonna: Minn., U.S.A.   44 06N 93 10W   98
Owel, Lough: Westmeath, Irish Republic   53 30N 07 15W   66
Owen, Mount: S.I., New Zealand   41 33S 172 33E   87
Owen Falls: Uganda   00 29N 33 11E   21 53
Owen Fracture Zone: Indian Ocean   13 00N 63 00E   1
Owensboro: Ky., U.S.A.   37 45N 87 05W   101 104
Owens Lake: salt lake, Calif., U.S.A.   36 26N 117 57W   91
Owen Sound: Ont., Canada   44 34N 80 56W   45 99
Owl: riv., Man., Canada   57 30N 93 45W   93
Owo: Nigeria   07 10N 05 39E   57
Owosso: Mich., U.S.A.   43 00N 84 11W   98
Owyhee: riv., U.S.A.   42 30N 117 15W   90
Owyhee Reservoir: Oreg., U.S.A.   43 38N 117 14W   90
Oxbow Dam: U.S.A.   44 58N 116 51W   90
Oxelösund: Sweden   58 40N 17 10E   75 105
Oxford: Oxon., England   51 46N 01 15W   26 59
Oxford: S.I., New Zealand   43 18S 172 11E   87
Oxford Canal: England   52 15N 01 15W   115
Oxford House: Man., Canada   54 58N 95 17W   93
Oxford Lake: Man., Canada   54 45N 95 30W   93
Oxfordshire: admin., England   51 45N 01 30W   59
Oxnard: Calif., U.S.A.   34 12N 119 11W   91
Oxted: Surrey, England   51 16N 00 01W   112
Oxus: riv. see Amudarja   41 00N 62 00E   8 29
Oykel: riv., Scotland   57 45N 04 30W   64
Oyo: Nigeria   07 50N 03 55E   57
Oyster Haven: bay, Cork, Irish Republic   51 30N 08 15W   67
Ozark Plateau: U.S.A.   37 00N 93 30W   17 45 98
Ozarks, Lake of the: Mo., U.S.A.   38 00N 92 45W   43 98
Ózd: Hungary   48 14N 20 15E   78 105
Ozero Aralsor: lake, U.S.S.R.   49 05N 48 12E   81
Ozero Baskunčak: lake, U.S.S.R.   48 12N 46 54E   81
Ozero Beloje, lake, U.S.S.R.   60 15N 37 30E   80
Ozero Botkul': lake, U.S.S.R.   48 46N 46 40E   81

Ozero Chanka (Lake Khanka): China/U.S.S.R.   45 00N 132 30E   37 86
Ozero El'ton: lake, U.S.S.R.   49 16N 46 35E   81
Ozero Gor'ko-Solenoje: lake, U.S.S.R.   49 20N 46 05E   81
Ozero Il'men': lake, U.S.S.R.   58 15N 31 15E   29 80
Ozero Imandra: lake, U.S.S.R.   67 30N 32 45E   74
Ozero Inder: lake, U.S.S.R.   48 27N 51 54E   81
Ozero Itmurynkol': lake, U.S.S.R.   49 30N 52 22E   81
Ozero Kubenskoje: lake, U.S.S.R.   59 45N 39 30E   80
Ozero Šalkar: lake, U.S.S.R.   50 33N 51 40E   81
Ozero Velikoje: lake, U.S.S.R.   55 13N 40 10E   80
Ozero Vože: lake, U.S.S.R.   60 30N 39 00E   80
Ozery: U.S.S.R.   54 51N 38 34E   80
Ōzu: Japan   33 30N 132 33E   86

Pa-an: Burma   16 51N 97 37E   35
Paarl: C.P., Rep. of S.Africa   33 45S 18 58E   55
Pabbay: is., Inv., Scotland   57 45N 07 00W   64
Pābna: Bangladesh   24 00N 89 15E   83
Pačelma: U.S.S.R.   53 20N 43 20E   80
Pacifica: Calif., U.S.A.   37 37N 122 29W   126
Pacific City: Oreg., U.S.A.   45 12N 123 57W   90
Pacific Grove: Calif., U.S.A.   36 38N 121 56W   91
Pacific Ocean   4
Packs Harbour: Nfld., Canada   53 52N 57 00W   97
Padang: Indonesia   01 00S 100 21E   38
Paderborn: W.Germany   51 43N 08 44E   72
Padiham: Lancs., England   53 49N 02 19W   114
Padma: riv., Bangladesh   23 45N 89 45E   83
Padova (Padua): Italy   45 24N 11 53E   26 78
Padrauna: India   26 54N 83 59E   83
Padre Island: Tex., U.S.A.   26 30N 97 15W   100
Padre Island National Seashore: Tex., U.S.A.   27 00N 97 15W   100
Padstow: Corn., England   50 33N 04 56W   61
Padua see Padova   45 24N 11 53E   26 78
Paducah: Ky., U.S.A.   37 03N 88 36W   45 100
Page: Ariz., U.S.A.   36 57N 111 27W   91
Pagwa River: Ont., Canada   50 02N 85 14W   98
Pahar-ganj: India   28 38N 77 12E   120
Paich'eng see Baicheng   45 38N 122 46E   37
Paide: U.S.S.R.   58 58N 25 32E   75
Paignton: Devon, England   50 26N 03 34W   61
Päijänne: lake, Finland   61 30N 25 30E   74
Painswick: Glos., England   51 48N 02 11W   61
Paintsville: Ky., U.S.A.   37 48N 82 50W   101
Paisley: Renf., Scotland   55 50N 04 26W   62 113
Paita: Peru   05 09S 81 08W   48
Pajakumbuh: Indonesia   00 10S 100 30E   38
Pakanbaru: Indonesia   00 33N 101 30E   38
Pakaraima Mountains: Guyana   05 00N 60 00W   48
PAKISTAN (West Pakistan)   1 10 34 82
Pakokku: Burma   21 20N 95 05E   35
Pākpattan: Pakistan   30 20N 73 27E   82
Pakse: Laos   15 07N 105 47E   38
Palaiseau: France   48 43N 02 14E   117
Pālanpur: India   24 12N 72 29E   82
Palatine: Ill., U.S.A.   42 05N 88 02W   124
Palatka: Fla., U.S.A.   29 38N 81 40W   101
Palau Islands: Caroline Island   07 30N 134 30E   12
Palawan: is., Philippines   09 30N 118 30E   12 28
Palembang: Indonesia   02 59S 104 45E   38
Palencia: Spain   42 01N 04 32W   77
Palermo: Sicily   38 08N 13 23E   27 79
Palestine: Tex., U.S.A.   31 46N 95 38W   100
Pāli: India   25 46N 73 26E   82
Palisade: Nev., U.S.A.   40 37N 116 12W   90
Palisades Dam: Idaho, U.S.A.   43 20N 111 12W   90
Palk Strait: India/Sri Lanka   10 00N 79 45E   34
Pallas-Ouinastunturin Kansallispuisto: na. rve., Finland   68 00N 24 00E   74
Pallasovka: U.S.S.R.   50 03N 46 53E   81
Palliser, Cape: N.I., New Zealand   41 37S 175 16E   87
Palma de Mallorca: Balearic Islands   39 35N 02 39E   26 77
Palmas, Cape: Liberia   04 25N 07 50W   57
Palm Beach: N.S.W., Australia   33 36S 151 19E   120
Palmer Land: reg., Antarctica   72 00S 65 00W   24
Palmer Station: rsch. stn., Antarctica   64 46S 64 05W   24

Types of map: Ocean pp. 1-5; Physical pp. 6-25; Human pp. 26-57; Topographic pp. 58-101; World pp. 102-111; Urban pp. 112-128.

Palmerston North: N.I., New Zealand   40 20S 175 39E   37 87
Palmira: Colombia   03 33N 76 17W   48
Palm Springs: Calif., U.S.A.   33 50N 116 33W   43
Palmyra: N.J., U.S.A.   40 00N 75 01W   122
Palmyra *Island*: N.Pacific Ocean   05 52N 162 05W   5
Palo Alto: Calif., U.S.A.   37 26N 122 10W   126
Paloh: Indonesia   01 46N 109 17E   38
Palomeras: Spain   40 24N 03 38W   116
Palopo: Indonesia   03 01S 120 12E   39
Palos, *Cabo de*: Spain   37 38N 00 40W   77
Palos Verde *Hills*: Calif., U.S.A.   33 45N 118 15W   127
Palouse *Hills*: U.S.A.   47 00N 117 00W   90
Palo Verde: Calif., U.S.A.   33 26N 114 44W   91
Pāltā: India   22 47N 88 22E   120
Palwal: India   28 08N 77 21E   82
Pamekasan: Indonesia   07 11S 113 30E   38
Pamiers: France   43 07N 01 36E   70
Pamirs: *mtns.*, Asia   37 45N 73 30E   8 29
Pamlico *Sound*: N.C., U.S.A.   35 10N 76 21W   45 101
Pampa: Tex., U.S.A.   35 32N 100 58W   95
Pampa: *geog. reg.*, Argentina   33 15S 62 45W   19 52
Pamplona: Spain   42 49N 01 39W   26 70 77
Panaji (Nova Goa, Panjim): India   15 29N 73 50E   34
PANAMA   09 00N 80 00W   18 47 106
Panamá: Panama   08 58N 79 32W   47
Panamá, *Golfo de*: Panama   08 30N 79 15W   47
Panama Canal Zone: Panama   09 15N 79 45W   47
Panama City: Fla., U.S.A.   30 10N 85 40W   45 101
Panay: *is.*, Philippines   11 00N 122 30E   12 39
Pančevo: Yugoslavia   44 52N 20 40E   27 79
Pāndhurna: India   21 35N 78 34E   82
Panevežys: U.S.S.R.   55 44N 24 24E   75
Pangbourne: Oxon., England   51 29N 01 05W   59
Pangfou *see* Bangbu   32 53N 117 29E   36 84
Pangkalanbuun: Indonesia   02 43S 111 38E   38
Pangkalpinang: Indonesia   02 05S 106 09E   38
Panguitch: Utah, U.S.A.   37 50N 112 26W   91
Pangutaran Group: *is.*, Philippines   06 00N 120 00E   39
Pānihāti: India   22 42N 88 23E   120
Pānīpat: India   29 23N 77 00E   34 82
Panjim *see* Panaji   15 29N 73 50E   34
Panke: *riv.*, E.Germany   52 31N 13 23E   117
Pankow: E.Germany   52 35N 13 25E   117
Panlong: China   31 12N 121 16E   121
Panmunjŏm: N.Korea   37 57N 125 40E   37
Panna: India   24 43N 80 11E   82
Pant: *riv.*, Essex, England   51 45N 00 15E   59
Pantelleria: *is.*, Mediterranean Sea   36 45N 12 00E   79
Panvel: India   18 59N 73 10E   82
Panyu: China   22 55N 113 23E   85
Paochi *see* Baoji   34 20N 107 14E   36 84
Paoshan *see* Baoshan   25 09N 99 09E   36
Paoting *see* Baoding   38 52N 115 29E   36 84
Paot'ou *see* Baotou   40 40N 109 59E   36 84 105
P'aozero: *lake*, U.S.S.R.   66 00N 31 00E   74
Paparoa *Range*: S.I., New Zealand   42 00S 171 15E   87
Papa Stour: *is.*, Shet. Is., Scotland   60 15N 01 30W   65
Papatoetoe: N.I., New Zealand   36 59S 174 52E   87
Papa Westray: *is.*, Ork. Is., Scotland   59 15N 02 45W   65
Papenburg: W.Germany   53 05N 07 25E   72
Paps, The: *mtns.*, Kerry, Irish Republic   52 00N 09 16W   67
PAPUA, TERRITORY OF   07 00S 142 00E   13 15
Pará *see* Belém   01 27S 48 29W   50
Pará: *admin.*, Brazil   03 45S 53 00W   50
Parabiago: Italy   45 34N 08 52E   116
Paradise: Ky., U.S.A.   37 16N 86 59W   101
Paragould: Ark., U.S.A.   36 03N 90 29W   100
Paragua: *riv.*, Bolivia   14 00S 61 45W   49
Paragua: *riv.*, Venezuela   06 45N 63 00W   48
Paraguai (Paraguay): *riv.*, S.America   26 45S 58 15W   18 51
PARAGUAY   18 51
Paraguay (Paraguai): *riv.*, S.America   26 45S 58 15W   18 51
Paraíba: *admin.*, Brazil   07 15S 36 30W   50
Paraíba do Sul: *riv.*, Brazil   22 15S 43 00W   51
Parakou: Dahomey   09 23N 02 40E   57
Paramaribo: Surinam   05 52N 55 14W   48
Paramus: N.J., U.S.A.   40 55N 74 04W   123
Paraná: Argentina   31 45S 60 30W   52
Paraná: *admin.*, Brazil   25 00S 51 00W   51
Paraná: *riv.*, S.America   26 45S 55 00W   19 51

Paranaguá: Brazil   25 32S 48 30W   51
Paranaíba: *riv.*, Brazil   18 15S 47 30W   18 51
Paranapanema: *riv.*, Brazil   22 30S 52 00W   51
Paranapiacaba, Serra do: *ra.*, Brazil   24 30S 49 15W   51
Paranatinga: *riv. see* Teles Pires   09 30S 56 30W   50
Parangaba: Brazil   03 45S 38 33W   50
Pārbati: *riv.*, India   25 30N 76 30E   82
Parbhani: India   19 16N 76 51E   82
Parchim: E.Germany   53 26N 11 51E   73
Pardubice: Czechoslovakia   50 03N 15 45E   73 78
Parecis, Serra dos: *ra.*, Brazil   13 00S 60 30W   18 49
Parent: Qué., Canada   47 55N 74 36W   96
Parepare: Indonesia   04 03S 119 40E   39
Parets: Spain   41 35N 02 14E   116
Parfino: U.S.S.R.   57 58N 31 41E   80
Paria, *Golfo de*: Trinidad &
    Tobago/Venezuela   10 15N 62 00W   1
Parícutin: *volc.*, Mexico   19 28N 102 15W   17 46
Paris: France   48 52N 02 20E   26 70 117
Paris: Tex., U.S.A.   33 40N 95 33W   100
Park City: Utah, U.S.A.   40 39N 111 30W   91
Parker *Dam*: U.S.A.   34 18N 114 08W   91
Parkersburg: W.Va., U.S.A.   39 17N 81 32W   99
Park *Range*: Colo., U.S.A.   40 00N 106 30W   94
Park Rapids: Minn., U.S.A.   46 45N 95 04W   98
Park Ridge: Ill., U.S.A.   42 01N 87 50W   124
Park Royal: Gt. Ldn., England   51 32N 00 17W   112
Parlākimidi: India   18 48N 84 10E   83
Parma: Italy   44 48N 10 19E   26 78
Parma: Ohio, U.S.A.   41 24N 81 44W   98
Parnaíba: Brazil   02 54S 41 47W   50
Parnaíba: *riv.*, Brazil   07 15S 45 00W   18 50
Parnassós: *mtn.*, Greece   38 32N 22 35E   79
Pärnu: U.S.S.R.   58 28N 24 30E   75
Pärnu: *riv.*, U.S.S.R.   58 45N 25 00E   75
Paro: Bhutan   27 26N 89 25E   83
Páros: *is.*, Greece   37 04N 25 06E   79
Parramatta: N.S.W., Australia   33 50S 150 57E   120
Parramatta: *riv.*, N.S.W., Australia   33 49S 151 05E   120
Parry Sound: Ont., Canada   45 21N 80 03W   44 99
Parsnip: *riv.*, B.C., Canada   55 30N 123 15W   89
Parsons: Kans., U.S.A.   37 20N 95 16W   95
Pārtabgarh: India   24 03N 74 50E   82
Parthenay: France   46 39N 00 15W   70
Partry *Mountains*: Mayo, Irish Republic   53 30N 09 30W   66
Pārvatīpuram: India   18 48N 83 28E   83
Pas, de: *riv.*, Qué., Canada   55 30N 65 15W   97
Paša: *riv.*, U.S.S.R.   60 29N 32 55E   80
Pasadena: Calif., U.S.A.   34 09N 118 09W   91 127
Pa Sak (Sak): *riv.*, Thailand   15 30N 101 00E   35
Pascagoula: Miss., U.S.A.   30 21N 88 33W   100 106
Pascagoula: *riv.*, Miss., U.S.A.   30 30N 88 30W   100 100
Pasco: Wash., U.S.A.   46 14N 119 06W   42 90
Pasewalk: E. Germany   53 30N 14 00E   73
Pasquia *Hills*: Sask., Canada   53 00N 103 00W   92
Passage West: Cork, Irish Republic   51 52N 08 20W   67
Passaic: N.J., U.S.A.   40 52N 74 08W   123
Passau: W.Germany   48 35N 13 28E   73 78
Passero, *Capo*: Sicily   36 42N 15 09E   79
Passo Fundo: Brazil   28 15S 52 24W   51
Passos: Brazil   20 43S 46 37W   51
Pastaza: *riv.*, Ecuador/Peru   04 15S 76 45W   48
Pasto: Colombia   01 12N 77 17W   48
Patagonia: *geog. reg.*, Argentina   47 00S 70 00W   19 52
Patan: India   23 51N 72 11E   34 82
Pat'ang *see* Batang   30 02N 99 02E   36
Patchway: Avon, England   51 32N 02 34W   61 113
Patea: N.I., New Zealand   39 45S 174 29E   87
Paternoster *Islands*: Indonesia   07 30S 117 30E   39
Paterson: N.J., U.S.A.   40 55N 74 10W   99 123
Pathfinder *Reservoir*: Wyo., U.S.A.   42 28N 106 51W   94
Patía: *riv.*, Colombia   01 45N 78 00W   48
Patiāla: India   30 21N 76 27E   34 82
P'atichatki: U.S.S.R.   48 24N 33 42E   80
Patience *Lake*: Sask., Canada   52 00N 106 30W   92
P'atigorsk (Pyatigorsk): U.S.S.R.   44 03N 43 04E   28
Pātipukur: India   22 36N 88 24E   120
Patna: India   25 37N 85 12E   35 83
Patnāgarh: India   20 42N 83 12E   83
Patos: Brazil   07 01S 37 16W   50
Patos, *Lagoa dos*: Brazil   31 00S 51 15W   51

Types of map: Ocean pp. 1-5; Physical pp. 6-25; Human pp. 26-57; Topographic pp. 58-101; World pp. 102-111; Urban pp. 112-128.

Pátrai (Patras): Greece   38 14N 21 44E   79
Patuākhāli: Bangladesh   22 20N 90 21E   83
Patuca: *riv.*, Honduras   15 15N 85 00W   47
Patutu: *mtn.*, N.I., New Zealand   39 15S 175 51E   87
Pau: France   43 18N 00 22W   70
Pauillac: France   45 12N 00 44W   70
Paulis *see* Isiro   02 48N 27 41E   54
Paul *Island*: Nfld., Canada   56 30N 61 20W   97
Paulistana: Brazil   08 09S 41 09W   50
Paulo Afonso: Brazil   09 21S 38 14W   50
Paungde: Burma   18 30N 95 30E   35
Pavia: Italy   45 12N 09 09E   71
Pavlodar: U.S.S.R.   52 18N 76 57E   29
Pavlovo: U.S.S.R.   55 58N 43 04E   80
Pawan: *riv.*, Indonesia   01 45S 110 15E   38
Pawtucket: R.I., U.S.A.   41 46N 71 23W   99
Payenk'ala Shan: *ra. see* Bayankalashanmai
    33 30N 98 00E   36
Payette: Idaho, U.S.A.   44 05N 116 56W   90
Payette: *riv.*, Idaho, U.S.A.   44 15N 116 00W   90
Paysandú: Uruguay   32 21S 58 05W   52
Paz de Ariporo: Colombia   05 53N 71 54W   48
Peace: *riv.*, Alta., Canada   58 30N 114 15W   16 42 92
Peacehaven: E.Sussex, England   50 48N 00 00E   59
Peace River: Alta., Canada   56 15N 117 18W   92
Peak District: *National Park*, England   53 15N 01 45W   58
Peake *Deep*: N.Atlantic Ocean   43 30N 20 15W   2
Peale, *Mount*: Utah, U.S.A.   38 26N 109 14W   91
Pea *Ridge*: Mo., U.S.A.   38 00N 91 00W   104
Pearl: *riv.*, China   23 00N 112 45E   85
Pearl: *riv.*, U.S.A.   31 00N 89 45W   100
Pearsall: Tex., U.S.A.   28 54N 99 06W   95
Pease: *riv.*, Tex., U.S.A.   34 15N 100 15W   95
Peć: Yugoslavia   42 40N 20 19E   79
Pečenga (Petsamo): U.S.S.R.   69 28N 31 12E   27 74
Peche *Island*: Ont., Canada   42 20N 82 55W   125
Pechora: *riv. see* Pečora   65 00N 54 00E   8
Pečora (Pechora): *riv.*, U.S.S.R.   65 00N 54 00E   8
Pečory (Petseri): U.S.S.R.   57 49N 27 36E   80
Pecos: Tex., U.S.A.   31 26N 103 30W   95
Pecos: *riv.*, U.S.A.   31 00N 102 15W   43 95
Pécs: Hungary   46 04N 18 15E   27 78
Pedreiras: Brazil   04 34S 44 39W   50
Peebles: Peeb., Scotland   55 39N 03 12W   62
Peeblesshire: *admin.*, Scotland   55 30N 03 15W   62
Pee Dee: *riv.*, U.S.A.   33 45N 79 15W   101
Peel: I. of M., United Kingdom   54 14N 04 42W   62
Peel: *riv.*, Yukon, Canada   66 00N 135 30W   88
Peel Fell: *mtn.*, Rox., Scotland   55 17N 02 35W   63
Peel *Plateau*: Canada   66 30N 134 15W   88
Peene: *riv.*, E.Germany   53 45N 13 50E   73
Pegasus *Bay*: S.I., New Zealand   43 15S 173 00E   87
Pegu: Burma   17 18N 96 31E   35
Pegu Yoma: *mtns.*, Burma   18 00N 96 00E   11 35
Peian *see* Beian   48 15N 126 30E   31
Peihai *see* Beihai   21 30N 109 10E   36 85
Peikang: Taiwan   23 35N 120 21E   85
Peine: W.Germany   52 19N 10 13E   73 105
Peip'ing *see* Beijing   39 55N 116 25E   36 84 121
Peipus, *Lake see* Čudskoje Ozero   58 45N 27 30E   28 80
Pekalongan: Indonesia   06 54S 109 37E   38
Pekan: Malaysia   03 29N 103 23E   38
Peking *see* Beijing   39 55N 116 25E   36 84 121
Peking *Municipality see* Beijing Shi   40 15N 116 00E   36 84
Pelado, Cerro: *mtn.*, Mexico   19 09N 99 13W   128
Pelee *Island*: Ont., Canada   41 45N 82 39W   98
Peleng: *is.*, Indonesia   01 15S 123 30E   39
Pelham Bay *Park*: N.Y., U.S.A.   40 52N 73 48W   123
Pelican: Alaska, U.S.A.   57 58N 136 14W   88
Pelican Narrows: Sask., Canada   55 12N 102 55W   92
Peljekajse *Nationalpark*: Sweden   66 15N 16 30E   74
Pelly: *riv.*, Yukon, Canada   62 00N 133 30W   42 88
Pelly Crossing: Yukon, Canada   62 48N 136 30W   88
Pelly *Mountains*: Yukon, Canada   61 30N 132 00W   88
Pelopónnisos: *is. & admin.*, Greece   37 45N 22 00E   79
Pematangsiantar: Indonesia   02 59N 99 01E   38
Pemba: *is.*, Tanzania   05 00S 39 45E   54
Pembina: *riv.*, Alta., Canada   53 15N 115 15W   92
Pembina: *riv.*, Canada/U.S.A.   48 45N 98 00W   93
Pembroke: Ont., Canada   45 49N 77 08W   99
Pembroke: Dyfed, Wales   51 41N 04 55W   61 107

Pembroke Dock: Dyfed, Wales   51 42N 04 56W   61
Pembrokeshire: *admin.*, Wales. Absorbed into new *admin.*
    of Dyfed, 1974   60
Pembrokeshire Coast *National Park*: Dyfed, Wales
    51 45N 04 30W   60
Peña Grande: Spain   40 29N 03 43W   116
Penang *see* Pinang   05 25N 100 20E   38
Penang: *is. see* Pinang   05 30N 100 15E   38
Peñarroya: Spain   38 19N 05 17W   77
Penarth: S.Glam., Wales   51 27N 03 11W   61 113
Penas, *Golfo de*: Chile   47 15S 75 15W   52
Pench'i *see* Benxi   41 18N 123 45E   37 105
Pendle *Hill*: Lancs., England   53 52N 02 17W   114
Pendleton: Oreg., U.S.A.   45 40N 118 47W   42 75 90
Pend Oreille *Lake*: Idaho, U.S.A.   48 10N 116 21W   90
P'enghu Liehtao (Pescadores): *is.*, Taiwan
    22 30N 119 30E   37 85
P'enghu Shuitao: *str.*, Taiwan   23 30N 120 00E   85
Penglai: China   37 48N 120 45E   84
Pengshui: China   29 18N 108 09E   85
Pengze: China   29 53N 116 39E   85
Penicuik: Midloth., Scotland   55 50N 03 14W   62
Penk: *riv.*, Staffs., England   52 30N 02 00W   115
Penmaenmawr: Gwyn., Wales   53 16N 03 54W   60
Pennant Hills: N.S.W., Australia   33 44S 151 04E   120
Penner: *riv.*, India   14 30N 79 30E   34
Penn Hills: Pa., U.S.A.   40 27N 79 49W   125
Pennine, *Alpi*: Switzerland   46 00N 07 45E   71
Pennines, The: *ra.*, England   53 30N 01 45W   63
Penn-Lincoln Parkway: *hwy.*, Pa., U.S.A.   40 15N 79 45W
    125
Pennsauken: N.J., U.S.A.   39 58N 75 03W   122
Pennsylvania: *admin.*, U.S.A.   41 00N 78 00W   45 99
Pennsylvania Turnpike: *hwy.*, Pa., U.S.A.   40 30N 79 45W
    125
Pennypack *Park*: Pa., U.S.A.   40 05N 75 04W   122
Penobscot: *riv.*, Maine, U.S.A.   45 15N 68 30W   99
Penobscot *Bay*: Maine, U.S.A.   44 00N 68 45W   99
Peñon, Cerro: *mtn.*, Mexico   19 19N 99 00W   128
Penong: S.A., Australia   31 55S 133 02E   40
Penrith: Cumbria, England   54 40N 02 44W   63
Penryn: Corn., England   50 09N 05 06W   61
Pensaco, *Rio*: N.Mex., U.S.A.   32 45N 104 30W   95
Pensacola: Fla., U.S.A.   30 25N 87 13W   45 101
Pensacola *Dam*: Okla., U.S.A.   36 20N 95 04W   95
Pensacola *Mountains*: Antarctica   83 45S 55 00W   24
Penticton: B.C., Canada   49 30N 119 35W   42 89
Pentire *Point*: Corn., England   50 36N 04 55W   61
Pentland Firth: *str.*, Scotland   58 30N 03 00W   65
Pentland *Hills*: Scotland   55 45N 03 15W   62
Pen-y-Ghent: *mtn.*, N.Yorks., England   54 10N 02 14W   63
Penza: U.S.S.R.   53 13N 45 00E   28 81
Penzance: Corn., England   50 07N 05 33W   61
People's *Park*: China   31 14N 121 28E   121
Peoria: Ill., U.S.A.   40 43N 89 38W   45 98 104
Perak: *admin.*, Malaysia   05 00N 101 00E   105
Perche, Collines du: *hills*, France   48 15N 00 45E   70
Perdido, *Monte*: France/Spain   42 40N 00 02E   70
Pereira: Colombia   04 49N 75 43W   48
Perejaslav-Chmel'nickij: U.S.S.R.   50 06N 31 30E   80
Perem'otnoje: U.S.S.R.   51 11N 50 49E   81
Pereslavl'-Zalesskij: U.S.S.R.   56 44N 38 51E   80
Pergamino: Argentina   33 55S 60 32W   52
Peribonca: *riv.*, Qué., Canada   49 00N 71 15W   96
Périgueux: France   45 12N 00 44E   70
Perijá, Sierra de: *ra.*, Colombia/Venezuela   10 00N 73 00W
    48
Perim: *is. see* Barīm *Island*   12 40N 43 24E   53
Perm' (Molotov): U.S.S.R.   58 00N 56 15E   29 81 105 107
Pernambuco *see* Recife   08 03S 34 54W   50
Pernambuco: *admin.*, Brazil   08 30S 37 45W   50
Pernik: Bulgaria   42 36N 23 03E   79
Pernis: Netherlands   51 54N 04 23E   107
Pero: Italy   45 31N 09 05E   116
Perovo: U.S.S.R.   55 44N 37 46E   119
Perpignan: France   42 42N 02 54E   26 71
Perry: *riv.*, Salop, England   52 45N 02 45W   60
Perryton: Tex., U.S.A.   36 23N 100 48W   95
Pershore: Here. & Worcs., England   52 07N 02 05W   59
Persia *see* Iran   10 33 107
Persian *Gulf*: Middle East   27 30N 51 00E   33

Types of map: Ocean pp. 1-5; Physical pp. 6-25; Human pp. 26-57; Topographic pp. 58-101; World pp. 102-111; Urban pp. 112-128.

Perth: W.A., Australia 31 58S 115 49E	40
Perth Amboy: N.J., U.S.A. 40 32N 74 17W	123
Perthshire: *admin.*, Scotland 56 30N 04 00W	64
PERU	18 49 106
Peru *Basin*: S.Pacific Ocean 15 00S 90 00W	5
Peru-Chile *Trench*: S.Pacific Ocean 23 00S 73 00W	5 18
Peru (Humboldt) *Current*: S.Pacific Ocean 20 00S 76 00W	5
Perugia: Italy 43 07N 12 23E	27 79
Pervomajsk: U.S.S.R. 48 04N 30 52E	80
Pervoural'sk: U.S.S.R. 56 54N 59 58E	29 81
Pes': U.S.S.R. 58 55N 34 19E	80
Pesaro: Italy 43 54N 12 54E	79
Pescadores: *is. see* P'enghu Liehtao 22 30N 119 30E	37 85
Peshāwar: Pakistan 34 01N 71 33E	29
Peskovka: U.S.S.R. 59 04N 52 22E	81
Pesqueira: Brazil 08 22S 36 42W	50
Pessac: France 44 49N 00 37W	70
Pestovo: U.S.S.R. 58 36N 35 48E	80
Petaluma: Calif., U.S.A. 38 13N 122 39W	91
Peterborough: Ont., Canada 44 19N 78 20W	99
Peterborough: Cambs., England 52 35N 00 15W	58
Peterhead: Aber., Scotland 57 30N 01 46W	65
Peterlee: Dur., England 54 46N 01 19W	63
Peter Pond *Lake*: Sask., Canada 56 00N 108 45W	92
Petersburg: Alaska, U.S.A. 56 48N 132 58W	89
Petersburg: Va., U.S.A. 37 14N 77 24W	101
Petersfield: Hants., England 51 00N 00 56W	59
Petitot: *riv.*, Canada 59 30N 120 30W	88
Petitsikapau *Lake*: Nfld., Canada 54 40N 66 25W	97
Petlād: India 22 29N 72 48E	82
Petoskey: Mich., U.S.A. 45 22N 84 59W	98
Petra Velikogo, *Zaliv*: *gulf*, U.S.S.R. 42 45N 132 00E	86
Petrel: *rsch. stn.*, Antarctica 63 28S 56 17W	24
Petrified Forest *National Park*: Ariz., U.S.A. 35 00N 109 45W	91
Petrila: Romania 45 27N 23 25E	78
Petrograd *see* Leningrad 59 55N 30 15E	28 80 105 119
Petropavlovsk: U.S.S.R. 54 54N 69 06E	29
Petrópolis: Brazil 22 30S 43 06W	51
Petroşeni: Romania 45 25N 23 22E	78
Petrovsk: U.S.S.R. 52 19N 45 23E	81
Petrovsk Zabajkal'skij: U.S.S.R. 51 20N 108 55E	30 105
Petrozavodsk: U.S.S.R. 61 47N 34 20E	28
Petsamo *see* Pečenga 69 28N 31 12E	27 74
Petseri *see* Pečory 57 49N 27 36E	80
Pevek: U.S.S.R. 69 42N 170 17E	31
Pevensey: E.Sussex, England 50 49N 00 20E	59
Pewsey, *Vale of*: Wilts., England 51 15N 01 45W	61
Pfalz: *admin.*, W.Germany 49 15N 07 45E	72
Pforzheim: W.Germany 48 53N 08 42E	72
Phagwāra: India 31 12N 75 46E	82
Phalodi: India 27 06N 72 22E	82
Phan Rang: S.Vietnam 11 34N 109 00E	38
Phan Thiêt: S.Vietnam 10 56N 108 06E	38
Phenix City: Ala., U.S.A. 32 28N 85 00W	101
Phet Buri: Thailand 13 05N 99 58E	35
Philadelphia: Pa., U.S.A. 40 00N 75 10W	45 99 106 122
Philippeville *see* Skikda 36 53N 06 54E	56 77
PHILIPPINES	12 39 107
Philippine *Sea*: 12 00N 129 00E	4 12 39
Philippine *Trench*: Philippine Sea 10 00N 127 00E	4
Philipsburg: Mont., U.S.A. 46 20N 113 18W	90
Phillipsburg: Kans., U.S.A. 39 45N 99 19W	94
Phitsanulok: Thailand 16 50N 100 15E	35
Phnom Penh: Khmer Rep. 11 35N 104 55E	38
Phoenix: Ariz., U.S.A. 33 27N 112 04W	43 91
Phoenix *Island*: S.Pacific Ocean 03 43S 171 25W	4
Phoenix *Islands*: S.Pacific Ocean 02 00S 172 00W	4
Phong Saly: Laos 21 40N 102 06E	35
Phra Nakhon *see* Krung Thep 13 44N 100 30E	35
Phuket: Thailand 07 52N 98 22E	35
Piacenza: Italy 45 03N 09 41E	71
Piassaguera: Brazil 23 50S 46 23W	104
Piatra-Neamţ: Romania 46 53N 26 23E	78
Piauí: *admin.*, Brazil 07 15S 42 30W	50
Picarde, *Plaine*: France 49 45N 02 30E	72
Pickering: N.Yorks., England 54 14N 00 46W	63
Pickering, *Vale of*: N.Yorks., England 54 00N 00 45W	63
Pickle Crow: Ont., Canada 51 30N 90 03W	93
Picton: S.I., New Zealand 41 17S 174 02E	87

Pidurutalagala: *mtn.*, Sri Lanka 07 01N 80 45E	11 34
Piedmont: Calif., U.S.A. 37 49N 122 13W	126
Piedras Negras: Mexico 28 42N 100 31W	46
Pieksämäki: Finland 62 18N 27 10E	74
Pielinen: *lake*, Finland 63 15N 29 30E	74
Pierre: S.D., U.S.A. 44 22N 100 21W	43 94
Pietarsaari: Finland 63 41N 22 40E	74
Pietermaritzburg: Natal, Rep. of S.Africa 29 36S 30 24E	55
Pietersburg: Trans., Rep. of S.Africa 23 54S 29 23E	55
Pigeon: *riv.*, Canada/U.S.A. 48 00N 90 00W	98
Piggott: Ark., U.S.A. 36 22N 90 11W	100
Pihlajarvesi: *lake*, Finland 61 44N 28 47E	74
Pihtipudas: Finland 63 24N 25 30E	74
Pihuamo: Mexico 19 15N 103 23W	104
Pikal'ovo: U.S.S.R. 59 31N 34 06E	80
Pikangikum *Lake*: Ont., Canada 51 45N 93 45W	93
Pikes *Peak*: Colo., U.S.A. 38 50N 105 03W	17 43 94
Pikeville: Ky., U.S.A. 37 29N 82 33W	101
Piła: Poland 53 09N 16 44E	73 78
Pilcomayo: *riv.*, S.America 22 00S 62 45W	49
Pīlībhīt: India 28 37N 79 48E	82
Pillar *Point*: Calif., U.S.A. 37 30N 122 30W	126
Pilsen *see* Plzeň 49 45N 13 22E	27 78 105
Pima: Ariz., U.S.A. 32 54N 109 50W	91
Pinang (Penang, George Town): Malaysia 05 25N 100 20E	38
Pinang (Penang): *is.*, Malaysia 05 30N 100 15E	38
Pinar del Río: Cuba 22 25N 83 42W	47
Pincher Creek: Alta., Canada 49 31N 113 53W	92
Píndhos Óros (Pindus *Mountains*): Greece 40 00N 21 00E	7 27 79
Pindus *Mountains see* Píndhos Óros 40 00N 21 00E	7 27 79
Pine: *riv.*, B.C., Canada 55 30N 122 00W	89
Pine Bluff: Ark., U.S.A. 34 13N 92 01W	100
Pine Falls: Man., Canada 50 33N 96 14W	93
Pinehouse *Lake*: Sask., Canada 55 30N 106 00W	92
Pine *Islands*: Fla., U.S.A. 24 45N 81 30W	101
Pine *Pass*: B.C., Canada 55 27N 122 39W	89
Pine Point: N.W.T., Canada 60 49N 114 28W	92
Pine *Point*: N.W.T., Canada 61 00N 114 15W	92
Pinerolo: Italy 44 53N 07 19E	71
Ping: *riv.*, Thailand 16 15N 99 45E	12 35
Pingchang: China 31 37N 106 59E	84
Pingdingshan: China 33 40N 113 12E	84
Pingdu: China 36 47N 119 54E	84
Pingfang: China 39 56N 116 32E	121
Pinggu: China 40 09N 117 07E	84
Pingguo: China 23 22N 107 31E	85
Pinghu: China 30 42N 121 06E	85
Pingjiang: China 28 44N 113 34E	85
Pingle: China 24 37N 110 30E	85
Pingli: China 32 30N 109 31E	84
Pingliang: China 35 22N 107 10E	36 84
Pingluo: China 38 57N 106 30E	84
Pingnan: China 26 50N 118 57E	85
Pingtan: China 25 31N 119 47E	85
Pingtang: China 25 53N 107 20E	85
P'ingtung: Taiwan 22 39N 120 31E	37 85
Pingxiang: Jiangxi, China 27 35N 113 50E	85 105
Pingyang: China 27 41N 120 38E	85
Pingyao: China 37 10N 112 10E	84
Pingyi: China 35 30N 117 42E	84
Pingyin: China 36 19N 116 32E	84
Pingyuan: China 37 11N 116 30E	84
Pinnau: *riv.*, W.Germany 53 41N 09 33E	119
Pinneberg: W.Germany 53 40N 09 49E	73 119
Pinos, *Isla de*: Cuba 21 30N 82 45W	47
Pinsk: U.S.S.R. 52 08N 26 01E	28 78
Pinto: Spain 40 15N 03 42W	116
Pioche: Nev., U.S.A. 37 56N 114 27W	91
Piombino: Italy 42 56N 10 32E	77 79 105
Pioneer *Fracture Zone*: N.Pacific Ocean 37 00N 140 00W	5
Piparia: India 22 46N 78 20E	82
Pipestone: *riv.*, Ont., Canada 52 15N 90 30W	93
Pipmuacan *Lake*: Qué., Canada 49 30N 70 15W	96
Piracicaba: Brazil 22 45S 47 40W	51
Piraeus *see* Piraiévs 37 57N 23 42E	27 79
Piraiévs (Piraeus): Greece 37 57N 23 42E	27 79
Pirapora: Brazil 17 21S 44 56W	50
Pir'atin: U.S.S.R. 50 15N 32 30E	80

Types of map: Ocean pp. 1-5; Physical pp. 6-25; Human pp. 26-57; Topographic pp. 58-101; World pp. 102-111; Urban pp. 112-128.

Pírgos: Greece 37 40N 21 27E 79
Piripiri: Brazil 04 16S 41 47W 50
Pirmasens: W.Germany 49 12N 07 37E 72
Pirna: E.Germany 50 58N 13 58E 73
Piru: Indonesia 03 01S 128 10E 39
Pisa: Italy 43 43N 10 24E 26 79
Pisco: Peru 13 46S 76 12W 49
Písek: Czechoslovakia 49 19N 14 10E 73
Pistoia: Italy 43 56N 10 55E 79
Pit: *riv.*, Calif., U.S.A. 41 15N 120 45W 90
Pitcairn *Islands*: S.Pacific Ocean 25 04S 130 06W 5
Piteälv: *riv.*, Sweden 66 15N 20 30E 74
Piteşti: Romania 44 51N 24 51E 78
Pithiviers: France 48 10N 02 15E 70
Pitlochry: Perth., Scotland 56 43N 03 45W 65
Pitt: *riv.*, B.C., Canada 49 15N 122 30W 126
Pitt *Island*: B.C., Canada 53 30N 129 45W 89
Pittsburg: Kans., U.S.A. 37 25N 94 42W 95
Pittsburg: Pa., U.S.A. 40 26N 80 00W 45 99 104 125
Pittsburg: Tex., U.S.A. 33 00N 94 58W 100
Pitt Water: *harb.*, N.S.W., Australia 33 37S 151 19E 120
Piura: Peru 05 15S 80 38W 48
Pižma: U.S.S.R. 57 52N 47 06E 81
Pižma: *riv.*, U.S.S.R. 57 30N 48 30E 81
Placentia: Nfld., Canada 47 15N 53 58W 97
Placentia *Bay*: Nfld., Canada 47 15N 54 15W 97
Pladju: Indonesia 02 59S 104 50E 107
Plainfield: N.J., U.S.A. 40 37N 74 25W 123
Plainview: Tex., U.S.A. 34 11N 101 43W 95
Planadas: Colombia 03 15N 75 45W 48
Plast: U.S.S.R. 54 22N 60 50E 81
Plata, Rio de la (Plate): *est.*, Argentina/Uruguay 35 00S 57 00W 52 128
Platte: *riv.*, Nebr., U.S.A. 40 45N 100 00W 17 43 94
Plattling: W.Germany 48 47N 12 53E 73
Platt *National Park*: Okla., U.S.A. 34 29N 96 58W 95 100
Plattsburgh: N.Y., U.S.A. 44 42N 73 29W 99
Plattsmouth: Nebr., U.S.A. 41 01N 95 53W 94
Plauen: E.Germany 50 29N 12 08E 73
Playgreen *Lake*: Man., Canada 54 15N 98 15W 93
Pleasant Hill: Calif., U.S.A. 37 58N 122 04W 126
Pleasant Hills: Pa., U.S.A. 40 20N 79 58W 125
Pleasanton: Tex., U.S.A. 28 58N 98 29W 95
Pleiku: S.Vietnam 13 57N 108 01E 38
Plenty, *Bay of*: N.I., New Zealand 38 45S 177 00E 87
Plentywood: Mont., U.S.A. 48 47N 104 34W 92
Pletipi *Lake*: Qué., Canada 51 45N 70 00W 96
Plettenberg: W.Germany 51 13N 07 52E 72
Pleven: Bulgaria 43 25N 24 40E 79
Plitivička Jezera *National Park*: Yugoslavia 44 45N 15 45E 78
Płock: Poland 52 32N 19 40E 78
Ploieşti (Ploesti): Romania 44 57N 26 01E 27 78 107
Plovdiv: Bulgaria 42 08N 24 45E 27 79
Plunge: U.S.S.R. 55 52N 21 49E 75
Pl'ussa: *riv.*, U.S.S.R. 58 30N 29 15E 80
Plym: *riv.*, Devon, England 50 15N 04 00W 61
Plymouth: Devon, England 50 23N 04 10W 26 61
Plymouth: Mich., U.S.A. 42 21N 83 27W 125
Plympton: Devon, England 50 23N 04 03W 61
Plynlimon: *mtn.*, Dyfed, Wales 52 28N 03 47W 60
Plzeň (Pilsen): Czechoslovakia 49 45N 13 22E 26 73 78 105
Po: *riv.*, Italy 44 45N 11 45E 27 78
Pobeda: *mtn.*, U.S.S.R. 65 12N 146 12E 9 31
Pobedy, *Peak*: U.S.S.R. 42 02N 80 05E 29
Pocatello: Idaho, U.S.A. 42 52N 112 27W 43 90
Počep: U.S.S.R. 52 56N 33 27E 80
Pochvistnevo: U.S.S.R. 53 38N 52 08E 81
Pocklington: Humb., England 53 56N 00 46W 63
Pocomoke City: Md., U.S.A. 38 04N 75 35W 99
Poços de Caldas: Brazil 21 48S 46 34W 51
Podborovje: U.S.S.R. 59 28N 34 43E 80
Podgorica *see* Titograd 42 28N 19 17E 27 79
Podol'sk: U.S.S.R. 55 26N 37 33E 28 80
Podor: Senegal 16 35N 15 02W 56
Pograniçnyj: U.S.S.R. 44 25N 131 24E 86
Point Comfort: Tex., U.S.A. 28 41N 96 33W 95
Pointe-à-Pierre: Trinidad & Tobago 10 18N 61 17W 106
Pointe-à-Pitre: Guadeloupe 16 14N 61 32W 47
Pointe-aux-Trembles: Qué., Canada 45 40N 73 30W 122

Pointe-Claire: Qué., Canada 45 27N 73 50W 122
Point Reyes *National Seashore*: Calif., U.S.A. 38 05N 122 49W 91
Poissy: France 48 56N 02 02E 117
Poitiers: France 46 35N 00 20E 70
Pojezierze Pomorskie: *geog. reg.*, Poland 53 30N 16 00E 73
Pokaran: India 27 57N 71 56E 82
Pokhara: Nepal 28 14N 83 58E 83
POLAND 52 45N 19 00E 7 27 78 107
Pol'arnyj: U.S.S.R. 69 12N 33 22E 75
Polegate: E.Sussex, England 50 49N 00 15E 59
Polevskoj: U.S.S.R. 56 26N 60 11E 81 105
Polillo *Island*: Philippines 14 45N 122 45E 39
Polist': *riv.*, U.S.S.R. 57 30N 31 00E 80
Polock: U.S.S.R. 55 31N 28 46E 80
Pologi: U.S.S.R. 47 29N 36 15E 80
Poltava: U.S.S.R. 49 35N 34 34E 28 80
Poluostrov Rybačij: *pen.*, U.S.S.R. 69 45N 32 30E 74
Polynesia: *geog. reg.*, Pacific Ocean 00 00 165 00W 4
Pomeranian *Bay*: E.Germany/Poland 54 00N 14 30E 78
Pomeroy: Ohio, U.S.A. 39 03N 82 03W 98
Pomona: Calif., U.S.A. 34 04N 117 45W 43 127
Pompey: France 48 46N 06 07E 105
Pompton Lakes: N.J., U.S.A. 41 01N 76 16W 123
Ponape: *is.*, N.Pacific Ocean 07 00N 158 00E 4
Ponca City: Okla., U.S.A. 36 42N 97 05W 95 106
Ponce: Puerto Rico 18 01N 66 36W 47
Pondicherry: India 11 59N 79 50E 34
Ponferrada: Spain 42 33N 06 35W 77
Ponoka: Alta., Canada 52 42N 113 33W 92
Pons: France 45 35N 00 32W 70
Ponta Grossa: Brazil 25 07S 50 09W 51
Pontardulais: W.Glam., Wales 51 43N 04 02W 61
Pontarlier: France 46 54N 06 22E 71
Pontchartrain, *Lake*: La., U.S.A. 30 00N 90 00W 100
Pontefract: W.Yorks., England 53 42N 01 18W 63 115
Ponteland: Northumb., England 55 03N 01 44W 63
Ponte Nova: Brazil 20 20S 41 57W 51
Pontevedra: Spain 42 25N 08 39W 77
Ponthierville *see* Ubundi 00 21S 25 29E 54
Pontiac: Mich., U.S.A. 42 39N 83 18W 98
Pontianak: Indonesia 00 05S 109 16E 38
Pontic *Mountains*: Turkey 41 45N 34 15E 10
Pontivy: France 48 04N 02 58W 70
Pontoise: France 49 03N 02 06E 117
Pont-Viau: Qué., Canada 45 34N 73 41W 122
Pontypool: Gwent, Wales 51 43N 03 02W 61
Pontypridd: M.Glam., Wales 51 37N 03 22W 61 113
Poole: Dorset, England 50 43N 01 59W 61
Poole *Bay*: Dorset, England 50 30N 01 45W 61
Poolewe: R.& Crom., Scotland 57 45N 05 37W 64
Poona *see* Pune 18 31N 73 54E 34
Poopó, *Lake*: Bolivia 18 45S 67 15W 49
Popayán: Colombia 02 27N 76 22W 48
Poplar: Gt. Ldn., England 51 31N 00 01W 112
Poplar: *riv.*, Man., Canada 52 45N 97 00W 93
Poplar Bluff: Mo., U.S.A. 36 16N 90 25W 100
Popocatépetl: *volc.*, Mexico 19 02N 98 38W 17
Porbandar: India 21 40N 69 40E 34
Porcher *Island*: B.C., Canada 54 00N 130 30W 89
Porchov: U.S.S.R. 57 46N 29 34E 80
Porcupine: Ont., Canada 48 15N 81 00W 99
Pordenone: Italy 45 58N 12 39E 78
Pori: Finland 61 28N 21 45E 27 75
Porirua: N.I., New Zealand 41 08S 174 52E 87
Porlamar: Venezuela 11 01N 63 54W 48
Porsangen: *fd.*, Norway 70 45N 26 00E 74
Porsgrunn: Norway 59 10N 09 40E 75
Portadown: Arm., N.Ireland 54 26N 06 27W 66
Portaferry: Down, N.Ireland 54 23N 05 33W 66
Portage la Prairie: Man., Canada 49 58N 98 20W 42 93
Port Alberni: B.C., Canada 49 14N 124 48W 89
Portalegre: Portugal 39 17N 07 25W 77
Portales: N.Mex., U.S.A. 34 11N 103 20W 95
Port Alexander: Alaska, U.S.A. 56 15N 134 39W 89
Port Alice: B.C., Canada 50 23N 127 24W 89
Port Angeles: Wash., U.S.A. 48 07N 123 27W 90
Port Antonio: Jamaica 18 10N 76 27W 47
Portarlington: Offaly, Irish Republic 53 10N 07 11W 67
Port Arthur: Canada *see* Thunder Bay 48 24N 89 14W 44 98

Types of map: Ocean pp. 1-5; Physical pp. 6-25; Human pp. 26-57; Topographic pp. 58-101; World pp. 102-111; Urban pp. 112-128.

Port Askaig: Argyll., Scotland   55 51N 06 07W   62
Port Arthur: China *see* Lüshun   38 47N 121 20E   37 84
Port Arthur: Tex., U.S.A.   29 54N 93 56W   43 100 106
Port Augusta: S.A., Australia   32 30S 137 46E   41
Port-au-Prince: Haiti   18 33N 72 20W   47
Port-aux-Basques: Nfld., Canada   47 35N 59 10W   44 97
Port Blandford: Nfld., Canada   48 21N 54 10W   97
Port Canning: India   22 19N 88 40E   83
Port Cartier: Qué., Canada   50 03N 66 46W   97
Port Chalmers: S.I., New Zealand   45 48S 170 38E   87
Port Chester: N.Y., U.S.A.   41 00N 73 40W   123
Port Chilkoot: Alaska, U.S.A.   59 14N 135 26W   88
Port Clarence: Dur., England   54 58N 01 12W   107
Port Coquitlam: B.C., Canada   49 16N 122 46W   126
Port-de-Bouc: France   43 25N 04 58E   71
Port Edward: B.C., Canada   54 11N 130 16W   89
Port Edward: China *see* Weihai   37 28N 122 07E   37 84
Port Elizabeth: C.P., Rep. of S.Africa   33 58S 25 36E   55
Port Ellen: Argyll., Scotland   55 39N 06 12W   62
Port Erin: I. of M., United Kingdom   54 05N 04 45W   62
Port Étienne: Mauritania   20 54N 17 01W   56
Port Francqui *see* Ilebo   04 19S 20 35E   54
Port Gentil: Gabon   00 40S 08 50E   57
Port Glasgow: Renf., Scotland   55 56N 04 41W   62 113
Portglenone: Antrim, N.Ireland   54 52N 06 29W   66
Port Hacking: *harb.*, N.S.W., Australia   34 04S 151 07E 120
Port Hacking *Point*: N.S.W., Australia   34 05S 151 10E 120
Port Harcourt: Nigeria   04 43N 07 05E   57
Port Hardy: B.C., Canada   50 41N 127 30W   89
Port Harrison: Qué., Canada   58 25N 78 15W   44
Port Hawkesbury: N.S., Canada   45 36N 61 22W   44
Porthcawl: M.Glam., Wales   51 29N 03 43W   61
Port Hedland: W.A., Australia   20 24S 118 36E   40
Port Huron: Mich., U.S.A.   42 59N 82 28W   98
Portimão: Portugal   37 08N 08 32W   77
Port Isaac: Corn., England   50 35N 04 49W   61
Portishead: Avon, England   51 30N 02 46W   61 113
Port Jackson: *harb.*, N.S.W., Australia
    33 51S 151 15E   120
Port Kembla: N.S.W., Australia   34 28S 150 54E   105
Portland: Maine, U.S.A.   43 41N 70 18W   44 99
Portland: Oreg., U.S.A.   45 32N 122 37W   42 90
Portland, Bill of: *cape*, Dorset, England   50 31N 02 27W 61
Portland, *Isle of*: Dorset, England   50 33N 02 27W   61
Portlaoise: Laois, Irish Republic   53 02N 07 17W   67
Port Lavaca: Tex., U.S.A.   28 37N 96 38W   95
Port Lincoln: S.A., Australia   34 43S 135 49E   41
Port Loko: Sierra Leone   08 50N 12 50W   57
Port Lyautey *see* Mina Hassan Tani   34 16N 06 36W   56
Port Madison: Wash., U.S.A.   47 41N 122 31W   126
Portmadoc: Gwyn., Wales   52 55N 04 08W   60
Port Menier: Qué., Canada   49 50N 64 20W   97
Port Moody: B.C., Canada   49 17N 122 51W   126
Port Moresby: Papua   09 30S 147 07E   15
Portnahaven: Argyll., Scotland   55 41N 06 31W   62
Port Nelson: Man., Canada   57 10N 92 35W   93
Port Nolloth: C.P., Rep. of S.Africa   29 17S 16 51E   55
Porto (Oporto): Portugal   41 09N 08 37W   26 77
Pôrto Alegre: Brazil   30 03S 51 10W   51
Porto Amélia: Mozambique   12 57S 40 30E   54
Port of Ness: R. & Crom., Scotland   58 30N 06 14W   64
Port of Spain: Trinidad & Tobago   10 38N 61 31W   1 48
Portola: Calif., U.S.A.   37 23N 122 13W   126
Porto-Novo: Dahomey   06 30N 02 47E   57
Port Orchard: Wash., U.S.A.   47 32N 122 39W   126
Porto Torres: Sardinia   40 50N 08 24E   77
Porto Vecchio: Corsica   41 35N 09 17E   77
Pôrto Velho: Brazil   08 46S 63 54W   49
Portoviejo: Ecuador   01 03S 80 27W   48
Port Pirie: S.A., Australia   33 11S 138 01E   41
Port Radium: N.W.T., Canada   66 04N 118 00W   88
Portree: Inv., Scotland   57 24N 06 12W   64
Portrush: Antrim, N.Ireland   55 12N 06 40W   66
Port Said *see* Būr Saʿīd   31 16N 32 18E   32
Port St. Joe: Fla., U.S.A.   29 49N 85 18W   101
Port Saunders: Nfld., Canada   50 40N 57 18W   97
Port Shepstone: Natal, Rep. of S.Africa   30 44S 30 28E 55
Port Simpson: B.C., Canada   54 32N 130 25W   89
Portsmouth: Hants., England   50 48N 01 05W   26 59
Portsmouth: N.H., U.S.A.   43 03N 70 47W   99
Portsmouth: Ohio, U.S.A.   38 45N 82 59W   98 104

Portsmouth: Va., U.S.A.   36 50N 76 20W   101
Portsoy: Banff., Scotland   57 41N 02 41W   65
Port Stanley: Ont., Canada   42 40N 81 14W   99
Port Stanley: Falkland Islands   51 45S 57 56W   52
Portstewart: Lon., N.Ireland   55 11N 06 43W   66
Port Sudan *see* Būr Sūdān   19 38N 37 07E   53
Port Sulphur: La., U.S.A.   29 29N 89 43W   100
Port Sunlight: Mers., England   53 21N 02 59W   114
Port Talbot: W.Glam., Wales   51 36N 03 47W   61 105
Porttipahta: *lake*, Finland   68 00N 26 30E   74
Port Townsend: Wash., U.S.A.   48 07N 122 45W   90
PORTUGAL   40 00N 08 00W   6 26 77
PORTUGUESE GUINEA   12 00N 15 00W   20 57
Portuguese Timor: *colony*, Timor   08 45S 126 00E 13 39
Portumna: Gal., Irish Republic   53 06N 08 13W   67
Port Washington: N.Y., U.S.A.   40 50N 73 32W   123
Porvoo (Borgå): Finland   60 24N 25 40E   75 107
Porz-am-Rhein: W.Germany   50 53N 07 04E   119
Posadas: Argentina   27 23S 55 53W   51
Pošechonje-Volodarsk: U.S.S.R.   58 30N 39 07E   80
Poshan *see* Boshan   36 30N 117 50E   36 84
Posiet: U.S.S.R.   42 39N 130 50E   86
Poso: Indonesia   01 23S 120 45E   39
Poso, *Lake*: Indonesia   02 00S 120 30E   39
Poste-de-la-Baleine *see* Great Whale
    River   55 20N 77 50W   96
Postillon *Island*: Indonesia   06 45S 119 00E   39
Postmasburg: C.P., Rep. of S.Africa   28 20S 23 05E   105
Postville: Nfld., Canada   54 54N 59 46W   97
Poteet: Tex., U.S.A.   29 02N 98 35W   95
Potenza: Italy   40 38N 15 48E   79
Potomac: *riv.*, U.S.A.   39 15N 77 30W   99
Potomac, *Great Falls of the*: Md., U.S.A.   39 00N 77 16W
                                                                         122
Potosí: Bolivia   19 35S 65 45W   49
Potsdam: E.Germany   52 24N 13 04E   73 117
Potsdam: N.Y., U.S.A.   44 40N 74 59W   99
Potters Bar: Herts., England   51 42N 00 11W   59 112
Potton: Beds., England   52 08N 00 14W   59
Pottstown: Pa., U.S.A.   40 15N 75 38W   99
Potwin: Kans., U.S.A.   37 56N 97 01W   95
Poughkeepsie: N.Y., U.S.A.   41 43N 73 56W   99
Poulsbo: Wash., U.S.A.   47 44N 122 38W   126
Poulton-le-Fylde: Lancs., England   53 51N 02 59W   114
Poverty *Bay*: N.I., New Zealand   38 45S 178 00E   87
Povorino: U.S.S.R.   51 12N 42 14E   80
Powder: *riv.*, U.S.A.   45 15N 105 30W   94
Powell: Wyo., U.S.A.   44 45N 108 46W   94
Powell, *Lake*: Utah, U.S.A.   37 00N 110 45W   43 91
Powell River: B.C., Canada   49 52N 124 33W   89
Powys: *admin.*, Wales   52 15N 03 15W   60
Poyang (Jaochou): China   29 00N 116 40E   36 85
Poyang, *Lake*: China   29 00N 116 15E   36 85
Poznań: Poland   52 25N 16 53E   27 73 78
Poznań: *admin.*, Poland   52 00N 17 30E   73
Prachuap Khiri Khan: Thailand   11 50N 99 49E   35
Prades: France   42 38N 02 25E   70
Prague: Czechoslovakia *see* Praha   50 05N 14 25E
                                                                    27 73 78
Praha (Prague): Czechoslovakia   50 05N 14 25E   27 73 78
Prairie Dog Town Fork: *riv.*, Tex., U.S.A.   34 30N 101 00W
                                                                           95
Prairies: *riv.*, Qué., Canada   45 30N 73 30W   122
Praslin *Island*: Seychelles   04 15S 55 45E   1
Prat de Llobregat: Spain   41 20N 02 06E   116
Prato: Italy   43 53N 11 06E   79
Pratt: Kans., U.S.A.   37 39N 98 44W   95
Prawle *Point*: Devon, England   50 12N 03 44W   61
Preeceville: Sask., Canada   51 58N 102 40W   92
Preesall: Lancs., England   53 55N 02 57W   63
Preissac, *Lake*: Qué., Canada   48 15N 78 15W   99
Prenzlau: E.Germany   53 19N 13 52E   73
Přerov: Czechoslovakia   49 27N 17 29E   73 78
Presa de Guadalupe: *res.*, Mexico   19 38N 99 16W 128
Prescot: Mers., England   53 26N 02 48W   114
Prescott: Ont., Canada   44 43N 75 31W   99
Prescott: Ariz., U.S.A.   34 33N 112 28W   91
Presidencia Roque Sáenz Peña: Argentina   26 47S 60 27W
                                                                           49
Presidente Frei: *rsch. stn.*, Antarctica   62 12S 58 55W   24
Presidente Prudente: Brazil   22 09S 51 24W   51

Presidio: Calif., U.S.A. 37 48N 122 28W 126
Prešov: Czechoslovakia 49 00N 21 13E 78
Prespa, *Lake*: Europe 40 55N 21 00E 79
Presque Isle: Maine, U.S.A. 46 42N 68 01W 99
Prestatyn: Clwyd, Wales 53 20N 03 24W 60
Presteigne: Powys, Wales 52 17N 03 00W 60
Preston: Lancs., England 53 46N 02 42W 63 114
Preston: Idaho, U.S.A. 42 06N 111 53W 90
Prestonpans: E.Loth., Scotland 55 57N 02 59W 63
Prestwich: Gt. Man., England 53 32N 02 17W 114
Prestwick: Ayr., Scotland 55 30N 04 37W 62
Pretoria: Trans., Rep. of S.Africa 25 45S 28 12E 55 105
Préveza: Greece 38 58N 20 45E 79
Préville: Qué., Canada 45 29N 73 29W 122
Priazovskaja Vozvyšennost': *hld.*, U.S.S.R. 47 30N 37 30E 80
Příbram: Czechoslovakia 49 42N 14 00E 73 78
Price: Utah, U.S.A. 39 36N 110 49W 91
Prichard: Ala., U.S.A. 30 44N 88 05W 100
Pridneprovskaja Nizmennost': *plain*, U.S.S.R. 49 30N 34 00E 80
Pridneprovskaja Vozvyšennost': *hld.*, U.S.S.R. 48 45N 31 30E 80
Prikaspijskaja Nizmennost': *plain*, U.S.S.R. 49 00N 52 00E 81
Prilep: Yugoslavia 41 20N 21 32E 79
Priluki: U.S.S.R. 50 36N 32 24E 80
Prima Porta: Italy 42 00N 12 29E 116
Primavalle: Italy 41 55N 12 25E 116
Primrose *Lake*: Sask., Canada 54 45N 109 30W 92
Prince Albert: Sask., Canada 53 13N 105 45W 42 92
Prince Albert *National Park*: Sask., Canada 54 00N 106 00W 92
Prince Edward Island: *admin.*, Canada 46 15N 63 00W 44 97
Prince Edward Island *National Park*: P.E.I., Canada 46 15N 62 30W 97
Prince Edward *Islands*: Indian Ocean 46 38S 37 55E 1
Prince George: B.C., Canada 53 55N 122 49W 42 89
Prince of Wales *Island*: Alaska, U.S.A. 55 30N 132 30W 89
Prince Rupert: B.C., Canada 54 09N 130 20W 42 89
Princes Risborough: Bucks., England 51 44N 00 51W 59
Princess Royal *Island*: B.C., Canada 53 00N 128 45W 89
Princeton: B.C., Canada 49 27N 120 31W 89
Princeton: N.J., U.S.A. 40 21N 74 40W 99
Príncipe: *is.*, Gulf of Guinea 01 30N 07 15E 57
Prineville: Oreg., U.S.A. 44 18N 120 51W 90
Priolo-Gargallo: Italy 37 09N 15 11E 107
Prip'at': *riv.*, U.S.S.R. 51 30N 24 00E 78
Pripet *Marshes*: U.S.S.R. 52 00N 28 00E 8 28
Priština: Yugoslavia 42 39N 21 10E 27 79
Privolžsk: U.S.S.R. 57 23N 41 17E 80
Privolžskaja Vozvyšennost': *hld.*, U.S.S.R. 53 00N 47 30E 81
Prizren: Yugoslavia 42 12N 20 43E 79
Procter: B.C., Canada 49 37N 116 57W 90
Prokopjevsk (Prokopyevsk): U.S.S.R. 53 53N 86 45E 30
Proletarij: U.S.S.R. 58 26N 31 44E 80
Prome *see* Pyè 18 50N 95 14E 35
Promyslovka: U.S.S.R. 43 00N 132 24E 86
Prophet: *riv.*, B.C., Canada 58 00N 122 45W 88
Prosna: *riv.*, Poland 52 00N 17 45E 73
Prospect Heights: Ill., U.S.A. 42 06N 87 56W 124
Prospect *Park*: N.Y., U.S.A. 40 40N 73 58W 123
Prospect *Reservoir*: N.S.W., Australia 33 50S 150 53E 120
Prosser: Wash., U.S.A. 46 12N 119 46W 90
Prötzeler *Forst*: E.Germany 52 39N 13 56E 117
Providence: R.I., U.S.A. 41 50N 71 25W 45 99
Providence, *Cape*: S.I., New Zealand 46 01S 166 28E 87
Provins: France 48 34N 03 18E 71
Provo: Utah, U.S.A. 40 14N 111 39W 43 91
Provost: Alta., Canada 52 24N 110 16W 92
Prudhoe: Northumb., England 54 58N 01 42W 63
Prudhoe *Bay*: Alaska, U.S.A. 70 15N 148 30W 22
Prudnik: Poland 50 20N 17 34E 73
Pruszków: Poland 52 10N 20 47E 78
Prut: *riv.*, Romania/U.S.S.R. 46 30N 28 15E 28 78
Przemyśl: Poland 49 48N 22 48E 78
Pskov: U.S.S.R. 57 50N 28 20E 28 80
Pskovskoje Ozero: *lake*, U.S.S.R. 58 00N 28 00E 80
Pucallpa: Peru 08 21S 74 33W 49
Puce: Ont., Canada 42 18N 82 47W 125
Pučež: U.S.S.R. 56 59N 43 11E 80
Pucheng: Fujian, China 27 58N 118 31E 84
Pucheng: Shănxī, China 34 58N 109 29E 85
Pudasjärvi: Finland 65 25N 26 50E 74
Pudožgora: U.S.S.R. 62 17N 35 54E 105
Pudsey: W.Yorks., England 53 48N 01 40W 63 115
Pudukkottai: India 10 23N 78 47E 34
Puebla de Zaragoza: Mexico 19 03N 98 12W 46
Pueblo: Colo., U.S.A. 38 14N 104 36W 43 95 104
Pueblo Nuevo: Spain 40 25N 03 38W 116
Puente *Hills*: Calif., U.S.A. 33 45N 117 45W 127
Puer: China 23 05N 101 06E 35
Puerco: *riv.*, U.S.A. 35 00N 109 30W 91
Puerto Barrios: Guatemala 15 43N 88 36W 46
Puerto Cabello: Venezuela 10 29N 68 02W 48
Puerto Cabezaz: Nicaragua 14 02N 83 24W 47
Puerto Carreño: Colombia 06 12N 67 22W 48
Puerto Cortés: Honduras 15 48N 87 56W 47
Puerto La Cruz: Venezuela 10 14N 64 40W 48 106
Puertollano: Spain 38 41N 04 07W 77
Puerto Madryn: Argentina 42 45S 65 02W 52
Puerto Maldonado: Peru 12 37S 69 11W 49
Puerto Montt: Chile 41 28S 73 00W 52
Puerto Ordaz: Venezuela 08 17N 62 44W 48
Puerto Peñasco: Mexico 31 20N 113 35W 46
Puerto Princesa: Philippines 09 46N 118 45E 39
PUERTO RICO 18 15N 66 30W 17 47 106
Puerto Rico *Trench*: N.Atlantic Ocean 20 00N 65 00W 2
Puerto Vallarta: Mexico 20 37N 105 15W 46
Puffin *Island*: Kerry, Irish Republic 51 45N 10 15W 67
Pugačov: U.S.S.R. 52 01N 48 50E 81
Puget *Sound*: Wash., U.S.A. 47 45N 122 15W 42 90
Pukaki, *Lake*: S.I., New Zealand 44 00S 170 00E 87
Pukekohe: N.I., New Zealand 37 12S 174 56E 87
Pukou: China 32 07N 118 43E 84
Pula: Yugoslavia 44 52N 13 52E 78
Pulaski: Va., U.S.A. 37 03N 80 47W 101
Pulborough: W.Sussex, England 50 58N 00 30W 59
Pulgaon: India 20 40N 78 22E 82
Puli: Taiwan 23 55N 120 58E 85
Pullman: Wash., U.S.A. 46 44N 117 10W 90
Pulog, *Mount*: Philippines 16 35N 120 54E 39
Puná *Island*: Ecuador 02 50S 80 08W 48
Pune (Poona): India 18 31N 73 54E 34
Punjab: *geog. reg.*, India/Pakistan 30 30N 73 00E 34
Punjabi Suba: *admin.*, India 31 00N 76 00E 34 82
Puno, Peru 15 53S 70 03W 49
Punta Arenas: Chile 53 10S 70 56W 52
Punta Cardón: Venezuela 11 38N 70 14W 106
Punta Gorda: British Honduras 16 07N 88 48W 46
Puntarenas: Costa Rica 09 58N 84 50W 47
Puqi: China 29 43N 113 53E 85
Purbeck, Isle of: *dist.*, Dorset, England 50 30N 02 00W 61
Puri: India 19 49N 85 54E 35 83
Purley: Gt. Ldn., England 51 21N 00 07W 112
Pūrna: *riv.*, India 20 00N 76 15E 82
Pūrna: *riv.*, India 20 45N 76 45E 82
Purnea: India 25 47N 87 28E 83
Pursat: Khmer Rep. 12 32N 103 55E 38
Purūlia: India 23 20N 86 24E 83
Purus: *riv.*, Brazil 07 30S 65 30W 18 48
Pusa: India 28 38N 77 10E 120
Pusan: S.Korea 35 06N 129 03E 37
Pusiano, *Lago di*: Italy 45 49N 09 17E 116
Puškin: U.S.S.R. 59 43N 30 25E 80
Putao (Fort Hertz): Burma 27 22N 97 27E 35
Putaruru: N.I., New Zealand 38 03S 175 48E 87
Putian: China 25 30N 119 05E 85
Putoran *Mountains*: U.S.S.R. 69 30N 96 00E 9 30
Puttgarden: W.Germany 54 31N 11 18E 73
Putumayo: *riv.*, S.America 02 15S 72 45W 48
Puulavesi: *lake*, Finland 61 50N 26 40E 74
Puyang: China 35 38N 114 59E 36 84
Pwllheli: Gwyn., Wales 52 53N 04 25W 60
Pyatigorsk *see* P'atigorsk 44 03N 43 04E 28
Pyè (Prome): Burma 18 50N 95 14E 35
Pyhäjärvi: Finland 63 41N 26 00E 74
Pyhäjärvi: *lake*, Finland 61 00N 22 20E 75
Pyhäselkä: *lake*, Finland 62 25N 29 55E 74
P'yŏngyang: N.Korea 39 01N 125 45E 37

Types of map: Ocean pp. 1-5; Physical pp. 6-25; Human pp. 26-57; Topographic pp. 58-101; World pp. 102-111; Urban pp. 112-128.

Pyramid *Lake*: Nev., U.S.A.   40 00N 119 35W   91
Pyrénées: *ra.*, France/Spain   42 30N 00 00   6 26 70

Qaşr al Burayqah (Marsa el Brega): Libya   30 25N 19 34E
     32
QATAR   25 30N 51 15E   10 33 107
Qattara *Depression*: Egypt   30 00N 27 30E   20 32
Qazvin: Iran   36 16N 50 00E   33
Qena *see* Qinā   26 10N 32 43E   32
Qian: *riv.*, China   23 30N 109 45E   85
Qibao: China   31 09N 121 20E   121
Qidong: Hunan, China   26 44N 112 01E   85
Qidong: Jiangsu, China   31 48N 121 45E   84
Qidong: Shandong, China   37 01N 117 29E   84
Qihe: China   36 42N 116 47E   84
Qijiang (Ch'ichiang): China   29 02N 106 39E   36
Qilianshan: *mtn.*, China   39 06N 98 40E   36
Qilianshanmai (Ch'ilien Shanmo): *ra.*, China
     39 30N 97 00E   36
Qilinhu (Qilin): *lake*, China   31 45N 89 00E   35 83
Qimen: China   29 50N 117 42E   85
Qinā (Qena): Egypt   26 10N 32 43E   32
Qinā *Wādī*: Egypt   27 15N 32 30E   32
Qingdao (Ch'ingtao, Tsingtao): China   36 02N 120 29E
     37 84 105
Qinghai (Chinghai): *admin.*, China   36 00N 96 00E   36
Qinghai (Koko Nor): *lake*, China   37 00N 100 30E   36
Qinghe: China   40 01N 116 20E   121
Qingjiang (Linchiang): China   28 00N 115 23E   36 85
Qingshui: China   34 37N 106 21E   84
Qingshui: *riv.*, China   36 30N 106 30E   84
Qingtian: China   28 09N 120 21E   85
Qingxian: China   38 37N 116 50E   84
Qingyang: Anhui, China   30 39N 117 45E   85
Qingyang: Gansu, China   36 01N 107 47E   85
Qingyuan (Ch'ingyüan): Guangdong, China
     23 43N 113 00E   36 85
Qingyuan: Hebei *see* Baoding   38 52N 115 29E   36 84
Qinhuangdao (Ch'inhuangtao): China   39 56N 119 39E
     37 84
Qinlingshan (Tsinling Shan): *mtns.*, China
     33 45N 107 45E   12 36 84
Qinshui: China   35 41N 112 15E   84
Qinshui (Ch'ingshui): *riv.*, China   26 30N 109 00E   36 85
Qinxian (Qinzhou): Guangxi Zhuang,
     China   22 01N 108 36E   85
Qinxian: Shānxī, China   36 48N 112 41E   84
Qinyang: Henan, China   32 48N 113 20E   84
Qinyang: Henan, China   35 06N 112 51E   84
Qinzhou *see* Qinxian   22 01N 108 36E   85
Qiqihaer (Ch'ich'ihaerh): China   47 19N 123 55E   31
Qixian: Henan, China   34 30N 114 45E   84
Qixian: Shānxī, China   37 20N 112 20E   84
Qiyang: China   26 33N 111 50E   85
Qom: Iran   34 39N 50 57E   33
Qu: *riv.*, China   31 30N 107 15E   84
Quadraro: Italy   41 52N 12 34E   116
Quang Ngãi: S.Vietnam   15 09N 108 50E   38
Quang Tri: S.Vietnam   16 46N 107 11E   38
Quan Long: S.Vietnam   09 11N 105 09E   38
Quannan: China   24 41N 114 23E   85
Quantocks: *hills*, Som., England   51 00N 03 15W   61
Quanzhou (Chinchiang): China   24 54N 118 35E   36 85
Qu' Appelle: *riv.*, Sask., Canada   50 30N 103 00W   42 92
Québec: Qué., Canada   46 50N 71 15W   44 96
Québec: *admin.*, Canada   44 96
Queen Charlotte: B.C., Canada   53 18N 132 04W   89
Queen Charlotte *Islands*: B.C., Canada   53 00N 132 00W
     16 89 104
Queen Charlotte *Sound*: B.C., Canada   51 30N 129 30W   89
Queen Charlotte *Strait*: B.C., Canada   50 45N 127 15W   89
Queen Elizabeth *Forest Park*: Stirl., Scotland
     56 00N 04 30W   64
Queen Elizabeth *Islands*: Canada   79 00N 100 00W   23
Queen Elizabeth *Park*: B.C., Canada   49 14N 123 06W   126
Queen Mary *Reservoir*: Surrey, England   51 24N 00 27W
     112
Queen Maud Land: *reg.*, Antarctica   78 00S 00 00   24

Queens: N.Y., U.S.A.   40 40N 73 45W   123
Queensbury: W.Yorks., England   53 46N 01 50W   115
Queensferry: W.Loth., Scotland   55 59N 03 25W   62
Queensland: *admin.*, Australia   41
Queen's *Park*: Ont., Canada   43 39N 79 23W   125
Queenstown: Tas., Australia   42 07S 145 33E   40
Queenstown: S.I., New Zealand   45 03S 168 41E   37 87
Queenstown: C.P., Rep. of S.Africa   31 54S 26 53E   55
Quelimane: Mozambique   17 51S 36 52E   55
Quemoy *see* Chinmen   24 27N 118 23E   85
Que Que: Rhodesia   18 55S 29 49E   55 105
Queshan: China   32 48N 114 03E   84
Quesnel: B.C., Canada   53 03N 122 31W   89
Quesnel *Lake*: B.C., Canada   52 30N 121 00W   89
Questa: N.Mex., U.S.A.   36 42N 105 36W   95
Quetico *Provincial Park*: Ont., Canada   48 15N 91 30W   98
Quetta: Pakistan   30 15N 67 00E   34
Quezaltenango: Guatemala   14 50N 91 31W   46
Quezon City: Philippines   14 39N 121 01E   39
Quibdó: Colombia   05 40N 76 40W   48
Quibell: Ont., Canada   49 58N 93 24W   93
Quickborn: W.Germany   53 44N 09 55E   119
Quillacollo: Bolivia   17 26S 66 17W   49
Quill *Lakes*: Sask., Canada   51 45N 104 15W   92
Quillota: Chile   32 54S 71 16W   52
Quilmes: Argentina   34 43S 58 15W   128
Quilon: India   08 53N 76 38E   34
Quimper: France   48 00N 04 06W   70
Quinag: *mtn.*, Suther., Scotland   58 13N 05 02W   64
Quincy: Ill., U.S.A.   39 55N 91 22W   98
Quincy: Mass., U.S.A.   42 17N 71 00W   122
Quincy *Bay*: Mass., U.S.A.   42 17N 71 00W   122
Quincy–sous–Sénart: France   48 40N 02 32E   117
Qui Nhon: S.Vietnam   13 47N 109 11E   38
Quintana Roo: *admin.*, Mexico   19 15N 88 15W   46
Quito: Ecuador   00 14S 78 30W   48
Quoich, *Loch*: Inv., Scotland   57 00N 05 15W   64
Quorn: Ont., Canada   49 25N 90 53W   98
Quseir *see* Al Quṣayr   26 06N 34 17E   32
Quxian: Sichuan, China   30 51N 106 58E   85
Quxian (Ch'ühsien): Zhejiang, China   28 58N 118 52E
     36 85
Quzhou: China   36 46N 114 51E   84

Raahe: Finland   64 42N 24 30E   75
Raasay: *is.*, Inv., Scotland   57 15N 06 00W   64
Raasay, *Sound of*: Inv., Scotland   57 30N 06 00W   64
Rába: *riv.*, Hungary   47 15N 17 15E   73
Rabat: Morocco   34 02N 06 51W   56
Raccoon: *riv.*, Iowa, U.S.A.   42 15N 94 45W   98
Race, *Cape*: Nfld., Canada   46 38N 53 10W   16 97
Rach Giá: S.Vietnam   10 02N 105 05E   38
Raciborz: Poland   50 05N 18 10E   78
Racine: Wis., U.S.A.   42 42N 87 50W   45 98
Radcliffe: Gt. Man., England   53 34N 02 20W   114
Radebeul: E.Germany   51 06N 13 41E   73
Radhanpur: India   23 52N 71 49E   82
Radisson: Sask., Canada   52 27N 107 24W   92
Radlinski, *Mount*: Antarctica   82 31S 103 34W   25
Radnor *Forest*: Powys, Wales   52 15N 03 00W   60
Radnorshire: *admin.*, Wales. Absorbed into new *admin.* of
     Powys, 1974.   60
Radom: Poland   51 26N 21 10E   27 78
Radomsko: Poland   51 04N 19 25E   78
Radstadt: Austria   47 23N 13 28E   73
Radstock: Avon, England   51 18N 02 28W   61
Radville: Sask., Canada   49 28N 104 19W   92
Rae: N.W.T., Canada   62 50N 116 00W   88
Rãe Bareli: India   26 14N 81 14E   83
Rafaela: Argentina   31 16S 61 44W   52
Rafael Castillo: Argentina   34 41S 58 37W   128
Ragusa: Sicily   36 56N 14 44E   79
Rahaeng *see* Tak   16 51N 99 08E   35
Rãhatgarh: India   23 47N 78 28E   82
Rahīmyār Khān: Pakistan   28 22N 70 20E   82
Rãichūr: India   16 15N 77 20E   34
Raiganj: India   25 38N 88 11E   83
Raigarh: India   21 53N 83 28E   83

Types of map: Ocean pp. 1-5; Physical pp. 6-25; Human pp. 26-57; Topographic pp. 58-101; World pp. 102-111; Urban pp. 112-128.

Rainford: Mers., England 53 30N 02 48W	114	
Rainier, *Mount*: Wash., U.S.A. 46 51N 121 46W	16 42 90	
Rainy: *riv.*, Canada/U.S.A. 48 30N 94 00W	98	
Rainy *Lake*: Canada/.U.S.A. 48 30N 93 15W	98	
Rainy River: Ont., Canada 48 44N 94 33W	98	
Raipur: India 21 16N 81 42E	34 83	
Raipur *Uplands*: India 20 45N 82 00E	83	
Raisio: Finland 60 30N 22 10E	75	
Rājahmundry: India 17 01N 81 52E	34	
Rajang: *riv.*, Malaysia 02 00N 112 30E	38	
Rājapālaiyam: India 09 26N 77 36E	34	
Rājāpur *Canal*: India 22 33N 88 07E	120	
Rājasthān: *admin.*, India 26 30N 74 00E	34 82	
Rajevskij: U.S.S.R. 54 04N 54 56E	81	
Rājgarh: Madhya Pradesh, India 24 01N 76 42E	82	
Rājgarh: Rājasthān, India 28 38N 75 23E	82	
Rājkot: India 22 18N 70 53E	34 82	
Rāj-Nāndgaon: India 21 06N 81 08E	82	
Rājpur: India 22 25N 88 25E	120	
Rājpura: India 30 29N 76 40E	82	
Rājshāhi: Bangladesh 24 24N 88 40E	35 83	
Rajula: India 21 01N 71 34E	82	
Rakvere: U.S.S.R. 59 22N 26 20E	75	
Raleigh: N.C., U.S.A. 35 46N 78 39W	45 101	
Raleigh *Bay*: N.C., U.S.A. 34 45N 76 00W	101	
Ramadi *see* Ar Ramādī 33 27N 43 19E	33	
Rāmānuj Ganj: India 23 48N 83 42E	83	
Rambouillet: France 48 39N 01 50E	117	
Rambouillet, *Forêt de*: France 48 30N 01 45E	117	
Ramechhāp: Nepal 27 19N 86 05E	83	
Rame *Head*: Corn., England 50 19N 04 13W	61	
Ramor, *Lough*: Cavan, Irish Republic 53 45N 07 00W	66	
Ramos Mejia: Argentina 34 39S 58 33W	128	
Rāmpur: Himachal Pradesh, India 31 26N 77 37E	82	
Rāmpur: Uttar Pradesh, India 28 48N 79 03E	34 82	
Rampur Hat: India 24 11N 87 51E	83	
Ramsbottom: Gt. Man., England 53 40N 02 19W	114	
Ramsey: Cambs., England 52 27N 00 07W	58	
Ramsey: I. of M., U.K. 54 19N 04 23W	62	
Ramsey *Island*: Dyfed, Wales 51 53N 05 20W	60	
Ramsgate: Kent, England 51 20N 01 25E	59	
Rānāghāt: India 23 11N 88 35E	83	
Rancagua: Chile 34 10S 70 45W	52	
Rancheria: Yukon, Canada 60 06N 130 40W	88	
Rānchī: India 23 22N 85 52E	35 83	
Rancooas *Creek*: N.J., U.S.A. 40 00N 74 45W	122	
Randalstown: Antrim, N.Ireland 54 45N 06 19W	66	
Randers: Denmark 56 28N 10 03E	75	
Randolph: Utah, U.S.A. 41 40N 111 11W	90	
Randwick: N.S.W., Australia 33 50S 151 14E	120	
Ranfurly: Renf., Scotland 55 52N 04 33W	113	
Rangiora: S.I., New Zealand 43 18S 172 38E	87	
Rangitoto *Range*: N.I., New Zealand 38 15S 175 30E	87	
Rangitukia: N.I., New Zealand 37 45S 178 30E	87	
Rangoon: Burma 16 47N 96 10E	35	
Rangpur: Bangladesh 25 45N 89 21E	83	
Rani Bagh: India 28 41N 77 07E	120	
Rānīganj: India 23 35N 87 07E	83	
Rannoch, *Loch*: Perth., Scotland 56 30N 04 15W	64	
Rannoch *Moor*: Scotland 56 30N 04 30W	64	
Rann of Kutch: *geog. reg.*, India 24 00N 70 00E	11 34 82	
Rānpur: India 20 04N 85 22E	83	
Rantauprapat: Indonesia 02 05N 99 46E	38	
Rantekombola, *Mount*: Indonesia 03 23S 120 02E	39	
Raoping: China 23 43N 116 59E	85	
Rapid City: S.D., U.S.A. 44 05N 103 14W	43 94	
Rāpti: *riv.*, India 27 00N 82 45E	83	
Raritan: *riv.*, N.J., U.S.A. 40 31N 74 27W	123	
Raritan *Bay*: N.J., U.S.A. 40 15N 74 00W	123	
Ra's at Tannūrah: *cape*, Saudi Arabia 26 40N 50 09E	107	
R'as aţ Ţīb (Bon, *cap*): Tunisia 37 05N 11 02E	79	
Ras Dashan: *mtn.*, Ethiopia 13 15N 38 27E	21 53	
Rashīd (Rosetta): Egypt 31 24N 30 25E	32	
Rasht (Resht): Iran 37 18N 49 38E	33	
Rasskazovo: U.S.S.R. 52 40N 41 53E	80	
Rastatt: W.Germany 48 51N 08 13E	72	
Rat: *riv.*, Man., Canada 56 00N 99 15W	93	
Ratangarh: India 28 02N 74 39E	82	
Rāth: India 25 36N 79 34E	82	
Rathdowney: Laois, Irish Republic 52 51N 07 35W	67	
Rathdrum: Wick., Irish Republic 52 56N 06 13W	67	

Rathenow: E.Germany 52 37N 12 21E	73	
Rathfriland: Down, N.Ireland 54 14N 06 10W	66	
Rathkeale: Lim., Irish Republic 52 32N 08 56W	67	
Rathlin *Island*: Antrim, N.Ireland 55 15N 06 00W	66	
Rath Luire: Cork, Irish Republic 52 21N 08 41W	67	
Ratingen: W.Germany 51 18N 06 50E	118	
Ratlām: India 23 18N 75 06E	34 82	
Ratnagiri: *admin.*, India 17 00N 73 30E	105	
Raton: N.Mex., U.S.A. 36 54N 104 24W	95	
Rat River: N.W.T., Canada 61 07N 112 35W	92	
Rattray: Perth., Scotland 56 36N 03 20W	65	
Ratz, *Mount*: B.C., Canada 57 22N 132 15W	89	
Rauma: Finland 61 09N 21 30E	75	
Raunds: Northants., England 52 21N 00 33W	59	
Raurkela: India 22 16N 85 01E	35 83 105	
Ravenglass: Cumbria, England 54 21N 03 24W	62	
Ravenna: Italy 44 25N 12 12E	26 79 107	
Ravensburg: W.Germany 47 47N 09 37E	72	
Ravi: *riv.*, Pakistan 30 45N 73 00E	34 83	
Rawalpindi: Pakistan 33 40N 73 08E	34	
Rawicz: Poland 51 38N 16 51E	73	
Rawlins: Wyo., U.S.A. 41 47N 107 14W	94	
Rawmarsh: S.Yorks., England 53 27N 01 21W	63	
Rawson: Chubut, Argentina 43 18S 65 06W	52	
Rawtenstall: Lancs., England 53 42N 02 18W	63 114	
Ray: Ariz., U.S.A. 33 11N 111 00W	91	
Ray, *Cape*: Nfld., Canada 47 38N 59 18W	97	
Rayleigh: Essex, England 51 36N 00 36E	59	
Raymond: Alta., Canada 49 30N 112 39W	92	
Raymond: Wash., U.S.A. 46 41N 123 44W	90	
Raymondville: Tex., U.S.A. 26 30N 97 48W	100	
R'azan' (Ryazan'): U.S.S.R. 54 38N 39 44E	28 80 107	
R'ažsk: U.S.S.R. 53 43N 40 04E	80	
Ré, *Ile de*: France 46 10N 01 26W	70	
Rea: *riv.*, Salop, England 52 30N 02 45W	60	
Rea, *Lough*: Irish Republic 53 00N 08 30W	67	
Reading: Berks., England 51 28N 00 59W	59	
Reading: Pa., U.S.A. 40 20N 75 55W	99	
Rechna Doāb: *geog. reg.*, Pakistan 31 15N 73 15E	82	
Rečica: U.S.S.R. 52 22N 30 25E	80	
Recife (Pernambuco): Brazil 08 03S 34 54W	50	
Recklinghausen: W.Germany 51 37N 07 11E	118	
Reconquista: *riv.*, Argentina 34 35S 58 41W	128	
Recovery *Glacier*: Antarctica 81 46S 163 05E	24	
Red: *riv.*, China/N.Vietnam *see* Song Hong; Yüan 21 45N 104 30E	12 36	
Red: *riv.*, U.S.A. 31 15N 92 00W	17 43 100	
Redange-sur-Attert: Luxembourg 49 46N 05 53E	105	
Red Bluff: Calif., U.S.A. 40 11N 122 16W	91	
Redbridge: Gt. Ldn., England 51 34N 00 05E	59	
Redcar: Cleve., England 54 37N 01 04W	63	
Redcar *see* Teesside 54 30N 01 15W	26 105	
Redcliff: Colo., U.S.A. 39 31N 106 22W	94	
Redcliffe: Rhodesia 19 00S 29 49E	105	
Red Deer: Alta., Canada 52 15N 113 48W	42 92	
Red Deer: *riv.*, Alta., Canada 51 15N 112 15W	92	
Red Deer: *riv.*, Canada 52 45N 103 15W	92	
Red Deer *Lake*: Man., Canada 52 45N 101 15W	92	
Redding: Calif., U.S.A. 40 35N 122 24W	91	
Redditch: Here.& Worcs., England 52 19N 01 56W	59 115	
Rede: *riv.*, Northumb., England 55 15N 02 15W	63	
Redfield: S.D., U.S.A. 44 53N 98 31W	94	
Redhill: Surrey, England 51 14N 00 11W	112	
Red Lake: *riv.*, Minn., U.S.A. 48 00N 95 15W	98	
Red Lake: Ont., Canada 51 00N 93 45W	93 104	
Red Mesa: Ariz., U.S.A. 36 50N 109 24W	91	
Redmond: Oreg., U.S.A. 44 17N 121 11W	90	
Redmond: Utah, U.S.A. 39 00N 111 52W	91	
Redmond: Wash., U.S.A. 47 40N 122 07W	126	
Rednitz: *riv.*, W.Germany 49 45N 11 00E	73	
Redon: France 47 39N 02 05W	70	
Redondo Beach: Calif., U.S.A. 33 50N 118 23W	127	
Red River of the North: *riv.*, Canada/U.S.A. 48 00N 97 00W	17 42 94	
Redruth: Corn., England 50 13N 05 14W	61	
Red *Sea* 20 45N 38 45E	10 33	
Red Sea *Hills*: Egypt 27 00N 33 15E	10 32	
Red Volta: *riv.*, W.Africa 11 30N 01 00W	57	
Redwater: Alta., U.S.A. 53 57N 113 06W	92	
Red Wing: Minn., U.S.A. 44 33N 92 31W	98	
Redwood City: Calif., U.S.A. 37 28N 122 15W	126	

Types of map: Ocean pp. 1-5; Physical pp. 6-25; Human pp. 26-57; Topographic pp. 58-101; World pp. 102-111; Urban pp. 112-128.

Redwood Falls: Minn., U.S.A.   44 30N 95 06W   98
Redwood *Regional Park*: Calif., U.S.A.   37 45N 122 00W
  126
Ree, *Lough*: Rosc., Irish Rep.   53 30N 08 00W   66
Reedy *Glacier*: Antarctica   85 30S 134 00W   25
Reefton: S.I., New Zealand   42 05S 171 51E   87
Reepham: Norf., England   52 46N 01 07E   58
Regen: *riv.*, W.Germany   49 00N 12 45E   73
Regensburg: W.Germany   49 01N 12 07E   73
Reggio di Calabria: Italy   38 06N 15 39E   27 79
Reggio nell' Emilia: Italy   44 42N 10 37E   78
Regina: Sask., Canada   50 30N 104 38W   42 92
Réidh, Rubha: *cape*, R. & Crom., Scotland   57 52N 05 49W
  64
Reidsville: N.C., U.S.A.   36 21N 79 40W   101
Reigate: Surrey, England   51 14N 00 13W   59 112
Reims (Rheims): France   49 15N 04 02E   26 71
Reina Adeleida *Archipelago*: Chile   52 15S 74 30W   52
Reinbek: W.Germany   53 31N 10 15E   119
Reindeer *Lake*: Canada   57 30N 102 15W   16 42 92
Reinosa (Reynosa): Mexico   26 07N 98 18W   46
Reinosa: Spain   43 01N 04 09W   70
Remiremont: France   48 01N 06 35E   71
Remscheid: W.Germany   51 10N 07 11E   118
Rendsburg: W.Germany   54 18N 09 40E   72 76
Renfrew: Ont., Canada   45 28N 76 44W   99
Renfrew: Renf., Scotland   55 53N 04 24W   62 113
Renfrewshire: *admin.*, Scotland   55 45N 04 30W   62 113
Renish *Point*: Inv., Scotland   57 43N 06 58W   64
Rennes: France   48 06N 01 40W   26 70
Reno: Nev., U.S.A.   39 32N 119 49W   43 91
Renton: Wash., U.S.A.   47 29N 122 12W   126
Répce: *riv.*, Hungary   47 15N 16 45E   73
Republic: Wash., U.S.A.   48 39N 118 44W   90
Republican: *riv.*, U.S.A.   40 00N 98 30W   94
Rescaldina: Italy   45 37N 08 57E   116
Resht *see* Rasht   37 18N 49 38E   33
Resistencia: Argentina   27 28S 59 00W   49
Reşiţa: Romania   45 16N 21 55E   78 105
Resolution *Island*: S.I., New Zealand   45 30S 166 45E   87
Réthimnon: Crete   35 23N 24 28E   79
Retiro: Argentina   34 36S 58 23W   128
Réunion: *is.*, Indian Ocean   21 06S 55 36E   1
Reus: Spain   41 10N 01 06E   77
Reutlingen: W.Germany   48 30N 09 13E   72
Reutov: U.S.S.R.   55 46N 37 52E   119
Revda: U.S.S.R.   56 48N 59 57E   81
Revel: U.S.S.R. *see* Tallinn   59 22N 24 48E   75
Revelstoke: B.C., Canada   51 02N 118 12W   89
Revere: Mass., U.S.A.   42 24N 71 00W   122
Revere *Beach*: Mass., U.S.A.   42 25N 70 59W   122
Revesby: N.S.W., Australia   33 57S 151 01E   120
Revilla Gigedos *Islands*: N.Pacific Ocean   19 00N 111 00W
  5
Rewa: India   24 32N 81 18E   34 83
Rewāri: India   28 14N 76 38E   83
Rexburg: Idaho, U.S.A.   43 49N 111 47W   90
Rey: *riv.*, Argentina   34 46S 58 26W   128
Reykjanes *Ridge*: N.Atlantic Ocean   59 00N 30 00W   2 6
Reynosa *see* Reinosa   26 07N 98 18W   46
Reż: U.S.S.R.   57 23N 61 24E   81
Rezā'īyeh: Iran   37 32N 45 02E   33
Rezé: France   47 12N 01 34W   70
Rēzekne: U.S.S.R.   56 30N 27 19E   80
Rhayader: Powys, Wales   52 18N 03 30W   60
Rheidol: *riv.*, Dyfed, Wales   52 15N 03 45W   60
Rheims *see* Reims   49 15N 04 02E   26 71
Rheinberg: W.Germany   51 33N 06 35E   118
Rheindahlen: W.Germany   51 10N 06 22E   118
Rheine: W.Germany   52 17N 07 26E   72
Rheinhausen: W.Germany   51 23N 06 41E   118
Rhein-Herne-*Kanal*: W.Germany   51 30N 07 00E   118
Rheinkamp: W.Germany   51 31N 06 38E   118
Rheinland-Pfalz: *admin.*, W.Germany   50 30N 06 45E
  72 72
Rheydt: W.Germany   51 10N 06 27E   118
Rhine: *riv.*, Europe   50 30N 07 30E   6 26 72 77
Rhinelander: Wis., U.S.A.   45 39N 89 23W   98
Rhinns, The: *dist.*, Wig., Scotland   54 45N 05 00W   62
Rhinns *Point*: Argyll., Scotland   55 41N 06 30W   62
Rhinog Fawr: *mtn.*, Gwyn., Wales   52 51N 04 00W   60

Rhiw: *riv.*, Powys, Wales   52 30N 03 15W   60
Rho: Italy   45 32N 09 02E   116
Rhode Island: *admin.*, U.S.A.   41 30N 71 30W   45 99
Rhodes *see* Ródhos   36 26N 28 14E   79
Rhodes; *is. see* Ródhos   36 15N 28 00E   27 79
RHODESIA   21 15S 30 00E   55 107
Rhodope *Mountains see* Rodopi Planina   41 30N 24 30E   79
Rhondda: M.Glam., Wales   51 40N 03 30W   61
Rhône: *riv.*, France/Switzerland   43 45N 04 30E   6 26 71
Rhuddlan: Clwyd, Wales   53 18N 03 27W   60
Rhum: *is.*, Inv., Scotland   57 00N 06 20W   64
Rhum, *Sound of*: Inv., Scotland   56 45N 06 15W   64
Rhyddhywel: *mtn.*, Powys, Wales   52 26N 03 25W   60
Rhyl: Clwyd, Wales   53 19N 03 29W   60
Rhymney: M.Glam., Wales   51 46N 03 18W   61 113
Rhymney: *riv.*, M.Glam., Wales   51 30N 03 00W   113
Riachuelo: *riv.*, Argentina   34 39S 58 22W   128
Riau *Archipelago*: Indonesia   00 45N 104 15E   38
Ribadavia: Spain   42 17N 08 08W   77
Ribadeo: Spain   43 32N 07 04W   77
Ribble: *riv.*, Lancs., England   53 45N 02 30W   63 114
Ribeirão Prêto: Brazil   21 10S 47 48W   51
Riberalta: Bolivia   10 59S 66 06W   49
Ribnitz: E.Germany   54 15N 12 26E   73
Richardson: *riv.*, Canada   58 00N 110 30W   92
Richardson *Island*: N.W.T., Canada   65 46N 118 20W   88
Richard-Toll: Senegal   16 25N 15 42W   56
Riche *Point*: Nfld., Canada   50 43N 57 25W   97
Richfield: Utah, U.S.A.   38 46N 112 05W   91
Richibucto: N.B., Canada   46 42N 64 54W   97
Richland: Wash., U.S.A.   46 17N 119 17W   90
Richlands: Va., U.S.A.   37 07N 81 48W   101
Richmond: B.C., Canada   49 10N 123 10W   126
Richmond: Gt. Ldn., England   51 28N 00 18W   112
Richmond: N.Yorks., England   54 24N 01 44W   63
Richmond: S.I., New Zealand   41 20S 173 10E   87
Richmond: Calif., U.S.A.   37 56N 122 20W   106 126
Richmond: Ind., U.S.A.   39 50N 84 51W   98
Richmond: Ky., U.S.A.   37 45N 84 19W   101
Richmond: N.Y., U.S.A.   40 30N 74 10W   123
Richmond: Va., U.S.A.   37 34N 77 26W   45 101
Richmond Beach: Wash., U.S.A.   47 46N 122 23W   126
Richmond *Gulf*: Qué., Canada   56 15N 76 15W   96
Richmond Highlands: Wash., U.S.A.   47 46N 122 22W   126
Richmond Hill: Ont., Canada   43 53N 79 26W   125
Richmond *Park*: Gt. Ldn., England   51 26N 00 16W   112
Richmond-San Rafael *Bridge*: Calif., U.S.A.
  37 56N 122 26W   126
Rich *Passage*: Wash., U.S.A.   47 35N 122 33W   126
Richwood: W.Va., U.S.A.   38 14N 80 33W   99
Rickmansworth: Herts., England   51 39N 00 29W   112
Rico: Colo., U.S.A.   37 52N 108 02W   95
Riddle: Oreg., U.S.A.   42 57N 123 22W   90
Ridgecrest: Calif., U.S.A.   35 38N 117 40W   91
Ridgewood: Ill., U.S.A.   41 33N 88 03W   124
Ridgewood: N.J., U.S.A.   40 58N 74 08W   123
Riding Mountain *National Park*: Man.,
  Canada   50 45N 100 15W   93
Riesa: E.Germany   51 18N 13 18E   73 105
Rifle: Colo., U.S.A.   39 32N 107 47W   94
Rif *Mountains*: Morocco   34 45N 04 15W   20 56
Rīga: U.S.S.R.   56 53N 24 08E   28 75
Riga, *Gulf of see* Rižskij Zaliv   57 45N 23 15E   28 75
Rigolet: Nfld., Canada   54 10N 58 30W   97
Rihadh *see* Ar Riyāḍ   24 39N 46 46E   33
Rihand *Reservoir*: India   24 00N 82 45E   83
Riihimäki: Finland   60 45N 24 45E   75
Rijeka: Yugoslavia   45 20N 14 27E   27 78
Rikeze (Shigatse): China   29 18N 88 50E   35 83
Rillito: Ariz., U.S.A.   32 25N 111 09W   91
Rimbey: Alta., Canada   52 39N 114 10W   92
Rimini: Italy   44 03N 12 34E   27 79
Rimouski: Qué., Canada   48 27N 68 32W   44 96
Ringkøbing: Denmark   56 06N 08 15E   75
Ringkøbing *Fjord*: Denmark   56 00N 08 15E   75
Ringvassøy: *is.*, Norway   69 55N 19 10E   74
Ringwood: Hants., England   50 51N 01 47W   59
Rinnes, Ben: *mtn.*, Banff., Scotland   57 24N 03 15W   65
Rinn *Lough*: Leit., Irish Republic   53 45N 07 45W   66
Riobamba: Ecuador   01 40S 78 38W   48
Rio Branco: Brazil   09 58S 67 48W   49

Río Cuarto: Argentina   33 08S 64 20W   52
Rio de Janeiro: Brazil   22 53S 43 17W   51 106
Rio de Janeiro: *admin.*, Brazil   22 45S 44 00W   51
Río de la Plata: *est.*, Argentina/Uruguay   35 00S 57 00W
                                               52 128
Río Gallegos: Argentina   51 35S 69 15W   52
Río Grande: Argentina   53 45S 67 46W   52
Rio Grande: Brazil   32 03S 52 08W   51
Rio Grande: *riv.*, Bolivia   16 15S 63 45W   49
Rio Grande: *riv.*, Brazil *see* Grande   19 45S 50 00W   18 51
Rio Grande: *riv.*, Mexico/U.S.A.   26 45N 99 15W   17 43 100
Rio Grande do Norte: *admin.*, Brazil   05 30S 36 45W   50
Rio Grande do Sul: *admin.*, Brazil   29 30S 53 30W   51
Rio Grande *Rise*: S.Atlantic Ocean   30 00N 35 00W   3 19
Ríohacha: Colombia   13 34N 72 58W   48
Rio Hondo: *riv.*, N.Mex., U.S.A.   33 15N 105 00W   95
Rioja, La: *admin.*, Argentina   30 00S 66 00W   52
Riom: France   45 54N 03 07E   71
Rio Muni: *admin.*, Equatorial Guinea   01 30N 10 30E   57
Riondel: B.C., Canada   49 46N 116 52W   90
Río Negro: *admin.*, Argentina   40 15S 66 45W   52
Rio Pensaco: *riv.*, N.Mex., U.S.A.   32 45N 104 30W   95
Ripley: Derby., England   53 03N 01 24W   58
Ripoll: *riv.*, Spain   41 30N 02 00E   116
Ripollet: Spain   41 29N 02 10E   116
Ripon: N.Yorks., England   54 08N 01 31W   63
Ripponden: W.Yorks., England   53 41N 01 57W   115
Risca: Gwent, Wales   51 37N 03 07W   61 113
Rishrã: India   22 43N 88 21E   120
Ritter, *Mount*: Calif., U.S.A.   37 40N 119 15W   91
Rivera: Uruguay   30 55S 55 33W   52
River Forest: Ill., U.S.A.   41 52N 87 48W   124
Riverhurst: Sask., Canada   50 53N 106 52W   92
River Rouge: Mich., U.S.A.   42 15N 83 09W   125
Riverside: Ont., Canada   42 20N 82 56W   125
Riverside: Calif., U.S.A.   33 59N 117 22W   91
Riverside: Ill., U.S.A.   41 50N 87 49W   124
Riverside: N.J., U.S.A.   40 02N 74 58W   122
Rivers Inlet: B.C., Canada   51 42N 127 15W   89
Riverstone: N.S.W., Australia   33 41S 150 52E   120
Riverton: Man., Canada   51 00N 97 00W   93
Riverton: Wyo., U.S.A.   43 02N 108 23W   94
Riverton Heights: Wash., U.S.A.   47 28N 122 17W   126
Rivière-du-Loup: Qué., Canada   47 49N 69 32W   44 96
Riyadh *see* Ar Riyāḍ   24 39N 46 46E   33
Rizhao: China   35 27N 119 29E   84
Rižskij Zaliv *see* Riga, *Gulf of*   57 45N 23 15E   28 75
Roanne: France   46 02N 04 05E   71
Roanoke: Va., U.S.A.   37 15N 79 58W   45 101
Roanoke: *riv.*, U.S.A.   36 45N 78 45W   45 101
Roanoke Rapids: N.C., U.S.A.   36 27N 77 40W   101
Roaringwater *Bay*: Cork, Irish Republic   51 30N 09 15W   67
Roatán: Honduras   16 18N 86 35W   47
Robe *River*: Australia   21 19S 115 40E   105
Robertsfield (Roberts International Airport): Liberia
    06 15N 10 22W   57
Roberval: Qué., Canada   48 31N 72 16W   96
Robin Hood's *Bay*: N.Yorks., England   54 15N 00 30W   63
Robinson: Yukon, Canada   60 24N 134 58W   88
Robson, *Mount*: B.C., Canada   53 08N 118 18W   16 42 89
Robstown: Tex., U.S.A.   27 47N 97 42W   100
Roby: Mers., England   53 25N 02 51W   114
Roçadas: Angola   16 43S 15 01E   55
Rocas *Island*: S.Atlantic Ocean   03 50S 33 50W   3
Roch: *riv.*, Gt. Man., England   53 30N 02 00W   114
Rocha: Uruguay   34 30S 54 22W   52
Rochdale: Gt. Man., England   53 38N 02 09W   63 114
Rochdale *Canal*: England   53 30N 02 00W   114
Rochefort: France   45 57N 00 58W   70
Rocher River: N.W.T., Canada   61 23N 112 45W   92
Rochester: Kent, England   51 24N 00 30E   59 112
Rochester: Minn., U.S.A.   44 01N 92 27W   43 98
Rochester: N.H., U.S.A.   43 18N 70 58W   99
Rochester: N.Y., U.S.A.   43 12N 77 37W   45 99
Rock: *riv.*, U.S.A.   41 45N 89 15W   98
Rockall *Plateau*: N.Atlantic Ocean   57 00N 14 00W   2
Rockaway *Beach*: N.Y., U.S.A.   40 33N 73 54W   123
Rockaway *Inlet*: N.Y., U.S.A.   40 34N 73 55W   123
Rock Creek *Park*: D.C., U.S.A.   38 58N 77 03W   122
Rockdale: N.S.W., Australia   33 57S 151 08E   120
Rockefeller *Plateau*: Antarctica   80 00S 135 00W   25

Rockford: Ill., U.S.A.   42 16N 89 06W   45 98
Rockhampton: Qld., Australia   23 22S 150 32E   41
Rock Hill: S.C., U.S.A.   34 55N 81 01W   101
Rock Island: Ill., U.S.A.   41 30N 90 34W   45 98
Rockland: Maine, U.S.A.   44 06N 69 08W   99
Rock Springs: Wyo., U.S.A.   41 35N 109 14W   43 94
Rockville Centre: N.Y., U.S.A.   40 40N 73 39W   123
Rockwood: Maine, U.S.A.   45 41N 69 46W   99
Rocky Ford: Colo., U.S.A.   38 03N 103 43W   95
Rocky Mount: N.C., U.S.A.   35 56N 77 48W   101
Rocky Mountain House: Alta., Canada   52 24N 114 52W   92
Rocky Mountain *National Park*: Colo.,
    U.S.A.   40 30N 105 45W   94
Rocky *Mountains*: Canada/U.S.A.   16 90
Rodez: France   44 21N 02 34E   70
Ródhos (Rhodes): Rhodes   36 26N 28 14E   79
Ródhos (Rhodes): *is.*, Mediterranean Sea   36 15N 28 00E
                                               27 79
Roding: *riv.*, Essex, England   51 30N 00 00   112
Rodniki: U.S.S.R.   57 06N 41 44E   80
Rodopi Planina (Rhodope *Mountains*):
    Bulgaria   41 30N 24 30E   79
Rodriguez: *is.*, Indian Ocean   19 45S 63 20E   1
Rodriguez *Fracture Zone*: Indian Ocean   20 00S 70 00E   1
Roermond: Netherlands   51 12N 06 00E   72
Roeselare: Belgium   50 57N 03 08E   72
Rogačov: U.S.S.R.   53 05N 30 03E   80
Rogagua, *Lake*: Bolivia   13 45S 66 45W   49
Rogers, *Mount*: Va., U.S.A.   36 39N 81 33W   101
Rogers City: Mich., U.S.A.   45 24N 83 50W   98
Roggan River: Qué., Canada   54 24N 79 27W   96
Rogoaguado, *Lake*: Bolivia   12 45S 65 45W   49
Rohtak: India   28 57N 76 38E   34 82
Rokan: *riv.*, Indonesia   01 30N 101 00E   38
Rokugo (Tama): *riv.*, Japan   35 31N 139 40E   121
Rolla: Mo., U.S.A.   37 56N 91 55W   98
Roma: Qld., Australia   26 32S 148 46E   41
Roma (Rome): Italy   41 53N 12 30E   27 79 116
Romain, *Cape*: S.C., U.S.A.   33 01N 79 23W   101
Romaine: *riv.*, Qué., Canada   51 00N 63 15W   97
Roman: Romania   46 56N 26 56E   78
Romanche *Fracture Zone*: Atlantic Ocean   02 00S 22 00W
                                                     3
ROMANIA   45 45N 24 30E   7 27 78 107
Romano, *Cape*: Fla., U.S.A.   26 50N 81 42W   101
Romanovka: U.S.S.R.   60 03N 30 42E   119
Romans-sur-Isère: France   45 03N 05 03E   71
Rome: Italy *see* Roma   41 53N 12 30E   27 79 116
Rome: Ga., U.S.A.   34 15N 85 10W   101
Romford: Gt. Ldn., England   51 35N 00 11E   112
Romney *Marsh*: Kent, England   51 00N 00 45E   59
Romny: U.S.S.R.   50 45N 33 30E   80
Romorantin: France   47 22N 01 44E   70
Rompin: Malaysia   02 42N 102 31E   105
Romsey: Hants., England   50 59N 01 30W   59
Romulus: Mich., U.S.A.   42 14N 83 23W   125
Rona: *is.*, Inv., Scotland   57 30N 05 45W   64
Ronay: *is.*, Inv., Scotland   57 30N 07 00W   64
Roncador, Serra do: *ra.*, Brazil   13 00S 51 45W   50
Ronda: Spain   36 45N 05 10W   77
Rondônia: *admin.*, Brazil   10 30S 63 30W   49
Rondorf: W.Germany   50 52N 06 58E   119
Rongan: China   25 15N 109 20E   85
Ronge, *Lac la*: Sask., Canada   55 00N 105 00W   92
Rongjiang: China   25 55N 108 39E   85
Rongxian: China   22 56N 110 32E   85
Ronne *Ice Shelf*: Antarctica   78 30S 60 00W   24
Ronsdorf: W.Germany   51 14N 07 12E   118
Ronse: Belgium   50 45N 03 36E   72
Roodepoort: Trans., Rep. of S.Africa   26 10S 27 53E   55
Roorkee: India   29 51N 77 54E   82
Roosendaal: Netherlands   51 32N 04 28E   72
Roosevelt Boulevard: *hwy.*, Pa., U.S.A.   40 00N 75 00W
                                                   122
Roosevelt *Dam*: Ariz., U.S.A.   33 42N 111 10W   91
Roosevelt *Island*: Antarctica   79 30S 162 00W   25
Root Portage: Ont., Canada   50 55N 91 23W   93
Rora *Head*: Ork. Is., Scotland   58 52N 03 26W   65
Roraima: *admin.*, Brazil   01 15N 61 00W   48
Roraima, *Monte*: S.America   05 14N 60 44W   48
Røros: Norway   62 35N 11 23E   74

Rošal': U.S.S.R. 55 40N 39 51E 80
Rosario: Argentina 33 00S 60 40W 52 104
Roscommon: Rosc., Irish Rep. 53 38N 08 11W 66 76
Roscommon: *admin.*, Irish Rep. 53 30N 08 00W 66
Roscrea: Tip., Irish Republic 52 57N 07 47W 67
Roseau: *riv.*, Canada/U.S.A. 48 45N 96 15W 98
Roseburg: Oreg., U.S.A. 43 13N 123 20W 90
Rosehearty: Aber., Scotland 57 42N 02 07W 65
Roseires *see* Ar-Ruṣayriṣ 11 51N 34 23E 53
Roselle: Ill., U.S.A. 41 57N 88 04W 124
Rosenheim: W.Germany 47 51N 12 07E 73
Rosetown: Sask., Canada 51 34N 107 59W 92
Rosetta *see* Rashīd 31 24N 30 25E 32
Roseville: Calif., U.S.A. 38 44N 121 19W 91
Roseville: Mich., U.S.A. 42 29N 83 05W 125
Roslavl': U.S.S.R. 53 57N 32 52E 80
Ross: *riv.*, Yukon, Canada 62 00N 131 45W 88
Ross & Cromarty: *admin.*, Scotland 57 30N 05 00W 64
Rossan *Point*: Don., Irish Republic 54 42N 08 48W 66
Rossendale, *Forest of*: Lancs., England 53 30N 02 15W 114
Ross *Ice Shelf*: Antarctica 81 30S 175 00W 25
Rossignol *Lake*: N.S., Canada 44 15N 65 00W 97
Ross *Island*: Antarctica 77 30S 168 00E 25
Rossland: B.C., Canada 49 03N 117 49W 89
Rosslare *Harbour*: Wex., Irish Republic 52 15N 06 15W 67
Rosslare *Point*: Wex., Irish Republic 52 20N 06 22W 67
Ross of Mull: *dist.*, Argyll., Scotland 56 15N 06 00W 64
Ross-on-Wye: Here. & Worcs., England 51 55N 02 35W 60
Rossoš': U.S.S.R. 50 12N 39 34E 80
Ross River: Yukon, Canada 62 02N 132 28W 88
Ross *Sea*: Antarctica 76 00S 175 00W 25
Rosthern: Sask., Canada 52 40N 106 20W 92
Rostock: E.Germany 54 06N 12 09E 26 73 78
Rostock: *admin.*, E.Germany 54 00N 12 30E 73
Rostov: U.S.S.R. 57 11N 39 25E 80
Rostov-na-Donu: U.S.S.R. 47 14N 39 42E 28 80
Roswell: N.Mex., U.S.A. 33 24N 104 32W 43 95
Rotbach: *riv.*, W.Germany 50 45N 06 45E 119
Rothaargebirge: *mtns.*, W.Germany 51 00N 08 15E 72
Rothbury: Northumb., England 55 19N 01 55W 63
Rother: *riv.*, England 51 00N 00 30E 59
Rotherham: S.Yorks., England 53 26N 01 20W 63 105
Rothes: Moray., Scotland 57 31N 03 13W 65
Rothesay: Bute., Scotland 55 51N 05 03W 62
Rothwell: Northants., England 52 25N 00 48W 58
Rothwell: W.Yorks., England 53 45N 01 29W 63 115
Rotorua: N.I., New Zealand 38 07S 176 17E 37 87
Rotterdam: Netherlands 51 55N 04 29E 26 72 107
Roubaix: France 50 42N 03 10E 72
Rouen: France 49 26N 01 05E 26 70
Rouge: *riv.*, Mich., U.S.A. 42 15N 83 00W 125
Roughty: *riv.*, Kerry, Irish Republic 51 45N 09 15W 67
Roundhay: W.Yorks., England 53 48N 01 26W 115
Roundup: Mont., U.S.A. 46 27N 108 33W 94
Rousay: *is.*, Ork. Is., Scotland 59 00N 03 00W 65
Rouyn: Qué., Canada 48 15N 79 00W 44 99
Rovaniemi: Finland 66 29N 25 40E 27 74
Rovelasca: Italy 45 40N 09 03E 116
Rovno: U.S.S.R. 50 37N 26 15E 28 78
Roxburgh: S.I., New Zealand 45 34S 169 21E 87
Roxburghshire: *admin.*, Scotland 55 15N 02 30W 63
Roxbury: Mass., U.S.A. 42 19N 71 03W 122
Roy, Glen: *val.*, Inv., Scotland 56 45N 04 45W 64
Royal Leamington Spa: War., England 52 18N 01 31W 59 115
Royal *National Park*: N.S.W., Australia 34 06S 151 06E 120
Royal Oak: Mich., U.S.A. 42 31N 83 08W 125
Royal Tunbridge Wells: Kent, England 51 08N 00 16E 59
Royan: France 45 38N 01 02W 70
Royston: Herts., England 52 03N 00 01W 59
Rožňava: Czechoslovakia 48 40N 20 32E 105
Rtiščevo: U.S.S.R. 52 16N 43 47E 80
Ruahine *Range*: N.I., New Zealand 40 00S 176 00E 87
Ruapehu, *Mount*: New Zealand 39 18S 175 36E 37 87
Rub 'al Khālī: *des.*, Saudi Arabia 20 00N 50 00E 10 33
Rubcovsk (Rubtsovsk): U.S.S.R. 51 33N 81 10E 29
Rubeženoje: U.S.S.R. 49 01N 38 23E 80
Rubha a' Mhail: *pt.*, Argyll., Scotland 55 56N 06 07W 64
Rubha Ardvule: *cape*, Inv., Scotland 57 15N 07 28W 64

Rubha Cóigeach: *cape*, R. & Crom., Scotland 58 06N 05 25W 64
Rubha Dubh: *cape*, Argyll., Scotland 56 32N 06 24W 64
Rubh' a' Geadha: *cape*, Argyll., Scotland 56 08N 06 09W 64
Rubha Hunish: *cape*, Inv., Scotland 57 42N 06 21W 64
Rubha Réidh: *cape*, R. & Crom., Scotland 57 52N 05 49W 64
Rubī: Spain 41 29N 02 02E 116
Rubtsovsk *see* Rubcovsk 51 33N 81 10E 29
Ruby *Ranges*: Yukon, Canada 61 00N 137 30W 88
Rucheng: China 25 34N 113 41E 85
Rüdersdorf: E.Germany 52 29N 13 50E 73
Rüdersdorf, Staatsforst: *for.*, E.Germany 52 15N 13 45E 117
Rudn'a: U.S.S.R. 50 48N 44 33E 80
Rudňany: Czechoslovakia 48 52N 20 40E 105
Rudnyj (Rudnyy): U.S.S.R. 52 57N 63 07E 29
Rudolf, *Lake*: Kenya 03 30N 36 00E 21 54
Rudolstadt: E.Germany 50 44N 11 20E 73
Rudong: China 32 19N 121 12E 84
Rueil: France 48 52N 02 11E 117
Ruffec: France 46 02N 00 12E 70
Rufiji: *riv.*, Tanzania 08 15S 37 45E 21 54
Rugao: China 32 23N 120 39E 84
Rugby: War., England 52 23N 01 15W 115
Rugeley: Staffs., England 52 46N 01 55W 58 115
Rügen: *is.*, E.Germany 54 30N 13 15E 73 78
Ruhr: *reg.*, W.Germany 7 26 118
Ruhr: *riv.*, W.Germany 51 15N 06 45E 118
Ruhrort: W.Germany 51 27N 06 44E 118
Ruhrschnellweg: *mtn.*, W.Germany 51 15N 07 15E 118
Ruian: China 27 49N 120 40E 85
Ruijin: China 25 47N 115 58E 85
Ruislip: Gt. Ldn., England 51 35N 00 25W 112
Rukwa, *Lake*: Tanzania 08 00S 32 15E 54
Rum: *riv.*, Minn., U.S.A. 46 00N 93 30W 98
Rumney: S.Glam., Wales 51 31N 03 07W 113
Rumoi: Japan 43 56N 141 39E 86
Ru'nan: China 33 01N 114 22E 84
Runcorn: Ches., England 53 20N 02 44W 58 114
Rupert: Idaho, U.S.A. 42 37N 113 41W 90
Rupert: *riv.*, Qué., Canada 51 15N 77 30W 96
Rupert House (Fort Rupert): Qué., Canada 51 29N 78 45W 96
Ruse: Bulgaria 43 50N 25 59E 27 79
Rush: Dublin, Irish Republic 53 32N 06 06W 66
Rushan: China 36 50N 121 29E 84
Rushden: Northants., England 52 17N 00 36W 59
Rushen, Slieve: *mtn.*, Ferm., N.Ireland 54 09N 07 37W 66
Russas: Brazil 04 56S 37 58W 50
Russell: Man., Canada 50 47N 101 17W 92
Russell: Kans., U.S.A. 38 54N 98 52W 94
Russellville: Ark., U.S.A. 35 17N 93 08W 100
Russian Soviet Federated Socialist Republic: *admin.*, U.S.S.R. 30 80 105
Rustavi: U.S.S.R. 41 33N 45 02E 28 105
Ruston: La., U.S.A. 32 32N 92 38W 100
Ruth: Nev., U.S.A. 36 17N 114 59W 91
Rutherglen: Lan., Scotland 55 50N 04 12W 62 113
Ruthin: Clwyd, Wales 53 07N 03 18W 60
Rutland: Vt., U.S.A. 43 37N 72 59W 99
Rutland: *admin.*, England. Absorbed into Leicestershire, 1974. 58
Ruvuma: *riv.*, Mozambique/Tanzania 11 30S 37 15E 21 54
Ruwenzori *Mountains*: Uganda 00 15N 30 00E 21 54
Ruzajevka: U.S.S.R. 54 04N 44 57E 81
RWANDA 01 45S 30 00E 21 54
Ryan, *Loch*: Scotland 55 00N 05 00W 62
Ryazan' *see* R'azan 54 38N 39 44E 28 80 107
Rybačij, Poluostrov: *pen.*, U.S.S.R. 69 45N 32 30E 74
Rybackoje: U.S.S.R. 59 50N 30 30E 119
Rybinsk (Shcherbakov): U.S.S.R. 58 03N 38 52E 28 80
Rybinskoje Vodochranilišče (Rybinskoye Vodokhranilishche): *res.*, U.S.S.R. 58 30N 38 30E 28 80
Rybnik: Poland 50 07N 18 30E 78
Ryde: N.S.W., Australia 33 49S 151 06E 120
Ryde: I. of W., England 50 44N 01 10W 59
Rye: E.Sussex, England 50 57N 00 44E 59
Ryhope: Tyne & Wear, England 54 52N 01 21W 63
Ryl'sk: U.S.S.R. 51 36N 34 43E 80

Types of map: Ocean pp. 1-5; Physical pp. 6-25; Human pp. 26-57; Topographic pp. 58-101; World pp. 102-111; Urban pp. 112-128.

Ryn-Peski: *des.*, U.S.S.R. 48 45N 50 00E 81
Ryōhaku Sanchi: *ra.*, Japan 36 00N 136 15E 86
Ryōtsu: Japan 38 05N 138 26E 86
Ryukyu *Islands*: E.China Sea 26 00N 127 00E 4 12 37
Ryukyu *Trench*: Philippine Sea 22 00N 130 00E 4
Rzeszów: Poland 50 04N 22 00E 78
Řžev (Rzhev): U.S.S.R. 56 16N 34 20E 28 80
Řžovka: U.S.S.R. 59 58N 30 30E 119

Saale: *riv.*, E.Germany 51 30N 11 45E 73
Saalfeld: E.Germany 50 39N 11 22E 73
Saarbrücken (Sarrebruck): W.Germany 49 15N 06 58E 26 72
Saaremaa (Ösel): *is.*, U.S.S.R. 58 15N 22 30E 75
Saariselkä: *hills*, Finland 68 15N 29 00E 74
Saarland: *admin.*, W.Germany 49 30N 06 45E 72
Saarlouis (Sarrelouis): W.Germany 49 19N 06 45E 72
Šabac: Yugoslavia 44 45N 19 41E 79
Sabadell: Spain 41 33N 02 07E 26 77 116
Sabah (British N.Borneo): *admin.*, Malaysia 05 15N 116 45E 39
Sabanalarga: Colombia 10 38N 74 55W 48
Sābarmati: *riv.*, India 23 15N 72 45E 82
Sabine: *riv.*, U.S.A. 31 15N 93 30W 100
Sabine, *Mount*: Antarctica 72 08S 169 10E 25
Sable, *Cape*: Fla., U.S.A. 25 08N 81 07W 101
Sabzi Mandi: India 28 41N 77 12E 120
Sachalin (Sakhalin): *is.*, U.S.S.R. 50 00N 143 00E 9 31
Sachigo: *riv.*, Ont., Canada 54 30N 90 45W 93
Sachsenwald: *wood*, W.Germany 53 30N 10 15E 119
Šachty (Shakhty): U.S.S.R. 47 42N 40 13E 28 80
Šachunja: U.S.S.R. 57 40N 46 37E 81
Saclay: France 48 44N 02 10E 117
Saco: Maine, U.S.A. 43 31N 70 26W 99
Sacramento: Calif., U.S.A. 38 32N 121 30W 43 91
Sacramento: *riv.*, Calif., U.S.A. 39 30N 121 45W 17 43 91
Sacramento *Mountains*: U.S.A. 33 00N 105 15W 95
Sá da Bandeira: Angola 14 55S 13 30E 55
Saddleback: *mtn.*, Cumbria, England 54 39N 03 03W 63
Sadiya: India 27 49N 95 38E 35
Sado: *is.*, Japan 38 00N 138 15E 37 86
Sado-kaikyō: *str.*, Japan 37 45N 138 30E 86
Saeki *see* Saiki 32 57N 131 54E 86
Şafaqis (Sfax): Tunisia 34 45N 10 43E 56
Säffle: Sweden 59 08N 12 55E 74
Safford: Ariz., U.S.A. 32 50N 109 43W 91
Saffron Walden: Essex, England 52 01N 00 15E 59
Safi: Morocco 32 20N 09 17W 56
Safonovo: U.S.S.R. 55 06N 33 15E 80
Saga: Japan 33 15N 130 18E 86
Sagami-nada: *gulf*, Japan 35 00N 139 15E 86
Sagami-wan: *bay*, Japan 35 15N 139 32E 121
Sägar: India 23 50N 78 44E 34 82
Sage: Wyo., U.S.A. 41 49N 110 58W 94
Saginaw: Mich., U.S.A. 43 25N 83 54W 45 98
Saginaw *Bay*: Mich., U.S.A. 43 45N 83 30W 98
Saguaro *National Monument*: Ariz., U.S.A. 32 00N 110 30W 91
Saguenay: *riv.*, Qué., Canada 48 15N 70 00W 17 44 96
Sagunto: Spain 39 41N 00 16W 104
Sahara *Desert*: N.Africa 20 56
Saharan Atlas: Algeria 33 00N 01 00E 20 56
Sahāranpur: India 29 58N 77 33E 34 82
Saharsa: India 25 54N 86 36E 83
Sahaswān: India 28 04N 78 45E 82
Sāhibganj: India 25 15N 87 38E 83
Sahiwāl (Montgomery): Pakistan 30 41N 73 11E 82
Saidpur: Bangladesh 25 48N 89 00E 35 83
Sài Gòn: S.Vietnam 10 46N 106 43E 38
Saiki (Saeki): Japan 32 57N 131 54E 86
Saimaa: *lake*, Finland 61 15N 28 00E 27 75
St. Abb's *Head*: Ber., Scotland 55 54N 02 08W 63
St. Agnes: Corn., England 50 18N 05 13W 61
St. Agnes: *is.*, I. of S., England 49 54N 06 21W 61
St. Agnes *Head*: Corn., England 50 19N 05 13W 61
St. Albans: Nfld., Canada 47 51N 55 50W 97
St. Albans: Herts., England 51 46N 00 21W 59 112
St. Albans: W.Va., U.S.A. 38 24N 81 53W 98

St. Alban's *Head*: Dorset, England 50 34N 02 04W 61
St. Amand-Mont-Rond: France 46 43N 02 29E 70
St. Andrews: Fife, Scotland 56 20N 02 48W 65
St. Andrews *Bay*: Fife, Scotland 56 15N 02 30W 65
St. Ann's *Head*: Dyfed, Wales 51 41N 05 10W 61
St. Anthony: Nfld., Canada 51 24N 55 37W 97
St. Anthony: Idaho, U.S.A. 43 58N 111 41W 90
St. Aubin: Channel Islands 49 12N 02 10W 61
St.-Augustin: *riv.*, Canada 51 45N 59 00W 96
St. Augustine: Fla., U.S.A. 29 54N 81 19W 101
St.-Augustin-Saguenay: Qué., Canada 51 14N 58 39W 97
St. Austell: Corn., England 50 20N 04 48W 61
St. Austell *Bay*: Corn., England 50 15N 04 30W 61
St. Bathans, *Mount*: S.I., New Zealand 44 44S 169 49E 87
St. Bees: Cumbria, England 54 29N 03 35W 62
St. Bees *Head*: Cumbria, England 54 31N 03 39W 62
St. Boniface: Man., Canada 49 54N 97 07W 42 93
St. Brides *Bay*: Dyfed, Wales 51 45N 05 00W 60
St. Brieuc: France 48 31N 02 45W 70
St. Catharines: Ont., Canada 43 10N 79 14W 99
St. Catherine's *Point*: I. of W., England 50 34N 01 18W 59
St. Christopher: *is. see* St. Kitts 17 30N 62 45W 47
St. Clair, *Lake*: Canada/U.S.A. 42 15N 82 30W 98
St. Clair Shores: Mich., U.S.A. 42 29N 82 54W 125
St. Cloud: France 48 51N 02 12E 117
St. Cloud: Minn., U.S.A. 45 34N 94 10W 43 98
St. Cloud, *Parc de*: France 48 50N 02 13E 117
St. Columb Major: Corn., England 50 26N 04 56W 61
Saint Croix: *is.*, Virgin Islands 17 45N 64 45W 47
St. Croix: *riv.*, U.S.A. 45 45N 92 30W 98
St. Cyr-l'École: France 48 48N 02 04E 117
St. David's: Dyfed, Wales 51 54N 05 16W 60
St. David's *Head*: Dyfed, Wales 51 55N 05 19W 60
St. David's *Island*: Bermuda 32 30N 64 45W 1
St. Denis: France 48 56N 02 21E 117
St. Dié: France 48 17N 06 57E 71
Ste.-Anne-de-Bellevue: Qué., Canada 46 24N 73 57W 122
Ste.-Geneviève: Qué., Canada 45 29N 73 52W 122
Ste. Geneviève-des-Bois: France 48 39N 02 19E 117
Ste. Hélène, *Île*: Qué., Canada 45 31N 73 32W 122
St. Elias *Mountains*: Yukon, Canada 60 30N 139 30W 88
Ste.-Rose: Qué., Canada 45 36N 73 47W 122
Saintes: France 45 44N 00 38W 70
Ste.-Thérèse: Qué., Canada 45 38N 73 50W 122
St. Étienne: France 45 26N 04 23E 26 71
St.-Félicien: Qué., Canada 48 38N 72 29W 96
St. Finan's *Bay*: Kerry, Irish Republic 51 45N 10 15W 67
St. Florent, *Golfe de*: Corsica, France 42 41N 09 18E 71
St. Flour: France 45 02N 03 05E 71
St. Francis: *riv.*, U.S.A. 35 30N 90 30W 100 100
St.-François: *riv.*, Qué., Canada 46 00N 72 45W 96
St.-François, *Lac*: Qué., Canada 45 45N 71 00W 96
St. Gallen: Switzerland 47 25N 09 23E 71
St. Gaudens: France 43 07N 00 44E 70
St. George: N.B., Canada 45 08N 66 50W 97
St. George: Utah, U.S.A. 37 06N 113 35W 91
St. George, *Cape*: Fla., U.S.A. 29 33N 85 00W 101
St. George's: Nfld., Canada 48 26N 58 31W 97
St. George's *Bay*: Nfld., Canada 48 15N 57 45W 97
St. George's *Channel*: Irish Republic/Wales 52 15N 05 45W 67
St. Germain, *Forêt de*: France 48 55N 02 05E 117
St.-Germain-en-Laye: France 48 53N 02 04E 70 117
St. Govan's *Head*: Dyfed, Wales 51 36N 04 55W 61
St. Helena: *is.*, S.Atlantic Ocean 15 58S 05 43W 3
St. Helena *Sound*: U.S.A. 32 15N 80 15W 101
St. Helens: Mers., England 53 28N 02 44W 63 114
St. Helens: Oreg., U.S.A. 45 52N 122 48W 90
St. Helier: Channel Islands 49 12N 02 07W 61
St.-Hyacinthe: Qué., Canada 45 38N 72 57W 96
St. Ignace, *Isle*: Ont., Canada 48 48N 87 55W 98
St. Ives: N.S.W., Australia 33 44S 151 10E 120
St. Ives: Cambs., England 52 20N 00 05W 59
St. Ives: Corn., England 50 12N 05 29W 61
St. James, *Cape*: B.C., Canada 51 58N 131 00W 89
St.-Jean: Qué., Canada 45 18N 73 16W 96
St. Jean-de-Luz: France 43 23N 01 39W 70
St. Jean-de-Maurienne: France 45 17N 06 21E 71
Saint John: N.B., Canada 45 16N 66 03W 44 97
Saint John: *riv.*, Canada/U.S.A. 46 30N 67 30W 96
St. John, *Cape*: Nfld., Canada 49 58N 55 29W 97

Types of map: Ocean pp. 1-5; Physical pp. 6-25; Human pp. 26-57; Topographic pp. 58-101; World pp. 102-111; Urban pp. 112-128.

St. John, *Lake*: Qué., Canada 48 30N 72 00W 44 96
St. John's: Nfld., Canada 47 34N 52 41W 44 97
St. Johns: *riv.*, Fla., U.S.A. 30 00N 81 30W 101
St. John's *Point*: Down, N.Ireland 54 14N 05 40W 66
St. Joseph: Mich., U.S.A. 42 05N 86 30W 98
St. Joseph: Mo., U.S.A. 39 45N 94 51W 43 94
St. Joseph: *riv.*, U.S.A. 42 00N 86 15W 98
St. Joseph, *Lake*: Ont., Canada 50 45N 90 45W 93
St. Junien: France 45 53N 00 54E 70
St. Just: Corn., England 50 07N 05 41W 61
St. Kilda: *is.*, Inv., Scotland 57 49N 08 36W 68
St. Kitts (St. Christopher): *is.*, Leeward Islands 17 30N 62 45W 47
St.-Lambert: Qué., Canada 45 29N 73 29W 122
St. Laurent: Qué., Canada 45 31N 73 42W 122
St. Laurent (St. Lawrence): *riv.*, Canada/U.S.A. 49 30N 73 30W 17 44 97 122
St. Lawrence (St. Laurent): *riv.*, Canada/U.S.A. 49 30N 66 30W 17 44 97 122
St. Lawrence, *Gulf of*: Canada 48 30N 62 00W 44 97
St. Lawrence *Island*: Bering Sea 63 15N 169 30W 22
St. Lawrence *Seaway*: Canada/U.S.A. 44 30N 75 30W 99
St. Lô: France 49 07N 01 05W 70
Saint-Louis: Senegal 16 01N 16 30W 57
St. Louis: Mo., U.S.A. 38 40N 90 15W 43 99
St. Louis, *Lac*: Qué., Canada 45 15N 73 45W 122
St. Lucia: *is.*, Windward Islands 13 45N 61 00W 47
St. Magnus *Bay*: Shet. Is., Scotland 60 15N 01 30W 65
St. Maixent-l'École: France 46 25N 00 12W 70
St. Malo: France 48 39N 02 00W 70
St. Malo, *Golfe de*: France 48 45N 02 30W 70
St. Martin, *Cape*: C.P., Rep. of S.Africa 32 42N 17 59E 55
St. Martin, *Lake*: Man., Canada 51 30N 98 15W 93
St. Martin's: *is.*, I. of S., England 49 58N 06 20W 61
St. Mary *Bay*: N.S., Canada 44 15N 66 00W 97
St. Marys: Pa., U.S.A. 41 27N 78 35W 99
St. Mary's: *is.*, I. of S., England 49 55N 06 20W 61
St. Mary's *Bay*: Nfld., Canada 46 45N 53 45W 97
St. Maur: France 48 48N 02 28E 117
St.-Maurice: *riv.*, Qué., Canada 47 15N 72 45W 96
St. Mawes: Corn., England 50 09N 05 01W 61
St. Médard-en-Jalles: France 44 54N 00 42W 70
St. Mellons: S.Glam., Wales 51 32N 03 07W 113
St. Michel: Qué., Canada 45 34N 73 37W 122
St. Mihiel: France 48 54N 05 33E 71
St. Moritz: Switzerland 46 30N 09 51E 71
St. Nazaire: France 47 17N 02 12W 70
St. Neots: Cambs., England 52 14N 00 17W 59
St. Ouen: France 49 02N 02 07E 117
St.-Pacôme: Qué., Canada 47 24N 69 58W 96
St. Paul: Alta., Canada 54 00N 111 18W 92
St. Paul: Minn., U.S.A. 45 00N 93 10W 43 98
St. Paul: *is.*, Indian Ocean 38 43S 77 29E 1
St.-Paul: *riv.*, Canada 52 15N 58 15W 97
St. Paul *Rocks*: N.Atlantic Ocean 00 23N 29 23W 3
St. Peter: Minn., U.S.A. 44 21N 93 58W 98
St. Peter Port: Channel Islands 49 27N 02 32W 61
St. Peter's: Channel Islands 49 13N 02 11W 61
St. Petersburg: Fla., U.S.A. 27 45N 82 40W 45 101
St. Pierre: *is.*, N.Atlantic Ocean 46 45N 56 15W 44 97
St. Pölten: Austria 48 12N 15 37E 73
St. Quentin: France 49 51N 03 17E 72
St. Servan-sur-Mer: France 48 38N 02 00W 70
St. Stephen: N.B., Canada 45 12N 67 18W 96
St. Thomas: Ont., Canada 42 46N 81 12W 99
St. Thomas: *is.*, Virgin Islands 18 30N 65 00W 47
St. Tropez: France 43 16N 06 39E 71
St. Vincent: *is.*, Windward Islands 13 15N 61 00W 47
St. Vincent, *Cape*, *see* São Vicente, *Cabo de* 37 01N 08 59W 26 77
Saipan: *is.*, Philippine Sea 15 12N 145 43E 4 12
Sajama: *mtn.*, Bolivia 18 06S 68 54W 49
Sajan *Mountains see* Eastern & Western Sayan *Mountains* 52 00N 96 00E 9 30
Sajnšand: Mongolia 44 55N 110 11E 36
Sak (Pa Sak): *riv.*, Thailand 15 30N 101 00E 35
Sakai: Japan 34 35N 135 28E 107
Sakai-minato: Japan 35 33N 133 15E 86
Sakākā: Saudi Arabia 29 59N 40 06E 33
Sakakawea, *Lake* (Garrison *Reservoir*): N.D., U.S.A. 47 30N 101 25W 17 42 94

Sakami: *riv.*, Qué., Canada 53 15N 75 30W 96
Sakami *Lake*: Qué., Canada 53 10N 77 00W 96
Sakata: Japan 38 55N 139 50E 86
Sakhalin: *is. see* Sachalin 50 00N 143 00E 9 31
Sakurai: Chiba, Japan 35 21N 139 55E 121
Sal: *riv.*, U.S.S.R. 47 30N 42 30E 80
Salado: *riv.*, Argentina 29 30S 61 15W 52
Salajar: *is.*, Indonesia 06 00S 120 30E 39
Salālah: Oman 17 00N 54 04E 33
Salamanca: Spain 40 58N 05 40W 26 77
Salaqi: China 40 38N 110 31E 84
Salavat: U.S.S.R. 53 21N 55 55E 29 81
Salawati: *is.*, Indonesia 01 00S 130 45E 39
Sala y Gomez: *is.*, S.Pacific Ocean 26 28S 105 28W 5
Sala y Gomez *Ridge*: S.Pacific Ocean 34 00S 97 00W 5
Salazar: Angola 09 18S 14 54E 54
Salcombe: Devon, England 50 13N 03 47W 61
Sale: Gt. Man., England 53 26N 02 19W 63 114
Salé: Morocco 34 04N 06 50W 56
Salechard (Salekhard): U.S.S.R. 66 33N 66 35E 30
Salem: India 11 38N 78 08E 34
Salem: Oreg., U.S.A. 44 56N 123 02W 42 90
Salem: Va., U.S.A. 37 17N 80 04W 101
Salembu *Islands*: Indonesia 05 45S 114 15E 38
Salen: Argyll., Scotland 56 43N 05 48W 64
Salerno: Italy 40 40N 14 46E 79
Salford: Gt. Man., England 53 30N 02 16W 63 114
Salgótarján: Hungary 48 05N 19 48E 79
Salgueiro: Brazil 08 04S 39 06W 50
Salida: Colo., U.S.A. 38 32N 106 00W 94
Salihli: Turkey 38 30N 28 09E 78
Salima: Malawi 13 47S 34 26E 54
Salina: Kans., U.S.A. 38 50N 97 37W 94
Salinas: Ecuador 02 13S 80 58W 48
Salinas: Calif., U.S.A. 36 40N 121 39W 91
Salinas Grandes: *salt lake*, Argentina 29 30S 65 00W 52
Saline: *riv.*, Ark., U.S.A. 33 15N 92 00W 100
Salisbury: Wilts., England 51 05N 01 48W 61
Salisbury: Rhodesia 17 50S 31 03E 55
Salisbury: Md., U.S.A. 38 22N 75 37W 99
Salisbury: N.C., U.S.A. 35 20N 80 30W 101
Salisbury *Plain*: Wilts., England 51 00N 01 45W 61
Salkar, Ozero: *lake*, U.S.S.R. 50 33N 51 40E 81
Sallyāna: Nepal 28 21N 82 11E 83
Sally Gap: *pass*, Wick., Irish Republic 53 08N 06 18W 67
Salmo: B.C., Canada 49 11N 117 16W 89
Salmon: Idaho, U.S.A. 45 11N 113 54W 90
Salmon: *riv.*, Idaho, U.S.A. 45 15N 115 30W 42 90
Salmon Arm: B.C., Canada 50 42N 119 16W 89
Salmon River *Mountains*: Idaho, U.S.A. 45 00N 115 00W 90
Salo: Finland 60 23N 23 10E 75
Salonika *see* Thessaloníki 40 38N 22 58E 27 79
Salop: *admin.*, England 52 30N 02 45W 60
Salpausselkä: *geog. reg.*, Finland 61 00N 26 30E 75
Salt: *riv.*, Ariz., U.S.A. 33 45N 110 30W 91
Salt: *riv.*, Mo., U.S.A. 39 45N 92 00W 98
Salta: Argentina 24 46S 65 28W 49
Salta: *admin.*, Argentina 25 15S 64 30W 49
Saltash: Corn., England 50 24N 04 12W 61
Saltcoats: Ayr., Scotland 55 38N 04 47W 62
Salt *Creek*: Ill., U.S.A. 41 51N 87 55W 124
Saltee *Islands*: Wex., Irish Republic 52 00N 06 30W 67
Salt Fork: *riv.*, Tex., U.S.A. 33 15N 100 30W 95
Salt Fork: *riv.*, U.S.A. 35 00N 100 15W 95
Saltillo: Mexico 25 03N 102 37W 46
Salt Lake City: Utah, U.S.A. 40 45N 111 53W 43 91
Salt *Lakes*: India 22 32N 88 27E 120
Saltney: Ches., England 53 10N 02 54W 114
Salto: Uruguay 31 27S 57 50W 52
Salton Sea: *lake*, Calif., U.S.A. 33 15N 115 45W 43 91
Salt River: N.W.T., Canada 60 04N 112 15W 92
Salt Wells: Nev., U.S.A. 39 23N 118 35W 91
Salur: India 18 31N 83 16E 83
Salvador (Bahia): Brazil 12 59S 38 31W 50
Salween (Ngo Chu): *riv.*, Burma/China 19 30N 97 30E 11 35
Salza: *riv.*, Austria 47 30N 15 00E 73
Salzburg: Austria 47 54N 13 03E 27 73
Salzgitter: W.Germany 52 20N 10 22E 73 105
Salzwedel: E.Germany 52 51N 11 10E 73

Sam: India   26 50N 70 30E   82
Sama de Langreo: Spain   43 18N 05 40W   77
Samar: *is.*, Philippines   12 00N 125 15E   12 38
Samara: *riv.*, U.S.S.R.   53 00N 51 45E   81
Samarinda: Indonesia   00 30S 117 09E   39
Samarkand: U.S.S.R.   39 40N 66 58E   29
Sâmarrâ': Iraq   34 12N 43 52E   33
Samâstipur: India   25 52N 85 47E   83
Sambalpur: India   21 28N 84 04E   83
Sambhal: India   28 35N 78 34E   82
Sâmbhar *Lake*: India   26 45N 75 00E   82
Sambor: U.S.S.R.   49 32N 23 11E   78
Sambre: *riv.*, Belgium/France   50 00N 03 45E   72
Sammamish, *Lake*: Wash., U.S.A.   47 30N 122 00W   126
Samoa *Islands*: S.Pacific Ocean   14 00S 171 00W   4
Sámos: *is.*, Greece   37 45N 26 58E   79
Samothráki (Samothrace): *is.*, Greece   40 15N 25 30E   79
Sampit: Indonesia   02 34S 112 59E   38
Samsun: Turkey   41 17N 36 22E   32
San'â': Yemen   15 23N 44 12E   33
Sanae: *rsch. stn.*, Antarctica   70 19S 02 22W   24
Sanaga: *riv.*, Cameroun   04 30N 10 45E   20
Sanana: *is.*, Indonesia   02 15S 126 00E   39
San Andreas *Fault*: Calif., U.S.A.   37 15N 122 15W   126
San Andreas *Lake*: Calif., U.S.A.   37 35N 122 25W   126
San Angelo: Tex., U.S.A.   31 28N 100 26W   95
San Antonio: Tex., U.S.A.   29 25N 98 30W   43 95
San Antonio: *riv.*, Tex., U.S.A.   28 30N 97 30W   95
San Antonio, *Cape*: Cuba   21 50N 84 57W   47
San Basilio: Italy   41 54N 12 35E   116
San Baudilio de Llobregat: Spain   41 21N 02 02E   116
San Bernardino: Calif., U.S.A.   34 07N 117 19W   43 91
San Bernardino Freeway: *hwy.*, Calif., U.S.A.
   34 00N 117 45W   127
San Blas, *Cape*: Fla., U.S.A.   29 40N 85 21W   46 101
San Bruno: Calif., U.S.A.   37 37N 122 24W   126
Sanbuzhen: China   22 20N 112 41E   85
San Carlos: Philippines   15 59N 120 22E   39
San Carlos: Calif., U.S.A.   37 30N 122 16W   126
San Carlos de Bariloche: Argentina   41 11S 71 23W   52
San Clemente *Island*: Calif., U.S.A.   32 53N 118 29W   91
San Cristóbal: Argentina   30 20S 61 14W   49
Sancti Spíritus: Cuba   21 56N 79 27W   47
San Cugat de Vallés: Spain   41 28N 02 05E   116
Sanda *Island*: Argyll., Scotland   55 18N 05 34W   62
Sandakan: Malaysia   05 52N 118 04E   39
Sanday: *is.*, Ork. Is., Scotland   59 15N 02 30W   65
Sanday *Sound*: Ork. Is., Scotland   59 00N 02 30W   65
Sandbach: Ches., England   53 09N 02 22W   58
Sandefjord: Norway   59 00N 10 15E   75
Sandhurst: Berks., England   51 19N 00 48W   59
San Diego: Calif., U.S.A.   32 43N 117 09W   43 91
Sandnes: Norway   58 51N 05 45E   74
San Donato Milanese: Italy   45 24N 09 16E   116
Sandoval: Ill., U.S.A.   38 38N 89 05W   98
Sandown: I. of W., England   50 39N 01 09W   59
Sand *Point*: Avon, England   51 22N 02 58W   113
Sandpoint: Idaho, U.S.A.   48 17N 116 33W   90
Sandray: *is.*, Inv., Scotland   56 45N 07 30W   64
Sandspit: B.C., Canada   53 14N 131 50W   89
Sand Springs: Okla., U.S.A.   36 09N 96 07W   95
Sandusky: Ohio, U.S.A.   41 27N 82 42W   98
Sandvika: Norway   59 54N 10 29E   75
Sandviken: Sweden   60 38N 16 50E   75
Sandwich: Kent, England   51 17N 01 20E   59
Sandwich *Bay*: Nfld., Canada   53 30N 57 15W   97
Sandy: Beds., England   52 08N 00 18W   59
Sandy: Utah, U.S.A.   40 36N 111 53W   91
Sandy: *riv.*, Qué., Canada   55 15N 68 30W   96
Sandy *Lake*: Ont., Canada   53 00N 92 45W   93
San Felipe: Chile   32 45S 70 30W   52
San Felipe: Mexico   31 03N 114 52W   46
San Felíu de Guixols: Spain   41 47N 03 02E   77
San Felix *Island*: S.Pacific Ocean   26 23S 80 05W   5
San Fermo: Italy   45 49N 09 02E   116
San Fernando: Argentina   34 26S 58 33W   128
San Fernando: Chile   34 40S 71 00W   52
San Fernando: Spain   36 28N 06 12W   77
San Fernando: Trinidad & Tobago   10 16N 61 28W   48
San Fernando de Apure: Venezuela   07 53N 67 15W   48
San Fernando de Henares: Spain   40 26N 03 32W   116

San Fernando *Reservoir*: Calif., U.S.A.   34 17N 118 28W
   127
San Fernando *Valley*: Calif., U.S.A.   34 15N 118 30W   127
Sanfjället *Nationalpark*: Sweden   63 00N 13 30E   74
Sanford: Fla., U.S.A.   28 49N 81 17W   101
Sanford: Maine, U.S.A.   43 25N 70 46W   99
Sanford: N.C., U.S.A.   35 29N 79 10W   101
San Francisco: Calif., U.S.A.   37 45N 122 27W   43 91 126
San Francisco: *riv.*, U.S.A.   33 30N 108 45W   95
San Francisco-Oakland Bay *Bridge*: Calif., U.S.A.
   37 49N 122 21W   126
San Gabriel: *riv.*, Calif., U.S.A.   33 45N 118 00W   127
San Gabriel *Mountains*: Calif., U.S.A.   34 15N 117 45W   127
Sangamner: India   19 37N 74 18E   82
Sangamon: *riv.*, Ill., U.S.A.   39 45N 89 15W   98
Sangay: *mtn.*, Ecuador   02 00S 78 20W   48
Sangerhausen: E.Germany   51 29N 11 18E   73
San Gervasio: Spain   41 24N 02 09E   116
Sanggan: *riv.*, China   39 45N 113 30E   84
Sangha: *riv.*, Congo   01 00N 16 45E   54
Sangihe: *is.*, Indonesia   03 30N 125 30E   39
San Giorgio Legnano: Italy   45 34N 08 55E   116
Sāngli: India   16 55N 74 37E   34
Sangre de Cristo *Mountains*: U.S.A.   37 15N 105 15W   95
Sangrūr: India   30 16N 75 50E   32
Sangüesa: Spain   42 34N 01 17W   70
Sanhe: China   39 59N 117 04E   84
Sanibel *Island*: Fla., U.S.A.   26 26N 82 10W   101
San Isidro: Argentina   34 29S 58 32W   128
Sanjianfang: China   39 55N 116 34E   121
Sanjiang: China   25 49N 109 30E   85
Sanjō: Japan   37 37N 138 57E   86
San Joaquin: *riv.*, Calif., U.S.A.   37 15N 120 45W   17 43 91
San Jorge: *Golfo*: Argentina   46 00S 66 00W   52
San José: Costa Rica   09 59N 84 04W   47
San Jose: Calif., U.S.A.   37 20N 121 55W   43 91
San Jose: *riv.*, N.Mex., U.S.A.   34 45N 107 15W   95
San José de Mayo: Uruguay   34 20S 56 42W   52
San Juan: Argentina   31 33S 68 31W   52
San Juan: Peru   15 22S 75 07W   49
San Juan: Puerto Rico   18 29N 66 08W   47
San Juan: *admin.*, Argentina   30 45S 68 30W   52
San Juan: *riv.*, U.S.A.   37 00N 110 00W   95
San Juan de los Morros: Venezuela   09 55N 67 21W   48
San Juan *Mountains*: U.S.A.   37 30N 106 45W   95
San Julián: Argentina   49 17S 67 45W   52
San Justo: Buenos Aires, Argentina   34 40S 58 32W   128
San Justo Desvern: Spain   41 23N 02 05E   116
Sankosh: *riv.*, Bhutan/India   26 45N 90 00E   83
Sānkrāil: India   22 33N 88 14E   120
Sankt Pauli: W.Germany   53 33N 09 58E   119
Sankt Pölten: Austria   48 12N 15 37E   78
Sankt Tönis: W.Germany   51 19N 06 29E   118
San Leandro: Calif., U.S.A.   37 43N 122 10W   126
San Lorenzo: Ecuador   01 17N 78 50W   48
San Lorenzo: Calif., U.S.A.   37 41N 122 08W   126
Sanlúcar de Barremeda: Spain   36 46N 06 21W   76
San Lucas, *Cape*: Mexico   22 50N 109 55W   17 46
San Luis: Argentina   33 20S 66 23W   52
San Luis: *admin.*, Argentina   34 00S 66 00W   52
San Luis, *Lake*: Bolivia   13 45S 64 15W   49
San Luis Obispo: Calif., U.S.A.   35 17N 120 40W   91
San Luis Obispo *Bay*: Calif., U.S.A.   35 00N 120 30W   91
San Luis Potosí: Mexico   22 09N 100 59W   46
San Luis Potosí: *admin.*, Mexico   23 00N 100 30W   46
San Manuel: Ariz., U.S.A.   32 36N 110 38W   91
San Marcos: Tex., U.S.A.   29 53N 97 56W   95
San Mateo: Calif., U.S.A.   37 33N 122 22W   126
San Mateo *Bridge*: Calif., U.S.A.   37 36N 122 12W   126
San Matías, *Golfo*: Argentina   41 30S 64 15W   52
San Miguel: Argentina   34 32S 58 42W   128
San Miguel: *riv.*, Bolivia   16 15S 62 45W   49
San Miguel de Tucumán: Argentina   26 49S 65 13W   49
San Miguel *Island*: Calif., U.S.A.   34 02N 120 23W   91
Sanming: China   26 15N 117 38E   85
Sannär (Sennar): Sudan   13 31N 33 38E   53
Sannazzaro de' Burgondi: Italy   45 06N 08 54E   107
San Nicolás de los Arroyos: Argentina   33 20S 60 13W   104
San Nicolas *Island*: Calif., U.S.A.   33 15N 119 30W   91
San Pablo: Mexico   19 40N 99 06W   128
San Pablo: Calif., U.S.A.   37 58N 122 21W   126

Types of map: Ocean pp. 1-5; Physical pp. 6-25; Human pp. 26-57; Topographic pp. 58-101; World pp. 102-111; Urban pp. 112-128.

San Pablo *Reservoir*: Calif., U.S.A.   37 55N 121 59W   126
San Patricio: N.Mex., U.S.A.   33 25N 105 20W   95
San Pédro: Ivory Coast   04 45N 06 37W   57
San Pedro: Mexico   19 16N 99 10W   128
San Pedro: Calif., U.S.A.   33 45N 118 19W   127
San Pedro: *riv.*, Ariz., U.S.A.   32 30N 110 30W   91
San Pedro, *Point*: Calif., U.S.A.   37 33N 122 33W   126
San Pedro *Bay*: Calif., U.S.A.   33 30N 118 00W   127
San Pedro *Channel*: Calif., U.S.A.   33 30N 118 30W   127
San Pedro Sula: Honduras   15 27N 88 02W   47
Sanquhar: Dumf., Scotland   55 22N 03 56W   62
San Rafael: Argentina   34 35S 68 24W   52
San Rafael: Calif., U.S.A.   37 58N 122 30W   126
San Rafael *Bay*: Calif., U.S.A.   37 57N 122 28W   126
San Remo: Italy   43 48N 07 46E   71
San Salvador: El Salvador   13 40N 89 10W   46
San Salvador de Jujuy: Argentina   24 11S 65 18W   49
San Sebastián: Spain   43 19N 01 59W   26 70 77
San Severo: Italy   41 41N 15 23E   79
Sansha: China   26 52N 120 15E   85
Sanshui: China   23 11N 112 53E   85
San Siro: Italy   45 29N 09 07E   116
Santa Ana: Bolivia   13 45S 65 35W   49
Santa Ana: El Salvador   14 00N 89 31W   46
Santa Ana: Calif., U.S.A.   33 46N 117 52W   91 127
Santa Ana: *riv.*, Calif., U.S.A.   33 45N 117 45W   127
Santa Ana Freeway: *hwy.*, Calif., U.S.A.   33 45N 118 00W
  127
Santa Barbara: Calif., U.S.A.   34 25N 119 42W   91
Santa Barbara *Channel*: Calif., U.S.A.   34 15N 120 00W   91
Santa Barbara *Island*: Calif., U.S.A.   33 29N 119 02W   91
Santa Barbara *Islands*: Calif., U.S.A.   33 30N 119 30W   91
Santa Catalina, *Gulf of*: Calif., U.S.A.   33 00N 118 00W   91
Santa Catalina *Island*: Calif., U.S.A.   33 23N 118 25W   91
Santa Catarina: *admin.*, Brazil   27 00S 51 30W   51
Santa Catarina, *Ilha de*: Brazil   27 30S 48 30W   51
Santa Clara: Cuba   22 25N 79 58W   47
Santa Clara: Mexico   19 32N 99 03W   128
Santa Clara: Calif., U.S.A.   37 21N 121 58W   91
Santa Coloma de Gramanet: Spain   41 27N 02 13E   116
Santa Cruz: Argentina   50 01S 68 31W   52
Santa Cruz: Bolivia   17 48S 63 10W   49
Santa Cruz: Calif., U.S.A.   36 58N 122 03W   91
Santa Cruz: *admin.*, Argentina   48 30S 70 15W   52
Santa Cruz: *riv.*, Argentina   50 15S 70 00W   52
Santa Cruz: *riv.*, Ariz., U.S.A.   32 30N 111 15W   91
Santa Cruz de Tenerife: Canary Islands   28 27N 16 14W
  6 56 106
Santa Cruz *Island*: Calif., U.S.A.   34 01N 119 43W   91
Santa Cruz *Islands*: S.Pacific Ocean   10 00S 166 30E   15
Santa Fe: Argentina   31 38S 60 43W   52
Santa Fe: N.Mex., U.S.A.   35 41N 105 57W   43 95
Santa Fe: *admin.*, Argentina   30 00S 60 45W   52
Santa Fe *Flood Control Basin*: Calif., U.S.A.
  34 07N 117 57W   127
Santa Isabel *see* Malabo   03 45N 08 48E   57
Santa Lucía: Mexico   19 21N 99 15W   128
Santa Maria: Brazil   29 40S 53 47W   51
Santa Maria: Calif., U.S.A.   34 57N 120 26W   91
Santa Maria di Leuca, *Capo*: Italy   39 48N 18 23E   79
Santa Marta: Colombia   11 18N 74 10W   48
Santa Marta, Sierra Nevada de: *mtns.*, Colombia
  10 45N 74 00W   48
Santa Monica: Calif., U.S.A.   34 01N 118 29W   127
Santa Monica Freeway: *hwy.*, Calif., U.S.A.
  34 00N 118 15W   127
Santa Monica *Mountains*: Calif., U.S.A.   34 00N 118 30W
  127
Santana do Livramento: Brazil   30 52S 55 30W   51
Santander: Spain   43 28N 03 48W   26 70 77
Santa Paula: Calif., U.S.A.   34 21N 119 04W   91
Santarém: Brazil   02 26S 54 42W   50
Santarém: Portugal   39 14N 08 40W   77
Santa Rosa: Argentina   36 37S 64 17W   52
Santa Rosa: Calif., U.S.A.   38 26N 122 43W   91
Santa Rosa: N.Mex., U.S.A.   34 57N 104 41W   95
Santa Rosa *Island*: Calif., U.S.A.   33 58N 120 06W   91
Santiago: Chile   33 30S 70 40W   52
Santiago: Dominican Rep.   19 30N 70 42W   47
Santiago de Compostela: Spain   42 52N 08 33W   26 77
Santiago de Cuba: Cuba   20 01N 75 49W   47

Santiago del Estero: Argentina   27 47S 64 16W   49
Santiago del Estero: *admin.*, Argentina   27 30S 63 30W   49
Santiago *Reservoir*: Calif., U.S.A.   33 47N 117 43W   127
Santi Nagar: India   28 40N 77 09E   120
Sāntipur: India   23 14N 88 29E   83
Santo Ângelo: Brazil   28 17S 54 15W   51
Santo Domingo (Ciudad Trujillo): Dominican Rep.
  18 30N 69 57W   47
San Tomé: Venezuela   08 58N 64 08W   104
San Tomé de Guayana *see* Ciudad Guayana
  08 22N 62 37W   48
Santoña: Spain   43 27N 03 26W   70
Sant' Onofrio: Italy   41 56N 12 21E   116
Santos: Brazil   23 56S 46 22W   51
Sanuki: Japan   35 15N 139 53E   121
San Vicente de Sarriá: Spain   41 22N 02 08E   116
Sanyuan: China   34 35N 108 54E   84
São Carlos: São Paulo, Brazil   22 02S 47 53W   51
Saoconago: Italy   45 36N 08 51E   116
São Francisco: *riv.*, Brazil   09 45S 38 00W   18 50
São João del Rei: Brazil   21 09S 44 16W   51
São José do Rio Prêto: Brazil   20 48S 49 23W   51
São José dos Campos: Brazil   23 07S 45 52W   51
São Leopoldo: Brazil   29 46S 51 09W   51
São Luís: Brazil   02 31S 44 16W   50
São Manuel: *riv.* see Teles Pires   09 30S 56 30W   50
Saône: *riv.*, France   46 15N 04 45E   26 71
São Paulo: Brazil   23 33S 46 39W   51 104
São Paulo: *admin.*, Brazil   22 30S 49 00W   51
São Roque, *Cabo*: Brazil   05 29S 35 16W   50
São Salvador do Congo: Angola   06 16S 14 15E   54
São Tomé: *is.*, Gulf of Guinea   00 15N 06 30E   57
São Vicente, *Cabo de* (St. Vincent, Cape): Portugal
  37 01N 08 59W   26 77
Sap, *Lake* (Tonle Sap): Khmer Rep.   12 45N 104 00E   12 38
Sapele: Nigeria   05 55N 05 46E   57
Sapporo: Japan   43 03N 141 21E   37 86
Sapulpa: Okla., U.S.A.   36 00N 96 07W   100
Saragossa *see* Zaragoza   41 39N 00 54W   26 77
Sarajevo: Yugoslavia   43 52N 18 26E   27 79
Saran': U.S.S.R.   49 46N 72 52E   29
Saranac: *riv.*, N.Y., U.S.A.   44 30N 73 45W   99
Saranac Lake: N.Y., U.S.A.   44 19N 74 10W   99
Saranap: Calif., U.S.A.   37 53N 122 06W   126
Sarandí: Argentina   34 41S 58 20W   128
Saransk: U.S.S.R.   54 11N 45 11E   28 81
Sarapul: U.S.S.R.   56 28N 53 48E   81
Sarasota: Fla., U.S.A.   27 20N 82 32W   45 101
Saratov: U.S.S.R.   51 34N 46 02E   28 81 107
Saravane: Laos   15 43N 106 25E   38
Sarawak: *admin.*, Malaysia   02 45N 112 45E   38
Sarbaj: U.S.S.R.   52 58N 63 07E   105
Sarcelles: France   49 00N 02 24E   117
Sarda: *riv.*, India   28 15N 80 30E   82
Sardanyola: Spain   41 29N 02 10E   116
Sardārshahr: India   28 30N 74 30E   82
Sardegna (Sardinia): *is.* & *Italian admin.*, Mediterranean
Sea   40 00N 09 00E   6 26 77
Sareks *Nationalpark*: Sweden   67 15N 17 45E   75
Sargans: Switzerland   47 03N 09 27E   71
Sargasso *Sea*: N.Atlantic Ocean   29 00N 64 00W   2
Sargodha: Pakistan   32 01N 72 40E   34 82
Sariwŏn: N.Korea   38 31N 125 44E   37 105
Šarja: U.S.S.R.   58 24N 45 30E   81
Sark: *is.*, Channel Islands   49 26N 02 22W   61
Sarmiento: Argentina   45 36S 69 05W   52
Sarnia: Ont., Canada   42 57N 82 24W   98 106
Saronno: Italy   45 38N 09 02E   116
Sarpinskaja Nizmennost': *plain*, U.S.S.R.   48 00N 46 00E   81
Sarpsborg: Norway   59 17N 11 06E   75
Sarrebourg: France   48 44N 07 03E   71
Sarrebruck *see* Saarbrücken   49 15N 06 58E   26
Sarreguemines: France   49 06N 07 03E   71
Sartène: Corsica   41 37N 08 59E   77
Sarthe: *riv.*, France   47 45N 00 30W   70
Sartrouville: France   48 57N 02 11E   117
Sasamat *Lake*: B.C., Canada   49 19N 122 53W   126
Sasarām: India   24 58N 84 01E   83
Sasebo: Japan   33 10N 129 43E   37 86
Saskatchewan: *admin.*, Canada   52 00N 105 00W   42 92
Saskatchewan: *riv.*, Canada   53 30N 103 30W   16 42 92

Types of map: Ocean pp. 1-5; Physical pp. 6-25; Human pp. 26-57; Topographic pp. 58-101; World pp. 102-111; Urban pp. 112-128.

Saskatoon: Sask., Canada 52 10N 106 40W	42 92	
Sasovo: U.S.S.R. 54 21N 41 54E	80	
Sassandra: Ivory Coast 04 58N 06 08W	57	
Sassandra: riv., Ivory Coast 05 30N 06 15W	57	
Sassari: Sardinia 40 43N 08 34E	26 77	
Sassnitz: E.Germany 54 32N 13 40E	73 75	
Satka: U.S.S.R. 55 03N 59 01E	81	
Satmala Hills: India 19 30N 79 00E	34	
Satna: India 24 33N 80 50E	34 82	
Sātpura Range: India 21 30N 77 00E	11 34 82	
SAUDI ARABIA 28 30N 35 15E	10 33 107	
Saugus: Mass., U.S.A. 42 27N 71 00W	122	
Saujon: France 45 41N 00 55W	70	
Sauk Centre: Minn., U.S.A. 45 43N 94 58W	98	
Saulte Ste. Marie: Ont., Canada 46 32N 84 20W	44 98 104	
Sault Ste. Marie: Mich., U.S.A. 46 29N 84 20W	44 98	
Saumlaki: Indonesia 07 59S 131 22E	39	
Saumur: France 47 16N 00 05W	70	
Sausalito: Calif., U.S.A. 37 51N 122 30W	126	
Sauveterre, Causse de: plat., France 44 15N 03 15E	71	
Sava: riv., Yugoslavia 44 45N 19 15E	27 79	
Savage River: Tas., Australia 41 38S 145 04E	105	
Savannah: Ga., U.S.A. 32 04N 81 07W	45 101	
Savannah: Tenn., U.S.A. 35 14N 88 15W	100	
Savannah: riv., U.S.A. 33 00N 81 30W	45 101	
Savannakhet: Laos 16 34N 104 45E	38	
Save: riv., Mozambique/Rhodesia 21 15S 34 00E	21 55	
Savona: Italy 44 18N 08 28E	71	
Savonlinna: Finland 61 52N 28 51E	74	
Savu Sea: Indonesia 09 30S 121 45E	13	
Sawai Mādhopur: India 26 00N 76 28E	82	
Sawbill: Nfld., Canada 53 37N 66 23W	97	
Sawel: mtn., Lon., N.Ireland 54 49N 07 03W	66	
Saxman: Alaska, U.S.A. 55 19N 131 36W	89	
Saxmundham: Suff., England 52 13N 01 29E	59	
Sazonovo: U.S.S.R. 59 04N 35 14E	80	
Sca Fell: mtn., Cumbria, England 54 27N 03 14W	62	
Scalasaig: Argyll., Scotland 56 04N 06 12W	64	
Scalloway: Shet. Is., Scotland 60 08N 01 17W	65	
Scalpay: is., Inv., Scotland 57 15N 05 45W	64	
Scapa Flow: bay, Ork. Is., Scotland	65	
Scarba: is., Argyll., Scotland 56 00N 05 30W	64	
Scarborough: Ont., Canada 43 44N 79 16W	125	
Scarborough: N. Yorks., England 54 17N 00 24W	63	
Scariff Island: Kerry, Irish Republic 51 44N 10 15W	67	
Scarp: is., R. & Crom., Scotland 58 00N 07 00W	64	
Scavaig, Loch: Inv., Scotland 57 00N 06 00W	64	
Sceaux: France 48 47N 02 18E	117	
Sceaux, Parc des: France 48 46N 02 18E	117	
Schaalsee: lake, E.Germany/W.Germany 53 30N 10 45E	73	
Schaffhausen: Switzerland 47 42N 08 38E	71	
Schaumburg: Ill., U.S.A. 42 02N 88 00W	124	
Schefferville (Knob Lake): Qué., Canada 54 50N 67 00W	44 96 104	
Schenectady: N.Y., U.S.A. 42 48N 73 57W	99	
Schiehallion: mtn., Perth., Scotland 56 40N 04 08W	65	
Schieldaig: R. & Crom., Scotland 57 31N 05 38W	64	
Schlei: riv., W.Germany 54 30N 09 45E	73	
Schleswig: W.Germany 54 32N 09 34E	72 76	
Schleswig-Holstein: admin., W.Germany 53 45N 09 00E	73	
Schönebeck: E.Germany 52 01N 11 45E	73	
Schulzendorf: E.Germany 52 22N 13 35E	117	
Schuyler: Nebr., U.S.A. 41 27N 97 04W	94	
Schuylkill: riv., Pa., U.S.A. 40 00N 75 15W	122	
Schuylkill Expressway: hwy., Pa., U.S.A. 40 00N 75 15W	122	
Schwäbisch Gmünd: W.Germany 48 49N 09 48E	73	
Schwäbisch Hall: W.Germany 49 07N 09 45E	73	
Schwandorf in Bayern: W.Germany 49 20N 12 07E	73	
Schwaner Mountains: Indonesia 00 15S 112 45E	14 39	
Schwarze Elster: riv., E.Germany 51 45N 13 15E	73	
Schwarzen Berge, Die: mtns., W.Germany 53 15N 09 45E	119	
Schwedt: E.Germany 53 04N 14 18E	107	
Schweinfurt: W.Germany 50 03N 10 16E	73	
Schwelm: W.Germany 51 17N 07 18E	118	
Schwenningen: W.Germany 48 03N 08 32E	72	
Schwerin: E.Germany 53 38N 11 25E	73	
Schweriner See: lake, E.Germany 53 30N 11 15E	73	

Schwerte: W.Germany 51 26N 07 34E	118	
Scilly, Isles of: England 49 45N 06 15W	26 61	
Ščokino: U.S.S.R. 54 01N 37 31E	80	
Ščolkovo: U.S.S.R. 55 55N 38 00E	80	
Ščors: U.S.S.R. 51 49N 31 59E	80	
Scotia Ridge: S.Atlantic Ocean 53 00S 48 00W	19	
Scotia Sea: Southern Ocean 56 00S 35 00W	37	
SCOTLAND	26 68	
Scott Base: rsch. stn., Antarctica 70 51S 166 46E	25	
Scott Islands: B.C., Canada 50 48N 128 38W	89	
Scottsbluff: Nebr., U.S.A. 41 52N 103 40W	94	
Scourie: Suther., Scotland 58 20N 05 08W	64	
Scrabster: Caith., Scotland 58 37N 03 34W	65	
Scranton: Pa., U.S.A. 41 25N 75 40W	45 99	
Scridain, Loch: Argyll., Scotland 56 15N 06 00W	64	
Scunthorpe: Humb., England 53 36N 00 38W	63 105	
Scurdie Ness: cape, Angus, Scotland 56 41N 02 25W	65	
Seadrift: Tex., U.S.A. 28 30N 96 47W	100	
Seaford: E. Sussex, England 50 46N 00 06E	59	
Seaford: Del., U.S.A. 38 39N 75 35W	99	
Seaforth, Loch: Scotland 57 45N 06 30W	64	
Seaham: Dur., England 54 52N 01 21W	63	
Sea Island: B.C., Canada 49 00N 123 00W	126	
Sea Islands: Ga., U.S.A. 31 30N 81 00W	101	
Seal: riv., Man., Canada 58 45N 95 30W	93	
Sealdah: India 22 32N 88 23E	120	
Seal Lake: Nfld., Canada 54 15N 61 30W	97	
Searsport: Maine, U.S.A. 44 27N 68 56W	99	
Seascale: Cumbria, England 54 24N 03 29W	62	
Seaside: Oreg., U.S.A. 46 00N 123 56W	90	
Seaton: Devon, England 50 43N 03 05W	61	
Seattle: Wash., U.S.A. 47 36N 122 20W	42 90 104 126	
Šebekino: U.S.S.R. 50 25N 36 56E	80	
Sechura Desert: Peru 05 54S 80 30W	48	
Secretary Island: S.I., New Zealand 45 00S 166 45E	87	
Sedalia: Mo., U.S.A. 38 42N 93 15W	98	
Sedan: France 49 42N 04 57E	71	
Sedbergh: Cumbria, England 54 20N 02 31W	63	
Seddonville: S.I., New Zealand 41 33S 172 00E	87	
Sedgley: W.Mid., England 52 33N 02 08W	115	
Ségou: Mali 13 28N 06 18W	57	
Segovia: Spain 40 57N 04 07W	77	
Segre: riv., Spain 42 00N 01 15E	77	
Segura: riv., Spain 38 15N 02 00W	77	
Sehore: India 23 12N 77 08E	82	
Seil: is., Argyll., Scotland 56 15N 05 30W	64	
Seinäjoki: Finland 62 45N 22 55E	74	
Seine: riv., France 49 15N 00 15E	6 26	
Seine, Baie de la: France 49 30N 00 30W	70	
Seis de Septiembre see Morón 34 39S 58 38W	128	
Seixal: Portugal 38 38N 09 06W	104	
Sekondi: Ghana 04 59N 01 43W	57	
Šeksna: U.S.S.R. 59 13N 38 30E	80	
Selatan, Cape: Indonesia 04 09S 114 36E	39	
Selb: W.Germany 50 11N 12 08E	73	
Selby: N.Yorks., England 53 48N 01 04W	63 115	
Sel'co: U.S.S.R. 53 22N 34 06E	80	
Selemdža (Selemdzha): riv., U.S.S.R. 52 30N 130 30E	31	
Selenge Mörön: riv., Mongolia 49 30N 102 30E	30	
Sélestat: France 48 16N 07 28E	71	
Šelichov (Shelikhov) Bay: U.S.S.R. 60 00N 158 00E	31	
Selkirk: Man., Canada 50 10N 96 52W	93	
Selkirk: Selk., Scotland 55 33N 02 50W	63	
Selkirkshire: admin., Scotland 55 30N 03 00W	63	
Selly Oak: W.Mid., England 52 24N 01 58W	115	
Selma: Ala., U.S.A. 32 25N 87 01W	101	
Selsey: W.Sussex, England 50 44N 00 48W	59	
Selsey Bill: cape, Sussex, England 50 43N 00 48W	59	
Selvas: geog. reg., Brazil 05 00S 64 15W	48	
Selwyn Lake: Canada 60 00N 104 15W	92	
Selwyn Mountains: Yukon, Canada 63 00N 131 00W	16 88	
Selwyn Range: Qld., Australia 21 30S 140 30E	41	
Semarang: Indonesia 06 58S 110 29E	38	
Semenovskoje: U.S.S.R. 55 41N 37 32E	119	
Seminoe Reservoir: Wyo., U.S.A. 42 10N 106 55W	94	
Seminole: Okla., U.S.A. 35 14N 96 41W	100	
Semipalatinsk: U.S.S.R. 50 28N 80 13E	29	
Semnān: Iran 35 30N 53 25E	33	
Senago: Italy 45 35N 09 07E	116	
Sénart, Forêt de: France 48 30N 02 15E	117	

Types of map: Ocean pp. 1-5; Physical pp. 6-25; Human pp. 26-57; Topographic pp. 58-101; World pp. 102-111; Urban pp. 112-128.

Sence: *riv.*, Leics., England   52 30N 01 30W   115
Sendai: Kagoshima, Japan   31 49N 130 18E   86
Sendai: Miyagi, Japan   38 15N 140 53E   37 86
Seneca *Lake*: N.Y., U.S.A.   42 30N 76 45W   99
SENEGAL   14 00N 14 00W   20 57 106
Sénégal: *riv.*, W.Africa   15 30N 13 00W   20 57
Senftenberg: E.Germany   51 31N 14 01E   73
Sengilej: U.S.S.R.   53 58N 48 46E   81
Senhor do Bonfim: Brazil   10 27S 40 11W   50
Senja: *is.*, Norway   69 15N 17 20E   74
Sennar *see* Sannār   13 31N 33 38E   53
Senneterre: Qué., Canada   48 24N 77 16W   99
Senno: U.S.S.R.   54 49N 29 43E   80
Sens: France   48 12N 03 18E   71
Sentinel *Range*: Antarctica   78 00S 87 00W   24
Seoni: India   22 06N 79 36E   82
Seoul *see* Sŏul   37 33N 126 58E   37
Šepetovka: U.S.S.R.   50 11N 27 04E   78
Sepik: *riv.*, Terr. of New Guinea   04 00S 142 45E   14
Septentrional, Meseta: *plat.*, Spain   41 15N 04 30W   77
Sept-Iles: Qué., Canada   50 12N 66 23W   44 97
Sept Iles, Les: *is.*, France   48 53N 03 28W   70
Sepulveda Dam *Recreation Area*: Calif., U.S.A.
    34 10N 118 29W   127
Sequoia *National Park*: Calif., U.S.A.   36 30N 118 30W   91
Seraing: Belgium   50 37N 05 31E   105
Serampore: India   22 45N 88 21E   120
Serang: Indonesia   06 07S 106 09E   38
Serdobsk: U.S.S.R.   52 28N 44 13E   80
Seregno: Italy   45 39N 09 12E   116
Seremban: Malaysia   02 42N 101 54E   38
Sergač: U.S.S.R.   55 32N 45 28E   81
Sergipe: *admin.*, Brazil   10 30S 37 30W   50
Seria: Brunei   04 39N 114 23E   38
Sérigny: *riv.*, Qué., Canada   55 45N 69 15W   96
Sernovodsk: U.S.S.R.   53 56N 51 17E   81
Serov: U.S.S.R.   59 29N 60 31E   29 81 105
Serowe: Botswana   22 25S 26 44E   55
Serpa Pinto: Angola   14 36S 17 48E   54
Serpentine: *riv.*, B.C., Canada   49 10N 122 45W   126
Serpuchov (Serpukhov): U.S.S.R.   54 55N 37 25E   28 80
Serra da Mantiqueira: *ra.*, Brazil   22 15S 45 15W   51
Serra de Maracaju: *ra.*, Brazil   23 45S 55 30W   51
Serra do Cachimbo: *ra.*, Brazil   08 45S 55 30W   50
Serra do Espinhaço: *ra.*, Brazil   18 15S 43 45W   51
Serra do Mar: *ra.*, Santa Catarina, Brazil   26 15S 49 15W   51
Serra do Paranapiacaba: *ra.*, Brazil   24 30S 49 15W   51
Serra do Roncador: *ra.*, Brazil   13 00S 51 45W   50
Serra dos Carajás: *ra.*, Brazil   05 15S 51 15W   50
Serra dos Parecis: *ra.*, Brazil   13 00S 60 30W   18 49
Serra do Tombador: *ra.*, Brazil   12 15S 57 30W   50
Sérrai: Greece   41 03N 23 33E   27 79
Serranias del Burro: *mtns.*, Mexico   29 00N 102 00W   95
Serra Paranapiacaba: *ra.*, Brazil   24 30S 49 15W   51
Sertão: *geog. reg.*, Brazil   10 00S 40 30W   50
Sesto (Sesto San Giovanni): Italy   45 32N 09 14E   71 116
Setagaya: Japan   35 37N 139 38E   121
Sète: France   43 25N 03 43E   71
Sete Lagoas: Brazil   19 27S 44 14W   51
Sétif: Algeria   36 11N 05 24E   56 77
Setiles: Spain   40 44N 01 37W   105
Seto-naikai (Inland *Sea*): Japan   34 00N 133 00E   86
Settecamini: Italy   41 56N 12 37E   116
Settle: N.Yorks., England   54 04N 02 16W   63
Setúbal: Portugal   38 31N 08 54W   77
Seul, *Lac*: Ont., Canada   50 15N 92 30W   93
Sevastopol': U.S.S.R.   44 36N 33 32E   28
Seven *Heads*: Cork, Irish Republic   51 34N 08 42W   67
Sevenoaks: Kent, England   51 16N 00 12E   59 112
Severn: *riv.*, Ont., Canada   54 30N 89 45W   44 93
Severn: *riv.*, England/Wales   51 45N 02 00W   61 113
Severnaja Zeml'a: *is.*, U.S.S.R.   79 00N 95 00E   23
Severočeský: *admin.*, Czechoslovakia   50 45N 15 30E   73
Severodvinsk: U.S.S.R.   64 34N 39 50E   7
Severomoravský: *admin.*, Czechoslovakia   49 45N 17 45E
    73
Severomorsk: U.S.S.R.   69 05N 33 30E   74
Severo-Zadonsk: U.S.S.R.   54 00N 38 23E   80
Seveso: *riv.*, Italy   45 38N 09 08E   116
Sevier: *riv.*, Utah, U.S.A.   39 15N 112 30W   91
Sevier *Lake*: Utah, U.S.A.   38 54N 113 09W   91

Sevilla: Colombia   04 16N 75 58W   48
Sevilla (Seville): Spain   37 24N 05 59W   26 77
Sèvres: France   48 50N 02 13E   117
Seward: Nebr., U.S.A.   40 55N 97 06W   94
Seward *Park*, Wash., U.S.A.   47 33N 122 15W   126
Seward *Peninsula*: Alaska, U.S.A.   65 30N 164 00W   16
Seychelles: *is.*, Indian Ocean   04 30S 55 30E   1 10
Seychelles–Mauritius *Plateau* (Seychelles *Ridge*): Indian
    Ocean   10 00S 60 00E   1
Seymour: Tex., U.S.A.   33 35N 99 16W   95
Seymour *Creek*: B.C., Canada   49 19N 123 00W   126
Seymour Heights: B.C., Canada   119 19N 123 00W   126
Sfax *see* Şafaqis   34 45N 10 43E   56
's-Gravenhage (Den Haag, The Hague): Netherlands
    52 05N 04 16E   26 72
Sgritheal, Ben: *mtn.*, Inv., Scotland   57 10N 05 33W   64
Sgurr Mór: *mtn.*, R. & Crom., Scotland   57 41N 04 59W   64
Sgurr na Ciche: *mtn.*, Inv., Scotland   57 01N 05 25W   64
Sha: *riv.*, China   39 58N 116 38E   121
Shabani: Rhodesia   20 20S 30 05E   55
Shackleton *Ice Shelf*: Antarctica   66 00S 100 00E   25
Shackleton *Range*: Antarctica   81 00S 26 00W   24
Shaftesbury: Dorset, England   51 01N 02 12W   61
Shāhābād: India   27 38N 79 57E   82
Shahdara: India   28 40N 77 17E   120
Shahdol: India   23 13N 81 32E   83
Shahe: China   36 50N 114 29E   84
Shāhjahānpur: India   27 53N 79 55E   34 82
Shāhpura: India   27 23N 75 58E   82
Shāhpura: India   25 38N 75 01E   82
Shāhrūd: Iran   36 25N 55 00E   33
Shājāpur: India   23 27N 76 21E   82
Shakhty *see* Šachty   47 42N 40 13E   28 80
Shaki: Nigeria   08 39N 03 25E   57
Shamattawa: Man., Canada   55 51N 92 05W   93
Shāmli: India   29 27N 77 18E   82
Shamrock: Tex., U.S.A.   35 13N 100 15W   95
Shandong (Shantung): *admin.*, China   36 00N 118 00E
    36 84
Shandong (Shantung) *Peninsula*: China   37 15N 121 30E
    37 84
Shangcheng: China   31 48N 115 24E   84
Shangch'iu *see* Shangqiu   34 23N 115 37E   36 84
Shangchuandao: *is.*, China   21 45N 112 45E   85
Shanggan: China   25 56N 119 29E   85
Sanggao: China   28 18N 114 54E   85
Shanghai: China   31 14N 121 30E   37 84 105 121
Shanghai Shi: *admin.*, China   30 45N 121 45E   37 85
Shanghang: China   25 02N 116 29E   85
Shanghe: China   37 19N 117 10E   84
Shangjao *see* Shangrao   28 28N 117 56E   36 85
Shangjin: China   33 12N 109 57E   84
Shanglin: China   23 28N 108 33E   85
Shangqiu (Shangch'iu): China   34 23N 115 37E   36 84
Shangrao (Shangjao): China   28 28N 117 56E   36 85
Shangshui: China   33 39N 114 39E   36 84
Shangsi: China   22 15N 108 05E   85
Shangxian: China   33 51N 109 44E   84
Shangyou: China   25 55N 114 30E   85
Shanhaiguan: China   40 00N 119 50E   84
Shanklin: I. of W., England   50 38N 01 10W   59
Shannon: *riv.*, Irish Rep.   53 00N 08 00W   26 67
Shannon, *Mouth of the*: Irish Republic   52 30N 09 30W   67
Shannon *Airport*: Clare, Irish Rep.   52 42N 08 57W   67
Shan *Plateau*: Burma   21 30N 98 45E   11 35
Shansi: *admin.*, *see* Shānxī   37 45N 112 15E   36 84
Shantou (Swatow): China   23 23N 116 41E   36 85
Shantung: *admin.*, *see* Shandong   36 00N 118 00E   36 84
Shantung *Peninsula see* Shandong *Peninsula*
    37 15N 121 30E   37 84
Shānxī (Shansi): *admin.*, China   37 45N 112 15E   36 84
Shānxī (Shensi): *admin.*, China   35 45N 109 30E   36 84
Shanyin: China   39 35N 112 51E   84
Shaoguan (Shaokuan): China   24 50N 113 31E   36 85
Shaohsing *see* Shaoxing   30 01N 120 30E   37 85
Shaokuan *see* Shaoguan   24 50N 113 31E   36 85
Shaowu: China   27 20N 117 28E   85
Shaoxing (Shaohsing): China   30 01N 120 30E   37 85
Shaoyang: China   27 12N 111 20E   36 85
Shap: Cumbria, England   54 32N 02 41W   63
Shapinsay: *is.*, Ork. Is., Scotland   59 00N 02 45W   65

Types of map: Ocean pp. 1-5; Physical pp. 6-25; Human pp. 26-57; Topographic pp. 58-101; World pp. 102-111; Urban pp. 112-128.

Shari-dake: *mtn.*, Japan 43 55N 144 50E	87	
Sharja *see* Ash Shāriqah 25 20N 55 26E	33	
Sharon: Pa., U.S.A. 41 16N 80 30W	99	
Sharpnose *Points*: Corn., England 50 55N 04 34W	61	
Sharp Park: Calif., U.S.A. 37 37N 122 29W	126	
Shashi: China 30 19N 112 20E	36 85	
Shasta, *Mount*: Calif., U.S.A. 41 25N 122 12W	17 43 90	
Shasta *Lake*: Calif., U.S.A. 40 45N 122 15W	91	
Shatsky *Rise*: N.Pacific Ocean 35 00N 160 00E	4	
Shattuck: Okla., U.S.A. 36 16N 99 53W	95	
Shaunavon: Sask., Canada 49 40N 108 25W	92	
Shaw: Gt. Man., England 53 35N 02 06W	114	
Shawinigan: Qué., Canada 46 33N 72 45W	44 96	
Shawnee: Okla., U.S.A. 35 20N 96 55W	100	
Shawville: Ont., Canada 45 36N 76 30W	104	
Shaxian: China 26 24N 117 42E	85	
Shayang, *Lake*: China 33 15N 119 45E	84	
Shcherbakov *see* Rybinsk 58 03N 38 52E	28 80	
Shebele: *riv.*, Ethiopia/Somali Rep. 06 15N 42 30E	53	
Sheboygan: Wis., U.S.A. 43 46N 87 44W	98	
Sheeffry *Hills*: Mayo, Irish Republic 53 30N 09 30W	66	
Sheelin, *Lough*: Irish Republic 53 45N 07 15W	66	
Sheep Haven: *bay*, Don., Irish Republic 55 00N 07 45W	66	
Sheet Harbour: N.S., Canada 44 56N 62 31W	97	
Sheffield: S.Yorks., England 53 23N 01 30W	26 63 105	
Sheffield: Ala., U.S.A. 34 46N 87 41W	100	
Shefford: Beds., England 52 02N 00 20W	59	
Shekhūpura: Pakistan 31 42N 74 08E	82	
Shelby: Mont., U.S.A. 48 30N 111 51W	90	
Shelbyville: Tenn., U.S.A. 35 29N 86 28W	101	
Sheldon: W.Mid., England 52 27N 01 47W	115	
Shelikhov *Bay see* Šelichov Bay 60 00N 158 00E	31	
Shelley: Idaho, U.S.A. 43 23N 112 07W	90	
Shellhaven: Essex, England 51 32N 00 31E	107 112	
Shelton: Wash., U.S.A. 47 13N 123 06W	90	
Shenandoah: *riv.*, U.S.A. 39 00N 77 45W	99	
Shenchi: China 39 05N 112 18E	84	
Shengxian: China 29 36N 120 48E	85	
Shengze: China 30 55N 120 39E	84	
Shenmu: China 38 52N 110 19E	84	
Shenqiu: China 33 24N 115 02E	84	
Shensi *see* Shānxī 35 45N 109 30E	36 84	
Shenyang (Fengt'ien, Mukden): China 41 48N 123 30E	37 105	
Sheopur: India 25 41N 76 42E	82	
Sheoraphuli: India 22 47N 88 19E	120	
Shepparton: Vic., Australia 36 25S 145 26E	41	
Sheppey, *Isle of*: Kent, England 51 25N 00 50E	59	
Shepshed: Leics., England 52 46N 01 17W	58 115	
Shepton Mallet: Som., England 51 12N 02 33W	61	
Sherborne: Dorset, England 50 57N 02 31W	61	
Sherbro *Island*: Sierra Leone 07 30N 12 30W	57	
Sherbrooke: Qué., Canada 45 24N 71 54W	44 96	
Sheridan: Wyo., U.S.A. 44 48N 106 58W	94	
Sheringham: Norf., England 52 57N 01 12E	59	
Sherkin *Island*: Cork, Irish Republic 51 15N 09 15W	67	
Sherman: Tex., U.S.A. 33 38N 96 36W	100	
Sherpur: Bogra, Bangladesh 24 40N 89 29E	83	
Sherpur: Mymensingh, Bangladesh 25 00N 90 01E	83	
Sherridon: Man., Canada 55 07N 101 05W	92	
's-Hertogenbosch: Netherlands 51 41N 05 19E	72	
Sheslay: B.C., Canada 58 16N 131 48W	88	
Shetland *Islands*: Scotland 60 15N 01 15W	26 65	
Shexian: China 29 50N 118 26E	85	
Sheyenne: riv., N.D., U.S.A. 47 45N 98 45W	94	
Shiant, *Sound of*: R. & Crom., Scotland 57 45N 06 15W	64	
Shiant *Islands*: Lewis, Scotland 57 54N 06 21W	64	
Shibetsu: Japan 44 10N 142 23E	86	
Shibh Jazīrat Sīnā (Sinai *Peninsula*): Egypt 29 15N 33 30E	10 32	
Shibīn al Kawm: Egypt 30 33N 31 01E	32	
Shibing: China 27 04N 108 08E	85	
Shibogama *Lake*: Ont., Canada 53 30N 88 15W	93	
Shibotsu-jima: *is.*, Japan 43 29N 46 09E	87	
Shibuya: Japan 35 39N 139 42E	121	
Shickshock *Mountains*: Qué., Canada 49 00N 66 00W	97	
Shidao: China 36 50N 122 25E	84	
Shiel: *riv.*, R. & Crom., Scotland 57 00N 05 15W	64	
Shiel, *Loch*: Scotland 56 45N 05 30W	64	
Shifnal: Salop, England 52 41N 02 22W	58	
Shifuhu: *lake*, China 31 30N 84 00E	83	

Shigatse *see* Rikeze 29 18N 88 50E	35 83	
Shihchiachuang *see* Shijiazhuang 38 03N 114 28E	36 84	
Shijiao *see* Fogang 23 54N 113 30E	85	
Shijiazhuang (Shihchiachuang): China 38 03N 114 28E	36 84	
Shijingshan: China 39 55N 116 09E	121	
Shikārpur: Pakistan 27 58N 68 42E	34	
Shiki: Japan 35 49N 139 35E	121	
Shikohābād: India 27 06N 78 35E	82	
Shikoku: *is.*, Japan 33 45N 133 30E	12 37 86	
Shikotan-tō: *is.*, Japan 43 45N 146 45E	87	
Shikotsu-toya-kokuritsu-kōen: *nat. park*, Japan 42 45N 141 00E	86	
Shillong: India 25 34N 91 53E	35 83	
Shilong: China 23 07N 113 50E	85	
Shilshole *Bay*: Wash., U.S.A. 47 41N 122 25W	126	
Shimen: China 29 36N 111 15E	85	
Shimizu: Japan 35 01N 138 29E	37 86	
Shimoga: India 13 56N 75 31E	34	
Shimonoseki: Japan 33 57N 130 57E	37 86	
Shin, *Loch*: Suther., Scotland 58 00N 04 30W	64	
Shinagawa: Japan 35 37N 139 44E	121	
Shinagawa-wan: *bay*, Japan 35 36N 139 49E	121	
Shinan: Cahina 22 53N 109 54E	85	
Shingū: Mie, Japan 33 44N 135 59E	86	
Shinjō: Japan 38 46N 140 18E	86	
Shinjuku: Japan 35 41N 139 42E	121	
Shiogama: Japan 38 19N 141 01E	86	
Shiono-zaki: *cape*, Japan 33 26N 135 45E	86	
Ship *Canal*: Wash., U.S.A. 47 39N 122 21W	126	
Shipki *Pass*: China/India 31 50N 78 50E	34	
Shipley: W.Yorks., England 53 50N 01 47W	63 115	
Shippigan *Island*: N.B., Canada 47 45N 64 30W	97	
Shiprock: N.Mex., U.S.A. 36 47N 108 41W	95	
Shipshaw: Qué., Canada 48 28N 71 15W	96	
Shipston-on-Stour: War., England 52 04N 01 37W	59	
Shiqi *see* Zhongshan 22 31N 113 22E	36 84	
Shiquan: China 33 05N 108 20E	84	
Shirakawa: Japan 37 07N 140 13E	86	
Shirako: Japan 35 46N 139 38E	121	
Shiranuka: Japan 41 08N 141 24E	87	
Shiraoi: Japan 42 33N 141 21E	86	
Shīrāz: Iran 29 38N 52 34E	33	
Shire: *riv.*, Malawi/Mozambique 16 15S 35 00E	55	
Shiretoko-kokuritsu-kōen: *nat. park*, Japan 44 00N 145 00E	87	
Shirpur: India 21 21N 74 56E	82	
Shirwa *Lake see* Chilwa *Lake* 15 15S 35 45E	55	
Shivagi Park: India 28 40N 77 08E	120	
Shivpuri: India 25 26N 77 39E	82	
Shixian: China 43 05N 129 47E	86	
Shixing: China 25 03N 114 03E	85	
Shizhu: China 30 03N 108 08E	85	
Shizunai: Japan 42 20N 142 22E	86	
Shizuoka: Japan 34 58N 138 23E	37 86	
Shkodër: Albania 42 03N 19 01E	79	
Shoebury Ness: *cape*, Essex, England 51 32N 00 48E	59	
Sholāpur: India 17 43N 75 56E	34	
Shoreham-by-Sea: W.Sussex, England 50 49N 00 16W	59	
Shotton: Clwyd, Wales 53 12N 03 02W	105 114	
Shouguang: China 36 59N 118 42E	84	
Shouxian: China 32 35N 116 47E	84	
Shouyang: China 37 50N 113 09E	84	
Shreveport: La., U.S.A. 32 31N 93 45W	43 100	
Shrewsbury: Salop, England 52 43N 02 45W	60	
Shropshire: *admin. see* Salop 52 45N 02 45W	60	
Shropshire Union *Canal*: England 52 45N 02 15W	115	
Shu: *riv.*, China 35 30N 118 45E	84	
Shuangfeng: China 27 30N 112 05E	85	
Shuangyashan: China 46 37N 131 22E	37	
Shucheng: China 31 27N 117 02E	84	
Shuiji: China 27 26N 118 20E	85	
Shule (Sulo): *riv.*, China 40 30N 94 45E	36	
Shulu (Xinji): China 37 50N 115 15E	84	
Shunchang: China 26 50N 117 46E	85	
Shunde: China 22 47N 113 19E	85	
Shuoxian: China 39 20N 112 28E	84	
Shuswap *Lake*: B.C., Canada 50 45N 119 00W	89 89	
Shuyang: China 34 08N 118 52E	84	
Shyamnagar: India 22 50N 88 24E	120	

Types of map: Ocean pp. 1-5; Physical pp. 6-25; Human pp. 26-57; Topographic pp. 58-101; World pp. 102-111; Urban pp. 112-128.

Si: *riv. see* Xi   23 30N 111 15E   36 85
Siålkot: Pakistan   32 29N 74 35E   34
Siam *see* Thailand   15 30N 102 30E   12 35 107
Siam, *Gulf of*: Indo-China   11 15N 100 45E   12 35
Šiauliai: U.S.S.R.   55 56N 23 19E   75
Sibaj: U.S.S.R.   52 42N 58 39E   81
Šibenik: Yugoslavia   43 45N 15 55E   79
Siberia: *geog. reg.*, U.S.S.R.   62 00N 120 00E   30
Siberut: *is.*, Indonesia   01 30S 98 45E   13 39
Sibi: Pakistan   29 31N 67 54E   34
Sibiu: Romania   45 46N 24 09E   27 78
Sibley: Iowa, U.S.A.   43 25N 95 43W   94
Sibolga: Indonesia   01 42N 98 48E   38
Sibpur: India   22 34N 88 19E   120
Sibu: Malaysia   02 18N 111 49E   38
Sibuyan *Sea*: Philippines   13 00N 122 00E   39
Sichote-Alin' (Sikhote Alin) *Range*: U.S.S.R.
    44 15N 135 00E   9 31 86
Sichuan (Szechwan): *admin.*, China   31 00N 107 45E   36 84
Sichuan, (Red) *Basin of*: China   30 45N 107 15E   36 85
Sicilia (Sicily): *is. & Italian admin.*, Mediterranean Sea
    37 30N 14 00E   7 27 79
Sicilian *Channel*: Sicily/Tunisia   37 15N 12 00E   79
Sicily: *is. see* Sicilia   37 30N 14 00E   7 27 79
Sicuani: Peru   14 21S 71 13W   49
Sidao: China   39 50N 116 28E   121
Sidcup: Gt. Ldn., England   51 26N 00 07E   112
Sidhpur: India   23 57N 72 28E   82
Sidi-bel-Abbès: Algeria   35 15N 00 39W   56
Sidi Ifni: Morocco   29 24N 10 12W   56
Sidlaw *Hills*: Angus, Scotland   56 30N 03 00W   65
Sidmouth: Devon, England   50 41N 03 15W   61
Sidney: Mont., U.S.A.   47 43N 104 09W   94
Sidney: Nebr., U.S.A.   41 08N 102 49W   94
Sidney Lanier, *Lake*: Ga., U.S.A.   34 15N 84 00W   101
Sidra, *Gulf of*: Libya   31 00N 19 00E   32
Siebengebirge, *Forst*: W.Germany   50 49N 07 13E   119
Siedlce: Poland   52 10N 22 18E   78
Siegburg: W.Germany   50 48N 07 13E   72 119
Siegen: W.Germany   50 52N 08 02E   72
Siegerland: *geog. reg.*, W.Germany   50 55N 08 05E   105
Siemensstadt: W.Germany   52 32N 13 16E   117
Siem Reap: Khmer Rep.   13 21N 103 50E   38
Siena: Italy   43 19N 11 19E   79
Sierra de Córdoba: *ra.*, Argentina   31 45S 64 45W   52
Sierra de Famatina: *ra.*, Argentina   28 30S 68 00W   52
Sierra de Perijá: *ra.*, Colombia/Venezuela   10 00N 73 00W
    48
SIERRA LEONE   08 30N 12 00W   20 57
Sierra Leone *Basin*: N.Atlantic Ocean   07 00N 17 00W   2
Sierra Madre del Sur: *ra.*, Mexico   17 15N 98 30W   17 46
Sierra Madre Occidental: *ra.*, Mexico   25 00N 105 45W
    17 46
Sierra Madre Oriental: *ra.*, Mexico   23 00N 100 00W   17 46
Sierra Morena: *ra.*, Spain   38 00N 05 00W   26 77
Sierra Nevada: *ra.*, Spain   36 45N 03 00W   77
Sierra Nevada: *ra.*, Calif., U.S.A.   38 00N 119 00W   17 43 91
Sierra Nevada de Cocuy (Chita): *mtn.*, Colombia
    06 25N 72 18W   48
Sierra Vista: Ariz., U.S.A.   31 33N 110 18W   91
Sighet Marmatier: Romania   47 56N 23 53E   79
Signy Island: *rsch. stn.*, Antarctica   60 43S 45 56W   24
Sigsbee *Knolls*: Gulf of Mexico   23 30N 92 00W   5
Sigüenza: Spain   41 04N 02 38W   77
Sihui: China   23 25N 112 39E   85
Sijing: China   31 07N 121 16E   121
Sikanni Chief: *riv.*, B.C., Canada   57 30N 122 00W   89
Sīkar: India   27 33N 75 12E   34 82
Sikasso: Mali   11 18N 05 38W   57
Sikeston: Mo., U.S.A.   36 52N 89 33W   100
Sikhote Alin *Range see* Sichote-Alin' *Range*
    44 15N 135 00E   9 31 86
SIKKIM   27 30N 88 30E   35 83
Silchar: India   24 49N 92 47E   35
Sil̃guri: India   26 41N 88 28E   35 83
Silistra: Bulgaria   44 06N 27 17E   79
Siljan: *lake*, Sweden   60 55N 14 50E   75
Sillamäe: U.S.S.R.   59 24N 27 45E   80
Silloth: Cumbria, England   54 52N 03 23W   62
Silong: China   23 54N 23 35E   85
Silsden: W.Yorks., England   53 55N 01 56W   63 115

Silva Porto (Bié): Angola   12 25S 16 56E   54
Silver Bay: Minn., U.S.A.   47 15N 91 17W   98
Silver Bell: Ariz., U.S.A.   32 26N 111 31W   91
Silver City: N.Mex., U.S.A.   32 46N 108 17W   95
Silvermine *Mountains*: Tip., Irish Republic
    52 45N 08 00W   67
Silver Peak: Nev., U.S.A.   37 46N 117 39W   91
Silver Spring: Md., U.S.A.   39 00N 77 01W   122
Silverstone: Northants., England   52 06N 01 02W   59
Silverton: Colo., U.S.A.   37 49N 107 40W   95
Sim: U.S.S.R.   54 59N 57 41E   81
Simanggang: Malaysia   01 10N 111 32E   38
Simcoe, *Lake*: Ont., Canada   44 23N 79 18W   99
Simeulue: *is.*, Indonesia   02 30N 95 45E   38
Simferopol': U.S.S.R.   44 57N 34 06E   28
Simla: India   31 07N 77 09E   34 82
Simoom Sound: B.C., Canada   50 44N 126 28W   89
Simplon *Pass*: Switzerland   46 15N 08 03E   71
Simpson *Desert*, N.T., Australia   25 15S 136 00E   14 41
Simpson *Island*: Ont., Canada   48 47N 87 40W   98
Sinai *Peninsula see* Shibh Jazīrat Sīnā   29 15N 33 30E
    10 32
Sinan: China   27 54N 108 20E   85
Sincelejo: Colombia   09 17N 75 23W   48
Sinclair's *Bay*: Caith., Scotland   58 30N 03 00W   65
Sind: *geog. reg.*, Pakistan   25 45N 68 45E   34
Sind Sāga Doāb: *geog. reg.*, Pakistan   30 00N 71 00E   82
Sinel'nikovo: U.S.S.R.   48 20N 35 31E   80
SINGAPORE   01 22N 103 48E   12 39 107
Singaradja: Indonesia   08 06S 115 07E   39
Singen: W.Germany   47 45N 08 50E   72
Singhbhum: *admin.*, India   22 30N 85 30E   105
Singora *see* Songkhla   07 12N 100 35E   35
Sinkiang: *admin. see* Xinjiang   42 15N 93 00E   36
Sinnar: India   19 52N 74 02E   82
Sinop: Turkey   42 01N 35 09E   28
Sintang: Indonesia   00 03N 111 31E   38
Sint-Niklaas: Belgium   51 10N 04 08E   72
Sinŭiju: N.Korea   40 05N 124 24E   37
Sion: Switzerland   46 14N 07 21E   71
Sion Mills: Tyr., N.Ireland   54 47N 07 30W   66
Sioux City: Iowa, U.S.A.   42 30N 96 28W   43 94
Sioux Falls: S.D., U.S.A.   43 33N 96 44W   43 94
Sioux Lookout: Ont., Canada   50 07N 91 54W   93
Siping (Ssup'ing): China   43 12N 124 20E   37
Sipiwesk *Lake*: Man., Canada   55 00N 97 30W   93
Siple, *Mount*: Antarctica   73 25S 122 50W   25
Sipora: *is. see* Sipura   02 15S 99 45E   13 38
Sipura (Sipora): *is.*, Indonesia   02 15S 99 45E   13 38
Sira: *riv.*, Norway   58 45N 06 45E   75
Siracusa (Syracuse): Sicily   37 04N 15 18E   32 79
Sirajganj: Bangladesh   24 27N 89 42E   83
Sir Alexander, *Mount*: B.C., Canada   53 56N 120 27W   89
Siretul: *riv.*, Romania   47 15N 26 15E   78
Sirhowy: *riv.*, Gwent, Wales   51 45N 03 00W   113
Sir James McBrien, *Mount*: N.W.T.,
    Canada   62 15N 128 01W   88
Sirohi: India   25 53N 72 58E   82
Sironj: India   24 05N 77 39E   82
Sirsa: India   29 32N 75 04E   82
Sirte, *Gulf of*: Libya/Tunisia   33 45N 15 30E   20
Sisak: Yugoslavia   45 30N 16 22E   78
Sishui: China   35 39N 117 20E   84
Sisseton: S.D., U.S.A.   45 40N 97 03W   94
Sistema Ibérico (Iberian *Mountains*):
    Spain   41 00N 01 00W   77
Sitāmarhi: India   26 36N 85 30E   83
Sitāpur: India   27 33N 80 40E   82
Sitka: Alaska, U.S.A.   57 05N 135 20W   88
Sittingbourne: Kent, England   51 21N 00 44E   59
Sittwe (Akyab): Burma   20 09N 92 54E   35
Situbondo: Indonesia   07 40S 114 01E   38
Sivas: Turkey   39 44N 37 01E   33
Siverskiy: U.S.S.R.   59 20N 30 03E   75
Siwalik *Range*: India   31 00N 77 30E   82
Siwān: India   26 14N 84 21E   83
Siwa *Oasis*: Egypt   29 15N 25 30E   32
Sixian: China   33 30N 117 56E   84
Sjælland (Zealand): *is. & admin.*, Denmark   55 15N 11 45E
    75
Skagerrak: *str.*, Denmark/Norway   57 45N 09 00E   26 75

Types of map: Ocean pp. 1-5; Physical pp. 6-25; Human pp. 26-57; Topographic pp. 58-101; World pp. 102-111; Urban pp. 112-128.

Skagway: Alaska, U.S.A.   59 23N 135 20W   88
Skanderborg: Denmark   56 02N 09 57E   75
Skåne: geog. reg., Sweden   55 45N 13 45E   74
Skeena: riv., B.C., Canada   54 15N 129 00W   89
Skeena Mountains: B.C., Canada   56 30N 129 00W   89
Skegness: Lincs., England   53 10N 00 21E   58
Skellefteå: Sweden   64 45N 21 10E   27 74
Skellefteälv: riv., Sweden   65 15N 19 00E   27 74
Skelmersdale: Lancs., England   53 33N 02 48W   63 114
Skelmorlie: Ayr., Scotland   55 51N 04 53W   113
Skerries: Dublin, Irish Republic   53 35N 06 07W   66
Ski: Norway   59 43N 10 52E   75
Skibbereen: Cork, Irish Republic   51 33N 09 15W   67
Skiddaw: mtn., Cumbria, England   54 40N 03 08W   63
Skien: Norway   59 14N 09 37E   75
Skikda (Philippeville): Algeria   36 53N 06 54E   56 77
Skinningrove: Cleve., England   54 34N 00 54W   105
Skipton: N.Yorks., England   53 58N 02 01W   63
Skiros: is., Greece   38 55N 24 34E   79
Skive: Denmark   56 34N 09 02E   75
Skokholm Island: Dyfed, Wales   51 42N 05 16W   61
Skokie: Ill., U.S.A.   42 01N 87 45W   124
Skokie: riv., Ill., U.S.A.   42 15N 87 45W   124
Skomer Island: Dyfed, Wales   51 45N 05 18W   61
Skopje: Yugoslavia   42 00N 21 28E   27 79
Skövde: Sweden   58 24N 13 52E   75
Skye: is., Inv., Scotland   57 15N 06 15W   64
Slagelse: Denmark   55 24N 11 23E   75
Slancy: U.S.S.R.   59 06N 28 04E   80
Slaney: riv., Irish Republic   52 30N 06 30W   67
Slate Islands: Ont., Canada   48 30N 87 00W   98
Slav'ansk (Slavyansk): U.S.S.R.   48 52N 37 37E   28 80
Slave: riv., Canada   59 15N 111 15W   16 42 92
Slavonski Brod: Yugoslavia   49 09N 18 02E   78
Slavyansk see Slav'ansk   48 52N 37 37E   28 80
Sleaford: Lincs., England   52 59N 00 24W   58
Slea Head: Kerry, Irish Republic   52 06N 10 27W   67
Sleat, Point of: Inv., Scotland   57 01N 06 01W   64
Sleat, Sound of: Inv., Scotland   57 00N 05 45W   64
Slessor Glacier: Antarctica   79 50S 28 30W   24
Slieve Anierin: mtn., Leit., Irish Republic   54 06N 07 58W   66
Slieve Aughty Mountains: Gal., Irish Republic   53 00N 08 30W   67
Slieve Beagh: mtns., Tyr., N.Ireland   54 21N 07 12W   66
Slieve Bloom: mtns., Laois, Irish Republic   53 00N 07 30W   67
Slieve Car: mtn., Mayo, Irish Republic   54 04N 09 39W   66
Slieve Donard: mtn., Down, N.Ireland   54 11N 05 55W   66
Slieve Elva: mtn., Clare, Irish Republic   53 05N 09 16W   67
Slievefelim Mountains: Irish Republic   52 30N 08 15W   67
Slieve Gallion: mtn., Lon., N.Ireland   54 45N 06 45W   66
Slieve Gamph: mtns., Irish Republic   54 00N 08 45W   66
Slieve Gullion: mtn., Arm., N.Ireland   54 06N 06 25W   66
Slieve Mish Mountains: Kerry, Irish Republic   52 00N 09 45W   67
Slievenaman: mtn., Tip., Irish Republic   52 25N 07 34W   67
Slieve Rushen: mtn., Ferm., N.Ireland   54 09N 07 37W   66
Slieve Snaght: mtn., Don., Irish Republic   55 12N 07 20W   66
Sligo: Sligo, Irish Rep.   54 17N 08 28W   22 66
Sligo: admin., Irish Rep.   54 00N 08 30W   66
Sligo Bay: Sligo, Irish Republic   54 15N 08 30W   66
Slioch: pk., R. & Crom., Scotland   57 39N 05 20W   64
Sliven: Bulgaria   42 40N 26 19E   79
Slobodskoj: U.S.S.R.   58 42N 50 12E   81
Slocan: B.C., Canada   49 46N 117 28W   89
Slonim: U.S.S.R.   53 05N 25 21E   75
Slough: Berks., England   51 31N 00 36W   59 112
Sl'ud'anka (Slyudyanka): U.S.S.R.   51 38N 103 42E   30
Słupsk: Poland   54 28N 17 00E   73 78
Slyne Head: Gal., Irish Republic   53 24N 10 13W   66
Slyudyanka see Sl'ud'anka   51 38N 103 42E   30
Smallbridge: Gt.Man., England   53 39N 02 07W   114
Smederevo: Yugoslavia   44 40N 20 56E   79
Smela: U.S.S.R.   49 14N 31 53E   80
Smethwick: W.Mid., England   52 30N 01 58W   115
Smith: Alta., Canada   55 10N 114 02W   92
Smith: riv., Mont., U.S.A.   47 00N 111 15W   94
Smith Arm: bay, N.W.T., Canada   66 15N 124 30W   88
Smithers: B.C., Canada   54 45N 127 10W   89

Smithfield: Utah, U.S.A.   41 50N 111 50W   90
Smith Mountain Reservoir: Va., U.S.A.   37 00N 79 30W   101
Smith River: B.C., Canada   59 56N 126 28W   88
Smiths Falls: Ont., Canada   44 54N 76 01W   99
Smith Valley: Nev., U.S.A.   39 00N 119 20W   104
Smoky: riv., Alta., Canada   54 45N 118 15W   89
Smoky Falls: Ont., Canada   50 04N 82 10W   98
Smoky Hill: riv., Kans., U.S.A.   38 30N 100 30W   94
Smøla: is., Norway   63 25N 08 00E   74
Smolensk: U.S.S.R.   54 47N 32 03E   28 80
Smolensko Moskovskaja Vozvyšennost': hld., U.S.S.R.   54 30N 34 00E   80
Smyrna: Turkey see Izmir   38 25N 27 10E   32 79
Snaefell: mt., I. of M., United Kingdom   54 16N 04 28W   62
Snag: Yukon, Canada   62 22N 140 22W   88
Snaght, Slieve: mtn., Don., Irish Republic   55 12N 07 20W   66
Snake: riv., Yukon, Canada   65 30N 133 30W   88
Snake: riv., U.S.A.   46 15N 117 00W   16 42 90
Snare: riv., N.W.T., Canada   63 45N 115 45W   88
Sneek: Netherlands   53 02N 05 40E   72
Śniardwy, Jezioro: lake, Poland   53 45N 21 45E   78
Snizort, Loch: Inv., Scotland   57 30N 06 15W   64
Snowbird Lake: N.W.T., Canada   60 30N 103 00W   92
Snowdon: mtn., Gwyn., Wales   53 04N 04 05W   60
Snowdonia National Park: Gwyn., Wales   52 45N 04 00W   60
Snowy: riv., Australia   37 00S 148 15E   15 41
Snyder: Tex., U.S.A.   32 44N 100 55W   95
Soaker, Mount: S.I., New Zealand   45 23S 167 14E   87
Soar: riv., England   52 45N 01 00W   58
Soasiu (Tidore): Indonesia   00 40N 127 25E   39
Soay Sound: Inv., Scotland   57 00N 06 00W   64
Sobat: riv., Ethiopia/Sudan   09 00N 32 30E   53
Sobral: Brazil   03 42S 40 21W   50
Soči (Sochi): U.S.S.R.   43 35N 39 45E   28
Society Islands: S.Pacific Ocean   17 00S 153 00W   5
Socorro: N.Mex., U.S.A.   34 04N 106 54W   95
Socotra: is. see Suqutra   12 30N 54 00E   10 33
Sodankylä: Finland   67 21N 26 31E   74
Soda Springs: Idaho, U.S.A.   42 39N 111 36W   90
Söderhamn: Sweden   61 19N 17 10E   75
Södertalje: Sweden   59 11N 17 39E   75
Soest: W.Germany   51 34N 08 06E   72
Sofija (Sofia): Bulgaria   42 40N 23 18E   27 79
Sognafjorden: fd., Norway   61 00N 05 30E   27 75
Sogndal: Norway   61 13N 07 05E   75
Sogne: fd., Norway   61 00N 05 30E   27 75
Soham: Cambs., England   52 20N 00 20E   59
Sohano: Terr. of New Guinea   05 26S 154 39E   15
Sōka: Japan   35 50N 139 49E   121
Söke: Turkey   37 45N 27 28E   79
Sokodé: Togo   08 59N 01 11E   57
Sokol: U.S.S.R.   59 28N 40 10E   80
Sokol'niki Park: U.S.S.R.   55 49N 37 40E   119
Sokolov: Czechoslovakia   50 10N 12 30E   73
Sokolovskaja: U.S.S.R.   53 05N 63 20E   105
Sokoto: Nigeria   13 02N 05 15E   57
Sokoto: riv., Nigeria   12 00N 04 00E   57
Sokskije Jary: mtns., U.S.S.R.   54 15N 51 30E   81
Sol, Costa del: coast, Spain   36 30N 04 00W   76
Solander, Cape: N.S.W., Australia   34 01S 151 14E   120
Solbiate Olona: Italy   45 40N 08 45E   116
Solent, The: str. Hants./I. of W., England   50 45N 01 30W   59
Soligorsk: U.S.S.R.   52 48N 27 32E   78
Solihull: W.Mid., England   52 25N 01 45W   58 115
Sol'-Ileck: U.S.S.R.   51 10N 54 59E   81
Solingen: W.Germany   51 10N 07 05E   72 118
Sollefteå: Sweden   63 09N 17 15E   74
Solnečnogorsk: U.S.S.R.   56 11N 36 59E   80
Solo see Surakarta   07 32S 110 50E   38
Solomon: riv., Kans., U.S.A.   39 15N 98 00W   94
Solomon Islands: S.Pacific Ocean   07 00S 157 00E   4 15
Solomon Rise: Pacific Ocean   00 00 152 00E   4
Solomon Sea: 08 30S 153 30E   15
Solothurn: Switzerland   47 13N 07 32E   71
Solway Firth: est., England/Scotland   54 45N 03 30W   62
Somali Basin: Indian Ocean   01 00N 52 00E   1 21
SOMALI REPUBLIC   01 00N 41 30E   21 53

Types of map: Ocean pp. 1-5; Physical pp. 6-25; Human pp. 26-57; Topographic pp. 58-101; World pp. 102-111; Urban pp. 112-128.

Sombor: Yugoslavia 45 46N 19 09E	27 78
Somerset: Ky., U.S.A. 37 05N 84 38W	101
Somerset: *admin.*, England 51 00N 02 45W	61
Somerton: Som., England 51 03N 02 44W	61
Somerville: Mass., U.S.A. 42 24N 71 07W	122
Someşul: *riv.*, Romania 47 15N 23 30E	78
Somme: *riv.*, France 50 00N 02 00E	72
Sompeta: India 18 58N 84 39E	83
Son: *riv.*, India 25 15N 84 30E	35 83
Sonārpur: India 22 27N 88 26E	120
Sønderborg: Denmark 54 55N 09 48E	75
Sondershausen: E.Germany 51 23N 10 52E	73
Song Da (Black): *riv.*, China/N.Vietnam 21 30N 103 30E	12 36
Sông Dông Nai (Dung): *riv.*, S.Vietnam 11 45N 107 30E	38
Songea: Tanzania 10 41S 35 39E	54
Song Hong (Red): *riv.*, China/N.Vietnam 21 45N 104 30E	12 36
Songhua (Sungari): *riv.*, China 45 30N 125 30E	37
Songhua, *Lake* (Sungari *Reservoir*): China 42 30N 127 00E	37
Sŏngjin *see* Kimch'aek 40 41N 129 12E	37 105
Songkan: China 28 35N 106 50E	85
Songkhla (Singora): Thailand 07 12N 100 35E	35
Songnim (Kyŏmip'o): N.Korea 38 44N 125 38E	105
Songtao: China 28 12N 109 10E	85
Songxian: China 34 07N 112 00E	84
Songzheng: China 27 33N 118 44E	85
SonĪpat: India 29 00N 77 01E	82
Sonneberg: E.Germany 50 22N 11 10E	73
Sonora: Tex., U.S.A. 30 34N 100 39W	95
Sonora: *admin.*, Mexico 29 30N 111 00W	46
Sonsorol *Islands*: Caroline Islands 05 15N 132 00E	12
Soochow *see* Suzhou 31 18N 120 45E	37 84
Sopot: Poland 54 27N 18 31E	78
Sopron: Hungary 47 40N 16 38E	73 78
Sorada: India 19 46N 84 29E	83
Sorel: Qué., Canada 46 03N 73 06W	96
Soria: Spain 41 46N 02 28W	77
Soro: India 21 18N 86 49E	83
Sorocaba: Brazil 23 30S 47 32W	51
Soročinsk: U.S.S.R. 52 26N 53 10E	81
Soroki: U.S.S.R. 48 09N 28 17E	78
Sorol: *is.*, Caroline Islands 08 08N 140 23E	12
Sorong: Indonesia 00 50S 131 17E	39
Soroti: Uganda 01 42N 33 37E	53
Sørøya: *is.*, Norway 70 35N 22 46E	74
Sorrento: Italy 40 37N 14 23E	27
Sorsele: Sweden 65 32N 17 34E	74
Sortavala: U.S.S.R. 61 40N 30 40E	74
Šostka: U.S.S.R. 51 52N 33 30E	80
Souillac: France 44 53N 01 29E	70
Sŏul (Kyŏngsŏng, Seoul): S.Korea 37 33N 126 58E	37
Souris: Man., Canada 49 38N 100 17W	93
Souris: P.E.I., Canada 46 22N 62 16W	97
Souris: *riv.*, Canada/U.S.A. 48 45N 110 45W	92
Sousse: Tunisia 35 50N 10 38E	26
SOUTH AFRICA, REPUBLIC OF	21 55 107
Southall: Gt. Ldn., England 51 31N 00 23W	112
Southam: War., England 52 15N 01 23W	59
Southampton: Hants., England 50 55N 01 25W	26 59
Southampton *Island*: N.W.T., Canada 64 30N 84 00W	16 44
South Atlantic *Ocean*	3
South Aulatsivik *Island*: Nfld., Canada 56 45N 61 30W	97
South Australia: *admin.*, Australia	41
South Australian *Basin*: S.Pacific Ocean 40 00S 125 00E	4 13
South Banda *Basin*: Banda Sea 06 30S 126 30E	13
South Bend: Ind., U.S.A. 41 40N 86 15W	45 98
South Benfleet: Essex, England 51 33N 00 34E	59 112
Southborough: Kent, England 51 10N 00 15E	59
South Boston: Va., U.S.A. 36 42N 78 58W	101
South Carolina: *admin.*, U.S.A. 34 00N 80 00W	45 101
South Cave: Humb., England 53 46N 00 35W	63
South China *Sea* (Nan Hai) 22 15N 115 45E	12 38 85
South Dakota: *admin.*, U.S.A. 44 30N 100 00W	43 94
South Dorset Downs: *hills*, Dorset, England 50 30N 02 15W	61
South Downs: *hills*, England 50 45N 00 30W	59
Southeast Indian *Basin*: Indian Ocean 32 00S 107 00E	

	1 13
Southeast Indian *Ridge*: Indian Ocean 45 00S 95 00E	1
Southeast Pacific *Basin*: S.Pacific Ocean	5 25
Southend: Sask., Canada	92
Southend-on-Sea: Essex, England 51 33N 00 43E	59
South Equatorial *Current*	1 3 4
Southern *Alps*: S.I., New Zealand 43 45S 170 00E	15 37 87
Southern Indian *Lakes*: Man., Canada 57 00N 98 30W	42
Southern Ocean	3 24
Southern *Uplands*: Scotland 55 15N 04 00W	62
Southfield: Mich., U.S.A. 42 28N 83 16W	125
South Fiji *Basin*: S.Pacific Ocean 25 00S 175 00E	4
South Foreland: *cape*, Kent, England 51 09N 01 23E	59
South Gate: Calif., U.S.A. 33 57N 118 11W	127
South Georgia: *is.*, S.Atlantic Ocean 54 15S 36 45W	3 19
South Glamorgan: *admin.*, Wales 51 15N 03 15W	61
South *Head*: N.S.W., Australia 33 50S 151 17E	120
South Henik *Lake*: N.W.T., Canada 61 15N 97 15W	93
South Honshu *Ridge*: Philippine Sea 20 00N 147 00E	4
South Indian *Basin*: Southern Ocean 57 00S 56 00E	1
South Indian Lake: Man., Canada 56 48N 98 56W	93
South *Island*: New Zealand 43 30S 171 00E	15 41 87
SOUTH KOREA 37 00N 129 00E	12 37 86 107
South *Magnetic Pole (I)*: Antarctica 60 05S 139 05E	25
South Melrose: Mont., U.S.A. 45 18N 107 57W	94
South Molton: Devon, England 51 01N 03 50W	61
South Nahanni: *riv.*, N.W.T., Canada 61 30N 125 30W	88
South Orkney *Islands*: Southern Ocean 60 30S 45 30W	3 19
South Pacific *Ocean*	5
South Pagai: *is.*, Indonesia 03 00S 100 15E	38
South *Park*: Pa., U.S.A. 40 19N 80 00W	125
South Platte: *riv.*, U.S.A. 40 45N 103 00W	94
South *Point*: Mich., U.S.A. 44 53N 83 18W	98
South *Pole*: Antarctica 90 00S 00 00	24
Southport: Mers., England 53 39N 03 01W	63 114
South *Riding*: *dist.*, Tip., Irish Republic 52 30N 07 45W	67
South Ronaldsay: *is.*, Ork. Is., Scotland 58 45N 03 00W	65
South Salmara: India 25 34N 90 01E	83
South Sandwich *Islands*: Southern Ocean 58 30S 27 00W	19
South Sandwich *Trench*: Southern Ocean 58 00S 23 00W	3 19
South San Francisco: Calif., U.S.A. 37 39N 122 25W	126
South San Gabriel: Calif., U.S.A. 34 04N 118 05W	127
South Saskatchewan: *riv.*, Canada 50 45N 109 30W	42 92
South Shetland *Islands*: Southern Ocean 56 00S 60 00W	3 19
South Shields: Tyne & Wear, England 55 00N 01 25W	63
South Sioux City: Nebr., U.S.A. 42 28N 96 24W	94
South *Sound*: Irish Republic 53 00N 09 15W	67
South Tyne: *riv.*, Northumb., England 54 45N 02 15W	63
South Uist: *is.*, Inv., Scotland 57 15N 07 15W	64
SOUTH VIETNAM 12 45N 108 15E	12 38 107
Southwark: Gt. Ldn., England 51 30N 00 06W	112
Southwell: Notts., England 53 05N 00 58W	58
SOUTH WEST AFRICA (Namibia)	21 55 107
Southwest *Cape*: Stewart I., New Zealand 47 17S 167 29E	87
Southwest Indian *Basin*: Indian Ocean 32 00S 66 00E	1
Southwest Indian *Ridge*: Indian Ocean 35 00S 57 00E	1
Southwest Monsoon *Current*: Indian Ocean	1
Southwest Pacific *Basin*: S.Pacific Ocean 35 00S 145 00E	5 25
Southwold: Suff., England 52 20N 01 40E	59
South Yorkshire: *admin.*, England 53 15N 01 15W	63
Sovetsk: U.S.S.R. 57 37N 48 58E	81
Spandau: W.Germany 52 32N 13 13E	73 117
Spanish: *riv.*, Ont., Canada 46 45N 81 45W	98
Spanish *Banks*: B.C., Canada 49 17N 123 00W	126
Spanish *Head*: I. of M., United Kingdom 54 03N 04 46W	62
SPANISH SAHARA 24 00N 14 00W	20 56
Sparks: Nev., U.S.A. 39 34N 119 46W	91
Sparrows Point: Md., U.S.A. 39 13N 76 28W	104
Sparta: Greece *see* Spárti 37 05N 22 25E	79
Spartanburg: S.C., U.S.A. 34 56N 81 57W	101
Spárti (Sparta): Greece 37 05N 22 25E	79
Spartivento, *Capo*: Italy 37 56N 16 04E	79
Spartivento, *Capo*: Sardinia 38 53N 08 50E	77

Types of map: Ocean pp. 1-5; Physical pp. 6-25; Human pp. 26-57; Topographic pp. 58-101; World pp. 102-111; Urban pp. 112-128.

Spas-Demensk: U.S.S.R.   54 25N 34 01E   80
Spassk-Dal'nij: U.S.S.R.   44 37N 132 48E   86
Spean, Glen: *val.*, Inv., Scotland   56 45N 04 45W   64
Spearfish: S.D., U.S.A.   44 30N 103 52W   94
Speed: Ind., U.S.A.   38 25N 85 54W   98
Speke: Mers., England   53 20N 02 51W   114
Spencer: Iowa, U.S.A.   43 08N 95 08W   94
Spencer *Gulf*: S.A., Australia   34 00S 137 15E   41
Spennymore: Dur., England   54 42N 01 35W   63
Spenser *Mountains*: S.I., New Zealand   42 15S 172 15E   87
Sperrin *Mountains*: N.Ireland   54 45N 07 00W   66
Spey: *riv.*, Scotland   57 15N 03 30W   65
Speyer: W.Germany   49 18N 08 26E   72
Spilsby: Lincs., England   53 11N 00 05E   58
Springburn: Lan., Scotland   55 53N 04 13W   113
Spirit River: Alta., Canada   55 46N 118 51W   89
Spittal an der Drau: Austria   46 48N 13 30E   78
Spitzbergen (Svalbard): *is.*, Arctic Ocean   78 00N 20 00E
                3 23
Split: Yugoslavia   43 31N 16 28E   27 79
Split Lake: Man., Canada   56 16N 96 08W   93
Split *Lake*: Man., Canada   56 00N 96 15W   93
Splügen: Switzerland   46 34N 09 21E   71
Spokane: Wash., U.S.A.   47 40N 117 24W   42 90
Spoleto: Italy   42 44N 12 44E   79
Sporádhes (Dodecanese): *is.*, Greece   36 30N 26 30E   79
Spot *Pond*: Mass., U.S.A.   42 27N 71 06W   122
Spree: *riv.*, W.Germany   52 30N 13 15E   117
Spring: *riv.*, U.S.A.   37 00N 94 30W   95
Springdale: Ark., U.S.A.   36 11N 94 08W   100
Springer: N.Mex., U.S.A.   36 22N 104 36W   95
Springfield: Colo., U.S.A.   37 24N 102 37W   95
Springfield: Ill., U.S.A.   39 49N 89 39W   45 98
Springfield: Mass., U.S.A.   42 07N 72 35W   45 99
Springfield: Mo., U.S.A.   37 11N 93 19W   43 98
Springfield: Ohio, U.S.A.   39 55N 83 48W   98
Springfield: Oreg., U.S.A.   44 03N 123 01W   90
Springfield: Pa., U.S.A.   39 56N 75 19W   122
Springhill: N.S., Canada   45 40N 64 04W   97
Springs: Trans., Rep. of S.Africa   26 15S 28 26E   55
Spring *Valley*: Minn., U.S.A.   43 41N 92 23W   104
Springville: Utah, U.S.A.   40 10N 111 37W   91
Spurn *Head*: Humb., England   53 36N 00 07E   63
Spy *Pond*: Mass., U.S.A.   42 24N 71 09W   122
Squamish: B.C., Canada   49 42N 123 09W   89
Srednekolymsk: U.S.S.R.   67 27N 153 41E   31
Srednerusskaja Vozvyšennost': *hld.*,
U.S.S.R.   53 30N 37 00E   80
Sri Gangānagar: India   29 54N 73 56E   34 82
SRI LANKA (Ceylon)   07 45N 80 45E   1 11 34 107
Środa: Poland   52 15N 17 15E   73
Ssup'ing *see* Siping   43 12N 124 20E   37
Staaken: E.Germany   52 32N 13 08E   117
Staatsforst Harburg: *for.*, W.Germany   53 15N 09 45E   119
Staatsforst Königsforst: *for.*, W.Germany   50 45N 07 00E
                119
Staatsforst Rüdersdorf: *for.*, E.Germany   52 15N 13 45E
                117
Stack, *Loch*: Suther., Scotland   58 15N 04 45W   64
Stacks *Mountains*: Kerry, Irish Republic   52 15N 09 30W   67
Stade: W.Germany   53 36N 09 28E   72
Stadtwald: *for.*, W.Germany   50 45N 06 45E   119
Stafford: Staffs., England   52 48N 02 07W   58 115
Staffordshire: *admin.*, England   52 30N 02 00W   58
Staffordshire & Worcester *Canal*: England   52 30N 02 00W
                115
Staines: Surrey, England   51 26N 00 31W   59 112
Stalbridge: Dorset, England   50 58N 02 23W   61
Stalinogorsk *see* Novomoskovsk   54 05N 38 13E   28 80
Stalinsk *see* Novokuzneck   53 45N 87 06E   30 105
Stalybridge: Gt. Man., England   53 29N 02 04W   114
Stamford: Lincs., England   52 39N 00 29W   58
Stamford Bridge: N.Yorks., England   53 59N 00 55W   63
Standish: Gt. Man., England   53 36N 02 41W   114
Stanford-le-Hope: Essex, England   51 31N 00 26E   112
Stanhope: Dur., England   54 45N 02 01W   63
Stanke Dimitrov: Bulgaria   42 15N 23 18E   79
Stanley: Dur., England   54 52N 01 42W   63
Stanley: W.Yorks., England   53 44N 01 28W   115
Stanley *Falls*: Zaïre   00 30N 25 12E   21 54
Stanley Mission: Sask., Canada   55 27N 104 33W   92

Stanley *Park*: B.C., Canada   49 18N 123 08W   126
Stanleyville *see* Kisangani   00 30N 25 12E   54
Stanlow: Ches., England   53 17N 02 52W   107 114
Stanovoj (Stanovoy) *Range*: U.S.S.R.   55 45N 128 00E   9 31
Stansted: Essex, England   51 54N 00 12E   59
Starachowice: Poland   51 03N 21 00E   78
Staraja Russa: U.S.S.R.   58 00N 31 23E   80
Stara Planina: *mtns.*, Bulgaria   42 45N 24 00E   79
Starav, Ben: *mtn.*, Argyll., Scotland   56 32N 05 03W   64
Stara Zagora: Bulgaria   42 25N 25 37E   27 79
Stargard Szczecinski: Poland   53 21N 15 01E   73 78
Starkville: Miss., U.S.A.   33 28N 88 49W   100
Starnberg: W.Germany   48 00N 11 20E   73
Starnberger See (Würm See): *lake*, W.Germany
47 45N 11 15E   73
Starogard Gdański: Poland   53 58N 18 30E   73 78
Start *Bay*: Devon, England   50 15N 03 30W   61
Start *Point*: Devon, England   50 13N 03 38W   61
Start *Point*: Ork. Is., Scotland   59 17N 02 24W   65
Staryj Oskol: U.S.S.R.   51 19N 37 51E   80
Stassfurt: E.Germany   51 51N 11 35E   73
State College: Pa., U.S.A.   40 48N 77 52W   99
State *Game Lands*: Pa., U.S.A.   40 38N 80 07W   125
Staten *Island*: N.Y., U.S.A.   40 30N 74 00W   123
Statesboro: Ga., U.S.A.   32 28N 81 47W   101
Statesville: N.C., U.S.A.   35 46N 80 54W   101
Staunton: Va., U.S.A.   38 10N 79 05W   99
Stavanger: Norway   58 58N 05 45E   26 75
Staveley: Derby., England   53 16N 01 20W   58
Stavropol' (Voroshilovsk): U.S.S.R.   45 02N 41 59E   28
Steamboat: B.C., Canada   58 41N 123 43W   88
Steamboat Springs: Colo., U.S.A.   40 29N 106 50W   94
Steep Rock Lake: Man., Canada   48 50N 91 38W   104
Stefanie, *Lake*: Ethiopia   04 45N 36 45E   53
Steinbach: Man., Canada   49 32N 96 40W   93
Steinkjer: Norway   64 00N 11 30E   74
Stelvio, *Parco Nazionale dello*: Italy   46 15N 10 30E   78
Stendal: E.Germany   52 36N 11 52E   73
Stenness, *Loch of*: Ork. Is., Scotland   59 00N 03 15W   65
Stephenville: Nfld., Canada   48 33N 58 34W   97
Stepney: Gt. Ldn., England   51 31N 00 04W   112
Steppes: *geog. reg.*, U.S.S.R.   52 00N 65 00E   8
Sterkrade: W.Germany   51 30N 06 50E   118
Sterling: Colo., U.S.A.   40 37N 103 13W   94
Sterling: Ill., U.S.A.   41 48N 89 43W   98 104
Sterlitamak: U.S.S.R.   53 37N 55 58E   29 81
Stettin *see* Szczecin   53 25N 14 32E   27 73 78
Stettiner Haff: *gulf*, E.Germany   53 45N 14 00E   73
Stettler: Alta., Canada   52 21N 112 40W   92
Steubenville: Ohio, U.S.A.   40 22N 80 39W   99 104
Stevenage: Herts., England   51 55N 00 14W   59
Stevens Point: Wis., U.S.A.   44 32N 89 33W   98
Stevenston: Ayr., Scotland   55 39N 04 45W   62
Steveston: B.C., Canada   49 08N 123 11W   126
Stewart: B.C., Canada   55 56N 130 01W   89
Stewart: *riv.*, Yukon, Canada   63 15N 138 30W   88
Stewart *County*: Ga., U.S.A.   32 10N 84 45W   104
Stewart *Island*: New Zealand   47 00S 168 00E   87
Stewarton: Ayr., Scotland   55 41N 04 31W   62 113
Stewart River: Yukon, U.S.A.   63 19N 140 26W   88
Stewartstown: Tyr., N.Ireland   54 35N 06 41W   66
Steyr: Austria   48 04N 14 26E   73 78
Stickney: Ill., U.S.A.   41 48N 87 57W   124
Stikine: *riv.*, B.C., Canada   57 45N 131 15W   89
Stillwater: Okla., U.S.A.   36 07N 97 04W   95
Stilton: Cambs., England   52 29N 00 17W   58
Štip: Yugoslavia   41 40N 22 12E   79
Stinchar: *riv.*, Ayr., Scotland   55 00N 04 45W   62
Stirling: Alta., Canada   49 34N 112 30W   92
Stirling: Stirl., Scotland   56 07N 03 57W   65
Stirlingshire: *admin.*, Scotland   56 00N 04 00W   64
Stockbridge: Hants., England   51 07N 01 29W   59
Stockerau: Austria   48 24N 16 13E   73
Stockholm: Sweden   59 20N 18 03E   27 75
Stockport: Gt. Man., England   53 25N 02 10W   63 114
Stocksbridge: S.Yorks., England   53 27N 01 34W   63
Stocks *Reservoir*: Lancs., England   54 00N 02 15W   62
Stockton: Calif., U.S.A.   37 59N 121 20W   43 91
Stockton: Utah, U.S.A.   40 27N 112 22W   91
Stockton Heath: Ches., England   53 22N 02 34W   114
Stockton-on-Tees: Cleve., England   54 34N 01 19W   63

Stockton *Plateau*: Tex., U.S.A.   30 30N 102 15W   95
Stoer, *Point of*: Suther., Scotland   58 16N 05 23W   64
Stokenchurch: Bucks., England   51 40N 00 55W   59
Stoke-on-Trent: Staffs., England   53 00N 02 10W   26 58
Stokesley: N.Yorks., England   54 28N 01 11W   63
Stone: Staffs., England   52 54N 02 10W   58
Stoneham: Mass., U.S.A.   42 27N 71 06W   122
Stonehaven: Kinc., Scotland   56 58N 02 13W   65
Stonehenge: *prehist. site*, Wilts., England   51 11N 01 50W   61
Stonehouse: Glos., England   51 45N 02 17W   61
Stonehouse: Lan., Scotland   55 43N 04 00W   113
Stone Mountain *Provincial Park*: B.C., Canada   58 15N 125 00W   88
Stonington Island: *rsch. stn.*, Antarctica   68 11S 67 00W   24
Stony Brook *Reservation*: Mass., U.S.A.   42 16N 71 09W   122
Stony *Creek*: Ill., U.S.A.   41 30N 87 45W   124
Stony *Lake*: Man., Canada   58 45N 98 15W   93
Stony Rapids: Sask., Canada   59 16N 105 50W   92
Stony Tunguska: *riv.*, U.S.S.R.   62 00N 95 00E   30
Stora Lulevatten: *lake*, Sweden   67 20N 19 00E   74
Størdalshalsen: Norway   63 27N 10 57E   74
Store Bælt: *str.*, Denmark   55 30N 11 00E   75
Stornoway: R. & Crom., Scotland   58 12N 06 23W   64
Storr, The: *mtn.*, Inv., Scotland   57 30N 06 11W   64
Storsjön: *lake*, Sweden   63 15N 14 15E   74
Stort: *riv.*, England   51 45N 00 00   112
Storuman: Sweden   65 05N 17 10E   74
Storuman: *lake*, Sweden   65 14N 16 50E   74
Stour: *riv.*, Dorset, England   50 45N 02 00W   61
Stour: *riv.*, Essex/Suff., England   51 45N 00 45E   59
Stour (Great Stour): *riv.*, Kent, England   51 15N 01 15E   59
Stour: *riv.*, Staffs./Worcs., England   52 15N 02 00W   115
Stourbridge: W.Mid., England   52 27N 02 09W   58 115
Stourport-on-Severn: Here. & Worcs., England   52 21N 02 16W   59
Stowmarket: Suff., England   52 11N 00 59E   59
Stow-on-the-Wold: Glos., England   51 56N 01 44W   60
Strabane: Tyr., N.Ireland   54 49N 07 28W   66
Stradbally: Laois, Irish Republic   53 10N 07 09W   67
Strakonice: Czechoslovakia   49 16N 13 55E   73
Stralsund: E.Germany   54 18N 13 06E   73 78
Strangford *Lough*: Down, N.Ireland   54 15N 05 30W   66
Stranorlar: Don., Irish Republic   54 48N 07 46W   66
Stranraer: Wig., Scotland   54 54N 05 02W   62
Strasbourg: France   48 35N 07 45E   26 71
Stratford: Ont., Canada   43 22N 81 00W   99
Stratford-upon-Avon: War., England   52 12N 01 41W   59
Stratford-upon-Avon *Canal*: War., England   52 15N 01 45W   115
Strathaven: Lan., Scotland   55 41N 04 05W   62 113
Strathblane: *val.*, Stirl., Scotland   55 59N 04 18W   113
Strathcona *Provincial Park*: B.C., Canada   49 30N 125 45W   89
Strathfield: N.S.W., Australia   33 52S 151 06E   120
Strathgryfe: *val.*, Renf., Scotland   55 45N 04 30W   113
Strathmore: Alta., Canada   51 05N 113 18W   92
Strathmore: *val.*, Scotland   56 30N 02 45W   65
Strath Tay: *val.*, Perth., Scotland   56 30N 03 30W   65
Strathy: *riv.*, Suther., Scotland   58 15N 04 00W   65
Strathy *Point*: Suther., Scotland   58 35N 04 01W   65
Stratton: Corn., England   50 50N 04 31W   61
Straubing: W.Germany   48 53N 12 35E   73
Strausberg: E.Germany   52 35N 13 54E   73 117
Strawberry *Mountain*: Oreg., U.S.A.   44 19N 118 43W   90
Streatham: Gt. Ldn., England   51 26N 00 07W   112
Středočeský: *admin.*, Czechoslovakia   50 00N 14 30E   73
Street: Som., England   51 08N 02 44W   61
Strel'na: U.S.S.R.   59 51N 30 02E   119
Stretford: Gt. Man., England   53 27N 02 19W   114
Strokestown: Rosc., Irish Republic   53 47N 08 06W   66
Stroma: *is.*, Caith., Scotland   58 30N 03 00W   65
Stromboli: *is. & volc.*, Sicily   38 48N 15 15E   79
Stromeferry: R. & Crom., Scotland   57 21N 05 34W   64
Strömsund: Sweden   63 51N 15 30E   74
Stronsay: *is.*, Ork. Is., Scotland   59 00N 02 30W   65
Stronsay Firth: *chan.*, Ork. Is., Scotland   59 00N 02 45W   65
Stroud: Glos., England   51 45N 02 12W   61
Strugi-Krasnyje: U.S.S.R.   58 17N 29 06E   80
Strumble *Head*: Dyfed, Wales   52 02N 05 04W   60

Strunino: U.S.S.R.   56 23N 38 34E   80
Stryj: U.S.S.R.   49 15N 23 51E   78
Stuart: *riv.*, B.C., Canada   54 00N 124 00W   89
Stuart *Lake*: B.C., Canada   54 30N 124 30W   89
Stuart *Range*: S.A., Australia   29 00S 134 30E   40
Stung Treng: Khmer Rep.   13 31N 105 59E   38
Stupino: U.S.S.R.   54 53N 38 05E   80
Stura di Demonte: *riv.*, Italy   44 15N 07 15E   71
Sturgeon: *riv.*, Sask., Canada   53 30N 106 30W   92
Sturgeon *Bank*: B.C., Canada   49 00N 123 15W   126
Sturgis: S.D., U.S.A.   44 45N 103 31W   94
Sturminster Newton: Dorset, England   50 56N 02 19W   61
Sturt *Desert*: Australia   29 30S 141 00E   14 41
Stuttgart: W.Germany   48 47N 09 12E   26 72
Stuttgart: Ark., U.S.A.   34 30N 91 33W   100
Styr: *riv.*, U.S.S.R.   51 15N 25 45E   78
Suárez, J.L.: Argentina   34 32S 58 35W   128
Subarharekha: *riv.*, India   22 00N 87 00E   83
Subotica: Yugoslavia   46 04N 19 41E   27 78
Sučan: U.S.S.R.   43 08N 133 09E   86
Suceava: Romania   47 37N 26 18E   78
Süchbaatar (Sühbaatar): Mongolia   45 30N 114 00E   30
Suchinići: U.S.S.R.   54 06N 35 20E   80
Suchoj Log: U.S.S.R.   56 55N 62 01E   81
Suchona (Sukhona): *riv.*, U.S.S.R.   60 15N 43 30E   28
Suchou *see* Suzhou   31 18N 120 45E   37 84
Suchumi (Sukhumi): U.S.S.R.   43 01N 41 02E   28
Suck: *riv.*, Irish Republic   53 30N 08 15W   67
Sucre: Bolivia   19 02S 65 17W   49
Sucunduri: *riv.*, Brazil   06 30S 59 00W   50
Sucy-en-Brie: France   48 46N 02 32E   117
SUDAN   04 15N 32 00E   20 53 107
Sudbury: Ont., Canada   46 30N 81 01W   44 99
Sudbury: Suff., England   52 02N 00 44E   59
Sudomskaja Vozvyšennost': *hld.*, U.S.S.R.   57 30N 29 30E   80
Suez *see* As Suways   29 58N 32 33E   32 107
Suez, *Gulf of see* Suways, Khalīj as   28 45N 32 45E   32
Suez *Canal see* Suways, Qanat as   30 30N 32 15E   20 32
Suffolk: Va., U.S.A.   36 44N 76 37W   101
Suffolk: *admin.*, England   52 00N 01 00E   59
Sugar Creek: Mo., U.S.A.   39 06N 94 27W   94
Suginami: Japan   35 41N 139 39E   121
Sühbaatar *see* Süchbaatar   45 30N 114 00E   30
Suhl: E.Germany   50 37N 10 43E   73
Suian: China   29 28N 118 44E   85
Suichang: China   28 34N 119 20E   85
Suichuan: China   26 22N 114 32E   85
Suide: China   27 33N 110 04E   84
Suining: Jiangsu, China   33 54N 118 00E   84
Suining: Sichuan, China   30 31N 105 34E   36
Suiping: China   33 10N 114 02E   84
Suir: *riv.*, Irish Republic   52 15N 07 15W   67
Suitland: Md., U.S.A.   38 51N 76 55W   122
Suixi: Anhui, China   33 54N 116 50E   84
Suixian: Henan, China   34 26N 115 05E   84
Suixian: Hubei, China   31 42N 113 22E   84
Suiyang: Guizhou, China   27 59N 107 14E   85
Suiyang: Heilongjiang, China   44 26N 130 53E   86
Suizhong: China   40 20N 120 21E   84
Sūjāngarh: India   27 43N 74 35E   82
Sukabumi: Indonesia   06 55S 106 50E   38
Sukagawa: Japan   37 17N 140 23E   86
Sukarnapura *see* Djajapura   02 32S 140 42E   13
Sukhona: *riv. see* Suchona   60 15N 43 30E   28
Sukhumi *see* Suchumi   43 01N 41 02E   28
Sukkur: Pakistan   27 42N 68 54E   34
Sulaiman *Range*: Pakistan   29 30N 69 45E   10 34
Sula *Islands*: Indonesia   01 45S 125 00E   39
Sulawesi: *is. see* Celebes   02 15S 120 30E   39
Sulgrave: Northants., England   52 07N 01 11W   59
Sullana: Peru   04 52S 80 39W   48
Sullivan *Lake*: Alta., Canada   52 00N 112 00W   92
Sullivan Station: B.C., Canada   49 07N 122 48W   126
Sulo: *riv. see* Shule   40 30N 94 45E   36
Sulphur: *riv.*, U.S.A.   33 15N 94 30W   100
Sulphur Springs: Tex., U.S.A.   33 08N 95 36W   100
Sultānpur: India   26 16N 82 05E   83
Sulu *Archipelago*: Philippines   05 45N 120 30E   39
Suluchi: *lake*, China   30 15N 86 15E   83
Sulu *Sea*   08 30N 120 30E   12 38

Sülz: W.Germany   50 55N 06 55E   119
Sülz: riv., W.Germany   50 45N 07 00E   119
Sulzbach-Rosenberg: W.Germany   49 30N 11 45E   73
Sumatra: is. & admin., Indonesia   00 00 101 00E   1 12 38
Šumava: mtns., Czechoslovakia   49 00N 13 30E   73 78
Sumba: is., Indonesia   09 45S 120 00E   13
Sumbawa: is., Indonesia   08 45S 117 30E   13 39
Sumburgh Head: Shet. Is., Scotland   59 51N 01 16W   65
Sumen: Bulgaria   43 16N 25 23E   79
Šumerl'a: U.S.S.R.   55 30N 46 26E   81
Sumgait: U.S.S.R.   40 36N 49 38E   28 105 107
Sumida: Japan   35 42N 139 50E   121
Summerland: B.C., Canada   49 36N 119 41W   89
Summerside: P.E.I., Canada   46 24N 63 46W   97
Summit: Ill., U.S.A.   41 46N 87 49W   124
Summit: N.J., U.S.A.   40 43N 74 23W   123
Summit Lake: B.C., Canada   58 39N 124 39W   88
Sumoto: Japan   34 21N 134 54E   86
Šumperk: Czechoslovakia   49 58N 17 00E   73
Sumter: S.C., U.S.A.   33 54N 80 22W   101
Sumy: U.S.S.R.   50 55N 34 45E   28 80
Sunagawa: Japan   43 29N 141 55E   86
Sunãm: India   30 07N 75 49E   82
Sunart, Loch: Argyll., Scotland   56 30N 05 45W   64
Sunbright: Tenn., U.S.A.   36 15N 84 40W   101
Sunbury: Gt. Ldn., England   51 24N 00 25W   59
Sunbury: Pa., U.S.A.   40 52N 76 47W   99
Sundarbans: geog. reg., Bangladesh   22 00N 89 45E   35 83
Sundargarh: admin., India   22 00N 84 00E   105
Sunda Strait: Indonesia   06 30S 105 30E   13 39
Sunderland: Tyne & Wear, England   54 55N 01 23W   63
Sundre: Alta., Canada   51 49N 114 46W   92
Sundsvall: Sweden   62 22N 17 20E   27 74
Sungari: riv. see Songhua   45 30N 125 30E   37
Sungari Reservoir see Songhua, Lake   42 30N 127 00E   37
Sunland: Calif., U.S.A.   34 16N 118 19W   127
Sunndalsøra: Norway   62 39N 08 37E   74
Sunnyside: Wash., U.S.A.   46 20N 120 00W   90
Sunrise: Wyo., U.S.A.   42 20N 104 42W   94
Sunset Beach: Calif., U.S.A.   33 43N 118 04W   127
Sunshine State Parkway: hwy., Fla., U.S.A.
  29 15N 82 15W   101
Sunti: riv., India   22 46N 88 27E   120
Sun Valley: Idaho, U.S.A.   43 42N 114 21W   90
Suoche (Yarkand): China   38 25N 77 16E   29
Suó-nada: sea, Japan   33 45N 131 15E   86
Suonenjoki: Finland   62 40N 27 06E   74
Superior: Ariz., U.S.A.   33 18N 111 06W   91
Superior: Nebr., U.S.A.   40 01N 98 04W   94
Superior: Wis., U.S.A.   46 42N 92 05W   44 98
Superior, Lake: Canada/U.S.A.   47 45N 88 00W   17 44 98
Suqian: China   33 53N 118 21E   84
Suqutra (Socotra): is., Arabian Sea   12 30N 54 00E   10 33
Sura: riv., U.S.S.R.   55 15N 46 30E   81
Surabaja: Indonesia   07 14S 112 45E   38
Surakarta (Solo): Indonesia   07 32S 110 50E   38
Surat: India   21 10N 72 54E   82
Surat Thani (Ban Don): Thailand   09 09N 99 20E   35
Suraż: U.S.S.R.   55 25N 30 44E   80
Surendranagar: India   22 44N 71 43E   82
Surgut: U.S.S.R.   61 14N 73 20E   29
Sũri: India   23 54N 87 32E   83
Surigao: Philippines   09 47N 125 29E   105
SURINAM (Netherlands Guiana):   04 30N 56 15W
  18 50 106
Suriname: riv., Surinam   03 45N 56 15W   48
Surovikino: U.S.S.R.   48 36N 42 51E   80
Surprise: B.C., Canada   59 37N 133 25W   88
Surrey: B.C., Canada   49 11N 122 52W   126
Surrey: admin., England   51 00N 00 30W   59
Sursk: U.S.S.R.   53 04N 45 42E   81
Surskoje: U.S.S.R.   54 30N 46 44E   81
Surtsey: is. & volc., Iceland   63 18N 20 37W   6
Susanville: Calif., U.S.A.   40 26N 120 40W   91
Sušary: U.S.S.R.   59 48N 30 23E   119
Susong: China   30 05N 116 08E   85
Sussex: N.B., Canada   45 43N 65 32W   97
Sussex: admin., England see East Sussex; West Sussex   59
Sussex, Vale of: England   50 45N 00 15W   59
Susuman: U.S.S.R.   62 47N 148 10E   31
Sutherland: N.S.W., Australia   34 02S 151 03E   120

Sutherland: admin., Scotland   58 15N 04 30W   64
Sutjeska National Park: Yugoslavia   43 30N 19 00E   79
Sutlej (Langchuhe): riv., Asia   30 00N 72 45E   82
Sutton: Gt. Ldn., England   51 22N 00 12W   112
Sutton Coldfield: W.Mid., England   52 34N 01 48W   58 115
Sutton-in-Ashfield: Notts., England   53 08N 01 15W   58
Suva: Fiji   18 08S 178 25E   1
Šuvalovo: U.S.S.R.   60 02N 30 18E   119
Suwa: Japan   36 02N 138 08E   86
Suwannee: riv., U.S.A.   29 30N 83 00W   101
Suways, Khalīj as (Suez, Gulf of): Egypt   28 45N 32 45E   32
Suways, Qanat as (Suez Canal): Egypt   30 30N 32 15E
  20 32
Suwŏn: S.Korea   37 17N 127 01E   37
Suxian: China   33 38N 117 02E   84
Suzhou (Suchou, Soochow): China   31 18N 120 45E   37 84
Suzhou (Wusong): riv., China   31 14N 121 22E   121
Suzuka: Japan   34 51N 136 35E   86
Suzu-misaki: cape, Japan   37 31N 137 21E   86
Svalbard: is. see Spitzbergen   78 00N 20 00E   3 23
Svatovo: U.S.S.R.   49 23N 38 13E   80
Svendborg: Denmark   55 04N 10 38E   75
Šventoji: riv., U.S.S.R.   55 15N 24 30E   75
Sverdlovsk: Rossijskaja S.F.S.R., U.S.S.R.   56 51N 60 36E
  29 81 105
Sverdlovsk: Ukrainskaja S.S.R., U.S.S.R.   48 05N 39 40E   80
Svetlogorsk: U.S.S.R.   52 38N 29 42E   80
Svetozarevo: Yugoslavia   44 00N 21 15E   79
Svitavy: Czechoslovakia   49 45N 16 30E   73
Svobodnyj (Svobodnyy): U.S.S.R.   51 24N 128 07E   31
Swadlincote: Derby., England   52 47N 01 34W   58 115
Swaffham: Norf., England   52 39N 00 41E   58
Swainsboro: Ga., U.S.A.   32 36N 82 21W   101
Swakopmund: S.W.Africa   22 40S 14 34E   55
Swale: riv., N.Yorks., England   54 00N 01 15W   63
Swale, The: chan., Kent, England   51 15N 00 45E   59
Swaledale: val., N.Yorks., England   54 15N 01 45W   63
Swampscott: Mass., U.S.A.   42 28N 70 55W   122
Swanage: Dorset, England   50 37N 01 58W   61
Swan Hills: Alta., Canada   54 45N 116 00W   92
Swan Lake: Man., Canada   52 30N 100 30W   93
Swanlinbar: Cavan, Irish Republic   54 12N 07 42W   66
Swan River: Man., Canada   52 06N 101 17W   92
Swansea: Ont., Canada   43 39N 79 29W   125
Swansea: W.Glam., Wales   51 38N 03 57W   26 61
Swansea Bay: W.Glam., Wales   51 30N 03 45W   61
Swatow see Shant'ou   23 23N 116 41E   36 85
SWAZILAND   26 30S 31 30E   21 55 107
SWEDEN   7 27 74 107
Sweeny: Tex., U.S.A.   29 03N 95 42W   106
Sweet Home: Oreg., U.S.A.   44 24N 122 44W   90
Sweetwater: Tex., U.S.A.   32 28N 100 25W   95
Świebodzin: Poland   52 15N 15 31E   73
Swift Current: Sask., Canada   50 17N 107 45W   92
Swift River: Yukon, Canada   60 00N 131 11W   88
Swilly, Lough: Don., Irish Rep.   55 10N 07 32W   66
Swindon: Wilts., England   51 34N 01 47W   61
Swinford: Mayo, Irish Republic   53 57N 08 57W   66
Świnoujście: Poland   53 55N 14 18E   73 78
Swistbach: riv., W.Germany   50 45N 06 45E   119
SWITZERLAND   46 30N 08 00E   6 26 71 107
Swords: Dublin, Irish Republic   53 28N 06 13W   66
Sybil Point: Kerry, Irish Republic   52 10N 10 27W   67
Syčovka: U.S.S.R.   55 50N 34 17E   80
Sydney: N.S.W., Australia   33 55S 151 10E   41 120
Sydney: N.S., Canada   46 10N 60 10W   44 97 104
Sydney Mines: N.S., Canada   46 16N 60 15W   97
Syktyvkar: U.S.S.R.   61 40N 50 46E   28
Sylacauga: Ala., U.S.A.   33 10N 86 15W   101
Syracuse: Sicily see Siracusa   37 04N 15 18E   32 79
Syracuse: N.Y., U.S.A.   43 03N 76 10W   45 99
Syrdarja (Syrdar'ya, Jaxartes): riv., U.S.S.R.
  45 30N 64 30E   8 29
SYRIA   35 00N 38 45E   10 32 107
Syrian Desert: Iraq   32 15N 39 00E   10 32
Syston: Leics., England   52 42N 01 04W   58
Syzran': U.S.S.R.   53 09N 48 27E   28 81 107
Szamotuły: Poland   52 36N 16 34E   73
Szczecin (Stettin): Poland   53 25N 14 32E   27 73 78
Szczecin: admin., Poland   53 30N 15 00E   73
Szczecinek: Poland   53 42N 16 41E   73 78

Szechwan: admin. see Sichuan   31 00N 107 45E   36 84
Szeged: Hungary   46 15N 20 09E   27 78
Székesfehérvár: Hungary   47 10N 18 24E   78
Szolnok: Hungary   47 10N 20 10E   78
Szombathely: Hungary   47 13N 16 38E   78

Tabaco: Philippines   13 21N 123 44E   39
Taber: Alta., Canada   49 48N 112 09W   92
Tablada: Argentina   34 42S 58 33W   128
Table Rock Reservoir: Mo., U.S.A.   36 38N 93 17W   98
Tábor: Czechoslovakia   49 25N 14 41E   73
Tabora: Tanzania   05 02S 32 50E   54
Tabou: Ivory Coast   04 28N 07 20W   57
Tabrīz: Iran   38 05N 46 18E   33
Tabūk (Tebuk): Saudi Arabia   28 23N 36 36E   33
Taché, Lac: N.W.T., Canada   64 00N 120 00W   88
Tacloban: Philippines   11 15N 125 01E   39
Tacna: Peru   18 00S 70 15W   49
Tacoma: Wash., U.S.A.   47 14N 122 26W   42 90
Taconite Harbor: Minn., U.S.A.   47 31N 90 56W   98
Tacuarembó: Uruguay   31 42S 56 00W   52
Tacuba: Mexico   19 27N 99 11W   128
Tacubaya: Mexico   19 24N 99 11W   128
Tadcaster: N.Yorks., England   53 53N 01 16W   63 115
Tademaït, Plateau du: Algeria   28 45N 02 00E   56
Tadoule Lake: Man., Canada   58 30N 98 15W   93
Tadoussac: Qué., Canada   48 09N 69 43W   96
Tadzhik S.S.R., admin., U.S.S.R.   38 30N 71 00E   29
Taegu: S.Korea   35 52N 128 35E   37
Taejŏn: S.Korea   36 20N 127 26E   37
Taf: riv., Dyfed, Wales   51 45N 04 30W   60
Tafalla: Spain   42 32N 01 41W   70
Taff: riv., Mid. Glam., Wales   51 30N 03 15W   113
Taf Fechan Reservoir: Powys, Wales   51 50N 03 23W   113
Taganrog: U.S.S.R.   47 12N 38 56E   28 80 105
Taganrogskij Zaliv: gulf, U.S.S.R.   47 00N 38 30E   80
Tagdempt: Algeria   35 20N 01 20E   56
Tagish Lake: Canada   60 00N 134 15W   88
Tagus (Tajo, Tejo): riv., Portugal/Spain   39 15N 08 30W
   26 77
Tahan, Mount: Malaysia   04 34N 102 17E   38
Tahat, Mount: Algeria   23 18N 05 33E   20 56
Tahiti: is., Society Is.   17 30N 149 30W   5
Tahoe, Lake: U.S.A.   39 00N 120 00W   91
Tahoua: Nigeria   14 57N 05 19E   57
Tahsinganling Shanmo see Great Khingan Mountains
   49 30N 122 00E   9 31
Tahsüeh Shan see Daxueshan   30 30N 101 30E   36
Ṭaḥṭā: Egypt   26 46N 31 30E   32
Tai, Lake: China   31 15N 120 15E   37 84
Taian: China   36 12N 117 07E   36 84
Taibaishan (T'aipai Shan): mtn., China   33 54N 107 39E
   36 84
T'aichou see Taizhou   32 25N 119 58E   37 84
T'aichung: Taiwan   24 09N 120 41E   37 85
Taigu: China   37 22N 112 30E   84
Taihape: N.I., New Zealand   39 40S 175 48E   87
Taihe: Anhui, China   33 09N 115 40E   85
Taihe: Jiangxi, China   26 47N 114 52E   84
Taihu: China   30 20N 116 21E   85
Taikang: China   34 00N 114 55E   84
Tain: R. & Crom., Scotland   57 48N 04 04W   65
T'ainan: Taiwan   23 00N 120 15E   37 85
Taínaron, Ákra (Matapan, Cape): Greece   36 23N 22 29E   79
Taining: China   26 52N 117 11E   85
T'aipai Shan: mtns. see Taibaishan   33 54N 107 39E   36 84
T'aipei: Taiwan   25 00N 121 35E   37 85
T'aipeihsien: Taiwan   24 58N 121 30E   85
Taiping: China   30 18N 118 12E   85
Taiping: Malaysia   04 54N 100 42E   38
Taira see Iwaki   37 03N 140 55E   37 86
Taisetsu-zan-kokuritsu-kōen: nat. park,
Japan   43 30N 143 00E   87
Taishan: China   22 16N 112 47E   85
Taishun: China   27 30N 119 45E   85
Taitao, Península de: Chile   46 30S 74 30W   52
Taito: Japan   35 43N 139 48E   121
T'aitung: Taiwan   22 45N 121 11E   85

TAIWAN (Formosa)   23 30N 120 45E   12 37 85 107
T'aiwan Haihsia see Formosa Strait   24 30N 119 30E
   12 37 85
Taixing: China   32 09N 120 01E   84
Taiyuan: China   37 50N 112 35E   36 84 105
Taizhou (T'aichou): China   32 25N 119 58E   37 84
Ta'izz: Yemen   13 38N 44 04E   33
Tajmyr (Taymyr), Lake: U.S.S.R.   74 45N 103 00E   9 30
Tajmyr (Taymyr) Peninsula: U.S.S.R.   75 00N 107 00E   9
Tajo (Tejo, Tagus): riv., Portugal/Spain   40 00N 03 15W
   26 77
Tajšet (Tayshet): U.S.S.R.   55 57N 98 00E   30
Tak (Rahaeng): Thailand   16 51N 99 08E   35
Takada: Japan   37 06N 138 15E   86
Takamatsu: Japan   34 20N 134 03E   37 86
Takaoka: Japan   36 45N 137 01E   37 86
Takatsu: Japan   35 35N 139 36E   121
Takeo: Khmer Rep.   11 00N 104 46E   38
Takeshita: Japan   35 33N 139 32E   121
Takikawa: Japan   43 33N 141 54E   86
Takingeun: Indonesia   04 37N 96 48E   38
Takla Lake: B.C., Canada   55 15N 125 45W   89
Takoradi: Ghana   04 55N 01 45W   57
Taku: B.C., Canada   59 40N 133 50W   88
Taku: China, see Dagu   38 58N 117 40E   84
Taku: riv., B.C., Canada   59 00N 133 00W   88
Talara: Peru   04 38S 81 18E   48
Talaud Islands: Indonesia   04 00N 126 45E   12 38
Talavera de la Reina: Spain   39 58N 04 50W   77
Talca: Chile   35 28S 71 40W   52
Talcahuano: Chile   36 40S 73 10W   52
Taldy-Kurgan: U.S.S.R.   45 00N 78 23E   29
Tali see Dali   34 42N 109 55E   84
Taliabu: is., Indonesia   02 00S 124 30E   39
Taliang Shan see Daliangshan: mtns.   28 00N 102 45E
   12 36
Talladega: Ala., U.S.A.   33 26N 86 06W   101
Tallaght: Dublin, Irish Republic   53 17N 06 22W   67
Tallahassee: Fla., U.S.A.   30 26N 84 19W   45 101
Tallinn (Revel): U.S.S.R.   59 22N 24 48E   75
Tallow: Wat., Irish Republic   52 05N 08 00W   67
Tallulah: La., U.S.A.   32 25N 91 11W   100
Talo: mtn., Ethiopia   10 44N 37 55E   53
Talovaja: U.S.S.R.   51 06N 40 44E   80
Taltal: Chile   25 24S 70 29W   49
Taltson: riv., N.W.T., Canada   60 30N 111 30W   92
Tama (Rokugo): riv., Japan   35 31N 139 30E   121
Tamale: Ghana   09 26N 00 49W   57
Tamanrasset: Algeria   22 50N 05 31E   56
Tamar: riv., England   50 30N 04 15W   61
Tamatave: Malagasy Rep.   18 10S 49 23E   55
Tamaulipas: admin., Mexico   23 30N 99 00W   46
Tambacounda: Senegal   13 45N 13 40W   57
Tambov: U.S.S.R.   52 43N 41 25E   28 80
Tame: Colombia   06 27N 71 42W   48
Tame: riv., England   52 30N 01 45W   115
Tamera: Tunisia   37 01N 09 09E   104
Tamgak Mountains: Niger   19 00N 09 00E   56
Tamil Nadu (Madras): admin., India   11 30N 78 00E   34
Tammerfors see Tampere   61 32N 23 45E   27 75
Tampa: Fla., U.S.A.   27 58N 82 38W   45 101 104
Tampa Bay: Fla., U.S.A.   27 30N 82 30W   101
Tampere (Tammerfors): Finland   61 32N 23 45E   27 75
Tampico: Mexico   22 13N 97 51W   46
Tamrida: Socotra   12 38N 54 02E   33
Tamworth: Staffs., England   52 39N 01 40W   58 115
Tana: fd., Norway   70 45N 28 30E   74
Tana: riv., Kenya   00 00 39 00E   54
Tana, Lake: Ethiopia   12 00N 37 15E   21 53
Tanabe: Japan   33 44N 135 22E   86
Tananarive (Antananarivo): Malagasy Rep.   18 55S 47 31E
   55
Tanashi: Japan   35 43N 139 30E   121
Tanat: riv., Wales   52 45N 03 15W   60
Tancheng: China   34 37N 118 23E   84
Tanch'ŏn: N.Korea   40 27N 128 54E   37 86
Tānda: India   26 33N 82 39E   83
Tandag: Philippines   09 04N 126 12E   39
Tanderagee: Arm., N.Ireland   54 22N 06 25W   66
Tandjungbalai: Indonesia   02 59N 99 46E   38
Tandjungpandan: Indonesia   02 44S 107 36E   38

Types of map: Ocean pp. 1-5; Physical pp. 6-25; Human pp. 26-57; Topographic pp. 58-101; World pp. 102-111; Urban pp. 112-128.

Tandula *Reservoir*: India   20 30N 81 00E   83
Tanezrouft: *geog. reg.*, Algeria   23 45N 00 30E   56
Tanga: Tanzania   05 07S 39 05E   54
Tangail: Bangladesh   24 15N 89 55E   83
Tanganyika, *Lake*: E.Africa   06 15S 29 30E   21 54
Tanger (Tangiers): Morocco   35 48N 05 45W   56 77
Tanggu: China   38 58N 117 40E   84
Tangguluha: *lake*, China   31 00N 85 30E   83
Tanghe: China   32 45N 112 48E   84
Tangiers *see* Tanger   35 48N 05 45W   56 77
Tangjiao: China   31 13N 121 31E   121
Tangshan: China   39 38N 118 11E   36 84
Tanimbar (Timorlaut) *Islands*: Indonesia   07 30S 131 15E   13 39
Tanjore *see* Thanjāvūr   10 46N 79 09E   34
Tanshui: Taiwan   25 10N 121 32E   85
Tantā: Egypt   30 48N 31 00E   32
Tantung *see* Andong   40 08N 124 20E   37
TANZANIA   04 30S 34 30E   21 54 107
Taohuaping *see* Longhui   27 10N 111 02E   85
Taole: China   38 44N 106 40E   84
Taos: N.Mex., U.S.A.   36 24N 105 35W   95
Taoyuan: China   28 50N 111 15E   85
Tapa: U.S.S.R.   59 16N 25 58E   80
Tapachula: Mexico   14 54N 92 17W   46
Tapajós: *riv.*, Brazil   05 15S 57 15W   18 50
Tapiales: Argentina   34 42S 58 29W   128
Tapieh Shan: *mtns. see* Dabieshan   31 15N 115 45E   36 84
Tappi-zaki: *cape*, Japan   41 15N 140 21E   86
Tapti: *riv.*, India   21 30N 74 00E   34 82
Tapuaenuku, *Mount*: S.I., New Zealand   42 00S 173 39E   37
Taquari: *riv.*, Mato Grosso, Brazil   18 15S 55 45W   51
Tarabuco: Bolivia   19 10S 64 57W   49
Tarābulus (Tripoli): Lebanon   34 27N 35 49E   32
Tarābulus (Tripoli): Libya   32 53N 13 12E   32
Tarakan: Indonesia   03 20N 117 38E   39
Taranaki: *geog. reg.*, New Zealand   39 15N 174 30E   87
Taransay: *is.*, Inv., Scotland   57 45N 07 00W   64
Taranto: Italy   40 28N 17 15E   27 79 105
Taranto, *Golfo di*: Italy   40 00N 17 15E   79
Tararua *Range*: N.I., New Zealand   40 45S 175 15E   87
Tarawa: *is.*, N.Pacific Ocean   01 30N 173 00E   4 15
Tarawera, *Mount*: N.I., New Zealand   38 14S 176 32E   87
Tarbat Ness: *cape*, R. & Crom., Scotland   57 52N 03 46W   65
Tarbert: Argyll., Scotland   55 52N 05 26W   62
Tarbert: Inv., Scotland   57 54N 06 49W   64
Tarbert, *East Loch*: Inv., Scotland   57 45N 06 45W   64
Tarbert, *West Loch*: Inv., Scotland   57 45N 06 45W   64
Tarbes: France   43 14N 00 05E   70
Târgu-Mureş *see* Tîrgu Mureş   46 33N 24 34E   27 78
Tarija: Bolivia   21 31S 64 45W   49
Tarim *Basin*: China   39 00N 84 00E   11
Tarkwa: Ghana   05 16N 01 59W   57
Tarlac: Philippines   15 29N 120 35E   39
Tarn: *riv.*, France   43 45N 01 15E   70
Târnovo: Bulgaria   43 04N 25 39E   79
Tarnów: Poland   50 01N 20 59E   78
Tarragona: Spain   41 07N 01 15E   77
Tarrasa: Spain   41 34N 02 00E   26 116
Tarsus: Turkey   36 52N 34 52E   32
Tartagal: Argentina   22 32S 63 49W   49
Tartary, *Gulf of*: U.S.S.R.   50 00N 141 00E   31
Tartu (Jurjev): U.S.S.R.   58 23N 26 43E   80
Tas: *riv.*, Norf., England   52 30N 01 15E   58
Tašauz (Tashauz): U.S.S.R.   41 50N 59 58E   29
Tashi Gang Dzong: Bhutan   27 19N 91 33E   83
Taškent (Tashkent): U.S.S.R.   41 20N 69 18E   29
Tasman, *Mount*: S.I., New Zealand   43 33S 170 10E   87
Tasman *Bay*: S.I., New Zealand   41 00S 73 15E   87
Tasmania: *admin. & is.*, Australia   42 15S 146 45E   15 40
Tasman *Mountains*: S.I., New Zealand   40 45S 72 45E   87
Tasman *Sea*   40 45S 169 00E   4 15 87
Tassili n'Ajjer: *hld.*, Algeria   25 30N 08 00E   20 56
Taštagol: U.S.S.R.   52 47N 87 53E   105
Tatabánya: Hungary   47 34N 18 25E   78
Tateyama: Japan   34 59N 139 52E   86
Tathlina *Lake*: N.W.T., Canada   60 30N 117 30W   88
Tatnam, *Cape*: Man., Canada   57 28N 90 43W   93
Tatry: *mtns.*, Czechoslovakia/Poland   49 15N 20 00E   78
Tat'ung *see* Datong   40 12N 113 15E   36 84

Taubaté: Brazil   23 00S 45 36W   51
Tauern: *mtns.*, Austria   47 00N 13 30E   78
Taufstein: *mtn.*, W.Germany   50 31N 09 16E   72
Taumarunui: N.I., New Zealand   38 53S 175 16E   87
Taunggyi: Burma   20 49N 97 01E   35
Taunton: Som., England   51 01N 03 06W   61
Taunton: Mass., U.S.A.   41 54N 71 06W   99
Taupo: N.I., New Zealand   38 42S 176 06E   87
Taupo, *Lake*: N.I., New Zealand   38 45S 175 45E   37 87
Tauranga: N.I., New Zealand   37 42S 176 11E   37 87
Taurus *Mountains*: Turkey   36 45N 32 45E   10 32
Tavda: *riv.*, U.S.S.R.   59 15N 63 15E   81
Tavistock: Devon, England   50 33N 04 08W   61
Tavoy: Burma   14 02N 98 12E   34
Taw: *riv.*, Devon, England   51 00N 03 45W   61
Tawas *Point*: Mich., U.S.A.   44 13N 83 28W   98
Tawau: Malaysia   04 16N 117 54E   39
Tawitawi *Group*: *is.*, Philippines   06 00N 121 00E   12 38
Tawu: Taiwan   22 17N 120 54E   85
Tay: *riv.*, Perth., Scotland   56 30N 03 30W   65
Tay, Firth of: *est.*, Scotland   56 15N 03 00W   65
Tay, *Loch*: Perth., Scotland   56 30N 04 00W   64
Tay, *Strath*: *val.*, Perth., Scotland   56 30N 03 30W   65
Taylor Flats: B.C., Canada   56 09N 120 40W   89
Taymyr, *Lake see* Tajmyr, *Lake*   74 45N 103 00E   9 30
Taymyr *Peninsula see* Tajmyr *Peninsula*   75 00N 107 00E   9
Tayshet *see* Tajšet   55 57N 98 00E   30
Tazin: *riv.*, Canada   60 15N 109 30W   92
Tazin *Lake*: Sask., Canada   59 45N 109 00W   92
Tbilisi: U.S.S.R.   41 43N 44 49E   28
Tczew: Poland   54 05N 18 46E   78
Teague: Tex., U.S.A.   31 38N 96 17W   100
Te Anau: S.I., New Zealand   45 24S 167 44E   87
Te Awamutu: N.I., New Zealand   38 00S 175 20E   87
Tébessa: Algeria   35 21N 08 06E   56
Tebuk *see* Tabūk   28 23N 36 36E   33
Techou *see* Dezhou   37 27N 116 18E   36 84
Tecomitl: Mexico   19 13N 98 59W   128
Tecuci: Romania   45 50N 27 27E   78
Tecumseh: Mich., U.S.A.   42 01N 83 56W   125
Tees: *riv.*, England   54 30N 01 30W   63
Teesdale: *val.*, Dur., England   54 30N 02 00W   63
Teesport: Yorks., England   54 36N 01 08W   106
Teesside (Middlesbrough, Redcar, Thornaby-on-Tees): England   54 30N 01 15W   26 105
Teesside: Cleve., England   54 35N 01 14W   63
Tegal: Indonesia   06 52S 109 07E   38
Tegeler See: *lake*, W.Germany   52 30N 13 15E   117
Tegucigalpa: Honduras   14 06N 87 13W   47
Tehrān (Teheran): Iran   35 40N 51 26E   33
Tehuantepec: Mexico   16 19N 95 13W   46
Tehuantepec, *Golfo de*: Mexico   16 00N 94 50W   17 47
Tehutli, Cerro del: *mtn.*, Mexico   19 13N 99 02W   128
Teifi: *riv.*, Dyfed, Wales   52 00N 04 15W   60
Teignmouth: Devon, England   50 33N 03 30W   61
Teixeira de Sousa: Angola   10 42S 22 12E   54
Tejkovo: U.S.S.R.   56 52N 40 34E   80
Tejo (Tajo, Tagus): *riv.*, Portugal/Spain   40 00N 03 15W   26 77
Tekapo, *Lake*: S.I., New Zealand   43 30S 171 00E   87
Tekeze: *riv.*, Ethiopia/Sudan   14 15N 36 45E   53
Tekirdağ: Turkey   40 59N 27 31E   79
Tela: Honduras   15 44N 87 27W   47
Teladuomu: China   29 38N 84 13E   35
Telanaipura (Djambi): Indonesia   01 36S 103 37E   38
Telaopengshashan: *mtn.*, China   30 33N 86 25E   83
Tel Aviv-Yafo (Jaffa-Tel Aviv): Israel   32 04N 34 46E   32
Telegraph Creek: B.C., Canada   57 56N 131 11W   42 89
Telen: *riv.*, Indonesia   01 30N 116 30E   39
Teles Pires (Paranatinga; São Manuel): *riv.*, Brazil   09 30S 56 30W   50
Telford: Salop, England   52 41N 02 29W   58
Tell Atlas: *mtns.*, Algeria   36 30N 06 30E   20 56
Teltow: E.Germany   52 24N 13 16E   117
Teltowkanal: *can.*, E.Germany/W.Germany   52 15N 13 00E   117
Telukbetung: Indonesia   05 28S 105 16E   38
Tema: Ghana   05 41N 00 00   57
Temangan: Malaysia   05 42N 102 09E   105
Teme: *riv.*, Here. & Worcs., England   52 00N 02 15W   59
Temesvár *see* Timişoara   45 45N 21 15E   27 78

Types of map: Ocean pp. 1-5; Physical pp. 6-25; Human pp. 26-57; Topographic pp. 58-101; World pp. 102-111; Urban pp. 112-128.

Temirtau: R.S.F.S.R., U.S.S.R.   53 08N 87 28E   105
Temirtau: Kazakh S.S.R., U.S.S.R.   50 05N 72 56E   29 105
Temperley: Argentina   34 47S 58 24W   128
Tempio Pausania: Sardinia   40 54N 09 06E   77
Temple: Tex., U.S.A.   31 06N 97 21W   95
Templemore: Tip., Irish Republic   54 48N 07 50W   67
Templin: E.Germany   53 07N 13 30E   73
Temuco: Chile   38 45S 72 40W   52
Temuka: S.I., New Zealand   44 12S 171 16E   87
Tenakee Springs: Alaska, U.S.A.   57 47N 135 13W   89
Tenāli: India   16 13N 80 36E   34
Tenas: riv., Spain   41 30N 02 15E   116
Tenasserim: Burma   12 05N 99 00E   35
Tenasserim: riv., Burma   12 45N 99 00E   35
Tenbury Wells: Here. & Worcs., England   52 19N 02 35W   60
Tenby: Dyfed, Wales   51 41N 04 43W   61
Tenerife: is., Canary Is.   28 15N 16 30W   56
Ténès: Algeria   36 34N 01 18E   77
Tengxian: Guangxi Zhuang, China   23 21N 110 53E   85
Tengxian: Shandong, China   35 08N 117 12E   84
Teniente Matienzo: rsch. stn., Antarctica   64 58S 60 02W   24
Tenkiller Ferry Reservoir: Okla., U.S.A.   35 35N 95 02W   100
Tennessee: admin., U.S.A.   43 101
Tennessee: riv., U.S.A.   34 30N 86 30W   45 101
Tenojoki: riv., Finland/Norway   70 30N 28 15E   74
Tenterden: Kent, England   51 05N 00 41E   59
Ten Thousand Islands: Fla., U.S.A.   25 45N 81 30W   101
Teófilo Otôni: Brazil   17 51S 41 30W   51
Tepepan: Mexico   19 16N 99 08W   128
Tepexpan: Mexico   19 37N 98 56W   128
Teplice: Czechoslovakia   50 40N 13 50E   73
Ter: riv., Spain   42 00N 02 30E   77
Teramo: Italy   42 40N 13 43E   79
Teresina: Brazil   05 05S 42 49W   50
Tereška: riv., U.S.S.R.   52 30N 47 30E   81
Termez: U.S.S.R.   37 14N 67 16E   29
Tern: riv., Salop, England   52 45N 02 30W   58
Ternate: Indonesia   00 48N 127 23E   39
Terni: Italy   42 34N 12 39E   27 79 105
Ternopol': U.S.S.R.   49 34N 25 36E   78
Terracina: Italy   41 17N 13 15E   79
Terre Haute: Ind., U.S.A.   39 27N 87 24W   45 98
Terrey Hills: N.S.W., Australia   33 41S 151 14E   120
Terror, Mount: volc., Antarctica   77 31S 168 33E   25
Terry: Mont., U.S.A.   46 37N 105 19W   94
Terschelling: is., Netherlands   53 25N 05 20E   72
Teruel: Spain   40 21N 01 06W   77
Teslin: Yukon, Canada   60 10N 132 42W   88
Teslin: riv., Canada   60 45N 134 00W   88
Teslin Lake: Canada   60 00N 132 30W   88
Test: riv., Hants., England   51 00N 01 30W   59
Tetbury: Glos., England   51 39N 02 10W   61
Tete: Mozambique   16 10S 33 36E   55
Tête Jaune: B.C., Canada   52 57N 119 25W   89
Teterev: riv., U.S.S.R.   51 00N 30 00E   80
Teterow: E.Germany   53 47N 12 35E   73
Tétouan (Tétuan): Morocco   35 34N 05 23W   56
Tetovo: Yugoslavia   42 00N 20 59E   79
Tétuan see Tétouan   35 34N 05 23W   56
Tetuan de las Victorias: Spain   40 28N 03 43W   116
Tet'uche (Tetyukhe): U.S.S.R.   44 35N 135 35E   37 86
Tet'uchePristan': U.S.S.R.   44 22N 135 48E   86
Tet'uši: U.S.S.R.   54 57N 48 50E   80
Tetyukhe see Tet'uche   44 35N 135 35E   37 86
Teuco (Bermejo): riv., Argentina   24 00S 62 30W   49
Tevere (Tiber): riv., Italy   42 15N 12 30E   79
Teviot: riv., Rox., Scotland   55 15N 02 45W   63
Teviotdale: val., Rox., Scotland   55 15N 02 45W   63
Te Waewae Bay: S.I., New Zealand   46 15S 167 30E   87
Tewkesbury: Glos., England   51 59N 02 09W   60
Texada Island: B.C., Canada   49 38N 124 30W   104
Texarkana: Ark., U.S.A.   33 26N 94 03W   100
Texarkana: Tex., U.S.A.   33 26N 94 03W   43 100
Texarkana Dam: Tex., U.S.A.   33 19N 94 10W   100
Texas: admin., U.S.A.   43 95
Texas City: Tex., U.S.A.   29 24N 94 54W   100 106
Texoco, Lago de (former site of): Mexico   19 30N 98 59W   128

Texel: is., Netherlands   53 00N 04 45E   72
Texoma, Lake: Okla., U.S.A.   33 50N 96 34W   43 100
Tezonco: Mexico   19 19N 99 04W   128
Tha-anne: riv., N.W.T., Canada   60 30N 95 30W   93
Thabana Ntlenyana: mtn., Lesotho   29 28S 29 16E   21 55
Thabazimbi: Trans., Rep. of S.Africa   24 41S 27 21E   105
THAILAND (Siam)   15 30N 102 30E   12 35 107
Thai Nguyen: N.Vietnam   21 31N 105 55E   36
Thakhek: Laos   17 22N 104 50E   38
Thal Desert: Pakistan   30 30N 71 15E   82
Thame: Oxon., England   51 45N 00 59W   59
Thame: riv., England   51 45N 00 45W   59
Thames: N.I., New Zealand   37 08S 175 35E   87
Thames: riv., Ont., Canada   42 30N 81 45W   98
Thames: riv., England   51 15N 00 00   59
Thames Estuary: England   51 30N 00 45E   59
Thāna: India   19 14N 73 02E   34 82
Thanjāvūr (Tanjore): India   10 46N 79 09E   34
Thar (Great Indian) Desert: India   28 00N 72 30E   11 34 82
Thásos: is., Greece   40 30N 24 30E   79
Thaton: Burma   16 56N 97 20E   35
Thebes see Thívai   38 19N 23 19E   79
The Bronx: N.Y., U.S.A.   40 50N 73 52W   123
The Dalles: Oreg., U.S.A.   45 36N 121 10W   90
The Hague see 's-Gravenhage, Den Haag   52 05N 04 16E   26 72
The Loop: Ill., U.S.A.   41 53N 87 37W   124
The North Sound: Ork. Is., Scotland   59 15N 02 45W   65
Theodore Roosevelt: riv., Brazil   10 30S 60 15W   50
Theodore Roosevelt National Memorial Park: N.D., U.S.A.   47 00N 103 15W   94
The Pas: Man., Canada   53 49N 101 14W   42 92
The Raven Point: Wex., Irish Republic   52 21N 06 22W   67
Thermopolis: Wyo., U.S.A.   43 39N 108 13W   94
Thessalon: Ont., Canada   46 15N 83 34W   98
Thessaloníki (Salonika): Greece   40 38N 22 58E   27 79
Thetford: Norf., England   52 25N 00 45E   58
Thetford Mines: Qué., Canada   46 06N 71 18W   96
Thiais: France   48 46N 02 23E   117
Thibodaux: La., U.S.A.   29 48N 90 49W   100
Thief River Falls: Minn., U.S.A.   48 07N 96 10W   98
Thiès: Senegal   14 49N 16 52W   57
Thiewiaza: riv., N.W.T., Canada   60 30N 98 00W   93
Thimbu: Bhutan   27 28N 89 39E   35 83
Thionville: France   49 22N 06 11E   71 105
Thíra: is., Greece   36 15N 25 15E   79
Thirsk: N.Yorks., England   54 14N 01 20W   63
Thívai (Thebes): Greece   38 19N 23 19E   79
Thoa: riv., N.W.T., Canada   61 45N 108 15W   92
Thom, Loch: Renf., Scotland   55 45N 04 45W   113
Thomaston: Maine, U.S.A.   44 04N 69 14W   99
Thomastown: Kilk., Irish Republic   52 31N 07 08W   67
Thomasville: Ala., U.S.A.   31 55N 87 44W   100
Thomasville: Ga., U.S.A.   30 50N 83 59W   101
Thompson: Man., Canada   55 45N 97 54W   42 93
Thompson: riv., B.C., Canada   50 30N 121 15W   89
Thomson: Ga., U.S.A.   33 28N 82 31W   101
Thomsons Falls: Kenya   00 04N 36 22E   54
Thon Buri: Thailand   13 43N 100 27E   35
Thonon-les-Bains: France   46 22N 06 30E   71
Thornaby-on-Tees see Teesside   54 30N 01 15W   26 105
Thornaby-on-Tees: Cleve., England   54 34N 01 18W   63
Thornbury: Avon, England   51 37N 02 32W   61 113
Thorne: S.Yorks., England   53 37N 00 58W   63
Thornhill: Dumf., Scotland   55 15N 03 46W   62
Thornton: Lancs., England   53 31N 03 01W   63
Thorp Arch: W.Yorks., England   53 55N 01 20W   115
Thouars: France   46 59N 00 13W   70
Thrapston: Northants., England   52 24N 00 32W   59
Three Kings Islands: N.I., New Zealand   34 00S 172 00E   87
Three Points, Cape: Ivory Coast   04 43N 02 06W   57
Three Rivers: Qué., Canada see Trois-Rivières   46 21N 72 34W   44 96
Thrushel: riv., Devon, England   50 30N 04 00W   61
Thule: Greenland   77 40N 69 00W   23
Thun: Switzerland   46 46N 07 38E   71
Thunder Bay (Fort William, Port Arthur): Ont., Canada   48 24N 89 14W   44 98
Thunder Bay: Ont., Canada   48 15N 89 00W   98
Thuner See: lake, Switzerland   46 30N 07 45E   71
Thüringer Wald: mtns., E.Germany   50 30N 10 45E   73

Types of map: Ocean pp. 1-5; Physical pp. 6-25; Human pp. 26-57; Topographic pp. 58-101; World pp. 102-111; Urban pp. 112-128.

Thurles: Tip., Irish Republic	52 41N 07 49W	67
Thurmaston: Leics., England	52 40N 01 05W	58
Thurso: Caith., Scotland	58 35N 03 32W	65
Thurso: riv., Caith., Scotland	58 15N 03 30W	65
Thurston Island: Antarctica	72 06S 99 00W	25
Thutade Lake: B.C., Canada	56 45N 127 00W	89
Thysville: Zaïre	05 15S 14 52E	54
Tiana: Spain	41 28N 02 16E	116
Tianchang: China	32 41N 119 00E	84
Tiandan: China	39 53N 116 26E	121
Tiandong (T'ientung): China	23 40N 107 09E	36 85
Tianjin (Tientsin): China	39 08N 117 12E	36 84
Tianjin (Tientsin): admin., China	39 00N 117 30E	84
Tianmen: China	30 35N 113 18E	85
Tianqiao: China	39 54N 116 24E	121
Tianshui (T'ienshui): China	34 30N 105 58E	36
Tiantai: China	29 09N 121 08E	85
Tianzhen: China	40 28N 114 06E	84
Tiaret: Algeria	35 20N 01 20E	77
Tĩb, R'as aṭ (Bon, Cap): Tunisia	37 05N 11 02E	79
Tibé, Pic de (Tio, Pic de): Guinea	08 52N 08 54W	20 57
Tiber: riv. see Tevere	42 15N 12 30E	79
Tiber Dam: Mont., U.S.A.	48 19N 111 06W	90
Tibesti: mtn. reg., Chad	21 00N 17 15E	20
Tibet: admin. see Xizang	29 00N 88 00E	35 83
Tibet, Plateau of: China	33 00N 85 00E	11
Tiburon: Calif., U.S.A.	37 53N 122 27W	126
Tiburón: is., Mexico	29 00N 112 30W	46
Tichmenevo: U.S.S.R.	58 00N 38 36E	80
Tichoreck (Tikhoretsk): U.S.S.R.	45 51N 40 09E	28
Tichvin: U.S.S.R.	59 39N 33 31E	80
Ticonderoga: N.Y., U.S.A.	43 51N 73 26W	99
Tidjikdja (Tidjikja): Mauritania	18 33N 11 25W	56
Tidore see Soasiu	00 40N 127 25E	39
Tien Shan: ra., China/U.S.S.R.	41 30N 78 00E	8 29
T'ienshui see Tianshui	34 30N 105 58E	36
Tientsin see Tianjin	39 08N 117 12E	36 84
Tientsin: admin. see Tianjin	39 00N 117 30E	84
T'ientung see Tiandong	23 40N 107 09E	36 85
Tiergarten: park, W.Germany	52 31N 13 21E	117
Tierra del Fuego: admin., Argentina	54 15S 67 15W	52
Tierra del Fuego: is., Argentina/Chile	54 00S 68 30W	
		19 52
Tietar: riv., Spain	40 00N 05 00W	77
Tietê: riv., Brazil	22 15S 48 45W	51
Tiffin: Ohio, U.S.A.	41 07N 83 11W	98
Tignish: P.E.I., Canada	46 58N 64 03W	97
Tigre: Argentina	34 25S 58 35W	128
Tigre: riv., Ecuador/Peru	03 00S 75 15W	48
Tigris: riv., Iraq/Turkey	35 15N 43 30E	10 32
Tijeras: N.Mex., U.S.A.	35 05N 106 23W	95
Tijuana: Mexico	32 29N 117 10W	91
Tikhoretsk see Tichoreck	45 51N 40 09E	28
Tiko: Cameroun	04 02N 09 19E	57
Tilaiya Reservoir: India	24 15N 85 30E	83
Tilak Nagar: India	28 39N 77 08E	120
Tilburg: Netherlands	51 34N 05 05E	26 72
Tilbury: Essex, England	51 28N 00 23E	112
Tilbury Island: B.C., Canada	49 08N 123 01W	126
Tile Hill: W.Mid., England	52 24N 01 33W	115
Tilhar: India	27 57N 79 45E	82
Tillamook: Oreg., U.S.A.	45 27N 123 51W	90
Tillicoultry: Clack., Scotland	56 09N 03 45W	65
Tilsit see Sovetsk	55 02N 21 50E	75
Tilt: riv., Perth., Scotland	56 45N 03 50W	65
Tilt Cove: Nfld., Canada	49 53N 55 44W	97
Timagami: Ont., Canada	47 04N 79 47W	99 104
Timaru: S.I., New Zealand	44 23S 171 14E	87
Timbuktu see Tombouctou	16 49N 02 59W	56
Timimoun: Algeria	29 15N 00 14E	56
Timiris, Cape (Mirik, Capel): Mauritania	19 21N 16 29W	56
Timirjazevskij Park: U.S.S.R.	55 49N 37 32E	119
Timiskaming: Qué., Canada	46 43N 79 06W	96
Timiskaming, Lake: Canada	47 00N 79 15W	99
Timişoara (Temesvár): Romania	45 45N 21 15E	27 78
Timmins: Ont., Canada	48 30N 81 20W	44 99
Timor: is., Timor Sea	09 15S 125 00E	13 39
Timorlaut: is. see Tanimbar Islands	07 30S 131 15E	13 39
Timor Sea	13 15S 123 15E	13 40
Tinicum Wildlife Preserve: Pa., U.S.A.	39 53N 75 15W	122
Tínos: is., Greece	37 32N 25 09E	79
Tinrhert, Plateau de: Algeria	28 00N 06 30E	56
Tintagel: Corn., England	50 40N 04 45W	61
Tintagel Head: Corn., England	50 41N 04 46W	61
Tintina Valley: Yukon, Canada	63 15N 137 00W	88
Tio, Pic de see Tibé, Pic de	08 52N 08 54W	20 57
Tipperary: Tip., Irish Rep.	52 29N 08 10W	67
Tipperary: admin., Irish Rep.	52 30N 07 45W	67
Tipton: W.Mid., England	52 32N 02 05W	115
Tiranë (Tirana): Albania	41 20N 19 49E	27 79
Tiraspol': U.S.S.R.	46 51N 29 38E	78
Tire: Turkey	38 04N 27 45E	79
Tiree: is., Argyll., Scotland	56 30N 06 45W	64
Tîrgovişte: Romania	44 56N 25 27E	78
Tîrgu-Jui: Romania	45 03N 23 17E	78
Tîrgu Mureş (Târgu-Mureş): Romania	46 33N 24 34E	
		27 78
Tirso: riv., Sardinia	40 00N 08 45E	77
Tiruchchiráppalli: India	10 50N 78 43E	34
Tirunelveli: India	08 45N 77 43E	34
Tiruppur: India	11 05N 77 20E	34
Tisdale: Sask., Canada	52 51N 104 01W	92
Tista: riv., Bangladesh/India	26 30N 88 45E	83
Tisza: riv., Hungary	48 15N 21 45E	27
Titagárh: India	22 44N 88 22E	120
Titicaca, Lake: Bolivia/Peru	16 00S 69 15W	18 49
Titograd (Podgorica): Yugoslavia	42 28N 19 17E	27 79
Titovo Užice (Užice): Yugoslavia	43 52N 19 50E	79
Titov Veles (Veles): Yugoslavia	41 43N 21 49E	79
Tiumpan Head: R. & Crom., Scotland	58 15N 06 10W	64
Tiverton: Devon, England	50 55N 03 29W	61
Tivoli: Italy	41 58N 12 48E	79
Tizi-Ouzou: Algeria	36 44N 04 05E	77
Tjilatjap: Indonesia	07 44S 109 00E	38
Tjirebon (Cheribon): Indonesia	06 46S 108 33E	38
Tlahuac: Mexico	19 16N 99 01W	128
Tlalnepantla: Mexico	19 33N 99 12W	128
Tlaloc, Cerro: mtn., Mexico	19 06N 99 02W	128
Tlálpan: Mexico	19 17N 99 10W	128
Tlaltenco: Mexico	19 17N 99 01W	128
Tlemcen: Algeria	34 53N 01 21W	56
Toad Hotsprings: B.C., Canada	58 55N 125 03W	88
Toad River: B.C., Canada	58 51N 125 14W	88
Toba, Lake: Indonesia	02 30N 98 45E	38
Tobago: is., Trinidad & Tobago	11 15N 60 45W	48
Toba Tek Singh: Pakistan	30 54N 72 30E	82
Tobelo: Indonesia	01 45N 127 59E	39
Tobercurry: Sligo, Irish Republic	54 03N 08 43W	66
Tobermore: Lon., N.Ireland	54 48N 06 42W	66
Tobermory: Ont., Canada	45 15N 81 39W	98
Tobermory: Argyll., Scotland	56 37N 06 05W	64
Tobique: riv., N.B., Canada	47 00N 67 00W	96
Tobol: riv., U.S.S.R.	54 45N 65 00E	29
Tobol'sk: U.S.S.R.	58 12N 68 16E	29
Tobruk see Tubruq	32 05N 23 58E	32
Tocantins: riv., Brazil	03 30S 49 30W	18 50
Toccoa: Ga., U.S.A.	34 34N 83 21W	101
Tocopilla: Chile	22 05S 70 12W	49
Tocorpuri: mtn., Bolivia	22 26S 67 55W	49
Todmorden: W.Yorks., England	53 43N 02 05W	63 115
Toe Head: Cork, Irish Republic	51 30N 09 12W	67
Toe Head: Inv., Scotland	57 50N 07 07W	64
Tofield: Alta., Canada	53 22N 112 39W	92
Tofino: B.C., Canada	49 05N 125 51W	89
TOGO	08 30N 01 00E	20 57
Togo Mountains: Togo	02 30N 00 45E	57
Tokelau (Union) Islands: S.Pacific Ocean	08 00S 172 00W	
		4
Tokmak: U.S.S.R.	47 15N 35 43E	80
Tokoroa: N.I., New Zealand	38 13S 175 53E	87
Tokorozawa: Japan	35 48N 139 28E	121
Tokushima: Japan	34 04N 134 34E	37 86
Tokuyama: Japan	34 03N 131 49E	86 105 121
Tōkyō: Japan	35 42N 139 46E	37 86 105 121
Tōkyō-wan (Tokyo Bay): Japan	35 26N 139 47E	121
Tolbuhin: Bulgaria	43 34N 27 50E	79
Toledo: Spain	39 52N 04 02W	77
Toledo: Ohio, U.S.A.	41 40N 83 35W	98 106
Toledo: Oreg., U.S.A.	44 37N 123 56W	98
Toledo, Montes de: Spain	39 30N 04 30W	77
Toledo Bend Reservoir: U.S.A.	31 30N 93 45W	43
Tolima, Nevado del: mtn., Colombia	04 40N 75 19W	48

Types of map: Ocean pp. 1-5; Physical pp. 6-25; Human pp. 26-57; Topographic pp. 58-101; World pp. 102-111; Urban pp. 112-128.

Töling *see* Zhada   31 29N 79 50E   34
Tolitoli: Indonesia   01 05N 120 50E   39
Toljatti (Tol'yatti): U.S.S.R.   53 31N 49 26E   28 81
Tollense See: *lake*, E.Germany   53 30N 13 15E   73
Tollygunge: India   22 30N 88 21E   120
Tolly's Nullah: *riv.*, India   22 28N 88 27E   120
Tolo, *Gulf of*: Indonesia   02 00S 122 00E   39
Tolsta *Head*: R. & Crom., Scotland   58 20N 06 10W   64
Tol'yatti *see* Toljatti   53 31N 49 26E   28 81
Tomakomai: Japan   42 38N 141 36E   86
Tomaszów Mazowiecki: Poland   51 33N 20 02E   79
Tomba di Nerone: Italy   41 54N 12 28E   116
Tombador, Serra do: *ra.*, Brazil   12 15S 57 30W   50
Tombigbee: *riv.*, Ala., U.S.A.   31 45N 88 00W   100
Tombouctou (Timbuktu): Mali   16 49N 02 59W   56
Tombstone: Ariz., U.S.A.   31 43N 110 04W   91
Tomelloso: Spain   39 09N 03 01W   77
Tomini: Indonesia   00 31N 120 30E   39
Tomini, *Gulf of*: Indonesia   00 00 122 00E   12 39
Tomo: *riv.*, Colombia   05 15N 68 00W   48
Tom Price, *Mount*: W.A., Australia   22 49S 117 51E   105
Tomsk: U.S.S.R.   56 30N 84 58E   30
Tonalá: Mexico   16 04N 93 45W   46
Tonbridge: Kent, England   51 12N 00 16E   59 112
TONGA   18 00S 175 00W   4 15
Tong'an: China   24 42N 118 10E   85
Tonga *Trench*: S.Pacific Ocean   20 00S 173 00W   4
Tongbai: China   32 22N 113 29E   84
Tongcheng: Anhui, China   31 03N 116 58E   84
Tongcheng: Hubei, China   29 14N 113 49E   85
Tongchuan: China   35 01N 109 01E   84
Tongdao: China   26 30N 109 30E   85
Tonggu: China   28 33N 114 19E   85
Tongguan: China   34 38N 110 21E   84
Tonghai (T'unghai): China   24 07N 102 49E   36
Tonghua (T'unghua): China   41 50N 125 55E   37 105
Tongjiang: China   31 58N 107 14E   84
Tongliao (T'ungliao): China   43 39N 122 14E   37
Tongling: China   30 53N 117 44E   85 105
Tonglu: China   29 48N 119 40E   85
Tongren: China   27 44N 109 10E   85
Tongtianhe: *riv.*, China   34 45N 95 00E   12 36
Tongue: Suther., Scotland   58 28N 04 25W   64
Tongue: *riv.*, U.S.A.   46 00N 106 00W   94
Tongue, Kyle of: *sea loch*, Suther., Scotland   58 30N 04 15W   64
Tongxian (T'unghsien): China   39 55N 116 39E   36 84 121
Tongxin: China   36 58N 106 09E   84
Tongzi: China   28 11N 106 45E   85
Tonk: India   26 10N 75 50E   82
Tonkin, *Gulf of*: China/N.Vietnam   19 45N 107 45E   12 36
Tonle Sap (Sap, *Lake*): Khmer Rep.   12 45N 104 00E   12 38
Tonopah: Nev., U.S.A.   38 04N 117 14W   91
Tønsberg: Norway   59 16N 10 25E   75
Tooele: Utah, U.S.A.   40 32N 112 18W   91
Toowoomba: Qld., Australia   27 35S 151 54E   41
Topeka: Kans., U.S.A.   39 03N 95 40W   43 94
Topozero: *lake*, U.S.S.R.   65 40N 32 00E   74
Toppenish: Wash., U.S.A.   46 23N 120 19W   90
Topsham: Devon, England   50 41N 03 27W   61
Torbat-e-Ḥehydarīyeh: Iran   35 15N 59 08E   33
Torbay: Devon, England   50 28N 03 30W   61
Torch: *riv.*, Sask., Canada   53 35N 105 00W   92
Tor di Quinto: Italy   41 56N 12 28E   116
Torgau: E.Germany   51 34N 13 01E   73
Torino (Turin): Italy   45 04N 07 40E   26 71 105
Torneälven: *riv.*, Sweden   67 00N 23 45E   27 74
Torne Lappmark: *geog. reg.*, Sweden   68 30N 21 00E   74
Torngat *Mountains*: Canada   59 30N 65 00W   44
Tornio: Finland   65 55N 24 10E   74
Toronto: Ont., Canada   43 42N 79 25W   45 99 125
Toropec: U.S.S.R.   56 30N 31 39E   80
Tororo: Uganda   00 42N 34 12E   53
Tor Pignattara: Italy   41 52N 12 33E   116
Torpoint: Corn., England   50 22N 04 11W   61
Torquay *see* Torbay   50 28N 03 30W   61
Torrance: Calif., U.S.A.   33 50N 118 19W   104 127
Torre Annunziata: Italy   40 45N 14 27E   79
Torrejón de Ardoz: Spain   40 27N 03 29W   116
Torrelavega: Spain   43 21N 04 03W   70 77
Torreón: Mexico   25 33N 103 26W   46

Torres *Strait*: Australia/New Guinea   10 15S 142 00E   14
Torridge: *riv.*, Devon, England   50 45N 04 15W   61
Torridon: R. & Crom., Scotland   57 33N 05 31W   64
Torridon, *Loch*: R. & Crom., Scotland   57 30N 05 30W   64
Torrington: Wyo., U.S.A.   42 04N 104 11W   94
Tortola: *is.*, Virgin Islands   18 30N 64 30W   47
Tortosa: Spain   40 49N 00 31E   77
Tortuguitas: Argentina   34 28S 58 45W   128
Toruń: Poland   53 01N 18 35E   27 78
Tõrva: U.S.S.R.   58 00N 25 56E   80
Tory *Island*: Don., Irish Republic   55 15N 08 00W   66
Tory *Sound*: Don., Irish Republic   55 00N 08 00W   66
Toržok: U.S.S.R.   57 03N 34 58E   80
Tosa-wan: *bay*, Japan   33 15N 133 30E   86
Toshima: Japan   35 43N 139 41E   121
Tosno: U.S.S.R.   59 33N 30 53E   80
Tot'ma: U.S.S.R.   59 57N 42 45E   80
Totsuka: Japan   35 23N 139 32E   121
Tottori: Japan   35 30N 134 14E   37 86
Toubkal, *Mount*: Morocco   31 03N 07 57W   20 56
Touggourt: Algeria   33 08N 06 04E   56
Toul: France   48 41N 05 54E   71
Toulnustouc: *riv.*, Qué., Canada   50 15N 68 00W   96
Toulon: France   43 07N 05 55E   26 71
Toulouse: France   43 37N 01 26E   26 70
Tounan: China   23 39N 120 31E   85
Tounassine, Hamada: *geog. reg.*, Algeria   28 30N 05 00W   56
Toungoo: Burma   18 57N 96 26E   35
Tourane *see* Dà Nang   16 04N 108 13E   38
Tourcoing: France   50 44N 03 10E   72
Tournai: Belgium   50 36N 03 24E   72
Tournus: France   46 33N 04 55E   71
Tours: France   47 23N 00 42E   26 70
Touside, *Pic*: Chad   21 04N 16 29E   20
Tovarkovskij (Kaganovich): U.S.S.R.   53 40N 38 14E   80
Tove: *riv.*, England   52 00N 01 00W   59
Towada-hachimantai-kokuritsu-kōen: *nat. park*, Japan   41 30N 141 45E   86
Towanda: Pa., U.S.A.   41 46N 76 27W   99
Towcester: Northants., England   52 08N 01 00W   59
Tow Law: Dur., England   54 45N 01 49W   63
Townsville: Qld., Australia   19 13S 146 48E   41
Towuti, *Lake*: Indonesia   03 00S 121 30E   39
Towyn: Gwyn., Wales   52 35N 04 05W   60
Toyama: Japan   36 41N 137 13E   37 86 105
Toyama-wan: *bay*, Japan   37 00N 137 15E   86
Toyohashi: Japan   34 46N 137 23E   37 86 105
Toyota (Koromo): Japan   35 05N 137 09E   37 86
Trabzon (Trebizond): Turkey   41 00N 39 43E   33
Tracadie: N.B., Canada   47 32N 64 57W   97
Tracy: Calif., U.S.A.   37 43N 121 27W   91
Tradate: Italy   45 43N 08 54E   116
Trafford Park: Gt. Man., England   53 15N 02 15W   114
Trail: B.C., Canada   49 04N 117 39W   42 89
Tralee: Kerry, Irish Rep.   52 16N 09 42W   67 76
Tralee *Bay*: Kerry, Irish Republic   52 15N 09 45W   67
Tramore: Wat., Irish Republic   52 10N 07 10W   67
Tramping *Lake*: Sask., Canada   52 00N 108 45W   92
Tranås: Sweden   58 03N 14 59E   75
Tranent: E.Loth., Scotland   55 57N 02 57W   63
Trang: Thailand   07 35N 99 35E   35
Tranninh, *Plateau du*: Laos   19 15N 103 00E   35
Transantarctic *Mountains*: Antarctica   77 00S 150 00E   25
Transcona: Man., Canada   49 56N 97 00W   93
Transkei: *reg.*, C.P., Rep. of S.Africa   31 00S 29 00E   55
Transylvanian Alps: *mtns.*, Romania   45 15N 23 30E   78
Trapani: Sicily   38 02N 12 32E   79
Trappes: France   48 47N 01 59E   117
Traun-See: *lake*, Austria   47 45N 13 45E   73
Traunstein: W.Germany   47 52N 12 39E   73
Travemünde: W.Germany   53 57N 10 53E   73
Travers, *Mount*: S.I., New Zealand   42 01S 172 44E   87
Traverse City: Mich., U.S.A.   44 46N 85 38W   45 98
Trawden, *Forest of*: Lancs., England   53 51N 02 08W   114
Třebíc: Czechoslovakia   49 13N 15 55E   73
Trebizond *see* Trabzon   41 00N 39 43E   33
Tredegar: Gwent, Wales   51 47N 03 16W   61 113
Treforest: M.Glam., Wales   51 36N 03 19W   113
Treharris: M.Glam., Wales   51 40N 03 18W   113
Treinta y Tres: Uruguay   33 14S 54 23W   52

Trelew: Argentina 43 13S 65 15W 52
Trelleborg: Sweden 55 22N 13 10E 75
Tremadoc *Bay*: Gwyn., Wales 52 45N 04 15W 60
Tremplinersee: *lake*, E.Germany 52 15N 13 00E 117
Trenčín: Czechoslovakia 48 54N 18 03E 78
Trent: *riv.*, England 53 15N 00 45W 58
Trent & Mersey *Canal*: England 53 15N 02 30W 114
Trento: Italy 46 04N 11 08E 78
Trenton: N.S., Canada 45 37N 62 38W 97
Trenton: Ont., Canada 44 07N 77 34W 99
Trenton: Mo., U.S.A. 40 04N 93 37W 98
Trenton: N.J., U.S.A. 40 15N 74 43W 45 99
Treptow: E.Germany 52 29N 13 27E 117
Tres Arroyos: Argentina 38 26S 60 17W 52
Tresco: *is.*, I. of S., England 49 57N 06 20W 61
Tres de Febrerro, *Parque*: Argentina 34 33S 58 26W 128
Três Marias *Reservoir*: Brazil 18 30S 45 15W 51
Tresnish *Islands*: Argyll., Scotland 56 30N 06 15W 64
Treviso: Italy 45 40N 12 15E 78
Trevose *Head*: Corn., England 50 33N 05 01W 61
Trichūr: India 10 32N 76 14E 34
Trident: Mont., U.S.A. 45 57N 111 28W 94
Trieg, *Loch*: Inv., Scotland 56 45N 04 30W 64
Trier: W.Germany 49 45N 06 39E 72
Trieste: Italy 45 39N 13 47E 27 78
Trikkala: Greece 39 33N 21 46E 79
Trim: Meath, Irish Republic 53 34N 06 47W 66
Trincomalee: Sri Lanka 08 34N 81 13E 34
Třinec: Czechoslovakia 49 41N 18 39E 105
Tring: Herts., England 51 48N 00 40W 59
Trinidad: Bolivia 14 47S 64 47W 49
Trinidad: Colo., U.S.A. 37 10N 104 31W 95
Trinidad: *is.*, S.Atlantic Ocean 20 30S 29 20W 3
Trinidad: *is.*, Trinidad & Tobago 10 30N 61 15W 48
TRINIDAD AND TOBAGO 11 00N 61 00W 17 48 106
Trinity: *riv.*, Tex., U.S.A. 31 15N 95 30W 100
Trinity *Bay*: Nfld., Canada 47 45N 53 30W 97
Tripoli: Lebanon *see* Țarābulus 34 27N 35 49E 32
Trípolis: Greece 37 31N 22 22E 79
Tripolitania: *geog. reg.*, Libya 30 45N 13 00E 32
Tripura: *admin.*, India 23 30N 91 15E 35 83
Tristan da Cunha: *is.*, S.Atlantic Ocean 37 15S 12 30W 3
Tristán Suárez: Argentina 34 53S 58 34W 128
Tri-State Tollway: *hwy.*, U.S.A. 42 00N 87 45W 124
Trivandrum: India 08 41N 76 57E 34
Trnava: Czechoslovakia 48 22N 17 36E 73 78
Troddi: *riv.*, Gwent, Wales 51 45N 02 45W 113
Troick (Troitsk): U.S.S.R. 54 06N 61 35E 29 81
Troisdorf: W.Germany 50 49N 07 09E 119
Trois-Rivières (Three Rivers): Qué., Canada 46 21N 72 34W 44 96
Troitsk *see* Troick 54 06N 61 35E 29 81
Trollhättan: Sweden 58 17N 12 20E 75
Trollheimen: *mtns.*, Norway 62 45N 09 00E 74
Trombetas: *riv.*, Brazil 01 00S 56 30W 50
Tromsø: Norway 69 42N 19 00E 27 74
Tromsøysund: Norway 69 40N 19 00E 74
Trondheim: Norway 63 36N 10 23E 27 74
Trondheimsfjorden: *fd.*, Norway 63 30N 10 45E 74 104
Troon: Ayr., Scotland 53 32N 04 40W 62
Trost'anec: U.S.S.R. 50 28N 34 59E 80
Troup *Head*: Banff., Scotland 57 41N 02 16W 65
Trout: *riv.*, N.W.T., Canada 61 00N 120 30W 88
Trout *Lake*: N.W.T., Canada 60 30N 121 00W 88
Trout *Lake*: Ont., Canada 51 00N 93 15W 93
Trowbridge: Wilts., England 51 20N 02 13W 61
Troy: Ala., U.S.A. 31 48N 85 58W 101
Troy: Mich., U.S.A. 42 36N 83 09W 125
Troy: N.Y., U.S.A. 42 43N 73 43W 99
Troyes: France 48 18N 04 05E 26 71
Trubč'ovsk: U.S.S.R. 52 37N 33 44E 80
Trucial States *see* United Arab Emirates 23 45N 53 45E 10 33 107
Trujillo: Honduras 15 55N 86 00W 47
Trujillo: Peru 08 06S 79 00W 49
Truk *Islands*: N.Pacific Ocean 09 00N 157 00E 4
Truro: N.S., Canada 45 24N 63 18W 97
Truro: Corn., England 50 16N 05 03W 61
Trutnov: Czechoslovakia 50 34N 15 55E 73
Truth or Consequences (Hot Springs): N.Mex., U.S.A. 33 08N 107 15W 95
Tselinograd *see* Celinograd 51 10N 71 30E 29
Tsiafajavona, *Mount*: Malagasy Rep. 19 21S 47 15E 55
Tsingtao *see* Qingdao 36 02N 120 29E 37 84 105
Tsinling Shan *see* Qinlingshan 33 45N 107 45E 12 36 84
Tsu (Tu): Japan 34 43N 136 31E 37 86
Tsuchiura: Japan 36 05N 140 12E 86
Tsugaru-kaikyō: *str.*, Japan 41 15N 140 15E 86
Tsukumi: Japan 33 04N 131 52E 86
Tsumeb: S.W.Africa 19 13S 17 42E 55
Tsunashima: Japan 35 31N 139 38E 121
Tsuni *see* Zunyi 27 42N 106 50E 36 85
Tsuruga: Japan 35 39N 136 04E 86
Tsuruoka: Japan 38 44N 139 50E 86
Tsushima-kaikyō: *str.*, Japan 34 15N 130 00E 86
Tsuyama: Japan 35 03N 134 00E 86
Tu *see* Tsu 34 43N 136 31E 37 86
Tuam: Gal., Irish Republic 53 31N 08 50W 66
Tuamotu *Archipelago*: S.Pacific Ocean 17 00S 142 00W 5
Tuapse: U.S.S.R. 44 07N 39 05E 28
Tuath, *Loch*: Argyll., Scotland 56 30N 06 15W 64
Tuba City: Ariz., U.S.A. 36 08N 111 14W 91
Tubarão: Brazil 28 29S 49 00W 51
Tübingen: W.Germany 48 32N 09 04E 72
Tubruq (Tobruk): Libya 32 05N 23 58E 32
Tubuai (Austral) *Islands*: S.Pacific Ocean 23 00S 151 00W 5
Tucson: Ariz., U.S.A. 32 13N 110 58W 43 91
Tucumán: *admin.*, Argentina 26 30S 65 15W 49
Tucumcari: N.Mex., U.S.A. 35 10N 103 44W 95
Tucupita: Venezuela 09 02N 62 04W 48
Tudela: Spain 42 04N 01 37W 77
Tudor, *Lac*: Qué., Canada 55 50N 65 25W 97
Tufts *Abyssal Plain*: N.Pacific Ocean 45 00N 140 00W 5
Tuguegarao: Philippines 17 36N 121 44E 39
Tuhai: *riv.*, China 36 45N 116 30E 84
Tujmazy: U.S.S.R. 54 36N 53 42E 81
Tukangbesi *Islands*: Indonesia 05 30S 123 45E 39
Tukums: U.S.S.R. 56 58N 23 10E 75
Tula: U.S.S.R. 54 12N 37 37E 28 80 105
Tulare: Calif., U.S.A. 36 13N 119 21W 91
Tularosa: N.Mex., U.S.A. 33 05N 106 01W 95
Tulcea: Romania 45 10N 28 50E 78
Tulear: Malagasy Rep. 23 21S 43 40E 55
Tulia: Tex., U.S.A. 34 32N 101 46W 95
Tullahoma: Tenn., U.S.A. 35 22N 86 13W 101
Tullamore: Offaly, Irish Rep. 53 16N 07 30W 67
Tulle: France 45 16N 01 46E 70
Tullow: Carlow, Irish Republic 52 48N 06 44W 67
Tuloma: *riv.*, U.S.S.R. 68 30N 32 15E 74
Tulpetlac: Mexico 19 35N 99 03W 128
Tulsa: Okla., U.S.A. 36 10N 95 55W 43 95 106
Tulsequah: B.C., Canada 58 39N 133 35W 88
Tultepec: Mexico 19 41N 99 08W 128
Tultitlán: Mexico 19 38N 99 10W 128
Tulfuá: Colombia 04 05N 76 12W 48
Tulun: U.S.S.R. 54 35N 100 33E 30
Tulyehualco: Mexico 19 15N 99 01W 128
Tumacacori *National Monument*: Ariz., U.S.A. 31 36N 111 02W 91
Tumaco: Colombia 01 51N 78 46W 48
T'umen' (Tyumen'): U.S.S.R. 57 09N 65 32E 29
Tummel: *riv.*, Perth., Scotland 56 30N 04 00W 65
Tumsar: India 21 24N 79 48E 82
Tumuc Humac *Mountains*: S.America 02 15N 54 45W 50
Tunbridge Wells, Royal: Kent, England 51 08N 00 16E 59
Tundža: *riv.*, Bulgaria 42 30N 26 00E 79
Tungchiang: Taiwan 22 26N 120 30E 85
T'unghai *see* Tonghai 24 07N 102 49E 36
T'unghsien *see* Tongxian 39 55N 116 39E 36 84 121
T'unghua *see* Tonghua 41 50N 125 55E 37 105
T'ungliao *see* Tongliao 43 39N 122 14E 37
Tungshih: Taiwan 24 10N 120 54E 85
Tungt'ing Hu *see* Dongting, *Lake* 28 45N 112 30E 36 85
Tunguska, Lower: *riv.*, U.S.S.R. 64 30N 93 00E 30
Tūnis: Tunisia 36 48N 10 11E 56
TUNISIA 34 00N 09 30E 20 56 106
Tunja: Colombia 05 33N 73 23W 48
Tunliu: China 36 10N 112 50E 84
Tunstall: Staffs., England 53 05N 02 13W 58
Tunungayualuk *Island*: Nfld., Canada 56 00N 61 00W 97
Tunxi: China 29 40N 118 21E 85

Tuobalage: China 31 37N 88 10E 83
Tuoketuo: China 40 22N 111 11E 84
Tupelo: Miss., U.S.A. 34 16N 88 43W 100
Tupiza: Bolivia 21 27S 65 43W 49
Tupungato: *mtn.*, Argentina/Chile 33 20S 69 50W 52
Tura: India 25 32N 90 14E 83
Tura: U.S.S.R. 64 17N 100 15E 30
Tura: *riv.*, U.S.S.R. 58 15N 63 00E 81
Turbat: Pakistan 26 00N 63 06E 34
Turbo: Colombia 08 06N 76 44W 48
Turda: Romania 46 35N 23 50E 78
Turdera: Argentina 34 47S 58 24W 128
Turfan *Depression*: China 42 30N 89 00E 11
Turgaj (Turgay): U.S.S.R. 49 38N 63 28E 29
Turgutlu: Turkey 38 31N 27 42E 79
Turin *see* Torino 45 04N 07 40E 26 71 105
Turinsk: U.S.S.R. 58 03N 63 42E 81
Turkestan: U.S.S.R. 43 18N 68 15E 29
TURKEY 39 00N 28 00E 7 27 79 107
Turkey: *riv.*, Iowa, U.S.A. 42 45N 91 15W 98
Turkmen S.S.R.: *admin.*, U.S.S.R. 39 30N 59 00E 29
Turku (Åbo): Finland 60 27N 22 15E 27 75
Turlock: Calif., U.S.A. 37 29N 120 50W 91
Turnagain: *riv.*, B.C., Canada 58 30N 128 30W 88
Turnagain, *Cape*: N.I., New Zealand 40 28S 176 38E 87
Turner *Lake*: Sask., Canada 56 30N 108 30W 92
Turner Valley: Alta., Canada 50 43N 114 19W 92
Turnhout: Belgium 51 19N 04 57E 72
Turnu-Măgurele: Romania 43 44N 24 53E 79
Turnu-Severin: Romania 44 36N 22 39E 79
Turramurra: N.S.W., Australia 33 44S 151 07E 120
Turriff: Aber., Scotland 57 32N 02 28W 65
Tuscaloosa: Ala., U.S.A. 33 12N 87 34W 45 100
Tušino: U.S.S.R. 55 50N 37 26E 119
Tutajev: U.S.S.R. 57 53N 39 32E 80
Tuticorin: India 08 48N 78 10E 34
Tuttle Creek *Reservoir*: Kans., U.S.A. 39 15N 96 36W 94
Tuttlingen: W.Germany 47 59N 08 49E 72
Tuxpan: Nayarit, Mexico 21 57N 105 18W 46
Tuxpan: Vera Cruz, Mexico 20 57N 97 24W 46
Tuxtla Gutiérrez: Mexico 16 45N 93 07W 46
Tuya: *riv.*, B.C., Canada 58 45N 130 45W 88
Tuy Hòa: S.Vietnam 13 08N 109 10E 38
Tuyün *see* Duyun 26 20N 107 29E 36 85
Tuz, *Lake*: Turkey 38 45N 33 30E 32
Tuzla: Yugoslavia 44 33N 18 41E 27 79
Tver' *see* Kalinin 56 52N 35 55E 28 80
Tweed: *riv.*, England/Scotland 55 30N 02 00W 63
Tweedsmuir *Provincial Park*: B.C., Canada 53 00N 126 15W 89
Twillingate: Nfld., Canada 49 38N 54 45W 97
Twin Bridges: Mont., U.S.A. 45 33N 112 20W 94
Twin Falls: Idaho, U.S.A. 42 34N 114 28W 90
Twin *Islands*: N.W.T., Canada 53 00N 80 00W 96
Twin *Peaks*: Calif., U.S.A. 37 45N 122 27W 126
Twitya: *riv.*, Canada 63 45N 129 15W 88
Two Harbors: Minn., U.S.A. 47 02N 91 40W 98
Two Rivers *Reservoir*: N.Mex., U.S.A. 33 18N 104 43W 95
Tyler: Tex., U.S.A. 32 21N 95 18W 43 100
Tyndrum: Perth., Scotland 56 27N 04 43W 64
Tyne: *riv.*, Tyne & Wear, England 54 45N 01 30W 63
Tyne: *riv.*, E.Loth., Scotland 55 45N 02 30W 63
Tyne and Wear: *admin.*, England 54 45N 01 30W 63
Tynemouth: Tyne & Wear, England 55 01N 01 24W 63
Tyrone: *admin.*, N.Ireland 54 30N 07 00W 66
Tyrrhenian *Sea* 40 00N 13 30E 7 26 79
Tyumen' *see* T'umen 57 09N 65 32E 29
Tywi: *riv.*, Dyfed, Wales 51 45N 04 00W 60
Tzukung *see* Zigong 29 22N 104 46E 36
Tzupo *see* Zibo 36 47N 118 01E 36 84

Ubangi: *riv. see* Oubangui, *riv.* 04 30N 21 15E 20 54
Ube: Japan 33 56N 131 15E 37 86
Uberaba: Brazil 19 45S 47 55W 51
Uberlândia: Brazil 18 56S 48 18W 51
Ubon Ratchathani: Thailand 15 14N 104 54E 38
Ubundi (Ponthierville): Zaïre 00 21S 25 29E 54
Ucayalí: *riv.*, Peru 06 30S 75 15W 48
Uchiura-wan: *bay*, Japan 42 15N 140 30E 86
Ucholovo: U.S.S.R. 53 47N 40 29E 80
Uckfield: E.Sussex, England 50 58N 00 06E 59
Ucluelet: B.C., Canada 48 57N 125 33W 104
Udaipur: India 24 36N 73 47E 34 82
Uddevalla: Sweden 58 20N 11 56E 75
Uddjaur: *lake*, Sweden 65 55N 17 50E 27 74
Udine: Italy 46 04N 13 14E 27 78
Udon Thani: Thailand 17 25N 102 45E 35
Ueda: Japan 36 24N 138 16E 86
Uele: *riv.*, Zaïre 03 30N 24 30E 21 54
Uelzen: W.Germany 52 58N 10 34E 73
Ueno *Park*: Japan 35 42N 139 46E 121
Ufa: U.S.S.R. 54 44N 55 56E 29 81 107
Uffculme: Devon, England 50 54N 03 19W 61
UGANDA 01 15N 32 30E 21 53
Uggiate: Italy 45 49N 08 58E 116
Ugie: *riv.*, Aber., Scotland 57 30N 02 00W 65
Uglič: U.S.S.R. 57 32N 38 19E 80
Uherské Hradiště: Czechoslovakia 49 05N 17 30E 73
Uil: U.S.S.R. 49 05N 54 40E 81
Uitenhage: C.P., Rep. of S.Africa 33 46S 25 25E 55
Ujiji: Tanzania 04 55S 29 41E 54
Uji-yamada *see* Ise 34 29N 136 42E 37 86
Ujjain: India 23 11N 75 50E 34 82
Ukiah: Calif., U.S.A. 39 09N 123 12W 91
Ukmergė: U.S.S.R. 55 14N 24 49E 75
Ukraine: *geog. reg.*, U.S.S.R. 48 00N 31 00E 8
Ukrainskaja S.S.R. (Ukrainian S.S.R.): *admin.*, U.S.S.R. 48 00N 34 00E 28 80
Ulaanbaatar (Ulan Bator): Mongolia 47 55N 106 53E 30
Ulanhoto *see* Wulanhaote 46 05N 122 05E 37
Ulan-Ude: U.S.S.R. 51 50N 107 37E 30
Ulhāsnagar: India 19 13N 73 07E 34 82
Ulithi: *is.*, Caroline Islands 09 58N 139 40E 12
Uljanovka: U.S.S.R. 59 38N 30 46E 80
Uljanovsk (Ul'yanovsk): U.S.S.R. 54 20N 48 24E 28 81
Ulla: U.S.S.R. 55 14N 29 15E 80
Ullapool: R. & Crom., Scotland 57 54N 05 10W 64
Ullswater: *lake*, Cumbria, England 54 30N 02 45W 63
Ulm: W.Germany 48 24N 10 00E 73
Ulsan: S.Korea 35 34N 129 19E 37 107
Ulubāria: India 22 28N 88 07E 120
Ulva: *is.*, Argyll., Scotland 56 30N 06 15W 64
Ulverston: Cumbria., England 54 12N 03 06W 63
Ul'yanovsk *see* Uljanovsk 54 20N 48 24E 28 81
Uman': U.S.S.R. 48 44N 30 14E 80
Umaria: India 23 30N 80 52E 82
Umeå: Sweden 63 50N 20 15E 74
Umeälv: *riv.*, Sweden 64 30N 18 30E 27 74
Umm Durmān (Omdurman): Sudan 15 37N 32 29E 53
Umreth: India 22 42N 73 07E 82
Umtali: Rhodesia 18 58S 32 40E 55
Umtata: C.P., Rep. of S.Africa 31 35S 28 47E 55
Unayzah (Anaiza): Saudi Arabia 26 06N 43 58E 33
Uneča: U.S.S.R. 52 50N 32 40E 80
Ungava *Bay*: Qué., Canada 59 30N 67 30W 16 44
Ungava *Peninsula*: Qué., Canada 61 00N 74 00W 16 44
Unggi: N.Korea 42 20N 130 24E 86
Union: N.J., U.S.A. 40 42N 74 16W 123
Union, *Lake*: Wash., U.S.A. 47 38N 122 20W 126
Union *Bay*: Wash., U.S.A. 47 39N 122 17W 126
Union City: Calif., U.S.A. 37 36N 122 01W 104 126
Union City: Tenn., U.S.A. 36 26N 89 03W 100
Union *Islands see* Tokelau *Islands* 08 00S 172 00W 4 15
UNION OF SOVIET SOCIALIST REPUBLICS 8 30 80
Uniontown: Pa., U.S.A. 39 54N 79 44W 99
UNITED ARAB EMIRATES (Trucial States) 23 45N 53 45E 10 33 107
UNITED KINGDOM 6 26 69 107
UNITED STATES OF AMERICA 17 43 106
Unity: Sask., Canada 52 27N 109 10W 92
Unjha: India 23 48N 72 23E 82
Unnão: India 26 32N 80 30E 82
Unst: *is.*, Shet. Is., Scotland 60 45N 00 55W 65
Unža: *riv.*, U.S.S.R. 58 00N 44 00E 80
Uozo: Japan 36 48N 137 24E 86
Upata: Venezuela 08 02N 62 25W 48
Uppington: C.P., Rep. of S.Africa 28 28S 21 14E 55
Upland: Calif., U.S.A. 34 06N 117 39W 127
Upper Arrow *Lake*: B.C., Canada 50 15N 117 45W 89

Types of map: Ocean pp. 1-5; Physical pp. 6-25; Human pp. 26-57; Topographic pp. 58-101; World pp. 102-111; Urban pp. 112-128.

Upper Crystal Springs *Reservoir*: Calif., U.S.A.
37 30N 122 20W   126
Upper Darby: Pa., U.S.A.   39 57N 75 16W   122
Upper Hutt: N.I., New Zealand   41 06S 175 06E   87
Upper Kapuas *Mountains*: Malaysia   01 45N 112 45E   38
Upper Klamath *Lake*: Oreg., U.S.A.   42 25N 122 00W   90
Upper Laberge: Yukon, Canada   60 54N 135 12W   88
Upper Lough Erne: *lake*, Ferm., N.Ireland   54 00N 07 30W
   66
Upper New York *Bay*: U.S.A.   40 30N 74 00W   123
Upper Red *Lake*: Minn., U.S.A.   48 04N 94 48W   98
Upper Rouge *Creek*: Mich., U.S.A.   42 15N 83 15W   125
UPPER VOLTA   12 30N 01 00W   20 57
Uppingham: Leics., England   52 35N 00 43W   58
Uppsala: Sweden   59 55N 17 38E   27 75
Upton: Ches., England   53 13N 02 52W   114
Upton upon Severn: Here. & Worcs., England
52 04N 02 13W   59
Uraga: Japan   35 14N 139 42E   121
Uraga-suido: *str.*, Japan   35 16N 139 46E   121
Urakawa: Japan   42 09N 142 47E   87
Ural: *riv.*, U.S.S.R.   47 45N 51 45E   28 81
Ural *Mountains* *see* Ural'skije Gory   55 00N 59 00E
   8 29 81 105
Ural'sk: U.S.S.R.   51 14N 51 22E   28 81
Ural'skije Gory (Ural *Mountains*): U.S.S.R.   55 00N 59 00E
   8 29 81 105
Uranium City: Sask., Canada   59 32N 108 43W   42 92
Uraricoera: *riv.*, Brazil   03 30N 61 00W   48
Urawa: Japan   35 51N 139 39E   86
Urayasu: Japan   35 40N 139 54E   121
Urbana: Ill., U.S.A.   40 07N 88 12W   98
Urdunn, Nahr al (Jordan): *riv.*, Israel/Jordan
32 00N 35 30E   32
Ure: *riv.*, N.Yorks., England   54 00N 01 30W   63
Urewera *National Park*: N.I., New Zealand   38 45S 177 00E
   87
Urfa: Turkey   37 08N 38 45E   32
Urgenč (Urgench): U.S.S.R.   41 33N 60 38E   29
Urick: U.S.S.R.   59 50N 30 11E   119
Urie: *riv.*, Aber., Scotland   57 15N 02 30W   65
Urlingford: Kilk., Irish Republic   52 43N 07 35W   67
Urmia, *Lake*: Iran   37 30N 45 30E   10 33
Urmston: Gt. Man., England   53 27N 02 21W   114
Urr Water: *riv.*, Kirkc., Scotland   55 00N 03 45W   62
Uruguai (Uruguay): *riv.*, S.America   33 15S 58 30W   19 51
Uruguaiana: Brazil   29 45S 57 05W   51
URUGUAY   19 52 106
Uruguay (Uruguai): *riv.*, S.America   33 15S 58 30W   19 51
Urumchi *see* Wulumuqi: China   43 48N 87 35E   9 105
Ur'upinsk: U.S.S.R.   50 47N 41 59E   80
Uržum: U.S.S.R.   57 08N 50 00E   81
Usa (Nagasu): Japan   33 31N 131 22E   86
Ušači: U.S.S.R.   55 11N 28 37E   80
Usedom: *is.*, E.Germany   54 00N 14 00E   73
Ushuaia: Argentina   54 48S 68 19W   52
Usk: Gwent, Wales   51 43N 02 54W   61
Usk: *riv.*, Wales   51 45N 03 00W   60 113
Usman': U.S.S.R.   52 02N 39 44E   80
Usolje-Sibirskoje (Usol'ye-Sibirskoye): U.S.S.R.
52 47N 103 38E   30
Uspallata *Pass* (La Cumbre *Pass*): Argentina
32 43S 69 24W   52
Ussuri (Wusuli): *riv.*, U.S.S.R./China   47 15N 134 00E   31
Ussurijsk (Ussuriysk; Voroshilov): U.S.S.R.
43 48N 131 59E   37 86
Usta: *riv.*, U.S.S.R.   57 00N 45 30E   81
Ústí: Czechoslovakia   50 41N 14 00E   73 78
Ust'-Kamenogorsk: U.S.S.R.   49 58N 82 38E   29
Ust'-Kut: U.S.S.R.   56 46N 105 40E   30
Ust'-Port: U.S.S.R.   69 44N 84 23E   30
Ust'-Urt *Plateau*: U.S.S.R.   44 00N 57 00E   8 29
Ust'užna: U.S.S.R.   58 51N 36 26E   80
Usuki: Japan   33 08N 131 49E   86
Usumbura *see* Bujumbura   03 22S 29 21E   54
Utah: *admin.*, U.S.A.   49 00N 112 00W   43 91
Utah *Lake*: Utah, U.S.A.   40 12N 111 48W   91
Utashinai: Japan   43 31N 142 03E   86
Ute *Creek*: N.Mex., U.S.A.   36 00N 103 45W   95
Utica: N.Y., U.S.A.   43 06N 75 15W   45 99
Utikuma *Lake*: Alta., Canada   55 45N 115 15W   92

Utila: *is.*, Honduras   16 06N 86 56W   47
Utraula: India   27 20N 82 25E   83
Utrecht: Netherlands   52 06N 05 07E   26 72
Utrera: Spain   37 10N 05 47W   77
Utsunomiya (Utunomiya): Japan   36 33N 139 52E   37 86
Uttarpāra: India   22 40N 88 21E   120
Uttar Pradesh: *admin.*, India   26 00N 80 00E   34 82
Uttoxeter: Staffs., England   52 54N 01 51W   58
Utunomiya *see* Utsunomiya   36 33N 139 52E   37 86
Uva: U.S.S.R.   56 59N 52 13E   81
Uvalde: Tex., U.S.A.   29 13N 99 47W   95
Uvarovo: U.S.S.R.   51 59N 42 15E   80
Uvs, *Lake*: Mongolia   50 15N 92 45E   30
Uwajima: Japan   33 13N 132 34E   86
Uxbridge: Gt. Ldn., England   51 33N 00 30W   112
Uyuni: Bolivia   20 28S 66 50W   49
Uyuni *Salt Flat*: Bolivia   20 15S 67 30W   49
Už: *riv.*, U.S.S.R.   51 15N 29 00E   80
Uza: *riv.*, U.S.S.R.   52 30N 46 00E   81
Uzbek S.S.R.: *admin.*, U.S.S.R.   42 00N 63 00E   29
Užgorod: U.S.S.R.   48 37N 22 18E   78
Užice *see* Titovo Užice   43 52N 19 50E   79
Uzlovaja: U.S.S.R.   53 59N 38 10E   80

Vaal: *riv.*, Rep. of S.Africa   28 15S 24 45E   21 55
Vaala: Finland   64 35N 26 50E   74
Vaasa: Finland   63 06N 21 36E   27 74
Vác: Hungary   47 46N 19 09E   78
Vaccarès, Étang de: *lag.*, France   43 32N 04 35E   71
Vachtan: U.S.S.R.   57 58N 46 42E   81
Vadsø: Norway   70 05N 29 43E   74
Vaduz: Liechtenstein   47 08N 09 32E   71
Váh: *riv.*, Czechoslovakia   48 30N 17 45E   78
Valamaz: U.S.S.R.   57 32N 52 05E   81
Valdaj: U.S.S.R.   57 59N 33 14E   80
Valdajskaja Vozvyšennost': *hld.*, U.S.S.R.   57 00N 33 00E
   80
Valdemoro: Spain   40 12N 03 40W   116
Valdepeñas: Spain   38 46N 03 24W   77
Valdés, *Peninsula*: Argentina   42 30S 64 00W   52
Valdivia: Chile   39 48S 73 14W   52
Val d' Or: Qué., Canada   48 07N 77 47W   44 99
Valdosta: Ga., U.S.A.   30 50N 83 17W   101
Valence: France   44 56N 04 54E   71
Valencia: Spain   39 29N 00 24W   26 77
Valencia: Venezuela   10 14N 67 59W   48
Valencia, *Golfo de*: Spain   39 30N 00 00   77
Valenciennes: France   50 22N 03 32E   72 105
Valentia *Island*: Kerry, Irish Rep.   51 55N 10 20W   67 76
Valentine: N.I., U.S.A.   42 52N 100 33W   94
Valera: Venezuela   09 21N 70 38W   48
Valga: U.S.S.R.   57 47N 26 02E   80
Valjevo: Yugoslavia   44 16N 19 56E   79
Valkeakoski: Finland   61 17N 24 05E   75
Valladolid: Spain   41 39N 04 45W   26 77
Vallecas: Spain   40 22N 03 37W   116
Valle de la Pascua: Venezuela   09 15N 66 00W   48
Vallejo: Calif., U.S.A.   38 05N 122 14W   91
Vallenar: Chile   28 36S 70 45W   52
Valletta: Malta   35 45N 14 32E   79
Valley: Gwyn., Wales   53 17N 04 34W   60
Valley City: N.D., U.S.A.   46 55N 98 00W   94
Valleyfield: Qué., Canada   45 14N 74 08W   96
Valley Forge *State Park*: Pa., U.S.A.   40 06N 75 26W   122
Valley Stream: N.Y., U.S.A.   40 40N 73 42W   123
Valleyview: Alta., Canada   55 04N 117 20W   92
Val Marie: Sask., Canada   49 15N 107 44W   92
Valmiera: U.S.S.R.   57 32N 25 29E   75
Valparaíso: Chile   33 05S 71 40W   52
Valujki: U.S.S.R.   50 13N 38 08E   80
Van, *Lake*: Turkey   38 30N 42 45E   10 32
Vancouver: B.C., Canada   49 16N 123 07W   42 89 126
Vancouver: Wash., U.S.A.   45 38N 122 40W   90
Vancouver *Island*: B.C., Canada   49 30N 126 00W   16 42 89
Vanda Station: *rsch. stn.*, Antarctica   77 32S 161 38E   25
Vanderbijlpark: Trans., Rep. of S.Africa   26 41S 27 50E   105
Vanderhoof: B.C., Canada   54 01N 124 01W   89
Vänern: *lake*, Sweden   58 45N 13 15E   26 75

Types of map: Ocean pp. 1-5; Physical pp. 6-25; Human pp. 26-57; Topographic pp. 58-101; World pp. 102-111; Urban pp. 112-128.

Vänersborg: Sweden   58 23N 12 19E   75
Vännäs: Sweden   63 56N 19 50E   74
Vannes: France   47 40N 02 44W   70
Vannøy: *is.*, Norway   70 10N 19 40E   74
Vanua Levu: *is.*, Fiji   16 30S 179 00E   4 15
Vanves: France   48 50N 02 17E   117
Var: *riv.*, France   43 45N 07 00E   71
Vārānasi (Benares): India   25 20N 83 00E   35 83
Varangerfjorden: *fd.*, Norway   70 00N 30 00E   74
Varangerhalvøya: *pen.*, Norway   70 22N 29 40E   74
Varaždin: Yugoslavia   46 18N 16 21E   78
Varberg: Sweden   57 06N 12 15E   75
Vardar: *riv.*, Yugoslavia   41 45N 22 30E   79
Vardø: Norway   70 22N 31 06E   74
Vareš: Yugoslavia   44 10N 18 20E   105
Varese: Italy   45 49N 08 49E   71 116
Varkaus: Finland   62 15N 27 45E   74
Varna: Bulgaria   43 13N 27 55E   27 79
Värnamo: Sweden   57 11N 14 03E   75
Varnsdorf: Czechoslovakia   50 57N 14 35E   73
Vartry *Reservoir*: Wick., Irish Republic   53 00N 06 00W   67
Vas: *admin.*, Hungary   47 00N 16 45E   73
Vashon *Island*: Wash., U.S.A.   47 15N 122 15W   126
Vasiljevo: U.S.S.R.   55 52N 48 42E   81
Vasil'kov: U.S.S.R.   50 12N 30 19E   80
Västerås: Sweden   59 36N 16 32E   27 75
Västerdalälven: *riv.*, Sweden   61 00N 13 15E   75
Västervik: Sweden   57 45N 16 40E   75
Vaternish *Point*: Inv., Scotland   57 37N 06 39W   64
Vatersay: *is.*, Inv., Scotland   56 45N 07 30W   64
VATICAN CITY (Città del Vaticano)   41 54N 12 27E   116
V'atka: *riv.*, U.S.S.R.   56 45N 50 45E   81
V'atskij Uval: *mtns.*, U.S.S.R.   56 45N 49 00E   81
Vättern: *lake*, Sweden   58 15N 14 30E   27 75
Vaucresson: France   48 50N 02 09E   117
Vaupés: *riv.*, Colombia   01 00N 72 00W   48
Vauréal: France   49 02N 02 02E   117
Växjö: Sweden   56 52N 14 50E   75
V'az'ma: U.S.S.R.   55 13N 34 18E   80
V'azniki: U.S.S.R.   56 15N 42 10E   80
Veendam: Netherlands   53 07N 06 53E   72
Vega: *is.*, Norway   65 38N 11 52E   74
Vegreville: Alta., Canada   53 30N 112 02W   92
Veinte de Junio: Argentina   34 46S 58 44W   128
Vejle: Denmark   55 43N 09 33E   75
Velbert: W.Germany   51 22N 07 03E   118
Veles *see* Titov Veles   41 43N 21 49E   79
Vélez: Colombia   06 02N 73 43W   48
Velikaja: *riv.*, U.S.S.R.   56 15N 29 00E   75
Velikije Luki (Velikiye Luki): U.S.S.R.   56 20N 30 32E   28 80
Velikij Ust'ug: U.S.S.R.   60 48N 46 18E   81
Velikiye Luki *see* Velikije Luki   56 20N 30 32E   28 80
Velikoje, Ozero: *lake*, U.S.S.R.   55 13N 40 10E   80
Veliž: U.S.S.R.   55 38N 31 12E   80
Vellore: India   12 56N 79 09E   34
Velsen: Netherlands   52 28N 04 39E   72
Velten: E.Germany   52 42N 13 12E   117
Venado Tuerto: Argentina   33 45S 61 56W   52
Vendée, Collines de: *hills*, France   46 45N 00 45W   70
Vendôme: France   47 48N 01 04E   70
Venezia (Venice): Italy   45 26N 12 20E   26 78
Venezia, *Golfo di* (Venice, *Gulf of*): Italy   45 15N 13 00E   78
VENEZUELA   18 48 106
Venezuela, *Golfo de*: Venezuela   11 15N 71 00W   48
Venezuelan *Basin*: Caribbean Sea   15 00N 70 00W   2
Venice: Italy *see* Venezia   45 26N 12 20E   26 78
Vénissieux: France   45 42N 04 46E   71
Venta: *riv.*, U.S.S.R.   56 00N 22 45E   75
Ventas Vicálvaro: Spain   40 25N 03 36W   116
Ventimiglia: Italy   43 47N 07 37E   71
Ventnor: I. of W., England   50 36N 01 11W   59
Ventspils: U.S.S.R.   57 22N 21 31E   75
Ventura Freeway: *hwy.*, Calif., U.S.A.   34 00N 118 30W   127
Vepsovskaja Vozvyšennost': *hld.*, U.S.S.R.   60 30N 35 30E   80
Ver: *riv.*, Herts., England   51 45N 00 15W   112
Veracruz: *admin.*, Mexico   20 00N 97 00W   46
Veracruz Llave: Mexico   19 12N 96 08W   46 104
Verāval: India   20 53N 70 28E   34
Verbania: Italy   45 56N 08 34E   71
Vercelli: Italy   45 19N 08 26E   71

Verchn'aja Pyšma: U.S.S.R.   56 55N 60 37E   81
Verchne-Kamskaja Vozvyšennost': *hld.*, U.S.S.R.   58 15N 53 30E   81
Verchnij Ufalej: U.S.S.R.   56 04N 60 14E   81
Verchojansk (Verkhoyansk): U.S.S.R.   67 35N 133 27E   31
Verchojansk (Verkhoyansk) *Range*: U.S.S.R.   67 00N 126 30E   9 31
Verchoturje: U.S.S.R.   58 52N 60 48E   81
Verde: *riv.*, Ariz., U.S.A.   34 15N 111 30W   91
Verden: W.Germany   52 56N 09 14E   72
Verdigris: *riv.*, U.S.A.   37 45N 95 45W   95
Verdun: Qué., Canada   45 28N 73 35W   122
Verdun-sur-Meuse: France   49 10N 05 24E   71
Vereeniging: Trans., Rep. of S.Africa   26 41S 27 56E   55 105
Vergara: Spain   43 07N 02 25W   70
Verkhoyansk *see* Verchojansk   67 35N 133 27E   31
Verkhoyansk *Range see* Verchojansk *Range*   67 00N 126 30E   9 31
Vermilion: Alta., Canada   53 21N 110 52W   92
Vermilion Chutes: Alta., Canada   58 22N 114 51W   92
Vermilion *Lake*: Minn., U.S.A.   47 45N 92 15W   98
Vermilion *Pass*: Canada   51 21N 116 05W   92
Vermilion *Range*: Minn., U.S.A.   47 45N 92 00W   98 104
Vermillion: S.D., U.S.A.   42 47N 96 56W   94
Vermillion: *riv.*, S.D., U.S.A.   43 45N 97 00W   94
Vermont: *admin.*, U.S.A.   44 00N 73 00W   44 99
Vernal: Utah, U.S.A.   40 27N 109 32W   91
Verneuil-sur-Seine: France   48 59N 01 59E   117
Vernon: B.C., Canada   50 16N 119 16W   89
Vernon: Tex., U.S.A.   34 09N 99 17W   95
Véroia: Greece   40 32N 22 11E   79
Verona: Italy   45 26N 11 00E   26 78
Verrières: France   48 45N 02 17E   117
Versailles: France   48 48N 02 08E   70 117
Verviers: Belgium   50 36N 05 52E   72
Veselovskoje Vodochraniliŝče: *res.*, U.S.S.R.   47 00N 41 15E   80
Vesjegonsk: U.S.S.R.   58 40N 37 16E   80
Vesoul: France   47 38N 06 09E   71
Vestfjorden: *fd.*, Norway   68 00N 14 30E   74
Vesuvio (Vesuvius): *volc.*, Italy   40 49N 14 26E   79
Vetlanda: Sweden   57 26N 15 05E   75
Vetl'anka: U.S.S.R.   52 52N 51 09E   81
Vetluga: U.S.S.R.   57 51N 45 47E   81
Vetluga: *riv.*, U.S.S.R.   56 30N 46 15E   81
Vevey: Switzerland   46 28N 06 51E   71
Viacha: Bolivia   16 39S 68 18W   49
Viana do Castelo: Portugal   41 41N 08 50W   77
Viborg: Denmark   56 28N 09 25E   75
Vicálvaro: Spain   40 24N 03 35W   116
Vicecomodoro Marambio: *rsch. stn.*, Antarctica   64 16S 56 45W   24
Vicente López: Argentina   34 32S 58 28W   128
Vicenza: Italy   45 33N 11 33E   78
Vichy: France   46 07N 03 25E   26 71
Vicksburg: Miss., U.S.A.   32 21N 90 51W   100
Victoria: Buenos Aires, Argentina   34 28S 58 32W   128
Victoria: Cameroun   04 01N 09 12E   57
Victoria: B.C., Canada   48 25N 123 22W   42 89
Victoria (Xianggang): Hong Kong   22 17N 114 13E   36 85
Victoria: Tex., U.S.A.   28 43N 97 00W   43 95
Victoria: *admin.*, Australia   37 00S 145 00E   41
Victoria, *Lake*: E.Africa   01 00S 33 00E   21 53
Victoria de Durango: Mexico   24 02N 104 40W   46 104
Victoria Falls: Rhodesia   17 56S 25 50E   55
Victoria *Falls*: Rhodesia/Zambia   17 55S 25 51E   21
Victoria *Island*: N.W.T., Canada   71 00N 110 00W   22
Victoria Land: *reg.*, Antarctica   73 00S 158 00W   25
Victoriaville: Qué., Canada   46 04N 71 57W   96
Vičuga: U.S.S.R.   57 13N 41 56E   80
Vidin: Bulgaria   44 00N 22 50E   79
Vidzeme: *hills*, U.S.S.R.   55 45N 25 30E   75
Viedma: Argentina   40 45S 63 00W   52
Vienna: Austria *see* Wien   48 13N 16 22E   27 73 78
Vienne: France   45 32N 04 54E   71
Vientiane: Laos   17 59N 102 38E   35
Vieques, *Isla de*: Puerto Rico   18 00N 65 15W   47
Vierlande: *geog. reg.*, W.Germany   53 15N 10 00E   119
Viersen: W.Germany   51 16N 06 24E   118
Vierzon: France   47 14N 02 03E   70

Types of map: Ocean pp. 1-5; Physical pp. 6-25; Human pp. 26-57; Topographic pp. 58-101; World pp. 102-111; Urban pp. 112-128.

Vietnam see North Vietnam and South Vietnam   12 38 107
Vigevano: Italy   45 19N 08 51E   71
Vigo: Spain   42 15N 08 44W   26 77
Vijayawāda (Bezwada): India   16 34N 80 40E   34
Viking: Alta., Canada   53 07N 111 50W   92
Vikna: is., Norway   64 55N 10 55E   74
Vila Cabral: Mozambique   13 18S 35 14E   54
Viladecans: Spain   41 19N 02 01E   116
Vilaine: riv., France   47 30N 02 00W   70
Vila Nova de Gaia: Portugal   41 08N 08 37W   77
Vila Real: Portugal   41 17N 07 45W   77
Vila Velha: Brazil   20 20S 40 17W   51
Vilhelmina: Sweden   64 38N 16 40E   74
Viljandi: U.S.S.R.   58 22N 25 30E   75
Villa Acuna: Mexico   29 18N 100 55W   95
Villa Ada: gdns., Italy   41 56N 12 30E   116
Villa Adelina: Argentina   34 31S 58 33W   128
Villa Ángela: Argentina   27 34S 60 45W   51
Villa Ballester: Argentina   34 33S 58 33W   128
Villa Borghese: gdns., Italy   41 55N 12 29E   116
Villach: Austria   46 37N 13 51E   78
Villa Cisneros: Spanish Sahara   23 43N 15 57W   56
Villa Dominico: Argentina   34 41S 58 19W   128
Villa Doria Pamphili: gdns., Italy   41 52N 12 26E   116
Villahermosa: Mexico   17 59N 92 55W   46
Villalba: Spain   43 17N 07 41W   77
Villa Madero: Argentina   34 41S 58 30W   128
Villa María: Argentina   32 25S 63 15W   52
Villa Montes: Bolivia   21 15S 63 30W   49
Villa Obregón: Mexico   19 21N 99 12W   128
Villarrica: Paraguay   25 45S 56 28E   51
Villavicencio: Colombia   04 09N 73 37W   49
Ville, Die: geog. reg., W.Germany   50 45N 06 45E   119
Villefranche-sur-Saône: France   46 00N 04 43E   71
Villejuif: France   48 47N 02 23E   117
Villemoisson-sur-Orge: France   48 40N 02 19E   117
Villeneuve: Qué., Canada   46 52N 71 11W   96
Villeneuve-St. Georges: France   48 44N 02 27E   70 117
Villeneuve-sur-Lot: France   44 25N 00 43E   70
Villeparisis: France   48 56N 02 38E   117
Villeurbanne: France   45 46N 04 54E   71
Villingen: W.Germany   48 03N 08 28E   72
Villmanstrand see Lappeenranta   61 04N 28 11E   75
Villoresi, Canale: Italy   45 30N 08 45E   116
Vilnius: U.S.S.R.   54 40N 25 19E   28 75
Vil'uj (Vilyuy): riv., U.S.S.R.   63 45N 120 00E   9 31
Vilyuy: riv. see Vil'uj   63 45N 120 00E   9 31
Viña del Mar: Chile   33 02S 71 35W   52
Vinaroz: Spain   40 29N 00 28E   77
Vincennes: France   48 51N 02 27E   117
Vincennes: Ind., U.S.A.   38 42N 87 30W   98
Vincennes, Bois de: woods, France   48 50N 02 26E   117
Vindelälven: riv., Sweden   65 00N 18 30E   74
Vindhya Range: India   23 00N 77 00E   11 34 82
Vineland: N.J., U.S.A.   39 29N 75 02W   99
Vinh Long: S.Vietnam   10 15N 105 59E   38
Vinkovci: Yugoslavia   45 16N 18 49E   78
Vinnica (Vinnitsa): U.S.S.R.   49 14N 28 29E   28 78
Virden: Man., Canada   49 50N 100 57W   93
Virgin: riv., U.S.A.   36 45N 113 45W   91
Virginia: Cavan, Irish Republic   53 50N 07 05W   66
Virginia: Minn., U.S.A.   47 30N 92 28W   98
Virginia: admin., U.S.A.   45 99
Virginia Falls: N.W.T., Canada   61 38N 125 48W   88
Virgin Islands: Caribbean Sea   18 30N 64 45W   47
Virudunagar: India   09 35N 77 57E   34
Visalia: Calif., U.S.A.   36 20N 119 18W   91
Visayan Sea: Philippines   11 45N 123 45E   39
Visby: Gotland, Sweden   57 38N 18 18E   75
Viscount Melville Sound: N.W.T., Canada   75 00N 105 00W   23
Viseu: Portugal   40 40N 07 55W   77
Vishākhapatnam (Vizagapatnam): India   17 42N 83 24E   35
Visnagar: India   23 41N 72 36E   82
Visp: Switzerland   46 18N 07 53E   71
Vistula: riv. see Wisła: riv.   53 30N 18 45E   7 27 78
Vitebsk: U.S.S.R.   55 12N 30 11E   28 80
Vitichi: Bolivia   20 13S 65 29W   49
Viti Levu: is., Fiji   17 45S 178 00E   4 15
Vitim: riv., U.S.S.R.   57 15N 115 45E   30
Vitória: Brazil   20 19S 40 21W   51

Vitoria: Spain   42 51N 02 40W   70 77
Vitória de Conquista: Brazil   14 51S 40 51W   51
Vitry-le-François: France   48 44N 04 36E   71
Vittuone: Italy   45 29N 08 57E   116
Vityaz Trench: S.Pacific Ocean   11 00S 170 00E   4
Vizagapatnam see Vishākhapatnam   17 42N 83 24E   35
Vizcaya: admin., Spain   43 15N 02 55W   105
Vizcaya, Golfo de: Spain   42 45N 02 00W   70
Vizianagaram: India   18 07N 83 30E   35
Vladimir: U.S.S.R.   56 10N 40 25E   28 80
Vladivostok: U.S.S.R.   43 10N 131 56E   37 86
Vlissingen (Flushing): Netherlands   51 27N 03 35E   72
Vlorë: Albania   40 27N 19 30E   79
Vochtoga: U.S.S.R.   58 47N 41 07E   80
Voerde: W.Germany   51 36N 06 41E   118
Vogelkop Peninsula: Indonesia   01 30S 132 30E   13
Vogel Peak: Nigeria   08 24N 11 47E   20
Voghera: Italy   44 59N 09 01E   71
Vohburg an der Donau: W.Germany   48 46N 11 37E   107
Vohwinkel: W.Germany   51 13N 07 05E   118
Vojnica: U.S.S.R.   65 10N 30 20E   74
Volčansk: U.S.S.R.   50 18N 36 57E   80
Volchov: U.S.S.R.   59 55N 32 20E   80
Volchov: riv., U.S.S.R.   58 45N 31 30E   80
Volga: U.S.S.R.   57 57N 38 24E   81
Volga: riv., U.S.S.R.   47 00N 47 30E   8 28 81
Volgodonsk: U.S.S.R.   47 33N 42 08E   80
Volgograd: U.S.S.R.   48 44N 44 25E   28 80 105 107
Volgogradskoje Vodochranilišče: res.,
   U.S.S.R.   51 00N 46 00E   81
Völklingen: W.Germany   49 15N 06 51E   72 105
Volme: riv., W.Germany   51 00N 07 30E   118
Vologda: U.S.S.R.   59 12N 39 55E   28 80
Vólos: Greece   39 22N 22 57E   32 79
Vol'sk: U.S.S.R.   52 02N 47 23E   28 81
Volta, Lake: Ghana   07 00N 00 00   20 57
Volta Redonda: Brazil   22 31S 44 05W   51 104
Volzhskiy see Volžskij   48 50N 44 44E   28 80
Volžsk: U.S.S.R.   55 53N 48 21E   81
Volžskij (Volzhskiy): U.S.S.R.   48 50N 44 44E   28 80
Vordingborg: Denmark   55 01N 11 55E   75
Voríai Sporádhes (Northern Sporades): is.,
   Greece   39 00N 24 00E   79
Vorkuta: U.S.S.R.   67 27N 63 58E   8
Vorlich, Ben: mtn., Perth., Scotland   56 21N 04 13W   64
Voronež (Voronezh): U.S.S.R.   51 40N 39 10E   28 80
Voronež (Voronezh): riv., U.S.S.R.   52 00N 39 15E   80
Voroshilov see Ussurijsk   43 48N 131 59E   37 86
Voroshilovgrad see Lugansk   48 34N 39 20E   28 80
Voroshilovsk see Kommunarsk   48 30N 38 47E   80 105
Voroshilovsk see Stavropol'   45 02N 41 59E   28
Vorst: W.Germany   51 18N 06 25E   118
Vørterkaka Nunatak: mtn., Antarctica   72 20S 27 29E   24
Võrts Järv: lake, U.S.S.R.   58 15N 26 00E   80
Võru (Vyru): U.S.S.R.   57 50N 27 01E   80
Vosges: mtns., France   48 00N 07 00E   71
Voskresensk: U.S.S.R.   55 19N 38 42E   80
Voss: Norway   60 38N 06 25E   75
Vostok: rsch. stn., Antarctica   78 28S 106 48E   25
Votkinsk: U.S.S.R.   57 03N 53 59E   81
Votkinskoje Vodochranilišče: res., U.S.S.R.   56 45N 55 00E   81
Vože, Ozero: lake, U.S.S.R.   60 30N 39 00E   80
Vožega: U.S.S.R.   60 29N 40 12E   80
Voznesensk: U.S.S.R.   47 34N 31 20E   80
Vraca: Bulgaria   43 12N 23 33E   79
Vrindāvan (Brindaban): India   27 36N 77 41E   82
Vršac: Yugoslavia   45 07N 21 19E   78
Vsevoložsk: U.S.S.R.   60 01N 30 40E   119
Vukovar: Yugoslavia   45 19N 19 01E   78
Vyborg: U.S.S.R.   60 45N 28 41E   27 75
Vyčegda (Vychegda): riv., U.S.S.R.   62 00N 52 00E   28
Východočeský: admin., Czechoslovakia   50 00N 16 00E   73
Vyksa: U.S.S.R.   55 18N 42 11E   80 105
Vyrnwy: riv., Powys, Wales   52 30N 03 15W   60
Vyrnwy, Lake: Powys, Wales   52 45N 03 30W   60
Vyru see Võru   57 50N 27 01E   80
Vyšnij Voloček (Vyshniy Volochëk): U.S.S.R.   57 35N 34 34E   28 80
Vytegra: U.S.S.R.   61 00N 36 24E   28

Types of map: Ocean pp. 1-5; Physical pp. 6-25; Human pp. 26-57; Topographic pp. 58-101; World pp. 102-111; Urban pp. 112-128.

Wa: Ghana 10 07N 02 28W 57
Wabana: Nfld., Canada 47 40N 52 58W 97 104
Wabasca: Alta., Canada 55 58N 113 56W 92
Wabasca: riv., Alta., Canada 56 45N 114 00W 92
Wabash: riv., U.S.A. 38 30N 87 30W 98
Wabowden: Man., Canada 54 57N 98 38W 93
Wabuk Point: Ont., Canada 55 20N 85 06W 93
Wabush, Lake: Nfld., Canada 53 02N 66 52W 97 104
Waccasassa Bay: Fla., U.S.A. 29 00N 82 45W 101
Waco: Tex., U.S.A. 31 33N 97 09W 43 95
Waddenzee: bay, Netherlands 53 15N 05 30E 72
Waddington, Mount: B.C., Canada 51 22N 125 14W 16 42 89
Wadebridge: Corn., England 50 32N 04 50W 61
Wadena: Sask., Canada 51 57N 103 58W 92
Wadena: Minn., U.S.A. 46 26N 95 08W 98
Wadhwān: India 22 44N 71 43E 82
Wādī Halfā: Sudan 21 56N 31 20E 32
Wad Madanī: Sudan 14 24N 33 32E 53
Waesch, Mount: Antarctica 77 10S 126 53W 25
Wagga Wagga: N.S.W., Australia 35 07S 147 24E 41
Wągrowiec: Poland 52 49N 17 11E 73
Waha: Libya 28 22N 19 52E 32
Wahai: Indonesia 02 48S 129 29E 39
Wahnbach Stausee: res., W.Germany 50 47N 07 16E 119
Wahner Heide: heath, W.Germany 50 45N 07 00E 119
Wahoo: Nebr., U.S.A. 41 13N 96 37W 94
Wahpeton: N.D., U.S.A. 46 16N 96 36W 94
Waidhān: India 24 04N 82 20E 83
Waigeo: is., Indonesia 00 15S 130 45E 39
Waiheke Island: N.I., New Zealand 36 48S 175 13E 37
Waikato: riv., N.I., New Zealand 37 45S 175 30E 15
Waimate: S.I., New Zealand 44 45S 171 03E 87
Wainfleet All Saints: Lincs., England 53 07N 00 14E 58
Wainwright: Alta., Canada 52 50N 110 51W 92
Waipara: S.I., New Zealand 43 03S 172 47E 87
Waipukurau: N.I., New Zealand 40 00S 176 33E 87
Wairoa: N.I., New Zealand 39 03S 177 25E 87
Waitara: N.I., New Zealand 38 59S 174 13E 87
Wajima: Japan 37 24N 136 54E 86
Wakamatsu see Aizuwakamatsu 37 30N 139 56E 86
Wakatipu, Lake: S.I., New Zealand 45 00S 168 30E 87
Wakaw: Sask., Canada 52 40N 105 45W 92
Wakayama: Japan 34 13N 135 11E 37 86
Wakayama: admin., Japan 33 45N 135 15E 105 107
Wakeeney: Kans., U.S.A. 39 01N 99 53W 94
Wakefield: W.Yorks., England 53 42N 01 29W 63 115
Wakefield: Mass., U.S.A. 42 29N 71 04W 122
Wake Island: N.Pacific Ocean 19 18N 166 36E 4
Wałbrzych: Poland 50 48N 16 19E 27 73 78
Wałcz: Poland 53 17N 16 29E 73
Walden Pond: Mass., U.S.A. 42 29N 71 00W 122
WALES 52 30N 03 30W 26 69
Walker Lake: Nev., U.S.A. 38 42N 118 43W 91
Wallachia: geog. reg., Romania 44 00N 24 30E 79
Wallasey: Mers., England 53 26N 03 03W 63 114
Walla Walla: Wash., U.S.A. 46 04N 118 20W 90
Walled Lake: Mich., U.S.A. 42 32N 83 29W 125
Walled Lake: Mich., U.S.A. 42 31N 83 29W 125
Wallingford: Oxon., England 51 37N 01 08W 59
Wallsend: Tyne & Wear, England 54 59N 01 31W 63
Walney Island: Cumbria, England 54 00N 03 15W 62
Walnut Creek: Calif., U.S.A. 37 55N 122 03W 126
Walsall: W.Mid., England 52 35N 01 58W 58 115
Walsenburg: Colo., U.S.A. 37 38N 104 47W 94
Walsrode: W.Germany 52 52N 09 35E 72
Walsum: W.Germany 51 32N 06 41E 118
Waltham: Mass., U.S.A. 42 23N 71 14W 122
Walthamstow: Gt. Ldn., England 51 34N 00 01W 112
Walton: N.S., Canada 45 14N 64 00W 97
Walton-on-Thames: Surrey, England 51 24N 00 25W 112
Walton-on-the-Hill: Staffs., England 52 47N 02 07W 115
Walton-on-the-Naze: Essex, England 51 51N 01 16E 59
Waltrop: W.Germany 51 37N 07 25E 118
Walvisbaai (Walvis Bay): S.W.Africa 22 59S 14 31E 55
Walvis Ridge: S.Atlantic Ocean 33 00S 04 00E 3
Wanaka: S.I., New Zealand 44 43S 169 10E 87

Wandsbek: W.Germany 53 34N 10 04E 119
Wandsworth: Gt. Ldn., England 51 27N 00 11W 59 112
Waneta: B.C., Canada 49 00N 117 37W 90
Wanganui: N.I., New Zealand 39 56S 175 00E 37 87
Wangjiang: China 30 09N 116 43E 85
Wangqing: China 43 20N 129 48E 86
Wanheim: W.Germany 51 23N 06 44E 118
Wanhsien: Sichau see Wanxian 30 52N 108 22E 36 85
Wani: India 20 03N 79 01E 82
Wānkāner: India 22 37N 70 56E 82
Wankie: Rhodesia 18 22S 26 29E 55
Wanne-Eickel: W.Germany 51 31N 07 09E 118
Wannian: China 28 40N 116 52E 85
Wansbeck: riv., Northumb., England 55 00N 01 45W 63
Wantage: Oxon., England 51 36N 01 25W 59
Wantagh: N.Y., U.S.A. 40 40N 73 30W 123
Wantashan: mtns., China 47 00N 132 00E 37
Wanxian (Wanhsien): Sichuan, China 30 52N 108 22E 36 85
Wanxian: Hebei, China 38 50N 115 00E 84
Wanyuan: China 32 04N 108 08E 84
Wanzai: China 28 04N 114 29E 85
Wapiti: riv., Canada 55 00N 119 45W 89
Warabi: Japan 35 50N 139 41E 121
Warangal: India 18 00N 79 35E 34
Ward: S.I., New Zealand 41 51S 174 10E 87
Wardha: India 20 41N 78 40E 82
Wardha: riv., India 19 30N 79 45E 82
Ware: B.C., Canada 57 26N 125 41W 89
Ware: Herts., England 51 49N 00 02W 59
Wareham: Dorset, England 50 41N 02 07W 61
Waren: E.Germany 53 32N 12 42E 73
Warendorf: W.Germany 51 57N 08 00E 72
Warley: W.Mid., England 52 30N 01 58W 58 115
Warman: Sask., Canada 52 19N 106 34W 92
Warminster: Wilts., England 51 13N 02 12W 61
Warner Robins: Ga., U.S.A. 32 35N 83 37W 101
Warren: Ariz., U.S.A. 31 25N 109 54W 95
Warren: Idaho, U.S.A. 45 16N 115 41W 90
Warren: Mich., U.S.A. 42 30N 83 02W 125
Warren: Minn., U.S.A. 48 12N 96 48W 98
Warren: Ohio, U.S.A. 41 15N 80 49W 99
Warren: Pa., U.S.A. 41 52N 79 09W 99 104
Warren Landing: Man., Canada 53 42N 97 54W 93
Warrenpoint: Down, N.Ireland 54 06N 06 15W 66
Warri: Nigeria 05 36N 05 46E 57
Warrington: Lancs., England 53 24N 02 37W 114
Warrnambool: Vic., Australia 38 23S 142 03E 41
Warroad: Minn., U.S.A. 48 54N 95 20W 98
Warsaw: Poland see Warszawa 52 15N 21 00E 27 78 105
Warszawa (Warsaw): Poland 52 15N 21 00E 27 78 105
Warta: riv., Poland 52 00N 17 15E 73 78
Warud: India 21 29N 78 22E 82
Warwick: War., England 52 17N 01 34W 59 115
Warwick: R.I., U.S.A. 41 42N 71 23W 99
Warwickshire: admin., England 52 15N 01 30W 59
Wasatch Range: Utah, U.S.A. 39 45N 111 30W 17
Wascana Creek: Sask., Canada 50 00N 104 15W 92
Wash, The: bay, England 53 00N 00 15E 58
Washington: Tyne & Wear, England 54 54N 01 31W 63
Washington: D.C., U.S.A. 38 55N 77 00W 45 99 122
Washington: Ind., U.S.A. 38 40N 87 10W 98
Washington: N.C., U.S.A. 35 33N 77 04W 101
Washington: admin., U.S.A. 47 00N 120 00W 42 90
Washington, Lake: Wash., U.S.A. 47 30N 122 15W 126
Washington, Mount: N.H., U.S.A. 44 17N 71 19W 17 44 99
Washington Park: Ill., U.S.A. 41 47N 87 36W 124
Watchet: Som., England 51 12N 03 20W 61
Waterbury: Conn., U.S.A. 41 33N 73 03W 99
Waterford: Wat., Irish Rep. 52 15N 07 06W 67
Waterford: admin., Irish Rep. 52 00N 07 30W 67
Waterford Harbour: Irish Republic 52 00N 06 45W 67
Waterhen Lake: Man., Canada 52 00N 99 30W 93
Waterloo: Iowa, U.S.A. 42 30N 92 20W 43 98
Waterton Glacier International Peace Park: Canada/U.S.A. 48 30N 114 00W 90
Waterton Lakes National Park: Alta., Canada 49 00N 114 00W 92
Watertown: Mass., U.S.A. 42 21N 71 11W 122
Watertown: N.Y., U.S.A. 43 57N 75 56W 99
Watertown: S.D., U.S.A. 44 54N 97 07W 94

Types of map: Ocean pp. 1-5; Physical pp. 6-25; Human pp. 26-57; Topographic pp. 58-101; World pp. 102-111; Urban pp. 112-128.

Watertown: Wis., U.S.A. 43 12N 88 46W	98	
Waterville: Maine, U.S.A. 44 34N 69 41W	99	
Waterways: Alta., Canada 56 41N 111 19W	92	
Watford: Herts., England 51 40N 00 25W	59 112	
Wathaman: *riv.*, Sask., Canada 57 00N 103 45W	92	
Watlington: Oxon., England 51 39N 01 01W	59	
Watson Lake: Yukon, Canada 60 07N 128 49W	88	
Watsonville: Calif., U.S.A. 36 53N 121 49W	91	
Watten, *Loch*: Caith., Scotland 58 30N 03 15W	65	
Wattenscheid: W.Germany 51 27N 07 07E	118	
Watton: Norf., England 52 34N 00 50E	58	
Waukegan: Ill., U.S.A. 42 21N 87 52W	98 124	
Waukesha: Wis., U.S.A. 43 01N 88 14W	98	
Wausau: Wis., U.S.A. 44 58N 89 40W	98	
Waveney: *riv.*, England 52 15N 01 15E	58	
Wawa: Ont., Canada 48 01N 84 49W	104	
Waxahachie: Tex., U.S.A. 32 24N 96 51W	100	
Waycross: Ga., U.S.A. 31 12N 82 22W	101	
Wayland: Mass., U.S.A. 42 22N 71 22W	122	
Wayne: Mich., U.S.A. 42 18N 83 13W	125	
Wayne: Nebr., U.S.A. 42 14N 97 01W	94	
Wayne: Pa., U.S.A. 40 03N 75 23W	122	
Waynesboro: Va., U.S.A. 38 04N 78 54W	99	
Weald, The: *geog. reg.*, England 51 00N 00 15E	59	
Wear: *riv.*, England 54 45N 02 00W	63	
Weaver: *riv.*, Ches., England 53 15N 02 30W	114	
Weaverville: Calif., U.S.A. 40 44N 122 57W	91	
Weber: *riv.*, Utah, U.S.A. 41 00N 111 45W	94	
Weda: Indonesia 00 30N 127 52E	39	
Weddell *Sea* 72 00S 40 00W	3 24	
Wednesbury: W.Mid., England 52 34N 02 00W	115	
Wednesfield: W.Mid., England 52 36N 02 04W	115	
Weed: Calif., U.S.A. 41 26N 122 23W	90	
Weedon Bec: Northants., England 52 14N 01 05W	59	
Wei: *riv.*, China 36 30N 115 30E	84	
Wei: *riv.*, Gansu, China 34 30N 106 00E	84	
Wei: *riv.*, Shandong, China 36 15N 119 30E	84	
Weiden in der Oberpfalz: W.Germany 49 40N 12 10E	73	
Weifang: China 36 42N 119 10E	36 84	
Weihai (Port Edward): China 37 28N 122 07E	37 84	
Weimar: E.Germany 50 59N 11 20E	73	
Weinan: China 34 27N 109 29E	84	
Weinheim: W.Germany 49 33N 08 40E	72	
Weirton: W.Va., U.S.A. 40 24N 80 37W	99 104	
Weiser: Idaho, U.S.A. 44 45N 116 58W	90	
Weishan, *Lake*: China 34 30N 117 15E	84	
Weishi: China 34 25N 114 11E	84	
Weissenfels: E.Germany 51 12N 11 58E	73	
Weixian: China 36 57N 115 15E	84	
Wejherowo: Poland 54 36N 18 12E	75	
Welkom: O.F.S., Rep. of S.Africa 27 59S 26 44E	55	
Welland: Ont., Canada 42 59N 79 14W	99	
Welland: *riv.*, England 52 45N 00 00	58	
Wellesley: Mass., U.S.A. 42 18N 71 18W	122	
Wellingborough: Northants., England 52 19N 00 42W	59	
Wellington: Salop, England 52 43N 02 31W	58	
Wellington: Som., England 50 59N 03 14W	61	
Wellington: N.I., New Zealand 41 17S 174 47E	37 87	
Wellington: Kans., U.S.A. 37 16N 97 24W	95	
Wellington: Tex., U.S.A. 34 51N 100 13W	95	
Wellington, *Isla*: Chile 49 20S 74 40W	52	
Wells: B.C., Canada 53 06N 121 34W	89	
Wells: Som., England 51 13N 02 39W	61	
Wells: Nev., U.S.A. 41 07N 114 58W	91	
Wells Gray *Provincial Park*: B.C., Canada 52 15N 120 00W	89	
Wells-next-the-Sea: Norf., England 52 58N 00 51E	58	
Wels: Austria 48 10N 14 02E	73 78	
Welshpool: Powys, Wales 52 40N 03 09W	60	
Welwyn Garden City: Herts., England 51 48N 00 13W	59 112	
Wem: Salop, England 52 51N 02 44W	60	
Wembley: Gt. Ldn., England 51 34N 00 18W	112	
Wen: *riv.*, China 36 15N 119 15E	84	
Wenan: China 38 52N 116 28E	84	
Wenatchee: Wash., U.S.A. 47 25N 120 19W	90	
Wencheng: China 27 50N 120 09E	85	
Wenchou *see* Wenzhou 28 00N 120 40E	37 85	
Wendeng: China 37 09N 122 02E	84	
Wendover: Bucks., England 51 46N 00 46W	59 112	
Wendover: Utah, U.S.A. 40 44N 114 02W	91	
Weng'an: China 27 03N 107 29E	85	
Wengbo: China 31 23N 86 40E	83	
Wengyuan (Longxianwei): China 24 31N 114 10E	85	
Wenling: China 28 22N 121 29E	85	
Wenlock Edge: *hills*, Salop, England 52 30N 02 45W	60	
Wenshan: China 23 30N 104 20E	36	
Wensleydale: *val.*, England 54 15N 02 15W	63	
Wensum: *riv.*, Norf., England 52 30N 01 00E	58	
Went: *riv.*, N.Yorks., England 53 30N 01 00W	115	
Wenxi: China 35 20N 111 01E	84	
Wenxiang: China 34 30N 110 45E	84	
Wenzhou (Wenchou): China 28 00N 120 40E	37 85	
Werden: W.Germany 51 23N 06 59E	118	
Wermelskirchen: W.Germany 51 08N 07 14E	118	
Wernecke *Mountains*: Yukon, Canada 64 45N 133 00W	88	
Werneuchen: E.Germany 52 38N 13 44E	117	
Wernigerode: E.Germany 51 51N 10 48E	73	
Werra: *riv.*, E.Germany/W.Germany 51 15N 09 45E	73	
Wesel: W.Germany 51 39N 06 37E	72	
Wesel-Datteln-*Kanal*: W.Germany 51 30N 07 00E	118	
Weser: *riv.*, W.Germany 53 30N 08 30E	72	
Wesseling: W.Germany 50 50N 06 58E	119	
West Atlantic-Indian *Basin*: Southern Ocean	3	
West Australian *Basin*: Indian Ocean 27 30S 106 00E	1 13	
West Bengal: *admin.*, India 27 30N 87 30E	35 83	
West Berlin: W.Germany 52 30N 13 20E	117	
West Bridgford: Notts., England 52 56N 01 08W	58	
West Bromwich: W.Mid., England 52 31N 01 59W	58 115	
Westbury: Wilts., England 51 16N 02 11W	61	
Westbury: N.Y., U.S.A. 40 46N 73 34W	123	
West Caroline *Basin*: N.Pacific Ocean 04 00N 137 00E	4	
Westchester: Ill., U.S.A. 41 50N 87 53W	125	
Western Australia: *admin.*, Australia	40	
Western Cordillera: *ra.*, Colombia *see* Cordillera Occidental 05 00N 76 00W	18 48	
Western Cordillera: *ra.*, Peru 13 00S 75 45W	49	
Western *Desert*: Egypt 26 45N 26 00E	20 32	
Western Dvina: *riv. see* Zapadnaja Dvina 55 15N 29 00E	28 80	
Western Ghats: *ra.*, India 15 00N 74 30E	11 34	
Western Rift *Valley*: Tanzania 08 00S 33 00E	21	
WESTERN SAMOA 13 00S 172 00W	4	
Western Sayan (Sajan) *Mountains*: U.S.S.R. 52 00N 93 00E	9 30	
Western Springs: Ill., U.S.A. 41 47N 87 53W	124	
Western Yamuna *Canal*: India 28 45N 77 08E	120	
Wester Ross: *dist.*, R. & Crom., Scotland 57 30N 05 15W	64	
West European *Basin*: Atlantic Ocean 46 00N 17 00W	2 6	
West Falkland: *is.*, Falkland Islands 51 30S 60 00W	52	
WEST GERMANY 52 00N 09 00E	7 26 72 76 107	
West Glamorgan: *admin.*, Wales 51 30N 03 45W	61	
West Greenland *Current*: N.Atlantic Ocean 68 00N 55 00W	2	
West *Ice Shelf*: Antarctica 67 00S 85 00E	24	
West Indies: *is.*, Caribbean Sea	17 47	
West Irian: *admin.*, Indonesia 05 00S 139 00E	13	
West Kilbride: Ayr., Scotland 55 42N 04 51W	62 113	
West Loch Tarbert: *lake*, Inv., Scotland 57 45N 06 45W	64	
Westlock: Alta., Canada 54 12N 113 50W	92	
West Looe: Corn., England 50 21N 04 28W	61	
West Lothian: *admin.*, Scotland 55 45N 03 30W	62	
West Malaysia: *admin.*, Malaysia 04 00N 102 00E	107	
West Mariana *Basin*: N.Pacific Ocean 15 00N 137 00E	4	
Westmeath: *admin.*, Irish Rep. 53 30N 07 30W	66	
West Memphis: Ark., U.S.A. 35 09N 90 11W	100	
West Midlands: *admin.*, England 52 15N 02 00W	58 115	
Westminster: Gt. Ldn., England 51 30N 00 09W	112	
Westminster: Calif., U.S.A. 33 47N 118 00W	127	
Westmorland: *admin.*, England. Absorbed into new *admin.* of Cumbria, 1974	63	
Westmount: Qué., Canada 45 30N 73 36W	122	
Weston: Ont., Canada 43 43N 79 32W	125	
Weston: W.Va., U.S.A. 39 03N 80 28W	99	
Weston-super-Mare: Avon, England 51 21N 02 59W	61	
West Pakistan *see* Pakistan	1 11 34 82	
West Palm Beach: Fla., U.S.A. 26 42N 80 05W	45 101	
West Plains: Mo., U.S.A. 36 44N 91 51W	100	
West Point: Nebr., U.S.A. 41 51N 96 43W	94	
Westport: Mayo, Irish Republic 53 48N 09 32W	66	
Westport: S.I., New Zealand 41 46S 171 38E	37 87	

Westray: *is.*, Ork. Is., Scotland 59 18N 03 00W 65
Westray Firth: *chan.*, Ork. Is., Scotland 59 00N 03 00W 65
West Scotia *Basin*: Southern Ocean 57 00S 48 00W 3 19
West Siberian *Plain*: U.S.S.R. 63 00N 78 00E 8 30
West Sussex: *admin.*, England 50 45N 00 30W 59
West Vancouver: B.C., Canada 49 22N 123 11W 126
Westview: B.C., Canada 49 50N 124 32W 89
West Virginia: *admin.*, U.S.A. 45 99
Westward Ho!: Devon, England 51 02N 04 15W 61
West Wind *Drift*: Indian Ocean 1
West Wind *Drift*: S.Atlantic Ocean 3
Westwood: Calif., U.S.A. 40 20N 121 00W 91
West Yorkshire: *admin.*, England 53 30N 01 30W 63
Wetar: *is.*, Indonesia 08 00S 126 15E 13 39
Wetaskiwin: Alta., Canada 52 45N 113 15W 92
Wetherby: W.Yorks., England 53 56N 01 23W 63 115
Wetter: W.Germany 51 23N 07 24E 118
Wewak: Terr. of New Guinea 03 34S 143 38E 14
Wexford: Wex., Irish Rep. 52 20N 06 27W 67
Wexford: *admin.*, Irish Rep. 52 30N 06 30W 67
Wexford *Bay*: Wex., Irish Republic 52 15N 06 15W 67
Wey: *riv.*, England 51 15N 00 15W 59 112
Weybridge: Surrey, England 51 23N 00 28W 59
Weyburn: Sask., Canada 49 39N 103 51W 92
Weymouth: Dorset, England 50 36N 02 28W 61
Weymouth: Mass., U.S.A. 42 14N 70 58W 122
Whakatane: N.I., New Zealand 37 56S 177 00E 37 87
Whale: *riv.*, Qué., Canada 57 00N 67 00W 97
Whaley Bridge: Derby., England 53 20N 01 59W 58
Whalsay: *is.*, Shet. Is., Scotland 60 15N 00 45W 65
Whangarei: N.I., New Zealand 35 43S 174 20E 37 87
Wharfe: *riv.*, N.Yorks., England 53 45N 01 00W 63 115
Wharfedale: *val.*, N.Yorks., England 53 45N 01 45W 63 115
Wharton *Basin*: Indian Ocean 17 00S 107 30E 1
Wheatley: Oxon., England 51 45N 01 09W 59
Wheaton: Ill., U.S.A. 41 54N 88 06W 124
Wheaton: Md., U.S.A. 39 02N 77 04W 99
Wheeler: *riv.*, Qué., Canada 56 00N 67 15W 96
Wheeler *Lake*: Ala., U.S.A. 34 48N 87 23W 101
Wheeling: W.Va., U.S.A. 40 05N 80 43W 45 99
Whipsnade: Beds., England 51 52N 00 33W 59
Whitburn: W.Loth., Scotland 55 52N 03 42W 62
Whitby: Ont., Canada 43 52N 78 56W 104
Whitby: N.Yorks., England 54 29N 00 37W 63
Whitchurch: Bucks., England 51 53N 00 51W 59
Whitchurch: Hants., England 51 14N 01 20W 59
Whitchurch: Salop, England 52 58N 02 41W 58
Whitchurch: S.Glam., Wales 51 32N 03 14W 113
White: *riv.*, Ont., Canada 48 30N 85 45W 98
White: *riv.*, Yukon, Canada 63 00N 140 00W 88
White: *riv.*, U.S.A. 43 30N 100 00W 94
White: *riv.*, U.S.A. 40 00N 108 45W 94
White: *riv.*, Ark., U.S.A. 35 00N 91 30W 100
White: *riv.*, Ind., U.S.A. 39 00N 86 45W 98
White *Bay*: Nfld., Canada 50 00N 56 30W 97
White Cart Water: *riv.*, Lan., Scotland 55 45N 04 15W 113
White Center: Wash., U.S.A. 47 31N 122 21W 126
Whitecourt: Alta., Canada 54 10N 115 38W 92
White East Fork: *riv.*, Ind., U.S.A. 38 30N 86 45W 98
Whitefish: Mont., U.S.A. 48 25N 114 20W 90
Whitegull *Lake*: Qué., Canada 55 30N 64 15W 97
Whitehall: Mont., U.S.A. 45 52N 112 06W 94
Whitehaven: Cumbria, England 54 33N 03 35W 62
Whitehead: Antrim, N.Ireland 54 46N 05 43W 66
Whitehorse: Yukon, Canada 60 41N 135 08W 88
White *Lake*: La., U.S.A. 29 44N 92 30W 100
White Mountain *Peak*: Calif., U.S.A. 37 38N 118 15W 17 43
Whiten *Head*: Suther., Scotland 58 34N 04 32W 64
White Nile: *riv. see* Al-Baḥr-al-Jabal 04 15N 31 30E 21 53
White Pine: Mich., U.S.A. 46 46N 89 36W 98
Whitesand *Bay*: Corn., England 50 00N 05 30W 61
White Sands *National Monument*: N.Mex., U.S.A. 32 45N 106 30W 95
White *Sea*: U.S.S.R. 67 00N 24 45E 8 74
Whiteshell *Provincial Park*: Man., Canada 50 15N 95 15W 93
White Volta: *riv.*, W.Africa 09 45N 01 00W 57
Whithorn: Wig., Scotland 54 44N 04 25W 62
Whiting: Ind., U.S.A. 41 41N 87 32W 106 124

Whitley Bay: Tyne & Wear, England 55 03N 01 25W 63
Whitmans *Pond*: Mass., U.S.A. 42 12N 70 56W 122
Whitney, *Mount*: Calif., U.S.A. 36 35N 118 18W 17 43 91
Whitney *Woods*: Mass., U.S.A. 42 14N 70 51W 122
Whitstable: Kent, England 51 22N 01 02E 59
Whittier: Calif., U.S.A. 33 58N 118 03W 127
Whittier Narrows Dam *Reservoir Area*: Calif., U.S.A. 34 02N 118 02W 127
Whittle, *Cape*: Qué., Canada 50 11N 60 05W 97
Whittlesey: Cambs., England 52 34N 00 08W 58
Whitwick: Leics., England 52 44N 01 21W 115
Wholdaia *Lake*: N.W.T., Canada 60 45N 104 00W 92
Whyalla: S.A., Australia 33 04S 137 34E 41 105
Wiay: *is.*, Inv., Scotland 57 15N 07 00W 64
Wichita: Kans., U.S.A. 37 41N 97 20W 43 95
Wichita: *riv.*, Tex., U.S.A. 33 45N 99 45W 95
Wichita Falls: Tex., U.S.A. 33 54N 98 30W 43 95
Wick: Caith., Scotland 58 26N 03 06W 65
Wickenburg: Ariz., U.S.A. 33 58N 112 44W 91
Wickford: Essex, England 51 38N 00 31E 112
Wickham Market: Suff., England 52 09N 01 22E 59
Wicklow: Wick., Irish Rep. 52 59N 06 03W 67
Wicklow: *admin.*, Irish Rep. 53 00N 06 30W 67
Wicklow *Head*: Wick., Irish Republic 52 58N 06 00W 67
Wicklow *Mountains*: Wick., Irish Rep. 53 00N 06 15W 67
Widnes: Ches., England 53 22N 02 44W 63 114
Wien (Vienna): Austria 48 13N 16 22E 27 73 78
Wiener Neustadt: Austria 47 49N 16 15E 73 78
Wiesbaden: W.Germany 50 05N 08 15E 26 72
Wigan: Lancs., England 53 33N 02 38W 114
Wight, Isle of *see* Isle of Wight 50 40N 01 15W 59
Wigston: Leics., England 52 36N 01 05W 58
Wigton: Cumbria, England 54 49N 03 09W 62
Wigtown: Wig., Scotland 54 52N 04 26W 62
Wigtown *Bay*: Scotland 54 45N 04 15W 62
Wigtownshire: *admin.*, Scotland 54 45N 04 45W 62
Wilde: Argentina 34 42S 58 18W 128
Wilhelmina: *mtn.*, Surinam 03 40N 56 30W 48
Wilhelmsburg: W.Germany 53 27N 09 57E 119
Wilhelmshaven: W.Germany 53 32N 08 07E 26 72
Wilkes-Barre: Pa., U.S.A. 41 15N 75 50W 45 99
Wilkes Land: *reg.*, Antarctica 68 00S 110 00E 25
Wilkie: Sask., Canada 52 27N 108 42W 92
Wilkinsburg: Pa., U.S.A. 40 26N 79 53W 125
Willamette: *riv.*, Oreg., U.S.A. 45 00N 123 00W 90
Willapa *Bay*: Wash., U.S.A. 46 30N 124 00W 90
Willcox: Ariz., U.S.A. 32 15N 109 50W 91
Willenhall: W.Mid., England 52 36N 02 02W 115
Willenhall: W.Mid., England 52 23N 01 28W 115
Williams: Ariz., U.S.A. 35 15N 112 11W 91
Williams Lake: B.C., Canada 52 08N 122 09W 89
Williamson: W.Va., U.S.A. 37 42N 82 16W 101
Williamsport: Pa., U.S.A. 41 16N 77 03W 99
Willich: W.Germany 51 16N 06 32E 118
Willington: Dur., England 54 43N 01 41W 63
Williston: N.D., U.S.A. 48 09N 103 37W 42 94
Williston *Reservoir*: B.C., Canada 56 00N 123 45W 89
Williton: Som., England 51 10N 03 20W 61
Willmar: Minn., U.S.A. 45 06N 95 03W 98
Willow Bunch: Sask., Canada 49 22N 105 39W 92
Willowdale: Ont., Canada 43 47N 79 26W 125
Willow Grove: Pa., U.S.A. 40 08N 75 07W 122
Willow *Lake*: N.W.T., Canada 62 00N 119 00W 88
Willowlake: *riv.*, N.W.T., Canada 62 30N 121 30W 88
Willows: Calif., U.S.A. 39 32N 122 10W 91
Will Rogers Turnpike: *hwy.*, Okla., U.S.A. 36 30N 95 00W 95
Wilmette: Ill., U.S.A. 42 04N 87 43W 124
Wilmington: Del., U.S.A. 39 46N 75 31W 45 99
Wilmington: N.C., U.S.A. 34 14N 77 55W 45 101
Wilmslow: Ches., England 53 20N 02 15W 58 114
Wilson: N.C., U.S.A. 35 43N 77 56W 101
Wilton: Wilts., England 51 05N 01 52W 61
Wiltshire: *admin.*, England 51 15N 01 45W 61
Wimbledon: Gt. Ldn., England 51 26N 00 12W 112
Wimborne Minster: Dorset, England 50 48N 01 59W 61
Wincanton: Som., England 51 04N 02 25W 61
Winchcombe: Glos., England 51 57N 01 58W 60
Winchelsea: E.Sussex, England 50 55N 00 42E 59
Winchester: Hants., England 51 04N 01 19W 59
Winchester: Ky., U.S.A. 38 00N 84 10W 101

Types of map: Ocean pp. 1-5; Physical pp. 6-25; Human pp. 26-57; Topographic pp. 58-101; World pp. 102-111; Urban pp. 112-128.

Winchester: Mass., U.S.A.   42 26N 71 08W   122
Winchester: Va., U.S.A.   39 11N 78 12W   99
Wind: *riv.*, Wyo., U.S.A.   43 15N 109 15W   94
Wind Cave *National Park*: S.D., U.S.A.   43 37N 103 30W   94
Windermere: Cumbria, England   54 23N 02 54W   63
Windermere: *lake*, Cumbria, England   54 15N 02 45W   63
Windfalls: *riv.*, Alta., Canada   53 45N 116 15W   92
Windhoek: S.W.Africa   22 34S 17 06E   55
Windigo *Lake*: Ont., Canada   52 30N 91 15W   93
Wind River *Range*: Wyo., U.S.A.   43 00N 109 30W   94
Windrush: *riv.*, England   51 45N 01 30W   59
Windsor: N.S., Canada   45 00N 64 09W   97
Windsor: Ont., Canada   42 18N 83 00W   45 125
Windsor: Berks., England   51 29N 00 38W   59 112
Windsor Great *Park*: Berks., England   51 29N 00 38W   112
Windward *Islands*: Caribbean Sea   14 00N 61 00W   47
Windward Passage: *str.*, Cuba/Haiti   19 45N 74 00W   47
Winfield: Kans., U.S.A.   37 15N 96 59W   95
Winifred: Mont., U.S.A.   47 34N 109 23W   94
Winisk: Ont., Canada   55 20N 85 15W   93
Winisk: *riv.*, Ont., Canada   54 30N 87 00W   93
Winisk *Lake*: Ont., Canada   52 45N 87 15W   93
Wink: Tex., U.S.A.   31 45N 103 09W   95
Winneba: Ghana   05 22N 00 38W   57
Winnebago, *Lake*: Wis., U.S.A.   44 00N 88 15W   98
Winnemucca: Nev., U.S.A.   40 58N 117 44W   91
Winnemucca *Lake*: Nev., U.S.A.   40 00N 119 15W   91
Winner: S.D., U.S.A.   43 22N 99 52W   94
Winnipeg: Man., Canada   49 53N 97 10W   42 93
Winnipeg: *riv.*, Man., Canada   50 30N 96 00W   93
Winnipeg, *Lake*: Man., Canada   52 30N 98 00W   16 42 93
Winnipegosis: Man., Canada   51 40N 99 56W   93
Winnipegosis, *Lake*: Man., Canada   52 30N 100 00W   42 93
Winona: Minn., U.S.A.   44 02N 91 37W   98
Winona: Miss., U.S.A.   33 29N 89 44W   100
Winsford: Ches., England   53 11N 02 31W   58 114
Winshill: Staffs., England   52 48N 01 37W   115
Winslow: Bucks., England   51 57N 00 54W   59
Winslow: Ariz., U.S.A.   35 02N 110 42W   91
Winslow: Wash., U.S.A.   47 36N 122 30W   126
Winston-Salem: N.C., U.S.A.   36 05N 80 18W   45 101
Winter Haven: Fla., U.S.A.   28 02N 81 46W   101
Winter *Hill*: Lancs., England   53 37N 02 31W   114
Winterset: Iowa, U.S.A.   41 20N 94 00W   98
Winterthur: Switzerland   47 30N 08 45E   71
Winterton: Humb., England   53 39N 00 35W   63
Winterton-on-Sea: Norf., England   52 43N 01 42E   58
Winthrop: Mass., U.S.A.   42 23N 70 59W   122
Winton: S.I., New Zealand   46 10S 168 20E   87
Wipper: *riv.*, W.Germany   51 00N 07 15E   118
Wipperfürth: W.Germany   51 07N 07 24E   118
Wirksworth: Derby., England   53 05N 01 34W   58
Wirral: *pen.*, England   53 15N 03 00W   60
Wisbech: Cambs., England   52 40N 00 10E   58
Wisconsin: *admin.*, U.S.A.   44 30N 90 00W   45 98
Wisconsin: *riv.*, Wis., U.S.A.   43 00N 90 30W   98
Wisconsin Rapids: Wis., U.S.A.   44 24N 89 50W   98
Wishaw: Lan., Scotland   55 47N 03 56W   62 113
Wisła (Vistula): *riv.*, Poland   53 30N 18 45E   7 27 78
Wismar: E.Germany   53 54N 11 28E   73
Wismarer Bucht: *bay*, E.Germany   54 00N 11 15E   73
Wissey: *riv.*, Norf., England   52 30N 00 30E   58
Witham: Essex, England   51 48N 00 38E   59
Witham: *riv.*, Lincs., England   53 00N 00 00   58
Withernsea: Humb., England   53 44N 00 02E   63
Witney: Oxon., England   51 48N 01 29W   59
Witten: W.Germany   51 27N 07 19E   118
Wittenberg: E.Germany   51 53N 12 39E   73
Wittenberge: E.Germany   52 59N 11 45E   73
Wivenhoe: Essex, England   51 52N 00 58E   59
Włocławek: Poland   52 39N 19 01E   79
Wnion: *riv.*, Gwyn., Wales   52 45N 03 45W   60
Woburn: Mass., U.S.A.   42 27N 71 09W   122
Woking: Surrey, England   51 20N 00 34W   59 112
Wokingham: Berks., England   51 25N 00 51W   59
Wolf: *riv.*, Wis., U.S.A.   44 45N 88 30W   98
Wolf Creek *Dam*: Ky., U.S.A.   36 50N 85 09W   101
Wolf *Lake*: U.S.A.   41 40N 87 31W   124
Wolf Point: Mont., U.S.A.   48 05N 105 39W   94
Wolfsburg: W.Germany   52 27N 10 49E   73
Wollaston *Lake*: Sask., Canada   58 15N 103 15W   42 92

Wollongong: N.S.W., Australia   34 25S 150 52E   41
Wolseley: Sask., Canada   50 25N 103 19W   92
Wolverhampton: W.Mid., England   52 36N 02 08W   58 115
Wolverton: Bucks., England   52 04N 00 50W   59
Wombourne: Staffs., England   52 32N 02 11W   115
Wŏnju: S.Korea   37 22N 127 58E   37
Wŏnsan: N.Korea   39 09N 127 25E   37
Woodbridge: Ont., Canada   43 47N 79 36W   125
Woodbridge: Suff., England   52 06N 01 19E   59
Wood Buffalo *National Park*: Canada   58 30N 113 00W   92
Woodbury: N.J., U.S.A.   39 50N 75 09W   122
Woodford: Gt. Ldn., England   51 37N 00 02W   112
Woodhall Spa: Lincs., England   53 09N 00 14W   58
Woodland: Calif., U.S.A.   38 40N 121 50W   91
Wood River: Ill., U.S.A.   38 54N 90 04W   106
Woodroffe, *Mount*: S.A., Australia   26 20S 131 42E   40
Woods, *Lake of the*: Canada/U.S.A.   49 15N 94 30W   44 98
Woodside: Calif., U.S.A.   37 26N 122 15W   126
Woodslee: Ont., Canada   42 13N 82 43W   125
Woodstock: Oxon., England   51 52N 01 21W   59
Woodville: N.I., New Zealand   40 20S 175 54E   87
Woodville: Tex., U.S.A.   30 47N 94 25W   100
Woodward: Okla., U.S.A.   36 26N 99 24W   95
Wooler: Northumb., England   55 33N 02 01W   63
Woollahra: N.S.W., Australia   33 53S 151 15E   120
Woolwich: Gt. Ldn., England   51 29N 00 05E   112
Woomera: S.A., Australia   31 11S 136 54E   41
Wootton Bassett: Wilts., England   51 33N 01 54W   61
Worcester: Here. & Worcs., England   52 11N 02 13W   59
Worcester: C.P., Rep. of S.Africa   33 39S 19 26E   55
Worcester: Mass., U.S.A.   42 17N 71 48W   45 99
Worcester & Birmingham *Canal*: England   52 15N 02 00W   115
Worcestershire: *admin.*, England *see* Hereford & Worcester
  52 15N 02 15W   60
Workington: Cumbria, England   54 39N 03 33W   62
Worksop: Notts., England   53 18N 01 07W   58
Worland: Wyo., U.S.A.   44 01N 107 57W   94
Worms: W.Germany   49 38N 08 23E   72
Worms *Head*: W.Glam., Wales   51 34N 04 20W   61
Woronora *Reservoir*: N.S.W., Australia   34 07S 150 56E   120
Worringen: W.Germany   51 04N 06 52E   118
Worth: Ill., U.S.A.   41 40N 87 48W   125
Worthing: W.Sussex, England   50 48N 00 23W   59
Worthington: Minn., U.S.A.   43 37N 95 36W   94
Wowoni: *is.*, Indonesia   04 00S 123 00E   39
Wrangel *Island*: U.S.S.R.   71 30N 179 30W   22
Wrangell: Alaska, U.S.A.   56 28N 132 23W   42 89
Wrath, *Cape*: Suther., Scotland   58 37N 05 01W   64
Wreake: *riv.*, Leics., England   52 45N 00 45W   58
Wrekin, The: *hill*, Salop, England   52 41N 02 34W   60
Wrexham: Clwyd, Wales   53 03N 03 00W   60
Wright *Peak*: Antarctica   73 40S 94 32W   25
Wrocław (Breslau): Poland   51 05N 17 00E   27 73 78
Wrocław: *admin.*, Poland   51 15N 16 30E   73
Wrotham: Kent, England   51 19N 00 19E   59
Wroughton: Wilts., England   51 32N 01 48W   61
Września: Poland   52 20N 17 32E   73
Wu: *riv.*, China   28 45N 117 15E   85
Wubao: China   37 33N 110 41E   84
Wuchang: China   30 30N 114 22E   85
Wuchih Shan: *mtn. see* Wuzhishan   18 57N 109 43E   12 36
Wuchou *see* Wuzhou   23 30N 111 21E   36 85
Wuchung *see* Wuzhong   37 55N 106 11E   36 84
Wuda: China   39 40N 106 40E   84
Wudi: China   37 44N 117 35E   84
Wufeng: China   30 11N 110 37E   85
Wugang: China   26 45N 110 37E   85
Wugong: China   34 21N 108 04E   84
Wugongshan: *mtns.*, China   27 15N 113 45E   85
Wuhan: China   30 35N 114 19E   36 85 105
Wuhe: China   33 07N 117 54E   84
Wuhsi *see* Wuxi: Siangsu   31 35N 120 19E   37 84
Wuhsing *see* Huzhou   30 55N 120 06E   37 85
Wuhu: China   31 21N 118 22E   36 84
Wuhua: China   23 49N 115 49E   85
Wuishan: *mtns.*, China   27 15N 117 00E   36 85
Wujiang: China   31 07N 120 40E   84
Wulanhaote (Ulanhoto): China   46 05N 122 05E   37
Wülfrath: W.Germany   51 17N 07 03E   118

Types of map: Ocean pp. 1-5; Physical pp. 6-25; Human pp. 26-57; Topographic pp. 58-101; World pp. 102-111; Urban pp. 112-128.

Wuli: China   22 09N 109 13E   85
Wuliang Shan: mtns., China   24 30N 100 45E   36
Wulumuqi (Urumchi): China   43 48N 87 35E   9 105
Wuming: China   23 12N 108 18E   85
Wuning: China   29 20N 115 06E   85
Wunnummin Lake: Ont., Canada   52 45N 89 00W   93
Wupatki National Monument: Ariz.,
    U.S.A.   35 30N 111 15W   91
Wuping: China   25 08N 116 11E   85
Wupper: riv., W.Germany   51 00N 07 15E   118
Wuppertal: W.Germany   51 15N 07 10E   72 118
Wuqi: China   37 08N 108 10E   84
Wuqiao: China   37 36N 116 20E   84
Wuqing: China   38 20N 117 04E   84
Würm See: lake see Starnberger See   47 45N 11 15E   73
Würzburg: W.Germany   49 48N 09 57E   26 73
Wushui: riv., China   27 30N 109 45E   85
Wusong: China   31 23N 121 31E   84 121
Wusong (Suzhou): riv., China   31 14N 121 19E   121
Wusuli (Ussuri): riv., China/U.S.S.R.   45 45N 133 30E   37
Wutai: China   38 44N 113 17E   84
Wutongqiao (Wut'ungch'iao): China   29 26N 103 51E   36
Wuwei: Gansu, China   37 58N 102 49E   36
Wuxi (Wuhsi): Siangsu, China   31 35N 120 19E   37 84
Wuxi: Sichuan, China   31 29N 109 34E   84
Wuxiang: China   36 49N 112 59E   84
Wuxuan: China   23 40N 109 39E   85
Wuyishan: mtn., China   27 40N 117 45E   85
Wuyuan: Jiangxi, China   29 15N 117 53E   85
Wuzhai: China   38 58N 111 50E   84
Wuzhishan (Wuchih Shan): mtn., China   18 57N 109 43E
    12 36
Wuzhong (Wuchung): China   37 55N 106 11E   36 84
Wuzhou (Wuchou): China   23 30N 111 21E   36 85
Wyandotte: Mich., U.S.A.   42 11N 83 11W   125
Wye: riv., England/Wales   52 00N 02 45W   61
Wylye: riv., Wilts., England   51 00N 02 00W   61
Wymondham: Norf., England   52 34N 01 07E   58
Wyndham: W.A., Australia   15 29S 128 05E   40
Wynyard: Sask., Canada   51 46N 104 10W   92
Wyoming: Del., U.S.A.   39 07N 75 34W   104
Wyoming: admin., U.S.A.   43 00N 107 30W   43 94
Wyre: riv., Lancs., England   53 45N 02 45W   114
Wyvis, Ben: mtn., R. & Crom., Scotland   57 40N 04 35W   64

Xánthi: Greece   41 07N 24 56E   79
Xi (Si): riv., China   23 30N 111 15E   36 85
Xiajin: China   36 55N 116 00E   84
Xiamen (Hsiamen, Amoy): China   24 28N 118 07E   36 85
Xi'an (Hsian): China   34 15N 108 52E   36 84 105
Xianfeng: China   29 45N 109 10E   85
Xiang (Hsiang): riv., China   28 15N 112 45E   36 85
Xiangcheng: China   33 50N 113 29E   84
Xiangfan (Hsiangfan): China   32 03N 112 01E   36 84
Xianggang see Victoria   22 17N 114 13E   36 85
Xiangshan: China   39 59N 116 10E   125
Xiangtan (Hsiangt'an): China   27 51N 112 47E   36 85
Xiangtang: China   28 26N 115 58E   85
Xiangxiang: China   27 43N 112 27E   85
Xiangyin: China   28 40N 112 48E   85
Xiangyuan: China   36 25N 113 11E   84
Xiangzhou: China   24 03N 109 40E   85
Xianju: China   28 52N 120 46E   85
Xianning: China   29 53N 114 21E   85
Xianyang (Hsienyang): China   34 22N 108 42E   36 84
Xianyou: China   25 23N 118 40E   85
Xiaogan: China   30 55N 113 57E   85
Xiaoqing: riv., China   37 15N 118 30E   84
Xiaoyi: China   37 04N 111 44E   84
Xiapu: China   26 52N 120 01E   85
Xiashi see Haining   30 32N 120 42E   85
Xiaxian: China   35 11N 111 05E   84
Xiayi: China   34 14N 116 14E   84
Xibahe: China   39 59N 116 25E   121
Xichuan: China   33 00N 111 25E   84
Xiegeer: China   28 38N 87 04E   83
Xielipuke: China   31 30N 82 45E   83
Xihua: China   33 47N 114 31E   84

Xin: riv., China   28 15N 117 45E   85
Xincai: China   32 44N 114 59E   84
Xinchang: China   29 30N 120 57E   85
Xincheng: China   24 10N 108 40E   85
Xindian: China   40 01N 116 25E   121
Xindu: China   23 59N 111 34E   85
Xinfeng: China   25 24N 114 48E   85
Xingguo: China   26 21N 115 05E   85
Xinghua: China   32 52N 119 50E   84
Xinglong: China   40 26N 117 30E   84
Xingning: China   24 05N 115 47E   85
Xingshan: China   31 13N 110 49E   84
Xingtai: China   37 04N 114 29E   84
Xingtang: China   38 26N 114 33E   84
Xingu: riv., Brazil   02 15S 52 15W   18 50
Xingxian: China   38 25N 111 00E   84
Xinhailian (Lienyünchiang): China   34 37N 119 16E   37 84
Xinhua: China   27 43N 111 22E   85
Xinhui: China   22 30N 113 02E   85
Xining (Hsining): China   36 38N 101 55E   36 105
Xinji see Shulu   37 50N 115 15E   84
Xinjiang: China   35 37N 111 13E   84
Xinjiang (Sinkiang): admin., China   42 15N 93 00E   36
Xinjin: China   39 24N 122 02E   84
Xinlonghua: China   31 10N 121 26E   121
Xinmin (Hsinmin): China   42 00N 122 48E   37
Xintai: China   35 54N 117 49E   84
Xintian: China   25 53N 112 05E   84
Xinxian: Henan, China   31 36N 114 44E   84
Xinxian: Shänxi, China   38 25N 112 45E   84
Xinxiang (Hsinhsiang): China   35 16N 113 51E   36 84
Xinyang (Hsinyang): China   32 10N 114 07E   36 84
Xinye: China   32 40N 112 21E   84
Xinyi: Guangdong, China   22 20N 110 54E   84
Xinyi: Jiangsu, China   34 21N 118 27E   85
Xinyu: China   27 49N 114 57E   85
Xiongyuecheng: China   40 06N 122 08E   84
Xiping: China   33 23N 114 02E   84
Xiqingshan: mtns., China   35 00N 102 30E   36
Xisanlintang: China   31 08N 121 29E   121
Xishui: China   30 27N 115 19E   85
Xiushan: China   28 29N 108 59E   85
Xiushi: riv., China   29 15N 114 45E   85
Xiushu: China   29 04N 114 33E   85
Xixia: China   33 29N 111 20E   84
Xixian: China   32 21N 114 50E   84
Xixiang: China   32 59N 107 35E   84
Xiyang: China   37 40N 113 39E   84
Xiyuan: China   40 00N 116 18E   121
Xizang (Tibet): admin., China   29 00N 88 00E   35 83
Xlukehu: lake, China   31 45N 89 30E   83
Xochiac: Mexico   19 19N 99 17W   128
Xochimilco: Mexico   19 16N 99 06W   128
Xu: riv., China   27 45N 116 30E   85
Xuancheng: China   30 57N 118 45E   85
Xuanhua: China   40 36N 115 01E   84
Xuchang (Hsüch'ang): China   34 03N 113 48E   36 84
Xujiawei: China   31 12N 121 25E   121
Xunwu: China   24 57N 115 28E   85
Xupu: China   27 55N 110 32E   85
Xuyi: China   33 01N 118 30E   84
Xuzhou: China   34 17N 117 18E   84

Yaan: China   30 03N 103 02E   36
Yablonovyy Range see Jablonovyj Range   54 00N 117 00E
    9 30
Yaheladazeshan: mtn., China   35 12N 95 20E   36
Yahk: B.C., Canada   49 05N 116 06W   90
Yakima: Wash., U.S.A.   46 36N 120 31W   42 90
Yakima: riv., Wash., U.S.A.   47 00N 120 45W   90
Yakumo: Japan   42 15N 140 16E   86
Yakutat: Alaska, U.S.A.   59 29N 139 49W   88
Yakutsk see Jakutsk   62 13N 129 49E   31
Yalong (Yalung): riv., China   30 30N 101 00E   36
Yalta see Jalta   44 30N 34 10E   28
Yalu (Amnok): riv., China/N.Korea   40 15N 125 00E   37
Yalung: riv. see Yalong   30 30N 101 00E   36
Yaluzangbujiang (Brahmaputra): riv., Asia   29 00N 86 15E
    11 35 83

Types of map: Ocean pp. 1-5; Physical pp. 6-25; Human pp. 26-57; Topographic pp. 58-101; World pp. 102-111; Urban pp. 112-128.

Yamagata: Japan   38 15N 140 15E   37 86
Yamantau, *Mount see* Jamantau, *Mount*   54 15N 58 06E
                                                   29
Yamato: Kanagawa, Japan   35 30N 139 28E   121
Yamethin: Burma   20 24N 96 08E   35
Yam Ḥā Melaḥ (Dead Sea): Israel   31 15N 35 15E   10 32
Yampa: *riv.*, U.S.A.   40 15N 107 30W   94
Yampi Sound: W.A., Australia   16 11S 123 40E   40
Yamuna: *riv.*, India   28 00N 77 30E   34 82
Yana: *riv. see* Jana: *riv.*   69 30N 134 15E   31
Yan'an: China   36 41N 109 20E   84
Yanbū (Yanbu'al Bahr): Saudi Arabia   24 07N 38 04E   32
Yanchang: China   36 40N 110 04E   84
Yancheng (Yench'eng): China   33 23N 120 10E   37 84
Yangambi: Zaïre   00 47N 24 28E   54
Yangcheng: China   35 30N 112 29E   84
Yangchou *see* Yangzhou   32 24N 119 26E   37 84
Yangch'uan *see* Yangquan   37 52N 113 29E   36 84
Yangchun: China   22 07N 111 43E   85 105
Yanggu: China   36 08N 115 49E   84
Yanghe: China   33 47N 118 33E   84
Yangjiang: China   21 52N 111 52E   85
Yangjiazhuang: China   31 23N 121 26E   121
Yangjizhen: China   31 22N 121 34E   121
Yangliuqing: China   39 08N 116 59E   84
Yangquan (Yangch'uan): China   37 52N 113 29E   36 84
Yangshan: China   24 23N 112 34E   85
Yangshuo: China   24 45N 110 20E   85
Yangtze (Chang): *riv.*, China   31 30N 118 15E   12 36 84
Yangtze, *Mouth of the*: China   31 30N 121 45E   37
Yangtze *Gorge* (Yichang *Gorge*): China   31 00N 110 00E
                                                   36 85
Yangxin: China   29 51N 115 08E   85
Yangyang: S.Korea   38 04N 128 38E   105
Yangyuan: China   40 05N 114 10E   84
Yangzhou (Yangchou): China   32 24N 119 26E   37 84
Yangzhuoyonghu: *lake*, China   29 00N 90 30E   83
Yanhe: China   28 30N 108 45E   85
Yankee Division *Highway*: Mass., U.S.A.   42 15N 71 00W
                                                   122
Yankton: S.D., U.S.A.   42 53N 97 23W   94
Yanqing: China   40 30N 115 58E   84
Yanshan: China   38 06N 117 13E   84
Yantai (Yent'ai, Chefoo): China   37 30N 121 22E   37 84
Yanzhou (Yenchou): China   35 35N 116 53E   36 84
Yaoundé: Cameroun   03 51N 11 31E   20
Yap: *is.*, Caroline Islands   09 31N 138 06E   12
Yar: *riv.*, I. of W., England   50 30N 01 15W   59
Yare: *riv.*, Norf., England   52 30N 01 15E   58
Yariga-take: *mtn.*, Japan   36 20N 137 39E   86
Yarkand *see* Suoche   38 25N 77 16E   29
Yarmouth: N.S., Canada   43 50N 66 08W   97
Yarmouth: I. of W., England   50 42N 01 29W   59
Yaroslavl' *see* Jaroslavl'   57 37N 39 52E   28 80 107
Yarrow Water: *riv.*, Selk., Scotland   55 30N 03 00W   63
Yarty: *riv.*, England   50 45N 03 00W   61
Yate: Avon, England   51 33N 02 25W   61
Yatsushiro: Japan   32 30N 130 36E   86
Yavatmāl: India   20 22N 78 11E   82
Yawatahama: Japan   33 27N 132 24E   86
Yazd: Iran   31 55N 54 22E   33
Yazoo: *riv.*, Miss., U.S.A.   32 30N 90 45W   100
Yazoo City: Miss., U.S.A.   32 51N 90 25W   100
Ye: Burma   15 15N 97 50E   35
Yeadon: W.Yorks., England   53 52N 01 41W   63 115
Yeerqiang: *riv.*, China   39 30N 78 00E   29
Yejiaji: China   31 52N 115 57E   84
Yelets *see* Jelec   52 37N 38 30E   28 80
Yell: *is.*, Shet. Is., Scotland   60 30N 01 00W   65
Yellowhead *Pass*: Canada   52 53N 118 13W   89
Yellowknife: N.W.T., Canada   62 30N 114 29W   42 88
Yellowknife: *riv.*, N.W.T., Canada   63 00N 114 00W 88
Yellow *River see* Huang   37 15N 118 00E   12 36 84
Yellow *Sea* (Huang Hai): China   33 30N 123 00E   12 37
Yellowstone: *riv.*, U.S.A.   46 00N 107 45W   17 42 94
Yellowstone *Lake*: Wyo., U.S.A.   44 27N 110 22W   43 94
Yellowstone *National Park*: U.S.A.
    44 30N 110 15W   94
Yellowtail: *dam*, Mont., U.S.A.   45 19N 107 57W   94
Yell *Sound*: Shet. Is., Scotland   60 30N 01 15W   65
YEMEN   14 45N 44 15E   10 33

YEMEN DEMOCRATIC REPUBLIC   16 00N 49 00E   10 33
Yenangyaung: Burma   20 28N 94 54E   35
Yench'eng *see* Yancheng   33 23N 120 10E   37 84
Yenchou *see* Yanzhou   35 35N 116 53E   36 84
Yengema: Sierra Leone   08 39N 10 58W   57
Yenisey: *riv. see* Jenisej   64 30N 87 30E   9 30
Yeniseysk *see* Jenisejsk   58 27N 92 10E   30
Yent'ai *see* Yantai   37 30N 121 22E   37 84
Yeo: *riv.*, Avon, England   51 15N 02 45W   113
Yeo: *riv.*, Devon, England   51 00N 03 30W   61
Yeo: *riv.*, Som., England   51 00N 02 45W   61
Yeola: India   20 02N 74 31E   82
Yeovil: Som., England   50 57N 02 39W   61
Yerevan *see* Jerevan   40 11N 44 30E   28
Yerington: Nev., U.S.A.   39 00N 119 10W   91
Yerres: *riv.*, France   48 45N 02 30E   117
Yerupajá: *mtn.*, Peru   10 16S 76 55W   49
Yerushalayim (Jerusalem): Israel   31 47N 35 14E   32
Yes Tor: *mtn.*, Devon, England   50 42N 04 01W   61
Yexian: Henan, China   33 30N 113 10E   84
Yexian: Shandong, China   37 10N 119 55E   84
Yeysk *see* Jejsk   46 42N 38 16E   28 80
Yi: *riv.*, China   34 45N 118 15E   84
Yiannitsá: Greece   40 46N 22 24E   79
Yibin (Ipin): China   28 47N 104 38E   36
Yichang (Ich'ang): China   30 42N 111 22E   36 85 105
Yichang *Gorge* (Yangtze *Gorge*, Hsiling Hsia): China
    30 45N 110 00E   36 85
Yicheng: Hubei, China   31 43N 112 17E   84
Yicheng: Shǎnxī, China   35 43N 111 42E   84
Yichuan: Henan, China   34 26N 112 15E   84
Yichuan: Shǎnxī, China   36 12N 110 05E   84
Yichun (Ich'un): China   27 42N 114 22E   36 85
Yidu: Hubei, China   30 22N 111 32E   85
Yidu: Shandong, China   36 41N 118 24E   84
Yifeng: China   28 22N 114 45E   85
Yiguqihu: China   30 10N 86 45E   83
Yihuang: China   27 36N 116 10E   85
Yinan: China   35 30N 118 30E   84
Yinchuan: China   38 30N 106 18E   36 84
Ying: *riv.*, China   33 00N 115 45E   84
Yingcheng: China   30 55N 113 31E   85
Yingde: China   24 12N 113 20E   85
Yingkou: Liaoning, China   40 40N 122 17E   37
Yingshan: China   30 40N 115 40E   84
Yingshang: Anhui, China   32 38N 116 19E   85
Yingshang: Sichuan, China   31 07N 106 31E   84
Yingtan: China   28 14N 116 58E   85
Yingxian: China   39 32N 113 15E   84
Yinhangzhen: China   31 21N 121 30E   121
Yining (Kuldja): China   43 55N 81 14E   29
Yinjiang: China   28 02N 108 33E   85
Yishan: China   24 35N 108 35E   84
Yishui: China   35 50N 118 39E   84
Yiwu (Chenyüeh): China   29 17N 120 03E   85
Yixian: Anhui, China   29 55N 117 57E   85
Yixian: Shandong, China   34 40N 117 38E   84
Yiyang (Iyang): Hunan, China   28 36N 112 10E   36 85
Yiyang: Kiangsi, China   28 21N 117 23E   85
Yizhang: China   25 24N 112 51E   85
Ylikitka: *lake*, Finland   66 00N 28 30E   75
Ylivieska: Finland   64 05N 24 30E   75
Yoho *National Park*: B.C., Canada   51 15N 116 30W 89
Yoichi: Japan   43 12N 140 41E   86
Yokkaichi: Japan   34 58N 136 37E   37 86 107
Yokohama: Japan   35 27N 139 29E   37 86 105 107 121
Yokosuka: Chiba, Japan   35 18N 139 40E   86
Yokosuka: Kamagawa, Japan   35 18N 139 39E   121
Yokote: Japan   39 18N 140 34E   86
Yonago: Japan   35 26N 133 20E   37 86
Yongchun: China   25 18N 118 13E   85
Yongding: China   24 45N 116 43E   85
Yongding: *riv.*, China   39 30N 116 30E   84 121
Yongdingmen: China   39 52N 116 23E   121
Yongfeng: China   27 19N 115 24E   85
Yongkang: China   28 50N 120 02E   85
Yongning: China   22 45N 108 26E   85
Yongshou: China   34 50N 108 05E   84
Yongtai: China   25 48N 118 54E   85
Yongxin: China   26 56N 114 28E   85
Yongxing: China   26 08N 113 06E   85

Types of map: Ocean pp. 1-5; Physical pp. 6-25; Human pp. 26-57; Topographic pp. 58-101; World pp. 102-111; Urban pp. 112-128.

Yongxiu: China   28 09N 115 47E   85
Yonkers: N.Y., U.S.A.   40 56N 73 54W   99 123
Yonne: *riv.,* France   48 15N 03 15E   71
York: Ont., Canada   43 55N 79 25W   125
York: N.Yorks., England   53 58N 01 05W   63 115
York: Nebr., U.S.A.   40 52N 97 36W   94
York: Pa., U.S.A.   39 57N 76 44W   99
York, *Vale of:* N.Yorks., England   54 15N 01 15W   63
York Factory: Man., Canada   57 08N 92 25W   42 93
Yorkshire: *admin.,* England *see* North Yorkshire; South
   Yorkshire; West Yorkshire   54 00N 01 00W   63
Yorkshire Dales *National Park:* England   54 00N 01 45W   63
Yorkshire Wolds: *hills,* N.Yorks., England   54 00N 00 30W   63
Yorkton: Sask., Canada   51 12N 102 29W   42 92
Yosemite *National Park:* Calif., U.S.A.   37 45N 119 30W   91
Yoshkar-Ola *see* Joškar-Ola   56 38N 47 52E   28 81
Yŏsu: S.Korea   34 46N 127 44E   37
You (Yu): *riv.,* China   23 15N 107 30E   12 36 85
Youghal: Cork, Irish Rep.   51 57N 07 50W   67
Youghal *Bay:* Cork, Irish Republic   51 45N 07 45W   67
Youghiogheny: *riv.,* U.S.A.   39 30N 79 30W   125
Young Nunataks: *mtn.,* Antarctica   66 44S 54 08E   24
Youngstown: Ohio, U.S.A.   41 05N 80 40W   45 99 104
Youxian: China   27 08N 113 20E   85
Youyang: China   28 48N 108 48E   85
Yr Eifl: *mtn.,* Gwyn., Wales   52 58N 04 25W   60
Yreka: Calif., U.S.A.   41 44N 122 39W   90
Ystad: Sweden   55 25N 13 50E   74
Ythan: *riv.,* Aber., Scotland   57 15N 02 00W   65
Yu: *riv. see* You   23 15N 107 30E   12 36 85
Yüan (Red): *riv.,* China/N.Vietnam   21 45N 104 30E   12 36
Yuan: *riv.,* Hunan, China   28 45N 110 45E   12 36 85
Yuan'an: China   31 04N 111 32E   84
Yuanling: China   28 31N 110 16E   85
Yuanping: China   38 42N 112 45E   84
Yuba City: Calif., U.S.A.   39 09N 121 36W   91
Yūbari: Japan   43 04N 141 59E   37 86
Yucatán: *admin.,* Mexico   20 45N 89 00W   46
Yucatan *Basin:* Caribbean Sea   20 00N 84 00W   2 17
Yucatán *Channel:* Cuba/Mexico   22 00N 86 00W   17 47
Yucatán *Peninsula:* Mexico   19 45N 89 00W   17 46
Yucheng: China   36 56N 116 39E   84
Yuci: China   37 40N 112 42E   84
Yudu: China   25 55N 115 24E   85
Yueyang: China   29 23N 113 03E   85
Yugan: China   28 41N 116 41E   85
YUGOSLAVIA   44 00N 19 00E   7 27 79 107
Yuhebao: China   38 01N 109 37E   84
Yukagir *Plateau see* Jukagir *Plateau*   66 00N 155 00E   9 31
Yukon: *riv.,* Canada/U.S.A.   61 45N 162 30W   16 88
Yukon Crossing: Yukon, Canada   62 20N 136 29W   88
Yukon Territory: *admin.,* Canada   42 88
Yulin: Guangxi Zhuang, China   22 37N 110 08E   84
Yulin: Hainan, China   18 20N 109 31E   36
Yulin: Shănxī, China   38 16N 109 29E   85
Yuling: *riv.,* China   29 30N 118 30E   85
Yuma: Ariz., U.S.A.   32 43N 114 37W   43 91
Yumen (Jade Hate): China   39 56N 97 51E   36
Yun: *canal,* China   33 45N 118 45E   84 121
Yunan (Ducheng): China   23 11N 111 29E   85
Yuncheng: Shandong, China   35 35N 115 54E   84
Yuncheng: Shănxī, China   34 59N 110 59E   84
Yungxiao: China   24 01N 117 20E   85
Yunnan: *admin.,* China   24 45N 101 45E   36
Yunnan *Plateau:* China   24 30N 102 45E   12 36
Yunxian (Yunyang): China   32 50N 110 45E   84
Yupanyang: *gulf,* China   30 30N 121 45E   85
Yuqing: China   27 13N 107 50E   85
Yurga *see* Jurga   55 42N 84 51E   30
Yurimaguas: Peru   05 54S 76 07W   48
Yushan: China   28 41N 118 15E   85
Yutian: China   39 53N 117 45E   84
Yuxian: China   34 10N 113 18E   84
Yuyao: China   30 04N 121 10E   85
Yuzhno-Sakhalinsk *see* Južno-Sachalinsk   46 58N 142 42E   31
Yverdon: Switzerland   46 47N 06 38E   71

Zabajkal'sk (Otpor): U.S.S.R.   49 38N 117 19E   30
Zabrze: Poland   50 18N 18 47E   27
Zacatecas: Mexico   22 47N 102 35W   46
Zacatecas: *admin.,* Mexico   23 30N 103 00W   46
Zadar: Yugoslavia   44 07N 15 14E   79
Zagań: Poland   51 37N 15 20E   73
Zagazig *see* Az Zaqāzīq   30 35N 31 31E   32
Zagorsk: U.S.S.R.   56 18N 38 08E   80
Zagreb: Yugoslavia   45 48N 15 58E   27 78
Zagros *Mountains:* Iran   31 45N 51 15E   10 32
Zāhedān: Iran   29 32N 60 54E   33
Zahlah: Lebanon   33 51N 35 53E   32
Zaīdpur: India   26 50N 81 20E   83
ZAÏRE (Congo, Rep. of)   00 00 24 45E   21 54 107
Zaïre (Congo): *riv.,* Zaïre/Congo   01 30N 23 00E   21 54
Zajsan, *Lake* (Zaysan, Lake): U.S.S.R.   48 00N 84 00E   29
Zákinthos: *is.,* Greece   37 45N 20 45E   78
Zakopane: Poland   49 17N 19 54E   78
Zalew Szczeciński: *gulf,* Poland   53 45N 14 30E   73
Zaliv Petra Velikogo: *gulf,* U.S.S.R.   42 45N 132 00E   86
Žamantau, Gora: *mtn.,* U.S.S.R.   48 20N 51 50E   81
Zambezi: *riv.,* Africa   15 30S 31 30E   21 55
ZAMBIA   13 45S 27 30E   21 54 107
Zamboanga: Philippines   06 55N 122 05E   39
Zamora: Spain   41 30N 05 45W   77
Zamość: Poland   50 44N 23 15E   78
Zanesville: Ohio, U.S.A.   39 55N 82 02W   98
Zanjān (Zenjan): Iran   36 40N 48 30E   33
Zanzibar: *admin. & is.,* Tanzania   06 10S 39 11E   1 10 54
Zaoyang: China   32 10N 112 43E   84
Zapadnaja Dvina (Western Dvina): *riv.,* U.S.S.R.
   55 15N 29 00E   28 80
Západočeský: *admin.,* Czechoslovakia   49 45N 13 00E   73
Zapala: Argentina   38 55S 70 09W   52
Zapla: Argentina   24 15S 65 08W   104
Zapl'usje: U.S.S.R.   58 26N 29 43E   80
Zaporožje (Zaporozh'ye): U.S.S.R.   47 50N 35 10E
   28 80 105
Zapotitlan: Mexico   19 17N 99 03W   128
Zaragoza (Saragossa): Spain   41 39N 00 54W   26 77
Zarajsk: U.S.S.R.   54 46N 38 53E   80
Zaraza: Venezuela   09 23N 65 20W   48
Zaria: Nigeria   11 01N 07 44E   57
Zarqa *see* Az-Zarqā'   32 04N 36 05E   32
Żary: Poland   51 40N 15 10E   73 78
Žatec: Czechoslovakia   50 20N 13 35E   73
Zavolžje: U.S.S.R.   56 37N 43 26E   80
Zavolžsk: U.S.S.R.   57 30N 42 10E   80
Zawiercie: Poland   50 30N 19 24E   105
Zāwiyat al Baydā' (Beida): Libya   32 46N 21 43E   32
Zaysan, Lake *see* Zajsan, *Lake*   48 00N 84 00E   29
Z Canyon *Dam:* Wash., U.S.A.   48 47N 117 22W   90
Ždanov (Zhdanov, Mariupol'): U.S.S.R.   47 06N 37 33E
   28 80 105
Zealand: *is. & admin. see* Sjælland   55 15N 11 45E   75
Zeballos: B.C., Canada   49 57N 126 10W   89 104
Zehdenick: E.Germany   52 59N 13 20E   73
Zehlendorf: W.Germany   52 26N 13 16E   117
Zeitz: E.Germany   51 03N 12 08E   73
Zeja (Zeya): *riv.,* U.S.S.R.   52 45N 128 00E   31
Zeja (Zeya) *reservoir:* U.S.S.R.   54 30N 127 45E   31
Zeleznogorsk: U.S.S.R.   52 22N 35 23E   80
Zel'onodol'sk: U.S.S.R.   55 51N 48 33E   81
Žemaitija: *geog. reg.,* U.S.S.R.   55 45N 22 30E   75
Zemetčino: U.S.S.R.   53 30N 42 38E   80
Zenica: Yugoslavia   44 11N 17 53E   79 105
Zenjan *see* Zanjān   36 40N 48 30E   33
Zepernick: E.Germany   52 39N 13 33E   117
Zeravšan (Zeravshan): *riv.,* U.S.S.R.   39 45N 68 00E   29
Žerdevka: U.S.S.R.   51 51N 41 28E   80
Zermatt: Switzerland   46 01N 07 45E   71
Zernez: Switzerland   46 43N 10 06E   71
Zernograd: U.S.S.R.   46 50N 40 19E   80
Zetland (Shetland Is.): *admin.,* Scotland   60 15N 01 15W
   65
Zeya: *riv. see* Zeja   52 45N 128 00E   31
Zeya *Reservoir see* Zeja *Reservoir*   54 30N 127 45E   31
Zgierz: Poland   51 52N 19 25E   78
Zhabei: China   31 15N 121 28E   121
Zhada (Töling): China   31 29N 79 50E   34
Zhaling, *Lake* (Chaling Hu): China   34 45N 98 00E   36

Types of map: Ocean pp. 1-5; Physical pp. 6-25; Human pp. 26-57; Topographic pp. 58-101; World pp. 102-111; Urban pp. 112-128.

Zhalinhu: *lake,* China 31 00N 88 00E 83
Zhang: *riv.,* China 36 15N 114 00E 84
Zhanghuang: China 22 03N 109 28E 85
Zhangjiakou (Changchiak'ou, Kalgan): China 40 50N 114 53E 36 84
Zhangjiangzha: China 31 12N 121 36E 121
Zhangping: China 25 19N 117 25E 85
Zhangpu: China 24 09N 117 36E 85
Zhangzhou (Changchou, Longxi): China 24 33N 117 39E 36 85
Zhanjiang (Chanchiang, Fort Bayard): China 21 16N 110 28E 36
Zhaoan: China 23 44N 117 15E 85
Zhaoping: China 24 03N 110 42E 85
Zhaoqing (Gaoyao): China 23 03N 112 27E 85
Zhaotong (Chaot'ung): China 27 12N 103 48E 36
Zhaoyuan: China 37 22N 120 24E 84
Zhasakeqi: China 39 21N 109 45E 84
Zhdanov *see* Ždanov 47 06N 37 33E 28 80 105
Zhecheng: China 34 06N 115 19E 84
Zhejiang (Chechiang): *admin.,* China 29 30N 120 00E 37 85
Zheng'an: China 28 25N 107 25E 85
Zhengding: China 38 10N 114 34E 84
Zhenghe: China 27 22N 118 50E 85
Zhengyang: China 32 37N 114 23E 84
Zhengzhou (Chengchou): China 34 40N 113 38E 36 84
Zhenjiang (Chenchiang): China 32 10N 119 30E 37 84
Zhenping: China 33 08N 112 10E 84
Zhenru: China 31 15N 121 23E 121
Zhenyuan: China 27 05N 108 22E 85
Zhide: China 30 04N 116 58E 85
Zhijiang: China 27 30N 109 39E 85
Zhitomir *see* Žitmoir 50 16N 28 40E 28
Zhongshan (Chungshan, Shiqi): China 22 31N 113 22E 36 85
Zhongxian: China 30 20N 108 00E 85
Zhongxiang: China 31 11N 112 40E 84
Zhoucun: China 36 47N 117 48E 84
Zhoujiadu: China 31 11N 121 29E 121
Zhoushan: China 30 02N 122 08E 85
Zhouzhi: China 34 12N 108 10E 84
Zhuansha: China 31 11N 121 41E 121
Zhucheng: China 36 00N 119 24E 84
Zhuji: China 29 43N 120 14E 85
Zhujia: China 31 16N 121 33E 121
Zhumadian: China 33 00N 114 01E 84
Zhuolu (Baoan): China 40 22N 115 05E 84
Zhuoxian: China 39 30N 115 58E 84
Zhushan: China 32 15N 110 19E 84
Zhuzhou (Chuchou): China 27 50N 113 07E 36 85
Zibo (Tzupo): China 36 47N 118 01E 36 84
Zielona Góra: Poland 51 57N 15 30E 73 78
Zielona Góra: *admin.,* Poland 52 00N 15 00E 73

Zigong (Tzukung): China 29 22N 104 46E 36
Ziguinchor: Senegal 12 35N 16 20W 57
Žigulevsk: U.S.S.R. 53 25N 49 27E 81
Ziiyang: China 32 45N 108 34E 84
Ziizhou: China 37 37N 109 41E 84
Zijin: China 23 36N 115 14E 85
Žilina: Czechoslovakia 49 13N 18 42E 78
Zimovniki: U.S.S.R. 47 08N 42 28E 80
Zinder: Niger 13 46N 08 58E 57
Zingst: *pen.,* E.Germany 54 26N 12 45E 73
Zion *National Park:* Utah, U.S.A. 37 15N 112 45W 91
Zishui: *riv.,* China 28 15N 111 15E 85
Žitomir (Zhitomir): U.S.S.R. 50 16N 28 40E 28
Zittau: E.Germany 50 55N 14 50E 73
Ziway, *Lake:* Ethiopia 08 00N 38 45E 53
Zixi: China 27 42N 117 08E 85
Ziya: *riv.,* China 38 30N 116 30E 84
Zlatoust: U.S.S.R. 55 10N 59 40E 29 81 105
Zlín *see* Gottwaldov 49 14N 17 40E 73 78
Žlobin: U.S.S.R. 52 54N 30 03E 80
Žmerinka: U.S.S.R. 49 02N 28 06E 78
Zmijov: U.S.S.R. 49 40N 36 19E 80
Znojmo: Czechoslovakia 48 52N 16 04E 73 78
Žodino: U.S.S.R. 54 06N 28 21E 80
Zoločov: U.S.S.R. 49 47N 24 52E 78
Zolotonoša: U.S.S.R. 49 40N 32 02E 80
Žoltyje Vody: U.S.S.R. 48 21N 33 31E 80
Zomba: Malawi 15 23S 35 20E 55
Zone *Point:* Corn., England 50 08N 05 00W 61
Zonguldak: Turkey 41 27N 31 49E 27
Zouxian: China 35 24N 117 00E 84
Žovtnevoje: U.S.S.R. 46 52N 32 02E 80
Zrenjanin: Yugoslavia 45 22N 20 23E 27 78
Zug: Switzerland 47 10N 08 31E 71
Zugersee: *lake,* Switzerland 47 00N 08 30E 71
Zujevka: U.S.S.R. 58 25N 51 10E 81
Žukovka: U.S.S.R. 53 32N 33 44E 80
Žukovskij: U.S.S.R. 55 35N 38 08E 80
Zülpicher Börde: *geog. reg.,* Germany 50 45N 06 45E 119
Zunhua: China 40 12N 117 58E 84
Zuni: *riv.,* U.S.A. 35 00N 108 30W 95
Zunyi (Tsuni): China 27 42N 106 50E 36 85
Zuo: *riv.,* China 22 45N 107 45E 36 85
Zuoshui: China 33 40N 109 01E 84
Zuoyun: China 40 02N 112 54E 84
Zürich: Switzerland 47 23N 08 33E 26 71
Zürichsee: *lake,* Switzerland 47 15N 08 30E 71
Zushi: Japan 35 17N 139 34E 121
Zwickau: E.Germany 50 43N 12 30E 73
Zwolle: Netherlands 52 31N 06 06E 72
Zyr'anka: U.S.S.R. 65 45N 150 51E 31
Zyr'anovsk: U.S.S.R. 49 43N 84 20E 29
Żyrardów: Poland 52 02N 20 28E 78